Contemporary Authors®

NEW REVISION SERIES

ISSN 0275-7176

Contemporary

Authors®

A Bio-Bibliographical Guide to
Current Writers in Fiction, General Nonfiction,
Poetry, Journalism, Drama, Motion Pictures,
Television, and Other Fields

NEW REVISION SERIES
volume **106**

STAFF

Library of Congress Catalog Card Number 62-52046
ISBN 0-7876-4615-6
ISSN 0275-7176
Printed in the United States of America

10 9 8 7 6 5 4 3 2 1

Contents

Indexing note: All *Contemporary Authors* entries are indexed in the *Contemporary Authors* cumulative index, which is published separately and distributed twice a year.

As always, the most recent Contemporary Authors cumulative index continues to be the user's guide to the location of an individual author's listing.

Preface

Contemporary Authors (*CA*) provides information on approximately 100,000 writers in a wide range of media, including:

- Current writers of fiction, nonfiction, poetry, and drama whose works have been issued by commercial publishers, risk publishers, or university presses (authors whose books have been published only by known vanity or author-subsidized firms are ordinarily not included)

- Prominent print and broadcast journalists, editors, photojournalists, syndicated cartoonists, graphic novelists, screenwriters, television scriptwriters, and other media people

- Authors who write in languages other than English, provided their works have been published in the United States or translated into English

- Literary greats of the early twentieth century whose works are popular in today's high school and college curriculums and continue to elicit critical attention

A *CA* listing entails no charge or obligation. Authors are included on the basis of the above criteria and their interest to *CA* users. Sources of potential listees include trade periodicals, publishers' catalogs, librarians, and other users.

How to Get the Most out of *CA*: Use the Index

The key to locating an author's most recent entry is the *CA* cumulative index, which is published separately and distributed twice a year. It provides access to *all* entries in *CA* and *Contemporary Authors New Revision Series* (*CANR*). Always consult the latest index to find an author's most recent entry.

For the convenience of users, the *CA* cumulative index also includes references to all entries in these Gale literary series: *Authors and Artists for Young Adults, Authors in the News, Bestsellers, Black Literature Criticism, Black Literature Criticism Supplement, Black Writers, Children's Literature Review, Concise Dictionary of American Literary Biography, Concise Dictionary of British Literary Biography, Contemporary Authors Autobiography Series, Contemporary Authors Bibliographical Series, Contemporary Dramatists, Contemporary Literary Criticism, Contemporary Novelists, Contemporary Poets, Contemporary Popular Writers, Contemporary Southern Writers, Contemporary Women Poets, Dictionary of Literary Biography, Dictionary of Literary Biography Documentary Series, Dictionary of Literary Biography Yearbook, DIS-Covering Authors, DISCovering Authors: British, DISCovering Authors: Canadian, DISCovering Authors: Modules* (including modules for Dramatists, Most-Studied Authors, Multicultural Authors, Novelists, Poets, and Popular/Genre Authors), *DISCovering Authors 3.0, Drama Criticism, Drama for Students, Feminist Writers, Hispanic Literature Criticism, Hispanic Writers, Junior DISCovering Authors, Major Authors and Illustrators for Children and Young Adults, Major 20th-Century Writers, Native North American Literature, Novels for Students, Poetry Criticism, Poetry for Students, Short Stories for Students, Short Story Criticism, Something about the Author, Something about the Author Autobiography Series, St. James Guide to Children's Writers, St. James Guide to Crime & Mystery Writers, St. James Guide to Fantasy Writers, St. James Guide to Horror, Ghost & Gothic Writers, St. James Guide to Science Fiction Writers, St. James Guide to Young Adult Writers, Twentieth-Century Literary Criticism, 20th Century Romance and Historical Writers, World Literature Criticism,* and *Yesterday's Authors of Books for Children.*

A Sample Index Entry:

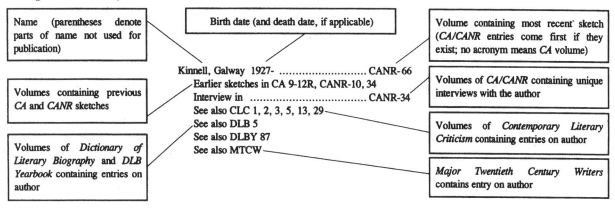

How Are Entries Compiled?

The editors make every effort to secure new information directly from the authors; listees' responses to our questionnaires and query letters provide most of the information featured in *CA*. For deceased writers, or those who fail to reply to requests for data, we consult other reliable biographical sources, such as those indexed in Gale's *Biography and Genealogy Master Index,* and bibliographical sources, including *National Union Catalog, LC MARC,* and *British National Bibliography.* Further details come from published interviews, feature stories, and book reviews, as well as information supplied by the authors' publishers and agents.

An asterisk (*) at the end of a sketch indicates that the listing has been compiled from secondary sources believed to be reliable but has not been personally verified for this edition by the author sketched.

What Kinds of Information Does An Entry Provide?

Sketches in *CA* contain the following biographical and bibliographical information:

- **Entry heading:** the most complete form of author's name, plus any pseudonyms or name variations used for writing

- **Personal information:** author's date and place of birth, family data, ethnicity, educational background, political and religious affiliations, and hobbies and leisure interests

- **Addresses:** author's home, office, or agent's addresses, plus e-mail and fax numbers, as available

- **Career summary:** name of employer, position, and dates held for each career post; resume of other vocational achievements; military service

- **Membership information:** professional, civic, and other association memberships and any official posts held

- **Awards and honors:** military and civic citations, major prizes and nominations, fellowships, grants, and honorary degrees

- **Writings:** a comprehensive, chronological list of titles, publishers, dates of original publication and revised editions, and production information for plays, television scripts, and screenplays

- **Adaptations:** a list of films, plays, and other media which have been adapted from the author's work

- **Work in progress:** current or planned projects, with dates of completion and/or publication, and expected publisher, when known

- **Sidelights:** a biographical portrait of the author's development; information about the critical reception of the author's works; revealing comments, often by the author, on personal interests, aspirations, motivations, and thoughts on writing

- **Interview:** a one-on-one discussion with authors conducted especially for *CA*, offering insight into authors' thoughts about their craft

- **Autobiographical essay:** an original essay written by noted authors for *CA*, a forum in which writers may present themselves, on their own terms, to their audience

- **Photographs:** portraits and personal photographs of notable authors

- **Biographical and critical sources:** a list of books and periodicals in which additional information on an author's life and/or writings appears

- **Obituary Notices** in *CA* provide date and place of birth as well as death information about authors whose full-length sketches appeared in the series before their deaths. The entries also summarize the authors' careers and writings and list other sources of biographical and death information.

Related Titles in the *CA* Series

Contemporary Authors Autobiography Series complements *CA* original and revised volumes with specially commissioned autobiographical essays by important current authors, illustrated with personal photographs they provide. Common topics include their motivations for writing, the people and experiences that shaped their careers, the rewards they derive from their work, and their impressions of the current literary scene.

Contemporary Authors Bibliographical Series surveys writings by and about important American authors since World War II. Each volume concentrates on a specific genre and features approximately ten writers; entries list works written by and about the author and contain a bibliographical essay discussing the merits and deficiencies of major critical and scholarly studies in detail.

Available in Electronic Formats

GaleNet. *CA* is available on a subscription basis through GaleNet, an online information resource that features an easy-to-use end-user interface, powerful search capabilities, and ease of access through the World-Wide Web. For more information, call 1-800-877-GALE.

Licensing. *CA* is available for licensing. The complete database is provided in a fielded format and is deliverable on such media as disk, CD-ROM, or tape. For more information, contact Gale's Business Development Group at 1-800-877-GALE, or visit us on our website at www.galegroup.com/bizdev.

Suggestions Are Welcome

The editors welcome comments and suggestions from users on any aspect of the *CA* series. If readers would like to recommend authors for inclusion in future volumes of the series, they are cordially invited to write the Editors at *Contemporary Authors*, Gale Group, 27500 Drake Rd., Farmington Hills, MI 48331-3535; or call at 1-248-699-4253; or fax at 1-248-699-8054.

Contemporary Authors Product Advisory Board

The editors of *Contemporary Authors* are dedicated to maintaining a high standard of excellence by publishing comprehensive, accurate, and highly readable entries on a wide array of writers. In addition to the quality of the content, the editors take pride in the graphic design of the series, which is intended to be orderly yet inviting, allowing readers to utilize the pages of *CA* easily and with efficiency. Despite the longevity of the *CA* print series, and the success of its format, we are mindful that the vitality of a literary reference product is dependent on its ability to serve its users over time. As literature, and attitudes about literature, constantly evolve, so do the reference needs of students, teachers, scholars, journalists, researchers, and book club members. To be certain that we continue to keep pace with the expectations of our customers, the editors of *CA* listen carefully to their comments regarding the value, utility, and quality of the series. Librarians, who have firsthand knowledge of the needs of library users, are a valuable resource for us. The *Contemporary Authors* Product Advisory Board, made up of school, public, and academic librarians, is a forum to promote focused feedback about *CA* on a regular basis. The seven-member advisory board includes the following individuals, whom the editors wish to thank for sharing their expertise:

- **Anne M. Christensen,** Librarian II, Phoenix Public Library, Phoenix, Arizona.

- **Barbara C. Chumard,** Reference/Adult Services Librarian, Middletown Thrall Library, Middletown, New York.

- **Eva M. Davis,** Teen Services Librarian, Plymouth District Library, Plymouth, Michigan.

- **Adam Janowski, Jr.,** Library Media Specialist, Naples High School Library Media Center, Naples, Florida.

- **Robert Reginald,** Head of Technical Services and Collection Development, California State University, San Bernadino, California.

- **Katharine E. Rubin,** Head of Information and Reference Division, New Orleans Public Library, New Orleans, Louisiana.

- **Barbara A. Wencl,** Media Specialist, Como Park High School, St. Paul, Minnesota.

International Advisory Board

Well-represented among the 100,000 author entries published in *Contemporary Authors* are sketches on notable writers from many non-English-speaking countries. The primary criteria for inclusion of such authors has traditionally been the publication of at least one title in English, either as an original work or as a translation. However, the editors of *Contemporary Authors* came to observe that many important international writers were being overlooked due to a strict adherence to our inclusion criteria. In addition, writers who were publishing in languages other than English were not being covered in the traditional sources we used for identifying new listees. Intent on increasing our coverage of international authors, including those who write only in their native language and have not been translated into English, the editors enlisted the aid of a board of advisors, each of whom is an expert on the literature of a particular country or region. Among the countries we focused attention on are Mexico, Puerto Rico, Germany, Luxembourg, Belgium, the Netherlands, Norway, Sweden, Denmark, Finland, Taiwan, Singapore, Spain, Italy, South Africa, Israel, and Japan, as well as England, Scotland, Wales, Ireland, Australia, and New Zealand. The thirteen-member advisory board includes the following individuals, whom the editors wish to thank for sharing their expertise:

- **Lowell A. Bangerter,** Professor of German, University of Wyoming, Laramie, Wyoming.

- **Nancy E. Berg,** Associate Professor of Hebrew and Comparative Literature, Washington University, St. Louis, Missouri.

- **David William Foster,** Regent's Professor of Spanish, Interdisciplinary Humanities, and Women's Studies, Arizona State University, Tempe, Arizona.

- **Frances Devlin-Glass,** Associate Professor, School of Literary and Communication Studies, Deakin University, Burwood, Victoria, Australia.

- **Hosea Hirata,** Director of the Japanese Program, Associate Professor of Japanese, Tufts University, Medford, Massachusetts.

- **Mark Libin,** Professor, University of Manitoba, Winnipeg, Manitoba, Canada.

- **Eloy E. Merino,** Assistant Professor of Spanish, Northern Illinois University, DeKalb, Illinois.

- **Linda M. Rodríguez Guglielmoni,** Associate Professor, University of Puerto Rico—Mayagüez, Puerto Rico.

- **Sven Hakon Rossel,** Professor and Chair of Scandanvian Studies, University of Vienna, Vienna, Austria.

- **Steven R. Serafin,** Director, Writing Center, Hunter College of the City University of New York, New York City.

- **Ismail S. Talib,** Senior Lecturer, Department of English Language and Literature, National University of Singapore, Singapore.

- **Dionisio Viscarri,** Assistant Professor, Ohio State University, Columbus, Ohio.

- **Mark Williams,** Associate Professor, English Department, University of Canterbury, Christchurch, New Zealand.

CA Numbering System and Volume Update Chart

Occasionally questions arise about the *CA* numbering system and which volumes, if any, can be discarded. Despite numbers like " 29-32R," " 97-100" and " 196," the entire *CA* print series consists of only 230 physical volumes with the publication of *CA* Volume 197. The following charts note changes in the numbering system and cover design, and indicate which volumes are essential for the most complete, up-to-date coverage.

CA **First Revision**	• 1-4R through 41-44R (11 books) *Cover:* Brown with black and gold trim. There will be no further First Revision volumes because revised entries are now being handled exclusively through the more efficient *New Revision Series* mentioned below.
CA **Original Volumes**	• 45-48 through 97-100 (14 books) *Cover:* Brown with black and gold trim. 101 through 197 (97 books) *Cover:* Blue and black with orange bands. The same as previous *CA* original volumes but with a new, simplified numbering system and new cover design.
CA **Permanent Series**	• *CAP*-1 and *CAP*-2 (2 books) *Cover:* Brown with red and gold trim. There will be no further Permanent Series volumes because revised entries are now being handled exclusively through the more efficient *New Revision Series* mentioned below.
CA **New Revision Series**	• CANR-1 through CANR-106 (106 books) *Cover:* Blue and black with green bands. Includes only sketches requiring significant changes; **sketches are taken from any previously published CA, CAP, or CANR volume.**

If You Have:	You May Discard:
CA First Revision Volumes 1-4R through 41-44R and *CA Permanent Series* Volumes 1 and 2	*CA* Original Volumes 1, 2, 3, 4 Volumes 5-6 through 41-44
CA Original Volumes 45-48 through 97-100 and 101 through 197	**NONE:** These volumes will not be superseded by corresponding revised volumes. Individual entries from these and all other volumes appearing in the left column of this chart may be revised and included in the various volumes of the *New Revision Series*.
CA New Revision Series Volumes *CANR*-1 through *CANR*-106	**NONE:** The *New Revision Series* does not replace any single volume of *CA*. Instead, volumes of *CANR* include entries from many previous *CA* series volumes. All *New Revision Series* volumes must be retained for full coverage.

A Sampling of Authors and Media People
Featured in This Volume

Iain M. Banks

Banks has sparked considerable controversy in British and American literary circles with his unique and highly imaginative brand of fiction. While the author is credited with crossing and redefining the boundaries of the thriller, fantasy, and science-fiction genres, he is probably best known for his macabre tales of horror, which have been compared by reviewers to the psychologically probing fiction of Franz Kafka and Edgar Allan Poe. His titles include the highly acclaimed 1984 novel *The Wasp Factory,* the novels *Canal Dreams* and *Complicity,* and the science fiction story *Look to Windward,* first published in 2000.

Laura Shaine Cunningham

Cunningham is an author and playwright who has written several critically successful novels and memoirs. In the humorous novel *Third Parties,* she describes the problems faced by descendants of the very rich. Cunningham's memoirs include *Sleeping Arrangements,* an autobiographical novel of the author's childhood in the Bronx during the 1950s, and *A Place in the Country,* which chronicles her purchase of a house in the Shawangunk Mountains of New York. Cunningham is also the author of the plays *Bang* and *The Man at the Door.*

William Goldman

An accomplished author of fiction and nonfiction, as well as a celebrated screenwriter, Goldman prefers to think of himself as a novelist who happens to write for films. He is the recipient of two Academy Awards, for the screenplays of the films *Butch Cassidy and the Sundance Kid* and *All the President's Men,* and has also authored several memoirs on working in the movie business, *Adventures in the Screen Trade: A Personal View of Hollywood and Screenwriting* and *Which Lie Did I Tell?: More Adventures in the Screen Trade.*

Ernst Jünger

One of modern Germany's foremost men of letters, Jünger is perhaps best known for his *In Stahlgewittern: Aus dem Tagebuch eines Strosstruppfuehrers,* translated as *The Storm of Steel: From the Diary of a German Storm-Troop Officer on the Western Front.* He has also published highly acclaimed travel books, diaries, and essays. Jünger, who continued to write well into his eighties and nineties, has created a body of work that reflects the longest life span of any major German literary figure. Indeed, many critics have considered Jünger to be the doyen of twentieth-century German letters.

Rem Koolhaas

Dutch architect Koolhaas "is known for designs that infuse modernist geometric forms with a lyrical, at times surrealist, spirit," according to a *New York Times* critic. Koolhaas, who heads the Office of Metropolitan Architecture (OMA) in Rotterdam is also renowned for his writings and lectures on the layout of contemporary urban centers. Like most architects, he has detractors who declare his buildings ugly. However, Koolhaas has also been a major influence in the last few decades. In April of 2000, he was awarded the Pritzker Prize for architecture.

Elisabeth Kübler-Ross

A physician, professor, and writer, Kübler-Ross has devoted her research to understanding the concerns of the terminally ill and thus better equip themselves to deal with this fear. *On Death and Dying,* Kübler-Ross's first book, became an enormously influential work for medical practitioners as well as for the general public. The book, which became a bestseller, outlines five stages of dying and discusses strategies for treating patients and their families as they negotiate these stages. The success of *On Death and Dying* prompted Kübler-Ross to devote her clinical practice to the treatment of dying patients.

Richard Selzer

Selzer draws upon his experience as a surgeon in his writing, both for the discipline it requires and for material. His stories and essays lead the reader through hospital wards, illuminating the world of medicine and surgery. Selzer's writing ranges from detailed descriptions of the human anatomy and operating techniques to discussions of patients' reactions to sickness and impending death. Among his works are *Mortal Lessons: Notes on the Art of Surgery,* a collection of essays, and *Letters to a Young Doctor,* which contains both essays and short fiction.

Diane Wakoski

Wakoski is frequently named among the foremost contemporary poets by virtue of her experiential vision and her unique voice. Her poems focus on intensely personal experiences, such as her unhappy childhood, on the painful relationships she has had with men and, perhaps most frequently, on the subject of being Diane Wakoski. The stylistic and structural aspects of Wakoski's poetry are as unique as her poetic statement. Often described as prosy, her poems are usually written in the first person. In 1989, she was the recipient of the William Carlos Williams Prize for *Emerald Ice: Selected Poems, 1962-1987.*

Acknowledgments

Grateful acknowledgment is made to those publishers, photographers, and artists whose work appear with these authors' essays. Following is a list of the copyright holders who have granted us permission to reproduce material in this volume of *CA*. Every effort has been made to trace copyright, but if omissions have been made, please let us know.

Photographs/Art

Reinaldo Arenas: Arenas, photograph. © Liaison Agency. Reproduced by permission.

Iain M. Banks: Banks, photograph. © Jerry Bauer. Reproduced by permission.

Alan Bennett: Bennett, photograph. Hulton-Deutsch Collection/Corbis. Reproduced by permission.

Judith P. Butler: Butler, photograph. © Jerry Bauer. Reproduced by permission.

Stephen L. Carter: Carter, photograph by Woodfin Camp & Associates. Reproduced by permission.

Laura Shaine Cunningham: Cunningham, photograph. © Jerry Bauer. Reproduced by permission.

Michael Dibdin: Dibdin, photograph by Mark Gerson. Reproduced by permission of Mark Gerson.

Allan Folsom: Folsom, photograph. © Jerry Bauer. Reproduced by permission.

Jane Gardam: Gardam, photograph. © Jerry Bauer. Reproduced by permission.

Alasdair Gray: Gray, photograph by Eric Thorburn. Reproduced by permission.

Frank Lentricchia: Lentricchia, photograph. The University of Chicago. Reproduced by permission.

H. P. Lovecraft: Lovecraft, photograph.

John McCabe: McCabe, photograph. Reproduced by permission.

John Cowper Powys: Powys, photograph. AP/Wide World Photos. Reproduced by permission.

Richard Selzer: Selzer, photograph. © Jerry Bauer. Reproduced by permission.

William Jay Smith: Smith, photograph by Rollie McKenna. Reproduced by permission.

Nancy Springer: Springer, photograph. Photo © Bison Studio. Reproduced by permission.

Iyanla Vanzant: Vanzant, photograph by Joyce Ravid. Reproduced by permission.

Diane Wakoski: Wakoski, photograph by Layle Silbert. Reproduced by permission.

C. K. Williams: Williams, photograph by Layle Silbert. Reproduced by permission.

A

ABELLA, Alex 1950-

PERSONAL: Surname is pronounced Ah-*beh*-ya; born November 8, 1950, in Havana, Cuba; immigrated to the United States in 1961, naturalized citizen, 1972; son of Lorenzo P. (a poet) and Elvira (Alvarez) Abella; married, 1976; married second wife, Armeen Kathleen, 1985; children: Veronica Lee. *Politics:* Democrat. *Religion:* Episcopalian. *Education:* Columbia University, B.A., 1972.

ADDRESSES: Home—Los Angeles, CA. *Agent*—c/o Simon & Schuster, 1230 Avenue of the Americas, New York, NY 10020.

CAREER: Ticketron Entertainment, New York, NY, general manager, assistant editor, restaurant reviewer, and feature writer, 1972-74; Gurtman, Murtha & Associates, New York, NY, public relations writer, 1974-75; Sullivan Associates, Menlo Park, CA, educational writer (in Spanish), 1975-76; KPOO-FM radio, San Francisco, CA, newscaster (in Spanish), beginning 1976; KEMO-TV, San Francisco, CA, newswriter for Spanish-language newscast and traffic assistant, 1975; Berlitz School of Languages, San Francisco, CA, Spanish interpreter and translator, 1975-77; *San Francisco Chronicle,* San Francisco, CA, general assignment reporter, 1977-78; KTVU-TV, Oakland, CA, writer for daily newscast and foreign affairs reporter, 1979—; Los Angeles Superior Court, court interpreter, 1985—.

MEMBER: San Francisco Press Club, San Francisco Media Alliance, World Affairs Council of Northern California, California Court Interpreters Association.

AWARDS, HONORS: Pulitzer Scholar at New York University, 1968-72; Emmy Award nomination for best

breaking news story, 1982; *The Killing of the Saints* was named a *New York Times* Notable Book, 1991.

WRITINGS:

The Total Banana (nonfiction), Harcourt (New York, NY), 1979.
The Killing of the Saints, Crown (New York, NY), 1991.
The Great American, Simon & Schuster (New York, NY), 1997.
Dead of Night, Simon & Schuster (New York, NY), 1998.
Final Acts, Simon & Schuster (New York, NY), 2000.

Also author of a play, *Camelia* (staged reading at the Actors Ensemble Theater in New York, NY). Contributor to *People's Almanac.* Contributor to periodicals, including *Oui.* Translator of *Saddleman's Review.*

ADAPTATIONS: Paramount Pictures owns film rights to *The Killing of the Saints.*

SIDELIGHTS: Alex Abella explores the dark world of cults in his novels featuring Charlie Morell, a lawyer, author, and private investigator who lives in Los Angeles. In his first adventure, *The Killing of the Saints,* Cuban-born Charlie is assigned to investigate the case of a Cuban refugee who is accused of killing hostages during a robbery. The refugee, Ramon Valdez, claims that he was ordered to carry out the killings by one of the gods of Santeria, a voodoo-like religion native to Cuba. As Charlie searches for witnesses and clues, he is forced to confront his own past, including the reasons he turned his back on his parents, wife, and child. A re-

1

viewer for *Publishers Weekly* praised *The Killing of the Saints* as an "atmospheric thriller" with a "splendid ethnic setting" enlivened by "Hispanic expressions, scenes of witchcraft and courtroom procedures." Santeria is again a key element of the plot in *Dead of Night*, which pits Charlie against his half-brother, Ricardo Diaz.

In *Final Acts*, Ricardo Diaz is dead, but his evil deeds live on—and Charlie is under suspicion for having committed them. He hires Rita Carr, a beautiful Mexican-Irish lawyer, to defend him. Rita suspects a connection between cult killings and the apparent suicide of a state senator. The case leads to a "surprisingly tense courtroom duel, followed by a climax that makes the rest of this wild, wooly tale look positively decorous," remarked a *Kirkus Reviews* contributor, who wondered about the target audience—"sensationalists who don't have enough time to make separate trips to the supernatural horror and courtroom drama shelves?" Alternating between Rita's first-person narration and Charlie's written account of events, the book is "thick in cult interest and suspense," according to Connie Fletcher in *Booklist. Los Angeles Magazine*'s Robert Ito praised Abella's depiction of "the city's creepier environs" and added that the author "can deliver a shocker ending with the best of them."

Abella's Cuban background also informs his novel *The Great American*, which concerns the involvement of a U.S. Marine, William Morgan, in the Castro revolution. Morgan is lured to Cuba by the promise of adventure; once there, he is caught up in the struggle to overthrow the dictator Batista. Hiding in the hills, he meets Fidel Castro and Che Guevara and lives through two star-crossed romances. This is a "heartfelt if flawed fictionalized account of [Cuba's] travails," according to Michele Leber in *Booklist*. Reviewing *The Great American* for *Library Journal*, Rebecca Sturm Kelm noted that "an action novel with a conscience is to be appreciated," but that Morgan's "political-religious soul searching often intrudes."

BIOGRAPHICAL/CRITICAL SOURCES:

PERIODICALS

Bloomsbury Review, December, 1991, review of *The Killing of the Saints,* p. 27.
Booklist, March 1, 1980, review of *The Total Banana,* p. 920; September 1, 1991, review of *The Killing of the Saints,* p. 33; March 1, 1997, Michele Leber, review of *The Great American,* p. 1108; December 1, 2000, Connie Fletcher, review of *Final Acts,* p. 694.

Book Report, January, 1994, review of *The Killing of the Saints,* p. 22.
Books, January, 1993, review of *The Killing of the Saints,* p. 13.
Hispanic, November, 1991, Martha Frase-Blunt, review of *The Killing of the Saints,* p. 70.
Kirkus Reviews, July 1, 1991, review of *The Killing of the Saints,* p. 802; January 15, 1997, review of *The Great American,* p. 74; June 15, 1998, review of *Dead of Night,* p. 824; October 1, 2000, review of *Final Acts,* p. 1372.
Kliatt Young Adult Paperback Book Guide, July, 1993, review of *The Killing of the Saints,* p. 524.
Library Journal, September 1, 1991, David Dodd, review of *The Killing of the Saints,* p. 227; January, 1997, Rebecca Sturm Kelm, review of *The Great American,* p. 141.
Locus, October, 1991, review of *The Killing of the Saints,* pp. 35, 43; June, 1993, review of *The Killing of the Saints,* p. 51.
Los Angeles Magazine, September, 1991, Steven Kane, "Names Under the Sun: Alex Abella," p. 32; December, 2000, Robert Ito, review of *Final Acts,* p. 48.
Los Angeles Times Book Review, September 8, 1991, review of *The Killing of the Saints,* p. 15.
Necrofile, spring, 1992, review of *The Killing of the Saints,* p. 25.
New York Times Book Review, September 29, 1991, Marilyn Stasio, review of *The Killing of the Saints,* p. 30.
Publishers Weekly, July 19, 1991, review of *The Killing of the Saints,* p. 47; August 23, 1991, review of *The Killing of the Saints,* p. S15; March 1, 1993, review of *The Killing of the Saints,* p. 53; January 6, 1997, review of *The Great American,* p. 63; November 6, 2000, review of *Final Acts,* p. 71.
Virginia Quarterly Review, autumn, 1997, review of *The Great American,* p. 131.
Washington Post Book World, September 15, 1991, review of *The Killing of the Saints,* p. 8.

OTHER

The Mysterious Realm of Alex Abella, http://www.alexabella.com (February 17, 2001).
Nocturne, http://www.nocturne.com/books/ (October 27, 1999), reviews of *The Killing of the Saints;* and of *Dead of Night.**

AINSWORTH, Ruth (Gallard) 1908-

PERSONAL: Full name Ruth Gallard Ainsworth Gilbert; born October 16, 1908, in Manchester, England; daughter of Percy Clough (a Methodist minister) and Gertrude (Fisk) Ainsworth; married Frank Lathe Gilbert (a managing director of chemical works), March 29, 1935; children: Oliver Lathe, Christopher Gallard, Richard Frank. *Education:* Attended Froebel Training Centre, Leicester, England. *Politics:* Labour.

ADDRESSES: Home—Field End, Corbridge, Northumberland NE45 5JP, England.

CAREER: Writer.

WRITINGS:

CHILDREN'S BOOKS

Tales about Tony, illustrated by Cora E. M. Paterson, Epworth, 1936.

Mr. Popcorn's Friends, Epworth, 1938.

The Gingerbread House, Epworth, 1938.

The Ragamuffins, Epworth, 1939.

Richard's First Term: A School Story, Epworth, 1940.

All Different (poems), illustrated by Linda Bramley, Heinemann, 1947.

Five and a Dog, Epworth, 1949.

"Listen with Mother" Tales (selected from *Listen with Mother* radio program, British Broadcasting Corporation), illustrated by Astrid Walford, Heinemann, 1951.

Rufty Tufty the Golliwog, illustrated by Dorothy Craigie, Heinemann, 1952.

The Ruth Ainsworth Readers (contains *The Cottage by the Sea; Little Wife Goody; The Robber; The Wild Boy; A Comfort for Owl; Sugar and Spice; Fun, Fires, and Friends; Black Bill; A Pill for Owl; Tortoise in Trouble; The Pirate Ship;* and *Hob the Dwarf*), Heinemann, 1953-55.

Rufty Tufty at the Seaside, illustrated by Dorothy Craigie, Heinemann, 1954.

Charles Stories, and Others from "Listen with Mother" (selected from *Listen with Mother* program), illustrated by Sheila Hawkins, Heinemann, 1954.

More about Charles, and Other Stories from "Listen with Mother" (selected from *Listen with Mother* program), illustrated by Sheila Hawkins, Heinemann, 1954.

Three Little Mushrooms: Four Puppet Plays (contains *Here We Go round the Buttercups, Lob's Silver Spoon, Hide-and-Seek,* and *Hay-Making*), Heinemann, 1955.

More Little Mushrooms: Four Puppet Plays (contains *Three Clever Mushrooms, Tick-Tock, Christmas Eve,* and *The White Stranger*), Heinemann, 1955.

The Snow Bear, illustrated by Rosemary Trew, Heinemann, 1956.

Rufty Tufty Goes Camping, illustrated by Dorothy Craigie, Heinemann, 1956.

Rufty Tufty Runs Away, illustrated by Dorothy Craigie, Heinemann, 1957.

Five "Listen with Mother" Tales about Charles (selected from *Listen with Mother* program), illustrated by Matvyn Wright, Adprint, 1957.

Nine Drummers Drumming (stories), illustrated by John Mackay, Heinemann, 1958.

Rufty Tufty Flies High, illustrated by D. G. Valentine, Heinemann, 1959.

Cherry Stones: A Book of Fairy Stories, illustrated by Pat Humphreys, Heinemann, 1960.

Rufty Tufty's Island, illustrated by D. G. Valentine, Heinemann, 1960.

Lucky Dip: A Selection of Stories and Verses, illustrated by Geraldine Spence, Penguin, 1961.

Rufty Tufty and Hattie, illustrated by D. G. Valentine, Heinemann, 1962.

Far-Away Children, illustrated by Felice Trentin, Heinemann, 1963, Roy, 1968.

The Ten Tales of Shellover, illustrated by Antony Maitland, Deutsch, 1963, Roy, 1968.

The Wolf Who Was Sorry, illustrated by Doritie Kettlewell, Heinemann, 1964, Roy, 1968.

(Editor) James H. Fassett, *Beacon Readers,* Ginn, 1964-65.

Rufty Tufty Makes a House, illustrated by D. G. Valentine, Heinemann, 1965.

Jack Frost, illustrated by Jane Paton, Heinemann, 1966.

Daisy the Cow, illustrated by Sarah Garland, Hamish Hamilton, 1966.

Horse on Wheels, illustrated by Janet Duchesne, Hamish Hamilton, 1966.

The Look about You Books, illustrated by Jennie Corbett, Heinemann, Book 1: *In Woods and Fields,* 1967, Book 2: *Down the Lane,* 1967, Book 3: *Beside the Sea,* 1967, Book 4: *By Pond and Stream,* 1969, Book 5: *In Your Garden,* 1969, Book 6: *In the Park,* 1969.

(Reteller) *My Monarch Book of Little Red Riding Hood,* Bancroft & Co., 1967, published as *Little Red Riding Hood,* Purnell, 1977.

(Reteller) *My Monarch Book of Goldilocks and the Three Bears,* Bancroft & Co., 1967, published as *Goldilocks and the Three Bears,* Purnell, 1980.

(Reteller) *My Monarch Book of Cinderella,* Bancroft & Co., 1967, published as *Cinderella,* Purnell, 1980.

Roly the Railway Mouse, illustrated by Leslie Atkinson, Heinemann, 1967, published as *Roly the Railroad Mouse,* F. Watts, 1969.

More Tales of Shellover, illustrated by Maitland, Roy, 1968.

The Aeroplane Who Wanted to See the Sea, Bancroft & Co., 1968.

Boris the Teddy Bear, Bancroft & Co., 1968.

Dougal the Donkey, Bancroft & Co., 1968.

Mungo the Monkey, Bancroft & Co., 1968.

The Old-Fashioned Car, Bancroft & Co., 1968.

The Rabbit and His Shadow, Bancroft & Co., 1968.

The Noah's Ark, illustrated by Elsie Wrigley, Lutterworth, 1969.

The Bicycle Wheel, illustrated by Shirley Hughes, Hamish Hamilton, 1969.

Look, Do, and Listen (anthology), illustrated by Bernadette Watts, F. Watts, 1969.

(Reteller) *My Monarch Book of Puss in Boots,* Purnell, 1969, published as *Puss in Boots,* 1977.

(Reteller) *My Monarch Book of Jack and the Beanstalk,* Purnell, 1969, published as *Jack and the Beanstalk,* 1977.

(Reteller) *My Monarch Book of Snow White and the Seven Dwarfs,* Purnell, 1969, published as *Snow White,* 1977.

(Reteller) *My Monarch Book of Beauty and the Beast,* Purnell, 1969, published as *Beauty and the Beast,* 1977.

(Editor) *Book of Colours and Sounds,* Purnell, 1969.

The Ruth Ainsworth Book (stories), illustrated by Shirley Hughes, F. Watts, 1970.

The Phantom Cyclist, and Other Stories, illustrated by Maitland, Deutsch, 1971, published as *The Phantom Cyclist, and Other Ghost Stories,* Follett, 1974.

Fairy Gold: Favourite Fairy Tales Retold for the Very Young, illustrated by Barbara Hope Steinberg, Heinemann, 1972.

Another Lucky Dip, illustrated by Shirley Hughes, Penguin, 1973.

Three's Company, illustrated by Prudence Seward, Lutterworth, 1974.

Ruth Ainsworth's Bedtime Book, Purnell, 1974.

The Phantom Fisherboy: Tales of Mystery and Magic, illustrated by Shirley Hughes, Deutsch, 1974.

Three Bags Full, illustrated by Sally Long, Heinemann, 1975.

The Bear Who Liked Hugging People, and Other Stories, illustrated by Maitland, Heinemann, 1976, Crane Russak, 1978.

(Reteller) *The Sleeping Beauty,* Purnell, 1977.

Up the Airy Mountain: Stories of Magic, illustrated by Eileen Browne, Heinemann, 1977.

The Phantom Roundabout, and Other Ghostly Tales, illustrated by Shirley Hughes, Deutsch, 1977, published in United States as *The Phantom Carousel, and Other Ghostly Tales,* Follett, 1978.

Mr. Jumble's Toyshop, illustrated by Paul Wrigley, Lutterworth, 1978.

The Talking Rock, illustrated by Joanna Stubbs, Deutsch, 1979.

(Reteller) *Hansel and Gretel,* Purnell, 1980.

(Reteller) *The Three Little Pigs,* Purnell, 1980.

(Reteller) *The Pied Piper of Hamelin,* Purnell, 1980.

(Reteller) *Rumplestiltskin,* Purnell, 1980.

The Mysterious Baba and Her Magic Caravan: Two Stories, illustrated by Joan Hickson, Deutsch, 1980.

Mermaids' Tales, illustrated by Dandi Palmer, Lutterworth, 1980.

The Pirate Ship and Other Stories, illustrated by Shirley Hughes, Heinemann, 1980.

The Little Yellow Taxi and His Friends, illustrated by Gary Inwood, Lutterworth, 1982.

(Contributor) *Tales of Horror and Mystery,* Dean, 1993.

(Contributor) *The Walker Book of Ghost Stories,* edited by Susan Hill, Walker, 1990.

EDUCATIONAL BOOKS WITH RONALD RIDOUT

Look Ahead Readers (eight books, with supplementary readers), illustrated by John Mackay, Heinemann, 1956-58.

Books for Me to Read, Red Series: *Jill and Peter, The House of Hay, Come and Play, A Name of My Own, The Duck That Ran Away,* and *Tim's Hoop,* illustrated by Ingeborg Meyer-Rey, Blue Series: *At the Zoo, What Are They?, Colours, Silly Billy, A Pram and a Bicycle,* and *Pony, Pony,* illustrated by Gwyneth Mamlock, Green Series: *Susan's House, What Can You Hear?, Tim's Kite, Flippy the Frog, Huff the Hedgehog,* and *A House for a Mouse,* illustrated by William Robertshaw, Bancroft & Co., 1965.

Dandy the Donkey, Bancroft & Co., 1971.

The Wild Wood, illustrated by Leslie Orriss, Bancroft & Co., 1971.

OTHER

The Evening Listens (adult poems), Heinemann, 1953.

Also wrote plays and stories for television; contributor of stories to BBC programs, including *Listen with Mother* and *English for Schools.*

SIDELIGHTS: British children's author Ruth Ainsworth spent her childhood by the sea in Suffolk, which accounts for the appearance of lonely beaches, mermaids, and sand dunes in many of her writings. "I am told that I began making up poems when I was three, and wrote an exercise book of fairy tales when I was eight," she recalled. "Throughout my childhood I enjoyed writing, whether diaries, school essays or stories." The numerous warm and gentle stories that fill Ainsworth's works are written primarily for younger readers, falling somewhere between picture books and books for more advanced readers. "It is like coming home, to open a book by Ruth Ainsworth," commented a *Junior Bookshelf* contributor. "Here is security, an affectionate welcome, and a warm happy tale without surprises or excessive excitement but with plenty of gentle fun."

Ainsworth continued writing throughout her childhood and into her teens, and by the age of fifteen was published in a national daily. She moved with her family to Leicester two years later, the large library there adding a new dimension to her life. Soon after, her poetry was published in a number of magazines and journals, including *Spectator* and *Country Life,* and when she won a Gold Medal for original work, the publication of more poems ensued as part of the prize. Her first break came when Heinemann published *All Different,* a book of her children's poetry. At the same time, Ainsworth began writing regularly for *Listen with Mother,* a BBC radio program, and Heinemann also published these stories in 1951 as *"Listen with Mother" Tales.* From then on, the books followed steadily.

Many of these books consisted of an assortment of short stories compiled in one volume. *The Ruth Ainsworth Book,* published in 1970, collects a number of Ainsworth's previously published short stories and adds a variety of new selections. The book contains a range of stories, from simple tales for the very young, to longer and more substantial narratives for older children. Everything from realism to fantasy is included; and a *Bulletin of the Center for Children's Books* contributor stated that "the collection on the whole has variety and is sturdy enough to be useful for reading aloud, particularly in home collections." In such works as *The Phantom Fisherboy: Tales of Mystery and Magic* and *The Phantom Cyclist, and Other Stories,* Ainsworth delved into the unknown and presents a number of modern ghosts. These spooky spirits appear to various young children, but like Ainsworth's other characters, they are gentle, kind, and even friendly. A *Times Literary Supplement* reviewer described the collection of stories in *The Phantom Cyclist* are "told in a simple and effective style." Catherine Storr, a contributor in *New Statesman,*

said, "Ainsworth will earn the gratitude of the children who always ask for ghost stories, and of parents who dread the waking and shrieking the following night, with her book of unalarming, but definitely inexplicable eerie tales."

In longer works, such as *The Talking Rock* and *The Mysterious Baba and Her Magic Caravan: Two Stories,* Ainsworth continued to mix elements of fantasy and reality. *The Talking Rock* revolves around six-year-old Jakes and his adventures on a beach in England. Quarantined with the measles, he must remain in England for a short time when his family moves to Nigeria. While staying by the sea with friends of the family, Jakes makes a boy in the sand who magically comes to life. Sand Boy, a young mermaid, and Jakes spend a few wonderful days on the beach until they, along with all the other sea creatures, are threatened by the sea monster Glumper. Jakes must climb to the top of Talking Rock to find out how to fight Glumper, and by the time he rejoins his family all is well. "This is a pleasant fantasy, not epic, but nicely written," remarked *School Library Journal* contributor Janice Giles. With *The Talking Rock,* stated a *Junior Bookshelf* reviewer, Ainsworth presented "her most ambitious, and in many ways her most successful, story."

The two stories that comprise *The Mysterious Baba and Her Magic Caravan* are set in the Left-Over Land, the place toys retire to when they are not sold. A doll family is among the inhabitants of this land, and they encounter a series of mysteries when they take in Baba, a homeless Russian doll. The other dolls are baffled by the size of some of her clothes and by the amount of food she eats until they find out that she is a Russian nested doll, with six other little Babas inside her. The family accepts Baba and her children, and the second story in the book picks up where the first left off, relating the adventures of the Baba children and their friends. *Baba and Her Magic Caravan* "is an amusing and ingenious story with a satisfying ending," commented Frances Ball in *British Book News Children's Supplement.* "Warmth and generosity distinguish all the characters, who retain their doll-like qualities along with their human traits," concluded *School Library Journal* contributor Susan Cain.

Ainsworth sees writing as a pleasure, and claims to "write from a top layer of happiness. . . . If I live long enough to write stories for my great-grandchildren," she continues, "I suppose my characters will behave much as they have always done, building sandcastles, making houses, and meaning well, though this sometimes turns out badly. They experience the anguish of separation and disappointment, but there is usually a comforting, solid figure near at hand, an eternal Mrs. Golliwog. Children find magic in the everyday life of play and family. My sources spring from just that. Only children and birds 'Know the sweetness of cherries, / The goodness of bread.'"

BIOGRAPHICAL/CRITICAL SOURCES:

PERIODICALS

British Book News Children's Supplement, autumn, 1980, Frances Ball, review of *The Mysterious Baba and Her Magic Caravan: Two Stories,* p. 15.
Bulletin of the Center for Children's Books, March, 1971, review of *The Ruth Ainsworth Book,* p. 101; December, 1979.
Junior Bookshelf, April, 1977; December, 1979, review of *The Talking Rock,* pp. 321-322; October, 1980, review of *The Mysterious Baba and Her Magic Caravan,* p. 236.
Library Journal, September 15, 1974.
New Statesman, November 12, Catherine Storr, "Fantasy, Fakes, and Fact," p. 663.
Newsweek, November 9, 1979.
Saturday Review, May 27, 1978.
School Library Journal, April, 1971; October, 1978; January, 1980, Janice Giles, review of *The Talking Rock,* p. 64; September, 1980, Susan Cain, review of *The Mysterious Baba and Her Magic Caravan: Two Stories,* p. 55; December, 1980.
Times Literary Supplement, October 22, 1971, review of *The Phantom Cyclist, and Other Stories,* p. 1321; December 2, 1977; November 21, 1980.*

*　　*　　*

ALBERTSON, Susan
See WOJCIECHOWSKI, Susan

*　　*　　*

ALEXANDER, Martha G. 1920-

PERSONAL: Born May 25, 1920, in Augusta, GA; daughter of Guy S. Alexander (an attorney, accountant, and woodworker) and Lillie Mae Camp; married, 1943 (divorced, 1959); children: Kim, Allen. *Education:* Graduated from Cincinnati Academy of Fine Arts, 1939. *Avocational interests:* Gardening of all kinds, pottery, and woodworking.

ADDRESSES: Home—P.O Box 1624, Yelm, WA 98597.

CAREER: Writer and illustrator; Honolulu Academy of Arts, Honolulu, HI, art teacher, 1946-49; children's art teacher; freelance artist; frequent lecturer on creating books to groups of children, parents, teachers, and librarians.

AWARDS, HONORS: New York Times Book Review outstanding book, 1969, for *Blackboard Bear; School Library Journal* best book, 1970, for *Bobo's Dream;* Children's Spring Book Festival honor book, 1971, for *Sabrina;* Children's Book Council Children's Book Showcase title, 1972, for *Nobody Asked Me if I Wanted a Baby Sister;* Christopher Award, 1973, for *I'll Protect You from the Jungle Beasts.*

WRITINGS:

SELF-ILLUSTRATED

Maybe a Monster, Dial, 1968.
Out! Out! Out!, Dial, 1968.
Blackboard Bear (also see below), Dial, 1969.
The Story Grandmother Told, Dial, 1969.
We Never Get to Do Anything, Dial, 1970.
Bobo's Dream, Dial, 1970.
Sabrina, Dial, 1970.
Nobody Asked Me if I Wanted a Baby Sister, Dial, 1971.
And My Mean Old Mother Will Be Sorry, Blackboard Bear (also see below) Dial, 1972.
No Ducks in Our Bathtub, Dial, 1973.
I'll Protect You from the Jungle Beasts, Dial, 1973.
(Editor) *Poems and Prayers for the Very Young* (also see below) Random House, 1973.
I'll Be the Horse if You'll Play with Me (Junior Literary Guild selection), Dial, 1975.
I Sure Am Glad to See You, Blackboard Bear (also see below), Dial, 1976.
Pigs Say Oink: A First Book of Sounds, Random House, 1978.
When the New Baby Comes, I'm Moving Out, Dial, 1979, reprinted, Econo-Clad Books (Minneapolis, MN), 1999.
We're in Big Trouble, Blackboard Bear (also see below), Dial, 1980.
Four Bears in a Box (contains *Blackboard Bear; And My Mean Old Mother Will Be Sorry, Blackboard Bear; I Sure Am Glad to See You, Blackboard Bear;* and *We're in Big Trouble, Blackboard Bear*), Dial, 1981.

Marty McGee's Space Lab, No Girls Allowed, Dial, 1981.

Move over, Twerp, Dial, 1981.

Maggie's Moon, Dial, 1982.

How My Library Grew, by Dinah, H. W. Wilson, 1983.

Three Magic Flip Books (contains *The Magic Hat, The Magic Picture,* and *The Magic Box*; also see below), Dial, 1984.

(Collection) *Poems and Prayers for the Very Young* appears in *Santa's Take-Along Library: Five Favorite Read-to-Me Books,* Random House, 1985.

Even That Moose Won't Listen to Me, Dial, 1988.

My Outrageous Friend Charlie, Dial, 1989.

Where Does the Sky End, Grandpa?, Harcourt, 1992.

Lily and Willy, Candlewick Press, 1993.

Where's Willy?, Candlewick Press, 1993.

Willy's Boot, Candelwick Press, 1993.

Good Night, Lily, Candlewick Press, 1993.

The Magic Hat, Puffin Books, 1994.

The Magic Picture, Puffin Books, 1994.

The Magic Box, Puffin Books, 1994.

ILLUSTRATOR

Charlotte Zolotow, *Big Sister and Little Sister,* Harper, 1966.

Janice Udry, *Mary Ann's Mud Day,* Harper, 1967.

Lois Wyse, *Grandmothers Are to Love,* Parents', 1967.

Lois Wyse, *Grandfathers Are to Love,* Parents', 1967.

La Verne Johnson, *Night Noises,* Parents', 1968.

Lois Hobart, *What Is a Whispery Secret?,* Parents', 1968.

Doris Orgel, *Whose Turtle?,* World, 1968.

Lillie D. Chaffin, *I Have a Tree,* White, 1969.

Louis Untermeyer, *You,* Golden, 1969.

Liesel Moak Skorpen, *Elizabeth,* Harper, 1970.

Liesel Moak Skorpen, *Charles,* Harper, 1971.

Dorothy Frances Canfield Fisher, *Understood Betsy,* Holt, 1972, new edition with an afterword by Peggy Parish, Dell, 1987.

Joan M. Lexau, *Emily and the Klunky Baby and the Next Door Dog,* Dial, 1972.

Carol K. Scism, *The Wizard of Walnut Street,* Dial, 1973.

Jean Van Leeuwen, *Too Hot for Ice Cream,* Dial, 1974.

Liesel Moak Skorpen, *Mandy's Grandmother* (Junior Literary Guild selection), Dial, 1975.

Amy Ehrlich, *The Everyday Train,* Dial, 1977.

Barbara Williams, *Jeremy Isn't Hungry* (Junior Literary Guild selection), 1978.

Judy Malloy, *Bad Thad,* Dutton, 1980.

Contributor to reviews in *Atlantic.*

ADAPTATIONS: A set of four filmstrips with cassettes based on the "Blackboard Bear" series, (including *Blackboard Bear, And My Mean Old Mother Will Be Sorry, Blackboard Bear, I Sure Am Glad to See You, Blackboard Bear,* and *We're in Big Trouble, Blackboard Bear*) was produced by Spoken Arts, 1984.

SIDELIGHTS: Martha Alexander has been an artist since childhood, trying her hand at ceramics, doll-making, fabric design, clothing design, portrait painting, children's murals and paintings, decorative collages and mosaics, and teaching art to adults and children. Alexander says she did not find her niche in the art world until, at the age of forty-five, she was given her first children's book to illustrate. She knew then that her long search for the right medium of expression had been more than justified. "I felt for the first time that here it *was,*" Alexander stated in *Junior Literary Guild.* "It was as though I had searched all my life to find me—or home." As Alexander went on to produce an impressive selection of picture books, her unique ability to make pictures tell the story and her insightful outlook on children combined to win her popular and critical acclaim.

Alexander was born in Georgia, but her family moved to Ohio when she was nine. Besides being shy and insecure by nature, she was sensitive about her Southern accent and a heritage that included slave-owning. Her books would later reflect her first-hand knowledge of some of childhood's uncertainties. Alexander's interest in art and her teachers' encouragement about her drawing provided her with a solid foundation during her school years.

After graduating from high school, Alexander entered the Cincinnati Academy of Fine Arts. Despite her aspirations to be a portrait painter, she soon found herself drawn into the world of modern art and "art for art's sake" by teachers and fellow-students. Her husband, an artist she met and married while at the academy, also influenced her. "Being married to a serious painter who, I believed, felt a certain disdain for anything other than 'fine arts,'" Alexander once commented, "I found it hard to find my way to a world of my own." The couple moved to Hawaii where, as they raised their two children, Alexander taught art classes and began to sell her paintings, murals, and collages to architects and decorators.

In 1960, after her marriage dissolved, Alexander moved to New York with her two teenaged children and began illustrating for magazines on a freelance basis. She described this pivotal stage of her career to *CA:* "After working for about five years freelancing for magazines and a bit in advertising, I felt extremely discouraged and frustrated and I was having a hard time making ends meet. One day I took the day off and did a whole series of drawings of children doing nonsensical things. I had such fun. I put them aside and went back to the grind until several weeks later I came across the drawings and decided 'if I'm going to be poor, I'll be poor doing what I want to do.' I put them together in a little book and went to Harper and Row." At the large publishing company, Alexander was almost immediately given a book to illustrate. With several more books closely following the first, Alexander's career as a children's book illustrator was established.

Alexander's training in the fine arts was invaluable to her new medium. While in art school, she was influenced greatly by three artists—modern Swiss painter Paul Klee, fifteenth-century Italian artist Leonardo da Vinci, and twentieth-century French painter Marc Chagall. The beauty of these artists' works impressed her, but she was particularly intrigued by the playfulness of Chagall and Klee and their ability to say so much without words. Alexander remarked in an autobiographical sketch in *Books for Schools and Libraries:* "By viewing their work I discovered how complete stories can be told through images . . . it was interesting to see that pictures themselves can enhance a story in ways that words can not. Now I take great pride in telling as much of the story as I can without text, but rather through gestures and expressions."

As she illustrated books for other authors, Alexander came up with ideas for books of her own. She once commented, "As I was working on my first book at Harper, I began to get ideas for books and told them to my editors, although I had no thought of writing them. My editor suggested I write them and my response was 'But I'm not a writer!' She chuckled and said, 'How do you know if you don't try?' My first efforts were very frustrating." Alexander's first publication as author and illustrator, *Out! Out! Out!,* was a wordless picture book, revealing not only Alexander's belief that pictures can tell a story without words, but also her initial insecurity as a writer. Alexander once stated that after making many efforts to write her own stories, "it seemed quite hopeless . . . they sounded good in my head but not on paper." She resolved her frustrations as a writer by developing a system of creating books that did not require her to separate the functions of writing and illustrating. Starting with a "dummy"—a book made up of thirty-two bound blank pages—she wrote her story with words and pictures simultaneously. "I found that as I worked

on a dummy, words and pictures began to come together as one, and I was hardly aware of the difference between them," she explained.

Alexander's third self-illustrated publication, the popular *Blackboard Bear,* is about a little boy who, rebuffed by the big boys for being too young, goes home and draws a large bear on his blackboard. He then takes his blackboard bear by the leash and parades it in front of the older boys, who long to hold the leash or ride the bear. With his creation of the bear, the little boy has turned the tables; it is his turn to cooly rebuff the big boys. This flight of childhood fantasy is "satisfying poetic justice," a *Horn Book* reviewer observed, summarizing that Alexander "has already shown the ingenuity of her wordless storytelling through pictures in *Out! Out! Out!* Now she proves just as imaginative with the same kind of eloquent drawings accompanied by a minimum of words." The three sequels to *Blackboard Bear: And My Mean Old Mother Will Be Sorry, Blackboard Bear; I Sure Am Glad to See You, Blackboard Bear;* and *We're in Big Trouble, Blackboard Bear,* have been very popular among readers and critics.

Interaction with the children in her family has been a great source of inspiration for Alexander's books. The idea for *Blackboard Bear* arose on a visit with her four-year-old nephew. "I was utterly fascinated by this child," she explained. "He lived in the country and had never had any children to play with. He had a fantasy world that was unbelievable. I watched him race around playing cops and robbers, cowboys and Indians, elephants, lions, and other games. Whatever he was playing, he became that part. He told me wild tales of how he once fell into a huge pit and how his brave father rescued him. It was endless. Once he handed me a dozen baby kangaroos to keep for him." Alexander believes that the imaginary worlds children create are very real and important aspects of their lives. "Adults should encourage, explore and be interested in the fantasy world of the child," she stated in *Publishers Weekly.*

Two picture books, *Nobody Asked Me if I Wanted a Baby Sister* and *When the Baby Comes I'm Moving Out,* originated when Alexander's two-year-old granddaughter indirectly expressed feelings of sibling rivalry about her new baby sister by telling her mother that the baby wanted to live with her grandmother. After thinking about the unvoiced resentment and jealousy that might be behind the two-year-old's statement, Alexander decided to write a story in which an older brother actually gives his baby sister away. She hoped that by reading about the basic, but often unspoken, resentments of sibling rivalry, her young readers will understand they are not alone in these feelings and find appropriate ways to resolve them.

Childhood frustration and powerlessness are also themes of *Even That Moose Won't Listen to Me,* a book in which a young girl, Rebecca, tries to tell her family that a moose is eating their garden. Her family, assuming that the moose is a figment of Rebecca's imagination, ignores her warnings. The moose, also ignoring Rebecca, continues to munch on the garden until there is nothing left to munch. When the family finally discovers that their garden has indeed been destroyed and comes to Rebecca for details, she lets them know that she is too busy to discuss it with them. "This book is about small children having power," Alexander stated in *Publisher's Weekly.* "I remember what it felt like in my own childhood when no one would listen to me. Children are so often misunderstood, not believed."

Critics have applauded the acute identification with children exhibited in Alexander's expressive drawings and humorously human stories. The author and illustrator says that her understanding of the child's world has been inspired by her children, grandchildren, and great-grandchildren and also by her own memories of childhood. But beyond these influences, Alexander is inspired by her readers, as she stated in *Books for Schools and Libraries:* "I want to give something to the child reading my book. The payoff comes when I receive a letter from one of my young readers, and it's evident that I've reached him or her. This affords me the deepest satisfaction of all. You see, I was once the timid, shy, and very insecure child for whom I am writing now."

BIOGRAPHICAL/CRITICAL SOURCES:

BOOKS

Books for Schools and Libraries, 1985.

PERIODICALS

Bulletin of the Center for Children's Books, September, 1969; March, 1977; December, 1979; July-August, 1980; December, 1982; April, 1988.
Horn Book Magazine, August, 1969, Ethel L. Heins, review of *Blackboard Bear,* p. 395; February, 1976; December, 1978; February, 1983.

Junior Literary Guild, September, 1975; March, 1975; September, 1978.
Publishers Weekly, February 26, 1988, p. 117; April 5, 1993, review of *Where's Willy?,* p.74.*

*   *   *

APPIGNANESI, Lisa 1946-
(Jessica Ayre)

PERSONAL: Born January 4, 1946, in Lodz, Poland; British citizen; daughter of Aron (a businessman) and Hena (Lipszyc) Borenstein; married Richard Appignanesi (a writer), January 3, 1967 (divorced, 1982); partner of John Forrester; children: (first marriage) Joshua; (with Forrester) Katrina Max. *Education:* McGill University, B.A., 1966, M.A., 1967; Sussex University, D.Phil., 1970.

ADDRESSES: Agent—Caradoc King, A. P. Watt, 20 John St., London NC1N 2DR, England. *E-mail*—L. Appignanesi@btinternet.com.

CAREER: Novelist and broadcaster. Centre for Community Research, New York, NY, staff writer, 1970-71; University of Essex, Colchester, Essex, England, lecturer in literature, 1971-73; New England College, Sussex, England, lecturer in literature, 1973-80; Institute of Contemporary Arts, London, England, director of seminars, 1981-86, deputy director, 1986-90; independent television producer of programs for Channel 4, British Broadcasting Corp., and French television, 1986—; full-time writer and lecturer, 1990—. Writers and Readers Publishing Cooperative, founding member and editorial director, 1975-81; Open University, visiting research fellow in brain and behavior laboratory, 2001.

MEMBER: PEN (member, writers in prison committee), Council of the Institute of Contemporary Arts.

AWARDS, HONORS: Losing the Dead was shortlisted for the Charles Taylor Literary Nonfiction Prize and the Wingate Literary Prize; Chevalier de l'Order des arts et des lettres, French Government.

WRITINGS:

(With Douglas and Monica Holmes) *Language of Trust,* Science House, 1972.
Femininity and the Creative Imagination: A Study of Henry James, Robert Musil, and Marcel Proust (criticism), Barnes & Noble (New York, NY), 1973.

The Cabaret (nonfiction), Studio Vista (London, England), 1975, Universe Books, 1976.

Simone de Beauvoir, Viking (New York, NY), 1988.

(With John Forrester) *Freud's Women,* Basic Books (New York, NY), 1992, new edition, Penguin (New York, NY), 2000.

Memory and Desire (novel), HarperCollins (London, England), 1991, Dutton (New York, NY), 1992.

Dreams of Innocence, HarperCollins (London, England), 1994, Dutton (New York, NY), 1995.

A Good Woman, HarperCollins (London, England), 1996, McArthur, 1999.

The Things We Do for Love, HarperCollins (London, England), 1997.

The Dead of Winter (novel), Bantam (London, England), 1998, McArthur, 1999.

Losing the Dead (memoir), McArthur, 1999.

Sanctuary (novel), Bantam (London, England), 1999, McArthur, 2000.

Paris Requiem, Bantam (London, England), 2001.

Contributor of articles and reviews to newspapers and magazines, including *Independent.* Regular contributor to television and radio programs, including *The Case of Sigmund Freud,* BBC-Radio 4, 2000. Works have been translated into various languages, including German, French, and Dutch.

UNDER PSEUDONYM JESSICA AYRE

Not to Be Trusted, Mills & Boon (London, England), 1981.

One-Man Woman, Mills & Boon (London, England), 1982.

Hard to Handle, Mills & Boon (London, England), 1983.

New Discovery, Mills & Boon (London, England), 1984.

EDITOR

Brand New York, Quartet Books (London, England), 1982.

(With Steven Rose) *Science and Beyond,* Basil Blackwell (Oxford, England), 1986.

(With Hilary Lawson) *Dismantling Truth: Reality in the Postmodern World,* St. Martin's Press (New York, NY), 1989.

Ideas from France: The Legacy of French Theory, Free Association Books (London, England), 1989.

Postmodernism: I.C.A. Documents, Institute of Contemporary Arts (London, England), 1986, new edition, Free Association Books (London, England), 1989.

(With Sara Maitland) *The Rushdie File,* Fourth Estate (London, England), 1989, Syracuse University Press (Syracuse, NY), 1990.

Editor of "ICA Documents" series for Institute of Contemporary Arts, 1985-88.

WORK IN PROGRESS: Kicking Fifty, a comic novel; a project on memory, with Steven Rose.

SIDELIGHTS: Lisa Appignanesi has written and edited books on a variety of subjects, including feminism, art history, and biography. She and Sara Maitland co-edited *The Rushdie File,* which was praised by *New York Times Book Review* contributor Edward Mortimer as "a very valuable sourcebook of documents" pertaining to author Salman Rushdie, who was condemned to death by the Ayatollah Khomeini after the publication of Rushdie's allegedly anti-Islamic novel *The Satanic Verses. The Rushdie File* provides a chronology of events pertaining to the book's publication and the uproar that followed; it also reprints reviews of the book, interviews with the author, samples of international reactions to Khomeini's death threat, and other related material.

Freud's Women, written in collaboration with John Forrester, examines Sigmund Freud's personal relationships with women and his theories on female psychology. Commenting in *Women's Review of Books,* Sheila Bienenfeld described *Freud's Women* as "detailed, scholarly and gracefully written." The authors address the oft-leveled charge that Freud was a misogynist who viewed women as nothing more than incomplete males. Appignanesi and Forrester argue that while some of the psychoanalyst's ideas about female sexuality may have been eccentric and old-fashioned, his relationships with women—particularly his mother, wife, daughter, and female patients and proteges—were, in Bienenfeld's words, "generally warm and long-lasting, free of the bitterness and acrimony that ended many of his friendships with men."

Appignanesi and Forrester further argue in *Freud's Women* that many of the best and brightest women of Freud's era subscribed to his theories, and that Freud routinely treated his female patients and students with all the respect he accorded their male counterparts. Bienenfeld summarized: "Wonderfully written throughout, [*Freud's Women*] is really two books in one: an intriguing collection of brief biographies of women . . . and also an intellectual history and close reading of the 'women's issue' as it has developed in psychoanalysis." Richard Wollheim, contributor to the *New York Times Book Review,* also found great merit in *Freud's Women,* calling it "a marvelously rich and engrossing work of intellectual history, deftly composed around the ambiguity in its title. Freud's women are in part the real women in his life and in part woman in the abstract, whose psychology he tried to reconstruct, never wholly to his satisfaction. The originality of this book lies in the many connections it traces between the two. . . . It is a relief to find two authors who are strong and free enough to recognize Freud's genius without falling into idolatry, and who can narrate its story in a fine cadenced prose."

Having established a solid reputation as an author of scholarly works, Appignanesi crossed into fiction with the 1992 novel *Memory and Desire.* Jennifer Selway, reviewer for the London *Observer,* called *Memory and Desire* "a thinking woman's block buster romance." Set in glamorous locations around Europe and in Manhattan, the multigenerational saga follows aristocrats and intellectuals through numerous adventures. A *Publishers Weekly* review noted Appignanesi's wide-ranging and diverse background in art, literature, and history and called *Memory and Desire* an "enjoyable if not particularly memorable read."

Appignanesi told *CA:* "Since [*Memory and Desire*] I have written six novels, several of them bestsellers in the United Kingdom and Canada. My fiction plays with genre, in the early books the saga and the romance, more recently the thriller, to explore deeper shades of characters and psychology, [such as in *The Dead of Winter* and *Sanctuary.*] My memoir of my parents' lives in Poland during World War II and the legacy of this experience across the generations, *Losing the Dead,* won high praise and was shortlisted for the Charles Taylor Literary Nonfiction Prize and the Wingate Literary Prize, as well as appearing on various book choices of the year."

BIOGRAPHICAL/CRITICAL SOURCES:

BOOKS

Twentieth-Century Romance and Historical Writers, third edition, St. James Press (Detroit, MI), 1994.

PERIODICALS

Choice, February, 1993, pp. 923-931.
Independent, April 2, 2000.

Guardian (London, England), April 15, 2000.
Kirkus Reviews, November 15, 1991, p. 1416.
Library Journal, April 1, 195, p. 122.
Library Quarterly, October, 1991, pp. 429-443.
London Review of Books, December 3, 1992, p. 17.
New Republic, October 8, 1990, pp. 31-39.
New Statesman & Society, May 26, 1989, p. 38.
New Yorker, February 8, 1993, p. 113.
New York Times Book Review, April 28, 1985; July 22, 1990, p. 3; January 24, 1993, p. 21; June 25, 1995, p. 20.
Observer (London, England), July 14, 1991, p. 63; December 12, 1993, pp. 22.
Publishers Weekly, January 6, 1992, p. 49; April 3, 1995, pp. 44-45.
Southern Humanities Review, fall, 1995, pp. 374-377.
Times Literary Supplement, July 19, 1991, p. 20; December 4, 1992, p. 11; December 18, 1992, p. 20; February 16, 1996, p. 24.
Women's Review of Books, April, 1993, pp. 21-22.

*   *   *

APPLETON, Lawrence
See LOVECRAFT, H(oward) P(hillips)

*   *   *

ARENAS, Reinaldo 1943-1990

PERSONAL: Born July 16, 1943, in Holguin, Cuba; immigrated to the United States, 1980; died of an apparent overdose of drugs and alcohol, December 7, 1990, in New York, NY; son of Antonio and Oneida (Fuentes) Arenas. *Education:* Attended Universidad de la Habana, 1966-68, and Columbia University.

CAREER: Writer. Jose Marti National Library, Havana, Cuba, researcher, 1963-68; Instituto Cubano del Libro (Cuban Book Institute), Havana, Cuba, editor, 1967-68; *La Gaceta de Cuba* (official Cuban monthly literary magazine), Havana, Cuba, journalist and editor, 1968-74; imprisoned by the Castro government, c. 1974-76, served time in State Security Prison, 1974, El Murro (prison), Havana, Cuba, 1974, and Reparto Flores (rehabilitation camp), 1976; visiting professor of Cuban literature at International University of Florida, 1981, Center for Inter-American Relations, 1982, and Cornell University, 1985; guest lecturer at Princeton University, Georgetown University, Washington University (St. Louis), Stockholms Universitet, Cornell University, and universities of Kansas, Miami, and Puerto Rico.

Reinaldo Arenas

MEMBER: Center for Inter-American Relations.

AWARDS, HONORS: First mention in Cirilo Villaverde contest for best novel from the Cuban Writers' Union, 1965, for *Celestino antes del alba;* French Prix Medici in 1969 for best foreign novel, for *Celestino antes del alba;* named best novelist published in France by *Le Monde,* 1969, for *El mundo alucinante;* fellow of the Cintas Foundation, 1980; fellow of the John Simon Guggenheim Memorial Foundation, 1982, and Wilson Center Foundation, 1988.

WRITINGS:

Celestino antes del alba (novel), Union de Escritores, 1967, translation by Andrew Hurley published as *Singing from the Well,* Viking (New York, NY), 1987.
El mundo alucinante (novel), Diogenes, 1969, translation by Gordon Brotherston published as *Hallucinations: Being an Account of the Life and Adventures of Friar Servando Teresa de Mier,* Harper

(New York, NY), 1971, new translation by Andrew Hurley published as *The Ill-Fated Peregrinations of Fray Servando,* Avon (New York, NY), 1987.
Con los ojos cerrados (short stories), Arca, 1972.
El palacio de las blanquisimas mofetas (novel), [France], 1975.
La Vieja Rosa (novel), Libreria Cruz del Sur, 1980, translation by Andrew Hurley, Grove (New York, NY), 1989.
Termina el desfile (short stories), Seix Barral, 1981.
El Central (poetry), Seix Barral, 1981, translation by Anthony Kerrigan published as *El Central: A Cuban Sugar Mill,* Avon (New York, NY), 1984.
Otra vez el mar (novel), Argos, 1982, translation by Andrew Hurley published as *Farewell to the Sea,* Viking (New York, NY), 1986.
Arturo, la estrella mas brillante, Montesinos, 1984, translation published by Grove (New York, NY), 1989.
Necesida de libertad (essays), Kosmos, 1985.
Persecucion: Cinco piezas de teatro experimental (plays), Ediciones, 1986.
La loma del angel (novel), translation by Alfred MacAdam published as *Graveyard of the Angels,* Avon (New York, NY), 1987.
El portero (novel), Presses de la Renaissensce, 1988, translation published as *The Doorman,* 1991.
El asalto (novel), 1990, translation by Andrew Hurley published as *The Assault,* Viking (New York, NY), 1994.
El color del verano (novel), Ediciones Universal, 1991, translation by Andrew Hurley published as *The Color of Summer; or, The New Garden of Earthly Delights,* Viking (New York, NY), 2000.
Antes que anochezca (autobiography), 1992, translation by Dolores Koch published as *Before Night Falls: A Memoir,* Viking (New York, NY), 1993.

Contributor of articles and short stories to numerous periodicals, including *El Universal* and *Miami Herald.* Editorial advisor to *Mariel Magazine, Noticias de arte, Unveiling Cuba, Caribbean Review,* and *Linden Lane Magazine.* Author's works have been translated into various languages, including English, French, Dutch, German, Italian, Japanese, Portuguese, and Turkish.

SIDELIGHTS: Internationally acclaimed writer Reinaldo Arenas was one of more than 140,000 Cuban citizens who left their Latin American homeland for the United States in 1980 during a mass exodus known as the Mariel boat lift. Cuban president Fidel Castro exported to the Florida coast certain natives of Cuba, including common criminals, artists, members of the literati, and other perceived adversaries of the state, in an effort to squelch opposition to his Communist regime. In an interview with F. O. Geisbut for *Encounter,* Arenas explained that, as a writer and a homosexual, he was considered "an enemy of the revolution," guilty of a twofold crime against his country. The author was imprisoned by the Castro government, he further explained to Geisbut, for his alleged display of disrespect "for the rules of the official literature [and] of conventional morality." Arenas reached the U.S. mainland on May 5, 1980, with nothing but pajamas and a spare shirt. His manuscripts were confiscated by the Cuban government before he left the island.

As a teenager Arenas had joined the resistance movement against the regime of Fulgencio Batista y Zaldivar, then president of Cuba. The author explained in the *Encounter* interview that the Cuban people wanted to topple Batista's totalitarian government and thus fought "against the tyrant in power rather than for Fidel Castro," the young revolutionary leader who had led an unsuccessful revolt against the president in 1953. By 1959 Batista had fled Cuba, and, within two years, Castro established a Communist state there, replacing the previous Batista dictatorship with his own brand of totalitarianism. It was in an atmosphere of fierce social and political scrutiny that Arenas composed his first novel, *Celestino antes del alba,* in the mid-1960s.

Translated in 1987 as *Singing from the Well,* the book is an evocation of the fantastic visions experienced by a mentally impaired boy growing up in Cuba's rural poverty. Illegitimate and raised in the turbulent environment created by his cruel grandparents, the child has trouble distinguishing fantasy from reality and imagines, among other things, that he can fly to the safety of the clouds when threatened by his axe-wielding grandfather. The boy finds consolation through his relationship with his cousin (or alter ego), a poet named Celestino who carves verses on trees. While several critics reported difficulty differentiating between dream sequences and periods of realism in the book, most regarded *Singing from the Well* as a novel of hope and an exceptional literary debut for Arenas. One *Times Literary Supplement* reviewer commented, "There is . . . a great deal of social significance in the child's pathetic longing for affection in so unsympathetic an environment." Commenting on his first novel in an interview with Ana Roca for *Americas,* Arenas referred to the story as "the revolt of a poet who wants to create in a completely violent medium."

Arenas's second novel, *El mundo alucinante,* also blends the fantastic with the real, this time in the form of a fictionalized biography. Translated in 1971 as *Hal-*

lucinations: Being an Account of the Life and Adventures of Friar Servando Teresa de Mier, the book chronicles the life of nineteenth-century Mexican monk and adventurer, Fray Servando Teresa de Mier, who suffered torture and persecution in his fight for Mexico's independence from Spain. Imprisoned for suggesting that Mexico was a Christian country prior to the arrival of the Spanish, Servando is sentenced to a lifelong quarantine in Spain. He manages an unbelievable series of escapes from his captors, only to fight in an ultimately doomed revolution. "Servando's real crime," theorized Alan Schwartz in *Washington Post Book World,* "is his refusal to be demoralized in a world completely jaded and dedicated to the exploitation of power and wealth."

Arenas defended *Hallucinations* against claims by several critics that the surrealistic rendering of Servando's exploits should have more closely approximated the monk's actual adventures. "True realism," the author told Roca, "is fantasy, the fantastic, the eclectic. It knows no bounds." Arenas further maintained that the depiction of Servando he envisioned could only be accomplished by weaving historical fact with fantasy: "My aim was to portray this compelling personality as a part of the American myth, the New World myth . . . part raving madman and part sublime, a hero, an adventurer, and a perennial exile." Schwartz felt that any flaws in Arenas's "ambitious technique" were "overshadowed by [the author's] madcap inventiveness, the acid satire, and the powerful writing."

The antirevolutionary implications of *Hallucinations* led to the banning of the book in Cuba by the Castro government. "What emerges [from the novel]," asserted a *Times Literary Supplement* reviewer, "is at least as much a disenchanted view of Man himself as of revolution in the abstract." Servando finds that the movement for Mexican independence meets with only token victory. By the end of the book, the ghosts of the old regime greet the new revolutionary leaders with a haunting, "We welcome you." Arenas implies that, as in Cuba, the new regime in Mexico will only perpetuate an unjust order. Yet in spite of the apparent bleakness of its vision, the *Times Literary Supplement* reviewer allowed, "The narrative . . . is an accomplished and bizarrely entertaining piece of work."

The manuscript of Arenas's 1982 novel, *Otra vez el mar,* translated as *Farewell to the Sea,* was twice confiscated by the Cuban authorities. After being arrested in 1974 for his supposed social deviancy, the author spent time in a reeducation camp; following unsuccessful attempts to reconstruct the novel's plot while in jail,

Arenas finally rewrote the book for the third time soon after reaching the United States in 1980. In the *Encounter* interview Arenas described *Farewell to the Sea* as a depiction of "the secret history of the Cuban people."

Set on a beach resort just outside of Havana, the novel describes Cuba's tumultuous political events, and the impact those events had on the nation's citizenry. Hector and his unnamed wife reflect on their lives, hopes, and disappointments since the fall of the Batista government. The first portion of the book is a lengthy interior monologue in which the woman expresses her feelings of emptiness and her desire for, as well as distance from, her husband. Speaking of life under Castro as well as life in a passionless marriage, she muses, "The terrible becomes merely monotonous." Hector's thoughts are documented in the second section through a long sequence of dreamlike poetry revealing his outrage over Cuba's failed revolution and his own homosexual longings. After engaging in a sexual encounter with a boy from a nearby beach cottage, Hector hurls seething invectives at his young lover: "You will live your whole life pleading, begging pardon of the whole world for a crime you haven't committed, and doesn't even exist. . . . You will be the world's shame." Hector's verbal abuse leads to the boy's suicide.

While several critics were disappointed by what Michael Wood, writing in the *New York Review of Books,* termed an overly "obsessive and . . . prolix" anticommunist demeanor in the book, virtually every critic acknowledged the power and beauty of Arenas's words. In an article for *Saturday Review,* Anthony DeCurtis called *Farewell to the Sea* "a stunning literary tour-de-force." And Jay Cantor stated in the *New York Times Book Review,* "Mr. Arenas is not interested in ordinary realistic drama. He wants to give the reader the secret history of . . . emotions, the sustaining victories of pleasure and the small dishonesties that callous the soul."

El color del verano—translated as *The Color of Summer; or, The New Garden of Earthly Delights*—is the phantasmagorical story of a Caribbean dictator celebrating fifty years in power by resurrecting his dead enemies so that they may pay homage to him before he kills them again. When he resurrects a famous woman poet, she refuses to participate in the pro-government farce and makes a run for the Florida coast. Told by a huge cast of real and imaginary characters, each of whom has multiple names, *The Color of Summer* is a "verbal whirlpool, spinning out stories, prayers, lists, tongue twisters, letters, taxonomies, lectures, vignettes, aphorisms, dreams, confessions, diatribes, and farces,"

as Lee Siegel wrote in the *New York Times Book Review.* Brad Hooper in *Booklist* explained that "this character-rich novel wraps its social and political criticism in an absurdly hilarious skin." In addition to being a biting attack on the Cuban regime's authoritarianism, its imprisonment of gays, and its suppression of liberty, the novel is also, as Sophia McLennan noted in the *Review of Contemporary Fiction,* a novel of "emotional intensity. . . . Fantastic humor is combined artfully with a profound sense of sadness, loss, and suffering." Jack Shreve of *Library Journal* called the book "magnificent," and "hilarious and savagely sarcastic." "The book is a pained affirmation of the uncanny pleasure of maintaining hope when all is profoundly hopeless," concluded Siegel.

Having emerged from a totalitarian milieu that he described in *Encounter* as one holding that "there's nothing more dangerous than new ideas," Arenas continues to garner worldwide attention and praise as an eminent writer who—in the tradition of fantastic Latin American fiction—depicts the reality of life in contemporary Cuba. Commenting in the Toronto *Globe and Mail* on the effect of the author's writings, Alberto Manguel observed, "Reinaldo Arenas' Cuba is a dreamworld of repeatedly frustrated passions." The critic further theorized that the writer's works have turned Castro into a "literary creation," rendering the dictator "immortal" and "condemn[ing him] to repeat [his] sins for an eternity of readers."

Arenas once told *CA*: "Being an isolated child growing up on a farm very far from people and civilization and under very poor conditions was an important motivating factor in my becoming a writer. In my books I try to communicate my happiness and my unhappiness, my solitude and my hope.

"Since the publication of my novel *El mundo alucinante* in Mexico in 1969, all of my writings have been prohibited in Cuba. In spite of Marxist censorship, however, I managed to keep on writing and was able to send four other novels out of Cuba. Though many of my works have been published all over the world and translated into French, English, Dutch, German, Italian, Japanese, Portuguese, and Turkish, I have not been able to receive any royalties, because Cuba does not have a copyright law." At the time of his death, Arenas had several works under contract for publication, including the novel *Journey to Havana.*

BIOGRAPHICAL/CRITICAL SOURCES:

BOOKS

Bejar, Edurdo, *La textualidad de Reinaldo Arenas,* [Madrid, Spain], 1988.

Contemporary Literary Criticism, Volume 41, Gale (Detroit, MI), 1987.

Nazario, Felix Lugo, *La Alucinacion y los recursos literarios en las novelas de Reinaldo Arenas,* Ediciones Universal Libreria & Dist., 1995.

Paulson, Michael G., *The Youth and the Beach: A Comparative Study of Thomas Mann's Der Tod in Venedig (Death in Venice) and Reinaldo Arenas's Otra vez el mar (Farewell to the Sea),* Ediciones Universal (Miami, FL), 1993.

Rozencvaig, Perla, *The Work of Reinaldo Arenas,* [Mexico], 1986.

Soto, Francisco, *Reinaldo Arenas: The Pentaonia,* University Press of Florida, 1994.

Soto, Francisco, *Reinaldo Arenas,* Twayne (Boston, MA), 1998.

PERIODICALS

Americas, September, 1981; January-February, 1982.

Booklist, June 1, 2000, Brad Hooper, review of *The Color of Summer; or, The New Garden of Earthly Delights,* p. 1807.

Chicago Tribune, January 26, 1986.

Chicago Tribune Book World, September 5, 1971.

Encounter, January, 1982, F. O. Geisbut, interview with Reinaldo Arenas.

Globe and Mail (Toronto), June 21, 1986.

Hispanic Review 53, autumn, 1985.

Library Journal, July, 2000, Jack Shreve, review of *The Color of Summer,* p. 136.

Listener, April 22, 1971.

New York Review of Books, March 27, 1986, Michael Wood, review of *Farewell to the Sea;* March 7, 1991; November 18, 1993.

New York Times Book Review, August 29, 1971; November 24, 1985, Jay Cantor, review of *Farewell to the Sea;* January 20, 1991; October 24, 1993; October 15, 2000, Lee Siegel, "A Disappearing Novel."

Publishers Weekly, May 22, 2000, review of *The Color of Summer,* p. 72.

Review of Contemporary Fiction, spring, 2001, Sophia McLennan, review of *The Color of Summer,* p. 186.

San Francisco Review of Books, May-June, 1985.

Saturday Review, November-December, 1985, Anthony DeCurtis, review of *Farewell to the Sea.*

Times Literary Supplement, April 30, 1970; May 7, 1971; May 30, 1986, review of *Singing from the Well.*

Washington Post Book World, September 5, 1971, Alan Schwartz, review of *Hallucinations: Being an Account of the Life and Adventures of Friar Servando Teresa de Mier.**

ASHER, R. E. 1926-

PERSONAL: Born July 23, 1926, in Gringley-on-the-Hill, Nottinghamshire, England; son of Ernest and Doris (Hurst) Asher; married, wife's name: Chin, 1960; children: David, Michael. *Education:* University of London, B.A., 1950, Ph.D., 1955; University of Edinburgh, D.Litt., 1992. *Religion:* Christian.

ADDRESSES: Home—Edinburgh, Scotland. *Office*—Department of Theoretical and Applied Linguistics, University of Edinburgh, Edinburgh EH8 9LL, Scotland. *E-mail*—rea@holyrood.ed.ac.uk.

CAREER: University of London, London School of Oriental and African Studies, London, England, assistant lecturer, 1953-56, lecturer in linguistics, 1956-67, lecturer in Tamil, 1957-65; University of Edinburgh, Edinburgh, Scotland, senior lecturer, 1965-70, reader, 1970-77, professor of linguistics, 1977-93, professor emeritus, 1993—, head of department, 1976-80, 1983-86, associate dean, Faculty of Arts, 1985-86, dean, 1986-89, associate director of Centre for Speech Technology Research, 1984-93, director, 1994, member of University Court, 1989-92, vice principal, 1990-93, curator of patronage, 1991-93. University of Chicago, visiting assistant professor, 1961-62; University of Illinois at Urbana-Champaign, visiting professor, 1967; Michigan State University, visiting professor, 1968; University of Minnesota—Twin Cities, visiting professor, 1969; College de France, *chaire des professeurs etrangers,* 1970; Tamil University, Subrahmaniya Bharati fellow, 1984; International Christian University, Tokyo, visiting professor, 1994-95; Mahatma Gandhi University, Vaikom Muhammad Basheer Chair, 1995-96; Tamil Sahitya Academy, Chennai, India, member of general council, 2000—.

MEMBER: International Association of Tamil Research (president, 1983-87, 1987-90), Linguistics Association of Great Britain, Philological Society (member of council, 1980-86, 1989-94, 1996-2000), Royal Asiatic Society (fellow), Dravidian Linguistics Association, Linguistic Society of India, Kerala Academy of Letters (fellow), Royal Society of Edinburgh (fellow).

AWARDS, HONORS: Gold Medal from Kerala Academy of Letters, 1983, for services to Malayalam language and literature.

WRITINGS:

(With R. Radhakrishnan) *A Tamil Prose Reader: Selections from Contemporary Tamil Prose, with Notes and Glossary,* Cambridge University Press (Cambridge, England), 1971.

Some Landmarks in the History of Tamil Prose, University of Madras (Madras, India), 1973.

(Translator from Malayalam) Thakazhi Sivasankara Pillai, *Scavenger's Son* (novel), [New Delhi, India], 1975, revised translation, Heinemann (Oxford, England), 1993.

(Translator from Malayalam, with Achamma Coilparampil) Vaikom Muhammad Basheer, *"Me Grandad 'ad an Elephant!" Three Stories of Muslim Life in South India,* Edinburgh University Press (Edinburgh, Scotland), 1980.

(Editor, with Eugenie A. J. Henderson) *Towards a History of Phonetics,* Edinburgh University Press (Edinburgh, Scotland), 1981.

Tamil, North-Holland (Amsterdam, Netherlands), 1982.

Malayala Bhasa-Sahitya Pathanangal (title means "Linguistic and Literary Studies"), D.C. Books (Kottayam, India), 1989.

National Myths in Renaissance France: Francus, Samothes, and the Druids, Edinburgh University Press (Edinburgh, Scotland), 1993.

(Editor, with Christopher Moseley) *Atlas of the World's Languages,* Routledge & Kegan Paul (New York, NY), 1994.

(Editor-in-chief) *The Encyclopedia of Language and Linguistics,* ten volumes, Pergamon (New York, NY), 1994.

(Editor, with E. F. Konrad Koerner) *Concise History of the Language Sciences: From the Sumerians to the Cognitivists,* Pergamon (Oxford, England), 1995.

Malayalam, Routledge & Kegan Paul (London, England), 1996.

Vaikom Muhammad Basheer (in Malayan), D.C. Books (Kottayam, India), 1999.

(Editor) Vaikom Muhammad Basheer, *Svatantryasamara kathakal* (title means "Stories of the Freedom Movement"), D.C. Books (Kottayam, India), 1999.

Several of Asher's books have been translated into Japanese.

SIDELIGHTS: R. E. Asher told *CA:* "Like most writers, I write because I am inwardly impelled to write. If I had the right sort of creative talent, I should doubtless have emulated my literary heroes and become a novelist, poet, or playwright. Instead I do what I can to make some of the things that fill me with enthusiasm more widely known and appreciated. Among the topics that have fascinated me sufficiently for me to write about them are the Renaissance of art and letters in sixteenth-century France and the development of historical writing in that period, the nature of language and language use, the structure of the languages of the Dravidian family, and the development of the novel and short story in Malayalam, an important member of this family."

*   *   *

AYRE, Jessica
   See APPIGNANESI, Lisa

B

BALLANTINE, David 1926-

PERSONAL: Born May 11, 1926, in Rochester, NY; son of Edward James (an actor) and Stella (Commins) Ballantine; separated; children: Lucy. *Education:* Attended Columbia University, 1947-51. *Politics:* None. *Religion:* None.

ADDRESSES: Home—P.O. Box 67, Bearsville, NY 12409.

CAREER: Armscraft House (mail-order gun business), West Hurley, NY, owner and manager, 1954-68; construction worker, 1969-77; freelance writer and book editor, 1977—. Gulf Coast shrimp fisherman, 1969—. Voting machine custodian of town of Woodstock, NY, 1977—. *Military service:* U.S. Army, 1944-46.

WRITINGS:

Lobo (novel), Ballantine (New York, NY), 1972.
(With Robert Haney) *Woodstock Handmade Houses,* photography by Jonathan Elliott, Ballantine (New York, NY), 1974.
(With Sylvia Weinberg) *The Book of Our House,* Overlook Press (Woodstock, NY), 1986.
Chalk's Woman (novel), Forge (New York, NY), 2000.

Editor of Bantam's "War Book" Series.

SIDELIGHTS: David Ballantine's novel *Chalk's Woman* tells the story of Ann Baxter, a sixteen-year-old girl who is orphaned and maimed during the battle of Vicks-

burg in 1863. Five years after her arm is amputated following a cannon volley that kills the rest of her family and destroys their home, Ann strikes out to establish a new life for herself on the western frontier. Although Ann is traveling under the protection of adoptive parents, they are mean-spirited people who ruthlessly exploit her. When she meets Jim, a fourteen-year-old orphan struggling to move his three younger siblings west, she teams up with him, and they form a makeshift family unit. After settling in Kansas, Ann meets Chalk, a hardworking, hard-drinking cowboy. Impressed by her courage, Chalk falls in love with Ann, and she gives birth to their child on the day he is arrested for shooting a notorious outlaw. Eventually he is given reward money for this act, and the whole group sets out to pan for gold in California.

Several reviewers praised *Chalk's Woman* for its interesting depiction of life in the late nineteenth century. A *Publishers Weekly* writer criticized the book for its "choppy prose and static characters who talk in platitudes," yet Harriet Klausner of *Whitestone Books* stated that "the engaging story line works because of the depth each important character contains, which allows the audience to feel what the prime cast feels." Klausner called *Chalk's Woman* "a powerful debut novel." Margaret Flanagan in *Booklist* described it as "a somber testament to the triumph of the pioneer spirit," and a *Kirkus Reviews* contributor termed it "a lively if not especially original debut about a gritty young frontierswoman," one "full of the sort of Old West derring-do that made A. B. Guthrie's *The Big Sky* so enthralling."

Ballantine once told *CA:* "Most of my thrust as a writer is in the direction of my own brand of pacifism. *Lobo* is a novel opposed to war. It is perhaps the only western novel in which no one gets killed." Although it cannot be said that no one dies in *Chalk's Woman,* Ballantine does explore related themes in his Reconstruction-era novel, a pioneer story set in the aftermath of the Civil War.

BIOGRAPHICAL/CRITICAL SOURCES:

PERIODICALS

Booklist, December 15, 2000, Margaret Flanagan, review of *Chalk's Woman,* p. 784.
Kirkus Reviews, October 1, 2000, review of *Chalk's Woman,* p. 1372.
Publishers Weekly, November 27, 2000, review of *Chalk's Woman,* p. 55.
Southern Living, November, 1987, review of *The Book of Our House,* p. 197.

OTHER

Whitestone Books, http://www.whitestone.com/ (February 17, 2001), Harriet Klausner, review of *Chalk's Woman.**

*   *   *

BANKS, Iain
   See BANKS, Iain M(enzies)

*   *   *

BANKS, Iain M(enzies) 1954-
   (Iain Banks)

PERSONAL: Born February 16, 1954, in Fife, Scotland; son of Thomas Menzies (an admiralty officer) and Euphemia (an ice skating instructor; maiden name, Thomson) Banks. *Education:* University of Stirling, B.A., 1975. *Politics:* Socialist. *Religion:* Atheist. *Avocational interests:* "Hillwalking, eating and drinking, and talking to friends."

ADDRESSES: Home—31 South Bridge, Flat 3, Edinburgh EH1 1LL, Scotland. *Agent*—c/o Macmillan Publishers Ltd., 4 Little Essex St., London WC2R 3LF, England.

CAREER: Writer. Nondestructive testing technician in Glasgow, Scotland, 1977; International Business Machines Corp. (IBM), Greenock, Scotland, expediter-analyzer, 1978; solicitor's clerk in London, England, 1980-84.

Iain M. Banks

MEMBER: Amnesty International, Campaign for Nuclear Disarmament.

WRITINGS:

UNDER NAME IAIN BANKS

The Wasp Factory, Houghton Mifflin (Boston, MA), 1984.
Walking on Glass, Macmillan (London, England), 1985, Houghton Mifflin (Boston, MA), 1986.
The Bridge, Macmillan (London, England), 1986.
Espedair Street, Macmillan (London, England), 1987.
Canal Dreams, Doubleday (New York, NY), 1991.
Complicity, Doubleday (New York, NY), 1995.
Whit, or Isis amongst the Unsaved, Little, Brown (London, England), 1995.
The Crow Road, Little, Brown (London, England), 1996.
A Song of Stone, Villard (New York, NY), 1998.
The Business: A Novel, Little, Brown (London, England), 1999.
Inversions, Orbit (London, England), 1998, Pocket Books (New York, NY), 2000.

SCIENCE FICTION; UNDER NAME IAIN M. BANKS

Consider Phlebas, St. Martin's Press (New York, NY), 1987.

The Player of Games, St. Martin's Press (New York, NY), 1989.

The State of the Art, M.V. Ziesing (Willimantic, CT), 1989.

Use of Weapons, Bantam (New York, NY), 1992.

Against a Dark Background, Spectra, 1993.

Feersum Endjinn, Bantam (New York, NY), 1995.

Excession, Orbit (London, England), 1996, Bantam (New York, NY), 1997.

Look to Windward, Orbit (London, England), 2000, Pocket Books (New York, NY), 2001.

SIDELIGHTS: Scottish novelist Iain M. Banks has sparked considerable controversy in British and American literary circles with his unique and highly imaginative brand of fiction. While the author is credited with crossing and redefining the boundaries of the thriller, fantasy, and science-fiction genres, he is probably best known for his macabre tales of horror, which have been compared by reviewers to the psychologically probing fiction of Franz Kafka and Edgar Allan Poe. Although Banks's books have received widely mixed reviews, many critics have conceded that the writer possesses a distinctive talent for structuring bold and compelling stories.

Banks was born in 1954 in Fife, Scotland, the son of an admiralty officer. He studied at Stirling University, and served as an extra in a battle scene for *Monty Python and the Holy Grail,* then filming nearby. He spent much of 1975 hitchhiking throughout Europe and North Africa, and then settled in London, where he worked as a "costing clerk" at a law firm. In a biography published on the *Iain Banks Web site,* the author explained that this job involved "drawing up narratives for enormous legal bills—arguably a good grounding in fiction writing."

Banks first captured the attention of critics in 1984 with his highly acclaimed novel, *The Wasp Factory.* A bizarre tale of murder and perversity, *The Wasp Factory* centers on Frank Cauldhame, a disturbed adolescent who narrates the sordid story of his life. Living on a remote Scottish island with his reclusive ex-professor father, Frank has developed a taste for killing children and ritualistically mutilating animals and insects. The book's plot turns on the escape from an asylum of Frank's insane half-brother, Eric, who was committed for his sadistic indulgences, which included setting dogs on fire and choking babies with maggots. Eric's return to the Cauldhame cottage and Frank's revelation of his father's ghastly secret bring the novel to its climax.

The Wasp Factory takes its title from a device that Frank concocted specifically for the systematic torture and execution of wasps, a process which, according to Frank, can reveal the future if correctly interpreted. In the novel Frank muses, "Everything we do is part of a pattern we at least have some say in. . . . The Wasp Factory is part of the pattern because it is part of life and—even more so—part of death. Like life it is complicated, so all the components are there. The reason it can answer questions is because every question is a start looking for an end, and the Factory is about the End—death, no less."

Some critics were outraged by the sadistic streak that runs through Banks's narrator. Commenting on the apparent delight Frank takes in his ghoulish acts of cruelty, Patricia Craig, writing in the *Times Literary Supplement,* deemed the book "a literary equivalent of the nastiest brand of juvenile delinquency." But in an article for *Punch,* Stanley Reynolds defended Banks's novel as "a minor masterpiece . . . red and raw, bleeding and still maybe even quivering . . . on the end of the fork." Much controversy surrounds the question of the author's intent in composing such a grizzly and fantastic tale; critics have attributed Banks's motivation to several varied forces, including the desire to expose the dark side of humanity, to experiment in the avant-garde, or simply to shock and revolt readers. Reynolds suggested that *The Wasp Factory* "is not an indictment of society" but "instead a toy, a game." This assessment was disputed by several other critics, including *Washington Post Book World* contributor Douglas E. Winter, who judged the novel "a literate, penetrating examination of the nature of violence and the dwindling value of life in the modern world."

Reviewers generally considered Banks's skillful use of black humor and mesmerizing narrative power more than enough compensation for the novel's few cited structural flaws, mainly the implausibility of plot and character. Winter felt that "Banks indulges too often in . . . insight beyond the years of his young narrator." Rosalind Wade echoed that sentiment in *Contemporary Review,* claiming that the tale "strain[s] credulity to the breaking point"; she nevertheless dubbed *The Wasp Factory* "a first novel of unusual promise."

Banks's second novel, *Walking on Glass,* consists of three separate but ultimately interwoven stories, each of which, upon interpretation, sheds light on the others.

Two of the tales are set in London, the first detailing young Graham Park's obsessive pursuit of the mysterious Sara ffitch and the second focusing on temperamental Steven Grout's paranoid belief that "They" are out to get him. The last story concerns Quiss and Ajayi, prisoners in a surreal castle who are doomed to play "One-Dimensional Chess" and "Spotless Dominoes" until they can correctly answer the riddle, "What happens when an unstoppable force meets an immovable object?" Banks ties the three narratives together in the book's closing pages, making *Walking on Glass* "a brilliant mind-boggler of a novel . . . [with] real kick," according to Jack Sullivan in the *Washington Post Book Review.*

Banks followed *Walking on Glass* with another complex story titled *The Bridge,* about an amnesiac's fantasy life. Following an accident, Orr (the central character, whose real name is Alexander Lennox), awakens in the world of the "Bridge," a land of social segregation arranged around an expansive railway that literally divides the classes. Dream and reality clash as Orr tries to make his escape. While some critics faulted Banks for his sketchy account of the narrator's life prior to the accident, the author was once again praised for his technical acumen. *The Bridge* drew comparisons to what Justin Wintle, in an article for *New Statesman,* termed "Banks's Kafka-Orwellian polity." Wintle further ventured that through his writings, the author strives "to make a point of pointlessness."

In 1987 Banks published his first science fiction novel, *Consider Phlebas,* one of two books he released that year. He refined his skill in the genre with his follow-up novel, *The Player of Games.* Although a few reviewers characterized both of these novels as overly extravagant, Tom Hutchinson, writing in the London *Times,* called *The Player of Games* "tremendous."

Gerald Jonas, a critic for the *New York Times Book Review,* noted that Banks's "passion for overwriting" was evident in another science fiction offering, *Use of Weapons,* but admitted that the flashback-laden narrative was worth reading just to get to the surprising denouement. Yet another science fiction novel, *Feersum Endjinn,* featured sections narrated by a character who can only spell phonetically, leading to sentences such as "Unlike evrybody els I got this weerd wirin in mi brane so I cant spel rite, juss-2 do eveythin foneticly." Gerald Jonas, again writing in the *New York Times Book Review,* explained: "I confess that I groaned inwardly each time this narrator took over. But despite the effort required, I was so caught up in the story and so eager to solve the

puzzle that I never for a moment considered giving up." *Analog* reviewer Tom Easton similarly noted that at times the book is "irritating," but went on to declare that "Banks proves quite convincingly that his imagination can beggar anyone else's. Wow. . . . If you can stand orthographic-phonetic-rebus overkill, yool find a grate deel hear 2 luv." Carl Hays concluded in *Booklist:* "Banks' skill at high-tech speculation continues to grow. Every page of this, his most ingenious work yet, seems to offer more dazzling, intriguing ideas." Summarizing Banks's work in the science fiction genre, Charles Shaar Murray wrote in *New Statesman:* "What comes through most clearly is just how much Banks loves SF. . . . He stuffs each novel to bursting point with everything he adores about the genre, and with everything his literary ancestors unaccountably left out. [His work proves] that 'fun' SF doesn't need to be either dumb or reactionary."

As his career has progressed, Banks's mainstream work has drawn increasingly positive reviews, despite his continued use of brutality and labyrinthine plots. In *Canal Dreams,* for example, he starts with a Japanese concert cellist whose fear of flying leads her to travel on her world tours by such unusual means as oil tankers. On one such cruise, she stumbles into the middle of a terrorist action, is raped, and then transformed into a grenade-carrying warrior. A *Publishers Weekly* writer called *Canal Dreams* a "stunning, hallucinatory, semi-surreal fable" and a "wrenching story, which can be read as a parable of the feminine principle reasserting itself and taking revenge on earth-destroying males." *Booklist* contributor Peter Robertson was so impressed with Banks's achievement in *Canal Dreams* that he declared, "Banks joins Martin Amis and Ian McEwan among the vanguard of the new British subversive novelist."

Banks's whodunit, *Complicity,* was, like much of his work, a cult bestseller in Britain but little-known in North America. The plot centers on a hermit in Scotland who enjoys visiting revenge on criminals who have gone undetected and are thus unpunished. Following the trail is an investigative journalist, but this "hero" is anything but, and instead reveals himself as a tortured masochist with a drug problem. *Complicity* proved to be, according to a *St. James Guide to Horror, Ghost, and Gothic Writers* contributor, "certainly his most horrific book."

A Song of Stone was described as "a morality tale and, ultimately, a passion play with startlingly twisted passions," by Thomas Gaughan in *Booklist.* Its plot shares a similarity with one of the stories in *Walking on Glass:*

a couple are held hostage at a castle. But Abel and Morgan, of noble birth, belong there, and have been taken into captivity by a group of soldiers while a mysterious war rages elsewhere. Abel narrates the tale, and wonders if the desperate band has deserted the army. The brutality with which they treat Abel and Morgan is horrendous, and the contemptuous Abel considers himself above such savagery. His elitist attitude, however, proves false, as the degradation of his days fills him with a rage that causes him to harbor barbaric thoughts himself. A *Publishers Weekly* review of the novel compared Banks to J. G. Ballard and Anthony Burgess. Banks's "impeccable prose undulates with a poetry and sensuality that transform the most ordinary movements of his tale into resonant images of beauty and terror," its reviewer stated. Barbara Hoffert, writing in *Library Journal,* called the novel "worthy, but nearly unbearable to read" for its "images [that] are astonishingly grim and forceful."

Much of Banks's science fiction is set in a utopian world known as "The Culture"; there is even a fanzine by that name devoted to his novels in the genre. In *Inversions,* Banks imagines a world without technology. The work seems at first to be two unrelated tales: the first centering upon Vosill, the female physician to a king. She becomes embroiled in court intrigues and finds herself in love with the monarch. The figure in the second tale, a bodyguard named DeWar, is also devoted to his employer. A *Publishers Weekly* review remarked that "the story of Vosill and DeWar and their unspoken connection unfolds with masterful subtlety," and predicted it would further enhance Banks's "reputation for creating challenging, intelligent stories." The author also won praise from Jackie Cassada in *Library Journal,* who stated that *Inversions* "demonstrates his considerable talent for subtle storytelling."

Look to Windward, published in North America in 2001, returns readers to the world of "The Culture." In this novel, government agents from the Culture unintentionally initiate a civil war on the planet Chel, which results in the deaths of billions of Chelgrians. Quilan, an ambassador from Chel, is sent to the Masaq' Orbital in an effort to avenge the killings. *Library Journal*'s Jackie Cassada called the book a "literate and challenging tale by one of the genre's master storytellers." Although Roland Green, reviewing the title in *Booklist,* characterized it as "no more than a thinking reader's space opera," a *Publishers Weekly* contributor praised "Banks's fine prose, complex plotting and well-rounded characters," and noted that readers "will find themselves fully rewarded when the novel reaches its powerful conclusion."

Banks skewered global multinational corporations in *The Business.* The work centers upon Kathryn Telman, who has worked as an executive for a very large, very secretive, but omnipresent corporation for much of her adult life. Known only as "The Business," it stretches back more than 2,000 years and appears to control much of the planet's resources. Kathryn was recruited when still a child in a Scotland slum; educated and groomed for an executive position, she now closes lucrative high-tech deals for her employer. Her personal life, however, is a bit more directionless: a prince from the tiny Himalayan nation of Thulahn courts her, but she is uninterested, favoring a romance with a married colleague instead. But when a few top executives at The Business become determined to buy a United Nations seat, and try to oust Thulahn's representative permanently, Kathryn is transferred to his small country in order to take care of the groundwork. To her surprise, she falls in love with the country and its peaceful way of life. A *Kirkus Reviews* contributor found it a novel "sprinkled with erudite puns" and described it as "smart, breezy entertainment." Other reviews were similarly positive. "Banks offers a hilarious look at international corporate culture and the insatiable avarice that drives it," stated a *Publishers Weekly* reviewer, "but he suggests the positive potential of globalization, too."

Banks once told *CA:* "I want to make people laugh and think, though not necessarily in that order."

BIOGRAPHICAL/CRITICAL SOURCES:

BOOKS

Contemporary Literary Criticism, Volume 34, Gale (Detroit, MI), 1985.
St. James Guide to Horror, Ghost, and Gothic Writers, first edition, St. James (Detroit, MI), 1998.

PERIODICALS

Analog, December, 1995, Tom Easton, review of *Feersum Endjinn,* pp. 183-184; October, 2000, Tom Easton, review of *Inversions,* p. 131.
Booklist, August, 1991, p. 2097; January 15, 1995, Emily Melton, review of *Complicity,* p. 899; July, 1995, p. 1865; February 1, 1997, Dennis Winters, review of *Excession,* p. 929; August, 1998, Thomas Gaughan, review of *A Song of Stone,* p. 1958; June 1, 2001, Roland Green, review of *Look to Windward,* p. 1855.

Books and Bookmen, February, 1984, pp. 22-23.

British Book News, April, 1984, p. 238.

Contemporary Review, April, 1984, Rosalind Wade, review of *The Wasp Factory,* pp. 213-224.

Globe and Mail (Toronto, Ontario, Canada), October 19, 1985.

Guardian, August 7, 1999, Colin Hughes, "Doing the Business," p. S6.

Kirkus Reviews, September 15, 2000, review of *The Business,* p. 1300.

Library Journal, August, 1991, Jackie Cassada, review of *Canal Dreams,* p. 150; June 15, 1995, p. 98; July, 1998, Barbara Hoffert, review of *A Song of Stone,* p. 132; February 14, 2000, Jackie Cassada, review of *Inversions,* p. 202; November 1, 2000, Marc Kloszewski, review of *The Business,* p. 132; August, 2001, Jackie Cassada, review of *Look to Windward,* p. 171.

Los Angeles Times, August 19, 1984, Charles Champlin, review of *The Wasp Factory,* p. 1; February 5, 1986.

Los Angeles Times Book Review, September 15, 1991, p. 6.

Magazine of Fantasy and Science Fiction, February, 1996, Charles De Lint, review of *Whit, or Isis amongst the Unsaved,* p. 37.

New Scientist, March 20, 1993.

New Statesman, April 5, 1985, Grace Ingoldby, review of *Walking on Glass,* p. 32; July 18, 1986; July 26, 1996, pp. 47-48.

New Statesman & Society, August 12, 1988; April 24, 1992, Brian Morton, review of *The Crow Road,* p. 37; September 3, 1993, John Williams, review of *Complicity,* p. 41; September 15, 1995, Roz Kaveney, review of *Whit,* p. 34.

New York Times Book Review, March 2, 1986, Samuel R. Delany, review of *Walking on Glass,* p. 37; May 3, 1992, Gerald Jonas, review of *Use of Weapons,* p. 38; February 19, 1995, Catherine Texier, review of *Complicity,* p. 26; September 10, 1995, Gerald Jonas, review of *Feersum Endjinn,* p. 46; January 7, 1996, p. 32; November 1, 1998, Margot Mifflin, review of *A Song of Stone,* p. 23; December 17, 2000, Peter Bricklebank, review of *The Business,* p. 23.

Observer (London, England), March 10, 1985; July 13, 1986; August 23, 1987.

Publishers Weekly, June 28, 1991, review of *Canal Dreams,* p. 88; November 7, 1994, review of *Complicity,* p. 66; January 27, 1997, review of *Excession,* p. 82; August 3, 1998, review of *A Song of Stone,* p. 73; January 3, 2000, review of *Inversions,* p. 61; September 25, 2000, review of *The Business,* p. 85; May 28, 2001, review of *Look to Windward,* p. 55.

Punch, February 29, 1984, Stanley Reynolds, review of *The Wasp Factory,* p. 42.

Sunday Times (London, England), February 12, 1984.

Times (London, England), February 16, 1984; March 7, 1985; September 24, 1988.

Times Literary Supplement, March 16, 1984; November 13, 1987; September 10, 1993, Will Eaves, review of *Complicity,* p. 22; September 1, 1995, Nicholas Lezard, review of *Whit,* p. 20; June 14, 1996; August 13, 1999, Robert Potts, review of *The Business,* p. 21.

Voice Literary Supplement, April, 1986.

Washington Post, March 17, 1986.

Washington Post Book World, September 9, 1984; July 31, 1988; October 29, 1989, p. 8; February 19, 1995, p. 7.

OTHER

James Thin-Iain Banks Page, http://www.jthin.co.uk/banks1.htm/ (January 2, 2001), "Iain Banks—Biography."*

* * *

BARROLL, John Leeds, III 1928-
(Leeds Barroll)

PERSONAL: Born July 20, 1928, in Lausanne, Switzerland; son of John Leeds and Mary Hargrove (Bellamy) Barroll; married Rayna Sue Klatzkin, March 17, 1951; children: John Leeds IV, James Edmonson, Ellen. *Education:* Harvard University, A.B. (cum laude), 1950; Princeton University, M.A., 1955, Ph.D., 1956. *Religion:* Episcopalian.

ADDRESSES: Office—Department of English, University of Pittsburgh, Pittsburgh, PA 15213. *E-mail*—barroll@umbc.edu.

CAREER: Teacher of classics at boys' school, 1950-52; English teacher at private school in New York, NY, 1952-53; Rutgers University, Douglass College, New Brunswick, NJ, instructor in English, 1955-56; University of Texas, Austin, TX, instructor, 1956-59, assistant professor of English, 1959-60; University of Cincinnati, Cincinnati, OH, associate professor, 1960-64, professor of English, 1964-67, assistant dean of graduate school, 1965-66, associate dean, 1966-67; University of Newcastle upon Tyne, Newcastle upon Tyne, England, visiting professor of English literature, 1967-68; Vanderbilt

University, Nashville, TN, professor of English, 1968-69; William Paterson College, Wayne, NJ, dean of arts and sciences, 1969-70; University of South Carolina, Columbia, SC, professor of English literature, 1970-74, director of Center for Shakespeare Studies, 1972-74; National Endowment for the Humanities, deputy director of Division of Research Grants, 1974-78; University of Pittsburgh, Pittsburgh, PA, Andrew W. Mellon Visiting Professor of English Literature, c. 1978; University of Maryland at Baltimore County, MD, Presidential Research Professor; Folger Shakespeare Library, Washington, DC, scholar-in-residence. Visiting associate professor at Washington University, St. Louis, MO, 1962. *Military service:* U.S. Army 1946-48.

MEMBER: International Association of University Professors, Shakespeare Council of America (chairman of board of trustees, 1970—), Shakespeare Association of America, Modern Language Association of America, Malone Society, Modern Humanities Research Association (England), Hasty Pudding Club (Harvard University).

AWARDS, HONORS: Huntington Library fellow, 1957-59; Folger Shakespeare Library fellow, 1958; Sachs Award from Cincinnati Institute of Fine Arts, 1966; University of Maryland Regents' Faculty Award, 1999-2000, for research, scholarship, or creative activity.

WRITINGS:

(Editor, with Austin M. Wright) *The Art of the Short Story: An Introductory Anthology,* Allyn & Bacon, 1969.
(Editor) William Shakespeare, *Hamlet,* W. C. Brown, 1970.
(Editor) Shakespeare, *Othello,* W. C. Brown, 1971.
Artificial Persons: The Formation of Character in the Tragedies of Shakespeare, University of South Carolina Press, 1974.
(With others) *Revels History of Drama in English,* Volume III: 1576-1613, Methuen, 1975.
Shakespearean Tragedy: Genre, Tradition, and Change in Antony and Cleopatra, Folger Books (Washington, DC)/Associated University Presses, 1984.
Politics, Plague, and Shakespeare's Theater: The Stuart Years, Cornell University Press (Ithaca, NY), 1991.
Anne of Denmark, Queen of England: A Cultural Biography, University of Pennsylvania Press (Philadelphia, PA), 2001.

Contributor to *Essays on Shakespeare,* edited by G. R. Smith, Pennsylvania State University Press, 1965.

General editor of "International Shakespeare," 1971—, and "The South Carolina Shakespeare," 1972; editor of "Shakespeare Studies" (monograph series), 1969—; founding editor *Medieval and Renaissance Drama in England.* Contributor to literature journals. Editor of *Shakespeare Studies,* 1965—.

SIDELIGHTS: John Leeds Barroll III is a scholar of the works of William Shakespeare. He has served as editor of *Shakespeare Studies* since the mid-1960s, and is affiliated with the Folger Shakespeare Library. After earning advanced degrees from Princeton University, Barroll began his career at Rutgers University in 1955. Since then he has held posts at the universities of Texas, Cincinnati, and South Carolina, where he also served as director of its Center for Shakespeare Studies in the early 1970s. Barroll's career has also taken him to Vanderbilt University, the University of Pittsburgh, and the University of Maryland at Baltimore County, where he was a presidential research professor.

Shakespeare Studies contains essays and book reviews presenting the latest efforts by scholars in the field of English Renaissance drama. In a review of volume 23, which appeared in 1998, Barbara L. Parker of *Renaissance Quarterly* stated that the "volume is far-ranging and impressively researched, illuminating Shakespeare's milieu no less than his works."

Barroll has also edited numerous scholarly tomes, and authored the titles *Artificial Persons: The Formation of Character in the Tragedies of Shakespeare, Politics, Plague, and Shakespeare's Theater: The Stuart Years,* and *Anne of Denmark, Queen of England: A Cultural Biography.* The latter examines the troubles and achievements of the much maligned consort to James I, the Scottish king who succeeded Elizabeth I on the English throne in 1603. Anne endured a troubled marriage, marked by conflict over their son Henry, heir to throne, and Barroll discusses matters both personal and public. The queen, he notes, was said to have ended a pregnancy herself in retaliation for transgressions by her husband, but left her mark as patron of several worthy artistic ventures. Anne held forth over her "alternative" court, as Barroll's account relates, and he gives special attention to the "masque" dramas that became popular during the reign of James I. Playwright Ben Jonson and set designer Inigo Jones were some of the genre's notable names, and Barroll makes the claim that Anna was the patron of such plays, not her husband, as scholars have previously maintained.

BIOGRAPHICAL/CRITICAL SOURCES:

PERIODICALS

Renaissance Quarterly, summer, 1998, Barbara L. Parker, review of *Shakespeare Studies,* p. 676.*

* * *

BARROLL, Leeds
   See BARROLL, John Leeds, III

* * *

BASHEVIS, Isaac
   See SINGER, Isaac Bashevis

* * *

BEDFORD, Sybille 1911-

PERSONAL: Born March 16, 1911, in Charlottenburg, Germany; British citizen; daughter of Maximilian von Schoenebeck and Elizabeth Bernard; married Walter Bedford, 1935. *Ethnicity:* "White European." *Education:* Privately educated in Italy, England, and France.

ADDRESSES: Agent—Lutyens & Rubinstein, 231 Westbourne Park Rd., London W11 1EB, England.

CAREER: Writer.

MEMBER: Society of Authors, PEN (vice president, 1979), Royal Society of Literature (fellow).

AWARDS, HONORS: Officer of the Order of the British Empire, 1981; elected Companion of Literature (C.Lit.), 1994; *Jigsaw* was shortlisted for the Booker Prize, 1989.

WRITINGS:

NONFICTION

The Sudden View: A Mexican Journey (travel book), introduction by Bruce Chatwin, Gollancz, 1953, revised edition, Atheneum, 1963, also published in England as *A Visit to Don Otavio: A Traveller's Tale from Mexico,* Collins, 1960, Eland, 1993.

The Best We Can Do: An Account of the Trial of John Bodkin Adams, Collins, 1958, published in the United States as *The Trial of Dr. Adams,* Simon & Schuster (New York, NY), 1959, reprinted, Penguin (New York, NY), 1989.
The Faces of Justice: A Traveller's Report, Collins (England), 1960, Simon & Schuster (New York, NY), 1961.
Aldous Huxley: A Biography, Collins/Chatto & Windus, Volume I, 1973, Volume II, 1974, omnibus volume, Knopf, 1974, reprinted with new introduction, Macmillan (London, England), 1993.
As It Was: Pleasures, Landscapes, and Justice, Sinclair-Stevenson, 1990.

NOVELS

A Legacy, Weidenfeld & Nicolson, 1956, Simon & Schuster (London, England), 1959, reprinted with an introduction by Bedford, Penguin (London, England), 1999.
A Favourite of the Gods, Simon & Schuster (London, England), 1963, reprinted with an introduction by Peter Vansittart, Virago, 1984, reprinted with an introduction by Bedford, Penguin (London, England), 2000.
A Compass Error, Collins, 1968, reprinted with an introduction by Bedford, Penguin (London, England), 2000.
Jigsaw: An Unsentimental Education (biographical novel), Sinclair-Stevenson, 1988, reprinted with new introduction, Penguin (London, England), 1999.

Contributor to periodicals, including *Chimera, Decision, Encounter, Esquire, Harper's Bazaar, Horizon, Life, New York Review of Books, Observer, Spectator, New Yorker,* and *Vogue.*

ADAPTATIONS: A Legacy was broadcast as a British Broadcasting Corporation (BBC) 3 radio program, 1958, a BBC Radio 4 program, 1960, and televised in 1975.

WORK IN PROGRESS: Quicksand: Perspectives of an Outsider, a nonfiction book, for Penguin (England) and Counterpoint (United States), 2002.

SIDELIGHTS: Although best known as a novelist, Sybille Bedford has also written a two-volume biography of Aldous Huxley, a number of food and travel essays, and several celebrated accounts of trials that she attended. In his introduction to a later edition of her second novel, *A Favourite of the Gods,* Peter Vansittart talked about the varied nature of Bedford's writing, calling her "an authority on law, a connoisseur of unusual houses and families, of manners, wit, social rituals, food and drink."

Bedford's novels have been praised by such distinguished authors as Evelyn Waugh and Aldous Huxley. Yet many critics consider her novels anachronistic because of her use of the aristocracy and upper classes as the central characters and the prevailing milieus of her fiction. Despite this criticism, however, many reviewers agree that Bedford has a graceful and lucid style of writing. In a discussion of Bedford's work published in the *Voice Literary Supplement,* David Leavitt characterized Bedford's literary strengths in the following manner: "Dry wit, careful attendance to detail, dialogue in which, as Elizabeth Bowen once wrote, there is 'more to be said than can come through,' are the hallmarks of Bedford's fiction."

Many of Bedford's novels are concerned with life in Europe from the turn of the twentieth century until the advent of World War II. Also characteristic of Bedford's writing is her extensive use of her own personal history. For example, in *A Legacy,* her first novel, Bedford tells the story of a German baron and his four sons. The basic facts of this narrative were drawn from Bedford's own family history. Reviewing the work in the *Times Literary Supplement,* Laura Marcus wrote that "the author successfully interweaves personal and political history and, although her characters are somewhat stylized, the hectic atmosphere of Edwardian Germany is convincingly portrayed." Bedford continued to draw upon her own history in her next two novels, *A Favourite of the Gods* and *A Compass Error.* Detailing the lives of three generations of European women, the works portray a lifestyle Bedford herself was part of while growing up in Europe. Commenting on these works in his *Voice Literary Supplement* essay, Leavitt said that these books were examples of Bedford's ability to portray individuals as they interact with society, a gift, said Leavitt, she shared with other writers of her generation. "If her works of fiction share a goal," he wrote, "it could probably best be stated as the determination to show the ways in which the private lives of individuals reflect the larger political life of their culture, and vice versa. . . . She portrays the evolution of Nazism and Fascism where it really took place—in living rooms, kitchens and on beaches."

In 1989 Bedford issued *Jigsaw: An Unsentimental Education.* The story of a nineteen-year-old girl named Billi, this work closely parallels Bedford's own childhood in Europe. The novel relates how, while living with her mother on the Cote d'Azur, Billi begins working on a novel. David R. Slavitt described *Jigsaw* in the *Chicago Tribune* as "a splendid book, lucid, balanced, humane and civilized, with an enchanting and depressing story of the author's mother, who is its central figure." He concluded, "This is a treasure of a book, one of the best I know about mothers and daughters."

In addition to her fiction writing, Bedford has also published a number of nonfiction titles. Notable among these is her two-volume biography of English author Aldous Huxley. Published first in two volumes, the work draws upon numerous letters and journals of Huxley and his first wife, Maria Nys, as well as Bedford's own recollection of her experiences with the couple. Bedford, who was a close friend of the Huxleys, uses the books to depict Huxley as a man rather than a writer, and she has gained much acclaim for her rendition of his life. In *Newsweek* Peter S. Prescott said that Huxley "has been well served in this vibrant and illuminating biography." The critic further noted that "Bedford knew the Huxleys intimately and brings a novelist's perceptions to her history of a novelist: Maria Huxley's death, for instance, is rendered as affectingly as any death in fiction."

Some critics, however, like R. Z. Sheppard of *Time* magazine, who said that Bedford "takes a rather protective and insular approach to her subject," felt that Bedford focuses too deeply on Huxley's personal life. Similarly, Stanley Weintraub's review of *Aldous Huxley* in the *New Republic* also criticized Bedford's highly personal approach to biography, saying that Bedford "forc[es] . . . the reader to pay a high price for her humanizing of Huxley, who—it is true—appears less than human from many of his books."

Yet, while critics were divided over Bedford's unwillingness to interpret events in Huxley's life, the biography was praised for its attention to accuracy and detail. Weintraub admitted that the work was a "crucial source of information about the man and fascinating reading in itself." And Diana Trilling, writing in the *New York Times Book Review,* said that despite Bedford's focus on the writer's private life, this book was the "first full-length study of Aldous Huxley's life and should do much to return this now little-read figure of the twenties to his proper standing in the literary history of the century." Others, like William Abrahams, admired Bedford's approach to the biography. In an essay published in the *Atlantic Monthly,* Abrahams said that "Mrs. Bedford, of course, is an artist, as anyone familiar with her novel *A Legacy* will know already. She has performed prodigies of research and mastered a staggering amount of material; *her* Aldous has indeed 'some kind of shape'; her biography is unquestionably a work of art; I admire it immensely." Prescott judged that Huxley "has been well served in this vibrant and illuminating biography."

Over the years, Bedford has also gained a reputation for writing well about both travel and legal trials. *As It Was: Pleasures, Landscapes, and Justice,* which Bedford issued in 1990, gathers her own writings from the 1950s and 1960s. The varied narratives that comprise the book range from sketches of different countries, like Denmark and Switzerland, to discussions of French cooking, to a reflection on notable court cases, including Jack Ruby's trial for murdering Lee Harvey Oswald, the man who assassinated former President John F. Kennedy. The assorted chronicles, said Peter Levi in the *Spectator,* make "the most ordinary journeys and shopping expeditions read like a crisp, unforgettable honeymoon." From her four novels to her Huxley biography to her journalistic essays, critics have noted that Bedford's ability to make characters—real or imagined—come to life is what distinguishes her work from that of other writers.

BIOGRAPHICAL/CRITICAL SOURCES:

BOOKS

Bedford, Sybille, *A Favourite of the Gods,* with an introduction by Peter Vansittart, Virago, 1984.
Contemporary Novelists, sixth edition, St. James Press (Detroit, MI), 1996.

PERIODICALS

American Scholar, summer, 1965.
Atlantic Monthly, March, 1957; April, 1969; January, 1975.
Chicago Tribune, June 11, 1989, p. 3.
Christian Science Monitor, January 31, 1957; October 21, 1969.
Commonweal, December 6, 1974; March 28, 1975.
Encounter, March, 1963.
Evening Standard, November 22, 1999.
Guardian Weekly, September 28, 1974.
Harper's, April, 1963; April, 1969; April, 1975.
Hudson Review, summer, 1975.
Listener, November, 1968; October 17, 1974.

Manchester Guardian, March 27, 1957.
Nation, March 28, 1953; March 31, 1956; May 4, 1963; February 1, 1975; December 30, 1991.
New Criterion, April, 1994.
New Republic, June 26, 1961; November 16, 1974, pp. 24-27.
New Statesman, January 17, 1959; May 26, 1961; October 18, 1968; September 20, 1974; May 12, 1989; September 14, 1990; March 27, 2000.
Newsweek, December 9, 1974, p. 109; December 30, 1974.
New Yorker, April 27, 1957; February 17, 1975.
New York Herald Tribune Book Review, January 10, 1954; February 3, 1957.
New York Review of Books, April 24, 1969; January 23, 1975; April 27, 1989, p. 22.
New York Times, January 17, 1954; February 3, 1957.
New York Times Book Review, March 23, 1969; November 24, 1974, pp. 1, 42; May 20, 1984; December 22, 1985; May 28, 1989; December 3, 1989.
Observer, September 16, 1969; September 15, 1974; April 20, 1975; May 31, 1987; May 7, 1989; September 9, 1990; March 8, 1992; March 14, 1993.
Observer Review, October 13, 1968.
Partisan Review, spring, 1976.
Saturday Review, February 9, 1957; March 16, 1963; November 16, 1974, pp. 16-18.
South Atlantic Quarterly, summer, 1975.
Spectator, April 13, 1956; November 14, 1958; May 26, 1961; October 25, 1968; September 28, 1974; February 18, 1984; May 20, 1989; November 25, 1989; September 15, 1990.
Time, December 2, 1974, p. 107.
Times (London, England), February 17, 1984; March 10, 1984; May 11, 1989; September 15, 1990.
Times Educational Supplement, December 21, 1984.
Times Literary Supplement, March 13, 1953; April 20, 1956; October 24, 1968; September 20, 1974; June 1, 1984; June 22, 1984; May 12, 1989; October 26, 1990.
Voice Literary Supplement, June, 1990, pp. 9-10.
Washington Post, December 11, 1968.
Washington Post Book World, November 17, 1974; November 17, 1985; April 2, 1989.

*   *   *

BENNETT, Alan 1934-

PERSONAL: Born May 9, 1934, in Leeds, England; son of Walter (a butcher) and Lilian Mary (Peel) Bennett. *Education:* Exeter College, Oxford, B.A. (with honors), 1957. *Religion:* Church of England.

Alan Bennett

ADDRESSES: *Agent*—Peters, Fraser & Dunlop, Drury House, 34-43 Russell Street, London WC2B 5HA, England.

CAREER: Playwright, screenwriter, and actor on stage and television, 1959—. Oxford University, Magdalen College, Oxford, England, temporary junior lecturer in history, 1960-62. President, North Craven Heritage Trust, 1968-93. *Military service:* Intelligence Corps, 1952-54.

MEMBER: British Actors' Equity Association, Actors' Equity Association, American Federation of Television and Radio Artists.

AWARDS, HONORS: London *Evening Standard* Drama Awards, 1961, for *Beyond the Fringe,* 1968, for *Forty Years On,* 1971, for *Getting On;* Antoinette Perry (Tony) Award, and New York Drama Critics Circle Award, both 1963, both for *Beyond the Fringe;* Guild of Television Producers award, 1967, for *On the Margin; Plays & Players* Award for best new play, 1977, for *The Old Country,* and 1986, for *Kafka's Dick;* Broadcasters Press Guild TV Award, 1983, British Academy of Film and Television Arts Writers Award, 1983, and Royal Television Society Award, 1984, all for *An Englishman*

Abroad; honorary fellow, Exeter College, 1987; Hawthornden Prize, 1989, for *Talking Heads;* Olivier Award for best comedy, 1989, for *Single Spies;* D.Litt., Leeds University, 1990.

WRITINGS:

PLAYS

(With Peter Cook, Jonathan Miller, and Dudley Moore) *Beyond the Fringe* (comedy revue; first produced in Edinburgh, Scotland, 1960; produced in the West End, 1961; produced in New York, NY, 1962), Random House (New York, NY), 1963.

(Coauthor) *Fortune,* produced in London, England, 1961.

(Coauthor) *Golden,* produced in New York, NY, 1962.

Forty Years On (two-act; first produced in Manchester, England, 1968; produced in the West End, 1968; also see below), Faber (London, England), 1969.

(With Caryl Brahms and Ned Sherrin) *Sing a Rude Song* (two-act), first produced in London, England, 1969.

Getting On (two-act; first produced in Brighton, England, 1971; produced in the West End, 1971; also see below), Faber (London, England), 1972.

Habeas Corpus (two-act; first produced in Oxford, England, 1973; produced in the West End, 1973; produced on Broadway, 1975; also see below), Faber (London, England), 1973, Samuel French (New York, NY), 1976.

The Old Country (first produced in Oxford, 1977; produced in the West End, 1977), Faber (London, England), 1978.

Enjoy (first produced at Richmond Theatre, 1980; produced in the West End, 1980), Faber (London, England), 1980.

Office Suite (adaptations of television plays *A Visit from Miss Prothero* and *Doris and Doreen* [also see below], produced in London, 1987), Faber (London, England), 1981.

Forty Years On, Getting On, Habeas Corpus, Faber (London, England), 1985.

Kafka's Dick (also see below), first produced at Royal Court Theatre, London, England, 1986.

Two Kafka Plays: Kafka's Dick [and] *The Insurance Man,* Faber (London, England), 1987.

(And director) *Single Spies* (two one-act plays; contains *A Question of Attribution* and *An Englishman Abroad;* also see below), first produced in London, England, 1988.

The Wind in the Willows (based on the novel by Kenneth Grahame; first produced in London, England, 1990), Faber (London, England), 1991.

The Madness of George III (first produced in London, England, 1991; produced in New York, NY, 1993), Faber (London, England), 1992.

Talking Heads (also see below; adapted from the teleplay by Bennett; first produced in London, 1992), Parkwest Publications (New York, NY), 1992.

Bed among the Lentils: A Monologue from 'Talking Heads,' Samuel French (New York, NY), 1998.

A Cream Cracker under the Settee: A Monologue from "Talking Heads," Samuel French (New York, NY), 1998.

Her Big Chance: A Monologue from "Talking Heads," Samuel French (New York, NY), 1998.

TELEPLAYS

On the Margin (television series), British Broadcasting Corp. (BBC-TV), 1966.

A Day Out (also see below), BBC-TV, 1972.

Sunset across the Bay, BBC-TV, 1975.

A Little Outing, BBC-TV, 1978.

A Visit from Miss Prothero, BBC-TV, 1978.

Me! I'm Afraid of Virginia Woolf (also see below), London Weekend Television, 1978.

Doris and Doreen, London Weekend Television, 1978.

The Old Crowd (also see below), London Weekend Television, 1979.

One Fine Day (also see below), London Weekend Television, 1979.

Afternoon Off (also see below), London Weekend Television, 1979.

All Day on the Sands (also see below), London Weekend Television, 1979.

Objects of Affection (contains *Our Winnie, A Woman of No Importance, Rolling Home, Marks,* and *Say Something Happened;* also see below), BBC-TV, 1982.

Intensive Care (also see below), BBC-TV, 1982.

An Englishman Abroad (also see below), BBC-TV, 1982.

Objects of Affection and Other Plays (includes *Intensive Care, A Day Out,* and *An Englishman Abroad*), BBC Publications (London, England), 1982.

The Writer in Disguise (includes *Me! I'm Afraid of Virginia Woolf, The Old Crowd, One Fine Day, Afternoon Off,* and *All Day on the Sands*), Faber (London, England), 1985.

The Insurance Man (also see below), BBC-TV, 1986.

Talking Heads (series), BBC-TV, 1987, published by BBC Publications (London, England), 1988.

Dinner at Noon (documentary), BBC-TV, 1988.

(And director) *Bed among the Lentils,* Public Broadcasting Service, 1989.

Poetry in Motion, Channel 4, 1990.

102 Boulevard Haussmann, BBC-TV, 1991.

A Question of Attribution, BBC-TV, 1991.

Poetry in Motion 2, Channel 4, 1992.

Portrait or Bust (documentary), BBC-TV, 1993.

The Abbey (documentary), BBC-TV, 1995.

Talking Heads 2, BBC-TV, 1998.

Telling Tales (autobiography), BBC-TV, 2000.

Also author of *An Evening with Alan Bennett, Famous Gossips, Ashenden, In My Defense,* and *A Chip in the Sugar.*

OTHER

A Private Function (screenplay), Handmade Films, 1984, Faber (London, England), 1985.

Uncle Clarence (radio talk), 1986.

Prick up Your Ears (screenplay; adapted from the biography by John Lahr; produced by Samuel Goldwyn, 1987), Faber (London, England), 1988.

The Lady in the Van (produced, 1990), Faber (London, England), 2001.

The Madness of King George (screenplay; based on his play *The Madness of George III;* produced by Samuel Goldwyn, 1994), Random House (New York, NY), 1995.

Writing Home (memoir and essays), Faber (London, England), 1994, Random House (New York, NY), 1995.

The Laying on of Hands (novel), Profile, 2000.

The Clothes They Stood up In (novel), Random House (New York, NY), 2001.

Contributor to periodicals, including *Listener* and the *London Review of Books.*

SIDELIGHTS: Alan Bennett is a playwright, screenwriter, and entertainer best known for his work on stage and in television in Great Britain. His contributions to *Beyond the Fringe* and *Talking Heads* have established him as one of the premiere satirists working in the United Kingdom today. "Whatever their ostensible subjects, Alan Bennett's plays consistently dramatize man's desire to define himself and his world through teasingly inadequate language, whether conventional adages, women's magazine prose, government jargon, or quotations from the 'Greats,'" Burton S. Kendle noted in *Contemporary Dramatists.* "The resulting parodies simultaneously mock and honor this impulse to erect linguistic safeguards in a frightening world." *Drama* critic

J. W. Lambert similarly observed: "Relaxed mockery is [the author's] line and detached affection, rather than any more intense emotion, informs his speculative eye. . . . They make a welcome counterpart to the assorted gobbets of half-baked romanticism which tend to be flung in our faces nowadays."

Bennett began his career as an actor, and *Beyond the Fringe,* his collaboration with Dudley Moore, Peter Cook, and Jonathan Miller, became a hit on both sides of the Atlantic. With its New York debut, the play became "the first British equivalent of American-type satire to reach our shores," Richard Brustein commented in the *New Republic.* Brustein described the series of sketches as having "all the qualifications of sick comedy. . . . It roasts all [the] categorical turkeys, it has no firm moral center, it is immoderate, irresponsible, and totally destructive, it affirms no changing world, and—if I may be permitted a . . . judgment of value—it is violently funny." As Matthew Wolf summarized in the *Chicago Tribune, Beyond the Fringe*'s "anarchic humor helped pave the way for *Rowan & Martin's Laugh-In* and *Saturday Night Live* in America and *Monty Python* in England, despite Bennett's assertion that these latter groups 'take it so much further.'"

Bennett's first solo creation, 1968's *Forty Years On,* is "a piece dripping with nostalgia for the Edwardian past and undercutting every satiric episode with expressions of affectionate regret," Irving Wardle reported in the London *Times.* Consisting of a play within a play, *Forty Years On* follows the changing of the guard at a boys' boarding school as the headmaster's retirement inspires the performance of a comic revue. A "fragmented, ambiguous, oddly interesting assortment of a play," as *Village Voice* writer Molly Haskell termed it, *Forty Years On* is "what [Bennett] needed to make the transition from revue-sketch writer to playwright," Wardle asserted, serving up a "brand of wry, negative patriotism." Highlighting the satire in *Forty Years On* is the author's flair for language; "as we know from [his previous work], Bennett has a mean ear for cliché and the verbal ingenuity to twist it into appealingly absurd shapes," Benedict Nightingale remarked in the *New Statesman.* In contrast, *New York Times* critic Clive Barnes felt that the satire is "fundamentally . . . cheap and nasty," and faulted the play for "pretentiousness and ineptness." Jeremy Kingston, however, praised *Forty Years On* for hitting its satirical targets, writing in *Punch* that Bennett "scores bull's-eyes and winners all down the line." "Ever since [*Beyond the Fringe*] we have been waiting for a full-scale mock-heroic pageant of modern British myth, and Mr. Bennett has now supplied it," Wardle concluded in a *New York Times* review; *Forty Years On* is "a lethally witty series of parodies."

In the 1970s and early 1980s, Bennett wrote more than fifteen television scripts, garnering many awards. During this time, he "made the change from satirist to writer of substance without losing a healthy talent for mockery and self-mockery," Andrew Hislop observed in the London *Times.* Despite critical acclaim for his teleplays, however, Bennett wished to return to writing for the stage, "yearning to get away from the naturalism he tends towards in his work for the small screen," Hislop added. In 1986 Bennett premiered *Kafka's Dick,* a "kind of leisurely vaudeville about the tormented Kafka of lit-crit and biographical legend," as *Observer* contributor Michael Ratcliffe put it. Investigating the relationships between biographers and their subjects, *Kafka's Dick* follows the investigations and trials of an insurance salesman who is obsessed with the famous Czech author, and the play includes characters such as Max Brod, Kafka's friend and literary executor, Kafka's father, and the author himself.

In the London *Times,* Wardle called the play a "head-on challenge to literary myth," and added: "There is a great deal more than that, too much in fact, to the play." Other reviewers likewise criticized the work as perhaps too ambitious; Ratcliffe observed that the work is "a mordant attack on twentieth-century trivialisation and barbarity by a playwright who cannot resist blunting the force and intensity of his attack by a constant stream of gags." "On the one hand, [Bennett] tilts at what Englishness stifles," Jim Hiley wrote in the *Listener,* and yet the playwright himself "refuses to get 'too' serious. He perches fretfully on the fence." Nevertheless, the critic believed that *Kafka's Dick* "provides a rewardingly inventive, provoking, often hilarious night out—a nutritious confection with pins in the cream." And Wardle likewise maintained that while Bennett "has taken more on board than he can deal with . . . there remains, of course, the Bennett dialogue, which is as rich as ever in exquisitely turned domestic banalities and literary give-aways."

Bennett's 1991 play, *The Madness of George III,* is "part court spectacle, part history lesson, part medical thriller," in the words of William A. Henry III of *Time.* The play is based on the life of the English king who reigned from 1760 to 1820. It focuses on two years during which time the king lost the American colonies and, later, his mind. "The uniqueness of [this] play," according to Robert Brustein in the *New Republic,* "lies in the way it manages to evoke an entire historical epoch . . . Before long we are deep in the intrigues of Georgian politics." As the king descends into madness, those about him—members of parliament, the Prince of Wales—scheme and vie for power. According to some critics, however, this portrayal of England's political intrigue is the play's chief weakness. Donald Lyons commented in the *New Criterion:* "Bennett writes these pols and docs on one note; once put on stage, they wrangle all too predictably. He has no Shavian knack for dramatizing ideas, or, better to describe what Shaw does, to play and toy articulately with ideas." Jonathan Yardley's *Washington Post* review offered a similar view. He suggested that "the [grand] production of the play cannot quite disguise the flimsiness of its superstructure." Yardley conceded that *The Madness of George III* "may possess in any single scene more wit and energy than most American playwrights or screenwriters can summon up in an entire evening, but in other respects it bears a striking similarity to the intermittent attempts that are made over here—mostly on television—to reinterpret history through dramatization."

Bennett translated his play about King George into a screenplay for the 1994 film, *The Madness of King George,* directed by Nicholas Hytner and produced by the Samuel Goldwyn Company. The film brought Bennett's talents to a much wider audience in the United States, but it was not his first screenplay. His first screenplay, *A Private Function,* was "as gently telling a treatment of the British class system as has been seen in years," in Wolf's opinion. The film follows a middle-class couple in postwar England as they attempt to ascend the social ladder by serving pork—forbidden by rationing laws—at a society banquet. According to *Chicago Tribune* critic Gene Siskel, "what Bennett has done is simply to throw one solitary wacky element—a pig—into what otherwise would be an entirely credible situation." The result, Siskel continued, is that "everything British is being skewered in a most delightful manner—especially the resentments that one always suspects lurk just beneath the incomparable British politeness." Paul Attanasio, however, believed that the movie doesn't measure up to the previous work of its star, Monty Python alumnus Michael Palin; the critic stated in the *Washington Post* that *A Private Function* "misses that touch of madness that Monty Python brought to the same comedic vein." Others, however, found the film a success; "not since the end of the collaboration between Roy and John Boulting . . . and the golden age of the Ealing Studios has there been a stylish English comedy of such high-hearted, self-interested knavery as *A Private Function,*" claimed *New York Times* critic Vincent Canby.

In 1986 Bennett took a more serious turn with *Prick up Your Ears,* a film biography of English playwright Joe Orton who, at age thirty-four, was murdered by his long-time male lover, who then committed suicide. *Los Angeles Times* film critic Sheila Benson termed it "a bracingly outrageous portrait of the playwright, his free-ranging life and remarkably constricted times." *Prick up Your Ears* follows Orton's life through a series of flashbacks framed by the investigations of the playwright's biographer, John Lahr. As director Stephen Frears told the *Chicago Tribune,* "Bennett's screenplay is very delicately written, a feast of words and aphorisms and linguistically very precise. We worked hard with the actors to get that precision." Some critics, however, thought that the film focuses too much on the details of Orton's life and not enough on his work; Canby commented that it "goes on to record little more than the facts of the Orton life, [and] the mere existence of the plays." But Benson, while expressing a similar criticism, commended the film for having "the rhythm and even the insolence of an Orton play, without its dialogue." And Desson Howe echoed previous praise of the author's work, asserting in a *Washington Post* review that Bennett's screenplay "is a case study in irony. He shows the beauty in 'dirtiness,' the humor in human anguish and the art of sarcasm in British culture. . . . Like *Casablanca, Diva, Clockwork Orange* and countless other quality-cult films," Howe concluded, "*Prick up Your Ears* has an indefinable idiosyncrasy that makes you want to come back for more."

The man behind the plays and movies, or at least his public persona, emerges in *Writing Home,* a collection of Bennett's diaries, essays, character sketches, and play prefaces. "Bennett has said," according to Peter Parker in the *Times Literary Supplement,* "that all writers play (rather than are) themselves in public, and *Writing Home* . . . a fragmentary but illuminating and engaging autobiography, is a classic performance." Evident in these occasional pieces are the characteristics that provide the basis for Bennett's work and account for his reception in the world of letters. Events from his unremarkable childhood in the north of England lie behind much of the writing in his television plays. Many of his insights into the supporting characters seem to be drawn from his own awkward experience. "Mr. Bennett talks a fair amount about himself," observed Ben Brantley in the *New York Times Book Review,* "but it is self as defined almost exclusively by self-consciousness, a free-floating, pained awareness of everything he isn't and of life as a minefield of potential embarrassments."

Also evident is the humor that permeates Bennett's work. At times, this humor comes from his command of language and timing. As Philip Hensher wrote in the *Spectator,* "What makes Bennett remarkable . . . is a linguistic spark, an unerring sense for the surprising, right word; the word which is going to slide like a ba-nana skin, at the point where the reader expects to place his foot." Humor also comes, noted Hensher, from Bennett's keen powers of observation. "Bennett's comedy never seems to try; it is addicted to the bathetic shrug after the laugh; it modestly tells us that its best lines are not invented but overheard; the pinpoint accuracy of its vocabulary is passed off as that of an *object trouvé*."

In the opinion of Richard Eder in the *Los Angeles Times Book Review,* not all of the pieces in *Writing Home* are of equal value. He maintained that the book "calls for prospecting, not straight reading; a vein of iron and more dazzling stuff are to be found under the topsoil." *New York Times* critic Michiko Kakutani admitted that "there are a few noticeable gaps in Mr. Bennett's book. . . . The reader notices these gaps, however, only because Mr. Bennett is such a delightful raconteur: this is a book you don't want to end." Fiona MacCarthy offered this evaluation in the *Observer:* "You finish this book liking Alan Bennett less than you imagined, but admiring him much more." For Peter Parker, what Bennett displays in *Writing Home* "is part of the reason why he is one of our most considerable, as well as one of our most popular, playwrights."

In 2001 Bennett turned to fiction, publishing a slender novel titled *The Clothes They Stood up In.* The darkly comic work examines the marriage of a middle-class British couple through the lens of a burglary and its aftermath. When Mr. and Mrs. Ransome return from a night at the opera to find their flat completely cleaned out by burglars, they each learn lessons about the power of possessions to shape and define their lives. In his *Washington Post* review of the work, Jonathan Yardley wrote: "To call it a novella borders on exaggeration. Yet there is more to it—more wit, more complexity and ambiguity, more depth, more sheer pleasure and satisfaction—than there is to just about any new novel of whatever length that I have read since Saul Bellow's *Ravelstein* or Michael Chabon's *The Amazing Adventures of Kavalier & Clay.*" Yardley called the book "absolutely delicious, near-perfect," and concluded: "You will read it in a couple of hours at most, but you will think about it for a long, long time."

With each new play, Bennett has furthered his standing in the eyes of many critics. "Alan Bennett is not as celebrated or prolific a playwright as his contemporaries Tom Stoppard and Simon Gray," admitted Richard Christiansen in the *Chicago Tribune,* "but he ranks right up there with them as a witty and humane observer of England in particular and of mankind in general." *New York Times* theater critic Ben Brantley called Bennett the "slyest and—along with Tom Stoppard—most elegant of contemporary British dramatists." David Nokes asserted in the *Times Literary Supplement,* "Alan Bennett's beguiling modesty has all but deflected recognition that he is probably our greatest living dramatist. His characteristic style is unpretentious, small-scale and domestic. His genius lies in an unerring ear for the idioms of lower-middle-class life, the verbal doilies of self-respect and self-repression."

BIOGRAPHICAL/CRITICAL SOURCES:

BOOKS

Contemporary Dramatists, 6th edition, St. James Press, Gale (Detroit, MI), 1999.
Wolfe, Peter, *Understanding Alan Bennett,* University of South Carolina Press (Columbia, SC), 1998.

PERIODICALS

America, September 9, 1989, p. 145.
Book, March, 2001, Paul Evans, review of *The Clothes They Stood up In,* p. 82.
Boston Globe, January 25, 1995, p. 35.
Chicago Tribune, April 12, 1985; April 21, 1985; February 18, 1986; November 16, 1986; May 20, 1987.
Christian Science Monitor, September 16, 1993, p. 10.
Commentary, April, 1978, p. 88.
Drama, spring, 1969; winter, 1977, p. 45.
Economist, February 23, 1991, p. 98; October 29, 1994, p. 105.
Guardian, February 17, 1989, p. 26.
Harper's, May, 1990, p. 36.
Harper's Bazaar, September, 1989, p. 46.
Hudson Review, winter, 1990, p. 629.
Library Journal, January 1, 2001, Judith Kicinski, review of *The Clothes They Stood up In,* p. 151.
Listener, October 2, 1986.
Los Angeles Times, May 1, 1987.
Los Angeles Times Book Review, September 24, 1995.
New Criterion, September, 1992, p. 59.
New Republic, December 15, 1962; April 20, 1987, p. 28; February 17, 1992, p. 28.
New Statesman, November 8, 1968; November 7, 1986; May 22, 1987, p. 23.
New Statesman and Society, December 6, 1991, p. 37.
Newsweek, April 20, 1987, p. 89; January 9, 1989, p. 53; January 21, 1991, p. 60; September 27, 1993, p. 74.

New York, April 20, 1987, p. 76; February 13, 1989, p. 71; September 27, 1993, p. 72.

New Yorker, May 4, 1987, p. 128; September 6, 1993, p. 92; October 11, 1993, p. 124.

New York Review of Books, September 24, 1987, p. 3A; April 13, 1989, p. 24; February 16, 1995, p. 15.

New York Times, November 5, 1968; July 26, 1969; March 1, 1985; April 17, 1987; May 17, 1987; March 3, 1992, p. C13; September 17, 1993, p. C1; September 26, 1995.

New York Times Book Review, October 15, 1995, p. 13.

New York Times Magazine, September 30, 1990, p. 36.

Observer, September 28, 1986; October 9, 1994, p. 20.

Publishers Weekly, December 4, 2000, review of *The Clothes They Stood up In,* p. 51.

Punch, November 6, 1968.

Sight and Sound, spring, 1979, p. 116; spring, 1984, p. 121.

Spectator, April 2, 1988, p. 27; October 8, 1994, p. 39; December 18, 1999, Sheridan Morley, review of *The Lady in the Van,* pp. 90-91; December 16, 2000, Paul Routledge, review of *Telling Tales,* pp. 78-79; October 6, 2001, Hilary Mantel, review of *The Laying on of Hands,* p. 63.

Time, September 13, 1993, p. 75.

Times (London), November 27, 1978, p. 7; May 4, 1984; September 6, 1986; p. 10; January 20, 1992, p. 10.

Times Literary Supplement, December 16, 1991, p. 18; October 7, 1994, p. 38; December 24, 1999, Robert Shore, review of *Lady in the Van,* p. 17.

Variety, February 3, 1992, p. 87; November 9, 1992, p. 66.

Village Voice, January 30, 1969.

Vogue, September, 1993, p. 324.

Wall Street Journal, December 29, 1994, p. A8.

Washington Post, April 29, 1985; May 15, 1987; May 16, 1987; February 19, 1992, p. C1; October 10, 1993, p. G4; October 18, 1993, p. D2; January 25, 2001, Jonathan Yardley, "Cleaned Out," p. C2.

*   *   *

BERG, Stephen (Walter) 1934-

PERSONAL: Born August 2, 1934, in Philadelphia, PA; son of Harry Sidney (a businessman) and Hilda (Wachansky) Berg; married Millie Lane, August 26, 1959; children: Clair, Margot. *Education:* Attended University of Pennsylvania, Boston University, and University of Indiana School of Letters; State University of Iowa, B.A., 1959.

ADDRESSES: Office—2005 Mt. Vernon St., Philadelphia, PA 19130.

CAREER: Temple University, Philadelphia, PA, instructor in English, beginning 1963; University of the Arts, Philadelphia, PA, professor of humanities, 1967—. Poet-in-residence, Princeton University, 1979-81; formerly instructor at Haverford College.

AWARDS, HONORS: Rockefeller-Centro Mexicano de Escritores grant, 1959-61; National Translation Center grant, 1969; Frank O'Hara Poetry Prize, 1970; Guggenheim fellow, 1974-75; National Endowment for the Arts fellow, 1976; Columbia University Translation Center Award, 1976; Pennsylvania Council grant, 1979; Philadelphia Mayor's Arts and Culture Award, 1991; Rockefeller fellow.

WRITINGS:

Berg-Goodman-Mezey, New Ventures Press (Philadelphia, PA), 1957.

Bearing Weapons (poems), Cummington Press (West Branch, IA), 1963.

(Editor, with Robert Mezey, and contributor) *Naked Poetry: Recent American Poetry in Open Forms,* Bobbs-Merrill (Indianpolis, IN), 1969.

The Queen's Triangle: A Romance, Cummington Press (West Branch, IA), 1970.

The Daughters: Poems, Bobbs-Merrill (Indianpolis, IN), 1971.

(Editor, with S. J. Marks, and contributor) *Between People: A Reader for Open Learning,* Scott, Foresman (Chicago, IL), 1972.

(Translator, with Steven Polgar and S. J. Marks) Miklos Radnoti, *Clouded Sky,* Harper (New York, NY), 1972.

Nothing in the Word: Versions of Aztec Poetry, Grossman (New York, NY), 1972.

(Editor, with S. J. Marks) *About Women: An Anthology of Contemporary Fiction, Poetry, and Essays,* Fawcett (New York, NY), 1973.

(Editor, with S. J. Marks) *Doing the Unknown,* Dell (New York, NY), 1974.

Grief: Poems and Versions of Poems, Viking (New York, NY), 1975.

(Editor, with Robert Mezey) *The New Naked Poetry,* Bobbs Merrill (Indianpolis, IN), 1976.

(Translator, with Diskin Clay) Sophocles, *Oedipus the King,* Oxford University Press (New York, NY), 1978.

With Akhmatora at the Black Gates: Variations, University of Illinois Press (Urbana, IL), 1981.

Sea Ice: Versions of Eskimo Songs, Cummington Press (Omaha, NE), 1985.

(Editor) *In Praise of What Persists,* Harper (New York, NY), 1983.

(Editor) *Singular Voices: American Poetry Today,* Avon Books (New York, NY), 1985.

In It, University of Illinois Press (Urbana, IL), 1986.

First Song, Bankei, 1653, Cummington Press (Omaha, NE), 1989.

Crow with No Mouth: Ikkyu, 15th-Century Zen Master: Versions, Copper Canyon Press (Port Townsend, WA), 1989.

Homage to the Afterlife, Cummington Press (Omaha, NE), 1991.

New and Selected Poems, Copper Canyon Press (Port Townsend, WA), 1992.

Oblivion: Poems, University of Illinois Press (Urbana, IL), 1995.

The Steel Cricket: Versions 1958-1997, Copper Canyon Press (Port Townsend, WA), 1997.

Shaving, Four Way Books (Marshfield, MA), 1998.

Footnotes to an Unfinished Poem, Orchises Press (Washington, DC), 2000.

Porno Diva Numero Uno: An Anonymous Confession, Hard Press, 2000.

Halo, Sheep Meadow Press (Riverdale-on-Hudson, NY), 2000.

(Editor, with David Bonanno and Arthur Vogelsang) *The Body Electric: America's Best Poetry from the American Poetry Review,* Norton (New York, NY), 2000.

Footnotes to an Unfinished Poem, Orchises Press (Washington, DC), 2000.

(Editor) *My Business Is Circumference,* Paul Dry Books, in press.

Contributor of poems to *Paris Review, New Yorker, Yale Review, Poetry, Prairie Schooner, Chicago Review,* and *Mademoiselle.* Poetry editor, *Saturday Evening Post,* 1961-62; founder and co-editor, *American Poetry Review,* 1972—.

SIDELIGHTS: Stephen Berg, wrote Linwood C. Powers in the *Dictionary of Literary Biography,* "is not a conventional poet. Full of free associations, surrealistic imagery, and harsh rhythms, his poetry is sensitive, imaginative, ambitious, and revelatory. His work requires careful scrutiny, but it frequently rewards that effort with a sudden awareness that compensates for any frustrations the reader may feel at its often difficult and elliptic nature." In a review of *The Daughters,* Laurence

Lieberman of *Yale Review* found that "Berg seems to be . . . taken with the sound of his own voice and the exhilarating process of juggling images . . . but his commitment to the tools of his craft, as well as to the most central human concerns, is total; and when these two rival espousals are balanced and matched . . . he can write masterful whole poems."

Berg's collection *Grief,* containing poems about the death of his father, was particularly well received. Richard Howard wrote in *Yale Review* that in this book Berg "is demonstrably a man of explicit affections, a husband and father of exemplary devotion [and] a compassionate teacher. . . . He cares, he mourns, he praises." In similar terms, Stanley Plumley of *Nation* stated that "Berg is perhaps the most passionate of his contemporaries." Plumley also found that Berg's "rhythms are free, searching, almost abrasive; they reveal the hard-working impatience of a poet determined to get down to it, no nonsense." Speaking of the book as a whole, Plumley maintained that "Berg's power builds line by line, poem by poem, and is really only achieved in the aggregate, when the poems' power to be beautiful transcends the local emotion."

The verse in *New and Selected Poems* shows how Berg "lives by seeking redemption for one's adult nature: the frailty, fallibility and fear," according to Stephen Dobyns in the *New York Times.* These poems, written over a twenty-year period, cover subjects ranging from the poet's daily life to the suffering brought about by the Stalin regime. The poems can be difficult, stated Dobyns, but not because of weak writing on Berg's part; rather, because they are "in a way too bright, the light is too sharply focused. By stripping away illusion and all the soft places, Mr. Berg gives us the skeleton with all its grimness. . . . We need poets like this. Mr. Berg relentlessly describes what we would often prefer to forget but can't allow ourselves to forget. To forget our very nature means to repeat our many blunders over and over again." Ten prose poems published in *New and Selected Poems* were later published as *Shaving,* a volume worthy of "our attention and, often, our applause," in the estimation of a *Publishers Weekly* reviewer. *Oblivion,* another volume of poetry, is a "technically brilliant" encounter with "fundamental metaphysical questions," according to *New York Times* contributor Philip Gambone, who further stated that the poems frequently give the reader "dazzling intimations of the possibility and mystery of a radically awakened consciousness."

With *In Praise of What Persists,* Berg presents essays by twenty-four prominent writers on what they believe were the most profound influences on their work. The answers range from witnessing brutality in Central America to realizing how distracting and all-consuming parenthood can be. The essays are "for the most part thoughtful, frank, generous, and often surprising," said Anne Tyler in *New Republic*. While she felt that all are not of equal value, "taken as a whole, *In Praise of What Persists* is an important book both for would-be writers and for literary scholars. It has something immensely valuable to say about the struggle into print—or more than that, about the struggle to find one's own voice, and to know why to write, as well as how and what to write."

BIOGRAPHICAL/CRITICAL SOURCES:

BOOKS

Contemporary Poets, St. James Press (Detroit, MI), 1996.
Dictionary of Literary Biography, Volume V: *American Poets since World War II*, Gale (Detroit, MI), 1980.

PERIODICALS

American Poetry Review, September, 1987, review of *In It*, p. 32.
Antioch Review, summer, 1983, review of *In Praise of What Persists*, p. 372; winter, 1993, Dan McGuiness, review of *New and Selected Poems*, p. 152.
Bloomsbury Review, March, 1996, review of *Oblivion*, p. 22.
Booklist, April 1, 1983, review of *In Praise of What Persists*, p. 1008; April 15, 1985, review of *Singular Voices: American Poetry Today*, p. 1153; April 15, 2000, Donna Seaman, review of *The Body Electric: America's Best Poetry from the American Poetry Review*, p. 1516.
Chicago, June, 1983, Marcia Froelke Coburn, review of *In Praise of What Persists*, p. 10.
Choice, October, 1983, review of *In Praise of What Persists*, p. 277.
Christian Science Monitor, November 28, 1983, review of *In Praise of What Persists*, p. 22; July 6, 1984, review of *In Praise of What Persists*, p. B8; March 1, 1985, review of *Singular Voices*, p. B8.
Georgia Review, spring, 1984, review of *In Praise of What Persists*, p. 196.
Hudson Review, spring, 1987, review of *In It*, p. 150.
Kirkus Reviews, February 15, 1983, review of *In Praise of What Persists*, p. 216.

Kliatt Young Adult Paperback Book Guide, fall, 1984, review of *In Praise of What Persists*, p. 36; spring, 1985, review of *Singular Voices*, p. 31; fall, 1986, review of *In It*, p. 32.
Library Journal, March 1, 1983, review of *In Praise of What Persists*, p. 501; May 1, 1985, Grace Bauer, review of *Singular Voices*, p. 64; February 15, 1992, Louis McKee, review of *New and Selected Poems*, p. 171; June 1, 1997, Tim Gavin, review of *The Steel Cricket: Versions 1958-1997*, p. 102; June 1, 2000, Fred Muratori, review of *The Body Electric*, p. 132.
Los Angeles Times Book Review, September 11, 1983, review of *In Praise of What Persists*, p. 10; June 10, 1984, review of *In Praise of What Persists*, p. 10.
Multicultural Review, October, 1992, review of *New and Selected Poems*, p. 66.
Nation, May 28, 1973; December 4, 1976.
New Republic, September 12, 1983, Anne Tyler, review of *In Praise of What Persists*, p. 32.
New York Times, December 13, 1992, Stephen Dobyns, review of *New and Selected Poems*; January 28, 1996, Philip Gambone, review of *Oblivion*.
New York Times Book Review, September 6, 1981; August 7, 1983, Martha Bayles, review of *In Praise of What Persists*, p. 15; January 28, 1996, review of *Oblivion*, p. 21.
North American Review, December, 1986, review of *In It*, p. 64.
Philadelphia Business Journal, August 7, 1989, Andrew W. Lehren, "Poetry Magazine Is Celebrating Itself," p. 1.
Philadelphia Magazine, May, 1983, Robert Leiter, review of *In Praise of What Persists*, p. 71.
Poetry, December, 1958; April, 1970; March, 1973; April, 1973; February, 1977; April, 1978.
Publishers Weekly, February 11, 1983, review of *In Praise of What Persists*, p. 60; February 15, 1985, review of *Singular Voices*, p. 98; April 25, 1986, John Mutter, review of *In It*, p. 89; January 6, 1992, review of *New and Selected Poems*, p. 63; March 31, 1997, review of *The Steel Cricket*, p. 71; August 31, 1998, review of *Shaving*, p. 70; March 27, 2000, review of *The Body Electric*, p. 71; November 20, 2000, review of *Porno Diva Numero Uno*, p. 65.
Reference and Research Book News, June, 1992, review of *New and Selected Poems*, p. 38; November, 1997, review of *The Steel Cricket*, p. 159.
Small Press, December, 1989, review of *Crow with No Mouth: Ikkyu, 15th Century Zen Master: Versions*, p. 52.
Southwest Review, autumn, 1969; spring, 1974.

Threepenny Review, summer, 1983, review of *With Akhmatova at the Black Gates: Variations,* p. 7.
Washington Post Book World, August 2, 1981.
Western Humanities Review, spring, 1972.
Times Literary Supplement, May 28, 1982.
TriQuarterly, fall, 1986, review of *In It,* p. 172.
Voice Literary Supplement, June, 1983, review of *In Praise of What Persists,* p. 3.
Wilson Quarterly, Number 3, 1985, review of *Singular Voices,* p. 139.
World Literature Today, spring, 1984, review of *In Praise of What Persists,* p. 276.
Yale Review, December, 1972; March, 1976.*

* * *

BERGMAN, Andrew 1945-
(Warren Bogle)

PERSONAL: Born 1945, in New York, NY. *Education:* Graduated from Harpur College (magna cum laude); University of Wisconsin, Ph.D.

ADDRESSES: Agent—Sam Cohn, International Creative Management, 40 West 57th St., New York, NY 10019.

CAREER: Writer. Director of motion pictures, including *So Fine,* 1981, *The Freshman,* 1990, *Honeymoon in Vegas,* 1992, *It Could Happen to You,* 1994, *Striptease,* 1996, and *Isn't She Great,* 2000. Executive producer of motion picture *Little Big League,* 1994. Made cameo appearance in motion picture *Big Trouble,* 1986.

WRITINGS:

We're in the Money: Depression America and Its Films (nonfiction), New York University Press (New York, NY), 1971.
James Cagney (monograph), Pyramid (New York, NY), 1973.
Social Security (two-act play), Doubleday (New York, NY), 1986.
Sleepless Nights (novel), Donald I. Fine (New York, NY), 1994.

"JACK LEVINE" MYSTERY NOVELS

The Big Kiss-off of 1944, Holt (New York, NY), 1974.
Hollywood and LeVine, Holt (New York, NY), 1975.
Tender Is LeVine, Thomas Dunne Books (New York, NY), 2000.

SCREENPLAYS

(With Mel Brooks, Richard Pryor, Alan Uger, and Norman Steinberg) *Blazing Saddles* (based on Bergman's story), Warner Bros., 1974.
The In-Laws, Warner Bros., 1979.
So Fine, Warner Bros., 1981.
Oh God! You Devil, Warner Bros., 1984.
Fletch (adapted from Gregory McDonald's novel), Universal, 1985.
(Under pseudonym Warren Bogle) *Big Trouble,* Columbia, 1986.
The Freshman, Tri-Star, 1990.
(With Robert Harling) *Soapdish,* Paramount, 1991.
Honeymoon in Vegas, Columbia, 1992.
(With Albert Brooks, Monica Johnson, and Lloyd Fonvielle) *The Scout* (based on a story by Roger Angell), Twentieth Century-Fox, 1994.
Striptease, Columbia, 1996.

SIDELIGHTS: Andrew Bergman is a versatile writer whose published volumes include a film history, novels, and a play; he has also written screenplays and has enjoyed success as a film director. He began his career in 1971 with the scholarly *We're in the Money: Depression America and Its Films,* and followed that volume with the monograph, *James Cagney.* In 1975 he published his first novel, *The Big Kiss-off of 1944,* which introduced readers to Jack LeVine, a tough-talking private investigator operating in New York City. The novel was well received and won comparisons with the works of genre master Raymond Chandler. Russell Davies wrote in the *Times Literary Supplement* that *The Big Kiss-off of 1944* constitutes a "thoroughly pleasant surprise for Raymond Chandler enthusiasts . . . The way Mr. Bergman manages to maintain both the spirit of affectionate parody and the impetus of his own story is remarkable." Bergman followed *The Big Kiss-off of 1944* with *Hollywood and LeVine,* in which the wisecracking hero uncovers murder and mayhem in the film capital.

By the time that *Hollywood and Levine* appeared in 1975, Bergman had already commenced his own involvement in filmmaking. He collaborated on the story and script for filmmaker Mel Brooks's *Blazing Saddles,* a rousing spoof of the western genre. In 1979, Bergman supplied the script for director Arthur Hiller's *The In-Laws,* a comedy in which a mild-mannered dentist (Alan Arkin) becomes embroiled in an ex-spy's (Peter Falk) plot to swindle a South American dictator out of a fortune, all just days before the two men's children are to be wed. *New York Times* critic Janet Maslin proclaimed *The In-Laws* an "altogether sidesplitting movie," and she declared that Bergman "has written one of those rare comedy scripts that escalates steadily and hilariously, without faltering or even having to strain for an ending."

In 1981 Bergman made his directorial debut with *So Fine,* a comedy in which an English literature professor returns to New York to assist in his family's faltering garment business and soon finds himself romantically involved with a gorgeous woman married to a mobster. In fleeing from the jealous husband, the professor, compelled to don his lover's too-tight jeans, inadvertently sparks a fashion trend when the seams split and his buttocks burst through the clothing. The film culminates in a madcap production of Verdi's opera *Othello,* replete with inappropriate scenery, the menacing mobster, and the professor's rope-swinging father; the opera, of course, is proclaimed a masterpiece. Maslin, who had been enthusiastic in her praise of the earlier *In-Laws,* acknowledged in the *New York Times* that *So Fine* also possesses "a consistently zany style," and she noted that Bergman's direction of his own script "is for the most part skillful and confident."

Bergman next received credit as the screenwriter for *Oh God! You Devil,* the third in a series of films featuring entertainer George Burns as God. In this entry, directed by Paul Bogart, a struggling musician unwittingly barters his soul for fame and riches; God and the devil—both played by Burns—then vie for ownership of the hero's soul. *Los Angeles Times* reviewer Kevin Thomas staunchly supported *Oh God! You Devil,* deeming it "fresh, fast and contemporary," and lauding it as "a consistently amusing, buoyant comedy."

Bergman also provided the script for *Fletch,* a 1985 vehicle for comic performer Chevy Chase. Directed by Michael Ritchie and derived from Gregory McDonald's popular mystery series, *Fletch* features Chase as a resourceful, flippant investigative reporter who dons a variety of disguises in his efforts to solve a mystery involving drug-dealing police and a business executive seemingly bent on ending his own life. Though it was considered inferior to the books on which it was based, *New York Times* critic Vincent Canby called *Fletch* "a lightweight, enjoyable experience," and *Chicago Tribune* reviewer Gene Siskel acknowledged it as "funny and exciting."

In the mid-1980s Bergman turned playwright, creating *Social Security,* a two-act comedy about an art-dealing couple saddled briefly with the wife's uncooperative

mother, who is prone to disturbing sloppiness and recklessness. Matters culminate during a dinner party in which the mother is drawn to the guest of honor, an aging artist about to be honored with an exhibition at the Museum of Modern Art. Directed by Mike Nichols, *Social Security* garnered generally positive reviews: David Richards, writing in the *Washington Post,* affirmed that *Social Security* "has an awareness of human idiosyncracy," and William H. Honan wrote in the *New York Times* that after watching *Social Security,* audiences "leave the theater refreshed and perhaps a little less fearful than before about having been deserted in a universe so lacking in common decency."

In 1986 Bergman adopted the pseudonym "Warren Bogle" to pen *Big Trouble,* the last film to be directed by John Cassavetes. The film reunites Alan Arkin and Peter Falk, stars of *The In-Laws,* and was originally meant to be the sequel to that film; also, Bergman had planned to direct. In the final version, directed by Cassavetes, Arkin gets caught in a scheme to kill Falk for insurance money in the manner of the 1944 film, *Double Indemnity.* "There are moments of comic brilliance in this film," wrote a *Motion Picture Guide* reviewer, "but as a whole *Big Trouble* was deemed unsatisfactory." The reviewer blamed director Cassavetes' tendency to emphasize character study over plot development—an approach that "just doesn't work" in this light comedy.

The 1990 comedy, *The Freshman,* marked Bergman's second effort as writer-director for the screen. A naive college student arrives in New York City and is soon immersed in organized crime hijinks involving an only slightly intimidating don (played by Marlon Brando). Reluctant to run afoul of the don and his rather more menacing henchmen, the student becomes drawn into a scheme for smuggling and cooking an endangered Komodo dragon. Maslin, in her *New York Times* appraisal, deemed *The Freshman* "a witty and enchanted comedy," and Joe Brown, writing in the *Washington Post,* contended that "Bergman gets away with nearly every goofy gag he goes for." Dave Kehr, meanwhile, observed in the *Chicago Tribune* that *The Freshman* "seems likely to become a classic."

Securing the services of the reclusive Brando for *The Freshman* was a major feat for Bergman, who exploits resemblances between the don of *The Freshman* and *The Godfather*'s Don Vito Corleone. Bergman told Maslin in the *New York Times* that adjusting the script to exploit Brando's presence "was the most delicious experience—that was heaven." But controversy flared when Brando, at the conclusion of filming, abruptly denigrated *The Freshman* as a likely failure; he later disclosed that his objections were actually with the film's producers rather than the film itself, remarking that *The Freshman* "contains moments of high comedy that will be remembered for decades."

Bergman next collaborated with Robert Harling on the script for *Soapdish,* a zany comedy directed by Michael Hoffman about the wacky behind-the-scenes intrigues among the cast and crew of a television soap opera. *Newsweek*'s David Ansen, while noting that the plot occasionally turns convoluted and the humor sometimes becomes tame, nonetheless declared, "a movie with this many belly laughs can be forgiven almost anything." He called *Soapdish* "uninhibited lunacy."

In 1992 Bergman completed *Honeymoon in Vegas,* his third film as both writer and director. In this comedy a private detective, Jack Singer, travels with his fiancé, a second-grade teacher, to Las Vegas for a quick wedding. But once there, he is drawn into a poker game in which he eventually incurs losses of more than sixty thousand dollars to dashing gambler Tommy Korman. Korman agrees to forego payment if he can have the company of Singer's fiancé for a weekend in Hawaii; Singer reluctantly agrees. *New Yorker* reviewer Michael Sragow described *Honeymoon in Vegas* as a "screwball idyll" and he observed that Bergman possesses "a refreshing satirical grasp of our native eclecticism." A reviewer for *Motion Picture Guide* noted that "Bergman is less concerned with plot than with simply putting his characters into bizarre, almost surrealistic situations to see how they'll squirm their way out," and described the writer-director as "one of the last of the true comic stylists."

Bergman returned to print in 1994 with *Sleepless Nights,* a comic novel about incest between a young man and his sister, a fashion model with whom he shares a bedroom. Upon reaching adulthood, the protagonist becomes a history professor, but he struggles to find happiness. David Murray, writing in the *New York Times Book Review,* described *Sleepless Nights* as "a first-rate work of fiction."

Bergman wrote the screenplay and directed actors Demi Moore and Burt Reynolds in *Striptease.* The story concerns a divorced mother, Erin, who works as a stripper to pay for court costs as she struggles to win custody of her young son. Her life is complicated when a lecherous old politician jumps onstage with her and is photographed by the press. *Striptease* was not a great critical success. In the opinion of Brian D. Johnson, a reviewer

for *Maclean's,* this film tries to be "a comedy, a morality tale and a titillating sideshow, [but] fails on all counts." Johnson felt the "flat-footed script bumps and grinds from dumb farce to dopey sentiment." Owen Gleiberman, a writer for *Entertainment Weekly,* also found the movie marked by an "amorphous, muzzy-headed tone." Reviewing *Striptease* for *Newsweek,* David Ansen decided that the film succeeded best as "a broad, ramshackle comedy" and noted, "Bergman has some fun tweaking the hypocrisies of . . . politicians."

Bergman next published a new Jack LeVine mystery, titled *Tender Is Levine.* This hard-boiled mystery puts LeVine in New York, Cuba, and Las Vegas as he searches for the great conductor, Arturo Toscanini, who has been kidnaped. The story is somewhat overblown, noted a *Publishers Weekly* writer, but "LeVine is so solidly set it time and place by the period details that the events seem believable, while the showbizzy shtick adds to the pleasure. The author proves again . . . that Jack's a great guy." Bill Ott, a contributor to *Booklist,* also found LeVine's persona the most satisfying part of Bergman's mystery. Ott stated: "The completely preposterous plot offers good, outlandish fun, but the real pleasure here is just listening to LeVine, who cracks wise as well as anyone."

BIOGRAPHICAL/CRITICAL SOURCES:

BOOKS

Motion Picture Guide, Cinebooks, *1987 Annual,* edited by Jay Robert Nash and Stanley Ralph Ross, 1987; *1993 Annual,* edited by John Miller-Monzon, 1993.

PERIODICALS

Booklist, December 15, 2000, Bill Ott, review of *Tender Is LeVine,* p. 789.
Chicago Tribune, September 30, 1981; November 9, 1984; June 3, 1985; July 27, 1990.
Los Angeles Times, November 9, 1984; July 20, 1990.
Los Angeles Times Book Review, July 3, 1994, p. 6.
Maclean's, July 8, 1996, Brian D. Johnson, review of *Striptease,* p. 49.
Nation, February 21, 2000, Stuart Klawans, review of *Isn't She Great?,* p. 34.
New Statesman, February 28, 1975, p. 284; April 9, 1976, p. 478.

Newsweek, June 24, 1991, p. 61; August 1, 1994, p. 56; July 8, 1996, David Ansen, review of *Striptease,* p. 67.

New York, July 12, 1996, Owen Gleiberman, review of *Striptease,* p. 38; February 7, 2000, Peter Rainer, review of *Isn't She Great?,* p. 52.

New Yorker, September 25, 1981, p. C8; September 7, 1992, pp. 86-87.

New York Times, September 4, 1975; June 15, 1979, p. C10; November 9, 1984; May 31, 1985; April 13, 1986; April 18, 1986; April 27, 1986; June 8, 1986; July 15, 1990; July 20, 1990; July 29, 1994, p. C10.

New York Times Book Review, March 31, 1974, p. 41; September 7, 1975, p. 39; September 11, 1994, p. 24.

People, July 8, 1996, Leah Rozen, review of *Striptease,* p. 19.

Premiere, February, 2000, review of *Isn't She Great,* p. 20.

Publishers Weekly, November 20, 2000, review of *Tender Is LeVine,* p. 49.

Time, April 28, 1986, p. 69; July 8, 1996, Richard Schickel, review of *Striptease,* p. 66; February 7, 2000, Richard Schickel, review of *Isn't She Great?,* p. 77.

Times Literary Supplement, March 7, 1975, p. 241.

Variety, June 24, 1996, Todd McCarthy, review of *Striptease,* p. 119; January 31, 2000, Emanuel Levy, review of *Isn't She Great?,* p. 31; February 7, 2000, Dave McNary, "'Great' Hopes Bowled Under," p. 9.

Video Business, June 5, 2000, Mayna Bergmann, review of *Isn't She Great,* p.14.

Washington Post, June 15, 1979, p. B2; September 25, 1981; May 31, 1985; March 10, 1986; July 27, 1990.*

*   *   *

BIDART, Frank 1939-

PERSONAL: Born, 1939; son of a farmer. *Education:* Graduated from University of California—Riverside; attended Harvard University.

ADDRESSES: Home—63 Sparts St., No. 3, Cambridge, MA 02138. *Office*—Wellesley College, Department of English, 106 Central St., Wellesley, MA 02481-8268.

CAREER: Poet. Wellesley College, Department of English, Wellesley, MA, faculty member, 1972—.

AWARDS, HONORS: Bernard F. Conners Prize, *Paris Review,* 1981, for "The War of Vaslav Nijinsky"; Lila Wallace Reader's Digest Foundation award, 1993; Morton Dauwen Zabel Award, American Academy of Arts and Letters, 1995; Rebekka Bobbitt Prize for poetry, Library of Congress, 1998, and Pulitzer Prize, National Book Award, and National Book Critics Circle Award nominations, all for *Desire;* Lannan literary fellowship, 1998; Wallace Stevens award, 2001; Shelley Award, Poetry Society of America; Guggenheim fellowship.

WRITINGS:

POETRY COLLECTIONS

Golden State, Braziller (New York, NY), 1973.

The Book of the Body, Farrar, Straus & Giroux (New York, NY), 1977.

The Sacrifice, Random House (New York, NY), 1983.

In the Western Night: Collected Poems, 1965-90, Farrar, Straus & Giroux (New York, NY), 1990.

Desire, Farrar, Straus & Giroux (New York, NY), 1997.

Music Like Dirt, Sarabande Books (Louisville, KY), 2002.

WORK IN PROGRESS: Editing a volume of poems by Robert Lowell.

SIDELIGHTS: Frank Bidart first gained the attention of critics with *Golden State* and *The Book of the Body,* introspective verse collections that were published during the 1970s. On the basis of Bidart's early work, David Lehman, in a *Newsweek* assessment, called him "a poet of uncommon intelligence and uncompromising originality." In the early 1980s Bidart wrote *The Sacrifice,* which furthered his reputation as a prominent voice in American poetry. Much of Bidart's work, critics suggest, focuses on the origins and consequences of guilt. Among his most notable pieces are dramatic monologues presented through such characters as Herbert White, a child-murderer, and Ellen West, an anorexic woman. "Part of his effectiveness comes simply from his ability as a storyteller," commented Michael Dirda in *Washington Post Book World.* "You long to discover what happens to his poor, doomed people."

Bidart grew up in California, where he developed a love for the cinema. He entertained thoughts of becoming an actor when he was young and later, at the time he enrolled in college, considered becoming a film director. His plans began to change, however, when he was introduced to literature at the University of California—Riverside. While an undergraduate, he was introduced to such critical works as *The Liberal Imagination* by Lionel Trilling and *The Idea of a Theater* by Francis Fergusson—both of which exerted a strong influence on his early attitudes toward literary expression. He also became familiar with the work of notable twentieth-century poets T. S. Eliot and Ezra Pound. In a 1983 interview with Mark Halliday, which is included in Bidart's *In the Western Night: Collected Poems, 1965-90,* the poet spoke of how reading Pound's cantos, long works which were first released in 1917, introduced him to the potential of poetry to encompass a wide range of subjects: "They were tremendously liberating in the way that they say that anything can be gotten into a poem, that it doesn't have to change its essential identity to enter the poem—if you can create a structure that is large enough or strong enough, *anything* can retain its own identity and find its place there."

After graduating from the University of California—Riverside, Bidart continued his education at Harvard University. He was not, however, certain of where his course of study would lead him. Bidart related in his interview with Halliday: "I took classes with half my will—often finishing the work for them months after they were over; and was scared, miserable, hopeful. I wrote a great deal. I wrote lugubrious plays that I couldn't see had characters with no character. More and more, I wrote poems." Bidart's first attempts at poetry were, by his own admission, failures. "They were terrible; no good at all," he continued in his interview. "I was doing what many people start out by doing, trying to be 'universal' by making the entire poem out of assertions and generalization about the world—with a very thin sense of a complicated, surprising, opaque world outside myself that resisted the patterns I was asserting. These generalizations, shorn of much experience, were pretty simple-minded and banal."

After honing his craft, Bidart submitted his work to Richard Howard, who was then editor of a poetry series at Braziller. Howard decided to publish Bidart's poetry in a volume titled *Golden State,* which was released in 1973. In the title poem to Bidart's debut collection, a son and father vainly attempt to understand and accept one another. The poem, presented as an address to the father, is divided into ten separate sections. Critics remarked on the autobiographical nature of the piece and on the sparse quality of the language that Bidart employs throughout the work. Other poems in the collection also touch upon the relationship between parent and child. In his interview Bidart discussed how he came upon the theme of family that enters into some of

the poems in *Golden State:* "When I first faced the central importance of 'subject matter,' I knew what I would have to begin by writing about. In the baldest terms, I was someone who had grown up obsessed with his parents. The drama of their lives dominated what, at the deepest level, *I* thought about."

Also included in *Golden State* is "Herbert White," a poem which is presented through the voice of a psychopathic child-murderer and necrophiliac. In his interview with Halliday Bidart stated that his intent in writing the piece was to present "someone who was 'all that I was not,' whose way of 'solving problems' was the *opposite* of that of the son in the middle of the book. The son's way . . . involves trying to 'analyze' and 'order' the past, in order to reach 'insight'; Herbert White's is to give himself a violent pattern growing out of the dramas of his past, a pattern that consoles him as long as he can feel that someone *else* has acted within it." According to several reviewers, the dramatic monologue, which opens the collection, is the most notable work in the book. Sharon Mayer Libera, in her *Parnassus* assessment, stated that "Bidart's achievement, even a *tour de force,* is to have made [Herbert White] human. The narrator's gruesome adventures become the least important aspect of the monologue—what is significant is his reaching out, in a language both awkward and alive, for the reasons he seeks power over his experience in peculiar and violent ways."

In Bidart's second collection, *The Book of the Body,* he includes several poems which feature characters who are struggling to overcome both physical and emotional adversity. The book opens with "The Arc," in which the author presents the musings of an amputee, who at the beginning of the poem provides instructions on how to care for his stump. Bidart also gives voice to Ellen West, a woman with anorexia, a condition which causes her to starve herself continuously because she is dissatisfied with the appearance of her body. Based on a case study by noted psychiatrist Ludwig Binswanger, "Ellen West" was regarded by Edmund White in *Washington Post Book World* as "a work that displays Bidart's talents at their most exacting, their most insistent."

In the opinion of several reviewers, Bidart's work gains strength by disregarding the conventions of poetry. In an appraisal of *The Book of the Body,* Helen Vendler of the *Yale Review* stated that "Bidart's method is not narrative; unlike the seamless dramatic monologues we are used to, his are spliced together, as harrowing bits of speech, an anecdote, a reminiscence, a doctor's journal notes, a letter, an analogy, follow each other in a cinematic progression." Reviewers have also often drawn attention to liberties that Bidart takes when spacing his words and lines in his poetry and when punctuating and capitalizing the English. In his interview with Halliday Bidart explained that "the only way I can sufficiently . . . express the relative weight and importance of the parts of a sentence—so that the reader knows where he or she is and the 'weight' the speaker is placing on the various elements that are being laid out—is [through] punctuation. . . . Punctuation allows me to 'lay out' the *bones* of a sentence visually, spatially, so that the reader can see the pauses, emphases, urgencies and languors in the voice."

The Sacrifice, released in 1983, received widespread praise from reviewers for its insightful poems, many with a guilt theme. Central to the volume is a thirty-page work titled "The War of Vaslav Nijinsky." The title character in the poem is a dancer who pays witness to World War I and eventually loses his sanity. Feeling responsible for the injustices inflicted upon humanity during the conflict, Nijinsky offers penance by performing a dance in which he enacts his own suicide. As with most of his poetry, "The War of Vaslav Nijinsky" went through a series of revisions with Bidart experimenting with language and punctuation throughout its development. "The Nijinsky poem was a nightmare," he remarked in his interview. "There is a passage early in it that I got stuck on, and didn't solve for two years. Undoubtedly there were a number of reasons for this; the poem scared me. Both the fact that I thought it was the best thing I had done, and Nijinsky's ferocity, the extent to which his mind is *radical,* scared me. But the problem was also that the movement of his voice is so mercurial, and paradoxical: many simple declarative sentences, then a long, self-loathing, twisted-against-itself sentence. The *volume* of the voice (from very quiet to extremely loud) was new; I found that many words and phrases had to be not only entirely capitalized, but in italics." In reviewing the poem, *Newsweek*'s Lehman offered praise for Bidart's technique of alternating portions of the dancer's monologue with prose sections on Nijinsky's life. According to Lehman, "the result combines a documentary effect with an intensity rare in contemporary poetry." Also included in Bidart's third collection is "Confessional," in which he presents the musings of a person who places himself in the role of a patient undergoing psychotherapy. The piece was regarded by Don Bogen of *Nation* as "one of the most intelligent and moving poems on family relations" to be published at the time.

Although he has written in a variety of forms, Bidart is best known for his dramatic monologues of troubled characters like Herbert White, Ellen West, and Vaslav Nijinsky. In his interview Bidart discussed how he is able to write dramatic monologues through voices different from his own: "Once I finally get the typed page to the point where it does seem 'right'—where it does seem to reproduce the voice I hear—something very odd happens: the '*being*' of the poem suddenly becomes the poem on paper, and no longer the 'voice' in my head. The poem on paper suddenly seems a truer embodiment of the poem's voice than what I still hear in my head. I've learned to trust this when it happens—at that point, the entire process is finished." Later in the interview he commented on his approach toward expression through language as a whole, remarking that "again and again, insight is dramatized by showing the conflict between what is ordinarily seen, ordinarily understood, and what now is experienced as real. Cracking the shell of the world; or finding that the shell is cracking under you."

Bidart's *Desire* was nominated for the triple crown of awards—the Pulitzer Prize, the National Book Award, and the National Book Critics Circle Award—and received the 1998 Rebekka Bobbitt Prize from the Library of Congress for the best book of poetry published during the previous two years. In reviewing the volume for the *Boston Phoenix* online, Elizabeth Schmidt wrote that "the use of autobiography in [Bidart's] work is a coded, highly intricate enterprise, and his poetry is some of the most difficult and painstakingly original written in America in the last thirty years, weaving quotes and philosophical fragments, vivid detail and stupefying abstraction, into a linguistic matrix that rarely follows the standard rules of punctuation and syntax." "Previously, most of Bidart's longer efforts were dramatic monologues," wrote Stephen Burt in the *New Leader.* "Here they are third-person narratives, unconfined by a persona's voice. Little else has changed, though, in his basic formula, least of all the initial shock of immersion that his poems occasion. To enter a Bidart poem is to enter a world of literal and figurative violence." Burt called "Adolescence," a found poem about sexual assault that Bidart created from anonymously published prose, "an extreme example."

The first part of *Desire* consists of thirteen short poems, including a memorial to artist Joe Brainard, who died of AIDS. Daphne Kutzer wrote in *Lambda Book Report* that this section "includes the few overtly homosexual poems in the volume, although the underlying premise of the entire volume—that we cannot choose what will bring us to ecstasy, it chooses us—certainly resonates for gay readers." William Logan said in *New Criterion* that these poems "prepare the psychology of 'The Second Hour of the Night,' a masterwork whose first part is as good as anything Bidart has done, juxtaposing the memoirs of Berlioz, whose wife died slowly and horribly, with the death of the poet's mother. The not-so-subtle merger of Bidart's mother and Berlioz's wife, in the erotics implicitly embraced, is the most important psychological gesture in these poems."

The second part is a recounting of Ovid's tale of Myrrha's incestuous love for her father, Cinyrus. In an *Antioch Review* article Molly Bendall compared Bidart's translation with that of Horace Gregory, saying that "characteristically, Bidart has chosen to make the psychological tension more available and succinct rather than allowing it to remain latent." *Nation* reviewer Langdon Hammer wrote that the poem "is, in a sense, the worst case that could be made against desire: Sex makes people miserable; it leads them to destroy others and themselves. Yet Bidart converts his poem into an affirmation of embodied love. The 'precious bitter resin' into which Myrrha's tears are changed tastes bitter and sweet, like *Desire* as a whole. That it is a gay man who has created this book, many years into the age of AIDS, makes the balm a little more bitter, a little more sweet." Hammer noted that the "pre-existing forms" in *Desire* include writing by Dante, Marcus Aurelius, and Catullus. "Bidart's mind," continued Hammer, "like Ezra Pound's, is full of writing. The experience he records is first of all the experience of a compassionate, intensive reader. What he cares about most is not the content of prior texts but what it feels like to enter them, and then to carry them inside you."

Poetry contributor David Yezzi wrote that Bidart's message is that "it's our inner struggles that inexorably define us." Kutzer said, "In a short review like this, I cannot possibly do justice to the beauty, horror, complexity, and passion of this poem, and indeed of all of Bidart's poetry." Adam Kirsch wrote in the *New Republic* that "while Bidart's poetry is, on the surface, about unpleasant things and people—monomaniacs, anorexics, transgressors—his treatment of them is not at all repellent; it is positively glamorous. His ostentatious violation of decorum and conventional morality is not shocking to the reader, but actually flattering to him, because it suggests that he, too, contains dark and tumultuous depths. The awe that the reader feels at Myrrha, or Nijinksy, or West, he is allowed to feel also at himself."

Bidart told *Lambda Book Report* interviewer Timothy Liu, "I think 'The Second Hour of the Night' is a poem I've been trying to write all my life. . . . I wanted to write a poem that questioned love, and in some sense, to punish love as far as one could—and see what

remained. Not out of the illusion that one could destroy the desire for love, but to devour as many sentimentalities and delusional aspects as possible, certainly to question the traditional assumptions about love."

Andrew Rathmann wrote in *Chicago Review* that *Desire* shows Bidart "to be perhaps less agonized and more resigned to the existential, erotic, and familial contradictions that had occasioned so many of his earlier works. These contradictions are no less intolerable than before (and his exposition of them is no less shockingly, daringly articulate), but Bidart in this book seems at least somewhat attracted to the idea of praising what cannot be altered. This takes the form of accepting desire as one's fate." *Booklist* reviewer Ray Olson called *Desire* "literature of the highest order, written to be carefully and slowly read and rewarding such reading with wonder-struck appreciation of human love."

BIOGRAPHICAL/CRITICAL SOURCES:

BOOKS

Bidart, Frank, *In the Western Night: Collected Poems, 1965-90,* Farrar, Straus & Giroux (New York, NY), 1990.
Contemporary Literary Criticism, Volume 33, Gale (Detroit, MI), 1985.
Contemporary Poets, 6th edition, St. James Press (Detroit, MI), 1996.

PERIODICALS

American Poetry Review, September, 1985, p. 14.
Antioch Review, summer, 1998, Molly Bendall, review of *Desire,* p. 380.
Bloomsbury Review, May, 1998, review of *Desire,* p. 7.
Booklist, October 1, 1997, Ray Olson, review of *Desire,* p. 301; January 1, 1998, review of *Desire.*
Chicago Review, fall, 1997, Andrew Rathmann, review of *Desire,* p. 148; fall, 2001, Andrew Rathmann and Danielle Allen, interview with Frank Bidart, p. 21.
Lambda Book Report, December, 1997, Jim Marks, "Editor's Corner," p. 4; April, 1998, Timothy Liu, "Punishing love: Tim Liu interviews Frank Bidart," p. 1, Daphne Kutzer, review of *Desire,* p. 9.
Library Journal, September 15, 1997, Graham Christian, review of *Desire,* p. 77.
Los Angeles Times, March 10, 1997, Mark Arax, "Coming Home, Coming Out" p. A3.

Nation, December 10, 1983, pp. 610-611; August 13, 1990, pp. 170-173; November 24, 1997, Langdon Hammer, review of *Desire,* p. 32.

New Criterion, June, 1998, William Logan, "Soiled Desires," p. 61.

New Leader, October 6, 1997, Stephen Burt, review of *Desire,* p. 16.

New Republic, October 27, 1997, pp. 38-41; October 27, 1997, Adam Kirsch, review of *Desire,* p. 38.

Newsweek, January 30, 1984, David Lehman, review of *The Sacrifice,* pp. 71-72.

New York Times Book Review, November 27, 1983, p. 13.

Parnassus, spring-summer, 1975, Sharon Mayer Libera, review of *Golden State,* pp. 259-269; February, 1993, review of *In the Western Night: Collected Poems, 1965-90,* p. 423.

Poetry, August, 1998, David Yezzi, review of *Desire,* p. 287.

Publishers Weekly, August 25, 1997, p. 66; August 25, 1997, review of *Desire,* p. 66.

Salmagundi, spring-summer, 1998, Cal Bedient, "Frank Bidart, Tragedian," p. 328.

Threepenny Review, summer, 1993, review of *In the Western Night,* p. 20; fall, 1999, review of *Desire,* p. 12.

Tribune Books (Chicago, IL), August 5, 1990, p. 3.

Virginia Quarterly Review, spring, 1998, review of *Desire,* p. 65.

Washington Post Book World, November 20, 1977, p. E5; October 9, 1983, p. 8; March 3, 1991, p. 6; January 25, 1998, Robert Hass, "Poet's Choice," p. 2; September 27, 1998, David Streitfeld, "Book Report," p. 15.

World Literature Today, summer, 1998, review of *Desire,* p. 628.

Yale Review, autumn, 1977, Helen Vendler, review of *The Book of the Body,* pp. 78-79; April, 1998, Stephen Yenser, review of *Desire,* p. 153.

OTHER

Boston Phoenix, http://www.bostonphoenix.com/ (October 27, 1997), Elizabeth Schmidt, "Frank Bidart: Mourning Glory."*

* * *

BLAISE, Clark 1940-

PERSONAL: Surname is pronounced "blezz"; born April 10, 1940, in Fargo, ND; Canadian/United States citizen; son of Leo Romeo Pierre (a furniture salesman) and Anne (a schoolteacher; maiden name, Vanstone) Blaise; married Bharati Mukherjee (a writer and professor), September 19, 1963; children: Bart Anand, Bernard Sudhir. *Education:* Denison University, B.A., 1961; University of Iowa, M.F.A., 1964.

ADDRESSES: Home—130 Rivoli St., San Francisco, CA 94117. *Agent*—Eric Simonoff, Janklow & Nesbit, 445 Park Ave., New York, NY 10022.

CAREER: Writer and teacher. University of Wisconsin-Milwaukee, Milwaukee, WI, acting instructor in English, 1964-65; Concordia University, Montreal, Quebec, assistant professor, 1968-73, associate professor, 1973-76, professor of English, 1976-78; York University, Toronto, Ontario, Canada, professor of humanities, 1978-80; Skidmore College, Saratoga Springs, NY, professor of English, 1980-84; David Thompson University Centre, Nelson, British Columbia, Canada, visiting professor, 1984; Columbia University and New York University, New York, NY, adjunct professor, 1985-89; Sarah Lawrence College, New York, NY, adjunct professor, 1987-90; University of Iowa, Iowa City, IA, director of International Writing Program and professor of English, 1990-98, professor emeritus, 1998—; University of California-Berkeley, Berkeley, CA, visiting professor of writing, 1998-2000; California College of Arts and Crafts, distinguished visiting professor, 2001—. Visiting teacher at summer writing workshops, including Bread Loaf, Squaw Valley, and Saratoga Springs, NY. Has conducted writing workshops in India, Singapore, Germany, Haiti, Holland, Argentina, Australia, and Estonia.

AWARDS, HONORS: President's Medal, University of Western Ontario, 1967, for best short story in a Canadian publication; Great Lakes College Association prize, 1973, for best first book of fiction; St. Lawrence Prize, 1974, for best book of short fiction; Fels Award, 1975, for best essay in a literary quarterly; Canada Council Sr. Arts grant, 1976-77; *Books in Canada* Prize, 1980, for best first novel; National Endowment for the Arts grant, 1981; Guggenheim fellowship, 1983; "book of the year" award from Canadian Booksellers' Association, 1995.

WRITINGS:

(With Dave Godfrey and David Lewis Stein) *New Canadian Writing, 1968: Stories by David Lewis Stein, Clark Blaise, and Dave Godfrey,* Irwin Clark (Toronto, Ontario, Canada), 1968.

A North American Education: A Book of Short Fiction, Doubleday (New York, NY), 1973.

Tribal Justice (short stories), Doubleday (New York, NY), 1974.

(With Bharati Mukherjee) *Days and Nights in Calcutta* (nonfiction), Doubleday (New York, NY), 1977.

(Editor, with John Metcalf) *Here and Now,* Oberon Press (Ottawa, Ontario, Canada), 1977.

Lunar Attractions (novel), Doubleday (New York, NY), 1979.

Lusts, Doubleday (New York, NY), 1983.

Resident Alien, Penguin Books (New York, NY), 1986.

(With Bharati Mukherjee) *The Sorrow and the Terror: The Haunting Legacy of the Air India Tragedy,* Viking (New York, NY), 1987.

The Border as Fiction, Borderlands (Orono, ME), 1990.

Man and His World (short stories), Porcupine's Quill (Erin, Ontario, Canada), 1992.

I Had a Father: A Post-modern Autobiography, Addison-Wesley (Reading, MA), 1993.

If I Were Me: A Novel, Porcupine's Quill (Erin, Ontario, Canada), 1997.

New and Selected Stories, Porcupine's Quill, Volume 1: *Southern Stories,* 2000, Volume 2: *Pittsburgh Stories,* 2001.

Time Lord: Sir Sanford Fleming and the Creation of Standard Time, Pantheon (New York, NY), 2001.

Work represented in more than ninety anthologies. Contributor of more than forty stories to magazines, including *Shenandoah, Tri-Quarterly, American Review, Tamarack Review,* and *Journal of Canadian Fiction.* Frequent book reviewer for newspapers and periodicals.

WORK IN PROGRESS: Two more volumes in the *New and Selected Stories,* Porcupine's Quill. *Montreal Stories,* 2002, and *International Stories,* 2003.

SIDELIGHTS: Clark Blaise wrote: "As a native-born American with foreign parents, and as a child who attended an average of two schools a year in twenty-five different cities, I grew up with an outsider's view of America and a romanticized exile's view of French-Canada. In 1965, for personal reasons having to do with a crisis of purpose and identity, I 'returned' to Montreal and claimed this area of the continent for my writings. I am a Canadian citizen. My interest is in 'tribalism' on the American continent, and in all groups who refuse amalgamation and prefer codes and taboos of their own."

Blaise's first two collections of short stories, *A North American Education* and *Tribal Justice,* reflect his concern with "tribalism." According to Val Clery in *Quill*

and Quire, the theme of both books is "the rough ambiguous justice meted out to the individual by the ethnic, geographical or religious tribes that inhabit North America." Clery believed this is an apt theme for Blaise, who was exposed to many "tribes" because of "his father's vagrant pursuit of a livelihood as a furniture salesman in the small towns of Florida and the cities of the American Middle West." Of *Tribal Justice,* a reviewer for the *New York Times Book Review* remarked that the stories "offer sudden, brilliant revelations of feeling or mood or character . . . [and] have the fresh, if apprehensive, vision of a new boy in a new place."

Days and Nights in Calcutta, coauthored by Bharati Mukherjee, is the result of Blaise and his wife's journey to visit her family in India. Each wrote approximately half the book, and while the two are observers of the same general scene, their observations reflect two very different points of view. *New York Times* reviewer Anatole Broyard commented: "Mr. Blaise brings to Calcutta the surprised eye of an outsider. . . . He is continually discovering India and is just as continually struck by its incongruities as seen through Western eyes. [His wife] is more immersed, tending to muse over her country, to mingle its history with her own." William Borders, writing in the *New York Times,* said that "the two have written an unusual book. . . . Its theme, not surprisingly, is cultural alienation."

For his first novel, *Lunar Attractions,* Blaise chose an outsider for his hero and again used alienation as a theme. David Greenwood is "a boy who doesn't quite fit the patterns established by society," observed Joseph McLellan in the *Washington Post.* McLellan continued: "This is all fairly standard material for a 'sensitive first novel.' . . . But there is a refreshing difference [because] David Greenwood is a real, three-dimensional human being. . . . the things that happen to him are believable." John Yohalem, writing in the *New York Times Book Review,* declared: "Mr. Blaise is a thoughtful and entertaining writer, a rediscoverer of childhood with a good memory for his reactions the first time he passed through. . . . [He] is a born storyteller and an easy writer to like, to savor."

The characteristic Blaise work is always autobiographical to some degree, and the author himself told *Contemporary Novelists,* "I would agree with critics who see my work as courting solipsism, and much of my own energy is devoted to finding ways out of the vastness of the first person pronoun." Indeed, the protagonists of Blaise's first two novels, *Lunar Attractions* and *Lusts,* are writers struggling in some sense with the role of the artist's life in his writings. Despite an avowed intention to steer clear of the first person in future writings—a declaration Blaise made in an interview with Barry Cameron conducted in 1980—his work instead became a more complex interweaving of points of view, including rather than avoiding the first person. "While *Lunar Attractions* proved that Blaise could master the novel form, it also demonstrated that his fundamental attraction to self-reflective writing remained central to his art," Robert Lecker commented in *Contemporary Novelists*. Similarly, *Lusts*, Blaise's second novel, centers on the correspondence exchanged between a Chinese-American biographer and the husband of her deceased subject, a poet who killed herself at the height of her success. Despite the surface dissimilarities, Mark Abley noted in his review in *Maclean's* that Blaise shares with his characters a sense of being the outsider, and thus, "Blaise . . . has turned his highly personal sense of displacement into a graphic metaphor for the experience of modern life in North America."

Resident Alien, a collection of short fiction and nonfiction pieces that followed *Lusts*, blurs the lines between autobiography and fiction even further, exploring the nature of identity, particularly as it relates to place. Blaise's stories and essays comment upon and undercut each other, making *Resident Alien* "both the most satisfying and the most provocative of his works" to date, according to David Jackel in the *Dictionary of Literary Biography*. Among Blaise's subsequent works is *I Had a Father: A Post-modern Autobiography*, a more straightforward look at the author's peripatetic youth. The book "provides much insight into how geography confers character," the reviewer for *Publishers Weekly* contended. The same reviewer singled out for praise the "geographic lushness and a sense of mystery" that pervade *I Had a Father*.

Time Lord: Sir Sandford Fleming and the Creation of Standard Time explores one Victorian entrepreneur's contribution to world culture, namely, the standardization of time through a twenty-four-hour day in which all clocks are set corresponding to Greenwich Mean Time. The book not only includes a biography of Sandford Fleming, the leading proponent of standard time, but also includes reflections on the way great novelists respond to time in their works, as well as ruminations on time in an age of computers. A *Publishers Weekly* critic found the book to be "an important history of ideas . . . [written] with perfect pitch and graceful narrative." John Bemrose in *Maclean's* also deemed the work "a dazzling meditation on social change . . . Blaise shows how new technologies . . . have shaped our perceptions of time, plunging us into a temporal

crisis from which we have never entirely emerged." A *Booklist* correspondent praised Blaise for taking readers "far beyond Fleming's nineteenth-century formula for keeping clocks into the mystery of time itself."

BIOGRAPHICAL/CRITICAL SOURCES:

BOOKS

Authors in the News, Volume 2, Gale (Detroit, MI), 1976.
Blaise, Clark, *I Had a Father: A Post-modern Autobiography*, Addison-Wesley (Reading, MA), 1993.
Cameron, Barry, *Clark Blaise and His Works*, ECW Press (Toronto, Ontario, Canada), 1983.
Contemporary Literary Criticism, Volume 29, Gale (Detroit, MI), 1984, pp. 69-77.
Contemporary Novelists, 6th edition, St. James Press (Detroit, MI), 1996.
Dictionary of Literary Biography, Volume 53: *Canadian Writers since 1960, First Series*, Gale (Detroit, MI), 1986, pp. 76-81.

PERIODICALS

Booklist, March 15, 2001, Bryce Christensen, review of *Time Lord: Sir Sandford Fleming and the Creation of Standard Time*, p. 1337.
Books in Canada, August-September, 1983, pp. 24-25.
Canadian Fiction Magazine, fall, 1980, pp. 46-64.
Canadian Forum, November-December, 1974, pp. 20-21; April, 1977, pp. 38-39.
Canadian Literature, autumn, 1973, pp. 114-116.
Essays on Canadian Writing, summer, 1981, pp. 154-168; spring, 1982, pp. 5-25; pp. 26-67.
Fiddlehead, summer, 1979, pp. 137-140.
Imperial Oil Review, Volume 58, number 6, 1974.
Journal of Canadian Fiction, fall, 1973, pp. 77-79.
Maclean's Magazine, August 15, 1983, p. 43; May 7, 2001, John Bemrose, "An Idea Whose Time Had Come: Sandford Fleming Invented Standard Time in Response to the Railway Revolution," p. 61.
New York Times, January 25, 1977; February 19, 1977.
New York Times Book Review, September 29, 1974; April 22, 1979, pp. 14, 32; April 22, 2001, Carla Davidson, "How Late It Was," p. 21.
Publishers Weekly, February 8, 1993, p. 65; March 12, 2001, review of *Time Lord: Sir Sandford Fleming and the Creation of Standard Time*, p. 74.
Quill and Quire, October, 1974.

Times Literary Supplement, May 14, 1976, p. 588.
Washington Post, February 24, 1979.

*   *   *

BLAKE, Jennifer
    See MAXWELL, Patricia

*   *   *

BLIGHT, David W. 1949-

PERSONAL: Born March 21, 1949, in Flint, MI; son of
George Franklin and Martha Ann Blight; married Karin
B. H. Beckett (a teacher), December 28, 1987; children:
(stepchild) Peter Beckett. *Education:* Michigan State
University, B.A., 1971, M.A., 1976; University of Wis-
consin—Madison, Ph.D., 1985.

ADDRESSES: Office—Box 2254, Department of History, Amherst College, Amherst, MA 01002.

CAREER: Affiliated with Northern High School, Flint,
MI, 1971-78; North Central College, Naperville, IL, assistant professor, 1982-87; Harvard University, Cambridge, MA, assistant professor of history and Afro-
American studies, 1987-89; Amherst College, Amherst,
MA, assistant professor, beginning in 1987 became associate professor of history and Afro-American studies;
writer.

MEMBER: American Historical Association, American
Studies Association, Organization of American
Historians.

AWARDS, HONORS: Senior Fulbright professorship at
University of Munich, 1992-93.

WRITINGS:

*Frederick Douglass's Civil War: Keeping Faith in Jubi-
    lee,* Louisiana State University Press (Baton Rouge,
    LA), 1989.
(Editor) Charles Harvey Brewster, *When This Cruel
    War Is Over: The Civil War Letters of Charles Har-
    vey Brewster,* University of Massachusetts Press
    (Amherst, MA), 1992.

(Editor) Frederick Douglass, *Narrative of the Life of
    Frederick Douglass, an American Slave,* St.
    Martin's Press (New York, NY), 1993.
Why the Civil War Came, edited by Gabor S. Boritt,
    Oxford University Press (New York, NY), 1996.
(Editor, with Brooks D. Simpson) *Union and Emanci-
    pation: Essays on Politics and Race in the Civil
    War Era,* Kent State University Press (Kent, OH),
    1997.
(Editor, with Robert Gooding-Williams) W. E. B.
    DuBois, *The Souls of Black Folk,* Bedford Books
    (Boston, MA), 1997.
(Editor and author of introduction) Caleb Bingham, *The
    Columbian Orator: Containing a Variety of Origi-
    nal and Selected Pieces Together with Rules, Which
    Are Calculated to Improve Youth and Others, in the
    Ornamental and Useful Art of Eloquence,* New York
    University Press (New York, NY), 1998.
Race and Reunion: The Civil War in American Memory,
    Harvard University Press (Cambridge, MA), 2001.

SIDELIGHTS: David W. Blight is a historian with particular expertise in the subject of African-American history during the Civil War era. Among his publications
is *Frederick Douglass's Civil War: Keeping Faith in Jubilee,* which he described to *CA* as "an intellectual biography of the nineteenth century's most important
black leader, focusing especially on the impact of the
Civil War on his life and thought." *New York Times* reviewer Herbert Mitgang wrote that *Frederick Douglass's
Civil War* "delves deeply into the character of the fugitive slave who became a renowned orator and newspaper editor."

In *Race and Reunion: The Civil War in American
Memory,* Blight reveals the ways in which the American national consciousness revised the Civil War in the
decades that followed it. The abolition of slavery was
the main issue that initiated the war between the North
and South. Yet once the conflict was over, the white
population turned its attention to healing the wounds of
a nation divided against itself. Rather than exacerbate
the ideological differences between the two sides in the
conflict, people chose to see the soldiers from both
armies as noble fighters caught up in a tragic struggle.
The issue of slavery was pushed aside as Southerners
framed the war as a quarrel over states' rights and
freedom. Northerners were willing to accept this palat-
able picture, even according respect to the Southerners
who fought bravely for their doomed cause. Northerners quickly brushed aside the challenges of ensuring
equal rights for the freed slaves, ignoring the corrupt
southern laws that were passed to ensure that African-

Americans remained subjugated. Although blacks were officially free citizens, some one hundred years passed without much change in their actual social status.

Blight "has distilled a mass of historical material into an impressive, clearly written volume that, however depressing, reads well and rings true," remarked a writer for *Kirkus Reviews*. Presenting material from a wealth of memoirs, magazines, and contemporary fiction, Blight shows how the nation chose to shape its perception of the devastating conflict. In so doing, he illuminates the "human capacity for evasion and self-delusion," reported Jonathan Yardley in *Washington Post Book World*. Yardley continued: "Individual memory is at best an imperfect, unreliable instrument. National memory, as David Blight amply demonstrates in this singular book, is even less reliable, and the consequences of its imperfections can be costly indeed."

Blight told *CA:* "My scholarly pursuits have combined three major interests in American history: the black experience, American intellectual and cultural history, and the causes, course, and consequences of the Civil War. I am drawn to the question of race and to the black experience in American history because of their importance. I am drawn to Afro-American history because it is a history full of moral predicament. At the same time, like all important histories, it forces us to confront the nature of power relations, as well as social and economic processes. And I am drawn to Afro-American cultural history, not merely because it is a source of metaphors about inclusion or exclusion in America, but because it moves and challenges me and because it is impossible to imagine our cultural landscape over the past century and a half without the influence of black expression.

"I approach history with the sensibilities and methodologies of intellectual history, in part because I think historians, like all scholars, are creatures of temperament. But I have long been persuaded by R. G. Collingwood's conception of the historical imagination as the search for the *ideas* within events, the thought within social process. Moreover, I believe that *events* really matter in history; they are the result of human agency, but they also shape human institutions and behavior.

"The Civil War and Reconstruction will always beckon the historical imagination; it will always draw its buffs, poets, writers, and filmmakers; and it will always draw me to keep trying to explain it as an event and as a legacy in American culture."

BIOGRAPHICAL/CRITICAL SOURCES:

PERIODICALS

Choice, October, 1997, review of *Union and Emancipation: Essays on Politics and Race in the Civil War Era,* p. 359.

Civil War History, June, 1998, William W. Giffin, review of *Union and Emancipation,* p. 147.

Journal of American History, March, 1998, Christopher Philips, review of *Union and Emancipation,* p. 1515.

Journal of Southern History, November, 1998, Stephen E. Maizlish, review of *Union and Emancipation,* p. 758.

Kirkus Reviews, November 15, 2000, review of *Race and Reunion: The Civil War in American Memory,* p. 1591.

Library Journal, December, 2000, John Carver, review of *Race and Reunion,* p. 158.

New York Times, August 24, 1989, p. C19.

Research & Reference Book News, August, 1997, review of *Union and Emancipation,* p. 39.

Reviews in American History, September, 1997, review of *Union and Emancipation,* p. 427.

Washington Post Book World, February 4, 2001, Jonathan Yardley, review of *Race and Reunion,* p. 2.

OTHER

PBS Web site, http://www.pbs.org/ (February 19, 2001), "David Blight on Slave Narratives and *Uncle Tom's Cabin*"; "David Blight on Racism in the Abolitionist Movement."*

*   *   *

BOGLE, Warren
See BERGMAN, Andrew

*   *   *

BOND, Edward 1934-

PERSONAL: Born July 18, 1934, in London, England; married Elizabeth Pable, 1971. *Education:* Attended state schools in England. *Politics:* Socialist. *Religion:* "Atheist".

ADDRESSES: Agent—c/o Casarotto Ramsay Ltd., 60-66 Walton St., London W1V 3HP, England.

CAREER: Writer. Worked previously in factories and offices; member of the writers group of the Royal Court Theater; University of Essex, resident theatre writer, 1982-83. *Military service:* British Army; served two years with the infantry.

AWARDS, HONORS: George Devine Award, English Stage Society, 1968, for *Early Morning;* co-recipient, with Peter Barnes, of the John Whiting Playwrights Award, Arts Council, 1969, for *Narrow Road to the Deep North;* Best New Play award, *Plays and Players,* 1976, for *The Fool,* and 1985, for *The War Plays;* Northern Arts Literary fellow, 1977-79; D.Litt., Yale University, 1977.

WRITINGS:

PLAYS

The Three Sisters (adapted from a play by Anton Chekhov), produced in London, England, 1967.
The Pope's Wedding and Other Plays (includes *The Pope's Wedding,* produced in the West End, 1962 and 1984; *Mr. Dog, The King with Golden Eyes,* and *Sharpeville Sequence*), Methuen (London, England), 1971.
Saved (produced in the West End at Royal Court Theater, 1965; produced in New Haven, CT, at Yale School of Drama Repertory Theater, on a triple bill with plays by David Epstein and Anthony Scully, 1968; produced Off-Broadway, 1970), Hill & Wang (New York, NY), 1966, Heinemann, 1984.
Early Morning (produced in the West End, 1968; produced Off-Broadway, 1970), Calder & Boyars (London, England), 1968, Hill & Wang (New York, NY), 1969.
Narrow Road to the Deep North (written for the Peoples and Cities Conference in Coventry and produced there at Belgrade Theater, 1968; produced in the West End, 1969; produced in Boston at Charles Playhouse, 1969; produced on Broadway, 1972), Methuen (London, England), 1968, Hill & Wang (New York, NY), 1969.
Black Mass, produced in Sheffield, England, at Sheffield Playhouse, 1970.
Lear (produced in the West End, 1971; produced at Yale School of Drama Repertory Theater, 1973), Hill & Wang (New York, NY), 1972, student edition with notes and commentary, Methuen (London, England), 1983.

Bingo: Scenes of Money and Death [and] *Passion* (contains *Passion,* produced in the West End, 1971, produced at Yale School of Drama Repertory Theater, 1972; and *Bingo,* produced in the West End, 1974; also see below), Eyre Methuen (London, England), 1974.
The Sea (comedy; produced in the West End, 1973; produced at Source Theater, 1984; also see below), Hill & Wang (New York, NY), 1973.
Bingo [and] *The Sea: Two Plays,* Hill & Wang (New York, NY), 1973.
The Fool (produced in London, 1975), Dramatic Club Publications (Chicago, IL), 1978.
(Author of libretto) *We Come to the River* (opera; produced in London at Covent Garden, 1976), music by Hans Werner Henze, published as *We Come to the River: Actions for Music,* Schott (New York, NY), 1976.
A-A-America! [and] *Stone* (two plays), Eyre Methuen (London, England), 1976, revised edition, 1981.
The Fool [and] *We Come to the River* (two plays), Eyre Methuen (London, England), 1976.
Plays, Methuen (London, England), 1977, published as *Plays One: Saved, Early Morning, The Pope's Wedding,* 1983.
Plays Two (includes *Lear, The Sea, Narrow Road to the Deep North, Black Mass,* and *Passion*), Methuen (London, England), 1978.
The Woman: Scenes of War and Freedom (produced in London at National Theater, 1978; produced in Baltimore, MD, at Center Theater, 1983), Hill & Wang (New York, NY), 1979.
The Bundle; or, New Narrow Road to the Deep North (produced in London by Royal Shakespearean Company, 1978; produced in New Haven, CT, at Yale Repertory Theater, 1979), Eyre Methuen (London, England), 1978, Dramatic Publishing (Chicago, IL), 1981.
The Worlds [and] *The Activists Papers* (two plays; includes *The Worlds,* produced by Newcastle University Theater Society, 1979), Eyre Methuen (London, England), 1980.
(Translator) Frank Wedekind, *Spring Awakening,* Methuen (London, England), 1980.
Restoration [and] *The Cat* (includes *Restoration: A Pastoral,* a musical, with music by Nick Bicat, produced in London at the Royal Court Theater, 1981, produced in Washington, DC, at Arena Theater, 1986; and *The Cat,* libretto for opera with music by Henze, performed by Stuttgart Opera, 1983), Eyre Methuen (London, England), 1982, 2nd edition, Methuen (London, England), 1982; *The Cat* (produced as *The English Cat,* Santa Fe, NM, 1985, and New York, 1986), published as *The English*

Cat: A Story for Singers and Instrumentalists, Schott (New York, NY), 1983.

Summer (produced in London at National Theater, 1982; produced in New York at Manhattan Theater Club, 1983), Methuen (London, England), 1982.

Summer [and] *Fables,* Methuen (London, England), 1983.

Derek [and] *Choruses from after the Assassinations,* Methuen (London, England), 1984.

The War Plays; Part 1: Red, Black, and Ignorant, Part 2: The Tin Can People, Part 3: Great Peace (produced by Royal Shakespeare Company, 1985), published in two volumes, Methuen (New York, NY), 1985, and in one volume, 1991.

Human Cannon (produced in Edinburgh), Methuen (New York, NY), 1985.

Jackets 2 (produced in double-bill with *Sugawara* [adapted from kabuki drama] in London, 1990), Methuen (London, England), 1990.

Two Post-Modern Plays (contains *Jackets 1, Jackets 2, In the Company of Men, September,* and "Notes on Post-Modernism"), Methuen (London, England), 1990.

At the Inland Sea: A Play for Young People (produced in Birmingham, England, 1995), Methuen (London, England), 1997.

Coffee (produced in London, 1997), Methuen (London, England), 1995.

Eleven Vests (also see below), produced in Birmingham, England, 1997.

The Children [and] *Have I None,* Methuen (London, England), 2000.

Existence, produced in London, 2002, Methuen (London, England), 2002.

The Crime of the Twenty-First Century, produced in Paris, France, London, England, and Bochum, Germany, 2000.

SCREENPLAYS

Blow-Up (based on a short story by Julio Cortazar), Premier Productions, 1969.

(With Clement Biddle-Wood and Schlondorff) *Michael Kohlhaas* (based on a novella by Heinrich Von Kleist), Columbia, 1969.

Laughter in the Dark (based on a novel by Vladimir Nabokov), Lopert, 1969.

Walkabout (based on a novel by James Vance Marshall), Twentieth Century-Fox, 1971.

(Author of additional dialogue) James Goldman, *Nicholas and Alexandra* (based on a book by Robert K. Massie), Columbia, 1971.

Fury, 1973.

OTHER

The Swing Poems, Inter-Action (London, England), 1976.

Theater Poems and Songs, edited by Malcolm Hay and Philip Roberts, Eyre Methuen (London, England), 1978.

Orpheus: A Story in Six Scenes (ballet scenario; produced in Stuttgart, Germany, and New York, NY, 1979), Schott (New York, NY), 1986.

Poems, 1978-1985, Methuen (New York, NY), 1987.

Olly's Prison (television play), Heinemann (London, England), 1993.

Tuesday (television play), Methuen (London, England), 1993, published in *Eleven Vests* [and] *Tuesday,* with teaching notes and an interview with the author by Jim Mulligan, Methuen (London, England), 1997.

Edward Bond Letters, selected and edited by Ian Stuart, Harwood (Philadelphia, PA), volume 1, 1994, volume 2, 1995, volume 3, 1996, volume 4, 1994, volume 5, 2001.

Selections from the Notebooks of Edward Bond, volumes 1 and 2, Methuen (London, England), 2000.

The Hidden Plot: Notes on Theatre and the State, Methuen (London, England), 2000.

Bond's plays have been translated into twenty-five languages.

SIDELIGHTS: "Edward Bond . . . is distinguished by his historical perspective and his social awareness. In his plays, a scrutiny of the past enables us to comprehend injustice of the present—and vice versa," Mel Gussow observed in the *New York Times.* In the 1970 play *Black Mass,* for example, which was written to commemorate the tenth anniversary of the Sharpeville Massacre in South Africa, Bond's Christ gives the South African prime minister poison at the communion table during the Eucharist. *Restoration* also addresses issues of freedom and interracial justice as they affect the lives of a wealthy murderer's valet and his black wife. And *The Woman,* set against the backdrop of the Trojan War, is an allegory about a state's abuses of power. Ruby Cohn, an essayist for *Contemporary Dramatists,* noted the rich language to be found in Bond's plays: "Bond writes the most lapidary language of today's English theatre, absorbing dialects, pastiches, metaphors, and questions into a rich mineral vein. Pithy phrases, swift scenes, and vivid characters are his building-blocks for what he calls Rational Theatre, dedicated to the creation of a rational society. . . . His plays range through history and legend, as well as the contemporary scene."

Writing in the *International Dictionary of Theatre,* John Bull called Bond "something of a paradox, a playwright with a world-wide reputation dealing with political debate on a global scale, but one with far less than the honour due him in his own country."

Bond made his debut as an original playwright in 1965 with *Saved,* a play in which a street gang stones an infant to death. Conceived in a casual affair between two working-class youths, the child has failed to elicit affection from its grandparents, who share their home with the couple. The child's father makes an attempt to establish meaningful communication with others in the household, but the young mother finds a gang leader less boring. The infanticide has little effect on the family, who have been numbed by years of repressed aggression and exploitation. "Although the stoning is meant to shock, and certainly succeeds, it is very clearly part of the fabric of life of these people," noted Frances A. Shirley in an essay for the *Reference Guide to English Literature.* And in a *New Criterion* review of the play's 2001 New York revival, Mark Steyn observed that "time passes and events occur but no matter how dramatic or life-changing they ought to be everything stays the same, as if the characters are unable to do anything but dig themselves deeper into their own decay."

With *Saved,* Bond's name quickly became associated with disturbing depictions of violence. His next play, *Early Morning,* was a farce in which Queen Victoria, a lesbian Florence Nightingale, Prince Albert, and Benjamin Disraeli destroy each other and continue to attack each other in the afterlife. The violence in *Saved* and *Early Morning* resulted in both plays being banned by the Lord Chamberlain; it was not until the fall of 1968, when official censorship of the English stage was ended, that Bond could even hope to produce his plays without difficulty.

Bond said the reception of *Saved* outraged him. During an interview with Ronald Bryden published in the London *Observer,* Bond remarked, "It didn't knock me out exactly, it surprised me. I was a very simple person. I'd spent a long time learning to write, and do it well. I knew I'd finally done it—written just what I intended; got it right. And suddenly all these people who set themselves up as custodians of art, of artistic opinion, were sounding off in every direction except that. They weren't involved with art at all. . . . But it didn't affect me as a writer. Art is the most private of all activities, and the theatre is the most private of all arts." In a letter published in the *Guardian,* Bond explained, "I

chose to show violence in an inarticulate, working-class group because this brings out clearly our general social position vis-a-vis violence. Socially we are as confused about our own larger use of violence as my characters are about theirs."

Bond's preface to the published play *Saved* explains that he believes people have been dehumanized by cultural institutions so that individuals try to reclaim some sense of personal power by acts of violence, which require energy and passion to execute. He also notes the acts of mass destruction perpetrated in wartime and the neglected state in which many children live, and asks the audience to compare the baby's death in *Saved* to those. Furthermore, he believes audiences desensitized by daily exposure to violence should be shocked awake by representations of violence on the stage; he reasons that feelings of outrage or disgust are better than no feeling at all. Indeed, some critics and viewers were appalled by the violence in his plays and denounced the playwright for portraying murder on stage.

In *Plays and Players,* John Russell Taylor observed that "in the 'Author's Note' [Bond] wrote for the published text of *Saved* . . . he offers what may well be the key to most of the difficulties people . . . have often found in his work. 'Like most people,' he says, 'I am a pessimist by experience, but an optimist by nature, and I have no doubt that I shall go on being true to my nature. Experience is depressing, and it would be a mistake to be willing to learn from it.'" Taylor believes that in Bond's early plays "some sort of hope gleams through, if only because some sort of basic goodness survives indestructibly the horrors of experience and steadfastly refuses to learn from them."

Commenting on Bond's career, Bryden stated: "Serious critics generally agree that he is the foremost of the new wave of dramatists who followed Osborne and his contemporaries in the 1960s. When his play *Saved* was staged at the Court in 1965, it was more or less howled down for its violence. . . . But when it was revived in 1969, in repertory with Bond's subsequent plays *Early Morning* and *Narrow Road to the Deep North,* recantations poured in and the consensus was that a formidable talent had been savagely misjudged. The conversion of the critics was completed by the arrival of Bond's *Lear* in 1971."

The evil that Bond's Lear suffers is more horrifying than that of his Shakespearean antecedent because it stems not from individual greed but from a society's collective renunciation of all natural human compassion. *Library Journal* reviewer J. H. Crouch related that Bond's skill "transmutes the stuff of classic tragedy into horrifying, yet splendid melodrama." A *Variety* reviewer, on the other hand, felt that "the play's psychopathy of stupidity and violence is repeated and repeated. There is apostrophized humor, but it's an otherwise unremittingly downbeat piece, a longish (almost three hours) and grueling evening of allegorical drama." Writing in the *New York Times,* Walter Kerr expressed a similar view: "There had been no controlling principle to account for the deeds being done, nothing intimately human or narratively necessary to engage us. We were only being invited to watch violence as violence, to accept it as the occasion's *sole* activity. . . . Mr. Bond, whose earlier *Saved* was a relatively realistic play . . . has here become so obsessed with the idea of violence that he has neglected to give it plausible, or even theatrically coherent, organization."

Bond's play *The Sea* centers around the passive indifference of a small village toward the drowning death of a young man. Critics appreciated two lively comic scenes and a wider emotional range than is found in Bond's earlier plays. Clive Barnes, reviewing *Bingo,* a 1971 production, in the *Times Literary Supplement,* wrote: "Mr. Bond's new play is about the death of Shakespeare. It is his most direct play since *Saved,* avoiding both absurdism and symbolism, and dealing with a man at the point of death, literally a man at point of accounting. The man happens to be William Shakespeare, and Mr. Bond is artistically honest with the basic facts known of the poet's life and character. But it could almost be any man of feeling, nervously aware of love and hate, and significance and insignificance of worldly goods, coming naked and fearful to that final summing up that is the only thing certain after birth."

Though Bond's plays received largely negative reviews when first produced because of misunderstandings about the presentation of violence, they won the respect of critics and audiences in the 1970s and 1980s. Because of different approaches to character, Bond's working relationships with actors also came under strain during the late '70s, culminating in his withdrawal from the Royal Shakespeare Company production of *The War Plays* in 1985 and a long sabbatical from the London stage. Instead, Bond produced his play about the Spanish Civil War, *Human Cannon,* with a group of amateur actors in South Wales. London *Times* reviewer Jim Hiley said of the play with which Bond returned to the London stage in 1990, "*Jackets 2* seems unlikely to diminish the combative aura that surrounds [Bond]. But his return to the London theatre is surely to be

welcomed. However abrasive his character and elusive his vision, Edward Bond's talent is too rare to be left in the wilderness."

Bond gained renewed attention in 2001 with the New York revival of *Saved.* "The play's clear-eyed observation of the interplay between need and neglect, and how people are warped by them, is as pertinent and powerful today as it was in 1965," commented Charles Isherwood in *Variety. New Criterion*'s Steyn thought that the play's "power is immediate, from the moment the curtain rises," while the production led *New Republic* critic Robert Brustein to call *Saved* "an extraordinary work that is possibly Bond's masterpiece, and that is certainly among the most potent English dramas of the century."

Speaking of his mission as a dramatist to a *Twentieth Century Literature* interviewer, Bond said, "It seems to me to be the job of rational people, of writers, of dramatists to plead for a just society, in their plays to rationally argue for a just society, to state clearly the conditions under which we live and try to make everybody understand that they must bear the consequences of the sort of life they lead. To show that our society is irrational and therefore dangerous—and that it maintains itself by denegating and corrupting human beings—that is what *Bingo* is about. If you are an unjust person it doesn't matter how cultured you are, how civilized you are, how capable you are of producing wonderful sayings, wonderful characters, wonderful jokes, you will still destroy yourself. And so a writer, nowadays, has to, as it were, put the cards on the table for the public and say: 'These are the consequences of your life; they are inescapable. If you want to escape violence you don't say "violence is wrong," you alter the conditions that create violence.' If you don't do that, then you are like somebody who says 'Well, the children in our village are dying of diphtheria, but we will not do anything about the drains!'"

Concerning his formal schooling, Bond once said that he is glad that his education was "deplorable." "It was marvellous for me. [Schools make] children . . . competitive, aggressive. People are not born violent by nature. Society . . . makes men animals in order to control them. I write because I want to change the structure of society. I think that society as it exists is primitive, dangerous and corrupt—that it destroys people. . . . I've no Utopia, no image of the society I want to see emerge. It would simply be people being themselves, happy in their own way—what could be more natural?"

Bond told CA that in the late 1990s and early years of the twenty-first century there was an explosion of interest in his plays in Europe. By the year 2000, Moliére was the only dramatist staged more often than Bond in France. French television also made a ninety minutes film about his international work in 2002.

BIOGRAPHICAL/CRITICAL SOURCES:

BOOKS

Contemporary Dramatists, St. James Press (Detroit, MI), 6th edition, 1999.
Contemporary Literary Criticism, Gale (Detroit, MI), Volume 4, 1975, Volume 6, 1976, Volume 13, 1980, Volume 23, 1983.
Coult, Tony, *The Plays of Edward Bond: A Study,* Eyre Methuen (London, England), 1977, revised edition, 1979.
Dictionary of Literary Biography, Volume 13: *British Dramatists since World War II,* Gale (Detroit, MI), 1982.
Donahue, Delia, *Edward Bond: A Study of His Plays,* Bulzoni (Rome, Italy), 1979.
Drama for Students, Gale (Detroit, MI), 1998.
Hay, Malcolm, and Philip Roberts, *Edward Bond: A Companion to the Plays,* TQ Publications (London, England), 1978.
Hay, Malcolm, and Philip Roberts, *Bond: A Study of His Plays,* Methuen (London, England), 1980.
Hirst, David L., *Edward Bond,* Macmillan (London, England), 1985, Grove Press (New York, NY), 1986.
International Dictionary of Theatre, Volume 2: *Playwrights,* St. James Press (Detroit, MI), 1993.
Lappin, Lou, *The Art and Politics of Edward Bond,* Peter Lang (New York, NY), 1987.
Reference Guide to English Literature, 2nd edition, St. James Press (Chicago, IL), 1991.
Roberts, Philip, editor, *Bond on File,* Methuen (London, England), 1985.
Scharine, Richard, *The Plays of Edward Bond,* Bucknell University Press (Cranbury, NJ), 1976.
Stuart, Ian, *Politics in Performance: The Production Work of Edward Bond, 1978-1990,* Peter Lang (New York, NY), 1996.
Trussler, Simon, *Edward Bond,* Longman (Harlow, Essex, England), 1976.

PERIODICALS

Choice, September, 1967.
Christian Science Monitor, July 6, 1968.
Cue, December 14, 1968.

Guardian, November 12, 1965; January, 1978.
Independent, May 21, 1997, p. S4.
Library Journal, December 1, 1972.
Listener, April 18, 1968; August 8, 1968; June 18, 1970.
Los Angeles Times, April 9, 1983.
Nation, November 16, 1970.
National Review, November 24, 1989.
New Criterion, April, 2001, Mark Steyn, "Policy Paper Plays," p. 38.
New Republic, February 17, 1992; April 9, 2001, Robert Brustein, "The Aesthetics of Violence," p. 32.
New Statesman, October 18, 1996, p. 34.
New Statesman & Society, November 6, 1992; January 26, 1996, p. 32.
Newsweek, November 9, 1970.
New York, November 9, 1970.
New York Times, November 26, 1970; October 24, 1971; January 7, 1972; April 29, 1973; May 13, 1973; August 19, 1974; August 25, 1974; March 11, 1979; June 3, 1979; February 11, 1983; February 20, 1983; February 2, 1986.
Observer Review, November 9, 1969.
Opera News, March 12, 1988.
Plays and Players, August, 1970.
Prompt, number 13, 1969.
Show Business, January 4, 1969.
Stage, October 7, 1971; May 31, 1973.
Stand, summer, 1989.
Time, November 9, 1970; January 17, 1972.
Times (London), July 27, 1985; February 23, 1987; February 28, 1990; March 5, 1990.
Twentieth-Century Literature, February 28, 1990; March 5, 1990.
Variety, December 18, 1968; January 29, 1969; March 12, 1969; November 18, 1970; October 20, 1971; March 1, 1972; July 4, 1973; March 5, 2001, Charles Isherwood, review of *Saved,* p. 52.
Washington Post, May 18, 1984; January 24, 1986.

*   *   *

BROCK, W(illiam) H(odson) 1936-

PERSONAL: Born December 15, 1936, in Brighton, Sussex, England; son of William Heron (a printer) and Phyllis (Hodson) Brock; married Elvina Hill, September 18, 1960; children: Gareth, Susannah, Benjamin. *Education:* University College, London, B.Sc., 1959; University of Leicester, M.Sc., 1961, Ph.D., 1966. *Politics:* Labour. *Religion:* Anglican. *Avocational interests:* Walking, music.

ADDRESSES: Home—56 Fitzgerald Ave., Seaford BN25 1AZ, England. *E-mail*—William.brock@btinternet.com.

CAREER: University of Leicester, Leicester, England, lecturer, 1961-74, reader, 1974-92, professor of history of science, 1992-98, professor emeritus, 1998—, head of history department, 1995-97, director of Victorian Studies Centre, 1974-90. University of Toronto, visiting fellow at Institute for History of Science and Technology, 1977; University of Melbourne, visiting fellow in history and philosophy of science, 1985 and 1989; University of Canterbury, honorary visiting professor, 1999-2002. Chemical Heritage Foundation, Philadelphia, PA, Edelstein international fellow in the history of chemical sciences, 1990-91, visiting fellow, 1993; Hebrew University of Jerusalem, Edelstein fellow, 1992; Dibner Institute for History of Science and Technology, Cambridge, MA, senior fellow, 1999; Science Museum, London, England, senior research fellow, 1999-2002; Max-Planck-Institut für Wissenschaftsgeschichte, Berlin, Germany, research visitor, 2000. Royal Society, member of British National Committee for the History of Science, 1970-75 and 1978-84; Royal Institution Centre for the History of Science and Technology, chair, 1984-90; Wellcome Trust, chair of grants and units panel for the history of medicine, 1988-93.

MEMBER: History of Science Society, British Society for the History of Science (president, 1978-80), Society for the History of Alchemy and Chemistry (chair, 1993—; member of council, beginning 1967), Victorian Society of Great Britain, Royal Institution of Great Britain, Liebig-Gesellschaft-Giessen.

AWARDS, HONORS: Grant for Germany, Deutsche-Akademische Austauschdienst, 1973; Dexter Award for History of Chemistry, American Chemical Society, 1995; Liebig-Wöhler-Freundschafts-Preis, Die Göttinger Chemische Gesellschaft, 1995; Justus von Liebig Medal, Medical Sciences Historical Society, 1997; History of the University Prize, University of Giessen, 2000, for German translation of *Justus von Liebig: The Chemical Gatekeeper.*

WRITINGS:

(Editor and contributor) *The Atomic Debates: Brodie and the Rejection of the Atomic Theory,* Leicester University Press (Leicester, England), 1967.
(Editor) *Science Case Histories,* 1972.
(Editor) *H. E. Armstrong and the Teaching of Science, 1880-1930,* Cambridge University Press (New York, NY), 1973.
(Editor, with N. D. McMillan and R. C. Mollan) *John Tyndall: Essays on a Natural Philosopher,* Royal Dublin Society (Dublin, Ireland), 1981.

(With A. J. Meadows) *The Lamp of Learning: Taylor & Francis and the Development of Science Publishing,* Taylor & Francis (Philadelphia, PA), 1984, revised edition published as *The Lamp of Learning: Two Centuries of Publishing at Taylor & Francis,* 1998.
(Editor) *Justus von Liebig und August Wilhelm Hofmann in ihren Briefen, 1841-1873,* Verlag Chemie (Deerfield Beach, FL), 1984.
From Protyle to Proton: William Prout and the Nature of Matter, 1785-1985, Adam Hilger (Boston, MA), 1985.
The Fontana History of Chemistry, Fontana/Collins (London, England), 1992, published as *The Norton History of Chemistry,* Norton (New York, NY), 1993, published as *The Chemical Tree: A History of Chemistry,* 2000.
(Associate editor for chemists) *New Dictionary of National Biography,* 1994—.
Science for All: Studies in the History of Victorian Science and Education, Variorum (Brookfield, VT), 1996.
Justus von Liebig: The Chemical Gatekeeper, Cambridge University Press (New York, NY), 1997.
(Editor, with Richard L. Hills) Wilfred Vernon Farrar, *Chemistry and the Chemical Industry in the Nineteenth Century: The Henrys of Manchester and Other Studies,* Variorum (Brookfield, VT), 1997.

Also editor, with Roy MacLeod, of *Natural Knowledge in Social Context: The Journals of Thomas Archer Hirst FRS* (microfiche), Mansell (London, England), 1980. Contributor of historical papers to *Isis, History of Science, Notes and Records of the Royal Society,* and other journals. *Ambix,* editor, 1968-83, book reviews editor, 1985-98; member of editorial board, *Medical History* and *Victorian Periodicals Review.*

Brock's writings have been translated into German, Spanish, Polish, and Japanese.

WORK IN PROGRESS: A biography of the life of Sir William Crookes, 1832-1919.

BIOGRAPHICAL/CRITICAL SOURCES:

PERIODICALS

American Historical Review, June, 1999, review of *Justus von Liebig: The Chemical Gatekeeper,* p. 1021.
Booklist, July, 1993, review of *The Norton History of Chemistry,* p. 1951.

Choice, February, 1994, review of *The Norton History of Chemistry*, p. 957; December, 1996, review of *Science for All: Studies in the History of Victorian Science and Education*, p. 632.

Isis, June, 1994, review of *The Fontana History of Chemistry*, p. 301; December, 1998, review of *Justus von Liebig*, p. 741.

Journal of Chemical Education, August, 1994, review of *The Norton History of Chemistry*, p. A214.

Library Journal, July, 1993, review of *The Norton History of Chemistry*, p. 112; March 1, 1994, review of *The Norton History of Chemistry*, p. 54.

Nature, April 15, 1993, review of *The Fontana History of Chemistry*, p. 677.

New York Times Book Review, September 26, 1993, review of *The Norton History of Chemistry*, p. 34; December 5, 1993, review of *The Norton History of Chemistry*, p. 76.

Reference & Research Book News, September, 1996, review of *Science for All*.

Science, August 6, 1982, David R. Wilson, review of *John Tyndall: Essays on a Natural Philosopher*, p. 529; May 13, 1994, review of *The Norton History of Chemistry*, p. 997; April 24, 1998, review of *Justus von Liebig*, p. 540.

Science Books & Films, January, 1994, review of *The Norton History of Chemistry*, p. 8.

Scientific American, February, 1994, review of *The Norton History of Chemistry*, p. 121.

SciTech Book News, August, 1996, review of *Science for All*, p. 20.

Technology and Culture, April, 1999, review of *Justus von Liebig*, p. 408.

Times Educational Supplement, January 8, 1993, review of *The Fontana History of Chemistry*, p. 10.

Victorian Studies, summer, 1998, review of *Justus von Liebig*, p. 659.*

* * *

BRODSKY, Joseph
  See BRODSKY, Iosif Alexandrovich

* * *

BRODSKY, Iosif Alexandrovich 1940-1996
  (Joseph Brodsky, Yosif Brodsky)

PERSONAL: Born May 24, 1940, in Leningrad (now St. Petersburg), Soviet Union (now Russia); became naturalized U.S. citizen, 1977; died of heart failure, January 28, 1996, in Brooklyn Heights, NY; son of Alexander I. and Maria M. (Volpert) Brodsky; married wife (an Italian-Russian translator), 1990; children: Andrei, Anna. *Religion:* Jewish. *Education:* Attended schools in Leningrad until 1956.

CAREER: Poet. Worked variously as a stoker, sailor, photographer, geologist's assistant on expedition to Central Asia, coroner's assistant, and farm laborer; poet-in-residence at University of Michigan, Ann Arbor, MI, 1972-73, 1974-79; adjunct professor, Columbia University, New York, NY; Mount Holyoke College, South Hadley, MA, educator, became Andrew W. Mellon Professor of Literature, 1990-96.

MEMBER: Bavarian Academy of Sciences (Munich; corresponding member), American Academy of Arts and Sciences, until 1987.

AWARDS, HONORS: D.Litt., Yale University, 1978, Dartmouth College, University of Keele, Amherst College, Uppsala University, University of Rochester, Williams College, Colchester University, and Oxford University; Mondello Prize (Italy), 1979; National Book Critics Circle Award nomination, 1980, for *A Part of Speech*, and award, 1986, for *Less than One: Selected Essays;* New York Institute for the Humanities fellowship; MacArthur fellowship, 1981; Guggenheim fellowship; Nobel Prize in Literature, 1987; Poet Laureate of the United States, 1991; Decorated Legion d'Honneur (France): Knight, Order of St. John of Malta.

WRITINGS:

Stikhotvoreniia i poemy (title means "Longer and Shorter Poems"), Inter-Language (Washington, DC), 1965.

Xol 'mi, translated by Jean-Jacques Marie and published in France as *Collines et autres poemes*, Editions de Seuil, 1966.

Ausgewahlte Gedichte, Bechtle Verlag, 1966.

(Under name Joseph Brodsky) *Elegy to John Donne and Other Poems*, selected, translated, and introduced by Nicholas Bethell, Longmans, Green, 1967.

Velka elegie, Edice Svedectvi (Paris, France), 1968.

Ostanovka v pustyne (title means "A Halt in the Wilderness"), Chekhov (New York, NY), 1970.

(Under name Joseph Brodsky) *Poems*, Ardis (Ann Arbor, MI), 1972.

(Under name Joseph Brodsky) *Selected Poems*, translated by George L. Kline, Harper (New York, NY), 1973.

(Editor, under name Joseph Brodsky, with Carl Proffer) *Modern Russian Poets on Poetry: Blok, Mandelstam, Pasternak, Mayakovsky, Gumilev, Tsvetaeva* (nonfiction), Ardis (Ann Arbor, MI), 1976.

Konets prekrasnoi epokhi: Stikhotvoreniia, 1964-1971 (title means "The End of A Wonderful Era: Poems"), Ardis (Ann Arbor, MI), 1977.

Chast' rechi: Stikhotvoreniia, 1972-1976 (title means "A Part of Speech: Poems"), Ardis (Ann Arbor, MI), 1977, translation published as *A Part of Speech,* Farrar, Straus (New York, NY), 1980.

V Anglii (title means "In England"), Ardis (Ann Arbor, MI), 1977.

Verses on the Winter Campaign 1980, translation by Alan Meyers, Anvil Press (London, England), 1981.

Rimskie elegii (title means "Roman Elegies"), [New York, NY], 1982.

Novye stansy k Avguste: Stikhi k M.B., 1962-1982 (title means "New Stanzas to Augusta: Poems to M.B."), Ardis (Ann Arbor, MI), 1983.

Uraniia: Novaia kniga stikhov (title means "Urania: A New Book of Poems"), Ardis (Ann Arbor, MI), 1984, translation published as *To Urania: Selected Poems, 1965-1985,* Farrar, Straus (New York, NY), 1988.

Mramor, Ardis (Ann Arbor, MI), 1984.

Less than One: Selected Essays, Farrar, Straus (New York, NY), 1986.

(Editor, under name Joseph Brodsky, with Alan Myers) *An Age Ago: A Selection of Nineteenth-Century Russian Poetry,* Farrar, Straus (New York, NY), 1988.

(Under name Joseph Brodsky) *Marbles: A Play in Three Acts,* Farrar, Straus (New York, NY), 1989.

(Under name Joseph Brodsky) *Watermark,* Farrar, Straus (New York, NY), 1992.

(With Alexander Liberman) *Campidoglio: Michaelangelo's Roman Capitol,* Random House (New York, NY), 1994.

(With Gianni Berengo Gardin) *Gli anni di Venezia,* F. Motta (Milan, Italy), 1994.

Isaak I Avraam, Izd-vo M.K. (St. Petersburg, Russia), 1994.

(Editor) *The Essential Hardy,* Ecco Press (Hopewell, NJ), 1995.

On Grief and Reason: Essays, Farrar, Straus (New York, NY), 1995.

So Forth: Poems, Farrar, Straus (New York, NY), 1995.

(With Seamus Heaney and Derek Walcott) *Homage to Robert Frost,* Farrar, Straus (New York, NY), 1996.

Brodskii o Tsvetaevoi, Nezavisimaia gazeta (Moscow, Russia), 1997.

Pis-mo Goratsiiu, Nash dom-L'age d'Homme, (Moscow, Russia), 1998.

Discovery, Farrar, Straus (New York, NY), 1999.

Gorbunov i Gorchakov, Pushkinskii fond (St. Petersburg, Russia), 1999.

Predstavlenie, Novoe literaturnoe obozrenie (Moscow, Russia), 1999.

Collected Poems in English, edited by Ann Kjellberg, Farrar, Straus (New York, NY), 2000.

Bol'shaia kniga interv'iu, Zakharov (Moscow, Russia), 2000.

Contributor to *Three Slavic Poets: Joseph Brodsky, Tymoteusz Karpowicz, Djordie Nikoloc,* edited by John Rezek, Elpenor Books, 1975.

Translations of Brodsky's poems appear in James Scully's *Avenue of the Americas,* University of Massachusetts Press, 1971, and in *New Underground Russian Poets: Poems by Yosif Brodsky and others.* Poems have been published in anthologies in twelve languages, and in *Russian Review, New York Review of Books, Nouvelle Revue Française, Unicorn Journal, Observer Review, Kultura, La Fiera Letteraria, New Yorker, New Leader,* and other journals. He also translated poetry from English and Polish into Russian, and from Russian into Hebrew.

SIDELIGHTS: Iosif Alexandrovich Brodsky was reviled and persecuted in his native Soviet Union, but the Western literary establishment lauded him as one of that country's finest poets. From the time he began publishing his verse—both under his own name, and under the name Joseph Brodsky—which was characterized by ironic wit and a spirit of fiery independence, Brodsky aroused the ire of Soviet authorities; he was also persecuted because he was a Jew. He was brought to trial for "parasitism," and a smuggled transcript of that trial helped bring him to the attention of the West, for he answered his interrogators with courageous and articulate idealism. Brodsky was condemned to a Soviet mental institution and later spent five years in Arkhangelsk, an Arctic labor camp. A public outcry from American and European intellectuals over his treatment helped to secure his early release. Forced to emigrate, he moved to Michigan in 1972, where, with the help of the poet W. H. Auden, he settled in at the University of Michigan in Ann Arbor as poet-in-residence. He then taught at several universities, including Queens College in New York and Mount Holyoke College in Massachusetts. He continued to write poetry, however, often writing in Russian and translating his own work into English, and eventually winning the Nobel Prize for his work. His predominant themes were exile and loss, and he was widely praised for his hauntingly eloquent writing style.

In many ways, Brodsky had lived as an exile before leaving his homeland. His father had lost a position of rank in the Russian Navy because he was Jewish, and the family lived in poverty. Trying to escape the ever-present images of Lenin, Brodsky quit school and embarked on a self-directed education, reading literary classics and working a variety of unusual jobs, which included assisting a coroner and a geologist in Central Asia. He learned English and Polish so that he would be able to translate the poems of John Donne and Czeslaw Milosz. His own poetry expressed his independent character with an originality admired by poets such as Anna Akhmatova.

According to a *Times Literary Supplement* reviewer, Brodsky's poetry "is religious, intimate, depressed, sometimes confused, sometimes martyr-conscious, sometimes elitist in its views, but it does not constitute an attack on Soviet society or ideology unless withdrawal and isolation are deliberately construed as attack: of course they can be, and evidently were." According to a reviewer in *Time,* the poet's expulsion from Russia was "the culmination of an inexplicable secret-police vendetta against him that has been going on for over a decade." Brodsky said: "They have simply kicked me out of my country, using the Jewish issue as an excuse." The vendetta first came to a head in a Leningrad trial in 1964, when Brodsky was charged with writing "gibberish" instead of doing honest work; he was sentenced to five years hard labor. Protests from artists and writers helped to secure his release after eighteen months, but his poetry still was banned. Israel invited him to immigrate, and the government encouraged him to go; Brodsky, though, refused, explaining that he did not identify with the Jewish state. Finally, Russian officials insisted that he leave the country. Despite the pressures, Brodsky reportedly wrote to Leonid Brezhnev before leaving Moscow asking for "an opportunity to continue to exist in Russian literature and on Russian soil."

Brodsky's poetry bears the marks of his confrontations with the Russian authorities. "Brodsky is someone who has tasted extremely bitter bread," wrote Stephen Spender in *New Statesman,* "and his poetry has the air of being ground out between his teeth. . . . It should not be supposed that he is a liberal, or even a socialist. He deals in unpleasing, hostile truths and is a realist of the least comforting and comfortable kind. Everything nice that you would like him to think, he does not think. But he is utterly truthful, deeply religious, fearless and pure. Loving, as well as hating."

Though one might expect Brodsky's poetry to be basically political in nature, this is not the case. "Brodsky's recurrent themes are lyric poets' traditional, indeed timeless concerns—man and nature, love and death, the ineluctability of anguish, the fragility of human achievements and attachments, the preciousness of the privileged moment, the 'unrepeatable.' The tenor of his poetry is not so much apolitical as antipolitical," wrote Victor Erlich. "His besetting sin was not 'dissent' in the proper sense of the word, but a total, and on the whole quietly undemonstrative, estrangement from the Soviet ethos."

Brodsky elaborated on the relationship between poetry and politics in his Nobel lecture, "Uncommon Visage," published in *Poets & Writers* magazine. Art teaches the writer, he said, "the privateness of the human condition. Being the most ancient as well as the most literal form of private enterprise, it fosters in a man . . . a sense of his uniqueness, of individuality, or separateness—thus turning him from a social animal into an autonomous 'I.'. . . A work of art, of literature especially, and a poem in particular, addresses a man tete-a-tete, entering with him into direct—free of any go-betweens—relations."

In addition, literature points to experience that transcends political limits. Brodsky observed, "Language and, presumably, literature are things that are more ancient and inevitable, more durable than any form of social organization. The revulsion, irony, or indifference often expressed by literature toward the state is essentially the reaction of the permanent—better yet, the infinite—against the temporary, against the finite. . . . The real danger for a writer is not so much the possibility (and often the certainty) of persecution on the part of the state, as it is the possibility of finding oneself mesmerized by the state's features which, whether monstrous or undergoing changes for the better, are always temporary."

Brodsky went on to say that creative writing is an essential exercise of individual freedom, since the writer must make many aesthetic judgments and choices during the process of composition. He pointed out, "It is precisely in this . . . sense that we should understand Dostoyevsky's remark that beauty will save the world, or Matthew Arnold's belief that we shall be saved by poetry. It is probably too late for the world, but for the individual man there always remains a chance. . . . If what distinguishes us from other members of the animal kingdom is speech, then literature—and poetry, in particular, being the highest form of locution—is, to put it bluntly, the goal of our species."

Even more compelling than the relationship between poetry and politics is the relationship between the writer and his language, Brodsky claimed. He explained that the first experience the writer has when taking up a pen to write "is . . . the sensation of immediately falling into dependence on language, on everything that has already been uttered, written, and accomplished in it." But the past accomplishments of a language do not impinge on the writer more than the sense of its vast potential. Brodsky added, "There are times when, by means of a single word, a single rhyme, the writer of a poem manages to find himself where no one has ever been before him, further, perhaps, than he himself would have wished for. . . . Having experienced this acceleration once . . . one falls into dependency on this process, the way others fall into dependency on drugs or alcohol."

In keeping with these views, Brodsky's poetry is known for its originality. Arthur C. Jacobs in the *Jewish Quarterly* noted that Brodsky is "quite apart from what one thinks of as the main current of Russian verse." A critic in *New Leader* wrote: "The noisy rant and attitudinizing rhetoric of public issues are superfluous to Brodsky's moral vision and contradictory to his craft. As with all great lyric poets, Brodsky attends to the immediate, the specific, to what he has internally known and felt, to the lucidities of observation heightened and defined by thought."

Though many critics agreed that Brodsky was one of the finest contemporary Russian poets, some felt that the English translations of his poetry are less impressive. Commenting on George L. Kline's translation of *Selected Poems, Joseph Brodsky,* Stephen Spender wrote: "These poems are impressive in English, though one is left having to imagine the technical virtuosity of brilliant rhyming in the originals. . . . One is never quite allowed to forget that one is reading a second-hand version." In *A Part of Speech,* Brodsky gathered the work of several translators and made amendments to some of the English versions in an attempt to restore the character of the originals. Brodsky's personal style remains somewhat elusive in that collection due to the subtle effects he achieves in the original Russian, Tom Simmons observed in the *Christian Science Monitor.* Brodsky, he said, "is a poet of dramatic yet delicate vision—a man with a sense of the increasingly obscured loftiness of human life. But under no circumstances is his poetry dully ethereal. . . . He can portray a luminous moment or a time of seemingly purposeless suffering with equal clarity."

Erlich also felt that some of the lines in *Selected Poems* are "strained or murky," but that Brodsky at his best had the "originality, incisiveness, depth and formal mastery which mark a major poet." Czeslaw Milosz felt that Brodsky's background allowed him to make a vital contribution to literature. Writing in the *New York Review of Books,* Milosz stated, "Behind Brodsky's poetry is the experience of political terror, the experience of the debasement of man and the growth of the totalitarian empire. . . . I find it fascinating to read his poems as part of his larger enterprise, which is no less than an attempt to fortify the place of man in a threatening world." This enterprise connected Brodsky to the literary traditions of other times and cultures. Erlich concluded that "the richness and versatility of his gifts, the liveliness and vigor of his intelligence, and his increasingly intimate bond with the Anglo-American literary tradition, augur well for his survival in exile, indeed for his further creative growth."

Exile was always difficult for Brodsky. In one poem, he described an exiled writer as one "who survives like a fish in the sand." Yet despite these feelings, Brodsky was largely unmoved by the sweeping political changes that accompanied the fall of the Soviet Union. He told David Remnick of the *Washington Post* that those changes were "devoid of autobiographical interest" for him, and that his allegiance was to his language. In the *Detroit Free Press,* Bob McKelvey cited Brodsky's declaration from a letter: "I belong to the Russian culture. I feel part of it, its component, and no change of place can influence the final consequence of this. A language is a much more ancient and inevitable thing than a state. I belong to the Russian language."

Shortly before his death, Brodsky completed *So Forth,* a collection of poems he wrote in English, or translated himself from poetry he wrote in Russian. *So Forth* was judged inferior to Brodsky's best work by several critics, including Michael Glover, who in *New Statesman* described the collection as "more failure than success." Glover felt that too often Brodsky "lapses into a kind of swashbuckling slanginess, a kind of raw muscularity that, at its worst, reads like embarrassing doggerel." Yet others found *So Forth* a powerful statement, such as the *Publishers Weekly* reviewer who called it "an astonishing collection from a writer able to mix the cerebral and the sensual, the political and the intimate, the elegiac and the comic. . . . Brodsky's death is a loss to literature; his final collection of poems is the best consolation we could ask for."

Collected Poems in English, published posthumously, is a definitive collection of Brodsky's translated work and his original work in English. It is "dramatic and ironic, melancholy and blissful," reported Donna Seaman in

Booklist. She claimed this volume "will stand as one of the twentieth century's tours de force." *Collected Poems in English* is "a highly accomplished, deft, and entertaining book, with a talent for exploitation of the richness of language and with a deep core of sorrow," in the estimation of Judy Clarence in *Library Journal.* It captures Brodsky's trademark sense of "stepping aside and peering in bewilderment" at life, according to Sven Birkerts in the *New York Review of Books.* Birkerts concluded: "Brodsky charged at the world with full intensity and wrestled his perceptions into lines that fairly vibrate with what they are asked to hold. There is no voice, no vision, remotely like it."

BIOGRAPHICAL/CRITICAL SOURCES:

BOOKS

Authors in the News, Volume 1, Gale (Detroit, MI), 1973.

Bethea, David, *Joseph Brodsky and the Creation of Exile,* Princeton University Press (Princeton, NJ), 1994.

Brodsky, Joseph, *A Part of Speech,* Farrar, Straus (New York, NY), 1980.

Contemporary Literary Criticism, Gale (Detroit, MI), Volume 4, 1975, Volume 6, 1976, Volume 36, 1986, Volume 50, 1988.

Speh, Alice J., *The Poet as Traveler: Joseph Brodsky in Mexico and Rome,* Peter Lang (New York, NY), 1996.

PERIODICALS

Agenda, winter, 1998, review of *On Grief and Reason: Essays* and *So Forth: Poems,* p. 140.

Antioch Review, winter, 1985; spring, 1996, Gerda Oldham, review of *On Grief and Reason: Essays,* pp. 247-248.

Bloomsbury Review, March, 1998, review of *Homage to Robert Frost,* p. 22.

Booklist, July, 1996, Donna Seaman, review of *So Forth,* p. 1797; August, 2000, Donna Seaman, review of *Collected Poems in English,* p. 2100.

Books in Canada, summer, 1996, review of *On Grief and Reason,* p. 12.

Book World, February 11, 1996, review of *On Grief and Reason,* p. 13.

Children's Book Review Service, December, 1999, review of *Discovery,* p. 42.

Choice, April, 1974; September, 1977.

Christian Century, November 11, 1987.

Christian Science Monitor, August 11, 1980, Tom Simmons, review of *A Part of Speech.*

Commonweal, November 5, 1999, review of *Discovery,* p. 24.

Contemporary Review, June, 1997, review of *Watermark,* p. 334.

Detroit Free Press, September 17, 1972; October 23, 1987.

Hungry Mind Review, fall, 1999, review of *Discovery,* p. 33.

Jewish Quarterly, winter, 1968-69.

Kirkus Reviews, July 1, 1996, review of *Homage to Robert Frost,* p. 940; September 15, 1999, review of *Discovery,* p. 1498.

Knight-Ridder/Tribune News Service, March 12, 1996; October 16, 1996.

Library Journal, June 1, 1996, Graham Christian, review of *So Forth,* p. 110; November 15, 1996, Denise S. Sticha, review of *Homage to Robert Frost,* p. 62; January, 1997, review of *So Forth,* p. 48; August, 2000, Judy Clarence, review of *Collected Poems in English,* p. 109.

Los Angeles Times, October 23, 1987; February 15, 1989.

Los Angeles Times Book Review, October 20, 1996, review of *Homage to Robert Frost,* p. 14; November 7, 1999, review of *Discovery,* p. 8.

Nation, October 4, 1980; February 12, 1996, Jessica Greenbaum, review of *On Grief and Reason,* pp. 32-33.

New Leader, December 10, 1973; December 14, 1987; October 31, 1988; September 9, 1996, John Simon, reviews of *So Forth* and *On Grief and Reason,* pp. 14 19; January 13, 1997, Phoebe Pettingell, review of *Homage to Robert Frost,* pp. 14-15.

New Republic, March 4, 1996, Stanislaw Baranczak, review of *On Grief and Reason,* pp. 39-42.

New Statesman, December 14, 1973; December 20, 1996, Michael Glover, reviews of *On Grief and Reason* and *So Forth,* pp. 119-120.

New Statesman and Society, June 19, 1992, p. 24.

Newsweek, November 2, 1987.

New Yorker, July 13, 1992, p. 84; December 16, 1996, review of *So Forth,* p. 107.

New York Review of Books, August 14, 1980, Czeslaw Milosz, review of *A Part of Speech;* January 21, 1988; November 24, 1988; February 1, 1996, J. M. Coetzee, review of *On Grief and Reason,* pp. 28-31; September 17, 2000, Sven Birkerts, review of *Collected Poems in English.*

New York Times, October 31, 1987.

New York Times Book Review, November 8, 1987; May 31, 1992; February 29, 1996, p. 7; March 3, 1996,

Seamus Heaney, "The Singer of Tales: On Joseph Brodsky," p. 31; April 14, 1996, Hugh Kenner, review of *On Grief and Reason*, p. 14; September 1, 1996, John Bayley, review of *So Forth*, p. 6; December 8, 1996, review of *So Forth*, p. 82; April 26, 1998, review of *So Forth*, p. 36; November 21, 1999, Deborah Hautzig, review of *Discovery*, p. 57.

Observer (London), October 27, 1996, review of *On Grief and Reason*, p. 15; September 28, 1997, review of *On Grief and Reason*, p. 18; January 4, 1998, review of *Homage to Robert Frost*, p. 15.

Partisan Review, fall, 1974.

Poetry, October, 1975; November, 1988; June, 1997, John Taylor, review of *So Forth*, pp. 169-172.

Poets & Writers, March-April, 1988.

Publishers Weekly, June 1, 1996, Graham Christian, review of *So Forth*, p. 110; June 24, 1996, review of *So Forth*, p. 51; July 15, 1996, review of *Homage to Robert Frost*, p. 60; July 21, 1997, review of *Homage to Robert Frost*, p. 199; October 18, 1999, review of *Discovery*, p. 80; June 26, 2000, review of *Collected Poems in English*, p. 71.

School Library Journal, November, 1999, review of *Discovery*, p. 168.

Sewanee Review, April, 1996, review of *On Grief and Reason*, p. 295.

Texas Studies in Literature and Language, number 17, 1975.

Time, June 19, 1972; August 7, 1972; April 7, 1986; November 2, 1987.

Times Literary Supplement, July 20, 1967; January 10, 1997, reviews of *So Forth* and *On Grief and Reason*, p. 6.

Translation Review Supplement, July, 1997, review of *So Forth*, p. 35.

Tribune Books (Chicago), February 11, 1996, review of *On Grief and Reason*, p. 3.

Village Voice Literary Supplement, winter, 1996, review of *So Forth*, p. 8.

Vogue, February, 1988.

Washington Post, October 23, 1987; March 21, 1996, Richard Cohen, "One of Them's a Poet," p. A17.

Washington Post Book World, August 24, 1980.

Wilson Quarterly, autumn, 1996, review of *Homage to Robert Frost*, p. 97.

World Literature Today, spring, 1996, Theodore Ziolkowsky, review of *On Grief and Reason*, p. 479; summer, 1997, Rosette C. Lamont, review of *So Forth*, pp. 592-593; autumn, 1997, William Pratt, review of *Homage to Robert Frost*, p. 801, "Peizazh S Navodneniem," p. 819; winter, 1997, David MacFadyen, "24 May 1996 in St. Petersburg, Russia: The Perceived Significance of Joseph Brodsky's Legacy," pp. 81-86; spring, 1998, "Brodskii o Tsvetaevoi," p. 406.

OTHER

Joseph Brodsky (1940-1996): In Memoriam, http://www.sharat.com.il/nosik/brodsky/ (October 23, 2001).

OBITUARIES:

PERIODICALS

Chicago Tribune, January 29, 1996, p. 6.

Los Angeles Times, January 29, 1996, p. A14.

New Republic, February 19, 1996, pp. 10-11.

New York Times, January 29, 1996, pp. A1, B5.

Washington Post, January 29, 1996, p. B4; January 30, 1996, p. D1.*

*   *   *

BROOK, Stephen 1947-

PERSONAL: Born June 20, 1947, in London, England; married Maria Lonstrup, 1987. *Education:* Trinity College, Cambridge, M.A., 1969. *Religion:* Jewish.

ADDRESSES: Home—34 Carlton Mansions, Randolph Ave., London W9 1NP, England; fax 020 7328 8807. *E-mail*—sbrook@mailbox.co.uk.

CAREER: Atlantic Monthly, Boston, MA, staff editor, 1971-73; David R. Godine, Inc. (publisher), Boston, MA, editorial director, 1973-75; Routledge & Kegan Paul Ltd. (publisher), London, England, editor, 1976-80; writer, 1982—. Also serves as contributing editor for *Decanter*, 1996—.

MEMBER: Circle of Wine Writers, Guild of Food Writers.

AWARDS, HONORS: André Simon Prize, 1987, for *Liquid Gold: Dessert Wines of the World;* Wines of France Award, 1995; Bunch Award for wine journalism, 1996; André Simon Special Commendation, 1999; Veuve Clicqot Wine Book of the Year award, 2000; Glenfiddich Awards for drink book of the year, 2000; Prix Lanson Award for best wine book of the year, 2000.

WRITINGS:

New York Days, New York Nights, Atheneum (New York, NY), 1983.

(Editor) *The Oxford Book of Dreams,* Oxford University Press (Oxford, England), 1983.

Honkytonk Gelato: Travels in Texas, Atheneum (New York, NY), 1984.

The Dordogne, G. Philip, 1985.

Maple Leaf Rag: Travels across Canada, Hamish Hamilton (London, England), 1987.

Liquid Gold: Dessert Wines of the World, Morrow (New York, NY), 1987.

The Double Eagle: Vienna, Budapest, Prague, Hamish Hamilton (London, England), 1988.

The Club: The Jews of Modern Britain, Constable, 1989.

Winner Takes All: A Season in Israel, Viking (New York, NY), 1990.

The Veneto, G. Philip, 1991.

Claws of the Crab: Georgia and Armenia in Crisis, Sinclair-Stevenson, 1992.

L.A. Lore, Sinclair-Stevenson, 1992.

Prague, G. Philip, 1992.

Sauvignon Blanc and Semillon, Viking (London, England), 1992.

(Editor) *The Penguin Book of Infidelities,* Viking/Penguin (London, England), 1994.

Vienna, Dorling Kindersley (London, England), 1994.

(Editor) *Opera: An Anthology,* Viking/Penguin (London, England), 1995.

Sauternes and the Other Sweet Wines of Bordeaux, Faber, 1995.

The Czech and Slovak Republics, Sun Tree, 1995.

Class: Knowing Your Place in Modern Britain, Gollancz, 1997.

Winelover's Companion to Southern France, Websters, 1997.

God's Army: The Salvation Army, Box Tree/Channel 3, 1998.

Pauillac, Mitchell Beazley, 1998.

The Wines of California, Farrar, Straus, Giroux (New York, NY), 1999.

(Editor) *A Century of Wine,* Mitchell Beazley, 2000.

(With John Radford) *Pocket Guide to Sweet and Fortified Wines,* Mitchell Beazley, 2000.

Wine columnist for *New Statesman,* 1985-88; *Vogue,* 1988-94, *Unique,* 1994-95, and *Conde Nast Traveller,* 1997—. Contributor of articles and reviews to periodicals and newspapers, including *Times, Sunday Times, Independent on Sunday, Wine Spectator, Wine & Spirit, Slow Magazine, Food Illustrated, Webster's Wine Guides, Webster's Wine CD-ROM, The Larousse Encyclopedia of Wine,* and *Oxford Companion to Wine.* Contributes gastronomy articles to *Caterer & Hotelkeeper, Cigar Aficionado, Financial Times, Decanter, Food & Travel,* and *Conde Nast Traveller.* Writes book reviews and travel articles for several publications, as well as wine and food articles for *Decanter.com* and *winetoday. com.*

*   *   *

BURK, Robert F(redrick) 1955-

PERSONAL: Born October 15, 1955, in Topeka, KS; son of Harry L. and Laura E. Burk; married Patricia K. Geschwent (a computer trainer), June 27, 1981; married Margaret L. Burk (associate professor of business, Muskingum College), 1996. *Education:* University of Kansas, B.A., 1977; University of Wisconsin—Madison, M.A., 1978, Ph.D., 1982. *Politics:* Democrat. *Religion:* None.

ADDRESSES: Home—890 Bald Hill Road, Zanesville, OH 43701. *Office*—Department of History, Muskingum College, New Concord, OH 43762.

CAREER: University of Wisconsin—Madison, Madison, WI, lecturer in history, 1983; University of Cincinnati, Cincinnati, OH, visiting assistant professor of history, 1983-84; Muskingum College, New Concord, OH, assistant professor, 1984-89, associate professor, 1989-95, professor of history, 1995—; college archivist, 1988-94, chairman of history department, 1994—.

MEMBER: American Historical Association, Organization of American Historians, Southern Historical Association, Ohio Academy of History, Phi Beta Kappa, Phi Alpha Theta.

WRITINGS:

The Eisenhower Administration and Black Civil Rights, University of Tennessee Press (Knoxville, TN), 1984.

Dwight D. Eisenhower: Hero and Politician, Twayne (Boston, MA), 1986.

The Corporate State and the Broker State: The duPonts and American National Politics, 1925-40, Harvard University Press (Cambridge, MA), 1990.

Never Just a Game: Players, Owners, and American Baseball to 1920, University of North Carolina Press (Chapel Hill, NC), 1994.

Much More than a Game: Players, Owners, and American Baseball since 1921, University of North Carolina Press (Chapel Hill, NC), 2001.

SIDELIGHTS: Robert F. Burk's companion volumes, *Never Just a Game: Players, Owners, and American Baseball to 1920* and *Much More than a Game: Players, Owners, and American Baseball since 1921,* offer a comprehensive treatment of baseball as a business. Burk argues that America's pastime has always been "more than a game," as players have struggled for competitive salaries and the protection of a union while owners have endeavored to keep the profits flowing into their own pockets. Burk divides the history of professional baseball into two eras: the "paternalistic era" in which owners set salaries at their whim and closely monitored players' behavior even in off-hours, and the "inflationary era" in which players' demands for rights led to unionization and extravagant salaries. In *Business History,* Robert J. Thornton praised *Never Just a Game* as "meticulously researched," and called it "a lively, highly readable volume filled with fascinating anecdotes." Thornton felt that the work "will appeal to both the serious student of business history and the layman with merely an interest in the game itself." A *Publishers Weekly* reviewer, commenting on *Much More than a Game,* noted that Burk's exploration of player grievances through the case histories of individual players themselves "significantly animates his heavily detailed narrative."

BIOGRAPHICAL/CRITICAL SOURCES:

PERIODICALS

American Historical Review, June, 1995, Steven A. Riess, review of *Never Just a Game: Players, Owners, and American Baseball to 1920,* p. 958.

Business History, January, 1995, Robert J. Thornton, review of *Never Just a Game,* p. 142.

Journal of American History, June, 1995, Benjamin G. Rader, review of *Never Just a Game,* p. 264.

New York Times Book Review, April 15, 1990, p. 10.

Publishers Weekly, February 12, 2001, review of *Much More than a Game: Players, Owners, and American Baseball since 1921,* p. 194.

Times Literary Supplement, July 13, 1990, p. 756.

BURKE, James Lee 1936-

PERSONAL: Born December 5, 1936, in Houston, TX; son of James Lee (a natural gas engineer) and Frances (Benbow) Burke; married Pearl Pai Chu, January 22, 1960; children: James, Andree, Pamela, Alafair. *Education:* Attended University of Southwest Louisiana, 1955-57; University of Missouri, B.A., 1959, M.A., 1960. *Politics:* "Jeffersonian Democrat." *Religion:* Roman Catholic. *Avocational interests:* Fishing, playing guitar, tennis, baseball, bluegrass music.

ADDRESSES: *Home*—Louisiana and Montana. *Agent*—Philip Spitzer, 50 Talmage Farm Ln., East Hampton, NY 11937.

CAREER: Writer. Worked variously as a surveyor, social worker in Los Angeles, CA, 1962-64, newspaper reporter in Lafayette, LA, 1964, and English instructor at colleges and universities, including University of Southern Illinois, University of Montana, Miami-Dade Community College, and Wichita State University; U.S. Forest Service, Job Corps Conservation Center, Frenchburg, KY, instructor, 1965-66.

AWARDS, HONORS: Breadloaf fellow, 1970; Southern Federation of State Arts Agencies grant, 1977; National Endowment grant, 1977; Pulitzer Prize nomination, 1987, for *The Lost Get-Back Boogie;* Edgar Allan Poe awards for Best Novel, Mystery Writers of America, 1989, for *Black Cherry Blues,* and 1998, for *Cimarron Rose;* Guggenheim fellow, 1989.

WRITINGS:

NOVELS

Half of Paradise, Houghton Mifflin (Boston, MA), 1965.

To the Bright and Shining Sun, Scribner (New York, NY), 1970.

Lay down My Sword and Shield, Crowell (New York, NY), 1971.

Two for Texas, Pocket Books (New York, NY), 1983, published as *Sabine Spring,* Watermark Press, 1989.

The Lost Get-Back Boogie, Louisiana State University Press (Baton Rouge, LA), 1986.

"DAVE ROBICHEAUX" CRIME NOVELS

The Neon Rain, Holt (New York, NY), 1987.

Heaven's Prisoners, Holt (New York, NY), 1988.

Black Cherry Blues, Little, Brown (Boston, MA), 1989.

A Morning for Flamingos, Little, Brown (Boston, MA), 1990.

A Stained White Radiance, Hyperion (New York, NY), 1992.

In the Electric Mist with Confederate Dead, Hyperion (New York, NY), 1993.

Dixie City Jam, Hyperion (New York, NY), 1994.

Burning Angel, Hyperion (New York, NY), 1995.

Cadillac Jukebox, Hyperion (New York, NY), 1996.

Sunset Limited, Doubleday (New York, NY), 1998.

Purple Cane Road, Doubleday (New York, NY), 2000.

Jolie Blon's Bounce, Simon and Schuster (New York, NY), 2002.

"BILLY BOB HOLLAND" CRIME NOVELS

Cimarron Rose, Hyperion (New York, NY), 1997.

Heartwood, Doubleday (New York, NY), 1999.

Bitterroot, Simon & Schuster (New York, NY), 2001.

OTHER

The Convict and Other Stories, Louisiana State University Press (Baton Rouge, LA), 1985.

(With Kenneth E. Davison) *Ohio's Heritage,* Peregrine Smith Books (Layton, UT), 1989.

Texas City, Nineteen Forty-Seven, Lord John Press (Northridge, CA), 1992.

Short story anthologized in *Best American Short Stories of 1986.* Also contributor of short stories to periodicals, including *Atlantic, Quarterly West, Antioch Review, Kenyon Review, New England Review,* and *Southern Review.*

ADAPTATIONS: Heaven's Prisoners was filmed in 1996; *To the Bright and Shining Sun* was released by the Turner Network.

SIDELIGHTS: James Lee Burke poetically evokes New Orleans and its rural bayous in his series of detective novels featuring Dave Robicheaux. An ex-New Orleans police officer, Vietnam veteran, and recovering alcoholic, Robicheaux is a human character, possessing as many faults as virtues. "Burke has created, in Dave Robicheaux, a complex and convincing protagonist, a deeply moral, but troubled and self-divided man who strikes us as the antithesis of the stereotypical macho detective of popular culture," Joyce Carol Oates stated in the *Washington Post Book World.* In addition to cre-

ating such an extraordinary character, Burke also fills his novels with a rich and fertile setting. "No one captures current Louisiana culture, or the feel of that very particular *place,* as well as James Lee Burke," maintained *Washington Post Book World* contributor James Sallis. Writing in the *St. James Guide to Crime and Mystery Writers,* David K. Jeffrey called Burke "a writer of extraordinary talent and power [whose novels] are well-plotted, suspenseful, and action-packed; their characters are complicated and psychologically real; their violence shocks and horrifies."

Born in Houston, Burke grew up on the Texas and Louisiana coast, writing his first short stories while attending the University of Southwestern Louisiana. It was when one of these stories won an honorable mention in a contest that Burke "got hooked" on writing. Following graduate school, where he earned a teaching degree, Burke worked for the Sinclair Oil Company, but he soon returned to the University of Southwestern Louisiana to teach. In 1965, four years after its completion, Burke's first novel was published.

Half of Paradise, written when Burke was twenty-four, interweaves three stories that are linked by time and geography. Although the three protagonists are from varying life situations in the South, the stories all begin and end in tragic circumstances. Wirt Williams, writing in the *New York Times Book Review,* pointed out that Burke's writing could be sharper, but concluded that "no reservations alter the important things about the book: it is an exciting piece of writing and a solid debut for a writer to be taken absolutely seriously."

Burke, who had given up hope for *Half of Paradise,* was surprised by the critical acclaim the novel received, but still felt restless with his life. "I guess it happens to a lot of guys who go from grad school into university teaching," explained Burke in an interview with W. C. Stroby of *Writer's Digest.* "You feel you're missing something. So I went from job to job. We bounced all over the country, literally." By the mid-1960s, Burke was teaching at the University of Montana, and his next novel, *To the Bright and Shining Sun,* was published in 1970.

Set in a mining town in Kentucky, *To the Bright and Shining Sun* is narrated by sixteen-year-old Perry Woodson Hatfield James, a loyal member of the union who knows nothing of the world outside his small town. Offered the chance to learn a trade, Perry's hopes are dashed when his father is killed in an explosion set by non-union miners. "Burke takes these harsh facts and brings them to life in a surging, bitter novel as authentic as moonshine," related Martin Levin in the *New York Times Book Review.* And a *Publishers Weekly* contributor asserted that Burke "has presented a powerful and cruel picture of the Appalachia many Americans would like to forget."

At the time *To the Bright and Shining Sun* was published, Burke had a falling out with the agent who negotiated the sales of his first two books. Confident from his early success, Burke quickly signed with the William Morris Agency and published his third book, *Lay down My Sword and Shield,* to less enthusiastic reviews. Angered over the advertising for this work, Burke elected to take his next novel, *The Lost Get-Back Boogie,* to a new publisher. Things then began to go downhill for him. "I found out I couldn't publish *The Lost Get-Back Boogie* anywhere," recalled Burke in his interview with Stroby. "I stayed with William Morris for six more years, but I couldn't sell a thing. After that, the agency returned all my material, cut me loose, and suddenly it was ground zero again."

It was not until thirteen years later that Burke published another novel. "I fell onto bad days," he said in his *Writer's Digest* interview. "By the time I was 34, I had published three novels, and I thought I was home free. I discovered I was just starting to pay dues." These dues came mostly in the form of short stories and unpublished novels, which Burke spent the next several years writing. Eventually Burke met New York agent Philip G. Spitzer, and finally sold another novel in 1983—*Two for Texas,* a paperback original. While his other manuscripts, including *The Lost Get-Back Boogie,* continued to circulate, Burke proceeded with his teaching career. In 1986, a year after publishing a collection of his short stories, the Louisiana State University Press finally published a revised version of *The Lost Get-Back Boogie,* a book which earned Burke a Pulitzer Prize nomination. "I owe those people at LSU Press a lot," Burke told Stroby. "They resurrected my whole career. Suddenly I was back in business."

Ironically, *The Lost Get-Back Boogie,* which racked up ninety-three rejection slips and went unpublished for more than a decade, became one of Burke's most successful books. The novel opens on the day Iry Paret gets out of a Louisiana prison after spending two years inside for manslaughter. A Korean War veteran and country musician, Paret ends up in Montana ranch country with the family of one of his prison friends, Buddy Riordan. Attempting to write a song that captures his life before the war and prison, Paret finds himself unwillingly drawn into a feud between Riordan's father and his neighbors. Set in the 1960s, the novel is filled with flashbacks, dreams, and drunken meditations that show a glimpse of Paret's past and point to the novel's tragic climax. Regina Weinreich, writing in the *New York Times Book Review,* found the language in *The Lost Get-Back Boogie* "exceptionally poetic: a muscular prose enlivened by lyric descriptions of the landscape and the lingo of the roughnecks Paret encounters in the American hinterland." A *Washington Post Book World* contributor similarly concluded that Burke's prose "is by turns taut and poetic and his portrait of a fundamentally decent man trying to do right—but too often only able to do wrong—is riveting."

Before *The Lost Get-Back Boogie* was published, Burke decided to try his hand at a crime novel. With the encouragement of fellow writers, he combined elements of two of his unpublished novels to create *The Neon Rain,* the first book in the "Dave Robicheaux" crime series. In the debut book, Robicheaux is a New Orleans Police homicide detective investigating the murder of a prostitute whose body is discovered in the bayou. The case ends up encompassing everything from a contract on Robicheaux's life to encounters with the Nicaraguan mafia. Eventually framed and suspended from his job, Robicheaux must clear his name, and his ability to do so is made difficult when he gives up and returns to drinking. "Mr. Burke has created a real character in Dave Robicheaux," pointed out Newgate Callendar in the *New York Times Book Review.* "This is a detective who is more than a lethal man of action." Alan Ryan, writing in the *Washington Post Book World,* also saw Robicheaux as a "human" character, concluding: "Burke's writing is masterful, catching the violence of words and attitudes as well as the dizzying action, the pain and the blood. I love this book."

Robicheaux's life is significantly changed in his next adventure, *Heaven's Prisoners.* No longer working for the police, he now runs a bait shop on the rural bayou and is happily married to Annie, the woman who helped pull him out of his depression in *The Neon Rain.* The couple's peaceful life is interrupted when they watch a plane crash into the sea. Going down to investigate, Robicheaux discovers four bodies and a little Latina girl who has managed to survive the crash (he eventually adopts her). When the newspaper accounts of the accident report only three bodies, Robicheaux tries to find out why. Discovering that there is a drug connection, he is warned off the case and severely beaten by two thugs. A tragic turn of events prompts Robicheaux to start drinking again, but in the end a form of justice is done.

Los Angeles Times Book Review correspondent Charles Champlin observed that in *Heaven's Prisoners* Burke mixes "hard-line action and terse dialogue with lyrical evocations of the bayou country and explorations of the deepest feelings of anger, revenge, love, compassion and understanding." Callendar, in his review of the book, similarly related that Burke "has the knack of combining action with reflection; he has pity for the human condition, and even his villains can have some sympathetic and redeeming qualities . . . *Heaven's Prisoners* is a long way from your average action novel."

After his wife is killed by hired killers and he makes a trip to Montana to help out an old friend in *Black Cherry Blues*, Robicheaux finds himself in debt and joins the small New Iberia police force in his fourth adventure, *A Morning for Flamingos*. While transferring prisoners for execution—Jimmy Lee Boggs, a cold-blooded killer, and Tante Lemon, the grandson of an old Creole woman—Robicheaux finds himself shot and lying in a ditch after the two prisoners escape. Once recovered, he agrees to go undercover to infiltrate a mafia gang in New Orleans, the same gang for which Boggs is a hit-man. Along the way, Robicheaux also meets up with an old sweetheart and undergoes an interior battle with his own fears. *A Morning for Flamingos*, maintained Champlin in his review of the book, is "a poetically expressed merging of melodramatic events and sensitive problems of character and relationship." Kevin Moore, writing in Chicago *Tribune Books*, related that in *A Morning for Flamingos* "the air always seems heavy with static electricity—and there is no telling when, or why, things may reach a flash point. This is gumshoe gumbo at its tastiest."

Robicheaux remains a member of the New Iberia sheriff's department in his next adventure, *A Stained White Radiance*. Having recently married his childhood sweetheart, he finds himself drawn into the affairs of the Sonnier family, which is made up of a wealthy oil-man, a politician with Klan connections, a television evangelist, and another of Robicheaux's old girlfriends. After a cop is killed while investigating a break-in at one of the Sonniers' homes, the other members of the secretive family are attacked one by one, and Robicheaux must find the killer. Chicago *Tribune Books* contributor John Fink declared: "Burke can write. He drops in local color and vibrant characters with masterly precision. His action scenes crackle." And a *Los Angeles Times Book Review* contributor observed that Burke "is an intricate plotter with all the narrative gifts of the born storyteller. Yet he is uncommonly concerned with and eloquent about the textures and stresses of his times."

Robicheaux faces more emotional turmoil in *Purple Cane Road*, a novel that revolves around the detective's uncovering of new information surrounding his mother's murder. As the investigation into his mother's past draws him into a web of corrupt police officers with ties to the state attorney general, Robicheaux must also contend with his adopted daughter's crush on a dangerous hired gun. In a starred review, a *Publishers Weekly* contributor called *Purple Cane Road* "a powerhouse of a thriller that shows Burke writing near the peak of his form." In *Booklist*, Bill Ott concluded: "Robicheaux battling the past instead of the present is only the latest example of Burke's continuing ability to mix the fresh with the familiar in just the right way."

Speaking of the "Robicheaux" series in general, Stroby pointed out that "the Robicheaux books are often as much explorations of faith and fear as they are tightly crafted thrillers about crime and punishment in southern Louisiana." The religious element in his fiction and Robicheaux's continuing battle with alcohol comes from Burke's own experience as an alcoholic and his rediscovery of his Roman Catholic faith. William Plummer in *People* reported that since he confronted his alcoholism in the early 1980s, Burke "attends mass every Sunday and a 12-step meeting twice a week."

In the 1997 novel *Cimarron Rose*, Burke began a new detective series featuring Billy Bob Holland. Holland is a former Texas Ranger who is now a lawyer in the small Texas town of Deaf Smith. In his first outing, Holland must defend his own illegitimate son who has been arrested on a murder charge. In the process of proving his son's innocence, Holland uncovers a web of corruption involving his community's most powerful citizens. Ace Atkins in the *Tampa Tribune* reassured longtime Burke readers that "all the elements that worked in his earlier mysteries are still there" in his latest. According to Megan Harlan in *Entertainment Weekly*, in this novel Burke "flexes a graceful artistry, with unabashedly lyrical prose and violence choreographed like a menacing ballet." "Along with an evocative sense of place rendered in the Burke tradition," wrote Susan A. Zappia in *Library Journal*, "Billy Bob's humanity suffuses every page with a warm, golden glow." J. D. Reed, in his review of *Cimarron Rose* for *People*, found that "with each new book, Burke moves closer to taking a place in the genre's front row with the likes of John le Carré and Dashiell Hammett. He already shares the masters' ability to make the pop form resonate with polyphonic literary riffs and lyrical intensity."

A *Publishers Weekly* reviewer of Burke's second Holland novel, *Heartwood*, noted that although Holland is a Texas lawyer, he "shares Robicheaux's sensibilities: he's brutally honest, haunted by his past, kind to children, protective of the underdog." *Booklist* contributor Bill Ott likewise characterized Holland as "a complex, tormented hero whose attraction to violence surfaces under the guise of protecting the weak." In another *Booklist* review, this one for *Bitterroot,* Ott commented that the Billy Bob Holland series has allowed Burke to inject "new life into many of the familiar themes—especially a good man's attraction to violence—from his Dave Robicheaux novels."

"James Lee Burke is one of the ablest crime novelists of the day, a remarkable combination of poetic sensibility and hard-muscled storyteller," contended Champlin. And Sallis maintained that "few other writers have ever obtained the delicate balance between action and contemplation that's a given in any James Lee Burke book. The sensuousness of descriptive and lyric passages would be remarkable in any novel, and in the context of thrillers, becomes truly astonishing. There simply aren't many writers who look this closely at things, who open themselves so fully to the sensual world; fewer still who so richly recreate such moments for the reader." "Burke," Jeffrey concluded, "is in the process of redefining the crime genre, and it is as exciting to witness this process as it is to read his novels." In *Booklist,* Ott suggested that the secret of Burke's success lies in his "ability to twist formula in new directions, always spicing the literary comfort food that is genre fiction with a distinctive new tang."

BIOGRAPHICAL/CRITICAL SOURCES:

BOOKS

Contemporary Southern Writers, St. James Press (Detroit, MI), 1999.
St. James Guide to Crime and Mystery Writers, 4th edition, St. James Press (Detroit, MI), 1996.

PERIODICALS

Armchair Detective, winter, 1989, p. 22.
Book, September, 2000, Randy Michael Signor, review of *Purple Cane Road,* p. 73.
Booklist, April 15, 1998, Bill Ott, review of *Sunset Limited,* p. 1376; April 15, 1999, Bill Ott, review of *Heartwood,* p. 1466; May 1, 2000, Bill Ott, review of *Purple Cane Road,* p. 1610; March 15, 2001, Bill Ott, review of *Bitterroot,* p. 1331.

BookPage, August, 1997.
Detroit News, August 11, 1997.
Entertainment Weekly, August 18, 1995, p. 51; August 9, 1996, p. 55; August 8, 1997, p. 74.
Esquire, October, 2000, Daniel Mendelsohn, "Quien es mas macho?," p. 100.
Library Journal, June 15, 1997, p. 94.
Los Angeles Times Book Review, April 10, 1988, p. 10; October 8, 1989; November 11, 1990, p. 15; April 12, 1992, p. 12.
New York Times, August 21, 2000, Richard Bernstein, "Born on the Bayou; Dying There, Too."
New York Times Book Review, March 14, 1965; August 9, 1970; January 16, 1972; January 11, 1987; June 21, 1987; June 26, 1988, p. 43; October 8, 1989, p. 20; November 4, 1990, p. 30; April 5, 1992, p. 14; July 5, 1998, Marilyn Stasio, review of *Sunset Limited,* p. 16.
People, October 7, 1996, p. 115; September 15, 1997, p. 51.
Publishers Weekly, June 1, 1970, p. 63; November 8, 1971, p. 47; June 10, 1996, p. 88; June 9, 1997, p. 35; April 27, 1998, review of *Sunset Limited,* p. 48; June 21, 1999, review of *Heartwood,* p. 59; July 24, 2000, review of *Purple Cane Road,* p. 72.
Tampa Tribune, September 20, 1997.
Tribune Books (Chicago), April 3, 1988; September 10, 1989; October 14, 1990; April 12, 1992.
Washington Post, June 10, 1998, Jonathan Yardley, "A Fun, Foul Romp through the Bayou," p. D2.
Washington Post Book World, May 17, 1987; October 4, 1987; September 10, 1989, p. 5; December 16, 1990, pp. 1, 8; April 5, 1992.
Writer's Digest, January, 1993, pp. 38-40.

*   *   *

BUTLER, Judith P. 1956-

PERSONAL: Born February 24, 1956, in Cleveland, OH; daughter of Dan and Lois (Lefkowich) Butler; partner of Wendy Brown; children: Isaac Daniel Butler-Brown. *Education:* Yale University, B.A., 1978, M.Phil., Ph.D. (philosophy), 1984.

ADDRESSES: Office—Department of Rhetoric, University of California, Berkeley, 2125 Dwinelle Hall, Berkeley, CA 94720-0001. *E-mail*—jpbutler@socrates.berkeley.edu.

CAREER: Wesleyan University, Middletown, CT, assistant professor, 1983-86; George Washington University, Washington, DC, assistant professor of philosophy,

Judith P. Butler

1986-89; Johns Hopkins University, Baltimore, MD, professor of humanities, 1989-93; University of California, Berkeley, CA, Maxine Elliot Professor of Rhetoric and Comparative Literature, 1993—. Donald M. Kramer visiting scholar in the humanities, Brooklyn College, 1994; advisor for English Institute, Pembroke Center for Research and Teaching, 1994; invited faculty member, Dartmouth School of Criticism and Theory, 1995. Board member and chair of the Modern Language Association executive council and the Human Research Institute at the University of California.

MEMBER: Modern Language Association (executive council, board, and chair), International Gay and Lesbian Human Rights Commission, American Philosophical Association, American Council of Learned Societies, University of California Humanities Research Institute (board and chair).

AWARDS, HONORS: Institute for Advanced Study award, 1987-88; American Council of Learned Societies award, 1988; fellow, Humanities Research Institute, 1992; Guggenheim fellowship, 1999; Rockefeller fellowship, 2001-02.

WRITINGS:

Subjects of Desire: Hegelian Reflections in Twentieth-Century France, Columbia University Press (New York, NY), 1987, republished with new preface, 1999.

Gender Trouble: Feminism and the Subversion of Identity, Routledge (New York, NY), 1990.

(Editor, with Joan Wallach Scott) *Feminists Theorize the Political,* Routledge (New York, NY), 1992.

Bodies That Matter: On the Discursive Limits of "Sex", Routledge (New York, NY), 1993.

(Editor, with Linda Singer and Maureen MacGrogan) *Erotic Welfare: Sexual Theory and Politics in the Age of Epidemic,* Routledge (New York, NY), 1993.

Subjection, Stanford University Press (Stanford, CA), 1996.

Excitable Speech: A Politics of the Performative, Routledge (New York, NY), 1997.

The Psychic Life of Power: Theories in Subjection, Stanford University Press (Stanford, CA), 1997.

Antigone's Claim: Kinship between Life and Death, Columbia University Press (New York, NY), 2000.

(With Ernesto Laclau and Slavoj Zizek) *Contingency, Hegemony, Universality: Contemporary Dialogues on the Left,* Verso (London, England), 2000.

SIDELIGHTS: Feminist theoretician and educator Judith P. Butler is the author of several books that attempt to reevaluate the social relationships involving sex and gender. Her major contributions to the area of so-called "queer theory" include 1993's *Bodies That Matter: On the Discursive Limits of "Sex"* and *Gender Trouble: Feminism and the Subversion of Identity,* the latter a 1990 work that has become a standard text in gender studies classes. In each of her works, Butler argues that the idea that men and women are in any way dissimilar is a cultural rather than a biological reality. As Georgette Fleischer noted in *Nation,* "From the start of her career, Judith Butler has been on a quest for a theory of the subject [of gender] that might work for 'those who live, or try to live, on the sexual margins.'"

First published in 1990, *Gender Trouble* has been hailed as "the foundational text of queer theory," wrote Fleischer. *Gender Trouble,* Butler told *CA:* "draws upon Simone de Beauvior's claim that 'one is not born, but rather becomes a woman.'" In the work, Butler talks about gender as a process of becoming rather than a static definition. In an essay posted on the University of Colorado Web site, Dr. Mary Klages wrote, "Butler wants to show that gender is not just a social construct, but rather a kind of performance, a show we put on, a set of signs we wear, as costume or disguise." In the work, Butler writes that the classification of a person according to "sex" and/or "gender" is only valid within a society that adheres to the definitions attached to those terms. Constance Jordan of *Women's Studies* explained, "The parodic stance toward identity depends on a de-mystified concept of discourse and culture, which are no longer to be seen as restrictive or foundational, but rather as permitting continuous and variable performances in which masculine and feminine, straight and lesbian/gay elements of gender are recombined at will and with an eye to the exigencies of the moment."

The title *Gender Trouble* refers not only to the trouble of gender definition, but also to the goal of the book: "The security of our gender categories [is] undermined," wrote Kathleen Lemmon of the *Journal of Applied Philosophy*. "Making such Gender Trouble is the aim of Judith Butler's book." Susan Bordo made a similar comment in her review for *Feminist Studies:* "Butler's aim is both to provoke 'gender trouble' in the mind of the reader—by 'denaturalizing' the categories of gender and of the 'natural' itself—and to suggest how 'gender trouble' is *culturally* stirred up through 'subversive bodily acts' that exhibit the artificiality of gender." Hilda L. Thomas, writing for *Canadian Literature* pointed out, "Making 'gender trouble' is risky business. For feminists battling the pronouncements of the pulpit and the perversions of the box office, the risk is worth it."

Gender Trouble is divided into three sections, each discussing a different collection of theorists. In the first section, Butler deconstructs the nature of sex and gender, questioning the politics of identity. In the second, Butler questions the assumption of heterosexual identity, and "brilliantly turns psychoanalytic argumentation on its head," according to Leora Auslander of *Radical History Review*. The third section, called "Subversive Bodily Acts," relates techniques used to combat the assumptions of gender definition. "*Gender Trouble* enacts the playful and exciting possibility that criticism can be disruptive, incisive and affirmative," wrote Margaret Nash of *Hypatia*. The critic continued, "Butler's voice . . . is indispensable for feminist theory at this historical juncture." Bordo remarked that *Gender Trouble* "is a striking example, both of the riches and reductions which have issued from the postmodern marriage of feminist scholarship and poststructuralist thought." In an article for *Feminist Review*, Margaret McIntosh noted that such writers as Harding, Haraway, Scott, and Spivak (all of whom are quoted on the book's cover) "have found it authoritative, brilliant, innovative, startling, lucid, witty, provocative, engaging, subver-

sive, powerful and constructive. With some reservations about its lucidity, I think I would agree with all of these." Fleischer praised, "What stands head and shoulders above Butler's illustrious collection of radical theories is *Gender Trouble's* overarching claim that gender, and possibly even sex itself, is not an expression of who one is but rather a performance." Susan Thackrey of the *San Francisco Review of Books* commented, "Judith Butler, like a good martial artist in a critical situation, goes for the most vulnerable spot. . . . She takes aim at our sexual identity, dealing a blow to our idea that it is either a natural or a permanent matter of fact." *French Review* contributor Elizabeth C. Goldsmith claimed, "Butler's analysis poses questions and unveils assumptions about the way we think about gender that will continue to provoke discussion for a long time to come." Jordan noted, "The force of these arguments on the future of feminist thought will be, I would guess, profound."

Butler continues her exploration of gender in *Bodies That Matter*. In this volume she focuses on the way power affects human sexuality, using such cultural manifestations as contemporary films and literature to reflect on the construction and enforcement of sexual hierarchies within society. Bryan S. Turner praised the book in a review for *Contemporary Sociology*, noting that "Butler's work will almost certainly become a major dimension of the current analysis of the body, particularly in feminist theory [in] the psychoanalytic tradition of Jacques Lacan."

Butler's work has come under attack from left-wing feminists who feel that her theories of the artificiality of gender roles erode women's attempts to gain equality in the political sphere. In 1999 Martha C. Nussbaum published a negative review of Butler's work in the *New Republic,* in which she criticized both the style and substance of Butler's writings and concluded that the author "collaborates with evil." Other scholars and philosophers defended Butler and welcomed her work as an extension of an important theoretical debate. "The questions, and ruptural projects of Judith Butler, especially, turn the ship of the scholar around 180 degrees on the turbulent waters of cultural, personal and political identities and rituals," wrote Ann R. Cacoullos in *American Studies International*. Cacoullos added: "Whether we sink or swim with 'feminist scholar-ship,' we can no longer evade its turnings for our research and for our pedagogy." In the *Journal of Women's History,* Lisa Duggan declared: "An undercurrent of hostility and suspicion of queer theories emerges from the writing of a number of leftist feminists who attack Theory as pretentious nonsense." Duggan observed that those same feminists see Butler "as having an almost magical power to destroy progressive activism." Duggan disagreed with that sentiment. "From another point of view," she concluded, "Butler's work has enabled forms of activism. Perhaps it is this queer activism . . . and not Theory alone that is the underlying target of some of the attacks." Cacoullos put it succinctly when she stated that Butler's writings "query business as usual."

BIOGRAPHICAL/CRITICAL SOURCES:

PERIODICALS

American Literature, December, 1995, p. 893.

American Studies International, October, 2000, Ann R. Cacoullos, "Feminist Ruptures in Women's Studies and American Studies," p. 89.

Canadian Literature, winter, 1995, p. 159; spring, 1996, Hilda L. Thomas, "Ungendering Ideas," pp. 189-192.

Choice, January, 1988, p. 780; October, 1990, R. W. Smith, review of *Gender Trouble,* p. 385.

Comparative Studies in Society and History, July, 1993, Fred Matthews, "Nature/Nurture, Realism/Nominalism: Our Fundamental Conflict over Human Identity," pp. 647-662.

Contemporary Sociology, May, 1995, p. 331.

Drama Review, fall, 1995, pp. 170-178.

Feminist Review, summer, 1991, Mary McIntosh, review of *Gender Trouble,* pp. 113-114.

Feminist Studies, spring, 1992, Susan Bordo, "Postmodern Subjects, Postmodern Bodies," pp. 159-175.

French Review, December, 1991, Elizabeth C. Goldsmith, review of *Gender Trouble,* pp. 297-298.

Hypatia, fall, 1990, Margaret Nash, review of *Gender Trouble,* pp. 171-175.

International Journal of Sexuality and Gender Studies, April, 2001.

Journal of Applied Philosophy, 1992, Kathleen Lennon, review of *Gender Trouble,* pp. 125-126.

Journal of Modern History, March, 1991, p. 124.

Journal of Women's History, spring, 1998, Lisa Duggan, "The Theory Wars, or, Who's Afraid of Judith Butler?," p. 9.

Library Journal, December, 1989, Mark P. Maller, review of *Gender Trouble,* p. 148.

London Review of Books, November 2, 2000, Bruce Robbins, "Dive In!," p. 33.

Nation, December 11, 2000, Georgette Fleischer, "Butler: Is It All Greek?," p. 40.

New Republic, February 22, 1999, Martha C. Nussbaum, "The Professor of Parody—The Hip Defeatism of Judith Butler," p. 37.

New Statesman and Society, July 10, 1992, Ellen Mizzell, "More Iron in the Spine," p. 36.

Philosophical Review, January, 1990, pp. 129-131.

Radical History Review, fall, 1992, Leora Auslander, "Feminist Theory and Social History: Explorations in the Politics of Identity," pp. 158-176.

San Francisco Review of Books, winter, 1989, Susan Thackery, "Ending Gender," pp. 9-10.

Signs, summer, 1992, E. Ann Kaplan, review of *Gender Troubles,* pp. 843-847.

Times Literary Supplement, June 1-7, 1990, Liam Hudson, "The Same but Different," p. 588.

Village Voice, June, 1992, "Speaking Queerly," p. 22.

Women's Studies, March, 1993, Constance Jordan, review of *Gender Trouble,* pp. 257-259.

OTHER

Lola Press, http://www.lolapress.org/elec2/artenglish/butl_e.htm, (February 7, 2002), Regina Michalik, interview with Judith Butler.

Theory.org, http://www.theory.org.uk/ctr-butl.htm, (February 7, 2002), "Judith Butler."

University of California, Berkley, Department of Rhetoric, http://cinemaspace.berkeley.edu/Film_Studies/Rhetoric/ (February 7, 2002).

University of Colorado, English 2010, http://www.colorado.edu/English/ENGL2012Klages/butler.html, (December 8, 1997), Mary Klages, review of *Gender Trouble.*

Wellek Library Lectures, http://sun3.lib.uci.edu/~scctr/Wellek/butler/ (May, 1998), Eddie Yeghiayan, bibliography of Butler's work.

C

CABLE, James (Eric) 1920-2001
(Grant Hugo)

PERSONAL: Born November 15, 1920, in London, England; died September 27, 2001, in Cambridge, England; son of Eric Grant (a consul-general) and Nellie Margaret (Skelton) Cable; married Viveca Hollmerus, 1954; children: Charles. *Education:* Corpus Christi College, Cambridge, Ph.D., 1973.

CAREER: Diplomat. British Diplomatic Service, London, England, joined Foreign Service, 1947, vice-consul in Batavia (now Djakarta, Indonesia), 1949, second secretary in Djakarta, 1950, charge d'affaires, 1951-52, second secretary in Helsinki, Finland, 1952, and in Foreign Office, London, England, 1953, became first secretary, 1953, member of British delegation to Geneva Conference on Indochina, 1954, first secretary in Budapest, Hungary, 1956, head of chancery and consul in Quito, Ecuador, 1959, charge d'affaires, 1959-60, in Foreign Office, 1961-63, head of Southeast Asia department, 1963-66, counselor in Beirut, Lebanon, 1966, charge d'affaires, 1967-69, head of western organizations department at Foreign and Commonwealth Office, 1970-71, counselor in contingency studies, 1971, head of planning staff, 1971-75, assistant under-secretary of state, 1972-75, ambassador to Finland in Helsinki, 1975-80; writer. Institute for Strategic Studies, research associate, 1969-70. *Military service:* British Army, 1941-46.

MEMBER: International Institute for Strategic Studies, British International Studies Association.

AWARDS, HONORS: Companion of Order of St. Michael and St. George, 1967; knight commander of Royal Victorian Order, 1976; Grand Cross of Order of Finnish Lion, 1976.

WRITINGS:

(Under pseudonym Grant Hugo) *Britain in Tomorrow's World,* Columbia University Press (New York, NY), 1969.

(Under pseudonym Grant Hugo) *Appearance and Reality in International Relations,* Columbia University Press (New York, NY), 1970.

Gunboat Diplomacy, Praeger (New York, NY), 1971, revised edition published as *Gunboat Diplomacy, 1919-1979,* St. Martin's Press (New York, NY), 1981, third edition published as *Gunboat Diplomacy, 1919-1991: Political Applications of Limited Naval Force,* 1994.

The Royal Navy and the Siege of Bilbao, Cambridge University Press (New York, NY), 1979.

Britain's Naval Future, Macmillan (New York, NY), 1983.

Diplomacy at Sea, Macmillan (New York, NY), 1985.

The Geneva Conference of 1954 on Indochina, Macmillan (New York, NY), 1986, second edition, 2000.

Political Institutions and Issues in Britain, Macmillan (New York, NY), 1987.

Navies in Violent Peace, Macmillan (New York, NY), 1989.

Intervention at Abadan: Plan Buccaneer, St. Martin's Press (New York, NY), 1991.

The Political Influence of Naval Force in History, St. Martin's Press (New York, NY), 1998.

Contributor to various journals.

SIDELIGHTS: James Cable's years of diplomatic service to Great Britain have resulted in several books examining political issues. One of these, *The Royal Navy and the Siege of Bilbao,* is "the story of how the British Government tried to cope at a stage in [the Spanish Civil War] which brought all these elements into play for the first time: the maintenance of trade and of food shipments and the evacuation of refugees in the face of a Nationalist blockade; the attempt to maintain the principles of Non-Intervention and, at the same time, to continue to act as a great power, with only minor interests at stake; all came together in a series of decisions and actions," as *Times Literary Supplement* critic Peter Nailor described it. "It is, of necessity, a tangled story," Nailor continued. "The records are not well preserved, and many recollections are partial. But James Cable . . . weaves the story deftly together and unravels many of its tangles to show how puzzled and uncertain, and fearful, many of the ideas and the agents of British policy-making then were."

Similarly, the essays in Cable's *Diplomacy at Sea,* while "the majority have a naval flavour," "draw more widely on [Cable's] diplomatic experience and views," Bryan Ranft observed in the *Times Literary Supplement.* Overall, the critic remarked, Cable's work "is marked by clarity and wit, and the subtlety of its conceptual differentiations, the aptness of its historical examples, and its telling references to his personal diplomatic experiences, show the author at his best." "As a retired ambassador, [Cable's] viewpoint is that of a professional observer and interpreter of politics who is neither a practitioner nor an academic," John Campbell noted in his *Times Literary Supplement* review of *Political Institutions and Issues in Britain.* "He is appropriately lucid, skeptical and, in the end, mildly elegiac." As a result, Campbell concluded, "in a discipline dominated by indigestible textbooks and arcane monographs his book . . . is a pleasure to read."

BIOGRAPHICAL/CRITICAL SOURCES:

PERIODICALS

Choice, February, 1999, review of *The Political Influence of Naval Force in History,* p. 1110.
Reference & Research Book News, April, 1992, review of *Intervention at Abadan: Plan Buccaneer,* p. 8; May, 1999, review of *The Political Influence of Naval Force in History,* p. 207.
Times (London, England), August 6, 1981.
Times Literary Supplement, February 15, 1980; May 27, 1983; November 8, 1985; November 13-19, 1987, John Campbell, review of *Political Institutions and*

Issues in Britain; November 17, 2000, David Carlton, review of *The Geneva Conference of 1954 on Indochina,* p. 33.*

*   *   *

CARD, Orson Scott 1951-
(Brian Green, Byron Walley)

PERSONAL: Born August 24, 1951, in Richland, WA; son of Willard Richards (a teacher) and Peggy Jane (a secretary and administrator; maiden name, Park) Card; married Kristine Allen, May 17, 1977; children: Michael Geoffrey, Emily Janice, Charles Benjamin, Zina Margaret, Erin Louisa. *Education:* Brigham Young University, B.A. (with distinction), 1975; University of Utah, M.A., 1981. *Politics:* "Moderate Democrat." *Religion:* Church of Jesus Christ of Latter-day Saints (Mormon).

ADDRESSES: Home—Greensboro, NC. *Agent*—Barbara Bova, 3951 Gulf Shore Blvd. #PH1B, Naples, FL 33940.

CAREER: Volunteer Mormon missionary in Brazil, 1971-73; operated repertory theater in Provo, UT, 1974-75; Brigham Young University Press, Provo, proofreader, 1974, editor, 1974-76; *Ensign* magazine, Salt Lake City, UT, assistant editor, 1976-78; freelance writer and editor, 1978—. Senior editor, Compute! Books, Greensboro, NC, 1983. Teacher at various writers workshops and universities, including University of Utah, 1979-80 and 1981, Brigham Young University, 1981, and Clarion Writers Workshop, East Lansing, MI, 1982. Local Democratic precinct election judge and Utah State Democratic Convention delegate.

MEMBER: Science Fiction Writers of America.

AWARDS, HONORS: John W. Campbell Award for best new writer of 1977, World Science Fiction Convention, 1978; Hugo Award nominations, World Science Fiction Convention, 1978, 1979, 1980, for short stories, and 1986, for novelette, "Hatrack River"; Nebula Award nominations, Science Fiction Writers of America, 1979, 1980, for short stories; Utah State Institute of Fine Arts prize, 1980, for epic poem "Prentice Alvin and the No-Good Plow"; Nebula Award, 1985, and Hugo Award, 1986, both for *Ender's Game;* Nebula Award, 1986, Hugo Award, and Locus Award, both 1987, all for *Speaker for the Dead;* World Fantasy Award, 1987, for novelette, "Hatrack River"; Hugo Award, and Locus

Award nomination, both 1988, both for novella "Eye for Eye"; Locus Award for best fantasy, Hugo Award nomination, World Fantasy Award nomination, and Mythopoeic Fantasy Award, Mythopoeic Society, all 1988, all for *Seventh Son;* Locus Award, 1989, for *Red Prophet;* Hugo Award, 1991, for *How to Write Science Fiction and Fantasy;* Israel's Geffen Award for Best Science Fiction Book, 1999, for *Pastwatch: The Redemption of Christopher Columbus;* Grand Prix de L'Imaginaire, 2000, for *Heartfire.*

WRITINGS:

"ENDER" SCIENCE FICTION SERIES

Ender's Game (also see below), Tor Books (New York, NY), 1985.
Speaker for the Dead (also see below), Tor Books (New York, NY), 1986.
Ender's Game [and] *Speaker for the Dead,* Tor Books (New York, NY), 1987.
Xenocide, Tor Books (New York, NY), 1991.
Children of the Mind, Tor Books (New York, NY), 1996.

"SHADOW" SCIENCE FICTION SERIES

Ender's Shadow, Tor Books (New York, NY), 1999.
Shadow of the Hegemon, Tor Books (New York, NY), 2001.
Shadow Puppets, Tor Books (New York, NY), 2001.

"TALES OF ALVIN MAKER" FANTASY SERIES

Seventh Son, St. Martin's (New York, NY), 1987.
Red Prophet, Tor Books (New York, NY), 1988.
Prentice Alvin, Tor Books (New York, NY), 1989.
Alvin Journeyman, Tor Books (New York, NY), 1995.
Heartfire, Tor Books (New York, NY), 1998.

"HOMECOMING" SCIENCE FICTION SERIES

The Memory of Earth (also see below), Tor Books (New York, NY), 1992.
The Call of Earth (also see below), Tor Books (New York, NY), 1993.
The Ships of Earth (also see below), Tor Books (New York, NY), 1993.

Homecoming: Harmony (contains *The Memory of Earth, The Call of Earth,* and *The Ships of Earth*), Tor Books (New York, NY), 1994.
Earthfall, Tor Books (New York, NY), 1995.
Earthborn, Tor Books (New York, NY), 1995.

SCIENCE FICTION/FANTASY NOVELS

Hot Sleep, Baronet, 1978.
A Planet Called Treason, St. Martin's (New York, NY), 1979, revised edition, Dell (New York, NY), 1980, published as *Treason,* St. Martin's (New York, NY), 1988.
Songmaster, Dial (New York, NY), 1980.
Hart's Hope, Berkley Publishing (New York, NY), 1982.
The Worthing Chronicle, Ace Books (New York, NY), 1983.
Wyrms, Arbor House (New York, NY), 1987.
The Abyss (novelization of screenplay by Jim Cameron), Pocket Books (New York, NY), 1989.
(With Lloyd Biggle) *Eye for Eye—The Tunesmith,* Tor Books (New York, NY), 1990.
Worthing Saga, Tor Books (New York, NY), 1990.
Lost Boys, HarperCollins (New York, NY), 1992.
(With Kathryn H. Kidd) *Lovelock,* Tor Books (New York, NY), 1994.
Pastwatch: The Redemption of Columbus, Donald M. Grant/Tor Books (New York, NY), 1996.
Magic Mirror, illustrated by Nathan Pinnock, Gibbs Smith (Salt Lake City, UT), 1999.
Enchantment, Del Rey (New York, NY), 1999.

SCIENCE FICTION/FANTASY SHORT STORY COLLECTIONS

Capitol, Ace Books (New York, NY), 1978.
Unaccompanied Sonata and Other Stories, Dial, 1981.
(Editor) *Dragons of Darkness,* Ace Books (New York, NY), 1981.
(Editor) *Dragons of Light,* Ace Books (New York, NY), 1983.
(With others) *Free Lancers,* Baen Books (Riverdale, NY), 1987.
The Folk of the Fringe, Phantasia Press, 1989.
Maps in a Mirror: The Short Fiction of Orson Scott Card, Tor Books (New York, NY), 1990, published in four volumes as *Flux,* 1992, *Cruel Miracles,* 1992, *The Changed Man,* 1992, and *Monkey Sonatas,* 1993.
(Editor) *Future on Fire,* Tor Books (New York, NY), 1991.

(Editor) *Future on Ice,* Tor Books (New York, NY), 1998.

(Editor) *Masterpieces: The Best Science Fiction of the Century,* Ace Books (New York, NY), 2001.

PLAYS

The Apostate, produced in Provo, Utah, 1970.

In Flight, produced in Provo, 1970.

Across Five Summers, produced in Provo, 1971.

Of Gideon, produced in Provo, 1971.

Stone Tables, produced in Provo at Brigham Young University, 1973.

A Christmas Carol (adapted from the story by Charles Dickens), produced in Provo, 1974.

Father, Mother, Mother, and Mom, produced in Provo, 1974, published in *Sunstone,* 1978.

Liberty Jail, produced in Provo, 1975.

Also author of (under pseudonym Brian Green) *Rag Mission,* published in *Ensign* magazine, July, 1977; (and director) *Fresh Courage Take,* produced in 1978; *Elders and Sisters* (adapted from a work by Gladys Farmer), produced in 1979; and *Wings* (fragment), produced in 1982.

OTHER

Listen, Mom and Dad, Bookcraft, 1978.

Saintspeak: The Mormon Dictionary, Signature Books (Salt Lake City, UT), 1982.

Ainge, Signature Books (Salt Lake City, UT), 1982.

A Woman of Destiny (historical novel), Berkley Publishing (New York, NY), 1983, published as *Saints,* Tor Books (New York, NY), 1988.

Cardography, Hypatia Press, 1987.

Characters and Viewpoint, Writer's Digest (Cincinnati, OH), 1988.

How to Write Science Fiction and Fantasy, Writer's Digest (Cincinnati, OH), 1990.

Lost Boys, HarperCollins (New York, NY), 1992.

Treasure Box, Deseret Book Co. (Salt Lake City, UT), 1996.

Stone Tables, Deseret Book Co. (Salt Lake City, UT), 1997.

Homebody, HarperCollins (New York, NY), 1998.

Sarah: Women of Genesis, Shadow Mountain (Salt Lake City, UT), 2000.

Rebekah, Deseret Book Co., (Salt Lake City, UT), 2001.

Also a contributor of articles and reviews to periodicals, including *Washington Post Book World, Short Form, Science Fiction Review,* and *Destinies.* Author of audio plays, beginning in 1978, and coauthor of animated videotapes for Living Scriptures, Ogden, UT. Contributor, sometimes under pseudonym Byron Walley, of stories to science fiction magazines. Author of regular review columns "You Got No Friends in This World," *Science Fiction Review,* 1979-86, "Books to Look For," *Magazine of Fantasy and Science Fiction,* 1987-94, and "Gameplay," *Compute!,* 1988— .

Some of Card's works have been translated into French, German, Italian, Japanese, Portuguese, Spanish, Dutch, Hebrew, and Polish. Card's manuscripts are housed at Brigham Young University.

ADAPTATIONS: Ender's Game, Seventh Son, Speaker for the Dead, The Memory of Earth, Lost Boys, and *The Call to Earth* have all been adapted for audio cassette; *Xenocide* has also been adapted into two audiocassettes, read by Mark Rolston, Audio Renaissance, 1991; *The Ender Wiggin Saga,* Card's "Ender" series, was adapted in nine cassettes, Audio Renaissance, 2000.

WORK IN PROGRESS: A fourth book in the "Shadow" series, *The Shadow of the Giant.*

SIDELIGHTS: Though usually thought of solely as a science fiction writer, award-winning author Orson Scott Card has penned over sixty books in genres as disparate as science fiction, fantasy, history, religious studies, and suspense. Best known for his "Ender" series of science fiction novels, he has also created other memorable series, including "Tales of Alvin Maker" and "Homecoming." His fantasy titles include the quest novel *Wyrms,* as well as *Enchantment,* a blend of Sleeping Beauty and Russian mythology. Writing more mainstream novels, the prolific Card has also produced contemporary novels with occult themes, such as *Lost Boys, Treasure Box,* and *Homebody.* Blending his own devout Mormon faith with an interest in history, the author has additionally written historical fiction, including *A Woman of Destiny, The Stone Tablets,* and *Sarah.* And, as if such a plethora of books in a diversity of styles is not enough for one imagination, Card is also a proficient playwright.

Card was born in Richland, Washington, in 1951, and became an early fan of both the theater and science fiction. Entering Brigham Young University at sixteen, he produced his first play while still an undergraduate.

His early work focused on the theater, for which he wrote dramas with religious and biblical themes. After a stint as a missionary in Brazil and working as the editor of a Mormon magazine, he finally turned his hand to science fiction, creating a healthy body of work in short stories. One such early story was "Ender's Game," which ultimately became the breakthrough novel of the same title.

Since publishing the story that evolved into his award-winning novel *Ender's Game,* Card has remained a prominent force in the science fiction and fantasy fields. In 1987, for example, he became the first writer to win the genre's top awards, the Nebula and the Hugo, for consecutive novels in a continuing series. The first of these two, *Ender's Game,* concerns the training of Ender Wiggin, a six-year-old genius who is the Earth's only hope for victory over invading "bugger" aliens. While this plot appears to be standard science fiction fare, *New York Times Book Review* critic Gerald Jonas observed that "Card has shaped this unpromising material into an affecting novel full of surprises that seem inevitable once they are explained." The difference, asserted Jonas and other critics, is in the character of Ender Wiggin, who remains sympathetic despite his acts of violence. A *Kirkus Reviews* contributor, for example, while noting the plot's inherent weakness, also admitted that "the long passages focusing on Ender are nearly always enthralling," and concluded that *Ender's Game* "is altogether a much more solid, mature, and persuasive effort" than the author's previous work. Dan K. Moran called *Ender's Game* "the best novel I've read in a long time" in the *West Coast Review of Books,* and added that "Ender Wiggin is a unique creation. Orson Scott Card has created a character who deserves to be remembered with the likes of Huckleberry Finn. *Ender's Game* is *that* good."

While *Ender's Game* garnered awards and popularity for Card, its sequel, *Speaker for the Dead,* "is the most powerful work Card has produced," claimed Michael R. Collings in *Fantasy Review.* "*Speaker* not only completes *Ender's Game* but transcends it. . . . Read in conjunction with *Ender's Game, Speaker* demonstrates Card's mastery of character, plot, style, theme, and development." Ender Wiggin, now working as a "Speaker for the Dead," travels the galaxy to interpret the lives of the deceased for their families and neighbors; as he travels, he also searches for a home for the eggs of the lone surviving "hive queen" of the race he destroyed as a child. When Ender is called to the colony planet of Lusitania, his visit coincides with the discovery of another intelligent race, re-opening the question of co-existence versus survival. Card "has woven a

constantly escalating storyline which deals with religion, alien/human viewpoints and perspectives on instinctual and cultural levels, the fate of three alien species . . . , and quite possibly the fate of mankind itself," according to *Science Fiction Review* editor Richard E. Geis. "Like *Game, Speaker* deals with issues of evil and empathy, though not in so polarized a way," observed Tom Easton in his *Analog* review. He concluded, "less brash than *Ender's Game, Speaker for the Dead* may be a much better book." In addition, critics found an extra element of complexity in the "Ender" books; *Washington Post Book World* contributor Janrae Frank saw "quasi-religious images and themes" in the conclusions of both novels.

Card continues his "Ender" series with 1991's *Xenocide,* picking up the story of Ender as he works feverishly with his adopted Lusitanian family to neutralize a deadly virus. Many critics venture that with *Xenocide* Card relies more on the scientific ruminations of a multitude of contemplative characters than on plot. "The real action is philosophical: long, passionate debates about ends and means among people who are fully aware that they may be deciding the fate of an entire species, entire worlds," observed Gerald Jonas in the *New York Times Book Review.* In 1996 Card published the final volume of the "Ender" quartet, *Children of the Mind.* In this novel, Ender is already moving off the stage, playing a relatively minor part in the hectic attempt to avoid destruction of the planet Lusitania by the Starways Congress. "Card's prose is powerful here," commented a reviewer for *Publishers Weekly,* "as is his consideration of mystical and quasi-religious themes." The same writer went on to wonder whether this book, "billed as the final Ender novel," would in fact be the last readers hear of Ender or his world. "This story leaves enough mysteries unexplored to justify another entry." *Booklist* contributor Roland Green called this novel "a worthy ending to what might be stylized a saga of the ethical evolution of humanity, a concept seldom attempted before and never realized with the success Card achieves here."

Card returned to the same themes with *Ender's Shadow* and its sequel, *Shadow of the Hegemon.* These titles feature the superhuman child, Bean, who is taken from the streets of Rotterdam to attend the Battle School and learn to fight the insect-like Buggers. At the school he not only learns how to battle the enemy, but also comes to understand what makes him human. A reviewer for *Publishers Weekly* called this an "immensely involving SF novel," and dubbed Card's portrait of Bean at once "strange and wonderful, tragic yet hopeful." In *Shadow of the Hegemon* Bean is a young man, and with the wars over he must make the crucial decision of which leader to support in creating a new world. Sally Estes, reviewing this title in *Booklist,* found it "so nicely integrated into the rest of the Ender canon that readers will be completely enthralled and left anxiously awaiting the next installment."

In 1987, while not yet finished with his "Ender" series, Card released *Seventh Son,* the first volume in his "Tales of Alvin Maker" series. A revision and expansion of an epic poem he wrote during graduate studies at the University of Utah, the series is set in an alternate pioneer America, a nation of inchoate states to which witches have been exiled by the Puritans. *Seventh Son* details the early years of the series' protagonist, Alvin Miller, a "Maker," or one endowed with magical powers because of his distinctive status as the seventh son of a seventh son. Though many people possess mystical powers in Card's America—such as dowsing, hexing, and healing—Alvin owns the supreme talent of being able to control reality. *Red Prophet,* the second novel in the series, shifts the focus away from Alvin to the issue of the interfacing between colonists and Native Americans. Three individuals are featured in the work: Ta-Kumsaw, a Shawnee who wishes to reserve all land east of the Mississippi River for the whites, who have "despoiled" it with their presence, and keep all land west for the Indians; William Henry Harrison ("White Murderer Harrison"), who desires to slaughter all Native Americans; and Lolla-Wossiky, Ta-Kumsaw's brother and the "Red Prophet," who preaches of a land where both peoples can live in harmony. In the course of the work, Alvin is drawn into the struggle. "His hands heal and bring together these seemingly disparate elements into a force to be reckoned with," contended Sue Martin in the *Los Angeles Times Book Review. Prentice Alvin,* the third volume in the series, follows Alvin as he matures to nineteen years of age under the watch of his guardian "torch," one who can see into the future. *Alvin Journeyman* continued the cycle, followed by *Heartfire.* Throughout the course of the series, Card presents "alternative American history," according to a reviewer for *Publishers Weekly.*

In 1992 Card introduced his "Homecoming" series with *The Memory of Earth,* a novel mixing philosophy, futuristic technology, and biblical lore. *Memory* opens on the planet Harmony, where for forty million years humans have been controlled by Oversoul, a powerful, global computer programmed to prevent humanity from destroying itself through needless wars. As the novel progresses, Oversoul falls into disrepair and requires restoration from Earth, a planet out of the reach of the citizens of Harmony, who have become technologically

stagnant and possess no concept of space travel. To save itself as well as Harmony, Oversoul engages the aid of Wetchik and his son Nafai, members of an extended family that "most closely resembles Biblical tribesmen," contended Faren Miller in *Locus.* "They are herders, small traders, semi-nomadic men." David E. Jones, in his Chicago *Tribune Books* appraisal of *Memory,* decided that "what Card gives us is an interaction between supreme intelligence and human mental capability that is at once an intellectual exercise, a Biblical parable and a thoroughly enjoyable piece of storytelling." "Card has recaptured the originality and grace that so enthralled readers of *Ender's Game,*" asserted reviewer Joel Singer in *Voice of Youth Advocates.* "He expertly weaves Biblical imagery, modern science, philosophy, and emotion in a tale of a young man, Nafai, growing and maturing."

Card continued the "Homecoming" series with *The Call of Earth.* As in *The Memory of Earth,* the Harmony city of Basilica is still occupied by the same families, yet semi-regulated by the powerful computer, Oversoul. Oversoul has deteriorated and desperately needs repair in order to save Harmony from its self-destruction. Oversoul uses the faith of its followers to communicate its demise—for without its power, humans will continue to regain their memories, which allowed technological advancement to occur and encouraged the re-creation of war and disorder. Singer, who continued to review the series in *Voice of Youth Advocates,* stated: "One of Card's major strengths as an author is characterization, and he introduces some extremely interesting and engaging ones in this novel."

The Ships of Earth, the third book in the "Homecoming" lineage, is the continuation of the story introduced in the first two novels. Rather than persevering with the demolition-of-a-society theme, Card explores the intricacies of man vs. man. Miller conveyed in *Locus* that "everything from religion to politics to sexuality is open to discussion as the arguing characters have at it, and the result is more open-minded than one might expect." Sherry Hoy, writing in *Voice of Youth Advocates,* similarly judged *The Ships of Earth* to be "classic Card—solid, careful character development and interplay plus a clearly defined setting."

Earthfall and *Earthborn* conclude the series, with the former novel seeing the travelers from Harmony coming back to Earth, the first humans to return in forty million years. "This action-packed, plot-rich installment features Card's typical virtues," wrote a contributor for *Publishers Weekly;* "well-drawn characters, and a story driven by complex moral issues." *Earthborn* concludes the saga.

Popular stand-alone fantasy titles from Card include *Wyrms* and *Enchantment. Wyrms* is a traditional quest adventure involving a deposed princess. "There is nothing trite about this book, nothing swollen and contrived," asserted *Los Angeles Times Book Review* contributor Ingrid Rimland. *Wyrms* "is many things at once: a parable, a heroic adventure, a philosophical treatise, a finely crafted masterpiece of stylistically honed paragraphs, [and] a careful and smart understatement on the rebellious theme that God might be evil and needs to be slain." *Enchantment* tells a story that blends Sleeping Beauty with the Russian folk tales about Baba Yaga. "In the hands of a gifted storyteller like Card," wrote *Booklist* reviewer Roberta Johnson, "this classic tale becomes a compelling adventure."

Though Card has established himself firmly as a writer of science fiction and fantasy, he has not limited himself to that genre. Throughout his career he has forged into nonfiction, adaptations, and, most notably, historical fiction. *A Woman of Destiny,* his novel set in the nineteenth century and revolving around the Mormon religion, is generally viewed by critics as his most significant work outside the field of science fiction. The volume turns on Dinah Kirkham, a courageous English woman who is converted to Mormonism by Joseph Smith, the founder of the religion, and then follows him to a Mormon community in Illinois, where she becomes his "secret" second wife. *Los Angeles Times Book Review* critic Kristiana Gregory pronounced *A Woman of Destiny* an "engrossing epic," stressing that Card "is a powerful storyteller."

Other more mainstream novels include *Treasure Box* and *Lost Boys,* each with elements of the supernatural and suspense. *Homebody* is another mainstream supernatural fantasy. It combines elements of spirituality, the occult, and psychological insight in a haunted house tale. *Homebody* tells the story of Don Lark, who, grieving the death of his two-year-old daughter, sets out to renovate the Bellamy House, a grand old Victorian mansion in a terrible state of disrepair. His three elderly neighbors warn him about the house's dark powers, but he goes forward with his project and becomes attached to a squatter who lives there. She is the occult key to the violent history of the house as a brothel and speakeasy. A writer for *Kirkus Reviews* assessed the novel as "solid but undistinguished work, not high in either tension or in depth." However, a *Publishers Weekly* reviewer found more to like, saying that the novel has "great potential that shines through its superfluous detail," and describing it as "a powerful tale of healing and redemption that skillfully balances supernatural horrors with spiritual uplift."

More religious in theme are *Stone Tablets,* Card's retelling of the story of Moses and the Exodus, and *Sarah* and *Rebekah,* the first titles of the "Women of Genesis" series. Reviewing *Sarah,* a contributor for *Publishers Weekly* noted that this "playfully speculative novel succeeds in bringing Sarah's often-overlooked character into vivid relief."

Card has long been praised for the moral messages delivered in his books, but he does not think of himself as a didactic author. As he told Laura Ciporen in a *Publishers Weekly* interview, "I hate black and white representations of good versus evil, that's so boring. . . . My characters wrestle with real moral dilemmas where all the choices have steep prices." Remarking on why he so often writes science fiction, Card concluded to Ciporen, "Mainstream literature is so stultifyingly rigid. I don't just want to talk to people who believed everything their English teacher told them. I want to reach people who read books for the sheer pleasure of it, because those are the people who are open to having their lives changed by what they read."

BIOGRAPHICAL/CRITICAL SOURCES:

BOOKS

Collings, Michael R., and Boden Clarke, *The Work of Orson Scott Card: An Annotated Bibliography & Guide,* Borgo Press (San Bernandino, CA), 1995.

Collings, Michael R., *Storyteller: The Official Orson Scott Card Bibliography and International Reader's Guide,* Overlook Connection Press (New York, NY), 2001.

Contemporary Literary Criticism, Gale (Detroit, MI), Volume 44, 1987, Volume 47, 1988, Volume 50, 1988.

Contemporary Popular Writers, St. James Press (Detroit, MI), 1997.

PERIODICALS

Analog, July, 1983, p. 103; July, 1985, p. 180; June, 1986, Tom Easton, review of *Speaker for the Dead,* p. 183; mid-December, 1987; September, 1988, p. 179; August, 1989, p. 175; January, 1990, p. 305; March, 1991, p. 184; mid-December, 1991; January, 1996, p. 277; June, 1996, p. 145; October, 1998, pp. 136-137; January, 2000, pp. 177-181.

Booklist, December 15, 1985, p. 594; December 15, 1987; December 1, 1995, p. 586; June 1 & 15, 1996, Roland Green, review of *Children of the Mind,* p. 1629; September 15, 1998, pp. 206, 219; March 1, 1999, Roberta Johnson, review of *Enchantment,* p. 1103; July, 1999, p. 1892; January 1, 2000, p. 819; April 1, 2000, p. 1448; November 1, 2000, Sally Estes, review of *Shadow of the Hegemon,* p. 490; February 1, 2001, p. 1064; October 1, 2001, Roland Green, review of *Masterpieces: The Best Science Fiction of the Century,* p. 306.

Economist, September 5, 1987, p. 92.

Fantasy Review, April, 1986, Michael R. Collings, "Adventure and Allegory," p. 20; June, 1987; July-August, 1987.

Kirkus Reviews, December 1, 1980, p. 1542; November 1, 1984, review of *Ender's Game,* p. 1021; May 1, 1994, p. 594; June 15, 1995, p. 864; June 15, 1996, p. 839; February 2, 1998, review of *Homebody.*

Library Journal, February 15, 1989, p. 179; November 15, 1990; September 1, 1991; October 15, 1991; January, 1994, p. 172; June 15, 1994, p. 99; May 15, 1995, p. 99; December, 1995, p. 163; July, 1996, p. 154; April 15, 1998, p. 111; August, 1998, p. 140; September 14, 1999, p. 115; November 1, 2000, p. 60; December, 2000, p. 196.

Locus, April, 1991, p. 15; February, 1992, Faren Miller, review of *The Memory of Earth,* pp. 17, 57; December, 1993, Faren Miller, review of *The Ships of Earth,* p. 19; May, 1994, p. 48; February, 1995, p. 17.

Los Angeles Times Book Review, September 28, 1980; March 6, 1983; July 22, 1984, Kristiana Gregory, review of *A Woman of Destiny,* p. 8; February 3, 1985; August 9, 1987, Ingrid Rimland, review of *Wyrms,* p. 11; February 14, 1988, Sue Martin, "Battling the Natives along the Mississippi"; July 20, 1990.

Magazine of Fantasy and Science Fiction, January, 1980, p. 35.

New York Times Book Review, June 16, 1985, Gerald Jonas, review of *Ender's Game,* p. 18; October 18, 1987, p. 36; September 1, 1991, Gerald Jonas, review of *Xenocide,* p. 13; March 15, 1992; May 8, 1994, p. 25; July 9, 1995, p. 18.

Publishers Weekly, December 4, 1978, p. 62; January 2, 1981, p. 49; January 24, 1986, p. 64; December 25, 1987, p. 65; September 16, 1988; May 19, 1989, p. 72; August 17, 1990, p. 55; November 30, 1990, Graceanne A. DeCandido and Keith R. A. DeCandido, "*PW* Interview: Orson Scott Card," pp. 54-55; June 14, 1991, p. 48; June 20, 1994, p. 97; January 30, 1995, review of *Earthfall,* p. 89; April 10, 1995, p. 58; August 7, 1995, p. 445; January 22, 1996,

pp. 61-62; June 24, 1996, review of *Children of the Mind,* pp. 45, 49; August 12, 1996, p. 20; February 2, 1998, review of *Homebody,* p. 79; June 29, 1998, review of *Heartfire,* p. 40; September 28, 1998, p. 77; March 8, 1999, review of *Enchantment,* p. 52; July 5, 1999, p. 63; November 1, review of *Ender's Shadow,* 1999, p. 48; September 11, 2000, review of *Sarah,* p. 71; November 20, 2000, Laura Ciporen, "*PW* Talks with Orson Scott Card," p. 51; November 20, 2000, review of *Shadow of the Hegemon,* p. 50.

School Library Journal, January, 1991, p. 123; November, 1991; March, 1999, p. 229; December, 1999, p. 163; June, 2001, p. 183.

Science Fiction and Fantasy Book Review, April, 1979, p. 27; December, 1979, p. 155; June, 1983, p. 21.

Science Fiction Review, August, 1979; February, 1986, Richard E. Geis, review of *Speaker for the Dead,* p. 14.

SF Chronicle, June, 1988, p. 50.

Tribune Books (Chicago, IL), March 1, 1990; March 1, 1992, David E. Jones, "Trapped in a Serial Universe."

Voice of Youth Advocates, October, 1992, Joel Singer, review of *The Memory of Earth,* p. 236; August, 1993, Joel Singer, review of *The Call of Earth,* p. 236; June, 1994, Sherry Hoy, review of *The Ships of Earth,* p. 98; August, 1995, p. 16.

Washington Post Book World, August 24, 1980, p. 6; January 25, 1981, March 27, 1983; February 23, 1986, Janrae Frank, "War of the Worlds," p. 10; August 30, 1987, John Clute, review of *Seventh Son;* February 28, 1988; March 19, 1992; September 25, 1994, p. 14; September 24, 1995.

West Coast Review of Books, March, 1984; July, 1986, Dan K. Moran, review of *Ender's Game,* p. 20; Number 2, 1987; Number 4, 1988.

Wilson Library Bulletin, February, 1994, p. 70.

Writer's Digest, October, 1986, p. 26; November, 1986, p. 37; December, 1986, p. 32; May, 1989, p. 31.

OTHER

Orson Scott Card Web site, http://www.hatrack.com (December 10, 2001).*

*   *   *

CARTER, Angela (Olive) 1940-1992

PERSONAL: Born May 7, 1940, in London, England; died of cancer, February 16, 1992, in London, England; daughter of Hugh Alexander (a journalist) and Olive (Farthing) Stalker; married Paul Carter, September 10,

1960 (divorced, 1972); partner of Mark Pearce, c. 1980; children: Alexander. *Education:* University of Bristol, B.A., 1965. *Politics:* Left. *Religion:* "None."

CAREER: Novelist, short story writer, teacher, and critic. Journalist for papers in Croyden, Surrey, England, 1958-61. Arts Council fellow in creative writing, University of Sheffield, 1976-78; visiting professor, Brown University, Providence, Rhode Island, 1980-81; writer-in-residence, University of Adelaide, Australia, 1984.

AWARDS, HONORS: John Llewllyn Rhys prize, 1968, for *The Magic Toyshop;* Somerset Maugham Award, 1969, for *Several Perceptions;* Cheltenham Literary Festival Award, 1979, for *The Bloody Chamber and Other Stories;* Kust Maschler Award, 1982, for *Sleeping Beauty and Other Favourite Fairy Tales;* James Tait Black Memorial Prize, 1986, for *Nights at the Circus.*

WRITINGS:

NOVELS

Shadow Dance, Heinemann (London, England), 1966, published as *Honeybuzzard,* Simon & Schuster (New York, NY), 1967.
The Magic Toyshop (also see below), Heinemann (London, England), 1967, Simon & Schuster (New York, NY), 1968.
Several Perceptions, Heinemann (London, England), 1968, Simon & Schuster (New York, NY), 1969.
Heroes and Villains, Heinemann (London, England), 1969, Simon & Schuster (New York, NY), 1970.
Love, Hart-Davis (London, England), 1971, revised edition, Chatto & Windus (London, England), 1987, Penguin (New York, NY), 1988.
The Infernal Desire Machines of Doctor Hoffman, Hart-Davis (London, England), 1972, published as *The War of Dreams,* Harcourt (New York, NY), 1974.
The Passion of New Eve, Harcourt (New York, NY), 1977.
Nights at the Circus, Chatto & Windus (London, England), 1984, Viking (New York, NY), 1985.
Wise Children, Chatto & Windus (London, England), 1991, Farrar, Straus (New York, NY), 1992.

JUVENILE

Miss Z, The Dark Young Lady, Simon & Schuster (New York, NY), 1970.
The Donkey Prince, Simon & Schuster (New York, NY), 1970.

(Translator) *Fairy Tales of Charles Perrault,* Gollancz (London, England), 1977, Avon (New York, NY), 1978.
Moonshadow, Gollancz (London, England), 1982, David & Charles (New York, NY), 1984.
(Editor) *Sleeping Beauty and Other Favourite Fairy Tales,* Gollancz (London, England), 1982, Schocken (New York, NY), 1984.

OTHER

Unicorn (poetry), Location Press (Leeds, England), 1966.
Fireworks: Nine Profane Pieces, Quartet Books (London, England), 1974, published as *Fireworks: Nine Stories in Various Guises,* Harper (New York, NY), 1981, revised edition, Chatto & Windus (London, England), 1987.
The Sadeian Woman and the Ideology of Pornography (nonfiction), Pantheon (New York, NY), 1979, published as *The Sadeian Woman: An Exercise in Cultural History,* Virago (London, England), 1979.
Comic and Curious Cats, illustrated by Martin Leman, Gollancz (London, England), 1979.
The Bloody Chamber and Other Stories, Gollancz (London, England), 1979, Harper (New York, NY), 1980.
(With Leslie Carter) *The Music People,* Hamish Hamilton (London, England), 1980.
Black Venus's Tale (short stories), Faber (London, England), 1980.
Nothing Sacred: Selected Journalism, Virago (London, England), 1982.
Black Venus (short stories), Chatto & Windus (London, England), 1985, published as *Saints and Strangers,* Viking (New York, NY), 1986.
Come unto These Yellow Sands (radio plays; includes *The Company of Wolves, Vampirella,* and *Puss in Boots*), Bloodaxe (Newcastle upon Tyne, England), 1985.
(With Neil Jordan) *The Company of Wolves* (screenplay), ITC Entertainment, 1985.
(Editor) *Don't Bet on the Prince: Contemporary Feminist Fairy Tales in North America and Europe,* Routledge, Chapman & Hall, 1987.
Artificial Fire (includes *Fireworks* and *Love*), McClelland & Stewart (Toronto, Ontario, Canada), 1988.
The Magic Toyshop (screenplay; based on novel of same title), Granada Television Productions, 1989.
(Editor) *Wayward Girls and Wicked Women: An Anthology of Subversive Women,* Penguin (New York, NY), 1989.

(Editor) *The Virago Book of Fairy Tales,* Virago (London, England), 1990, published as *The Old Wives' Fairy Tale Book,* Pantheon (New York, NY), 1990.

Expletives Deleted: Selected Writings, Chatto & Windus (London, England), 1992.

(Editor) *The Second Virago Book of Fairy Tales,* Virago (London, England), 1992, published as *Strange Things Sometimes Still Happen: Fairy Tales from Around the World,* Faber (Boston, MA), 1993.

American Ghosts and Old World Wonders, Chatto & Windus (London, England), 1993.

Burning Your Boat: The Complete Short Stories, introduction by Salman Rushdie, Holt (New York, NY), 1996.

Curious Room: Collected Dramatic Works, Chatto & Windus (London, England), 1996.

Shaking a Leg: Collected Writings, edited by Jennifer S. Uglow and introduced by Joan Smith, Chatto & Windus (London, England), 1997, Penguin (New York, NY), 1998.

Also author of the radio play *A Self-Made Man,* 1984. Contributor to periodicals, including *New Society* and *Vogue.*

SIDELIGHTS: Angela Carter's prolific but relatively short career spanned less than three decades but covered many genres, including novels, short stories, screenplays, and nonfiction. Her writing is noted for its vivid prose, Gothic settings, eroticism, violence, use of fantasy and fairy tales, and surrealism that combine to form what Victoria Glendinning of the *New Statesman* called "the world of Freudian dream and futuristic fiction and pornography." As an essayist, Carter's most influential work is *The Sadeian Woman and the Ideology of Pornography,* an exploration of the Marquis de Sade's depiction of women and their modern-day counterparts. As an editor and translator, she produced several collections of fairy tales, and as a fiction writer, she wrote her own fairy tales that were mired in her own theories of sexual dominance and violence. Carter won many awards for her writing, including the James Tait Black Memorial Award for her novel *Nights at the Circus.* By the time of her death from cancer in 1992, Carter was hailed as one of Britain's foremost writers. "Her books show her preoccupation with the frankly erotic," wrote Margaret B. McDowell in *Contemporary Novelists,* "with the sadistic linking of sex with pain, and with the struggles for mastery between the powerful individual and the vulnerable."

These elements are apparent in Carter's first novel, *Shadow Dance,* published in the United States as *Honeybuzzard,* which is set in an English junk shop that sells newly fashionable Victorian antiques. Morris, the demented owner of the shop, and his girlfriend Honeybuzzard—whose face Morris has disfigured with a knife—prowl condemned houses at night, stripping them of items to sell in their shop. "The fantasy motifs lurking in the background in *Shadow Dance* come into their own in *Magic Toyshop* [Carter's second novel]," wrote Lorna Sage in the *Dictionary of Literary Biography. The Magic Toyshop,* which won Britain's John Llewllyn Rhys prize, is a "Freudian fairy tale," according to Sage, complete with "something of a fairy-tale's happy-ever-after promise." Characteristically featuring an adolescent protagonist on the cusp of womanhood, *The Magic Toyshop* is narrated by fifteen-year-old Melanie, who is sent with her two siblings to live above their sadistic uncle's toyshop after the death of their parents. In a claustrophobic space where mirrors are forbidden, Melanie loses her self-identity and is sexually assaulted and psychologically tormented. Eventually Melanie escapes, but the damage is done and her freedom becomes a kind of Pyrrhic victory.

Carter won the Somerset Maugham Award for her third novel, *Several Perceptions.* Set in England during the late 1960s, the novel tells the story of Joseph Harker, a suicidal young man ensconced in a carnival-like milieu. Plagued by hallucinations and macabre images that are reminiscent of a surrealist vaudeville nightmare, Joseph gradually comes to terms with his life through his interaction with his eccentric neighbors. According to Sage, the story is essentially a Christmas tale with a "puppet-master theme," which is "constructed rather like a strip cartoon or a flicker-book, in which the motion of the pages turning sets the different characters into illusory motion." Characters include "a geriatric music-hall artiste playing an imaginary fiddle, [and] a bisexual self-appointed master of the revels, an analyst who tells Joseph, 'You're wedged in the gap between art and life,'" wrote Sage.

With *Heroes and Villains,* Carter abandoned the English settings that characterized her previous novels in favor of a more fantasy-like science fiction setting. Set in a post-World War III world of barbarians and scattered remnants of civilization, the novel is largely a fable about the nature of "civilized" society. "The fantasy is made to work through the use of detail and the firmly established individuality of the characters," noted a reviewer in the *Times Literary Supplement.*

Nights at the Circus returns to surrealism in its depiction of the seamy world of a travelling circus during the Belle Époque. Fevvers, a trapeze artist known for her beautiful wings, convinces an American reporter that she was hatched from an egg and abandoned on a brothel doorstep at birth. The reporter is smitten with the beguiling, winged Fevvers and joins the circus to be with her. As much a tale about the deceptions of women as of the transfiguration of men, *Nights at the Circus* "blends the real and the surreal, makes unbelievable Dickensian eccentrics credible for the moment, and creates scenes of comic violence in fires and explosions and scenes of gothic horror and grotesque sexual encounter," wrote McDowell. "What is new in this novel," she continued, "is the joy, the sympathetic development of a male, and the use of Fevvers as a symbol of the 'New Woman' who may emerge in the approaching 20th century."

Carter's interest in fairy tales and mythology, explored in her works as an editor and translator, is also apparent in her short story collection *The Bloody Chamber and Other Stories,* which includes adult retellings of such fairy tales as "Snow White" and "Little Red Riding Hood." The title story in *The Bloody Chamber and Other Stories* is a retelling of the Bluebeard legend, in which a virgin bride is tempted to disobey her mysterious husband with tragic consequences. Many elements of Carter's version are familiar—a castle, a dungeon, an admonition to not go snooping around when her husband is gone. "Carter's story—and indeed all the earlier versions—are about women's masochistic complicity in the male sexual aggression," wrote Patricia Duncker in *Literature and History.* But what is unfamiliar about her version is the mother/daughter relationship, which proves to be stronger than the bond between the young woman and her voracious husband. Her "retelling of European folk and fairy tales has the power, not only to cause us to think again, and deeply, . . . but to plunge us into hackle-raising speculation about aspects of our human/animal nature," remarked Susan Kennedy in the *Times Literary Supplement.* Kennedy went on to say that "with her ability to blend reality with the bizarre to create imaginary worlds, Carter's oeuvre stretches the boundaries of contemporary fiction." As James Brockway commented in *Books and Bookmen,* Carter, "like all geniuses . . . walks the tightrope on one side of which yawns the chasm of madness, and the other the chasm of bathos. . . . Our Lady Edgar Allan Poe."

As an academic, Carter's concern with violence and sexuality is explored in her nonfiction work *The Sadeian Woman and the Ideology of Pornography.* The first of Carter's books to cause a stir in the United States, *The Sadeian Woman and the Ideology of Pornography* is a feminist study of pornography in which Carter argues that the Marquis de Sade created in his porno-

graphic novels truthful portraits of the status of women in society. His two most popular fictional creations, Justine and Juliette, represent the dichotomies of the Madonna and the whore, says Carter. She examines the possibility of a "moral pornographer" who confronts the brutality of sexual mythology and uses it as a means to liberate the imagination, rather than to oppress it. Carter imagines such a figure to be "a terrorist of the imagination, a sexual guerilla," who offers up only what is deeply rooted in our unconscious. What makes Sade unusual as a pornographer, and of special interest to feminists, according to Carter, was his "claiming rights of free sexuality for women, and in installing women as beings of power in his imaginary worlds. This sets him apart from all other pornographers at all times and most other writers of his period." But Carter refuses to embrace Sade wholeheartedly. Acknowledging that freedom is a meaningful concept only in the presence of prohibition, "Carter is bitterly disappointed that freedom has no savor for him unless the prohibited woman is in chains, unconscious of her sexuality," wrote Ann Snitow in *Nation.* Michael Wood, writing in *British Writers,* viewed *The Sadeian Woman and the Ideology of Pornography* as a nonfiction companion to *The Bloody Chamber and Other Stories,* which, taken together, present "the full range of Carter's irreverence and intelligence, and the play of a considerable moral courage, which suggests that even our monsters, those figments of Goya's sleep of reason, will help us if we help ourselves."

Feminist themes are also significant in Carter's last novel, *Wise Children,* which depicts a pair of twins who have made their living first as vaudeville performers and later as actresses in Hollywood. The novel satirically parallels many of the conventions of Shakespearean comedy, such as mistaken identity and a happy ending. "Carter sets herself to demonstrate that the jungle law of the casting couch and the tawdry world of stage and screen can nonetheless be pure at heart, peopled not by tigers but by does and fauns, creatures who may be grotesque but are also endearing," summarized John Bayley in *New York Review of Books.*

Carter's numerous short stories have been collected in a single volume titled *Burning Your Boats: The Complete Short Stories.* Distinguishing the style of Carter's stories from the realism that characterizes much contemporary fiction, a reviewer in *Publishers Weekly* observed that Carter's short fiction consists of "tales, legends, [and] variations on mythic themes." "What becomes ever clearer as one reads these tales . . . is that short fiction was a laboratory in which [Carter] remade herself over and over again," commented Roz Kaveney in *New Statesman & Society.*

Carter's literary essays are collected in *Expletives Deleted: Selected Writings.* The volume articulates her feminist perspective and highlights her incisive commentary on a wide variety of books. "Angela Carter writes with wild grace, like a dandy, as is demonstrated by the best . . . of these articles. She can never forego the wicked pleasures of a joke, of a literary reference, of dancing on the pomposities of dullards." Another posthumous volume, *American Ghosts and Old World Wonders,* presents several of Carter's previously uncollected stories and prose writings, each of which is concerned in some way with the subject of myths and legends. While discussions and renderings of fairy tales inform such pieces as "Ashputtle or The Mother's Ghost," in which Carter expounds upon the story of Cinderella, "some of the most fertile ground in this collection is found . . . where American ghosts and Old World wonders meet, where the 'mirth, anarchy and terror' of Europe clash with the airy, mysterious promise of the New World," asserted Candice Rodd in *Times Literary Supplement.*

Six years after Carter's death another volume of her essays appeared, *Shaking a Leg: Collected Writings.* Reviewers often took as their point of departure what Carter's work had meant to them personally. "Reading Carter in one's teens and twenties," wrote Kaveney in the *New Statesman & Society,* "was to be told that there was a vibrant world out there of polymorphous perversity and gilded roundabout horses and Japanese comic books and late-night continental movies and wonderfully withering scorn for anything second-rate or puritanical." Wendy Steiner in the *New York Times Book Review* described Carter as "equal parts esthetician and folklorist" who "used Kant to explain industrial blight and the Greeks' golden section to advocate high heels and long skirts."

With regard to the structure of *Shaking a Leg,* organized by editor Jennifer S. Uglow into various groupings in order (in her words) to "define and separate but also to please and provoke," Steiner wrote, "Had this book been organized chronologically, from its first entries in the 1960's until her death in 1992, [Carter] would have emerged as a faultless barometer of the shifting pressures of her era. As it is, this Borgesian mishmash is the structural equivalent of Carter's truculent whimsy." Melanie Phillips, who worked with Carter on *New Society* magazine, wrote in the *Times Literary Supplement* that "her best essay period was the 1970s, which was in a way more 60s than the 1960s themselves were, since it took a while for the sexual and cultural upheavals of that decade to translate into a recognizable style of the self." In Phillips's view, Carter

did not simply celebrate the countercultural revolution of that era; particularly in retrospect, her attitude was skeptical: "The new order produced a narcissistic culture which she dissected with vivid wit." "There is brilliance in these essays," wrote Kaveney, "and much wisdom about books and life, but there is also a healthy vein of malice—just to remind us that no one, even Carter, is beyond reproach."

Sage found that despite Carter's literary awards, "her preoccupations as a writer—deepened and defined over the years—remain radically at odds with the puritanism and the conventional realism that characterize much of British fiction." Carter, who regarded the fantasy element of her work as "social satire" or "social realism of the unconscious," explained in a *Publishers Weekly* interview, "I have always felt that one person's fantasy is another person's everyday life. It has its own logic as well. I got more and more into it as I got older, because it's a genre with its own rigorous logic." Carter expounded on this idea in the collection *On Gender and Writing:* "I become mildly irritated when people . . . ask me about the 'mythic' quality of work I've written lately. . . . I'm in the demythologising business. I'm interested in myths . . . just because they are extraordinary lies designed to make people unfree."

BIOGRAPHICAL/CRITICAL SOURCES:

BOOKS

Bristow, Joseph, and Trev Lynn Broughton, editors, *The Infernal Desires of Angela Carter: Fiction, Femininity, Feminism,* Longman (New York, NY), 1997.
British Writers, Supplement 3, Scribner, 1996.
Carter, Angela, *The Sadeian Woman and the Ideology of Pornography,* Pantheon (New York, NY), 1979.
Contemporary Issues in Criticism, Volume 1, Gale (Detroit, MI), 1982.
Contemporary Literary Criticism, Gale (Detroit, MI), Volume 5, 1976, Volume 41, 1987, Volume 76, 1993.
Contemporary Novelists, 5th edition, St. James Press (Detroit, MI), 1991.
Day, Aidan, *Angela Carter: The Rational Glass,* Manchester University Press (Manchester, England), 1998.
Dictionary of Literary Biography, Gale (Detroit, MI), Volume 14: *British Novelists since 1960,* 1983, Volume 207: *British Novelists since 1960, Third Series,* 1999.
Feminist Writers, St. James (Detroit, MI), 1996.

Gamble, Sarah, *Angela Carter: Writing from the Front Line,* Edinburgh University Press, 1997.

Lee, Alison, *Angela Carter,* G. K. Hall (New York, NY), 1997.

Michael, Magali Cornier, *Feminism and the Postmodern Impulse: Post-World War II Fiction,* State University of New York Press (Albany, NY), 1996.

Peach, Linden, *Angela Carter,* St. Martin's Press (New York, NY), 1998.

Robinson, Sally, *Engendering the Subject: Gender and Self-Representation in Contemporary Women's Fiction,* State University of New York Press (Albany, NY), 1991.

Sage, Lorna, *Angela Carter,* Northcote House/British Council (Plymouth, England), 1994.

Sage, Lorna, editor, *Flesh and the Mirror: Essays on the Art of Angela Carter,* Virago Press (London, England), 1994.

Short Story Criticism, Volume 13, Gale (Detroit, MI), 1993.

St. James Guide to Fantasy Writers, St. James (Detroit, MI), 1996.

Tucker, Lindsey, editor, *Critical Essays on Angela Carter,* G. K. Hall (New York, NY), 1998.

Wandor, Michelene, editor, *On Gender and Writing,* Pandora Press, 1983.

PERIODICALS

Booklist, December 1, 1998, Jim O'Laughlin, review of *Shaking a Leg: Collected Writings,* p. 646.

Books and Bookmen, February, 1975, James Brockway, review of *Fireworks: Nine Profane Pieces,* pp. 55-56.

Chicago Tribune, April 22, 1985; September 26, 1986; February 23, 1992, p. 6.

Commonweal, November 20, 1998, review of *Old Wives' Fairy Tale Book,* p. 22.

Critique, spring, 1999, p. 248.

Entertainment Weekly, December 4, 1998, review of *Shaking a Leg,* p. 94.

Kirkus Reviews, October 15, 1998, review of *Shaking a Leg,* p. 1504.

Listener, May 20, 1971; September 26, 1974.

Literature and History, spring, 1984, Patricia Duncker, "Re-imagining the Fairy Tales: Angela Carter's *Bloody Chambers,*" pp. 3-14.

London Review of Books, June 13, 1991, p. 3.

Los Angeles Times Book Review, March 16, 1980.

Nation, October 4, 1986, Ann Snitow, "The Post-Lapsarian Eve," pp. 315-317; April 20, 1992, p. 526.

New Review, June-July, 1977.

New Statesman, July 8, 1968; November 14, 1969; August 16, 1974, Victoria Glendinning, "Real Cities," p. 229; March 25, 1977; May 25, 1979, Patricia Craig, review of *The Bloody Chambers and Other Stories,* p. 762; October 18, 1985; July 18, 1997, pp. 46-47.

New Statesman & Society, April 10, 1992, p. 38; July 31, 1992; July 21, 1995, pp. 39-40.

New York Review of Books, April 23, 1992, John Bayley, review of *Wise Children,* p. 9.

New York Times Book Review, January 19, 1992, p. 7; May 19, 1996, p. 11; December 27, 1998, review of *Shaking a Leg,* p. 6; June 6, 1999, review of *Shaking a Leg,* p. 41; December 5, 1999, review of *Shaking a Leg,* p. 97.

Observer (London), January 31, 1993; September 5, 1999, review of *Nights at the Circus,* p. 14.

Publishers Weekly, January 14, 1985; June 17, 1986; January 8, 1996, p. 57; November 16, 1998, review of *Shaking a Leg,* p. 66.

Saturday Review, February 18, 1967.

Science-Fiction Studies, November, 1999, review of *Shaking a Leg,* p. 473.

Spectator, March 26, 1977.

Times Educational Supplement, July 18, 1997, p. 21; July 3, 1998, review of *Shaking a Leg,* p. 9.

Times Literary Supplement, August 1, 1968; November 20, 1969; June 18, 1974; February 8, 1980; July 4, 1981; September 28, 1984; October 18, 1985; June 19, 1992, p. 5; April 2, 1993, p. 20; August 4, 1995, p. 20; August 15, 1997, p. 24.

Washington Post Book World, August 18, 1974; February 24, 1980; June 28, 1981; February 3, 1985.

World Literature Today, summer, 1998, Elin Elgaard, review of *Shaking a Leg,* pp. 627-628.

Yale Review, April, 1992, p. 227.

OBITUARIES:

PERIODICALS

Chicago Tribune, February 17, 1992, section 1, p. 10.
Los Angeles Times, February 22, 1992, p. A22.
New York Times, February 19, 1992, p. D21.
Times (London), February 17, 1992, p. 15.
Washington Post, February 18, 1992, p. B4.*

*   *   *

CARTER, Stephen L(isle) 1954-

PERSONAL: Born 1954. *Education:* Stanford University, B.A., 1976; Yale University Law School, J.D., 1979.

Stephen L. Carter

ADDRESSES: Office—Yale University Law School, P.O. Box 1303a, New Haven, CT 06520.

CAREER: Educator and writer. Admitted to the Bar of Washington, DC, 1981. U.S. Court of Appeals, District of Columbia Circuit, law clerk, 1979-80; U.S. Supreme Court, Washington, DC, law clerk for Justice Thurgood Marshall, 1980-81; Shea & Gardner (law firm), Washington, DC, associate, 1981-82; Yale University Law School, New Haven, CT, assistant professor, 1982-84, associate professor, 1984-85, professor, 1985—, William Nelson Cromwell Professor of Law.

AWARDS, HONORS: Named one of Ten Outstanding Young Americans, United States Jaycees, 1987.

WRITINGS:

Reflections of an Affirmative Action Baby, Basic Books (New York, NY), 1991.
The Culture of Disbelief: How American Law and Politics Trivialize Religious Devotion, Basic Books (New York, NY), 1993.
Integrity, Basic Books (New York, NY), 1996.
Civility: Manners, Morals, and the Etiquette of Democracy, Basic Books (New York, NY), 1998.
The Dissent of the Governed: A Meditation on Law, Religion, and Loyalty, Harvard University Press (Cambridge, MA), 1998.
God's Name in Vain: How Religion Should and Should Not Be Involved in Politics, Basic Books (New York, NY), 2000.
The Emperor of Ocean Park (novel), Knopf (New York, NY), in press.

WORK IN PROGRESS: A second novel.

SIDELIGHTS: Stephen L. Carter's controversial nonfiction works on race and religion in contemporary America have brought him recognition as "one of our nation's most intriguing and noteworthy public intellectuals," according to *Commonweal* contributor Don Wycliff. Carter's books have been praised for their thought-provoking arguments, independent perspective, honesty, and engaging style. In his first book, *Reflections of an Affirmative Action Baby,* Carter examines the racial prejudice hidden within affirmative action programs, which aid African Americans on the theory that social and economic forces prevent them from competing on an equal level with whites. An affirmative-action beneficiary himself, Carter asserts that, because of affirmative action, accomplished African Americans are denied the satisfaction of being acknowledged as the "best," and are instead set apart as the "best blacks." The author also points out that affirmative action programs have helped college-educated, middle-class blacks the most, whereas the poorest and neediest have not benefitted.

In addition, Carter rejects the common argument that affirmative action programs increase diversity in education and the workplace, because he feels the assertion is based on the premise that blacks have a special, unified perspective to offer. "The ideals of affirmative action," Carter writes in *Reflections of an Affirmative Action Baby,* "have become conflated with the proposition that there is a *black way to be*—and the beneficiaries of affirmative action are nowadays supposed to be people who will be black the right way."

According to David J. Garrow of the *New York Times Book Review, Reflections of an Affirmative Action Baby* "is Mr. Carter's powerfully written and persuasive attempt to illuminate both the significant personal costs that accrue even to those like himself who are acknowledged beneficiaries of affirmative action programs . . . as well as what he correctly terms 'the deepening divisions in the black community over the issue of affirmative action.'" Some reviewers noted that while a few of Carter's ideas may make him sound like what Garrow defined as "some sort of neoconservative advocate or apologist," Carter is in fact not so easily categorized. In *Reflections of an Affirmative Action Baby,* for instance, Carter argues that racial discrimination pervades the administration of the death penalty and notes that "the Republican Party is now . . . a natural and evidently comfortable home for white racism in the United States."

Though most reviews of *Reflections of an Affirmative Action Baby* were favorable, Roy L. Brooks asserted in the *Washington Post Book World* that Carter's reliance on his personal experiences for the volume deprives the reader of "a more studied analysis of such an important and complex topic." Brooks concluded: "While no doubt the book is a catharsis for the author . . . the seriousness and complexity of these topics warrant a more sophisticated and less meandering analysis than the book provides." Other reviewers praised the force and clarity of Carter's arguments. A *New Yorker* critic concluded: "Carter is shrewd, subtle, and funny; he is also earnest in maintaining that a black who seeks intellectual freedom . . . is not disloyal to his race."

In *The Culture of Disbelief: How American Law and Politics Trivialize Religious Devotion,* Carter examines the shift away from the encouragement of religious discourse by mainstream, and particularly liberal, political forces in the years since the Supreme Court legalized abortion in 1973. Prior to that decision, the left had welcomed religious support for such liberal causes as civil rights; after it, religion in the American political sphere increasingly belonged to right-wing activists protesting abortion or gay and lesbian rights. According to *New York Times Book Review* contributor Peter L. Berger, Carter "argues that since most Americans derive their moral values from their religious beliefs, to bar the political expression of religiously derived values is not only contrary to the basic assumptions of democracy, it is futile. The banning of religion from political discourse would reduce God to a sort of hobby. No genuinely religious person will accept such a reduction, he argues, and no democratic polity should make the attempt."

"Though some of Mr. Carter's assertions are highly debatable, though some of his arguments are easily assailable," wrote *New York Times* critic Michiko Kakutani, "*The Culture of Disbelief* is a provocative and thought-ful book about an important aspect of our national life that's all too often the subject of knee-jerk thinking and reaction." Although some critics pointed out a tendency toward overgeneralization on the part of the author, several also asserted the importance of Carter's arguments. In a *New York Times* article, Peter Steinfels wrote: "Carter plunges into deep legal and philosophical waters here, and it is one of his virtues not to pretend that he has resolved them completely. In fact, it is often the open, probing quality of his mind as much as his specific arguments that makes this a winning book."

Integrity offers an account of a moral quality Carter defines as "1) discerning what is right and what is wrong; 2) acting on what you have discerned, even at personal cost; and 3) saying openly that you are acting on your understanding of right from wrong." Carter argues that integrity is often in short supply in contemporary American life and, in seven broad scenarios, discusses how individuals in key social institutions can act with integrity. Though reviewers respected the book's sincerity and seriousness, some found Carter's approach oversimplified. "The very inclusiveness of Carter's integrity makes it alarmingly content-free," wrote Barbara Ehrenreich in *Time.* Loren E. Lomasky, in *Reason,* suggested that "the virtue central to Carter's discussion isn't really integrity at all but rather moderation" and that the book "occasionally borders on the simplistic," as in its treatment of the O. J. Simpson trial. "Carter only occasionally illuminates what is distinctive about integrity," Lomasky concluded, "but . . . the advice he proffers is sensible and, even where disputable, deserves to be taken seriously." Though *New Republic* contributor Alan Wolfe noted that Carter "wrote with integrity long before he wrote about it," he concluded that "it is not so simple to make a case for simple virtues. Carter's book is full of integrity, and it is an improvement over the way politicians treat these matters, but it fails to persuade me to join him in peering into the national soul."

In *Civility: Manners, Morals, and the Etiquette of Democracy,* a sequel to *Integrity,* Carter confronts America's "civility crisis" and discusses the appropriate measures for introducing and supporting civility regardless of political differences among individuals. Indeed, Carter sees the book as a "prayer" for the nation's ability to construct a society governed by true respect; the religious basis of much of his argument, in fact, caused some consternation among critics. "The burden of Carter's argument is to show that his religious doctrine is better equipped than any other to further democratic life," observed Rochelle Gurstein in the *New Republic.* "Unfortunately, Carter makes no serious effort to make his vision come alive for the non-believers in this democracy, nor does he demonstrate its necessity for democracy generally. Is Carter calling for more civility or for more religion in America? They are not the same thing." In *Washington Monthly,* Adam Goodheart faulted Carter for ignoring the rich tradition of American secularism in favor of "a return to traditional, unobjectionable Judeo-Christian values." Finding this approach basically nostalgic, Goodheart concluded "Perhaps 'incivility' isn't a bad description of our predicament. But exhortations that we all just be nice to each other only trivialize a complicated set of problems, and an even more complicated history."

Others, however, found *Civility* an important and timely work. *American Prospect* contributor Randall Kennedy considered it the best of several recent books on the subject, though he expressed skepticism about the author's tendency to romanticize a past era and to exaggerate present notions of moral decline. A. Javier Trevino in *Society* commended the book as an impressive work that "contribute[s] immeasurably to a public discussion . . . of some of the weighty issues that must be considered in our understanding of how to share community." And Molly Marsh in *Nieman Reports* pronounced the book "thoughtful and thought-provoking."

Carter delves into social and political controversy once more in *The Dissent of the Governed: A Meditation on Law, Religion, and Loyalty.* The book is an edited version of his 1995 Massey Lectures in American Government delivered at Harvard University; like Carter's previous works, it drew spirited but mixed response. The book's theme, in the words of *America* reviewer Patrick H. Samway, is "the conflict between loyalty and disobedience and the recognition of a sovereign's possibly faulty authority." Religious freedom, especially, receives significant attention in the book; among Carter's more controversial subjects is his consideration of support for public funding of religious schools. "Carter deserves credit for thinking the unthinkable about law, revolution and religion in a liberal society," commented *New York Times Book Review* contributor Michael Lind, who found Carter's criticism of liberal dogma on the separation of church and state especially convincing. Noting that Carter's points need not conflict with liberal values, Lind concludes that "Carter not only defends the legitimacy of religious argument but provides an impressive example of how a believer may engage in civil debate with fellow citizens who do not share his faith. His meditations on the tensions between democracy and religion display the eloquence and independence of mind that have made [him] one of America's leading public intellectuals."

National Review contributor Lino A. Graglia, however, was among those critics who found Carter's argument compromised by his unwillingness to take a more conservative stand. "Carter is unable or unwilling to take a squarely pro-religion position on almost any issue," Graglia complained. Similarly, *Commentary* reviewer Gary Rosen observed that "this tension, between rightly identifying problems and offering responsible solutions to them, is very much on display" in *The Dissent of the Governed.* "The real problem for Carter," in Rosen's view, "is that the political agenda embraced by his would-be constituency is a conservative one; here as elsewhere in his writings, he will not allow himself to keep such company." However, Rosen concluded that the book is an "important contribution to a heated, ongoing debate."

In *God's Name in Vain: How Religion Should and Should Not Be Involved in Politics,* Carter addresses a question implied but not fully answered in *The Culture of Disbelief:* What is the proper role of religion in politics? His answer, according to *American Prospect* contributor Mark Silk, is "that religion should maintain a strong, principled voice on issues of public concern but should steer clear of political entanglements." Carter argues that religion often encourages productive political debate—as it did with abolitionism, labor and temperance crusades, and the civil rights movement—but that involving it in politics can have a negative effect on individuals' commitment to religion. Commending Carter's elegant prose and subtle arguments, a reviewer for *Publishers Weekly* hailed Carter's "sane, fresh voice in the too-often stale debate about religion and public life." Brent Staples, in the *New York Times Book Review,* offered a more negative assessment. Staples felt that Carter "regards even the slightest challenge to a statement of faith . . . as a blatant insult to religious people generally," and exaggerates the sense that religion in America is under siege. The critic further suggested that Carter's argument ignores the fact that "religion is by its very nature a group activity. . . . To stay alive and prosper, religions must keep abreast of a messy, nondenominational world that is dominated at the moment by religious flexibility. The retreat 'into the garden,' as Stephen Carter terms it, is a moribund strategy that would feed institutional decline." Though *Commentary* contributor Terry Eastland raised some objections to *God's Name in Vain,* particularly its omission of such questions as whether a pastor should run for office or whether some religions are incompatible with democracy, Eastland found that the book "intelligently addresses a wide variety of matters" and serves as a "useful, if not especially original, believer's brief in behalf of a religious America."

Though some critics have speculated that Carter will write more books on religion, many in the publishing world were surprised when the publisher Alfred Knopf offered Carter a $4 million advance for two novels. The manuscript for Carter's first novel, *The Emperor of Ocean Park,* sparked one of the most intense literary auctions in recent times and resulted in one of the highest advances ever paid for a first novel; according to a *New York Times* report, publishers were struck by the novel's combination of thriller pacing, literary thoughtfulness, and unique insight into the lives of African American professionals.

BIOGRAPHICAL/CRITICAL SOURCES:

BOOKS

Carter, Stephen L., *Civility: Manners, Morals, and the Etiquette of Democracy,* Basic Books (New York, NY), 1998.

Carter, Stephen L., *Integrity,* Basic Books (New York, NY), 1996.

Carter, Stephen L., *Reflections of an Affirmative Action Baby,* Basic Books (New York, NY), 1991.

Contemporary Black Biography, Volume 4, Gale (Detroit, MI), 1994.

PERIODICALS

America, April 27, 1996, T. Howland Sanks, review of *Integrity,* p. 22; March 21, 1998, Patrick H. Samway, *The Dissent of the Governed: A Meditation on Law, Religion, and Loyalty,* p. 29.

American Prospect, November 6, 2000, Mark Silk, review of *God's Name in Vain: How Religion Should and Should Not Be Involved in Politics,* p. 54.

Booklist, February 15, 1996, Bonnie Smothers, review of *Integrity,* p. 969; March 1, 1998, Ray Olson, review of *The Dissent of the Governed,* p. 1072.

Book Report, November-December, 1996, Ron Marinucci, review of *Integrity,* p. 55.

Christianity Today, January 8, 2001, Terry Mattingly, review of *God's Name in Vain,* p. 88.

Civil Rights Journal, fall, 1997, Donald F. Beisswenger, review of *Integrity,* p. 63.

Commentary, August, 1998, Gary Rosen, review of *The Dissent of the Governed,* p. 66; December, 2000, Terry Eastland, review of *God's Name in Vain,* p. 75.

Commonweal, May 17, 1996, Don Wycliff, review of *Integrity,* p. 22; November 3, 2000, Alan Wolfe, review of *God's Name in Vain,* p. 29.

Current, October, 1996, Loren E. Lomasky, review of *Integrity,* p. 35.

Emerge, March, 1996, Robert L. Joiner, review of *Integrity,* p. 59.

Forbes, November 30, 1998, Steve Forbes, review of *The Dissent of the Governed,* p. 31.

Library Journal, February 1, 1996, Jerry E. Stephens, review of *Integrity,* p. 88.

National Catholic Reporter, November 6, 1998, Mark Chmiel, review of *Civility: Manners, Morals, and the Etiquette of Democracy,* p. 23.

National Review, December 25, 1995, Mayer Schiller, review of *Integrity,* p. 54; May 4, 1998, Lino A. Graglia, review of *The Dissent of the Governed,* p. 52.

New Republic, March 18, 1996, Alan Wolfe, review of *Integrity,* p. 34; October 5, 1998, Rochelle Gurstein, review of *Civility,* p. 40.

New Yorker, October 21, 1991, pp. 134-135.

New York Times, September 4, 1993; September 28, 1993, p. C18; February 20, 2001, David D. Kirkpatrick, "Knopf Pays a $4 Million Advance to a First-Time Novelist."

New York Times Book Review, September 1, 1991, pp. 1, 16; September 19, 1993, p. 15; March 3, 1996, Richard Brookhiser, review of *Integrity,* p. 12; May 10, 1998, Michael Lind, review of *The Dissent of the Governed,* p. 19; November 26, 2000, Brent Staples, review of *God's Name in Vain.*

Nieman Reports, fall, 1998, Molly Marsh, review of *Civility,* p. 61.

Public Administration Review, March, 1999, Robert C. Zinke, review of *Civility,* p. 170; March, 1999, Ralph Clark Chandler, review of *The Culture of Disbelief: How American Law and Politics Trivialize Religious Devotion,* p. 179.

Publishers Weekly, December 11, 1995, review of *Integrity,* p. 61; March 16, 1998, review of *Civility,* p. 41; March 23, 1998, reviews of *The Dissent of the Governed,* p. 88 and p. 94; October 16, 2000, review of *God's Name in Vain,* p. 70; March 5, 2001, John F. Baker, "*The Emperor of Ocean Park,*" p. 18.

Reason, August-September, 1996, Loren E. Lomasky, review of *Integrity,* p. 62.

Society, July, 2000, A. Javier Trevino, review of *Civility,* p. 78.

Time, March 25, 1996, Barbara Ehrenreich, review of *Integrity,* p. 73.

Washington Monthly, May, 1998, Adam Goodheart, review of *Civility,* p. 50; November, 2000, Ben Soskis, review of *God's Name in Vain,* p. 50.

Washington Post Book World, September 8, 1991, pp. 4, 14.

World and I, July, 1998, Lloyd Eby, review of *Civility,* p. 269.*

CASPER, Leonard Ralph 1923-

PERSONAL: Born July 6, 1923, in Fond du Lac, WI; son of Louis and Caroline (Eder) Casper; married Belinda Velasquez-Ty, 1956; children: Gretchen Gabrielle, Kristina Elise. *Education:* University of Wisconsin, B.A., 1948, M.A., 1949, Ph.D., 1953.

ADDRESSES: Home—54 Simpson Dr., Framingham, MA 01701.

CAREER: Cornell University, Ithaca, NY, instructor, 1952-53; University of the Philippines and Ateneo de Manila, Quezon City, visiting professor, 1953-56; Boston College, Chestnut Hill, MA, professor, 1956-99; Retired and Senior Volunteer Program (RSVP; under Domestic Peace Corps: Metro West), professor, 2001—. Fulbright lecturer in Philippines, 1962-63 and 1973; University of Rhode Island, Kingston, director of summer writing program, 1958. *Military service:* U.S. Army, Field Artillery, 1943-46.

MEMBER: Asia Society, American Association of University Professors, University of the Philippines Writers Club (honorary member), Catholic Playwrights' Circle.

AWARDS, HONORS: Stanford creative writing fellowship, 1951-52; grants from Ford Foundation, 1960, American Council of Learned Societies, 1965, Asia Society, 1965, and American Philosophical Society, 1968-69; Bread Loaf scholar, 1961; Fulbright lectureships, 1962-63 and 1973; National Council on the Arts, 1970; Rockefeller writing grant, 1994.

WRITINGS:

(Editor) *Six Filipino Poets,* Benipayo Press (Manila, Philippines), 1955.
Robert Penn Warren: The Dark and Bloody Ground, University of Washington Press, 1960.
The Wayward Horizon: Essays on Modern Philippine Literature, Community Press (Manila, Philippines), 1961.
(Editor, with others) *The World of Short Fiction: An International Collection,* Harper (New York, NY), 1962.
(Editor) *Modern Philippine Short Stories,* University of New Mexico Press (Albuquerque, NM), 1962.
The Wounded Diamond: Studies in Modern Philippine Literature, Bookmark (Manila, Philippines), 1964.

New Writing from the Philippines: A Critique and Anthology, Syracuse University Press (Syracuse, NY), 1966.
A Lion Unannounced: Twelve Stories and a Fable, Southern Methodist University Press (Dallas, TX), 1971.
(Editor) Bienvenido N. Santos, *Distances: In Time* (poems), Ateneo University Press (Quezon City, Philippines), 1984.
Firewalkers: Concelebrations 1964-1984, New Day (Quezon City, Philippines), 1987.
In Burning Ambush: Essays 1985-1990, New Day (Quezon City, Philippines), 1991.
The Opposing Thumb: Decoding Philippine Literature of the Marcos Regime, Giraffe (Manila, Philippines), 1995.
Sunsurfers Seen from Afar: Critical Essays 1991-1996, Anvil (Manila, Philippines), 1996.
The Blood-Marriage of Earth and Sky: Robert Penn Warren's Later Novels, Louisiana State University Press (Baton Rouge, LA), 1997.
The Circular Firing Squad (novella), Giraffe (Manila, Philippines), 1999.

Contributor of short stories, poems, and reviews to periodicals, including *Wisconsin Studies in Contemporary Literature, Philippine Studies, College English, Pacific Affairs, Solidarity, Antigonish Review, Amerasia, South Carolina Review, Columbia Journal of American Studies, Southwest Review,* and *Popular World Fiction.* Author of a verse play. Contributor to books, including *Americana Encyclopedia,* 1969-92, *Encyclopedia of World Literature in the Twentieth Century,* and *Encyclopedia of Post-Colonial Literatures in English;* contributor of prefaces to books by Filipino authors. Guest editor of *Literary Review,* summer, 1960, and *Literature East and West,* spring, 1965 and winter, 1969.

SIDELIGHTS: Leonard Ralph Casper told *CA:* "As the seventh child in a family of eight, during the Great Depression I found that words made more readily available playthings than did expensive toys. That predisposition was reinforced by the love of reading inherited from an Alsatian mother, herself compensating for an orphaned infancy and a Kansas farm schooling that ended with the eighth grade. There also was endless access to the town's Carnegie library, the natural ease that I always felt in the classroom, and after three years' wartime service, the G. I. Bill which carried me all the way to my doctorate at Madison.

"Critical analysis of other person's writing never seemed irrelevant to my own desire to capture experience in poetry and short fiction. It seemed only natural that my dissertation should focus on Robert Penn Warren, novelist, poet, playwright, critic, and teacher. In 1960 I published the pioneer study of his work and never let him go until my sequel in 1997. Meanwhile I learned more about the diversity of thematics and themetrics, available in any writer, by teaching contemporary American literature at Cornell and in the Philippines where in writing workshops I tried to induce the same respect for the 'disciplined free flow' of words which I continued to enjoy.

"Though an alien abroad during five (unconsecutive) years, I easily became a compatriot of writers in the Philippines, encouraged students there to respect and emulate their own literature, and eventually was considered a 'world-class critic' of their culture—for reading their works more constantly than they themselves, under the influence of 'colonial mentality,' and by publishing ten volumes on their distinguished branch of the English language Union, despite censorship under Ferdinand Marcos' dictatorship.

"Most of all, it was my great fortune to marry Linda Velasquz-Ty, valedictorian of her 1955 University of the Philippines law class and future LL.M. at Harvard, whose native/trained sensibility was devoted to writing several collections of short stories and historical novels which I continue to envy to this day. The decision of our daughters to become, respectively, a (published) professor of Third World political science and an instructor in cultural/physical anthropology, has broadened our common ground as a family, even as distances have otherwise separated us."

*   *   *

CASTEL, J(ean) G(abriel) 1928-

PERSONAL: Born September 17, 1928, in Nice, France; Canadian citizen; son of Charles (in business) and Simone (Ricour) Castel; children: Christopher, Maria, Marc, Matthew. *Ethnicity:* "French." *Education:* University of Aix-Marseille, B.Sc. and Phil., 1947; University of Paris, LL.B. and LL.M., 1950; University of Michigan, J.D., 1953; Harvard University, S.J.D., 1958. *Religion:* "Roman Catholic (Minister of caze)." *Avocational interests:* "Travel, skiing, scuba diving, music, and painting."

ADDRESSES: Home—R.R. #5, Orangeville, Ontario L9W 2Z2, Canada; Mas de la Font, Quartier du Clos, Claviers, 83830 France; fax: 011-33-4-94-76-69-32. *Of-

fice—Osgoode Hall Law School York University, 4700 Keele St., Toronto, Ontario M3J 1P3, Canada; fax: 416-736-5736. *E-mail*—jgcastel@sympatico.ca.

CAREER: Attorney, educator, and author. United Nations, Department of Economic Affairs, New York, NY, legal research assistant/intern, 1952; employed with Dewey, Ballantine, Busby, Palmer, & Wood (law firm), New York, NY, 1953; McGill University, Montreal, Quebec, assistant professor of law, 1954-55, associate professor of law, 1955-59, secretary of the Faculty of Law, 1956-59; York University, Osgoode Hall Law School, Toronto, Ontario, Canada, professor of law, 1959-99, distinguished research professor, 1986, professor emeritus and senior scholar, 1999—; called to the Bar, Ontario, Canada, June 1960, appointed to Queen's Court, 1980, retired; international arbitrator and consultant, including work with Department of External Affairs, 1962, 1971-72 and 1985-87, Canadian Government, Canada Law Reform Commission, 1977-78 and 1984, Canada-US Free Trade Agreement, 1989-93, and Regional Centre for Commercial Arbitration (Kuala, Lumpur, Malaysia), 1979-89. Lecturer, University of Toronto, 1956 and 1974-79, Hague Academy of International Law, 1969 and 1983, University of San Diego, 1984 and 1986, various universities in Japan, 1985, Glendon College, 1991 and 1992, International Law and International Relations Association of the Republic of Romania, 1984, and University of Western Australia, 1989; visiting professor, Laval University and University of Montreal, both 1959-70, National University of Mexico, 1963, University of Lisbon, 1964, University of Montreal, 1964-65, 1966-67, 1970-71, 1976-77, and 1979, University of Nice, 1969, University of Ottawa, 1970, 1979-81 and 1984, University of Puerto Rico, 1973, McGill University, 1977-83 and 1985, University of Aukland, 1981, University of Paris I (Sorbonne) and Paris II (Assas), 1981-82, University of Moncton, New Brunswick, 1982, and University of Aix-Marseille, 1983-99; academic in residence, Department of Foreign Affairs and International Trade, 1979-80; Killam Senior Research Fellow, 1986-88; Robinson Cox Visiting Fellow (Australia), 1989. Council of the Canadian Association of Comparative Law, secretary general, treasurer and president, 1960-65 and 1970-74; Union des Français de l'Estranger, Ontario section, president, 1986-91; president, committee on private international law, Office for the Revision of the Civil Code, Quebec; president, Association of French War Veterans residing in Ontario. *Military service:* Served with French resistance, 1943-45; received Croix du Combattant, Croix du Combattant de l'Europe, Médaille du Combattant Volontaire de la Résistance, Médaille Commémorative de la Guerre 1939-45, and Medal of 40th anniversary of Hiroshima, 1985.

MEMBER: Canadian Bar Association (council, 1957-86), Association of Canadian Law Teachers, Canadian Association of University Teachers, Canadian Council on International Law, Canadian Council for International Business, Royal Society of Canada (fellow), Association des juristes d'expression française de l'Ontario, Académie du Var (France), Fondation Internationale pur l'Eseignement du Droit des Affaires (Aix-Marseille), Faculté Internationale pour l'Eseignement du Droit Comparé (Strasbourg), Couseil Supérieur des Français de l'Etranger (Paris, France).

AWARDS, HONORS: Fulbright scholar, 1950; Commonwealth Scholar, 1960; British Commonwealth fellow, 1962; honorary diplomas, Institute of Comparative Law (Mexico), 1963, and International Faculty of Comparative Law, Strasbourg, 1971; Killam scholar, 1986; honorary doctorate, University of Aix-Marseille, 1988; Officer of Order of Canada; Order of Ontario; Chevalier de la Légion d'Honneur; Officer de l'Ordre national du Mérite, Chevalier de l'Ordre des Palmes Académiques; Medal of Confederation 1867-1967; Medal of Confederation 1867-1992; Medal of Silver Jubilee of Her Majesty the Queen; Medal of 100th anniversary of the Supreme Court of Canada 1875-1975; medal, Law Society of Upper Canada; John E. Read medal for distinguished contribution to international law and organizations.

WRITINGS:

Foreign Judgments: A Comparative Study, McGill University Press (Montreal, Canada), 1956.

Private International Law. A Comparative Study of the Rules Prevailing in Canada and the United States, Canada Law Book (Toronto, Ontario, Canada), 1960.

Cases, Notes, and Materials on the Conflict of Laws, Butterworths (Toronto, Ontario, Canada), 1960, 6th edition published as *Conflict of Laws: Cases, Notes, and Materials,* 1986.

The Civil Law System of Quebec, Osgoode Hall Law School (Toronto, Ontario, Canada), 1961, 2nd edition, Butterworths (Toronto, Ontario, Canada), 1962.

Droit international privé québéçois. Recueil de textes choisis, University of Montreal Press (Montreal, Quebec, Canada), 1964.

International Law Chiefly as Interpreted and Applied in Canada, University of Toronto Press (Toronto, Ontario, Canada), 1965, 3rd edition, Butterworths (Toronto, Ontario, Canada), 1975, 4th edition with others, Emond & Montgomery (Toronto, Ontario, Canada), 1987, 6th edition, 1994.

Canadian Conflict of Laws, Butterworths (Toronto, Ontario, Canada), Volume 1, 1975, Volume 2, 1977, supplement, 1995, 5th edition, 2002.

(With S. A. Williams) *International Criminal Law: Cases, Notes, and Materials,* Osgoode Hall Law School (Toronto, Ontario, Canada), 1974, 2nd edition, 1975.

Introduction to Conflict of Laws, Butterworths (Toronto, Ontario, Canada), 1978, 3rd edition, 1998.

Droit international privé québéçois, Butterworths (Toronto, Ontario, Canada), 1980.

(With Armand de Mestral) *Legal Problems in Foreign Direct Investment,* 3rd edition revised, Osgoode Hall Law School (Toronto, Ontario, Canada), 1980, 4th edition revised, 1982.

(With S. A. Williams) *Canadian Criminal Law: International and Transnational Aspects,* Butterworths (Toronto, Ontario, Canada), 1981.

(With Armand de Mestral and William C. Graham) *International Business Transactions and Economic Relations: Cases, Notes, and Materials on the Law as It Applies to Canada,* Emond & Montgomery (Toronto, Ontario, Canada), 1986.

Extraterritoriality in International Trade, Canada and United States of America Practices Compared, Butterworths (Toronto, Ontario, Canada), 1988.

(With Armand de Mestral and William C. Graham) *The Canadian Law and Practice of International Trade with Particular Emphasis on Export and Import of Goods and Services,* Emond & Montgomery (Toronto, Ontario, Canada), 1991, 2nd edition also with S. Hainsworth and M. A. A. Warner, 1997.

Also, author of reports and other publications, including *Index to the Canadian Bar Review,* Canadian Bar Association (Ottawa, Ontario, Canada), 1973, 2nd edition, 1984; *Civil Code Revision Office: Report on Private International Law* and *Civil Code Revision Office: Report on the Domicile of Human Persons,* both with others, both 1975; *International Judicial Co-operation in Civil, Commercial, Administrative, and Criminal Matters,* Department of Foreign Affairs, Government of Canada, 1980; *Legal Services Provided by the Department of Foreign Affairs with Respect to International Judicial Co-operation and Other Matters,* Department of Foreign Affairs, Government of Canada, 1987; *Market Place North America,* 1990; and *Les Français de l'Etranger, Répertoire de Droit international, Dalloz,* Paris, 1998. Contributor of chapters to books, including *Antitrust Laws. A Comparative Symposium,* edited by W. Friedmann, Carswell Company Limited (Toronto, Ontario, Canada), 1956; *Problèmes de droit contemporain. Principes généraux de droit international privé québéçois,* University of Montreal Press

(Montreal, Quebec, Canada), 1972; *Canadian Perspective on International Law,* edited by R. St. J. Macdonald & Gerald L. Morris, University of Toronto Press (Toronto, Ontario, Canada), 1974; and *Liber Memorialis François Laurent, The Unification of Private International Law Rules in Canada,* University of Gent, 1989.

Also contributor of numerous articles, comments, and book reviews to journals and other periodicals, including *Journal of Patent Society, Canadian Bar Review, McGill Law Journal, Review du Barreau, American Journal of Comparative Law, Revue du Notariat, Alberta Law Review, Kōbe University Law Review, Osgoode Hall Law School Journal, University of Toronto Law Journal, Netherlands International Law Review,* and *Canadian Yearbook of International Law.* Editor, *Canadian Bar Review,* 1957-83; faculty advisor, *MacGill Law Journal,* 1956-59; editorial board, *Canadian Yearbook of International Law,* 1960-99; Canadian editor, *Boletin del Instituto de Derecho Comparado de Mexico,* 1963-68, *Journal du Droit International* (Paris), 1970-99; French language consulting editor, Ontario Reports.

SIDELIGHTS: J. G. Castel once told *CA:* "There are no shortcuts to scholarship."

*   *   *

CHESEBRO, James William 1944-

PERSONAL: Born June 24, 1944, in Minneapolis, MN; son of Floyd J. and Jeanette M. Chesebro. *Ethnicity:* "American." *Education:* University of Minnesota, B.A., 1966, Ph.D., 1972; Illinois State University, M.S., 1967.

ADDRESSES: Home—Forest Hills, NY. *Office*—Department of Communication Arts and Sciences, Queens College of the City University of New York, Flushing, NY 11367.

CAREER: Illinois State University, teaching assistant of Speech Communication, 1966-67; Concordia College, Moorhead, MN, instructor in speech communication, 1967-69; University of Minnesota, teaching associate of Speech Communication, 1969-72; Temple University, Philadelphia, PA, assistant professor, 1972-76, associate professor of speech communication, 1977-81; Queens College of the City University of New York, Flushing, NY, associate professor of communication arts and sci-

ences, 1981-86, professor, 1987-89; George Mason University, adjunct professor of Communication, 1989-92; National Communication Association, director of Education Services, 1989-92; Indiana State University, professor of Communication, 1992—. Visiting professor, University of Puerto Rico, fall, 1980.

MEMBER: Speech Communication Association of America, Rhetoric Society of America, American Institute for Political Communication, Central States Speech Communication Association, Eastern Communication Association (vice president, 1981-82, president, 1982-83, immediate past president, 1983-84).

AWARDS, HONORS: Fellow of National Endowment for the Humanities, 1974; Distinguished Service Award, Speech Communication Association of Puerto Rico, 1982; Golden Anniversary Prize Fund Award (Monograph), National Communication Association, 1985, for "The Media Reality: Epistemological Functions of Media in Cultural Systems"; Everett Lee Hunt Scholarship Award, Eastern Communication Association, 1989, for "Epistemology and Ontology as Dialectical Modes in the Writings of Kenneth Burke," and 1997, for *Analyzing Media: Communication Technologies as Symbolic and Cognitive Systems;* Distinguished Service Award, Eastern Communication Association, 1989; Jose De Diego Award for Outstanding Service to SCAPR and to the Hispanic Community, Speech Communication Association of Puerto Rico, 1990; Distinguished Service Award, National Kenneth Burke Society, 1993; Alumnus of Notable Achievement award, University of Minnesota College of Liberal Arts, 1994; Distinguished Research Fellow, Eastern Communication Association, 1996; Samuel L. Becker Distinguished Service Award, National Communication Association, 1997; selected one of three "ECA Scholars," Everett Lee Hunt Award for Outstanding Scholarship Selection Committee of the Eastern Communication Association, 1983-84, and 1998-99; Distinguished Teaching Fellow, Eastern Communication Association, 1998; Lifetime Achievement Award, National Kenneth Burke Society, 1999.

WRITINGS:

(With Bernard L. Brock, J. F. Cragan, and J. F. Klumpp) *Public Policy Decision-making: Systems Analysis and Comparative Advantages Debate,* Harper (New York, NY), 1973.
(Editor) *Gayspeak: Gay Male and Lesbian Communication,* Pilgrim Press of the United Church (New York, NY), 1981.

(With D. G. Bonsall) *Computer-Mediated Communication: Human Relationships in a Computerized World,* University of Alabama Press (Tuscaloosa, AL), 1989.

(Editor) *Methods of Rhetorical Criticism: A Twentieth-Century Perspective,* Wayne State University Press (Detroit, MI), 1990.

(Editor) *Extensions of the Burkeian System,* University of Alabama Press, 1993.

(With Dale A. Bertelsen) *Analyzing Media: Communication Technologies as Symbolic and Cognitive Systems,* Guilford Publications (New York, NY), 1996.

(Editor, with B. L. Brock and D. Bertelsen) *Methods of Rhetorical Criticism: A Twentieth-Century Perspective,* 4th revised edition, Wayne State University Press (Detroit, MI), 2001.

Contributor to professional journals, including *Quarterly Journal of Speech, Critical Studies in Mass Communication, Communication Monographs, Communication Education, Text and Performance Quarterly, Journal of Popular Culture, Innovator,* and *Information and Behavior.* Editor of *Moments in Contemporary Rhetoric and Communication,* 1971-73, and of *Communication Quarterly,* 1985-87.

WORK IN PROGRESS: Masculinity as a Social and Symbolic Construction.

SIDELIGHTS: James William Chesebro told *CA:* "In the discipline of communication, I specialize in the study of culture and media as symbolic systems. Since 1966, I have maintained a sustained focus on dramatistic theory, methods, and criticism, with specific applications to contemporary culture, particularly television. Since 1981, this orientation has been extended to include all media systems, with conceptual attention devoted to media literacy and media technologies as communication and cognitive systems, which are reflected in both my teaching and research."

BIOGRAPHICAL/CRITICAL SOURCES:

PERIODICALS

Southern Communication Journal, spring, 1994, Frank Harmon, review of *Extensions of the Burkeian System,* pp. 269-270; fall, 1994, Elizabeth Newton, review of *Extensions of the Burkeian System,* p. 88.

*   *   *

CLAY, Rosamund
    See OAKLEY, Ann (Rosamund)

COHEN, I. Bernard 1914-

PERSONAL: Born March 1, 1914, in Far Rockaway, NY; son of Isador and Blanche (Bernstein) Cohen; married Frances Parsons Davis, June 23, 1944; children: Frances. *Education:* Harvard University, B.S. (cum laude), 1937, Ph.D., 1947.

ADDRESSES: Office—235 Science Center, Harvard University, Cambridge, MA 02138.

CAREER: Carnegie Institution, Washington, DC, fellow in the history of science, 1938-41; Harvard University, Cambridge, MA, instructor in physics, 1942-46, instructor in physical science, 1946-47, instructor, 1947-49, assistant professor, 1949-53, associate professor, 1953-59, professor of the history of science, 1959—. University of London, special lecturer, 1959; Lowell lecturer, 1961; Queen's University, Belfast, Wiles lecturer, 1966; Cambridge University, visiting fellow at Clare Hall, 1965, visiting overseas fellow at Churchill College, 1968.

MEMBER: International Union for the History and Philosophy of Science (first vice president, 1962-68; president, 1968-71), International Academy for the History of Science (chair of membership committee, 1961-62), U.S. National Committee for the History and Philosophy of Science (chair, 1961-62), Institute for Early American History and Culture (member of council, 1957-60), History of Science Society (member of executive council, 1945-58; president, 1961, 1962), American Association for the Advancement of Science (fellow; vice president, 1959-60), American Association for the History of Medicine, American Antiquarian Society, American Academy of Arts and Sciences (vice president), American Historical Association, Royal Astronomical Society (fellow), Massachusetts Historical Society, Colonial Society of Massachusetts, Athenaeum Club (London, England), Club of Odd Volumes (member of council, 1965-69), Phi Beta Kappa, Sigma Xi.

AWARDS, HONORS: Guggenheim fellowship, 1956; postdoctoral fellowship, National Science Foundation, 1960-61; LL.D., Polytechnic Institute of Brooklyn, 1964; George Sarton Medal, History of Science Society.

WRITINGS:

Benjamin Franklin's Experiments, Harvard University (Cambridge, MA), 1941.

Roemer and the First Determination of the Velocity of Light, Burndy Library (Norwalk, CT), 1942.

Science, Servant of Man: A Layman's Primer for the Age of Science, Little, Brown (Boston, MA), 1948.

Some Early Tools of American Science: An Account of the Early Scientific Instruments and Mineralogical and Biological Collections in Harvard University, foreword by Samuel Eliot Morison, Harvard University Press (Cambridge, MA), 1950.

Ethan Allen Hitchcock: Soldier, Humanitarian, Scholar, Discoverer of the "True Subject" of the Hermetic Art, American Antiquarian Society, 1952.

Benjamin Franklin: His Contribution to the American Tradition, Bobbs-Merrill (New York, NY), 1953.

Franklin and Newton: An Inquiry into Speculative Newtonian Experimental Science and Franklin's Work in Electricity as an Example Thereof, American Philosophical Society (Philadelphia, PA), 1956, revised edition, Harvard University Press (Cambridge, MA), 1973.

Isaac Newton's Papers on Natural Philosophy, Harvard University Press (Cambridge, MA), 1957.

The Birth of a New Physics, Doubleday (New York, NY), 1960, revised edition, W. W. Norton (New York, NY), 1985.

Science and American Society in the First Century of the Republic, Department of Physics and Astronomy and Graduate School, Ohio State University (Columbus, OH), 1961.

Introduction to Newton's "Principia," Harvard University Press (Cambridge, MA), 1971.

The Newtonian Revolution: With Illustrations of the Transformation of Scientific Ideas, Burndy Library (Norwalk, CT), 1980.

From Leonardo to Lavoisier, 1450-1800, Scribner (New York, NY), 1980.

(With others) *Transformation and Tradition in the Sciences,* Cambridge University Press (New York, NY), 1984.

Revolution in Science, Belknap Press (Cambridge, MA), 1985.

The Newtonian Revolution, Burndy Library (Norwalk, CT), 1987.

Benjamin Franklin's Science, Harvard University (Cambridge, MA), 1990.

Interactions: Some Contacts between the Natural Sciences and the Social Sciences, MIT Press (Cambridge, MA), 1994.

Science and the Founding Fathers: Science in the Political Thought of Jefferson, Franklin, Adams, and Madison, W. W. Norton (New York, NY), 1995.

Howard Aiken: Portrait of a Computer Pioneer, MIT Press (Cambridge, MA), 1999.

EDITOR

(With F. Watson) *General Education in Science,* Harvard University Press (Cambridge, MA), 1952.

Benjamin Franklin, *Some Account of the Pennsylvania Hospital,* Johns Hopkins University Press (Baltimore, MD), 1954.

(With Howard Mumford Jones) *A Treasury of Scientific Prose: A Nineteenth-Century Anthology,* Little, Brown (Boston, MA), 1963.

(With A. Koyre and Anne Whitman) *Issac Newton's Philosophiae Mathematica, the Third Edition (1926) with Variant Readings,* Harvard University Press (Cambridge, MA), 1972.

Issac Newton's "Theory of the Moon's Motion" (1702) with a Bibliographical and Historical Introduction, Dawson's of Pall Mall, 1975.

Isaac Newton's Papers and Letters on Natural Philosophy and Related Documents, Harvard University Press (Cambridge, MA), 1978.

Index Rafinesquianus: The Plant Names Published by C. S. Rafinesquianus with Reductions, and a Consideration of His Methods, Objectives, and Attainments (revision of 1949 edition), Ayer (Salem, NH), 1980.

The Chequered Career of Ferdinand Rudolph Hassler: First Superintendent of the U.S. Coast Survey (revision of 1929 edition), Ayer (Salem, NH), 1980.

Quantum Physics in America, Ayer (Salem, NH), 1980.

(With John F. Herschel) *Essays from the Edinburgh and Quarterly Reviews, with Addresses and Other Pieces,* Ayer (Salem, NH), 1981.

François Magendie (revision of 1944 edition), Ayer (Salem, NH), 1981.

Puritanism and the Rise of Modern Science: The Merton Thesis, Rutgers University Press (New Brunswick, NJ), 1990.

The Natural Sciences and the Social Sciences: Some Critical and Historical Perspectives, Dordrecht (Boston, MA), 1993.

(With Richard S. Westfall) *Newton: Texts, Backgrounds, Commentaries,* W. W. Norton (New York, NY), 1993.

(With Gregory W. Welch and Robert V. D. Campbell) *Makin' Numbers: Howard Aiken and the Computer,* MIT Press (Cambridge, MA), 1999.

(And translator, with Anne Whitman, and contributor of guide) Isaac Newton, *The Principia: Mathematical Principles of Natural Philosophy,* University of California Press (Berkeley, CA), 1999.

(With Jed Z. Buchwald) *Isaac Newton's Natural Philosophy,* MIT Press (Cambridge, MA), 2001.

(With George E. Smith) *The Cambridge Companion to Newton,* Cambridge University Press (New York, N), 2002.

Editor of book series, including "Three Centuries of Science in America" *series,* Ayer (Salem, NH), 1980; and "The Development of Science" series, Arno Press (New York, NY), 1981.

OTHER

Author of *Album of Science,* 1998. Contributor of introductions to books, including Jean Baptiste Joseph Delambre, *Histoire de l'astronomie moderne,* Johnson Reprint (New York, NY), 1969; Walter William Rouse Ball, *An Essay on Newton's Principia,* Johnson Reprint, 1972; Stephan Peter Rigaud, *Historical Essay on the First Publication of Sir Isaac Newton's Principia,* Johnson Reprint, 1972; and William Whiston, *Sir Isaac Newton's Mathematick Philosophy More Easily Demonstrated,* Johnson Reprint, 1972.

Contributor of articles and reviews to professional journals. *Isis,* managing editor, 1947-52, editor and chair of editorial committee, 1953-58; editorial advisor to the "Papers of Benjamin Franklin" book series.

SIDELIGHTS: The author or editor of over one hundred texts, American science historian and physicist I. Bernard Cohen writes about the theories and the theorists who have shaped modern scientific knowledge. In addition, several of his books provide detailed examinations of the history of scientific thought since the 1500s. In Cohen's *Revolution in Science,* the author poses the question as to whether science is "primarily evolutionary . . . or revolutionary," according to a reviewer for the *New York Times Book Review.* Many of the volumes Cohen edited in the "Three Centuries of Science" and "The Development of Science" book series are reprints of earlier editions from the nineteenth through the mid-twentieth century.

"The main narrative content of *Revolution in Science* is the history of physical science from the 17th through the 20th centuries, culminating in the theory of relativity, quantum theory and the theory of plate tectonics," noted *New York Times Book Review* contributor Joshua Lederberg. Praising the anthology as being "carefully documented and told in a straightforward, comprehensive style," Lederberg went on to praise Cohen for his ability to "tease . . . out what is revolutionary about the people whose works have become mile-stones." As the critic explained, the author maintains that there are "four stages in a revolution. It begins with an intellectual insight. The scientist then makes a private record of his commitment to its pursuit. He then communi-

cates his ideas privately with colleagues before he formally publishes them. Finally, his theory is incorporated into the theoretical fabric and practice of consensual science. Instead of giving a precise definition of a revolution . . . he lists four tentative criteria for identifying one: There must be testimony of contemporary witnesses that a revolution has occurred."

Eighteenth-century scientific thought and the desire to achieve consensus on the scientific credentials of Benjamin Franklin are central themes of *Benjamin Franklin's Science.* Esmond Wright noted in a *New York Times Book Review* appraisal of the work that Cohen "writes with total authority and renews his now familiar thesis: Franklin was not just a practical inventor but a scientific thinker . . . and it was as a theorist that he won election to a fellowship of the Royal Society. Mr. Cohen contends that . . . it was [Franklin's] standing as a scientist that eased his later path as a diplomat in London and Paris, where he was well known and respected for his science."

Comprised of learned articles originally published between 1943 and 1956, *Benjamin Franklin's Science* reflects "a period when Professor Cohen and others were fighting to establish the relevance of the history of science to a fuller understanding of eighteenth-century society, and of its multi-faceted individuals such as Franklin," explained *Times Literary Supplement* reviewer Stephen Pumfrey. "Chapters Four and Five . . . remind us of how influential Cohen has been in establishing the methodological principle that mature scientific accomplishments must be traced to their micro-context. [Cohen] has an enviable capacity to introduce eighteenth-century problems simply and succinctly, in a literary style which would have pleased Franklin himself."

In summing up Cohen's contribution to the history of science, Pumfrey pointed out that "claims by historians of science for close connections between political and scientific revolutions are quite recent, and Cohen himself broached the subject in his *Revolutions in Science.* [Cohen's] claim made here is . . . that we should study Franklin's science because it was his scientific reputation that went before him, opening the doors of the influential."

BIOGRAPHICAL/CRITICAL SOURCES:

PERIODICALS

American Historical Review, June, 1997, review of *Science and the Founding Fathers: Science in the Political Thought of Jefferson, Franklin, Adams, and Madison,* p. 884.

American Scientist, November, 1999, review of *Howard Aiken: Portrait of a Computer Pioneer,* p. 566.

Business History, July, 2000, Geoffrey Tweedale, review of *Howard Aiken,* p. 178.

Business History Review, winter, 1999, Nathan L. Ensmenger, reviews of *Howard Aiken* and *Makin' Numbers: Howard Aiken and the Computer,* p. 761.

Contemporary Review, November, 1997, review of *Science and the Founding Fathers,* p. 273.

History Today, May, 1997, review of *Science and the Founding Fathers,* p. 53.

Isis, September, 1997, review of *Science and the Founding Fathers,* p. 543.

Journal of Economic Literature, December, 1999, reviews of *Makin' Numbers* and *Howard Aiken,* p. 1749.

London Review of Books, November 16, 2000, Simon Schaffer, "Somewhat Divine," pp. 30-31.

Nature, February 20, 1997, review of *Science and the Founding Fathers,* p. 693.

New York Times Book Review, April 21, 1985, Joshua Lederberg, review of *Revolution in Science;* August 16, 1987; September 30, 1990, Esmond Wright, review of *Benjamin Franklin's Science;* September 12, 1999, Lawrence Hunter, review of *Howard Aiken.*

Science Books & Films, special edition, 1998, review of *Album of Science,* p. 44; November, 1999, review of *Makin' Numbers,* pp. 248, 264, review of *Howard Aiken,* p. 252.

Times Literary Supplement, September 13, 1985; January 18, 1991, Stephen Pumfrey, review of *Benjamin Franklin's Science.**

*   *   *

COONTS, Stephen (Paul) 1946-

PERSONAL: Born July 19, 1946, in Morgantown, WV; son of Gilbert Gray (an attorney) and Violet (a teacher; maiden name, Gadd) Coonts; married Nancy Quereau, February 19, 1971 (divorced, 1984); married Deborah Buell, April 12, 1995; children: Rachael, Lara, David. *Education:* West Virginia University, A.B., 1968; University of Colorado, J.D., 1979.

ADDRESSES: Home—Clarksville, MD. *Agent*—Robert Gottlieb, William Morris Agency, 1350 Avenue of the Americas, New York, NY 10019.

CAREER: Cab driver and police officer, 1977-81; Hymes & Coonts Attorneys, Buckhannon, WV, private practice, 1980-81; Petro-Lewis Corporation (oil and gas company), Denver, CO, in-house counsel, 1981-86; writer, 1986—. Trustee, West Virginia Wesleyan College. *Military service:* U.S. Navy, 1968-77, served as aviator in Vietnam, 1971-73; became lieutenant; worked as flying instructor; received Distinguished Flying Cross.

MEMBER: Naval Institute Foundation.

AWARDS, HONORS: Author award of merit, U.S. Naval Institute, 1986, for *Flight of the Intruder;* inducted into Academy of Distinguished Alumni, West Virginia University, 1992.

WRITINGS:

FICTION

Fortunes of War, St. Martin's (New York, NY), 1998.
Saucer, St. Martin's (New York, NY), 2002.

"JAKE GRAFTON" SERIES

Flight of the Intruder, U.S. Naval Institute Press (Annapolis, MD), 1986.
Final Flight, Doubleday (New York, NY), 1988.
The Minotaur, Doubleday (New York, NY), 1989.
Under Siege, Pocket Books (New York, NY), 1990.
The Red Horseman, Pocket Books (New York, NY), 1993.
The Intruders, Pocket Books (New York, NY), 1994.
Cuba, St. Martin's (New York, NY), 1999.
Hong Kong, St. Martin's (New York, NY), 2000.
America, St. Martin's (New York, NY), 2001.

OTHER

The Cannibal Queen: An Aerial Odyssey across America (nonfiction), Pocket Books (New York, NY), 1992.
(Editor) *War in the Air: True-Life Accounts of the 20th Century's Most Dramatic Air Battles—by the Men Who Fought Them,* Pocket Books (New York, NY), 1996.
(Editor and author of introduction) *Combat,* Forge (New York, NY), 2001.

Several of Coonts's novels, as well as *The Cannibal Queen: An Aerial Odyssey across America,* were recorded in full by Books on Tape, and in abridged versions by Bantam and Simon & Schuster.

ADAPTATIONS: Flight of the Intruder was adapted into a Paramount film starring Willem Dafoe, Danny Glover, and Brad Johnson in 1991, and the novel was made into a computer video game.

SIDELIGHTS: Stephen Coonts is the best-selling author of a series of thriller novels, including *Flight of the Intruder, Final Flight, The Minotaur,* and *Under Siege,* that feature naval aviator Jake Grafton. Grafton has evolved from a fighter pilot in Coonts's early novels to a commander and something of a sleuth in more recent works such as *Cuba* and *Hong Kong.* Like the fictional Grafton, Coonts has flown sophisticated planes for the U.S. Navy, such as the A-6 Intruder. However, Coonts has always insisted that Grafton is not his fictional counterpart, that Grafton is more of a military Everyman who has orders to follow. Coonts described his popular hero in *People* as "not handsome, not wise, not witty, not smart. Just average." Whatever his fictive origins, Grafton has proven to be a publishing success story, even though his role in Coonts's novels has changed over time.

Born and raised in the Appalachian mountains of West Virginia, Coonts earned his bachelor's degree from West Virginia University in 1968. He was then commissioned an Ensign in the Navy, and he was trained to fly the A-6 Intruder aircraft in Pensacola, Florida. As part of an attack squadron, he performed two combat cruises aboard the USS *Enterprise* during the Vietnam War. His naval duties also included stints as a flight instructor and an officer aboard the USS *Nimitz.* Coonts completed his military service in 1977, attended law school, and worked as an attorney for an oil company in the early 1980s. Finding himself with "no money but plenty of time" after undergoing a divorce in 1984, he began writing *Flight of the Intruder,* his first Jake Grafton novel. The book was turned down by thirty-four publishers before being accepted by the Naval Academy Press, the same small house that first published Tom Clancy's *The Hunt for Red October.*

Flight of the Intruder was only the second work of fiction (Clancy's was the first) ever released by the Naval Institute Press during its more than one hundred years of publishing history. The novel achieved best-seller status even sooner than *The Hunt for Red October,* and it went on to become one of the longest running best-sellers in 1987, according to *Publishers Weekly. Flight of the Intruder,* a realistic portrayal of naval aviators who fought in the Vietnam War, features Grafton as an average pilot who tires of the seemingly pointless and dangerous missions of hitting minor targets, such as

mud huts and bombed-out barracks. Convinced that military leaders are not making the right decisions to end the war quickly, Grafton decides to fly off on his own and attack what he thinks may be the communist headquarters in Hanoi. He struggles with this decision because it represents an act of disobedience similar to the antiwar protests—which he hates—going on at home.

Reviewers praised *Flight of the Intruder* for its vivid descriptions of life in the cockpit. "When Grafton is at the controls of his Intruder, the novel comes alive with a jolt," remarked Reid Beddow in the *Washington Post Book World.* Some critics, however, felt the novel had its weak moments. For example, David Holahan in Chicago *Tribune Books* faulted the "obligatory 'love interest' chapters, which are unconvincing and distracting." Holahan nonetheless applauded the author's "compelling tale of aerial warfare" and affirmed that "Coonts' accounts of the riveting drama of combat flights are first rate, as are the scenes of wise-cracking camaraderie aboard ship and on leave ashore." Beddow, moreover, concluded that "Coonts . . . has written a first novel of impressive power and authority."

Grafton returns to action in Coonts's next three novels, *Final Flight, The Minotaur,* and *Under Siege.* The first concerns Grafton's attempt to thwart an international terrorist plot led by an Arab named Colonel Qazi, whose followers converge on an Italian harbor to hijack a U.S. aircraft carrier containing nuclear missiles. The second is set in the United States and revolves around Grafton's efforts to prevent a Pentagon double agent from learning about the "Athena" stealth bomber. And *Under Siege* finds Grafton countering an attack on top officials in Washington, D.C., by Colombian terrorists who want to free an imprisoned drug kingpin. Critics generally praised the intensity of the flight and battle scenes in these books but found other portions less engaging. Still, George C. Wilson commented in the *Washington Post Book World:* "If you liked the authentic flying and carrier scenes in *The Flight of the Intruder,* you will find enough fresh ones in *Final Flight* to make you glad you bought the book." In addition, *Washington Post Book World* contributor Rory Quirk found considerable merit in *The Minotaur:* "What unfolds is a fast-paced, graphic thriller that combines equal parts high tech and high adventure, laced with harrowing insights into the thankless, razor-edge world of the Navy test pilot and the labyrinth of superpower espionage." Quirk also affirmed in a review for the *Washington Post* that *Under Siege* "is a disquieting story, told by a first-rate storyteller who, so far, has resisted grinding out formulaic bestsellers."

Later books that feature Jake Grafton include *The Red Horseman*—in which Jake and his assistant, Toad Tarkington, dismantle the nuclear weapons of the former Soviet Union, as well as a cabal of evil CIA agents—and *The Intruders,* which is set in 1973 and deals with Jake's disillusionment with the Vietnam War. International espionage—and its more immediate concerns for Grafton's safety—figure prominently in *Cuba* and *Hong Kong.* The latter work in particular represents a new phase in Grafton's career, as he is no longer in the cockpit, but instead must foil a conspiracy and rescue his wife from kidnappers. *Cuba* presents Grafton in a new role: as a rear admiral tracking a cargo of biological weapons. A *Booklist* reviewer observed that the novel "mines the original Cuban missile crisis for source material" even though it is set in the near future. The same reviewer credited *Cuba* with "dramatic, diverting action. . . . Coonts delivers the anticipated excitement." In *Publishers Weekly,* Tim Warren wrote: "*Cuba* demonstrates Coonts's growth as a writer. . . . He has always been strong at building characters and incorporating a mass of technical information into the story; *Cuba* is also more intricately plotted."

Although Coonts has written a number of novels that do not include Grafton, only one has been released to date. *Fortunes of War* is a speculative techno-thriller set in a near future threatened by Russian corruption and the collapse of the Japanese economy. Bob Cassidy, an Air Force officer, must help the Russians to foil Japanese attempts to seize Siberian oil reserves. Unfortunately, the Russian military is beset with aging equipment, while the Japanese have developed sophisticated, radar-invisble fighter jets. In his *Denver Post Online* review of the work, Edward P. Smith called the book "a tribute to [Coonts's] imagination," adding: "In a world short on bigger-than-life villains, Coonts creates some that we can only hope we never see in real life." A *Kirkus Reviews* critic observed that, in *Fortunes of War,* Coonts "rewrites the near-future-war formula with splendid results. . . . A stirring examination of the courage, compassion, and profound nobility of military professionals under fire."

With *The Cannibal Queen: An Aerial Odyssey across America,* Coonts ventures into nonfiction to recount his summer-long journey to each of the contiguous forty-eight American states in a fifty-year-old open-cockpit biplane. Most critics responded positively to his obvious enthusiasm and love of flying. Some commentators, however, sensed the book was a bit self indulgent, and a few were put off by the author's frequent discourses on political issues. A writer in *Kirkus Reviews* concluded: "Middle-class, upbeat to a fault, and

unmeditative. Yet the descriptions of flight and the portrait of an America seemingly trapped in a time-warp are arresting."

Coonts has always spoken candidly about the aims of his writing and what he hopes to accomplish with each novel. In an interview with *Writers Write,* he said that his fans "want to read Jake Grafton stories, and they make it known to me. They also make it known at the bookstore too! . . . I think a writer that doesn't give his fans what they want to read is taking severe risks with his own career. I think you owe it to the fans to give them what they want. It's all just entertainment. I'm not in the running for the Pulitzer Prize. I don't write literature; I just write entertainment, commercial fiction. It's a proud profession and I'm quite happy with that, but I think I've got to give the public what they want, or else I won't be in this business very long."

In 2000, Coonts returned to the character of Jake Grafton in *America,* a techno-thriller about a hijacking. He also edited an anthology of original novellas by several authors who focus on themes similar to Coonts—the work is titled *Combat.*

An interview with Coonts can be found in *Contemporary Authors,* Volume 133.

BIOGRAPHICAL/CRITICAL SOURCES:

PERIODICALS

Booklist, May 1, 1992, p. 1562; April 15, 1993, p. 1470; June 1, 1999, Gilbert Taylor, review of *Cuba;* July 2001, Roland Green, review of *America,* p. 949.
Detroit Free Press, September 25, 1988.
Detroit News, November 27, 1988.
Entertainment Weekly, October 21, 1994, p. 60.
Kirkus Reviews, March 1, 1998, review of *Fortunes of War.*
Library Journal, February 15, 2001, Robert Conroy, review of *Combat,* p. 198; August, 2001, Robert Conroy, review of *America,* p. 159.
New York Times, November 1, 1986.
New York Times Book Review, October 22, 1989, p. 37; November 18, 1990, p. 41; May 23, 1993, p. 21; October 30, 1994, p. 26.
People, January 19, 1987.
Publishers Weekly, January 8, 1988; August 22, 1994, p. 41; January 1, 2001, review of *Combat,* p. 69; July 23, 2001, review of *America,* p. 51; August 13, 2001, Daisy Maryles, "'America' the Dangerous," p. 161.

School Library Journal, February, 1991, p. 104.
Tribune Books (Chicago), November 23, 1986.
Wall Street Journal, October 8, 1990.
Washington Post, October 29, 1990.
Washington Post Book World, October 5, 1986; October 23, 1988; October 12, 1989; July 4, 1993.

OTHER

About Stephen Coonts, http://www.coonts.com/ (September 7, 2000).
About: The Human Internet, http://www.usmilitary. about.com/ (August 7, 1999), interview with Coonts.
CNN.com, http://www.cnn.co.uk/books/news/ (August 20, 1999), interview with Coonts.
Denver Post Online: Books & Authors, http://www. denverpost.com/ (May 10, 1999), Edward P. Smith, review of *Fortunes of War.*
Publishers Weekly.com, http://www.publishersweekly. com/ (August 9, 1999), Tim Warren, "Stephen Coonts: Ace of Suspense."
Stephen Coonts Online, http://www.stephencoonts.com (September 7, 2000).
Time.com, http://www.time.com/ (May 13, 1998), interview with Coonts.
Writers Write, http://www.writerswrite.com/ (January, 2000), Claire E. White, interview with Coonts.*

*   *   *

CUNNINGHAM, Laura Shaine 1947-

PERSONAL: Born January 25, 1947, in New York, NY; daughter of Laurence Moore (an aviator) and Rose Weiss; married Barry Cunningham (a journalist), December 4, 1966 (separated, 1994); children: Alexandra Rose, Jasmine Sou Mei (both adopted). *Education:* New York University, B.A., 1966.

ADDRESSES: Home—New York, NY. *Agent*—Owen Laster, William Morris Agency, 1350 Avenue of the Americas, New York, NY 10019.

CAREER: Author.

MEMBER: Authors League of America, Dramatists Guild, Authors Guild, Writers Guild of America, Girl Scouts of America, Poets and Writers, New Dramatists, Writer's Community.

Laura Shaine Cunningham

AWARDS, HONORS: Nationwide journalism award for best profile, for cover story in *Newsday,* 1984; National Endowment for the Arts grant, 1987, for playwriting, and 1990, for creative nonfiction; New York Foundation of the Arts grant, 1987, for theater, and 1990, for nonfiction literature.

WRITINGS:

Sweet Nothings (novel), Doubleday (New York, NY), 1977.
Third Parties (novel), Coward (New York, NY), 1980.
Sleeping Arrangements (memoir), Knopf (New York, NY), 1989.
A Place in the Country (memoir), Putnam/Riverhead (New York, NY), 2000.

PLAYS

Bang, first produced in Chicago, IL, by Steppenwolf Theatre Company, 1986.
Beautiful Bodies, first produced in Montclair, NJ, by Whole Theatre Company, 1987.

I Love You, Two (related one-act plays; contains *Where She Went, What She Did,* first produced at the Manhattan Punchline, 1988, and *The Man at the Door,* first produced at the Renegade Theatre, Hoboken, NJ, 1991), Samuel French (New York, NY), 1988.

Also author of unpublished play *Cruising Close to Crazy.*

Contributor of articles, short stories, and reviews to periodicals, including *New Yorker, New York Times, Atlantic, Vogue, Mirabella,* and *Newsday.*

SIDELIGHTS: Laura Shaine Cunningham has written several critically successful novels and memoirs, including *Third Parties, Sleeping Arrangements,* and *A Place in the Country.* Cunningham describes the problems faced by descendants of the very rich in her humorous novel, *Third Parties.* The novel is set in Darton's Wood, an extravagant playground built by turn-of-the-century robber barons. Their third-generation descendants struggle to maintain the grand estates in spite of twentieth-century maintenance costs. Into this scene moves Isaac Katcher, a songwriter from the Bronx who finds peace in the beauty of Darton's Wood. When a corporation threatens to transform the country retreat into modern developments, Katcher, "in a hilarious show of strength . . . musters an army of ex-wives and social misfits who share his views and, in a brilliantly engineered filibuster, literally bores the opposition into surrender," related Elizabeth Forsythe Hailey in the *New York Times Book Review. Los Angeles Times Book Review* contributor Joan Reardon rated *Third Parties* "definitely one of a kind" and called it "a wonderful blend of fantasy and funk . . . a just-right blend of snappy and sassy satire."

Sleeping Arrangements is an autobiographical novel of Cunningham's childhood in the Bronx during the 1950s. Novelist Ann Tyler, reviewing the book for the *Baltimore Sun,* noted, "*Sleeping Arrangements* is so funny and quirky, and it's written with such a deft touch, that at first you may not recognize its underlying seriousness." Young Lily—the fictional stand-in for author Cunningham—lives in circumstances most would call unusual. She is left an orphan at age eight by the death of her mother. She has never known her father; he was (according to her mother) killed while fighting the Germans, with his noble boxer, Butch, by his side. Into Lily's life sweep her two bachelor uncles to care for her. Uncle Gabe, a music teacher, writes love songs that rhyme "river" with "liver." Uncle Len aspires to be

a detective and travels on mysterious errands with a change of clothes in a manila envelope. Together they create a surreal version of "normal" life that includes allowing Lily to decorate the living room to her own taste (orange and white stripes, like her favorite Good Humor bar).

But critics found Cunningham's story more than a catalog of wacky characters. Cunningham proves to be an affectionate and sharp chronicler of a time and place some might recall as lacking in excitement. In a *New York Times* review, Michiko Kakutani quoted a passage where Lily describes what it is like to live in the shadow of Yankee stadium: "To an extent, I lead a baseball-dominated life. Not only does the stadium emit strange lights and sounds—my mother and I soon become accustomed to the twilights, accept them as naturally as Norsemen must have tolerated their endless days in the land of the midnight sun—but the entire neighborhood is designed around the sport. . . . In season, the streets are clogged with fans; the entire neighborhood is redolent of frankfurter." In Kakutani's judgment, "*Sleeping Arrangements* stands as a model memoir—at once funny and sad, irreverent and generous."

In the memoir *A Place in the Country,* Cunningham chronicles her purchase of a house in the Shawangunk Mountains of New York, something she had always dreamed of having. She "recounts with wry humor her conversion from innocent newcomer to country sophisticate," according to a reviewer for *Publishers Weekly.* Detailing not only the joys of country life but the many unexpected complications as well, Cunningham presents "hilarious and cautionary anecdotes," Ellie Barta-Moran noted in *Booklist.* Among the problems are an ill-fated attempt at raising chickens, uncooperative water pipes in the aged house, and the appearance of a swami's community as new neighbors. "Cunningham's lovely portrait of country scenes will engage readers," the writer for *Publishers Weekly* stated. Barta-Moran concluded that *A Place in the Country* is an "ode to all things green and earthy."

Cunningham once told *CA:* "I have a typical writer's personal history, that is: atypical. I am of Jewish-Southern Baptist descent, was orphaned at age eight, and raised by two unmarried uncles (both writers). I'm a third-generation author: my grandparents also wrote stories and books. Motivation? I didn't know there was anything else to be. Had I known, I would have been a ballerina."

BIOGRAPHICAL/CRITICAL SOURCES:

PERIODICALS

Baltimore Sun, November 26, 1989, Ann Tyler, review of *Sleeping Arrangements.*
Booklist, June 1, 2000, Ellie Barta-Moran, review of *A Place in the Country,* p. 1834.
Chicago Magazine, December, 1986.
Entertainment Weekly, July 21, 2000, review of *A Place in the Country.*
Library Journal, September 1, 2000, Michael Rogers, review of *Sleeping Arrangements,* p. 257.

Los Angeles Times Book Review, October 12, 1980, Joan Reardon, review of *Third Parties.*
New York Post, July 9, 2000, review of *A Place in the Country.*
New York Times, November 7, 1989, Michiko Kakutani, review of *Sleeping Arrangements.*
New York Times Book Review, October 26, 1980, Elizabeth Forsythe Hailey, review of *Third Parties.*
Publishers Weekly, June 5, 2000, review of *A Place in the Country,* p. 81.
Redbook, October, 2000, review of *A Place in the Country.*
San Francisco Chronicle, January 28, 1990.*

D

DAVIES, Christie
See DAVIES, John Christopher Hughes

*   *   *

DAVIES, John Christopher Hughes 1941-
(Christie Davies)

PERSONAL: Surname pronounced "*Day*-viss"; born December 25, 1941, in Sutton, Surrey, England; son of Christopher G. H. (an inspector of schools) and Marian (a teacher; maiden name, Johns) Davies. *Ethnicity:* "British." *Education:* Emmanuel College, Cambridge, B.A. (with first class honors), 1964, M.A., Ph.D.

ADDRESSES: Home—Reading, England. *Office*—Department of Sociology, University of Reading, Whiteknights, P.O. Box 218, Reading, Berkshire RG6 6AA, England. *Agent*—Laurence Pollinger Ltd., 9 Staple Irish, London WC1V 7QM, England. *E-mail*—J.C.H.Davies@Reading.ac.uk.

CAREER: British Broadcasting Corporation, London, England, radio producer for *Third Programme,* 1967-69; University of Leeds, Leeds, England, lecturer in sociology, 1969-72; University of Reading, Reading, England, lecturer, 1972-75, senior lecturer, 1975-81, reader, 1981-84, professor of sociology, 1984—, acting department head, 1976-77, department head, 1982-94, department chair, 1990. Visiting lecturer at University of Bombay and Delhi University, both 1973-74, Jagiellonian University Kraków, 1991; Distinguished Scholars Interdisciplinary Lecturer at George Mason University, 1986; lecture tours for British Council.

MEMBER: Union Society, Cambridge (president, 1964).

AWARDS, HONORS: Salzburg Seminar in American Studies, fellow, 1977.

WRITINGS:

AS CHRISTIE DAVIES

(With Ruth Brandon) *Wrongful Imprisonment: Mistaken Convictions and Their Consequences,* Allen & Unwin (London, England), 1973.
(With Russell Lewis) *The Reactionary Joke Book,* Wolfe, 1973.
Permissive Britain: Social Change in the Sixties and Seventies, Pitman (London, England), 1975.
(Editor, with Rajeev Dhavan and author of introduction) *Censorship and Obscenity,* Martin Robertson (Oxford, England), 1978.
Welsh Jokes, John Jones (Cardiff, UK), 1978.
Ethnic Humor around the World: A Comparative Analysis, Indiana University Press (Bloomington, IN), 1990.
Jokes and Their Relation to Society, Mouton de Gruyter (New York, NY), 1998.
The Mirth of Nations, a Social and Historical Study, Transaction (New Brunswick, NJ), 2002.

Also contributor to books, including *The Boundaries of the State in Modern Britain,* edited by Simon Green and Richard Whiting, Cambridge University Press, 1995, and *Contemporary Issues in the Sociology of Death, Dying, and Disposal,* edited by Glennys Howarth and Peter Jupp, Macmillan, 1995. Contributor to periodicals in India, Bulgaria, Switzerland, Ireland, Wales, Canada, United States, and England, including *Quest, Irish Independent, Le Devoir, Vingt Quatre Heures, New*

Quest, Daily Telegraph, Straits Times, National Post, National Review, Spectator, and *Wall Street Journal.* Contributor to academic journals, including *American Journal of Sociology, Australian Journal of Comedy, British Journal of Sociology, Journal of Strategic Studies, Policy Review, Humor, International Journal of Human Research, Annual Review of the Social Sciences of Religion, British Journal of Sexual Medicine,* and *Stylistika.* Member of editorial board, *International Journal of Humor Research* and *Sociological Papers.* Also author of a number of radio and television scripts, and contributor of humorous fiction to various periodicals.

WORK IN PROGRESS: The Strange Death of Moral England, a work on the sociology of morality; a book on the social position of those born out of wedlock who have come to occupy high positions.

*   *   *

DIBDIN, Michael 1947-

PERSONAL: Born March 21, 1947, in Wolverhampton, Staffordshire, England; son of Frederick John (a lecturer in science) and Peggy (a health visitor; maiden name, Taylor) Dibdin; married Benita Mitbrodt, 1971 (marriage dissolved, 1979); married Sybil Sheringham, 1986 (marriage ended); married Kathrine "K.K." Beck (a writer); children: (first marriage) Moselle Benita; (second marriage) Emma Yvette. *Education:* University of Sussex, Brighton, B.A. (English literature), 1968; University of Alberta, Edmonton, M.A. (English literature), 1969.

ADDRESSES: Agent—Pat Kavanagh, Peters Fraser & Dunlop Group Ltd., Drury House, 34-43 Russell Street, London WC2B 5HA, England.

CAREER: Mystery novelist. College of Technology, Belfast, Northern Ireland, part-time lecturer, 1968; held a variety of jobs in western Canada, 1969-75; International House, Perugia, Italy, English teacher, 1980-82; University of Perugia, language assistant, 1982-84.

AWARDS, HONORS: Gold Dagger Award, Crime Writers Association, 1988, for *Ratking; New York Times* notable book citation, 1991, for *Dirty Tricks.*

WRITINGS:

NOVELS

The Last Sherlock Holmes Story, J. Cape (London, England), 1978, Pantheon Books (New York, NY), 1979.

Michael Dibdin

A Rich Full Death, J. Cape (London, England), 1986, Vintage Books (New York, NY), 1999.
The Tryst, Faber (London, England), 1989, Summit Books (New York, NY), 1990.
Dirty Tricks, Summit Books (New York, NY), 1991.
The Dying of the Light, Pantheon Books (New York, NY), 1993.
Dark Specter, Pantheon Books (New York, NY), 1995.
The Last Sherlock Holmes Story, Vintage Books (New York, NY), 1996.
Thanksgiving, Pantheon Books (New York, NY), 2001.

"AURELIO ZEN" SERIES

Ratking, Faber (London, England), 1988, Vintage Crime (New York, NY), 1997.
Vendetta, Faber (London, England), 1990, Bantam Books (New York, NY), 1991.
Cabal, Faber (London, England), 1992, Doubleday (New York, NY), 1993.
Dead Lagoon, Pantheon Books (New York, NY), 1994.
Cosi Fan Tutti, Pantheon Books (New York, NY), 1997.
A Long Finish, Pantheon Books (New York, NY), 1998.
Blood Rain, Pantheon Books (New York, NY), 1999.

OTHER

(Editor) *The Picador Book of Crime Writing,* Picador (London, England), 1993.
(Editor) *The Vintage Book of Classic Crime,* Vintage Books (New York, NY), 1997.

Contributor of short story "A Death in the Family" to *Best Short Stories 1991,* Heinemann, 1991; contributor of stories to *Granta* and *Modern Painters,* and of book reviews to the *Independent on Sunday.*

SIDELIGHTS: Novelist Michael Dibdin has achieved success on two fronts. His series of crime novels featuring Italian detective Aurelio Zen have drawn praise for their comedy, deft plotting, and reflections on Italian politics, while his suspense stories are cited for their dark atmosphere and troubling conclusions about modern culture. A native of Great Britain who now lives in America, Dibdin has numerous fans on both sides of the Atlantic. A *Publishers Weekly* correspondent called the author "an erudite crime writer" who "places complex characters into exacting plot puzzles that unfold in evocative prose rich in historical and geographic color." In *New Statesman and Society,* Bill Greenwell noted of Dibdin: "If this is formula writing, then most contemporary novelists should indulge in a little theft. It has the knack of heisting the reader's imagination into its territory and holding it there."

Dibdin's first novel, *The Last Sherlock Holmes Story,* brings together the fictional detective Sherlock Holmes and the real-life Jack the Ripper in a plot involving a showdown between Holmes and his arch-rival, James Moriarty. Enhanced by Freudian innuendo and narrated by the dogged, confused Watson, the story features an ending with a twist. The novel gained wide attention, although some reviewers noted significant flaws. Novelist Kingsley Amis, writing in the *New Statesman,* disliked the book's stylistic modernisms and added, "The plot is wrong too: Holmes called in by Lestrade to catch Jack the Ripper. The horror of those real crimes . . . won't blend with the undistressing fictions of the Holmes-Watson-Doyle world." In the *New York Review of Books,* crime novelist and critic Julian Symons described Dibdin's novel as emblematic of its subgenre, and noted, "[The] book is a fair example, in kind and quality, of the current Sherlock Holmes fiction. . . . The language is pastiche, not bad of its kind but still 'an alloy of literary pretense,' and the story drags distinctly after a lively opening." David Pietrusza remarked in the *National Review* that "Dibdin's tale proceeds at a

brisk gallop. Yet his thesis is definitely un-Conanical; his research shows signs of a fatal sloppiness; his depiction of Holmes's attitude toward the Yard is not at all on the mark; and his plot's denouement is certain to breed contempt among all true Holmesians."

A Rich Full Death casts British poet Robert Browning as an amateur detective in Florence, Italy, in 1855. Multiple murders, spiritualism, and Dante's *Inferno* play roles in the book, narrated in the form of letters written by a young American, Robert Booth, to his friend, Professor Prescott. Booth, an admirer of the then-obscure Browning, observes the poet investigating the apparent suicide of the woman with whom Booth was in love, as well as later deaths. Walter Nash, writing in the *London Review of Books,* deemed *A Rich Full Death* "a wonderful warren of literary devices," commenting that "a pastiche running to two hundred pages, immediately characterising the English of an educated 19th-century American, and more distantly yet pervasively evoking the speech-style of Browning's monologists, is no mean achievement. . . . What is totally pleasing is the ingenuity of the book as a literary game with ethical consequences. . . . It raises, in the most engaging way, such problems of mind and matter as were formulated by the mandarin who, waking from a dream, said he did not know whether he was a man dreaming about a butterfly or a butterfly dreaming about a man." In view of such strengths, Nash was relatively untroubled by his perception that "the whodunnit is not such a mystery." In a London *Times* review of *A Rich Full Death,* John Nicholson observed that "clever plotting, witty writing, and a well-judged display of historical background should provide Mr. Dibdin with another well-deserved success."

Ratking, Dibdin's third novel, marked a departure from historical pastiche and introduced the character of Police Commissioner Aurelio Zen. The complex plot deals with the kidnapping of a rich industrialist in Perugia, where Dibdin lived for several years. Marcel Berlins explained in the London *Times* that the plot ingredients "combine splendidly in a convincing tale reeking of authentic Italian atmosphere and politics," while Frederick Busch, reviewing for Chicago *Tribune Books,* applied the adjective "wonderful" to the book's dialogue, atmosphere, and detective hero.

Dibdin's fourth novel, *The Tryst,* is a still more ambitious departure, a psychological fable in the manner of Patricia Highsmith or Ruth Rendell. The plot revolves around Aileen Mackin, an unhappily married female psychiatrist with an LSD-soaked past, and her involvement with a disturbed boy named Gary Dunn, who may remind her of a child she lost. Gary's troubled life is narrated in a story-within-the-story. In another framed narrative, the reader becomes acquainted with an old man haunted by a possible fratricide he witnessed fifty years earlier. Reviewers acknowledged the complexity and ambitiousness of the novel, sometimes approvingly and sometimes not. In the London *Times,* Lisanne Radice called *The Tryst* "a subtle, absorbing novel of despair and menace." Marcel Berlins, also in the London *Times,* described the book as an "extraordinary portrayal of squalid, half-real existence (the boy's) and psychological disintegration (hers) with a gripping build-up to a stunning, eerie climax." Joseph Coates in the *Chicago Tribune* remarked, "*The Tryst* is a novel of sly psychological suspense that for much of its length reads like a superior whodunit and then, on the last page, reveals itself to have been a ghost story—or maybe science fiction." A critic for the *Bloomsbury Review* termed the novel "a gripping story of the struggle with the tricks that time and memory can play," while a reviewer for *Washington Post Book World* wrote: "This is an odd but fascinating suspense novel. . . . A Chinese box full of interwoven stories." In the *New York Times Book Review,* Candia McWilliam explained that the "scope and ambition of the novel are well beyond any comfortable formula," but added that "as a record of that unregarded and growing population recently accorded a title—'the underclass'—it is honorable and unnerving." McWilliam also felt that Dibdin did not fully flesh out any of the characters, but observed that given Dibdin's skill, he might have done so intentionally. *London Review of Books* critic Walter Nash wrote that although he is a fan of Dibdin's, he found *The Tryst* "an uneven book," comparing it unfavorably to *Ratking* and *A Rich Full Death.*

Detective Aurelio Zen returns in *Vendetta,* another mystery set in Italy, in which Zen is sent to Sardinia to investigate the videotaped murder of a security-conscious architect. In the *London Review of Books,* Stephen Wall stated, "Michael Dibdin writes convincingly where locale is concerned and, as a thriller, *Vendetta* is a superior and well-informed performance. At times, however, the dialogue reads as if it has been subtitled into gangsterese." Wall also expressed the opinion that Zen is not an absorbing character. Marcel Berlins, however, writing in the London *Times,* described Zen as "quiet" and "endearingly human," saying, "the joy of Zen lies as much in his daily work as in his occasional violent activities."

Dibdin's next novel, *Dirty Tricks,* continues his tradition of experimentation. *Dirty Tricks* uses the crime novel form as a medium through which to satirize Brit-

ain during the tenure of Prime Minister Margaret Thatcher. Set at Oxford, it is narrated by Tim, a teacher of English as a second language who faces extradition charges in Latin America. At a dinner party, Tim meets Karen, the wife of an affluent accountant, and an affair begins. Her husband dies, and Tim, vowing never to work again, marries Karen and lives off the estate. Patricia Craig wrote in the *Times Literary Supplement,* "You are riveted (if appalled) by the unabashed self-interest of Michael Dibdin's central character, intrigued by his vicissitudes, and struck by the deftness with which a reckoning (of a kind) is arranged." A reviewer for the *Washington Post Book World* commented, "The author's thinly disguised commentary on the readjusted class lines of contemporary Britain makes this more than just a crime novel." Robert Plunket in the *New York Times Book Review* observed that the work is "just like James M. Cain, only funny. . . . Come to think of it, maybe it's more just like Nabokov. Only fun." Plunket added, "*Dirty Tricks* has a few too many phony climaxes. . . . toward the end, and they dilute the impact of what could have been some real emotion. This, however, is but a minor annoyance considering the highly sophisticated entertainment the book offers."

Dibdin's third Aurelio Zen mystery, *Cabal,* opens with the corpse of Prince Ludovico Ruspanti crashing from the cupola of St. Peter's Church to the pavement during Mass. *Cabal* includes a series of deaths, revelations about Italian political corruption, and is a satire of the Milan fashion world. *Times Literary Supplement* reviewer Jonathan Keates expressed impatience with the aspects of the book derived from genre conventions, such as the narration of the murderer's motive—"a clot in the narrative artery which the advanced technology of the whodunit seems unable, or perhaps unwilling, to remove." Regarding the author's personal contribution to the novel, however, Keates was much more complimentary. "Dibdin's skill," he observed, "lies in revitalizing these ancient mechanisms by rooting them within a series of chillingly authentic scenes from contemporary Italian life." Suggesting that even Italian readers might find pleasure in studying Dibdin's "perfectly" understood Italy, Keates concluded, "Dibdin, a more naturally gifted writer than the medium needs or deserves, can wrap even the most banal piece of plot engineering . . . within an atmosphere of gamey, tangible immediacy."

Dibdin published two more books in the Aurelio Zen series, *Dead Lagoon* and *Cosi Fan Tutti,* in quick succession. *New York Times Book Review* critic Marilyn Stasio noted of *Dead Lagoon,* "The author has transcended his own superb craftsmanship by working [two] story lines into a structure of pure steel—and by making it the foundation of a serious study of modern-day Venice." In *Dead Lagoon* Zen is working undercover in his native Venice, in order to discover the whereabouts of a kidnapped American businessman. *Cosi Fan Tutti*, on the other hand, finds Zen transferred to Naples in order to sidestep a demotion in Rome. There he tries unsuccessfully to fade into anonymity, eventually becoming embroiled in an attempt to put an end to a series of gangland-style murders. *BookPage* reviewer Cynthia Riggs noted of *Cosi Fan Tutti*, "Dibdin obviously had fun writing this book. He combines suspense and rapid pace with a remarkable sense of place, exquisitely drawn characters, and a joyful sense of farce." In the *Houston Chronicle*, Steven E. Alford remarked, "*Cosi Fan Tutti* finds Dibdin at the top of his witty and entertaining form. For readers new to Aurelio Zen, this novel will make a good starting place; then they will want to go back to Zen's first appearance in *Ratking* and work their way forward. To Dibdin fans, this will mark a fresh and diverting encounter with an old and trusted friend."

The darker side of Dibdin's imagination found free rein in *Dark Specter*. The story revolves around a pathological cult leader in the Pacific Northwest and his followers, who stage a series of seemingly random violent acts in far-flung American cities. Into this milieu wanders Phil, a college professor seeking to understand the disappearance of his son and his wife's suicide. "Dibdin's fans may decry his having exchanged elegant, dark Venice for this glossy, plastic-colored U.S. setting," noted a *Publishers Weekly* reviewer, "but his deft plotting and reliable characterization are fully present in this top-notch thriller." *New Statesman and Society* correspondent Douglas Kennedy found the novel "deeply disturbing," adding: "Brilliantly constructed, mutedly written with chilling finesse, *Dark Spectre* is a contemporary house of horrors—a grim journey into the great American nowhere. . . . [Dibdin] comprehends the disjointed rhythms of American life—the way that society is haunted by the spectre of random malevolence, especially from those who have decided to withdraw and create their own little Utopia with apocalyptic aspirations." In *BookPage*, Gary Crawford concluded, "By the time I finished *Dark Specter*, the idea of random violence without any meaning was preferable to the alternative: a madman planning scores of murders just to settle a philosophical argument."

Dibdin returned to the Zen series with *A Long Finish* and *Blood Rain*. The former, set in the Piedmont region of northern Italy, has Zen dealing with deadly infighting among members of a tightly knit community; it shows

that "this series remains a must for Italy buffs and followers of murder continental style," related Bill Ott in *Booklist*. In *Blood Rain*, the Interior Ministry posts Zen to Sicily so he can gather information on another crime-fighting force, the state police anti-Mafia squad. One member of the squad is a woman who claims to be his daughter; some others prove as corrupt as the criminals they are ostensibly pursuing. Amid murders of mobsters and police, and not knowing whom to trust, Zen finds Sicily to be his "most dangerous assignment yet," in the words of a *Publishers Weekly* reviewer. *Booklist*'s Ott noted that *Blood Rain* differed significantly from *Cosi Fan Tutti* and *A Long Finish*, in which "Zen took on an almost-comic persona." He explained, "In the heart of organized crime, the comic tone disappears." The *Publishers Weekly* reviewer thought *Blood Rain* showed off Dibdin's "manifold gifts as a storyteller," while Ott called the novel "crime fiction at its multifaceted best."

Dibdin ventured back outside the series with *Thanksgiving*, which is both a crime story and a study of obsession and grief. The novel's protagonist, Anthony, is a British journalist, now living in Seattle—where Dibdin settled after marrying Seattle-based mystery writer Kathrine "K.K." Beck in the 1990s. Anthony's wife, Lucy, has recently been killed in a plane crash, and he is driven to discover details of her life before she met him, a topic about which she was secretive. He meets her first husband, Darryl Bob, who lives in Nevada in an isolated trailer, where he keeps salacious photographs of Lucy and recordings that provide evidence of her infidelity. Soon afterward, Darryl Bob is murdered, and Anthony becomes a suspect. A *Publishers Weekly* commentator found Anthony an underdeveloped character, but thought the novel "perceptively questions the boundaries of intimacy and love." The reviewer, however, predicted that fans "will surely clamor for the speedy return of Aurelio Zen." *Booklist* critic Michael Spinella, on the other hand, deemed *Thanksgiving* "a wonderful departure for Dibdin," adding that the author "keeps his psychodrama suspenseful and chilling."

Some critics have pointed out that Dibdin's books transcend the limitations of the crime novel genre. Stasio offered the opinion that the Aurelio Zen novels are "so delicately complex they might have been spun by spiders." A *Publishers Weekly* contributor called Dibdin "a supremely skilled author able to fashion the mystery form into an endless series of deft variations." According to *Entertainment Weekly* reviewer Daneet Steffens, reading a Dibdin novel "brings not only the satisfaction of a mystery solved, but the culmination of an intense, exploratory journey."

BIOGRAPHICAL/CRITICAL SOURCES:

BOOKS

St. James Guide to Crime & Mystery Writers, 4th edition, St. James Press (Detroit, MI), 1996.

PERIODICALS

American Libraries, September, 1995, p. 804.
Bloomsbury Review, January, 1990.
Booklist, August, 1998, Bill Ott, review of *A Long Finish,* p. 1974; March 15, 2000, Bill Ott, review of *Blood Rain,* p. 1333; March 1, 2001, Michael Spinella, review of *Thanksgiving,* p. 1226.
BookPage, February, 1996; May, 1997.
Chicago Tribune, January 4, 1990.
Entertainment Weekly, March 17, 1995, p. 84; March 30, 2001, Cherise Bakersfield, review of *Thanksgiving,* p. 64.
Houston Chronicle, July 23, 1997.
Library Journal, May 1, 1997, p. 144; June 1, 1999, Rex E. Klett, review of *A Rich Full Death,* p. 186.
London Review of Books, December 18, 1986, pp. 19-20; April 21, 1988, pp. 22-23; May 4, 1989, pp. 22-23; June 28, 1990, p. 18.
National Review, August 18, 1978.
New Statesman, June 30, 1978, pp. 889-890.
New Statesman and Society, April 22, 1994, p. 41; September 1995, p. 38; September 20, 1996, p. 45.
New York Review of Books, August 17, 1978, pp. 14-15.
New York Times Book Review, March 11, 1990, p. 21; October 6, 1991, p. 10; March 21, 1993; January 9, 1994; January 8, 1995; October 11, 1998, Marilyn Stasio, review of *A Long Finish,* p. 28; April 2, 2000, Marilyn Stasio, review of *Blood Rain,* p. 28.
Observer, July 2, 1995, p. 21.
Publishers Weekly, January 18, 1993, p. 453; November 7, 1994, p. 68; November 27, 1995, p. 50; April 7, 1997, p. 77; May 17, 1999, review of *A Rich Full Death,* p. 59; March 27, 2000, review of *Blood Rain,* p. 57; January 29, 2001, review of *Thanksgiving,* p. 62.
Time, July 31, 1978.
Times (London), October 24, 1986; May 5, 1988; March 10, 1989; May 20, 1989; April 21, 1990; July 12, 1990.
Times Literary Supplement, June 14, 1991, p. 27; June 5, 1992, p. 21; September 18, 1998, Alessia Del Guido, review of *A Long Finish,* p. 28; September 24, 1999, Caroline Moorehead, review of *Blood Rain,* p. 22.
Tribune Books (Chicago), March 5, 1989.
Washington Post Book World, March 10, 1991, p. 12; September 20, 1992, p. 12.*

* * *

DICKSON, Gordon R(upert) 1923-2001

PERSONAL: Born November 1, 1923, in Edmonton, Alberta, Canada; died January 31, 2001, in Richfield, MN; came to United States in 1936; naturalized citizen; son of Gordon Fraser (a mining engineer) and Maude Leola (a teacher; maiden name, Ford) Dickson. *Education:* University of Minnesota, B.A., 1948, graduate study, 1948-50.

CAREER: Writer. *Military service:* U.S. Army, 1943-46.

MEMBER: Authors Guild, Authors League of America, Mystery Writers of America, Science Fiction Writers of America (president, 1969-71), Science Fiction Research Association, Minnesota Science Fiction Society.

AWARDS, HONORS: Hugo Award, 1965, for *Soldier, Ask Not;* Nebula Award, Science-Fiction Writers of America, 1966, for short story "Call Him Lord"; E. E. Smith Memorial Award for imaginative fiction, 1975; August Derleth Award, British Fantasy Society, 1976, for *The Dragon and the George;* Jupiter Award, 1978, for *Time Storm;* Hugo Award nomination, 1978, for *Time Storm,* and 1979, for *The Far Call;* Hugo Award, 1980, for *Lost Dorsai;* Hugo Award for Best Novelette, World Science Fiction Society, 1981, for *The Cloak and The Staff.*

WRITINGS:

SCIENCE FICTION AND FANTASY NOVELS

Alien from Arcturus (bound with *The Atom Curtain,* by Nick Boddie Williams), Ace Books (New York, NY), 1956, revised edition published as *Arcturus Landing,* 1979.
Mankind on the Run (bound with *The Crossroads of Time,* by Andre Norton), Ace Books (New York, NY), 1956, published as *On the Run,* 1979.
Time to Teleport [and] *The Genetic General,* Ace Books (New York, NY), 1960, expanded edition of the latter published as *Dorsai!* (also see below), DAW Books (New York, NY), 1976.

Delusion World [and] *Spacial Delivery,* Ace Books (New York, NY), 1961, reprinted, 1978.

Naked to the Stars, Pyramid Publications (New York, NY), 1961, reprinted, Ace Books (New York, NY), 1980.

Necromancer (also see below), Doubleday (New York, NY), 1962, published as *No Room for Man,* Macfadden, 1963, reprinted under original title, DAW Books (New York, NY), 1978.

The Alien Way, Bantam (New York, NY), 1965.

Mission to Universe, Berkley Publishing (New York, NY), 1965, revised edition, Ballantine (New York, NY), 1977.

(With Keith Laumer) *Planet Run,* Doubleday (New York, NY), 1967.

Soldier, Ask Not, Dell (New York, NY), 1967.

The Space Swimmers, Berkley Publishing (New York, NY), 1967.

None but Man, Doubleday (New York, NY), 1969.

Spacepaw, Putnam (New York, NY), 1969.

Wolfing, Dell (New York, NY), 1969.

Hour of the Horde, Putnam (New York, NY), 1970.

Sleepwalker's World, Lippincott (Philadelphia, PA), 1971.

Tactics of Mistake (also see below), Doubleday (New York, NY), 1971.

The Outposter, Lippincott (Philadelphia, PA), 1972.

The Pritcher Mass, Doubleday (New York, NY), 1972.

The R-Master, Lippincott (Philadelphia, PA), 1973, revised edition published as *The Last Master,* Tor Books (New York, NY), 1984.

Three to Dorsai! (contains *Necromancer, Dorsai!,* and *Tactics of Mistake*), Science Fiction Book Club, 1975.

(With Harry Harrison) *The Lifeship,* Harper (New York, NY), 1976, published as *Lifeboat,* Futura (London, England), 1978.

The Dragon and the George, Ballantine (New York, NY), 1976.

Time Storm, St. Martin's (New York, NY), 1977, reprinted as *Timestorm,* Baen (New York, NY), 1992.

The Far Call, Dial (New York, NY), 1978.

Pro, Ace Books (New York, NY), 1978.

Home from the Shore, Ace Books (New York, NY), 1978.

Spirit of Dorsai, Ace Books (New York, NY), 1979.

Masters of Everon, Ace Books (New York, NY), 1980.

Lost Dorsai, Ace Books (New York, NY), 1980, revised edition, Sphere (London, England), 1988, new revised edition published as *Lost Dorsai: The New Dorsai Companion,* Tor Books (New York, NY), 1993.

The Cloak and The Staff (novelette), published in *Analog Science Fiction and Fact,* Stanley Schmidt, 1980.

Love Not Human, Ace Books (New York, NY), 1981.

(With Roland Green) *Jamie the Red,* Ace Books (New York, NY), 1984.

Beyond the Dar al-Harb Tor Books (New York, NY), 1985.

The Dorsai Companion, Ace Books (New York, NY), 1986.

The Forever Man, Ace Books (New York, NY), 1986.

Way of the Pilgrim, Ace Books (New York, NY), 1987.

The Chantry Guild, Ace Books (New York, NY), 1988.

The Earth Lords, Ace Books (New York, NY), 1988.

(With Troy Denning and Cory Glaberson) *Dorsai's Command,* Ace Books (New York, NY), 1989.

Wolf and Iron, Tor Books (New York, NY), 1990.

The Dragon Knight, Tor Books (New York, NY), 1990.

Young Bleys, Tor Books (New York, NY), 1991.

The Dragon on the Border, Ace Books (New York, NY), 1992.

The Dragon at War, Ace Books (New York, NY), 1992.

The Dragon, the Earl, and the Troll, Ace Books (New York, NY), 1994.

Other, Tor Books (New York, NY), 1994.

The Magnificent Wilf, Baen (New York, NY), 1995.

The Dragon and the Djinn, Ace Books (New York, NY), 1996.

The Dragon and the Gnarly King, Tor Books (New York, NY), 1997.

The Dragon in Lyonesse, Tor Books (New York, NY), 1998.

The Right to Arm Bears (collection including *Special Delivery, Spacepaw,* and "The Law-Twister Shorty"), Baen (New York, NY), 2000.

The Dragon and the Fair Maid of Kent, Tor Books (New York, NY), 2000.

YOUNG ADULT SCIENCE-FICTION NOVELS

Secret under the Sea (also see below), Holt (New York, NY), 1960.

Secret under Antarctica (also see below), Holt (New York, NY), 1963.

Secret under the Caribbean (also see below), Holt (New York, NY), 1964.

Space Winners, Holt (New York, NY), 1965.

Alien Art, Dutton (New York, NY), 1973.

(With Ben Bova) *Gremlins, Go Home!,* St. Martin's (New York, NY), 1974.

(With Poul Anderson) *Star Prince Charlie,* Putnam (New York, NY), 1975.

Secrets of the Deep (includes *Secret under the Sea, Secret under Antarctica,* and *Secret under the Caribbean*), Critic's Choice Paperbacks (New York, NY), 1985.

COLLECTIONS OF SHORT SCIENCE FICTION

(With Poul Anderson) *Earthman's Burden,* Gnome Press (New York, NY), 1957.

(With others) *Five Fates,* Doubleday (New York, NY), 1970.

Danger—Human, Doubleday (New York, NY), 1970, published as *The Book of Gordon R. Dickson,* DAW Books (New York, NY), 1973.

Mutants: A Science Fiction Adventure, Macmillan (New York, NY), 1970.

(With Poul Anderson and Robert Silverberg) *The Day the Sun Stood Still: Three Original Novellas of Science Fiction* (contains *A Chapter of Revelation* by Anderson, *Thomas the Proclaimer* by Silverberg, and *Things Which Are Caesar's*" by Dickson), Nelson (Nashville, TN), 1972.

The Star Road, Doubleday (New York, NY), 1973.

Ancient, My Enemy, Doubleday (New York, NY), 1974.

Gordon R. Dickson's SF Best, Dell (New York, NY), 1978, revised edition published as *In the Bone: The Best Science Fiction of Gordon R. Dickson,* Ace Books (New York, NY), 1987.

In Iron Years, Doubleday (New York, NY), 1980.

(With Poul Anderson) *Hoka!,* Simon & Schuster (New York, NY), 1983.

Survival!, Pocket Books (New York, NY), 1984.

Forward!, Baen (New York, NY), 1985.

Invaders!, Baen (New York, NY), 1985.

Dickson!, NESFA (Boston, MA), 1984, revised edition published as *Steel Brother,* Tor Books (New York, NY), 1985.

The Last Dream, Baen (New York, NY), 1986.

The Man the Worlds Rejected, Tor Books (New York, NY), 1986.

Mindspan, Baen (New York, NY), 1986.

Stranger, Tor Books (New York, NY), 1987.

Beginnings, Baen (New York, NY), 1988.

Ends, Baen (New York, NY), 1988.

Guided Tour, Baen (New York, NY), 1988.

EDITOR

Rod Serling's Triple W: Witches, Warlocks and Werewolves, Bantam (New York, NY), 1963.

Rod Serling's Devils and Demons, Bantam (New York, NY), 1967.

(With Poul Anderson and Robert Silverberg) *The Day the Sun Stood Still,* Nelson (Nashville, TN), 1972.

1975 Annual World's Best Science Fiction, DAW Books (New York, NY), 1975.

Combat SF, Doubleday (New York, NY), 1975.

Nebula Award Winners Twelve, Harper (New York, NY), 1979.

The Harriers, Baen (New York, NY), 1991.

(With Martin G. Greenberg and Charles G. Waugh) *Robot Warriors,* Ace Books (New York, NY), 1991.

(With Martin Harry Greenberg and Charles G. Waugh) *Bootcamp 3000,* Ace Books (New York, NY), 1992.

(With Martin Harry Greenberg and Charles G. Waugh) *Space Dogfights,* Ace Books (New York, NY), 1992.

Harriers #2: Blood and Honor, Baen (Riverdale, NY), 1993.

OTHER

Dickson!, NESFA Press (Cambridge, MA), 1984.

The Final Encyclopedia, Tor Books (New York, NY), 1984.

(Creator, with David Drake, Chelsea Quinn Yarbro, Christopher Stasheff) *Blood and War,* Baen (Riverdale, NY), 1993.

Author of about 200 short stories and novelettes, some of which appear in anthologies. Also author of radio plays.

SIDELIGHTS: Gordon R. Dickson was a prolific and accomplished author of science fiction and fantasy. He is best known for his humorous series beginning with *The Dragon and the George* and also for his uncompleted "Childe Cycle," a lengthy series of books intended to explore the evolutionary potential of mankind. In his early career, Dickson wrote numerous radio plays, westerns, and lots of science fiction. Gradually his work moved into the more magical realm of fantasy. His work is notable for its skillful blend of serious, even tragic, issues and a light, comic tone. He frequently used the standard plot devices of a youth's initiation, or a gifted hero battling to save his society.

Dickson's Childe Cycle is a multi-volume epic which was intended to span a period of time from the early fourteenth century to the late twenty-fourth century. Begun in 1956, the cycle was never completed, but the books within it, which include *Dorsai!, Necromancer, Soldier, Ask Not,* and *The Chantry Guild*—present Dickson's vision of humanity's evolutionary potential. It is the "principal showcase for [Dickson's] ideas and artistry," observed a contributor to *St. James Guide to Science Fiction Writers.* In it, the same hero is reincarnated as a Warrior, to develop his intuition; as a Man

Philosopher, to develop his empathy; and as a Faith-Holder, to develop his creativity. Ultimately, he must find and assimilate his "Twin Enemy," in order to achieve his fullest potential.

Discussing the Childe Cycle in an interview with *Science Fiction Review*'s Clifford McMurray, Dickson stated, "I'm making the argument that a type of characteral, moral—spiritual, if you like—evolution began with the Renaissance, is presently continuing unnoticed, and will culminate 500 years from now in what I call the Responsible Man." In Dickson's vision, three successful lines, which he calls Splinter Cultures, have evolved: the warrior (the Dorsai), the philosopher (the Exotics of Mara and Kultis), and the faith-holder (the Friendlies of Harmony and Association). Dickson continued: "My assumption is that the Splinter Cultures have only one character-facet, instead of being full spectrum in character like you and me and the people of old Earth. Concentrated in this way, they are nonviable. If all the rest of the human race was killed off and they were left alone they would eventually die off, too, because they don't have the full spectrum of humanity in them—yet."

Although the series beginning with *The Dragon and the George* is superficially more lighthearted than the Childe Cycle, at times it "hovers close to tragedy," according to a writer for *St. James Guide to Fantasy Writers*. The fantasy kicks off with an unassuming, twentieth-century mathematics professor being launched back to medieval times, in a place where magic is a force to be reckoned with. The professor, Jim Eckert, also finds that he can occasionally transform himself into a dragon. His discomfort with this power, and with life in the Middle Ages in general, form the ongoing joke of the series, a joke Dickson sustains admirably, according to many commentators. "Dickson walks an impossibly thin line between showing medieval life as it really was (short, dangerous, hard on peasants) and a gloriously romantic vision of noble deeds done for noble reasons," wrote the contributor to *St. James Guide to Fantasy Writers*. The tragic element comes from the knights' callous treatment of those really in need, with all their nobility devoted to an inhuman set of ideals. Taken as a whole, the books are "funny, charming, satirical, melancholic and generous."

Dickson's work frequently made the point that apparent opposites must learn to cooperate, whether that was in the form of humans and aliens, darkness and light, or some other halves of a duality. One of the most unusual manifestations of this was in his book *Wolf and Iron.*

Set in the near future, when economic collapse has ruptured society, a man called Jeebee is crossing the United States trying to reach his brother's ranch in Montana. Along the way, Jeebee meets and befriends a captive wolf, then begins bonding and traveling with the animal. "Dickson's meticulous research and the breadth of his imagination are manifested in the absorbing, credible details," praised Sybil Steinberg in *Publishers Weekly*. The author has "created the most human, best-realized character of his career," she concluded.

BIOGRAPHICAL/CRITICAL SOURCES:

BOOKS

Dictionary of Literary Biography, Volume 8: *Twentieth-Century American Science-Fiction Writers,* Gale (Detroit, MI), 1981.
St. James Guide to Fantasy Writers, St. James Press (Detroit, MI), 1996.
St. James Guide to Science Fiction Writers, St. James Press (Detroit, MI), 1996.
Thompson, Raymond H., *Gordon R. Dickson: A Primary and Secondary Bibliography,* G. K. Hall (Boston, MA), 1983.

PERIODICALS

Analog Science Fiction and Fact, August, 1984, review of *The Man from Earth,* p. 282; October, 1984, review of *The Last Master,* p. 145; May, 1987, review of *The Forever Man,* p. 179; May, 1989, review of *The Chantry Guild,* p. 178; November, 1990, review of *Wolf and Iron,* p. 177; May, 1991, review of *The Dragon Knight,* p. 1991; September, 1991, Tom Easton, review of *Young Bleys,* p. 161; July, 1993, Tom Easton, review of *Dragon at War,* p. 266; March, 1995, review of *The Dragon, the Earl, and the Troll,* p. 162; July, 1995, Tom Easton, review of *The Dragon, the Earl, and the Troll,* p. 306; October, 1996, Tom Easton, review of *The Dragon and the Djinn,* p. 145. *Bloomsbury Review,* September, 1989, review of *The Chantry Guild,* p. 22.
Booklist, August, 1983, review of *The Man from Earth,* p. 1447; September 1, 1986, review of *The Forever Man,* p. 34; September 1, 1987, review of *Way of the Pilgrim,* p. 30; October 1, 1998, review of *The Chantry Guild,* p. 220; January 1, 1989, review of *The Earth Lords,* p. 754; April 1, 1990, review of *Wolf and Iron,* p. 1532; February 1, 1991, review of

Young Bleys, p. 1099; April 15, 1991, review of *The Harriers,* p. 1627; February 15, 1992, Roland Green, review of *The Dragon on the Border,* p. 1065; November 1, 1992, Sally Estes, review of *The Dragon at War,* pp. 492, 495; September 15, 1994, Roland Green, review of *Other,* pp. 118, 121; December 1, 1994, review of *The Dragon, the Earl, and the Troll,* pp. 657, 660; June 1, 1995, Roland Green, review of *The Magnificent Wilf,* pp. 1736, 1741; January 1, 1996, reviews of *The Dragon and the Djinn,* pp. 798, 802; August, 1997, Roland Green, review of *The Dragon and the Gnarly King,* p. 1886; October 1, 1998, Roland Green, review of *The Dragon in Lyonesse,* p. 313; December 15, 2000, Roland Green, review of *The Dragon and the Fair Maid of Kent,* p. 794.

Book Report, March, 1992, review of *The Dragon Knight,* p. 60.

Bookwatch, August, 1990, review of *Wolf and Iron,* p. 3.

Bulletin of the Science Fiction Writers of America, fall, 1979.

Destinies, February-March, 1980.

Extrapolation, winter, 1995, review of *The Final Encyclopedia,* p. 360; fall, 1979.

Fantasy Review, December, 1985, review of *Beyond the Dar Al-Harb,* p. 17; January, 1986, review of *Invaders!,* p. 18; February, 1986, review of *The Steel Brother,* p. 20; July, 1986, review of *The Dorsal Companion,* p. 24; March, 1986, review of *The Outposter,* p. 18; June, 1986, review of *The Last Dream,* p. 19; October, 1986, review of *The Forever Man,* p. 23; January, 1987, review of *The Man the Worlds Rejected,* p. 35; May, 1987, review of *The Stranger,* p. 39; June, 1987, reviews of *In the Bone* and *Way of the Pilgrim,* p. 35.

Kirkus Reviews, August 15, 1984, review of *The Final Encyclopedia,* p. 779; July 15, 1986, review of *The Forever Man,* p. 1068; March 15, 1987, review of *Way of the Pilgrim,* pp. 423; April 15, 1990, review of *Wolf and Iron,* p. 541; October 1, 1990, review of *The Dragon Knight,* p. 1344; March 15, 1991, review of *Young Bleys,* p. 365; November 1, 1994, review of *The Dragon, the Earl, and the Troll,* p. 1448; July 1, 1997, review of *The Dragon and the Gnarly King,* p. 992; August 15, 1998, review of *The Dragon in Lyonesse,* p. 1162; November 15, 2000, review of *The Dragon and the Fair Maid of Kent,* p. 1583.

Kliatt Young Adult Paperback Book Guide, spring, 1986, review of *Invaders!,* p. 20; April, 1992, review of *The Dragon Knight,* p. 14; September, 1993, review of *The Dragon on the Border,* p. 16; January, 1994, review of *The Dragon at War,* p. 14; May, 1996, review of *The Dragon, the Earl and the Troll,* p. 14; September, 1996, review of *The Magnificent Wilf,* p. 16; May, 1998, review of *The Dragon and the Djinn,* p. 20.

Library Journal, September 15, 1986, Jackie Cassada, review of *The Forever Man,* p. 103; May 15, 1987, Jackie Cassada, review of *Way of the Pilgrim,* p. 101; November 15, 1988, review of *Three to Dorsal,* p. 27; April 15, 1990, Jackie Cassada, review of *Wolf and Iron,* p. 127; November 15, 1990, Jackie Cassada, review of *The Dragon Knight,* p. 94; March 15, 1991, review of *Young Bleys,* p. 119; March 15, 1992, Jacki Cassada, review of *The Dragon on the Border,* p. 129; May, 1992, review of *Soldier, Ask Not,* p. 48; November 15, 1992, review of *The Dragon at War,* p. 104; January, 1993, review of *Time Storm,* p. 44; April, 1993, review of *Dorsal!,* p. 46; July, 1993, review of *Lost Dorsai,* p. 40; September, 1993, review of *Blood and Honor,* p. 64; April, 1994, review of *Wolf and Iron,* p. 48; December, 1994, review of *The Dragon, the Earl, and the Troll,* p. 56; December, 1995, Jackie Cassada, review of *The Dragon and the Djinn,* p. 164; August, 1997, Susan Hamburger, review of *The Dragon and the Gnarly King,* p. 140; October 15, 1998, Jackie Cassada, review of *The Dragon in Lyonesse,* p. 104; December, 2000, Jackie Cassada, review of *The Dragon and the Fair Maid of Kent,* p. 196.

Locus, February, 1989, reviews of *The Earth Lords* and *None but Man,* p. 48; May, 1989, review of *Invaders!,* p. 46; January, 1990, review of *The Far Call,* p. 50; September, 1990, review of *Wolf and Iron,* p. 58; November, 1990, review of *The Dragon Knight,* p. 17; December, 1990, review of *The Dragon Knight,* p. 52; February, 1991, review of *Wolf and Iron,* p. 36; March, 1991, review of *Wolf and Iron,* p. 46; review of *Wolfling,* p. 57; April, 1991, review of *Young Bleys,* p. 19, review of *Naked to the Stars,* p. 41; May, 1991, reviews of *Wolf and Iron, Young Bleys,* and *The Harriers,* p. 46; October, 1991, review of *Steel Brother,* p. 45; December, 1991, reviews of *The Dragon Knight* and *Tactics of Mistake,* p. 51; January, 1992, review of *Necromancer,* p. 56; February, 1992, review of *Space Dogfights,* p. 56.

Los Angeles Times Book Review, June 26, 1983, review of *The Man from Earth,* p. 10; July 29, 1990, review of *Wolf and Iron,* p. 6.

Minneapolis Star Tribune, February 2, 2001.

New York Times Book Review, August 2, 1987, Gerald Jonas, review of *Way of the Pilgrim,* p. 25.

Publishers Weekly, September 2, 1983, Sally A. Lodge, review of *Hoka!,* p. 73; February 24, 1984, review of *Jamie the Red,* p. 138; September 7, 1984, review of *The Final Encyclopedia,* p. 74; August 23,

1985, review of *The Final Encyclopedia,* p. 70; November 1, 1985, Sybil Steinberg, review of *Steel Brother,* p. 63; May 23, 1986, John Mutter, review of *The Dorsai Companion,* p. 100; August 15, 1986, Sybil Steinberg, review of *The Forever Man,* p. 73; January 30, 1987, John Mutter, review of *In the Bone,* p. 379; March 27, 1987, Sybil Steinberg, review of *Way of the Pilgrim,* p. 39; September 2, 1988, Sybil Steinberg, review of *The Chantry Guild,* p. 90; November 11, 1988, Penny Kaganoff, review of *The Earth Lords,* p. 50; April 14, 1989, review of *The Chantry Guild,* p. 65; April 20, 1990, Sybil Steinberg, review of *Wolf and Iron,* p. 61; October 5, 1990, Sybil Steinberg, review of *The Dragon Knight,* p. 93; March 1, 1991, Sybil Steinberg, review of *Young Bleys,* p. 61; August 29, 1994, review of *Other,* p. 64; November 14, 1994, review of *The Dragon, the Earl, and the Troll,* p. 56; June 26, 1995, review of *The Magnificent Wilf,* p. 91; December 11, 1995, review of *The Dragon and the Djinn,* p. 60; July 14, 1997, review of *The Dragon and the Gnarly King,* p. 69; September 28, 1998, review of *The Dragon in Lyonesse,* p. 78; November 27, 2000, review of *The Dragon and the Fair Maid of Kent,* p. 59.

Rapport, April, 1994, review of *Other,* p. 33.

School Library Journal, May, 1984, Olive Hull, review of *Gremlins Go Home,* p. 76; September, 1990, John Lawson, review of *Wolf and Iron,* p. 266; October, 1996, Charlotte Bradshaw, review of *The Dragon and the Djinn,* p. 162; June, 1991, Pat Royal, review of *The Dragon Knight,* p. 135.

Science Fiction Chronicle, January, 1987, review of *The Forever Man,* p. 39; May, 1987, review of *Space Winners,* p. 50; September, 1990, review of *Wolf and Iron,* p. 37; March, 1991, review of *Wolf and Iron,* p. 28; June, 1991, review of *The Harriers,* p. 32; July, 1991, review of *Young Bleys,* p. 31; December, 1991, review of *Robot Warriors,* p. 34; February, 1992, review of *Space Dogfights,* p. 32; March, 1992, review of *Young Bleys,* p. 20; January, 1993, review of *Bootcamp 3000,* p. 33; September, 1993, review of *Blood and War,* p. 34; September, 1995, review of *Other,* p. 35.

Science Fiction Review, July, 1978; February, 1985, review of *Survival,* p. 62.

Times Literary Supplement, May 25, 1967.

Tribune Books (Chicago), January 18, 1987, review of *The Forever Man,* p. 6.

Wilson Library Bulletin, June, 1989, review of *None but Man,* p. 108.

Voice of Youth Advocates, December, 1982, review of *Outposter,* p. 36; December, 1983, review of *The Man from Earth,* p. 282; April, 1985, review of *Hour of the Horde,* p. 55; December, 1985, review

of *Forward!,* p. 324; April, 1986, review of *Invaders!,* p. 39; August, 1986, review of *Steel Brother,* p. 160; December, 1986, reviews of *The Dorsai Companion* and *The Last Dream,* p. 236; February, 1987, review of *The Man the Worlds Rejected,* p. 291; August, 1987, review of *The Stranger,* p. 129; October, 1987, review of *Way of the Pilgrim,* p. 176; April, 1989, reviews of *Beginnings* and *Ends,* p. 40; June, 1989, review of *The Chantry Guild,* p. 116; April, 1998, review of *The Dragon and the Gnarly King,* p. 54; October, 1989, review of *Earth Lords,* p. 222; August, 1989, review of *None but Man,* p. 164; June, 1991, review of *The Dragon Knight,* p. 107; October, 1991, review of *Young Bleys,* p. 238; April, 1992, review of *The Dragon Knight,* p. 9; June, 1992, review of *The Dragon on the Border,* p. 108, review of *Young Bleys,* p. 143; February, 1993, review of *Dragon at War,* p. 346; April, 1993, review of *The Dragon on the Border,* p. 10; April, 1995, review of *The Dragon, the Earl, and the Troll,* p. 32.

OTHER

About.com, http://fantasy.about.com/arts/fantasy/ (February 23, 2001), Gryph Clarke, "Remembering Gordon R. Dickson, Part I: Fond Memories."

The Dragon Knight, http://www-personal.umich.edu/~pkretsch/dragon/ (February 23, 2001).

Science Fiction and Fantasy Writers of America Web site, http://www.sfwa.org/ (February 23, 2001), "Gordon R. Dickson (1923-2001)."

Two Moons, http://www.twomoons.com/books/dickson. htm (February 23, 2001).*

*   *   *

DONALDSON, Julia 1948-

PERSONAL: Born September 16, 1948, in London, England; daughter of James (a geneticist) and Elizabeth (Ede) Shields; married Malcolm Donaldson (a pediatrician), September 30, 1972; children: Hamish, Alastair, Jesse. *Ethnicity:* "British." *Education:* Bristol University, degree in drama and French, 1970. *Politics:* "Labour voter." *Religion:* "Agnostic."

ADDRESSES: Home—2 Chapelton Ave., Glasgow G61 2RE, Scotland.

CAREER: Writer.

AWARDS, HONORS: Smarties Prize, 1999, and Blue Peter Book Award, 2000, both for *The Gruffalo.*

WRITINGS:

FOR CHILDREN

A Squash and a Squeeze (rhyming picture book), illustrated by Axel Scheffler, M. K. McElderry (New York, NY), 1993.

Birthday Surprise (play), Ginn (London, England), 1994.

Names and Games (play), Ginn (London, England), 1995.

The Gruffalo, illustrated by Axel Scheffler, Dial Books for Young Readers (New York, NY), 1999.

Room on the Broom, illustrated by Axel Scheffler, Dial Books for Young Readers (New York, NY), 2001.

Follow the Swallow, illustrated by Martin Ursell, Crabtree (New York, NY), 2002.

Also, author of books published by Macmillan: *Monkey Puzzle* (rhyming picture book), *Postman Bear* (board book), *Fox's Socks* (board book), *Hide-and-Seek Pig* (board book), *Rabbit's Nap* (board book), *The Gruffalo Song;* other books published by Ginn (London, England): *Turtle Tug* (play based on traditional story), *The Magic Twig* (play based on traditional story), *The Boy Who Cried Wolf* (play based on traditional story; also published as "Big Book"), *The Three Billy Goats Guff* (play based on traditional story; also published as "Big Book"), *The Wonderful Smells* (play), *Top of the Mops* (play), *The King's Porridge* (traditional Scottish story), *Counting Chickens* (traditional tale), *The Town Mouse and the Country Mouse* (traditional tale), *The False Tooth Fairy* (published with two other titles by different authors), *Mr Snow* (short narrative poem), *Spacegirl Sue* (short narrative poem), *BZZZ Splat—The Impact Poetry Book* (with others; comic verse; for reluctant teenage readers); *Steve's Sandwiches* (play), *Clever Katya* (traditional tale from Russia), *The Noises Next Door* (traditional tale from China), *The Monster in the Cave* (play based on traditional fable), *Stop Thief!* (play based on a Japanese story); other books published by Heinemann Educational: *Waiter! Waiter!* (comic verse story), *The Brownie King* (comic verse story), and Problem Page (play; for juveniles); books published by Rigby Heinemann: *All Gone* (play; for reluctant teenage readers), *One Piece Missing* (fantasy story), *Jumping Jack* (fantasy story), *The Giant Jumperee* (play), *Books and Crooks* (play; for reluctant teenage readers); and three books based on traditional British tales, published by Oxford University Press: *The King's Ears, The Boy Who Talked to the Birds,* and *The Strange Dream.* Author of songs, scripts, and stories for BBC television and radio (mainly children's programs); and of the produced but unpublished musicals *King Grunt's Cake* and *Pirate on the Pier.* Contributor to *The Nursery Collection,* Egmont Children's Books; *The Alien and Other Plays,* Heinemann Educational; and *Christmas Poems,* Oxford University Press. Author of songs, scripts, and stories for BBC television and radio (mainly children's programs). Author of unpublished musicals, *King Grunt's Cake* and *Pirate on the Pier.*

SIDELIGHTS: Julia Donaldson once commented: "I am principally a songwriter, performing my own material (for adults and children) with my guitar-playing husband, Malcolm, and also writing songs for other performers on children's T.V. and radio. My book *A Squash and a Squeeze* started life as a song on a television programme. I also visit a lot of schools and libraries (doing songs, drama, and storytelling), and have written two musicals for children (unpublished but often performed), *King Grunt's Cake* and *Pirate on the Pier. Birthday Surprise* and *Names and Games* are both short plays for schoolchildren to read and/or perform."

Donaldson's book *The Gruffalo* is a story about one smart little mouse. Every time Mouse meets a predator in the woods, he scares the predator away by describing to them a frightful creature called the gruffalo, who has "terrible tusks, and terrible claws, and terrible teeth in his terrible jaws." To the fox, Mouse says that the gruffalo's favorite food is roasted fox; when he is speaking to the owl, it's owl ice cream, and its scrambled snake when dealing with Snake. Each time, when the predator runs away, Mouse chants, "Doesn't he know? There's no such thing as a gruffalo." Except there is a gruffalo, and it wouldn't mind having Mouse for dinner. The intelligent mouse rapidly outsmarts the gruffalo as well. Mouse tells the gruffalo that he, Mouse, is the scariest creature in the woods. He convinces the gruffalo to walk with him and see how all of the animals run away, which, of course, they do. In a review for *Booklist,* Stephanie Zvirin called this "a clever, exuberant story," while a *Publishers Weekly* contributor praised her use of rhyme and repetition.

Room on the Broom was dubbed "a surefire read-aloud hit" by Pamela K. Bomboy, who reviewed the book for *School Library Journal.* In this "lightweight, witty" tale, in the words of a *Publishers Weekly* contributor, an unfortunate witch keeps losing things as she flies along on a windy night. Each time, the item is rescued by a friendly animal who then humbly asks, "Is there room on the broom for a [fill in the blank] like me?" When the witch has been joined by a cat, a dog, a bird, and a frog, the overloaded broom snaps and they are all plunged into a swamp. A dragon comes along, intent on eating the witch, but the quick-thinking, mud-coated animals stand on each other's backs and make as much noise as they can. The dragon, convinced that they are some strange and fearful monster, flees, and the grateful witch conjures up a larger and more comfortable broom, complete with a nest for the bird and a tiny pond for the frog. "The wart-nosed witch and her passengers make magic that is sure to please," commented a *Kirkus Reviews* contributor who also praised Donaldson's "fluid rhyming and smooth rhythm."

BIOGRAPHICAL/CRITICAL SOURCES:

BOOKS

Donalson, Julia, *The Gruffalo,* illustrated by Axel Scheffler, Dial Books for Young Readers (New York, NY), 1999.

PERIODICALS

Booklist, July, 1999, Stephanie Zvirin, review of *The Gruffalo,* p. 1950; September 1, 2001, Grace Anne A. DeCandido, review of *Room on the Broom,* p. 120.
Childhood Education, Fall, 1999, Kelly Krawczyk, review of *The Gruffalo,* p. 44.
Children's Book Review Service, August, 1993, p. 158.
Horn Book Guide, fall, 1993, p. 325.
Kirkus Reviews, August 1, 2001, review of *Room on the Broom,* p. 1121.
Times (London, England), November, 1993, p. 45.
Los Angeles Times Book Review, May 2, 1993, p. 7.
Publishers Weekly, April 26, 1993, p. 78; June 21, 1999, review of *The Gruffalo,* p. 67; September 10, 2001, review of *Room on the Broom,* p. 92.
School Library Journal, April, 1993, p. 95; August, 1999, Marianne Saccardi, review of *The Gruffalo,* pp. 132-133; September, 2001, Pamela K. Bomboy, review of *Room on the Broom,* p. 187.*

*   *   *

DONOVAN, Josephine (Campbell) 1941-

PERSONAL: Born March 10, 1941, in Manila, Philippines; United States citizen; daughter of William N. (a physician) and Josephine (Devigne) Donovan. *Education:* Bryn Mawr College, A.B. (cum laude), 1962; University of Wisconsin—Madison, M.A., 1967, Ph.D, 1971.

ADDRESSES: Home—294 Dennett St., Portsmouth, NH 03801. *Office*—Department of English, 5752 Neville Hall, University of Maine, Orono, ME 04469-5752. *E-mail*—Josephine.Donovan@umit.maine.edu.

CAREER: University of Kentucky, Lexington, assistant professor in honors program, 1971-76; University of New Hampshire, Durham, coordinator of women's studies program, 1977-80; University of Tulsa, Tulsa, OK, visiting scholar, 1982; George Washington University, Washington, DC, visiting associate professor, 1983-84; University of Maine, Orono, professor of English, 1987—. Consultant to numerous university presses.

MEMBER: Modern Language Association of America, Women's Caucus for the Modern Languages, National Women's Studies Association.

AWARDS, HONORS: Outstanding academic book citation, *Choice* magazine, 1986, for *Feminist Theory: The Intellectual Traditions of American Feminism.*

WRITINGS:

(Editor and contributor) *Feminist Literary Criticism: Explorations in Theory,* University Press of Kentucky (Lexington, KY), 1975, revised edition, 1989.
Sarah Orne Jewett, Ungar (New York, NY), 1980, revised Internet edition, Cybereditions, 2001.
New England Local Color Literature: A Women's Tradition, Ungar (New York, NY), 1983.
Feminist Theory: The Intellectual Traditions, Ungar (New York, NY), 1985, 3rd edition, 2000.
(Editor, with Charles G. Waugh and Martin H. Greenberg, and author of introduction) Sarah Orne Jewett, *Best Stories of Sarah Orne Jewett,* illustrated by Peter Farrow, L. Tapley (Augusta, ME), 1988.
After the Fall: The Demeter-Persephone Myth in Wharton, Cather, and Glasgow, Pennsylvania State University Press (University Park, PA), 1989.
Gnosticism in Modern Literature: A Study of the Selected Works of Camus, Sartre, Hesse, and Kafka, Garland Publishing (New York, NY), 1990.
Uncle Tom's Cabin: Evil, Affliction, and Redemptive Love, Twayne (Boston, MA), 1991.
(Editor, with others) *Animals and Women: Feminist Theoretical Explorations,* Duke University Press (Durham, NC), 1995.
(Editor, with others, and contributor) *Beyond Animal Rights: A Feminist Caring Ethic for the Treatment of Animals,* Continuum (New York, NY), 1996.

(Editor and contributor) William N. Donovan, *P.O.W. in the Pacific: Memoirs of an American Doctor in World War II*, Scholarly Resources (Wilmington, DE), 1998.

Women and the Rise of the Novel, 1405-1726, St. Martin's Press (New York, NY), 1998.

Contributor to books, including *Aesthetics in Feminist Perspective*, edited by Hilde Hein and Carolyn Korsmeyer, Indiana University Press (Bloomington, IN), 1993; *Ecofeminism*, edited by Greta Gaard, Temple University Press (Philadelphia, PA), 1993; *The (Other) American Traditions*, edited by Joyce Warren, Rutgers University Press (New Brunswick, NJ), 1993; *History and Theory*, edited by Barbara Laslett and others, University of Chicago Press (Chicago, IL), 1997; and *Ecofeminist Literary Criticism*, edited by Greta Gaard and Patrick J. Murphy, University of Illinois Press (Urbana, IL), 1998. Contributor of articles and reviews to literature journals, including *American Literature, Critical Inquiry, Massachusetts Review, Signs,* and *Tulsa Studies in Women's Literature*.

WORK IN PROGRESS: A memoir; fiction.

BIOGRAPHICAL/CRITICAL SOURCES:

PERIODICALS

Choice, October, 2000, review of *Women and the Rise of the Novel, 1405-1726.*

*   *   *

D'ORSO, Michael 1953-

PERSONAL: Born October 12, 1953, in Portsmouth, VA; son of James and Claire D'Orso; divorced; children: Jamie (daughter). *Education:* College of William and Mary, B.A. (philosophy), 1975, M.A. (English), 1981. *Avocational interests:* Basketball, pocket billiards, movies, music.

ADDRESSES: Agent—Black Literary Agency, 156 Fifth Ave., Suite 608, New York, NY 10010.

CAREER: Author and journalist. *Commonwealth Magazine*, Richmond, VA, staff writer, 1981-84; *Virginian-Pilot*, Norfolk, VA, features writer, 1984-93.

AWARDS, HONORS: National Headliner Award citation; Penney-Missouri Prize; National Association of Black Journalists Award citation; three awards, Best Sports Stories, *The Sporting News;* International Reading Association Award; American Association of Sunday and Feature Editors award; two awards, American Academy of Family Physicians National Journalism Award; National Unity Awards in Media; fifteen awards, Virginia Press Association; Virginia College Stores Association Book of the Year, 1988, for *Somerset Homecoming;* Gustavus Myers Center for the Study of Human Rights citation, 1992, and *Library Journal*'s Best Book of the Year list, both 1992, for *The Cost of Courage;* Gold Medallion Book Award finalist, 1993, for *Rise and Walk;* Lillian Smith Book Award, American Library Association Notable Book of the Year, and New York Public Library "Books to Remember" list, all 1996, for *Like Judgment Day;* Christopher Award, Lillian Smith Book Award, *Booklist* "Top of the List" award, and *New York Times* Notable Book of the Year, all 1998, and Robert F. Kennedy Book Award, 1999, for *Walking with the Wind.*

WRITINGS:

(With Dorothy Spruill Redford) *Somerset Homecoming: Recovering a Lost Heritage*, Doubleday (New York, NY), 1988.

(As Mike D'Orso) *Fast Takes: Slices of Life through a Journalist's Eye*, Hampton Roads (Norfolk, VA), 1990.

(With Carl Elliott) *The Cost of Courage: The Journey of an American Congressman*, Doubleday (New York, NY), 1992.

(With Madeline Cartwright) *For the Children: Lessons from a Visionary Principal—How We Can Save Our Public Schools*, Doubleday (New York, NY), 1993.

(With Dennis Byrd) *Rise and Walk: The Trial and Triumph of Dennis Byrd*, HarperCollins (New York, NY), 1993.

(As Mike D'Orso) *Pumping Granite, and Other Portraits of People at Play*, Texas Tech University Press (Lubbock, TX), 1994.

(As Michael D'Orso) *Like Judgment Day: The Ruin and Redemption of a Town Called Rosewood*, Grosset/Putnam (New York, NY), 1996.

(With Dee Hakala) *Thin Is Just a Four-Letter Word*, Little, Brown (Boston, MA) 1997.

(With John Lewis) *Walking with the Wind: A Memoir of the Movement*, Simon & Schuster (New York, NY), 1998.

(With Leigh Steinberg) *Winning with Integrity: Getting What You're Worth without Selling Your Soul*, Villard (New York, NY), 1998.

(With Bill Phillips) *Body-for-Life: 12 Weeks to Mental and Physical Strength,* HarperCollins (New York, NY), 1999.

(With Joseph I. Lieberman) *In Praise of Public Life,* Simon & Schuster (New York, NY), 2000.

Contributor of articles to periodicals, including *Sports Illustrated, Fortune, Oxford American, Studies in American Fiction, Oklahoma Today, Reader's Digest, Self,* and *People Weekly.*

WORK IN PROGRESS: Darwin's Garden: the Hand of Man on the Galapagos Islands, for HarperCollins.

ADAPTATIONS: Rise and Walk: The Trial and Triumph of Dennis Byrd was adapted as a television movie by the Fox Television Network; *Like Judgment Day: The Ruin and Redemption of a Town Called Rosewood* was a source for a motion picture titled *Rosewood* by Warner Brothers, directed by John Singleton.

SIDELIGHTS: Journalist Michael D'Orso has coauthored several autobiographical works, as well as his *Like Judgment Day: The Ruin and Redemption of a Town Called Rosewood,* a 1996 account of the destruction of an African-American community in Florida in 1923. Among his collaborations are the 1993 volumes, *Rise and Walk: The Trial and Triumph of Dennis Byrd,* which chronicles the recovery of an injured professional football player, and *For the Children: Lessons from a Visionary Principal—How We Can Save Our Public Schools,* comprising the case study of a dedicated educator who transforms a troubled school into a community haven.

Somerset Homecoming: Recovering a Lost Heritage was written by D'Orso with Dorothy Spruill Redford, a single mother and social worker in Portsmouth, Virginia, who, inspired by the 1977 telecast of Alex Haley's *Roots,* set out on a journey to discover her own ancestral heritage. That journey, which would last nine years, led her to the remains of a decrepit plantation in North Carolina, where she found the records of the first slaves brought to that estate in the eighteenth century to plant rice: her ancestors. Redford's subsequent efforts to locate living descendants of those slaves and their owners and to bring them together for a reunion resulted in the 1986 event for which the book is named. Alex Haley, who wrote the book's foreword, called it "the best, most beautifully researched and most thoroughly presented black family history that I know of." Carl Senna,

writing in the *New York Times Book Review,* called it "moving . . . as much about a remarkable woman as about an American people."

In *The Cost of Courage: The Journey of an American Congressman,* coauthored with John F. Kennedy Profiles in Courage Award recipient Carl Elliott, Sr., D'Orso recounts Elliott's career from tenant farmer to rural lawyer to the U.S. Congress, where he participated in passing the National Defense of Education Act and served on the House rules committee during the Kennedy administration. Ultimately unseated by advocates of racial segregation in the charged political atmosphere of the civil rights movement in Alabama during the 1960s, Elliott retired from public life after an unsuccessful bid for the governor's office. In a *Publishers Weekly* review of *The Cost of Courage,* praise of the work centered on the narrative as "rich in portrayals of political figures, including the 'fearsome magnetism' of a ruthless [then-Governor George] Wallace." Alex Raksin of the *Los Angeles Times Book Review* called the book "refreshing . . . thanks to the richly evocative text shaped by co-writer Michael D'Orso."

For the Children, written by D'Orso and Madeline Cartwright, details Cartwright's experiences as an elementary school principal in Philadelphia's Strawberry Mansion district, an inner city neighborhood plagued by poverty and violence. Taking an active role in maintaining high standards of instruction, physical cleanliness, and parental involvement, Cartwright restored the school to a central position within the community. Reviewing *For the Children* in *Library Journal,* Arla Lindgren called it "a powerful book" which "should be required reading for politicians, sociologists, educators, and anyone interested in the future of this country."

Rise and Walk, which John Maxymuk of *Library Journal* characterized as "very moving and inspirational" was also published in 1993. This nonfiction work treats the recovery of New York Jets defensive lineman Dennis Byrd, who was paralyzed after colliding with another player during a football game in November, 1992. Informed that he would never walk again, Byrd relied on a combination of medical treatment, physical therapy, Christian faith, and a supportive family to overcome his injuries. According to Andrea Cooper in *New York Times Book Review,* Byrd's story is "undeniably gripping." The Fox Television Network made *Rise and Walk* into a movie of the same name, which premiered on the Fox network in January 1994.

Like Judgment Day documents the destruction of the town of Rosewood, Florida, in January, 1923. Incited by a white woman's accusation of rape, members of a white community murdered a number of black inhabitants of nearby Rosewood and drove others away from the area through repeated acts of arson and intimidation. With survivors scattered, the incident lay buried for six decades until the descendant of one of the victims began a personal investigation into the episode, a quest that would culminate in a successful damage suit against the State of Florida. Tracing both the perpetrators and the victims of the incident, D'Orso "vividly captures each figure and event, resisting the impulse to gloss over inconvenient material," according to reviewer Nell Irvin Painter in *Washington Post Book World.* A *Publishers Weekly* contributor called the account "a significant contribution to American history." A reviewer for *New Yorker* credited D'Orso for writing this book "with the insight of a serious novelist." The 1997 motion picture, *Rosewood,* directed by John Singleton, relied on D'Orso's book as a reference, and Singleton wrote an introduction to the paperback edition of the book, which was published as a tie-in to the Warner Brothers film.

D'Orso wrote *Walking with the Wind: A Memoir of the Movement* with John Lewis, an Atlanta congressman since 1986 when he defeated Julian Bond, and a leader in the civil rights movement of the 1960s. A *Kirkus Reviews* contributor called the autobiography "well-paced history fired by moral purpose and backed by the authority of hard time in the trenches." Mary Carroll, writing in *Booklist,* called it "a thoughtful, illuminating 'insider' history of the movement and its aftermath." *New Leader* reviewer Joseph Dolman expressed similar enthusiasm. "This book, beautifully written with Michael D'Orso, really tells two stories simultaneously," he wrote. "The first focuses on Lewis, a man of extraordinary character. . . . The second story is a chronicle of the civil rights movement through Lewis's eyes, and the theme here is more melancholy than triumphant. For inherent in the movement was a wicked paradox: The stronger it grew, the more fragile it became, and, for leaders like Lewis and the Reverend Martin Luther King Jr., the more distant were its goals."

Lewis, the son of Alabama sharecroppers, was educated in a one-room schoolhouse and was the victim of segregation in the Deep South. He later became chairman of the Student Nonviolent Coordinating Committee and spoke at the 1963 March on Washington. Lewis was arrested more than forty times and beaten in South Carolina and Alabama. He was knocked unconscious during the Montgomery Freedom Rides and suffered a fractured skull in Selma on Bloody Sunday at the hands of Alabama state troopers. Ten days after this infamous day, President Lyndon B. Johnson sent voting rights legislation to Congress, and it passed as the Voting

Rights Act of 1965. Lewis eventually lost his leadership positions to the more militant members of the movement, such as Stokely Carmichael. Lewis worked with Robert F. Kennedy and was in the Senator's room in the Ambassador Hotel when Kennedy was shot in the kitchen. In *Walking with the Wind,* Lewis stresses the importance of the churches and the clergy in the civil rights movement. A *USA Today* reviewer called his memoir "evocative and vividly personal."

A *Publishers Weekly* contributor wrote that Lewis "notes that people often take his quietness for meekness. His book . . . makes clear that such an impression is entirely inaccurate." Jack E. White said in *Time* that of the survivors of the civil rights movement, John Lewis "remains most committed to its original creed." "The strength of Lewis's powerful new book . . . is not only the witness he bears but also the simplicity of his voice," said Jon Meacham in *Newsweek. Library Journal* reviewer Thomas H. Ferrell felt Lewis's account of the lunch counter sit-ins in Nashville, Tennessee, in 1960 to be "the most valuable" of his reminiscences. "Lewis knows how far we've come—and senses how far we have to go," wrote Meacham in the *Washington Monthly.* "To his credit, Lewis has stayed the integrationist course as well, remaining faithful to the spirit of the March on Washington in a world more interested in Malcolm than in Martin. He understands, too, that the ground on which liberalism must fight now includes class as well as race: 'There hasn't been a time in America—certainly not since World War II—that the classes have been pushed as far apart as they are today.' He's right, and solutions will only result from the kind of interracial effort that characterized the movement of the 1950s and early 1960s, not the separatism that became so fashionable in the late '60s."

Leigh Steinberg and D'Orso collaborated on *Winning with Integrity: Getting What You're Worth without Selling Your Soul.* Steinberg is a top sports agent whose clients include Steve Young, Troy Aikman, Drew Bledsoe, Kordell Stewart, and Warren Moon. His contracts total more than two billion dollars, and he has maintained a high standard of ethics over his twenty-five years as an agent. His manner of doing business was a model for the film *Jerry Maguire.* Steinberg lists twelve points to follow in any negotiation, and includes his own experiences. A *Publishers Weekly* reviewer said that Steinberg's philosophy, "'that it is always more advantageous to act ethically, to take the high road,' is what makes his book a useful guide."

D'Orso coauthored Connecticut Senator Joseph I. Lieberman's *In Praise of Public Life.* Lieberman, chair of the Democratic Leadership Council, advised a reform of the political process and advocated more involvement by voters, especially younger voters. *Washington Monthly* contributor Phil Keisling declared that "by most accounts, Senator Joe Lieberman (D-Conn.) is a decent, devout, likable, and occasionally courageous politician. He's bucked his own party leaders on issues like the Persian Gulf War and cutting capital gains taxes. He's publicly upbraided Hollywood for its excessive taste for sex and violence; his pointed (and timely) September 1998 speech excoriating President Clinton for his 'disgraceful and immoral' conduct in the Lewinsky matter also received widespread kudos." Though Keisling recognized the senator's "sincerity, idealism, and native optimism," he went on to point out that "the problem is that when Lieberman finally gets around to discussing what his life as a U.S. senator is really like—in the book's second, less interesting half—the picture is resoundingly ambivalent. Yes, he's helped pass some worthy legislation, and he derives genuine satisfaction from some of his case work. But then there's having to deal with special interest groups, excessive partisanship, raising campaign cash, the long hours, commuting back and forth between Connecticut and Washington, and the struggles of juggling family, religious, and community obligations."

Keisling felt that Lieberman's book "underscores, yet again, the need for comprehensive campaign finance reform . . . a system of public financing that gives credible candidates the option of focusing exclusively on ideas . . . and not on cross-country fund-raising jaunts and multi-million dollar media buys that resort to empty rhetoric, distortions of opponents' records, and funny cartoon characters." *Library Journal* reviewer Michael A. Genovese said that in the book's final sections, Lieberman "returns to the theme of the value of public service, offering some important reform proposals." In *Publishers Weekly,* a reviewer concluded "It is refreshing to hear the point of view of someone who still finds politics a noble calling."

BIOGRAPHICAL/CRITICAL SOURCES:

PERIODICALS

Atlantic, November, 1988, Phoebe-Lou Adams, review of *Somerset Homecoming: Recovering a Lost Heritage,* p. 99.

Booklist, February 15, 1996, review of *Like Judgment Day: The Ruin and Redemption of a Town Called Rosewood,* pp. 984, 997; April 1, 1997, review of *Like Judgment Day,* p. 1285; April 15, 1998, Mary Carroll, review of *Walking with the Wind: A Memoir of the Movement,* p. 1355; September 1, 1998, Wes Lukowsky, review of *Winning with Integrity: Getting What You're Worth without Selling Your Soul,* p. 54; January 1, 1999, review of *Walking with the Wind,* p. 775.

Journal of American History, September, 1999, Kathryn L. Nasstrom, review of *Walking with the Wind,* p. 849.

Journal of Southern History, February, 2000, John Salmond, review of *Walking with the Wind,* p. 167.

Kirkus Reviews, April 15, 1998, review of *Walking with the Wind.*

Kliatt, May, 1997, review of *Like Judgment Day,* p. 28.

Library Journal, June 15, 1993, pp. 79, 82; October 1, 1993, p. 100; March 15, 1996, review of *Like Judgment Day,* p. 89; May 15, 1998, Thomas H. Ferrell, review of *Walking with the Wind,* p. 100; March 1, 2000, Michael A. Genovese, review of *In Praise of Public Life,* p. 110.

Los Angeles Times, January 26, 1992.

New Leader, June 29, 1998, Joseph Dolman, review of *Walking with the Wind,* p. 20.

Newsweek, June 1, 1998, Jon Meacham, "A Storm in the Streets," p. 69.

New Yorker, June 17, 1996, review of *Like Judgment Day,* p. 100.

New York Review of Books, June 25, 1998, Garry Wills, review of *Walking with the Wind,* p. 27.

New York Times, December 28, 1996, Dinitia Smith, "Town's 1923 Horror Haunts a Book and Two Films," p. 12.

New York Times Book Review, November 13, 1988, Carl Senna, review of *Somerset Homecoming,* p. 35; October 3, 1993, Andrea Cooper, review of *Rise and Walk: The Trial and Triumph of Dennis Byrd,* p. 25; November 14, 1993, John Allen Paulos, review of *For the Children: Lessons from a Visionary Principal—How We Can Save Our Public Schools,* p. 15; September 24, 2000, Douglas A. Sylva, review of *In Praise of Public Life,* p. 23.

Publishers Weekly, January 6, 1992, p. 60; January 1, 1996, review of *Like Judgment Day,* p. 65; April 13, 1998, review of *Walking with the Wind,* p. 57; August 3, 1998, review of *Winning with Integrity,* p. 69; January 31, 2000, review of *In Praise of Public Life,* p. 96.

Reference & Research Book News, March, 1995, review of *Pumping Granite and Other Portraits of People at Play,* p. 18.

Sojourners, November, 1999, review of *Walking with the Wind,* p. 56.

Time, June 22, 1998, Jack E. White, review of *Walking with the Wind,* p. 76.

USA Today, December 2, 1999, review of *Walking with the Wind.*

Voice of Youth Advocates, December, 1997, review of *Like Judgment Day,* p. 305.

Washington Monthly, May, 1998, John Meacham, review of *Walking with the Wind,* p. 38; March, 2000, Phil Keisling, review of *In Praise of Public Life,* p. 44.

Washington Post, October 31, 1993, Sara Mosle, review of *For the Children,* p. ER15.

Washington Post Book World, February 4, 1996, review of *Like Judgment Day,* pp. 3, 6.

*   *   *

DOUGLASS, Sara
    See WARNEKE, Sara

*   *   *

DUNNING, John H(arry) 1927-

PERSONAL: Born June 26, 1927, in Sandy, Bedfordshire, England; son of John Murray (a Baptist minister) and Anne Florence (Baker) Dunning; married Ida Teresa Bellamy, 1948 (divorced, 1975); married Christine Mary Brown, August 4, 1975; children: (first marriage) one son. *Education:* University College, London, B.S. (with first-class honors), 1951; University of Southampton, Ph.D., 1957.

ADDRESSES: Office—Department of Economics, University of Reading, Whiteknights Park, Reading RG6 2AH, England; fax: 44-1491-628902.

CAREER: University of Southampton, Southampton, England, lecturer, then senior lecturer in economics, 1952-64; University of Reading, Reading, England, Foundation Professor of Economics, 1964-74, head of department, 1964-87, Esmee Fairbairn Professor of International Investment and Business Studies, 1975-87, ICI Professor of International Business, 1987-92, professor emeritus of international business, 1992—. Visiting professor at University of Western Ontario and University of California, Berkeley, 1968-69, Boston University, 1976, Stockholm School of Economics, 1978, and University of Montreal, 1980; Walker Ames Professor of Economics at University of Washington, Seattle, 1981; Seth Boyden Distinguished Professor of International Management, 1987, and State of New Jersey Professor of International Business, 1989-99, both

Rutgers University. Chair, Economists Advisory Group Ltd.; member, South East Economic Planning Council, 1965-69, and Chemical Economic Development Committee, 1970-77; adviser to committee on invisible exports; consultant to international agencies, national governments, and business enterprises, including United Nations, World Bank, and Department of Trade and Industry (United Kingdom).

MEMBER: Academy of International Business (fellow; president, 1986-88), International Trade and Finance Association (president, 1994), Royal Economic Society (member of council, 1969-73).

AWARDS, HONORS: D.Phil., University of Uppsala, 1975, Universidad Autonoma de Madrid, 1990, and University of Antwerp, 1997.

WRITINGS:

American Investment in British Manufacturing Industry, Allen & Unwin (London, England), 1958, Arno (New York, NY), 1976.

(With C. J. Thomas) *British Industry: Change and Development in the Twentieth Century,* Hutchinson (London, England), 1961.

Economic Planning and Town Expansion: A Case Study of Basingstoke, Workers Education Association, 1963.

(With P. G. Hall and others) *A New Town in Mid-Wales,* H.M.S.O. (London, England), 1966.

(With D. Lees and others) *The Economics of Advertising,* Hutchinson (London, England), 1967.

The Role of American Investment in the United Kingdom Economy, Political and Economic Planning, 1969.

Studies in International Investment, Allen & Unwin (London, England), 1970.

(With E. V. Morgan) *The City of London: An Economic Study,* Allen & Unwin (London, England), 1971.

Problems of the Small Firm in Raising External Finance, H.M.S.O. (London, England), 1971.

Insurance and the Economy, Institute of Economic Affairs, (London, England) 1971.

The Location of International Firms in an Enlarged E.E.C., Manchester Statistical Society (Manchester, England), 1972.

(With R. D. Pearce) *Profitability and Performance of the World's Leading Companies,* Financial Times (London, England), 1975.

U.S. Industry in Britain, Wilton House (Aldershot, England), 1976.

(With T. Houston) *British Industry Abroad,* Financial Times (London, England), 1976.

United Kingdom Enterprises in Manufacturing Industry in LDC's and Their Effect on Trade Flows, United Nations Conference on Trade and Development, 1977.

(With G. Norman) *Factors Influencing the Location of Offices of Multinational Enterprises,* Location of Offices Bureau, 1979.

(With J. Stopford and K. Haverich) *The World Directory of Multinational Enterprises,* Macmillan (London, England), 1980.

International Production and the Multinational Enterprise, Allen & Unwin (London, England), 1981.

(With R. D. Pearce) *The World's Largest Industrial Enterprises,* Gower Press (Aldershot, England), 1981.

(With M. Burstall and A. Lake) *The Impact of Multinational Enterprises on National Scientific and Technological Capacity: The Pharmaceutical Industry,* Organization for Economic Cooperation and Development, 1981.

(With M. McQueen) *Transnational Corporations in the International Tourist Industry,* United Nations Center on Transnational Corporations, 1981.

(With John Black) *International Capital Movements,* Macmillan (London, England), 1982.

(With others) *The World Directory of Multinational Enterprises, 1982-83,* Gale (Detroit, MI), 2nd edition, 1982-1983.

(With others) *The World's Largest Industrial Enterprises, 1962-1983,* St. Martin's Press (New York, NY), 1985.

Japanese Participation in British Industry, Croom Helm (Beckenham, England), 1986.

Decision-making Structures in U.S. and Japanese Manufacturing Affiliates in the U.K.: Some Similarities and Contrasts, International Labour Office (London, England), 1986.

IRM Directory of Statistics of International Investment and Production, New York University Press, 1987.

Multinationals, Technology, and Competitiveness, Unwin Hyman (London, England), 1988.

Explaining International Production, Unwin Hyman (London, England), 1988.

Multinational Technology and Competitiveness, Unwin Hyman (London, England), 1988.

Transnational Corporations and the Growth of Services: Some Conceptual and Theoretical Issues, United Nations, 1989.

(With others) *Foreign Privatization in Central & Eastern Europe,* Central and Eastern European Privatization Network, 1993.

Globalisation: The Challenge for National Economic Regimes, Economic and Social Research Institute (Dublin, Ireland), 1993.

Multinational Enterprises and the Global Economy, Addison Wesley (Wokingham, England), 1993.

The Globalisation of Business, Routledge (London, England), 1993.

Alliance Capitalism and Global Business, Routledge (London, England), 1997.

American Investment in British Manufacturing Industry, Routledge (London, England), revised edition, 1998.

Global Capitalism at Bay, Routledge (London, England), 2001.

EDITOR, EXCEPT AS NOTED

The Multinational Enterprise, Allen & Unwin (London, England), 1971.

International Investment: Selected Readings, Penguin (London, England), 1972.

Readings in International Investment, Penguin (London, England), 1972.

Economic Analysis and the Multinational Enterprise, Allen & Unwin (London, England), 1974.

Multinational Enterprises, Economic Structure, and International Competitiveness, Wiley (Chichester, England), 1985.

(With others) *Economic Interdependence,* St. Martin's Press (New York, NY), 1987.

(With others) *Multinationals and the European Community,* Basil Blackwell (London, England), 1988.

(With others) *Structural Change in the World Economy,* Routledge (London, England), 1992.

The Theory of Transnational Corporations, Routledge (London, England), 1993.

(General editor) *Co-operative Forms of Transnational Corporation Activity,* United Nations Transnational Corporations and Management Division (London, England), 1994.

(General editor) *Transnational Corporations and Human Resources,* Routledge (London, England), 1994.

(General editor) *Market Structure and Industrial Performance,* Routledge (London, England), 1994.

(General editor) *Transnational Corporations: Transfer Pricing and Taxation,* Routledge (London, England), 1994.

(With others) *The New Globalism and Developing Countries,* United Nations (New York, NY), 1997.

(With others) *Foreign Direct Investment and Governments: Catalysts for Economic Restructuring,* Routledge (London, England), 1998.

Globalization, Trade, and Foreign Direct Investment, Elsevier (New York, NY), 1998.

(With others) *Structural Change and Cooperation in the Global Economy,* Edward Elgar (New York, NY), 1999.

Governments, Globilization, and International Business, Oxford University Press (New York, NY), 1999.

Regions, Globalization, and the Knowledge-based Economy, Oxford University Press (New York, NY), 2000.

Founding editor of *Business Ratios;* member of editorial board of *Journal of International Business Studies, Journal of Business Research, Global Economy Quarterly, International Business Review,* and *World Development.*

OTHER

Contributor to books, including *Economic Integration in Europe,* Weidenfeld & Nicolson (London, England), 1969; *Foreign Investment: The Experience of Host Countries,* Praeger (New York, NY), 1970; *North American and Western European Policies,* Macmillan (London, England), 1970; *Recent Research on the Internationalisation of Business,* Almqvist & Wiksell (Stockholm, Sweden), 1979; *Transnational Corporations and China's Open-Door Policy,* Heath (Lexington, MA), 1988; *Transferimenti di Tecnologie e Finanziamenti ai Paesi in Via di Sviluppo,* Franco Angeli (Milan, Italy), 1989; *Services in World Economic Growth,* Mohr (Tübingen, Germany), 1989; *International Trade: Existing Problems and Prospective Solutions,* Taylor & Francis (London, England), 1989; *Multinationals and Europe 1992,* Routledge (London, England), 1990; *The Nature of the Transnational Firm,* Routledge, 1991; *Europe and America 1992: US-EC Economic Relations in the Single European Market,* Manchester University Press (Manchester, England), 1991; *Multinationals in the New Europe and Global Trade,* Springer-Verlag (New York, NY), 1992; *Comparative Work Practices of Multinational Firms,* Oxford University Press (New York, NY), 1993; *The Globalisation of Professional Services,* Routledge, 1993; *Globalization, Foreign Direct Investment, and Technology Transfer,* Routledge, 1998; *The Americanisation of European Business,* Routledge, 1998; *The Globalization of Multinational Enterprise Activity and Economic Development,* Macmillan, 2000; and to *Collier's Encyclopedia.* Also, contributor of over two hundred articles to business and economic journals.

SIDELIGHTS: John H. Dunning told *CA:* "I am one of the pioneers in the study of international direct investment and the multinational enterprise. I have maintained a lively interest in the subject since the mid-1950s. I am equally at home with theoretical issues as policy-oriented research, and am currently advising the United Nations Conference on Trade and Development (UNCTAD) on matters relating to multinational enterprises. I describe myself as a 'moderate' in my political attitude to multinational enterprises: I believe strongly that they can make an important contribution to economic development, particularly those of advanced developing countries, but that it is the responsibility of governments to manage their own affairs so that the net benefits of foreign direct investment can be maximized. I believe also that governments and multinational enterprises are learning to live with each other and that this augurs well for international economic relations in the 1990s. More recently, I have become interested in, and writing on, the moral imperatives of (sustainable) global capitalism."

*   *   *

DUONG, Thu Huong 1947-

PERSONAL: Born in 1947, in Thai Binh, Vietnam; daughter of Duong Dinh Chau (a radio specialist and North Vietnamese military officer) and Ngo Thuy Cham (a primary schoolteacher); married, 1968 (divorced, 1981); children: Minh (son), Ha (daughter). *Education:* Cultural Theory College, graduated, 1968.

ADDRESSES: Home—Hanoi, Vietnam. *Agent*—c/o Phan Huydong, 82 Rue Prosper Legoute, 92160 Antony, France.

CAREER: Cultural activities guide in Vietnam, until 1975; Hanoi Feature Film Studio, Hanoi, Vietnam, screenwriter, beginning 1975.

MEMBER: Association of Vietnamese Filmmakers.

AWARDS, HONORS: Paradise of the Blind was shortlisted for the Prix Femina Etranger, 1992; Hammett-Hellman Grant for Persecuted Writers, 1992; Chevalier des Arts et des Lettres, 1994.

WRITINGS:

Paradise of the Blind, translated by Phan Huy Duong and Nina McPherson, Morrow (New York, NY), 1993.

Novel without a Name, translated by Phan Huy Duong and Nina McPherson, Morrow (New York, NY), 1994.

Memories of a Pure Spring, translated by Phan Huy Duong and Nina McPherson, Hyperion East, 2000.

Author of three other novels written in Vietnamese, some of which have been translated into French, including *Au-dela des illusions,* 1997.

SIDELIGHTS: Dissident and novelist Duong Thu Huong is among the most popular writers in contemporary Vietnam even though her writings are officially banned in her homeland. Her widely praised novels, which include *Paradise of the Blind* and *Novel without a Name,* were first translated into French for France's thriving Vietnamese expatriate community and later into English. Her works explore not only the political realities of post-war Vietnam, but also the quest to find meaning in daily life through art and love. Recognized internationally for her contribution to literature, Duong was awarded France's Chevalier des Arts et des Lettres in 1994. After a bitter battle to obtain a passport to attend the awards ceremony, Duong chose to return to Vietnam rather than seek political asylum in France. "I want to stay here to insult those in power," she told Brian Eads of *Reader's Digest.*

Born in 1947, Duong grew up the daughter of a North Vietnamese military official, and she herself worked for several years as a member of a performing arts group that entertained Vietcong troops at the front. Now a resident of Hanoi, Duong is a favorite, albeit underground, writer among the poor, but highly literate, Vietnamese. The author's frequently unflattering fictional portrayals of Vietnamese Communist Party functionaries have made her the target of official harassment, arrest, and incarceration in her native country. She was expelled from the Vietnamese Communist Party in 1989 and arrested in 1991 for attempting to "smuggle 'reactionary' documents out of the country," according to Philip Shenon in the *New York Times.* "The documents turned out to be her own writings." Duong subsequently spent seven months in prison, and was released only after the collapse of the Soviet Union's Communist government and a campaign by Amnesty International.

In *Paradise of the Blind,* which in 1993 became the first of her works to appear in English, Duong creates a disastrously divided family. Hang, the novel's protagonist, is the daughter of a teacher who was financially ruined when communists seized his farmland. Hang's mother works as a street vendor, living a life of service to her brother, the Communist Party official who drove Hang's father to eventual suicide. Hang's aunt—the sister of her father—has cannily managed to win back the family land and lives comfortably, although through somewhat illicit means. The title of the work refers to the author's intimation "that humankind has invented a Marxist paradise which, though cleverly made attractive and appetizing, is reserved solely for 'blind people,'" wrote *World Literature Today* reviewer Dinh-Hoa Nguyen. The novel recounts Hang's personal struggle for identity and purpose as she is torn between conflicting family and political loyalties. Much as Laura Esquivel did with Latin cuisine in her novel *Like Water for Chocolate,* Duong weaves a culinary portrait of Vietnam throughout the text of her book; there is even a glossary at the end of *Paradise of the Blind* to help readers further understand the making of such Vietnamese delicacies as blood pudding. Dan Duffy of the *Nation* stated that *Paradise of the Blind* is "a book to read for the story and remember for the food."

Paradise of the Blind won high praise from reviewers. "Duong Thu Huong is a social panoramist who writes with a tight focus on individual consciousness and personal relations," maintained Duffy. In the *New York Times,* Herbert Mitgang declared that what makes Duong's novel unique for American audiences is the fact "that it humanizes a Vietnamese family and turns its members into individuals. . . . *Paradise of the Blind* describes the problems of ordinary people and the contradictions of political reform openly." Marilyn B. Young, critiquing *Paradise of the Blind* for the *Women's Review of Books,* lauded the "political allegory disguised as a family chronicle" and judged it "a difficult, compelling, not always very attractive novel about the nature and limits of sacrifice." A *Publishers Weekly* contributor called the book a "staunchly unsentimental, evocative novel," a "narrative rich in detail and free of cliche."

In 1994, Duong's second work in English translation appeared. In *Novel without a Name,* Duong portrays Vietnam's long and bloody war for independence and socialism. The book's disillusioned protagonist, Quan, has spent ten years as a soldier in the North Vietnamese Army during its conflict with Western-financed South Vietnamese troops and American forces. Unlike the U.S. soldiers, who were drafted for a year's service and then, if lucky, returned home alive, the Vietnamese combatant can imagine no such end; his tour of duty in the fight against imperialism will last until the bitter end. Quan recounts the madness and near-starvation he and his fellow soldiers encountered in the jungle, as well as the ways in which they outwitted the stubborn, often naïve American enemy with no experience in jungle-based guerrilla conflict. In a brief respite from the fighting, Quan journeys back to his village, en route encountering the many faces of hypocrisy that his country's battle for sovereignty wears.

Like *Paradise of the Blind, Novel without a Name* also won praise from reviewers, although Michiko Kakutani of the *New York Times* faulted some of its lesser characters as bordering "on stereotype or caricature, a problem that is not helped [by a translation that] often feels stilted and clichéd." Nevertheless, Kakutani commended Duong's characterization of Quan as "a sort of resolutely non-mythic Ulysses," and pointed out that the book "underscores the commonality of the war experience." Critiquing *Novel without a Name* for the *New York Times Book Review,* Nicholas Proffitt asserted that Duong "reminds us that war grants no immunity, that it is the most universal of experiences, a cross-cultural disaster that leaves none of its participants unscarred."

Memories of a Pure Spring continues to mine the territory of Duong's previous novels. Taking place primarily after the triumph of the Communists, the story follows Hung, a composer who rises to fame during the war with America but who is ruined, physically and spiritually, by the Marxist bureaucrats he once fought for. Hung's wife, Suong, also achieves renown as a singer during the couple's tours with a state-sponsored cultural troupe to military encampments. Afterward, Hung is captured on a boat that is leaving Vietnam and falsely accused of trying to flee the country. He is sent to a "re-education camp," and is released as a broken man, afflicted with venereal disease and addicted to opium. Suong continues to sing and tries to keep the family together as long as she can, but eventually she attempts suicide. Hung, having lost all faith and pleasure in the music he once loved, recognizes that he can do nothing but play "the role of the dead man."

As with Duong's previous novels, critics applauded her unflinching depiction of life in post-war Vietnam. Duong "deftly employs flashbacks, multiple points of view and a haunting interplay of narrative and interior voices to construct her sadly beautiful tale," wrote Philip Gambone in the *New York Times Book Review.* Richard Bernstein, also writing in the *New York Times Book Review,* said the book is more than just a political statement. "One reads it certainly for its politics," Bernstein wrote, "but even more for the depth and complex-

ity of its characters who strive to define themselves in a world that still puts everything and everybody in one or another category of ideology and national aspiration."

Many reviewers also praised Duong's language and her exploration of the themes of beauty and art. Donna Seaman of *Booklist* called the novel "a work of exceptional lyricism. . . . [that] skillfully illuminates the human spirit's capacity for brutality and compassion, betrayal and beauty." Noting a scene in which a character carefully tends to his injured hand moments before hanging himself, Terry McCarthy of *Time* praised the book's "exquisite writing that constantly hovers on the border of pain, dark irony that threatens to weep."

The plot of *Memories of a Pure Spring* has many parallels to Duong's own life, which are outlined in an appendix to the novel. She herself was an organizer of cultural events for the troops during the early 1970s, and much has been written about her imprisonment in 1991. While her works are still banned in Vietnam, she continues to be outspoken about the government, who are, she told a *People* interviewer, "a bunch of liars."

Duong once told *CA:* "My official job in the late sixties was to guide mass cultural activities; namely, to organize amateur art units (song and dance, pantomime) for mass entertainment. After graduating from the Cultural Theory College in 1968, I carried out this task in Quang Binh, the hardest-hit province in the north during the air war, where I served army and 'shock youth' units. At that time, the spirit of this work was epitomized by the slogan 'Let's drown the explosion of bombs by our singing.' After 1975, I came back to Hanoi and worked as a screenwriter at the Hanoi Feature Film Studio.

"I never intended to become a writer. As I always tell others, it just happened to me, because of the pain. Pain is the precise word. My novels are cries of pain. My work is inseparable from the society in which I have lived, the country, Vietnam, that has forged me. As an adolescent, I did not like literature. I was fond of free gymnastics, uneven parallel bars, ping pong. I enjoyed those games very much until I was fourteen years of age. At fifteen, because of my family's financial difficulties, I had to leave my playground. I went to school to become a government employee.

"I served my fatherland devotedly like a soldier, an exemplary citizen. During that time, I hoarded my feelings, impressions, ideas. I weighed my reflections, recorded the different fates of my compatriots. This became an obsession for me, and eventually, I had no other alternative but to take up my pen. I share the view of Henry Miller, which I read in a translated version as 'To write is to emit toxin.'

"My personal struggle—and it is one shared by many others—is to gain respect for my rights as a free citizen, here in my own country. Writing is the way I free myself, the way I make myself a free woman. I could have gone to the United States in 1980 at the invitation of my relatives, but I wanted to stay in Vietnam. I have decided to devote my life to writing and making films about my country. If they decide to put me in prison again, I'm ready."

BIOGRAPHICAL/CRITICAL SOURCES:

PERIODICALS

Booklist, February 1, 2000, Donna Seaman, review of *Memories of a Pure Spring*, p. 1007.

Nation, April 12, 1993, Dan Duffy, review of *Paradise of the Blind*, pp. 491-494.

New Yorker, June 7, 1993, p. 113.

New York Review of Books, September 21, 1995, pp.58-62; May 25, 2000, Jonathan Mirsky, review of *Memories of a Pure Spring*, p. 54.

New York Times, May 19, 1993, p. C19; April 12, 1994, p. A4; May 30, 1995, p. C15.

New York Times Book Review, February 12, 1995, pp. 13-14; January 30, 2000, Philip Gambone, review of *Memories of a Pure Spring;* February 9, 2000, Richard Bernstein, "After the War Is Won, Another Struggle Begins."

People, May 1, 2000, "Enemy of the State: Novelist Duong Thu Huong Rails against Her Country's Communist Rulers," p. 99.

Publishers Weekly, January 18, 1993, p. 451; December 19, 1994, p. 45.

Reader's Digest, October, 1998, Brian Eads, "She Dares to Live Free: Vietnam's Most Famous Novelist Writes What Others Only Think," p. 158.

Time, March 20, 2000, Terry McCarthy, "A Tale of Disillusionment: Duong Thu Huong's Latest Novel Drifts Gracefully through a Vietnam Plagued by Soulless Ideologues," p. 48.

Women's Review of Books, July, 1993, Marilyn B. Young, review of *Paradise of the Blind*, p. 24.

World Literature Today, spring, 1992, p. 410; summer, 1997, Bettina L. Knapp, review of *Au-dela des illusions*, p. 656.*

E

EARLE, Sylvia A(lice) 1935-

PERSONAL: Born August 30, 1935, in Gibbstown, NJ; daughter of Lewis Read and Alice Freas (maiden name Richie) Earle; married Jack Taylor (a naturalist), c. 1957 (divorced); married Giles W. Mead (a scientist), December, 1966 (divorced); married Graham Hawkes (an engineer), May, 1986 (divorced); children: (first marriage) Elizabeth, John; (second marriage) Gale. *Education:* St. Petersburg Junior College, A.A., 1952; Florida State University, B.S., 1955; Duke University, M.A., 1956, Ph.D., 1966.

ADDRESSES: Home—12812 Skyline Boulevard, Oakland, CA 94619-3125. *Office*—c/o National Geographic Society, 1145 17th St. NW, Washington, DC 20036-4688.

CAREER: Research marine biologist and oceanographer. Cape Haze Marine Laboratories, Sarasota, FL, resident director, 1966; Radcliffe Institute, research scholar; Farlow Herbarium, Harvard University, Cambridge, MA, research fellow, 1975; California Academy of Sciences, research biologist and curator, 1976; Natural History Museum, University of California, Berkeley, fellow, 1976; National Oceanic and Atmospheric Administration (NOAA), chief scientist, 1990-92; Deep Ocean Technology and Deep Ocean Engineering, Oakland, CA, founder, president, and CEO, 1981-90; National Geographic Society's Sustainable Seas Expeditions (SSE), explorer-in-residence, 1998—.

MEMBER: World Wildlife Fund (trustee, 1976-82), World Wildlife Fund, International, (trustee 1979-81), Charles A. Lindbergh Fund (president, 1990—), Center for Marine Conservation, (trustee, 1992—), Perry Foundation, (chairman, 1993—), International Union for Conservation of Nature, Woods Hole Oceanographic Institute, National Advancement Commission on Oceans and Atmosphere, International Phycological Society, Phycological Society of America, American Society of Ichthyologists and Herpetologists, American Institute of Biological Scientists, British Phycological Society, Ecology Society of America, International Society of Plant Taxonomists, Explorer's Club.

AWARDS, HONORS: Conservation Service Award, United States Department of Interior, 1970; Woman of the Year, Los Angeles Times, 1970; Boston Sea Rovers Award, 1972 and 1979; Nogi Award, Underwater Society of America, 1976; Order of Golden Ark, Prince, Netherlands, 1980; Lowell Thomas Award, Explorer's Club, 1980; Scientist of the Year, California Museum of Science and Industry, 1981; Conservation Service Award, California Academy of Science, 1989; David B. Stone Medal, New England Aquarium, 1989; gold medalist, Society of Women Geographers, Radcliffe College, 1990; Pacon International Award, 1992; Directors Award, Natural Resources County Administration, 1992; named one of *Time* magazine's Hero for the Planet, 1998. Fellow, AAAS, Marine Technological Society, California Academy of Scientists. Honorary degrees conferred from Monterey Institute of International Studies, 1990; Ball State University, 1991; George Washington University, 1992; D.Sc., Duke University, 1993; Ripon College, 1994; and University of Connecticut, 1994.

WRITINGS:

Humbrella, a New Red Alga of Uncertain Taxonomic Position from the Juan Fernandez Islands, Harvard University Press (Cambridge, MA), 1969.

(With Joyce Redemsky Young) *Siphonoclathrus, A New Genus of Chlorophyta (Siphonales: Codiaceae) from Panama,* Harvard University Press (Cambridge, MA), 1972.

(Editor with Bruce C. Collette) *Results of the Tektite Program: Ecology of Coral Reef Fishes,* Natural History Museum (Los Angeles, CA), 1972.

(Editor with Robert J. Lavenberg) *Results of the Tektite Program, Coral Reef Invertebrates and Plants,* Natural History Museum (Los Angeles, CA), 1975.

(With Al Giddings) *Exploring the Deep Frontier: The Adventure of Man in the Sea,* National Geographic Press (Washington, DC), 1980.

Sea Change: A Message of the Oceans, Putnam (New York, NY), 1995.

Dive!: My Adventures in the Deep Frontier, National Geographic Society (Washington, DC), 1999.

Hello, Fish, photographs by Wolcott Henry, National Geographic Society (Washington, DC), 1999.

(With Wolcott Henry) *Wild Ocean: America's Park under the Sea,* National Geographic Society (Washington, DC), 1999.

(With Ellen J. Prager) *The Oceans,* McGraw-Hill (New York, NY), 2000.

Sea Critters, photographs by Wolcott Henry, National Geographic Society (Washington, DC), 2000.

SIDELIGHTS: Sylvia A. Earle is a former chief scientist of the National Oceanic and Atmospheric Administration and a leading American oceanographer. She was among the first underwater explorers to make use of modern self-contained underwater breathing apparatus (SCUBA) gear, and identified many new species of marine life. With her former husband, Graham Hawkes, Earle designed and built a submersible craft that could dive to unprecedented depths of three thousand feet.

Sylvia Alice Reade Earle was born in Gibbstown, New Jersey on August 30, 1935, the daughter of Lewis Reade and Alice Freas (Richie) Earle. Both parents had an affinity for the outdoors and encouraged her love of nature after the family moved to the west coast of Florida. As Earle explained to *Scientific American,* "I wasn't shown frogs with the attitude 'yuk,' but rather my mother would show my brothers and me how beautiful they are and how fascinating it was to look at their gorgeous golden eyes." However, Earle pointed out, while her parents totally supported her interest in biology, they also wanted her to get her teaching credentials and learn to type, "just in case."

She enrolled at Florida State University and received her bachelor of science degree in the spring of 1955. That fall she entered the graduate program at Duke University and obtained her master's degree in botany the following year. The Gulf of Mexico became a natural laboratory for Earle's work. Her master's dissertation, a detailed study of algae in the Gulf, is a project she still follows. She has collected more than twenty thousand samples. "When I began making collections in the Gulf, it was a very different body of water than it is now—the habitats have changed. So I have a very interesting baseline," she noted in *Scientific American.*

In 1966, Earle received her Ph.D. from Duke University and immediately accepted a position as resident director of the Cape Haze Marine Laboratories in Sarasota, Florida. The following year, she moved to Massachusetts to accept dual roles as research scholar at the Radcliffe Institute and research fellow at the Farlow Herbarium, Harvard University, where she was named researcher in 1975. Earle moved to San Francisco in 1976 to become a research biologist at and curator of the California Academy of Sciences. That same year, she also was named a fellow in botany at the Natural History Museum, University of California, Berkeley.

Although her academic career could have kept her totally involved, her first love was the sea and the life within it. In 1970, Earle and four other oceanographers lived in an underwater chamber for fourteen days as part of the government-funded Tektite II Project, designed to study undersea habitats. Fortunately, technology played a major role in Earle's future. A self-contained underwater breathing apparatus had been developed in part by Jacques Cousteau as recently as 1943, and refined during the time Earle was involved in her scholarly research. SCUBA equipment was not only a boon to recreational divers, but it also dramatically changed the study of marine biology. Earle was one of the first researchers to don a mask and oxygen tank and observe the various forms of plant and animal habitats beneath the sea, identifying many new species of each. She called her discovery of undersea dunes off the Bahama Islands "a simple Lewis and Clark kind of observation." But, she said in *Scientific American,* "the presence of dunes was a significant insight into the formation of the area."

In 1979, Earle made the deepest dive ever made without a cable to the surface when she went down 1,250 feet about six miles off the coast of Oahu, Hawaii. This record-breaking dive earned her the title "Her Deepness" from colleagues. Outfitted in a "Jim suit," named after the first person to wear it, Jim Jarratt, she plunged into the ocean going at times more than one hundred feet per minute strapped to the front of a submarine. She told Peggy Orenstein in the *New York Times Magazine,* "When I got to the bottom, I stepped off and walked on the ocean floor for two and a half hours. It was a nice parallel: That's about how long Buzz Aldrin and Neil Armstrong were on the moon. It took them longer to get there, of course, and it cost more. But I had the fun of seeing all kinds of critters out there."

Though Earle set the unbelievable record of freely diving to a depth of 1,250 feet, there were serious depth limitations to SCUBA diving. To study deep-sea marine life would require the assistance of a submersible craft that could dive far deeper. Earle and her former husband, British-born engineer Graham Hawkes, founded Deep Ocean Technology, Inc., and Deep Ocean Engineering, Inc., in 1981, to design and build submersibles. Using a paper napkin, Earle and Hawkes rough-sketched the design for a submersible they called *Deep Rover,* which would serve as a viable tool for biologists. "In those days we were dreaming of going to thirty-five thousand feet," she told *Discover* magazine. "The idea has always been that scientists couldn't be trusted to drive a submersible by themselves because they'd get so involved in their work they'd run into things."

Deep Rover took its first voyage in 1984 and soon set the record for the world's deepest solo dive when it went to 3,000 feet with Hawkes aboard. Later, Earle took it down to that depth as well. Since then, several scientists, including Earle, have used the vessel for exploration. The company's most successful product, though, was a remote submersible called the *Phantom* used for inspecting nuclear reactors, dams, oil rigs and pipelines; drug interdiction; mine detection; and other exploration.

In 1990, Earle was named the first woman to serve as chief scientist at the National Oceanic and Atmospheric Association (NOAA), the $1.5-billion agency that conducts underwater research, oversees the weather service, manages fisheries, and responds to marine spills. Eighteen months later, though, she left because she felt she could do more on her own. She also admitted she might have irked some in the fishing industry because of her position against eating sea creatures. While there, though, she also became involved in assessing the damage done to the Persian Gulf after massive oil spills there when Iraq destroyed several hundred Kuwaiti wells.

After leaving the NOAA Earle in 1992, continued work on "Ocean Everest," a project she had started with Hawkes. She hoped to visit the deepest spot on the ocean floor—the marine equivalent of climbing to the summit of Mount Everest. In 1998, she began serving as an explorer-in-residence for the National Geographic Society, serving a five-year stint as leader of their Sustainable Seas Expeditions.

During this time, Earle used a new, more maneuverable submarine to study the deepest waters of the twelve national marine sanctuaries. She also used this position to step up her efforts on educating the public about overfishing and pollution of the seas, becoming an ardent spokesperson on maintaining the health of the oceans. She pointed out to Josie Glausiusz in *Discover,* "More than 70 percent of the oxygen in the atmosphere is generated by life in the sea, which also absorbs carbon dioxide. The oceans are in trouble—and if they are, we are." She cited pesticides and heavy metals as the biggest offenders, and warned that over-extraction of fish and sea creatures threaten the survival of several species.

BIOGRAPHICAL/CRITICAL SOURCES:

BOOKS

Encyclopedia of World Biography, 2nd edition, Gale (Detroit, MI), 1998.
Newsmakers, Gale (Farmington Hills, MI), 2001.
Notable Women Scientists, Gale (Farmington Hills, MI), 2000.

PERIODICALS

Animals, March, 1999, p. 36.
Discover, February, 1986, Shannon Brownlee, "Explorers of the Dark Frontiers," pp. 60-67; April, 2000, Josie Glausiusz, "Earle of the Sea," p. 16.
Life, June, 1987, p. 47.
Modern Maturity, September-October, 1995, p. 46.
National Wildlife, April-May, 1999, Mark Wexler, "Sylvia Earle's Excellent Adventure."
New Yorker, July 3, 1989, p. 41.
New York Times Magazine, June 23, 1991, p. 14.
People, May 25, 1981, p. 50; March 6, 2000, William Plummer, "Depth Charger: First Lady of the Sea Sylvia Earle Dives in to Save the World's Polluted Oceans," p. 159.
Popular Science, April, 1995, p. 67.
PR Newswire, April 10, 2000, "National Geographic: Seven Pioneers Gather to Redefine Exploration," p. 2463.

Publishers Weekly, March 6, 1995, review of *Sea Change: The Message of the Oceans,* p. 47; February 1, 1999, review of *Dive! My Adventures in the Deep Frontier,* p. 85; April 24, 2000, review of *The Oceans,* p. 78.

Scientific American, April, 1992, Marguerite Holloway, "Fire in Water," pp. 37-40.

Skin Diver, December, 1999, p. 42; January, 2000, p. 49.

Time, October 5, 1998, Roger Rosenblatt, "Call of the Sea," p. 58.

USA Today, February 2, 1999, p. 1D.*

* * *

ELLIS, Ella Thorp 1928-

PERSONAL: Born July 14, 1928, in Los Angeles, CA; daughter of William Dunham (a film writer) and Marion (Yates) Thorp; married Leo H. Ellis (a construction engineer), December 17, 1949; children: Steven, David, Patrick. *Education:* University of California—Los Angeles, B.A. (English literature), 1966; San Francisco State University, M.A. *Politics:* Democrat. *Religion:* Protestant. *Avocational interests:* Reading, gardening, listening to music, attending plays, travel.

ADDRESSES: Home—1438 Grizzly Peak, Berkeley, CA 94708. *Agent*—Patricia Myrer, McIntosh & Otis, Inc., 353 Lexington Ave., Ste. 1500, New York, NY 10016-0900.

CAREER: Writer of children's books. Teacher of English at Acalanes Adult School, 1971-76. Lecturer, University of California—Berkeley Extension, 1972-77, 1987-94; San Francisco State University, San Francisco, CA, 1974-80; and University of Women's Studies, Buenos Aires, Argentina, 1981-85.

MEMBER: Authors Guild, Authors League of America, American Civil Liberties Union, Sierra Club, California Writers' Club.

AWARDS, HONORS: American Library Association Honor Book designation, 1967, for *Roam the Wild Country.*

WRITINGS:

Roam the Wild Country, Atheneum (New York, NY), 1967.

Riptide, Atheneum (New York, NY), 1969.

Celebrate the Morning, Atheneum (New York, NY), 1972.

Where the Road Ends, Atheneum (New York, NY), 1974.

Hallelujah (science fiction), illustrated by Ginny McWilliams, Atheneum (New York, NY), 1976.

Sleepwalker's Moon, Atheneum (New York, NY), 1980.

Hugo and the Princess Nena, Atheneum (New York, NY), 1983.

Swimming with the Whales, Holt (New York, NY), 1995.

The Year of My Indian Prince, Delacorte (New York, NY), 2001.

Work has been anthologized in *And Everywhere Children,* Greenwillow, 1979. Contributor of short fiction to *Mademoiselle.*

WORK IN PROGRESS: "A story of coming to terms with jealousy between a mother and daughter over an older daughter who died ten years before."

SIDELIGHTS: Ella Thorp Ellis has penned several novels for middle-grade readers that shows the importance of family connection and strong relationships between generations. Often featuring unusual family situations and protagonists who live far from normal lifestyles, Ellis has been praised by critics for creating vivid, complex teen characters whose journey to adulthood is compelling due to its uniqueness. Among Ellis's novels are *Where the Road Ends, Hugo and the Princess Nena,* and *Roam the Wild Country,* the last an American Library Association Honor book that takes place in Argentina.

"I have always been a vagabond," Ellis once remarked. Born in 1928, Ellis's unusual upbringing has provided the basis for many of her books for preteen readers. "My father was a freelance writer," she explained, "and during the Depression [of the 1930s] we lived up and down the coast of California: in a commune on the beach; with the only doctor in a small town; in South Berkeley; in San Francisco's Richmond District; and in Washington, D.C., with an uncle who was a painter. I had the chance to know different kinds of people well. But every summer I returned to Oceano, California, the small town where my mother lived. . . . This is my home." Several of Ellis's early novels, including *Riptide* and *Celebrate the Morning,* are set in Oceano.

When Ellis was a high school student of seventeen, she contracted tuberculosis, "I spent the next three years reading, watching, and waiting. I try to bring to my books the capacity for precise observation that I learned during those years, so that my readers will be able to read my descriptions of the places I have been and feel that they have been there too." Ellis's 2001 novel *The Year of My Indian Prince* is based on that period of the author's life, as a teen at a sanatorium in the mid-1940s gains the romantic attention of fellow patient Ravi, son of an Indian maharajah. Karen Simonetti praised *The Year of My Indian Prince,* describing it in *Booklist* as an "inspiring profile of a teen's courage to thrive, not merely survive, while coping with a deadly disease."

Married in 1949 to an electrical engineer working in the construction trade, Ellis found herself on the move again. "The first five years of our marriage we moved a dozen times, following construction jobs. When our three sons started school, we developed a home base— Berkeley, California—and left only a year or two at a time." Ellis and her family traveled to Argentina for two years during this period, spending summers on a horse ranch there, and the trip inspired both *Roam the Wild Country* and *Swimming with the Whales.* In *Swimming with the Whales,* Ellis's story of a young Argentinian boy named Paolo, who is forced to move from the home of his father to that of his mother, the author "paints realistic scenes of a different way of life," according to *Voice of Youth Advocates* contributor Cynthia Brown, "including quite a bit of information about . . . [the] natural life of Argentina."

Despite her frequent traveling and her need to care for her growing family, Ellis also found a way to continue her education. "Whenever we lived in a town that had one, I went to college. Eight colleges and universities later, I graduated in English literature from the University of California Los Angeles in 1966. This educational meandering made headaches for the people who had to evaluate my credits but I could savor each course and often share them with growing sons." She eventually went on to complete her master's degree at San Francisco State University.

Ellis's first novel for young readers, *Roam the Wild Country,* was published in 1967, the year after she graduated from college at age thirty-seven. "Like most people, I have always wanted to write, to share adventure and insight with a reader," she once stated. With stretches of time now available to her while her children were in school, she began to write poems and stories. She also had sons who were good critics. "The main problem was finding a quiet place to work and my husband solved this by getting me a small house trailer which we park about a mile from our house."

Ellis's 1974 novel, *Where the Road Ends,* is characteristic of her work. Fifteen-year-old Pete pals up with fel-

low runaway Barney after leaving his California foster home to search for a blood relative living in the Virgin Islands. Among their adventures, the two young men join a circus in Texas before traveling to Florida and going their separate ways. While some critics noted the novel's slow pace, Beryl Robinson praised *Where the Road Ends* in *Horn Book,* calling it a "realistic novel enlivened by tense situations, touches of humor, and effective characterization." In *Booklist,* a reviewer complimented Ellis for "calling up a sense of her various settings," finding the novel s "a thoughtful, thorough portrayal of a young boy seeking security and fulfillment."

Young people leaving home in search of a more positive home life are also the focus of *Sleepwalker's Moon* and *Hugo and the Princess Nena.* In *Sleepwalker's Moon,* a young teen named Anna, living with family friends while her father is away fighting in World War II, decides to run away to her aunt and uncle's home thousands of miles away when she realizes she has been raised in a far more permissive home. Also with a female protagonist, *Hugo and the Princess Nena* finds eleven-year-old Nena sent to California to live temporarily with her eighty-year-old uncle Hugo. A free spirit, Hugo lives a colorful life in a low-rent trailer park, and his way of living provides his granddaughter with increased toleration of difference. A contributor to *Kirkus Reviews* dubbed *Sleepwalker's Moon* "an interesting novel that, like its heroine, is heavy-hearted and rough-edged," while in *School Library Journal* Anne Connor called *Hugo and the Princess Nena* an "evocative book [that] will appeal to sensitive readers." In a *Booklist* review, Ilene Cooper also noted that the character of Hugo "will expand readers' perceptions about older people," much as he did those of his granddaughter, Nena.

BIOGRAPHICAL/CRITICAL SOURCES:

BOOKS

Ward, Martha E., and others, *Authors of Books for Young People,* 3rd edition, Scarecrow Press (Metuchen, NJ), 1990.

PERIODICALS

Booklist, May 1, 1974, review of *Where the Road Ends,* p. 1001; March 15, 1983, Ilene Cooper, review of *Hugo and the Princess Nena,* p. 965; July, 1995,

Mary Harris Veeder, review of *Swimming with the Whales,* p. 1873; June 1, 2001, Karen Simonetti, review of *The Year of My Indian Prince,* p. 1862.

Christian Science Monitor, November 6, 1969.

Horn Book, December, 1972; August, 1974, Beryl Robinson, review of *Where the Road Ends,* p. 384.

Kirkus Reviews, September 15, 1976, review of *Hallelujah,* p. 1039; March 15, 1980, review of *Sleepwalker's Moon,* p. 370; February 15, 1983, review of *Hugo and the Princess Nena,* p. 184.

Library Journal, September 15, 1974, Carol Sebastian, review of *Where the Road Ends,* p. 2288.

New York Times Book Review, November 9, 1969.

Publishers Weekly, May 22, 1995, review of *Swimming with the Whales,* p. 60; June 11, 2001, review of *The Year of My Indian Prince,* p. 86.

School Library Journal, October, 1976, Sarajean Marks, review of *Hallelujah,* p. 116; April, 1980, Cyrisse Jaffee, review of *Sleepwalker's Moon,* p. 123; October, 1983, Anne Connor, review of *Hugo and the Princess Nena,* p. 166; July, 1995, Connie Tyrrell Burns, review of *Swimming with the Whales,* p. 95; June, 2001, Susan Riley, review of *The Year of My Indian Prince,* p. 148.

Voice of Youth Advocates, October, 1995, Cynthia Brown, review of *Swimming with the Whales,* pp. 216-217.

Washington Post Book World, January 28, 1968; November 9, 1969.

OTHER

Ella Thorp Ellis Web site, http://www.geocities.com/ellathorpellis/ (December 5, 2001).*

F-G

FLORES, Dan Louie 1948-

PERSONAL: Born October 19, 1948, in Vivian, LA; son of Willie Clyde, Jr., and Kathryn (Hale) Flores. *Ethnicity:* "White." *Education:* Northwestern State University of Louisiana, B.A., 1971, M.A., 1972; Texas A & M University, Ph.D., 1978.

ADDRESSES: Home—P.O. Box 746, Florence, MT 59833. *Office*—Department of History, University of Montana, Missoula, MT 59812. *E-mail*—dflores@ selway.umt.edu.

CAREER: Freelance writer, columnist, and conservation editor for various outdoor and environmental magazines, 1971—; Texas Tech University, Lubbock, professor of history, 1978-92; University of Montana, Missoula, Hammond Professor of Western History, 1992—. Visiting professor, University of Wyoming, 1986.

MEMBER: American Association for Environmental History, American Historical Association, Western History Association, Montana State History Association, Texas Institute of Letters.

AWARDS, HONORS: Townshend Whelen Prize, Digest Books, 1976; "best book on the West" citation, Westerners International, and "best book on Texas" citation, Texas State Historical Association, both 1984, for *Jefferson and Southwestern Exploration: The Freeman and Custis Accounts of the Red River Expedition of 1806;* Ray Allen Billington Prize, Western History Association, and H. Bailey Carroll Prize, Texas State Historical Association, both 1984, for "Ecology of the Red River in 1806"; Wrangler Award, National Cowboy Hall of Fame, 1997, for magazine article; finalist, best western short nonfiction, Western Writers, 1998; finalist citation, best contemporary nonfiction book, Western Writers, 2000, for *Horizontal Yellow.*

WRITINGS:

Jefferson and Southwestern Exploration: The Freeman and Custis Accounts of the Red River Expedition of 1806, University of Oklahoma Press (Norman, OK), 1984, 2nd edition revised, 2002.

Journal of an Indian Trader: Anthony Glass and the Texas Trading Frontier, 1790-1810, Texas A & M University Press (College Station, TX), 1985.

(With Amy Winton) *Canyon Visions: Photographs and Pastels of the Texas Plains,* Texas Tech University (Lubbock, TX), 1989.

Caprock Canyonlands: Journeys into the Heart of the Southern Plains, University of Texas Press (Austin, TX), 1990.

(With Eric Bolen) *The Mississippi Kite: Portrait of a Southern Hawk,* University of Texas Press (Austin, TX), 1993.

Horizontal Yellow: Nature and History in the Near Southwest, University of New Mexico, 1999.

The Natural West: Environmental History in the Great Plains and Rocky Mountains, University of Oklahoma Press (Norman, OK), 2001.

Contributor to history journals, environmental periodicals, nature writing anthologies; associate editor of *Ethno-history,* 1984-86.

WORK IN PROGRESS: "A book on the art of the Northern Rockies and Plains," 2003; "a book on bison and Plains Indians," for Yale University Press, 2003.

SIDELIGHTS: Dan Louie Flores once told *CA:* "My work on the history of the Southwest originates in my family's long interrelationship with the area—my French and Spanish ancestors have been in western Louisiana since the early eighteenth century—and in the strong sense of history and landscape that yet affects me. The latter is probably the reason I do what scholars now call environmental history. My discovery early in graduate school that Thomas Jefferson had dispatched into 'my' country a southwestern counterpart to the Lewis and Clark expedition and that since 1806 no one had bothered to assemble the documents and write the story of that Jeffersonian probe was tantamount to having my first book choose me to write it."

Flores more recently told *CA:* "As I look back over my work in light of current projects, I realize that the thread that strings through all of it is some instinctive (I don't think it is learned) fascination with the evolving historical relationships between human cultures and specific kinds of landscapes. To one degree or another, most of my articles and essays and all of my books have had something to do with regional ecologies (the Red River Valley, the Great Plains, the American West) and the endlessly intriguing ways that people have interacted with them across time. This approach has always involved a personal relationship with the land, as my early books were about the historical and environmental circumstances of the places where I lived. But more recently it has led me in something of an autobiographical direction, as I have explored my own reaction to place. So my recent and present work has become an experimental type of environmental and personal history, often (as with *Caprock Canyonlands, Horizontal Yellow,* and *The Natural West*) written in first-person. Thus my books and articles have combined the personal essay with historical research, the study of cultures with an effort to understand the ecological history of places.

"When I look at much of what I've written, I can't help but think that the country made me do it. Using words like 'sense of place' and 'continuum' makes it sound as if the environmentalist bent of my work has mystical origins; I rather think the sources lie in the concreteness of geology, landforms, skies, and the topophilic pull these have on all of us in some genetic way. Particularized environmental history related through closely observed personal essays that also feature social criticism thus seems to be my current direction."

FOLSOM, Allan (R.) 1941-

PERSONAL: Born December 9, 1941, in Orlando, FL; son of Edwin W. and Ada (Ott) Folsom; married Karen Glick (an executive search consultant), 1979. *Education:* Boston University, B.S., 1963. *Avocational interests:* Skiing, travel.

ADDRESSES: Home—Santa Barbara, CA. *Agent*—Robert Gottlieb, Trident Media Group, 488 Madison Ave., 17th Flr., New York, NY 10022. *E-mail*—belfond@aol. com.

CAREER: Worked in Los Angeles, CA, as a delivery driver, film editor, and camera operator; author of television scripts, screenplays, and novels.

MEMBER: Writers Guild of American West.

AWARDS, HONORS: Richard and Hinda Rosenthal Award in Screenwriting, 1963; Premio Internazionale Flaiano, per la narrativa, 1995; alumni award, Boston University, 1995.

WRITINGS:

The Day after Tomorrow (novel), Little, Brown (Boston, MA), 1994.
Day of Confession (novel), Little, Brown (Boston, MA), 1998.

Author of television scripts for series, including *Untamed World,* 1968 and 1969; *Hart to Hart,* 1981 and 1982; and *Sable,* 1987. Also author of unproduced screenplays.

WORK IN PROGRESS: A third novel.

SIDELIGHTS: Author Allan Folsom was making headlines even before the publication of his first novel, *The Day after Tomorrow.* The book, a fast-paced and multiplotted thriller, made history by garnering the biggest offer ever for the rights to a first novel. Made jointly by Little, Brown & Company and Warner Books, the offer paid Folsom approximately two million dollars, with an additional $500,000 to be paid when sales of the book reached 400,000 copies. Maureen O'Brien in *Publishers Weekly* quoted agent Aaron M. Priest, who had sent

Allan Folsom

relished the street activity, an innocuous thought flickered languidly through Folsom's mind: 'What if someone walked by who was important in my life thirty years ago?'" Thus *The Day after Tomorrow* begins with its protagonist, American surgeon Paul Osborn, sitting in a French café. Suddenly, he realizes that a man sitting nearby is the man he saw murder his father many years before. Osborn embarks upon a mission to find out why the man did it and then kill him; along the way he becomes entangled in a series of grisly decapitation murders and an international neo-Nazi plot.

When *The Day after Tomorrow* was published in 1994, most reviewers agreed that the book lived up to its advance publicity. Chris Petrakos in *Chicago Tribune Books* observed that the novel "seamlessly blends more plotlines than some writers do in a half-dozen books," and hailed Folsom as "an enthusiastic storyteller with a talent for vivid characterization." Robert Ward in the *Los Angeles Times Book Review* praised *The Day after Tomorrow* in glowing terms, comparing it to such books as *The Manchurian Candidate, The First Deadly Sin, The Exorcist,* and *The Shining.* Ward lauded Folsom's "particular brilliance" in marrying "the novel of revenge with the political thriller and grafted the whole thing seamlessly onto a brilliant updating of the Frankenstein story." The reviewer concluded: "I defy you to put it down."

copies of Folsom's manuscript to several publishers: "People were . . . calling in preemptive bids like crazy. . . . Initially I was prepared to accept a much, much smaller offer, but as the weekend progressed and these publishers began calling off the wall, tracking me down [on vacation] in Barbados, it became clear it was going to go for a great deal more."

Before his record-breaking book deal, Folsom had struggled to make a career for himself in Hollywood. He began as a delivery driver, then graduated to film editing and camera work; meanwhile, he worked on his own screenplays. He occasionally wrote for television series, including *Hart to Hart.* Folsom came close to fame when actress Natalie Wood agreed to take the lead role in a screenplay he had written about the life of poet Anne Sexton, whom he had known in Boston. However, following Wood's death in a boating accident, Folsom turned to other projects.

As Bob Sipchen reported in the *Los Angeles Times,* Folsom found inspiration for his novel during a trip to Paris in 1990. While he and his wife "sipped coffee and

BIOGRAPHICAL/CRITICAL SOURCES:

PERIODICALS

Chicago Tribune Books, April 17, 1994, p. 6.
Los Angeles Times, February 25, 1993, pp. E1, E8.
Los Angeles Times Book Review, April 10, 1994, pp. 1, 8.
New York Times, February 4, 1993, p. C24.
New York Times Book Review, May 22, 1994, p. 36.
Publishers Weekly, February 8, 1993, p. 12; March 7, 1994, pp. 46-47.

*   *   *

GARDAM, Jane 1928-

PERSONAL: Born July 11, 1928, in Coatham, Yorkshire, England; daughter of William (a schoolmaster) and Kathleen Mary (Helm) Pearson; married David Hill Gardam (a Queen's counsel), April 20, 1952; children: Timothy, Mary, Thomas. *Education:* Bedford College,

Jane Gardam

London, B.A. (with honors), 1949, graduate study, 1949-52. *Politics:* "Ecology." *Religion:* Anglo-Catholic. *Avocational interests:* Growing roses.

ADDRESSES: *Agent*—Bruce Hunter, David Higham Associates, 5-8 Lower John Street, London W1R 4HA, England.

CAREER: Writer. *Weldons Ladies Journal,* London, England, sub-editor, 1952-53; *Time and Tide,* London, assistant literary editor, 1953-55. Organizer of hospital libraries for Red Cross, 1950.

MEMBER: PEN, Royal Society of Literature (fellow), Arts Club, University Womens Club.

AWARDS, HONORS: *Book World's* Spring Book Festival award, 1972, for *A Long Way from Verona; Boston Globe-Horn Book* honor book for text, 1974, for *The Summer after the Funeral;* David Higham Prize for fiction and Winifred Holtby Award, both 1977, both for *Black Faces, White Faces;* runner-up citation, Booker

Prize, 1978, for *God on the Rocks;* Whitbread Award, 1983, for *The Hollow Land,* and 1991, for *The Queen of the Tambourine;* Carnegie Medal "highly recommended" award, for *The Hollow Land* and "commended" award, for *Bridget and William,* both 1983; Katherine Mansfield Award, 1984, for *The Pangs of Love;* Phoenix Award, 1991, for *A Long Way from Verona;* Heywood Hill Prize, 1999, for lifetime achievement in literature.

WRITINGS:

JUVENILE FICTION

A Few Fair Days (short stories), illustrated by Peggy Fortnum, Macmillan (New York, NY), 1971.
A Long Way from Verona (novel), Macmillan (New York, NY), 1971.
The Summer after the Funeral (novel), Macmillan (New York, NY), 1973.
Bilgewater (novel), Hamish Hamilton (London, England), 1976.
God on the Rocks (novel), Morrow (New York, NY), 1978.
Bridget and William, illustrated by Janet Rawlings, Julia MacRae (New York, NY), 1981.
The Hollow Land (stories), illustrated by Janet Rawlings, Julia MacRae (New York, NY), 1981.
Horse, illustrated by Janet Rawlings, Julia MacRae (New York, NY), 1982.
Kit, illustrated by William Geldart, Julia MacRae (New York, NY), 1984.
Kit in Boots, Julia MacRae (New York, NY), 1986.
Swan, Julia MacRae (New York, NY), 1986.
Through the Dolls' House Door (novel), Julia MacRae (New York, NY), 1987.
Going into a Dark House (stories), Sinclair-Stevenson (London, England), 1994.
Faith Fox: A Nativity, Sinclair-Stevenson (London, England), 1996.
(With Mary Fedden) *The Green Man,* Windrush, 2000.
The Flight of the Maidens, Chatto & Windus (London, England), 2000.

ADULT FICTION

Black Faces, White Faces (stories), Hamish Hamilton (London, England), 1975, published as *The Pineapple Bay Hotel,* Morrow (New York, NY), 1976.
The Sidmouth Letters (stories), Morrow (New York, NY), 1980.

The Pangs of Love (stories; also see below), Hamish Hamilton (London, England), 1983.

Crusoe's Daughter (novel), Atheneum (New York, NY), 1986.

Showing the Flag (stories), Penguin (New York, NY), 1989.

The Queen of the Tambourine (novel), Sinclair-Stevenson (London, England), 1991, St. Martin's Press (New York, NY), 1995.

Missing the Midnight: Hauntings & Grotesques, Sinclair-Stevenson (London, England), 1997.

Also author of scripts for television films, including *The Easter Lilies,* based on the author's book *The Pangs of Love,* and *God on the Rocks,* ITV, 1992. Contributor of short stories to magazines.

SIDELIGHTS: Hailed in Great Britain as a writer of talent and originality, Jane Gardam has enjoyed success with children's fiction as well as with short stories and novels written expressly for adults. In the *Dictionary of Literary Biography,* Patricia Craig argued that categorizing Gardam's fiction strictly as "juvenile" or "adult" does the writer's work a disservice. The appeal of Gardam's fiction, wrote Craig, "should not be restricted by any factor of age in the reader. . . . All of Gardam's work is marked by certain admirable characteristics: economy of style, exuberance and humor, a special relish for the startling and the unexpected."

Proof of Gardam's ability to touch readers of various ages can be found in the awards she has won: the David IIigham Prize for *Black Faces, White Faces,* a collection of short stories for adults; the prestigious Whitbread Award for *The Hollow Land,* a work ostensibly for juveniles; and for *The Queen of the Tambourine,* a novel for adults. Jane Miller outlined Gardam's strengths in a *Times Literary Supplement* review: "[She] has a spectacular gift for detail, of the local and period kind, and for details which make characters so subtly unpredictable that they ring true, and her humor is tough as well as delicate."

Young teens on the brink of adulthood are often the central characters in Gardam's juvenile fiction. Craig believed that Gardam's works "recreate directly the sensations and impressions of childhood." Craig also noted a slightly autobiographical cast in a number of the juvenile novels: "Although to an extent transformed in the course of writing, certain elements of Gardam's early life seem to have made a fairly consistent pattern in her books: the girl with a much younger brother; the

schoolmaster or clergyman father; the Yorkshire or Cumbria locations. Each book, however, has a distinctive feeling, a mood and atmosphere all its own. Gardam repeats her motifs but not her effects. . . . The narrative is charged as well with a kind of muted fairytale glamour." A contributor to *St. James Guide to Young Adult Writers* found that "Gardam's work as a whole is distinguished by a clearly delineated, often satiric representation of historical and cultural moments of English life and British educational, religious, and class institutions. . . . She offers us a perspective on changes in English culture, moments in time now lost. A sense of history, and of history within the lives of particular persons and groups, structures the progression of the narrative in works such as *The Hollow Land, Through the Dolls' House Door,* and *Crusoe's Daughter.*"

Gardam received critical acclaim for her first three children's books, but she was still virtually unknown as an author when she published *Black Faces, White Faces,* released in the United States as *The Pineapple Bay Hotel.* Craig noted that the stories in Gardam's story collections are interrelated within each volume, but "what is important is not the classification [as novel or collection] but the degree of acuity brought to bear on a theme." Indeed, publication of *Black Faces, White Faces* expanded Gardam's critical audience considerably and accorded her highly favorable reviews.

Among her critically acclaimed works is the novel *The Queen of the Tambourine,* which tells the story of Eliza Peabody, a middle-aged woman whose marriage is dull and unsatisfying. The novel consists of Eliza's letters to her friend Joan, who has left her husband to live in the Far East. As Jonathan Yardley stated in the *Washington Post,* the letters "describe a woman slipping slowly into lunacy." These letters, Michael Harris reported in the *Los Angeles Times Book Review,* "are full of delusions, often not sent and never answered." Commenting on the novel's structure, Frances Spalding wrote in the *Times Educational Supplement* that the narrative strays from the "demands of a traditional plot" and "has an improvisatory air." Eliza's experiences, Spalding continued, "form a series of vignettes which ornament the thread of her mental journeying." Several critics also remarked on Gardam's ability to create a character who, although unreliable as a narrator because of her delusions, is nonetheless likeable. Calling *The Queen of the Tambourine* "funny and moving," Nina Sonenberg of the *New York Times Book Review* praised Gardam's "devilish wit" and described Eliza as another heroine driven insane by "splendid suburban isolation." Barbara Hardy, however, writing for the *Times Literary Supplement,* questioned the efficacy of Gardam's portrayal of

Eliza's insanity. "Everything is explained by Eliza's madness," Hardy stated, "but there are too many ways in which she is sane to the point of banality, and the mad bits are hardly ever thoroughly mad." Yardley recommended the novel to "readers with a taste for psychological portraiture and subtle wit."

In the story collection *Missing the Midnight: Hauntings & Grotesques,* Gardam gathers several of her Christmas and ghost stories. Graeme Harper, writing in the *Dictionary of Literary Biography,* found that the stories are "sometimes based on the everyday, sometimes fantastical, and often involve allegorical structures." Speaking of Gardam's approach to writing stories, Harper noted: "She treads the line cleverly between reality and fantasy, eccentricity and ordinariness, without being overwhelmed, or overwhelming the reader, with the complexities of this movement."

Several critics have discussed Gardam's ability to write with wit and sharpness about the English upper class without resorting to polemics. In a review for *Room of One's Own,* Carroll Klein explained that Gardam's approach in her stories is subtle, and that "the subtlety of her writing salvages and often enhances her reticence in making direct statements. She sets up a situation, creates brilliantly realistic dialogue, and lets the reader conclude what she will." Victoria Glendinning described Gardam in the *Times Literary Supplement* as "a very English writer, in that her observation is at its sharpest on matters of class and status, and her most poisonous darts reserved for the upper middle classes, or rather for the female residue who no longer have servants to exploit and are ending their days in seedy stinginess." "Her manifold traps are hidden away under glass and satin," noted Raymond Sokolov in the *Washington Post Book World.* "The voice you hear is an odd combination of girl and grande dame, a voice that trills out the most sinister truths as if they were part of the court circular." In a London *Times* review of *The Pangs of Love,* Elaine Feinstein suggested that Gardam "is a spare and elegant master of her art, which is neither genteel nor gentle, and she spares the well-bred less than the vulgar, and the predictably English abroad least of all."

Gardam's penchant for writing about the English middle class is clearly evident in her story collection, *Going into a Dark House.* Writing in the *Spectator,* Anita Brookner described the world Gardam creates as "cautious, middle-class, respectable, and capable of extreme wildness." The majority of the characters are middle-aged or elderly, and themes of death and chance are prominent in many of the stories. "Death is everywhere," stated Alex Clark of the *Times Literary Supplement,* "and it provides the dominant motif through which character, motivation and story are revealed." Brookner considered the collection a tribute to Gardam's talent as a writer and stated that though "robustly English and eschewing post-modern tricks, [Gardam's writing] conquers by stealth, as all good fiction should, and surprises one with a convincing account of eccentricities triumphing over the most mundane of circumstances."

Throughout Gardam's fiction, juvenile and adult alike, the author explores eccentric behavior. Klein noted that "Gardam peoples her stories with ineffectual, occasionally absurd, characters, with the walking wounded, the intellectually incompetent, and with those hovering on the edge of social approbation." A *Times Literary Supplement* reviewer also noted that Gardam's characters, "young and old, are observed with unwavering directness, their emotional hang-ups and outlets quietly understated so that the adolescent reader can take or leave the undertones." In Craig's view, Gardam "is interested in the discrepancy between the face one presents to the world and one's actual feelings, and the comedy which results from lack of face." Gardam's eccentric characters are matched by her eye for finding the strange hidden among the everyday. "She can pick on the small incident and find that behind it lies the bizarre, or the chilling, uncomfortable edge," wrote Simon Blow in the *New Statesman.* According to Craig, however, "the fanciful and highly colored in Gardam's work are always disciplined by a northern toughness and plainness of expression."

"Gardam," Harper concluded, "writes both for adults and for children, moving between these two readerships, and seems to find her own fascination with the theme of childhood a useful bridge between the two. . . . Her writing is quiet, wry, sometimes pleasantly archaic, and unsentimental but emotive; writing in which things are often slightly askew or hidden beneath the surface of otherwise unassuming narrative." In the years since Gardam began publishing fiction, wrote Craig, she "has shown herself to be a novelist of rare inventiveness and power."

BIOGRAPHICAL/CRITICAL SOURCES:

BOOKS

Children's Literature Review, Volume 12, Gale (Detroit, MI), 1987.
Contemporary Literary Criticism, Volume 43, Gale (Detroit, MI), 1987.

Dictionary of Literary Biography, Gale (Detroit, MI), Volume 14: *British Novelists since 1960,* 1982, Volume 161: *British Children's Writers since 1960,* 1996, Volume 231: *British Novelists since 1960, Fourth Series,* 2000.

St. James Guide to Young Adults Writers, 2nd edition, St. James Press (Detroit, MI), 1999.

Something About the Author Autobiography Series, Volume 9, Gale (Detroit, MI), 1990.

PERIODICALS

Booklist, October 1, 1987.
Horn Book, October, 1978; December, 1978.
Los Angeles Times Book Review, December 21, 1980; October 22, 1995.
New Statesman, November 12, 1971; October 13, 1978; April 11, 1980, p. 558.
New Statesman & Society, April 12, 1996, p. 39.
New York Times, December 19, 1980.
New York Times Book Review, May 7, 1972; February 17, 1974; August 11, 1974; May 2, 1976; April 27, 1986; August 27, 1995, p. 18.
Observer (London, England), February 13, 1983; October 9, 1994.
Publishers Weekly, September 25, 1987, p. 111; July 8, 1988, p. 57.
Room of One's Own, Volume 8, number 3, 1983.
School Librarian, May, 1987, pp. 131-132.
Spectator, November 13, 1971; December 22, 1973; November 29, 1975; December 11, 1976; November 25, 1978; May 3, 1980; February 19, 1983; September 3, 1994, p. 36.
Times (London, England), February 10, 1983; February 9, 1985.
Times Educational Supplement, November 20, 1981; November 21, 1986, p. 31; September 18, 1987, p. 34; November 27, 1987, p. 45; January 6, 1989, p. 26; May 3, 1991, p. 23.
Times Literary Supplement, November 22, 1971; December 3, 1971; November 23, 1973; September 19, 1975; December 10, 1976; October 13, 1978; April 18, 1980; March 27, 1981; September 18, 1981; February 10, 1984; May 31, 1985; July 10, 1987, p. 751; July 7, 1989; April 12, 1991, p. 18; August 26, 1994, p. 20; September 29, 2000, David Nokes, "A Sepia Society," p. 24.
Washington Post, April 21, 1986; August 23, 1995, p. C3.
Washington Post Book World, May 2, 1976; January 8, 1978.*

*   *   *

GARNETT, Isobel
  See WADDINGTON, Patrick (Haynes)

GIBSON, William (Ford) 1948-

PERSONAL: Born March 17, 1948, in Conway, SC; emigrated to Canada; son of William Ford (a contractor) and Otey (a homemaker; maiden name, Williams) Gibson; married Deborah Thompson (a language instructor), June, 1972; children: Graeme Ford Gibson, Claire Thompson Gibson. *Education:* University of British Columbia, B.A., 1977.

ADDRESSES: Home—Vancouver, British Columbia, Canada. *Agent*—Martha Millard Literary Agency, 293 Greenwood Ave., Florham Park, NJ 07932; (for film and television) Martin S. Shapiro, Shapiro-Lichtman Talent, 8827 Beverly Blvd., Los Angeles, CA 90048.

CAREER: Writer.

AWARDS, HONORS: Nebula Award nomination from Science Fiction Writers of America, c. 1983, for short story "Burning Chrome"; Hugo Award for best novel of 1984 from World Science Fiction Society, Philip K. Dick Award for best U.S. original paperback of 1984 from Philadelphia Science Fiction Society, Nebula Award for best novel of 1984 from Science Fiction Writers of America, and Porgie Award for best paperback original novel in science fiction from *West Coast Review of Books,* all 1985, and Ditmar Award from Australian National Science Fiction Convention, all for *Neuromancer.*

WRITINGS:

"CYBERSPACE" TRILOGY

Neuromancer Ace (New York, NY), 1984.
Count Zero, Arbor House (New York, NY), 1986.
Mona Lisa Overdrive, Bantam (New York, NY), 1988.

OTHER

(With John Shirley, Bruce Sterling, and Michael Swanwick) *Burning Chrome* (short stories; includes "Burning Chrome," "Johnny Mnemonic," and "New Rose Hotel," introduction by Bruce Sterling, Arbor House (New York, NY), 1986.
Dream Jumbo (text to accompany performance art by Robert Longo), produced at UCLA Center for the Performing Arts, Los Angeles, CA, 1989.

(With Bruce Sterling) *The Difference Engine* (novel), Gollancz (London, England), 1990, Bantam (New York, NY), 1991.

Virtual Light (novel; first in trilogy), Viking (New York, NY), 1993.

Johnny Mnemonic (screenplay; based on Gibson's short story of the same title), TriStar, 1995.

Idoru (novel; second in trilogy), Putnam (New York, NY), 1996.

All Tomorrow's Parties (novel; third in trilogy), Putnam, 1999.

Work represented in anthologies, including *Shadows 4*, Doubleday, 1981; *Nebula Award Stories 17*, Holt, 1983; and *Mirrorshades: The Cyberpunk Anthology*, edited with an introduction by Sterling, Arbor House, 1986. Contributor of short stories, articles, and book reviews to periodicals, including *Omni, Rolling Stone, Wired*, and *Science Fiction Review*. Scriptwriter for "Kill Switch," an episode of *The X-Files*, 1999. Contributor to Fox Network series, *Harsh Realm*, 2000.

ADAPTATIONS: Neuromancer has been optioned for production as a feature film to be directed by Chris Cunningham.

SIDELIGHTS: Science-fiction author William Gibson had published only a handful of short stories when he stunned readers with his debut novel, *Neuromancer.* Published in 1984, *Neuromancer* became the first work ever to sweep the major honors of science fiction—the Hugo, Nebula, and Philip K. Dick awards. Combining the hip cynicism of the rock music underground and the dizzying powers of high technology, the novel was hailed as the prototype of a new style of writing, promptly dubbed "cyberpunk." Gibson, who was also earning praise as a skillful prose stylist, disliked the trendy label but admitted that he was challenging science fiction traditions. "I'm not even sure what cyberpunk means," he told the *Philadelphia Inquirer,* "but I suppose it's useful as a tip-off to people that what they're going to read is a little wilder."

The surface features of Gibson's allegedly cyberpunk style—tough characters facing a tough world, frantic pacing, and bizarre high-tech slang—alienated some reviewers. "Like punk rock . . . Cyberpunk caters to the wish-fulfillment requirements of male teenagers," explained science-fiction novelist Thomas M. Disch in *New York Times Book Review,* "and there is currently no more accomplished caterer than William Gibson." In *Science Fiction Review,* Andrew Andrews criticized the

"style and execution" of *Count Zero,* a novel typical of Gibson's work during the 1980s. "It is hodgepodge; spastic; incomprehensible in spots, somehow just *too much,*" the reviewer declared. "I prefer a novel that is concise, with fleshy, human characters." Beneath the flash, however, some admirers detected a serious purpose. Writers like Gibson, suggested J. R. Wytenbroeck in *Canadian Literature,* are really describing the world "in which we live today, with all its problems taken to their logical extreme." In particular, the advance of technology is shown to cause as many problems as it solves. "Technology has *already* changed us, and now we have to figure out a way to stay sane," Gibson observed in *Rolling Stone.* "If you were to put this in terms of mainstream fiction and present readers with a conventional book about modern postindustrial anxiety, many of them would just push it aside. But if you put it in the context of science fiction, maybe you can get them to sit still for what you have to say." Along with "adrenalin verve and random pyrotechnics," wrote Colin Greenland in the *Times Literary Supplement,* Gibson's work is "intellectually substantial." "His style," Greenland wrote, "is deadpan and precise, with the tone of the classic crime thriller: canny, cool and undeceived, yet ultimately the very opposite of the callousness it imitates, because motivated by a desire for justice."

Gibson grew up in a small town in southwest Virginia, on the edge of the Appalachian Mountains. "It was a boring, culturally deprived environment," he recalled in the *Sacramento Union.* "The library burned down in 1910, and nobody bothered to rebuild it." In such a place, he told *Interview,* "science-fiction books were the only source I had for subversive information." By his late teens Gibson had left behind the conventional authors who filled the genre with shining cities and benevolent scientists. Instead he began to prefer iconoclasts, such as J. G. Ballard and Philip K. Dick, who described a grim and frightening future. Some of his favorites might not qualify with purists as science-fiction writers at all: both William S. Burroughs and Thomas Pynchon were intricate stylists whose core following was among literary intellectuals. Such writers used the fantastic element of science fiction as a device to explore the ugly potentials of the human heart. Science fiction, Gibson realized, was a way to comment on the reality of the present day.

The 1960s youth culture also drew Gibson's attention; a long-term rock fan, he counts the hard-edged music of Lou Reed as a major influence. In 1967 he dropped out of high school and journeyed to Canada, ending up in Toronto, which had a thriving hippie scene. "We had our own version of the Summer of Love there," he said in the *Sacramento Union.* "If I'd gone to New York or San Francisco, I can't imagine what would have happened to me." Reluctant to be drafted into the Vietnam War, he remained in Canada and eventually married. The couple settled in Vancouver, where their lives soon centered around the University of British Columbia (UBC). Gibson's wife was a teacher and he was a "permanent pseudo-grad student" who earned his bachelor's degree shortly before he turned thirty. After graduating, "I was clueless," he recalled in *Chicago Tribune.* "A lot of my friends were becoming lawyers and librarians, things that filled me with horror." So he became a science fiction writer, even though at the time "it seemed like such a goofy, unhip thing to do," as he told *Rolling Stone.* Gibson began his career almost in spite of himself, after enrolling in a science fiction course at UBC in hope of an easy credit. Unwilling to submit a term paper, he accepted the teacher's challenge to compose a short story—an ordeal that lasted three months. As Gibson settled into life as a househusband, however, he realized that writing more stories was the best way he could earn money while watching over his children.

His writing blossomed with amazing speed. By the early 1980s he was a favorite of fiction editor Ellen Datlow, who helped make *Omni* magazine a showcase of rising science fiction talent. In *Omni* stories such as "Johnny Mnemonic" and "Burning Chrome," Gibson began to sketch his own grim version of the future, peopled with what *Rolling Stone* called "high-tech lowlifes." The title character of "Johnny Mnemonic," for instance, stashes stolen computer data on a microchip in his brain. He is marked for murder by the Yakuza, a Japanese syndicate that has moved into high-tech crime, but he is saved by Molly Millions, a bionic hitwoman with razors implanted under her fingernails. "I thought I was on this literary kamikaze mission," Gibson informed *Rolling Stone.* "I thought my work was so disturbing it would be dismissed and ignored by all but a few people." Instead, on the basis of a few short stories, he began to gain a powerful reputation: "Burning Chrome" was nominated for a Nebula Award, and Ace Books editor Terry Carr encouraged him to expand his vision into a novel. Meanwhile, "cyberpunk" was becoming a trend throughout the science-fiction world. After writing a third of his novel, *Neuromancer,* Gibson went to see the 1982 film *Blade Runner,* director Ridley Scott's stylish, punked-out interpretation of a book by Philip K. Dick. "It looked so much like the inside of my head," reported Gibson in *Saturday Night,* "that I fled the theatre after about thirty minutes and have never seen the rest of it."

Neuromancer, together with its sequels, *Count Zero* and *Mona Lisa Overdrive,* fleshes out the future society of Gibson's short stories. Here technology is the main source of power over others, and the multinational corporations that develop and control technology are more important than governments. The world is a bewildering splatter of cultures and subcultures; Gibson skirts the issue of whether the United States or Canada are still viable countries, but his multinationals are generally based in Europe or Japan. While shadowy figures run the world for their own benefit, a large underclass—the focus of Gibson's interest—endures amid pollution, overcrowding, and pointlessness. People commonly drug themselves with chemicals or with "simstims," a form of electronic drug that allows users to experience vicariously the life of another, more glamorous, human being.

Though the future envisioned by Gibson may seem hopeless, he remains in some sense a romantic, observers note, for he chronicles the efforts of individuals to carve out a life for themselves in spite of hostile surroundings. His misfit heroes often exist on the crime-infested fringes of society, thus lending his works some of the atmosphere of a traditional crime thriller. Along with the expected cast of smugglers, prostitutes, murderers, and thieves, Gibson celebrates a distinctly modern freebooter, the computer hacker. Computers of the future, Gibson posits, will be linked worldwide through "cyberspace"—an electronically generated alternate reality in which all data, and the security programs that protect it, will appear as a palpable three-dimensional universe. Computer operators will access cyberspace by plugging into it with their brains, and hackers—known as "cowboys"—will sneak in to steal data, fill their bank accounts with electronic money, or suffer death when a security program uses feedback to destroy their minds. Gibson wrote in *Rolling Stone,* "The Street finds its own uses for things—uses the manufacturers never imagined."

Gibson's wandering youth did not hinder—and may have helped—his ability to create such a world. "I didn't invent most of what's strange in the [books'] dialogue," Gibson told the *Mississippi Review,* as quoted in *Whole Earth Review.* "There are so many cultures and subcultures around today that if you're willing to listen, you start picking up different phrases, inflections, metaphors everywhere you go. A lot of stuff in *Neuromancer* and *Count Zero* that people think is so futuristic is probably just 1969 Toronto dope-dealers' slang, or bikers' slang." Gibson lacked an education in computers, but he knew about computer people. "They have this whole style of language. . . . which attracted me simply for the intensity with which they talked about their machines," he said in *Rolling Stone.* "I immediately heard in that a real echo of the teenagers I grew up with talking about cars." Cyberspace came from watching a new generation of youth in video arcades. "I could see in . . . their postures how *rapt* these kids were," Gibson informed *Mississippi Review,* adding: "Everyone who works with computers seems to develop an intuitive faith that there's some kind of actual *space* behind the screen."

The plots of Gibson's works, some reviewers suggest, are less important than the way of life he describes: even admirers find the narratives rather complicated and difficult to summarize. As Gibson told *Interview,* he doesn't "really start with stories" but prefers to assemble images, "like making a ball out of rubber bands." *Neuromancer* centers on Henry Case, a skilled computer "cowboy" who has been punished for his exploits by being given a powerful nerve poison that leaves him unable to plug into cyberspace. As the book opens he is scrounging a living on the seamy side of Japan's Chiba City, when a mysterious patron offers him restorative surgery in exchange for more computer hacking. Case assents, and in the company of Molly Millions (one of Gibson's many recurring characters) he travels from one bizarre setting to the next in pursuit of a goal he cannot even understand. Finally Case arrives on a space station controlled by the wealthy Tessier-Ashpool clan, a family of genetic clones that owns two Artificial Intelligences—powerful computers which, like humans, have self-awareness and free will. Case realizes that one of the computers, named Wintermute, has hired him to help it take control of the other, named Neuromancer; the combined Artificial Intelligence that would result could break free of its human masters.

"*Neuromancer* was a bit hypermanic—simply from my terror at losing the reader's attention," Gibson recalled in *Rolling Stone.* For the sequel, *Count Zero,* "I aimed for a more deliberate pace. I also tried to draw the characters in considerable detail. People have children and dead parents in *Count Zero,* and that makes for different emotional territory." Thus instead of taking one main character on a manic ride throughout human society, *Count Zero* tells the stories of three more fleshed-out individuals whose lives gradually intertwine. The "Count Zero" of the title is really Bobby Newmark, a poor teenage computer "cowboy" with dreams of greatness. On his first illicit run into cyberspace, he finds it much more colorful than Henry Case had found it a few years earlier: the Artificial Intelligences of *Neuromancer* seem to have broken apart into many cyberspace entities, some of which manifest themselves as voodoo gods. The "gods" have human worshippers who take custody of Bobby after he apparently has a reli-

gious experience while he is hacking. Meanwhile, art dealer Marly Krushkova tries to find an artist with mysterious powers, only to encounter an old "cowboy" who also believes that God lives in cyberspace. And Turner, a mercenary who rounds up scientists for multinationals, finds himself the protector of a strange young woman named Angie Mitchell. Angie has a unique gift: her scientist father placed microchips in her brain that give her direct access to cyberspace and sometimes make her the mouthpiece for its ghostly inhabitants. "The resolution [of the plot] is figuratively left in the hands of the Haitian Computer Gods," wrote Dorothy Allison in the *Village Voice.* "They are particularly marvelous, considering that the traditional science-fiction model of an intelligent computer has been an emotionless logician."

Gibson's third novel, *Mona Lisa Overdrive,* "brilliantly pyramids the successes of its predecessors," wrote Edward Bryant in *Bloomsbury Review.* The book is set several years after *Count Zero,* using a similar structure of plot-lines that slowly interconnect. When *Mona Lisa Overdrive* opens, Bobby Newmark has grown up into an accomplished cowboy. Now he leaves his body in a coma so that he can explore the electronically generated universe inside a unique and costly microchip that he stole from the Tessier-Ashpool clan. Angie Mitchell, Bobby's sometime girlfriend, has become a simstim star, struggling against drug abuse and unsure of her future. In *Mona Lisa Overdrive,* wrote Richard Mathews of the *St. Petersburg Times,* "Gibson employs the metaphor of addiction as the central fact of existence. Addictions to drugs, information, and sensuality permeate society and form the basis of all economic transactions." The drug-abusing Angie, for example, is herself a "mere fix . . . piped to millions of simstim addicts to enrich [her producers]." Bobby is also a junkie—"a metaphor for society, increasingly techno-dependent, and hopelessly addicted to the excitement of high-tech power trips and head games."

As *Mona Lisa Overdrive* unfolds amid complex intrigues, the power of technology looms so large as to challenge the meaning of human identity itself. Characters seek friendship and advice from the personalities recorded on microchips; Angie comes face-to-face with "Mona Lisa," a confused teenage junkie who has been surgically altered to resemble Angie herself as part of a bizarre abduction plot. In the violent climax of the novel, during which Angie dies of a brain hemorrhage, the simstim producers stumble upon Mona and gladly recruit her as a new star. Then, in an astonishing burst of fantasy, Gibson shows Angie reunited with Bobby in his microchip universe—a computer-generated heaven.

By then, Mathews observed, "Gibson has us re-evaluating our concepts of 'life,' 'death' and 'reality,' all of which have been redefined by the impact of the information matrix. What makes Gibson so exceptional a writer is that you haven't just seen or thought about this future; you've been there."

Increasingly Gibson was hailed as a master of observant, evocative, economical prose. Paul Kincaid of the *Times Literary Supplement* observed, "If the pace [of *Mona Lisa Overdrive*] is rather less frantic than in the earlier books, it is because Gibson's writing has improved, and the space given to more vividly presenting mood, place and character slows the action." Even the skeptical Thomas Disch quoted a passage from *Mona Lisa Overdrive* and, as other reviewers have done, observed how deftly Gibson could suggest a whole society with a handful of words. "Gibson is writing brilliant prose," declared Ellen Datlow in the *Philadelphia Inquirer,* "work that can be compared to anything being written inside or outside the science-fiction field."

Gibson at first seemed bemused by his new life as a best-selling novelist. At book signings he was greeted by disparate groups of hackers and punks whom he termed "M & M's" (for "modems and Mohawks"). As a soft-spoken, conservatively dressed father of two, Gibson realized that his wilder fans were sometimes disappointed to see him in person. "There was a classic case in San Francisco when two huge motorcyclists came screeching up," he continued in the *Chicago Tribune.* "One of them looked at me, picked up a book and shook his head and said, 'You can sign it anyway.'" To Gibson's surprise he quickly attracted the attention of the Hollywood film industry, and two years after *Neuromancer* was published he sold the film rights for $100,000. Soon he was recruited as screenwriter for the projected third film in the highly profitable *Aliens* series. But after he wrote several drafts, the film studio had a management shuffle and he lost his job. Paradoxically, the very fact that he was involved with such a high-profile effort made it easy for him to find more film work. Though Gibson stresses that *Mona Lisa Overdrive* is not autobiographical, he admits that the simstim subplot was inspired by his introduction to America's film capital. As he told the *Philadelphia Inquirer:* "Sitting in the Polo Lounge talking to 20-year-old movie producers with money coming out of their ears—*that's* science fiction, boy."

By the time *Mona Lisa Overdrive* was published in 1988, Gibson and many reviewers were glad to say farewell to the cyberpunk era. "It's becoming fashion-able now to write 'cyberpunk is dead' articles," he noted in the *Bloomsbury Review.* The author teamed with fellow novelist Bruce Sterling to write *The Difference Engine,* a sort of retroactive science-fiction novel set in Victorian England. The book is named for one of several mechanical computers that were designed during the nineteenth century by mathematician Charles Babbage. Babbage failed to build his most sophisticated machines, for their manufacture was beyond his budget and he was unable to secure public funding. Gibson and Sterling, however, imagine what might have happened had he succeeded. With the help of mechanical computers, the Victorians develop airplanes, cybernauts, and a huge steam-powered television. *The Difference Engine,* Gibson warned, "sounds cuter than it is. It's really a very, very chilly semi-dystopia." In this novel, as in most of Gibson's work, technology proves to be corrupting, and society is painfully divided between the haves and have-nots. "One of the reasons we cooked this up was so people wouldn't be able to say it was more cyberpunk writing," Gibson told the *Chicago Tribune.* "There won't be one guy with a silver Mohawk in the whole book."

After the short vacation from cyberpunk that *The Difference Engine* afforded him, Gibson returned to a familiar dystopian future with his next novel, *Virtual Light.* Set in the geographic conglomerate known as the Sprawl (most likely a fusion of most of North America), the novel centers on the adventures of an unlikely pair of allies who are thrown together by circumstance. While Gibson's trademarks are still present: biotechnology, evil corporate empires, and ghosts in the machines, *Virtual Light* was perceived by critics as more character-driven than the author's previous cyberpunk work. The technology serves the advancement of the plot rather than existing as the locus of the narrative.

In addition to his return to cyberpunk writing, Gibson also revisited the arena of Hollywood scriptwriting. Although his efforts for *Alien 3* were fruitless, he returned to produce a screenplay in 1995. Adapting his short tory "Johnny Mnemonic," Gibson worked closely with director and artist Robert Longo (who had previously collaborated with the author on a performance art piece titled *Dream Jumbo*) to bring his vision of the near future to the screen. With slight alterations to the original story—the remorselessly fierce Molly Millions character was turned into a softer, more accessible female mercenary—the film was released to mixed reviews. While many credited the work with faithfully creating the "look" of the Gibson universe, there were numerous complaints regarding the film's pacing and the acting of Keanu Reeves, who played Johnny.

The world of *Virtual Light* has been elaborated on in two subsequent Gibson novels, *Idoru* and *All Tomorrow's Parties*. Both are tales of "the techno-decadent 21st century" that find "semi-innocents wading hip-deep into trouble," to quote a *Publishers Weekly* reviewer. In *Idoru,* the second novel of the trilogy, "Gibson excels . . . in creating a warped but comprehensible future saturated with logical yet unexpected technologies," according to the reviewer. One of the central characters, the "idoru" of the title, exists only in virtual reality but is the love object of a flesh-and-blood American rock star. *Booklist* contributor Benjamin Segedin noted of the story: "Gibson remains on the cutting edge, but his vision does not now seem far-fetched. Indeed, often *Idoru* seems not to be set in the future at all. It resonates with startling realism as it presents a future not unlike the present, part hell and part paradise." In *Entertainment Weekly,* Ty Burr observed that *Virtual Light* and *Idoru* "reminded readers of what makes Gibson so damned good: a love of Raymond Chandler-esque pulp poetry, a knack for visionary squalor, a bone-dry wit, and an insistence that the technology we create will inevitably evolve beyond us. "The final novel of the trilogy, *All Tomorrow's Parties,* picks up the trail of Colin Laney, a freakish interpreter of computer data, who has possession of the projector which holds the idoru. Laney and a host of other characters—some original to this title, others returning from its two predecessors—must try to thwart the ambitions of nano-technology billionaire Cody Harwood. "Gibson's prose, as always, is portentous, crosscutting tough-guy understatement and poetic vagary," wrote Tom LeClair in a *New York Times Book Review* piece on the novel. Nevertheless, the critic added: "Compared to 'Idoru' and 'Virtual Light,' the world of 'All Tomorrow's Parties' is lo/rez, but the author appears to have been highly resolved to compose a trilogy, even if the result is 'Virtual Lite.'" Conversely, *Booklist* correspondent Benjamin Segedin noted that *All Tomorrow's Parties* "is less a cyberpunk novel about virtual reality than one that realizes an almost recognizable future filled with new and exciting technologies. . . . Gibson's vision is inextricably linked to the advent of the Internet, whose possibilities he envisioned in the book that made him a big sf name, *Neuromancer.*"

Gibson has extended his narrative vision to realms beyond the printed page. His work is often exchanged and discussed on the Internet and he has contributed to television series such as *The X-Files.* Much as he envisioned back in 1984, information and communication has become the fastest growth industry of the new millennium. But despite the prophetic aura one can bestow upon Gibson's ideas, it is his storytelling ability that continues to hold his readers' interests.

Gibson's *Neuromancer* has become one of the most anticipated science-fiction films in the history of the genre. In 1998, the book—called "the Rosetta stone of modern sci-fi" by *Entertainment Weekly*'s Noah Robischon—seemed to be on its way to the screen when a director, Chris Cunningham, signed on to work with Gibson on the project. Though Cunningham was a special-effects expert in the entertainment industry and had never directed a feature film before, he had drawn storyboards for *Neuromancer* after he read it as a teen, which impressed Gibson. Both writer and director were determined to make "an intelligent, human film rather than just another sci-fi blockbuster," noted Robischon, who predicted that the big-screen *Neuromancer* was likely "years away" from fruition. "Then again, when the book was first published in 1984, cyberspace seemed a long way off too."

BIOGRAPHICAL/CRITICAL SOURCES:

BOOKS

Contemporary Novelists, 6th edition, St. James Press (Detroit, MI), 1996.
Contemporary Popular Writers, St. James Press (Detroit, MI), 1997.
Contemporary Literary Criticism, Volume 39, Gale (Detroit, MI), 1986.
McCaffery, Larry, editor, *Across the Wounded Galaxies: Interviews with Contemporary American Science Fiction Writers,* University of Illinois Press (Champaign, IL), 1990.
St. James Guide to Science Fiction Writers, 4th edition, St. James Press (Detroit, MI), 1996.
St. James Guide to Young Adult Writers, 2nd edition, St. James Press (Detroit, MI), 1999.
Sterling, Bruce, editor, *Mirrorshades: The Cyberpunk Anthology,* Arbor House (New York, NY), 1986.

PERIODICALS

Analog, November, 1984, p. 167; December, 1986, p. 179; January, 1987, p. 182; April, 1989, p. 178; October, 1989, p. 93; January, 1994, p. 304; September, 1995, p. 160; March, 1997, Tom Easton, review of *Idoru,* p. 147.
Austin American-Statesman, November 27, 1988.
Best Sellers, July, 1986.
Bloomsbury Review, September, 1988.
Booklist, June 1, 1993, p. 1734; March 15, 1995, p. 1301; August, 1996, Benjamin Segedin, review of *Idoru,* p. 1853; September 1, 1999, Benjamin Segedin, review of *All Tomorrow's Parties,* p. 7.

Canadian Forum, October, 1994, p. 40.

Canadian Literature, summer, 1989.

Chicago Tribune, November 18, 1988; November 23, 1988.

College English, November, 2000, Daniel Punday, "The Narrative Construction of Cyberspace: Reading *Neuromancer,* Reading Cyberspace Debates," p. 194.

Entertainment Weekly, January 31, 1992, p. 54; August 13, 1993, p. 66; August 26, 1994, p. 106; November 17, 1995, Ty Burr, review of *Johnny Mnemonic,* p. 86; February 13, 1998, Ken Tucker, review of "Kill Switch" episode of *The X-Files,* p. 48; October 8, 1999, Noah Robischon, "Virtual Celebrity," pp. 10, B16; October 29, 1999, Ty Burr, "Slight of Hand," p. 104.

Fantasy Review, July, 1984; April, 1986.

Film Comment, January, 1990, p. 60.

Fortune, November 1, 1993.

Guardian, October 7, 1999, Jim McClellan, "Cyperpunk 2000," p. S14; April 26, 2001, Sean Dodson, "The Original Cyperpunk," p. S16.

Heavy Metal, May, 1985.

Impulse, winter, 1989.

Interview, January, 1989, p. 84.

Isaac Asimov's Science Fiction Magazine, August, 1986.

Library Journal, August, 1993, p. 159; August, 1996, p. 120; October 15, 1999, Jackie Cassada, review of *All Tomorrow's Parties,* p. 110.

Listener, October 11, 1990.

Locus, August, 1988.

Los Angeles Times Book Review, January 29, 1989.

Maclean's, April 29, 1991, p. 63; September 6, 1993, p. 52; June 5, 1995, Brian D. Johns, "Mind Games with William Gibson," p. 60.

Magazine of Fantasy and Science Fiction, August, 1985, p. 28; August, 1986, p. 64; October, 1990, p. 31; February, 1997, Charles de Lint, review of *Idoru,* p. 40.

Mississippi Review, Volume 16, numbers 2 and 3, 1988.

Mosaic, March, 1999, Tony Fabijancic, "Space and Power: 19th-Century Urban Practice and Gibson's Cyberworld," p. 105.

Nation, May 8, 1989, p. 636; May 6, 1991, p. 598; November 5, 1993, p. 580.

National Review, June 26, 1995, John Simon, review of *Johnny Mnemonic,* p. 65.

New Statesman, June 20, 1986; September 26, 1986; September 24, 1993, p. 55; October 11, 1996, Charles Shaar Murray, review of *Idoru,* p. 44.

New Yorker, August 16, 1993, p. 24; June 12, 1995, p. 111.

New York Times Book Review, November 24, 1985, p. 33; October 30, 1988, p. 40; December 11, 1988,
p. 23; March 10, 1991, p. 5; August 29, 1993, p. 12; September 12, 1993, p. 36; September 8, 1996, Laura Miller, review of *Idoru,* p. 6; November 21, 1999, Tom LeClair, review of *All Tomorrow's Parties,* p. 15.

Oregonian (Portland), November 24, 1988.

People Weekly, December 12, 1988, p. 49; June 10, 1991, p. 103; October 25, 1993, p. 45; July 10, 1995, p. 33.

Philadelphia Inquirer, April 15, 1986; October 30, 1988.

Pittsburgh Press, October 19, 1986.

Playboy, August, 1993, p. 32.

Popular Science, October, 2001, "Q&A: William Gibson," p. 63.

Publishers Weekly, July 12, 1993, p. 72; September 6, 1993, p. 70; August 5, 1996, review of *Idoru,* p. 435; December 2, 1996, review of *Idoru* cassette recording, p. 30; October 11, 1999, review of *All Tomorrow's Parties,* p. 59.

Punch, February 6, 1985.

Reason, November, 1991, p. 61.

Rolling Stone, December 4, 1986, p. 77; June 15, 1989.

Sacramento Union, October 26, 1988.

St. Petersburg Times, December 18, 1988.

San Francisco Chronicle, January 1, 1987.

Saturday Night, March, 1989, p. 69.

Science Fiction Review, fall, 1985; summer, 1986; winter, 1986.

Science-Fiction Studies, March, 1995, Istvan Sciscery-Ronay, Jr., "Antimancer: Cybernetics and Art in Gibson's 'Count Zero,'" p. 63; November, 1998, Ross Farnell, "Posthuman Topologies: William Gibson's 'Architexture' in *Virtual Light* and *Idoru,*" p. 459.

Seattle Times, October 24, 1988.

Spin, December, 1988.

Time, spring, 1995, p. 4; December 6, 1999, Michael Krantz, review of *All Tomorrow's Parties,* p. 120.

Times Literary Supplement, December 7, 1984; June 20, 1986; August 12, 1988; September 27, 1996, Paul Quinn, review of *Idoru,* p. 25; October 15, 1999, Keith Miller, review of *All Tomorrow's Parties,* p. 25.

Utne Reader, July, 1989, p. 28.

Variety, November 20, 2000, Ken Eisner, review of *No Maps for These Territories,* p. 19.

Village Voice, July 3, 1984; July 16, 1985; May 6, 1986; January 17, 1989.

Washington Post Book World, July 29, 1984; March 23, 1986; October 25, 1987; November 27, 1988.

West Coast Review of Books, September, 1985.

Whole Earth Review, January, 1985, p. 39; summer, 1989, p. 78.

OTHER

No Maps for These Territories (documentary film) Mark Neal Productions (London, England), 2000.*

*   *   *

GIGERENZER, Gerd 1947-

PERSONAL: Born September 3, 1947, in Wallersdorf, West Germany (now Germany); son of Franz (a businessman) and Rosemarie (a singer; maiden name, Engl) Gigerenzer; married Lorraine J. Daston (a professor of history and science), October 25, 1985; children: Thalia. *Education:* University of Munich, diploma in psychology, 1974, Ph.D., 1977, Habilitation, 1982. *Religion:* Roman Catholic.

ADDRESSES: Office—Max Planck Institute for Human Development, Lentzeallee 94, 14195 Berlin, Germany. *E-mail*—Gigerenzer@mpib-berlin.mpg.de.

CAREER: University of Munich, Munich, West Germany (now Germany), assistant professor of psychology, 1974-82; University of Bielefeld, Center of Interdisciplinary Research, Bielefeld, West Germany (now Germany), research fellow, 1982-83; University of Konstanz, Konstanz, West Germany (now Germany), professor of psychology, 1984-90; University of Saltzberg, professor of psychology, 1990-92; University of Chicago, professor of psychology, 1992-95; Max Planck Institute for Psychological Research, Munich, Germany, director of Center for Adaptive Behavior and Cognition, 1995-97; Max Planck Institute for Human Development, Berlin, Germany, director of Center for Adaptive Behavior and Cognition, 1997—. Visiting scholar, Princeton University, 1984-86, Brandeis University, 1987, Harvard University, 1987-89; fellow, Stanford University Center for Advanced Studies in the Behavioral Sciences, 1989-90; visiting professor, Queen's University, Kingston, Ontario, 1985; John M. Olin Distinguished Visiting Professor, University of Virginia School of Law, 1999. *Theory and Psychology,* coeditor. Musician and band leader, 1964-77. *Military service:* West German Army, 1967-69.

MEMBER: Deutsche Gesellschaft für Psychologie, American Psychological Association, American Psychological Society.

AWARDS, HONORS: The Probabilistic Revolution was named best book in the social and behavioral sciences by Association of American Publishers, 1987; AAAS prize for behavioral science research, 1992; fellow, Berlin Brandenburg Academy of Science, 2000.

WRITINGS:

Messung und Modellbildung in der Psychologie (title means "Measurement and Modeling in Psychology"), Reinhardt (Munich, Germany), 1981.
(Editor) *Psychophysik heute, Aktuelle Probleme und Ergebnisse,* Volume 1, 1982, Volume 2, 1984.
(With David J. Murray) *Cognition as Intuitive Statistics,* Laurence Erlbaum (Hillsdale, NJ), 1987.
(Editor, with L. Krueger and M. S. Morgan) *The Probabilistic Revolution,* Volume 2: *Ideas in the Sciences,* MIT Press (Cambridge, MA), 1987.
(With wife, Lorraine Daston, Z. Swijtink, T. Porter, and others) *The Empire of Chance: How Probability Changed Science and Everyday Life,* Cambridge University Press (New York, NY), 1989.
(With Peter M. Todd and the ABC Research Group) *Simple Heuristics That Make Us Smart,* Oxford University Press (New York, NY), 1999.
Adaptive Thinking: Rationality in the Real World, Oxford University Press (New York, NY), 2000.
(Editor, with R. Selten) *Bounded Rationality: The Adaptive Toolbox,* MIT Press (Cambridge, MA), 2001.
Calculated Risks: How to Know When Numbers Deceive You, Simon & Schuster (New York, NY), 2002.

Contributor to academic journals, including *Psychology Review* and *Science.*

WORK IN PROGRESS: A book with wife, Lorraine Daston, on changing ideas about female intelligence from the time of Greek philosopher Aristotle to the present.

SIDELIGHTS: Psychologist Gerd Gigerenzer is a noted educator and author as well as director of the Max Planck Institute for Human Development, a research institute located in Berlin, Germany. In *Science News,* contributor Bruce Bower noted that, "for the past decade, in scientific papers and in lectures at U.S. and European universities, Gigerenzer has tried to yank heuristics off their throne. Although not the first critic of the idea that highly fallible assumptions rule human thought, he is perhaps the most aggressive, and he comes armed with alternative theories to explain human reasoning. As a result, the German scientist has attracted both ardent supporters and detractors, and his wake has roiled the waters of psychological research." *Adaptive Thinking: Rationality in the Real World* is a collection of Gigerenzer's papers, with new prefaces and afterwords, that *Library Journal* reviewer Mary Ann Hughes called "of obvious importance." However, noted Hughes, the volume is written in very technical language and, therefore, understandable only by specialists.

Gigerenzer once told *CA:* "I am performing research on how scientists' tools (computers, statistics) turn into metaphors of the mind and on how people deal with uncertainty, unpredictability of behavior, and randomness in their lives."

BIOGRAPHICAL/CRITICAL SOURCES:

PERIODICALS

Library Journal, October 1, 2000, Mary Ann Hughes, review of *Adaptive Thinking: Rationality in the Real World,* p. 128.
Science News, July 13, 1996, Bruce Bower, "Rational Mind Designs: Research into the Ecology of Thought Treads on Contested Terrain," p. 24.

*   *   *

GILBERT, Ruth Gallard Ainsworth
    See AINSWORTH, Ruth (Gallard)

*   *   *

GILBERT, Sandra M(ortola) 1936-

PERSONAL: Born December 27, 1936, in New York, NY; daughter of Alexis Joseph (a civil engineer) and Angela (Carvso) Mortola; married Elliot Lewis Gilbert (a professor of English), December 1, 1957 (died, 1991); children: Roger, Katherine, Susanna. *Education:* Cornell University, B.A., 1957; New York University, M.A., 1961; Columbia University, Ph.D., 1968.

ADDRESSES: Office—Department of English, 272 Voorhies Hall, University of California, Davis, CA 95616. *E-mail*—sgilbert@ucdavis.edu.

CAREER: Queens College of the City University of New York, Flushing, NY, lecturer in English, 1963-64, 1965-66; Sacramento State College (now California State University, Sacramento, CA), lecturer in English, 1967-68; California State College (now California State University), Hayward, CA, assistant professor of English, 1968-71; St. Mary's College, Moraga, CA, lec-

turer in English, 1972; Indiana University, Bloomington, IN, associate professor of English, 1973-75; University of California, Davis, CA, 1975-85, began as associate professor, became professor of English; Princeton University, Princeton, NJ, professor of English, 1985-89, Charles Barnwell Strout Class of 1923 professor, 1989; University of California, Davis, CA, professor of English, 1989—. Literary Classics in the United States (member of board of advisors), 1979-82. Visiting professor, Indiana University, Bloomington, IN, fall, 1980, Williams College, fall, 1984, Stanford University, winter, 1985, Johns Hopkins University, Baltimore, MD, fall, 1986. Barnard College, Gildersleeve professorship, fall, 1982. Mt. Holyoke Project on Gender Context, director, 1983 and 1984. Northwestern University, School of Criticism and Theory, faculty, summer, 1984. Humanities Institute (member of executive committee), 1983-87. Hebrew University, Jerusalem, Israel, Paley Lecturer, 1990. University of Washington, Seattle, WA, Danz Lecturer, 1992.

MEMBER: Modern Language Association of America (nominating committee, 1985-87; second vice president, first vice president, president-elect, 1994—), D. H. Lawrence Society.

AWARDS, HONORS: Morrison Poetry Prize; National Endowment for the Humanities fellowship, 1980-81; Rockefeller Foundation fellowship, 1982; Guggenheim fellowship, 1983; Woman of the Year Award, *Ms.* magazine, 1986; University of California-Davis Humanities Institute fellowship, 1987-88; Charity Randall Award, International Poetry Foundation, 1990; University of California President's fellowship, 1991-92; Eugene Tiegens Memorial Prize, *Poetry Magazine;* honorary D.Litt., Wesleyan University, 1988.

WRITINGS:

Shakespeare's "Twelfth Night," Thor Publishing (Ventura, CA), 1964.
Two Novels by E. M. Forster, Thor Publishing (Ventura, CA), 1965.
D. H. Lawrence's "Sons and Lovers," Thor Publishing (Ventura, CA), 1965.
The Poetry of W. B. Yeats, Thor Publishing (Ventura, CA), 1965.
Two Novels by Virginia Woolf, Thor Publishing (Ventura, CA), 1966.
In the Fourth World: Poems, University of Alabama Press (Tuscaloosa, AL), 1978.

(With Susan Gubar) *The Madwoman in the Attic: The Woman Writer and the Nineteenth-Century Literary Imagination,* Yale University Press (New Haven, CT), 1979, new edition with expanded introduction, 2000.

(Editor, with Susan Gubar) *Shakespeare's Sisters: Feminist Essays on Women Poets,* Indiana University Press (Bloomington, IN), 1979.

The Summer Kitchen: Poems, Heyeck (Woodside, CA), 1983.

Emily's Bread: Poems, Norton (New York, NY), 1984.

(Editor, with Susan Gubar) *The Norton Anthology of Literature by Women: The Tradition in English,* Norton (New York, NY), 1985, 2nd edition, 1996.

Blood Pressure: Poems, Norton (New York, NY), 1988.

(With Susan Gubar) *No Man's Land: The Place of the Woman Writer in the Twentieth Century,* Yale University Press (New Haven, CT), Volume 1: *The War of the Words,* 1988, Volume 2: *Sexchanges,* 1989, Volume 3: *Letters from the Front,* 1994.

Acts of Attention: The Poems of D. H. Lawrence, Cornell University Press (Ithaca, NY), 1990.

Ghost Volcano: Poems, Norton (New York, NY), 1995.

(With Susan Gubar) *Masterpiece Theatre: An Academic Melodrama,* Rutgers University Press (New Brunswick, NJ)), 1995.

(With Susan Gubar and Diana O'Hehir) *Mothersongs: Poems for, by, and about Mothers,* Norton (New York, NY), 1995.

Wrongful Death: A Medical Tragedy, Norton (New York, NY), 1995.

Kissing the Bread: New and Selected Poems, 1969-1999, Norton (New York, NY), 2000.

(Editor and author of introduction) *Inventions of Farewell: A Book of Elegies,* Norton (New York, NY), 2001.

Also editor of Kate Chopin's *The Awakening and Other Stories,* Peter Smith. Contributor to anthologies, including *Best Little Magazine Fiction,* 1971, *Bicentennial Poetry Anthology,* 1976, *Contemporary Women Poets,* 1978, and *The Poetry Anthology,* 1978. Contributor of fiction and poetry to *Mademoiselle, Poetry, Epoch, Nation, New Yorker,* and other magazines.

WORK IN PROGRESS: The Tidal Wave: Poems; Mother Rights: Studies in Maternity and Creativity; The Fate of the Elegy: History, Memory, and the Mythology of Modern Death, a booklength study of the contemporary poetry of grief.

SIDELIGHTS: Sandra M. Gilbert has earned acclaim as a literary critic and as a poet. Her study, *The Madwoman in the Attic: The Woman Writer and the*

Nineteenth-Century Literary Imagination, which she cowrote with Susan Gubar, was credited with breaking important new ground in the field of women's studies, and has become a classic. The book, according to Le Anne Schreiber in *New York Times Book Review,* offers a "bold new interpretation of the great 19th-century woman novelists, [which] . . . present[s] the first pervasive case for the existence of a distinctly female imagination." As Carolyn See noted in *Los Angeles Times Book Review,* the authors examine how attitudes toward women and woman writers shaped the literature of Jane Austen, Charlotte and Emily Bronte, Emily Dickinson, George Eliot, and Mary Shelley. See explained that Gilbert and Gubar reveal how these women novelists used the "essentially destructive myth [that a woman writer was an aberration, 'the Devil Herself']—and their own fears about it to create their own myths, their own world views." Nineteenth century women writers, note Gilbert and Gubar, found themselves "trapped in the specifically literary constructs of what Gertrude Stein was to call 'patriarchal poetry.'" In response, these writers created what critic Kate Arneson, writing in *English Notes,* described as "subversive, displaced expressions of their own frustration," such as the madwoman of the title—a reference to Bertha Mason in *Jane Eyre.* As Arneson pointed out, "the powerful madwoman in the attic is an alter-ego of the gentle and submissive Jane Eyre. . . . a personification of Jane's hidden anger and unconscious resentment of her powerless . . . state."

The Madwoman in the Attic attracted significant notice from critics, many of whom appreciated its critique of the male-dominated literary canon, and its efforts to create a female literary canon. Some, however, found fault with the book. Rosemary Ashton, in *Times Literary Supplement,* described it as a "purposefully written book essentially without a thesis," whose "authors exhaust the reader with . . . formidable but unconvincing rhetoric." She added, "It is hard not to suspect that they found just what they were looking for, and equally hard to give acceptance to their 'findings.'" Yet, in a *Washington Post Book World* review, Carolyn G. Heilbrun wrote, "At last, feminist criticism, no longer capable of being called a fad, is clearly and coherently mapped out." Heilbrun concluded that *The Madwoman in the Attic,* by revealing the past, will profoundly alter the present, making possible, at last, for women writers to create their own texts." The book has remained on college reading lists since it first appeared and has become, in Arneson's estimation, "perhaps the most famous text of feminist critics."

Gilbert and Gubar also produced a three-volume series of feminist criticism titled *No Man's Land: The Place of the Woman Writer in the Twentieth Century*. In a *Globe and Mail* review of the first volume, *The War of the Words*, which appeared in 1988, Janice Kulyk Keefer called the study a "thoroughly provocative (and provocatively thorough) revisioning of the genesis of modernism." Noting that *No Man's Land* was written to be a sequel to *The Madwoman in the Attic*, *New York Times Book Review* contributor Walter Kendrick remarked that if this subsequent work "achieves its complementary goal, it will set the direction of feminist criticism for the next generation of students and scholars."

The third and final volume of the *No Man's Land* series, *Letters from the Front*, appeared in 1994. While the first volume provided an overview of writers from Tennyson forward and the second ended in the years between the two World Wars, the third offers analysis of female writers from the 1920s to the 1980s, including Marianne Moore, Virginia Woolf, Edna St. Vincent Millay, Zora Neale Hurston, and Sylvia Plath. Here Gilbert and Gubar argue that twentieth-century women writers became the subject of "feminizing publicity" and consequent fetishization that antagonized their male contemporaries and led women to assume a self-conscious false femininity. The authors examine the reaction of women writers to the Second World War, contemporary feminism, and the transformation of the "mother-poet" figure, particularly through their own revisions of the Snow White story.

Elaine Showalter observed in *London Review of Books*, "Now, they argue, all the sex roles are so scrambled, the family romance so open-ended, and the epistemological certainties so undermined that it is no longer possible to propose a 'monolithic' tale about the female imagination." In *Sexchanges*, according to *Belles Lettres* contributor Roberta Rubenstein, "the authors consider the disjunctions between *self* and *self-representation* in writers who feel compelled to become, in the interests of their art, what Gilbert and Gubar term 'female-female impersonators.'" Though finding weaknesses in their coverage of homosexuality, race, and class, Helen Carr concluded in *New Statesman and Society*, "This packed history helps to clear the rich and varied contribution made by women writers to the modernist movement, something hardly acknowledged when the first volume appeared seven years ago."

Gilbert experienced an unexpected personal tragedy in 1991 when her husband, Elliot, died after routine surgery for prostate cancer performed at the hospital of the university where he taught English. Gilbert suspected negligence and eventually settled a wrongful death lawsuit out of court. Four years later she published a prose memoir, *Wrongful Death: A Medical Tragedy*, in which she offers both a bitter indictment of medical malpractice and a tender eulogy for her husband of more than thirty years. In her effort to reconstruct circumstances surrounding her husband's death, Gilbert describes evasive physicians, crass lawyers, and her own deep sorrow. Lisa Alther wrote in *Women's Review of Books*, "In *Wrongful Death* [Gilbert] draws on both her creative and her critical skills. The poet in her conveys the depth of her love for her husband and the agony of his loss, often in very touching images." The book's "power," according to a *Publishers Weekly* review, "lies in [Gilbert's] anger and her grief, and in her all-consuming determination."

Gilbert produced *Ghost Volcano*, a book of poetry in memory of her late husband, in the same year. In this volume Gilbert explores her despair and the grieving process while struggling to come to terms with her husband's permanent absence. Diane Wakoski, in *Women's Review of Books*, praised Gilbert's rare "Orphic voice," adding that "*Ghost Volcano* is one of the most satisfying kinds of book a reader can discover. It is an unfolding, the telling of a secret story. Gilbert has organized it so that we follow the progress of her feelings as she embarks on the quest to bring her husband back from the dead by the sheer power of her lyric voice." A *Publishers Weekly* reviewer described the work as "vulnerable, bitter and courageous," concluding that "Gilbert confronts grief directly—and endures." As Miriam Levine wrote in *American Book Review*, "There is a circle that encompasses both the fall and the quest. . . . The widow in *Ghost Volcano* circles and comes back to herself, her solitary grief."

Kissing the Bread: New and Selected Poems, 1969-1999 is a collection that, according to *Women's Review of Books* contributor Rita Signorelli-Pappas, reveals Gilbert as "a poet of intense, informed feeling and unusual technical virtuosity," with a "formidable" range of subject. "Poems that might wobble and fall to earth in the hands of another poet," commented the reviewer, "are kept aloft by the sheer effervescent force of [Gilbert's] personality and thought."

Gilbert, who is the author of several other poetry collections, once told *CA:* "I see myself as a poet, a critic, and a feminist, hoping that each 'self' enriches the others. As a poet, however, I'm superstitious about becoming too self-conscious; as a critic, I want to stay close to the sources of poetry; and as a feminist, I try to keep my priorities clear without sermonizing. Those *caveats* mean that a statement like this one necessarily has to be short—at least for now."

BIOGRAPHICAL/CRITICAL SOURCES:

BOOKS

Dictionary of Literary Biography, Volume 120: *American Poets since World War II, Third Series,* Gale (Detroit, MI), 1992.
Gilbert, Sandra M., and Gubar, Susan, *The Madwoman in the Attic: The Woman Writer and the Nineteenth-Century Literary Imagination,* Yale University Press (New Haven, CT), 1979.

PERIODICALS

American Book Review, December, 1995, Mirian Levine, review of *Ghost Volcano.*
American Literature, March, 1990, Linda Wagner-Martin, review of *Sexchanges,* p. 107; March, 1998, Jane Lilienfeld, review of *Letters from the Front,* p. 218.
Belles Lettres, spring, 1995, Roberta Rubenstein, review of *Sexchanges,* p. 30.
Choice, September, 1995, p. 166.
Chronicle of Higher Education, December 17, 1999, Scott Heller, "The Book That Created a Canon," p. A20.
Comparative Literature, spring, 1991, Margot Norris, review of *No Man's Land: The Place of the Woman Writer in the Twentieth Century,* p. 199.
English Notes, fall, 1998, Kate Arneson, "Shakespeare's Sister and the Madwoman in the Attic: Updating the Literary Canon."
Globe and Mail (Toronto), February 13, 1988, Janice Kulyk Keefer, review of *The War of the Words.*
Journal of the American Medical Association, November 8, 1995, John C. Kruse, review of *Wrongful Death: A Medical Tragedy,* p. 1478.
Journal of American Studies, April, 1991, Peter Nicholls, review of *No Man's Land,* Volumes 1-1, p. 101; August, 1995, Kate Fullbrook, review of *Letters from the Front,* p. 320.
Lancet, September 2, 1995, Paul A. Volberding, review of *Wrongful Death,* p. 624.
Library Journal, June 1, 1995, p. 122.

London Review of Books, October 20, 1994, Elaine Showalter, review of *No Man's Land,* p. 36.
Los Angeles Times Book Review, March 2, 1980; May 12, 1985; March 26, 1995, p. 6.
Modern Fiction Studies, winter, 1988, Elizabeth Boyd Thompson, review of *The War of the Words,* p. 747; winter, 1989, Elizabeth Boyd Thompson, review of *Sexchanges,* p. 867.
Modern Language Quarterly, March, 1996, Sydney Janet Kaplan, review of *Letters from the Front,* p. 115.
National Review, October 28, 1988, Jane Larkin Crain, review of *The War of the Words,* 0. 46.
New Statesman and Society, October 7, 1994, Helen Carr, review of *Sexchanges,* p. 45.
Newsweek, July 15, 1985.
New York Review of Books, May 31, 1990, p. 23.
New York Times Book Review, December 9, 1979; August 17, 1980, review of *The Madwoman in the Attic,* p. 27; April 28, 1985; February 7, 1988, Caryn James, "What's Bothering Virginia Woolf?," p. 12; February 7, 1988, Christine Froula, review of *The War of the Words,* p. 12; February 19, 1989, Walter Kendrick, review of *Sexchanges,* p. 9; March 12, 1989, Bruce Bennett, "Blood Pressure," p. 38; November 6, 1994, Mark Hussey, review of *Letters From the Front,* p. 27; March 19, 1995, James S. Kunen, review of *Wrongful Death,* p. 28.
Publishers Weekly, December 5, 1994, p. 59; March 27, 1995, review of *Mothersongs: Poems for, by, and about Mothers,* p. 79; May 29, 1995, p. 78; June 26, 2000, review of *Kissing the Bread,* p. 72.
Review of English Studies, November, 1996, Judy Simons, review of *Letters from the Front,* p. 632.
Studies in the Novel, spring, 1989, Katherine Fishburn, review of *The War of the Words,* p. 104; winter, 1990, Katherine Fishburn, review of *Sexchanges,* p. 472.
Times Higher Education Supplement, February 17, 1995, Lorna Sage, review of *Letters from the Front,* p. 23.
Times Literary Supplement, August 8, 1980; April 18, 1986; June 3, 1988; June 2, 1989, Terry Castle, review of *Sexchanges,* p. 607; June 30, 1995, Gillian Beer, review of *Letters from the Front,* p. 6; June 14, 1996, Elaine Showalter, review of *Masterpiece Theater: An Academic Melodrama,* p. 9.
Washington Post Book World, November 25, 1979; June 2, 1985; January 17, 1988.
Women's Review of Books, July, 1995, pp. 18, 27; November, 2000, Rita Signorelli-Pappas, review of *Kissing the Bread,* pp. 16-17.
World Literature Today, summer, 1995, Sandra P. Cookson, review of *Letters from the Front,* p. 590.

OTHER

Poetry Daily, http://www.poems.com/ (January 4, 2001), "Sandra Gilbert."
Sandra Gilbert Web site, http://wwwenglish.ucdavis. edu/ (January 18, 2002).*

* * *

GOLDEN, Christopher 1967-

PERSONAL: Born July 15, 1967, in Framingham, MA; son of J. Laurence Golden, Jr. (an attorney) and Roberta Poulos (an attorney; maiden name, Pendolari); married Connie Russo (a paralegal), May 5; children: two. *Ethnicity:* "Irish American." *Education:* Tufts University, B.A. (cum laude), 1989. *Avocational interests:* Theater.

ADDRESSES: Agent—c/o Author Mail, Pocket Books, Simon & Schuster, 1230 Avenue of the Americas, New York, NY 10020.

CAREER: Writer. *Billboard,* New York, NY, licensing manager; also worked as marketing and publicity consultant for firms such as the William Morris Agency and Marvel Comics.

AWARDS, HONORS: Bram Stoker Award for *CUT!: Horror Writers on Horror Film;* American Library Association Best Books for Young Readers award for *Body Bags.*

WRITINGS:

NOVELS

Of Saints and Shadows, Berkley (New York, NY), 1994.
Angel Souls and Devil Hearts (sequel to *Of Saints and Shadows*), Berkley (New York, NY), 1995.
Hellboy: The Lost Army, Dark Horse (Milwaukie, OR), 1997.
Of Masques and Martyrs, Ace (New York, NY), 1998.
Strangewood, Signet Books (New York, NY), 1999.
Straight on 'til Morning, Signet (New York, NY), 2001.
Hellboy: The Bones of Giants, Dark Horse (Milwaukie, OR), 2001.
(With Tom Sniegoski) *Force Majeure,* Pocket Books (New York, NY), 2002.

The Ferryman, Signet (New York, NY), 2002.
Four Dark Nights, Leisure (New York, NY), 2002.

"BUFFY THE VAMPIRE SLAYER" SERIES

(With Nancy Holder) *Halloween Rain,* Pocket Books (New York, NY), 1997.
(With Nancy Holder) *Blooded,* Pocket Books (New York, NY), 1998.
(With Nancy Holder) *Child of the Hunt,* Pocket Books (New York, NY), 1998.
(With Nancy Holder) *Out of the Madhouse* (first in "Gatekeeper" trilogy), Pocket Books (New York, NY), 1999.
(With Nancy Holder) *Ghost Roads* (second in "Gatekeeper" trilogy), Pocket Books (New York, NY), 1999.
(With Nancy Holder) *Sons of Entropy* (third in "Gatekeeper" trilogy), Pocket Books (New York, NY), 1999.
(With Nancy Holder) *Immortal,* Pocket Books (New York, NY), 1999.
Sins of the Father, Pocket Books (New York, NY), 1999.
Spike and Dru: Pretty Maids All in a Row, Pocket Books (New York, NY), 2000.
Prophecies: The Lost Slayer, Part One, Pulse, 2001.
Dark Times: The Lost Slayer, Part Two, Pulse, 2001.
Oz: Into the Wild, Pocket Books (New York, NY), 2002.
The Wisdom of War, Pocket Books (New York, NY), 2002.

"PROWLERS" SERIES

Prowlers, Pocket Books (New York, NY), 2001.
Laws of Nature, Pocket Books (New York, NY), 2001.
Predator and Prey, Pocket Books (New York, NY), 2001.
Wild Things, Pocket Books (New York, NY), 2002.

"BODY OF EVIDENCE" SERIES

Body Bags, Pocket Books (New York, NY), 1999.
Meets the Eye, Pocket Books (New York, NY), 2000.
(With Rick Hautala) *Skin Deep,* Pocket Books (New York, NY), 2000.
(With Rick Hautala) *Burning Bones,* Pocket Books (New York, NY), 2001.
(With Rick Hautala) *Brain Trust,* Pocket Books (New York, NY), 2001.

"SUPERHEROES" SERIES

Daredevil: Predator's Smile, Boulevard (New York, NY), 1996.

X-Men: Mutant Empire Book One: Siege, Boulevard (New York, NY), 1996.

X-Men: Mutant Empire Book Two: Sanctuary, Boulevard (New York, NY), 1996.

X-Men: Mutant Empire Book Three: Salvation, Boulevard (New York, NY), 1997.

X-Men: Codename Wolverine, illustrated by Darick Robertson, Boulevard (New York, NY), 1998.

(With Jeff Mariotte) *Gen13: Netherwar,* Boulevard (New York, NY), 1999.

"STAR WARS" SERIES

Star Wars: Shadows of the Empire, Bantam (New York, NY), 1996.

Star Wars: Choose Your Own Adventure—A New Hope, Bantam (New York, NY), 1998.

Star Wars: Choose Your Own Adventure—The Empire Strikes Back, Bantam (New York, NY), 1998.

Star Wars: Choose Your Own Adventure—Return of the Jedi, Bantam (New York, NY), 1998.

COMIC BOOKS

Wolverine '95 Special, Marvel (New York, NY), 1995.

(With Tom Sniegoski) *Vampirella: Death and Destruction,* Harris Publications (New York, NY), 1996.

Thundergod, Crusade, 1996, Caliber, 1997.

(With Tom Sniegoski) *Daredevil/Shi,* Marvel-Crusade (New York, NY), 1996.

The Crow: Waking Nightmares, Kitchen Sink (Northampton, MA), 1997-98.

Shi: Rekishi, Crusade, 1997.

(With Tom Sniegoski) *Waterworld: Children of Leviathan,* Acclaim, 1997.

Shi: Night Stalkers, Crusade, 1997.

Wildworld Halloween Special, Wildstorm (New York, NY), 1997.

X-Man '97 Annual, Marvel (New York, NY), 1997.

Shi: The Series, Crusade, 1997.

(With Tom Sniegoski) *Shi: Masquerade,* Crusade, 1998.

Blade: Crescent City Blues, Marvel (New York, NY), 1998.

Spider-Man Unlimited # 20 & #21, Marvel (New York, NY), 1998.

(With Tom Sniegoski) *The Punisher,* Marvel Knights (New York, NY), 1998.

Buffy the Vampire Slayer: The Origin, Dark Horse (Milwaukie, OR), 1999.

Spike & Drusilla: Paint the Town Red, Dark Horse (Milwaukie, OR), 1999.

Buffy the Vampire Slayer #1/2, Dark Horse (Milwaukie, OR), 1999.

TV Guide/Buffy the Vampire Slayer, TV Guide, 1998.

The Crow #0, Kitchen Sink (Northampton, MA), 1999.

(With Tom Sniegoski) *Night Tribes,* Wildstorm (New York, NY), 1999.

Angel: The Hollower, Dark Horse (Milwaukie, OR), 1999.

(With Tom Sniegoski) *Buffy the Vampire Slayer Annual #1,* Dark Horse (Milwaukie, OR), 1999.

Buffy the Vampire Slayer #12 & #16, Dark Horse (Milwaukie, OR), 1999-2000.

(With Tom Sniegoski) *Wolverine/Punisher: Revelation,* Marvel (New York, NY), 1999.

Spike & Drusilla: Queen of Hearts, Dark Horse (Milwaukie, OR), 1999.

(With Tom Sniegoski) *Angel #1-#17,* Dark Horse (Milwaukie, OR), 1999-2001.

Buffy the Vampire Slayer #21-#25, #29, #30, Dark Horse (Milwaukie, OR), 2000.

(With Tom Sniegoski) *Star Trek: Embrace the Wolf,* Wildstorm (New York, NY), 2000.

(With Tom Sniegoski) *Batman: Realworlds,* DC (New York, NY), 2000.

(With Tom Sniegoski) *Batman Chronicles #22,* DC (New York, NY), 2000.

(With Tom Sniegoski) *Dark Horse Presents #153-#155,* Dark Horse (Milwaukie, OR), 2000.

(With Tom Sniegoski) *Buffy the Vampire Slayer: Giles,* Dark Horse (Milwaukie, OR), 2000.

Spike & Drusilla: All's Fair, Dark Horse (Milwaukie, OR), 2000.

(With Tom Sniegoski) *Jade #1-#4,* Chaos (Scottsdale, AZ), 2001.

(With Amber Benson) *Buffy the Vampire Slayer: Willow & Tara,* Dark Horse (Milwaukie, OR), 2001.

Buffy the Vampire Slayer: Oz #1-#3, Dark Horse (Milwaukie, OR), 2001.

(With Tom Sniegoski) *Jade: Redemption #1-#4,* Chaos (Scottsdale, AZ), 2001.

(With Tom Sniegoski) *Mike Mignola's BPRD: The Hollow Earth,* Dark Horse (Milwaukie, OR), 2002.

(With Ton Sniegoski) *Chastity: Heartbreaker #1,* Chaos (Scottsdale, AZ), 2002.

(With Amber Benson) *Buffy the Vampire Slayer: Willow & Tara—Wilderness,* Dark Horse (Milwaukie, OR), 2002.

OTHER

(Editor) *CUT!: Horror Writers on Horror Film,* Berkley (New York, NY), 1992.

Sophomore Slumps: Disastrous Second Movies, Singles, Books, and Other Stuff, Carol Publishing (Secaucus, NJ), 1995.

The 10-Minute Detective: 25 Scene-of-the-Crime Mystery Puzzles You Can Solve Yourself, Prima (Rocklin, CA), 1997.

(With Richard Hatch) *Battlestar Galactica: Armageddon,* Pocket Books (New York, NY), 1997.

(With Nancy Holder and Keith R. A. DeCandido) *The Watcher's Guide: The Official Buffy the Vampire Slayer Companion,* Pocket Books (New York, NY), 1998.

(With Nancy Holder) *The Sunnydale High Yearboook,* Pocket Books (New York, NY), 1999.

(Editor) *Hellboy: Odd Jobs,* Dark Horse (Milwaukie, OR), 1999.

(With Stephen R. Bissette and Tom Sniegoski) *Buffy the Vampire Slayer: The Monster Book,* Pocket Books (New York, NY), 2000.

(With Stanley Wiater and Hank Wagner) *The Stephen King Universe: A Tale-by-Tale Examination of the Interconnected Elements in His Work,* Renaissance (Los Angeles, CA), 2000.

Author of the young adult suspense novels *Bikini* and *Beach Blanket Psycho,* and the screenplay for *Beach Blanket Psycho.* Columnist for BPI Entertainment News Wire. Contributor to comic books, including *The Crow, Wolverine* and *Vampirella.* Contributor to periodicals, including *Boston Herald, Starlog,* and *Disney Adventures.*

WORK IN PROGRESS: Batman: Dark Worlds for DC Comics; *The Gathering Dark* (novel), Berkley, 2003; scripts for *Buffy the Vampire Slayer* and *Buffy the Vampire Slayer: Chaos Bleeds* (video games).

SIDELIGHTS: Horror writer Christopher Golden's body of work includes several books that tie in to the *Buffy the Vampire Slayer* TV series, the "Body of Evidence" novels for young adults, and several nonseries projects. *Buffy the Vampire Slayer: The Watcher's Guide,* written by Golden and Nancy Holder, with Keith R. A. DeCandido, is a comprehensive companion to the program, which concerns a teenage girl who battles the forces of evil. The book features episode summaries, biographies of show regulars and guest stars, the geography of the fictional town of Sunnydale (where the series is set), and more. "Sure, it's excessive. . . . but addicts will no doubt suck this trivia-laden tome dry with fanatic ferocity," observed Kristen Baldwin in *Entertainment Weekly.* Meanwhile, Mark Graham of Denver's *Rocky Mountain News* advised *Buffy* fans, "Don't miss this book." *Buffy The Vampire Slayer: The Monster Book,* a collaboration with Tom Sniegoski and Stephen Bissette, is a guide to the supernatural beings who have figured in the program, either as Buffy's adversaries or her allies. It includes interviews with the show's creator and several of its scriptwriters, plus information on the role otherworldly creatures have played in the culture overall. The "behind-the-scenes info" will appeal to regular watchers of the series, while the background data will be valuable to new viewers, remarked Kristine Huntley in *Booklist.* Two of *Buffy*'s monsters, vampires Spike and Drusilla, star in Golden's novel *Spike and Dru: Pretty Maids All in a Row.* This book finds the two vampires trying to acquire a magical necklace from an evil demon, who orders the pair to kill all the world's Slayers-in-Waiting, young women who are prepared to become Slayers in the event of another Slayer's death. A *Publishers Weekly* reviewer thought the novel "at times unnecessarily gruesome" and the characters "marginally developed," but added that "the narrative's swift momentum and engaging action sequences make for breezy entertainment."

The "Body of Evidence" series focuses on Jenna Blake, a college student who works in a medical examiner's office, a setting that allows her to become involved in solving mysteries. The first entry, *Body Bags,* has Jenna trying to thwart a global conspiracy, and being pursued by a killer "whose technique demonstrates Golden's sense of the truly morbid," noted a *Publishers Weekly* critic. In *Meets the Eye,* Jenna sees a dead student come back to life during his autopsy, and she then finds that other people thought to be dead are alive and committing crimes. *Skin Deep* adds the issue of racism to the plot, as Jenna goes on the trail of a killer who has the power to change his skin color. Golden's writing style is "a cross between horror and mystery," reported *School Library Journal* contributor Michele Snyder, who found some elements of *Skin Deep* "far-fetched" but the book "involving" overall.

Straight on 'til Morning, an effort outside of Golden's series books, is a coming-of-age tale with echoes of the never-aging boy, Peter Pan. The protagonist, thirteen-year-old Kevin Murphy, has a crush on a slightly older girl, Nikki French, who is more interested in Peter Starling, a mysterious young man who eventually spirits her off to a place called Neverland. Kevin, aided by his brother and friends, sets out to bring her back. The novel is "a horrific and ultimately sorrowful thriller," commented a *Publishers Weekly* reviewer.

BIOGRAPHICAL/CRITICAL SOURCES:

PERIODICALS

Booklist, August, 2000, Kristine Huntley, review of *Buffy The Vampire Slayer: The Monster Book,* p. 2095.

Entertainment Weekly, October 9, 1998, Kristen Baldwin, review of *Buffy the Vampire Slayer: The Watcher's Guide,* p. 78.

Publishers Weekly, September 28, 1998, review of *X-Men: Codename Wolverine,* p. 78; March 29, 1999, review of *Body Bags,* p. 101; October 2, 2000, review of *Spike and Dru: Pretty Maids All in a Row,* p. 64; March 12, 2001, review of *Straight on 'til Morning,* p. 67.

Rocky Mountain News (Denver), November 8, 1998, Mark Graham, "*Watcher's Guide* Scares up *Buffy* Junkies," p. 5E.

School Library Journal, July, 2000, Molly S. Kinney, review of *Meets the Eye,* p. 104; January, 2001, Michele Snyder, review of *Skin Deep,* p. 130.

OTHER

Christopher Golden (author Web site), http://www. christophergolden.com (September 10, 2001).

*   *   *

GOLDMAN, William (W.) 1931-

PERSONAL: Born August 12, 1931, in Chicago, IL; son of Maurice Clarence (a businessman) and Marion (Weil) Goldman; married Ilene Jones, April 15, 1961; children: Jenny Rebecca, Susanna. *Education:* Oberlin College, B.A., 1952; Columbia University, M.A., 1956. *Avocational interests:* Tennis, swimming, mysteries, basketball, and baseball.

ADDRESSES: Home—50 East 77th St., New York, NY 10021. *Agent*—Morton Janklow Associates, 598 Madison Ave., New York, NY 10022 (books); Creative Artists Agency, 1888 Century Park East, 14th Floor, Los Angeles, CA 90067 (films).

CAREER: Freelance writer. *Military service:* U.S. Army, 1952-54.

AWARDS, HONORS: Academy of Motion Picture Arts and Sciences Award (Oscar) for best original screenplay, 1970, for *Butch Cassidy and the Sundance Kid;* Academy of Motion Picture Arts and Sciences Award (Oscar) for best screenplay based on material from another medium, 1976, for *All the President's Men;* Laurel Award, 1983, for lifetime achievement in screenwriting.

WRITINGS:

NOVELS

The Temple of Gold, Knopf (New York City), 1957.

Your Turn to Curtsy, My Turn to Bow, Doubleday (New York City), 1958.

Soldier in the Rain, Atheneum (New York City), 1960.

Boys and Girls Together, Atheneum, 1964.

(Under pseudonym Harry Longbaugh) *No Way to Treat a Lady,* Gold Medal (New York City), 1964, published under own name, Harcourt, 1968.

The Thing of It Is . . . , Harcourt (New York City), 1967.

Father's Day, Harcourt, 1971.

The Princess Bride: S. Morgenstern's Classic Tale of True Love and High Adventure, the "Good Parts" Version, Abridged by William Goldman, Harcourt, 1974.

Wigger (juvenile), Harcourt, 1974.

Marathon Man, Macmillan (New York City), 1975.

Magic, Delacorte (New York City), 1976.

Tinsel, Delacorte, 1979.

Control, Delacorte, 1982.

(Under pseudonym S. Morgenstern) *The Silent Gondoliers,* Ballantine (New York City), 1983.

The Color of Light, Warner Books (New York City), 1984.

Heat, Warner Books, 1985.

Brothers, Warner Books, 1987.

William Goldman: Four Screenplays with Essays, Applause Books (New York City), 1995.

NONFICTION

The Season: A Candid Look at Broadway, Harcourt, 1969.

Adventures in the Screen Trade: A Personal View of Hollywood and Screenwriting, Warner Books, 1983.

(With Mike Lupica) *Wait till Next Year: The Story of a Season When What Should've Happened Didn't and What Could've Gone Wrong Did!,* Bantam (New York City), 1988.

Hype and Glory, Villard Books (New York City), 1990.

Which Lie Did I Tell?: More Adventures in the Screen Trade, Pantheon, 2000.

The Big Picture: Who Killed Hollywood? and Other Essays, Applause, 2000.

PLAYS

(With brother, James Goldman) *Blood, Sweat, and Stanley Poole* (produced on Broadway at Morosco Theatre, October 5, 1961), Dramatists Play Service, 1962.

(With Goldman and John Kander) *A Family Affair* (musical), produced on Broadway at Billy Rose Theatre, January 27, 1962.

Mr. Horn (teleplay), produced by Columbia Broadcasting System (CBS), 1979.

SCREENPLAYS

(With Michael Relph) *Masquerade,* United Artists, 1965.

Harper, Warner Brothers, 1966.

Butch Cassidy and the Sundance Kid (produced by Twentieth Century-Fox, 1969), Bantam, 1971.

The Hot Rock, Twentieth Century-Fox, 1972.

The Stepford Wives, Fadsior/Palomar, 1974.

The Great Waldo Pepper (produced by Universal, 1975), Dell, 1975.

All the President's Men (based on book of same title by Bob Woodward and Carl Bernstein), Warner Brothers, 1976.

Marathon Man (based on Goldman's novel of same title), Paramount, 1976.

A Bridge Too Far (produced by United Artists, 1977), published as *William Goldman's Story of A Bridge Too Far,* Dell, 1977.

Magic (based on Goldman's novel of same title), Twentieth Century-Fox, 1978.

The Princess Bride (based on Goldman's novel of same title), Twentieth Century-Fox, 1987.

Heat (based on Goldman's novel of same title), New Century/Vista, 1987.

Misery, 1990.

(With Robert Collector and Dana Bodner) *Memoirs of an Invisible Man,* 1992.

Absolute Power (based on novel of same title by David Baldacci), 1997.

The General's Daughter, Paramount Pictures, 1999.

Hearts in Atlantis, Castle Rock, 2001.

OTHER

Contributor to periodicals, including *Transatlantic Review, Rogue, Esquire,* and *New World Writing.*

ADAPTATIONS: Soldier in the Rain was filmed by Allied Artists, 1963; *No Way to Treat a Lady* was filmed by Paramount, 1968; a musical play based on *No Way to Treat a Lady* was produced on Broadway at the Hudson Guild Theatre, May 27, 1987.

SIDELIGHTS: William Goldman is "just about the biggest, the best, the most successful writer in movies today," according to Bruce Cook in the *Chicago Tribune Book World.* Goldman, who has won two Academy Awards for his screenplays, prefers to think of himself as a novelist who happens to write for films; indeed, his fiction has found as wide an audience as any movie he has written. In the *Dictionary of Literary Biography,* Botham Stone calls Goldman "an instinctive writer who works very quickly and with little revision. His extremely popular screenplays and books have a quality of humanity that sets them apart from formula bestsellers and other, more calculated 'blockbuster' films. . . . There is no small amount of skill in [his works'] creation." Goldman is "not only prolific and versatile," concludes Bob Ellison in the *Chicago Tribune Book World,* "he's one of only a handful of earthlings who can write and screenplays and novels—and excel at both." Richard Andersen in *Contemporary Novelists* describes Goldman as "an extraordinarily talented and prolific writer whose incorporation of cinematic techniques with conventional narrative forms mark a significant contribution to the novel tradition."

Summing up his career for *CA,* Goldman said: "I've only been a writer. My first novel was taken the summer I finished graduate school, so I've never known anything else." Part of the reason for Goldman's consistent success through thirty years of writing is his rather unconventional attitude toward his work. He goes to an office every day, even though his home is quiet and comfortable, because an office environment encourages him to apply himself. "I grew up in a businessman's town [Chicago]," he told the *New York Times,* "and it's essential that I maintain a sense that what I'm doing is as important as what an insurance man or businessman is doing. That's why I have an office." Stone describes Goldman as "normally unenthusiastic about his work, no matter how flamboyant or comic it might appear." While this may not necessarily be the case, Goldman is satisfied to leave his projects behind at the end of a working day while he relaxes elsewhere. "The sooner I'm done," he told Stone, "the sooner I can go to the movies."

Goldman enjoyed attending films as a youngster, so it is perhaps not surprising that he also claims to enjoy writing for the medium. In the *New York Times* he said: "I have a theory that we gravitate toward affection. I have a facility for screenwriting. It's gone very well. I needed something else to write besides novels, which are physically hard and take time. Since nobody wanted my stories and people seemed to want my screenplays, I gravitated toward that affection." Before he ventured into screenwriting, however, Goldman had established himself as an author of "well-crafted, moderately interesting, psychological novels[with] a distinctive talent for creating characters through dialogue," to quote *New York Times Book Review* contributor Sheldon Frank. Between 1957, when he published his first novel, *The Temple of Gold,* until 1966, when he penned his first solo screenplay, Goldman wrote five full-length works of fiction and two Broadway plays.

According to Stone, Goldman's novels are "blunt and direct, and he avoids symbolism and elaborate detail. His narrative voice is rarely intrusive, but he will occasionally step away from his omniscient stance and deliver a few words of his own. . . . He constructs scenes efficiently and with a deliberate punch line, as if determining the weight and flow of scenes from the very start of the writing process. He very rarely thinks in visual terms, preferring to work with plot and character action as a way of building his themes." Cook also observes that Goldman's adventure stories "are written rather casually, as though shot from the hip right onto the page." This is not to suggest, though, that Goldman's work lacks psychological depth. In a full-length study titled *William Goldman,* Richard Andersen describes the author's main theme as an investigation of "the illusions men and women live by, which often make human existence more miserable than it need be." Andersen detects a tendency for Goldman's protagonists to seek escape from a society that encroaches on their desire for personal freedom. Ironically, he adds, "what they escape to is more often than not other illusions."

In *Season of Promise: Spring Fiction 1967,* Warren French contends that Goldman's fiction is "particularly timely, because [it deals] with conditions that are specifically characteristic of our affluent time. The depression and World War II caught Americans unprepared. To survive, they were forced to develop psychological expedients for dealing with these catastrophic events. By the time, however, that these expedients have hardened into conventions—as expedients have a way of doing—conditions have changed enough so that people are once again unprepared to deal with their immediate situation." Goldman's protagonists often survive the be-

wildering times by developing bonds of camaraderie—a "closeness that transcends individual backgrounds and differences," to quote Stone. Otherwise, in Andersen's view, what slight affirmation Goldman's heroes can achieve "seems to be the small but valuable awareness that life is simply better than death."

Goldman entered the screenwriting business quite by chance when actor Cliff Robertson saw the typescript for one of Goldman's novels, *No Way to Treat a Lady.* Unexpectedly, Robertson offered Goldman some screen work; a first project, an adaptation of the short story "Flowers for Algernon," was eventually turned over to someone else. Goldman did earn a screen credit, however, for his contribution to the British film *Masquerade,* released in 1965. Armed with that experience, Goldman was able to land other film work relatively easily. In 1966 he wrote his first solo screenplay, *Harper,* a detective story based on a Ross Macdonald novel. Paul Newman starred in the film, and Stone notes that the association between Newman and Goldman "signaled the start of an acting/writing collaboration that would perfectly mesh."

Newman also starred with Robert Redford in the film from Goldman's second solo screenplay, *Butch Cassidy and the Sundance Kid.* The movie follows the adventures of two affable bank robbers who must outrun a posse hired to track and kill them. Stone states that the film "was one of the best received in the 1960s. Goldman won his first Academy Award for the screenplay, which continues to be one of the most influential works in Hollywood, still defining a standard for entertainment movies." Stone adds: "It was a breakthrough film, not just for Goldman, but for screenwriters in general; Goldman received $400,000 for his script, the first time a screenwriter had ever received so high a payment."

With the success of *Butch Cassidy and the Sundance Kid,* Goldman began to alternate between novels and screenplays; several of his subsequent films, including *The Hot Rock, A Bridge Too Far, The Great Waldo Pepper,* and *All the President's Men,* featured the popular Redford in leading roles. Goldman won his second Oscar for *All the President's Men,* a script he based on the Watergate-era book by Bob Woodward and Carl Bernstein.

Stone writes: "Goldman has often suggested in his work that friendship is the only comfort in an absurd universe in which individual lives are ultimately meaningless, but for commercial reasons this darker slant to the material is usually missing from the final product on the screen. Two of Goldman's scripts do deal effectively with this darker theme, however." Stone is referring to *Marathon Man* and *Magic,* two movies Goldman adapted from his own novels. In the novel and film *Marathon Man,* a meek graduate student becomes the target of a brutal team of ex-Nazi diamond smugglers simply because his murdered brother had been a spy. Eventually the student adopts the ruthless techniques of his tormentors in order to free himself from their grasp. Addressing his comments to the novel, *Best Sellers* contributor William R. Evans states: "Unlike many thrillers, *Marathon Man* has some serious implications. Upon finishing it, the reader finds that the issues of hatred, war, destruction, and revenge focus in the mind. Are these things naturally part of humankind? Are we condemned to go on making the same mistakes, year after year, decade after decade? If such a thing as a timely, relevant, thoughtful novel of suspense exists, this is it." *Magic* explores the psychological dangers of an uncontrollable alter ego through the person of a ventriloquist who is dominated by his puppet. *Best Sellers* reviewer Edward F. Warner finds the novel "a fascinating[work] about the dark world of a man's mind driven to its inevitable end." As films, both *Marathon Man* and *Magic* did well at the box office, and as books they signalled a new direction for Goldman's writing: the adventure-thriller with psychological or satirical undertones.

Goldman's more recent screenplays include *The Princess Bride,* based on a fractured fairy tale he wrote in 1973. Speaking of the original novel, the essayist for the *St. James Guide for Fantasy Writers* explained: "The words 'rollicking' and 'swashbuckling' might have been invented to describe *The Princess Bride,* yet in it Goldman also manages to satirize New York life, the publishing industry, critics, and the whole fantasy genre. Along the way he pulls off a feat of alienation that would have made Bertolt Brecht proud. He does this by pretending that he is presenting the 'good parts' version of an older book—*The Princess Bride* by S. Morgenstern—based on the true story of Buttercup and Westley, two citizens of the ancient mid-European country of Florin."

The film, like the book, is framed around an old adventure story by "S. Morgenstern" (actually a Goldman pseudonym), from which the "boring parts" have been extracted. What remains is a simple tale of swashbuckling rescue and true romance, peopled by evil princes, giants, and miracle workers. According to S. K. Oberbeck in *Newsweek,* Goldman has concocted "a 'classic' medieval melodrama that sounds like all the Saturday

serials you ever saw feverishly reworked by the Marx brothers." Most reviewers have praised the film treatment for its balance of sincerity and tongue-in-cheek parody. *New York Times* contributor Janet Maslin writes: "The material might easily have lent itself to broad parody or become too cute for its own good. But Mr. Reiner [the director] presents it as a bedtime story, pure and simple. The film's style is gentle, even fragile, with none of the bold flourishes that might be expected but with none of the silliness either. . . . Mr. Reiner seems to understand exactly what Mr. Goldman loves about stories of this kind, and he conveys it with clarity and affection."

In the 1997 film *Absolute Power,* based on the bestselling novel by David Baldacci, Goldman tells the story of Luther Whitney, a jewel thief who, while robbing a mansion, witnesses the murder of the lady of the house. The problem is that the killer is the president of the United States. "Which President?" Stuart Klawans asks in his review of the film for the *Nation.* "As we gradually learn, this one keeps his fly unzipped, owes his power to a liberal backer and generally allows the country to be run by a tough broad who wears her hair in bangs." Starring Clint Eastwood in the role of Whitney, the film won acclaim particularly for its depiction of the aging Whitney's desperate bid to reestablish a close relationship with his daughter. As Richard Corliss writes in *Time:* "The plot is a doomsday version of Bill Clinton's Paula Jones problem, but the theme is impending mortality—settling scores before time's up. " Corliss concludes: "The warming, nicely played relationship of the burglar and his lawyer daughter . . . is the source of the film's absolute power." Brian D. Johnson in *Maclean's* finds that "the suspense is taut, the humor is dry and the whole thing goes down with the cool kick of a double martini."

Many writers who have worked for Hollywood have subsequently written about life and business there. Goldman is no exception. His novel *Tinsel* and his nonfiction memoirs *Adventures in the Screen Trade: A Personal View of Hollywood and Screenwriting* and *Which Lie Did I Tell?: More Adventures in the Screen Trade* detail "how Hollywood [has] alchemied literary gold into commercial dross," to quote *Los Angeles Times Book Review* correspondent Nancy Yanes Hoffman. *Tinsel,* according to Andersen, "tells the story of three women who desperately try to escape from the boredom of their daily lives to the fame and fortune of movie stardom, which, like all illusions, eludes them." In *Film Comment,* John Sayles observes that *Adventures in the Screen Trade* is "split between descriptions of studio and star politics and discussions of writing technique. In this way it mirrors the life of the screenwriter. Ask any screenwriter why a certain moment exists in a movie he's worked on and you're as likely to hear an anecdote about the producer's wife or the cost of camel wranglers as you are to hear about plot, dialogue, or pacing. The tension between these two—between what you hope for when you start a screenplay and what you settle for when it smacks up against the reality of film production—runs up and down the spine of Goldman's book." Maslin explains in the *New York Times Book Review* that the work "is not the most complex or sophisticated analysis of moviemaking," but that it "does take a nuts-and-bolts approach very like Hollywood's own. This is a savvy, gossipy book by someone with considerable insight into the tricks of the trade." Sayles concludes: "Like listening to a much-traveled sailor before your first time at sea, Goldman offers horror stories, tales of hardship, and plenty of warnings, but through it all he weighs anchor in the exhilaration and transcendent moments that get you hooked on the idea in the first place."

In 2000, Goldman released *Which Lie Did I Tell?: More Adventures in the Screen Trade.* In this follow-up, he reveals secrets of his success in Hollywood, which he sums up by claiming the only important element is to have a good story. He also dispatches his analyses of favorite scenes and offers more insider tidbits about actors and actresses. In addition, he bemoans the direction in which entertainment is going, blaming MTV specifically for having a negative impact on movies with all of its quick-cutting and complaining that most movies are mass-produced and formulaic. Goldman also mentions instances in which his instincts have failed him. For example, in *Misery,* though Goldman insisted on keeping novelist King's scene of the hero having his feet chopped off, director Rob Reiner changed it to show his ankles being broken instead. The scene became a determining moment in the picture and later, Goldman admitted Reiner was right. A *Library Journal* reviewer of *Which Lie Did I Tell?* called the book "an engaging expose that is not mean-spirited." Steve Kurtz, reviewing the book for *Reason,* called it "a worthy successor to *Adventures in the Screen Trade.*"

When he talks about screenwriting, Goldman does not tend to dwell upon the "exhilaration and transcendent moments." His approach to the work is both modest and pragmatic. "No one has ever heard me use the word 'good' about any of my screenplays," he said in *Esquire.* "I would never attribute that kind of quality—good, bad, or beautiful—to a screenplay. A screenplay is a piece of carpentry, and except in the case of Ingmar Bergman, it's not an art, it's a craft. And you want to be

as good as you can at your craft, and you want to give them what they need within the limits of your talents—and the only reason I am 'hot' now has nothing to do with the quality of the films that I have been involved with. It has to do with two things: some of the films have been successful, but more important, *they have been made.*" Goldman has also expressed relief that screenwriting is not his sole professional and creative outlet—too many people, he says, have a hand in producing a finished movie script. "My feeling is that you must have something else, something you create that won't get altered for reasons that have nothing to do with quality," he told *Publishers Weekly.* "If what you want to do is to bring something into being, and you want to have control over the final product, you must have another outlet." That outlet for Goldman is fiction. Assessing that aspect of Goldman's career, Andersen concludes: "Goldman may be considered an accomplished and inventive storyteller, and, in thematic terms, a serious artist. Though his angle of vision has become increasingly more violent and absurd, he has not give way to despair or cynicism, but has managed to deal with his resignation about the human condition without losing his sense of humor or concern for humanity. . . . Goldman's works provide an unassailable argument against the novel-is-dead critics and effectively contribute to the life span of our literature's most popular and therefore most important genre."

BIOGRAPHICAL/CRITICAL SOURCES:

BOOKS

Andersen, Richard, *William Goldman,* Twayne (Boston), 1979.

Brady, John, *The Craft of the Screenwriter,* Touchstone, 1982.

Contemporary Literary Criticism, Gale (Detroit), Volume 1, 1973, Volume 48, 1988.

Contemporary Novelists, 6th edition, St. James Press (Detroit), 1996.

Dictionary of Literary Biography, Volume 44: *American Screenwriters, Second Series,* Gale, 1986.

French, Warren, *Season of Promise: Spring Fiction 1967,* University of Missouri Press, 1968.

Goldman, William, *Adventures in the Screen Trade: A Personal View of Hollywood and Screenwriting,* Warner Books, 1983.

Goldman, William, *Hype and Glory,* Villard Books, 1990.

Kael, Pauline, *Reeling,* Little, Brown, 1972.

Newsmakers, Gale (Farmington Hills, MI), 2001.

St. James Guide to Fantasy Writers, St. James Press (Detroit, MI), 1996.

PERIODICALS

Atlantic Monthly, August, 1960.
Best Sellers, May 1, 1967; September 15, 1969; March 15, 1971; November 1, 1974; December, 1976.
Books and Bookmen, January, 1968.
Book World, April 18, 1971.
Chicago Sunday Tribune, October 13, 1957.
Chicago Tribune, November 13, 1978; March 13, 1987; October 9, 1987.
Chicago Tribune Book World, August 12, 1979; May 16, 1982; June 30, 1985.
Christian Science Monitor, April 27, 1967; October 9, 1969.
Commonweal, November 29, 1957.
Detroit News, May 20, 1984.
Entertainment Weekly, February 14, 1997, p. 39.
Esquire, October, 1981.
Film Comment, June, 1983.
Globe and Mail (Toronto), July 4, 1987.
Library Journal, February 15, 2000, review of *What Lie Did I Tell?,* p. 164.
Life, October 31, 1969.
Los Angeles Times, March 13, 1987; September 25, 1987.
Los Angeles Times Book Review, July 15, 1979; June 6, 1982; April 3, 1983; May 20, 1984; June 2, 1985; May 17, 1987.
Maclean's, February 17, 1997, p. 72.
Nation, March 17, 1997, p. 43.
New Leader, September 15, 1969.
New Republic, March 17, 1997, p. 28.
Newsweek, September 17, 1973; August 13, 1979; October 5, 1987; February 17, 1997, p. 67.
New Yorker, May 20, 1967.
New York Herald Tribune Book Review, November 3, 1957.
New York Times, November 17, 1957; August 31, 1969; September 19, 1969; November 8, 1978; November 12, 1978; July 24, 1979; April 12, 1982; March 17, 1983; February 5, 1987; March 13, 1987; June 12, 1987; September 25, 1987.
New York Times Book Review, November 17, 1957; July 17, 1960; July 26, 1964; April 19, 1967; April 14, 1968; September 28, 1969; January 31, 1971; December 23, 1973; October 27, 1974; September 12, 1976; August 26, 1979; September 16, 1979; April 25, 1982; March 20, 1983; April 15, 1984; May 19, 1985; February 15, 1987.
People, August 20, 1979; March 30, 1987; September 28, 1987; February 17, 1997, p. 19.
Publishers Weekly, March 18, 1983; January 31, 2000, Kevin Howell, "PW Talks with William Goldman," pp. 90-91.

Reason, August, 2000, Steve Kurtz, "It's the Story, Stupid," p. 61.
Saturday Review, October 19, 1957; July 25, 1964; September 13, 1969.
Spectator, March 12, 1965; October 16, 1982.
Time, April 4, 1983; September 12, 1987; February 24, 1997, p. 67.
Tribune Books (Chicago), February 15, 1987; February 28, 1988.
Variety, August 13, 1969; July 19, 1999, Peter Bart, "Egos on the Line," p. 2; February 14, 2000, p. 51.
Washington Post, November 11, 1978; May 1, 1982; April 14, 1984; October 9, 1987.
Washington Post Book World, August 19, 1979; June 5, 1983; June 16, 1985; February 15, 1987.
Writer's Digest, July, 1997, p. 37.*

*　　*　　*

GORMLEY, Beatrice 1942-

PERSONAL: Born October 15, 1942, in Glendale, CA; daughter of Louis Kirk and Elizabeth (Fisher) LeCount; married Robert J. Gormley (a college textbook publisher), September 4, 1966; children: Catherine, Jennifer. *Education:* Pomona College, B.A. (magna cum laude), 1964.

ADDRESSES: Home—Ossining, NY. *Agent*—Aladdin Books, 1230 Avenue Of The Americas, New York, NY 10020. *E-mail*—bgormley@bestweb.net.

CAREER: Addison-Wesley Publishing Co., Menlo Park, CA, assistant English editor, 1966-67; freelance editor, 1968-77; full-time writer.

MEMBER: Society of Children's Book Writers and Illustrators.

WRITINGS:

FOR CHILDREN

Mail-Order Wings, illustrations by Emily Arnold McCully, Dutton (New York, NY), 1981.
Fifth Grade Magic, illustrations by Emily Arnold McCully, Dutton (New York, NY), 1982.
Best Friend Insurance, Dutton (New York, NY), 1983.
The Ghastly Glasses, Dutton (New York, NY), 1985.
Paul's Volcano, Houghton (Boston, MA), 1987.

Richard and the Vratch, Avon (New York, NY), 1987.

More Fifth Grade Magic, Dutton (New York, NY), 1989.

Wanted, UFO, Dutton (New York, NY), 1990.

Sky Guys to White Cat, Dutton (New York, NY), 1991.

Ellie's Birthstone Ring, Dutton (New York, NY), 1992.

Maria Mitchell: The Soul of an Astronomer, Eerdmans (Grand Rapids, MI), 1995.

First Ladies: Women Who Called the White House Home, Scholastic (New York, NY), 1997.

C. S. Lewis: Christian and Storyteller, Eerdmans (Grand Rapids, MI), 1998.

Miriam, Eerdmans (Grand Rapids, MI), 1999.

Louisa May Alcott: Young Novelist, Aladdin (New York, NY), 1999.

Amelia Earhart: Young Aviator, Aladdin (New York, NY), 2000.

Adara, Eerdmans (Grand Rapids, MI), 2001.

President George W. Bush: Our Forty-third President, Aladdin (New York, NY), 2001.

Laura Ingalls Wilder: Young Pioneer, Aladdin (New York, NY), 2001.

Also a contributor to magazines and newspapers.

SIDELIGHTS: Beatrice Gormley is the author of books for young readers, including novels that blend fantasy and reality, as well as biographies of famous writers, scientists, and politicians. With novels such as *Mail-Order Wings, Fifth Grade Magic* and its sequel, *More Fifth Grade Magic, Paul's Volcano, Wanted, UFO,* and *Richard and the Vratch,* Gormley serves up entertaining mixtures of magic and humor for middle-grade readers. Working in nonfiction, Gormley has written inspiring biographies of pioneering women, such as in her *Maria Mitchell: The Soul of an Astronomer, Louisa May Alcott: Young Novelist,* and *Amelia Earhart: Young Aviator,* as well as a biography of the author of the "Narnia" books, C. S. Lewis, and of the forty-third president of the United States, George W. Bush. And with her *Miriam* she moved into new writing territory with the fictionalized biography of the biblical Miriam, sister of Moses.

Born in Glendale, California, in 1942, Gormley decided at an early age what she wanted to do when she grew up. "When I was eight," the author once commented, "I wanted to become a cowgirl when I grew up. By the time I was ten I had changed my mind, deciding to become a writer instead. That has been my heart's desire ever since." Gormley passed a happy childhood in California, as she once described: "In my spare time, when I wasn't reading, I was playing in the sagebrush-covered

hills behind my family's house in Burbank, California. Sometimes I explored the canyons and ridges and their absorbing variety of wildflowers and shrubs and trees. Sometimes I played fantasy games in which I was shipwrecked or captured by Indians. Sometimes I just sat under a bush and smelled the pungent sage and felt peaceful and happy."

Despite her evident love of nature, her fist love remained writing. "All through school I was encouraged in my ambition," Gormley once noted. "My teachers were enthusiastic about my writing; I even won awards for writing. So, I was confident that I would know, when the time came, *how* to become a writer. But I graduated from college with my final prize for student fiction and still no idea of how to go about earning my living as a professional writer. Instead I went into textbook publishing, and edited and rewrote other people's prose. This was interesting work, but not exactly what I had in mind when I was ten. I wrote short stories now and then, dreary, aimless stories that I would never want to read myself, and sent them to the *New Yorker.* They were always sent back with printed rejection slips."

Finally, however, Gormley decided that if she really wanted to become a writer, she had to get radical about it. "It began to dawn on me that perhaps I hadn't worked hard enough at becoming a writer," Gormley remarked. "Maybe I had to give it more time and effort—maybe I had to risk failing. So I worked up my courage, stopped accepting freelance editing jobs (I was lucky to have this option, because my husband could support us on his salary) and spent that time on my own writing. At first I concentrated on articles and essays, and I was delighted to see my work in print in newspapers and magazines. But I couldn't stop trying to write fiction, even though I was still totally unsuccessful in getting it published. Then, in the year that my two daughters were eight and ten, I began to write stories for children. They were the kind of stories I liked to read at that age—adventure stories, especially with some magic or science fiction.

"I enjoyed writing these stories so much I couldn't understand why I'd never tried them before. In June of 1979 I took my latest attempt, *Mail-Order Wings,* to a writer's conference. To my great good fortune, Jane Langton was teaching the 'Writing for Children' section. She encouraged me, helped me revise *Mail-Order Wings,* and advised me to send it to Ann Durell at Dutton. I felt that my fairy godmother had appeared! Ann Durell thought my manuscript was promising, but outlined major revisions, and I saw right away that the story could be ten times better if I did what she said. Sweating to make these revisions, I had my first revelation about how hard one has to work to write a good story."

Published in 1981, *Mail-Order Wings* tells the magical story of young Andrea who has a great desire to fly. Purchasing a pair of WondaWings through the post, she is surprised that, when donning them, she actually can fly. Even greater is her surprise, however, when she discovers her wings are impossible to remove and that in fact feathers are beginning to sprout on her back. "This book is exciting, believable, sometimes comic, and it shows real feeling for the lives of birds, and what it might be like to be one," wrote Rodie Sudbery in a *School Librarian* review of this debut novel. A contributor for *Publishers Weekly* called Gormley's first effort a "neat mixture of reality and fantasy."

"After writing *Mail-Order Wings* in a haphazard way, and with a great deal of advice," Gormley once commented, "I knew that I would have to find a more organized method of working if I was going to make a career out of this. I did some painful and unsuccessful trial-and-error work, and then a friend told me about Phyllis Whitney's *Writing Juvenile Stories and Novels*. I began to keep a notebook, as Whitney advises, with sections for outline, theme, characters, and so on. Her method has been invaluable to me."

Reprising the characters from her first book, Gormley has Andrea fitted for glasses in *The Ghastly Glasses*. But instead of the eye doctor's office, Andrea and her Aunt Bets wind up in a psychic research laboratory, where Andrea receives some very peculiar glasses—ones that allow her to focus inside an individual's personality and change it. Initially, she enjoys "improving" the people around her, but soon she tires of such powers and destroys the glasses, returning everyone to their former selves. Reviewing the title in *School Library Journal*, Lisa Smith noted that the "ethical conflict in meddling with other's personalities is keenly felt." *Horn Book* reviewer Anita Silvey thought that the "humor, drama, and suspense of the story make it a delightful page-turner," adding that the "characters are as eccentric and engaging as the plot."

Another pair of companion books also fit into the fantasy genre: *Fifth Grade Magic* and *More Fifth Grade Magic*. In the former title, Gretchen Nichols gets help from her fairy godmother, Errora, when she is passed over as the lead in her school play, a part given to her rival, Amy, instead. But then Errora solves the problem: she casts a spell to put Gretchen inside Amy's skin. Mistakes and miscalculations abound before the eventual happy ending. In the sequel title, Amy and Gretchen are now friends, but Amy is forced to use the magic powers she discovers in a calendar to cope with her new career as a child model, despite Gretchen's warnings. Reviewing *More Fifth Grade Magic* in *Booklist*, Carolyn Phelan concluded that "fast-paced action," as well as "believable magic" and "touches of humor," combine to make this an "appealing book for young readers."

More friends are featured in *Best Friend Insurance*, in which Maureen, made unhappy by the defection of her best buddy, follows the advice of an odd insurance salesman and takes out a policy for friend insurance. Maureen, however, is less than pleased when she finds that this replacement friend is in fact her own mother, transformed into a fifth-grader named Kitty. *Booklist* reviewer Barbara Elleman remarked that Gormley's "understanding of fifth-graders' woes and excitements is evident," while George Gleason, writing in *School Library Journal*, lauded the "wacky, occasionally humorous situations."

Gormley once commented on her use of fantasy in her novels for young readers: "I have always enjoyed reading fantasy (C. S. Lewis's "Narnia" books, the Tolkien trilogy, Ursula LeGuin's "Earthsea" trilogy), but it wasn't until I started to write it myself that I learned, from the inside out, that this most fanciful fiction must be based on the most solid psychological truth. I was amazed that I had to be so honest with myself in order to write a good story."

Further adventures in fantasy are delivered up in *Richard and the Vratch*, *Paul's Volcano*, *Wanted, UFO*, and *Sky Guys to White Cat*. Animals figure in many of Gormley's plot. In *Richard and the Vratch*, an adopted dog turns out to be a supposedly extinct critter, while *Sky Guys to White Cat* features an extraterrestrial feline, which is exploring the earth for the out-of-this-world Aldebarans. "Readers will laugh out loud at this outrageous adventure," wrote *Booklist* critic Chris Sherman in a review of *Sky Guys to White Cat*. More aliens appear in *Wanted, UFO*, in which an eager science student gets more than she bargained for in her quest to spot a UFO—namely, aliens in the backyard. Ruth Smith, reviewing this novel in *School Library Journal*, pointed to Gormley's "knack for short dramatic sentences" that "makes this a real page-turner." *Booklist* contributor Kay Weisman noted of the same book that "young sf fans will be caught up in the mystery." In *Paul's Volcano,* the young members of a club worship their model volcano, calling up an evil spirit. "As is her habit, Gormley adds a dash of the supernatural to this expertly concocted farce," noted John Peters in *School Library Journal.*

Gormley turned her hand to fiction of a different order in *Ellie's Birthstone Ring* and *Miriam.* The former, a realistic tale, deals with questions of friendship when Ellie, who is about to turn seven, must decide whom to invite to her party. A ring she sees in a store downtown compounds the decision in this book that is, according to a contributor for *Kirkus Reviews,* "likable, perceptive, [and] easily read." *Miriam,* on the other hand, is an experiment in historical fiction, telling the story of Moses's sister, Miriam, who struggles to remain loyal to both her people and religion while living in the Pharaoh's palace. "*Miriam* is far more than a biblical retelling," wrote Barbara Auerbach in *School Library Journal.* "Gormley gives readers the universal struggle between mother and daughter." "Gormley's novel not only imparts many interesting details but may well send children back to the original Bible passages that were its inspiration," predicted a reviewer for *Publishers Weekly.* And writing in *Kliatt,* Claire M. Dignan found *Miriam* to be "an engaging historical fiction about one girl's coming of age during the time of the pharaohs."

Actual rather than fictional history is provided in other works from Gormley. Her biography *Maria Mitchell: The Soul of an Astronomer* introduces this first female science professor at Vassar and the first to become an astronomer in America. Phyllis Graves, reviewing the book in *School Library Journal,* noted Gormley's "smoothly flowing and lively style" in this study of the discoverer of Comet Mitchell and the first woman inducted into the American Academy of Arts and Sciences. A contributor for *Kirkus Reviews* found this same biography "Inspiring and incisive." Other biographies from Gormley include studies of the writers C. S. Lewis and Louisa May Alcott, as well as the aviation pioneer Amelia Earhart. With *President George W. Bush,* Gormley relates the life story of the forty-third president in a "brisk and informative biography," according to William McLoughlin in *School Library Journal.*

"The writing of each [book] has evoked surprisingly strong feelings," Gormley once noted, "strong enough to distort the story if I don't face up to them. The core of each book is something important to me. Of course it is equally important to entertain my readers; I think a dull or dreary novel is worthless."

BIOGRAPHICAL/CRITICAL SOURCES:

BOOKS

Science Fiction and Fantasy Literature, Gale (Detroit, MI), 1992.

PERIODICALS

Booklist, February 1, 1984, Barbara Elleman, review of *Best Friend Insurance,* p. 813; May 15, 1987, p. 1445; December 15, 1987, p. 714; August, 1989, Carolyn Phelan, review of *More Fifth Grade Magic,* p. 1976; July, 1990, Kay Weisman, review of *Wanted, UFO,* p. 2089; December 1, 1991, Chris Sherman, review of *Sky Guys to White Cat,* p. 697; December 15, 1992, p. 736; September 1, 1995, p. 53; March 15, 1997, p. 1236; March 15, 1998, p. 1231; April 1, 1999, p. 1424; May 15, 2001, p. 1747.
Book Report, September-October, 1996, p. 50.
Books for Keeps, September, 1987, review of *Mail-Order Wings,* p. 25.
Horn Book, October, 1982, p. 516; March-April, 1986, Anita Silvey, review of *Ghastly Glasses,* pp. 200-201.
Kirkus Reviews, April 1, 1987, p. 552; November 15, 1992, review of *Ellie's Birthstone Ring,* pp. 1442-1443; June 15, 1995, review of *Maria Mitchell,* p. 857.
Kliatt, July 1999, Claire M. Dignan, review of *Miriam,* p. 16.
Publishers Weekly, July 17, 1981, p. 94; April 13, 1984, review of *Mail-Order Wings,* p. 72; November 1, 1985, p. 65; November 16, 1992, p. 64; January 25, 1999, review of *Miriam,* p. 89.
School Librarian, November, 1987, Rodie Sudbery, review of *Mail- Order Wings,* p. 330.
School Library Journal, February, 1984, George Gleason, review of *Best Friend Insurance,* p. 70; January, 1986, Lisa Smith, review of *The Ghastly Glasses,* pp. 66-67; March, 1987, John Peters, review of *Paul's Volcano,* p. 158; July, 1990, Ruth Smith, review of *Wanted, UFO,* p.76; December, 1991, p. 114; January, 1993, p. 76; January, 1995, Phyllis Graves, review of *Maria Mitchell,* pp. 132, 134; June, 1998, pp. 158, 160; May, 1999, Barbara Auerbach, review of *Miriam,* p. 125; June, 2001, William McLoughlin, review of *President George W. Bush,* p. 172.

OTHER

Beatrice Gormley Web site, http://www.webcom.com/bgormley (December 8, 2001).*

GRAY, Alasdair (James) 1934-

PERSONAL: Born December 28, 1934, in Glasgow, Scotland; son of Alex Gray (a machine operator) and Amy (Fleming) Gray (a homemaker); children: Andrew. *Education:* Glasgow Art School, diploma (design and printmaking), 1957. *Politics:* "Socialist. Supporter of Scottish home rule and Campaign for Nuclear Disarmament." *Religion:* "Rational pantheism."

ADDRESSES: Home—2 Marchmont Terrace, Glasgow G12 9LT, Scotland. *Agent*—Giles Gordon, 6 Ann St., Edinburgh EH 4 1PJ, Scotland.

CAREER: Part-time art teacher in Lanarkshire and Glasgow, Scotland, 1958-62; theatrical scene painter in Glasgow, 1962-63; freelance playwright and painter in Glasgow, 1963-75; People's Palace (local history museum), Glasgow, artist-recorder, 1976-77; University of Glasgow, writer-in-residence, 1977-79, professor of creative writing, 2001—; freelance painter and maker of books in Glasgow, 1979-2001.

MEMBER: Society of Authors, Glasgow Print Workshop, various organizations supporting trade unions and nuclear disarmament.

AWARDS, HONORS: Bellahouston Travelling Scholarship, 1957; Three grants from Scottish Arts Council, between 1968 and 1981; Booker Prize nomination, Book Trust (England), 1981, award from Saltire Society, 1982, and Niven Novel Award, all for *Lanark: A Life in Four Books;* award from Cheltenham Literary Festival, 1983, for *Unlikely Stories, Mostly;* award from Scottish branch of PEN, 1986; Whitbread Prize, and Guardian Fiction Prize, both 1992, both for *Poor Things.*

WRITINGS:

(And illustrator) *Lanark: A Life in Four Books* (novel), Harper (New York, NY), 1981, revised edition, Braziller (New York, NY), 1985.

(And illustrator) *Unlikely Stories, Mostly* (short stories; includes "The Star," "The Spread of Ian Nicol," and "Five Letters from an Eastern Empire"), Canongate (Edinburgh, Scotland), 1983, revised edition, Penguin (London, England), 1984.

1982 Janine (novel), J. Cape (London, England), 1984, revised edition, Penguin, 1985.

Alasdair Gray

The Fall of Kelvin Walker: A Fable of the Sixties (novel; adapted from his television play of the same title; also see below), Canongate (Edinburgh, Scotland), 1985, Braziller (New York, NY), 1986.

(With James Kelman and Agnes Owens) *Lean Tales* (short story anthology), J. Cape, (London, England), 1985.

Saltire Self-Portrait 4, Saltire Society Publications (Edinburgh), 1988.

(And illustrator) *McGrotty and Ludmilla; or, The Harbinger Report: A Romance of the Eighties,* Dog and Bone (Glasgow, Scotland), 1989.

(And illustrator) *Old Negatives: Four Verse Sequences,* J. Cape (London, England), 1989.

Something Leather (novel), Random House (New York, NY), 1990.

Poor Things: Episodes from the Early Life of Archibald McCandless, M.D., Scottish Public Health Officer (novel), Harcourt (New York, NY), 1992.

Why Scots Should Rule Scotland, Canongate Press (Edinburgh, Scotland), 1992.

(And illustrator) *Ten Tales Tall and True: Social Realism, Sexual Comedy, Science Fiction, and Satire,* Harcourt (New York, NY), 1993.

(And illustrator) *A History Maker,* Canongate Press (Edinburgh, Scotland), 1994, Harcourt (New York, NY), 1996.

(And illustrator) *Mavis Belfrage: A Romantic Novel with Five Shorter Tales,* Bloomsbury (London, England), 1996.

The Artist in His World: Prints, 1986-1997 (poetry; prints by Ian McCulloch), Argyll (Gelndaruel, Argyll, Scotland), 1998.

(And illustrator) *The Book of Prefaces,* Bloomsbury (London, England), 2000.

Sixteen Occasional Poems, Morag McAlpine (Glasgow, Scotland), 2000.

A Short Survey of Classical Scottish Writing, Canongate (Edinburgh, Scotland), 2001.

The British Book of Popular Political Songs, Bloomsbury (London, England), 2002.

STAGE PLAYS

Dialogue (one-act; first produced in Edinburgh, Scotland, at Gateway Theatre, 1971), Scottish Theatre (Kirknewton, Scotland), 1971.

The Fall of Kelvin Walker (two-act; adapted from his television play of the same title; also see below), first produced in Stirling, Scotland, at McRoberts Centre, University of Stirling, 1972.

The Loss of the Golden Silence (one-act), first produced in Edinburgh, Scotland, at Pool Theatre, 1973.

Homeward Bound (one-act), first produced in Edinburgh, Scotland, at Pool Theatre, 1973.

(With Tom Leonard and Liz Lochhead) *Tickly Mince* (two-act), first produced in Glasgow, Scotland, at Tron Theatre, 1982.

(With Liz Lochhead, Tom Leonard, and James Kelman) *The Pie of Damocles* (two-act; also see below), first produced in Glasgow, Scotland, at Tron Theatre, 1983.

McGrotty and Ludmilla, first produced in Glasgow, Scotland, at Tron Theatre, 1987.

(And illustrator) *Working Legs: A Play for People without Them* (first produced by Birds of Paradise Company, 1998), Dog and Bone Press (Glasgow, Scotland), 1997.

RADIO PLAYS

Quiet People, British Broadcasting Corporation (BBC), 1968.

The Night Off, BBC, 1969.

Thomas Muir of Huntershill, BBC, 1970.

The Loss of the Golden Silence, BBC, 1974.

McGrotty and Ludmilla, BBC, 1976.

The Vital Witness (documentary), BBC, 1979.

Near the Driver, translation into German by Berndt Rullkotter broadcast by Westdeutsche Rundfunk, 1983, original text broadcast by BBC, 1988.

TELEVISION PLAYS

The Fall of Kelvin Walker, BBC, 1968.

Dialogue, BBC, 1972.

Triangles, Granada, 1972.

The Man Who Knew about Electricity, BBC, 1973.

Honesty (educational documentary), BBC, 1974.

Today and Yesterday (series of three twenty-minute educational documentaries), BBC, 1975.

Beloved, Granada, 1976.

The Gadfly, Granada, 1977.

The Story of a Recluse, BBC, 1987.

OTHER

(Designer and illustrator) Wilma Paterson, *Songs of Scotland,* Mainstream, 1995.

Author and reader of *Some Unlikely Stories* (audiocassette), Canongate Audio, 1994, and *Scenes from Lanark, Volume 1* (audiocassette), Canongate Audio, 1995.

WORK IN PROGRESS: A Life in Pictures: Paintings, Murals, and Graphic Work, for Canongate, 2003; *The Ends of Their Tethers: Eight Song Stories.*

SIDELIGHTS: After more than twenty years as a painter and a scriptwriter for radio and television, Alasdair Gray rose to literary prominence with the publication of several of his books in the 1980s. His works have been noted for their mixture of realistic social commentary and vivid fantasy, augmented by the author's own evocative illustrations. Jonathan Baumbach wrote in the *New York Times Book Review* that Gray's work "has a verbal energy, an intensity of vision, that has been mostly missing from the English novel since D. H. Lawrence." And David Lodge of the *New Republic* said that Gray "is that rather rare bird among contemporary British writers—a genuine experimentalist, transgressing the rules of formal English prose . . . boldly and imaginatively."

In his writing Gray often draws upon his Scottish background, and he is regarded as a major force in the literature of his homeland. Author Anthony Burgess, for instance, said in the London *Observer* that he considered Gray the best Scottish novelist since Sir Walter Scott became popular in the early nineteenth century. Unlike Scott, who made his country a setting for historical romance, Gray focuses on contemporary Scotland, where the industrial economy is deteriorating and many citizens fear that their social and economic destiny has been surrendered to England. Critics praised Gray for putting such themes as Scotland's decline and powerlessness into a larger context that any reader could appreciate. "Using Glasgow as his undeniable starting point," Douglas Gifford wrote in *Studies in Scottish Literature,* "Gray . . . transforms local and hitherto restricting images, which limited [other] novelists of real ability. . . . into symbols of universal prophetic relevance."

As noted above, Gray became prominent as a writer only after several years of working as an artist and illustrator. Gray traces his own literary and artistic development to the early years of his life, explaining to *CA* in a 1987 written interview that "as soon as I could draw and tell stories, which was around the age of four or five, I spent a lot of time doing these or planning to do them. My parents were friendly to my childish efforts, as were most of my teachers, though they also told me I was unlikely to make a living by either of these jobs. . . . I was delighted to go to art school, because I was a maturer draftsman and painter than writer. My writings while at art school were attempts to prepare something I knew would take long to finish: though I didn't know how long."

Gray went on to say that although his first novel took years to complete, the story-line of what would become his now acclaimed first novel, *Lanark: A Life in Four Books,* had essentially been worked out in his mind by the time he was eighteen. A long and complex work that some reviewers considered partly autobiographical, *Lanark* opens in Unthank, an ugly, declining city explained in reviews as a comment on Glasgow and other Western industrial centers. As in George Orwell's *Nineteen Eighty-four,* citizens of Unthank are ruled by a domineering and intrusive bureaucracy. Lanark is a lonely young man unable to remember his past. Along with many of his fellow-citizens, he is plagued with "dragonhide," an insidious, scaly skin infection seen as symbolic of his emotional isolation. Cured of his affliction by doctors at a scientific institute below the surface of the Earth, Lanark realizes to his disgust that the staff is as arrogant and manipulative as the ruling elite on the surface. Before escaping from this underworld, Lanark has a vision in which he sees the life story of a young man who mysteriously resembles him—Duncan Thaw, an aspiring artist who lives in twentieth-century Glasgow.

Thaw's story, which comprises nearly half the book, is virtually a novel within a novel. It echoes the story of Lanark while displaying a markedly different literary technique. As William Boyd explained in the *Times Literary Supplement,* "The narration of Thaw's life turns out to be a brilliant and moving evocation of a talented and imaginative child growing up in working-class Glasgow. The style is limpid and classically elegant, the detail solidly documentary and in marked contrast to the fantastical and surrealistic accoutrements of the first 100 pages." Like Gray, Thaw attends art school in Glasgow, and, as with Lanark, Thaw's loneliness and isolation are expressed outwardly in a skin disease, eczema. With increasing desperation, Thaw seeks fulfillment in love and art, and his disappointment culminates in a violent outburst in which he kills—or at least thinks he kills—a young woman who had abandoned him. Bewildered and hopeless, he commits suicide. Boyd considered Thaw's story "a minor classic of the literature of adolescence," and Gifford likened it to James Joyce's novel *A Portrait of the Artist as a Young Man.* The last part of Gray's book focuses once more on Lanark, depicting his futile struggle to improve the world around him. Readers have often remarked on the various diseases the characters in *Lanark*'s Unthank suffer from: dragonhide, mouths, twittering rigor, softs. When *CA* asked Gray if these diseases had allegorical significance, he responded: "Probably, but I came to that conclusion after, not before, I imagined and described them. And it would limit the reader's enjoyment and understanding of my stories to fix on one 'allegorical significance' and say 'This is it.'"

Critics have generally lauded *Lanark,* although some expressed concern that it was hampered by its size and intricacy. Boyd, for instance, felt that the parallel narratives of Thaw and Lanark "do not happily cohere." *Washington Post Book World*'s Michael Dirda said that Lanark was "too baggy and bloated," but he stressed that "there are such good things in it that one hardly knows where it could be cut." Many critics echoed Boyd's overall assessment that "*Lanark* is a work of loving and vivid imagination, yielding copious riches." Moreover, Burgess featured *Lanark* in his book *Ninety-nine Novels: The Best in English since 1939—A Personal Choice,* declaring, "It was time Scotland produced a shattering work of fiction in the modern idiom. This is it."

Although *Lanark* rapidly achieved critical recognition in Britain, it was Gray's second novel, *1982 Janine,* that was the first to be widely known in the United States. When asked why his work had now attained critical notice in the United States, Gray replied to *CA:*

"*Lanark* was the first novel I had published in the U.S. A., by Harper & Row in 1981. It was speedily remaindered, because Harper & Row classified it as science fiction, only sent it to sci-fi magazines for review, and the sci-fi reviewers were not amused. . . . I suppose my books have been published in the United States because they sold well in Britain, and were praised by authors of *A Clockwork Orange* [Anthony Burgess] and *The History Man* [Malcolm Bradbury]."

1982 Janine records the thoughts of Jock McLeish, a disappointed, middle-aged Scottish businessman, during a long night of heavy drinking. In his mind Jock plays and replays fantasies in which he sexually tortures helpless women, and he gives names and identities to his victims, including the Janine of the title. Burgess spoke for several reviewers when he wrote in the *Observer* that such material was offensive and unneeded. But admirers of the novel, such as Richard Eder of the *Los Angeles Times*, felt that Jock's sexual fantasies were a valid metaphor for the character's own sense of helplessness. Jock, who rose to a managerial post from a working-class background, now hates himself because he is financially dependent on the ruling classes he once hoped to change.

As Eder observed, Jock's powerlessness is in its turn a metaphor for the subjugation of Scotland. Jock expounds on the sorry state of his homeland in the course of his drunken railings. Scotland's economy, he charges, has been starved in order to strengthen the country's political master, England; what is more, if war with the Soviet Union breaks out, Jock expects the English to use Scotland as a nuclear battlefield. As the novel ends, Jock resolves to quit his job and change his life for the better. Eder commended Gray for conveying a portrait of helplessness and the search for self-realization "in a flamboyantly comic narrator whose verbal blue streak is given depth by a winning impulse to self-discovery, and some alarming insight."

Gray's short-story collection, *Unlikely Stories, Mostly,* is "if anything more idiosyncratic" than *1982 Janine,* according to Jonathan Baumbach of the *New York Times Book Review.* Many reviewers praised the imaginativeness of the stories while acknowledging that the collection, which includes work dating back to Gray's teenage years, is uneven in quality. As Gary Marmorstein observed in the *Los Angeles Times Book Review,* some of the stories are "slight but fun," including "The Star," in which a boy catches a star and swallows it, and "The Spread of Ian Nicol," in which a man slowly splits in two like a microbe reproducing itself.

By contrast, "Five Letters from an Eastern Empire" is one of several more complex tales that received special praise. Set in the capital of a powerful empire, the story focuses on a talented poet. Gradually readers learn the source of the poet's artistic inspiration: the emperor murdered the boy's parents by razing the city in which they lived, then ordered him to write about the destruction. "The tone of the story remains under perfect control as it darkens and deepens," according to Adam Mar-Jones in the *Times Literary Supplement,* "until an apparently reckless comedy has become a cruel parable about power and meaning." While responding to a *CA* question about *Lanark* and the possible allegorical significance of its characters, Gray related an anecdote about the story "Five Letters from an Eastern Empire": "I wrote [the story] when [I was] writer-in-residence at Glasgow University. When I finished, it occurred to me that the Eastern Empire was an allegory of modern Britain viewed from Glasgow University by a writer-in-residence. A year ago I met someone just returned from Tokyo, who said he had heard a Chinese and a Japanese academic having an argument about my Eastern empire story. The Chinese was quite sure the empire was meant to be China, the Japanese that it was Japan. My only knowledge of these lands is from a few color prints, Arthur Waley's translation of the novel *Monkey* [by Wu Ch'eng-en] and some translated poems."

Gray's third novel, *The Fall of Kelvin Walker: A Fable of the Sixties,* was inspired by personal experience. Still struggling to establish his career several years after his graduation from art school, Gray was tapped as the subject of a documentary by a successful friend at the British Broadcasting Corporation (BBC). Gray, who had been living on welfare, suddenly found himself treated to airline flights and limousine rides at the BBC's expense. In *The Fall of Kelvin Walker* the title character, a young Scotsman with a burning desire for power, has a similar chance to use the communications media to fulfill his wildest fantasies. Though Kelvin arrives in London with little besides self-confidence and a fast-talking manner, his persistence and good luck soon win him a national following as an interviewer on a television show. But in his pride and ambition Walker forgets that he exercises such influence only at the whims of his corporate bosses, and when he displeases them his fall from grace is as abrupt as his rise.

The Fall of Kelvin Walker, which Gray adapted from his 1968 teleplay of the same title ("I sent it to a [BBC] director I know. He gave it to a producer who liked it"), is shorter and less surrealistic than his previous novels. The *Observer*'s Hermione Lee, though she stressed that

Gray "is always worth attending to," felt that this novel "doesn't allow him the big scope he thrives on." By contrast, Larry McCaffery of the *New York Times Book Review* praised *The Fall of Kelvin Walker* for its "economy of means and exquisite control of detail." Gray "is now fully in command of his virtuoso abilities as a stylist and storyteller," McCaffery said, asserting that Gray's first four books—"each of which impresses in very different ways—indicate that he is emerging as the most vibrant and original new voice in English fiction."

As reviewers became familiar with Gray's work, they noticed several recurring features in it: illustrations by the author, typographical eccentricities, and an emphasis on the city of Glasgow. Asked by *CA* about the illustrations, Gray explained a little about the process of creating this kind of manuscript: "The illustrations and cover designs of my books are not essential to them, being thought of after the text is complete. I add them because they make the book more enjoyable. The queer typography, in the three stories which use it, was devised in the act of writing, not added after, like sugar to porridge."

As Gray continued to write, critical reception of his work varied widely. Many reviewers acknowledged his genius in such works as *Lanark,* while books such as *Something Leather* and *McGrotty and Ludmilla; or, The Harbinger Report: A Romance of the Eighties* were criticized for lacking the intensity of his earlier work. Gray himself was remarkably candid about the quality and intent of some of these efforts. For example, he described *McGrotty and Ludmilla; or, The Harbinger Report* as an Aladdin story set in modern Whitehall, "with the hero a junior civil servant, wicked uncle Abanizir a senior one, and the magic lamp a secret government paper which gave whoever held it unlimited powers of blackmail." And works such as *Something Leather,* said Gerald Mangan in the *Times Literary Supplement,* placed Gray in "an unfortunate tradition in Scottish fiction, whereby novelists have tended to exhaust their inspiration in the effort of a single major achievement." That *Lanark* was a major achievement Mangan had no doubt. "*Lanark* is now so monumental a Scottish landmark," he wrote, "that few readers would have reproached him if a decade of silence had followed it." Instead, Gray brought out "a good deal of inferior material that had evidently subsidized or distracted him during the composition of his epic." A *New York Times Book Review* article by John Kenny Crane further explained the circumstances under which Gray composed *Something Leather.* According to Crane, a publisher had been pushing Gray for years to produce a new novel.

Getting nowhere and needing money, Gray shuffled around in his rejected short-story manuscripts and came up with one about a conventional working woman in Glasgow who decides to shave off her hair and begin dressing in leather clothing. The publisher sent Gray a substantial advance, and the tale of the bald, leather-clad Glaswegian woman became his first chapter, "One for the Album." Other unpublished stories, unstaged plays, and early radio and TV scripts were also pressed into service and ultimately published as *Something Leather.* Lamented Crane in his review, "Gray, who has published some very creditable works of fiction, shamelessly admits to absolutely everything in his epilogue." Yet, the critic added, "Taken on their own, some of the interior chapters have artistry and merit. I particularly liked the reflections on war in one titled 'In the Boiler Room' and the comical friction caused by the divergent life styles of boarders in 'Quiet People.' As short stories, some are quite fine. I would recommend the reader take them as such, even though Mr. Gray insists they are part of a novel." And despite his own criticism of *Something Leather,* Mangan said that in the five stories that comprise the work, Gray's "prose is generally notable for its refusal of second-hand definitions; and it is not surprising to find, among other consolations, a divertingly cynical diatribe on Glasgow's current status as culture-capital."

With the publication of *Poor Things: Episodes from the Early Life of Archibald McCandless, M.D., Scottish Public Health Officer,* purportedly edited by Gray, the author returns to form, suggested Philip Hensher in the *Spectator,* "after a rather sticky patch." The work drew comparisons to such authors as Daniel Defoe and Laurence Sterne, partly because of its eccentric humor and setting and partly because of Gray's skillful use of the traditions of Victorian novels, which, according to Barbara Hardy in the *Times Literary Supplement,* "embodied their liberal notions of providence and progress in realistic narratives which often surge into optimistic or melioristic visions on the last page."

Set in Glasgow during the 1880s, the novel is narrated by Archie McCandless, a young medical student, who befriends the eccentric Godwin Baxter, another medical student. Baxter has been experimenting on the body of a beautiful and pregnant young woman who committed suicide to escape her abusive husband, and has created "Bella" by transplanting the brain of the fetus into its mother's skull. Bella is sexually mature and wholly amoral, and McCandless wants to marry her. She, however, runs off with a wicked playboy whom she soon drives to insanity and death. Bella then works for a time in a Parisian brothel before returning to Scotland.

Here she runs into her ex-husband just as she is preparing to marry McCandless. A happy ending is combined with a clever final twist to produce a book that, said Hensher, becomes "a great deal more than entertaining only on finishing it. Then your strongest urge is to start reading it again."

Gray uses his visual and writing talents in *Ten Tall Tales and True: Social Realism, Sexual Comedy, Science Fiction, and Satire.* He illustrates the cover with ten animal tails, then showing each animal in its entirety within the covers. A critic for *Review of Contemporary Fiction* asked: "Is Gray suggesting perhaps the fragmented and nonhuman character of our life when we do not exist in a state of wholeness?" Set in present-day Scotland, the stories explore human relationships with humor and feeling. "[Gray's] stories most often dramatize those symbioses of oppression in which people find just the right partner, family or group to dominate or be dominated by," wrote Ron Loewinsohn in the *New York Times Book Review.* Observed Christopher Bray in the *Spectator,* "Stories and characters like these ought to make you downcast, and they would, were it not for the pithy intensity with which Gray sketches things in."

Gray expresses his concern for modern society in *A History Maker,* a political allegory set in a twenty-third-century Scotland that seems reminiscent of more ancient times. Society has become matriarchal, and men have little to do but kill each other; their war games are televised as entertainment. When warrior Wat Dryhope becomes clan chieftain in the Ettrick Forest, he also becomes the leader of a mass militaristic movement. Furthermore, he becomes the darling of the media and one of Scotland's most desirable men. But he gives up war after meeting the evil Delilah Puddock, who infects him with a virus that threatens to destroy the world's food supply. *A History Maker* is presented as Wat's memoir of seven critical days in his life. "Gray's touch is light and wry, and there is enough strangeness in his future to whet conventional SF appetites. But there is no mistaking the relevance of his allegory to the situation of nation-states in today's uneasy post-Cold War peace," maintained a *Village Voice Literary Supplement* reviewer. A *Publishers Weekly* reviewer stated that *A History Maker* succeeds on "all of its many levels" and is a fine work of social satire: "The wit is sharp, the social commentary on target and, most important, the quirky, arch-voiced storytelling is unfailingly entertaining."

Gray's *The Book of Prefaces* is an unusual volume, which took him years to compile and edit. It is, as the title suggests, a collection of what he considers the greatest prefaces in works of literature written in English. It begins with the seventh-century author Caedmon and progresses through the twentieth century. Michael Kerrigan in the *Times Literary Supplement* had mixed feelings about *The Book of Prefaces;* while crediting Gray with choosing "prefaces that motivate the reader to seek out in their entirety the works they introduce, and to acknowledge the alternative futures that past achievements have made," he criticized the book for adhering too closely to a "rigid and restrictive" selection of works, and calls it "striking in its portentousness." A very different point of view was expressed by Peter Dollard in *Library Journal;* he found *The Book of Prefaces* to be "a delightfully original, ironic, and humorous compilation," a genuine "work of literature" in its own right, thanks to the "fascinating and often idiosyncratic commentary" by Gray.

Despite the author's success with later works, *Lanark* remains Gray's masterpiece. In the *New York Review of Books,* Gordon A. Craig summed up Gray's achievement in *Lanark,* praising its "masterful evocation . . . of an adolescence and young manhood in post-1945 Glasgow, of early friendships and first love, of the stirring of artistic genius and its frustration, and of the subtle social prejudices that had to be learned as one grew up." "In a larger sense," Craig continued, "the novel is an attempt to expose the ills that threaten modern society, an elaboration on a text in one of Gray's plates: 'Let Glasgow flourish' any and all Glasgows 'by telling the truth.'"

BIOGRAPHICAL/CRITICAL SOURCES:

BOOKS

Bernstein, Stephen, *Alasdair Gray,* Associated University Presses, 1999.

Burgess, Anthony, *Ninety-nine Novels: The Best in English since 1939—A Personal Choice,* Allison & Busby (London, England), 1984.

Contemporary Literary Criticism, Volume 41, Gale (Detroit, MI), 1987.

Crawford, R., and T. Naim, editors, *The Arts of Alasdair Gray,* Edinburgh University Press (Edinburgh, Scotland), 1991.

Dictionary of Literary Biography, Volume 194: *British Novelists since 1960, Second Series,* Gale (Detroit, MI), 1998.

Moore, Phil, editor, *Alasdair Gray: Critical Appreciations and Bibliography,* British Library, 2001.

PERIODICALS

Booklist, March 1, 1994, Gilbert Taylor, review of *Ten Tales Tall and True: Social Realism, Sexual Comedy, Science Fiction, and Satire,* p. 1180; October 1, 2000, Mary Ellen Quinn, review of *The Book of Prefaces,* p. 374.

Books, September, 1993, p. 9.

Christian Science Monitor, October 5, 1984.

Daily Telegraph, August 30, 1992, Kate Chisholm, review of *Poor Things: Episodes from the Early Life of Archibald McCandless, M.D., Scottish Public Health Officer,* December 17, 1994, David Profumo, review of *A History Maker;* November 11, 1995, Candida Clark and Jason Thompson, review of *A History Maker;* January 18, 1997, Miranda France, interview with Alasdair Gray.

Guardian, September 2, 1992, Francis Spufford, interview with Alasdair Gray; June 18, 1998, Jonathan Jones, interview with Alasdair Gray.

Kirkus Reviews, February 1, 1994, review of *Ten Tales Tall and True,* p. 87; February 15, 1996, review of *A History Maker,* p. 247.

Library Journal, May 1, 1991, Francis Poole, review of *Library Journal,* p. 108; August, 2000, Peter Dollard, review of *The Book of Prefaces,* p. 102.

Los Angeles Times, November 21, 1984.

Los Angeles Times Book Review, December 9, 1984.

New Republic, November 12, 1984.

New Statesman, November 25, 1994, p. 48.

New Statesman & Society, September 11, 1992, Christopher Harvie, review of *Poor Things,* p. 38; November 25, 1994, Boyd Tonkin, review of *A History Maker,* p. 48.

Newsweek, March 22, 1993, Malcolm Jones, Jr., review of *Poor Things,* p. 70.

New York, March 8, 1993, Rhoda Koenig, review of *Poor Things,* p. 84.

New Yorker, April 12, 1993, review of *Poor Things,* p. 121.

New York Review of Books, April 25, 1991.

New York Times Book Review, October 28, 1984; May 5, 1985; December 21, 1986; August 4, 1991, John Kenny Crane, review of *Something Leather,* p. 15; March 28, 1993, review of *Poor Things,* p. 8; March 6, 1994, Ron Loewinsohn, review of *Ten Tales Tall and True,* p. 11; August 18, 1996, Nicholas Birns, review of *A History Maker,* p. 18.

Observer (London), April 15, 1984; March 31, 1985; September 27, 1994, p. 21; December 10, 1995, p. 15.

Publishers Weekly, April 19, 1991, Sybil Steinberg, review of *Something Leather,* p. 58; January 25, 1993, review of *Poor Things,* p. 78; January 31, 1994, review of *Ten Tales Tall and True,* p. 76; March 4, 1996, review of *A History Maker,* p. 61.

Review of Contemporary Fiction, fall, 1994, p. 204.

Spectator, February 28, 1981; September 5, 1992; October 30, 1993, p. 35.

Stage, November 30, 1972.

Studies in Scottish Literature, Volume 18, 1983.

Sunday Times (London), December 11, 1994, Andro Linklater, review of *A History Maker.*

Times (London), April 1, 1986.

Times Literary Supplement, February 27, 1981; March 18, 1983; April 13, 1984; March 29, 1985; May 10, 1985; July 6-12, 1990; April 3, 1992; August 28, 1992; December 9, 1994, p. 22; August 11, 2000, Michael Kerrigan, review of *A Book of Prefaces,* p. 10.

Village Voice Literary Supplement, December, 1984; April, 1996, p. 8.

Washington Post Book World, December 16, 1984; August 31, 1986; June 16, 1991.

Whole Earth Review, December 22, 1995, James Donnely, review of *Ten Tales Tall and True.*

*   *   *

GREEN, Brian
See CARD, Orson Scott

*   *   *

GURR, Andrew (John) 1936-

PERSONAL: Surname rhymes with "fur"; born December 23, 1936, in Leicester, England; son of John V. and Elsie R. (Dow) Gurr; married Elizabeth Ann Gordon (a teacher), July 1, 1961; children: Robin, Douglas, Corin. *Education:* University of Auckland, B.A., 1957, M.A., 1958; Cambridge University, Ph.D., 1963.

ADDRESSES: Office—Department of English, University of Reading, Whiteknights Park, Reading RG6 2AA, England.

CAREER: Victoria University of Wellington, Wellington, New Zealand, lecturer in English, 1959; University of Leeds, Leeds, England, lecturer in English, 1962-69; University of Nairobi, Kenya, lecturer in English and head of department, 1969-73; University of Reading, Reading, England, professor of English, 1976—, department chairman, 1979-86. Chief academic advisor to

Globe Project, London, England, 1981—, director of Globe research, 1998—. Judith E. Wilson Drama Lecturer, 1985; visiting fellow, Folger Shakespeare Library, 1986, 1990, 1994; distinguished visiting professor, University of California, Los Angeles, CA, 1989.

MEMBER: Association of Commonwealth Literature and Language Studies.

WRITINGS:

(Editor) Francis Beaumont, *The Knight of the Burning Pestle,* University of California Press (Berkeley, CA), 1968.

(Editor) Francis Beaumont and John Fletcher, *The Maid's Tragedy,* University of California Press (Berkeley, CA), 1969.

(Editor) Francis Beaumont and John Fletcher, *Philaster,* Methuen (New York, NY), 1969.

The Shakespearean Stage, 1574-1642, Cambridge University Press, 1970, 3rd revised edition, 1992.

(Editor, with Pio Zirimu) *Black Aesthetics: Papers from a Colloquium Held at the University of Nairobi, June, 1971,* East African Literature Bureau (Nairobi, Kenya), 1973.

(Editor, with Angus Calder) *Writers in East Africa,* East African Literature Bureau (Nairobi, Kenya), 1974.

Hamlet and the Distracted Globe, Scottish Academic Press (Edinburgh, Scotland), 1978.

(With Clare Hanson) *Katherine Mansfield,* St. Martin's (New York, NY), 1981.

Writers in Exile: The Identity of Home in Modern Literature, Humanities Press (Atlantic Highlands, NJ), 1981.

(Editor) William Shakespeare, *King Richard II,* Cambridge University Press (New York, NY), 1984.

Studying Shakespeare: An Introduction, Edward Arnold (Baltimore, MD), 1988.

(With John Orrell) *Rebuilding Shakespeare's Globe,* Routledge (New York, NY), 1989.

William Shakespeare: The Extraordinary Life of the Most Successful Writer of All Time, photographs by Dominic Clemence, Harper (New York, NY), 1995.

Playgoing in Shakespeare's London, Cambridge University Press (New York, NY), 1996.

(Advisory editor and contributor) *Shakespeare's Globe Rebuilt,* Cambridge University Press (New York, NY), 1997.

(Editor) *The First Quarto of King Henry V,* Cambridge University Press (New York, NY), 2000.

Director. "Northern House Pamphlet Poets."

SIDELIGHTS: Andrew Gurr is a Shakespearean scholar who, since 1981, has been the academic advisor to the Globe Project in England. The Globe Project has used archaeological and written source material to assist in the reconstruction of the Globe Theatre in London, the venue where many of Shakespeare's plays made their debut. In *Early Modern Literary Studies,* Bryan S. Gooch wrote: "Clearly, one of this century's most significant events in the realm of Shakespearean theatre—and one of the most spectacular recent results of careful scholarship—is the building of a replica of Shakespeare's Globe in Southwark." Gurr has written about the efforts in two works, *Rebuilding Shakespeare's Globe* and *Shakespeare's Globe Rebuilt.* He was the advisory editor of the latter title and contributed an essay on staging in the confines of the Globe. Gooch called *Shakespeare's Globe Rebuilt* "a first-rate volume which recounts a stunning story. . . . We are much in debt to . . . Gurr . . . and all the members of the Globe team who have so energetically and conscientiously pursued to a brilliant conclusion the building of our new wooden O, and this book is a happy tribute to their collective endeavor."

Gurr is also editor of Shakespeare's plays and the author of several texts on Shakespeare and his work. His *The Shakespearean Stage, 1574-1642* is in its third edition and is widely used by students who want not only analysis of the plays but also information on how they were produced and staged.

BIOGRAPHICAL/CRITICAL SOURCES:

PERIODICALS

Early Modern Literary Studies, January, 1998, Bryan S. Gooch, review of *Shakespeare's Globe Rebuilt,* p. 10.

Times Literary Supplement, December 29, 2000, H. R. Woudhuysen, review of *The First Quarto of King Henry V,* p. 29.

OTHER

University of Reading, http://www.rdg.ac.uk/globe/siteinfo/Andy/ (June 7, 2001), "Andrew Gurr."

*   *   *

GUTKIND, Lee 1945-

PERSONAL: Surname is pronounced "goodkind"; born January 3, 1945, in Pittsburgh, PA; son of Jack R. (a merchant) and Mollie (Osgood) Gutkind; married Pamela Johnson (a teacher), March 30, 1969 (divorced

March, 1975). *Education:* University of Pittsburgh, B.A. (cum laude), 1968. *Religion:* Jewish. *Avocational interests:* Backpacking, hiking.

ADDRESSES: Home—623 Ivy St., Pittsburgh, PA 15232. *Office*—Department of English, University of Pittsburgh, Pittsburgh, PA 15260. *Agent*—Amanda Urban, International Creative Management, 40 West 57th St., New York, NY 10019. *E-mail*—gutkind@ creativenonfiction.org; lgu+@pitt.edu.

CAREER: Account executive and copywriter, Osgood-McCullough, Inc., 1965-67, and Lando, Inc., 1967-69; University of Pittsburgh, Pittsburgh, PA, instructor, 1970-71, assistant professor, 1972-77, associate professor, 1977-90, professor of English, 1990—, director of creative writing program, 1980-81, founder and director of writer's conference. Community College of Allegheny County, PA, instructor, 1969-72; Carnegie-Mellon University, Pittsburgh, PA, visiting professor, 1972, judge of creative writing competition. Virginia Center for the Creative Arts at Sweet Briar College, Virginia, resident, 1979; Yaddo resident, 1984. *Pennsylvania Review,* founder; *Creative Nonfiction* (literary journal), founder and editor. Has conducted writing and editing seminars throughout the United States. Consultant to the Aluminum Company of America, Pennsylvania Humanities Council, Ketchum, Inc., Mid-Atlantic States Arts Consortium, and United States Information Agency. Once performed as a circus clown. *Military service:* U.S. Coast Guard, 1962-63.

MEMBER: Omicron Delta Kappa, Phi Delta Epsilon.

AWARDS, HONORS: Creative writing fellowship, National Endowment for the Humanities, 1978, for *God's Helicopter;* grants from the Pennsylvania Humanities Council, 1977, University of Pittsburgh Center for International Studies, 1983, and the Bowman Fund of the University of Pittsburgh, 1983; Golden Eagle Award, Council on International Nontheatrical Events, 1981; Golden Quill Award, Pittsburgh Press Club, 1982; Merit Service Award, American Council on Transplantation; Blakeslee Award, American Heart Association; Maurice Falk Medical Fund grant; Lila Wallace grant; Ray Springle Memorial Award, Carnegie Mellon University, for creative writing.

WRITINGS:

Bike Fever, Follett (Chicago, IL), 1973.
The Best Seat in Baseball, but You Have to Stand: The Game as Umpires See It, Dial (New York, NY), 1975, with new foreword by Eric Rolfe Greenberg, Southern Illinois University Press (Carbondale, IL), 1999.

(Also producer, narrator, and on-screen interviewer) *A Place Just Right* (16-mm documentary film), Pennsylvania State University, 1980.
God's Helicopter (novel), Slow Loris Press (Pittsburgh, PA), 1983.
The People of Penn's Woods West, University of Pittsburgh Press (Pittsburgh, PA), 1984.
Our Roots Grow Deeper than We Know, University of Pittsburgh Press (Pittsburgh, PA), 1985.
Many Sleepless Nights: The World of Organ Transplantation, Norton (New York, NY), 1988.
One Children's Place: A Profile of Pediatric Medicine, Grove Weidenfeld (New York, NY), 1990.
Stuck in Time: The Tragedy of Childhood Mental Illness, Henry Holt (New York, NY), 1993.
Creative Nonfiction: How to Live It and Write It, Chicago Review Press (Chicago, IL), 1996.
The Art of Creative Nonfiction: Writing and Selling the Literature of Reality, Wiley (New York, NY), 1997.
An Unspoken Art: Profiles of Veterinary Life, Henry Holt (New York, NY), 1997.
(Editor) *Surviving Crisis: Twenty Prominent Authors Write about Events That Shaped Their Lives,* Jeremy P. Tarcher/Putnam (New York, NY), 1997.
The Veterinarian's Touch: Profiles of Life among the Animals, Henry Holt (New York, NY), 1998.
(Editor) *Connecting: Twenty Prominent Authors Write about the Relationships That Shaped Our Lives,* Jeremy P. Tarcher/Putnam (New York, NY), 1998.
(Editor) *A View from the Divide: Creative Nonfiction on Health and Science* (special double issue of the journal *Creative Nonfiction*), University of Pittsburgh Press (Pittsburgh, PA), 1998.
(Editor) *The Essayist at Work: Profiles of Creative Nonfiction Writers,* Heinemann (Portsmouth, NH), 1998.
(Editor) *Lessons in Persuasion: Creative Nonfiction/ Pittsburgh Connections,* University of Pittsburgh Press (Pittsburgh, PA), 2000.
(Editor) *Healing: Twenty Prominent Authors Write about Inspirational Moments of Achieving Health and Gaining Insight,* Jeremy P. Tarcher/Putnam (New York, NY), 2001.

Contributor to newspapers, magazines, and syndicates.

SIDELIGHTS: Lee Gutkind is a professor of English and an author and editor. He also produced one film, *A Place Just Right,* which profiles several rural Pennsylvania residents, some of whom voluntarily traded a metropolitan life for one in the country.

Among Gutkind's books is *Many Sleepless Nights: The World of Organ Transplantation,* about the "God Squad" (the University of Pittsburgh's transplant team), the patients who lived at Family House while awaiting organs, and those who died before they could be helped. The book was reviewed in *Journal of the American Medical Association* by Robert E. McCabe, who said that "it is a story of camaraderie and disappointment. . . . Lee Gutkind has expressed a humility and understanding about the patients and doctors that only a journalist can appreciate. . . . Only a journalist would capture such warmth and esteem for the squad while also reporting the many ethical and moral issues they have faced."

Gutkind spent two years working out of the Children's Hospital of Pittsburgh, researching *One Children's Place: A Profile of Pediatric Medicine.* He writes in detail about the hospital's day-to-day activities, and records the special compassion and care accorded to the children, some of whom suffer from the most difficult maladies and injuries. A *Publishers Weekly* reviewer wrote that Gutkind "justifiably argues that the distinctive nature of children's medical care is underrated." Harrison C. Spencer said in *Journal of the American Medical Association* that Gutkind "shows talent in investigative reporting, but does so with a special humanistic touch in revealing the individual emotions of the people and patients."

Stuck in Time: The Tragedy of Childhood Mental Illness details the years during which Gutkind followed the cases of three adolescents as they were passed through the system of group homes, shelters, and psychiatric institutions. He notes that $2 million was spent on one of these young people without result, but also that four fifths of mentally ill children and teens, many of whom have learning disabilities, receive no treatment or service at all. A *Publishers Weekly* reviewer said that Gutkind "accuses government, social service professionals, and media of ignoring this 'national disgrace.'"

Gutkind's *An Unspoken Art: Profiles of Veterinary Life* describes the life of vets in such variable locations as a Manhattan facility, a clinic that treats race horses, and the Pittsburgh Zoo. He notes that seven of ten admissions to veterinary schools are now women, and describes the love of owners for their pets. *Booklist* contributor Nancy Bent said Gutkind "affords an appealing and well-written profile of veterinary life." A *Publishers Weekly* reviewer said that Gutkind "knows how to tell animal tales that are endearing without being cloying."

Gutkind founded and is editor of the literary journal *Creative Nonfiction,* and has published a number of nonfiction anthologies. The first, *Surviving Crisis:*

Twenty Prominent Authors Write about Events That Shaped Their Lives, includes life events such as trauma, divorce, mental and physical illness, and approaching death. Caroline Mitchell wrote in *Library Journal* that while some readers will find the essays in this anthology "brave and inspiring; others will find them undignified and wish the authors had kept their personal troubles private." Contributors include Annie Dillard, John McPhee, Richard Rodriguez, and John Edgar Wideman. "These courageously candid essays are not for casual reading," wrote Donna Seaman in *Booklist*. "So searing are many of the essays there that one reads them more for technique than for pleasure," said a *Publishers Weekly* contributor.

Connecting: Twenty Prominent Authors Write about the Relationships That Shaped Our Lives includes contributions by Raymond Carver, Alec Wilkinson, Deborah Tannen, Judy Ruiz, and Joyce Carol Oates. In reviewing this second anthology, Seaman called Gutkind "the tireless apostle of this dynamic and diverse genre." Many of the essays revolve around family and friends. B. J. Nelson writes of assisting with his mother's suicide, and Alice Hoffman reflects on the wit and insight of her grandmother. "Each writer's style is unique, and the collection provides a rich variety of compelling stories," wrote Denise J. Stankovics in *Library Journal*.

Gutkind has authored a number of books on nonfiction writing, including *A View from the Divide: Creative Nonfiction on Health and Science,* which is a double issue of Gutkind's journal and contains essays by eighteen writers on a variety of topics. *Journal of the American Medical Association* reviewer Larry R. Kirkland said that "all are extremely personal, some almost diary-like, and the quality of the writing fits the mode of many anthologies, i.e., some interesting and informative, some prosaic." Five of the essays deal with the authors' own illnesses, and three with the illnesses or deaths of family members. Kirkland felt that Mara Gorman's "Proud Flesh," about her mother's breast cancer, was one of the best of the collection. "By the end of the fifteen pages," wrote Kirkland, "you care what happens to these people, a reaction not easy to elicit in such a short piece."

In a *Library Journal* review, Lisa J. Cihlar called Gutkind's *The Essayist at Work: Profiles of Creative Nonfiction Writers* an "exciting compilation." Writers include Gay Talese, Ellen Gilchrist, and Tracy Kidder. Cihlar felt that Scott Chisholm's essay about William Least Heat Moon is "worth the price of the book."

Another of the author's "creative nonfiction" books is *Healing: Twenty Prominent Authors Write about Inspi-*

rational Moments of Achieving Health and Gaining Insight. Contributors include Leonard Kreigel, who lost the use of his legs to polio as a child; Oliver Sacks, who talks of the time he spent with a surgeon suffering from Tourette's Syndrome; and Raphael Campo, who writes of his work with AIDS patients, and who Seaman said "presents an extraordinarily candid and moving rumination on touch, healing, desire, homosexuality, and . . . fears." Lucy Grealy reveals how during years of reconstructive surgery to her face beginning at age fifteen, she avoided looking into mirrors. A *Publishers Weekly* reviewer called Grealy's essay "an exceptionally moving memoir," and said the collection "will offer sustenance and support to anyone attempting to deal with illness and physical or emotional healing."

BIOGRAPHICAL/CRITICAL SOURCES:

PERIODICALS

Bloomsbury Review, January, 1998, reviews of *Surviving Crisis: Twenty Prominent Authors Write about Events That Shaped Their Lives, Creative Nonfiction: How to Live It and Write It,* and *The Art of Creative Nonfiction: Writing and Selling the Literature of Reality,* p. 13.

Booklist, June 15, 1988, review of *Many Sleepless Nights: The World of Organ Transplantation,* p. 1699; July, 1990, review of *One Children's Place: A Profile of Pediatric Medicine,* p. 2056; July, 1993, Mary Carroll, review of *Stuck in Time: The Tragedy of Childhood Mental Illness,* p. 1933; July, 1997, Nancy Bent, review of *An Unspoken Art: Profiles of Veterinary Life,* p. 1785; August, 1997, Donna Seaman, review of *Surviving Crisis,* p. 1870; April 15, 1998, Donna Seaman, review of *Connecting: Twenty Prominent Authors Write about the Relationships That Shaped Our Lives,* p. 1413; March 1, 2001, Donna Seaman, review of *Healing: Twenty Authors Write about Inspirational Moments of Achieving Health and Gaining Insight,* p. 1216.

Contemporary Psychology, August, 1995, review of *Stuck in Time,* p. 788.

Journal of the American Medical Association, June 9, 1989, Robert E. McCabe, review of *Many Sleepless Nights,* p. 3313; March 20, 1991, Harrison C. Spencer, review of *One Children's Place,* p. 1465; August 18, 1999, Larry R. Kirkland, review of *A View from the Divide: Creative Nonfiction on Health and Science,* p. 695.

Kirkus Reviews, May 1, 1988, review of *Many Sleepless Nights,* p. 668; May 15, 1990, review of *One Children's Place,* p. 707; May 15, 1993, review of *Stuck in Time,* p. 642; June 1, 1997, review of *An Unspoken Art,* p. 851.

Kliatt, September, 1990, review of *Many Sleepless Nights,* p. 35; July, 1998, review of *The Essayist at Work: Profiles of Creative Nonfiction Writers,* p. 23.

Library Journal, September 1, 1988, David A. Buehler, review of *Many Sleepless Nights,* p. 178; March 1, 1989, Ellis Mount, Barbara A. List, review of *Many Sleepless Nights,* p. 43; June 1, 1990, Mary Hemmings, review of *One Children's Place,* p. 162; June 15, 1993, Linda Beck, review of *Stuck in Time,* p. 87; April 15, 1996, Cathy Sabol, review of *Creative Nonfiction,* p. 96; October 15, 1997, Caroline Mitchell, review of *Surviving Crisis,* p. 62; February 15, 1998, Lisa J. Cihlar, review of *The Essayist at Work,* p. 142; April 15, 1998, Denise J. Stankovics, review of *Connecting,* p. 78.

New England Journal of Medicine, Jonathan D. K. Trager, review of *One Children's Place,* p. 590.

Pittsburgh Post-Gazette, May 12, 1980.

Pittsburgh Press, May 5, 1980, November 8, 1980.

Publishers Weekly, May 13, 1988, Genevieve Stuttaford, review of *Many Sleepless Nights,* p. 261; May 18, 1990, Genevieve Stuttaford, review of *One Children's Place,* p. 74; September 27, 1991, review of *One Children's Place,* p. 55; May 24, 1993, review of *Stuck in Time,* p. 73; May 27, 1996, review of *Creative Nonfiction,* p. 75; June 23, 1997, review of *An Unspoken Art,* p. 77; July 7, 1997, review of *Surviving Crisis,* p. 57; December 15, 1997, review of *The Essayist at Work,* p. 46; February 26, 2001, review of *Healing,* p. 73.

Readings: A Journal of Reviews and Commentary in Mental Health, December, 1991, review of *One Children's Place,* p. 13.

Reference & Research Book News, December, 1993, review of *Stuck in Time,* p. 52.

School Library Journal, January, 1994, Yvonne Reeder-Tinsley, review of *Stuck in Time,* p. 146.

SciTech Book News, March, 1991, review of *Many Sleepless Nights,* p. 19.

Small Press Review, October, 1996, review of *Creative Nonfiction,* p. 13.

Washington Post, September 21, 1993, Ann Waldron, review of *Stuck in Time,* p. 18.

Washington Post Book World, September 12, 1993, review of *Stuck in Time,* p. 13.

OTHER

Creative Nonfiction, http://www.cnf.edu/ (June 7, 2001).*

H

HALL, Donald (Andrew Jr.) 1928-

PERSONAL: Born September 20, 1928, in New Haven, CT; son of Donald Andrew (in business) and Lucy (Wells) Hall; married Kirby Thompson, September 13, 1952 (divorced, 1969); married Jane Kenyon (a poet; died 1995), April 25, 1972; children: (first marriage) Andrew, Philippa. *Education:* Harvard University, B.A., 1951; Oxford University, B. Litt., 1953; attended Stanford University, 1953-54.

ADDRESSES: Home—Eagle Pond Farm, Box 29, Route 4, Wilmot, NH 03287. *Agent*—Gerald McCauley Agency, Inc., Box 844, Katonah, NY.

CAREER: Harvard University, Cambridge, MA, junior fellow in the Society of Fellows, 1954-57; University of Michigan, Ann Arbor, MI, 1957-75, began as assistant professor, became professor of English; full-time writer, 1975—. Poetry editor for *Paris Review,* 1953-61; broadcaster on several British Broadcasting Corp. (BBC) radio programs, 1959-80; host of *Poets Talking,* a series of television interviews with poets, broadcast nationally on more than eighty stations, 1974-75; judge of contests including the Lamont Poetry Competition, the National Book Awards, and the National Poetry Series; has given poetry readings at more than 1,500 colleges, universities, schools, libraries, prisons, and community centers. Consultant, Harper & Row (now HarperCollins) (New York, NY), 1964-81. Deacon, South Danbury Church, NH.

MEMBER: PEN, American Academy of Arts and Letters, Authors Guild.

AWARDS, HONORS: Newdigate Prize, Oxford University, 1952, for poem "Exile"; Lamont Poetry Prize, Academy of American Poets, 1955, for *Exiles and Marriages;* Edna St. Vincent Millay Award, Poetry Society of America, 1956; National Book Award nominee, 1956, 1979, and 1993; Longview Foundation award, 1960; Guggenheim fellowship, 1963-64, 1972-73; Caldecott Medal, American Library Association, 1980, for *Ox-Cart Man;* Sarah Josepha Hale Award, 1983, for writings about New England; *Horn Book* Honor List, 1986, for *The Oxford Book of Children's Verse in America;* Lenore Marshall Poetry Prize, 1986, for *The Happy Man;* National Book Critics Circle Award for poetry, 1988, Pulitzer Prize nominee in poetry, 1989, and *Los Angeles Times* Book Prize in poetry, 1990, all for *The One Day;* named Poet Laureate of New Hampshire, 1984-89, 1995—; Robert Frost Silver Medal, Poetry Society of America, 1991; New England Booksellers Association Award, 1993; Ruth Lilly Prize, 1994. D.Litt., Presbyterian College, Colby-Sawyer College, Franklin Pierce College, New England College, Bates College, Daniel Webster College, University of New Hampshire, University of Michigan; L.H.D., Plymouth State College.

WRITINGS:

String Too Short to Be Saved: Recollections of Summers on a New England Farm (autobiography), illustrated by Mimi Korach, Viking Press (New York, NY), 1961, expanded edition, David R. Godine (Boston, MA), 1979.
Henry Moore: The Life and Work of a Great Sculptor, Harper (New York, NY), 1966.
As the Eye Moves: A Sculpture by Henry Moore, illustrated with photographs by David Finn, Abrams, 1970.
Marianne Moore: The Cage and the Animal, Pegasus Press (Asheville, NC), 1970.

The Pleasures of Poetry, Harper (New York, NY), 1971.

Writing Well, Little, Brown (New York, NY), 1974, 8th edition, Harper (New York, NY), 1994.

(With others) *Playing Around: The Million-Dollar Infield Goes to Florida,* Little, Brown (New York, NY), 1974.

(With Dock Ellis) *Dock Ellis in the Country of Baseball,* Coward, 1976.

Goatfoot Milktongue Twinbird: Interviews, Essays, and Notes on Poetry, 1970-76, University of Michigan Press (Ann Arbor, MI), 1978.

Remembering Poets: Reminiscences and Opinions—Dylan Thomas, Robert Frost, T. S. Eliot, Ezra Pound, Harper (New York, NY), 1978, revised edition published as *Their Ancient Glittering Eyes,* Ticknor & Fields, 1992.

To Keep Moving: Essays, 1959-1969, Hobart & William Smith Colleges Press, 1980.

To Read Literature, Holt, 1980, 3rd edition, 1992.

The Weather for Poetry: Essays, Reviews, and Notes on Poetry, 1977-81, University of Michigan Press (Ann Arbor, MI), 1982.

Fathers Playing Catch with Sons: Essays on Sport (Mostly Baseball), North Point Press, 1985.

(With Clifton C. Olds) *Winter* (essays), University Press of New England (Hanover, NH), 1986.

Seasons at Eagle Pond, illustrated by Thomas W. Nason, Ticknor & Fields, 1987.

The Ideal Bakery (short stories), North Point Press, 1987.

Poetry and Ambition, University of Michigan Press (Ann Arbor, MI), 1988.

Life Work, Beacon Press (Boston, MA), 1993.

Death to the Death of Poetry: Essays, Reviews, Notes, Interviews, University of Michigan Press (Ann Arbor, MI), 1994.

The Farm Summer, 1942, Dial (New York, NY), 1994.

Old Home Day, Harcourt, Brace (Orlando, FL), 1994.

Principal Products of Portugal: Prose Pieces, Beacon Press (Boston, MA), 1995.

Donald Hall in Conversation with Ian Hamilton, edited by Ian Hamilton, Peter Dale, Philip Hoy, and J. D. McClatchy, photographs by Linden Frederick, Between the Lines (London, England), 2000.

Contributor of short stories and articles to numerous periodicals, including *New Yorker, Esquire, Atlantic, Playboy, Transatlantic Review,* and *American Scholar.*

POETRY

Fantasy Poets No. 4, Fantasy Press, 1952.

Exile, Fantasy Press, 1952.

To the Loud Wind and Other Poems, Pegasus Press (Asheville, NC), 1955.

Exiles and Marriages, Viking Press (New York, NY), 1955.

The Dark Houses, Viking Press (New York, NY), 1958.

A Roof of Tiger Lilies, Viking Press (New York, NY), 1964.

The Alligator Bride: Poems, New and Selected, Harper (New York, NY), 1969.

The Yellow Room: Love Poems, Harper (New York, NY), 1971.

The Gentleman's Alphabet Book (limericks), illustrated by Harvey Kornberg, Dutton (New York, NY), 1972.

The Town of Hill, David R. Godine (Boston, MA), 1975.

A Blue Wing Tilts at the Edge of the Sea: Selected Poems, 1964-1974, Secker & Warburg, 1975.

Kicking the Leaves: Poems, Harper (New York, NY), 1978.

The Toy Bone, BOA Editions (Rochester, NY), 1979.

Brief Lives: Seven Epigrams, William B. Ewart, 1983.

The Twelve Seasons, Deerfield Press, 1983.

Great Day in the Cows' House, illustrated with photographs by T. S. Bronson, Ives Street Press, 1984.

The Happy Man, Random House (New York, NY), 1986.

The One Day, Ticknor & Fields, 1988.

Old and New Poems, Ticknor & Fields, 1990.

Here at Eagle Pond, Houghton Mifflin (Boston, MA), 1992.

The Museum of Clear Ideas, Ticknor & Fields, 1993.

The Old Life, Houghton Mifflin (Boston, MA), 1996.

Without, Houghton Mifflin (Boston, MA), 1998.

The Painted Bed, Houghton Mifflin (Boston, MA), 2002.

Contributor of poetry to numerous periodicals, including *New Yorker, New Republic, New Criterion, Kenyon Review, Iowa Review, Georgia Review, Ohio Review, Gettysburg Review, Nation,* and *Atlantic.*

JUVENILE

Andrew and the Lion Farmer, illustrated by Jane Miller, F. Watts, 1959, illustrated by Ann Reason, Methuen, 1961.

Riddle Rat, illustrated by Mort Gerber, Warner (New York, NY), 1977.

Ox-Cart Man, illustrated by Barbara Cooney, Viking Press (New York, NY), 1979.

The Man Who Lived Alone, illustrated by Mary Azarian, David R. Godine (Boston, MA), 1984.

Summer of 1944, illustrated by Barry Moser, Dial (New York, NY), 1994.

I Am the Dog, I Am the Cat, Dial (New York, NY), 1994.

Lucy's Christmas, Harcourt (Orlando, FL), 1994.

Lucy's Summer, Harcourt (Orlando, FL), 1995.

When Willard Met Babe Ruth, illustrated by Barry Moser, Browndeer Press (San Diego, CA), 1996.

Old Home Day, Harcourt (Orlando, FL), 1996.

The Milkman's Boy, Walker (New York, NY), 1997.

PLAYS

An Evening's Frost, first produced in Ann Arbor, MI; produced Off-Broadway at the Theatre de Lys, 1965.

Bread and Roses, produced in Ann Arbor, MI, 1975.

Ragged Mountain Elegies, produced in Peterborough, NH, 1983, revised as *The Bone Ring* (produced in New York, NY, at the Theater of the Open Eye, 1986), Story Line, 1987.

EDITOR

The Harvard Advocate Anthology, Twayne (New York, NY), 1950.

(With Robert Pack and Louis Simpson) *The New Poets of England and America,* Meridian Books, 1957.

Whittier, Dell, 1961.

Contemporary American Poetry, Penguin (Harmonsworth, England), 1962, Penguin (Baltimore, MD), 1963.

(With Robert Pack) *New Poets of England and America: Second Selection,* Meridian Books, 1962.

A Poetry Sampler, F. Watts, 1962.

(With Stephen Spender) *The Concise Encyclopedia of English and American Poets and Poetry,* Hawthorn, 1963.

(With Warren Taylor) *Poetry in English,* Macmillan (New York, NY), 1963.

The Faber Book of Modern Verse, revised edition, Faber & Faber (New York, NY), 1965.

A Choice of Whitman's Verse, Faber & Faber (New York, NY), 1968.

Man and Boy, F. Watts, 1968.

The Modern Stylists: Writers on the Art of Writing, Free Press (New York, NY), 1968.

American Poetry: An Introductory Anthology, Faber & Faber (New York, NY), 1969.

(With D. L. Emblen) *A Writer's Reader,* Little, Brown (New York, NY), 1969, 9th edition, Longman (New York, NY), 2001.

The Pleasures of Poetry, Harper (New York, NY), 1971.

Galway Kinnell, Walking down the Stairs, University of Michigan Press (Ann Arbor, MI), 1978.

William Stafford, Writing the Australian Crawl, University of Michigan Press (Ann Arbor, MI), 1978.

The Oxford Book of American Literary Anecdotes, Oxford University Press (New York, NY), 1981.

To Read Literature: Fiction, Poetry, Drama, Holt, Rinehart & Winston (Austin, TX), 1981, 3rd edition, Harcourt (Orlando, FL), 1992.

Claims for Poetry, University of Michigan Press (Ann Arbor, MI), 1982.

To Read Poetry, Holt, Rinehart & Winston (Austin, TX), 1982, revised edition published as *To Read a Poem,* Harcourt (Orlando, FL), 1992.

The Contemporary Essay, St. Martin's (New York, NY), 1984, 3rd edition, 1995.

The Oxford Book of Children's Verse in America, Oxford University Press (New York, NY), 1985.

To Read Fiction, Holt, Rinehart & Winston (Austin, TX), 1987.

The Best American Poetry, Scribner (New York, NY), 1989.

(With Pat Corrington Wykes) *Anecdotes of Modern Art: From Rousseau to Warhol,* Oxford University Press (New York, NY), 1990.

Science Fiction and Fantasy, Gale (Detroit, MI), 1991.

Peter Davison, One of the Dangerous Trades: Essays on the Work and Workings of Poetry, 1963-1990, University of Michigan Press (Ann Arbor, MI), 1991.

Andrew Marvell, The Essential Marvell, Ecco Press (New York, NY), 1991.

Edwin *Arlington Robinson, The Essential Robinson,* Ecco Press (New York, NY), 1993.

The Oxford Illustrated Book of American Children's Poems, Oxford University Press (New York, NY), 1999.

Poetry editor, *Paris Review,* 1953-62; member of editorial board for poetry, Wesleyan University Press, 1958-64.

OTHER

Names of Horses was recorded and released by Watershed Tapes, 1985, and Audiobooks published a two-cassette volume titled *Donald Hall Poetry and Prose in 1997.* Hall has also recorded several albums of poetry by other writers.

SIDELIGHTS: Over the course of his career as a poet, Donald Hall has gone from writing formal, metrical verse, to free verse, to a combination of the two, all the while developing a distinctive voice that speaks movingly of the influences of family and history. Hall has also published works of autobiography, a successful instructional guide, *Writing Well,* children's stories, and has edited numerous collections of poems and stories.

In "Finally Only the Art of Love," an essay in the *New York Times Book Review,* Hall spoke of the childhood influences on his writing career and two of the houses he remembered living in as a boy. "When I was in my snooty teens I would have denied it," he wrote, "but these houses were bookish." The reading matter consisted of Book-of-the-Month-Club "masterpieces," *Reader's Digest* and *Collier's.* "I felt superior," the poet confessed, realizing only later his good fortune in living with "people who continually gazed at print," having a mother who read poems to him, and a grandfather who, during Hall's summers at his New Hampshire farm, recited poems "all day long without repeating himself." Other literary relatives included a great-uncle who wrote devotional verses and an aunt who wrote light verse for greeting cards.

This poetic influence led Hall to try his own hand at poetry; by the age of twelve, he was writing. Poems and stories came first, novels and dramatic verse later. He recalled being under the spell of Edgar Allan Poe: "I wanted to be mad, addicted, obsessed, haunted and cursed. I wanted to have deep eyes that burned like coals—profoundly melancholic, profoundly *attractive.*" Less horrific discoveries were T. S. Eliot and H. D. He wrote through prep school at Exeter and attended the Bread Loaf Writers' Conference at the age of sixteen, the same year he had his first work published. Going on to Harvard, he wrote in the company of Robert Bly, Adrienne Rich, Kenneth Koch, John Ashbery, Frank O'Hara, and other poets who are well known today. Archibald MacLeish was Hall's teacher for a year.

"Over the four years at college," Hall recalled in the *Contemporary Authors Autobiography Series,* "some things increased: sophistication, competence, literary knowledge, cynicism. Nothing altered shape or direction; and when I went to Oxford for two years after Harvard, again nothing much altered; as I look back I sense my complacency. At Harvard I won prizes for poetry; at Oxford I kept on winning them." While he was at Oxford, his poem "Exile," submitted to the Newdigate contest, made Hall the first American to win the coveted award. The prize made his poems easier to sell to magazines at home.

Back in the States, Hall spent three years in the Society of Fellows at Harvard, where he put *Exiles and Marriages* together and edited *The New Poets of England and America* with Robert Pack and Louis Simpson. In 1957 he settled in Ann Arbor to teach at the University of Michigan and, except for two year-long sojourns in England, he remained there until 1975, when he bought the New Hampshire farm that had belonged to his grandparents and moved there with his second wife, the poet and translator Jane Kenyon, to make writing his full-time occupation.

Some of Hall's feelings about his move to New Hampshire were expressed in *Kicking the Leaves,* which Brent Spencer described in *Poet and Critic* as "mostly poems about memory, yet not mere reminiscence. The effort in these poems is to look for that part of the past that lives on into the present. They are, for the most part, poems about the gifts the past brings to us, the gifts of the dead." *String Too Short to Be Saved* contains stories or reminiscences about Hall's boyhood summers on the farm. "Ultimately the prose book expresses a moral imperative that goes beyond mere nostalgia and personal need," Barry Wallenstein elaborated in *American Book Review.* "The author realizes the insight that 'to be without history is like being forgotten.'" "The stories show both of the main characteristics of Hall's poetry—the attention to language and to detail," Spencer wrote. "And they show a real storyteller at work, something we get a taste of in *Kicking the Leaves.* Each book throws light on the other, both coming as they do from the same source."

The Happy Man, winner of the Lenore Marshall Prize, also centers on Hall's life on the family farm. As William Logan explained in the *New York Times Book Review,* the poems in this collection "continue [the] New Hampshire pastoral" of *Kicking the Leaves,* "but in a landscape of reversion and collapse. . . . The tone of these poems veers wildly between mania and depression. . . . Living through, and living out, a heritage of householding, [Hall] is haunted by the ghosts of family and the familiarity of aging." Alicia Ostriker also acknowledged this quality. "Where *Kicking the Leaves* was elegiac," she wrote in the *Nation,* "this book begins to grapple with monsters: fear, guilt, despair." Ostriker praised the collection for its depiction of rural New England life, exclaiming that "Hall . . . paints scenes with the reverent earthliness of a Dutch master, getting all the textures right." The slim collection of essays titled *Seasons at Eagle Pond* provides a prose counterpart to a book of poetry. In this book Hall evokes his native New England "as eloquently as any living writer," in the opinion of Frank Levering in the *Washington Post Book World,* who praised the author for taking on picture-postcard characteristics of rural New England and making them fresh for the reader.

Hall's 1988 book of poetry, *The One Day,* was published on his sixtieth birthday and won the National Book Critics Circle Award for poetry, the *Los Angeles Times* Book Prize in poetry, and a Pulitzer Prize nomination. Composed of 110 ten-line stanzas divided into three parts, *The One Day* is an ambitious work about mid-life, in which Hall speaks in several narrative voices. Reviewing the book for the *Los Angeles Times Book Review,* Liam Rector claimed that "Hall has long kept his eye and ear upon what is old, what is historical, what seems *behind* us yet is still living with us, and with *The One Day* he moves out into a different terrain from his recent mature books, *Kicking the Leaves* and *The Happy Man.*"

In an *American Poetry Review* interview with Rector, Hall explained that *The One Day* "began with an onslaught of language back in 1971. Over a period of weeks I kept receiving messages. I filled page after page of notebooks. . . . It was inchoate, sloppy, but full of *material:* verbal, imaginative, recollected." After approaching this material in several different ways over a period of seventeen years, Hall went on, he developed the 110 ten-line stanzas and worked with them for about four more years before he thought of structuring the long narrative poem into three parts.

The One Day, Daniel Mark Epstein wrote in *America,* is "Donald Hall's poem of the mid-life crisis, a painful time for men and women alike." Epstein observed that Hall "uses mid-life [in the poem] as a metaphor that works on several levels—personal, historical and mythic." Both a male and a female voice speak in *The One Day,* but they appear to be aspects of one voice—perhaps the poet's persona, as Stephen Sandy suggests in the *Boston Review*—that works through despair, rage, and cynicism before settling into a calm that embodies acceptance of inevitable death. In the *Washington Post Book World,* David Lehman praised the book as "loud, sweeping, multitudinous, an act of the imperial imagination," and declared that "high on Hall's thematic agenda are age and aging, rage and raging against the dying of the light, but his powerful rhetorical gestures and dazzling juxtapositions communicate a pleasure even beyond the skillful treatment of such themes."

Two years after the success of *The One Day,* Hall's *Old and New Poems* was published. Richard Tillinghast, writing in the *New York Times Book Review,* labeled the book a "magnificent collection" and called "Praise for Death," the closing poem, "perhaps the finest sustained evocation of death in American poetry." Reviewing the book in the *Times Literary Supplement,* Dick Davis declared that "few writers could have taken such apparently slight anecdotes of country life and made them, so unobtrusively but surely, into such profoundly authoritative icons of human experience."

Hall concluded "Finally Only the Love of Art" with these words: "If you continue to write, you go past the place where praise, publication or admiration sustains you. . . . You arrive at a point where only the possibilities of poetry provide food for your desires." Eventually, Hall explained, you find "repose only in the love of the art, and in the desire, if not precisely the hope, that you may make something fit to endure with the old ones."

The Museum of Clear Ideas was published in 1993 and includes Hall's "Baseball," his ode to the game. The poem is based on the nine innings of a baseball game: marked by nine stanzas and nine syllables per line. John Skott of *Time* noted of Hall: "He is besotted by baseball and, like all the other writers who crowd the box seats, assumes dreamily that everyone will accept this." The collection also includes poetry on other topics such as love, sex, family, aging, and poetry. As Susanne Keen commented in *Commonweal,* "Hall does not eschew the ordinary; he inhabits it. Books and poems and language belong in this poet's everyday world, so we find poems about old affairs or old friends cheek by jowl with his criticism of contemporary poetry." High praise came from Vernon Shetley of the *Yale Review:* "Hall's latest book should encourage us all: live long enough, work hard and sincerely, and eventually the muse will pay you back by giving you poems as wonderful as these."

While best known for his poetry, Hall also had a successful career as a children's book writer, penning *Lucy's Christmas, The Farm Summer 1942, When Willard Met Babe Ruth,* and *I Am the Dog, I Am the Cat,* among other titles. As within his poetry, Hall infuses his own loves—family, writing, baseball—into his writing for children. In *I Am the Dog, I Am the Cat,* Hall alternates the animals' voices in a free-verse poem that cleverly describes the pets' true natures. Several reviewers commented favorably on the nostalgia Hall evokes in *Lucy's Christmas, The Farm Summer 1942,* and *When Willard Met Babe Ruth,* each based on elements of Hall's life or his family's. Hall uses his skills as an editor in *The Oxford Illustrated Book of American Children's Poems,* which includes works by fifty-seven American poets, including Emily Dickinson, Sandra Cisneros, and Carl Sandburg. Indicating that the poems are intended to be read aloud to young children, Hall writes in the book's foreword that "poetry is most poetry when it makes noise."

In Hall's poetry collection *Without,* he writes about his wife's losing battle with leukemia. Published three years after Jane Kenyon's death, the poems in *Without* explore the course of Kenyon's illness and of Hall's loss following her death. The longest poem in the collection, "Her Long Illness," provides a focal point to the other twenty works, some written during her illness, and some written just after her death and over the ensuing year. Most of the poems explore Hall's grief as he continues to live in the house they shared together for decades. "For all the heartache pressed into these poems," wrote John Boening in *World Literature Today,* "there is a fearless honesty about them." Praising the collection, Boening concluded, "It is a measure of his great, good heart and his consummate skill that we never feel intrusive as we share this most personal of tragedies."

Assessing *Without* in the *American Book Review,* critic Robert Buttel praised both Hall's tone and structure: "It requires a delicate balancing act to get the tone right, to avoid self-pity or exploitation. . . . and Hall achieves this partly by the third person narration . . . and partly by the formal measure of the alternating short and long syllabic lines." Buttel examined how the poems move from "clinical precision" in the beginning, with their focus on the illness's assault on Jane's body, to "an affecting elegiac closure" with Hall's letters to her in the days and months after her death. Buttel concluded that "the aims of traditional elegy have been fulfilled in a new key—and superbly."

In *Life Work,* Hall provides readers with insight into both his writing practice and his life practice. Hall begins his work day at 4:30 am, writing until 10 am, and spending the rest of the day doing dictation, reading, and writing again. The book also relates Hall's discovery of his own cancer, which has spread to his liver, threatening the balance of his work and life. Of the title and the book, Robert Kelly in the *New York Times Book Review* wrote, "we can almost feel the ampersand between the words. He really is telling us about the life and work of Donald Hall, and in a lovely, delicate sense, this is, in fact, an autobiography." Scott Donaldson in *Washington Post Book World* observed, "Reading *Life Work* is enough to make anyone short of John Updike feel unproductive. . . . But forgive him we do, and gladly, for this extended essay is winning in its honesty and charm." Vincent Sherry in the *Sewanee Review* praised the work, noting that "if one moral can be attached to the story told in *Life Work,* the lesson is that it is only through work that ideas come at all: discipline is the one effort we can make at wisdom."

More insight into Hall's philosophy of writing can be found in *Donald Hall in Conversation with Ian Hamil-* ton, published by Between the Lines, which includes a bibliography of Hall's numerous publications, along with a sampling of his recent work and an interview with Hall, conducted by the prominent poetry critic Ian Hamilton. Patrick Crotty in the *Times Literary Supplement* related the book's assessment of Hall's career: "Even-tempered and meticulous, he exemplifies a contented subservience to the work ethic. Poetry, for Hall, is a craft which can be laboured at in expectation of success proportionate to investment of effort." Crotty also complimented Hall's "stoic grace" in his work following the death of his wife.

BIOGRAPHICAL/CRITICAL SOURCES:

BOOKS

Contemporary Authors Autobiography Series, Volume 7, Gale (Detroit, MI), 1988.
Contemporary Literary Criticism, Gale (Detroit, MI), Volume 1, 1973, Volume 13, 1980, Volume 37, 1986, Volume 59, 1990.
Dictionary of Literary Biography, Volume 5: *American Poets since World War II,* Gale (Detroit, MI), 1980.
Hall, Donald, editor, *The Oxford Illustrated Book of American Children's Poems,* Oxford University Press (New York, NY), 1999.
Rector, Liam, editor, *The Day I Was Older: Collected Writings on the Poetry of Donald Hall,* Story Line Press, 1989.

PERIODICALS

America, June 17-24, 1989.
American Book Review, March-April, 1981; May-June, 1999, Robert Buttel, "Love Letters to the Dead," pp. 21, 24.
American Poetry Review, January-February, 1989.
Antioch Review, fall, 2000, Barbara Beckerman Davis, a review of *Without,* p. 524.
Booklist, June 1, 1994; August, 1994; February 1, 1998, Ray Olson, a review of *Without,* p. 894.
Boston Globe Magazine, May 26, 1985.
Boston Review, October, 1988.
Christian Science Monitor, October 2, 1958.
Commonweal, September 24, 1993, p. 21; December 2, 1994, p. 29.
Encounter, March, 1965.
Horn Book, July-August, 1994; September-October, 1994, p. 577; November-December, 1994, p. 711.
Iowa Review, winter, 1971.

Kirkus Reviews, May 15, 1994, p. 698; August 15, 1994, p. 1129; October 15, 1994, p. 1420; March 1, 1996, p. 374.

Library Journal, March 15, 1995, p. 69; March 15, 1998, Barbara Hoffert, a review of *Without,* p. 68.

Los Angeles Times Book Review, February 5, 1989; April 30, 1995, p. 6.

Nation, August 30, 1986.

New Republic, February 14, 1994.

New Statesman, November 27, 1964.

New Yorker, June 28, 1993; October 11, 1993.

New York Review of Books, March 24, 1994; July 16, 1998, John Bayley, a review of *Without,* p. 41.

New York Times Book Review, November 30, 1958; December 11, 1966; December 31, 1978; January 16, 1983; January 18, 1987; February 24, 1991; October 3, 1993; April 30, 1995, p. 22.

Poet and Critic, Volume 12, number 3, 1980.

Poetry, May, 1971; February, 1999, Leslie Ullman, a review of *Without,* p. 312.

Publishers Weekly, August 28, 1981; April 11, 1994; July 18, 1994; September 19, 1994; April 29, 1996, p. 63; January 26, 1998, a review of *Without,* p. 87.

School Library Journal, June, 1994; September, 1994, p. 185; October, 1994, p. 40; May, 1996, p. 113.

Sewanee Review, summer, 1994.

Tennessee Poetry Journal (special Donald Hall issue), winter, 1971.

Time, December 5, 1955; March 22, 1993, p. 70.

Times Literary Supplement, November 1, 1991; October 27, 2000, Patrick Crotty, "Poets on the Parish," p. 27.

Virginia Quarterly Review, spring, 1965; spring, 1970.

Washington Post Book World, December 17, 1987; August 28, 1988; September 12, 1993, p. 4; January 22, 1995, p. 12.

World Literature Today, summer, 1995, p. 593; summer, 1999, John Boening, a review of *Without,* p. 533-534.

Yale Review, October, 1993, p. 151.

*   *   *

HALLAM, Elizabeth M. 1950-

PERSONAL: Born November 5, 1950, in Somerset, England; married, 1976; children: two. *Education:* Westfield College, London, B.A. (with first class honors), 1972, Ph.D., 1975.

ADDRESSES: Office—Public Record Office, Ruskin Ave., Kew, Richmond, Surrey TW9 4DU, England. *E-mail*—elizabeth-hallam-smith@pro.gov.uk.

CAREER: University of Reading, Reading, England, tutor, 1975-76; Public Record Office, London, England, assistant keeper of public records, 1976—, director of public services, 1994—. Open University, part-time tutor for London Region, 1974-78.

MEMBER: Royal Historical Society (fellow), Royal Society of Arts (fellow), Society of Antiquaries of London (fellow).

WRITINGS:

Capetian France, 987-1328, Longman (London, England), 1980, 2nd edition (with J. Everard), 2000.

The Itinerary of Edward I and His Household, 1307-1328, List and Index Society (London, England), 1984.

The Domesday Project Book, Hodder & Stoughton (London, England), 1986.

Domesday Book through Nine Centuries, Thames & Hudson (London, England), 1986.

Domesday Souvenir Guide, Pro Publications (London, England), 1999.

EDITOR

The Plantagenet Chronicles, Weidenfeld & Nicolson (London, England), 1986.

Chronicles of the Age of Chivalry, Weidenfeld & Nicolson (London, England), 1987.

Chronicles of the Wars of the Roses, Weidenfeld & Nicolson (London, England), 1988.

Chronicles of the Crusades, Weidenfeld & Nicolson (London, England), 1989.

The Plantagenet Encyclopaedia, Weidenfeld & Nicolson (London, England), 1990.

Saints: More than 150 Patron Saints for Today, Simon & Schuster (New York, NY), 1994.

Gods and Goddesses, Macmillan (New York, NY), 1997.

(Editor, with others) *The British Inheritance: A Treasury of Historic Documents,* University of California Press (Berkeley, CA), 1999.

OTHER

Author of museum pamphlet *English Royal Marriages,* Public Record Office, HMSO (London, England), 1981. Contributor to books, including (author of introduction) *Domesday Heritage: Towns and Villages of Norman*

England through Nine Hundred Years, Arrow Books (London, England), 1986; (author of introduction) *The Domesday Book: England's Heritage, Then and Now,* edited by Thomas Hinde, Hutchinson (East Sussex, England), 1986; (author of introduction) *Eleanor of Castile, 1290-1990,* edited by D. Parsons, Paul Watkins (Stamford), 1991; (author of transcriptions and translations) *Domesday Book, Middlesex,* Alecto Historical Editions (London, England), 1992; and *Sir Robert Cotton and His Circle,* edited by C. Wright, British Library Publications (London, England), 1997. Contributor to periodicals, including *Journal of Medieval History, History Today, Studies in Church History, Journal of Ecclesiastical History, Bulletin of the Institute of Historical Research, Journal of the Society of Archivists,* and *Museums Journal.* Some of Hallam's work has been translated into French and Japanese.

WORK IN PROGRESS: Further research on Domesday Book and medieval ecclesiastical history.

SIDELIGHTS: Elizabeth M. Hallam once told *CA:* "My work in the Public Record Office (particularly in the departments which help members of the public with their historical and genealogical studies) has convinced me of the importance of producing carefully researched but widely intelligible history, which appeals to an audience beyond that of the specialized scholar. At the same time, meticulously researched monographs and editions of texts are vital to the continuation of historical studies as an academic discipline."

Much of Hallam's writing has been connected to the Domesday Book, which was begun at the order of William the Conqueror in the year 1086. This record of England's government administration was used continuously until the sixteenth century; it has also served the needs of British property holders into the twentieth century. H. R. Loyn praised Hallam's *Domesday Book through Nine Centuries* in the *Times Literary Supplement* as "an attractive and well-illustrated book . . . alive with information." The reviewer added: "It is good to have the antiquarian details so well presented." Loyn also described *Domesday Heritage* as a popular survey of sites that housed the Domesday Book at various times in its nine-hundred-year history.

Hallam's *The Plantagenet Chronicles* is a lavishly illustrated work covering the English Plantagenet kings of the twelfth and thirteenth centuries. In the first volume of this book, she supports her historical entries with numerous excerpts from contemporary accounts.

BIOGRAPHICAL/CRITICAL SOURCES:

PERIODICALS

Times Literary Supplement, May 16, 1986, H. R. Lyon, review of *Domesday Book through Nine Centuries.*

*   *   *

HARRIS, Thomas 1940(?)-

PERSONAL: Born c. 1940, in Jackson, MS; son of William Thomas (an electrical engineer and farmer) and Polly (a high-school teacher) Harris; children: Anne. *Education:* Baylor University, B.A., 1964.

CAREER: Writer. Worked as a night police reporter for the Waco *News-Tribune,* Waco, TX; *Associated Press,* New York City, assistant editor, general assignment reporter, and night editor, 1968-74.

AWARDS, HONORS: Bram Stoker Award for Best Novel, Horror Writers Association and Anthony Award, Novel, 1989, for *Silence of the Lambs.*

WRITINGS:

Black Sunday, Putnam (New York, NY), 1975.
Red Dragon, Putnam (New York, NY), 1981, published as *Manhunter,* Bantam (New York, NY), 1986.
The Silence of the Lambs, St. Martin's (New York, NY), 1988.
Hannibal, Delacorte (New York, NY), 1999.

ADAPTATIONS: Black Sunday was filmed by John Frankenheimer for Paramount, 1977; *Red Dragon* was filmed as *Manhunter* by Michael Mann for De Laurentiis Entertainment Group, 1986; *The Silence of the Lambs* was filmed by Jonathan Demme for Orion, 1991; *Hannibal* was filmed in 2001.

SIDELIGHTS: Thomas Harris is known for his novels that combine detailed examination of police procedure with spellbinding suspense. Writing in the *St. James Guide to Horror, Ghost, and Gothic Writers,* S. T. Joshi noted that Harris's *Red Dragon* and *The Silence of the Lambs* "are certainly among the more successful works of popular fiction in recent years." The essayist for

Contemporary Southern Writers found that all of Harris's novels "are crime-thrillers: fast-paced, intricately plotted, suspense-charged narratives fueled by the urgency of a countdown to catastrophe."

Much of Harris's personal history is cloaked in mystery. Having judiciously avoided interviews, Harris has made it difficult to find or confirm biographical information about him. He has also reportedly made it very clear to his friends, acquaintances, and even childhood neighbors that he would appreciate their restraint as well; fond as they are of their places in his inner circle, they have for the most part complied. Still, over the years some information has surfaced. Harris grew up in Rich, Mississippi, a small farming town, and was reportedly an outcast. His father went off to war and left his wife and young son to manage on their own, and proved to be a less than adequate farmer after his return. Many of the difficulties of Harris's childhood are related in his books through the experiences of various characters, according to off-the-record accounts from people who knew his family. Stanley Gaines, Harris's best friend in high school and one of the few who has consented to an interview, told Meg Laughlin of the *Knight Ridder/ Tribune News Service* that "in high school, Tom blossomed. Sometimes, the things that make you an outcast as a kid make you cool when you get older." Whatever it was that Harris may have been trying to get back at the townsfolk for, several have acknowledged that he succeeded in the best possible way: As one Rich resident told Laughlin, "He left and got wealthy and famous." Another implied that however poorly Harris may have been treated as a youth, he is now the pride of his former hometown: "One of the things we love about Tom is that he is so gracious we know he has forgiven everyone."

While his childhood may have provided much of Harris's characterization and even story lines (serial killer and cannibal William Coyner did his deeds in nearby Cleveland, Mississippi), many of the gruesome details came from his years as a journalist. After high school, Harris earned a bachelor's degree in English from Baylor University in Waco, Texas, and took a job as a night police reporter with the local newspaper. After several years, he screwed up his courage and set out for New York. "It took guts for a boy from Mississippi to go to the big city," Bob Sadler, Harris's former editor, told Laughlin. "You can be talented and be too afraid to do something about it. Tom wasn't." Harris left behind his old life in more ways than one: His wife, whom he had married while in college, and his daughter remained in Waco. In 1968 Harris found a job as an assistant editor with the Associated Press (AP)

news service, again working the night shift and handling crime stories. A fellow reporter, Nicholas Pileggi, recalled to Cathleen McGuigan of *Newsweek* that Harris's demeanor did not portend his future works. "Tom was very quiet and cheery," Pileggi commented. "He did cover a lot of bloody stuff, but we all did." It was at this time that Harris began to develop his work ethic for extensive research, at the same time sating his thirst for knowledge. Those close to Harris mark a distinction between interest and obsession, however. "He has this imagination that's just unbridled," Walter Stovall, an old AP colleague, told McGuigan. "But it's not anything that roils around in his brain."

Harris's first book, *Black Sunday,* was conceived during his tenure with the AP. During slow periods, Harris and two colleagues passed the time by cooking up plots for novels; among these was the story that became *Black Sunday.* In the novel, Harris pits a crazed Vietnam veteran and a group of Arab extremists—who plan to bomb the Super Bowl stadium as a protest of the United States' support of Israel—against cunning FBI and Israeli agents whose mission is to stop them. The president of the United States is among the 100,000 spectators in the stadium, and all are unaware that the blimp flying overhead may attack them at any second. *Black Sunday* received mixed reviews from critics. Newgate Callendar of the *New York Times Book Review,* for example, found *Black Sunday* to be "written in a stolid, expository, unimaginative style," while L. W. Lindsay in the *Christian Science Monitor* labeled the book "a dud." But the critic for *Library Journal* was enthusiastic: "The action is up-to-date, . . . very violent . . . , and the plot is packed with business. Not a bit believable, but successful entertainment." Joshi called *Black Sunday* "a mere potboiler" but admitted that one sequence, a psychological history of one of the terrorists, was quite interesting: "It is written in a clinical, almost emotionless manner, but it nevertheless provides the necessary psychological motivation for the entire novel." John Frankenheimer's movie adaptation of the book also met with mixed critical reaction, but was well-liked by the movie-going public.

Harris's second effort was the bestseller *Red Dragon,* about Will Graham, an FBI agent searching for a deformed murderer who calls himself Red Dragon. Graham attempts "to hunt down [the] serial killer by adopting the mind-set of the criminal." This novel was more warmly received than *Black Sunday,* with a *New York Times* reviewer declaring that Harris's "depiction of police technology is comprehensive and compelling. . . . For all the gruesome nature of his subject, he writes with taste and with a high intelligence and verve." Critic

Jospeh Amie, writing in the *Saturday Review,* observed: "The suspense is sustained by deft characterizations, fascinating crime-lab details, and a twisting plot, and understated prose," while *Newsweek*'s Jean Strouse deemed *Red Dragon* "gruesome, appalling, occasionally formulaic and mechanical," but "guaranteed to terrify and succeed." In the *New York Times Book Review* Thomas Fleming recommended the book for "those who like their flesh to crawl." *Miami Vice* creator Michael Mann filmed *Red Dragon* as *Manhunter* in 1986. "*Manhunter . . .* is a snappy police procedural," noted Walter Goodman of the *New York Times.* The critic added: "The movie drives along with such intensity for much of the time that you can just let it work on your senses without worrying about whether it makes sense."

Harris produced *The Silence of the Lambs* in 1988. Like *Red Dragon, The Silence of the Lambs* deals with an FBI hunt for a serial killer. Utilizing some of the characters and themes of its predecessor, the novel presents the search through the eyes of female agent Clarice Starling. "It is a superlative mystery," exclaimed Douglas Winters in the *Washington Post Book World.* "Harris tells the story with the stunning and unflinching eye of the combat photographer . . . as remarkable as its predecessor in mingling the horror story with the police procedural." Christopher Lehmann-Haupt of the *New York Times* termed the novel "superb," adding that "Mr. Harris doesn't fool around or settle for trite effects. He goes straight for the viscera." Joshi ranked *The Silence of the Lambs* higher than *Red Dragon,* "in fullness of characterization, in intricacy of plot, and in cumulative suspense."

With *Silence of the Lambs,* Harris's reputation as well as his value as a commodity in the world of fiction writing were assured. The film version of *Silence of the Lambs,* directed by Jonathan Demme and starring Jodie Foster as Starling and Anthony Hopkins as a riveting Lecter, all of whom received Oscar Awards for their work, served to enhance Harris's reputation and left readers and moviegoers alike waiting breathlessly for the next installment. After heated sparring among New York's largest publishing houses, Harris accepted a contract for $5.25 million for his next two works. When he failed to produce a *Silence* sequel after several years, some observers questioned whether Delacorte had indeed gotten the bargain it had at first anticipated. Such doubts were laid to rest when, more than a decade later, Harris finally delivered. There has been no word on when the second contracted work should be expected. Observers looking to rationalize Harris's sparse output point to a remark he once made to Thomas McCormack, his editor at St. Martin's Press: "I can't write it until I believe it."

Eleven years after *The Silence of the Lambs* enthralled critics and readers, Harris ended a long sabbatical by producing the psychological thriller *Hannibal.* "*Hannibal* is entirely different in tone from either *Silence* or *Manhunter,* " Stephen Hunter wrote in the *Washington Post.* "Where they were gritty, journalistically researched pieces that turned on, and demanded, reality in their making, *Hannibal* is more like an extremely grim fairy tale combined with a cookbook." In *Hannibal,* Harris revisits the mind of the cannibal with cultivated tastes whom *Denver Post* critic Tom Walker has declared "the best literary villain since Iago." In this third installment of the Lector trilogy, Harris introduces the character of Mason Verger, whose encounter with Lector has left him hideously disfigured. As he lies in a darkened room, attached to a respirator, Verger plots a vicious revenge and attempts to use FBI agent Clarice Starling, a character who featured prominently in *The Silence of the Lambs,* to bait the brilliant, elusive Lector. Harris addresses his central theme when he wrote in *Hannibal:* "Now that ceaseless exposure has calloused us to the lewd and the vulgar, it is instructive to see what still seems wicked to us. What still slaps the clammy flab of our submissive consciousness hard enough to get our attention?"

Critics were divided in their reception of *Hannibal. New York Times* critic Christopher Lehmann-Haupt observed that "Mr. Harris seems determined to top himself in monstrosity at any and all cost. . . . The result shades toward the stuff of comic boks." Owen Gleiberman of *Entertainment Weekly* was another critic who found it difficult to take the novel seriously, commenting that *Hannibal* was Harris's "gaudiest, most lavishly over-the-top book yet . . . —Hitchcock by way of the Marquis de Sade." Lehmann-Haupt did admit that "*Hannibal* remains full of wonderful touches, typical of Mr. Harris's grasp of arcane detail." Some critics criticized *Hannibal* for its gratuitous violence, and others felt that the book was somewhat less inventive than *The Silence of the Lambs.* A reviewer for the *Economist* noted that *Hannibal* "is less a sequel than a baroque variation, transposed in part to Italy, in which Lecter is more gourmet than cannibal." Stephen King, however, writing for the *New York Times,* praised Harris's work by placing it in a category of "novels that so bravely and cleverly erase the line between popular fiction and literature."

BIOGRAPHICAL/CRITICAL SOURCES:

BOOKS

Contemporary Southern Writers, St. James Press (Detroit, MI), 1999.

Magistrale, Tony, and Michael A. Morrison, editors, *A Dark Night's Dreaming: Contemporary American Horror Fiction,* University of South Carolina Press (Columbia, SC), 1996.

St. James Guide to Horror, Ghost, and Gothic Writers, St. James Press (Detroit, MI), 1998.

PERIODICALS

Best Sellers, March 1, 1975.
Christian Science Monitor, January 10, 1975, p. 10.
Critic, May/June, 1975.
Denver Post, June 13, 1999.
Economist, July 17, 1999, review of *Hannibal.*
Entertainment Weekly, May 7, 1999, p. 22; June 25, 1999, p. 123.
Journal of American Culture, spring, 1995, Joseph Grixti, "Consuming Cannibals: Psychopathic Killers as Archetypes and Cultural Icons."
Knight Ridder/Tribune News Service, June 10, 1999, p. K4078; August 4, 1999, p. K6478.
Library Journal, April 1, 1975; November 1, 1981; July, 1999, p. 131.
London Review of Books, July 29, 1999, p. 10-11.
Los Angeles Times Book Review, July 17, 1988.
National Review, July 12, 1999, p. 53.
New Statesman, June 21, 1999.
Newsweek, November 9, 1981; June 7, 1999, p. 72; June 21, 1999, p. 75.
New York Times, August 15, 1988; March 25, 1990; June 10, 1999; June 13, 1999.
New York Times Book Review, February 2, 1975, p. 14; November 15, 1981, p. 14.
Notes on Contemporary Literature, January, 1995, "Thomas Harris Issue."
People, April 12, 1999, p. 12.
Publishers Weekly, June 14, 1999, p. 46; July 5, 1999, p. 34.
Saturday Review, November, 1981.
Time, June 21, 1999, p. 72.
Times (London), May 25, 1991.
Tribune Books (Chicago), August 14, 1988.
Washington Post, July 18, 1999, Stephen Hunter, review of *Hannibal,* p. G1.
Washington Post Book World, August 21, 1988; May 21, 1989.*

*   *   *

HAYDEN, Patrick Nielsen
  See NIELSEN HAYDEN, Patrick (James)

HAYNES, W. P.
  See WADDINGTON, Patrick (Haynes)

*   *   *

HERSHMAN, Marcie 1951-

PERSONAL: Born May 2, 1951, in Cleveland, OH; daughter of Eugene (in real estate and business) and Phyllis (a homemaker; maiden name, Weiss) Hershman; companion of Rebecca Blunk (an arts administrator). *Education:* Boston University, B.A. (summa cum laude), 1973; University of Massachusetts, Boston, M.A., 1978. *Politics:* "Democratic." *Religion:* Jewish.

ADDRESSES: Home—Brookline, MA. *Agent*—Ellen Levine, Ellen Levine Literary Agency, 15 East 26th St., No. 1801, New York, NY 10010. *E-mail*—marcie.hershman@tufts.edu.

CAREER: Boston Globe, Boston, MA, arts and books correspondent, 1975-82; Tufts University, Medford, MA, lecturer in English, 1981—; Emerson College, Boston, instructor in M.F.A. writing program, 1982-99. Cambridge Women's School, instructor in creative writing, 1974-76; Boston Center for Adult Education, Boston, instructor in fiction, 1974-76; Fisher Junior College, Boston, instructor in department of continuing education, 1975-78; Young Women's Christian Association, Boston, writer and community liaison in nontraditional jobs program, 1977; Lesley College, Cambridge, MA, instructor in American literature, 1978-80; Massachusetts College of Pharmacy and Allied Health Sciences, Boston, visiting assistant professor of English, 1980; Simmons College, New England Writers' Conference, visiting faculty, 1993; Fannie Hurst Writer-in-Residence, Brandeis University, 1999-2001; Fine Arts Work Center, Provincetown, MA, summer faculty, 1999—; University of Minnesota, Split Rock Arts Program, summer faculty, 2002; Bennington College, Bennington, VT, visiting associate faculty in M.F.A. writing program, 2002. Served as judge for numerous writing awards and contests, including Oregon literary awards, State of Connecticut grants, and Massachusetts Cultural Council grants.

MEMBER: PEN New England (member of executive board, 1996—), Society of Bunting Fellows, Phi Beta Kappa.

AWARDS, HONORS: Brace Award for Fiction, Boston University, 1973; People to Watch award, *Boston Magazine,* 1992; St. Botolph Club Foundation grant for artistic achievement, and Laurence L. Winship Book Award, distinguished honorable mention, *Boston Globe,* both 1992, both for *Tales of the Master Race;* fellow, Corporation of Yaddo, Saratoga Springs, NY, 1992, 1993, and 1994, Bunting Institute, Radcliffe College, 1992-93, and MacDowell Colony, 1993.

WRITINGS:

Tales of the Master Race, HarperCollins (New York, NY), 1991.

Safe in America, HarperCollins (New York, NY), 1995.

Speak to Me: Grief, Love, and What Endures, Beacon Press (Boston, MA), 2001.

Work represented in anthologies, including *Amazon Poetry,* Persephone Press (Watertown, MA), 1976; *Vrowen Houden,* Boche en Keuning (a Dutch translation), 1978; *Ourselves and Our Children,* Random House (New York, NY), 1978; *American Fiction,* Birch Lane, 1990; *Sororophobia: Differences among Women in Literature and Culture,* Oxford University Press (New York, NY), 1992; *Expect a Miracle,* HarperCollins (New York, NY), 1994; *Wrestling with the Angel: Jewish Insights on Death and Mourning,* Schlocken (New York, NY), 1995; *A Place Called Home,* St. Martin's Press (New York, NY), 1996; and *Beacon Best of 1999,* Beacon Press (Boston, MA), 2000. Contributor to periodicals, including *Boston Globe, Tikkun, Agni, Ploughshares, Ms., New York Times Magazine, Massachusetts Review,* and *Bellingham Review.* Contributing writer for *Goodlife,* 1985-86; fiction editor for *Tikkun,* 1990-91.

SIDELIGHTS: Marcie Hershman's first novel, *Tales of the Master Race,* was written in honor of her grandmother, whose family was destroyed in the Holocaust; among the members killed was Hershman's great-grandmother, who died in Auschwitz, the site of the largest concentration camp. Hershman's novel is a collection of interconnected stories about Aryan Germans living in the fictional German city of Kreiswald during World War II. Through the lives of her characters Hershman shows how people rationalized the events around them and made the Holocaust possible.

Michiko Kakutani noted in a *New York Times* review that although Hershman rarely refers to the Nazis directly, "each person [in the book] is in some way touched by [Nazi leader Adolf] Hitler's policy of genocide or implicated in it, even if most of them try to ignore the shocking realities by focusing willfully on the

minutiae of their daily lives." According to Kakutani, Hershman's tool is understatement, and the book presents "a searing portrait of the consequences of moral laziness and self-absorption." Bob Allen's *Washington Post Book World* review called the book "vividly rendered" and said "it portrays with chilling insight the gradual moral corrosion of Germany's Aryan middle classes." Robert DiAntonio, discussing the book in a *Jerusalem Post* review, wrote that Hershman's novel combines "the sweep of social and political history with revelations about individual lives." He deemed *Tales of the Master Race* unique in its treatment of the Holocaust because of its focus not on the "victims," but on German men and women who countenance the horrors of Hitler's laws by deliberately ignoring the true nature of the events taking place in front of them. Bridget Frost, in a *Writers' Monthly* review, felt that the structure of the book as a collection of interconnected stories reflects its theme. For Frost, each tale is "part of an unruly whole; just as each Kreiswald inhabitant is but a part of a sickeningly wayward city."

In an interview with Thomas Lee for *Bay Windows,* Hershman said: "I wanted to put a face on the enemy; I wanted to find out what it's like when your eyes, mind and heart are completely closed." Lee felt that this denial on the part of the characters is "a chilling refrain heard throughout" *Tales of the Master Race* that effectively exposes the true nature of the characters. Talking about her reasons for writing the book in a *Boston Globe* interview with Charles E. Claffey, Hershman said that when she visited Bavaria in 1987, "the air seemed to be full of voices. . . . It seemed so calm but I kept hearing echoes that I couldn't ignore." The result was *Tales of the Master Race.*

For Lee, *Tales of the Master Race* defines the Holocaust more effectively than any historical account, and he saw Kreiswald as "Anytown in Anycountry, where people who cling to an illusory sense of conformity continue to turn their backs on those who suffer." Elaine Kendall in a *Los Angeles Times* review maintained that *Tales* forces readers to reflect on what their responses would be in the same situation. By doing this, asserted Kendall, Hershman "effectively shifts the burden of knowledge from them to us."

Hershman's second novel, *Safe in America,* continues her close engagement with the Holocaust. As she did with *Tales of the Master Race,* she places historical documents, both actual and fictional, within chapters to bring to the fore questions about historical accuracy and literary truth. The novel centers on three generations of a family, from the mid-1930s through the early 1990s. Although the family in *Safe in America* lives a comfortable, middle-class existence in Cleveland, Ohio, during World War II, they cannot escape the European horrors. Their extended family is stuck in Eastern Europe, thwarted by an indifferent U.S. government while attempting to immigrate to the United States. Despite the parents' calm facade, the children growing up in Cleveland feel the pulls between their parents' "old country" responsibilities and their own "first-generation" American lives. Ultimately, even those who are "safe in America" lose loved ones in the war and suffer the consequences of sheltering others from its effects. In his *Booklist* review of *Safe in America*, George Needham declared that Hershman "is a spellbinding storyteller." Noting in *People Weekly* that the novel "is unerring in [its] depiction of grief," Kim Hubbard added that *Safe in America* "is about transcendence as much as tragedy." A *Publishers Weekly* critic found the work to be "a penetrating study of loss" and "an intimate, unsparing and psychologically profound portrait of a Jewish family in crisis."

In 2001 Hershman published *Speak to Me: Grief, Love, and What Endures.* This nonfiction memoir consists of essays that meditate on the power of memory and the human voice, the bonds between siblings, homosexual attraction, mystical and religious faith, and the loss of a brother to Acquired Immune Deficiency Syndrome (AIDS). A *Publishers Weekly* reviewer praised the book as "a wise, lyrical and deeply moving auscultation of a mourning heart and its possibilities for solace." In a review for the *Cleveland Plain Dealer*, a contributor found *Speak to Me* to be "an intense reading experience," "one of those rare books that leave you feeling it has contributed to your life." Amanda Heller, in a *Boston Globe* critique, noted that "the human voice is the most poignant medium of memory for Hershman" and called *Speak to Me* "a passionate meditation on the sound of others' voices, on the way they can come to us through the magic of technology or the mystery of dreams . . . communicating the mystical faiths we create for ourselves when the framework of received faith is not enough to support us." In an interview for the *Boston Globe*, David Mehegan quoted Hershman as saying: "The silence didn't win. My brother's voice has now reached other people. What more could I ask for but that the conversation continue?"

BIOGRAPHICAL/CRITICAL SOURCES:

PERIODICALS

Bay Windows, April 30, 1992, pp. 18, 25.
Booklist, May 15, 1995, George Needham, review of *Safe in America,* p. 1631.
Boston Globe, February 18, 1992, p. 49; July 16, 2001, David Mehegan, interview with Hershman, pp. B9, B11; July 22, 2001, review of *Speak to Me: Grief, Love, and What Endures.*
Cleveland Plain Dealer, May 6, 2001, review of *Speak to Me.*
Forward, January 3, 1992, pp. 9-10.
Jerusalem Post, March 7, 1992.
Los Angeles Times, December 27, 1991, p. E5.
New York Times, December 17, 1991, p. C19; December 10, 1995, A. G. Mojtabai, review of *Safe in America.*
People Weekly, February 17, 1992; August 21, 1995, Kim Hubbard, review of *Safe in America,* p. 29.
Philadelphia Gay News, August 24-30, 2001, review of *Speak to Me.*
Publishers Weekly, April 3, 1995, review of *Safe in America,* p. 45; February 19, 2001, review of *Speak to Me,* p. 76.
Radcliffe Quarterly, summer, 2001, interview with Hershman, p. 19.
Washington Post Book World, November, 3, 1991, p. 10.
Writers' Monthly (London), December, 1991, p. 23.

*   *   *

HICKMAN, Janet 1940-

PERSONAL: Born July 8, 1940, in Kilbourne, OH; daughter of Bernard Franklin (a plumber) and Pauline (Williams) Gephart; married John D. Hickman (a teacher), January 14, 1961; children: John H., Holly. *Education:* Ohio State University, B.Sc., 1960, M.A. Ed., 1964, Ph.D., 1979. *Religion:* Presbyterian.

ADDRESSES: Home—356 Gudrun Rd., Columbus, OH 43202.

CAREER: Junior high school teacher in public schools of Whitehall, OH, 1961-64; Ohio State University, Columbus, part-time instructor in children's literature, 1968-73, lecturer, 1979—.

MEMBER: National Council of Teachers of English, Ohio Historical Society.

WRITINGS:

FOR CHILDREN

The Valley of the Shadow, Macmillan (New York, NY), 1974.
The Stones, Macmillan (New York, NY), 1976.

Zoar Blue, Macmillan (New York, NY), 1978.
The Thunder-Pup, Macmillan (New York, NY), 1981.
Jericho: A Novel, Greenwillow (New York, NY), 1994.
Susannah, Greenwillow (New York, NY), 1998.
Ravine, Greenwillow (New York, NY), 2002.

OTHER

(Editor, with Bernice E. Cullinan) *Children's Literature in the Classroom—Weaving Charlotte's Web,* Christopher-Gordon Publishers (Needham Heights, MA), 1989.
(With Charlotte S. Huck and Susan Hepler) *Children's Literature in the Elementary School,* 5th edition, Harcourt Brace Jovanovich College Publishers (Fort Worth, TX), 1993.

Contributor to professional journals, including *Theory into Practice, Research in the Teaching of English, Language Arts,* and *Ohio Reading Teacher,* and to *Ingenue* and *Teen* magazine.

SIDELIGHTS: Janet Hickman has written a number of novels for middle-grade readers that focus on American history. The stresses that occur during wartime are the subject of several of Hickman's books, among them *The Stones* and *Zoar Blue,* although each work focuses on the way war affects members of an unusual community. And in her 1994 novel *Jericho,* Hickman depicts the ties between family members across several generations, creating what *Horn Book* contributor Nancy Vasilakis dubbed a "haunting coming-of-age novel set in both the present and the past." *Jericho* is particularly compelling for its portrait of four generations of women, their stories interwoven against the frustrated grumblings of a modern fourteen-year-old girl forced to take care of her invalid great-grandmother who gradually comes to understand the connection between the old woman and herself. Noted for her avoidance of melodrama and sentimentalism, Hickman was praised by a *Publishers Weekly* contributor for possessing a "sharp eye for detail, a profound understanding of the aging process and a deep love for humanity."

Born in 1940, Hickman was raised in Ohio, where she continues to live. "When I was little I liked to read and tell myself stories," she stated, "but I never thought seriously about writing for children. Then when I became a teacher one of the first assignments in my eighth graders' history book was to write a short story based on the information in the chapter they had just read.

They complained so much that I promised I would do the assignment too, just to prove it wasn't so bad." The story Hickman penned that evening was not only popular with her students; it also became her first published fiction when it was sold to a magazine. "Nothing since has been that easy," Hickman was quick to add.

Hickman published her first book for young readers, *The Valley of the Shadow,* in 1974. Two years later she released *The Stones,* which takes place in the Midwest during World War II. In the novel, eleven-year-old Garrett McKay channels his concern over his father, missing in action at the front, into participation in a local gang. The gang's harassment of an elderly man with a German-sounding name results in tragedy, as fire and then concern over Garrett's missing little sister quickly make Garrett realized what is truly important. *The Stones* was praised by *School Library Journal* contributor Jean Lambert Ross as "tightly plotted." The critic further praised Hickman for her vivid characters and realistic setting. While noting that the ending is predictable, a contributor to *Kirkus Reviews* also had positive comments about the novel, writing that the characters "fit naturally into the sticky, dust-choked midwestern scene where summer boredom is a more present villain than the World War itself."

Zoar Blue takes readers back to the 1860s and the U.S. Civil War, as Hickman spins a story about the effects of war on a small Midwestern town whose residents are members of the Society of the Separatists of Zoar. While the European-born elders are pacifists—many immigrants remember with horror their own experiences in the wars fought throughout Europe—idealistic young men like seventeen-year-old John Keffer decide to join the Union Army, only to meet with tragedy at the Battle of Gettysburg. John's girlfriend, the orphaned fourteen-year-old Barbara, also decides to leave. Her travels outside of Zoar in search of her uncle and her own experience of the war as a nurse in an army hospital making her realize the security she has left behind. *School Library Journal* critic Sara Miller praised the novel for its depiction of an "isolated, ingrown community" of refugees, calling *Zoar Blue* "compassionate and detailed, moving slowly but firmly into a full view of that life."

A community of Shakers *circa* 1810 is the setting for Hickman's 1998 novel *Susannah,* which finds the fourteen-year-old protagonist an unhappy participant in a strict religious lifestyle. Susannah is still suffering from the death of her mother, a death her father has dealt with by moving the family to a community of religious zealots in Lebanon, Ohio. Forced to live apart from her father in a building that houses all the community's children, Susannah finds that she is not alone in her discontent, and she and her new friend Mary begin to plot their escape at the same time that the Shakers are being attacked by nearby residents. While noting that Hickman effectively handles "the complexities of portraying a religious utopian community," *Horn Book* reviewer Maeve Visser Knoth added that the novel also addresses such modern themes as dealing with blended families and the complex emotions of children following a divorce. Calling *Susannah* "suspenseful and insightful," a *Publishers Weekly* contributor added that the "down-to-earth, accessible prose captures the flavor of 19th-century English without appearing stilted."

Being the author of historical fiction "requires as much groundwork as it does writing," Hickman once explained. "But I have discovered that I, who once barely tolerated history courses, truly enjoy this research—the reading, the puzzling, the discovery of odd facts that fit." Hickman's family wholeheartedly supports her quests for information: "My family shares the search for authentic backgrounds; they always serve as willing taste-testers for period recipes, and they seem to welcome the excuse for vacation when I need to see for myself what a particular mountain or battlefield looks like." In the Hickman household, most family vacations were actually research trips in disguise, a fact that the author views as "a bonus" of her job as the creator of historical fiction for young readers.

BIOGRAPHICAL/CRITICAL SOURCES:

PERIODICALS

Booklist, December 15, 1976, Denise M. Wilms, review of *The Stones,* p. 608; November 1, 1978, D. Wilms, review of *Zoar Blue,* p. 479; September 1, 1994, Chris Sherman, review of *Jericho,* p. 41; October 15, 1998, Carolyn Phelan, review of *Susannah,* p. 422.

Horn Book, February, 1982, Ethel R. Twitchell, review of *The Thunder-Pup,* p. 43; November-December, 1994, Nancy Vasilakis, review of *Jericho,* p. 731; January, 1999, Maeve Visser Knoth, review of *Susannah,* p. 62.

Kirkus Reviews, July 15, 1976, review of *The Stones,* p. 794; September 15, 1978, review of *Zoar Blue,* p. 1021; December 15, 1981, review of *The Thunder-Pup,* p. 1519.

Publishers Weekly, August 8, 1994, review of *Jericho,* p. 436; October 26, 1998, review of *Susannah,* p. 67; January 1, 2001, review of *Susannah,* p. 94.

School Library Journal, October, 1976, Jean Lambert Ross, review of *The Stones,* p. 107; October, 1978, Sara Miller, review of *Zoar Blue,* p. 155; November, 1981, Karen Stang Handley, review of *The Thunder-Pup,* p. 92; September, 1994, review of *Jericho,* p. 436; October, 1998, Carolyn Noah, review of *Susannah,* p. 136.*

*   *   *

HOLMES, Barbara Ware 1945-

PERSONAL: Born September 2, 1945, in Roanoke, VA; daughter of Cecil O. (an air force pilot who died in Korea) and Dorris (a homemaker; maiden name, Vest) Savoy; stepdaughter of Robert H. Savoy; married David J. Holmes (a manuscript and autograph dealer), November 30, 1968; children: Sarah Anne. *Education:* In conjunction with studies at Springfield College, attended Institute of European Studies, Vienna, Austria, 1965-66, and Exeter College, Oxford, 1966; Springfield College, B.A., 1967; Northeastern University, M.A., 1986; graduate study at Connecticut College for Women (now Connecticut College), 1969.

ADDRESSES: Home—2051 Spring St., Hamilton, NY 13346.

CAREER: Springfield City Library, Springfield, MA, reference librarian and desk clerk, 1968; Connecticut College, New London, CT, secretary to the dean, 1969; elementary school librarian in Montville, CT, 1969-70, and Ketchikan, AK, 1970-72; National Association of Independent Schools, Boston, MA, advertising manager and assistant to editor of *Independent School Bulletin,* 1973-75; writer, 1975—.

MEMBER: Authors Guild, Authors League of America, Franklin Inn Club (Philadelphia, PA), Society of Children's Book Writers and Illustrators.

WRITINGS:

Charlotte Cheetham: Master of Disaster, illustrated by John Himmelman, Harper (New York, NY), 1985.
Charlotte the Starlet, illustrated by John Himmelman, Harper (New York, NY), 1988.

Charlotte Shakespeare and Annie the Great, illustrated by John Himmelman, Harper (New York, NY), 1989.

Letters to Julia, HarperCollins (New York, NY), 1997.

My Sister the Sausage Roll, illustrated by Karen Lee Schmidt, Hyperion (New York, NY), 1997.

Following Fake Man, illustrated by Sarah Hokanson, Knopf (New York, NY), 2001.

Contributor of adult stories to magazines, including *Redbook, Janus, Samisdat, Moving Out,* and *Pig Iron.*

SIDELIGHTS: Beginning her children's writing career with three books about the fib-telling Charlotte Cheetham, Barbara Ware Holmes has produced an additional book for young readers, *My Sister the Sausage Roll,* as well as two young adult works, *Letters to Julia* and *Following Fake Man.* In the "Charlotte Cheetham" series, Holmes follows the exploits of an elementary-school girl who has a problem telling the truth. In *Charlotte Cheetham: Master of Disaster,* this tendency to lie gets Charlotte into a difficult situation after bragging to her friends that she can get them a tour of a non-existent sticker factory. The next entry in the series, *Charlotte the Starlet,* shows the young protagonist stirring up trouble with a book she writes, while *Charlotte Shakespeare and Annie the Great* finds the now sixth grader becoming envious of the attention her best friend Annie receives after trying out for a school play.

My Sister the Sausage Roll features another character given to exaggeration, Eloise Trombly. When a new baby sister joins the family, Eloise is not thrilled with her arrival, but nonetheless decides to help her father—away on an extended business trip—learn more about his new daughter by writing him letters about Mary Alice's progress. Along with her friend, Eloise decides to teach the infant about her father by showing Mary Alice a picture of Mr. Trombly everyday. The two hope that when Eloise's father returns from his trip, Mary Alice will recognize her father from the photo. However, things do not go as planned when the infant sees her father for the first time, and Eloise realizes that despite her best intentions, it will take a bit of time for Mary Alice to warm up to Mr. Trombly. According to *School Library Journal* reviewer Carrie A. Guarria, Holmes "portrays the feelings of the main character in a truthful, sometimes endearing way."

In a book for older readers, *Letters to Julia,* Holmes uses an epistolary format to tell the story of fifteen-year-old Liz Beech. After a teacher suggests that she send the first chapter of her novel to a publisher, Liz develops a close relationship with the editor who receives her manuscript. This editor, Julia Steward Jones, becomes, for Liz, not only a mentor for her writing, but also a counselor for the stress in her family life. While her life in the suburbs appears comfortable, in reality she is miserable, living with divorced parents who still reside in the same house. Throughout *Letters to Julia,* both editor and student use their correspondence to work through the difficulties in each of their respective lives, though with mixed results. "The voices of all the characters are very true," commented *Booklist* reviewer GraceAnne A. DeCandido, who went on to predict that "those who have thought about writing themselves will find an honest glimpse" at the craft.

Reviewers widely praised Holmes' 2001 work *Following Fake Man.* Twelve-year-old Homer desperately wishes to know something of his father who died when Homer was only a toddler. However, the boy's linguist mother, Dr. Winthrop, never wishes to discuss her dead husband, remaining cold and aloof towards her only son. One summer, Homer, his mother, and their warm and generous housekeeper take a vacation to the family's former home in Maine. While there, Homer finds his first real friend and decides to discover the story of his seemingly forgotten father. Eventually, Homer tracks down an acquaintance of his father and tries to find a way to reach his emotionally distant mother. "Using strong visual imagery and occasionally alternating points of view," remarked a *Publishers Weekly* reviewer, "Holmes adroitly conveys the discord in a household haunted by the past." *School Library Journal* contributor Leigh Ann Jones found the novel "a genuinely satisfying book about friendship and family," while a *Horn Book* critic thought that "Homer's observations of his affecting metamorphosis have a freshness and spontaneity that give them the ring of truth."

Holmes once stated, "I spent much of my childhood following relatives from room to room, entertaining them with readings from my works in progress and, like [Charlotte Cheetham], telling a fair share of tall tales. It wasn't until the success of my riveting sixth-grade play on coffee beans in Brazil, however, that I began to consider the career of writing seriously. From there it was simply a matter of working for twenty-two more years to ready myself for publication.

"*Charlotte Cheetham: Master of Disaster* is the story of a fifth-grader who tells lies. How can she not when the lies are there, waiting to be told, and seeming, to Charlotte, exactly like the truth? It is only later, when classmates demand she prove them true, that Charlotte is forced to distinguish between fantasy and truth. She decides to write, storing up her fictions for future books. The "Charlotte Cheetham" trilogy follows Charlotte's career as a writer of books and producer of a play which stars her unpredictable classmates.

"Surely the subject of lying is dear to any writer's heart, believing, as we must, that good fiction is truer than 'truth.' Children, I think, know this too, for they see that the world as it *is* is not the world as it should be, and only the imagination can set it straight."

BIOGRAPHICAL/CRITICAL SOURCES:

PERIODICALS

Booklist, July, 1997, GraceAnne A. DeCandido, review of *Letters to Julia,* p. 1812; June 1, 2001, Hazel Rochman, review of *Following Fake Man,* p. 1883.

Horn Book, July, 2001, review of *Following Fake Man,* p. 451.

Kirkus Reviews, March 1, 1997, review of *Letters to Julia,* p. 381; April 15, 1997, review of *My Sister the Sausage Roll,* p. 640.

Publishers Weekly, January 15, 1988, review of *Charlotte the Starlet,* p. 97; May 21, 2001, review of *Following Fake Man,* p. 108.

School Library Journal, February, 1986, Eleanor K. MacDonald, review of *Charlotte Cheetham: Master of Disaster,* p. 86; August, 1997, Carrie A. Guarria, review of *My Sister the Sausage Roll,* p. 135; May, 2001, Leigh Ann Jones, review of *Following Fake Man,* p. 150.

*　　*　　*

HOUDINI
See LOVECRAFT, H(oward) P(hillips)

*　　*　　*

HUGO, Grant
See CABLE, James (Eric)

*　　*　　*

HUMPHREYS, Susan L.
See LOWELL, Susan

J

JOHNSON, Herbert A(lan) 1934-

PERSONAL: Born January 10, 1934, in Jersey City, NJ; son of Harry Oliver and Magdalena (Diemer) Johnson; married Jane McCue, June 4, 1983. *Ethnicity:* "Mixed." *Education:* Columbia University, A.B., 1955, M.A., 1961, Ph.D., 1965; New York Law School, LL.B., 1960.

ADDRESSES: Home—615 La Bruce Lane, Columbia, SC 29205. *Office*—School of Law, University of South Carolina, Columbia, SC 29208; fax: 803-777-8613. *E-mail*—hjohnson@law.law.sc.edu.

CAREER: Hunter College of the City University of New York, New York, NY, lecturer in history, 1964-65, assistant professor, 1965-67; Institute of Early American History and Culture, Williamsburg, VA, associate editor, 1967-70, co-editor, 1970-71, editor, *The Papers of John Marshall,* 1971-77; University of South Carolina, Columbia, professor of history and law, 1977-90, professor of constitutional law, 1991—. *Military service:* U.S. Air Force, 1955-57; became first lieutenant.

MEMBER: American Historical Association, Historical Society, American Society for Legal History.

WRITINGS:

(Editor with Charles T. Cullen) *The Papers of John Marshall,* University of North Carolina Press (Chapel Hill, NC), volume 1, 1974, volume II, 1977.

Imported-Eighteenth Century Law Treatises in American Law Libraries, 1700-1799, University of Tennessee Press (Knoxville, TN), 1978.

(Editor) *South Carolina Legal History,* Reprint Co. (Spartanburg), 1980.

(With George L. Haskins) *Foundations of Power—John Marshall, 1801-1815,* Volume 2: *History of the Supreme Court of the United States,* edited by Paul A. Freund, Macmillan (New York, NY), 1981.

Essays on New York Colonial Legal History, Greenwood Press (Westport, CT), 1981.

History of Criminal Justice, Anderson (Cincinnati, OH), 1988, 2nd edition, with Nancy Travis Wolfe, 1995, third edition, 2002.

American Legal and Constitutional History: Cases and Materials, Austin & Winfield (San Francisco, CA), 1994, 2nd edition revised, 2000.

The Chief Justiceship of John Marshall, 1801-35, University of South Carolina Press (Columbia, SC), 1997.

Wingless Eagle: U.S. Army Aviation from 1907-1918, University of North Carolina Press (Chapel Hill, NC), 2001.

Contributor of chapters to *Punishment: Transactions of the Jean Bodin Society for Comparative Institutional History,* LVIII, DeBoeck-Universite (Brussels), 1991; and, with James K. Lehman, *South Carolina Jurisprudence,* XXVII, South Carolina Bar (Columbia, SC), 1996. Contributor of articles to *American Journal of Legal History, Air University Review, New York History,* and *Melbourne University Law Review.*

WORK IN PROGRESS: English and American Constitutional Thought, 1607-1776.

JONES, Charles M(artin) 1912-2002
(Chuck Jones)

PERSONAL: Born September 21, 1912, in Spokane, WA; died of congestive heart failure, February 22, 2002, in Corona del Mar, CA; son of Charles Adams and Mabel (Martin) Jones; married Dorothy Webster, January 31, 1935 (died, 1978); married Marian Dern (a writer), January 14, 1983; children: Linda Jones Clough. *Education:* Chouinard Art Institute (now California Institute of the Arts), diploma, 1931. *Politics:* Democrat. *Religion:* Unitarian-Universalist.

ADDRESSES: Office—c/o Screen Cartoonist Guild, 1616 West Ninth St., Suite 300, Los Angeles, CA, 90015-1007.

CAREER: Warner Brothers, Inc., Hollywood, CA, animator, 1933-38, director of animated films, 1938-63; freelance writer, producer, and director of television specials, 1962-2002. Metro-Goldwyn-Mayer, Inc., producer of "Tom and Jerry" cartoon series, beginning in 1963, head of animation department, beginning in 1966; founder of Tower Twelve Productions, 1965; American Broadcasting Companies (ABC-TV), vice president of children's programming, beginning in 1970, and creator of the program *The Curiosity Shop,* 1971-73; founder of Chuck Jones Enterprises (film company). Co-producer, writer, and director of *The Bugs Bunny Show* for ABC-TV, 1960-62, and *The Bugs Bunny/Road Runner Hour* for Columbia Broadcasting System (CBS-TV), 1968-71; television specials include *How the Grinch Stole Christmas,* 1970, and *The Cricket in Times Square,* 1973, both for ABC-TV, and the CBS-TV specials *Rikki-Tikki-Tavi,* 1975, *Bugs Bunny in King Arthur's Court,* 1978, *Raggedy Ann and Andy in the Great Santa Claus Caper,* 1978, and *The Pumpkin Who Couldn't Smile,* 1979; animator for *Gremlins,* 1984, *Gremlins 2,* 1990, and animation consultant, *Who Framed Roger Rabbit?,* 1988. Teacher and lecturer at colleges and universities in the United States and abroad. Work exhibited at Gallery Lainzberg and Circle Fine Art Galleries; film retrospectives at Museum of Modern Art, British Film Institute, American Film Institute, New York Cultural Center, Harvard University, Ottawa Art Center, London Film School, Filmex Festival, Deauville Festival of American Films, Moscow Film Festival, and Montreal Film Festival. *Military service:* U.S. Army, worked on training films during World War II.

MEMBER: Academy of Motion Picture Arts and Sciences, Screen Writers Guild, Academy of Television Arts and Sciences, National Council on Children and Television, Screen Actors Guild.

AWARDS, HONORS: Award for the best animated cartoon of the year from Newsreel Theatre, 1940, for *Old Glory*; Academy Awards from Academy of Motion Picture Arts and Sciences, 1950, for best animated cartoon *For Scentimental Reasons* and best documentary short subject *So Much for So Little,* and 1965, for best animated cartoon *The Dot and the Line*; CINE Eagle Certificates for animated films from Council on International Non-Theatrical Events in 1966 for *The Dot and the Line,* in 1973 for *The Cricket in Times Square,* in 1976 for *Rikki-Tikki-Tavi* and *The White Seal,* and in 1977 for *Mowgli's Brothers*; Peabody Award for Television Programming Excellence, 1971, for *How the Grinch Stole Christmas* and *Horton Hears a Who*; tributes from American Film Institute, 1975 and 1980, and British Film Institute and New York Film Institute, both 1979; Best Educational Film Award from Columbus Film Festival (Columbus, Ohio), 1976; first prize from Tehran Festival of Films for Children, 1977; Parents' Choice Award for videos from Parents' Choice Foundation, 1985, for *Rikki-Tikki-Tavi* and *Mowgli's Brothers*; Great Director Award from U.S. Film Festival, 1986; Academy Award for lifetime achievement, 1996.

WRITINGS:

SELF-ILLUSTRATED BOOKS FOR CHILDREN, UNDER NAME CHUCK JONES

(Adapter) Rudyard Kipling, *Rikki-Tikki-Tavi,* Ideals Publishing, 1982.
(Editor) Rudyard Kipling, *The White Seal,* Ideals Publishing, 1982.
(Adapter) George Selden, *The Cricket in Times Square,* Ideals Publishing, 1984.
William the Backwards Skunk, Crown, 1987.
Chuck Amuck (autobiography), with foreword by Steven Spielberg, Farrar, Straus (New York, NY), 1989.
Chuck Jones (art instruction), with foreword by Robin Williams, Warner (New York, NY), 1996.
(Author of foreword) Stefan Kanfer, *Cartoons and America, from Betty Boop to Toy Story,* Scribner (New York, NY), 1997.

OTHER, UNDER NAME CHUCK JONES

Gay Purr-ee (film), United Producers of America, 1962.
(Co-author) *The Phantom Toll Booth* (screenplay), Metro-Goldwyn-Mayer, 1971.

Creator of syndicated comic strip "Crawford," beginning in 1978. Contributor to periodicals.

SIDELIGHTS: Chuck Jones was considered one of the most gifted studio cartoonists of Hollywood's so-called "golden age" of animated shorts, with a name eclipsed only by that of Walt Disney. During his seven-decade-long career, Jones either created or gave verve to such classic characters as Bugs Bunny, Daffy Duck, Porky the Pig, Elmer Fudd, the Road Runner, Wile E. Coyote, and Pepé Le Pew, all of which have become essential assets of American pop culture. Jones did some of his best work between 1938 and 1962, when he made shorts starring these characters for Warner Brothers. "They all share certain characteristics: high energy, expressive eyes, exquisite comic timing, and the ability to surprise us," wrote Lloyd Rose in an *Atlantic* article that called Jones "our greatest invisible actor."

After leaving Warner in the early 1960s, Jones worked on the Tom and Jerry series for Metro Goldwyn-Mayer, but also began to explore the emerging medium of television as a vehicle for his creative energies. He worked with longtime friend Theodore Geisel, also known as Dr. Seuss, on the animated children's specials *Horton Hears a Who* and *How the Grinch Stole Christmas.* When a feature film remake of The Grinch appeared in theaters in late 2000, the 88-year-old Jones was still working, and still in possession of his sharp sense of humor. Discussing his return to Warner Brothers after a long absence, he explained to *New York Times* writer John Canemaker that he was now under a lifetime contract with the studio, which means "they can't fire me 'til I'm dead."

Jones was born Charles Martin Jones on September 21, 1912, in Spokane, Washington. When he was around six, his family moved to southern California, where his father hoped to make his fortune. Jones was the third of four children of Charles Adams Jones and Mabel Martin Jones, and the family lived in a series of rented homes, some of them pleasantly close to the ocean. But Charles Jones's entrepreneurial schemes usually failed spectacularly. He published a book titled *Fifty Ways to Serve Avocados,* owned a vineyard during Prohibition, and once tried to start a geranium farm on a parcel of land near Long Beach called Signal Hill; frustrated, he sold it, and the land was later discovered to be rich in crude oil. As a result, there were reams of unused business stationery in the Jones house, which the children were heartily encouraged to use for drawing paper. They were even forbidden to use both sides of a sheet of paper to draw, so that the letterhead might disappear all the more quickly. Jones loved to draw from an early age, and his first character studies were made of the family cat, Johnson, who liked to swim and had an inexplicable passion for grapefruit. The cat would tear an entire one apart and eat it, which sometimes left him with a helmet of rind on his head. "And so Johnson's first lesson to me as a future animator was this: Eschew the ordinary, disdain the commonplace," Jones wrote in his richly illustrated 1989 autobiography, *Chuck Amuck.*

Jones grew up in a literary household, and he picked up a fascination for the coyote from reading Mark Twain's book *Roughing It.* "The coyote is a living, breathing allegory of Want," Jones quoted the book in his autobiography. "He is *always* hungry. He is always poor, out of luck and friendless." Later, he would recall this description in creating one of his most memorable cartoon characters, the Road Runner's omnipresent predator. Jones was also an avid filmgoer, and loved the silent films of the era from comics like Buster Keaton and Charlie Chaplin. Some of the film studios were near his home, and he even appeared in a few himself as an extra for director Mack Sennett. But as a teen, Jones was an indifferent student, and his poor grades frustrated his father to the point where he was taken out of high school and enrolled in Chouinard Art Institute, now California Institute of the Arts. He graduated in 1930, hoping to move to Paris to paint, but the Great Depression thwarted his plans. After looking for work as a janitor, the nearly indigent Jones found work in 1931 as a cel-washer at an animation studio owned by Ub Iwerks, a former Disney associate. Cel-washing was the lowliest job in animation, and involved wiping the drawings off hundreds of sheets of celluloid so they could be re-used. He eventually moved up to the status of in-betweener, the artist who drew the hundreds of small frames that, when filmed, actually "animated" the character. As Jones said about his career in the *New York Times* interview, "I just kind of fell uphill."

Jones credited his wife, Dorothy Webster, for finding him the job with the Leon Schlesinger Studio around 1933. Jones soon felt at home among the jocular animation staff, and began to find his own style. His first credit was for the 1934 Friz Freleng short "The Miller's Daughter." By 1936, he was working for famed director Tex Avery, whose animated shorts were known for their verve and flawless comic timing. Jones and his colleagues were involved with some of the early Porky the Pig shorts, and then helped create two of the most timeless cartoon anti-heroes, Daffy Duck and Bugs Bunny, in the late 1930s. Daffy was a hapless black duck who could never succeed. "Daffy was Jones's richest subject," declared Pope Brock in *People.* "Originally a flat-out wacko, hopping around a lake on his head, the duck became in Jones's hands a resilient, greedy, insecure dynamo with big plans. Jones often cast him in heroic roles, like the Scarlet Pumpernickel, for which the duck considered himself fabulously well suited. Greeting each challenge with a volcanic surge of ego, he suffered endless humiliations."

Jones borrowed Daffy's catchword, "despicable," from recollections of his father's ire over President Warren G. Harding's mangling of the English language in his speeches. But Jones and his colleagues gave Daffy a raspy lisp in imitation of the arrogant Leon Schlesinger, whom they detested. "What we forgot," Jones recalled in a *People* interview with Brock, "was that Leon would have to see it. We figured when he heard his own voice coming out of this screwball duck, we'd all get fired. Leon came in and sat on the gold-painted throne that he'd probably stolen from some Theda Bara picture. We rolled it, praying. At the end he jumped up in the air and cried, 'Jethuth Chritht, where'd you get that great voith?'"

All of the Schlesinger studio shorts were created for the big screen, as part of a program of short features played before the billed film. Daffy Duck and his travails were an instant hit, and Jones began directing his own shorts. Bugs Bunny, another character that also came alive under Jones's direction, had been created by a man named Charles Thorson from an idea of an animator, Ben "Bugs" Hardaway, and the rabbit's wisecracking Brooklynite personality was the work of Tex Avery. But when Jones began directing the Bugs shorts, he gave the rabbit a very distinct personality. "His movements give the sense that he has real mass and inertia, that he weighs something, and Jones has frankly borrowed for him gestures from the great silent comedians (Keaton's eye movements, Chaplin's one-legged hopping turn)," noted Rose in the *Atlantic*. "His Bugs also has sophistication—he is less the loudmouthed wise guy, more the gentleman anarchist." The dimwit rabbit hunter Elmer Fudd became a staple of the Bugs shorts, and in others, Daffy and Bugs would do battle with one another. "Some of his funniest cartoons result from matching the unflappable and ironic Bugs with the desperate and treacherous Daffy," declared Rose. "Daffy plots against Bugs; Bugs eludes him with lazy ease. Daffy, through greed, falls into trouble; Bugs, sighing, rescues him."

In the late 1940s—after a stint as a cartoonist making military training films for the U.S. Army, where he worked with Geisel—Jones and a gag writer named Michael Maltese created the classic Road Runner cartoons. Both had worked at the Schlesinger studio, which was sold to Warner Brothers outright in 1944, and wanted to make an animated short with no dialogue. What emerged from Jones's drawing board was the de-

termined Road Runner, a creature constantly on the run from his nemesis, Wile E. Coyote. *People* journalist Brock described the Coyote as "the luckless predator who defines failure, whether he is raising a forlorn umbrella in the spreading shade of an incoming boulder or falling victim to Acme products through his own ineptness."

The first Road Runner cartoon was 1949's *Fast and Furry-ous,* and was set in the southwestern United States desert. Studio executives at Warner didn't like it, primarily because it had no dialogue, and they were already paying Mel Blanc to do the voices for the cartoons; the Road-runner said only "Beep, beep." But when they learned that U.S. Navy pilots liked to call this out to each other over their radios, they changed their mind, and Jones and Maltese were given the go-ahead. They made twenty-six in all in the series, all set in a bleak landscape devoid of anything save desert sand, a road, some train tracks, a tunnel, and the inevitable cliff. There was usually a mailbox, which the Coyote used to send away for products from the Acme Company with which he might capture his prey. The "Acme" name served as homage to the maker of their camera crane at the studio.

Jones went on to make numerous other short animated works outside of the character-centered series. Like his Road Runner cartoons, others without dialogue are termed especially brilliant by critics. In 1952's *Feed the Kitty,* a large bulldog becomes unnaturally attached to the tiny kitten in his household, and allows it to ride on his back. One day, he mistakenly thinks it has been baked, and "The sight of the distraught bulldog, eyes red and cheeks tear-stained, carrying a cat-shaped cookie on his back, is both touching and absurd," declared Canemaker in the *New York Times*. Jones also won praise for the 1957 short *What's Opera, Doc?,* that reduces nineteenth-century German Romantic composer Richard Wagner's sixteen-hour *Der Ring des Nibelungen* cycle to a six-minute musical confrontation between Bugs Bunny and Elmer Fudd.

Warner closed its animation studio in 1963, and Jones and many of his team went to Metro Goldwyn-Mayer, where they created shorts for the "Tom and Jerry" series. Then Jones began finding work in a new medium—television. With Geisel, he collaborated on the 1967 holiday classic, *How the Grinch Stole Christmas,* and 1971's *Horton Hears a Who.* He also directed animated TV specials like 1975's *The White Seal,* based on a Rudyard Kipling tale. Even in his sixties, Jones continued to work, for he never earned more from his

Warner days than the contractual salary he was paid as an animator or director. He even won two Oscars for best animated short—the first in 1940 for *Old Glory,* and again a decade later with the Pepé Le Pew vehicle *For Scentimental Reasons,* but the producers accepted both and took them home. The studios kept all royalties when such works found a new generation of fans via television, and Jones and his colleagues were also left out of the lucrative licensing deals that Warner and MGM signed for merchandise.

At the start of the new century, Jones was under contract once again with Warner, but this time in a far wiser arrangement. He was creating a new character for their Internet site, *Entertaindom.com,* called Timber Wolf. "People say, 'But you don't know anything about all that,'" Jones told the *New York Times* about his foray into cyberspace. "I agree with them. But I didn't know about how an animated cartoon was made either. No kidding! I never went into the camera room. I would try to figure out what I wanted to see on the screen."

Jones died of congestive heart failure at his home in Corona Del Mar on February 22, 2002.

BIOGRAPHICAL/CRITICAL SOURCES:

BOOKS

International Dictionary of Films and Filmmakers, St. James Press (Detroit, MI), 1996.
Newsmakers, Gale (Farmington Hills, MI), 2001.
Peary, Danny, and Gerald Peary, editors, *The American Animated Cartoon,* Dutton (New York, NY), 1980.

PERIODICALS

American Film, July-August, 1985.
Atlantic, December, 1984, p. 124.
Christian Science Monitor, November 2, 1970.
Film Comment, January/February, 1975; December, 1985.
Films and Filming, September, 1982.
Funnyworld, spring, 1971.
Houston Chronicle, April 15, 1979.
Los Angeles Herald Examiner, January 21, 1985.
Los Angeles Times, August 27, 1978.
Newsweek, October 21, 1985.
New York Times, February 8, 1976; October 7, 1979; November 19, 2000, p. 37.

Observer (London), April 8, 1979.
Opera News, November, 2000, Harry Bicket, "On the Beat," p. 10.
People, November 13, 1989, p. 103.
Publishers Weekly, August 12, 1996, "Chuck Reducks: Drawing from the Fun Side of Life," p. 71.
Take One, September, 1978.
Time, December 17, 1973; September 9, 1985.
Video, March, 1986.*

*   *   *

JONES, Chuck
  See JONES, Charles M(artin)

*   *   *

JONES, John J.
  See LOVECRAFT, H(oward) P(hillips)

*   *   *

JONES, Stuart 1933-1998

PERSONAL: Born March 29, 1933, in Manchester, England; died April 17, 1998, in South Africa. *Education:* Degrees from Oxford University, 1955 and 1958, Victoria University of Manchester, 1962, and University of British Columbia, 1968. *Politics:* Conservative. *Religion:* Anglican.

CAREER: University of the Witwatersrand, Johannesburg, South Africa, began as lecturer, became senior lecturer in economic history and head of division, 1969-93; University of South Africa, Pretoria, professor of economics, 1993-98.

MEMBER: Economic History Society of South Africa (president, 1986-88, 1994-98).

WRITINGS:

(With Andre Muller) *The South African Economy, 1910-90,* St. Martin's (New York, NY), 1992.
The Great Imperial Banks: Standard Bank and Barclays in South Africa, 1862-1961, Unisa Press (Pretoria), 1997.
(With Jon Inggs)*The South African Economy in Decline: 1970-2000,* Edward Elgar (Cheltenham), 2001.

EDITOR

Banking and Business in South Africa, Macmillan (London, England), 1988.

Financial Enterprise in South Africa since 1950, Macmillan (London, England), 1988.

Economic Interpretations of Nineteenth-Century Imperialism, Economic History Society of Southern Africa, 1992.

(With Jon Inggs) *Entrepreneurs of the Industrial Revolution,* Economic History Society of Southern Africa, 1993.

(With Jon Inggs) *The South African Economy in the 1980s,* Economic History Society of Southern Africa, 1994.

(With Jon Inggs) *Business Imperialism in South Africa,* Economic History Society of Southern Africa, 1997.

(With Jon Inggs) *The South African Economy in the 1970s,* Economic History Society of Southern Africa, 1999.

Also editor of *South African Journal of Economic History,* 1986-94.*

*   *   *

JONNES, Jill 1952-

PERSONAL: Surname is pronounced "Jones"; born April 5, 1952, in Bern, Switzerland; American citizen born abroad; daughter of Lloyd (an epigrapher) and Marilyn (Alley) Jonnes; married Christopher A. Ross (a scientist and physician), December 26, 1980. *Education:* Barnard College, B.A., 1974; Columbia University, M.S., 1977; Johns Hopkins University, Ph.D., 1992.

ADDRESSES: Home and office—2526 East Baltimore St., Baltimore, MD 21224. *Agent*—Arthur Klebanoff, Scott Meredith Literary Agency, 845 Third Ave., 15th floor, New York, NY 10022.

CAREER: Record (newspaper), Troy, NY, journalist, 1975-76; *Record* (newspaper), Hackensack, NJ, journalist, 1977-79; freelance writer, 1979—.

WRITINGS:

We're Still Here: The Rise, Fall, and Resurrection of the South Bronx, Atlantic Monthly Press (New York, NY), 1986.

Hep-cats, Narcs, and Pipe Dreams: A History of America's Romance with Illegal Drugs, Scribner (New York, NY), 1996.

(With John C. Ball) *Fame at Last: Who Was Who according to the New York Times Obituaries,* Andrews McMeel (Kansas City, MO), 2000.

Contributing editor of *Baltimore* magazine, 1985—.

SIDELIGHTS: Journalist Jill Jonnes has written about American society from various perspectives. Her first book, *We're Still Here: The Rise, Fall, and Resurrection of the South Bronx,* documents the fall and rise of one of the worst areas of urban blight in modern times. As she once told *CA:* "I have always been an American but lived overseas because of my father's career with the U.S. State Department. The South Bronx was justly famous as the most devastated urban area ever destroyed during peacetime. As a journalist I thought the story of how this happened would be fascinating. The Bronx was a perfect slice of urban America with all its worst problems concentrated and magnified."

While doing research on the South Bronx, Jonnes was struck by the devastating impact of street drugs in the area. The subject of drugs became the focus of her second book, *Hep-cats, Narcs, and Pipe Dreams: A History of America's Romance with Illegal Drugs.* The book traces the history of three distinct waves of drug use: patent medicines in the nineteenth century; marijuana, heroin, and psychedelic drugs from the 1950s through the 1970s; and cocaine and crack in the 1990s. As Jonnes indicates, she believed at first that legalization of street drugs would help solve drug abuse problems; after researching the book, however, she was convinced that "no society can afford to be conciliatory on drugs."

The book generated significant attention and discussion. Dan Baum in *Washington Post Book World* commented that it "lays down some hard truths" about the relationship between drug availability and addiction, and the relative danger of drugs compared to alcohol. *Reason* reviewer Jacob Sullum, however, disputed Jonnes's "hackneyed, simplistic policy recommendations," and criticized her tendency in the book to generalize about all addicts in harshly negative terms. "Jonnes not only assumes that every addict is a menace," Sullum observed, "she implies that every drug user is an addict in the making. . . . She presents the worst cases—Charlie Parker, Billie Holiday, Len Bias—as if they were typical." Sullum went on to point out that statistics show a strong analogy between alcohol use and drug use, which he felt Jonnes neglected to cover. Similar objections were raised by *Washington Monthly* writer David C. Morrison, who felt that the book "fails . . . to truly illuminate this dark topic, thanks to the narrowness of Jonnes's analytical vision." Morrison particularly questioned the author's dismissal of the role of cultural and racial factors in the shaping of popular attitudes toward drugs, as well as her "unwillingness to distinguish between intoxicants save on the basis of over-the-counter availability."

Many reviewers, though, saw the book in a more positive light. A *Publishers Weekly* contributor called the it a "sweeping, highly colorful, riveting narrative" that "culminates with a compelling argument against legalization or decriminalization." Joseph A. Califano in *America* proclaimed the book "a classic, as fine a history of America's experience with illegal drugs as we are likely to see and a delight to read. The author writes with such pace and excitement that you cannot wait to find out what's on the next page." In *Johns Hopkins Magazine*, Dale Keiger appreciated Jonnes's attention to the middle-class origins of today's drug problems, pointing out that she "is tough on the baby-boom generation" and that she "draws a direct line of responsibility from white middle-class marijuana smokers of the 1960s to the Colombian cocaine cartels." *Booklist*, hailing Jonnes as a "consummate researcher," named *Hep-cats, Narcs, and Pipe Dreams* one of their Editors' Choice books for 1996.

In *Fame at Last: Who Was Who according to the New York Times Obituaries*, Jonnes and co-author John C. Ball examine that newspaper's obituaries from 1993 to 1999. According to Mike Albo in *Salon.com*, the emerging patterns are not surprising: "Men predominate, minorities are marginalized, the rich are prevalent." Jonnes's and Ball's "Overall Apex of Fame," which includes the twenty-eight longest obituaries they studied, is headed by Richard M. Nixon, followed by Frank Sinatra. Others whose deaths were chronicled in the *Times* include the inventors of kitty litter and of Day-Glo, the creator of Sesame Street's Cookie Monster, and the founder of the Women's Professional Surfing Association. Critical opinion of the book was mixed. Albo suggested that the topic offered rich opportunities that Jonnes and Ball failed to exploit. They do not "cheekily poke fun, examine the history of obituaries or shed light on the power structures that might reveal what's behind the *Times*' selections," he complained. "Nor do they even consider the nature of our desperate fascination with fame." *Baltimore City Paper* writer Loren Glass, however, found the study insightful and

well-researched. And a reviewer for *Publishers Weekly* deemed the book an "absorbing study of what constitutes success and fame in the United States."

Jonnes told CA: "I have spent my life in cities and find them endlessly interesting. I am writing another urban book, which focuses more on Baltimore, where I live now, than New York."

BIOGRAPHICAL/CRITICAL SOURCES:

PERIODICALS

America, April 26, 1997, Joseph A. Califano, review of *Hep-cats, Narcs, and Pipe Dreams: A History of America's Romance with Illegal Drugs*, p. 27.
Booklist, July 1996, Donna Seaman, review of *Hep-cats, Narcs, and Pipe Dreams*, p. 1784.
Johns Hopkins Magazine, June 1996, Dale Keiger, review of *Hep-cats, Narcs, and Pipe Dreams*.
Journal of American History, March 1997, John c. Burnham, review of *Hep-cats, Narcs, and Pipe Dreams*, p. 1493.
Library Journal, March 1, 1986, Kevin M. Rosswurm, review of *We're Still Here: The Rise, Fall, and Resurrection of the South Bronx*, p. 87; August 1996, Suzanne W. Wood, review of *Hep-cats, Narcs, and Pipe Dreams*, p. 96.
New York Times Book Review, February 16, 1986, review of *We're Still Here*, p. 25.
Publishers Weekly, January 3, 1986, review of *We're Still Here*, p. 44; June 10, 1996, review of *Hep-cats, Narcs, and Pipe Dreams*, p. 78; October 16, 2000, review of *Fame at Last: Who Was Who according to the New York Times Obituaries*, p. 57.
Reason, July 1997, Jacob Sullum, review of *Hep-cats, Narcs, and Pipe Dreams*, p. 60.
Washington Monthly, October 1996, David C. Morrison, review of *Hep-cats, Narcs, and Pipe Dreams*, p. 53.

OTHER

Baltimore City Paper, http://www.citypaper.com/2000 (August 30, 2001), Loren Glass, review of *Fame at Last*.
Salon.com, http://www.salon.com/books (November 29, 2000), Mike Albo, review of *Fame at Last*.*

*   *   *

JUENGER, Ernst
  See JÜNGER, Ernst

JÜNGER, Ernst 1895-1998

PERSONAL: Born March 29, 1895, in Heidelberg, Germany; died February 16, 1998, in Wilflingen, Germany; son of Ernst (a chemist and pharmacist) and Lily (Lampl) Jünger; married Gretha von Jeinsen, August 3, 1925 (died, 1960); married Liselotte Lohrer, March 3, 1962; children: Ernstel (died, 1944), Alexander J. *Education:* Attended University of Leipzig, 1923-25.

CAREER: Writer. Honorary member, International Nomenclature Committee—Division of Literature, 1982; honorary president, Societe allemande-togolaise, 1985. *Military service:* German Army, 1914-23; became lieutenant; wounded seven times; received Pour le merite; German Army, 1939-44; became captain.

MEMBER: Society for Bloy Studies (honorary member).

AWARDS, HONORS: Literary awards from cities of Bremen and Goslar, West Germany, both 1955; Grand Order of Merit, Federal Republic of Germany, 1959; Federal League of German Industry Literature Prize, 1960; Immermann Prize, City of Düsseldorf, 1965; Freiherr vom Stein Gold Medal, 1970; Schiller Gedächtnispreis, 1974; Star of the Grand Cross of Merit, Federal Republic of Germany, 1977; Golden Eagle, City of Nice, 1977; Peace Medal, City of Verdun, 1979; Order of Merit, Baden-Württemberg, 1980; Prix Europa-Litterature, Fondation Internationale pour le Rayonnement des Arts et des Lettres, 1981; Prix Mondial Cino-del-Duca, 1981; Goethe Prize, City of Frankfurt, 1982; Diplome d'Honneur and Medal, City of Montpellier, 1983; Premio Circeo, Association for Italian-German Friendship, 1983; Schulterband, highest distinction of Grand Cross of Merit, 1985; Premio Mediterraneo, Center of Mediterranean Culture (Palermo), 1986; Bayerischer Maximiliansorden, 1986; Dante Alighieri Prize, Accademia Casentinese, 1987; Premio Internazionale Tevere (Rome), 1987; honorary doctorate, University of Bilbao, 1989; Oberschwäbischer Kunstpreis, 1990; Robert Schuman Prize, F. V. S. Foundation, 1993; Gran Premio Cultura, Venice Biennial, 1993.

WRITINGS:

IN ENGLISH TRANSLATION

In Stahlgewittern: Aus dem Tagebuch eines Strosstruppführers, E. S. Mittler (Berlin, Germany), 1922, published as *In Stahlgewittern: Ein Kriegstagbuch,* [Hamburg, Germany], 1934, translation by Basil Creighton published as *The Storm of Steel: From the Diary of a German Storm-Troop Officer on the Western Front,* Doubleday (New York, NY), 1929.

Das Wäldchen 125: Eine Chronik aus den Grabenkaempfen 1918, E. S. Mittler (Berlin, Germany), 1925, translation by Basil Creighton published as *Copse One Hundred Twenty-five: A Chronicle from the Trench Warfare of 1918,* Chatto & Windus (London, England), 1930.

Afrikanische Spiele, Hanseatische Verlagsanstalt (Hamburg, Germany), 1936, translation by Stuart Hood published as *African Diversions,* Lehmann (London, England), 1954.

Auf den Marmorklippen (novel), Hanseatische Verlagsanstalt (Hamburg, Gemany), 1939, translation by Stuart Hood published as *On the Marble Cliffs,* New Directions (New York, NY), 1947.

Der Friede: Ein Wort an die Jugend Europas, und an die Jugend der Welt (essay), Hanseatische Verlagsanstalt (Hamburg, Germany), 1945, translation by Stuart Hood published as *The Peace,* Regnery (Hinsdale, IL), 1948.

Glaeserne Bienen (novel), E. Klett, 1957, translation by Louise Bogan and Elizabeth Mayer published as *The Glass Bees,* Noonday Press (New York, NY), 1960.

Eumeswil, E. Klett, 1977, translation by Joachim Neugroschel, Marsilio (New York, NY), 1993.

Aladins Problem (novel), Klett-Cotta (Stuttgart, Germany), 1983, translation by Joachim Neugroschel published as *Aladdin's Problem,* Marsilio (New York, NY), 1992.

Eine gefährliche Begegnung (novel), Klett-Cotta (Stuttgart, Germany), 1985, translation by Hilary Barr published as *A Dangerous Encounter,* Marsilio (New York, NY), 1993.

IN GERMAN; HISTORY

Der Kampf als inneres Erlebnis (title means "Struggle as Inner Experience"), E. S. Mittler (Berlin, Germany), 1922.

Feuer und Blut: Ein kleiner Ausschnitt aus einer grossen Schlacht, Stahlhelm, 1925, fifth edition, Hanseatische Verlagsanstalt (Hamburg, Germany), 1941.

Gärten und Strassen: Aus den Tagebüchern von 1939 und 1940 (autobiography), E. S. Mittler (Berlin, Germany), 1942.

(With Armin Mohler) *Die Schleife: Dokumente zum Weg,* Arche (Zurich, Switzerland), 1955.

Jahre der Okkupation (title means "Years of Occupation"), E. Klett, 1958.

IN GERMAN; TRAVEL

Dalmatinischer Aufenthalt, 1934.

Atlantische Fahrt, Kriegsgefangenenhilfe des Weltbundes der YMCA in England (London, England), 1947.

Ein Inselfrühling: Ein Tagebuch aus Rhodes, Arche (Zurich, Switzerland), 1948.

Aus der goldenen Muschel, 1948.

Am Kieselstrand, V. Klostermann (Frankfurt am Main, Germany), 1951.

Am Sarazenenturm, V. Klostermann (Frankfurt am Main, Germany), 1955.

Serpentara, 1957.

San Pietro, 1957.

Zwei Inseln: Formosa, Ceylon, Olten, 1968.

IN GERMAN; ESSAYS

Der Arbeiter: Herrschaft und Gestalt (title means "The Worker"), Hanseatische Verlagsanstalt (Hamburg, Germany), 1932.

Blätter und Steine (title means "Leaves and Stones"), Hanseatische Verlagsanstalt (Hamburg, Germany), 1934.

Geheimnisse der Sprache: Zwei Essays, Hanseatische Verlagsanstalt (Hamburg, Germany), 1939.

Über die Linie (title means "Across the Line"), V. Klostermann (Frankfurt am Main, Germany), 1950.

Der Waldgang, V. Klostermann (Frankfurt am Main, Germany), 1951.

Der gordische Knoten, V. Klostermann (Frankfurt am Main, Germany), 1953.

Das Sanduhrubuch, V. Klostermann (Frankfurt am Main, Germany), 1954.

An der Zeitmauer (title means "At the Time Barrier"), E. Klett, 1959.

Der Weltstaat: Organismus und Organisation, E. Klett, 1960.

Essays, E. Klett, 1960.

Sgraffiti, E. Klett, 1960.

Typus, Name, Gestalt, E. Klett, 1963.

Grenzgänge, Olten, 1965.

Grenzgänge: Essays, Reden, Traeume, E. Klett, 1966.

Zahlen und Götter, Philemon und Baucis: Zwei Essays, E. Klett, 1974.

(With Wolf Jobst Sieder) *Bäume: Gedichte und Bilder,* Propylaeen, 1976.

IN GERMAN; EDITOR

Die Unvergessenen, W. Andermann, 1928.

Der Kampf um das Reich (title means "The Struggle for the Empire"), Rhein & Ruhr, c. 1929.

Das anlitz des Weltkrieges, Neufeld & Henius, 1930.

Franz Schauwecker, *Der feurige Weg,* Frundsberg, 1930.

Krieg und Krieger, Junker & Dünnhaupt, 1930.

Antoine Rivarol, *Rivarol,* V. Klostermann (Frankfurt am Main, Germany), 1956.

IN GERMAN; OTHER

Das abenteuerliche Herz: Aufzeichnungen bei Tag und Nacht, Frundsberg, 1929, second edition published as *Das abenteuerliche Herz: Figuren und Capriccios,* Hanseatische Verlagsanstalt (Hamburg, Germany), 1938.

Luftfahrt ist not!, W. Andermann, 1930.

Sprache und Körperbau, Arche (Zurich, Switzerland), 1947.

Heliopolis: Rückblick auf eine Stadt (novel), Heliopolis, 1949.

Strahlungen (personal narrative; title means "Radiations"), Heliopolis, 1949.

Besuch auf Godenholm (short stories; title means "Visit in Godenholm"), V. Klostermann (Frankfurt am Main, Germany), 1952.

Capriccios: Eine Auswahl, Reclam, 1953.

Erzählende Schriften, E. Klett, 1960.

Werke, ten volumes, E. Klett, 1960.

(Compiler, with Klaus Ulrich Leistikow) *Mantrana: Ein Spiel,* E. Klett, 1964.

Subtile Jagden (memoirs; title means "The Subtle Chase"), E. Klett, 1967.

Ad hoc, E. Klett, 1970.

Annaeherungen: Drogen und Rausch, E. Klett, 1970.

Sinn und Bedeutung: Ein Figurenspiel, E. Klett, 1971.

Die Zwille (semi-autobiographical; title means "The Slingshot"), E. Klett, 1973.

Ausgewählte Erzaehlungen, E. Klett, 1975.

(With Alfred Kubin) *Eine Begegnung* (letters), Propylaeen, 1975.

Collected Works, eighteen volumes, Klett-Cotta (Stuttgart, Germany), 1978-83.

Siebzig verweht, two volumes, Klett-Cotta (Stuttgart, Germany), 1980-81.

Autor und Autorschaft (title means "Author and Authorship"), Klett-Cotta (Stuttgart, Germany), 1984.

Zwei Mal Halley (title means "Halley Revisited"), Klett-Cotta (Stuttgart, Germany), 1987.

Zeitsprünge (title means "Time-Fissures"), Klett-Cotta (Stuttgart, Germany), 1990.

Die Schere (title means "The Shears"), Klett-Cotta (Stuttgart, Germany), 1990.

Siebzig verweht III, Klett-Cotta (Stuttgart, Germany), 1993.

Ernst Junger, Rudolf Schlichter: Briefe 1935-1955, edited and with commentary by Dirk Heisserer, Klett-Cotta (Stuttgart, Germany), 1997.

Briefe 1930-1983: Ernst Junger, Carl Schmitt, edited and with commentary by Helmuth Kiesel, Klett-Cotta (Stuttgart, Germany), 1999.

Coeditor of *Standarte, Arminius, Widerstand, Der Vormarsch,* and *Die Kommenden* magazines, late 1920s-early 1930s. Coeditor and cofounder, *Antaios: Zeitschrift fuer eine freie Welt,* 1959. Some of Juenger's work has appeared in French and Swiss editions.

ADAPTATIONS: Edgardo Cozarinsky's film *One Man's War* is based on Juenger's Parisian diaries; in 1995 Johan Kresnik and Hans Haacke created a dance production called "Ernst Junger," based on the author's life and works.

SIDELIGHTS: One of modern Germany's foremost men of letters, Ernst Jünger is best known for his *In Stahlgewittern: Aus dem Tagebuch eines Strosstruppfuehrers,* translated as *The Storm of Steel: From the Diary of a German Storm-Troop Officer on the Western Front.* He has also published highly acclaimed travel books, diaries, and essays. Speaking of the diversity of Jünger's accomplishment, Carl Steiner described Jünger in the *Dictionary of Literary Biography* as a "soldier-philosopher, a combination with which ancient civilizations such as those of Greece and Rome were quite comfortable. . . . If one adds the categories of naturalist, writer, and essayist, one moves into even more rarified circles. Ernst Jünger, blending the courage of the soldier with the curiosity of the student of life forms, the skill and imagination of the literary stylist with the probing intellect of the researcher, is such an exceptional individual." Jünger, who continued to write well into his eighties and nineties, has created a body of work that reflects the longest life span of any major German literary figure. Indeed, many critics have considered Jünger to be the doyen of twentieth-century German letters.

As a young man, Jünger was fascinated by warfare and the military life. His longing to experience battle firsthand asserted itself at the age of sixteen when he ran away from home to join the French Foreign Legion. Jünger's father did not share his son's enthusiasm, however, and with the help of the authorities, located and returned the underage boy to his home. But when World War I erupted, Jünger immediately enlisted in the German Army. He distinguished himself on the Western Front, received Germany's highest military honor, and was wounded seven times. From his World War I experiences came his first book, *The Storm of Steel,* which was based on the diaries he kept at the time. The book was praised across the United States as a significant and revealing insight into the mind of a German officer.

In his introduction to *The Storm of Steel,* R. H. Mottram asserts that the work was profound and meaningful because the author did not shy away from depicting events and feelings exactly as they occurred; he censored nothing. Mottram's description of Jünger reveals much of the tone of the work: "He was no middle-aged civilian, unwillingly taking up arms and finding all his worst preconceptions abundantly fulfilled. He was nearly as good a specimen as ever worshipped Mars [the Roman god of war], and to what did he come? To that unescapable doom that brings to meet violence precisely such resistance as shall cancel and annul it." Mottram concludes that "on this point the strength and finality of the testimony cannot be missed."

Jünger did not apologize in *The Storm of Steel* for the bloodshed and violence of warfare, but rather reveled in the glories of battle. As he wrote in the book: "War means the destruction of the enemy without scruple and by any means. War is the harshest of all trades, and the masters of it can only entertain humane feelings as long as they do no harm." A reviewer for *New Statesman* declared: Jünger "has a remarkable gift for describing certain emotions, complex and hard of analysis, which beset, and still have power to bewilder, the man of even average sensibility who was brought by war into abrupt contact with the most primitive of human experiences."

In addition to recommending it to the general public, several reviewers considered *The Storm of Steel* a book imperative for pacifists to read and study. As F. Van de Water of the *New York Evening Post* observed, the book "presents a view of battle not generally recognized, yet too logical to be overlooked." A reviewer for *Spectator* also advised pacifists to heed "this fine book," commenting, "It is even better propaganda than [Erich M. Remarque's] *All Quiet on the Western Front,* for there is a certain horrible lure in the completeness of that work of genius, whereas this is a ghastly, gripping story whose truth and whose horror stand out all the plainer for the author's psychic blindness."

After World War I, Jünger attended the University of Leipzig where he studied both philosophy and zoology, becoming interested particularly in entomology, the study of insects. Hilary Barr, who translated Jünger's *Eine gefährliche Begegnung* as *A Dangerous Encounter*, told *CA* that "the [German] term 'Subtiler Jagd,' which Jünger uses throughout his works, refers to his entomological excursions (primarily beetle-chasing) as well as to his practice (more a second vocation) of observing close-up the wonders of the animal and plant kingdoms. He is also a passionate collector and renowned entomologist (coleopterist)." Numerous reviewers, in fact, attributed Jünger's probing and analytical approach in writing to his university training in the sciences. It was while a student that he first became politically active and participated in radical right-wing organizations that supported his view that a democracy of all the people could never retain order in the world. Jünger looked forward to the rise of the new "Federation" and the coming of the new man, an industrial individual who would restore order in a chaotic world. He defined and explained these ideas in his 1932 work, *Der Arbeiter: Herrschaft und Gestalt.*

When Hitler came to power, Jünger dropped out of the political scene due to his disillusionment with the Nazi Party. Although the Nazis were striving for totalitarianism, he felt that their interpretation was a mockery of the "true system" he advocated. With this in mind, in 1939 he wrote *Auf den Marmorklippen,* an allegorical novel based on Nazi practices and later translated as *On the Marble Cliffs.* A major turning point in his literary career, this work offers a more humanistic and, some insist, almost Christian point of view.

On the Marble Cliffs depicts the annihilation of a peaceful and gentle country by "barbarian hordes." Quickly recognized as anti-Nazi when released to English-speaking audiences, the book miraculously escaped the censor's eye when published in Germany in 1939. By the time the German government realized the novel's true meaning and halted further publication, tens of thousands of copies were already in circulation. Jünger's honor was not seriously questioned, however, for he was loyally serving with the German Army at the time.

Alfred Werner of the *New York Times* praised the novel, but complained that "despite its poetical merits and its unmistakable challenge to Hitlerism, [*On the Marble Cliffs*] fails to uplift the reader because of its impotent hopelessness." A reviewer for the *New Yorker* claimed that Jünger's "allegory, which is full of the same sort of hobgoblinism that the Nazis themselves went in for— skulls, torches, midnight revels, and so on—is so murky that most readers are likely to miss the point."

As an appeal for humanist values, Jünger wrote *Der Friede: Ein Wort an die Jugend Europas, und an die Jugend der Welt,* translated as *The Peace,* in late 1941. Jünger began to draft the essay in the fall of 1941, when German arms were most successful. Working on in through the following winter, he kept it hidden in a reinforced safe so that the Gestapo, who had him under continual surveillance, would not find it. Dedicated to the memory of his son Ernstel, who was killed in action in 1944, the 1945 work is an acknowledgement of Germany's guilt and a plea for world peace to end the senseless sacrifice of human life. Although he still repudiated liberalism, Jünger called for a renunciation of nationalism and the affirmation of the individual, and lobbied actively for a politically united Europe. Erik von Kuehnelt-Leddihn of *Catholic World* observed that *The Peace* "is not only a highly prophetic piece of writing in the finest literary style . . . but it is also a blueprint for the sound peace which should have followed this terrible massacre."

Jünger employed a fantastic and dream-like style of writing in his next book, *Glaeserne Bienen,* published in English translation as *The Glass Bees.* This allegorical novel tells of a former cavalryman, Captain Richard, who must perform extensive feats of strength and endurance in the magical garden of political dictator Zapparoni in order to secure employment. The garden is filled with thousands of glass bees, tiny mechanized robots able to lay waste to all civilization if summoned. According to E. S. Pisko of the *Christian Science Monitor,* the glass bees symbolize "the destruction Jünger sees modern technology wreaking upon human society." Siegfried Mandel of the *New York Times Book Review* commended the novel as "harrowing and thought-disturbing," asserting that it "contributes not only to prophetic and nihilistic literature but also to an understanding of the inner and outer forces that shape many a man's attitude toward tyranny."

Jünger's third novel to be released in English translation was *Aladins Problem,* or *Aladdin's Problem.* Reaching U.S. audiences in 1992, almost a decade after its publication in Germany, the metaphysical novel follows thirty-seven-year-old Friedrich Baroh. Born in Poland into an aristocratic family and drafted into the Polish army during World War II, Baroh rises in rank in the military, but ultimately deserts his post and defects to the West. After the war he moves to Germany, and goes to work for his uncle, a mortician. While on a visit to the vast cemetery at Verdun, he becomes fascinated with the idea of constructing a giant mausoleum in Turkey that he calls Terrestra, wherein could be housed all the world's dead. With the help of a friend, Baroh puts his idea into practice, and soon find that "he has aroused a 'primal instinct,' a desire for some sense of permanence amid the planet's endless upheavals," in the words of *New York Times Book Review* contributor Eils Lotozo. Unfortunately, as the novel progresses, Baroh's successful venture begins to drive him to madness. The novel's title, "Aladdin's Problem," refers to the lamp which, although roughly hewn and constructed from a simple substance, held the potential to control the world. Aladdin, as possessor of this power, wields it without concern for the human consequences of his actions. In the *Washington Post Book World*, contributor Thomas McGonigle praised Jünger's epigrammatic novel as an effective vehicle for recalling the author's personal history and making readers "take with appropriate seriousness his [nihilistic] observations about the modern world." And Lotozo concluded of the novel that "Readers will be stirred by its persistent and intriguing questions about the conflicts between nature and technology, the individual and the state, and by its examination of humanity's place in this wasteland of a world that we are rapidly creating."

Taking place in Paris in 1888, *A Dangerous Encounter*—first published in German in 1985 as *Eine gefährliche Begegnung*—also finds aristocratic protagonists attempting to grapple with an increasingly mechanized world. Captain Kargane, an officer in the Germany navy, is married to an unfaithful wife; Ducasse is a wealthy decadent, reduced by the "soulless age of steam and light" in which he lives "to being a mischievous arbiter of elegance at the doubtful tables of rich strangers," according to *New York Review of Books* contributor Ian Buruma. Arranging a tryst between Kargane's wife and a young German student, Ducasse inadvertently brings about the woman's murder. The event forces a duel between Kargane and the student's second, an old soldier, that restores the sense of traditional honor of both men.

Jünger's 1977 novel *Eumeswil* was translated into English in 1993 and received good reviews from American critics. Eumeswil is a land controlled by the dictator Condor on the shores of north Africa in a dystopic time following the collapse of a world government in the third millennium. The story is narrated by Martin Venator, a history professor who claims to have no political allegiance, and who moonlights as a servant to the dictator. Venator, who in his spare time revisits historical events via his time machine, takes copious notes regarding Eumeswil's history as it has valiantly struggled to save itself from the doom of democracy. Eventually, an overthrow of Condor's regime becomes imminent, and Venator escapes with Condor and his allies into the woods, leaving his journals behind as a legacy. Jack Byrne of the *Review of Contemporary Fiction* wrote that Jünger's "style is overpowering with lit-

erary, philosophical, and historical references," which make *Eumeswil* "a veritable handbook on political power, dictatorship, and the inevitable corruption that follows in their wake." A critic for *Publishers Weekly* called the book a "labyrinthine study of a compromised individual [which] telescopes past and present, playing over the sweep of Western history and culture with a dazzling range of allusions from Homer and Nero to Poe and Lenin."

Reviewing particularly Jünger's later works of fiction, Philip Brantingham noted in Chicago's *Tribune Books* that the philosopher-novelist's "beautifully written and challenging works as a whole provoke much rethinking on subjects often thought to be closed and settled. Aside from his literary artistry, that is perhaps the greatest heritage Jünger will leave us." But in his later years, Jünger gained a semblance of a different kind of notoriety after discussing his extensive drug experimentation—including the use of LSD with the drug's inventor, Albert Hofmann—in his book *Annaeherungen: Drogen und Rausch.* Nevertheless, key political figures continued to recognize his importance in German letters. He appeared publicly with German Chancellor Helmut Kohl and French President François Mitterand in 1984 in a ceremony to commemorate casualties of both world wars, and both leaders visited him at his home in Wilflingen on the occasion of his ninetieth birthday in 1985. When Jünger died at the age of 102 in 1998, he was eulogized in the *Economist* by a contributor who noted that "writers of obituaries in German newspapers have agonised in their efforts to be honest about Mr Junger. Some have looked at his long life covering the blackest period of German history . . . and note that he never lost his contempt for democracy." The *Economist* writer concluded that "others say he was simply a patriotic German trying to make the best of the times. The important thing, say his defenders, is that he was one of the finest writers of the century, a great stylist, a master of German, and don't writers make their own rules?"

BIOGRAPHICAL/CRITICAL SOURCES:

BOOKS

Arnold, Heinz Ludwig, editor, *Wandlung und Wiederkehr: Festschrift zum 70. Geburtstag Ernst Juenger,* Georgi (Aachen, Germany), 1965.
Arnold, Heinz Ludwig, *Ernst Juenger,* Steglitz (Berlin, Germany), 1966.
Baumer, Franz, *Ernst Juenger,* Colloquium (Berlin, Germany), 1967.

Bohrer, Karl Heinz, *Die Asthetik des Schreckens: Die pessimistische Romantik und Ernst Juengers Frühwerk,* Hanser (Munich. Germany), 1978.

Brock, Erich, *Ernst Juenger und die Problematik der Gegenwart,* Schwabe (Basel, Switzerland), 1943.

Contemporary Literary Criticism, Volume 125, Gale (Detroit, MI), 2000.

Decombis, Marcel, *Ernst Juenger: L'homme et l'oeuvre jusqu'en 1936,* Aubier (Paris, France), 1943.

Dictionary of Literary Biography, Volume 56: *German Fiction Writers, 1914-1945,* Gale (Detroit, MI), 1987.

Figal, Gunter, and Heimo Schwilk, *Magie der Heiterkeit: Ernst Junger zum Hundersten,* Klett-Cotta (Stuttgart, Germany), 1995.

Hietala, Marjatta, *Der neue Nationalismus in der Publizistik Ernst Juengers und des Kreises um ihn 1920-1933,* Suomalaison Tiedeakatemian Toimituksia (Helsinki, Finland), 1975.

Jünger, Ernst, *The Storm of Steel: From the Diary of a German Storm-Troop Officer on the Western Front,* translation by Basil Creighton, Doubleday (New York, NY), 1929.

Katzmann, Volker, *Ernst Juengers magischer Realismus,* Olms (Hildesheim), 1975.

Kerker, Arnim, *Ernst Juenger—Klaus Mann: Gemeinsamkeit und Gegensatz in Literatur und Politik,* Bouvier (Bonn, Germany), 1974.

Kiesel, Helmuth, *Wissenschaftliche Diagnose und dichterische Vision der Moderne: Max Weber und Ernst Junger,* Manutius (Heidelberg, Germany), 1994.

Konitzer, Martin, *Ernst Junger,* Campus, 1993.

Konrad, Helmut, *Kosmos: Politische Philosophie im Werk Ernst Juengers,* Blasaditsch (Vienna, Austria), 1972.

Kunicki, Wojciech, *Projektionen des Geschichtlichen,* P. Lang, 1993.

Loose, Gerhard, *Ernst Juenger,* Twayne (New York, NY), 1974.

Martin, Alfred von, *Der heroische Nihilismus und seine Uberwindung: Ernst Juengers Weg durch die Krise,* Scherpe (Krefeld), 1948.

Mohler, Arnim, editor, *Die Schleife: Dokumente zum Weg von Ernst Juenger,* Arche (Zurich, Switzerland), 1955.

Muehleisen, H., and H. P. des Coudres, *Bibliographie der Werke Ernst Juengers,* Klett-Cotta (Stuttgart, Germany), 1985.

Mueller-Schwefe, Hans-Rudolf, *Ernst Juenger,* Barmen (Wuppertal), 1951.

Muller, Hans-Harald, and Harro Segeberg, *Ernst Junger im 20. Jahrhundert,* Wilhelm Fink (Munich, Germany), 1995.

Nebel, Gerhard, *Ernst Juenger und das Schicksal des Menschen,* Marees (Wuppertal), 1948.

Paetel, Karl O., *Ernst Juenger: Eine Bibliographie,* Lutz & Meyer, 1953.

Paetel, Karl O., *Ernst Juenger in Selbstzeugnissen und Bilddokumenten,* Rowohlt (Hamburg, Germany), 1962.

Sader, Jorg, *Im Bauche des Leviathan: Tagebuch und Maskerade, Anmerkungen zu Ernst Jungers "Strahlungen,"* Konigshausen & Neumann (Wurzburg), 1996.

Schieb, Roswitha, *Das teilbare Individuum: Korperbilder bei Ernst Junger, Hans Henny Jahnn, und Peter Weiss,* M. & P. (Stuttgart, Germany), 1997.

Schroter, Olaf, *Es ist am Technischen viel Illusion: Die Technik im Werk Ernst Jungers,* Koster (Berlin, Germany), 1993.

Schwartz, Hans Peter, *Der konservative Anarchist: Politik und Zeitkritik Ernst Juengers,* Rombach (Freiburg, Germany), 1962.

Stern, Joseph Peter, *Ernst Juenger: A Writer of Our Time,* Yale University Press (New Haven, CT), 1953.

Treher, Wolfgang, *Transzendenz und Katastrophe: Ernst Junger im Spiegel der Hegelschen Philosophie; Eine psychopathologische Studie,* Oknos (Emmendingen-Maleck), 1993.

Woods, Roger, *Ernst Juenger and the Nature of Political Commitment,* Heinz (Stuttgart, Germany), 1982.

PERIODICALS

Art in America, June, 1995, Brigitte Werneburg and Christopher Phillips, "The Armored Male Exposed," pp. 44-47.

Atlantic, May, 1961.

Bloomsbury Review, March, 1994, p. 4.

Booklist, April 1, 1994, John Shreffler, review of *Eumeswil,* pp. 1423-1424.

Catholic World, November, 1948, Erik von Kuehnelt-Leddihn, review of *The Peace.*

Chicago Tribune, May 1, 1994, Thomas McGonigle, "Deadly Details and Rules for Living," p. 6.

Christian Science Monitor, March 2, 1961, E. S. Pisko, review of *The Glass Bees.*

Journal of European Studies, March, 1999, Thomas Pekar, "Ernst Junger's Thematic Use of the Orient and Asia," p. 27.

Library Journal, April 1, 1994, Michael T. O'Pecko, review of *Eumeswil,* p. 132.

Nation, March 27, 1948, Louis Clair, review of *On the Marble Cliffs,* pp. 357-358.

New Statesman, August 17, 1929.

New Yorker, March 20, 1948, review of *On the Marble Cliffs.*

New York Evening Post, September 28, 1929, F. Van de Water, review of *The Storm of Steel: From the Diary of a German Storm-Troop Officer on the Western Front.*

New York Review of Books, June 24, 1993, Ian Buruma, review of *A Dangerous Encounter,* pp. 27-30.

New York Times, April 4, 1978, Alfred Werner, review of *On the Marble Cliffs.*

New York Times Book Review, February 19, 1961; November 22, 1992, Eils Lotozo, "A Booming Necropolis," p. 24.

Observer, December 5, 1993, p. 23.

Publishers Weekly, June 21, 1993, p. 85; May 9, 1994, review of *Eumeswil,* p. 64; March 25, 1996, review of *Aladdin's Problem,* p. 80.

Review of Contemporary Fiction, fall, 1994, Jack Byrne, review of *Eumeswil,* p. 230.

Spectator, June 22, 1929, review of *The Storm of Steel.*

Texas Studies in Literature and Language, winter, 1965.

Tribune Books (Chicago), August 1, 1993, p. 4.

Washington Post Book World, February 7, 1993, Thomas McGonigle, review of *Aladdin's Problem,* p. 11.

Yale Review, June, 1961.

OTHER

Ernst Juenger in Cyberspace, http://www.juenger.org/ (August 24, 2001).

Scorpion Magazine Web site, http://www.stormloader.com/thescorpion/ (October 31, 2001).

OBITUARIES:

PERIODICALS

Economist, February 28, 1998, p. 89.

New York Times, February 18, 1998, David Binder, "Ernst Junger, Contradictory German Author Who Wrote about War, Is Dead at 102," p. D22.*

K

KALLEN, Stuart A(rnold) 1955-

PERSONAL: Born August 24, 1955, in Cleveland, OH; son of Edward Samuel (a salesperson) and Ruth (a secretary) Kallen; married P. Marlene Boekhoff (a writer). *Education:* Attended Ohio University. *Politics:* "Frankly, I'm appalled." *Religion:* Jewish. *Avocational interests:* Playing music, art photography, travel, cooking, reading, humor.

ADDRESSES: Home—3253 Via Arcilla, San Diego, CA 92111.

CAREER: Freelance writer and musician.

AWARDS, HONORS: Mid-American Publishers Association award, for *Recycle It! Once Is Not Enough.*

WRITINGS:

NONFICTION; FOR CHILDREN

Recycle It! Once Is Not Enough ("We Can Save the Earth" series), Abdo & Daughters (Minneapolis, MN), 1990.
Before the Communist Revolution: Russian History through 1919 ("Rise and Fall of the Soviet Union" series), Abdo & Daughters (Minneapolis, MN), 1992.
The Brezhnev Era, 1964-1982 ("Rise and Fall of the Soviet Union" series), Abdo & Daughters (Minneapolis, MN), 1992.

Exploring the Origins of the Universe ("Secrets of Space" series), Twenty-first Century (New York, NY), 1997.
Egypt ("Modern Nations of the World" series), Lucent (San Diego, CA), 1999.
The Rolling Stones ("People in the News" series), Lucent (San Diego, CA), 1999.
Rosie O'Donnell ("People in the News" series), Lucent (San Diego, CA), 1999.
The Salem Witch Trials ("World History" series), Lucent (San Diego, CA), 1999.
(Editor) *The 1950s* ("America's Decades"), Greenhaven Press (San Diego, CA), 2000.
(Editor) *The 1990s* ("America's Decades"), Greenhaven Press (San Diego, CA), 2000.
Witches ("Mystery Library"), Lucent (San Diego, CA), 2000.
(With wife, P. M. Boekhoff) *Leonardo da Vinci* ("Importance Of" series), Lucent (San Diego, CA), 2000.
The War at Home ("American War Library"), Lucent (San Diego, CA), 2000.
The Home Front: Americans Protest the War ("American War Library"), Lucent (San Diego, CA), 2001.
(Editor) *The 1400s* ("Headlines in History" series), Greenhaven Press (San Diego, CA), 2001.
(Editor) *The 1700s* ("Headlines in History" series), Greenhaven Press (San Diego, CA), 2001.
(Editor) *Sixties Counterculture,* Greenhaven Press (San Diego, CA), 2001.
(With P. M. Boekhoff) *Lasers,* Kidhaven Press (San Diego, CA), 2001.
The Mayans ("Lost Civilizations" series), Lucent (San Diego, CA), 2001.
Spiders ("Nature's Predators" series), Kidhaven Press (San Diego, CA), 2001.

Understanding "The Catcher in the Rye" ("Understanding Great Literature" series), Lucent (San Diego, CA), 2001.

The Gold Rush, Kidhaven Press (San Diego, CA), 2001.

Shintoism ("Religions of the World" series), Lucent (San Diego, CA), 2001.

The Baby Boom ("Turning Points" series), Greenhaven Press (San Diego, CA), 2001.

(Editor) *Roaring Twenties,* Greenhaven Press (San Diego, CA), 2002.

Alligators ("Nature's Predators" series), Kidhaven Press (San Diego, CA), 2002.

John Lennon ("Importance Of" series), Lucent (San Diego, CA), 2002.

Dolphins and Porpoises ("Endangered Animals and Habitats" series), Lucent (San Diego, CA), 2002.

(Editor) *The Age of Revolution,* Greenhaven Press (San Diego, CA), 2002.

(With P. M. Boekhoff) *Plains Indian Village* ("Daily Life" series), Kidhaven Press (San Diego, CA), 2002.

(With P. M. Boekhoff) *Dr. Seuss* ("Inventors and Creators" series), Kidhaven Press (San Diego, CA), 2002.

(With P. M. Boekhoff) *Mercury* ("Eyes on the Sky" series), Kidhaven Press (San Diego, CA), 2002.

"HISTORY OF ROCK 'N' ROLL" SERIES

Roots of Rock, two volumes, Abdo & Daughters (Minneapolis, MN), 1989.

Renaissance of Rock: The British Invasion, Abdo & Daughters (Minneapolis, MN), 1989.

Renaissance of Rock: The Sixties-Sounds of America, Abdo & Daughters (Minneapolis, MN), 1989.

The Revolution of Rock: The 1970s, Abdo & Daughters (Minneapolis, MN), 1989.

Rock in Retrospect: The 1980s, Abdo & Daughters (Minneapolis, MN), 1989.

"BUILDING A NATION" SERIES

Newcomers to America, 1400-1650, Abdo & Daughters (Minneapolis, MN), 1990.

Life in the Thirteen Colonies, 1650-1750, Abdo & Daughters (Minneapolis, MN), 1990.

The Road to Freedom, 1750-1783, Abdo & Daughters (Minneapolis, MN), 1990.

A Nation United, 1780-1850, Abdo & Daughters (Minneapolis, MN), 1990.

A Nation Divided, 1850-1900, Abdo & Daughters (Minneapolis, MN), 1990.

A Modern Nation, 1900-1990, Abdo & Daughters (Minneapolis, MN), 1990.

"BLACK HISTORY" SERIES

The Lost Kingdoms of Africa, Abdo & Daughters (Minneapolis, MN), 1990, revised as *Kingdoms of Africa,* Abdo Publishing (Edina, MN), 2001.

Days of Slavery: A History of Black People in America, 1619-1863, Abdo & Daughters (Minneapolis, MN), 1990, revised, Abdo Publishing (Edina, MN), 2001.

The Civil War and Reconstruction: A History of Black People in America, 1830-1880, Abdo & Daughters (Minneapolis, MN), 1990, revised, Abdo Publishing (Edina, MN), 2001.

The Twentieth Century and the Harlem Renaissance, Abdo & Daughters (Minneapolis, MN), 1990, revised as *The Harlem Renaissance,* Abdo Publishing (Edina, MN), 2001.

The Civil Rights Movement: The History of Black People in America, 1930-1980, Abdo & Daughters (Minneapolis, MN), 1990, revised, Abdo Publishing (Edina, MN), 2001.

The Struggle into the 1990s: A History of Black People from 1968 to the Present, Abdo & Daughters (Minneapolis, MN), 1990, revised as *Striving into 2000,* Abdo Publishing (Edina, MN), 2001.

"GHASTLY GHOST STORIES" SERIES

How to Catch a Ghost, Abdo & Daughters (Minneapolis, MN), 1991.

(And illustrator) *Haunted Hangouts of the Undead,* Abdo & Daughters (Minneapolis, MN), 1991.

Phantoms of the Rich and Famous, Abdo & Daughters (Minneapolis, MN), 1991.

Vampires, Werewolves, and Zombies, Abdo & Daughters (Minneapolis, MN), 1991.

Monsters, Dinosaurs, and Beasts, Abdo & Daughters (Minneapolis, MN), 1991.

Ghosts of the Seven Seas, Abdo & Daughters (Minneapolis, MN), 1991.

World of the Bizarre, Abdo & Daughters (Minneapolis, MN), 1991.

Witches, Magic, and Spells, Abdo & Daughters (Minneapolis, MN), 1991.

"WORLD RECORD LIBRARY"

Human Oddities, Abdo & Daughters (Minneapolis, MN), 1991.

Spectacular Sports Records, Abdo & Daughters (Minneapolis, MN), 1991.

Incredible Animals, Abdo & Daughters (Minneapolis, MN), 1991.

Awesome Entertainment Records, Abdo & Daughters (Minneapolis, MN), 1991.

Super Structures, Abdo & Daughters (Minneapolis, MN), 1991.

Amazing Human Feats, Abdo & Daughters (Minneapolis, MN), 1991.

"SECOND REVOLUTION" SERIES

Princes, Peasants, and Revolution, Abdo & Daughters (Minneapolis, MN), 1992.

The Rise of Lenin, Abdo & Daughters (Minneapolis, MN), 1992.

Stalin: Man of Steel, Abdo & Daughters (Minneapolis, MN), 1992.

Khrushchev: The Coldest War, Abdo & Daughters (Minneapolis, MN), 1992.

Brezhnev: Before the Dawn, Abdo & Daughters (Minneapolis, MN), 1992.

Gorbachev-Yeltsin: The Fall of Communism, Abdo & Daughters (Minneapolis, MN), 1992.

"FABULOUS FUN LIBRARY"

Ridiculous Riddles (Giggles, Gags, and Groaners), illustrated by Terry Boles, Abdo & Daughters (Minneapolis, MN), 1992.

Tricky Tricks (Simple Magic Tricks), Abdo & Daughters (Minneapolis, MN), 1992.

Mad Scientist Experiments (Safe, Simple Science Experiments), Abdo & Daughters (Minneapolis, MN), 1992.

Math-a-Magical Fun (Fun with Numbers), Abdo & Daughters (Minneapolis, MN), 1992.

Puzzling Puzzles (Brain Teasers), Abdo & Daughters (Minneapolis, MN), 1992.

Silly Stories (Funny, Short Stories), Abdo & Daughters (Minneapolis, MN), 1992.

Funny Answers to Foolish Questions, Abdo & Daughters (Minneapolis, MN), 1992.

The Giant Joke Book, Abdo & Daughters (Minneapolis, MN), 1992.

"TARGET EARTH" SERIES

If the Clouds Could Talk, Abdo & Daughters (Minneapolis, MN), 1993.

If Trees Could Talk, Abdo & Daughters (Minneapolis, MN), 1993.

If the Sky Could Talk, Abdo & Daughters (Minneapolis, MN), 1993.

If the Waters Could Talk, Abdo & Daughters (Minneapolis, MN), 1993.

If Animals Could Talk, Abdo & Daughters (Minneapolis, MN), 1993.

Eco-Games, Abdo & Daughters (Minneapolis, MN), 1993.

Precious Creatures A-Z, Abdo & Daughters (Minneapolis, MN), 1993.

Eco-Fairs and Carnivals: A Complete Guide to Raising Funds for the Environment, Abdo & Daughters (Minneapolis, MN), 1993.

Earth Keepers, Abdo & Daughters (Minneapolis, MN), 1993.

Eco-Arts and Crafts, Abdo & Daughters (Minneapolis, MN), 1993.

"I HAVE A DREAM" SERIES

Maya Angelou: Woman of Words, Deeds, and Dreams, Abdo & Daughters (Minneapolis, MN), 1993.

Arthur Ashe: Champion of Dreams and Motion, Abdo & Daughters (Minneapolis, MN), 1993.

Martin Luther King Jr.: A Man and His Dream, Abdo & Daughters (Minneapolis, MN), 1993.

Thurgood Marshall: A Dream of Justice for All, Abdo & Daughters (Minneapolis, MN), 1993.

Quincy Jones, Abdo Publishers (Edina, MN), 1996.

"FAMOUS ILLUSTRATED SPEECHES AND DOCUMENTS" SERIES

The Statue of Liberty: "The New Colossus," Abdo & Daughters (Minneapolis, MN), 1994.

The Gettysburg Address, Abdo & Daughters (Minneapolis, MN), 1994.

Pledge of Allegiance, Abdo & Daughters (Minneapolis, MN), 1994.

Star-Spangled Banner, Abdo & Daughters (Minneapolis, MN), 1994.

The Declaration of Independence, illustrated by Michael Birawer, Abdo & Daughters (Minneapolis, MN), 1994.

"IF THE DINOSAURS COULD TALK" SERIES

Brontosaurus, illustrated by Kristen Copham, Abdo & Daughters (Minneapolis, MN), 1994.

Stegosaurus, illustrated by Kristen Copham, Abdo & Daughters (Minneapolis, MN), 1994.

Tyrannosaurus Rex, illustrated by Kristen Copham, Abdo & Daughters (Minneapolis, MN), 1994.

Pterandon, illustrated by Kristen Copham, Abdo & Daughters (Minneapolis, MN), 1994.

Plesiosaurus, illustrated by Kristen Copham, Abdo & Daughters (Minneapolis, MN), 1994.

Triceratops, illustrated by Kristen Copham, Abdo & Daughters (Minneapolis, MN), 1994.

"THE HOLOCAUST" SERIES

The History of a Hatred: 70 A.D. to 1932, Abdo & Daughters (Minneapolis, MN), 1994.

The Nazis Seize Power: 1933-1939, Abdo & Daughters (Minneapolis, MN), 1994.

The Holocaust: 1939-1945, Abdo & Daughters (Minneapolis, MN), 1994.

Bearing Witness: Liberation and the Nuremberg Trials, Abdo & Daughters (Minneapolis, MN), 1994.

Holocausts in Other Lands, Abdo & Daughters (Minneapolis, MN), 1994.

The Faces of Resistance, Abdo Publishing (Edina, MN), 1994.

"DOGS" SERIES

German Shepherds, Abdo Publishing (Edina, MN), 1995.

Cocker Spaniels, Abdo Publishing (Edina, MN), 1996.

Dalmatians, Abdo Publishing (Edina, MN), 1996.

Golden Retrievers, Abdo Publishing (Edina, MN), 1996.

Poodles, Abdo Publishing (Edina, MN), 1996.

Labrador Retrievers, Abdo Publishing (Edina, MN), 1996.

Mutts, Abdo Publishing (Edina, MN), 1996.

Yorkshire Terriers, Abdo Publishing (Edina, MN), 1996.

Beagles, Abdo Publishing (Edina, MN), 1998.

Collies, Abdo Publishing (Edina, MN), 1998.

Dachshunds, Abdo Publishing (Edina, MN), 1998.

Old English Sheepdogs, Abdo Publishing (Edina, MN), 1998.

"CATS" SERIES

Abyssinian Cats, Abdo Publishing (Edina, MN), 1995.

Maine Coon Cats, Abdo Publishing (Edina, MN), 1996.

Manx Cats, Abdo Publishing (Edina, MN), 1996.

Persian Cats, Abdo Publishing (Edina, MN), 1996.

Russian Blue Cats, Abdo Publishing (Edina, MN), 1996.

Tabby Cats, Abdo Publishing (Edina, MN), 1996.

Siamese Cats, Abdo Publishing (Edina, MN), 1996.

American Curl Cats, Abdo Publishing (Edina, MN), 1998.

Balinese Cats, Abdo Publishing (Edina, MN), 1998.

Devon Rex Cats, Abdo Publishing (Edina, MN), 1998.

Exotic Shorthair Cats, Abdo Publishing (Edina, MN), 1998.

Oriental Shorthair Cats, Abdo Publishing (Edina, MN), 1998.

"BEARS" SERIES

Black Bears, Abdo Publishing (Edina, MN), 1996.

Alaskan Brown Bears, Abdo Publishing (Edina, MN), 1998.

Giant Pandas, Abdo Publishing (Edina, MN), 1998.

Grizzly Bears, Abdo Publishing (Edina, MN), 1998.

Polar Bears, Abdo Publishing (Edina, MN), 1998.

Sun Bears, Abdo Publishing (Edina, MN), 1998.

"GIANT LEAPS" SERIES

The Apollo Moonwalkers, Abdo Publishing (Edina, MN), 1996.

The Gemini Spacewalker, Abdo Publishing (Edina, MN), 1996.

The Mercury Seven, Abdo Publishing (Edina, MN), 1996.

The Race to Space, Abdo Publishing (Edina, MN), 1996.

Space Shuttles, Abdo Publishing (Edina, MN), 1996.

"FIELD TRIPS" SERIES

The Farm, Abdo Publishing (Edina, MN), 1997.

The Museum, Abdo Publishing (Edina, MN), 1997.

The Fire Station, Abdo Publishing (Edina, MN), 1997.

The Police Station, Abdo Publishing (Edina, MN), 1997.

The Airport, Abdo Publishing (Edina, MN), 1997.

The Zoo, Abdo Publishing (Edina, MN), 1997.

"THE WAY PEOPLE LIVE" SERIES

Life among the Pirates, Lucent (San Diego, CA), 1999.

Life on the American Frontier, Lucent (San Diego, CA), 1999.

Life in the Amazon Rain Forest, Lucent (San Diego, CA), 1999.

Life on the Underground Railroad, Lucent (San Diego, CA), 2000.

Life in America during the 1960s, Lucent (San Diego, CA), 2001.
Life in Tokyo, Lucent (San Diego, CA), 2001.
Life During the American Revolution, Lucent (San Diego, CA), 2002.

"CULTURAL HISTORY OF THE UNITED STATES" SERIES

The 1950s Lucent (San Diego, CA), 1999.
The 1980s, Lucent (San Diego, CA), 1999.
The 1990s, Lucent (San Diego, CA), 1999.

"HISTORY MAKERS" SERIES

Native American Chiefs and Warriors, Lucent (San Diego, CA), 1999.
Great Composers, Lucent (San Diego, CA), 2000.
Great Male Comedians, Lucent (San Diego, CA), 2000.

"INDIGENOUS PEOPLES OF NORTH AMERICA" SERIES

Native Americans of the Northeast, Lucent (San Diego, CA), 2000.
Native Americans of the Great Lakes, Lucent (San Diego, CA), 2000.
Native Americans of the Southwest, Lucent (San Diego, CA), 2000.
The Pawnee, Lucent (San Diego, CA), 2001.

"FOUNDING FATHERS" SERIES

Alexander Hamilton, Abdo Publishing (Edina, MN), 2001.
Benjamin Franklin, Abdo Publishing (Edina, MN), 2001.
George Washington, Abdo Publishing (Edina, MN), 2001.
James Madison, Abdo Publishing (Edina, MN), 2001.
James Monroe, Abdo Publishing (Edina, MN), 2001.
John Adams, Abdo Publishing (Edina, MN), 2001.
John Hancock, Abdo Publishing (Edina, MN), 2001.
John Jay, Abdo Publishing (Edina, MN), 2001.
Thomas Jefferson, Abdo Publishing (Edina, MN), 2001.
John Marshall, Abdo Publishing (Edina, MN), 2001.
John Marshall, Abdo Publishing (Edina, MN), 2001.
Patrick Henry, Abdo Publishing (Edina, MN), 2001.
Samuel Adams, Abdo Publishing (Edina, MN), 2002.

"SEEDS OF A NATION" SERIES; WITH P. M. BOEKHOFF

California, Kidhaven Press (San Diego, CA), 2001.
New York, Kidhaven Press (San Diego, CA), 2001.
Illinois, Kidhaven Press (San Diego, CA), 2001.
Minnesota, Kidhaven Press (San Diego, CA), 2001.
Delaware, Kidhaven Press (San Diego, CA), 2001.
Ohio, Kidhaven Press (San Diego, CA), 2002.
Indiana, Kidhaven Press (San Diego, CA), 2002.

FOR ADULTS

Beer Here: A Traveler's Guide to American Brewpubs and Microbreweries, Citadel Press, 1995.
The Fifty Greatest Beers of the World: An Expert's Ranking of the Very Best, Carol Publishing (Secaucus, NJ), 1997.
The Complete Idiot's Guide to Beer, Alpha (New York, NY), 1997.

OTHER

Also author of numerous articles for magazines.

SIDELIGHTS: Prolific children's author Stuart A. Kallen, with dozens of books for young readers to his credit, has allowed his curiosity as a writer to lead him to gather information about a variety of topics, from history to science to fun and games. One case in particular, Kallen's award-winning *Recycle It! Once Is Not Enough,* which identifies ways to reduce waste, piqued his writer's curiosity more than usual; further study led Kallen to write a ten-book series, "Target Earth," which focuses on ecology and the natural world.

In his "The History of Rock 'n' Roll" series, Kallen offers a chronological look at the story of rock music. The sounds of the 1950s are represented in the two-volume *Roots of Rock.* The two volumes of *Renaissance of Rock,* covering the 1960s, are separated into American music and the sounds of the British Invasion. The music of the 1970s is discussed in *Revolution of Rock,* and Kallen closes his series with *Rock in Retrospect: The 1980s,* a look at the nostalgic influences that shaped much of the popular rock and roll of the 1980s.

American history is another subject to which Kallen has devoted dozens of books. His "Building of a Nation" series is a collection of books that covers the American experience from the age of exploration and colonialism through the Revolutionary and Civil War periods to the twentieth century. In *The Salem Witch Trials,* Kallen begins with a discussion of goddess cults before describing how the European tradition of witch-hunting made its way to colonial Massachusetts, his attention to detail prompting *School Library Journal* contributor Laura Glaser to recommend the book as "an excellent resource." Figures such as Thomas Jefferson, George Washington, and John Jay receive attention in Kallen's "Founding Fathers" series. Praising the author for his "highly readable" text, *Booklist* reviewer Ilene Cooper remarked that in the volume *The 1950s,* Kallen "does an excellent job of surveying the decade and placing it in the larger context of American history." The history of African Americans is covered in even greater detail in "Black History and the Civil Rights Movement," a six-volume series. And Kallen's "I Have a Dream" books contain biographies of notable black Americans such as civil rights activist Martin Luther King, Jr., author Maya Angelou, tennis player Arthur Ashe, and Supreme Court Justice Thurgood Marshall.

In books such as *Native Americans of the Northeast* and *Native American Chiefs and Warriors,* Kallen addresses the life of North America's indigenous peoples, illustrating for young readers the daily life, religion, social habits, and warring habits of the tribes that inhabited the American continent prior to the arrival of white Europeans. *Native American Chiefs and Warriors* recounts the biographies of such warriors as Wampanoag chief King Philip, Ottawa chief Pontiac, Apache leader Geronimo, and Sioux leader Crazy Horse, "cover[ing] basic information in an interesting and genuine manner," according to *School Library Journal* contributor Sarah O'Neal. *Booklist* reviewer Susan Dove Lempke also had praise for the volume, citing in particular Kallen's use of primary source materials. Calling Kallen "sympathetic to, yet realistic about, Indian causes," Cris Riedel noted in a *School Library Journal* review of *Native Americans of the Northeast* that "while the ideas presented are occasionally complex, the writing is straightforward." In *Native Americans of the Great Lakes,* *Booklist* contributor Karen Hutt noted that "detailed descriptions . . . illustrate the differences as well as the similarities between the tribes," and recommended Kallen's book for its "wealth of information."

Kallen's curiosity has also led him to examine conflicts on distant shores, as in *The Nazis Seize Power: 1933-39* and *Bearing Witness: Liberation and the Nuremberg Trials,* two of the books in his series describing the torments endured by millions of European Jews and others during the Holocaust of World War II. The volumes in "The Second Revolution" series allow readers to ex-

plore the rise and fall of yet another world power, the Communist empire of the former Soviet Union, from its prerevolutionary days as Mother Russia through the Cold War era and *glasnost* to the fall of the Soviet Union and the efforts of small Eastern European nations to create free-market democracies after achieving independence. Focusing on a different kind of violence, Kallen's *Life in the Amazon Rainforest* describes the way of life in this endangered region before discussing the destruction wrought by sixteenth-century European explorers, and modern-day gold miners, rubber tapers, and those whose cut-and-burn policy has provided the region more farmland at a cost to the entire planet.

Subjects of scientific interest also benefit from Kallen's curiosity. In *Exploring the Origins of the Universe,* the author reviews several ancient theories about the creation of the universe before embarking on a discussion that stretches from Pythagoras through the development of the telescope to the theories of Stephen Hawking. His "Giant Leaps" series describes the history of the U.S. space program through such titles as *The Apollo Moonwalkers, The Mercury Seven,* and *The Race to Space.*

In addition to his many volumes of nonfiction, Kallen has written a number of books in a much lighter vein. *Witches, Magic, and Spells, Haunted Hangouts of the Undead,* and *Phantoms of the Rich and Famous* are just a few of the titles in Kallen's "Ghastly Ghost Stories" series. And the books he has compiled for his "The Fabulous Fun Library" series provide young readers with a host of ideas for fun and games that include brain teasers, magic tricks, riddles, jokes, math games, and simple science experiments.

A writer who tries to project his great enthusiasm for learning beyond the pages of his books, Kallen has strong feelings about his readers. "I believe there are only three solutions to the problem facing America today," he once stated. "Education, education, and education. But learning must be exciting and fun. I believe in piquing a reader's curiosity with humor to generate interest in the topic at hand. I was not the greatest student back in the 1960s, but books have been some of my best friends since childhood. I read the 'Lord of the Rings' trilogy in sixth grade, all the while getting low marks in English class. As my list of published works can attest, one is never too old to keep learning and growing. Writing is a gift, but it is also one that needs to be nurtured and fed with an open book and an open mind."

BIOGRAPHICAL/CRITICAL SOURCES:

PERIODICALS

Booklist, January 1, 1999, Ilene Cooper, review of *The 1950s,* pp. 866, 868; August, 1999, Ilene Cooper, review of *Rosie O'Donnell,* p. 2054; January 1, 2000, Susan Dove Lempke, review of *Native American Chiefs and Warriors,* and Mary Romano Marks, review of *War at Home,* pp. 890, 896; March 1, 2000, Karen Hutt, review of *Native Americans of the Great Lakes,* p. 1235; June 1, 2000, Roger Leslie, review of *The 1990s,* p. 1876; September 1, 2000, Anne O'Malley, review of *Witches,* p. 73; February 15, 2001, Carolyn Phelan, review of *Sixties Counterculture,* pp. 1124, 1126.

Library Journal, May 1, 1995, review of *Beer Here,* p. 121.

School Library Journal, May, 1993; February, 1995; March, 1995, Cathryn A. Camper, review of *Brontosaurus,* p. 198; April, 1995, Sharon Grover, reviews of *The Nazis Seize Power* and *Holocausts in Other Lands,* p. 143; June, 1997, John Peters, review of *Exploring the Origins of the Universe,* p. 132; March, 1999, Andrew Medlar, review of *Life among the Pirates,* and Cindy Darling Codel, review of *The 1950s,* pp. 222-223; July, 1999, Kathy Piehl, review of *Life in the Amazon Rain Forest,* p. 109; September, 1999, Laura Glaser, review of *The Salem Witch Trials,* p. 236; October, 1999, Steve Matthews, review of *Egypt,* p. 170; January, 2000, Sarah O'Neal, review of *Native American Chiefs and Warriors,* p. 148; May, 2000, Cris Riedel, review of *Native Americans of the Northeast,* and Starr E. Smith, *A Live on the Underground Railroad,* p. 184; September, 2000, Susan Shaver, review of *The 1950s,* Sean George, review of *Native Americans of the Southwest,* and Ann G. Brouse, review of *Witches,* pp. 249-250; April, 2001, Jane Halsall, review of *Sixties Counterculture,* p. 162, Eldon Younce, *The Home Front: Americans Protest the War,* p. 162, and Herman Sutter, review of *Understanding* The Catcher in the Rye, p. 162; May, 2001, Carol Wichman, review of *The Mayans,* p. 166; June, 2001, DeAnn Tabuchi, review of *Life in Tokyo,* p. 174.

*   *   *

KANTER, Rosabeth Moss 1943-

PERSONAL: Born March 15, 1943, in Cleveland, OH; daughter of Nelson Nathan (an attorney) and Helen (a teacher; maiden name, Smolen) Moss; married Stuart A. Kanter, June 15, 1963 (died March 24, 1969); married Barry A. Stein (a management consultant), July 2, 1972; children: Matthew Moss Kanter Stein. *Education:* Attended University of Chicago, 1962-63; Bryn Mawr College, B.A. (magna cum laude), 1964; University of Michigan, M.A., 1965, Ph.D., 1967; post-doctoral study at Harvard University, 1975-76.

ADDRESSES: Home—Cambridge and Edgartown, MA. *Office*—Harvard Business School, Graduate School of Business Administration, Soldiers Field Rd., Boston, MA 02163.

CAREER: University of Michigan—Ann Arbor, instructor in sociology, 1967; Brandeis University, Waltham, MA, assistant professor of sociology, 1967-73; Harvard University, Cambridge, MA, associate professor of administration, 1973-74; Brandeis University, associate professor of sociology, 1974-77; Yale University, New Haven, CT, associate professor, 1977-78, professor of sociology, 1978-86, chairman of department, 1982, chairman of University Council on Priorities and Planning, 1982-83; Harvard University Business School, Cambridge, MA, professor, 1986—, Ernest L. Arbuckle professor of business administration, 2000—. Visiting professor of organizational psychology and management, Massachusetts Institute of Technology, Sloan School of Management, 1979-80; visiting scholar at Newberry Library, 1973, Harvard University, 1975—, and Norwegian Research Council on Science and Humanities, September, 1980; faculty member at Young President's Organization of International University (Hong Kong), 1976; Sigma Chi scholar-in-residence, Miami University (Oxford, OH), October, 1978; editor, *Harvard Business Review,* 1989-92; Goodmeasure, Inc., Cambridge, MA, founding partner, 1977—, (former chairman of the board).

Director, American Center for Quality of Work Life, 1978-82, Educational Fund for Individual Rights, 1979-84, and National Organization for Women, Legal Defense and Education Fund, 1979-86, 1993-95; member of planning task force of Cambridge Institute's New City Project, 1969-71; expert witness before Equal Employment Opportunities Commission, 1976-77; American Leadership Forum, Houston, TX, 1982-86 (trustee, 1981—); President's Commission on Industrial Competitiveness (member of work group on entrepreneurship), 1984; College Retirement Equities Fund, trustee, 1985-89; Massachusetts Governor's Economic Council (former co-chair of International Trade Task Force), 1986-95; member of board of directors of New Democracy, Washington, DC, 1985-88, American Production and Quality Center, Houston, TX, 1989,

Economic Policy Institute, 1994, Alliance for the Commonwealth, 1995, and City Year (national urban youth service corps), 1995—. Incorporater, Babson College, 1984-87, Boston Children's Museum, 1984, and Mt. Auburn Hospital, 1991; member of the board of overseers of the Malcolm Baldridge National Quality Award, U.S. Dept. of Commerce, 1994; consultant to Russell Sage Foundation, Ford Foundation, and U.S. Department of State; judge for the Ron Brown Award for Corporate Leadership; co-chair of the Youth Service Advisory Board for Colin Powell's America's Promise. Consultant, speaker and lecturer.

MEMBER: International Association of Applied Social Scientists, Academy of Management, American Association for Higher Education, World Productivity Congress, World Economic Forum (fellow), American Society of Quality and Participation, Society for the Advancement of Socio-Economics, American Sociological Association (member of executive council, 1982-85), American Orthopsychiatric Association, American Legal Studies Association, National Training Laboratories Institute for Applied Behavioral Science (dean, 1973—), Society for the Study of Social Problems, Society for the Psychological Study of Social Issues, Sociologists for Women in Society, Law and Society Association, International Women's Forum Council on Foreign Relations, Eastern Sociological Society (member of executive committee, 1975-78), Committee of 200 (founding member, 1982), Yale Club (New York, NY and New Haven, CT).

AWARDS, HONORS: U.S. Office of Education grant, 1969-72; National Institute of Mental Health grant, 1973-74; Guggenheim fellowship, 1975-76; C. Wright Mills Award of 1977, 1978, for *Men and Women of the Corporation;* I. Peter Gellman Award, Eastern Sociological Society, 1978; William F. Donner Foundation grant, 1979-80; McKinsey Award, 1979, for article, "Power Failure in Management Circuits," in *Harvard Business Review;* Athena Award, Intercollegiate Association of Women Students, 1980; Professional Woman of the Year award, International Association of Personnel Women, 1981; Woman of the Year award, New England Women Business Owners Association, 1981; award for best article, *Hospital Forum,* 1982; Russell Sage Foundation grant, 1983-84; named to Cleveland Heights High School Hall of Fame, 1986, Working Woman Hall of Fame, AT&T and *Working Woman* magazine, 1986, and Ohio Women's Hall of Fame, 1990; Gold Medal, Big Sisters Association of Greater Boston, 1985; Women Who Make a Difference award, International Women's Forum, 1988; Richard M. Cyert award for professional excellence, Carnegie-Mellon

University Graduate School of Industrial Administration, 1989; Project Equality award, 1990; Crohn's and Colitis Foundation award, 1993, 1994; distinguished scholar award, Academy of Management, 1994; McFeeley award, YMCA, 1995; leadership award, New England Council, 1995. Honorary degrees from Yale University, 1978, Bucknell University, 1980, Antioch University, 1984, Westminster College, 1984, Babson College, 1984, Harvard University, 1986, Bryant College, 1986, Suffolk University, 1987, North Adams State College, 1987, Union College, 1987, Regis College, 1987, Colby-Sawyer College, 1988, University of New Haven, 1989, Bentley College, 1990, Florida International University, 1990, State University of New York Institute of Technology, 1991, Dowling College, 1991, Claremont College, 1992, Monmouth College, 1994, University of Massachusetts, Boston, 1996. Named one of the hundred most important women in America by the *Ladies Home Journal* and one of the fifty most powerful women in the world by the London *Times.*

WRITINGS:

Commitment and Community: Communes and Utopias in Sociological Perspective, Harvard University Press (Boston, MA), 1972.

(Editor and contributor) *Communes: Creating and Managing the Collective Life,* Harper (New York, NY), 1973.

(Editor with Marcus Millman, and contributor) *Another Voice: Feminist Perspectives on Social Life and Social Science,* Doubleday (New York, NY), 1975.

Work and Family in the United States: A Critical Review and Research and Policy Agenda, Russell Sage Foundation (Washington, DC), 1976.

Men and Women of the Corporation, Basic Books (New York, NY), 1977.

(Editor) *Life in Organizations,* Basic Books (New York, NY), 1979.

A Tale of "O", Harper (New York, NY), 1980.

The Change Masters: Innovation for Productivity in the American Corporation, Simon & Schuster (New York, NY), 1983.

(With Michael S. Dukakis) *Creating the Future: The Massachusetts Comeback and Its Promise for America,* Summit Books (New York, NY), 1988.

When Giants Learn to Dance: Mastering the Challenge of Strategy, Management, and Careers in the 1990s, Simon & Schuster (New York, NY), 1989.

(Compiler with Barry A. Stein and Todd D. Jick) *The Challenge of Organizational Change: How Companies Experience It and Leaders Guide It,* Free Press (New York, NY), 1992.

Men and Women of the Corporation, Basic Books (New York, NY), 1993.

World Class: Thriving Locally in the Global Economy, Simon & Schuster (New York, NY), 1995.

(Editor with John Kao and Fred Wiersema) *Innovation: Breakthrough Ideas at 3M, DuPont, GE, Pfizer, and Rubbermaid,* HarperBusiness (New York, NY), 1997.

Rosabeth Moss Kanter on the Frontiers of Management, Harvard Business School Press (Boston, MA), 1997.

Evolve!: Succeeding in the Digital Culture of Tomorrow, Harvard Business School Press (Boston, MA), 2001.

Contributor to books, including *Internal Labor Markets,* edited by P. Osterman, MIT Press, 1984; *New Futures: The Challenge of Transition Management,* edited by J. Kimberly and R. Quinn, Irwin-Dorsey, 1984; and *Handbook of Nonprofit Organizations,* edited by W. Powell and P. DiMaggion, Yale University Press, 1985. Contributor of articles and reviews to business, sociology, education, psychology, and psychiatry journals. Member of editorial boards of *Journal of Applied Behavioral Science,* 1970-73, "Rose Monograph Series," American Sociological Association, 1973-76, *American Sociologist,* 1976-78, *Administrative Science Quarterly,* 1979-82, *Human Resource Management,* 1982—, and *Organizational Dynamics,* 1983—. Associate editor, *Sociological Symposium,* 1972-76, *Sociological Inquiry,* 1973-76, and *American Sociological Review,* 1978-81. Consulting editor, *Journal of Voluntary Action Research,* 1972-76, and *American Journal of Sociology,* 1975-77; contributing editor, *Working Papers for a New Society,* 1977-80.

SIDELIGHTS: Rosabeth Moss Kanter is a sociologist, professor, internationally recognized business leader, and author. As a speaker, she has addressed conventions and trade and civic groups across the United States and in more than twenty countries. As a consultant, she has served clients that include Bell Atlantic, General Electric, IBM, and Volvo, as well as United States agencies and foreign governments. She has had a leadership role in dozens of initiatives and served as editor of the *Harvard Business Review* and on the editorial boards of other well-regarded publications.

"All her adult life, Kanter, a highly respected management consultant, has studied that traditionally amorphous institution, the corporation, trying to understand it, to explain it, and, ultimately, to make it a better place for everyone," wrote Carol Kleiman in the *Chicago Tribune.* Kanter's *The Change Masters: Innovation for Productivity in the American Corporation* is "an effort to discover why some firms succeed in maintaining innovation and growth while others retard individual initiative." Tom Redburn, commenting in the *Los Angeles Times,* said that the book "provides some of the most revealing glimpses into the day-to-day workings of several successful companies." "To the layman," stated Anatole Broyard in the *New York Times,* "The Change Masters* explains a great deal and does it very persuasively." He added, "Though Miss Kanter sometimes uses the word innovation as if it were a mantra, it may well be."

Kanter's main point, in both her work as a consultant and her writings, is that most corporate structures impede communication between upper echelon executives and workers. Workers feel cut off from decision making and problem solving. Believing they are powerless, they end up as either "movers," those obviously slated for promotion to positions of increasing power, or "stuck" workers, who continue to perform (often less and less productively) but realize the future holds no more than an automatic raise every twelve months. Management, while wielding power in the eyes of the workers, actually is caught in the middle. Managers are in the position of passing along information and enforcing decisions with which they had little or nothing to do. They appear powerful but usually don't know what the future holds. Kanter told Kleiman that "to her, the ideal corporate state is one in which executives in lofty positions get to know their employees, where they can relax and communicate with them—and where employees can do the same. 'We are all people,' says Kanter, 'people of the organization.'" The author explains, "I realized very early in college that corporations are among the most powerful entities in society, and if you care about how the world is run, you have to find out about them. My interest has always been in how a complex world is put together."

Kanter's earliest books are an examination of communal dynamics, while her later volumes take into account technology and the global economy. John Kay reviewed *World Class: Thriving Locally in the Global Economy* in *Management Today.* Kay wrote that "the true substance of the book is a sober perspective on how superficial is the impact of internationalisation on American life." Kay noted that for many of Kanter's interviewees (who hail from small communities), "integration into the world economy has not gone much beyond the discovery that foreigners are not an alien species, and sometimes not as far as that: 'We're building a new Kroger's supermarket with Japanese signs, because

Honda was coming.'" As Kanter points out, boundaries are still there—most foreign companies maintain their offices in their home countries, and the few transnational companies tend to be American companies with European operations. "Almost every page displays this tension between the rhetoric of globalisation and the reality of substantial cultural differences," wrote Kay.

Rosabeth Moss Kanter on the Frontiers of Management is a collection of her articles taken from the *Harvard Business Review* over the previous fifteen years. They cover her familiar subjects of community responsibility, strategic alliances, innovation, and customer empowerment. Tim Dickson, who reviewed the book for *Strategy & Business* online, called Kanter "one of America's best-known management thinkers" and noted that in spite of her accomplishments, Kanter "is most unguru-like in her modesty, approachability, and charm." Dickson wrote that Kanter has "a rare ability to champion the cause of the manager at the sharp end of business while rightly retaining her academic detachment. She revels in the detail of case studies and nitty-gritty examples, yet never loses the bigger picture."

Strategy & Business interviewer Joel Kurtzman said, "In a way, Professor Kanter is now returning to her roots as a sociologist. Recently, she wrote an article in the *Harvard Business Review* on change and innovation. In the article she looked at the examples of certain social agencies as beta sites for corporate change." Kanter spoke of "thinking globally" and the internet as a force in connectivity. She also stressed the importance of developing a company culture that reaches out beyond the local market. "What I'm trying to convey," Kanter told Kurtzman, "is that your global strategies must take account of differences in the various countries where your company operates, and then, with that knowledge, you must build local country relationships that are strong and deep so that you're seen as being an insider wherever you are. You will be constantly balancing your need for uniformity with the acknowledgment of differences. That is one of the big challenges companies have, both in terms of their strategy and management of people."

Kanter's theme of internet-based business is the topic of *Evolve!: Succeeding in the Digital Culture of Tomorrow.* In this work, Kanter draws on anecdotal information from companies like eBay, but her opinion that shares of online companies that experience little or no profit will continue to enjoy high valuations has been disproved by the drop in these stocks after the

book was published. Kanter advises managers who rely on the Web and notes how technology will transform the way in which we work. A *Publishers Weekly* reviewer wrote that Kanter "argues convincingly that the biggest obstacles to change are management and employee attitudes, not the technological tools they employ."

BIOGRAPHICAL/CRITICAL SOURCES:

PERIODICALS

Booklist, March 1, 1989, review of *When Giants Learn to Dance: Mastering the Challenge of Strategy, Management, and Careers in the 1990s,* p. 1052; September 1, 1995, review of *World Class: Thriving Locally in the Global Economy,* p. 22; November 1, 1998, review of *The Change Masters: Innovation for Productivity in the American Corporation,* p. 474; September 1, 1997, review of *Rosabeth Moss Kanter on the Frontiers of Management,* p. 43.

Chicago Tribune, May 6, 1979, Carol Kleiman, review of *The Change Masters.*

Choice, March, 1996, review of *World Class,* p. 1180; January, 1998, review of *Rosabeth Moss Kanter on the Frontiers of Management,* p. 865.

Christian Science Monitor, December 28, 1995, review of *World Class,* p. 8.

Contemporary Sociology, September, 1993, review of *The Challenge of Organizational Change: How Companies Experience It and Leaders Guide It,* p. 718.

Economist, September 9, 1995, review of *World Class,* p. 85.

Far Eastern Economic Review, June 27, 1996, review of *World Class,* p. 52.

Fortune, November 2, 1992, review of *The Challenge of Organizational Change,* p. 144.

HR, September, 1997, review of *Rosabeth Moss Kanter on the Frontiers of Management,* p. 144.

Industrial and Labor Relations Review, July, 1994, review of *The Challenge of Organizational Change,* p. 724.

Journal of Economic Literature, June, 1994, review of *Men and Women of the Corporation,* p. 808.

Library Journal, March 15, 1990, review of *When Giants Learn to Dance,* p. 43; August, 1995, review of *World Class,* p. 22; March 15, 1996, review of *World Class,* p. 40; September 1, 1997, review of *Rosabeth Moss Kanter on the Frontiers of Management,* p. 192.

Los Angeles Times, October 20, 1983, Tom Redburn, review of *The Change Masters.*

Management Today, February, 1996, John Kay, review of *World Class,* p. 24.

New York Times, August 27, 1983, Anatole Broyard, review of *The Change Masters.*

New York Times Book Review, October 16, 1983; February 24, 1985, review of *The Change Masters,* p. 34; October 29, 1989, review of *When Giants Learn to Dance,* p. 40.

Public Administration Review, November, 1994, review of *The Challenge of Organizational Change,* p. 577.

Publishers Weekly, July 3, 1995, review of *World Class,* p. 40; June 2, 1997, review of *Innovation: Breakthrough Ideas at 3M, DuPont, GE, Pfizer, and Rubbermaid,* p. 62; February 5, 2001, review of *Evolve!: Succeeding in the Digital Culture of Tomorrow,* p. 80.

Signs, spring, 1988, review of *Men and Women of the Corporation,* p. 529.

Wall Street Journal, October 2, 1992, review of *The Challenge of Organizational Change,* p. A12; July 10, 1997, review of *Innovation,* p. A13.

Washington Post Book World, July 3, 1977.

OTHER

NewsHour Online, http://www.pbs.org/ (November 1, 1995), David Gergen, "Corporate Communities" (interview).

Peter F. Drucker Foundation for Nonprofit Management, http://www.pfdf.org/ (summer, 1999), Rosabeth Moss Kanter, "The Enduring Skills of Change Leaders."

Rosabeth Moss Kanter Web site, http://www.rosabeth. com (September 12, 2001).

Strategy & Business, http://www.stragegy-business.com/ (September 12, 2001), Tim Dickson, review of *Rosabeth Moss Kanter on the Frontiers of Management;* Joel Kurtzman, "An Interview with Rosabeth Moss Kanter."*

*   *   *

KARR, Kathleen 1946-

PERSONAL: Born April 21, 1946, in Allentown, PA; daughter of Stephen (a mechanical engineer) and Elizabeth (a homemaker; maiden name, Szoka) Csere; married Lawrence F. Karr (a physicist and computer consultant), July 13, 1968; children: Suzanne, Daniel.

Education: Catholic University of America, B.A., 1968; Providence College, M.A., 1971; further study at Corcoran School of Art, 1972.

ADDRESSES: Home—Washington, DC. *Agent*—McIntosh & Otis, 353 Lexington Ave., Rm. 1500, New York, NY 10016-0900.

CAREER: Novel and screenplay writer. Barrington High School, Barrington, RI, English and speech teacher, 1968-69; Rhode Island Historical Society Film Archives, curator, 1970-71; American Film Institute, Washington, DC, archives assistant, 1971-72, member of catalog staff, 1972; Washington Circle Theater Corporation, Washington, DC, general manager, 1973-78; Circle/Showcase Theaters, Washington, DC, advertising director, 1979-83, director of public relations, 1984-88; Circle Management Company/Circle Releasing, Washington, DC, member of public relations staff, 1988-93. Assistant professor at George Washington University, summer, 1979, and 1980-81. Lecturer or instructor in film and communications at various institutions, including Providence College, 1969-70, University of Rhode Island, 1971, University of Maryland, 1972, Catholic University of America, 1973-77, New Line Presentations Lecture Bureau, 1974-76, American Film Institute, 1979-80, and Trinity College, 1985-86, 1995; lecturer at film and writing conferences, 1973-89. Juror, American Film Festival, 1971, and Rosebud Awards, 1991.

MEMBER: Washington Romance Writers (member of board of directors, 1985-86; president, 1986-87), Children's Book Guild of Washington, DC (member of board of directors, 1998-2002; president, 2000-01), Society of Children's Book Writers and Illustrators, Children's Literature (member of advisory board, 1994—).

AWARDS, HONORS: Golden Medallion Award for best inspirational novel, Romance Writers of America, 1986, for *From This Day Forward;* finalist, outstanding emerging artist, Washington, DC Mayor's Arts Awards, 1986; "100 Books for Reading and Sharing" citation, New York Public Library, 1990, for *It Ain't Always Easy;* Parents' Choice Story Book citation, 1992, for *Oh, Those Harper Girls!;* Books for the Teen Age selection, New York Public Library, for *The Cave;* Notable Children's Trade Book in the Field of Social Studies, National Council for the Social Studies/Children's Book Council (NCSS/CBC), 1999, Notable Children's Book in the Language Arts, National Council of Teachers of English, 1999, and Prix de Bernard Verselo

(Brussels, Belgium), 2000-01, all for *The Great Turkey Walk;* Best Book for Young Adults selection, American Library Association (ALA), 2000, for *Man of the Family;* Golden Kite Award, Society of Children's Book Writers and Illustrators, Notable Children's Trade Book in the Field of Social Studies, NCSS/CBC, Books for the Teen Age selection, New York Public Library, Best Book for Young Adults selection, ALA, all 2001, all for *The Boxer.*

WRITINGS:

FICTION FOR CHILDREN

It Ain't Always Easy, Farrar, Straus & Giroux (New York, NY), 1990.
Oh, Those Harper Girls!; or, Young and Dangerous, Farrar, Straus & Giroux (New York, NY), 1992.
Gideon and the Mummy Professor, Farrar, Straus & Giroux (New York, NY), 1993.
The Cave, Farrar, Straus (New York, NY), 1994.
In the Kaiser's Clutch, Farrar, Straus & Giroux (New York, NY), 1995.
Spy in the Sky, illustrated by Thomas F. Yezerski, Hyperion (New York, NY), 1997.
The Great Turkey Walk, Farrar, Straus & Giroux (New York, NY), 1998.
The Lighthouse Mermaid, illustrated by Karen Lee Schmidt, Hyperion (New York, NY), 1998.
The White House Book, Hyperion (New York, NY), 1999.
Man of the Family, Farrar, Straus & Giroux (New York, NY) 1999.
Skullduggery, Hyperion (New York, NY), 2000.
The Boxer, Farrar, Straus & Giroux (New York, NY), 2000.
It Happened in the White House: Extraordinary Tales from America's Most Famous Home, illustrated by Paul Meisel, Hyperion (New York, NY), 2000.
Playing with Fire, Farrar, Straus & Giroux (New York, NY), 2001.
Dear Mr. President—Dwight D. Eisenhower: Letters from a New Jersey Schoolgirl, Winslow Press (New York, NY), 2002.
Bone Dry, Hyperion (New York, NY), 2002.

Some of Karr's novels have been translated into French, Danish, Catalan, and Italian.

"PETTICOAT PARTY" SERIES; FICTION; FOR CHILDREN

Go West, Young Women!, HarperCollins (New York, NY), 1996.
Phoebe's Folly, HarperCollins (New York, NY), 1996.

Oregon, Sweet Oregon, HarperCollins (New York, NY), 1998.
Gold-Rush Phoebe, HarperCollins (New York, NY), 1998.

ROMANCE NOVELS; FOR ADULTS

Light of My Heart, Zondervan (Grand Rapids, MI), 1984.
From This Day Forward, Zondervan (Grand Rapids, MI), 1985.
Chessie's King, Zondervan (Grand Rapids, MI), 1986.
Destiny's Dreamers Book I: Gone West, Barbour (Uhrichsville, OH), 1993.
Destiny's Dreamers Book II: The Promised Land, Barbour (Uhrichsville, OH), 1993.

OTHER

(Editor) *The American Film Heritage: Views from the American Film Institute Collection,* Acropolis Press (Washington, DC), 1972.

Also author of various short films, including *The Elegant Mr. Brown and I* (and director), 1969; *Mayor Tom Bradley,* 1973; *Profile: Tom Bradley,* 1974; and *No Smoking, Spitting, or Molesting,* 1976. Contributor to numerous journals, including *Film Society Review, Film News, Journal of Popular Film, Providence Journal,* and *Rhode Island History;* contributor to texts, including *Cartoon: A Celebration of American Comic Art,* 1975, and *Magill's Survey of Cinema,* annual editions. Contributing editor, *Media and Methods,* 1970-72; editor, *ASFE News,* March, 1976; member of advisory board, *Children's Literature,* 1994—.

ADAPTATIONS: The Great Turkey Walk was recorded as an audiobook, Recorded Books, 1999.

SIDELIGHTS: Kathleen Karr's historical novels for young teens are noted for their humorous and suspenseful plots and boldly drawn characters. Besides their settings, which range from the streets of New York City to the "Wild West" of the late 1800s, Karr's works also feature compelling portrayals of young people confronting adult-sized challenges, their efforts to deal with these challenges rendered in an upbeat prose that many critics have found engaging. Among Karr's books are the historical novels *The Cave, In the Kaiser's Clutch,* and *Playing with Fire,* as well as the "Petticoat Party" series about women moving westward along the Oregon Trail during the early 1800s.

Born in 1946 in Allentown, Pennsylvania, Karr began writing fiction "on a dare from my husband," as she once stated. "Tired of hearing me complain about not being able to find a 'good read,' he suggested I write a book myself." In 1984 she sold her third attempt, the romance novel *Light of My Heart,* and, as Karr described it, "entered the world of women's fiction." It was her two children who convinced her to switch genres, however; "They asked me to write a book for them." Karr agreed, penning *It Ain't Always Easy,* which, in 1990, would become her first published children's novel. Along the way she discovered a new vocation as an author of children's historical novels.

It Ain't Always Easy follows the efforts of two New York City orphans—eleven-year-old Jack and eight-year-old Mandy—who move out West in the hope of finding a family to take care of them. Despite the odds, they stay together and, after many adventures, manage to find a home and family. While acknowledging the entertaining aspect of the children's adventures, some critics found the events and dialogue unrealistic; Gail Richmond pointed out in *School Library Journal* that Jack's character is "too good to be true, and loses some credibility as a result." Describing the book as "powerful," a *Publishers Weekly* writer concluded that "the spirit and perseverance of the protagonists are uplifting." Other critics cited authentic period details and well-rounded characterizations in praising *It Ain't Always Easy;* as *Horn Book* writer Elizabeth S. Watson observed, even "lesser characters are three-dimensional," making for "an extremely appealing" story.

Karr uses the setting of the nineteenth-century American West to a more comic effect in *Oh, Those Harper Girls!; or, Young and Dangerous.* In this novel, the six daughters of a hapless rancher try a number of foolhardy and illegal schemes to save their West Texas homestead from bankruptcy and eventually land on the New York stage, reenacting their famous escapades. Centered on the youngest daughter, Lily, the brains behind the girls' schemes, the story also comments on the restricted roles available to women in the nineteenth century. *Booklist* contributor Mary Romano Marks commented favorably on this aspect of Karr's work, adding: "The girls' hilarious escapades and good-natured sibling rivalry make the novel an enjoyable read." "Characterization is quite strong," Rita Soltan remarked in a *School Library Journal* review, dubbing *Oh, Those Harper*

Girls! "fast paced and satisfying." A contributor to *Kirkus Reviews* called the novel "a happy, rip-roaring adventure, capped by a whirlwind of marriages, family reunions, and wishes fulfilled."

The world of the American West is also the focus of the "Petticoat Party" series, which features a group of pioneers on their way west in 1846. In *Go West, Young Women!,* twelve-year-old Phoebe Brown finds herself part of a wagon train led by women after the men in their party are killed or seriously disabled during a buffalo stampede. Despite numerous hardships, the determined women lead the wagon train nearly 1,400 miles by the novel's end. Elizabeth Mellett found *Go West, Young Women!* to be a "light, entertaining tale of adventure on the trail to Oregon," in her *School Library Journal* assessment of the series, while in *Kirkus Reviews,* a critic praised the novel as a "good adventure tale . . . and a real consciousness-raiser to boot." In the second novel, *Phoebe's Folly,* Phoebe learns how to pull her weight on the journey by becoming knowledgeable about firearms, her perky, positive attitude prompting *Booklist* contributor Lauren Peterson to call her a "likeable, spunky heroine who will attract a loyal following." *Oregon, Sweet Oregon* finds Phoebe reaching her destination, only to discover disappointment when she is expected to retire to an appropriately subservient "woman's place" in the growing society. The lure of riches prompts her to continue her travels, and in *Gold-Rush Phoebe,* Karr's protagonist joins with fellow teen Robbie Robson to make the trek to California, where they encounter further adventures and develop a romantic relationship. Calling Phoebe's saga in *Oregon, Sweet Oregon* "more entertainment than history," *Booklist* contributor Peterson praised the series as "a nice alternative to lengthier and more challenging historical fiction" about America's westward expansion.

Karr returns to New York City in her 2000 novel, *Skullduggery.* In 1839 medicine still has many advances left to make, and quacks and unsound medical practices abound. For twelve-year-old Matthew, orphaned after a cholera epidemic, getting a job with a doctor seems like a way of helping others avoid his family's terrible fate. However, Dr. Cornwall is no ordinary doctor: he is a phrenologist who determines people's personalities by feeling the lumps and bumps on their head. Cornwall's efforts to develop his "science" requires skulls, and Matthew finds his job description includes sneaking into cemeteries and digging up graves in order to provide them. This grave robbing eventually takes the pair to Europe, in search of the skulls of great men such as the French philosopher Voltaire and Napoleon Bonaparte. Praising the novel's plot as "fast-paced,"

School Library Journal contributor Steven Engelfried added that the discussion of phrenology and the creepiness of grave robbing combine to make *Skullduggery* attractive to "curious readers not ordinarily drawn to historical fiction." A *Kirkus Reviews* critic called the novel "rich in period color and good old-fashioned derring do."

Moving half a century closer to the present, Karr sets her novel *The Boxer* in 1885. Johnny Woods is a fifteen year old who boxes at a local saloon as a way to make some extra money to supplement the small wage he earns for working grueling hours at a New York City sweatshop in order to support his fatherless family. Unfortunately, boxing is illegal in New York, and Johnny is arrested and sent to prison for six months. There he is aided by a fellow inmate, a former pro boxer named Michael O'Shaunnessey, who teaches Johnny not only the finer points of boxing, but also how to turn his life around after his release from prison and start his climb to the top of the professional prizefighting circuit. Praising Karr's "clarity of purpose" in writing *The Boxer,* Carolyn Phelan cited the novel as unique due to its "focus on a lower-class character during peace time." In *Horn Book,* a contributor commended the inclusion of actual people of the period and described the novel's tenacious, determined protagonist as "a highly sympathetic, ultimately admirable character. . . . In or out of the ring, this kid is a fighter." Edward Sullivan praised *The Boxer* as a "wonderful blend of fascinating history and compelling drama," adding in his *School Library Journal* review that Karr succeeds admirably in "creating a vivid sense of time and place." The novel's "one-two-punch pacing and warmhearted resolutions will keep the pages turning," promised a *Publishers Weekly* reviewer.

Karr draws readers into the dustbowl era with *The Cave,* which is set in drought-burdened South Dakota during the Great Depression of the 1930s. The lack of rain poses many difficulties for pre-teen Christine, for it has threatened the livelihood of her family's farm and aggravates her younger brother Michael's asthma. Her father is considering moving the family to California when Christine unearths a cave in the foothills near the farm, complete with crystals, stalactites—and water. Although she wants to stay on the farm, Christine tries to keep her discovery from her father, afraid that in rescuing the farm he will destroy the cave's beauty. With numerous period details, "Karr excels in re-creating time and place," Cindy Darling Codell noted in *School Library Journal.* In addition, the critic wrote, the ecological conflict enhances the "sweet, well-crafted story of a family forced to be tough by the extremities of nature."

Comparing the book to the children's classic *Caddie Woodlawn,* *Booklist* critic Mary Harris Veeder observed that "Karr creates an active and believable girl in the throes of both physical and emotional change" and praised the author's child's-eye view of the era. A *Kirkus Reviews* writer concluded: "Fine period detail and masterful writing grace Karr's story of quiet courage during hard times."

"After a number of years working in the 'real' worlds of motion pictures and education, I find it a pleasure to be able to create my own worlds in fiction," Karr once commented regarding her developing career as a novelist. "To watch a character come alive—become real flesh and blood and take the reins of a story in hand—is an exhilarating experience. It's also hard work."

"As for my penchant for historical settings, well, I've discovered that I feel quite comfortable in the nineteenth century. It's a challenge to try to recreate a specific time and place, with its specific language patterns. Short of inventing a time machine, this is my way of reentering the past and attempting to show my readers that while events may change, the nature of human beings is fairly constant. Courage and common decency against difficult odds have always existed."

BIOGRAPHICAL/CRITICAL SOURCES:

PERIODICALS

Booklist, April 15, 1992, Mary Romano Marks, review of *Oh, Those Harper Girls!,* p. 1523; September 15, 1994, review of *The Cave,* p. 92; December 1, 1996, Lauren Peterson, review of *Phoebe's Folly,* p. 654; June 1, 1998, Chris Sherman, review of *The Great Turkey Walk,* p. 1748, and Ilene Cooper, review of *The Lighthouse Mermaid,* p. 1767; July, 1998, Lauren Peterson, review of *Oregon, Sweet Oregon,* p. 1881; September 15, 1999, Hazel Rochman, review of *Man of the Family,* p. 257; April 1, 2000, John Peters, review of *Skullduggery,* p. 1477; September 1, 2000, Carolyn Phelan, review of *The Boxer,* p. 116; April 1, 2001, Ilene Cooper, review of *Playing with Fire,* p. 1483.

Bulletin of the Center for Children's Books, February, 1991, p. 143; July-August, 1992, p. 297; September, 1993, pp. 12-13.

Children's Book Review Service, review of *In the Kaiser's Clutch,* p. 33.

Horn Book, March, 1991, Elizabeth S. Watson, review of *It Ain't Always Easy,* pp. 199-200; May-June, 1992, Maeve Visser Knoth, review of *Oh, Those*

Harper Girls!, p. 341; September-October, 1993, Elizabeth S. Watson, review of *Gideon and the Mummy Professor*, p. 599; November, 1999, Mary M. Burns, review of *Man of the Family*, p. 742; May, 2000, review of *Skullduggery*, p. 315; September, 2000, review of *The Boxer*, p. 573.

Journal of Adolescent & Adult Literacy, September, 2001, Rosie Kerin, review of *The Boxer*, p. 84.

Kirkus Reviews, April 15, 1992, review of *Oh, Those Harper Girls!*, p. 539; May 15, 1993, p. 663; July 15, 1994, review of *The Cave*, p. 987; October, 1, 1995, review of *In the Kaiser's Clutch*, p. 1430; December 1, 1995, review of *Go West, Young Women!*, p. 1703; March 15, 1997, review of *Spy in the Sky*, pp. 463-464; December 15, 1999, review of *Skullduggery*, pp. 1958-1959.

Kliatt, September, 1995, Barbara Shepp, review of *Oh, Those Harper Girls!*, pp. 10-11.

Publishers Weekly, September 28, 1990, review of *It Ain't Always Easy*, p. 103; March 23, 1992, review of *Oh, Those Harper Girls!*, p. 73; May 24, 1993, review of *Gideon and the Mummy Professor*, p. 89; September 12, 1994, review of *The Cave*, p. 92; February 12, 1996, review of *Go West, Young Women!*, p. 78; April 20, 1998, review of *The Great Turkey Walk*, p. 67; October 4, 1999, review of *Man of the Family*, p. 76; February 7, 2000, review of *Skullduggery*, p. 86; October 30, 2000, review of *The Boxer*, p. 76; January 22, 2001, review of *Playing with Fire*, p. 325.

School Library Journal, December, 1990, Gail Richmond, review of *It Ain't Always Easy*, p. 104; May, 1992, Rita Soltan, review of *Oh, Those Harper Girls!*, p. 133; June, 1993, Beth Tegart, review of *Gideon and the Mummy Professor*, p. 107; September, 1994, Cindy Darling Codell, review of *The Cave*, p. 218; January, 1996, Kelly Dillery, review of *In the Kaiser's Clutch*, p. 128; May, 1996, Elizabeth Mellett, review of *Go West, Young Women!*, p. 114; August, 1997, Linda L. Plevak, review of *Spy in the Sky*, p. 136; March, 1998, Coop Renner, review of *The Great Turkey Walk*, p. 214; August, 1998, Elaine Lesh Morgan, review of *The Lighthouse Mermaid*, p. 141; January, 1999, Shawn Brommer, review of *Gold Rush Phoebe*, p. 128; March, 2000, Carol Katz, review of *The Great Turkey Walk* (audio version), p. 166, and Steven Engelfried, review of *Skullduggery*, p. 239; November, 2000, Edward Sullivan, review of *The Boxer*, p. 157; May, 2001, Patricia B. McGee, review of *Playing with Fire*, p. 154.

Voice of Youth Advocates, April, 1985, p. 44; February, 1991, p. 352; June, 1992, p. 96; December, 1994, pp. 275-276.

OTHER

Children's Book Guild of Washington, DC, http://www. childrensbookguild.org/ (December 8, 2001), biography of Kathleen Karr.

*   *   *

KENISON, Katrina 1958-

PERSONAL: Born October 3, 1958, in Philadelphia, PA; daughter of John Burton (a dentist) and Marilyn (an office manager; maiden name, Stancerfield) Kenison; married James Harker, 1980 (divorced, 1985); married Steven Moore Lewers (a publisher), September 12, 1987; children: (second marriage) Henry Joseph. *Education:* Graduate of Smith College (cum laude), 1980.

ADDRESSES: Office—Houghton Mifflin Co., 222 Berkeley St., Boston, MA 02166.

CAREER: Houghton Mifflin Co., Boston, MA, editor, 1981-88, 1990—.

MEMBER: Phi Beta Kappa.

WRITINGS:

(Editor) *The Best American Short Stories*, Houghton Mifflin (Boston, MA), published annually, 1991—.
(Editor and author of introduction, with Kathleen Hirsch) *Mothers: Twenty Stories of Contemporary Motherhood*, North Point Press (New York, NY), 1996.
(Editor, with John Updike) *The Best American Short Stories of the Century*, Houghton Mifflin (Boston, MA), 2000.
Mitten Strings for God: Reflections for Mothers in a Hurry, Warner Books (New York, NY), 2000.

Author of "A Remembrance," a 150-page biographical essay included in Olive Ann Burns's book of memoirs, *Leaving Cold Sassy*, Ticknor & Fields, 1992.

SIDELIGHTS: As editor of Houghton Mifflin's annual "Best American Short Stories" series, Katrina Kenison has helped to bring outstanding fiction to a wide readership. In *The Best American Short Stories of the Cen-*

tury, which Kenison coedited with John Updike, the task of judging the best stories was monumental. Kenison picked semifinalists from thousands of stories submitted to the publisher's "Best of" series, out of which only fifty-five made Updike's final cut. Reviewers found the volume notable for its diversity: while classics by such writers as Sherwood Anderson, Ernest Hemingway, John Cheever, and Raymond Carver are included, almost half the stories are by women, and the perspectives of black, Jewish, gay, and immigrant writers abound. In Kenison's words, the anthology's stories "are an invaluable record of our century."

Critics welcomed the volume with great enthusiasm. *Booklist* reviewer Brad Hooper noted that the anthology "brims with significance," and a contributor to *Publishers Weekly* observed that "life on this continent may be brutal, but this extraordinary collection offers up dazzling writing that salves wounds, as well as stories full of the pleasures of life."

Kenison mined more specialized material for *Mothers: Twenty Stories of Contemporary Motherhood,* coedited with Kathleen Hirsch. The anthology, which a *Publishers Weekly* reviewer considered "well-chosen," presents stories that, in the editors' words, show "the complexities of mothering in America today." The book includes stories by Perri Klass, Barbara Kingsolver, Kate Braverman, Mary Gordon, Sue Miller, and Alice Elliott Dark.

In *Mitten Strings for God: Reflections for Mothers in a Hurry,* Kenison presents a volume of her own personal essays on the themes of family and spirituality. A reviewer for *Publishers Weekly* found it a "heartfelt" collection of "richly anecdotal musings" that, though occasionally treacly, nevertheless "resonate with honesty and wisdom."

BIOGRAPHICAL/CRITICAL SOURCES:

BOOKS

Kenison, Katrina, and John Updike, editors, *The Best American Short Stories of the Century,* Houghton Mifflin (Boston, MA), 2000.
Kenison, Katrina, and Kathleen Hirsch, editors, *Mothers: Twenty Stories of Contemporary Motherhood,* North Point Press (New York, NY), 1996.

PERIODICALS

Booklist, November 1, 1995, Brad Hooper, review of *The Best American Short Stories 1995,* p. 453; November 15, 1996, Jim O'Laughlin, review of *The*

Best American Short Stories 1996, p. 569; September 1, 1998, Brad Hooper, review of *The Best American Short Stories 1998,* p. 56B; April 1, 1999, review of *The Best American Short Stories of the Century,* p. 1384; November 1, 2000, Bonnie Smothers, review of *The Best American Short Stories 2000,* p. 511.
Christian Science Monitor, December 30, 1996, Carl Wood, review of *The Best American Short Stories 1996,* p. 13.
Entertainment Weekly, April 16, 1999, Mark Harris, review of *The Best American Short Stories of the Century,* p. 12.
Family Circle, April 1, 2000, excerpt from *Mitten Strings for God: Reflections for Mothers in a Hurry,* p. 24.
Kirkus Reviews, September 1, 2000, review of *The Best American Short Stories 2000,* p. 1303.
Insight on the News, July 26, 1999, Rex Roberts, review of *The Best American Short Stories of the Century,* p. 36.
Library Journal, February 1, 1994, Eleanor Mitchell, review of *The Best American Short Stories 1993,* p. 114; November 1, 1994, Eleanor Mitchell, review of *The Best American Short Stories 1994,* p. 113; May 1, 1996, Helen Rippier Wheeler, review of *Mothers: Twenty Stories of Contemporary Motherhood,* p. 94; October 1, 1996, Adam Mazmanian, review of *The Best American Short Stories 1996,* p. 129; September 1, 1999, Christine DeZelar-Tiedman, review of *The Best American Short Stories 1999,* p. 235.
New York Times Book Review, May 9, 1999, Michael Gorra, review of *The Best American Short Stories of the Century,* p. 8.
Publishers Weekly, September 19, 1994, review of *The Best American Short Stories 1994,* p. 65; September 18, 1995, review of *The Best American Short Stories 1995,* p. 123; April 15, 1996, review of *Mothers,* p. 48; September 8, 1997, review of *The Best American Short Stories 1997,* p. 56; August 24, 1998, review of *The Best American Short Stories 1998,* p. 49; March 8, 1999, review of *The Best American Short Stories of the Century,* p. 47; August 30, 1999, review of *The Best American Short Stories 1999,* p. 47; p. April 3, 2000, review of *Mitten Strings for God: Reflections for Mothers in a Hurry,* p. 74; May 1, 2000, review of *Mitten Strings for God* (audio version), p. 32; August 28, 2000, review of *The Best American Short Stories 2000,* p. 53.

OTHER

New York Times on the Web, http://www.nytimes.com/books/ (August 10, 1999), author interview.*

KENNAN, George F(rost) 1904-
(X)

PERSONAL: Born February 16, 1904, in Milwaukee, WI; son of Kossuth Kent and Florence (James) Kennan; married Annelise Sorensen, 1931; children: Grace Kennan Warnecke, Joan Elisabeth, Christopher James, Wendy Antonia Pfaeffli. *Education:* Princeton University, A.B., 1925; Berlin Seminary for Oriental Languages, diploma, 1930.

ADDRESSES: Office—School of Historical Studies, Institute for Advanced Study, Princeton, NJ 08540.

CAREER: U.S. Foreign Service, officer, 1926-27, served as vice-consul, Geneva, Switzerland and Hamburg, Germany, 1927, Berlin, Germany and Tallinn, Estonia, 1928, served as language officer, Berlin, 1929, served as third secretary, Riga, Latvia, 1929, 1931, Moscow, USSR, 1934, consul, Vienna, Austria, 1935, second secretary, Prague, 1935, Czechoslovakia, 1938, Berlin, 1939, first secretary, 1940, counselor of legation, Lisbon, Portugal, 1942, counselor, American delegation to European Advisory Commission, London, England, 1943, minister-counselor, Moscow, 1944; National War College, Washington, DC, deputy for foreign affairs, 1946; U.S. Department of State, director of policy planning staff, 1947, counselor, 1949-50; U.S. ambassador to USSR, 1952; U.S. ambassador to Yugoslavia, 1961-63. Assisted U.S. ambassador to Moscow in reopening American Embassy, 1933. University of Chicago, Charles R. Walgreen Foundation lecturer, 1951; Princeton University, Stafford Little lecturer, 1954, professor, 1963-64; Institute for Advanced Study, Princeton, NJ, professor, 1956-74, professor emeritus, 1974—. Balliol College, Oxford, George Eastman visiting professor, 1957-58; Harvard University, visiting lecturer, 1960, university fellow, 1965-69. Kennan Institute for Advanced Russian Studies, Washington, DC, founder, 1975. Member of National Advisory Council for the W. Averell Harriman Institute for Advanced Study of the Soviet Union at Columbia University; member of Council on Foreign Relations.

MEMBER: American Philosophical Society, National Institute of Arts and Letters (president, 1965-67; director), American Academy of Arts and Letters (president, 1968-72), Order of Pour le Mérite for Arts and Sciences (Germany), American Academy of Diplomacy (member emeritus, 1985—), Century Association, British Academy for the Promotion of Historical, Philosophical, and Philological Studies, Royal Society for the Encouragement of Arts, Manufactures, and Commerce (Benjamin Franklin fellow, 1968—).

AWARDS, HONORS: Freedom House Award, 1951, for *American Diplomacy, 1900-1950;* Pulitzer Prize in history, National Book Award, Bancroft Prize, and Francis Parkman Prize, all 1957, for *Russia Leaves the War;* Pulitzer Prize in biography, National Book Award, and Overseas Press Club of America award, all 1968, for *Memoirs, 1925-1950;* All Souls College fellow, Oxford, 1969; Director General's Cup, American Foreign Service Association, 1973; Emory Buckner Medal, Federal Bar Council of New York, 1973; Knight Commander's Cross, Federal Republic of Germany, 1973; John F. Lewis Prize, American Philosophical Society, 1974; Woodrow Wilson International Center for Scholars fellow, 1974-75; Woodrow Wilson Award, Princeton University, 1976; American Book Award nomination, 1980, for *The Decline of Bismarck's European Order: Franco-Russian Relations, 1875-1890;* Albert Einstein Peace Prize, 1981; Grenville Clark Prize, 1981; Pacem in Terris Peace and Freedom Award, Quad City Peace and Justice Coalition, 1982; Börsenverein Peace Prize, Frankfurt, 1982; Peace Prize, German Book Trade, 1982; Union Medal, Union Theological Seminary, 1982; Charles E. Merriam Award, American Political Science Association, 1984; Gold Medal for History, American Academy and Institute of Arts and Letters, 1984; National Book Critics Circle nomination, 1984, for *The Fateful Alliance: France, Russia, and the Coming of the First World War;* James Madison Award, Whig-Cliosophic Society, Princeton University, 1985; Literary Lion Award, New York City Public Library, 1985; Creative Arts Award for Nonfiction, Brandeis University, 1986; Freedom from Fear Award, Four Freedoms Foundation of the Franklin and Eleanor Roosevelt Institute, 1987; Physicians for Social Responsibility Award, 1988; Toynbee Prize, 1988; Encyclopaedia Britannica Award, 1989; Presidential Medal of Freedom, 1989; Woodrow Wilson Public Service Award, 1990; Coalition for Nuclear Disarmament Tribute, 1990; honored by 'George F. Kennan Week,' City of Milwaukee, May 7 to 12, 1990; Outstanding Achievement Award, Wisconsin Library Association, 1990; Distinguished Service Award, 1993; Decorated Officer Order, Federal Republic of Germany, for merit.

Received numerous honorary degrees from colleges and universities, including Princeton University, LL.D., 1956; Yale University, LL.D., and Dartmouth College, LL.D., both 1950; Colgate University, LL.D., 1951; University of Notre Dame, LL.D., 1953; Kenyon College, LL.D., 1954; New School of Social Research, LL.D., 1955; University of Michigan, LL.D., and Northwestern University, LL.D., both 1957; Brandeis University, LL.D., 1958; University of Wisconsin—Madison, LL.D., and Harvard University, LL.D., both

1963; Rutgers University, LL.D., and Denison University, LL.D., both 1966; Ripon College, LL.D., 1968; Oxford University, D.C.L., 1969; Marquette University, LL.D., 1972; Catholic University of America, LL.D., 1976; Duke University, LL.D., 1977; Dickinson College, LL.D., 1979; Lake Forest College, LL.D., 1982; Clark University, LL.D., Oberlin College, LL.D., and Brown University, LL.D., all 1983; New York University, LL.D., 1985; Columbia University, LL.D., College of William and Mary, LL.D., and University of Helinski, all 1986; New York University, 1987; and Rider College, 1988.

WRITINGS:

American Diplomacy, 1900-1950, University of Chicago Press (Chicago, IL), 1951, expanded edition with new foreword published as *American Diplomacy,* 1984.

Das amerikanisch-russische Verhältnis, Deutsche Verlags-Anstalt, 1954.

Realities of American Foreign Policy, Princeton University Press (Princeton, NJ), 1954.

Soviet-American Relations, 1917-1920, Princeton University Press (Princeton, NJ), Volume 1: *Russia Leaves the War,* 1956, Volume 2: *The Decision to Intervene,* 1958.

Russia, the Atom, and the West, Harper (New York, NY), 1957.

Soviet Foreign Policy, 1917-1941, Van Nostrand (Princeton, NJ), 1960.

Russia and the West under Lenin and Stalin, Little, Brown (Boston, MA), 1961.

On Dealing with the Communist World, Harper (New York, NY), 1964.

Memoirs, 1925-1950, Little, Brown (Boston, MA), 1967.

Democracy and the Student Left, Little, Brown (Boston, MA), 1968.

From Prague after Munich: Diplomatic Papers, 1938-1940, Princeton University Press (Princeton, NJ), 1968.

The Marquis de Custine and His "Russia in 1839," Princeton University Press (Princeton, NJ), 1971.

Memoirs, 1950-1963, Little, Brown (Boston, MA), 1972.

The Cloud of Danger: Current Realities of American Foreign Policy, Little, Brown (Boston, MA), 1977.

The Decline of Bismarck's European Order: Franco-Russian Relations, 1875-1890, Princeton University Press (Princeton, NJ), 1979.

The Nuclear Delusion: Soviet-American Relations in the Atomic Age, Pantheon (New York, NY), 1982, revised edition, 1983.

The Fateful Alliance: France, Russia, and the Coming of the First World War, Pantheon (New York, NY), 1984.

On Russian Diplomacy in the 19th Century and the Origins of World War I, Kennan Institute for Advanced Russian Studies (Washington, DC), 1986.

George F. Kennan on Russian Society and U.S.-Soviet Relations, Kennan Institute for Advanced Russian Studies (Washington, DC), 1987.

Sketches from a Life, Pantheon (New York, NY), 1989.

The German Problem: A Personal View, American Institute for Contemporary German Studies (Washington, DC), 1989.

Measures Short of War: The George F. Kennan Lectures at the National War College, 1946-47, edited by Giles D. Harlow and George C. Maerz, National Defense University Press (Washington, DC), 1991.

Around the Cragged Hill: A Personal and Political Philosophy, Norton (New York, NY), 1992.

At a Century's Ending: Reflections, 1982-1995, Norton (New York, NY), 1996.

George F. Kennan and the Origins of Containment, 1944-46: The Kennan-Lukacs Correspondence, University of Missouri Press (Columbia, MO), 1997.

An American Family: The Kennans—the First Three Generations, Norton (New York, NY), 2000.

Also contributor to *South Africa: Three Visitors Report,* Munger Africana Library (Pasadena, CA), 1971. Contributor to numerous periodicals, sometimes under the psuedonym "X," including *Foreign Affairs.*

SIDELIGHTS: George F. Kennan is an internationally renowned historian and former high-ranking diplomat whose contributions to American policy have been both scholarly and immediate. As one of the nation's foremost kremlinologists—and for a time the leading authority on the former Soviet Union—Kennan helped to define and describe the issues dividing America and the Soviet Union at the beginning of the Cold War. Kennan's controversial views on "containment" of Soviet aggression formed a basis for U.S. diplomatic and military efforts for two decades, although Kennan himself deplored nuclear proliferation and the wars in Korea and Vietnam. As a writer uniquely positioned to view, influence, and comment upon important moments in twentieth-century history, his worldview "has great merit as an explanatory tool for the past and as a guiding principle for the present and the future," according to Mary Ann Heiss in *Historian.*

Kennan entered the fledgling Foreign Service after graduating from Princeton University and spent the next two decades working as a diplomat in Europe. He elected to study Russian and, in 1933, became assistant to William C. Bullitt, the first American ambassador to the Soviet Union. At a time when Americans were unaware of the abuses practiced by Joseph Stalin, Kennan viewed them firsthand, and the experience influenced his view of Soviet political philosophy and Soviet intentions outside Russia. Kennan served in a variety of important positions during World War II, spending time in Prague, Berlin, Lisbon, and London. He returned to the Soviet Union in 1944 as aide to U.S. ambassador W. Averell Harriman.

Kennan made his mark on history in February of 1946, when he authored the celebrated "Long Telegram" from Moscow. In the 8,000-word document, he urged U.S. officials to treat the Soviet regime with extreme suspicion and caution. He warned that America would have to assume a role of "Great Power" in order to thwart the international expansionist aims of the Soviet Union. Lastly, he spoke candidly about the Stalin administration's contempt for Western treaties and capitalist values. The Long Telegram found its way to the desk of President Harry Truman and most of his closest advisors. When Kennan followed that work a year later with a *Foreign Affairs* piece called "The Sources of Soviet Conduct," published under the pseudonym "X," he gained national renown. It was in the *Foreign Affairs* piece that he proposed the idea of "containing" Soviet expansion—but he advocated using diplomatic and economic means, while American leaders commenced the military buildup that became known as the Cold War.

In November of 1952 Kennan retired from government service and took a position with Princeton University's Institute for Advanced Study. It was there that he prepared his books and lectures on U.S.-Soviet relations and on other aspects of Russian diplomatic history. His works have aroused considerable debate, particularly as he questioned the central tenets of democracy and integration. According to Gabriel Schoenfeld in *Commentary*, by the 1980s Kennan "was still an advocate of containment—no longer, however, of the USSR, but of a country he had come to regard as even more dangerous to peace on earth, namely, the United States."

Commenting on *The Fateful Alliance: France, Russia, and the Coming of the First World War, Los Angeles Times Book Review* critic Peter deLeon wrote of Kennan: "His discussions of contemporary United States-Soviet Union relations and his more recent warnings of an unremitting nuclear arms race mark him as an august man of letters. *The Fateful Alliance* amply demonstrates his skills as a diplomatic historian blessed with literary

deftness." Even from those who disagreed with his views, Kennan received praise for his far-reaching knowledge as well as for his ability to make complex political issues accessible to the average reader. H. Stuart Hughes noted in a *Nation* review of *American Democracy, 1900-1950,* "It is a rare event when a book appears that exactly fills a long-recognized need—a book dealing with a subject of critical importance and written by a man uniquely qualified to speak with authority. It is even more remarkable when the book in question proves to be brief, well written, and so simple and direct in presentation that it can be read with ease by any reasonably informed citizen." A reviewer for the *Times Literary Supplement* described *Russia Leaves the War* as "one of those intensive and highly specialized works of original historical research which are becoming increasingly rare in our time and are therefore all the more welcome."

"For more than half a century, the diplomatic dispatches and political and historical writings of George F. Kennan have enriched and enlivened American public debates and our intellectual and academic scenes," Don Cook stated in the *Los Angeles Times Book Review,* "It is difficult to name another American writer who has been so intellectually stimulating over such a long period, and who has commanded such constant attention on the great problems of the nuclear age." Jerome B. Wiesner, reviewing *The Nuclear Delusion: Soviet-American Relations in the Atomic Age* for the *Washington Post Book World,* asserted that Kennan "not only knows about nuclear weapons, he knows Soviet society, its history, and its driving forces well and is perhaps *the* person in the United States best qualified to discuss the complex issues that must be faced if the nation is to make rational decisions about future weapons systems."

Many reviewers have strongly disagreed with Kennan's views, yet praised him at the same time. In the *New York Times Book Review,* John Kenneth Galbraith, while disputing Kennan's views of Congress, Senator Joseph McCarthy, and the Korean War, concluded, "All of this is to say that not even Kennan is infallible. But it remains a privilege, nonetheless, to argue with this most brilliant and civilized of students of the public scene."

Kennan's views have often gone against the grain of United States political policy, particularly in his abhorrence of nuclear weaponry. *New York Review of Books* critic Ronald Steel noted this in a review of *Sketches from a Life,* one of Kennan's autobiographical works. "Over the years," Steel said, "Kennan was opposed to a considerable number of 'responsible' positions," among them the division of Germany, development of the H-bomb, support for the wars in Korea and Vietnam, and the reliance on nuclear weapons for national defense. "His campaign against instruments of mass destruction has made him a hero of the antinuclear movement," Steel continued. "His eloquent plea for the abolition of such weapons is perhaps his most famous peroration. 'For the love of God, of your children, and of the civilization to which you belong, cease this madness,' he exhorted the great powers in 1980. 'You have a duty not just to the generation of the present— you have a duty to civilization's past, which you threaten to render meaningless, and to its future, which you threaten to render nonexistent.'"

In reviewing *Sketches from a Life,* Cook noted: "In his observations Kennan reveals himself as a kind of Nineteenth-Century figure continuously saddened and lonely in the turmoil and waste and mindless profligate decay and deterioration of the way of life in the Twentieth Century." Indeed, in his epilogue to *Sketches,* Kennan wrote: "I am startled to note the bleakness of the impressions of my own country. . . . I view the United States of these last years of the Twentieth Century as essentially a tragic country, endowed with magnificent natural resources which it is rapidly wasting and exhausting, and with an intellectual and artistic intelligentsia of great talent and originality of which the dominant political forces of the country have little understanding or regard. Its voice is normally silenced or outshouted by the commercial media. It is probably condemned to remain indefinitely, like the Russian intelligentsia in the 19th Century, a helpless spectator of the disturbing course of a nation's life."

Kennan himself was a somewhat helpless spectator in the years preceding 1990, according to *Washington Post* writer Mary McGrory, who noted in 1989 that Kennan "has not been consulted by the last two or three administrations, for reasons not immediately apparent." She surmised that it may have been Kennan's tendency to be "prematurely and unfashionably right" or that his views could have been perceived as "politically inconvenient during [Ronald Reagan's]'evil empire' period." However, Kennan's insight was validated with the demise of the Cold War in the early 1990s. In a 1991 *Los Angeles Times* editorial, William Pfaff claimed, "At a time when the [George] Bush [Sr.] administration and Western leaders are arguing about the character of Boris Yeltsin and the other reform figures emerging in what used to be the Soviet Union, and attempting to analyze how to influence the upheaval there, advice from the man who foresaw the collapse of the USSR forty years ago deserves attention."

Kennan maintains great respect outside the United States, even from the leader of a country formerly hostile to his own. In *Sketches,* Kennan relates an anecdote from the 1987 summit, during which Soviet General Secretary Mikhail Gorbachev approached Kennan, grasped him by the elbows, and said, "Mr. Kennan, we in our country believe that a man may be the friend of another country and remain, at the same time, a loyal and devoted citizen of his own; and that is the way we view you." Kennan wrote, "I reflected that if you cannot have this sort of recognition from your own government to mark the end of your involvement in such a relationship, it is nice to have it at least from the one-time adversary."

Following that writing, however, Kennan's theories continued to be a guiding force in U.S. relations with the former Soviet Union. "In this, his 87th year," Pfaff observed in 1991, "he has the right to reflect, as few men can, that history has justified him."

Kennan has continued to write well into his nineties, publishing a collection of essays titled *At a Century's Ending: Reflections 1982-1995* and a history of his colonial family, *An American Family: The Kennans—The First Three Generations.* A writer for *Contemporary Review* called *An American Family* "a charming history," and "an important chapter of American history told through the annals of one family."

"As a diplomat," Schoenfeld concluded, "there can be no question that George F. Kennan made a significant contribution to the security of our country at a particularly parlous moment. As the author of a shelf-ful of historical books, some of them excellent, he has added much to our understanding of Russia in the modern era. . . . By virtue of these considerable accomplishments, he long ago gained a solid reputation with the public and the respect—better, the adulation—of many in the opinion-making elite." In *Insight on the News,* Charles M. Lichenstein commended Kennan for his "manifold contributions to unlocking the mysteries of diplomacy and of Soviet totalitarianism, and on his ability to infer lessons from the richness and specificity of contextual reality."

BIOGRAPHICAL/CRITICAL SOURCES:

BOOKS

Bucklin, Steven J., *Realism and American Foreign Policy: Wilsonians and the Kennan-Morgenthau Thesis,* Praeger (Westport, CT), 2001.

Deibel, Terry L., and John Lewis Gaddis, editors, *Containing the Soviet Union: A Critique of U.S. Policy,* Pergamon-Brassey (Washington, DC), 1987.

Encounters with Kennan: The Great Debate, Biblio Distribution Centre (Totowa, NJ), 1979.

Encyclopedia of World Biography, Gale (Detroit, MI), 1998.

Findling, John E., *Dictionary of American Diplomatic History,* Greenwood Press (Westport, CT), 1989.

Frankel, Benjamin, editor, *The Cold War, 1945-1991,* Gale (Detroit, MI), 1992.

Franklin, Laurel F., *George F. Kennan: An Annotated Bibliography,* Greenwood Press (Westport, CT), 1997.

Gellman, Barton, *Contending with Kennan: Toward a Philosophy of American Power,* Praeger (New York, NY), 1984.

Grose, Peter, *Operation Rollback: America's Secret War behind the Iron Curtain,* Houghton (Boston, MA), 2000.

Harper, John Lamberton, *American Visions of Europe: Franklin D. Roosevelt, George F. Kennan, and Dean G. Acheson,* Cambridge University Press (New York, NY), 1994.

Herz, Martin F., editor, *Decline of the West?: George Kennan and His Critics,* Ethics and Public Policy Center, Georgetown University (Washington, DC), 1978.

Hixson, Walter L., *George F. Kennan: Cold War Iconoclast,* Columbia University Press (New York, NY), 1989.

Jeepersen, T. Christopher, editor, *Interviews with George F. Kennan,* University Press of Mississippi (Jackson, MS), 2002.

Jensen, Kenneth M., and Elizabeth P. Faulkner, editors, *Morality and Foreign Policy: Realpolitik Revisited,* United States Institute of Peace (Washington, DC), 1991.

Kennan, George F., *Memoirs, 1925-50,* Little, Brown (Boston, MA), 1967.

Kennan, George F., *Memoirs, 1950-63,* Little, Brown (Boston, MA), 1972.

Kennan, George F., *Sketches from a Life,* Pantheon (New York, NY), 1989.

Mayers, David Allan, *George Kennan and the Dilemmas of U.S. Foreign Policy,* Oxford University Press (Oxford, England), 1988.

Miscamble, Wilson, *George F. Kennan and the Making of American Foreign Policy 1947-50,* Princeton University Press (Princeton, NJ), 1992.

Russell, Richard L., *George F. Kennan's Strategic Thought: The Making of an American Political Realist,* Praeger (Westport, CT), 2000.

Stephanson, Anders, *George F. Kennan and the Art of Foreign Policy,* Harvard University Press (Cambridge, MA), 1989.

PERIODICALS

America, December 10, 2001, Steven F. Spahn, "Lessons from Memories Grown Cold," p. 9.

Contemporary Review, July, 2001, review of *An American Family: The Kennans,* p. 60.

Commentary, June, 1996, Gabriel Schoenfeld, review of *At a Century's Ending: Reflections 1982-1985,* p. 59.

Foreign Affairs, July, 1947; April, 1951; July, 1955; January, 1959; January, 1960; January, 1964; October, 1964; April, 1970; January, 1971; October, 1972; July, 1976; spring, 1982; winter, 1984; winter, 1985; spring, 1987; spring, 1990; winter, 1990; July-August, 1996, David C. Hendrickson, review of *At a Century's Ending,* p. 145; September-October, 1997, David C. Hendrickson, "American Diplomacy," p. 222.

Historian, fall, 2000, Mary Ann Heiss, review of *George F. Kennan's Strategic Thought: The Making of an American Political Realist,* p. 167.

Insight on the News, February 8, 1993, Charles M. Lichenstein, review of *Around the Cragged Hill: A Personal and Political Philosophy,* p. 21.

Library Journal, February 15, 1997, James Holmes, review of *George F. Kennan and the Origins of Containment, 1944-1946: The Kennan-Lukacs Correspondence,* p. 149.

Los Angeles Times, July 15, 1991, p. 8.

Los Angeles Times Book Review, November 18, 1984, pp. 1, 14; May 14, 1989, pp. 1, 7.

Nation, October 6, 1951; December 11, 1967, p. 634.

National Review, September 6, 1985, "Kennan's Mind."

New Republic, January 28, 2002, Isaiah Berlin, "On Human Dignity—A Letter to George Kennan," p. 23.

Newsweek, October 22, 1984, p. 93.

New Yorker, November 13, 2000, Nicholas Lemann, "The Provocateur," p. 94.

New York Review of Books, August 17, 1989, Ronald Steel, review of *Sketches from a Life,* pp. 3-5; August 8, 1996, Walter J. Zimmerman, "Prophet without Honor," p. 4; August 12, 1999, "The U.S. and the World: An Interview with George Kennan," p. 4.

New York Times, October 26, 1982, p. 26; October 17, 1984; May 1, 1989.

New York Times Book Review, October 8, 1972, pp. 1, 12; January 3, 1993, George F. Will, review of *Around the Cragged Hill,* p. 7; April 7, 1996, Fareed Zakaria, review of *At a Century's Ending,* p. 6; December 17, 2000, Michael Lind, "Roots," p. 12.

Political Science Quarterly, winter, 1993, Anders Stephanson, review of *Around the Cragged Hill,* p. 758.

Publishers Weekly, January 29, 1996, review of *At a Century's Ending: Reflections, 1982-1995,* p. 93.

Times (London), January 12, 1984; January 17, 1985.

Times Literary Supplement, January 4, 1957, p. 1; August 25, 1961.

Washington Post, April 9, 1989; November 16, 2000, Jonathan Yardley, "Slivers from the Family Tree," p. C2.

Washington Post Book World, November 21, 1982, Jerome B. Wiesner, review of *The Nuclear Delusion: Soviet-American Relations in the Atomic Age,* p. 5.*

* * *

KONIGSBURG, E(laine) L(obl) 1930-

PERSONAL: Born February 10, 1930, in New York, NY; daughter of Adolph (a businessman) and Beulah (Klein) Lobl; married David Konigsburg (a psychologist), July 6, 1952; children: Paul, Laurie, Ross. *Education:* Carnegie Mellon University, B.S., 1952; graduate study, University of Pittsburgh, 1952-54. *Religion:* Jewish.

ADDRESSES: Office—c/o Atheneum Books for Young Readers, 1230 Avenue of the Americas, New York, NY 10020.

CAREER: Writer. Shenango Valley Provision Co., Sharon, PA, bookkeeper, 1947- 48; Bartram School, Jacksonville, FL, science teacher, 1954-55, 1960-62. Worked as manager of a dormitory laundry, playground instructor, waitress, and library page while in college; research assistant in tissue culture lab while in graduate school at the University of Pittsburgh.

AWARDS, HONORS: Honor book, *Book Week,* Children's Spring Book Fair, 1967, and Newbery Honor Book, American Library Association (ALA), 1968, both for *Jennifer, Hecate, Macbeth, William McKinley, and Me, Elizabeth;* Newbery Medal, ALA, 1968, Lewis Carroll Shelf Award, 1968, and William Allen White Award, 1970, all for *From the Mixed-up Files of Mrs. Basil E. Frankweiler;* Carnegie Mellon Merit Award, 1971; Notable Children's Book, ALA, and National Book Award finalist, both 1974, both for *A Proud Taste for Scarlet and Miniver;* Notable Children's Book, ALA, and American Book Award nomination, both 1980, both for *Throwing Shadows; Jennifer, Hecate, Macbeth, William McKinley, and Me, Elizabeth, About the B'nai Bagels, A Proud Taste for Scarlet and Miniver,* and *Journey to an 800 Number* were all chosen Children's Books of the Year by the Child Study Association of America; Notable Children's Book, ALA, Parents' Choice Award for Literature, and Notable Children's Trade Book for the Language Arts, National Council of Teachers of English, all 1987, all for *Up from Jericho Tel;* Special Recognition Award, Cultural Council of Greater Jacksonville, FL, 1997; Newbery Medal, ALA, 1997, for *The View from Saturday;* Best Books for Young Adults selections, ALA, for *The Second Mrs. Giaconda* and *Father's Arcane Daughter.*

WRITINGS:

FOR CHILDREN; SELF-ILLUSTRATED

Jennifer, Hecate, Macbeth, William McKinley, and Me, Elizabeth, Atheneum (New York, NY), 1967, published as *Jennifer, Hecate, MacBeth, and Me,* Macmillan (London, England), 1968.

From the Mixed-up Files of Mrs. Basil E. Frankweiler, Atheneum (New York, NY), 1967.

About the B'nai Bagels, Atheneum (New York, NY), 1969.

(George), Atheneum (New York, NY), 1970, published as *Benjamin Dickenson Carr and His (George),* Penguin (Harmondsworth, England), 1974.

A Proud Taste for Scarlet and Miniver, Atheneum (New York, NY), 1973.

The Dragon in the Ghetto Caper, Atheneum (New York, NY), 1974.

Samuel Todd's Book of Great Colors, Macmillan, 1990.

Samuel Todd's Book of Great Inventions, Atheneum (New York, NY), 1991.

Amy Elizabeth Explores Bloomingdale's, Atheneum (New York, NY), 1992.

FOR CHILDREN

Altogether, One at a Time (short stories), illustrated by Gail E. Haley, Mercer Meyer, Gary Parker, and Laurel Schindelman, Atheneum (New York, NY), 1971, second edition, Macmillan, 1989.

The Second Mrs. Giaconda, illustrated with museum plates, Atheneum (New York, NY), 1975.

Father's Arcane Daughter, Atheneum (New York, NY), 1976.

Throwing Shadows (short stories), Atheneum (New York, NY), 1979.

Journey to an 800 Number, Atheneum (New York, NY), 1982, published as *Journey by First Class Camel,* Hamish Hamilton (London, England), 1983.

Up from Jericho Tel, Atheneum (New York, NY), 1986.

T-Backs, T-Shirts, COAT, and Suit, Atheneum (New York, NY), 1993.

The View from Saturday, Atheneum (New York, NY), 1996.

Silent to the Bone, Atheneum (New York, NY), 2000.

FOR ADULTS; NONFICTION

The Mask beneath the Face: Reading about and with, Writing about and for Children, Library of Congress, 1990.

TalkTalk: A Children's Book Author Speaks to Grown-Ups, Atheneum (New York, NY), 1995.

OTHER

Also author of promotional pamphlets for Atheneum and contributor to the Braille anthology, *Expectations 1980,* Braille Institute, 1980; subject of a videocassette interview by Tim Podell Productions, *Good Conversation!: A Talk with E. L. Konigsburg,* 1995.

Collections of E. L. Konigsburg's manuscripts and original art are held at the University of Pittsburgh, PA.

ADAPTATIONS: From the Mixed-up Files of Mrs. Basil E. Frankweiler was adapted for a record and cassette, Miller-Brody/Random House, 1969; a motion picture, starring Ingrid Bergman, Cinema 5, 1973, released as *The Hideaways,* Bing Crosby Productions, 1974; and a television movie, starring Lauren Bacall, 1995. *Jennifer, Hecate, Macbeth, William McKinley, and Me, Elizabeth* was adapted for a television movie titled *Jennifer and Me,* NBC-TV, 1973, and for a cassette, Listening Library, 1986. *The Second Mrs. Giaconda* was adapted for a play, first produced in Jacksonville, FL, 1976. *Father's Arcane Daughter* was adapted for television as *Caroline?,* for the Hallmark Hall of Fame, 1990. *About the B'nai Bagels* and *From the Mixed-up Files of Mrs. Basil E. Frankweiler* are available as Talking Books. *From the Mixed-up Files of Mrs. Basil E. Frankweiler* is also available in Braille.

SIDELIGHTS: An impressive figure in children's literature, E. L. Konigsburg is the only author to have had two books on the Newbery list at the same time. *From the Mixed-up Files of Mrs. Basil E. Frankweiler* won the 1968 Newbery Medal and *Jennifer, Hecate, Macbeth, William McKinley, and Me, Elizabeth* was a runner-up for the award in the same year. Konigsburg

has also won not one but two of the coveted Newbery Medals, capturing the 1997 award for *The View from Saturday.* Known for her witty and often self-illustrated works for young people, Konigsburg has carved out a unique niche with her score of published books, generally writing out of personal experience, but sometimes also verging far afield to the medieval world and the Renaissance. As Perry Nodelman noted in *Dictionary of Literary Biography,* Konigsburg is an innovator and tireless experimenter, "a creator of interesting messes." The term "messes" is for Nodelman hardly pejorative; rather, it is an indication of a truly artistic temperament at work.

Konigsburg did not set her sights on writing as a career until later in life. Born in New York City, in 1930, she was the middle of three daughters. She grew up in small towns in Pennsylvania, not only absorbing books such as *The Secret Garden* and *Mary Poppins,* but also much unabashed "trash along the lines of *True Confessions,*" as she once reported in *Saturday Review.* "I have no objection to trash. I've read a lot of it and firmly believe it helped me hone my taste." Konigsburg also mentioned that as a child she did much of her reading in the bathroom because "it was the only room in our house that had a lock on the door." She also drew often as a child and was a good student in school, graduating valedictorian of her class. Yet for a young person growing up in the small mill towns of Pennsylvania as Konigsburg did, college was not necessarily the next step. There were advantages to such an upbringing, however. As Konigsburg has commented, "Growing up in a small town gives you two things: a sense of place and a feeling of self-consciousness—self-consciousness about one's education and exposure, both of which tend to be limited. On the other hand, limited possibilities also means creating your own options. A small town allows you to grow in your own direction, without a bombardment of outside stimulation."

And that is precisely what Konigsburg did—she grew in her own way and decided to head for college. Completely ignorant of such things as scholarships, she devised a plan whereby she would alternate working for a year with a year of school. The first year out of high school she took a bookkeeping job at a local meat plant where she met the brother of one of the owners—the man who would become her husband, David Konigsburg. The following year, Konigsburg enrolled in Carnegie Mellon University in Pittsburgh, choosing to major in chemistry. She survived not a few laboratory accidents to eventually take her degree in chemistry. Early in her college career, however, a helpful instructor directed her to scholarships and work-study assistance, so that she was able to continue her studies without break. Konigsburg noted that college was "a crucial 'opening up'" period. "I worked hard and did well. However, the artistic side of me was essentially dormant." She graduated with honors, married David Konigsburg, and went on for graduate study at the University of Pittsburgh. Meanwhile, her husband was also studying, preparing himself for a career in industrial psychology. When her husband won a post in Jacksonville, Florida, Konigsburg picked up and moved with him, working for several years as a science teacher in an all-girls school. The teaching experience opened up a new world for her, giving her insight into the lives of these young girls whom she expected to be terribly spoiled. But she quickly learned that economic ease did nothing to ease inner problems.

Konigsburg left teaching in 1955 after the birth of her first child, Paul. A year later a daughter, Laurie, was born, and in 1959 a third child, Ross. Konigsburg became a full-time mom, taking some time out, however, to pursue painting. She returned to teaching from 1960-1962 until her husband's work required a move to New York. With all the children in school, Konigsburg then started her writing career. She employed themes and events close to her family life for her books. She also used her children as her first audience, reading them her morning's work when they came home for lunch. Laughter would encourage her to continue in the same vein; glum faces prompted revision and rewrites. Konigsburg once commented that she had noticed that her kids were growing up very differently from the way she did, but that their growing up "was related to this middle-class kind of child I had seen when I had taught at the private girls' school. I recognized that I wanted to write something that reflected their kind of growing up, something that addressed the problems that come about even though you don't have to worry if you wear out your shoes whether your parents can buy you a new pair, something that tackles the basic problems of who am I? What makes me the same as everyone else? What makes me different?"

Such questions led Konigsburg to her first two books, *Jennifer, Hecate, Macbeth, William McKinley, and Me, Elizabeth,* inspired by her daughter's experience making friends in their new home in Port Chester, New York, and *From the Mixed-up Files of Mrs. Basil E. Frankweiler,* which was inspired by the finicky manner in which her kids behaved on a picnic. Konigsburg also illustrated both these books, as she has many of her titles, using her children as models. The first novel tells the story of Elizabeth, who is new in town, and her at-

tempts at finding friendship. It does not help that she is small for her age, and Cynthia, the cool kid in school, is quick to dismiss her. But then Elizabeth meets Jennifer, another classic outsider who styles herself as a witch. Elizabeth soon becomes her apprentice, and suddenly life is full of adventures. Jennifer is a source of mystery for Elizabeth: she never lets the new girl know where or how she lives, and this is just fine for Elizabeth, smitten by Jennifer to the point of declaring that even if she "discovered that Jennifer lived in an ordinary house and did ordinary things, I would know it was a disguise."

Nodelman noted that, baldly told, the story sounds like a "typical wish-fulfillment novel. . . . [But] as its title suggests this is no ordinary novel. It is too witty." As Nodelman pointed out, Elizabeth comes face to face with the important issue of what it means to be "normal," and decides not to worry about that. "The idea that it is better to be yourself than to be 'normal' and accepted by others transcends the cheap egocentricity of most wish-fulfillment fantasies," according to Nodelman. It is this extra dimension of story-telling that has set Konigsburg apart from other children's writers from the outset of her career. She eschews the easy solution and turns cliches on their head. Critical reception for this first book was quite positive. *Booklist* contributor Ruth P. Bull called it "a fresh, lively story, skillfully expressed," and a contributor for *Publishers Weekly* warned against allowing a too-cute title scare readers away from "one of the freshest, funniest books of the season." This same reviewer went on presciently to say that the reader will have "the smug pleasure" of saying in later years—when the author would surely make a name for herself—that he or she had read Konigsburg when she was just beginning. Writing in *Horn Book,* Ruth Hill Viguers also praised the book, noting that the story "is full of humor and of situations completely in tune with the imaginations of ten-year-old girls."

Konigsburg's second novel, *From the Mixed-up Files of Mrs. Basil E. Frankweiler,* was published shortly after her first. Following a family picnic in Yellowstone Park in which Konigsburg's children complained of the insects and the warm milk and the general lack of civilization, Konigsburg came to the realization that if they should ever run away from home, they would surely carry with them all the stuffy suburban ways that were so inbred in them. This started her thinking of a pair of children who run away from home to the Metropolitan Museum of Art, a safe sort of imitation of far-away places. Claudia, tired of being taken for granted at home, plans to run away and takes her younger brother

Jamie—the one with a sense for finances—with her on this safe adventure. Together they elude guards at the Met, sleep on royal beds, bathe in the cafeteria pool, and hang about lecture tours during the day. Their arrival at the museum coincides with the showing of a recent museum acquisition, a marble angel believed to have been sculpted by Michelangelo. Soon they are under the spell of the angel and want to know the identity of the carver, and this brings them to the statue's former owner, Mrs. Frankweiler. The story is narrated in the form of a letter from Mrs. Frankweiler to her lawyer, and it is she who confronts Claudia with the truth about herself. "Returning with a secret is what she really wants," says Mrs. Frankweiler. "Claudia doesn't want adventure. She likes baths and feeling comfortable too much for that kind of thing. Secrets are the kind of adventure she needs. Secrets are safe, and they do much to make you different. On the inside, where it counts."

Booklist reviewer Bull concluded that this second novel was "fresh and crisply written" with "uncommonly real and likable characters," and Bull praised the humor and dialogue as well. Viguers, writing in *Horn Book*, noted that the novel violated every rule of writing for children, yet was still "one of the most original stories of many years." A *Kirkus Reviews* critic commented that whereas Konigsburg's first title is a "dilly," this one is a "dandy—just as fast and fresh and funny, but less spoofing, more penetrating." Plaudits continued from Alice Fleming, who noted in the *New York Times Book Review* that Konigsburg "is a lively, amusing and painlessly educational storyteller," and from *Washington Post Book World* reviewer Polly Goodwin, who commented that the book is "an exceptional story, notable for superlative writing, fresh humor, an original theme, clear-eyed understanding of children, and two young protagonists whom readers will find funny, real and unforgettable." Award committees agreed with the reviewers, and for the first time in its history, the Newbery list contained two titles by the same author.

In Konigsburg's acceptance speech for her first Newbery, she talked about her overriding feeling of owing kids a good story. "[I try to] let the telling be like fudge-ripple ice cream. You keep licking the vanilla, but every now and then you come to something richer and deeper and with a stronger flavor." Her books all explore this richer and deeper territory, while employing humor in large doses. However, instant success is a hard act to follow, and her third book, *About the B'nai Bagels,* a Little League baseball story with a Jewish Mother twist, was not as well received as the first two. A further suburban tale is *(George),* Konigsburg's "most unusual, messiest, and most interesting book," according to

Nodelman. Ben is a twelve-year-old with an inner voice he calls George who acts as a sort of higher intelligence and conscience for the boy. When Ben, who is a bright student, is placed in a high school chemistry class, George starts acting out, causing a crisis of identity.

A fascination for medieval times led Konigsburg to a major departure from suburban themes with her *A Proud Taste for Scarlet and Miniver,* a historical fantasy—told from the participants' points of view in heaven— about the life of Eleanor of Aquitaine. Though some critics found the book to be too modern for the subject, in the *Bulletin of the Center for Children's Books* Zena Sutherland called it "one of the most fresh, imaginative, and deft biographies to come along in a long, long time." Paul Heins, writing in *Horn Book,* also noted that Konigsburg's drawings "are skillfully as well as appropriately modeled upon medieval manuscript illuminations and add their share of joy to the book." Following in this historical vein is *The Second Mrs. Giaconda,* the story of Leonardo da Vinci's middle years. Konigsburg posits a solution to the riddle of the Mona Lisa and serves up a "unique bit of creative historical interpretation" with a glimpse of Renaissance culture she has "artfully and authentically illumined," according to Shirley M. Wilton in *School Library Journal.* Another more experimental novel—though in theme rather than period—is *Father's Arcane Daughter,* a mystery. The novel tells of the return of Caroline after having been kidnapped and presumed dead seventeen years earlier. The story focuses on the effects of Caroline's reappearance on her father, his new wife, and their children in a "haunting, marvelously developed plot," according to a reviewer in *Publishers Weekly.*

Konigsburg returned to more familiar ground with *The Dragon in the Ghetto Caper* and *Throwing Shadows,* the latter a group of short stories nominated for an American Book Award. Both *Journey to an 800 Number* and *Amy Elizabeth Explores Bloomingdale's* are vintage Konigsburg, the second of which tells the story of a girl and her grandmother trying to find the time to see Bloomingdale's. A reviewer for *Publishers Weekly* called the book a "vivid portrait of a distraction-filled city—and of a most affectionate relationship." *Up from Jericho Tel* relates the encounter between the ghost of a dead actress and two children, who are turned invisible and sent out with a group of street performers to search for a missing necklace. "A witty, fast-paced story," is how a reviewer in *Publishers Weekly* characterized the novel. A contributor to the *Bulletin of the Center for Children's Books,* reviewing *Up from Jericho Tel,* provided a summation of Konigsburg's distinctive gift to children's literature: "Whether she is writing a realistic or a fanciful story, Konigsburg always provides fresh ideas, tart wit and humor, and memorable characters."

With *T-Backs, T-Shirts, COAT, and Suit,* Konigsburg proved that she not only still had the knack for a weird title but also for telling a story. Young Chloe spends the summer in Florida with her stepfather's sister, who runs a meals-on-wheels van and becomes involved in a controversy over T-back swimming suits. Rachel Axelrod, reviewing the book in *Voice of Youth Advocates,* concluded that Konigsburg "has produced another winner!"

The View from Saturday tells the story of four members of a championship quiz bowl team and the paraplegic teacher who coaches them. A series of first-person narratives from the students display links between their lives in a story that is "glowing with humor and dusted with magic," according to a critic in *Publishers Weekly.* Julie Cummins concluded in *School Library Journal* that "brilliant writing melds with crystalline characterizations in this sparkling story that is a jewel in the author's crown of outstanding work." Konigsburg won the 1997 Newbery Medal for this novel, her second in three decades of writing. Commenting on the connection between *The View from Saturday* and Konigsburg's previous medal winner, *The Mixed-up Files of Mrs. Basil E. Frankweiler,* the author's daughter, Laurie Konigsburg Todd, noted in *Horn Book:* "Although the inspiration for these Newbery books was as disparate as the three decades which separate their publication, their theme is the same. In fact, every one of E. L. Konigsburg's . . . novels are about children who seek, find, and ultimately enjoy who they are. Despite this common denominator, [her] writing is the antithesis of the formula book. Her characters are one-of-a-kind."

More one-of-a-kind characters are served up in *Silent to the Bone,* the story of a thirteen-year-old wrongly accused of injuring his baby sister. Branwell, shocked by such an accusation, loses the power of speech, and it is left to his friend Connor to reach out to him and discover the truth about what really happened. Accused by the English au pair of dropping and shaking his infant half-sister, Branwell cannot defend himself and is confined at a juvenile center. Employing handwritten flash cards, Connor is able to piece together the events leading up to the 911 call that opens the book. By the end of this journey of discovery, not only is the real villain revealed, but both Bran and Connor have come to grips with larger truths in their own lives, including the dynamics of stepfamilies. "No one is better than Konigsburg at plumbing the hearts and minds of smart, savvy kinds," commented *Horn Book* critic Peter D. Sieruta,

who called *Silent to the Bone* an "edgy, thought-provoking novel . . . written with Konigsburg's characteristic wit and perspicuity." *Booklist's* Hazel Rochman pleaded for a second reading of the book, not simply for clues to the identity of the real perpetrator, but for "the wit, and insight, the farce, and the gentleness of the telling." Reviewing the novel in the *New York Times Book Review,* Roger Sutton commented that Konigsburg "is one of our brainiest writers for young people, not only in the considerable cerebral powers she brings to her books but in the intellectual demands she makes on her characters."

Some of Konigsburg's characters, such as Jennifer, Elizabeth, and Claudia, have become not only best friends to readers, but also telegraphic symbols of complex emotions and adolescent conditions. "The strong demands Konigsburg makes of her characters and the fine moral intelligence she gives them imply much respect for children, a respect she has continued to express in all of her books," asserted Nodelman. A writer who takes her craft seriously yet who manages to avoid heavy-handed thematic writing, Konigsburg views children's books as "the primary vehicle for keeping alive the means of linear learning," as she wrote in *TalkTalk: A Children's Book Author Speaks to Grown-Ups.* "[Children's books] are the key to the accumulated wisdom, wit, gossip, truth, myth, history, philosophy, and recipes for salting potatoes during the past 6,000 years of civilization. Children's books are the Rosetta Stone to the hearts and minds of writers from Moses to Mao. And that is the last measure in the growth of children's literature as I've witnessed it—a growing necessity."

BIOGRAPHICAL/CRITICAL SOURCES:

BOOKS

Children's Literature Review, Volume 1, Gale (Detroit, MI), 1976.
Dictionary of Literary Biography, Volume 52: *American Writers for Children from 1960, Fiction,* Gale (Detroit, MI), 1986.
Hanks, Dorrel Thomas, *E. L. Konigsburg,* Twayne, 1992.
Konigsburg, E. L., *From the Mixed-up Files of Mrs. Basil E. Frankweiler,* Atheneum, 1967.
Konigsburg, E. L., *Jennifer, Hecate, Macbeth, William McKinley, and Me, Elizabeth,* Atheneum, 1967.
Konigsburg, E. L., *TalkTalk: A Children's Book Author Speaks to Grown-Ups,* Atheneum, 1995.

Schwartz, Narda, *Articles on Women Writers,* Volume 2, ABC-Clio, 1986.

Twentieth-Century Children's Writers, fourth edition, St. James Press (Detroit, MI), 1995.

PERIODICALS

Booklist, June 1, 1967, Ruth P. Bull, review of *Jennifer, Hecate, Macbeth, William McKinley, and Me, Elizabeth,* p. 1048; October 1, 1967, Ruth P. Bull, review of *From the Mixed-up Files of Mrs. Basil E. Frankweiler,* p. 199; May 1, 1986, p. 1313; December 15, 1998, p. 751; March 15, 1999, pp. 1349-1350; August, 2000, Hazel Rochman, review of *Silent to the Bone,* p. 2135.

Bulletin of the Center for Children's Books, June, 1967, p. 155; February, 1971, p. 94; September, 1971, pp. 10-11; September, 1973, Zena Sutherland, review of *A Proud Taste for Scarlet and Miniver,* pp. 10-11; January, 1976, p. 80; September, 1976, p. 12; September, 1979, p. 10; March, 1982, p. 133; March, 1986, review of *Up from Jericho Tel,* p. 131; May, 1990, p. 216; September, 1992, p. 16; November, 1993, p. 88.

Growing Point, November, 1983, pp. 4161-4164.

Horn Book, March-April, 1967, Ruth Hill Viguers, review of *Jennifer, Hecate, Macbeth, William McKinley, and Me, Elizabeth,* pp. 206-207; September-October, 1967, Ruth Hill Viguers, review of *From the Mixed-up Files of Mrs. Basil E. Frankweiler,* p. 595; July-August, 1968, E. L. Konigsburg, "Newbery Award Acceptance," pp. 391-395; June, 1969, p. 307; September-October, 1973, Paul Heins, review of *A Proud Taste for Scarlet and Miniver,* pp. 466-467; September-October, 1975, pp. 470-471; May-June, 1982, pp. 289-290; May-June, 1986, p. 327; March-April, 1996, p. 229; January-February, 1997, p. 60; July-August, 1997, pp. 404-414; July- August, 1997, Laurie Konigsburg Todd, "E. L. Konigsburg," pp. 415-417; May-June, 1999, p. 3; November-December, 2000, Peter D. Sieruta, review of *Silent to the Bone,* p. 756.

Kirkus Reviews, July 1, 1967, review of *From the Mixed-up Files of Mrs. Basil E. Frankweiler,* p. 740; July 1, 1973, p. 685; February 1, 1986, p. 209.

New York Times Book Review, November 5, 1967, Alice Fleming, review of *From the Mixed-up Files of Mrs. Basil E. Frankweiler,* p. 44; March 30, 1969, p. 29; June 8, 1969, p. 44; October 20, 1974, p. 10; November 7, 1976, p. 44; July 5, 1980, p. 19; May 25, 1986, p. 25; April 10, 1994, p. 35; November 10, 1996, p. 49; November 19, 2000, Roger Sutton, "In the Blink of an Eye," p. 54.

Publishers Weekly, April 10, 1967, review of *Jennifer, Hecate, Macbeth, William McKinley, and Me, Elizabeth,* p. 80; September 28, 1970, pp. 78-79; July 19, 1976, review of *Father's Arcane Daughter,* p. 13; April 25, 1986, review of *Up from Jericho Tell,* p. 80; July 22, 1996, review of *The View from Saturday,* p. 242; November 11, 1997, review of *The View from Saturday,* p. 30; September 6, 1999, p. 106; September 13, 1999, review of *Amy Elizabeth Explores Bloomingdale's,* p. 86; February 14, 2000, p. 98.

Saturday Review, November 9, 1968, E. L. Konigsburg, "A Book Is a Private Thing," pp. 45-46.

School Library Journal, September, 1975, Shirley M. Wilton, review of *The Second Mrs. Giaconda,* p. 121; September, 1979, p. 141; May, 1982, p. 72; April, 1983, p. 122; May, 1986, p. 93; March, 1990, p. 208; October, 1991, p. 98; September, 1992, p. 206; October, 1993, p. 124; December, 1993, p. 26; February, 1996, p. 42; May, 1996, p. 69; September, 1996, Julie Cummins, review of *The View from Saturday,* p. 204; December, 2000, p. 54.

Teaching and Learning Literature, May-June, 1997, p. 75.

Voice of Youth Advocates, December, 1986, p. 219; December, 1993, Rachel Axelrod, review of *T-Backs, T-Shirts, COAT, and Suit,* p. 254; December, 1995, p. 335.

Washington Post Book World, November 5, 1967, Polly Goodwin, review of *From the Mixed-up Files of Mrs. Basil E. Frankweiler,* p. 22.

OTHER

Authors Online Library, http://teacher.scholastic.com/ (June 23, 2001).

E. L. Konigsburg, http://slis-two.fsu.edu/ (June 23, 2001).*

*   *   *

KOOLHAAS, Rem(ment) 1944-

PERSONAL: Born 1944 in Rotterdam, Netherlands; married Madelon Vriesendorp; children: one daughter, one son. *Education:* Architectural Association, London, England; Institute for Architecture and Urban Studies, New York, NY.

ADDRESSES: Agent—Monacelli Press, 10 East 92nd St., New York, NY 10128.

CAREER: Writer. Harvard University, Graduate School of Design, Cambridge, MA, professor of practice of architecture and urban design, 1995—. Has also taught at Columbia University, University of California, Los Angeles, Technical University of Delft, and London's Architectural Association.

AWARDS, HONORS: Harkness fellowship; Pritzker Prize, 2000.

WRITINGS:

IN ENGLISH

Delirious New York: A Retroactive Manifesto for Manhattan, Oxford University Press (New York, NY), 1978.

(With Bruce Mau) *S, M, L, XL: Office for Metropolitan Architecture,* edited by Jennifer Sigler, photography by Hans Werlemann, Monacelli Press (New York, NY), 1995.

Rem Koolhaas: Conversations with Students, edited by Sanford Kwinter, Rice University School of Architecture (Houston, TX)/Princeton Architectural Press (New York, NY), 1996.

Yves Brunier: Landscape Architect, Birkhauser, 1996.

OMA Rem Koolhaas, Birkhauser, 1998.

(With Bruce Mau) *Living,* Monacelli Press, 1999.

OMA@Work: 1972-2000, Gingko Press, 2000.

(With Norman Foster and Alessandro Mendini) *Colours,* Princeton Architectural Press, 2001.

(With others) *Mutations,* ACTAR, 2001.

(Author of introduction) *Projects for Prada Part 1,* Fondazione Prada, 2001.

Harvard Design School Guide to Shopping, TASCHEN America, 2002.

(With others) *Great Leap Forward,* TASCHEN America, 2002.

Also author of *Four Spaces, Four Architects* and *Exodus; or, The Voluntary Prisoners of Architecture.*

UNTRANSLATED WORKS

(With others) *Hoe Modern is de Nederlandse Architectuur?,* Uitgeverij 010 (Rotterdam, Netherlands), 1990.

Lille, edited by Patrice Goulet, Institut Français d'Architecture, Editions Carte Segrete (Paris, France), 1990.

Rem Koolhaas: Projectes Urbans (1985-1990), Collegi d'Arquitectes de Catalunya (Barcelona, Spain), 1990.

Six Projets/O.M.A., edited by Patrice Goulet, Institut Français d'Architecture, Editions Carte Segrete (Paris, France), 1990.

OTHER

Also author of film *The White Slave* and of unproduced screenplay. Contributor to *Atlanta,* Art Publishers, 1996.

SIDELIGHTS: Dutch architect Rem Koolhaas "is known for designs that infuse modernist geometric forms with a lyrical, at times surrealist, spirit," according to Herbert Muschamp in the *New York Times.* In addition, Koolhaas is "regarded as one of the profession's most inventive thinkers," according to a reporter for *PR Newswire.* Koolhaas, who heads the Office of Metropolitan Architecture (OMA) in Rotterdam—with offices in London and Athens—is also renowned for his writings and lectures on the layout of contemporary urban centers. Like most architects, he has detractors who flat-out deem his buildings ugly. However, he has also been a major influence in the last few decades. In April of 2000, he was awarded the Pritzker Prize for architecture.

Martin Filler wrote in *Harper's Bazaar,* "During a period where mainstream architects opportunistically embraced the historical bric-a-brac of postmodernism, Koolhaas never wavered from his high-modernist vision of the city—all gleaming glass towers and glittering steel bridges, a radiant lodestar where people would always be stimulated and the future would always be bright." Long before Koolhaas had built anything, though, he became admired for his designs and ideas; two of his books have become "talismans for young architects looking for a vision," stated Belinda Luscombe in *Time International.*

In addition, Koolhaas is praised for his constant flow of fresh ideas. "At a certain point, certain architects begin to capitalize on their success, to kind of do it again, rather than look to new territory," commented Terence Riley, a curator at the Museum of Modern Art, to Arthur Lubow in the *New York Times Magazine.* "I've never seen Rem attracted to that. Instead, there is an unbelievable willingness to keep the thing as a series of new questions."

The eldest of three children, Koolhaas was born in Rotterdam, Netherlands, in 1944. His father, Anton Koolhaas, edited a left-wing newspaper that advocated independence for Indonesia. After the nation successfully broke away, Koolhaas at age eight moved with his family to the new state, where his father served as director of a cultural institute.

In Jakarta, Indonesia, Koolhaas witnessed a shift from a rigid colonialism to a more chaotic world stemming from the budding independence. He noted to Lubow, "It was a strange coexistence between very ordered sections and disordered sections. That is the source of a kind of fundamental division of loyalties or stretch of extremes in my work."

Koolhaas began his career as a journalist, working for a weekly newspaper in Amsterdam. At the same time, he began socializing with film aficionados and tried his hand at screenwriting. He had one script produced by Dutch director Rene Daalder; it was a contemporary social commentary on Europe using old footage from B-movies called *The White Slave.* Koolhaas also wrote a screenplay for Russ Meyer, known for his low-budget films starring buxom actresses, but it never came to fruition.

At age 24, Koolhaas decided on a career change. His maternal grandfather had been an architect, so that had always been an option in his mind. After giving a speech about movies to a group of architecture students at the University of Delft, he realized he wanted to build. However, he told Lubow that he believes the two fields have much in common. "You are considering episodes, and you have to construct the episodes in a way that is interesting and makes sense or is mysterious," he explained. "It's about montage also—whether it's making a book, a film or a building."

After training at the Architectural Association in London, Koolhaas completed a controversial paper titled "The Berlin Wall as Architecture." This was "deliberately designed to unsettle his 'flower power' teachers at the Association," according to Richard Vine in *Art in America.* Two years later, in 1972, he and his future OMA partners Elia and Zoe Zenghelis and his future wife, Madelon Vriesendorp, published another unconventional architectural work. *Exodus, or the Voluntary Prisoners of Architecture,* proposed walling off certain portions of London and making residents decide whether they wanted to be inside or outside of this physical border.

Subsequently, Koolhaas received a Harkness Fellowship, which allowed him to go to New York and attend the Institute for Architecture and Urban Studies. There,

he studied under Peter Eisenman and became friends with peers such as Frank Gehry, Philip Johnson, and Kenneth Frampton.

In 1974, Koolhaas opened the Office for Metropolitan Architecture (OMA) in London. The acronym was typically clever of him; it means "grandmother" in Dutch. Later the office was moved to Rotterdam, and as of 2000 employed 90 architects. Koolhaas ended his professional relationship with the Zenghelises in 1985. The year the office opened, one of Koolhaas's students asked him to design a home for her parents in Miami. Though it was never built, it won a Progressive Architecture award. The student, Laurinda Spear, and her husband, Bernardo Fort-Brescia, in 1977 cofounded an architecture firm of their own, Arquitectonica, which some have said built Koolhaas's principles into reality even before he did so himself.

Indeed, much of Koolhaas's work was theoretical for some time. OMA entered and won several international competitions and even had a show at the Guggenheim in 1978, but did not start to complete their first buildings until the late 1980s. Some of Koolhaas's major commissions have been the Netherlands Dance Theater in the Hague, 1987; the Kunstahl, a major art exhibition space in Rotterdam, 1992; 24 innovative homes in Fukuoka, Japan, under the name Nexus Housing, 1994; and the Educatorium building at Utrecht University in the Netherlands, 1997.

Koolhaas's *Delirious New York: A Retroactive Manifesto for Manhattan* was first published in 1978. Walter Clemons reviewed the first edition in *Newsweek,* saying the book contains "forgotten historical details, . . . and startling, hallucinatory drawings." Paul Goldberger said in the *New York Review of Books* that it is "a book which takes its place in the long line of works by Europeans, from Dickens to Le Corbusier, who, for all their sophistication, seem stunned by New York's energy. *Delirious New York* celebrates bigness and power and drama and congestion, all of which, in Koolhaas's view, are crucial to the city's identity. . . . The gospel of Manhattan's 'culture of congestion,' as Koolhaas calls it, must be spread quickly," Goldberger continued, ". . . for we may already be doomed to another kind of city, a city of sterile boxes without any of the wild and mad power of Manhattan in its heyday."

Goldberger agreed with Koolhaas in his observation that New York's style was threatened in the 1950s with the introduction of modern European architecture.

"Koolhaas suggests that the 'delirious' architecture of New York . . . was irrational—fantasy was more important to the designers of New York's great early skyscrapers than any sort of principles of structural honesty or form following function." Goldberger said Rockefeller Center "comes closest" to Koolhaas's ideal of "massive, powerful, exuberant towers mixing all kinds of function, all kinds of human experience, so as to permit us 'to exist in a world totally fabricated by man; i.e., to live inside fantasy.'" Goldberger concluded by calling *Delirious New York* "a morality play masquerading as architectural history."

When publisher Monacelli planned the 1995 reissue of *Delirious New York,* it paid four hundred dollars to a rare book store for one of the original seven thousand five hundred copies. A *New Yorker* reviewer called the book "part love poem, part psychological thriller, part polemical manifesto on Manhattan's history of excess." In reviewing *Delirious New York* in *Newsweek,* Peter Plagens called Koolhaas "the R.E.M. of architecture," and said the book has reached "cult status." Plagens called it an "ode to the raucous, sexy collage of congestion that's the island of Manhattan. Koolhaas's celebration of New York's geewhiz gigantism and ego-driven skyscrapers was ahead of its time: in the 70's people still thought that modern rationalism could bring order to the essential messiness of cities. Now *Delirious* pushes all the right buttons." Richard Vine wrote in *Art in America* that a factor "tainting Koolhaas's treatment of the collective sphere is his evident condescension toward 'the masses,' as he repeatedly calls ordinary citizens in *Delirious New York.* His attempt to create social arenas by default, like his conviction that most people seek only distraction (rather than elevation and intimate community), exacerbates a contemporary crisis of faith."

Vine described a number of Koolhaas's projects, including the Villa dall'Ava (1991) in Saint-Cloud near Paris. "Its two corrugated box forms are stacked askew and conjoined by a rooftop swimming pool. . . . A maddeningly placed wall runs through the main living area. . . . The house's basic components are rendered in steel and concrete, but the pool is bordered on one side by astroturf and a loop of orange plastic fencing. The Lemoine House (1993) in Bordeaux features a huge external roof beam that looks like a piece from an oversized erector set. . . . Inside, a major section of floor can be raised or lowered one story. . . . By contrast, Holten House (1994) in the Netherlands, seems a mild instance of classic modernism." Vine said the Kunsthal, completed in Rotterdam in 1992, "presents a glass facade that seductively discloses much of the structure

and activity within. (This is a possible allusion to the windows in Holland's red-light districts, where ladies of the evening sit, visible from the street. . . . Or it may simply reflect the Dutch custom of keeping ground-level curtains open, day and night."

"OMA at MOMA: Rem Koolhaas and the Place of Public Architecture" opened at the Museum of Modern Art in 1994 after the reissue of *Delirious.* In 1988, Koolhaas was included in the museum's "Deconstructivist Architecture," and OMA was the focus of a Guggenheim show in 1978. Koolhaas's first American project was the three-billion-dollar expansion of MCA-Universal studios. Belinda Luscombe wrote in *Time* that "the MCA commission . . . caps an amazing 18 months. His 1994 exhibition . . . drew big crowds and critical plaudits. He was photographed, celebrity-style, in his midnight blue Maserati by *Vogue* and *Harper's Bazaar.* His first book, *Delirious New York,* was rereleased and sold 28,000 copies (not bad for a theoretical treatise on the American city written in the '70's)."

Luscombe called Koolhaas's second book *S, M, L, XL,* which refers to the sizes of his projects, a "curious tome. . . . A dense, not always coherent conglomeration of photos, plans, essays, fiction, cartoons and alphabetized ephemera, it's the ultimate coffee-table book for a generation raised on both MTV and Derrida." The book contains twenty years of history and over two thousand illustrations. "The theory that architecture should do rather than be has made Koolhaas the hero of students but not necessarily of his elders," wrote Luscombe. "Koolhaas has also been criticized for his apparent embrace of the rapid, mall-filled expansion that has scarred many American cities. 'Get away from Paris and Amsterdam and go see Atlanta,' says Koolhaas in *S, M, X, XL.* In his defense, Koolhaas says he is critical of untrammeled urban growth but it should be understood before being judged." Fiona MacCarthy wrote in the *Observer Review* that the book "is roomy, stimulating, barbed and funny, visually beautiful and verbally poetic. Intellectually, Koolhaas is the Colossus in whose shadow Richard Rogers and Norman Foster stutter platitudes. . . . It's the bigness of things that most delight him. He sees architecture's salvation in the freedom of operating on a truly giant scale. . . . The Nineties have been glorious surrender time for Koolhaas, in which the all-too-obvious failure of modern urban architecture has offered 'a pretext for Nietzschean frivolity.'"

"He has organized the book's contents according to the scale of his architectural projects," noted Brendan Gill in the *New Yorker,* "ignoring chronology, tossing in obiter dicta wherever it has pleased him to do so, and providing along the margin of nearly every page of text a curious alphabetical grab bag of quotations from diverse sources." Gill noted that *S, M, L, XL* contains thirteen hundred and seventy-six pages and weights over five pounds. "The sheer physical gorgeousness of *S, M, L, XL* greatly increases the usual difficulty of judging architecture from photographs," said Gill. "I was often unable to tell whether the pictures were of a model or of the real thing, much less whether I found the project, in either case, admirable." Gill wrote that Koolhaas "is no less gifted as a writer than he is as an architect. He also demonstrates that he possesses an attribute rare in both occupations: an invincibly merry view of life." "Mr. Koolhaas has always been an astute social observer," wrote Martin Filler in the *New York Times Book Review*. "His ability to penetrate and interpret even arcane human interactions is evident in this book's most sharply drawn segment, 'Learning Japanese,' a poem based on his experiences during the design and construction of his Nexus World Housing complex of 1991 in Fukuoka, Japan. This is a highly perceptive account of what it is like to do business with the Japanese." Filler said Koolhaas portrays these details "with pinpoint accuracy." Filler wrote in *Harper's Bazaar* "In an age of diminished civic expectations and urban hopelessness Koolhaas . . . clings to the romantic early-twentieth-century idea of the architect as superhero. . . . The provocative prose and unforgettable images he has published have deeply influenced a young generation of designers."

A long-range project of OMA was Lilli's International Business Center in France. The fifteen-year project, begun in 1989, transforms three hundred acres into a station for high-speed trains and includes six high-rise buildings, a world trade center, and ten million square feet of cultural facilities, retail outlets, offices, parks, residential buildings, parks, hotels, and offices. Using the new, fast trains, over fifty million people will be able to travel to the center from either London or Paris in less than ninety minutes.

Koolhaas became a professor at Harvard University in 1995 on the condition that he would not have to teach design. Instead, he joined the staff in order to direct one graduate seminar each year on a topic about which he desired to learn more. For his first research study, he chose to investigate China's Pearl River Delta, which includes Hong Kong and the area to the north. It was expected to triple in population from 2000 to 2020, to 36 million people. Koolhaas is intrigued by the effect of this super-rapid urbanization on the area's architecture, especially given the scarcity of Chinese architects and the quantities they must produce.

Subsequently, *Time* magazine recognized Koolhaas for the "Best Design for '98." It was a home in France on a hillside overlooking Bordeaux for a newspaper editor who had been confined to a wheelchair following an accident in the early 1990s. "He wanted a very complex house, so he could participate in the life of his family," Koolhaas commented in the *Christian Science Monitor.* "He wanted the house to help him transcend his handicap." To do this, Koolhaas created a large room in the center of the building that functioned as an elevator so that the owner could reach every level without leaving his desk. In addition, the nature of the house changes depending on where the elevator is stopped.

In 1999, Koolhaas designed the 296-seat Second Stage Theater in Manhattan in collaboration with Richard Gluckman of New York. It was his second work for the city, his first being the Lehmann Maupin Gallery in SoHo in 1996, which was also his first work in the United States overall. Unlike many architects, Koolhaas readily works in conjunction with other designers.

Koolhaas was selected as winner of the largest award in architecture, the Pritzker Prize, in April of 2000 and accepted the honor and its corresponding purse of $100,000 in Jerusalem that May. The jury chose him because they wanted to recognize an architect who represented the future. According to Benjamin Forgey in the *Washington Post,* the panel specifically applauded Koolhaas for his "rare combination of visionary and implementer, philosopher and pragmatist, theorist and prophet."

Koolhaas began several new projects in 2000. That year his firm signed on to create three new Prada stores in Los Angeles, San Francisco, and Manhattan. Koolhaas had never before designed a retail store but had recently advised his students on a book they published titled *The Harvard Guide to Shopping,* an examination of the effect shopping has had on modern life. Koolhaas also unveiled plans for the new downtown Seattle Public Library. For that, he proposed an exterior of copper-colored steel tubing encased in glass that would change color in response to sunlight. "It will engage in a very interesting dialogue with the weather," Koolhaas noted, according to an *American Libraries* article. To prepare for the commission, the architect traveled the United States for three months compiling a study of "everything from first impressions to what is wrong with libraries," as he noted to Lubow in the *New York Times.* He conducted a similar investigation before working on the Prada stores.

Also in 2000, Koolhaas began work on a New York hotel and the Dutch Embassy in Berlin. However, a proposed student union for the Illinois Institute of Technology in Chicago came into dispute due to protests by the Illinois Historical Preservation Agency. They were concerned about its impact on the structure, which was designed by another seminal architect, modernist guru Ludwig Mies van der Rohe. Other projects included redesigning the Los Angeles County Museum of Art and an addition for the Whitney Museum in New York city.

BIOGRAPHICAL/CRITICAL SOURCES:

BOOKS

Cuito, Aurora, and Cristina Montes, editors, *Rem Koolhaas: Archipockets,* te Neues Publishing, 2002.
Euralille: The Making of a New City Center: Koolhaas, Nouvel, Portzamparc, Vasconi, Duthilleul, Architects, Birkhauser, 1996.
Leupen, Bernard, *IJ-Plen, Amsterdam: Een Speurtocht naar Nieuwe Compositorische Middelen: Rem Koolhaas, Office for Metropolitan Architecture,* Uitgeverij 010 (Rotterdam), 1989.
Lucan, Jacques, *OMA-Rem Koolhaas: Pour une Culture de la Congestion,* Electa Moniteur (Paris), 1990.
Marco, Tabet, *La Terrifiante Beaute de la Beaute: Naturalisme et Abstraction dans l'Architecture de Jean Nouvel et Rem Koolhaas,* Sens & Tonka (France), 1996.
Puglisi, Luigi Prestinenza, *Rem Koolhaas: Trasparenze Metropolitane,* Testo & Immagine (Torino, Italy), 1997.
Richardson, Sara, *Remment Koolhaas: Office of Metropolitan Architecture,* Vance Bibliographies (Monticello, IL), 1988.
Stark, Ulrike, *Architekten, Rem Koolhaas und OMA,* IRB Verlag (Stuttgart), 1993.

PERIODICALS

American Artist, September, 2001, Kathleen Baxter, "Slot Machines, Show Girls, and Chagall," p. 64.
American Libraries, February, 2000, p. 16.
Architectural Review, June, 2000, "The Station Not the Airport," p. 44.
Architectural Record, March, 1993, p. 66; March, 1995, p. 88; March, 1996, p. 19.
Architecture, January, 1995, pp. 24-25; August, 1998, p. 25; February, 2000, Lawrence W. Cheek, "Seattle Gives Koolhaas the Cold Shoulder," p. 23; December, 2001, "Rem Koolhaas/OMA's Proposed (and Controversial) San Francisco Prada Store Is No More."

Art in America, May, 1979, p. 19; April, 1988, p. 27; April, 1995, p. 35; July, 2000, pp. 23, 128; August, 2001, p. 43.
ARTnews, November, 1995, p. 228; summer, 1998, p. 79.
Booklist, October 15, 1978, p. 344.
Chicago Tribune, December 11, 1994, p. 9.
Choice, March, 1988, p. 1056.
Christian Science Monitor, April 20, 2000, p. 18.
Harper's Bazaar, November, 1994, pp. 194-195, 197.
House & Garden, June, 1983, p. 121; April, 1988, p. 38; March, 1992, p. 158.
Independent, August 11, 1999, p. 9.
Interview, January, 1992, p. 59; October, 2000, Ingrid Sischy, "If He Builds It, They Will Come," p. 204.
Library Journal, March 15, 1979, p. 719; April 1, 1995, p. 130; June 15, 2001, Eric Bryant, review of *Mutations,* p. 68.
Observer, December 9, 1979, p. 35.
Observer Review, February 18, 1996, p. 16.
New Perspectives Quarterly, summer, 1996, p. 4.
New Statesman and Society, July 26, 1999, Hugh Aldersey-Williams, "Utopian Visions," p. 40.
Newsweek, December 11, 1978, p. 92; January 16, 1995, p. 68; January 28, 2002, Cathleen Mcguigan, "How Kool Is Rem: The Hot Dutch Architect Has Landed in the U.S. with a Fistful of Projects and a Head Full of Radical Ideas," p. 56.
New Yorker, December 26, 1994, p. 147; February 12, 1996, pp. 76, 78-79.
New York Review of Books, June 14, 1979, pp. 15-17; November 28, 1996, p. 42.
New York Times, September 11, 1994, sec. 2, p. 45; November 4, 1994, p. C1; February 15, 1996, p. C12; September 19, 1996, p. C4; April 8, 1999, p. E1; April 17, 2000, p. E1; April 18, 2000, p. B9.
New York Times Book Review, August 24, 1980, p. 27; March 17, 1996, p. 12.
New York Times Magazine, July 9, 2000, p. 30.
PR Newswire, December 4, 2001, "Architects Named for the Dallas Center for the Performing Arts"; December 6, 2001, "Los Angeles County Museum of Art Selects Architect Rem Koolhaas to Redesign Museum."
Progressive Architecture, November, 1994, p. 80.
Publishers Weekly, January 22, 1996, p. 54; February 12, 1996, p. 17.
Time, April 8, 1996, p. 62.
Tribune Books (Chicago), December 11, 1994, p. 9.
U.S. News & World Report, May 1, 2000, p. 59.
Village Voice, November 6, 1978, p. 123; December 11, 1978, p. 112.
Voice Literary Supplement, May, 1996, p. 17; June, 1998, p. 76.

Vogue, November, 1994, p. 330.
Wall Street Journal, May 12, 1999, p. B16.
Washington Post, April 17, 2000, p. C1.*

*   *   *

KÜBLER-ROSS, Elisabeth 1926-

PERSONAL: Born July 8, 1926, in Zurich, Switzerland; daughter of Ernst and Emmy (Villiger) Kübler; married Emanuel Robert Ross (a physician), February 7, 1958; children: Kenneth Lawrence, Barbara Lee. *Education:* University of Zurich, M.D., 1957.

ADDRESSES: Agent—c/o Simon & Schuster Author Mail, 1230 Avenue of the Americas, New York, NY 10020.

CAREER: Physician and writer. Did relief work in post-war Europe, and practiced as country doctor in Switzerland; Community Hospital, Glen Cove, NY, intern, 1958-59; Manhattan State Hospital, Ward's Island, NY, research fellow, 1959-61; Montefiore Hospital, New York, NY, resident, 1961-62; Psychopathic Hospital, Denver, CO, fellow, 1962-63; University of Colorado Medical School, Denver, CO, instructor in psychiatry and psychophysiology, 1963-65; University of Chicago Medical School, Chicago, IL, assistant professor of psychiatry and assistant director of psychiatric consultation and liaison service, 1965-71. Consulting psychiatrist, Chicago Lighthouse for the Blind, 1965-71; consultant to the Peace Corps, 1965-71, and Illinois State Psychiatric Institute 1965-71; founder, Shanti Nilaya healing center, Escondido, CA, 1977.

MEMBER: American Psychiatric Association, American Psychosomatic Society, Society for Psychophysiological Research, American Association for the Advancement of Science, Academy of Religion and Mental Health, Schweizerischer Hochschulverein, Society of Swiss Physicians.

AWARDS, HONORS: Honorary degrees include: Doctor of Science from Albany Medical College, 1974, and Smith College, 1975; Doctor of Law from University of Notre Dame, 1974, and Hamline University, 1975; Ph.D., Medical College of Pennsylvania, 1975.

WRITINGS:

On Death and Dying, Macmillan (New York, NY), 1969.
Questions and Answers on Death and Dying, Macmillan (New York, NY), 1972.

Death: The Final Stage, Prentice-Hall (Englewood Cliffs, NJ), 1974.
(Author of foreword) Raymond Moody, Jr., *Life after Life,* Mockingbird Press, 1975, new edition, Harper San Francisco (San Francisco, CA), 2001.
To Live Until We Say Good-Bye, photographs by Mal Warshaw, Prentice-Hall (Englewood Cliffs, NJ), 1978.
Living with Death and Dying, Macmillan (New York, NY), 1981.
Remember the Secret, illustrated by Heather Preston, Celestial Arts (Berkeley, CA), 1982.
Working It Through, photographs by Mal Warshaw, Macmillan (New York, NY), 1982.
On Children and Death, Macmillan (New York, NY), 1983.
AIDS: The Ultimate Challenge, Macmillan (New York, NY), 1987.
On Life after Death, Celestial Arts (Berkeley, CA), 1991.
Death Is of Vital Importance: On Life, Death, and Life after Death, Station Hill Press (Barrytown, NY), 1995, selections edited by Göran Grip and published as *The Cocoon and the Butterfly, Healing in Our Time, The Meaning of Suffering,* and *Say Yes to It,* Barrytown, Ltd. (Barrytown, NY), 1997.
The Wheel of Life: a Memoir of Living and Dying, Scribner (New York, NY), 1997.
The Tunnel and the Light: Essential Insights on Living and Dying, compiled and edited by Göran Grip, photographs by Ken Ross, Marlowe & Co. (New York, NY), 1999.
(With David Kessler) *Life Lessons: Two Experts on Death and Dying Teach Us about the Mysteries of Life and Living,* Scribner (New York, NY), 2000.

Contributor to books, including *The Dying Patient,* edited by Orville G. Brim, Howard E. Freeman, Jr., Sol Levine, and Norman A. Scotch, Russell Sage Foundation, 1970; *The Vestibule,* edited by Jess E. Weiss, Ashley Books, 1972; *The Phenomenon of Death,* edited by Edith Wyschogrod, Harper, 1973; *Emergency Psychiatric Care: The Management of Mental Health Crisis,* by H.L.P. Resnick and H. L. Ruben, Charles Press, 1974.

Also author of *Images of Growth and Death.* Contributor to *Encyclopaedia Britannica;* also contributor of articles on dying and death to professional journals.

SIDELIGHTS: In a paper for the Chicago Theological Seminary *Register,* psychiatrist Elisabeth Kübler-Ross wrote: "The fear of death is the most inescapable fear of human beings and the most unavoidable one. . . .

Dying is still a distasteful but inevitable happening which is rarely spoken about. One might think that the scientific man of the twentieth century would have learned to deal with this uniform fear as successfully as he has been able to add years to his life-span, or to replace human organs, or to produce children through artificial insemination. Yet, when we compare dying in less civilized and less sophisticated countries, we cannot help but see that we, in the so-called advanced civilization, die less easily. Advancement of science has not contributed to but rather detracted from man's ability to accept death with dignity."

Her preoccupation with death is understandable: "Whoever has seen the horrifying appearance of the [postwar European] concentration camps," she explained, would be similarly preoccupied. But Kübler-Ross decided to act on her primary concern in a most unique way. In 1965, she founded a teaching seminar at the Billings Hospital of the University of Chicago in which she proposed "a series of conversations with the terminally ill which would make it possible for them to talk about their feelings and thoughts in this crisis situation. [By] these conversations . . . others would learn too how better to work with the dying." Suprisingly, perhaps, most dying patients are eager to talk about death. "They welcome a breakthrough of their defenses," Kübler-Ross wrote. "They welcome a frank, unemotional, honest discussion, and a sharing of their feelings. Other factors contributing to their willingness may include a break in the lonely monotony of waiting, a feeling of being 'useful or worthwhile for something' and, for a few perhaps, a gratification of exhibitionist needs, to show 'how strong' they are, or some may just be unable to say no to the chance to gratify some dependency needs."

But more important, the dying are helping Kübler-Ross and her many followers to understand the concerns of the terminally ill and thus better equip themselves to deal with this fear, "in spite of the almost uniform attempts of this culture and this country to deny the reality of death." "It is a gratifying experience," she wrote, "to sit and listen to these patients who can teach us so much. It is a challenge to share with a human being his most difficult hours—and sometimes his finest."

On Death and Dying, Kübler-Ross's first book, became an enormously influential work for medical practitioners as well as for the general public. The book, which became a bestseller, outlines five stages of dying: denial, anger, bargaining, depression, and acceptance. The book also discusses strategies for treating patients and

their families as they negotiate these stages. The book became a standard reference for those who work with the terminally ill; its success prompted Kübler-Ross to devote her clinical practice to the treatment of dying patients.

Kübler-Ross grew up with an awareness of death that is relatively rare in much of the contemporary western world. The oldest of triplet daughters born to a middle-class Swiss family, she had been dangerously ill as a young child and, at age five, witnessed the death of her hospital roommate. She also remembered seeing a neighbor who was dying of a broken neck reassure his family about his impending death. When Kübler-Ross was thirteen, the Nazi invasion of Poland at the beginning of World War II captured her attention; she worked in various ways to help treat refugees and, after the war, volunteered to help rebuild ravaged areas of Poland. These experiences confirmed her desire to spend her life healing others, and she became convinced that spiritual and mental health were crucial to physical healing.

Against her father's wishes, Kübler-Ross enrolled in medical school at the University of Zurich. After marrying an American physician and moving with him to New York City in 1958, she completed an internship and residency in psychiatry. Her work in psychiatric hospitals convinced her of the importance of treating patients with more sympathy and compassion than was ordinarily the case; her approach showed improvement even among those patients with the most difficult conditions. In 1965, Kübler-Ross moved to Chicago, where she began working with the terminally ill. Her work became the focus of several seminars among health care professionals, and resulted in the publication of *On Death and Dying.* She followed this seminal work with *Questions and Answers on Death and Dying, Death: The Final Stage of Growth,* and *To Live until We Say Good-bye.* In 1977, Küler-Ross opened the Shanti Nilaya ("Home of Peace") healing center near Escondido, California.

During the 1980s Kübler-Ross began to explore particular issues on dying. *Children and Death* focuses on children's concepts of dying and discusses ways in which their families can help them cope with terminal disease. *AIDS: The Ultimate Challenge* discusses how caregivers and loved ones can help AIDS patients deal not only with the stages of dying, but also with the cruel social stigma of the disease. At the same time, Kübler-Ross became more interested in spiritual life after death. In *On Life after Death,* she revises her earlier thesis that death is the final stage of life, and suggests instead that death is a transition to a new kind of life. Though this position drew heavy skepticism from the medical establishment, Kübler-Ross has continued to write about such topics as near-death experiences, out-of-body experiences, and visitations from spirit guides.

After suffering a serious stroke in her seventies, Kübler-Ross wrote *The Wheel of Life: A Memoir of Living and Dying,* in which she confronts her own death and reflects on her life. This book did not receive the acclaim of her earlier works. Karen McNally Bensing, in a *Library Journal* review, found it a "puzzling combination of hastily sketched reminiscence and the worst of New Age ramblings." *Booklist* contributor Ilene Cooper considered the book relatively light, but added that Kübler-Ross's "forthrightness and enthusiasm are undeniable."

Though Kübler-Ross believed that *The Wheel of Life* would be her final book, she recovered after her stroke, and went on, though her health was much diminished, to write *Life Lessons: Two Experts on Death and Dying Teach Us about the Mysteries of Life and Living* with coauthor David Kessler, a leader of the hospice movement. The book is composed of alternating entries, written separately, and some reviewers found this a drawback. Yet, as Whitney Scott observed in *Booklist,* the authors' voices sometimes complement each other "very powerfully." Their message: that life lessons are opportunities to free ourselves from the negative emotions that prevent us from seeing what is best in others and ourselves. A reviewer for *Publishers Weekly* wrote that "such lessons may be true and useful, but here they come off as trite." Scott, however, pointed out that Kübler-Ross and Kessler "teach that true healing extends beyond physical repair to the mending of spirits and souls."

BIOGRAPHICAL/CRITICAL SOURCES:

BOOKS

Encyclopedia of World Biography, 2nd edition, Gale Research (Detroit, MI), 1999.

Gill, Derek, *Quest: The Life of Elisabeth Kübler-Ross,* Harper & Row (New York, NY), 1980.

PERIODICALS

America, February 23, 1974; September 27, 1975; June 4, 1988, John S. Sullivan, review of *AIDS: the Ultimate Challenge,* p. 588.

Booklist, May 15, 1997, Ilene Cooper, review of *The Wheel of Life: A Memoir of Living and Dying,* p. 1538; October 15, 2000, Whitney Scott, review of *Life Lessons: Two Experts on Death and Dying Teach Us about the Mysteries of Life,* p. 392.

Chicago Theological Seminary Register, December, 1966.

Christian Century, September 15, 1976; May 20, 1981, review of *Living with Death and Dying,* p. 598; February 15, 1984, William A. Sadler, Jr., review of *On Children and Death,* p. 64; May 11, 1988, Joseph A. Edelheit, review of *AIDS,* p. 483.

Commonweal, January 3, 1975.

Cosmopolitan, February 1980, Ann Nietzke, "The Miracle of Kübler-Ross," p. 206.

Library Journal, October 15, 1980, E. Mansell Pattison, review of *Quest: The Life of Elisabeth Kübler-Ross,* p. 2196; November 15, 1980, Anneliese Schwarzer, review of *On Death and Dying,* p. 2386; September 1, 1983, Catherine G. Atwood, review of *On Children and Death,* p. 1710; March 1, 1988, David A. Buehler, review of *AIDS,* p. 73.

Life, November 21, 1969.

Mother Earth News, May-June 1983, "Elisabeth Kübler-Ross on Living, Dying . . . and Beyond," p. 16.

New England Journal of Medicine, January 19, 1989, Harrison G. Pope, Jr., review of *AIDS,* p. 191.

New Statesman, July 9, 1982, Anne Karpf, review of *Living with Death and Dying,* p. 24.

New York Times Book Review, July 21, 1974; January 11, 1981, Jennifer Dunning, review of *Quest,* p. 14; April 10, 1988, Stephen S. Hall, review of *AIDS,* p. 3.

New York Times Magazine, January 22, 1995, Jonathan Rosen, "Rewriting the End: Elisabeth Kübler-Ross," p. 22.

Publishers Weekly, September 26, 1980, review of *Quest,* p. 111; January 23, 1981, review of *Living with Death and Dying,* p. 112; September 2, 1983, review of *On Children and Death,* p. 64; May 19, 1997, review of *The Wheel of Life,* p. 61; October 9, 2000, review of *Life Lessons,* p. 80.

Vanity Fair, June 1997, Leslie Bennetts, "Elisabeth Kübler-Ross's Final Passage," p. 70.

Vogue, January 1988, Susan Bolotin, review of *AIDS,* p. 97.*

*   *   *

KUEBLER-ROSS, Elisabeth
See KÜBLER-ROSS, Elisabeth

KUPPERMAN, Karen Ordahl 1939-

PERSONAL: Born April 23, 1939, in Devil's Lake, ND; daughter of Stafford Newell and Grace (Swanson) Ordahl; married Joel J. Kupperman (a professor of philosophy), 1964; children: Michael, Charles. *Education:* University of Missouri, B.A., 1961; Harvard University, M.A., 1962; Cambridge University, Ph.D., 1978.

ADDRESSES: Office—53 Washington Square South, New York, NY 10012-1098. *E-mail*—karen.kupperman@nyu.edu.

CAREER: Teacher at private school in New York, NY, 1962-64; University of Connecticut, Storrs, CT, lecturer, 1976-77, assistant professor, 1978-81, associate professor, beginning 1981, became professor of history; New York University, New York, NY, professor of history, 1995—.

MEMBER: American Historical Association, Organization of American Historians, American Society for Ethnohistory, Southern Historical Association.

AWARDS, HONORS: Mellon fellow at Harvard University, 1980-81; Binkley-Stephenson Award from Organization of American Historians, 1980, for article "Apathy and Death in Early Jamestown"; American Philosophical Society fellow, 1981; American Council of Learned Societies research fellow, 1984-85; National Humanities Center fellow, 1984-85; Rockefeller Foundation fellow, 1988; National Endowment for the Humanities fellow, 1989; Albert J. Beveridge Award, American Historical Association, 1995, for *Providence Island, 1630-1641: The Other Puritan Colony;* Times-Mirror Foundation distinguished fellow, 1995-96.

WRITINGS:

Settling with the Indians: The Meeting of English and Indian Cultures in America, 1580-1640, Rowman & Littlefield, 1980.
Roanoke: The Abandoned Colony, Rowman & Allenheld (Totowa, NJ), 1984.
(Editor) *Captain John Smith: A Select Edition of His Writings,* University of North Carolina Press/Institute of Early American History and Culture (Williamsburg, VA), 1988.
North America and the Beginnings of European Colonization, American Historical Association (Washington, DC), 1992.

(Editor) *Major Problems in American Colonial History: Documents and Essays,* D. C. Heath (Lexington, MA), 1993, 2nd edition, Houghton Mifflin (Boston, MA), 2000.
Providence Island, 1630-1641: The Other Puritan Colony, Cambridge University Press (New York, NY), 1993.
(Editor) *America in European Consciousness, 1493-1750,* University of North Carolina Press/Institute of Early American History and Culture (Williamsburg, VA), 1995.
Indians and English: Facing off in Early America, Cornell University Press (Ithaca, NY), 2000.

Contributor to *New Perspectives in Seventeenth-Century New England History,* edited by David G. Allen and David Hall, University of Virginia Press, 1984. Also contributor to history journals.

SIDELIGHTS: Karen Ordahl Kupperman has written extensively on early American colonial history. *Providence Island, 1630-1641: The Other Puritan Colony* recounts the little-known history of an English Puritan settlement on a small island off the coast of Nicaragua in the early 1600s. The short-lived colony was beset by many problems, including ignorance of tropical agriculture and the hostility of the neighboring Spanish, who ultimately took over the settlement. *Wilson Library Bulletin* contributor Stephanie Martin deemed the study an "excellent" book and noted that Kupperman "adds greatly to the already fascinating saga by comparing Providence Island to Massachusetts and showing how the differences in their social and political arrangements worked in Massachusetts's favor."

In *Indians and English: Facing off in Early America,* Kupperman provides an overview of the often complex relationships between the early English colonists and explorers and the native peoples they encountered. Rejecting the idea that it was simply a confrontation between an advanced culture and a more primitive one, Kupperman argues instead that both the English and the native Americans learned much from each other. The English, for example, were dependent upon the Indians for information about the New World. Both cultures learned from each other new ways of looking at the world. Kupperman also dispels common misperceptions about the relationship between early colonists and the native tribes, including the idea that native cultures were egalitarian in nature. She points out that the hierarchical structure of native society made the English more comfortable with them. Though he pointed out some minor shortcomings in the book, Michael P. Winship in the *Times Literary Supplement* concluded that Kupperman's "emphases on cultural contexts and the recovery of Indian agency and endurance make her book representative of much recent work in this field." Charles K. Piehl, reviewing the book for *Library Journal,* found it to be an "exceedingly well-argued and well-presented work, with many interdisciplinary insights."

Kupperman also received praise for *America in European Consciousness: 1493-1750,* a collection of scholarly papers that she edited. The book, which *English Historical Review* contributor John Lynch cited favorably for its "precise focus," explores the impact of the American continent on European consciousness from the late fifteenth through the mid-eighteenth centuries.

BIOGRAPHICAL/CRITICAL SOURCES:

PERIODICALS

American Historical Review, June, 1985, Bernard W. Sheehan, review of *Roanoke,* p. 750; December, 1995, David Eltis, review of *Providence Island, 1630-1641: The Other Puritan Colony,* p. 1663.
American History Illustrated, March, 1985, review of *Roanoke: The Abandoned Colony,* p. 7.
English Historical Review, June, 1997, John Lynch, review of *American in European Consciousness: 1493-1750,* p. 756.
Journal of American History, March, 1995, Virginia DeJohn Anderson, review of *Providence Island,* p. 1671; June, 1996, Richard Middleton, review of *America in European Consciousness: 1493-1750,* p. 173.
Journal of Southern History, February, 1996, Virginia Bernhard, review of *Providence Island,* p. 112; May, 1996, Michael L. Oberg, review of *America in European Consciousness,* p. 353.
Library Journal, May 1, 1984, review of *Roanoke,* p. 898; May 1, 2000, Charles K. Piehl, review of *Indians and English: Facing off in Early America,* p. 132.
Times Literary Supplement, September 22, 2000, Michael P. Winship, review of *Indians and English,* p. 33.
Wilson Library Bulletin, May, 1994, Stephanie Martin, review of *Providence Island,* p. 89.*

*   *   *

KURTZ, Katherine (Irene) 1944-

PERSONAL: Born October 18, 1944, in Coral Gables, FL; daughter of Fredrick Harry Kurtz (an electronics technician) and Margaret Frances Carter (a paralegal); married Scott Roderick MacMillan (an author and producer), March 9, 1983; children: Cameron Alexander Stewart. *Education:* University of Miami, B.S., 1966; University of California—Los Angeles, M.A., 1971. *Religion:* "Nominally Church of Ireland (Anglican)."

ADDRESSES: Home and office—Holybrooke Hall, Bray, County Wicklow, Ireland. *Agent*—Russell Galen, Scovil, Chichak, Galen Literary Agency, 381 Park Ave. S., New York, NY 10016.

CAREER: Writer. Los Angeles Police Department, Los Angeles, CA, instructional technologist, 1969-81.

MEMBER: Authors Guild, Authors' League, SFFWA.

AWARDS, HONORS: Edmund Hamilton Memorial Award, 1977, for *Camber of Culdi;* Balrog Award, 1982, for *Camber the Heretic; The Legacy of Lehr* was cited as a best science-fiction title, *Voice of Youth Advocates,* 1986; named dame of the Military and Hospitaller Order of St. Lazarus of Jerusalem, dame grand officer of the Supreme Military Order of the Temple of Jerusalem, dame of honour of the Hospitaller Order of St. John of Jerusalem, dame of the Noble Company of the Rose, and companion of the Royal House of O'Conor; fellow of Augustan Society and Octavian Society.

WRITINGS:

"DERYNI" SERIES

Deryni Rising, Ballantine (New York, NY), 1970.
Deryni Checkmate, Ballantine (New York, NY), 1972.
High Deryni, Ballantine (New York, NY), 1973.
Camber of Culdi ("Legends of Camber of Culdi," vol. 1), Ballantine (New York, NY), 1976.
Saint Camber ("Legends of Camber of Culdi," vol. 2), Ballantine (New York, NY), 1978.
Camber the Heretic ("Legends of Camber of Culdi," vol. 3), Ballantine (New York, NY), 1981.
The Bishop's Heir ("Histories of King Kelson," vol. 1), Ballantine (New York, NY), 1984.
The King's Justice ("Histories of King Kelson," vol. 2), Ballantine (New York, NY), 1985.
The Chronicles of the Deryni (includes *Deryni Rising, Deryni Checkmate,* and *High Deryni*), Science Fiction Book Club, 1985.

The Deryni Archives (stories), Ballantine (New York, NY), 1986, hardcover edition, Science Fiction Book Club, 1987.

The Quest for Saint Camber ("Histories of King Kelson," vol. 3), Ballantine (New York, NY), 1986.

The Harrowing of Gwynedd ("Heirs of St. Camber," vol. 1), Ballantine (New York, NY), 1989.

Deryni Magic: A Grimoire, Del Rey (New York, NY), 1991.

King Javan's Year ("Heirs of St. Camber," vol. 2), Ballantine (New York, NY), 1992.

The Bastard Prince ("Heirs of St. Camber," vol. 3), Ballantine (New York, NY), 1994.

(Compiler and editor, with Robert Reginald) *Codex Derynianus: Being a Comprehensive Guide to the Peoples, Places, and Things of the Derynye and the Human Worlds of the XI Kingdoms*, Borgo Press (San Bernardino, CA), 1998.

King Kelson's Bride, Ace (New York, NY), 2000.

"ADEPT" SERIES; WITH DEBORAH TURNER HARRIS

The Adept, Ace (New York, NY), 1991.

The Lodge of the Lynx, Ace (New York, NY), 1992.

The Templar Treasure, Ace (New York, NY), 1993.

Dagger Magic, Ace (New York, NY), 1995.

Death of an Adept, Ace (New York, NY), 1996.

OTHER

Lammas Night (novel), Ballantine (New York, NY), 1983, hardcover edition, Severn, 1986.

The Legacy of Lehr (science-fiction novel), Walker (New York, NY), 1986.

(Editor) *Tales of the Knights Templar*, Warner (New York, NY), 1995.

Two Crowns for America, Bantam (New York, NY), 1996.

(With Deborah Turner Harris) *The Temple and the Stone*, Warner (New York, NY), 1998.

(Editor) *On Crusade: More Tales of the Knights Templar*, Warner (New York, NY), 1998.

St. Patrick's Gargoyle, Ace (New York, NY), 2001.

(With Deborah Turner Harris) *The Temple and the Crown*, Warner (New York, NY), 2001.

Contributor of stories to anthologies, including *Flashing Swords #4*, edited by Lin Carter, Dell (New York, NY), 1977; *Hecate's Cauldron*, edited by Susan Shwartz, DAW (New York, NY), 1982; *Nine Visions*, edited by Andrea LaSonde Melrose, Seabury Press (New York, NY), 1983; *Moonsinger's Friends*, edited by Shwartz, Bluejay, 1985; *Once upon a Time*, edited by Lester del Rey and Risa Kessler, Ballantine (New York, NY), 1991; *Crafter I*, edited by Bill Fawcett and Christopher Stasheff, Ace (New York, NY), 1991; *Gods of War*, edited by Fawcett, Baen (New York, NY), 1992; and *Battlestation II*, edited by Fawcett and Stasheff, Ace, 1992. Contributor of stories to periodicals, including *Fantasy Book*.

Kurtz's works have been translated into Dutch, German, Italian, Polish, Swedish, Japanese, Spanish, and Romanian.

SIDELIGHTS: Katherine Kurtz's love of history has helped to shape the medieval worlds of her fantasy novels, as well as her books set in twentieth-century England and Scotland. Her "Deryni" series, composed of four base trilogies plus additional novels, focuses on the land of Gwynedd in the Eleven Kingdoms, a world based on medieval Wales. There the Deryni, a race of beings with unusual psychic powers, struggle against persecution by humans and attempt to preserve their powers and their culture. In a review of *The Quest for Saint Camber*, a *Publishers Weekly* critic dubbed Kurtz "queen of the proliferating fantasy subgenre that adds a magical element to dynastic historical romances." Kurtz's ability to weave historical detail with themes of magic and sorcery has made her books popular with both adults and young adults. A *Publishers Weekly* contributor declared Kurtz "a master of epic fantasy." Kurtz has also produced the thriller *Lammas Night*, authored a science fiction novel, and, with Deborah Turner Harris, has written the popular "Adept" series of contemporary mysteries. Comparing Kurtz to British fantasy writer J. R. R. Tolkien in her approach to her imaginary world, an essayist in *St. James Guide to Fantasy Writers* commented that Kurtz's "magic is well realized, the characters [in her novels] much better drawn than in most modern fantasies, and, for anyone with a romantic interest in the Middle Ages, [her 'Deryni'] saga will inevitably have a great deal of fascination."

Born in 1944, in Coral Gables, Florida, during a hurricane, Kurtz once described her first moments on earth as "a whirlwind entry into the world which I like to think was a portent of exciting things to come." Kurtz began her love affair with books at an early age, and since elementary school proved dull, she smuggled library books to school, secreting them "in my lift-top desk or under the book I was supposed to be reading. I also read under the covers at night by flashlight," Kurtz confessed.

During her fourth-grade year, Kurtz discovered her first science fiction novel, *Lodestar.* "After that, no science fiction book in any library was safe from eye-tracking by 'The Kurtz,'" she recalled. Even though, after graduating from high school, Kurtz earned her B.S. in chemistry at the University of Miami, "my tastes always leaned toward humanities rather than hard science. It was during my undergraduate years at the University of Miami that I consciously fell in love with history, and it was to history that I returned when I decided, after one year of medical school, that I would rather write about medicine than practice it." In 1971 she graduated from the University of California—Los Angeles, with an M.A. in English history. "More important than the piece of paper," Kurtz explained, "was the formal knowledge of the medieval and renaissance world that I gained and the sharpening of research skills which would stand me in good stead as I continued writing medievally set fantasy."

After working for over a decade for the Los Angeles Police Department as a technical writer and curriculum designer—and writing what would become the first six "Deryni" novels in her spare time—Kurtz embarked on her full-time career as a fiction writer in 1980. "I can't imagine a more satisfying life than to be making a living doing what I love," she once admitted. "Far too few people get the opportunity to do that, and especially at a relatively young age."

Her first "Deryni" novel, *Deryni Rising,* was published in 1970. The first installment in the three-volume "Chronicles of the Deryni" trilogy, it introduces the reader to the kingdom of Gwynedd and its culture, which is laced with magic. The other trilogies that comprise the "Deryni" series include "Legends of St. Camber," which follows the life of a nobleman as he is first sainted then deemed a heretic; "Histories of King Kelson," which continues the events from the "Chronicles of the Deryni"; and "Heirs of St. Camber," where the magical kingdom suffers a dark age between the time of St. Camber and the rise to power of King Kelson. While *Voice of Youth Advocates* contributor Diane G. Yates expressed personal dismay that in the second part of the "Heirs of St. Camber" trilogy, *King Javan's Year,* "so many of the characters that [readers of the series] have grown to love, lose their lives in an unceasing struggle with the forces of evil," she nonetheless added: "the book is up to Kurtz's usual high standards, is beautifully written, and should appeal to teens as well as adults." In *The Bastard Prince,* the concluding volume in "Heirs of St. Camber," the efforts of the heir to the throne "reflects the atmospheric gloom of a dark and secret land, full of treachery and cruelty but

shot through with light and a promise of hope," in the opinion of a *Publishers Weekly* contributor who went on to praise Kurtz for her ability to sustain tension and create vivid characters.

In addition to the "Deryni" novels, Kurtz has made what she terms "several literary forays outside the medieval world of the Eleven Kingdoms." Her historical thriller *Lammas Night,* published in 1983, takes place in England during World War II. As Kurtz explained, "British folk tradition has it that England has been saved from invasion more than once by the magical intervention of those appointed to guard her, Napoleonic and Armada times being cited as two specific examples. Less well-known tradition has it that similar measures were employed to keep Hitler from invading Britain during that fateful summer of 1940, with its sagas of Dunkirk and the Battle of Britain. Whether or not what was done actually had any effect we will never know for certain, but the fact remains that Hitler never did invade, even though he was poised to do so for many months. *Lammas Night* is the story of how and why that might have been."

Together with fellow author Deborah Turner Harris, Kurtz has written several volumes in the "Adept" series. Set in the twentieth century, the novels features members of a secret, three-member brotherhood known as the Adept: former members of the ancient Knights Templar who, now based in Scotland, have sworn to uphold cosmic laws in their reincarnated form. In *The Templar Treasure,* the trio search for the treasured Seal of Solomon, only to discover a host of horrors. And in *Dagger Magic,* the Adept must foil efforts by a reincarnated Tibetan magician to gain absolute power by way of a collection of ancient texts confiscated by the Nazis decades ago and now discovered to exist in a German U-boat hidden in a cave along the northern coast of Ireland. "The plot, though somewhat convoluted, has a Wangerian intensity and a profound moral message chillingly told," maintained *Voice of Youth Advocates* contributor Mary Anne Hoebeke in her review of *Dagger Magic.*

Other works by Kurtz include the science-fiction novels *The Legacy of Lehr,* several collections of short stories focusing on the Knights Templar, and an historical novel set during the American Revolutionary War, titled *Two Crowns for America.* Positing an alternate history, in *Two Crowns for America* Kurtz shows what would have happened had America adopted a monarchy, with factional Jacobites and Freemasons attempting to crown their preferred king while an occult Master has a plan of his own for the new country's future. Calling *Two Crowns for America* an "engrossing and elegant tale," *Booklist* reviewer Roland Green praised the author for her "vivid portrayals" of such characters as Prince Charles Stuart, otherwise known as Bonnie Prince Charlie, George Washington, and Benjamin Franklin. *St. Patrick's Gargoyle,* which *Booklist* contributor Ray Olson predicted would become a "Christmas perennial," finds a guardian gargoyle and a member of the Knights of Malta determined to find those responsible for vandalizing St. Patrick's Cathedral in the days before Christmas.

Kurtz has several interests outside history and writing, although, as she noted, "most of them do tend to relate to my writing or medieval background in some way." A voracious reader, she tackles history, religion, and other books related to her research, while saving time to dip into "the occasional Brother Cadfael mystery for fun." Other hobbies take her away from the printed page; as Kurtz explained: "I delight in counted cross-stitch embroidery and needlepoint, will occasionally crochet, but am totally indifferent to knitting. I can sew just about anything, including medieval costumes and horse bardings." Together with her husband, who she met at a Scottish country dance in Santa Monica, California, she is restoring a historic country house which she bought in County Wicklow, Ireland, in 1986.

BIOGRAPHICAL/CRITICAL SOURCES:

BOOKS

Clarke, Boden, and Mary A. Burgess, *The Work of Katherine Kurtz: An Annotated Bibliography and Guide,* Borgo Press (San Bernardino, CA), 1993.
St. James Guide to Fantasy Writers, St. James Press (Detroit, MI), 1996.
St. James Guide to Science-Fiction Writers, 4th edition, St. James Press (Detroit, MI), 1996.

PERIODICALS

Booklist, May 1, 1994, Roland Green, review of *The Bastard Prince,* p. 1583; February 1, 1996, Roland

Green, review of *Two Crowns for America,* p. 920; December 1, 1996, Roland Green, review of *Death of an Adept,* p. 643; February 1, 2001, Ray Olson, review of *St. Patrick's Gargoyle,* p. 1042.
Kirkus Reviews, April 1, 1998, review of *On Crusade,* p. 452.
Kliatt, September, 1995, Judith H. Silverman, review of *Tales of the Knights Templar,* p. 23.
Library Journal, June 15, 2000, Jackie Cassada, review of *King Kelson's Bride,* p. 121; February 15, 2001, review of *St. Patrick's Gargoyle,* p. 205.
Publisher Weekly, April 10, 1972, p. 60; July 9, 1973, p. 48; May 31, 1976, p. 197; September 11, 1978, review of *Saint Camber,* p. 77; September 25, 1981, p. 87; September 21, 1984, p. 92; July 5, 1985, p. 66; review of *The Quest for Saint Camber,* August 8, 1986; September 26, 1986, p. 69; December 2, 1988, p. 48; December 21, 1990, p. 50; February 8, 1991, p. 54; June 21, 1993, review of *The Templar Treasure,* p. 102; May 23, 1994, review of *The Bastard Prince,* p. 82; November 27, 1995, review of *Two Crowns for America,* pp. 52-53; April 13, 1998, review of *On Crusade,* p. 57; July 27, 1998, review of *The Temple and the Stone,* pp. 58-59; May 29, 2000, review of *King Kelson's Bride,* p. 57.
School Library Journal, January, 1985, p. 92; February, 1986, p. 103; November, 1986, p. 116; December, 1986, p. 126; September, 1991, p. 298; September, 1992, p. 29.
Voice of Youth Advocates, December, 1986, p. 238; April, 1987, p. 38; August, 1989, p. 166; April, 1993, Diane G. Yates, review of *King Javan's Year,* p. 42; October, 1993, Faye H. Gottschall, review of *The Templar Treasure,* p. 230; October, 1995, Mary Anne Hoebeke, review of *Dagger Magic,* p. 234.

OTHER

Katherine Kurtz Web site, http://www.deryni.net/ (September 26, 2001).*

L

LEES, Gene 1928-

PERSONAL: Born February 8, 1928, in Hamilton, Ontario, Canada; son of Harold (a musician, later a construction engineer) and Dorothy (Flatman) Lees; married Carmen Lister, 1951 (marriage ended); married Micheline A. Ducreux, July, 1955 (marriage ended); married Janet Suttle, 1971; children: (second marriage) Philippe. *Education:* Attended Ontario College of Art, Toronto.

ADDRESSES: Home and office—P.O. Box 240, Ojai, CA 93024-0240; fax: 805-640-0253. *E-mail*—jazzlet@ix.net.com.

CAREER: Journalist and musician. Reporter for *Hamilton Spectator,* Hamilton, Ontario, Canada, *Toronto Telegram,* Toronto, Ontario, Canada, and *Montreal Star,* Montreal, Quebec, Canada, 1948-55; *Louisville Times,* Louisville, KY, classical music critic and film and drama editor, 1955-58; *Down Beat* (jazz magazine), Chicago, IL, editor, 1959-61; *Hi Fi/Stereo Review,* New York, NY, contributing editor, 1962-65; *High Fidelity,* columnist, 1965-79; *Jazzletter,* Ojai, CA, founder and principal writer, 1981—. Lecturer at colleges and universities, including Lawrence University, Columbia College, and Louisiana State University. Lyricist, composer, and collaborator with other composers on songs; toured Latin America under the auspices of U.S. Department of State as manager of jazz sextet, 1962; thirty songs with his lyrics, among them "Waltz for Debby," "Song of the Jet," "Paris Is at Her Best in May," and "Someone to Light up My Life," were released in a Richmond Organization portfolio, 1968. Radio and television writer and singer for the Canadian Broadcasting Corp. and various independent Canadian radio stations.

MEMBER: Society of Composers, Authors and Music Publishers of Canada.

AWARDS, HONORS: Reid fellowship, 1958-59; Deems Taylor awards, American Society of Composers, Authors, and Publishers, 1978, for articles in *High Fidelity,* and 1989, for *Meet Me at Jim and Andy's* and for *Waiting for Dizzy.*

WRITINGS:

And Sleep until Noon (novel), Simon & Schuster (New York, NY), 1966.
The Modern Rhyming Dictionary: How to Write Lyrics, Cherry Lane (Port Chester, NY), 1981.
Singers and the Song (essays), Oxford University Press (New York, NY), 1987.
Meet Me at Jim and Andy's, Oxford University Press (New York, NY), 1988.
Oscar Peterson: The Will to Swing (biography), Lester & Orpen Dennys, 1988.
(With Henry Mancini) *Did They Mention the Music* (autobiography), Contemporary Books (Chicago, IL), 1989.
Inventing Champagne: The Worlds of Lerner and Loewe (biography), St. Martin's Press (New York, NY), 1990.
Waiting for Dizzy, Oxford University Press (New York, NY), 1991.
Jazz Lives, photographs by John Reeves, McClelland & Stewart (Toronto, Ontario, Canada), 1992.
Cats of Any Color: Jazz Black and White, Oxford University Press (New York, NY), 1994.
Leader of the Band: The Life of Woody Herman, Oxford University Press (New York, NY), 1995.

Singers and the Song II (essays), Oxford University Press (New York, NY), 1998.

Arranging the Score: Portraits of the Great Arrangers, Cassell (London, England), 1999.

You Can't Steal a Gift: Dizzy, Clark, Milt, and Nat, introduction by Nat Hentoff, Yale University Press (New Haven, CT), 2001.

Contributor of articles and short stories to the *Jazz Times, New York Times, Los Angeles Times, Globe and Mail* (Toronto), *Saturday Review, American Film,* and other periodicals in the United States, Canada, and Europe.

WORK IN PROGRESS: Biographies of Glenn Miller and songwriter Johnny Mercer; another collection of essays originally published in *Jazzletter.*

SIDELIGHTS: A distinguished lyricist known for his words to "Quiet Nights of Quiet Stars" and other bossa nova songs, Gene Lees helped introduce the bossa nova in North America and has translated the Portuguese lyrics of many Brazilian songs into English. His songs have been recorded by Frank Sinatra, Tony Bennett, and others, and he has collaborated with such composers as Charles Aznavour of France, Antonio Carlos Jobim of Brazil, and Lalo Schifrin of Argentina. In 1976 Lees collaborated with Roger Kellaway on the musical score for the film *The Mouse and His Child.*

In 1983 Lees adapted to music an English version of a group of poems by Pope John Paul II, which Sarah Vaughan recorded in concert the following year. The resulting album, a suite of songs pleading for world peace, was released internationally under the title *The Planet Is Alive: Let It Live* and was well received critically. In 1984 Choice Records released an album of Lees singing his own songs, and in 1985 Stash Records released *Gene Lees Sings the Gene Lees Song Book,* a performance with orchestra of songs Lees wrote with Jobim and other composers.

Also known as one of the finest jazz writers of his generation, Lees launched *Jazzletter* in 1980, and he has collected his essays from his newsletter into several published volumes. Interviewing Lees for a review of the first collection of *Jazzletter* essays, *Singers and the Song,* for the *New York Times Book Review,* Peter Keepnews wrote: "The singers closest to [Lees'] heart belong to a tradition he feels is fading, and he acknowledged that most of the essays have a nostalgic tone, as

does the newsletter itself: 'It's not so much a news publication as a historical publication. And let's face it, most people in history are dead.'"

Lees once told *CA* that *Jazzletter* has been a useful vehicle for his work: "Since I do not have to submit material to editors, I can determine for myself the importance of the subject matter, the nature of the treatment, and the length of it. I don't have to answer to anyone but my readers." He later added: "I am amazed to find that the *Jazzletter* has survived into its twenty-first year. Several times I announced that I was closing it down, but the reader protest was so strong that each time I decided to go another year. This has been tremendously heartening, as have the reviews of the books compiled of *Jazzletter* essays, thus far seven volumes with an eighth in progress. I don't think any other writer on jazz and allied subjects, excepting my friend Whitney Balliett of the *New Yorker,* has ever been so extensively anthologized.

"The *Jazzletter* and the support of the musicians who are its primary subscribers have permitted me to find my own voice like nothing in my previous experience. I think my previous work as an editor has given me a measure of objectivity about my own stuff, including the critical cutting process. And of course it heightens one's disciplines to have to meet deadlines set by yourself.

"I always found magazine writing restrictive. With the *Jazzletter,* I have the luxury of extending an essay over several issues. This has resulted in some pieces running as much as 30,000 words.

"I have been doing a number of concerts of my songs coupled with master classes at various institutions, including Lawrence University, Columbia College, and Louisiana State University, and I found myself telling aspirant writers about a process I went through when I was nineteen and thinking about wanting to write. I thought I was pathetic, dejected, and lonely. I would type out passages of writers I admired, among them James M. Cain, John Dos Passos, John Steinbeck, and the vastly underrated Morley Callaghan. I thought it would somehow bring me closer to them. I now realize I was right. It did. And this process—which is not unlike the valuable copying process in music and graphic art—gives you the feel of the writers' rhythms, the way they construct paragraphs, pages, and longer structures, down to the details of punctuation. So I tell young people now to give it a try.

"As for songwriting, the best training I know is to sing—and study the works of the great writers such as Johnny Mercer, Cole Porter, and Harold Arlen, who gave us an astonishing body of masterpieces before rock-and-roll brought our musical culture crashing down."

BIOGRAPHICAL/CRITICAL SOURCES:

BOOKS

Lees, Gene, *You Can't Steal a Gift: Dizzy, Clark, Milt, and Nat,* Yale University Press (New Haven, CT), 2001.

PERIODICALS

BMI (publication of Broadcast Music, Inc.), November, 1967.
Jazztimes, August 24, 1986.
Los Angeles Times Book Review, January 17, 1982.
New York Times Book Review, November 15, 1987, Peter Keepnews, review of *Singers and the Song.*

*   *   *

LENTRICCHIA, Frank (Jr.) 1940-

PERSONAL: Surname is pronounced Len-*trick*-ya; born May 23, 1940, in Utica, NY; son of Frank John and Ann (Yacovella) Lentricchia; married Karen Young (a teacher), June 24, 1967 (divorced, 1973); married Melissa Christensen, 1973; children: two. *Education:* Utica College of Syracuse University, B.A., 1962; Duke University, M.A., 1963, Ph.D., 1966.

ADDRESSES: Office—Department of English, Duke University, Durham, NC 27706. *E-mail*—frll@acpub.duke.edu.

CAREER: University of California, Los Angeles, CA, assistant professor of English and comparative literature, 1966-68; University of California, Irvine, CA, assistant professor, 1968-70, associate professor, 1970-76, professor, 1976-82; Rice University, Houston, TX, Autrey Professor of Humanities, 1982-84; Duke University, Durham, NC, member of faculty, 1984—, named Katherine Everett Gilbert Professor of English and Literature.

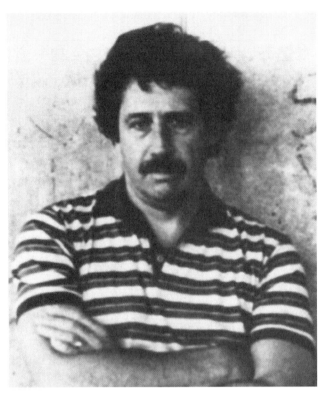

Frank Lentricchia

MEMBER: Modern Language Association of America.

WRITINGS:

The Gaiety of Language: An Essay on the Radical Poetics of W. B. Yeats and Wallace Stevens, University of California Press (Berkeley, CA), 1968.
Robert Frost: Modern Poetics and the Landscapes of Self, Duke University Press (Durham, NC), 1975.
(Compiler, with Melissa Christensen Lentricchia) *Robert Frost: A Bibliography, 1913-1974,* Scarecrow (Metuchen, NJ), 1976.
After the New Criticism, University of Chicago Press (Chicago, IL), 1980.
Criticism and Social Change, University of Chicago Press (Chicago, IL), 1983.
Ariel and the Police: Michel Foucault, William James, Wallace Stevens, University of Wisconsin Press (Madison, WI), 1988.
(Editor) *Introducing Don DeLillo,* Duke University Press (Durham, NC), 1991.
(Editor) *New Essays on White Noise,* Cambridge University Press (New York, NY), 1991.
(Contributor) *Situational Tensions of Critic-Intellectuals Thinking through Literary Politics with Edward W. Said and Frank Lentricchia,* Peter Lang (New York, NY), 1992.

The Edge of Night: A Confession, Random House (New York, NY), 1994.

Modernist Quartet, Cambridge University Press (New York, NY), 1994.

(Coeditor) *Critical Terms for Literary Study,* University of Chicago Press (Chicago, IL), 1995.

Johnny Critelli; and, The Knifemen, Scribner (New York, NY), 1996.

The Music of the Inferno, State University of New York Press (Albany, NY), 1999.

Lucchesi and the Whale, Duke University Press (Durham, NC), 2001.

Contributor to *Poetry, Yale Review,* and other journals.

SIDELIGHTS: Frank Lentricchia is "a star in the galaxy of cultural theory," to quote a *Publishers Weekly* reviewer. The son of a house painter, Lentricchia has become one of the best known literary critics in the United States, and has received notice for writing novels and fiction/criticism hybrids nearly unique to his pen. *National Review* correspondent Jeffrey Hart wrote of Lentricchia: "He is a denizen of the infamous Duke University English Department, a major center of the brand of literary 'theory' allied with ideology that a large and aggressive segment of the professoriate has substituted for literature. Indeed, Mr. Lentricchia has been known as one of the foremost exponents of theory."

According to Terence Hawkes in the *Times Literary Supplement,* Lentricchia's book, *After the New Criticism,* is "a tough-minded account of some of the major theoretical preoccupations of literary criticism [of the late twentieth century]. . . . Its anti-idealist commitment, openly presented and tellingly deployed, gives it an attractive bite. The result is a demanding and compelling work, spirited in its deflation of a number of established reputations, and implacable in its raising of the crucial questions concerning historical consciousness which any new New Criticism must be prepared to answer." Peter Rudnytsky observed in *World Literature Today* that *After the New Criticism* "is a landmark book. Combining a masterful gift for exposition with incisive analytical rigor . . . Lentricchia offers a mapping of the contemporary critical scene on axes at once historical and theoretical."

In addition to his numerous critical works, Lentricchia has written several works of fiction that reveal "the once-detached scholar no longer hiding, or hiding behind, his judgments and values," in the words of a

Kirkus Reviews critic. Lentricchia bases his fiction closely on his youth in Utica, New York, but he is also well versed in a postmodern aesthetic that revels in crossing genres and bending the rules of character, plot, and purpose. A *Publishers Weekly* contributor candidly noted that *The Edge of Night: A Confession* "may be indigestible for the average reader." According to other critics, more demanding readers can find rewards in Lentricchia's work. In his *New York Times Book Review* piece on *The Edge of Night,* John Sutherland maintained that the book is "absorbing . . . because Mr. Lentricchia is an interesting and ultimately rather elusive man. In a competitive field where traditionally the cards are stacked against sons of Italian-American house painters, he has succeeded brilliantly. . . . He has refused to conform, assimilate or show his origins. It is a remarkable achievement." In the *Review of Contemporary Fiction,* Irving Malin deemed *Johnny Critelli; and, The Knifemen* "an ambitious attempt to use language as matter to make it bleed." A *Publishers Weekly* review of the same work noted that Lentricchia's fiction displays "a rousing capacity for language and a gritty sense of the contemporary male mind."

For Sutherland, both Lentricchia's fiction and his critical work reveal a unique mind at work. The critic declared: "Think of 'college professor' or 'Eliot scholar' and a tweedy, pipe-puffing, upper-class WASP (or would-be WASP) comes to mind. Mr. Lentricchia is a new breed—one for whom 'don' evokes Al Pacino playing Michael Corleone rather than C. S. Lewis."

BIOGRAPHICAL/CRITICAL SOURCES:

BOOKS

Situational Tensions of Critic-Intellectuals: Thinking through Literary Politics with Edward W. Said and Frank Lentricchia, Peter Lang (New York, NY), 1992.

PERIODICALS

America, May 7, 1994, Paul Wilkes, review of *The Edge of Night: A Confession,* p. 18.
Choice, November, 1975; December, 1980; July-August, 1984.
Kirkus Reviews, December 15, 2000, review of *Lucchesi and the Whale,* p. 1710.
Library Journal, June 15, 1980.

National Review, November 21, 1994, Jeffrey Hart, review of *Modernist Quartet,* p. 68.

New England Quarterly, June, 1976.

New York Times Book Review, February 6, 1994, John Sutherland, "The Don of Duke," p. 24; December 29, 1996, Lorna Sage, "The Messy Stuff of Memory," p. 7.

Publishers Weekly, January 10, 1994, review of *The Edge of Night: A Confession,* p. 51; November 4, 1996, review of *Johnny Critelli; and, The Knifemen,* p. 64; December 11, 2000, review of *Lucchesi and the Whale,* p. 62.

Review of Contemporary Fiction, summer, 1997, Irving Malin, review of *Johnny Critelli; and, The Knifemen,* p. 294.

Times Literary Supplement, April 17, 1981; June 22, 1984.

Village Voice Literary Supplement, March 26, 1984.

Voice Literary Supplement, March, 1984.

World Literature Today, spring, 1981.

*   *   *

LESCROART, John T. 1948-

PERSONAL: Surname is pronounced "*Les*-qua"; born January 14, 1948, in Houston, TX; son of Maurice E. and Loretta (a homemaker; maiden name, Gregory) Lescroart; married Leslee Ann Miller, June 13, 1976 (divorced July, 1979); married Lisa M. Sawyer (an architect), September 2, 1984; children: (second marriage) Justine Rose, John Jack Sawyer. *Education:* Attended University of California—Santa Cruz, 1966, College of San Mateo, 1967, University of San Francisco, 1967-68; University of California—Berkeley, B.A. (with honors; English literature), 1970. *Avocational interests:* Baseball, food and wine, fishing.

ADDRESSES: Home—El Macero, CA. *Office*—426 D St., Davis, CA 95616-4131. *Agent*—Barney Karpfinger, The Karpfinger Agency, 357 West 20th St., New York, NY 10011.

CAREER: Computer room supervisor, 1970-72; professional singer and guitarist in Los Angeles and San Francisco, CA, 1972-77; *Guitar Player,* Cupertino, CA, editor and advertising director, 1977-79; Guardians of the Jewish Homes for the Aging, Los Angeles, CA, associate director, 1979-83; A. T. Kearney, Inc. (consulting firm), Alexandria, VA, technical writer and associate consultant, 1982-85; Pettit & Martin (law firm), Los Angeles, CA, word processor and legal administrator, 1985-91. Writer, 1991—.

MEMBER: Mystery Writers of America, El Macero Country Club, Authors Guild, PEN, International Association of Crime Writers.

AWARDS, HONORS: Joseph Henry Jackson Award, San Francisco Foundation, 1978, for novel *Sunburn.*

WRITINGS:

"DISMAS HARDY" MYSTERY SERIES

Dead Irish, Donald I. Fine (New York, NY), 1989.

The Vig, Donald I. Fine, (New York, NY), 1990.

Hard Evidence, Donald I. Fine (New York, NY), 1993.

The 13th Juror, Donald I. Fine (New York, NY), 1994.

The Mercy Rule, Delacourt Press (New York, NY), 1998.

Nothing but the Truth, Dutton (New York, NY), 2000.

The Hearing, Dutton (New York, NY), 2001.

The Oath, Dutton (New York, NY), 2002.

OTHER

(Editor) Craig Anderton, *Home Recording for Musicians,* GPI Publications, 1975.

(Editor) Rusty Young, *The Pedal Steel Handbook,* GPI Publications, 1976.

Sunburn (novel), Pinnacle Books, 1982.

Son of Holmes ("Auguste Lupa" series), Donald I. Fine (New York, NY), 1986.

Rasputin's Revenge: The Further Startling Adventures of Auguste Lupa—Son of Holmes ("Auguste Lupa" series), Donald I. Fine (New York, NY), 1987.

Son of Holmes and Rasputin's Revenge: The Early Works of John T. Lescroart, Donald I. Fine (New York, NY), 1995.

A Certain Justice ("Abe Glitsky" series), Donald I. Fine (New York, NY), 1995.

Guilt ("Abe Glitsky" series), Delacorte Press (New York, NY), 1997.

Writer of more than 500 songs; recorded (with Amy Tan and Norman Mailer) *Lit Rock Sampler #1,* "Don't Quit Your Day Job" Records, San Francisco, CA.

ADAPTATIONS: Novels adapted as audio recordings include *Nothing but the Truth* (abridged; four cassettes), BDD, 2000; *The Hearing* (unabridged), Brilliance Audio; and *The Oath* (unabridged), Brilliance Audio, 2002.

SIDELIGHTS: John T. Lescroart worked at a variety of jobs, his last at a law firm, before he quit to become a full-time writer. The event that changed his life was a near-death experience when he contracted spinal meningitis from contaminated sea water and lay in a coma for eleven days before making an unexpected recovery. Since that time, his list of novels has grown, notably his popular series featuring the evolving character Dismas Hardy.

Richard G. La Porte, writing in *St. James Guide to Crime and Mystery Writers,* noted, "After a Joseph Henry Jackson Award-winning and veiled autobiographical *Sunburn . . .* Lescroart went on to a two-step experiment in the creation of a literary linkage between the Sherlock Holmes/Irene Adler liaison and Nero Wolfe called John Hamish Adler-Holmes who appears in *Son of Holmes* and *Rasputin's Revenge: The Further Startling Adventures of Auguste Lupa—Son of Holmes* as Auguste Lupa. Lupa, a British Secret Service agent with a penchant for Roman Imperial aliases works for Mycroft Holmes the original 'M' of the Service but carries an American passport. After The Great War Lupa retired to New York City and apparently took up orchid culture. Both of these relatively brief novels are well planned and researched and are believable pastiches. Lescroart is not, of course, the first to determine Nero Wolfe's parentage."

Lescroart's second series features the wayward Dismas Hardy of San Francisco's corporate culture. "In *Dead Irish,*" stated La Porte, Dismas Hardy is "a failed cop, husband, lawyer, and parent. He [is] a part-time barkeep, nursing his Guinness and darts in the Little Shamrock, catty-cornered across 9th and Lincoln from the Hall of Flowers in Golden Gate Park." A *Library Journal* reviewer deemed the book "a full-bodied, substantive, and stylistic effort of the first order [with] full attention to character . . . a sympathetic protagonist, and a satisfying conclusion." Peter Robertson, writing in *Booklist,* called it "An unusual and powerful mystery." In the same *Booklist* review of *The Vig* ("vig" or "vigorish" is street slang for the interest a loan shark charges), Robertson said, "Details are all in Lescroart's compelling vision of a world made up of dark bars, dark drinks, and dark lives."

In a *Publishers Weekly* review of *The 13th Juror* the critic stated that "the story gets off to a slow start . . . and [Lescroart] . . . comes close to telegraphing the solution to the mystery, and much of his writing about characters' personal lives is hamfisted. Despite these flaws, however, an intricate story and satisfying court-

room scenes carry the day." Dan Bogey, writing in *Booklist,* called the novel "very readable . . . with engaging characters and a riveting plot that fans of Scott Turow and John Grisham will love."

Regarding the protagonist of Lescroart's "Abe Glitsky" series novels *A Certain Justice* and *Guilt,* La Porte summarized: "Back before *Dead Irish* when Hardy was a cop, his partner was Abe Glitsky. Abe stayed in the SFPD and is on his way up the promotional ladder with its treacherous snakes of political reform. Affirmative action policies posed a double-ended problem to Abe. Glitsky senior is an orthodox Jew and Abe's mother was black. Although his appearance is strongly African-American, his commitments are not."

Dawn L. Anderson, writing in *Library Journal,* called *A Certain Justice* a "heart-stopping thriller" that "will keep readers riveted to their chairs." *Chicago Tribune* reviewer Chris Petrakos agreed, noting that "Lescroart does a masterly job juggling politics and justice, demonstrating along the way that the two rarely mix." A *Kirkus Reviews* critic surmised that it is not as humorous as Tom Wolfe's *Bonfire of the Vanities,* but it is "just as mordant and electric." Steve Brewer, writing in *Mostly Murder,* called *Guilt* "a blockbuster of a trial. . . . [Lescroart] establishes the main characters carefully."

La Porte stated, "Although the Hardy/Glitsky books are part of the mystery/detection genre, they are far more fully developed than most of the earlier series character studies. For one thing, the greater length gives Lescroart more time for detailing the fauna and flora of the mean streets of San Francisco and their effects on the people in the story. For another, they are primarily plot-driven, character-development studies. They are not stories of how the protagonist, The Master Detective, brings his acute powers to bear on a single problem but more the reverse. The crime and its manifestations are brought to bear on the protagonist forcing him to rise, change, and challenge himself to prove his beliefs."

La Porte summarized, "All of this [writing] is done with a smooth literary style with a padding of truth and a verisimilitude that makes you feel that you are right there where it is happening. There may not be an old bar with its dartboard on that corner of 9th and Lincoln but it seems as if there should be one. This is one of the strongest points in Lescroart's writing; the believability, not only the places, but also the people."

In *The Mercy Rule,* called a "satisfying legal thriller" by Melissa Kuzma Rokicki in *Library Journal,* Graham Russo asks defense attorney Dismas to represent him when Graham is accused of murdering his father, Sal, who had been suffering from Alzheimer's disease and a brain tumor. Graham admits to Dismas that had assisted his father with his morphine injections, but denies that he ended his father's life. Homicide detective Sarah Evans and Dismas believe that Sal was murdered, but not by Graham. A *Publishers Weekly* reviewer called the courtroom scenes "little masterpieces of battlefield maneuvering," but added that "because the book's only overarching concerns are plot-related . . . the added level of depth and concern that would create a truly great courtroom thriller are absent." *Booklist* contributor Gilbert Taylor said Lescroart "has the technical clues of the plot perfectly arranged . . . but it's his credible characters who cement this entertaining, front-rank whodunit."

Nothing but the Truth finds Dismas and his wife, Frannie, drifting apart, which explains why Dismas didn't know that Frannie had been subpoenaed to appear before the grand jury to testify when her friend, Ron Beaumont, is suspected in the death of his wife, Bree, who had been a political advisor and the possible lover of a gubernatorial candidate. Ron has shared a secret with Frannie, which she refuses to relate, and now Frannie faces contempt charges and jail time. Dismas steps in to help Frannie and vows to find the actual murderer, but the first officer assigned to the case has already been murdered, and trouble comes at Dismas from all directions. A *Publishers Weekly* contributor wrote that "it's the close-to-home secrets affecting Hardy and his marriage that resonate most," and concluded by calling the novel a "winning thriller." *Booklist* reviewer Emily Melton commented on the many elements of the plot, but said that Lescroart "keeps his potboiler under control, and the result is a riveting if over-the-top thriller." Thea Davis reviewed *Nothing but the Truth* for the *Mystery Reader* online, saying that "scenes shift swiftly, although the pace is slowed by an extraordinary amount of detail."

A *Kirkus Reviews* contributor wrote that in *The Hearing,* Lescroart "lays on the political intrigue as fearlessly as if he were writing exposé journalism." Junkie Cole Burgess is found by the body of Elaine Wager, a former assistant district attorney and the daughter of a deceased female senator. Cole, who was holding the murder weapon and whose pockets were filled with Elaine's jewelry, is coerced into making a full confession with the promise of a fix, and a friend asks Dismas to defend Cole, who has obviously been railroaded. Cole is swiftly prosecuted by a district attorney who wants the death penalty, and also by Abe Glitsky, who was actually Elaine's unacknowledged father. Abe is

suspended for leaking Cole's confession and changes sides, opposing the district attorney when he sees holes in the case against Cole. The cast of *The Hearing* is large, but a *Publishers Weekly* reviewer said that its "richness and diversity . . . neither slows the pace nor confuses the narrative, as even minor characters take on memorable presence and depth." *Library Journal* reviewer Nancy McNicol called the plot "tightly constructed."

In Joe Hartlaub's review of *The Hearing* for *Bookreporter.com,* he commented that Lescroart's descriptions of San Francisco are "just right." Hartlaub called the plot "intriguing, complex. . . . Lescroart's unrushed and thoughtful narrative expertly and meticulously begins to paint each piece of the puzzle and slowly put them together, one-by-one. While he does this, we really get to know and care about the people involved." Hartlaub concluded by calling *The Hearing* "an all encompassing feast for the senses with enough mystery, drama, and characterization to fill three books."

Lescroart once told *CA:* "I have always been intrigued with the written word. I viewed my creative writing assignments as early as the sixth grade as great fun, and I continue to feel pretty much the same way. After experimenting with short stories, poetry, and song lyrics (and continuing to do so), when I was twenty-two I took the plunge and began my first novel, which no one will ever see.

"Six years later, my novel *Sunburn* won the Joseph Henry Jackson Award from the San Francisco Foundation. That award gave me the confidence to continue my pursuit of novel-writing as a career. Though it hasn't to this day proven especially lucrative, I still love writing books. I work daily first thing in the morning for two to four hours and also work full-time (currently as a word processor, though I have done the proverbial 'everything' they say every writer needs to do, from singing to bartending to house painting to consulting). I don't consider this an ideal situation, and I would very much like to be able to devote more time to writing. Still, I have finished two novels in the past year and continue to keep busy and hopeful. I am blessed with my wife Lisa, who is incredibly and consistently supportive of my pursuit of my dreams and my art.

"My heroes, disparate though they may be, are Ernest Hemingway, Lawrence Durrell, and John Fowles. I like Larry McMurtry and James Clavell. I am also a big fan of several mystery writers, including Arthur Conan Doyle, Rex Stout, John D. MacDonald, P. D. James, and Elmore Leonard. And I continue to believe, naively I'm sure, that if more people would read quality fiction, it would do more good for them and for the world than all the how-to and self-help books ever published."

BIOGRAPHICAL/CRITICAL SOURCES:

BOOKS

St. James Guide to Crime and Mystery Writers, 4th edition, Gale (Detroit, MI), 1996.

PERIODICALS

Booklist, January 15, 1990, pp. 804, 976; September 1, 1994, Dan Bogey, review of *The 13th Juror,* p. 27; July, 1998, Gilbert Taylor, review of *The Mercy Rule,* p. 1830; November 15, 1999, Emily Melton, review of *Nothing but the Truth,* p. 580.
Books, summer, 1999, review of *Nothing but the Truth,* p. 20.
Chicago Tribune, July 16, 1995, Chris Petrakos, review of *A Certain Justice,* p. 6.
Kirkus Reviews, June 1, 1995, review of *A Certain Justice,* p. 731; August 1, 1998, review of *The Mercy Rule,* p. 132; November 15, 1999, review of *Nothing but the Truth,* p. 1764; February 1, 2001, review of *The Hearing,* p. 132.
Library Journal, January, 1990, p. 151; July, 1994, p. 127; July, 1995, p. 121; January, 1998, review of *Guilt,* p. 176; August, 1998, Melissa Kuzma Rokicki, review of *The Mercy Rule,* p. 132; November 15, 1999, Nancy McNicol, review of *Nothing but the Truth,* p. 100; January 1, 2001, Nancy McNicol, review of *The Hearing,* p. 155.
Mostly Murder, May-June, 1997, Steve Brewer, review of *Guilt.*
New York Law Journal, January 5, 2001, Pamela Aucoin, review of *The Hearing,* p. 2
Publishers Weekly, June 20, 1994, review of *The 13th Juror,* pp. 93-94; August 17, 1998, review of *The Mercy Rule,* p. 48; December 13, 1999, review of *Nothing but the Truth,* p. 64; March 12, 2001, review of *The Hearing,* p. 60.

OTHER

Bee Book Club, http://www.sacbee.com/ (March 29, 2000), Alison Roberts, "In Character."
Bookreporter.com, http://www.bookreporter.com/ (September 12, 2001), Joe Hartlaub, review of *The Hearing.*

John Lescroart Web site, http://www.johnlescroart.com/ (September 12, 2001).
Mystery Reader, http://www.themysteryreader.com/ (September 12, 2001), Thea Davis, review of *Nothing but the Truth.*

*   *   *

LIPSET, Seymour Martin 1922-

PERSONAL: Born March 18, 1922, in New York, NY; son of Max (a printer) and Lena (Lippman) Lipset; married Elsie Braun, December 26, 1944; children: David, Daniel, Carola. *Education:* City College of New York (now City College of the City University of New York), B.S., 1943; Columbia University, Ph.D., 1949. *Religion:* Jewish.

ADDRESSES: Office—Institute of Public Policy, Pohick Module 306, George Mason University, 4400 University Dr., Fairfax, VA 22030-4444. *E-mail*—slipset@gmu.edu.

CAREER: University of Toronto, Toronto, Ontario, Canada, lecturer in sociology, 1946-48; University of California, Berkeley, CA, assistant professor, 1948-50; Columbia University, New York, NY, 1950-56, began as assistant professor, became associate professor of sociology, assistant director of Bureau of Applied Social Research, 1954-56; University of California, Berkeley, CA, professor of sociology, 1956-66, director of Institute of International Studies, 1962-66; Harvard University, Cambridge, MA, professor of government and social relations, 1966-75, George D. Markham Professor of Government, 1974-75; Stanford University, Stanford, CA, professor of political science and sociology, 1975-92, Caroline S. G. Munro Professor, 1981-92, senior fellow, Hoover Institution, 1975—; George Mason University, Fairfax, VA, Hazel Professor of Public Policy, 1990—. Visiting professor, Yale University, New Haven, CT, 1960-61; visiting scholar, Russell Sage Foundation, New York, NY, 1988-89.

Member, Board of Foreign Scholarships, 1968-71; national chair, B'nai B'rith Hillel Foundation, 1975-79, chair of national executive committee, 1979-84; associate president, American Professors for Peace in the Middle East, 1976-77, national president, 1977-81; chair of national faculty cabinet, United Jewish Appeal, 1981-84; co-chair of executive committee, International Center for Peace in the Middle East, 1982-92; chair of Aurora Foundation, 1985—; president, Progressive Foundation, 1991-95; chair, U.S. Institute for Peace, 1996—.

MEMBER: International Sociological Association (chair of committee on political sociology, 1959-71), International Society of Political Psychology (president, 1979-80), American Sociological Association (member of council, 1958-61), American Political Science Association (member of council, 1972-74), Sociological Research Association, American Academy of Arts and Sciences (fellow; vice president, 1974-78), National Academy of Science, National Academy of Education, American Association for the Advancement of Science (fellow; chair of section on economics and social sciences, 1975), Finnish Academy of Science, Institute of Political Studies (Spain; honorary member).

AWARDS, HONORS: Fellow, Social Science Research Council, 1945-46; fellow, Center for Advanced Study in Behavioral Sciences, 1955, 1972; MacIver Award for outstanding work in sociology, 1962, for *Political Man;* M.A., Harvard University, 1966; Gunnar Myrdal Prize, 1970, for *The Politics of Unreason;* Townsend Harris Medal, 1971; Guggenheim fellowship, 1972-73; 125th Anniversary Alumni Medal, City College of the City University of New York, 1973; L.L.D., Villanova University, 1973; M. B. Rawson Award, 1986; Northern Telecommunications gold medal for Canadian studies, 1987; Leon Epstein Prize, American Political Science Association, 1989; Marshall Sklare Award, Association for Social Scientific Study of Jewry, 1993; Woodrow Wilson Center for International Scholars fellow, 1995-96; Helen Dinnerman Prize, World Association for Public Opinion Research, 1997; National Book Award nomination for *The First New Nation;* Margaret Byrd Dawson Medal.

WRITINGS:

Agrarian Socialism, University of California Press (Berkeley, CA), 1950, revised edition, 1972.

(Editor, with R. Bendix) *Class, Status, and Power,* Free Press (New York, NY), 1953.

(With M. Trow and J. S. Coleman) *Union Democracy,* Free Press (New York, NY), 1956.

(With R. Bendix) *Social Mobility in Industrial Society,* University of California Press (Berkeley, CA), 1959, 3rd edition, Transaction Books (New Brunswick, NJ), 1992.

Political Man, Doubleday (Garden City, NY), 1960, expanded edition published as *Political Man: The Social Bases of Politics,* Johns Hopkins University Press (Baltimore, MD), 1981.

(Editor, with W. Galenson) *Labor and Trade Unionism,* Wiley (New York, NY), 1960.

(Editor, with L. Lowenthal) *Culture and Social Character,* Free Press (New York, NY), 1961.

(Editor, with Neil Smelser) *Sociology: Progress of a Decade,* Prentice-Hall (Englewood Cliffs, NJ), 1961.

(Editor and author of introduction) Harriet Martineau, *Society in America,* Doubleday (Garden City, NY), 1962, 2nd edition, Transaction Books (New Brunswick, NJ), 1981.

The First New Nation: The U.S. in Historical and Comparative Perspective, Basic Books (New York, NY), 1963, 2nd edition, Norton (New York, NY), 1979.

(Editor) Moisei Ostrogorskii, *Democracy and the Organization of Political Parties,* Quadrangle (New York, NY), 1964.

(Editor, with Sheldon Wolin) *The Berkeley Student Revolt,* Doubleday (Garden City, NY), 1965.

(Editor, with Neil Smelser) *Social Structure and Social Mobility in Economic Growth,* Aldine (Hawthorne, NY), 1966, reprinted as *Social Structure and Mobility in Economic Development,* Irvington (New York, NY), 1983.

(Editor, with Aldo Solari) *Elites in Latin America,* Oxford University Press (Oxford, England), 1967.

(With S. Rokkan) *Party Systems and Voter Alignments,* Free Press (New York, NY), 1967.

(Editor) *Student Politics,* Basic Books (New York, NY), 1968.

(With Richard Hofstadter) *Turner and the Sociology of the Frontier,* Basic Books (New York, NY), 1968.

Revolution and Counterrevolution, Basic Books (New York, NY), 1968, revised edition, Transaction Books (New Brunswick, NJ), 1988.

(Contributor) Daniel Bell and Irving Kristol, editors, *Confrontation: The Student Rebellions and the Universities,* Basic Books (New York, NY), 1969.

(Editor) *Politics and the Social Sciences,* Oxford University Press (New York, NY), 1969.

(Editor, with P. G. Altbach) *Students in Revolt,* Houghton (Boston, MA), 1969.

(With Earl Raab) *The Politics of Unreason: Right Wing Extremism in America,* Harper (New York, NY), 1970, 2nd edition, University of Chicago Press (Chicago, IL), 1979.

Rebellion in the University: A History of Student Activism in America, Little, Brown (Boston, MA), 1972, 2nd edition, University of Chicago Press (Chicago, IL), 1976.

(With Gerald M. Schaflander) *Passion and Politics,* Little, Brown (Boston, MA), 1972.

Opportunity and Welfare in the First New Nation, American Enterprise Institute for Public Policy Research (Washington, DC), 1974.

(With David Riesman) *Education and Politics at Harvard,* McGraw (New York, NY), 1975.

(With Everett Carll Ladd, Jr.) *The Divided Academy: Professors and Politics,* Norton (New York, NY), 1976.

(Editor) *The Third Century: America as a Post-Industrial Society,* Hoover Institution (Stanford, CA), 1979.

(Editor) *Emerging Coalitions in American Politics,* Institute for Contemporary Studies (San Francisco, CA), 1979.

(Editor) *Party Coalitions in the 1980s,* Institute for Contemporary Studies (San Francisco, CA), 1981.

(Editor) Moisei Ostrogorski, *Democracy and the Organization of Political Parties,* Transaction Books (New Brunswick, NJ), 1982.

The Confidence Gap: Business, Labor, and Government in the Public Mind, Free Press (New York, NY), 1983.

(Editor, with John H. M. Laslett) *Failure of a Dream?: Essays in the History of American Socialism,* University of California Press (Berkeley, CA), 1984.

Consensus and Conflict: Essays in Political Sociology, Transaction Books (New Brunswick, NJ), 1985.

Unions in Transition: Entering the Second Century, Institute for Contemporary Studies (San Francisco, CA), 1986.

Continental Divide: The Values and Institutions of the United States and Canada, Canadian-American Committee (Washington, DC), 1989.

(Editor) *American Pluralism and the Jewish Community,* Transaction Books (New Brunswick, NJ), 1990.

(Editor, with Larry Diamond and Juan J. Linz) *Politics in Developing Countries: Comparing Experiences with Democracy,* L. Rienner (Boulder, CO), 1990, 2nd edition, 1995.

North American Cultures: Values and Institutions in Canada and the United States, Borderlands Project (Orono, ME), 1990.

Passion and Politics [and] *Rebellion in the University,* Transaction Books (New Brunswick, NJ), 1993.

(Editor-in-chief) *The Encyclopedia of Democracy,* Congressional Quarterly (Washington, DC), 1995.

(With Earl Raab) *Jews and the New American Scene,* Harvard University Press (Cambridge, MA), 1995.

American Exceptionalism: A Double-edged Sword, Norton (New York, NY), 1996.

(With Gary Marks) *It Didn't Happen Here: Why Socialism Failed in the United States,* Norton (New York, NY), 2000.

(Editor, with Terry Nichols Clark) *The Breakdown of Class Politics: A Debate on Post-industrial Stratification,* Johns Hopkins University Press (Baltimore, MD), 2001.

Contributor to *Encounter, New Republic, Commentary, New York Times Magazine, Reporter,* and other periodicals. Co-editor, *Public Opinion,* 1978—.

SIDELIGHTS: Seymour Martin Lipset is "an internationally renowned political scientist and sociologist," according to David Rouse in *Booklist.* Lipset has devoted decades of academic study to the peculiarities of American political culture and how that culture impacts upon sub-groups within the American populace. A sociologist, historian, and political scientist, Lipset has compared American society to that of Canada and various developed nations; he is an authority on the way in which democratic political ideals have shaped the United States; and in his books he has written on the subject of American exceptionalism and its influence upon Jews in particular. According to J. M. Cameron in the *New York Review of Books,* Lipset's works provide "a way of coming to know more about one's own culture and to measure the qualities of one's own society." In *Commonweal,* Thomas Massaro concluded that the author's books "make sound contributions to our understanding of American political culture."

Lipset's academic career began in Canada following World War II, and included joint appointments at the Hoover Institute and George Mason University. His more recent research has focused on the ways in which the ideals of the American Revolution—"live free or die," for instance—have shaped the American character and dictated the American social agenda. In *The Continental Divide: The Values and Institutions of the United States and Canada* and *American Exceptionalism: A Double-edged Sword,* the author incorporates history, political philosophy, and sociological data in search of what is exceptional—not necessarily what is *good*—about America. A reviewer for *Economist* suggested that, in *American Exceptionalism,* Lipset "comes up with explanations for all sorts of American oddities: low turnout at elections, extremes of income, intolerance towards ethnic minorities and high crime rates." Massaro argued that *American Exceptionalism* "[goes] beyond merely expounding a set of predetermined conclusions or recommendations and [provides] readers with analytic tools for use in the assessment of American political culture."

American Exceptionalism identifies and defines an American Creed, based upon liberty, egalitarianism, individualism, populism, and laissez-faire. These ideals, the scholar demonstrates, have led to a distrust of socialism, lower per capita taxes than other developed nations, higher rates of litigation, and a belief in upward mobility—among other American attributes. Comparisons to Canada, which also appear in *Continental Divide,* help to clarify the exceptional nature of American society. In *Washington Post Book World,* Martin Walker called *American Exceptionalism* a "masterpiece," observing: "Seymour Martin Lipset is one of America's most useful intellectuals. . . . More than any other figure, with the possible exception of John Kenneth Galbraith, he plausibly explains to us baffled aliens why you Americans are so very odd."

It is the "double-edged sword" that preoccupies Lipset in his book, *Jews and the New American Scene,* coauthored with Earl Raab. The writers argue that America's tolerance for ethnic and religious minorities has created a climate in which American Jews thrive economically and feel less inclined to remain within the bounds of their faith. "Pessimism regarding Jewish life is usually associated with a deep concern about anti-Semitism, but this is not what animates Lipset and Raab," maintained David Singer in *Commentary.* "Indeed, as they see it, anti-Semitism is at present a marginal phenomenon in American society. What preoccupies these writers is not the external but the internal threat: a sharp fall-off in Jewish identity and a serious weakening of Jewish commitment. Lipset and Raab argue forcefully that American Jews have become victims of their own success, achieving integration and acceptance in the larger American society at the price of a declining sense of their own Jewishness."

Critics of *Jews and the New American Scene* applauded Lipset and Raab, despite the fact that their conclusions paint a grim picture of the future of Judaism in America. Singer noted that the book "gives flesh to the anguished concern voiced by many over 'Jewish continuity.'" *Times Literary Supplement* contributor Anne Swidler deemed the work "a courageous and unsettling book," from authors with "a long, unbroken commitment to Jewish continuity in the United States and Israel." In the *Wall Street Journal,* Jay P. Lefkowitz concluded that Lipset and Raab "have written an important book, and their pessimism about the future of American Jewry is well-founded."

In *It Didn't Happen Here: Why Socialism Failed in the United States,* Lipsett and coauthor Gary Marks examine why the United States has never become a socialist country or developed a strong socialist movement. In the late nineteenth and early twentieth centuries, many socialists predicted that the United States would be the first country to adopt socialism. In 1912, the Socialist Party won only six percent of the vote, the party's best showing in a national election. While European socialist parties exerted strong influence in their countries, American socialists were marginal figures. According to David Glenn in *New York Times Book Review, It Didn't Happen Here* "provides a systematic overview of the

plausible explanations for the American left's weakness." Chief among the reasons that Lipsett and Marks cite for socialism's failure in America are "the absence . . . of rigid class distinctions or of a popular resentment of capitalism and the presence . . . of a highly individualistic ethos," as Arch Puddington explained in *Commentary.* Duncan Stewart in *Library Journal* found *It Didn't Happen Here* to be "a great leap forward in scholarship about socialism in America." Puddington concluded that "in skillfully illuminating the roots of this ineffectual tradition, *It Didn't Happen Here* makes a valuable contribution to historical understanding."

BIOGRAPHICAL/CRITICAL SOURCES:

PERIODICALS

American History Review, June, 1997, reviews of *American Exceptionalism,* pp. 749-769.
American Political Science Review, December, 1999, review of *Jews and the New American Scene,* p. 935.
American Spectator, April, 1995, pp. 66-67.
Booklist, July, 2000, David Rouse, review of *It Didn't Happen Here,* p. 1981.
Christian Science Monitor, August 22, 1968; April 29, 1996.
Commentary, April, 1995, pp. 64-67; October, 2000, Arch Puddington, review of *It Didn't Happen Here,* p. 78.
Commonweal, September 13, 1996, pp. 38-39.
Contemporary Sociology, May, 1976.
Detroit News, February 6, 1972.
Economist, February 24, 1996, p. 90; June 3, 2000, "Blame the Steaks," p. 83.
Journal of American Studies, August, 1997, review of *American Exceptionalism,* p. 322.
Journal of Social History, fall, 1997, review of *American Exceptionalism,* p. 196.
Library Journal, July, 2000, Duncan Stewart, review of *It Didn't Happen Here,* p. 115.
Nation, May 6, 1996, pp. 28-34; September 4, 2000, March Chandler, "Creeping Socialism?," p. 38.
National Review, February 23, 1971; October 14, 1983, pp. 1286-1287; August 14, 2000, Fred Siegel, "The Statist Temptation."
New England Quarterly, June, 1976.
New Leader, December 4, 1967.
New Statesman, December 22, 1967.
New York Review of Books, April 28, 1977; August 16, 1990, pp. 25-27.

New York Times, October 10, 1966.

New York Times Book Review, April 10, 1983, p. 7; May 13, 1990, p. 41; March 26, 1995, p. 20; February 11, 1996, p. 7; September 3, 2000, David Glenn, "Waiting for Lefty."

Political Science Quarterly, fall, 1997, review of *American Exceptionalism,* p. 506.

Publishers Weekly, June 19, 2000, review of *It Didn't Happen Here,* p. 68.

Quarterly Journal of Speech, December, 1972.

Religious Studies Review, January, 1998, review of *Jews and the New American Scene,* p. 119.

Society, September, 1997, review of *American Exceptionalism,* p. 72.

Times Literary Supplement, August 29, 1969; November 2-8, 1990, p. 1189; August 4, 1995, p. 10.

Tribune Books (Chicago), June 1, 1997, review of *American Exceptionalism,* p. 8.

Virginia Quarterly Review, summer, 1999, review of *A Double-edged Sword,* p. 599.

Wall Street Journal, May 10, 1995.

Washington Post, October 7, 1970.

Washington Post Book World, May 6, 1990, p. 6; April 7, 1996, pp. 4-5.

OTHER

Seymour Martin Lipset's Web site, http://www.hoover.stanford.edu/bios/lipset.html/ (January 28, 2002).*

*   *   *

LITTLE, Bentley 1960-
(Phillip Emmons)

PERSONAL: Born 1960, in Mesa, AZ; son of Larry (a teacher) and Roseanne (an artist; maiden name Dobrinin) Little; married Wai Sau Li (a librarian), 1995. *Education:* California State University, Fullerton, B.A., 1994, M.A., 1996. *Politics:* "Liberal."

ADDRESSES: Home—Fullerton, CA. *Agent*—Dominick Abel, 146 West 82nd St., Suite 1B, New York, NY 10024.

CAREER: Writer. Worked as a journalist.

AWARDS, HONORS: Bram Stoker Award for best first novel, Horror Writers of America, 1990, for *The Revelation.*

WRITINGS:

HORROR NOVELS

The Revelation, St. Martin's Press (New York, NY), 1989.

The Mailman, Onyx (New York, NY), 1991.

(As Phillip Emmons) *Death Instinct,* Signet Books (New York, NY), 1992, published under name Bentley Little as *Evil Deeds,* Headline (London, England), 1994.

The Summoning, Zebra (New York, NY), 1993.

Night School, Headline (London, England), 1994, published as *University,* Signet Books (New York, NY), 1995.

Dark Dominion, Headline (London, England), 1995, published as *Dominion,* Signet Books (New York, NY), 1996.

The Store, Headline (London, England), 1996, Signet Books (New York, NY), 1998.

Houses, Headline (London, England), 1997.

The Ignored, Signet Books (New York, NY), 1997.

Guests, Headline (London, England), 1997.

The Town, Signet Books (New York, NY), 2000.

The Walking, Signet Books (New York, NY), 2000.

The Association, Signet Books (New York, NY), 2001.

Contributor of short stories to anthologies. Also contributor of short stories to periodicals, including *Cemetery Dance, Grue Magazine, Gauntlet, The Horror Show,* and *Eldritch Tales.*

SIDELIGHTS: Horror author Bentley Little attracted notice and praise with his debut novel, *The Revelation,* which received the Bram Stoker Award for best first novel. Many of Little's works are set in rural areas in the American Southwest, and this book is among them, detailing bizarre happenings in the small town of Randall, Arizona. These include the unexplained pregnancy of an elderly woman, a rash of deaths of farmers and their livestock, the disappearance of a local clergyman (while obscene writings appear in blood in his church and home), and the arrival of a strange new minister who seems to know everything about the townspeople and seeks their help in a battle he says is forthcoming. This all adds up to an apocalyptic tale: "Obviously, forces as old as the sun have converged on Randall, Arizona," observed an essayist for the *St. James Guide to Horror, Ghost, and Gothic Writers.*

Little's follow-up novel, *The Mailman,* may be his "*tour de force* to date," the same essayist remarked. "Again, in a small community, a form of hell breaks out—but it is a very strange version indeed. Showing the flip-side of *The Revelation*'s overtly supernatural and *faux-religious* horrors, *The Mailman* is squarely built on a foundation of paranoia." The eponymous mailman, John Smith, is able to control and frighten the town's entire population by misdirecting the mail. "Inch by inch," the *St. James Guide* contributor related, "he manages to make the townspeople drift from a happy-go-lucky *joie de vivre*, to a sense of mutual suspicion, to outright hatred." Eventually, the essayist added, "the scene is set for a form of fiery apocalypse."

Among Little's other works is *The Summoning*, a 1993 tale that concerns an extraordinary vampire capable of great evil and mayhem. In the novel, this vampire settles in a small town and proceeds to terrorize and dominate the population. A reviewer for *Science Fiction Chronicle* commented that the book is both "a good old fashioned vampire story and an innovative new one." That reviewer expressed regret that "this excellent book" might not get the attention it deserved, due to an influx of books in the vampire genre. In *The Ignored*, a new employee finds himself increasingly ignored by co-workers. He therefore determines to arrive at work dressed as a knife-wielding clown. A *Publishers Weekly* reviewer called *The Ignored* a "nightmarishly brilliant tour de force."

The Town concerns a man, Gregory Tomasov, who wins the California state lottery and decides to move with his wife and three young children to his boyhood hometown of McGuane, Arizona. The Tomasovs do not realize the house they move into is haunted, having been the site of a murder-suicide. The Tomasovs begin behaving strangely and are blamed for numerous peculiar and horrifying events around McGuane—the birth of a cactus-baby and the violent deaths of several townspeople among them. A *Publishers Weekly* commentator praised the novel's "terrifying finale" and noted that "what, in a lesser writer's hands, would have been an obvious conclusion remains a mystery until the end."

The Walking finds a dead man reanimated and appearing to his son, Miles Huerdeen, a private investigator trying to determine the forces behind a series of mysterious deaths. Miles then discovers that there are numerous other members of the walking dead about, and that they are headed for a canyon in the Arizona desert, "formerly a government sponsored witch colony, where a vengeful resident's evil powers have yet to be fully unleashed," a *Publishers Weekly* critic reported. The critic thought that "readers will gladly suspend disbelief for Little's deft touch for the terrifying." Meanwhile, *Library Journal* contributor Jackie Cassada praised Little's "uncanny sense of horror."

Snob zoning and luxury real estate get satiric horror treatment in *The Association*. In this novel, a couple who move to an exclusive gated community in a fictional Utah town find themselves living in what a reviewer for *Publishers Weekly* described as "the kind of deranged world" that protagonist Barry, a horror writer, "once believed existed only within the safety of his imagination." Behind this nightmare environment is the community's powerful Homeowners' Association, which creates and brutally enforces all manner of strict rules for residents. The reviewer judged *The Association* to be "an incredibly credible tale" and a worthy addition to Little's impressive horror opus.

Little has won comparisons with and accolades from Stephen King and other prominent writers of horror fiction. "That Bentley Little has been praised liberally by writers as non-diverse as Richard Laymon, Stephen King and Gary Brandner (by generic horror writers, in other words) gives the reader two matters to think about," commented the *St. James Guide* essayist. "The first is that there should be no doubt as to what is in store (or even in Store) with a Bentley Little novel: his writing is one-hundred per cent horror, and he is clearly at ease with this. And the second is that he offers additions to the small-town-under-threat canon that the aforementioned trio have contributed to in the past. Bentley Little is on his way to achieving—perhaps surpassing—their critical stature."

BIOGRAPHICAL/CRITICAL SOURCES:

BOOKS

Reginald, Robert, *Science Fiction & Fantasy Literature, 1975-1991*, Gale (Detroit, MI), 1992.
St. James Guide to Horror, Ghost, and Gothic Writers, St. James Press (Detroit, MI), 1998.

PERIODICALS

Library Journal, January, 1990, pp. 148-149; November 15, 2000, Jackie Cassada, review of *The Walking*, p. 101.
Locus, August, 1993, p. 46.
Publishers Weekly, January 5, 1990, p. 62; April 14, 1997, p. 71; April 17, 2000, review of *The Town*, p. 58; October 16, 2000, review of *The Walking*, p. 55; August 27, 2001, review of *The Association*, p. 62.
Science Fiction Chronicle, August, 1993, p. 38.*

LITTLEWIT, Humphrey, Gent.
    See LOVECRAFT, H(oward) P(hillips)

*   *   *

LONGBAUGH, Harry
    See GOLDMAN, William (W.)

*   *   *

LOVECRAFT, H(oward) P(hillips) 1890-1937
    (Lawrence Appleton, Houdini, John J. Jones, Humphrey Littlewit, Gent., Henry Paget-Lowe, Ward Phillips, Richard Raleigh, Ames Dorrance Rowley, Edgar Softly, Edward Softly, Augustus Swift, Lewis Theobald, Jr., Frederick Willie, Zoilus)

H. P. Lovecraft

PERSONAL: Born August 20, 1890, in Providence, RI; died of cancer and Bright's disease, March 15, 1937, in Providence, RI; son of Winfield Scott (a traveling salesman) and Sarah (Phillips) Lovecraft; married Sonia H. Greene, 1924 (divorced, 1929). *Education:* Self-educated.

CAREER: Short story writer, novelist, poet, and essayist. Worked as a ghostwriter, revisionist, and amateur journalist; *Evening News,* Providence, RI, astrology columnist, 1914-18; publisher of *The Conservative,* 1915-19 and 1923. President of United Amateur Press Association, 1917-18 and 1923.

WRITINGS:

FICTION

The Shadow over Innsmouth, illustrated by Frank A. Utpatel, Visionary Publishing (Everett, PA), 1936.
The Outsider and Others, collected by August Derleth and Donald Wandrei, Arkham (Sauk City, WI), 1939.
Beyond the Wall of Sleep (includes *The Dream Quest of Unknown Kadath* [also see below] and *The Case of Charles Dexter Ward* [also see below]), collected by August Derleth and Donald Wandrei, Arkham (Sauk City, WI), 1943.
The Weird Shadow over Innsmouth, and Other Stories of the Supernatural, Bartholomew House, 1944.
The Dunwich Horror, [New York, NY], 1945.
(With August Derleth) *The Lurker at the Threshold,* Arkham (Sauk City, WI), 1945.

Best Supernatural Stories of H. P. Lovecraft, edited with introduction by August Derleth, World Publishing, 1945.
The Lurking Fear, and Other Stories, Avon (New York, NY), 1948, published under title *Cry Horror!,* 1958, reprinted under original title, Ballantine (New York, NY), 1971.
Something about Cats, and Other Pieces, collected by August Derleth, Arkham (Sauk City, WI), 1949.
The Dream Quest of Unknown Kadath, introduction by George T. Wetzel, Shroud (Buffalo, NY), 1955, reprinted, edited with new introduction by Lin Carter, Ballantine (New York, NY), 1970.
(With August Derleth) *The Survivor and Others,* Arkham (Sauk City, WI), 1957.
The Shuttered Room, and Other Pieces, collected by August Derleth, Arkham (Sauk City, WI), 1959.
Dreams and Fancies, Arkham (Sauk City, WI), 1962.
(With August Derleth) *The Shadow out of Space,* introduction by Sam Moskowitz, [New York], 1962.
The Dunwich Horror, and Others: The Best Supernatural Stories of H. P. Lovecraft, collected with introduction by August Derleth, Arkham (Sauk City, WI), 1963, revised edition, edited by S. T. Joshi, 1985.
At the Mountains of Madness, and Other Novels, collected with introduction by August Derleth, Arkham

(Sauk City, WI), 1964, revised edition, edited by S. T. Joshi, introduction by James Turner, 1985.

Dagon and Other Macabre Tales, collected with introduction by August Derleth, Arkham (Sauk City, WI), 1965, revised edition, edited by S. T. Joshi, 1987.

The Case of Charles Dexter Ward, complete edition, Belmont Books, 1965.

The Dark Brotherhood, and Other Pieces, Arkham (Sauk City, WI), 1966.

Three Tales of Horror, illustrated by Lee Brown Coye, Arkham (Sauk City, WI), 1967.

The Colour out of Space, and Others, Lancer Books, 1967.

(With August Derleth) *The Shadow out of Time, and Other Tales of Horror,* Gollancz (London, England), 1968.

At the Mountains of Madness, and Other Tales of Terror, Panther, 1968, Beagle Books, 1971.

The Haunter of the Dark, and Other Tales of Horror, edited with introduction by August Derleth, Gollancz (London, England), 1969.

(With others) *Tales of the Cthulhu Mythos,* collected by August Derleth, Arkham (Sauk City, WI), 1969.

The Tomb and Other Tales, collected by August Derleth, Panther, 1969, Ballantine (New York, NY), 1970.

(With August Derleth) *The Shuttered Room, and Other Tales of Horror,* Panther, 1970.

(With others) *The Horror in the Museum, and Other Revisions,* Arkham (Sauk City, WI), 1970, 3rd revised and enlarged edition, edited by S. T. Joshi, 1989.

The Doom That Came to Sarnath, edited with introduction by Lin Carter, Ballantine (New York, NY), 1971.

Nine Stories from "The Horror in the Museum and Other Revisions," Beagle Books, 1971.

(With others) *The Spawn of Cthulhu,* edited with introduction by Lin Carter, Ballantine (New York, NY), 1971.

(With August Derleth) *The Watchers out of Time, and Others,* foreword by April Derleth, Arkham (Sauk City, WI), 1974.

(With others) *The Horror in the Burying Ground, and Other Tales,* Panther, 1975.

Herbert West: Reanimator, edited by Marc A. Michaud, Necronomicon Press (West Warwick, RI), 1977.

Writings in the Tryout, edited by Marc A. Michaud, foreword by S. T. Joshi, Necronomicon Press (West Warwick, RI), 1977.

(With others) *New Tales of the Cthulhu Mythos,* Arkham (Sauk City, WI), 1980.

The Best of H. P. Lovecraft: Bloodcurdling Tales of Horror and the Macabre, introduction by Robert Bloch, Ballantine (New York, NY), 1982.

The H. P. Lovecraft Christmas Book, edited by Susan Michard, Necronomicon Press (West Warwick, RI), 1984.

The Night Ocean, Necronomicon Press (West Warwick, RI), 1986.

Cthulhu 2000: A Lovecraftian Anthology, Arkham (Sauk City, WI), 1995.

The Dream Cycle of H. P. Lovecraft: Dreams of Terror and Death, Ballantine (New York, NY), 1995.

Miscellaneous Writings, Arkham (Sauk City), WI, 1995.

The Transition of H. P. Lovecraft: The Road to Madness, Ballantine (New York, NY), 1996.

The Annotated H. P. Lovecraft, edited by S. T. Joshi, Dell (New York, NY), 1997.

Tales of H. P. Lovecraft: Major Works, selected and introduced by Joyce Carol Oates, Ecco Press (Hopewell, NJ), 1997.

The Call of Cthulhu and Other Weird Stories, edited by S. T. Joshi, Penguin Books (New York, NY), 1999.

More Annotated H. P. Lovecraft, edited by Peter Cannon and S. T. Joshi, Dell (New York, NY), 1999.

Author of about sixty stories, many of which were first published in magazines *Weird Tales,* beginning in 1923, *Amazing Stories,* and *Astounding Stories.* Stories have also been published in various multiwork volumes, including *Eleven Great Horror Stories,* 1969, *Ghosts,* 1971, *Summoned from the Tomb,* 1973, *Cries of Terror,* 1976, and *Feast of Fear,* 1977.

Ghostwriter and revisionist under pseudonyms Lawrence Appleton, Houdini, John J. Jones, Humphrey Littlewit, Gent., Henry Paget-Lowe, Ward Phillips, Richard Raleigh, Ames Dorrance Rowley, Edgar Softly, Edward Softly, Augustus Swift, Lewis Theobald, Jr., Frederick Willie, and Zoilus.

POETRY

Collected Poems, illustrated by Frank Utpatel, Arkham (Sauk City, WI), 1963, published under title *Fungi from Yuggoth, and Other Poems,* Ballantine (New York, NY), 1971.

The Prose Poems of H. P. Lovecraft, 4 volumes, Roy Squires (Glendale, CA), 1969-70.

Four Prose Poems, Necronomicon Press (West Warwick, RI), 1987.

The Fantastic Poetry, edited by S. T. Joshi, Necronomicon Press (West Warwick, RI), 1990.

Contributor of poetry to amateur publications.

OTHER

The Notes and Commonplace Book, Futile Press, 1938, reprinted, Necronomicon Press (West Warwick, RI), 1978.

Marginalia, collected by August Derleth and Donald Wandrei, Arkham (Sauk City, WI), 1944.

Supernatural Horror in Literature (essay), introduction by August Derleth, Ben Abramson, 1945, reprinted with new introduction by E. F. Bleiler, Dover (New York, NY), 1973.

Autobiography: Some Notes on a Nonentity, annotated by August Derleth, Arkham (Sauk City, WI), 1963.

Selected Letters, Volume 1: *1911-1924,* Volume 2: *1925-29,* Volume 3: *1929-31,* Volume 4: *1932-34,* Volume 5: *1934-37,* Volumes 1-3 edited by August Derleth and Donald Wandrei, Volumes 4 and 5 edited by August Derleth and J. Turner, Arkham (Sauk City, WI), 1965-76.

(With Willis Conover) *Lovecraft at Last,* foreword by Harold Taylor, Carrollton, Clark, 1975.

The Conservative: Complete, 1915-1923, edited by Marc A. Michaud, foreword by Frank Belknap Long, Necronomicon Press (West Warwick, RI), 1976.

To Quebec and the Stars, edited by L. Sprague de Camp, D. M. Grant (West Kingston, RI), 1976.

First Writings: Pawtuxet Valley Gleaner, 1906 (essays), edited by Marc A. Michaud, foreword by Ramsey Campbell, Necronomicon Press (West Warwick, RI), 1976.

A Winter Wish (essays and poetry), edited by Tom Collins, Whispers Press (Binghamton, NY), 1977.

(With R. H. Barlow) *Collapsing Cosmoses,* Necronomicon Press (West Warwick, RI), 1977.

Memoirs of an Inconsequential Scribbler, Necronomicon Press (West Warwick, RI), 1977.

Uncollected Prose and Poetry, edited by S. T. Joshi and Marc A. Michaud, Necronomicon Press (West Warwick, RI), 1978.

(With J. F. Hartmann) *Science versus Charlatanry: Essays on Astrology,* edited with introduction and notes by S. T. Joshi and Scott Connors, The Strange Company, 1979.

H. P. Lovecraft in "The Eyrie," edited by S. T. Joshi and Marc A. Michaud, Necronomicon Press (West Warwick, RI), 1979.

Juvenilia, 1897-1905, introduction by S. T. Joshi, Necronomicon Press (West Warwick, RI), 1984.

Lord of a Visible World: An Autobiography in Letters, edited by S. T. Joshi and David E. Schultz, Ohio University Press (Athens, OH), 2000.

Annotated Supernatural Horror in Literature, edited by S. T. Joshi, Hippocampus Press (New York, NY), 2000.

Contributor of nonfiction to amateur publications.

ADAPTATIONS: The Case of Charles Dexter Ward was adapted for a film titled *The Haunted Palace,* directed by Roger Corman, 1963, and for a film titled *The Res-*urrected, directed by Dan O'Bannon, 1992; "The Colour out of Space" was adapted for a film titled *Die, Monster, Die!,* directed by Daniel Haller, 1965; "The Shuttered Room" was adapted for a film directed by David Greene, 1968; "The Dunwich Horror" was adapted for a film directed by Daniel Haller, 1970; *Herbert West: Reanimator* was adapted for a film titled *Re-Animator,* directed by Stuart Gordon, 1985; "From Beyond" was adapted for a film of the same name, directed by Stuart Gordon, 1986; "The Unnameable" was adapted for a film of the same name, directed by Jean-Paul Ouellette, 1988; *Necronomicon: Book of the Dead* is a film based on Lovecraft's stories, directed by Christopher Gans, Shusuke Kaneko, and Brian Yuzna, 1994; "Dagon" was adapted for a film of the same name, directed by Stuart Gordon, 2001; "The Haunter of the Dark" was adapted for a film of the same name, directed by Alexander Weimer, 2001.

SIDELIGHTS: H. P. Lovecraft is widely considered the twentieth century's most important writer of supernatural horror fiction. Forging a unique niche within the horror genre, he created what became known as "weird tales," stories containing a distinctive blend of dreamlike imagery, Gothic terror, and elaborate concocted mythology. During his lifetime Lovecraft published work almost exclusively in pulp magazines, and only after his death in 1937 did he receive a wide readership and critical analysis. While many disparage his writings as verbose, melodramatic, and inconsequential, others extol his precise narrative skills and capacity to instill the unsettling. He has been placed among the ranks of such storytellers as Lord Dunsany, Arthur Machen, and Edgar Allan Poe, but, as August Derleth pointed out in *H. P. L.: A Memoir,* "Lovecraft was an original in the Gothic tradition; he was a skilled writer of supernatural fiction, a master of the macabre who had no peer in the America of his time." According to Curt Wohleber in *American Heritage,* Lovecraft was "the man who brought the . . . thriving genre of supernatural fiction into the twentieth century. . . . Lovecraft abandoned the demons, ghosts, and vampires of his nineteenth-century predecessors in favor of modern horrors inspired by Darwinian evolution and Einsteinian physics."

Born in 1890 in Providence, Rhode Island, Lovecraft grew up in the affluent and intellectual surroundings of his grandfather's Victorian mansion. Sickly as a child and only able to attend school sporadically, he was an avid reader, fascinated by eighteenth-century history and Gothic horror stories. He was particularly interested in science and began to write about it at an early age. Following the death of his grandfather in 1904, Lovecraft and his mother moved from the family mansion to a nearby duplex (his father, a virtual stranger to Lovecraft, had died some years earlier after spending the last years of his life in a sanitorium). Lovecraft would later relate that, raised by a sensitive and overprotective mother, he grew up in relative isolation, believing he was unlike other people.

Chronic sickness as a teenager prevented Lovecraft from finishing high school or attending college. He continued his self-education and supported himself by working as a ghostwriter and revisionist—vocations that, though disliked by Lovecraft, would financially sustain him throughout his life. An admirer of Poe, he had begun writing horror tales but, deeming them meager efforts, devoted himself to amateur journalism. In addition, he contributed nonfiction and poetry to magazines. In 1914 Lovecraft joined the United Amateur Press Association, a group of nonprofessional writers who produced a variety of publications and exchanged letters, and one year later he began publishing his own magazine, *The Conservative.* His numerous letters and essays written during this time focus on his deep respect for scientific truth, his love of the past, and his relative disdain for a present-day world populated by non-Anglo-Nordic citizens. Lovecraft developed the belief, to quote Darrell Schweitzer in *The Dream Quest of H. P. Lovecraft,* "that only by clinging to tradition could we make life worth living amidst the chaos of modern civilization."

Lovecraft resumed writing fiction in 1917 and, at the behest of friends, began submitting stories to *Weird Tales,* a pulp magazine that would serve as the major publisher of Lovecraft's writings during his lifetime. Critics note that many of his early tales are heavily influenced by Irish fantasist Lord Dunsany. Such stories as "Dagon," "The White Ship," "The Silver Key," "The Doom That Came to Sarnath," and "The Cats of Ulthar" stem from fairy tale tradition, exhibiting rich dreamlike descriptions and imaginary settings. "This early cycle culminated in the extraordinary short novel Lovecraft called *The Dream Quest of Unknown Kadath,*" stated Lin Carter in his introduction to Ballantine's edition of the work. The story of protagonist Randolph Carter's search for a magnificent city he once envisioned, *The Dream Quest of Unknown Kadath* depicts Carter's voyage into the world of his dreams, where wondrous landscapes and fantastic creatures exist. "Few more magical novels of dream-fantasy exist than this phantasmagoric adventure," declared Carter. "[Never have] the fluid and changing landscapes, the twilit and mysterious silences, and the spire-thronged and opulent Oriental cities of the dreamworld been so lovingly explored."

Contrasting to these relatively innocuous stories of fantasy are Lovecraft's tales of horror, remarkable for their bizarre supernatural conceptions rooted in the realism of a New England setting. Lovecraft was captivated by what he considered the ideal beauty of New England's traditional landscape and architecture. However, he was also intrigued by a perceived darker dimension. His stories "The Unnameable" and "The Picture in the House," for example, depict corruption and superstition that persist in secluded New England areas. "The Festival" illustrates unearthly rituals practiced in the picturesque town of Kingsport—a village Lovecraft modeled after Marblehead, Massachusetts, and "Pickman's Model" focuses on a group of ghouls inhabiting modern Boston. Similar to these stories is the novel *The Case of Charles Dexter Ward,* in which the title character engages in magic to resurrect a seventeenth-century ancestor named Curwen. A practitioner of the black arts in Salem, Curwen is determined to inflict his evil on modern Massachusetts and consequently takes over the identity of Ward, who is later saved by the family doctor.

The best known of Lovecraft's stories are his later ones centering on the "Cthulhu Mythos," a term critics use to describe a distinctive universe of landscape, legends, and mythology completely of Lovecraft's invention. Like his earlier tales, the Cthulhu Mythos works are inspired by New England locales, but their settings are extensively recast to form Arkham, Innsmouth, and Dunwich, fictional worlds overseen by Cthulhu, Yog-Sothoth, and other gods. These stories, explained Lovecraft as quoted by August Derleth, "are based on the fundamental lore or legend that this world was inhabited at one time by another race who, in practising black magic, lost their foothold and were expelled, yet live on the outside ever ready to take possession of this earth again." Tales governed by this principle include "The Nameless City," "The Call of the Cthulhu," "The Whisperer in the Darkness," and *At the Mountains of Madness.*

In addition to writing weird tales, Lovecraft maintained an extensive correspondence and continued to generate a number of essays. Through these nonfiction outlets, he expounded on the aesthetics of supernatural horror fiction and on such philosophies as "mechanistic materialism" and "cosmic indifferentism"—the idea that the universe is a purposeless mechanism wherein humankind is largely insignificant. Lovecraft also produced a relatively large body of poetry, mostly imitative of eighteenth-century masters. Though he wrote prolifically, only one book, 1936's *The Shadow over Innsmouth,* realized publication during his lifetime. When Lovecraft died of intestinal cancer at the age of forty-six, the bulk of his writings remained either scattered in magazines or unpublished.

Later, Lovecraft's friends and fellow writers August Derleth and Donald Wandrei brought his writings to a wide readership. Establishing the publishing house of Arkham expressly to bring Lovecraft's work into book form, Derleth and Wandrei edited such early collections as *The Outsider and Others* in 1939 and *Beyond the Wall of Sleep* in 1943. Numerous volumes of the horror writer's work have been collected by Arkham and other publishers over subsequent decades, and this broader circulation has spawned an extensive and diverse body of analysis.

Admirers of Lovecraft point to several elements in his fiction that distinguish him as a master of supernatural horror. Foremost is his ability to evoke terror through the creation of an unseen and unearthly presence. Lovecraft once explained in his lengthy essay, *Supernatural Horror in Literature,* that in order for fiction to instill fear, "a certain atmosphere of breathless and unexpected dread of outer, unknown forces must be present." Particularly impressed by Lovecraft's capacity to induce anxiety in this way was Angela Carter, who described in an essay appearing in George Hay's *The Necronomicon:* "The twisted shapes of the trees in the woods above Arkham are emanations of the menace they evoke—menace, anguish, perturbation, dread. The cities themselves, whether those of old New England or those that lie beyond the gates of dream, present the dreadful enigma of a maze, always labyrinthine and always, the Minotaur at the heart of this labyrinth, lies the unspeakable in some form or else in some especially vile state of formlessness—the unspeakable, a nameless and unnameable fear."

While some critics have been satisfied that Lovecraft effectively arouses fear solely through developing a sense of imminent dread, others pointed to an extra element in his fiction that creates a more powerful terror. Donald Burleson explained in *H. P. Lovecraft: A Critical Study:* "The horror, ultimately, in a Lovecraft tale is not some gelatinous lurker in dark places, but rather the realization, by the characters involved, of their helplessness and their insignificance in the scheme of things—their terribly ironic predicament of being sufficiently well-developed organisms to perceive and feel the poignancy of their own motelike unimportance in a blind and chaotic universe which neither loves them nor even finds them worthy of notice, let alone hatred or hostility." Steven J. Mariconda, writing in *Lovecraft Studies,* expressed a similar sentiment, calling Lovecraft's tales "cosmic horror . . . the horror of unknowable forces or beings which sweep men aside as indifferently as men do ants."

Other uncommon components marking Lovecraft's work include his manner of combining sterile scientific facts with arcane mysticism. Lovecraft "was uniquely able to link the inner substance of former spiritual beliefs with the most recent scientific discoveries," explained Schweitzer. "He used a rational, mechanistic context to get his readers to the edge of the abyss—and then dropped them over. The result was an irrational horror grimmer than anything a Puritan could conjure up." Critics also admired Lovecraft's ability to agitate his readers by creating an atmosphere of chaos. Lovecraft's universe, according the Maurice Levy in *Lovecraft: A Study in the Fantastic,* is a place of "bizarre dimensions . . . where time and space stretch or contract in incomprehensible ways." These various features of Lovecraft's fiction lead many reviewers to conclude, as Dirk Mosig did in *Whispers,* that "[Lovecraft's] *oeuvre*] is a work of genius, a cosmic-minded *oeuvre* embodying a mechanistic materialist's brilliant conception of the imaginary realms and frightful reality 'beyond the fields we know,' a literary rhapsody of the cosmos and man's laughable position therein. . . . The Lovecraft *oeuvre* can be regarded as a significant contribution to world literature."

Despite extensive praise, controversy exists over Lovecraft's position in American letters. "At his best . . . [Lovecraft] was a superior literary technician," wrote Schweitzer. "At his worst, he was one of the more dreadful writers of this century who is still remembered." Other critics have been less gentle. Deeming Lovecraft "a totally untalented and unreadable writer" as well as "a hopeless and rather pitiful literary crank," Larry McMurtry dismissed Lovecraft in the *Washington Post* as "the master of the turgid and the inflated." Colin Wilson, in *Strength to Dream: Literature and the Imagination,* further attacked the author's prose, claiming, "Lovecraft hurls in the adjectives ('monstrous,' 'slithering,' 'ghoulish,' 'thunder-crazed') until he seems to be a kind of literary dervish who gibbers with hysteria as he spins. . . . [It] must be admitted that Lovecraft is a very bad writer." Even more scornful was Ursula Le Guin, who announced in the *Times Literary Supplement* that Lovecraft "was an exceptionally, almost impeccably, bad writer. . . . Derivative, inept, and callow, his tales can satisfy only those who believe that a capital letter, some words, and a full stop make a sentence."

Curt Wohleber described Lovecraft's prose as "florid" and "Gothic," but the reviewer nevertheless concluded that Lovecraft "explored the territories of alienation surveyed with much different instruments by Sartre, Kafka, and Beckett." Lovecraft himself made no pretensions of possessing great writing talent. "No one is more acutely conscious than I of the inadequacy of my work. . . . I am a self-confessed amateur and bungler, and have not much hope of improvement," the author confessed in

"The Defense Reopens!," an article later collected in S. T. Joshi's *In Defense of Dagon*. He did, however, consider himself a serious artist, practitioner, and theorist. Lovecraft "demanded that the fantastic tale be treated as art, not just a frivolous parlor game or an easy way to make a buck," wrote Schweitzer.

Placing himself among those whom he considered "imaginative artists," such as Poe, Dunsany, William Blake, and Ambrose Bierce, Lovecraft explained in "The Defense Reopens!": "The imaginative writer devotes himself to art in its most essential sense. . . . He is the painter of moods and mind-pictures—a capturer and amplifier of elusive dreams and fancies—a voyager into those unheard-of lands which are glimpsed through the veil of actuality but rarely, and only by the most sensitive. . . . Most persons do not understand what he says, and most of those who do understand object because his statements and pictures are not always pleasant and sometimes *quite impossible*. But he exists not for praise, nor thinks of his readers. His only [goal is] to paint the scenes that pass before his eyes."

BIOGRAPHICAL/CRITICAL SOURCES:

BOOKS

Burleson, Donald, *H. P. Lovecraft: A Critical Study,* Greenwood Press (Westport, CT), 1983.

Carter, Lin, *Lovecraft: A Look behind the "Cthulhu Mythos,"* Ballantine (New York, NY), 1972, updated, 1996.

Carter, Paul A., *The Creation of Tomorrow: Fifty Years of Magazine Science Fiction,* Columbia University Press (New York, NY), 1977.

Davis, Sonia H., *The Private Life of H. P. Lovecraft,* Necronomicon Press (West Warwick, RI), 1985.

De Camp, L. Sprague, *Lovecraft: A Biography,* Doubleday (Garden City, NY), 1975.

Derleth, August, *H. P. L.: A Memoir,* Ben Abramson, 1945.

Faig, Kenneth W., Jr., *H. P. Lovecraft: His Life, His Work,* Necronomicon Press (West Warwick, RI), 1979.

Hay, George, editor, *The Necronomicon,* Neville Spearman (London, England), 1978.

Joshi, S. T., *H. P. Lovecraft; A Life,* Necronomicon Press (West Warwick, RI), 1996.

Joshi, S. T., editor, *H. P. Lovecraft: Four Decades of Criticism,* Ohio University Press (Athens, OH), 1980.

Joshi, S. T., *H. P. Lovecraft and Lovecraft Criticism: An Annotated Bibliography,* Kent State University Press (Kent, OH), 1981.

Joshi, S. T., editor, *In Defense of Dagon,* Necronomicon Press (West Warwick, RI), 1985.

Joshi, S. T., *A Subtler Magick: The Writings and Philosophy of H. P. Lovecraft,* Borgo Press (San Bernardino, CA), 1995.

Levy, Maurice, *Lovecraft: A Study in the Fantastic,* translated by S. T. Joshi, Wayne State University Press (Detroit, MI), 1988.

Long, Frank Belknap, *Howard Phillips Lovecraft: Dreamer on the Nightside,* Arkham (Sauk City, WI), 1975.

Lovecraft, H. P., *Supernatural Horror in Literature,* introduction by August Derleth, Ben Abramson, 1945.

Lovecraft, H. P., *The Dream Quest of Unknown Kadath,* edited by Lin Carter, Ballantine (New York, NY), 1970.

Price, Robert M., editor, *H. P. Lovecraft and the Cthulhu Mythos: Essays on America's Classic Writer of Horror Fiction,* Borgo Press (San Bernardino, CA), 1995.

Schweitzer, Darrell, *The Dream Quest of H. P. Lovecraft,* Borgo Press (San Bernardino, CA), 1978.

Schweitzer, Darrell, editor, *Discovering H. P. Lovecraft,* Starmont House (Mercer Island, WA), 1987, revised, Borgo Press (San Bernardino, CA), 1996.

Short Story Criticism, Volume 3, Gale (Detroit, MI), 1989.

Turner, Jim, editor, *Eternal Lovecraft: The Persistence of HPL in Popular Culture,* Golden Gryphon Press (Collinsville, IL), 1998.

Twentieth-Century Literary Criticism, Gale (Detroit, MI), Volume 4, 1981, Volume 22, 1987.

Weinberg, Robert E., and Martin H. Greenberg, editors, *Lovecraft's Legacy,* Tor Books (New York, NY), 1996.

Wilson, Colin, *The Strength to Dream: Literature and the Imagination,* Houghton Mifflin (Boston, MA), 1962.

PERIODICALS

American Heritage, December, 1995, Curt Wohleber, "The Man Who Can Scare Stephen King," p. 82.

Chicago Tribune, October 25, 1985.

Kirkus Reviews, July 1, 1997, review of *Tales of H. P. Lovecraft.*

Library Journal, July, 2000, Alicia Graybill, review of *Lord of a Visible World: An Autobiography in Letters,* p. 92.

Lovecraft Studies, spring, 1986.

Publishers Weekly, September 2, 1996, review of *The Transition of H. P. Lovecraft: The Road to Madness,* p. 120.

Times Literary Supplement, March 26, 1976.

Village Voice, March 19, 1985.

Washington Post, February 17, 1975; October 25, 1985.

Whispers, December, 1976.

OTHER

Alan Gullette, http://www.creative.net/~alang/(December 13, 2000), "H. P. Lovecraft."*

* * *

LOVELACE, Merline (A.) 1946-

PERSONAL: Born September 9, 1946, in Northampton, MA; daughter of Merlin (in military) and Alyce (a homemaker; maiden name, Griggs) Thoma; married Cary A. Lovelace (in the military), May 2, 1970. *Education:* Ripon College, B.A. (magna cum laude), 1968; Troy State University, M.S. (cum laude), 1975; attended Middlebury College, Princeton University, and Air War College; graduate of Harvard University's Kennedy School of Government, 1991. *Avocational interests:* Reading, golf, old film musicals.

ADDRESSES: Home and office—2325 Tuttington, Oklahoma City, OK 73170; P.O. Box 892717, Oklahoma City, OK 73189. *Agent*—Pam Hopkins, Elaine Davie Literary Agency, 620 Park Ave., Rochester, NY 14607. *E-mail*—merline@merlinelovelace.com.

CAREER: Entered U.S. Air Force in 1968, commissioned, 1968, served at the Pentagon on the staff of a presidential appointee and on the Joint Staff, served in Vietnam and China, commander of Eglin Air Force Base, participated in support service for U.S. invasion of Panama and for the Gulf War, retired with rank of colonel, 1991; novelist, 1991—. Lecturer on women in the military at national and local level.

MEMBER: Romance Writers of America (president, Oklahoma Chapter).

AWARDS, HONORS: Southwest Writer's Workshop prize for Best Historical Novel, and finalist, Romance Writers of America Golden Heart Contest, both 1992, both for *Alena; Bits and Pieces* named Best Kismet Romance by *Romantic Times,* 1993; *Dreams and Schemes, Somewhere in Time, Night of the Jaguar,* and *Cowboy and the Cossack* all appeared on Waldenbooks Bestseller lists; *Undercover Man* appeared on *USA Today* Bestseller list.

WRITINGS:

ROMANCE NOVELS

Bits and Pieces, Meteor/Kismet (Bensalem, PA), 1993.
Maggie and Her Colonel (novella), Harlequin (New York, NY), 1994.

Alena, Harlequin (New York, NY), 1994.
Sweet Song of Love, Harlequin (New York, NY), 1994.
Dreams and Schemes, Silhouette (New York, NY), 1994.
Siren's Call, Harlequin (New York, NY), 1994.
Somewhere in Time, Silhouette (New York, NY), 1994.
His Lady's Ransom, Harlequin (New York, NY), 1995.
Lady of the Upper Kingdom, Harlequin (New York, NY), 1996.
Line of Duty, Dutton/Signet (New York, NY), 1996.
The Harder They Fall, Silhouette (New York, NY), 1996.
Mistaken Identity, Silhouette (New York, NY), 1996.
Beauty and the Bodyguard, Silhouette (New York, NY), 1996.
Halloween Honeymoon, Silhouette (New York, NY), 1996.
Thanksgiving Honeymoon, Silhouette (New York, NY), 1996.
Wrong Bride, Right Groom, Silhouette (New York, NY), 1996.
(With others) *The Gifts of Christmas,* Silhouette (New York, NY), 1996.
Valentine's Honeymoon, Silhouette (New York, NY), 1997.
Duty and Dishonor, Dutton/Signet (New York, NY), 1997.
Above and Beyond, Dutton/Signet (New York, NY), 1997.
Countess in Buckskin, Harlequin (New York, NY), 1997.
White Tiger/Green Dragon, Harlequin (New York, NY), 1997.
The 14th and Forever, Silhouette (New York, NY), 1997.
Call of Duty, Onyx, 1998.
Return to Sender, Onyx, 1998.
If a Man Answers, Silhouette (New York, NY), 1998.
The Tiger's Bride, Harlequin (New York, NY), 1998.
The Mercenary and the New Mom, Silhouette (New York, NY), 1999.
(With others) *Holiday Honeymooners: Two Tickets to Paradise,* Silhouette (New York, NY), 1999.
A Man of His Word, Silhouette (New York, NY), 1999.
River Rising, Roc (New York, NY), 1999.
Undercover Groom, Silhouette (New York, NY), 1999.
Brides by Arrangement, Harlequin (New York, NY), 2000.
(With Maggie Price and Debra Covan) *Special Report: Final Approach. . . to Forever/Cover Me!/Midnight Seduction,* Silhouette (New York, NY), 2000.
The Horse Soldier, Mira Books (New York, NY), 2001.
Dark Side of Dawn, Signet (New York, NY), 2001.
The Spy Who Loved Him, Silhouette (New York, NY), 2001.
Twice in a Lifetime, Silhouette (New York, NY), 2001.

(With others) *The Officer's Bride,* Harlequin (New York, NY), 2001.

The Colonel's Daughter, Mira Books (New York, NY), 2002.

Also author of *Daughters of Destiny* and *Some Like It Hot* (Online novel). Contributor to *Rogue Knight* (anthology), Harlequin, 1995.

Author's works have been translated into several languages, including Spanish.

"CODE NAME: DANGER" SERIES

Night of the Jaguar, Silhouette (New York, NY), 1995.

The Cowboy and the Cossack, Silhouette (New York, NY), 1995.

Undercover Man, Silhouette (New York, NY), 1995.

Perfect Double, Silhouette (New York, NY), 1996.

Dangerous to Hold (includes *Night of the Jaguar* and *Cowboy and the Cossack*), Silhouette (New York, NY), 2002.

Hot as Ice, Silhouette (New York, NY), 2002.

SIDELIGHTS: Merline Lovelace completed a distinguished career as an Air Force officer before trying her hand at writing romances. She retired as a colonel in 1991, and her first novel, *Bits and Pieces,* was published in 1993. *Bits and Pieces* won Lovelace an award from *Romantic Times,* and she has gone on to write numerous romance novels, including *Somewhere in Time, Perfect Double,* and *Lady of the Upper Kingdom.* In 1996, she broke into the mainstream lists with *Line of Duty,* a novel of romance and military suspense. A *Publishers Weekly* reviewer described Lovelace's work as "adventurous and delightful," adding that the author writes "with such humor and passion that the most jaded romance reader will be sated."

Lovelace was born in 1946 to a military family. Her father's Air Force career took her to numerous states and many foreign countries during her childhood. In college, Lovelace studied several languages, including German, Russian, and Mandarin Chinese; these skills helped her greatly during her own career in the Air Force. Her assignments ranged in location from the Pentagon, to Vietnam and China, and to Eglin Air Force Base in Florida, which she commanded for a time. She married another colonel, Cary A. Lovelace, in 1970.

Somewhere in Time, which was published by Silhouette in 1994, was Lovelace's first time-travel romance. Its protagonist, Aurora Durant, a female pilot of the U.S.

Air Force, crashes her plane in a desert in the Middle East. Somehow the crash allows Aurora to defy the laws of time; she finds herself in 180 A.D. and is captured by Lucius Antonius, an important centurion of the Roman Army. Despite many differences in their mutual cultures, the pair are deeply attracted to each other. A *Library Journal* reviewer judged that "Lovelace handles nicely a rarely used time period for romances."

Lovelace features Maggie Sinclair as the central character for the novels comprising her "Code Name: Danger" series, which includes titles such as *Night of the Jaguar, The Cowboy and the Cossack,* and *Perfect Double.* In *Perfect Double,* Sinclair stands in as a double for the first female vice president of the United States. She also finds love. The *Romantic Times* hailed *Perfect Double* as "a big hit."

Egypt under Alexander the Great is the setting for Lovelace's historical romance, *Lady of the Upper Kingdom.* The book's hero is Philip Tauron, a friend of Alexander's, who is first attracted to, and then marries the Egyptian Lady Farah, a priestess who is assigned to protect a sacred desert cat. Although the pair find love early, marriage is not a guarantee of their happiness, and they have much to overcome before they can achieve their happy ending. A reviewer from the *Romance Reader* Web site felt that *Lady of the Upper Kingdom* was hindered by the "numbness" Lady Farah experiences after a family tragedy, but praised the book as "quite a nice afternoon's diversion from the modern day world."

Moving a few centuries forward in time, Lovelace finds a suitable setting for her adventurous protagonists in the American west. In *The Horse Soldier* Major Andrew Garrett patrols the Dakota territory, keeping the region safe for the men and women braving the American frontier. It is on one of these westward-bound wagons that he comes face to face with his wife, Julia, who, believing Andrew to be dead, married again and how has a daughter, Suzanne. The couple draws close during the hardships that follow in a novel *BookBrowser* critic Harriet Klausner praised as "a powerful western romance starring two interesting characters." Lovelace "gracefully goes historical," Klausner added, "with her expertise and flourishes by providing fans with an invigorating Americana novel." *The Colonel's Daughter* continues the story, as Suzanne, now grown, rides into the Dakotas to aid an Arapaho friend. As luck would have it, she is waylaid by an outlaw gang whose leader, Black Jack Sloan, becomes her lover. Praising the "powerful look at the times" provided by Lovelace's historical romance, Klausner added that the "fast-paced" sto-ryline and "genuine" cast of *The Colonel's Daughter* provide readers with a genuine view of the late nine-teenth century.

Lovelace began a series of three mainstream military suspense novels with *Line of Duty,* in which Brenna Duggan, a lieutenant colonel, must investigate the death of one of the enlisted men under her command. Some of Brenna's worst difficulties arise while dealing with the dead man's widow, Janeen Lang, after Brenna de-termines that Lang's husband did not die in the line of duty. In the course of her investigations, Brenna meets Dave Sanderson, an ex-military man who now works for U.S. Customs. While she responds to his magne-tism, she also feels he is connected to the death of Staff Sergeant Lang. Dede Anderson, commenting in the *Ro-mance Reader,* found Janeen to be the novel's most sympathetic character, and felt that "this is definitely a book for readers interested in the military."

Lovelace enjoyed further success with her military ro-mance *Call of Duty.* In this novel, military computer specialist Jennifer Varga finds herself the target of a se-cret paramilitary group. Jennifer must also contend with her growing passion for her superior, Lieutenant Colo-nel Mike Page. A *Publishers Weekly* correspondent de-clared the "fast-paced thriller" to be "both a gripping as well as a timely read." *Dark Side of Dawn* features a strong military heroine, Jo West, who must fight for her life after becoming involved with a wealthy and well-connected stalker. Reviewing the 2001 novel, a *Pub-lishers Weekly* reviewer commended it as a "satisfying tale with an original heroine who appeals both as a woman and an officer."

Lovelace once told *CA* that she is "an unabashed ro-mantic" who "loves happy endings, no matter how many lost babies, murders, civil wars, or sizzling bed-room scenes it takes to get them." She feels that ro-mance novels "celebrate the fundamental relationship between a man and a woman, yet still combine ele-ments of suspense, drama, and/or historical detail." The author also confessed that she "loves strong, aggressive heroes and heroines who reach out and grab hold of their fate," and she believes "warriors make great heroes. It doesn't matter whether they're wearing the short skirts of a Roman toga or an Air Force flight suit, they all possess the same basic qualities—the ability to command both men and respect, to think fast and make tough decisions, and a bod that really sets off a uniform." As for her heroines, she likes them "strong and adventurous. . . . Whether in a historical or con-temporary setting, they are women who live within the cultural framework of their times and find the inner strength to achieve their goals."

BIOGRAPHICAL/CRITICAL SOURCES:

PERIODICALS

Library Journal, August, 1994, pp. 66, 68.
Publishers Weekly, June 29, 1998, review of *Call of Duty,* p. 56; July 27, 1998, review of *The Tiger's Bride,* p. 74; December 18, 2000, review of *Dark Side of Dawn,* p. 62.
Romantic Times, February, 1996.

OTHER

BookBrowser, http://www.bookbrowser.com/ (April 13, 1999) Harriet Klausner, review of *Rising River;* (October 7, 2000) Harriet Klausner, review of *The Horse Soldier;* (December 12, 2001) Harriet Klaus-ner, review of *The Colonel's Daughter.*
Merline Lovelace Web site, http://home.swbell.net/merline (January 29, 2002).
Romance Reader, http://www.theromancereader.com/ (June 13, 1996), review of *Lady of the Upper King-dom;* (November 18, 1996) review of *Line of Duty.**

*   *   *

LOWELL, Susan 1950-
(Susan L. Humphreys)

PERSONAL: Born October 27, 1950, in Chihuahua, Mexico; daughter of J. David (a geologist) and Edith (a rancher; maiden name, Sykes) Lowell; married William Ross Humphreys (a management consultant), March 21, 1975; children: Anna, Mary. *Education:* Stanford Uni-versity, A.B., 1972, A.M., 1974; Princeton University, M.A., Ph.D., 1979. *Religion:* Episcopalian. *Avocational interests:* Reading, cooking, hiking, horseback riding.

ADDRESSES: Home—Tucson, AZ. *Agent*—Jean V. Nag-gar Literary Agency, Inc., 216 East 75th St., New York, NY 10021.

CAREER: Freelance writer, 1980—. University of Texas at Dallas, visiting assistant professor of English, 1979-80; University of Arizona, Tucson, adjunct lecturer of creative writing, 1989.

MEMBER: Society of Children's Book Writers and Illustrators, Southern Arizona Society of Authors, Phi Beta Kappa.

AWARDS, HONORS: Milkweed National Fiction Award, Milkweed Editions, 1988, for *Ganado Red: A Novella and Stories;* children's regional book award, Mountains and Plains Booksellers' Association, 1993, and distinguished children's book of 1993 citation, *Hungry Mind Review,* both for *I Am Lavina Cumming;* 1994 Arizona Young Readers' Award for picture books, and Reading Rainbow selection, 1994, both for *The Three Little Javelinas;* Arizona Children's Author of the Year, Arizona Library Association, 1994.

WRITINGS:

Ganado Red: A Novella and Stories, Milkweed Editions (Minneapolis, MN), 1988.

FOR CHILDREN

The Three Little Javelinas, illustrated by Jim Harris, Northland (Flagstaff, AZ), 1992, paperback with audiotape edition, Scholastic (New York, NY), 1993.
I Am Lavina Cumming (novel), Milkweed Editions (Minneapolis, MN), 1993.
The Tortoise and the Jackrabbit, illustrated by Jim Harris, Northland (Flagstaff, AZ), 1994.
The Boy with Paper Wings, Milkweed Editions (Minneapolis, MN), 1995.
Little Red Cowboy Hat, illustrated by Randy Cecil, Holt (New York, NY), 1997.
The Bootmaker and the Elves, illustrated by Tom Curry, Orchard Books (New York, NY), 1997.
Cindy Ellen: A Wild Western Cinderella, illustrated by Jane Manning, HarperCollins (New York, NY), 2000.
Dusty Locks and the Three Bears, illustrated by Randy Cecil, Holt (New York, NY), 2001.
(With Anna Humphreys) *Saguaro: The Desert Giant,* Rio Nuevo Publishers (Tucson, AZ), 2002.

Contributor, under name Susan L. Humphreys, of scholarly articles to literature journals.

SIDELIGHTS: Children's author Susan Lowell is known for her original stories for young readers as well as for her retellings of traditional fairy tales from a South-western point of view. Lowell patterned her first children's book, *The Three Little Javelinas,* after the familiar story of "The Three Little Pigs," but she recreated the tale in a desert setting. The three javelinas, or peccaries, are pursed by the coyote, the traditional trickster in Southwestern lore. While the first little javelina builds his house out of tumbleweed, and the second builds his house out of the ribs of the saguaro tree, their sister is the one who provides an adequate shelter made of mud adobe bricks. The text is accompanied by explanatory notes. According to a critic for *Bloomsbury Review,* *The Three Little Javelinas* "is a funny and clever retelling of a familiar tale," and a *Publishers Weekly* reviewer called it "sprightly fun."

I Am Lavina Cumming is based on the story of Lowell's grandmother and is infused with folktales. In this novel, the father of ten-year-old Lavina decides that, since her mother has died, she must learn the manners of a lady from her aunt. Lavina is sent alone from the Arizona Territory to Santa Cruz, California. While Lavina misses Arizona and her family and has trouble coping with a younger girl, Aggie, she begins to appreciate her aunt and the lessons she learns in her home. A reviewer for *Publishers Weekly* wrote that "Lavina is both likable and believable, her credibility enhanced by the author's skillful use of period details."

In 1994, Lowell again teamed up with illustrator Jim Harris for a new take on the "Tortoise and the Hare" fable. Featuring a Southwestern theme, *The Tortoise and the Jackrabbit* puts a mature, white-gloved tortoise in a race against a flashy, bandana-topped jackrabbit. As the duo travel across the desert, Lowell introduces young readers to the unique and varied plant life there, identifying saguaro cacti and mesquite trees, as well as other vegetation native to the Southwest. Calling the book "a merry blend of play, allegory, and environmentalism," a *Publishers Weekly* reviewer wrote that "precise and punchy, Lowell's undated prose turns hip alongside Harris's comical characterizations." *School Library Journal* reviewer Donna L. Scanlon described the work as a "sprightly, fresh approach," while *Booklist* reviewer Ellen Mandel believed that Lowell's tale was "fetchingly told."

Little Red Riding Hood becomes transformed by Lowell into Little Red Cowboy Hat in a title of the same name. Here, Little Red dons a sheriff's badge and keeps an eye out for rattlesnakes in her dusty Southwest town. One day, however, a bigger threat appears in the form of a wolf who blocks her path. Raised to be polite, Little Red feels obliged to talk to the wolf who asks many questions. Later, she again encounters the wolf at her grandmothers house and thinks that the wolf has done something terrible to her granny. Instead of running off, Little Red tries to figure out what happened to Grandma who, as it tuns out, was out chopping wood. When the missing relative finally rescues Little Red from the "low-life lobo," Little Red learns that sometimes "a girl's gotta stick up for herself." Writing in *School Library Journal,* critic Ruth Semrau called *Little Red Cowboy Hat* "an amusing addition to the growing collection of fairy-tale spoofs."

Cinderella meets the Southwest in *Cindy Ellen: A Wild Western Cinderella.* Instead of keeping a house clean while her mean stepmother and stepsisters relax as in the traditional tale, Cindy Ellen must make repairs on the family's ranch, from fixing the fences to mucking out the corral. After she is forbidden to attend a neighbor's rodeo, Cindy Ellen receives a visit from her fairy godmother. Presenting her with a golden six-shooter, the fairy godmother insists that her magic is useless without a bit of Cindy Ellen's spunk. With that advice, the young girl sets out to win the rodeo and the heart of Joe Prince, her wealthy neighbor's son. "Lowell's savory slang adds punch to this tale," claimed a *Publishers Weekly* reviewer. Starr LaTronica, a contributor to *School Library Journal,* found that "an abundance of action combined with humor and high-spirited hyperbole make this a rip-roaring rendition" of the traditional Cinderella tale.

Goldilocks receives the Wild West treatment too, as Lowell sets her story about the young trespasser and the three bears in the American West. *Dusty Locks and the Three Bears* features a cowboy-boot-wearing girl who comes across an empty cabin in the woods. Hungry for a good meal, Dusty Locks walks inside and tests the biggest bear's beans, much too spicy for her taste. Although Lowell has the young heroine follow the traditional storyline, breaking the cub's stool, falling asleep in his bed, and being woken by the bears, she adds a twist at the end when Dusty Locks's mother finally catches up with her. *School Library Journal* critic Adele Greenlee described the story as a "humorous and fresh retelling," while a *Publishers Weekly* reviewer predicted that "with its zippy lines and range of voices . . . this should be a read-aloud hit."

Lowell once commented about her life in the southwest: "I was born in Chihuahua, Mexico. I have lived on both sides of the border since then, and in many other places, too, but my real home, and my family's home for five generations, is southern Arizona. A giant

saguaro cactus is my favorite kind of tree, and I love to see sand-colored coyotes sneak through the desert outside my kitchen window. Sometimes we also see hairy, pig-like javelinas snuffling along, hungry for cactus (which they eat thorns and all).

"My husband and daughters and I own a small ranch at the base of a high mountain called Baboquivari, a sacred peak to the Tohono O'odham Nation, our neighbors on the other side of the mountain. For them, Baboquivari is the center of the universe. For me this is also true. My books, which I write for adults as well as children, have all grown from my lifelong experience of the West. Family stories, some handed down to me from pioneer days, fascinate me, and I am also particularly interested in the rich mixture of Native American, Mexican, and Anglo cultures in my region. Flying coyotes, lost treasures, bandit ghosts, tiny rubies in the sand—there are many stories here to tell, and I hope to keep on writing them down. Yet they are not necessarily all Southwestern stories. A center is not a limit. It's a beginning, a heart. The wide world lies open all around it."

BIOGRAPHICAL/CRITICAL SOURCES:

BOOKS

Lowell, Susan, *Little Red Cowboy Hat,* illustrated by Randy Cecil, Holt (New York, NY), 1997.

PERIODICALS

Bloomsbury Review, October, 1992, review of *The Three Little Javelinas,* p. 25.
Booklist, January 1, 1993, p. 809; January 15, 1995, Ellen Mandel, review of *The Tortoise and the Jackrabbit,* p. 937; April 15, 1997, Ilene Cooper, review of *Little Red Cowboy Hat,* p. 1436; September 15, 1997, Julie Corsaro, review of *The Bootmaker and the Elves,* p. 242; July, 2001, Hazel Rochman, review of *Dusty Locks and the Three Bears,* p. 2014.
Horn Book, July, 2001, review of *Dusty Locks and the Three Bears,* p. 464.
Los Angeles Times Book Review, September 11, 1988, Georgia Jones-Davis, review of *Ganado Red: A Novella and Stories,* p. 3.
New York Times Book Review, October 2, 1988, p. 26.
Publishers Weekly, September 14, 1992, review of *The Three Little Javelinas,* p. 123; July 5, 1993, review of *I Am Lavina Cumming,* p. 74; November 7, 1994,

review of *The Tortoise and the Jackrabbit,* p. 77; November 20, 1995, review of *The Boy with Paper Wings,* p. 78; March 3, 1997, review of *Little Red Cowboy Hat,* p. 75; September 22, 1997, review of *The Bootmaker and the Elves,* p. 80; June 19, 2000, review of *Cindy Ellen: A Wild Western Cinderella,* p. 78; May 21, 2001, review of *Dusty Locks and the Three Bears,* p. 107.

School Library Journal, February, 1995, Donna L. Scanlon, review of *The Tortoise and the Jackrabbit,* p. 76; May, 1997, Ruth Semrau, review of *Little Red Cowboy Hat,* pp. 104-105; June, 2000, Starr LaTronica, review of *Cindy Ellen: A Wild Western Cinderella,* p. 134; July, 2001, Adele Greenlee, review of *Dusty Locks and the Three Bears,* p. 96.*

*   *   *

LUSTBADER, Eric Van 1946-

PERSONAL: Born December 24, 1946, in New York, NY; son of Melvin Harry (a state social security bureau director) and Ruth (Aaronson) Lustbader; married Victoria Schochet (a freelance editor), May, 1982. *Education:* Columbia University, B.A., 1968. *Avocational interests:* Japanese and Mayan history, history of prewar Shanghai, music, landscaping, Japanese pruning, ballet.

ADDRESSES: Office—c/o Random House Inc., 201 East 50th St., New York, NY 10022. *Agent*—Henry Morrison, Inc., Box 235, Bedford Hills, NY 10507.

CAREER: Writer, 1978—. CIS-TRANS Productions (music producers), New York, NY, owner, 1963-67; elementary school teacher in New York, NY, 1968-70; *Cashbox* (music trade journal), New York, NY, associate editor, 1970-72; Elektra Records, New York, NY, director of international artists and repertory and assistant to the president, 1972-73; Dick James Music, New York, NY, director of publicity and creative services, 1974-75; Sweet Dream Productions, New York, NY, owner, 1975-76; NBC-TV, New York, NY, writer and field producer of news film on Elton John, 1976; CBS Records, New York, NY, designer of publicity and album covers and manager of media services, 1976-78.

MEMBER: Nature Conservancy, Save the Manatee Club, Historical Preservation Society, Cousteau Society, World Wildlife Fund, Smithsonian Institution, Metropolitan Museum of Art, Museum of Modern Art, South Street Seaport Museum.

WRITINGS:

NOVELS

Sirens, M. Evans (New York, NY), 1981.
Black Heart, M. Evans (New York, NY), 1982.
Jian, Random House (New York, NY), 1985.
Shan (sequel to *Jian*), Fawcett (New York, NY), 1987.
Zero, Random House (New York, NY), 1988.
French Kiss, Fawcett (New York, NY), 1988.
Angel Eyes, Fawcett (New York, NY), 1991.
Black Blade, Fawcett (New York, NY), 1993.
Batman: The Last Angel, DC/Warner (New York, NY), 1994.
The Ring of Five Dragons (volume one in "The Pearl" series), Tor (New York, NY), 2001.
Art Kills, Carroll & Graf (New York, NY), 2002.
Veil of a Thousand Tears, Tor (New York, NY), 2002.

"SUNSET WARRIOR" CYCLE

The Sunset Warrior, Doubleday (New York, NY), 1977.
Shallows of Night, Doubleday (New York, NY), 1978.
Dai-San, Doubleday (New York, NY), 1978.
Beneath an Opal Moon, Doubleday (New York, NY), 1980.

"NICHOLAS LINNEAR" SERIES

The Ninja, M. Evans (New York, NY), 1980.
The Miko, Villard Books (New York, NY), 1984.
White Ninja, Fawcett (New York, NY), 1989.
The Kaisho, Pocket Books (New York, NY), 1993.
The Floating City, Pocket Books (New York, NY), 1994.
Second Skin, Pocket Books (New York, NY), 1995.
Dark Homecoming, Pocket Books (New York, NY), 1997.

OTHER

Also author of introduction, *Batman & Dracula: Red Rain,* by Doug Moench, illustrated by Kelley Jones, DC Comics (New York, NY), 1997. Contributor to popular music magazines, including *Crawdaddy, Good Times,* and *Rock.*

SIDELIGHTS: The novels of Eric Van Lustbader are steeped in the culture and traditions of Japan. Though he first translated his fascination with the Far East into a series of science-fiction/fantasy books known as the "Sunset Warrior" cycle, he attained international success with his 1980 novel *The Ninja,* the first of what would become a long string of bestsellers interweaving sex, intrigue, murder, and, of course, the traditions of the Far East. Lustbader's subject matter has divided reviewers into two very distinct groups: those who view his novels as too violent and often clichéd, and those who praise their well-researched and intricately wrought plots, and their heart-pounding suspense.

As a young man, Lustbader decided to pursue a career in the music industry. While still a student at Columbia University, he produced several local New York City acts. Not long after attaining his degree, he took a position as an associate editor for the music magazine *Cashbox,* and from there he climbed the ladder to publicist and media-service manager for Elektra and CBS Records. Though his job enabled him to hobnob with such artists as Pink Floyd and Elton John, Lustbader became increasingly disillusioned with the music industry. "It was no longer what it was when I first came in," he recalled in *Publishers Weekly.* "People who knew nothing about music were handling the money end, and the business was mired in the elephantine tracks of big conglomerates. . . . I was at a dead end." He had, over the previous few years, completed a trilogy of fantasy books, writing mostly on weekends, and in 1978 he sold the trilogy to Doubleday, thus beginning his career as a writer.

The trilogy, comprised of *The Sunset Warrior, Shallows of Night,* and *Dai-San,* served two important functions for its author. First, it gave him the freedom to leave the music industry. Second, it allowed him to explore a subject that had fascinated him since he was a teenager: the Samurai of ancient Japan. This fascination had been sparked by the artwork of nineteenth-century artist Ando Hiroshige. Lustbader described in *Publishers Weekly* his introduction to Hiroshige's art: "Falling in love is not even the term for it. . . . I looked at Hiroshige's work, and I was there. His prints speak to me more of the Japanese sensibility—of honor, friendship and the code of the samurai—than any photography ever could."

Using this vision of sensibility and honor as a framework, Lustbader's "Sunset Warrior" trilogy chronicles the adventures of the Bladesman Ronin in a future world rich in Eastern tradition. To this backdrop, the author adds the fast-paced action associated with martial arts,

giving a new look to the fantasy-adventure story. The trilogy did very well, and Lustbader was commissioned by Doubleday to write a fourth book, *Beneath an Opal Moon.* From there he has gone on to write several other books that feature sword-bearing aggressors, including 1993's *Black Blade.* The novel, which John Mort called "Bruce Lee, with a twist or two" in his *Booklist* review, finds a secret Japanese society poised to control the world through a series of secret murders, political machinations, and other mayhem that has been carried out for decades. In addition to the martial arts, fantasy elements, artificial intelligence, industrial tycoons, spies, and a sexy heroine with psychic abilities also serve to fuel what a *Kirkus Reviews* critic dubbed "midair double-somersault reverse plotting."

Despite the success of the "Sunset Warrior" cycle, Lustbader temporarily abandoned the fantasy genre in favor of a suspense-thriller titled *The Ninja. The Ninja* was rejected by a number of publishers before being picked up by M. Evans. Recognizing the novel's immense potential, the editors at M. Evans set into motion an ambitious—and expensive—publicity campaign. They stirred interest in the book by quickly selling the paperback and film rights; this impressed such booksellers as Waldenbooks and Barnes & Noble, whose advance-copy orders funded even more publicity. By the time *The Ninja*'s "official" release date arrived it had already spent three weeks on the best seller list, marking M. Evans's first best seller ever and making Lustbader a millionaire almost overnight.

The Ninja introduces Nicholas Linnear, a half-English, half-Asian businessman who, as a young man in Japan, was trained in the semi-mystical ways of ninjutsu. Linnear, now a player in New York City's world of high finance, becomes enmeshed in a series of martial arts-style murders. Recognizing the killing style as that of a ninja, Linnear surreptitiously investigates the murders, discovering ultimately that the killer is a boyhood rival with whom he had trained. By that time, though, Linnear has been marked as the assassin's next target. "Somewhere inside this sprawling novel . . . there is an exciting thriller trying to break out," stated a *Publishers Weekly* reviewer, who called the plot "implausible." *Los Angeles Times Book Review* writer Don G. Campbell also found the story too fast-paced at times, occasionally leaving the reader behind; however, he ultimately pronounced Lustbader "a fluid storyteller," claiming that "few can match him in creating a mood that something terrible is just about to happen." The immense popularity of *The Ninja* eventually sparked several more novels featuring Nicholas Linnear: 1984's *The Miko,* and *White Ninja,* published in 1989.

Beginning in the fall of 1993, Lustbader began a second three-book sequence featuring the further adventures of protagonist Linnear; the series includes *The Kaisho, The Floating City,* and 1995's *Second Skin.* "Although all three novels are entirely separate, their overall theme is the exploration of Nicholas's father's role in the creation of the new post-war Japan and Linnear's role in tomorrow's Japan," Lustbader once explained to *CA.* In *The Kaisho,* Linnear fulfills a family duty to the Japanese mafia—the Kaisho—whose members are being painstakingly eliminated by a Vietnamese assassin called Du Doc. While his debt to the Kaisho—who helped Linnear's diplomat father lead Japan toward democracy after World War II—comes at a bad time for businessman Linnear, the hero rises to the task, puts his business expansion on hold, and hones up on the latest occult-laced martial arts skills to battle the fearless Du Doc.

The Floating City finds Linnear battling Saigon's underground drug trade while still working to repay his father's debt to the Japanese mob, in a novel that a *Publishers Weekly* contributor claimed is for "fans of the Teenage Mutant Ninja Turtles." Mafia wars and nuclear wars serve as backdrop to protagonist Linnear's characteristic penchant for violent interludes and exotic love interests. The action climaxes in *Second Skin,* as mob wars merge with the battles of big business and Linnear finds his own company—which has developed a cellular phone that transmits clear pictures and threatens to monopolize Japan's technology industry through its creation of the Transrim CyberNet internet highway—the focus of industrial espionage by his arch rival, mobster Mick Leonforte. "At its root," noted Chris Petrakos in *Chicago Tribune Books,* "*Second Skin* is a story of meeting one's own dark side, and while the pace is sometimes too frenetic and the plot is overwhelmed by wildly excessive characters, Lustbader can leave the reader exhilarated as well as exhausted."

In *Dark Homecoming,* Lustbader turns his attention from Asia, setting this crime thriller in a crime-ridden, blood-soaked Miami. Cop Lewis Cloaker reappears as the hero of this novel, though this time he has retired from the police and become the captain of a charter boat. Cloaker gets snared in a sinister network of villains involved in black-market organ "donations," as he struggles against the clock to find a kidney for his dying, drug addicted fifteen-year-old niece. A *Kirkus Reviews* critic wrote that "Lustbader's intense flow of invention is wonderful to watch: Wild, gory, over-the-top entertainment throughout."

The Ring of Five Dragons inaugurates Lustbader's "Pearl" saga, a new series that is a return to the fantasy realm for the author. Giyan and Bartta are twin sisters, priestesses of the goddess Miina, who seek to find Dar Sala-at, a man prophesized to save their people, the Kundalans, who have been enslaved by the V'ornn race for over a century. As the Kundalans lose faith in Miina, the sisters study ancient teachings, hoping to unravel the mystery behind the ring of Five Dragons, which will enable its bearer to unlock the secrets of Kundala. The Gyrgon, the ruling class of the V'ornn, know of the ring and are seeking it so they can further subjugate the Kundalans. The sisters head a large cast of characters in this "richly detailed tapestry," as a reviewer for *Publishers Weekly* described it. The book's complexity is highlighted by appendices listing the story's major characters and a pronunciation guide to the V'ornn language. While a writer for *Kirkus Reviews* took issue with the book's complicated dialogue, the same reviewer concluded that "this midnight dish will leave many disembodied with rapture." Paula Luedtke of *Booklist* called the novel "enthralling and exciting reading, full of unexpected twists and surprises," and the *Publishers Weekly* contributor concluded that "newcomers to Lustbader and his ardent admirers will champion this novel as a potent portal to fabulous mythic realms."

Lustbader's novels continue to receive a variety of reviews. His 1988 novel *Zero,* for example, is described by a writer for *West Coast Review of Books* as an "action-paced, contemporary adventure" that will "undoubtedly please readers," while the *New York Times Book Review*'s William J. Harding labeled the work "ponderous," "unimaginative," and "bloated." Critics such as Harding often point to the graphic sex and violence that pervade Lustbader's writing. "I suppose that's all true," the author responded in *Publishers Weekly.* "But my novels are about the most uncalculatedly written books possible. I never know what's going to happen in them from day to day. The whole excitement about writing. . . . is not knowing what's going to happen." His main concern is for his readers—not his critics. "I'm not out to get good reviews," he commented in the *New York Times Book Review.* "I'm out to sell books and entertain people."

BIOGRAPHICAL/CRITICAL SOURCES:

PERIODICALS

Booklist, July 15, 1980, p. 1658; December 15, 1992, p. 699; April 15, 2001, Paula Luedtke, review of *The Ring of Five Dragons,* p. 1510.
Economist, August 20, 1983, p. 83.

Entertainment Weekly, August 19, 1994, p. 57.

Kirkus Reviews, November 15, 1992, p. 1400; August 1, 1993, p. 957; May 15, 1994, p. 652; April 15, 1995, pp. 497-498; May 15, 1997; April 1, 2001, review of *The Ring of Five Dragons,* p. 446.

Library Journal, June 15, 2001, Jackie Cassada, review of *The Ring of Five Dragons,* p. 106.

Los Angeles Times Book Review, June 22, 1980; April 10, 1983, p. 2; February 2, 1986, p. 6; May 15, 1988, p. 12; January 22, 1989; February 10, 1991, p. 6; May 19, 1991, p. 14.

New York Times Book Review, May 18, 1980, p. 44; June 7, 1981, p. 15; April 10, 1983, p. 29; September 23, 1984; February 1, 1987; June 26, 1988; February 12, 1989; February 25, 1990, p. 35.

People, October 29, 1984, p. 117.

Publishers Weekly, April 11, 1980, p. 71; August 17, 1984, p. 70; December 15, 1989, p. 58; December 14, 1990, p. 55; December 14, 1992, pp. 39-40; August 16, 1993, pp. 85-86; June 20, 1994, p. 95; May 22, 1995, p. 49; April 23, 2001, review of *The Ring of Five Dragons,* p. 54; November 12, 2001, review of *Art Kills,* p. 38.

Tribune Books (Chicago, IL), January 22, 1989, p. 7; June 18, 1995, p. 6.

Washington Post Book World, September 1, 1985, p. 8; October 3, 1993, p. 11.

West Coast Review of Books, June, 1983, p. 29; Volume 12, number 5, 1987, p. 32; Volume 15, number 5, 1990, p. 36; Volume 16, number 2, 1991, p. 30.*

*   *   *

LYNN, Loretta (Webb) 1932(?)-

PERSONAL: Born April 14, 1932(?), in Butcher Hollow, KY; daughter of Melvin (a coal miner) and Carla (Butcher) Webb; married Oliver Vanetta Lynn (a business manager), January 10, 1948; children: Betty Sue (Mrs. Paul Markworth), Jack Benny, Carla (Mrs. Gary Lyell), Ernest Ray, Peggy and Patsy (twins). *Education:* Attended public schools in Van Lear, KY.

ADDRESSES: Home—Hurricane Mills, TN 37078. *Office*—903 16th Ave. S., Nashville, TN 37213. *Agent*—Jimmy Jay United Talent, Inc., 1907 Division, Nashville, TN 37203.

CAREER: Professional country and western vocalist and composer, 1963—; guest on various television programs, including *Bobby Lord Show, Flatt and Scruggs Show, Eddie Hill Show, Ralph Emery Show, Porter Wag-* oner *Show, Today Show, Dinah Shore Show, David Frost Show, To Tell the Truth, Hee Haw, Dean Martin's Music Country,* and NBC's *Midnight Special.* Organized her own ensemble, Blue Kentuckians; founder and secretary-treasurer of Loretta Lynn Enterprises, and Loretta Lynn Championship Rodeo; founder and vice president of United Talent Inc.; founder and honorary board chair of Loretta Lynn Western Stores; founder of Loretta Lynn Dude Ranch, and Loretta Lynn Museum.

Musical recordings include: *Loretta Lynn Sings,* Decca, 1963; *Before I'm over You,* Decca, 1964; *Songs from My Heart,* Decca, 1965; *Ernest Tubb & Loretta Lynn,* Decca, 1965; *Hymns,* MCA, 1965; *I Like 'Em Country,* Decca, 1966; *A Country Christmas,* MCA, 1966; *You Ain't Woman Enough,* MCA, 1966; *Singin' with Feelin',* Decca, 1967; *Ernest Tubb & Loretta Lynn Singin' Again,* Decca, 1967; *Don't Come Home a Drinkin',* MCA, 1967; *Fist City,* Decca, 1968; *Here's Loretta Lynn,* Columbia, 1968; *Who Says God Is Dead!,* MCA, 1968; *Your Squaw Is on the Warpath,* Decca, 1969; *A Woman of the World,* Decca, 1969; *If We Put Our Heads Together,* Decca, 1969; *Loretta Lynn Writes 'Em and Sings 'Em,* Decca, 1970; *Wings upon Your Horns,* Decca, 1970; *I Wanna Be Free,* Decca, 1971; *One's on the Way,* Decca, 1971; *You're Lookin' at Country,* Decca, 1971; *Coal Miner's Daughter,* MCA, 1971; *We Only Make Believe,* MCA, 1971; *Lead Me On,* MCA, 1971; *God Bless America Again,* Decca, 1972; *Here I Am Again,* Decca, 1972; *Alone with You,* MCA, 1972; *Louisiana Woman/Mississippi Man,* MCA, 1973; *Country Partners,* MCA, 1974; *Back to the Country,* MCA, 1975; *Blue-eyed Kentucky Girl,* Decca, 1976; *I Remember Patsy,* MCA, 1977; *Lookin' Good,* MCA, 1980; *Two's a Party,* MCA, 1981; *Making Love from Memory,* MCA Special, 1982; *Lyin' Cheatin' Woman Chasin' Honky Tonkin'. . .,* MCA, 1983; *Loretta Lynn,* MCA, 1984; *Just a Woman,* MCA, 1985; *Making Believe,* MCA, 1988; *Who Was That Stranger,* MCA, 1989; *I'll Just Call You Darlin',* MCA, 1989; *Peace in the Valley,* MCA, 1990; *The Old Rugged Cross,* MCA, 1992; *Sings Patsy Cline's Favorites,* MCA Special, 1992; *Hey Good Lookin,* MCA Special, 1993; *An Evening with Loretta Lynn,* Musketeer, 1995; *Loretta Lynn & Patsy Cline on Tour,* Volume 1 (live album), MCA Special, 1996; *Loretta Lynn & Patsy Cline On Tour,* Volume 2 (live album), MCA Special, 1996; and *Still Country,* Audium, 2000.

AWARDS, HONORS: Country Music Association Grammy awards, 1967, 1972, and 1973, for female vocalist of the year; TNN/*Music City News* awards, best female vocalist, 1967-78 and 1980; Academy of Country Music top female vocalist, 1971, 1973-75; Academy of Country Music best vocal group and/or duet, (with Conway Twitty), 1971, 1974-76; Grammy Award (with Twitty) for best country vocal performance by a duo, 1971, for *After the Fire Is Gone;* TNN/*Music City News* Country Awards, best vocal duo (with Twitty), 1971-78, 1980-81; Country Music Association entertainer of the year award, 1972; Country Music Association vocal duo of the year award (with Twitty), 1972-75; Academy of Country Music entertainer of the year, 1975; American Music Award country favorite duo or group, (with Twitty) 1975, 1977, 1978; TNN/*Music City News* Country Award, best album, 1976, for *When a Tingle Becomes a Chill;* American Music Awards country favorite female vocalist, 1977, 1978; Grammy Award for best children's recording (with others, for *Sesame Country* album), 1981; American Music Awards special award of merit, 1985; TNN/*Music City News* living legend award, 1986; named to Country Music Association Hall of Fame, 1988; received honorary doctorate from the University of Kentucky, 2002; earned gold album for *Don't Come Home A-Drinkin (with Lovin on Your Mind);* named top country female vocalist by *Record World,* favorite female vocalist by *Billboard,* female country singer of the year by *Music Business,* and most programmed female vocalist by *Cash Box;* twice voted number-one female country singer in Europe.

WRITINGS:

(With George Vecsey) *Coal Miner's Daughter: An Autobiography,* Regnery (Washington, DC), 1976.
(With Patsy Bale Cox) *Still Woman Enough: A Memoir,* Hyperion (New York, NY), 2002.

Author of numerous songs.

SIDELIGHTS: With twenty-six number-one songs to her credit and a career that spanned more than four decades, singer-songwriter Loretta Lynn has been hailed as the Queen of Country. Many of the feisty performer's works appeal to a female fan base because of their gritty but often upbeat tales of betrayal, hard times, raising kids, and other real-life topics. With a hardscrabble upbringing, a devoted yet troubled marriage, chronic illness and exhaustion due to her hectic pace, and several tragedies through the years, Lynn's own life often provided the grist for her popular tunes. Her best-selling 1976 autobiography, *Coal Miner's Daughter,* was made into a hit Oscar-winning film starring Sissy Spacek and Tommy Lee Jones. Though she was out of the loop for a few years while taking care of her husband, who died in 1996, Lynn returned to touring in 1998. In 2000 she released her first album since 1988 to contain original solo material.

Born Loretta Webb in Butcher Hollow, Tennessee, Lynn's birthday is April 14, but she is secretive about the year. Some sources put it at 1935, while others have said 1932, 1936, or 1938. She grew up during the Depression. Her father, Melvin, whom everyone knew as Ted, worked on road construction for the Works Progress Administration during the Depression, but when the economy improved, he found a job in the coal mines. Her mother, Clara (Butcher) Webb, was Irish and Cherokee and raised eight children. Lynn was the second child; the youngest, Brenda, changed her name to Crystal Gayle and went on to a successful singing career of her own.

Lynn grew up in a rustic home in the mountains with no electricity or water. Later, after getting a job in the mines, her father was able to buy a four-room home in a big clearing down in the hollow, or "holler," as she calls it. Each week, the family listened to the Grand Ole Opry on a battery-powered radio. "I can't say that I had big dreams of being a star at the Opry," Lynn wrote in *Coal Miner's Daughter.* "It was another world to me. All I knew was Butcher Holler—didn't have no dreams that I knew about." She was twelve years old before she rode in a car.

While growing up, Lynn helped her mother take care of her siblings, and that is how she began singing. "I'd sit on the porch swing and rock them babies and sing at the top of my voice," she recalled in her autobiography. She got an education in a one-room schoolhouse, and met her husband there at a pie social one night when she was thirteen. He had already served in World War II, and was dressed in his uniform. He bid a whopping $5 for her pie, which she baked with salt instead of sugar by accident. Despite the mix-up, he walked her home and asked for a kiss, and she fell in love immediately.

Oliver Vanetta Lynn was nicknamed "Mooney" because he once ran moonshine, but Lynn called him "Doo" because of his other nickname, "Doolittle," which he had since age two. "Nobody knows why—maybe because he was always a little feller," she noted in *Coal Miner's Daughter.* She pointed out that it was not because he was a layabout; she wrote that he worked hard running their ranch and managing her career and touring schedule.

The pair married on January 10, 1948, a few weeks before Lynn turned fourteen. She noted in *Newsweek,* "I told Momma, 'I'm getting married so I won't have to rock all them babies.' Momma cried all night. Then bang, bang, bang, bang, I had four children in four years—before I was 18." After having Betty Sue, Jack Benny, Carla, and Ernest Ray, Lynn later gave birth to twins Peggy and Patsy. By age thirty, she became a grandmother when her eldest daughter married and had a child.

Soon after they married, Lynn and her husband moved to Washington state, where he had lived when he was young. The coal industry was declining and he found a better job in the timber industry. She helped support the family by picking strawberries with migrant workers and doing laundry. Thanks to the farming family they worked and lived with, she learned how to cook. Doo later worked as an auto mechanic.

When their oldest daughter was ten, Lynn's husband bought her a guitar. Her brother and two of her sisters were already performing in clubs in Indiana, where the family had moved after her father was laid off from the mines. Doo Lynn had heard his wife singing along with the radio and thought she was talented. "I was proud to be noticed, to tell you the truth, so I went right to work on it," she commented in her autobiography.

At first, Lynn sang Kitty Wells tunes, but soon started writing her own material. After a couple months, her husband suggested she could earn some money by playing for patrons at the local bars. Though she was extremely bashful, she went along with it. "He said I could do it, and he said he'd set me up at some club," Lynn wrote in *Coal Miner's Daughter.* "So I did it—because he said I could. He made all the decisions in those days." She added, "Now that's what I mean when I say my husband is responsible for my career. It wasn't my idea: he told me I could do it. I'd still be a housewife today if he didn't bring that guitar home and then encourage me to be a singer."

Lynn's career began at Delta Grange Hall, where she first appeared at a party with the governor of Washington in attendance. She then started appearing with the Penn Brothers. Soon, with help from her husband, formed her own group, Loretta's Trail Blazers. Before long, she was playing six nights a week at a tavern and on Sundays would perform at Air Force bases and mental hospitals. After winning first prize at the Northwest Washington District Fair, she and her husband decided to try to make it in Nashville.

A lucky break came after Lynn won an amateur contest on Buck Owens's television show when he was just starting out himself. A Vancouver businessman saw the

show and offered to put up the money to cut a record. She went to Los Angeles and managed to get into a studio, where they recorded "Honky Tonk Girl." Doo Lynn took a picture of his wife and mailed 3,500 copies of the single and Lynn's photo to radio stations around the country. The song made it to number 14 on *Billboard*'s country charts on July 25, 1960. She soon took off on a cross-country promotional tour to talk herself up at radio stations.

By October of 1960, Lynn was performing with the Grand Ole Opry. She signed a contract with Decca Records and moved to Nashville in 1961. She became good friends with Patsy Cline, one of the reigning country stars of the time, and the two shared secrets and went shopping together. Cline died in 1963 in a plane crash, the year that Lynn's first album, *Loretta Lynn Sings,* went to number one and became the first album by a female country artist to be certified gold. It featured the hit single, "Don't Come Home A-Drinkin' (with Lovin' on Your Mind)."

This song was indeed a tribute to Lynn's husband, whom she admits had problems with alcohol. "I think one of the reasons he drinks is he's lonesome when I'm away so much," she told Phyllis Battelle in *Ladies' Home Journal.* He even showed up drunk at the premiere of *Coal Miner's Daughter,* and Lynn has hinted that he was not always faithful. But not all of her songs are directly about her life. She admitted that the tune "Fist City," about a woman who plans to fight to keep her man from another woman's attentions, was autobiographical, but said that another, "You Ain't Woman Enough (to Take My Man)" was actually about a distraught fan she met one night backstage.

Indeed, Lynn recounts many tender stories about her husband in *Coal Miner's Daughter.* Just after signing with Decca, Lynn and her husband bought a sprawling 1,450-acre ranch about sixty-five miles outside Nashville. It was actually an old mill town called Hurricane Mills, and the house on the property reminded Lynn of the house "Tara" in *Gone with the Wind.* Her husband discovered it was structurally unsound, but he worked diligently to get it back into shape because he knew how much she wanted it. But there were other problems, too. "Right after we moved in [in April, 1967], I found out the place was haunted," Lynn told Battelle in *Ladies' Home Journal.* She refused to be alone in the home after seeing spirits. In 1975, they opened a dude ranch on the property.

Meanwhile, by the mid-1960s, Lynn had racked up several number-one hits and best-selling albums. From the late 1960s to the late 1970s she amassed numerous country awards, including many for duets with Conway Twitty. Rumors abounded that Lynn was responsible for breaking up Twitty's marriage, but in her autobiography she steadfastly denied ever having an affair.

In 1972, Lynn was honored as entertainer of the year by the Country Music Association. Before the televised ceremonies, some warned that if she won, she should not to touch presenter, Charley Pride, in order to maintain her "image in rural white America," as George Vecsey wrote in the *New York Times.* She disregarded the advice and embraced him. In 1973, Lynn became the first country artist to appear on the cover of *Newsweek.*

In another controversial move, Lynn released the song "The Pill" in 1975, which touted the benefits that birth control pills can have on women's lives. Many radio stations refused to play it. Incidentally, Lynn in her typical candor noted in her book that she had never taken the Pill, but did use a diaphragm until her husband had a vasectomy. She noted in *Coal Miner's Daughter,* "I'm glad I had six kids because I couldn't imagine my life without 'em. But I think a woman needs control over her own life, and the pill is what helps her do it."

By the late 1970s, spending ten months a year of the road appeared to be catching up with Lynn. She suffered from exhaustion, illness, high blood pressure, ulcers, and chronic migraines, and began to pass out on stage. Rumors flew that she was drinking heavily or addicted to pills. In her book, she has insisted her troubles were due to an allergy to aspirin, but Dalma Heyn reported in *McCall's* that she was addicted to Valium. Lynn denied this to Bob Allen in *Country Music,* telling him that she did, however, take Librium for nerves. She also has had trouble with unexplained seizures but has said doctors ruled out epilepsy. Also, in 1972 doctors found tumors in her breast and she was in the hospital a total of nine times for that.

As her career was building, Lynn's husband took care of the children for the most part. They had babysitters, too, because he was often on the road with her. She wrote in her book, "If I could start over again, I would still go into show business. But if I could change just one thing, I would be with my children more."

Lynn was devastated in 1984 when her son Jack drowned in an accident on her family ranch. He went out horseback riding, and the police later found the horse standing beneath a river bluff with Jack's body nearby. She was in intensive care at the time after having one of her seizures on tour. This followed on the heels of plenty of other bad news for the family. The same year, Lynn's other son had a kidney removed, and the previous year, his wife gave birth to stillborn twins. In addition, two of her daughters, including one who married at fifteen, got divorced.

.

After the death of her son, Lynn did not record anything for two years and she cut back on her touring. The album *Just a Woman,* which was recorded before the accident, came out in 1985, but then she went back to the studio and released *Who Was That Stranger* in 1988. That same year, she was inducted into the Country Music Hall of Fame as the most-awarded female in country music history. Subsequently, though, Lynn dropped out of circulation for a few years to take care of Doo Lynn, who had heart surgery in the early 1990s.

Lynn returned to the public eye in 1993 with the trio album *Honky Tonk Angels,* recorded with Dolly Parton and Tammy Wynette, and the following year released a three-CD boxed set chronicling her career. Also, in 1995 she taped a seven-week series on the Nashville Network (TNN) titled *Loretta Lynn & Friends,* and performed about fifty dates that year as well. Doo Lynn died in August of 1996, after suffering from heart disease and diabetes. He had both legs amputated by the time he died.

Afterward, in 1998 Lynn went back on the road, and in 1999 signed a contract to co-write another memoir, *Still Woman Enough,* which picks up where *Coal Miner's Daughter* left off. In 2000, she released her first collection of solo original songs in twelve years, *Still Country.* The release features her trademark twang and homespun lyrics. Though some felt her rootsy music was out of place in the new, glitzier Nashville atmosphere, she told Miriam Longino in the *Atlanta Journal and Constitution,* "I never left country music; everybody else did. It's made me a good livin'. Why should I go in another direction?"

BIOGRAPHICAL/CRITICAL SOURCES:

BOOKS

Contemporary Musicians, Volume 2, Gale (Detroit, MI), 1989.
Krishef, Robert K., *Loretta Lynn,* Lerner, 1978.

Lynn, Loretta, and George Vecsey, *Coal Miner's Daughter: An Autobiography,* Regnery (Washington, DC), 1976.

Newsmakers, Gale (Farmington Hills, MI), 2001.

Zanderbergen, George, *Nashville Music: Loretta Lynn, Mac Davis, Charley Pride,* Crestwood House, 1976.

Zwisohn, Laurence J., *Loretta Lynn's World of Music, Including an Annotated Discography and Complete List of Songs She Composed,* Laurence Zwisohn, 1980.

PERIODICALS

Atlanta Journal and Constitution, September 10, 2000, p. L1.

Book Digest, December, 1976.

Country Music, November-December, 1985, p. 40; September-October, 1988, p. 30.

Dallas Morning News, June 9, 1997, p. 21A.

Entertainment Weekly, November 1, 1999, Alanna Nash, "Loretta Lynn: Country's First Daughter Spun Tales of Backwoods Perseverence into Music and Movie Gold," p. 134.

Ladies' Home Journal, June, 1984, Phyllis Battelle, "The Haunting of Loretta Lynn," p. 36.

McCall's, March, 1985, p. 88; June, 1988, p. 86.

Ms., May, 1980, p. 37.

National Observer, April 26, 1971.

News, January 19, 1973.

Newsday, March 6, 1971; October 7, 1973.

Newsweek, June 18, 1973.

New York Times, October 25, 1972.

People, June 5, 1975.

Reader's Digest, January, 1977, p. 83.

Star Tribune (Minneapolis, MN), August 24, 1996.

USA Today, July 21, 1997, p. 5D.*

M

MAGEE, Bryan 1930-

PERSONAL: Born April 12, 1930, in London, England; son of Frederick (a shop assistant) and Sheila (Lynch) Magee; divorced; children: Gunnela. *Education:* Oxford University, B.A., 1952, M.A., 1956; Yale University, graduate study, 1955-56. *Politics:* Socialist. *Avocational interests:* Music.

ADDRESSES: Home—12 Falkland House, Marloes Rd., London W8 5LF, England. *Agent*—Peters Fraser Dunlop Group Ltd., Drury House, 34-43 Russell St., London WC2B 5HA, England.

CAREER: Folk University, Lund, Sweden, lecturer in English, 1953-54; British Council, visitors' officer in Oxford, England, 1954-55; Guinness, brewer, 1956-57; freelance writer and broadcaster, 1957—. Former resident reporter on television program, *This Week;* conducted network television series on the arts, music, and philosophy for the British Broadcasting Corporation (BBC-TV); drama critic of *Listener,* 1966—. Socialist candidate for Parliament, 1959, 1960; member of Parliament for Leyton, 1974-83. Correspondent for *Guardian* at international music festivals, 1959, 1960, 1961, 1963, and for London *Times,* 1959. Visiting fellow, All Souls' College, Oxford, England, 1973-74, King's College, London, England, 1984-94; visiting professor, King's College, London, England, 1994—; visiting fellow, Wolfson College, Oxford, England, 1993-94, New College, Oxford, England, 1995, Merton College, Oxford, England, 1998, St. Catherine's College, Oxford, England, 2000, Peterhouse College, Cambridge, England, 2001. Judge, Evening Standard Opera Award, 1973-84, Laurence Olivier Opera Award, 1990-91 and

1993-95, Royal Philharmonic Society Annual Opera Award, 1991-2001. *Military service:* British Intelligence Corps, 1948-49; served on Austro-Yugoslav frontier.

MEMBER: Society of Authors, Edinburgh University Philosophy Society (president, 1987-88), Critics Circle of Great Britain (president, 1983-84), Royal Philharmonic Society, Garrick Club, Savile Club.

AWARDS, HONORS: Silver Medal, RTS, 1978; honorary fellow, Keble College, Oxford, 1994.

WRITINGS:

Crucifixion, and Other Poems, Fortune, 1951.
Go West, Young Man, Eyre & Spottiswoode (London, England), 1958.
To Live in Danger, Hutchinson (London, England), 1960.
The New Radicalismm Secker & Warburg (London, England), 1962, St. Martin's (New York, NY), 1963.
The Democratic Revolution, Bodley Head (London, England), 1964.
Towards 2000, Macdonald & Co. (London, England), 1965.
One in Twenty: A Study of Homosexuality in Men and Women, Stein & Day (London, England), 1966, new edition, 1968.
The Television Interviewer, Macdonald & Co. (London, England), 1966.
Aspects of Wagner, Stein & Day (London, England), 1968.

Modern British Philosophy, St. Martin's (New York, NY), 1971.

Popper, Viking (New York, NY), 1973.

Facing Death (novel), Kimber, 1977.

Men of Ideas, Viking (New York, NY), 1979.

Philosophy and the Real World: An Introduction to Karl Popper, Open Court (LaSalle, IL), 1985.

Misunderstanding Schopenhauer, University of London (London, England), 1990.

On Blindness: Letters between Bryan Magee and Martin Milligan, Oxford University Press (New York, NY), 1995.

The Philosophy of Schopenhauer, Oxford University Press (New York, NY), 1997.

Confessions of a Philosopher: A Journey through Western Philosophy, Random House (New York, NY), 1999.

The Story of Philosophy, Dorling Kindersley (New York, NY), 1999.

(Editor) *The Great Philosophers: An Introduction to Western Philosophy,* Oxford University Press (New York, NY), 2000.

Wagner and Philosophy, Penguin (London, England), 2000, published as *The Tristan Chord: Wagner and Philosophy,* Holt (New York, NY), 2001.

Contributor to *Poetry from Oxford,* edited by Dennis Williamson, Fortune Press, 1950; *Club Voltaire II,* edited by Gerhard Szezesny, Szezesny Verlag (Munich, Germany), 1965.

Also contributor to *Observer, Spectator, New Society, Encounter, New Statesman,* and newspapers in England. Regular columnist, London *Times,* 1974-76.

SIDELIGHTS: By virtue of his television series and books for general readers, Bryan Magee has helped to popularize philosophy, especially in his native Great Britain. Magee has served as host of such British Broadcasting Corporation (BBC-TV) series as *Men of Ideas, Thinking Aloud,* and *The Great Philosophers,* and has followed up this line of work with books such as *Modern British Philosophy, The Story of Philosophy,* and *The Great Philosophers: An Introduction to Western Philosophy.* A *Fountain* Web site reviewer wrote: "For all of his life Magee has sought the answers to life's big questions. . . . He quite deliberately avoided an academic career on the grounds that academic philosophy only studies about philosophy—it is not doing philosophy." In *Forbes* magazine, Adam Bresnick suggested that Magee "makes this dusty subject relevant again."

To explore the role that the senses play in knowing, Magee engaged in a correspondence with philosopher Martin Milligan, who had been blind since childhood. The resulting book, *On Blindness: Letters between Bryan Magee and Martin Milligan,* probes questions about how sight might structure our knowledge, and whether sightlessness might significantly alter one's experience of the world. *Times Literary Supplement* reviewer Rosemary Dinnage found the book "unusual, moving, and sometimes exasperating." In particular, she criticized Magee's assumption that sightlessness significantly diminishes experience, as when he suggests to Milligan that the blind man's world must be "pale, grey, thin, second-hand stuff." When Milligan explains that this is not the case, Magee welcomes the exchange as a "learning experience." Noting that Magee is a "beautifully lucid writer" if somewhat naive about the experience of blindness, Dinnage concluded that *On Blindness* is a work by "two honest and clever writers" who "have managed to strike some fine sparks."

One of Magee's better-known books is *Confessions of a Philosopher: A Journey through Western Philosophy,* in which he blends memoir with a sweeping commentary on two millennia of Western philosophical inquiry. *Booklist* correspondent Jim O'Laughlin found the work to be "a highly detailed and engagingly readable explanation of . . . philosophical issues," and the *Fountain* reviewer also praised the book as "full of interesting arguments and discussions, written in Magee's highly readable and lucid style." Anthony O'Hear in *Times Literary Supplement* considered the book an "engaging account of one man's intense and personal journeying in philosophy." This journeying, O'Hear added, led to Magee's rejection of "the tendency of academics in philosophy . . . to engage in increasingly laboured, obscure and self-referential disquisitions on less and less" in favor of a type of transcendental idealism that is influenced by scientific thought. In *Publishers Weekly,* a critic commended *Confessions of a Philosopher* for its "restless intellect and independent outlook," concluding that the book "reclaims philosophy as a bulwark against . . . wishful thinking."

A critic of theater and music in addition to philosophy, Magee has also written *The Tristan Chord: Wagner and Philosophy,* in which he argues that Wagner's music was significantly influenced by the composer's study of philosophy. A writer for *Kirkus Reviews* concluded that Magee offers a "mellow, lucid" and "highly persuasive" interpretation of how Wagner's intellectual life informed his operas.

BIOGRAPHICAL/CRITICAL SOURCES:

PERIODICALS

Booklist, February 15, 1998, Jim O'Laughlin, review of *Confessions of a Philosopher: A Journey through Western Philosophy,* p. 950; December 1, 1998, Bryce Christensen, review of *The Story of Philosophy,* p. 621; October 1, 2001, Bryce Christensen, review of *The Tristan Chord: Wagner and Philosophy,* p. 291.

Economist, August 6, 1983, review of *The Philosophy of Schopenhauer,* p. 72; April 20, 1996, review of *On Blindness: Letters between Bryan Magee and Martin Milligan,* p. S12.

Forbes, November 16, 1998, Adam Bresnick, "The Consolations of Philosophy," p. 279.

History Today, December, 1998, review of *The Story of Philosophy,* p. 59.

Kirkus Reviews, August 1, 1995, review of *On Blindness,* p. 1084; January 1, 1998, review of *Confessions of a Philosopher,* p. 38; October 1, 2001, review of *The Tristan Chord,* p. 1404.

Library Journal, October 1, 1983, review of *The Philosophy of Schopenhauer,* p. 1879; August 1, 1999, review of *The Great Philosophers,* p. 59; August 1, 1999, review of *Confessions of a Philosopher,* p. 59; August 1, 1999, review of *The Story of Philosophy,* p. 59; November 1, 2001, Larry Lipkis, review of *The Tristan Chord,* p. 95.

London Review of Books, January 2, 1997, review of *On Blindness,* p. 9.

New Scientist, July 5, 1997, review of *Confessions of a Philosopher,* p. 43.

New Statesman & Society, November 11, 1988, Sean French, review of *Aspects of Wagner,* p. 32; November 11, 1988, review of *The Great Philosophers,* p. 32.

Observer, August 7, 1983, review of *The Philosophy of Schopenhauer,* p. 24.

Publishers Weekly, December 22, 1997, review of *Confessions of a Philosopher,* p. 45; October 5, 1998, "I Think, Therefore," p. 75.

Spectator, June 14, 1997, review of *Confessions of a Philosopher,* p. 43.

Times Educational Supplement, December 25, 1987, review of *The Great Philosophers,* p. 21; February 5, 1999, review of *The Story of Philosophy,* p. 26.

Times Literary Supplement, January 12, 1996, Rosemary Dinnage, review of *On Blindness;* August 22, 1997, Anthony O'Hear, review of *Confessions of a Philosopher,* p. 7; November 17, 2000, Jerry Fodor, review of *Wagner and Philosophy,* p. 6.

Washington Post Book World, October 30, 1988, review of *Aspects of Wagner,* p. 16.

Wilson Quarterly, spring, 1998, review of *Confessions of a Philosopher,* p. 104.

OTHER

Fountain, http://www.fountain.btinternet.co.uk/philosophy/ (March 6, 2001), "The Life of Bryan: A Review of Bryan Magee's Book *Confessions of a Philosopher.*"*

*   *   *

MARRIN, Albert 1936-

PERSONAL: Born July 24, 1936, in New York, NY; son of Louis and Frieda (Funt) Marrin; married Yvette Rappaport, November 22, 1959. *Education:* City College (now City College of the City University of New York), B.A., 1958; Yeshiva University, M.Ed., 1959; Columbia University, M.A., 1961, Ph.D., 1968. *Avocational interests:* Travel in Europe.

ADDRESSES: Home—750 Kappock St., Bronx, NY 10463. *Office*—Department of History, Yeshiva University, 500 West 185th St., New York, NY 10033. *Agent*—Toni Mendez, Inc., 141 East 56th St., New York, NY 10022.

CAREER: William Howard Taft High School, New York, NY, social studies teacher, 1959-68; Yeshiva University, New York, NY, assistant professor of history, 1968-78, professor and chairman of history department, 1978—; writer, 1968—. Visiting professor, Yeshiva University, 1967-68, and Touro College, 1972-74.

MEMBER: Western Writers of America.

AWARDS, HONORS: Notable Children's Trade Book selection, National Council for Social Studies and Children's Book Council, and *Boston Globe/Horn Book* Honor Book, both 1985, both for *1812: The War Nobody Won;* Western Heritage Award for best juvenile nonfiction book, National Cowboy Hall of Fame, and Spur Award, Western Writers of America, both 1993, both for *Cowboys, Indians, and Gunfighters: The Story of the Cattle Kingdom; Boston Globe/Horn Book* Honor Book, 1994, Dorothy Canfield Fisher Children's Book Award, 1995, and Association of Christian Public

School Teachers and Administrators Honor Award, 1995, all for *"Unconditional Surrender": U. S. Grant and the Civil War;* Children's Book Guild and *Washington Post* Nonfiction Award for contribution to children's literature, 1995; *Boston Globe/Horn Book* Honor Book, 2000, for *Sitting Bull and His World.*

WRITINGS:

FOR CHILDREN; NONFICTION

Overlord: D-Day and the Invasion of Europe, Atheneum (New York, NY), 1982.

The Airman's War: World War II in the Sky, Atheneum (New York, NY), 1982.

Victory in the Pacific, Atheneum (New York, NY), 1983.

War Clouds in the West: Indians and Cavalrymen, 1860-1890, Atheneum (New York, NY), 1984.

The Sea Rovers: Pirates, Privateers, and Buccaneers, Atheneum (New York, NY), 1984.

The Secret Armies: Spies, Counterspies, and Saboteurs in World War II, Atheneum (New York, NY), 1985.

1812: The War Nobody Won, Atheneum (New York, NY), 1985.

The Yanks Are Coming: The United States in the First World War, Atheneum (New York, NY), 1986.

Aztecs and Spaniards: Cortes and the Conquest of Mexico, Atheneum (New York, NY), 1986.

Struggle for a Continent: The French and Indian Wars, 1690-1760, Atheneum (New York, NY), 1987.

Hitler, Viking (New York, NY), 1987.

The War for Independence: The Story of the American Revolution, Atheneum (New York, NY), 1988.

Stalin: Russia's Man of Steel, Viking (New York, NY), 1988.

Inca and Spaniard: Pizarro and the Conquest of Peru, Atheneum (New York, NY), 1989.

Mao Tse-tung and His China, Viking (New York, NY), 1989.

Napoleon and the Napoleonic Wars, Viking (New York, NY), 1990.

The Spanish-American War, Atheneum (New York, NY), 1991.

America and Vietnam: The Elephant and the Tiger, Viking (New York, NY), 1992.

Cowboys, Indians, and Gunfighters: The Story of the Cattle Kingdom, Atheneum (New York, NY), 1993.

"Unconditional Surrender": U. S. Grant and the Civil War, Atheneum (New York, NY), 1993.

Virginia's General: Robert E. Lee and the Civil War, Atheneum (New York, NY), 1994.

The Sea King: Sir Francis Drake and His Times, Atheneum (New York, NY), 1995.

Plains Warrior: Chief Quanah Parker and the Comanches, Atheneum (New York, NY), 1996.

Empires Lost and Won: The Spanish Heritage in the Southwest, Atheneum (New York, NY), 1997.

Commander in Chief: Abraham Lincoln and the Civil War, Dutton (New York, NY), 1997.

Terror of the Spanish Main: Sir Henry Morgan and His Buccaneers, Dutton (New York, NY), 1999.

Sitting Bull and His World, Dutton (New York, NY), 2000.

George Washington and the Founding of a Nation, Dutton (New York, NY), 2001.

Secrets from the Rocks: Dinosaur Hunting with Roy Chapman Andrews, Dutton (New York, NY), 2002.

Dr. Jenner and the Speckled Monster: The Story of the Conquest of Smallpox, Dutton (New York, NY), 2002.

Oh Rats!, The Story of Rats and People, Dutton (New York, NY), in press.

FOR ADULTS; NONFICTION

War and the Christian Conscience: Augustine to Martin Luther King Jr., Gateway (Chicago, IL), 1971.

The Last Crusade: The Church of England in the First World War, Duke University Press (Durham, NC), 1974.

Nicholas Murray Butler: An Intellectual Portrait, Twayne (Boston, MA), 1976.

Sir Norman Angell, Twayne (Boston, MA), 1976.

WORK IN PROGRESS: Old Hickory, a book about Andrew Jackson.

SIDELIGHTS: Albert Marrin is a professor of history who has attempted to make the past accessible to young readers via the many books he has authored. In award-winning books such as *1812: The War Nobody Won, Cowboys, Indians, and Gunfighters: The Story of the Cattle Kingdom,* and *"Unconditional Surrender": U. S. Grant and the Civil War,* Marrin has created an intriguing tapestry of U.S. history by focusing on dramatic moments and famous personalities. With biographies of leaders and tyrants from Napoleon Bonaparte to Adolf Hitler, Marrin has also interpreted the events of a larger world stage for juvenile readers. Additionally, his several books on World Wars I and II provide introductions to many aspects of those struggles. Marrin's books for young readers complement his academic duties as chair of the history department at New York's Yeshiva University.

One of Marrin's first books intended for a young audience, 1983's *Victory in the Pacific,* is indicative of Marrin's approach to history. Writing in *Voice of Youth Advocates,* Michael Wessells commented on his "straightforward account," highlighted by "lucid capsule descriptions of selected topics" interspersed in the otherwise chronologically organized narrative which follows the war through major battles, from Pearl Harbor to Midway and Guadalcanal and the bombing of Japan. Marrin's treatment, anecdotal rather than detailed, would appeal, the reviewer noted, to "hi/lo readers." And Kate M. Flanagan, writing in *Horn Book,* pointed out Marrin's "fast-paced" accounts of various battles and his balanced narration, looking at history from both sides of the conflict to "provide an understanding of the warrior heritage that made the Japanese such a formidable enemy."

Marrin has dealt with various other aspects of World War II, from the invasion of Europe by the Allies to a history of spies and a study of the air war. With his *The Yanks Are Coming,* he also examines U.S. involvement in World War I. His concentration on military subjects enhanced an even more domestic topic in his *War Clouds in the West: Indians and Cavalrymen, 1860- 1890,* which chronicles, battle by battle, the thirty-year war of destruction of the Plains Indians and Apache by the U.S. Cavalry. "The breadth of coverage," along with detailed diagrams and photos "all recommend this book for general readers," noted George Gleason in a *School Library Journal* review. *Horn Book* critic Nancy C. Hammond found Marrin's book to be a "dramatic readable account," with enlightening cultural and historical perspectives on the struggle, such as the pressures ensuing from demands for buffalo brought on by a new hide-tanning process.

The history of the Native Americans of the Great Plains also figures in several titles by Marrin: *Cowboys, Indians, and Gunfighters: The Story of the Cattle Kingdom, Sitting Bull and His World,* and *Plains Warrior: Chief Quanah Parker and the Comanches.* The award-winning *Cowboys, Indians, and Gunfighters* is a history of the Old West, from the earliest Spanish settlers who introduced horses and cattle to the region to the struggle between buffalo and cattle for the open range. Divided into six chronological chapters, the book includes "minority viewpoints," according to Julie Halverstadt in *School Library Journal,* in its listing of contributions of African-American and Mexican cowboys. "A dynamic look at one of the most exciting and dangerous periods in U.S. history," Halverstadt concluded. With his *Plains Warrior,* Marrin focuses on the Comanche and their losing battle in the nineteenth century for their traditional life on the Great Plains. Providing at once an overview of Comanche history as well as a dramatic representation of the last tragic years of fighting under Chief Quanah Parker, son of a kidnaped settler, *Plains Warrior* "brings the period to life," according to a reviewer in *Bulletin of the Center for Children's Books.* The reviewer also praised Marrin for his even-handed treatment of both parties in the battle. While noting that Marrin's "vivid writing occasionally strays into sensationalism," *Horn Book* contributor Mary M. Burns praised *Plains Warrior* for building on both the "major differences between the Comanche and the white points of view and the tragedy inherent in those differences." In *Booklist,* Chris Sherman commented favorably on Merrin's use of "vivid description" and "compelling anecdotes" in telling his "engrossing" story. In *Sitting Bull and His World,* Marrin frames his biography of the Lakota warrior within "both the nature and substance of one man's resistance to and witness of his nation's ethnocide," according to a contributor to *Horn Book.*

Marrin also investigated an earlier conflict between Europeans and Native Americans in the New World—the wars between the British and French and their Indian allies. *Struggle for a Continent: The French and Indian Wars, 1690- 1760,* once again demonstrates Marrin's use of accurate research as well as the use of anecdotes to create a "retelling of history that young people find accessible and appealing," according to Elizabeth S. Watson in *Horn Book.* Paula Nespeca Deal, writing in *Voice of Youth Advocates,* called *Struggle for a Continent* a "fascinating, easy to read overview," and noted that Marrin brings this little-understood battle for power alive with "vivid details of the cultural and social background." Deal also pointed out that Marrin includes the accomplishments of women in the struggle.

A logical chronological companion piece to *Struggle for a Continent* is *The War for Independence: The Story of the American Revolution,* which provides a "detailed account" of the American war for independence, according to Anne Frost in *Voice of Youth Advocates.* "This engrossing narrative gives the reader rare insight," Frost wrote. "Highly recommended." Marrin divides his narrative into eight chapters dealing with various topics such as causes, spies, naval battles, and the front-line skirmishes along the frontier. A contributor in *Kirkus Reviews* remarked particularly on Marrin's use of details that "engage the reader's senses," and a *Bulletin of the Center for Children's Books* reviewer called the work a "spirited and thoughtful account."

Marrin turned to the U.S. Civil War with titles profiling generals on opposing sides. *"Unconditional Surrender": U. S. Grant and the Civil War* uses Union General Ulysses S. Grant to focus on the war years, though it also includes information about the general before and after that conflict. Marrin confines his chronicle to battles and strategies that Grant was personally involved in. Thus Gettysburg and Bull Run are not included, but detailed accounts of Shiloh and Petersburg are, along with a plethora of facts and anecdotes. Neither Grant's racism nor his drinking are glossed over in this account, and the extensive bibliography appended "will be much appreciated by both history students and Civil War buffs," noted Elizabeth M. Reardon in *School Library Journal.*

A view from the other side of the battle lines is provided in *Virginia's General: Robert E. Lee and the Civil War.* Beginning with a brief account of the subject's life before and after the Civil War, it focuses on the war years through the Confederate general's eyes as well as through the eyes of a score of other witnesses. The extensive use of quotations from Lee and his generals, as well as plentiful detail, provides a "vivid picture of the war, its participants, and its effects," according to Deborah Stevenson in *Bulletin of the Center for Children's Books.* Carolyn Phelan, writing in *Booklist,* concluded that *Virginia's General* was "well researched and readable," and Connie Allerton in *Voice of Youth Advocates* noted that Marrin tells "an exciting story." Marrin extended his series on the Civil War with a volume focusing on Abraham Lincoln, *Commander in Chief: Abraham Lincoln and the Civil War.*

With *The Spanish-American War* and *America and Vietnam: The Elephant and the Tiger,* Marrin tackles two bloody chapters in U.S. history. In *The Spanish-American War* he creates "a fine sense of intimacy in his text," according to Margaret A. Bush in *Horn Book,* as he details the events that led up to the war that President McKinley did not want. Raymond E. Houser, writing in *Voice of Youth Advocates,* called *The Spanish-American War* "a good YA history," and a contributor in *Kirkus Reviews* labeled the same work "fresh (and timely)."

Marrin's history of America's longest war, *America and Vietnam,* was both praised for even-handedness and criticized for bias, demonstrating the deep rifts still apparent in U.S. society as a result of that conflict. Initially, Marrin provides an overview of Vietnamese history as one of struggle, beginning with Chinese control of the nation and continuing through the French colonial system, occupation by the Japanese, renewed conflict with the French, and U.S. involvement in the region. The author also provides a lengthy account of

the early life of the leader, Ho Chi Minh, who established Communism in the northern regions of the country following World War II. But the centerpiece of the book is the U.S. presence in Vietnam and the ensuing war. "Marrin covers the Vietnam Conflict in a sweeping fashion," according to Raymond E. Houser in *Voice of Youth Advocates.* "This is an excellent history book. . . . If a YA reader had but one book to read on this subject, this should be the one." Margaret A. Bush in *Horn Book* also found Marrin's account "remarkably even- handed."

Marrin has also written a quartet of biographies on world leaders, including portraits of Hitler, Stalin, Mao Tse-tung, Sir Henry Morgan, and Napoleon, as well as books on the influence of the Spanish in the Americas. A *Kirkus Reviews* critic deemed Marrin's *Hitler* "a dramatic account," and drew attention to the author's inclusion of various topics of recent interest, such as the White Rose resistance group and the fate of Josef Mengele. Margaret A. Bush, writing in *Horn Book,* termed the work a "riveting account that is informative, illuminating, and inescapably painful." Marrin continues his series on world leaders with *Stalin,* dubbed "another fine biography" by Elizabeth S. Watson in *Horn Book,* and with *Mao Tse-tung and His China.* In the latter, Marrin interweaves Mao's life with the history of China from 1911 to his death. From Mao's troubled childhood through the Long March and the days of the Cultural Revolution, Marrin traces the major turning points in the life of one of China's most controversial leaders. "A vivid but inconsistent account," noted Marsha L. Wagner in the *New York Times Book Review.* "This book is actually less a biography than a highly readable historical overview of modern China. . . . Sadly, Mao himself never emerges as a clear historical personalty," Wagner concluded.

With *Napoleon and the Napoleonic Wars,* Marrin took on a project that has been attempted by many other biographers. Marrin's book puts Napoleon's life into the context of his times, and also has the "particular talent for selecting an incident or anecdote" that sums up an individual, according to Margaret Miles in *Voice of Youth Advocates.* "The text is readable, dramatic, and well documented," noted Elizabeth S. Watson in *Horn Book.* And in *Terror of the Spanish Main: Sir Henry Morgan and His Buccaneers* Marrin "has created a narrative of epic proportions," in the opinion of *Horn Book* reviewer Mary M. Burns. Beginning with a history of Spain on the high seas, Marrin focuses on the Welsh-born Morgan as he builds his career from that of lowly pirate to almost- respectable businessman, creating a book that Burns dubbed "addictive reading." In *Booklist*

Randy Meyer praised Marrin for doing "a top- notch job of bringing [the seventeenth-century Jamaican] setting to life, describing colonial life in all its grit and glory."

In *George Washington and the Founding of a Nation,* Marrin presents what *School Library Journal* contributor Steven Engelfried called an "engaging" portrait of both Washington and the times in which he lived. Covering General Washington's military campaigns in detailed fashion, Marrin captures Washington's courage and character by including the words of his contemporaries. Although, as Engelfried pointed out, the author "clearly admires his subject," he "carefully discusses [Washington's] . . . flaws and errors . . . [and] raises questions and presents different views," among them questions about Washington's ownership of slaves. Washington becomes, through Marrin's lens, "a man of his time," according to *Booklist* reviewer Randy Meyer, "one who could never reconcile his public philosophy of freedom with his private actions."

With *Inca and Spaniard: Pizarro and the Conquest of Peru, Aztecs and Spaniards: Cortes and the Conquest of Mexico,* and *Empires Lost and Won: The Spanish Heritage in the Southwest,* Marrin examines Spanish incursions in the New World and the clash of cultures such incursions brought about. Kathryn Pierson in *Bulletin of the Center for Children's Books* commented particularly on Marrin's novelistic treatment of *Inca and Spaniard,* which might limit the research value of his book, "but has probably enhanced its appeal," while Zena Sutherland in *Bulletin of the Center for Children's Books* described his *Aztecs and Spaniards* "as dramatic as fiction but well-grounded in fact."

BIOGRAPHICAL/CRITICAL SOURCES:

BOOKS

Children's Literature Review, Volume 53, Gale (Detroit, MI), 1999.

PERIODICALS

Booklist, December 15, 1982, p. 565; February 1, 1983, Ilene Cooper, review of *Overlord: D-Day and the Invasion of Europe,* p. 725; June 15, 1983, review of *Victory in the Pacific,* p. 1340; September 1, 1984, p. 68; August, 1985, p. 1668; May 1, 1986,

p. 1322; July, 1987, p. 1681; December 15, 1988, p. 700; October 15, 1989, p. 460; December 15, 1989, p. 823; July, 1991, p. 2039; March 1, 1992, p. 1269; August, 1993, p. 2046; April 1, 1994, p. 1440; December 15, 1994, Carolyn Phelan, review of *Virginia's General: Robert E. Lee and the Civil War,* p. 746; March 15, 1996, review of *Virginia's General,* p. 1274; June 1, 1996, Chris Sherman, review of *Plains Warrior,* p. 1723; January 1, 1998, review of *Commander in Chief Abraham Lincoln and the Civil War,* p. 744; January 1-15, 1999, Randy Meyer, review of *Terror of the Spanish Main,* p. 849; January 1, 2001, Randy Meyer, review of *George Washington and the Founding of a Nation,* p. 951.

Bulletin of the Center for Children's Books, April, 1986, Zena Sutherland, review of *Aztecs and Spaniards: Cortes and the Conquest of Mexico,* p. 153; April, 1988, review of *The War for Independence: The Story of the American Revolution,* p. 161; February, 1990, Kathryn Pierson, review of *Inca and Spaniard: Pizarro and the Conquest of Peru,* p. 142; March, 1994, Deborah Stevenson, review of *"Unconditional Surrender": U. S. Grant and the Civil War,* p. 227; January, 1995, Deborah Stevenson, review of *Virginia's General: Robert E. Lee and the Civil War,* p. 173; May, 1996, review of *Plains Warrior: Chief Quanah Parker and the Comanches,* p. 308.

Horn Book, April, 1983, Kate M. Flanagan, review of *Victory in the Pacific,* p. 184; June, 1984, p. 349; March-April, 1985, Nancy C. Hammond, review of *War Clouds in the West: Indians and Cavalrymen, 1860- 1890,* pp. 195-196; September, 1986, p. 610; April, 1986, Zena Sutherland, review of *Aztecs and Spaniards: Cortes and the Conquest of Mexico,* pp. 153-154; September-October, 1987, Margaret A. Bush, review of *Hitler,* p. 630; January-February, 1988, Elizabeth S. Watson, review of *Struggle for a Continent: The French and Indian Wars, 1690-1760,* p. 87; March-April, 1989, Elizabeth S. Watson, review of *Stalin,* p. 234; January, 1990, p. 89; July-August, 1991, Margaret A. Bush, review of *The Spanish-American War,* p. 481; September-October, 1991, Elizabeth S. Watson, review of *Napoleon and the Napoleonic Wars,* p. 617; September-October, 1992, Margaret A. Bush, review of *America and Vietnam: The Elephant and the Tiger,* pp. 600-601; September, 1993, p. 625; July, 1994, p. 473; September, 1996, Mary M. Burns, review of *Plains Warrior,* p. 621; March, 1999, Mary M. Burns, review of *Terror of the Spanish Main,* p. 227; July, 2000, review of *Sitting Bull and His World,* p. 474.

Kirkus Reviews, May 15, 1987, review of *Hitler,* pp. 796-797; April 15, 1988, review of *The War for In-*

dependence: The Story of the American Revolution, p. 621; February 15, 1991, review of The Spanish-American War, p. 250; April 1, 1992, review of America and Vietnam: The Elephant and the Tiger, p. 463.

New York Times Book Review, February 25, 1990, Marsha L. Wagner, review of Mao Tse-tung and His China, p. 33; August 17, 1997, review of Empires Lost and Won, p. 19; August 13, 2000, review of Sitting Bull and His World, p. 16.

School Library Journal, November, 1982, p. 88; April, 1983, p. 126; August, 1984, p. 76; March, 1985, George Gleason, review of War Clouds in the West: Indians and Cavalrymen, 1860-1890, p. 180; August, 1986, p. 104; June, 1987, p. 110; December, 1987, p. 108; June, 1988, p. 124; November, 1989, p. 132; February, 1990, p. 116; May, 1991, p. 192; August, 1993, Julie Halverstadt, review of Cowboys, Indians, and Gunfighters: The Story of the Cattle Kingdom, p. 199; July, 1994, Elizabeth M. Reardon, review of "Unconditional Surrender": U. S. Grant and the Civil War, p. 1122; December, 1994, p. 25; July, 2000, review of Sitting Bull and His World, p. 15; January, 2001, Steven Engelfried, review of George Washington and the Founding of a Nation, p. 150.

Voice of Youth Advocates, October, 1983, Michael Wessells, review of Victory in the Pacific, p. 226; October, 1987, Paula Nespeca Deal, review of Struggle for a Continent: The French and Indian Wars, 1690-1760, p. 189; June, 1988, Anne Frost, review of The War for Independence: The Story of the American Revolution, p. 103; June, 1991, Raymond E. Houser, review of The Spanish-American War, p. 127; October, 1991, Margaret Miles, review of Napoleon and the Napoleonic Wars, p. 265; June, 1992, Raymond E. Houser, review of America and Vietnam: The Elephant and the Tiger, p. 130; April, 1995, Connie Allerton, review of Virginia's General: Robert E. Lee and the Civil War, p. 50; August, 1996, review of The Sea King, p. 181; February, 1998, review of Empires Lost and Won, p. 365.

*　*　*

MARSDEN, Alexander Marsden
See WADDINGTON, Patrick (Haynes)

*　*　*

MARSTON, Hope Irvin 1935-

PERSONAL: Born January 31, 1935, in Fishing Creek (now Mill Hall), PA; daughter of Charley (a dairy farmer) and Orpha (a homemaker; maiden name, Harber) Irvin; married Arthur Wakefield Marston, Jr. (a farmer), August 28, 1961. Education: Milligan College, B.A., 1956; State University of New York College at Geneseo, M.A., 1972. Politics: Republican. Religion: "Christian—CMA." Hobbies and other interests: Reading, cooking new recipes, walking, directing the North Country Writing Workshop.

ADDRESSES: Home—P.O. Box 710, Black River, NY 13612. E-mail—amarston@twcny.rr.com.

CAREER: Secondary school teacher and librarian in Maryland, Maine, and New York, beginning in 1956; Case Junior High School, Watertown, NY, library media specialist, c. 1967-90; freelance writer.

MEMBER: Society of Children's Book Writers and Illustrators (founder and director of North Country Writing Workshop), Black River Valley Writers Club (founder), Adirondack Mountain Club (Black River Chapter).

AWARDS, HONORS: Notable Children's Trade Book in the Field of Social Studies, National Council for the Social Studies/Children's Book Council, 1996, for Isaac Johnson: From Slave to Stonecutter; Professional Excellence Award, Milligan College, 2000.

WRITINGS:

Do You Love Jesus?, Child Evangelism Fellowship (Warrenton, MO), 1972.

Trucks, Trucking, and You, Dodd (New York, NY), 1978.

Big Rigs (Junior Literary Guild selection), Dodd (New York, NY), 1980, revised edition, Cobblehill/Dutton (New York, NY), 1993.

Machines on the Farm, Dodd (New York, NY), 1982.

Fire Trucks, Dodd (New York, NY), 1984, revised edition, Cobblehill/Dutton (New York, NY), 1995.

Snowplows, Dodd (New York, NY), 1986.

Load Lifters, Putnam (New York, NY), 1989.

To the Rescue, Cobblehill/Dutton (New York, NY), 1991.

Journey to Joy, Christian Publications (Harrisburg, PA), 1994.

The Promise, Christian Publications (Harrisburg, PA), 1994.

(With Claire Coughlin) Santanoni Sunrise (adult romance novel), Barbour (Uhrichsville, OH), 1994.

By an Unfamiliar Path, Christian Publications (Harrisburg, PA), 1995.

To Viet Nam with Love, Christian Publications (Harrisburg, PA), 1995.
Isaac Johnson: From Slave to Stonecutter, illustrated by Maria Magdalena Brown, Dutton (New York, NY), 1996.
My Little Book of Wood Ducks, illustrated by Maria Magdalena Brown, NorthWord (Minocqua, WI), 1996.
My Little Book of Burrowing Owls, illustrated by Maria Magdalena Brown, NorthWord (Minocqua, WI), 1996.
My Little Book of Painted Turtles, illustrated by Maria Magdalena Brown, NorthWord (Minocqua, WI), 1997.
My Little Book of Timber Wolves, illustrated by Maria Magdalena Brown, NorthWord/Cowles (Minocqua, WI), 1998.
My Little Book of River Otters, illustrated by Maria Magdalena Brown, NorthWord/Cowles (Minocqua, WI), 1998.
Wings in the Water: The Story of a Manta Ray, Soundprints (Norwalk, CT)/Smithsonian, 1998.
Salmon River Odyssey: The Story of Pulaski, Syracuse University Press (Syracuse, NY), in press.

WORK IN PROGRESS: Two teen biographies, one of a teen from Scots Martyr who died in the seventeenth century, and the other of a female Civil War spy; a nonfiction book on accelerant detection dogs.

SIDELIGHTS: Hope Irvin Marston once stated: "Writing is my joy as well as my livelihood. I used to consider a rejection letter a sign of failure. Now I realize it is merely a stepping stone to my next publication."

"I've loved books since I was a child and first learned to read. As a librarian in a junior high school, it was a joy to be working with kids and books. I retired from that position in 1990 so I could write full-time. I miss the interaction with students and the pleasure of handling new books as well as old ones at Case Junior High School in Watertown, New York. I enjoy sharing my books with children as I do school presentations, and I keep alert to their questions and suggestions for new titles."

"I am thrice blessed. The Lord has blessed me with a talent for writing. He has guided me in finding publishers for my works. He has given me a wonderful illustrator for my picture books, Maria Magdalena Brown. My desire is to brighten the lives of the children who read my books."

BIOGRAPHICAL/CRITICAL SOURCES:

PERIODICALS

Owls, fall, 1996, review of *My Little Book of Burrowing Owls.*
Provident Book Finder, March-May, 1999, review of *Wings in the Water: The Story of a Manta Ray.*
School Library Journal, September, 1995, review of *Isaac Johnson: From Slave to Stonecutter.*

*   *   *

MARTIN, Ann M. 1955-

PERSONAL: Born August 12, 1955, in Princeton, NJ; daughter of Henry Read (a cartoonist) and Edith Aiken (a teacher; maiden name, Matthews) Martin. *Education:* Smith College, A.B. (cum laude), 1977. *Politics:* Democrat. *Avocational interests:* "Reading and needlework, especially smocking and knitting."

ADDRESSES: Agent—Amy Berkower, Writers House, Inc., 21 West 26th St., New York, NY 10010.

CAREER: Elementary school teacher in Noroton, CT, 1977-78; Pocket Books, Inc., New York, NY, editorial assistant for Archway Paperbacks, 1978-80; Scholastic Book Services, New York, NY, copywriter for Teen Age Book Club, 1980-81, associate editor, 1981-83, editor, 1983; Bantam Books, Inc., New York, NY, senior editor of Books for Young Readers, 1983-85; writer and freelance editor, 1985—. Co-founder of Lisa Novak Community Libraries; founder of Ann M. Martin Foundation.

MEMBER: PEN, Authors Guild, Society of Children's Book Writers.

AWARDS, HONORS: New Jersey Author awards, New Jersey Institute of Technology, 1983, for *Bummer Summer,* 1987, for *Missing since Monday;* Children's Choice, 1985, for *Bummer Summer;* Child Study Association of America's Children's Books of the Year selection, 1986, for *Inside Out,* 1987, for *Stage Fright, With You and without You,* and *Missing since Monday;* Keystone State Reading Award, 1998, for *Leo the Magnificat;* California Young Reader Medal nomination, 2000, and Washington Sasquatch Reading Award nomination, 2001, both for *P.S. Longer Letter Later.*

WRITINGS:

Bummer Summer, Holiday House (New York, NY), 1983.

Just You and Me, Scholastic, Inc. (New York, NY), 1983.

(With Betsy Ryan) *My Puppy Scrapbook,* illustrated by father, Henry Martin, Scholastic, Inc. (New York, NY), 1983.

Inside Out, Holiday House (New York, NY), 1984.

Stage Fright, illustrated by Blanche Sims, Holiday House (New York, NY), 1984.

Me and Katie (the Pest), illustrated by Blanche Sims, Holiday House (New York, NY), 1985.

With You and without You, Holiday House (New York, NY), 1986.

Missing since Monday, Holiday House (New York, NY), 1986.

Just a Summer Romance, Holiday House (New York, NY), 1987.

Slam Book, Holiday House (New York, NY), 1987.

Yours Turly, Shirley, Holiday House (New York, NY), 1988.

Ten Kids, No Pets, Holiday House (New York, NY), 1988.

Fancy Dance in Feather Town, illustrated by Henry Martin, Western Publishing, 1988.

Ma and Pa Dracula, illustrated by Dirk Zimmer, Holiday House (New York, NY), 1989.

Moving Day in Feather Town, illustrated by Henry Martin, Western Publishing, 1989.

Eleven Kids, One Summer, Holiday House (New York, NY), 1991.

Enchanted Attic, Bantam (New York, NY), 1992.

Rachel Parker, Kindergarten Show-off, illustrated by Nancy Poydar, Holiday House (New York, NY), 1992.

Chain Letter, Scholastic, Inc. (New York, NY), 1993.

(With Margot Becker) *Ann M. Martin: The Story of the Author of the Baby-Sitters Club,* Scholastic, Inc. (New York, NY) 1993.

Leo the Magnificat, illustrated by Emily A. McCully, Scholastic, Inc. (New York, NY), 1996.

(With Paula Danziger) *P.S. Longer Letter Later,* Scholastic, Inc. (New York, NY), 1998.

(With Laura Godwin) *The Doll People,* Hyperion (New York, NY), 1999.

(With Paula Danziger) *Snail Mail No More,* Scholastic, Inc. (New York, NY), 2000.

Belle Teal, Scholastic, Inc. (New York, NY), 2001.

"BABY-SITTERS CLUB" SERIES

Kristy's Great Idea, Scholastic, Inc. (New York, NY), 1986.

Claudia and the Phantom Phone Calls, Scholastic, Inc. (New York, NY), 1986.

The Truth about Stacey, Scholastic, Inc. (New York, NY), 1986.

Mary Anne Saves the Day, Scholastic, Inc. (New York, NY), 1987.

Dawn and the Impossible Three, Scholastic, Inc. (New York, NY), 1987.

Kristy's Big Day, Scholastic, Inc. (New York, NY), 1987.

Claudia and Mean Janine, Scholastic, Inc. (New York, NY), 1987.

Boy-Crazy Stacey, Scholastic, Inc. (New York, NY), 1987.

The Ghost at Dawn's House, Scholastic, Inc. (New York, NY), 1988.

Logan Likes Mary Anne!, Scholastic, Inc. (New York, NY), 1988.

Kristy and the Snobs, Scholastic, Inc. (New York, NY), 1988.

Claudia and the New Girl, Scholastic, Inc. (New York, NY), 1988.

Good-bye Stacey, Good-bye, Scholastic, Inc. (New York, NY), 1988.

Hello, Mallory, Scholastic, Inc. (New York, NY), 1988.

Little Miss Stoneybrook . . . and Dawn, Scholastic, Inc. (New York, NY), 1988.

Jessi's Secret Language, Scholastic, Inc. (New York, NY), 1988.

Mary Anne's Bad-Luck Mystery, Scholastic, Inc. (New York, NY), 1988.

Stacey's Mistake, Scholastic, Inc. (New York, NY), 1988.

Claudia and the Bad Joke, Scholastic, Inc. (New York, NY), 1988.

Kristy and the Walking Disaster, Scholastic, Inc. (New York, NY), 1989.

Mallory and the Trouble with the Twins, Scholastic, Inc. (New York, NY), 1989.

Jessi Ramsey, Pet-Sitter, Scholastic, Inc. (New York, NY), 1989.

Dawn on the Coast, Scholastic, Inc. (New York, NY), 1989.

Kristy and the Mother's Day Surprise, Scholastic, Inc. (New York, NY), 1989.

Mary Anne and the Search for Tigger, Scholastic, Inc. (New York, NY), 1989.

Claudia and the Sad Good-bye, Scholastic, Inc. (New York, NY), 1989.

Jessi and the Superbrat, Scholastic, Inc. (New York, NY), 1989.

Welcome Back, Stacey!, Scholastic, Inc. (New York, NY), 1989.

Mallory and the Mystery Diary, Scholastic, Inc. (New York, NY), 1989.

Mary Anne and the Great Romance, Scholastic, Inc. (New York, NY), 1990.

Dawn's Wicked Stepsister, Scholastic, Inc. (New York, NY), 1990.

Kristy and the Secret of Susan, Scholastic, Inc. (New York, NY), 1990.

Claudia and the Great Search, Scholastic, Inc. (New York, NY), 1990.

Mary Anne and Too Many Boys, Scholastic, Inc. (New York, NY), 1990.

Stacey and the Mystery of Stoneybrook, Scholastic, Inc. (New York, NY), 1990.

Jessi's Baby-Sitter, Scholastic, Inc. (New York, NY), 1990.

Dawn and the Older Boy, Scholastic, Inc. (New York, NY), 1990.

Kristy's Mystery Admirer, Scholastic, Inc. (New York, NY), 1990.

Poor Mallory, Scholastic, Inc. (New York, NY), 1990.

Claudia and the Middle School Mystery, Scholastic, Inc. (New York, NY), 1991.

Mary Anne vs. Logan, Scholastic, Inc. (New York, NY), 1991.

Jessi and the Dance School Phantom, Scholastic, Inc. (New York, NY), 1991.

Stacey's Emergency, Scholastic, Inc. (New York, NY), 1991.

Dawn and the Big Sleepover, Scholastic, Inc. (New York, NY), 1991.

Kristy and the Baby Parade, Scholastic, Inc. (New York, NY), 1991.

Mary Anne Misses Logan, Scholastic, Inc. (New York, NY), 1991.

Mallory on Strike, Scholastic, Inc. (New York, NY), 1991.

Jessi's Wish, Scholastic, Inc. (New York, NY), 1991.

Claudia and the Genius of Elm Street, Scholastic, Inc. (New York, NY), 1991.

Dawn's Big Date, Scholastic, Inc. (New York, NY), 1992.

Stacey's Ex-Best Friend, Scholastic, Inc. (New York, NY), 1992.

Mary Anne and Too Many Babies, Scholastic, Inc. (New York, NY), 1992.

Kristy for President, Scholastic, Inc. (New York, NY), 1992.

Mallory and the Dream Horse, Scholastic, Inc. (New York, NY), 1992.

Jessi's Gold Medal, Scholastic, Inc. (New York, NY), 1992.

Keep out, Claudia!, Scholastic, Inc. (New York, NY), 1992.

Dawn Saves the Planet, Scholastic, Inc. (New York, NY), 1992.

Stacey's Choice, Scholastic, Inc. (New York, NY), 1992.

Mallory Hates Boys (and Gym), Scholastic, Inc. (New York, NY), 1992.

Mary Anne's Makeover, Scholastic, Inc. (New York, NY), 1993.

Jessi and the Awful Secret, Scholastic, Inc. (New York, NY), 1993.

Kristy and the Worst Kid Ever, Scholastic, Inc. (New York, NY), 1993.

Claudia's Friend, Scholastic, Inc. (New York, NY), 1993.

Dawn's Family Feud, Scholastic, Inc. (New York, NY), 1993.

Stacey's Big Crush, Scholastic, Inc. (New York, NY), 1993.

Maid Mary Anne, Scholastic, Inc. (New York, NY), 1993.

Dawn's Big Move, Scholastic, Inc. (New York, NY), 1993.

Jessi and the Bad Baby-Sitter, Scholastic, Inc. (New York, NY), 1993.

Get Well Soon, Mallory, Scholastic, Inc. (New York, NY), 1993.

Stacey and the Cheerleaders, Scholastic, Inc. (New York, NY), 1993.

Claudia and the Perfect Boy, Scholastic, Inc. (New York, NY), 1994.

Dawn and the We Love Kids Club, Scholastic, Inc. (New York, NY), 1994.

Mary Anne and Miss Priss, Scholastic, Inc. (New York, NY), 1994.

Kristy and the Copycat, Scholastic, Inc. (New York, NY), 1994.

Jessi's Horrible Prank, Scholastic, Inc. (New York, NY), 1994.

Stacey's Lie, Scholastic, Inc. (New York, NY), 1994.

Dawn and Whitney, Friends Forever, Scholastic, Inc. (New York, NY), 1994.

Claudia and Crazy Peaches, Scholastic, Inc. (New York, NY), 1994.

Mary Anne Breaks the Rules, Scholastic, Inc. (New York, NY), 1994.

Mallory Pike, #1 Fan, Scholastic, Inc. (New York, NY), 1994.

Kristy and Mr. Mom, Scholastic, Inc. (New York, NY), 1995.

Jessi and the Troublemaker, Scholastic, Inc. (New York, NY), 1995.

Stacey vs. the BSC, Scholastic, Inc. (New York, NY), 1995.

Dawn and the School Spirit War, Scholastic, Inc. (New York, NY), 1995.

Claudia Kishi, Live from WSTO, Scholastic, Inc. (New York, NY), 1995.

Mary Anne and Camp BSC, Scholastic, Inc. (New York, NY), 1995.

Stacey and the Bad Girls, Scholastic, Inc. (New York, NY), 1995.

Farewell, Dawn, Scholastic, Inc. (New York, NY), 1995.

Kristy and the Dirty Diapers, Scholastic, Inc. (New York, NY), 1995.

Welcome to the BSC, Abby, Scholastic, Inc. (New York, NY), 1995.

Claudia and the First Thanksgiving, Scholastic, Inc. (New York, NY), 1995.

Mallory's Christmas Wish, Scholastic, Inc. (New York, NY), 1995.

Mary Anne and the Memory Garden, Scholastic, Inc. (New York, NY), 1996.

Stacey McGill, Super Sitter, Scholastic, Inc. (New York, NY), 1996.

Kristy + Bart = ?, Scholastic, Inc. (New York, NY), 1996.

Abby's Lucky Thirteen, Scholastic, Inc. (New York, NY), 1996.

Claudia and the World's Cutest Baby, Scholastic, Inc. (New York, NY), 1996.

Dawn and Too Many Sitters, Scholastic, Inc. (New York, NY), 1996.

Stacey's Broken Heart, Scholastic, Inc. (New York, NY), 1996.

Kristy's Worst Idea, Scholastic, Inc. (New York, NY), 1996.

Claudia Kishi, Middle School Drop Out, Scholastic, Inc. (New York, NY), 1996.

Mary Anne and the Little Princess, Scholastic, Inc. (New York, NY), 1996.

Happy Holidays, Jessi, Scholastic, Inc. (New York, NY), 1996.

Abby's Twin, Scholastic, Inc. (New York, NY), 1997.

Stacey the Match Whiz, Scholastic, Inc. (New York, NY), 1997.

Claudia, Queen of the Seventh Grade, Scholastic, Inc. (New York, NY), 1997.

Mind Your Own Business, Kristy!, Scholastic, Inc. (New York, NY), 1997.

Don't Give up, Mallory, Scholastic, Inc. (New York, NY), 1997.

Mary Anne to the Rescue, Scholastic, Inc. (New York, NY), 1997.

Abby the Bad Sport, Scholastic, Inc. (New York, NY), 1997.

Stacey's Secret Friend, Scholastic, Inc. (New York, NY), 1997.

Kristy and the Sister War, Scholastic, Inc. (New York, NY), 1997.

Claudia Makes up Her Mind, Scholastic, Inc. (New York, NY), 1997.

The Secret Life of Mary Anne Spier, Scholastic, Inc. (New York, NY), 1997.

Jessi's Big Break, Scholastic, Inc. (New York, NY), 1997.

Abby and the Best Kid Ever, Scholastic, Inc. (New York, NY), 1997.

Claudia and the Terrible Truth, Scholastic, Inc. (New York, NY), 1997.

Kristy Thomas, Dog Trainer, Scholastic, Inc. (New York, NY), 1997.

Stacey's Ex-Boyfriend, Scholastic, Inc. (New York, NY), 1997.

Mary Anne and the Playground Fight, Scholastic, Inc. (New York, NY), 1997.

Abby in Wonderland, Scholastic, Inc. (New York, NY), 1997.

Kristy in Charge, Scholastic, Inc. (New York, NY), 1997.

Claudia's Big Party, Scholastic, Inc. (New York, NY), 1998.

Stacey McGill . . . Matchmaker?, Scholastic, Inc. (New York, NY), 1998.

Mary Anne in the Middle, Scholastic, Inc. (New York, NY), 1998.

The All-New Mallory Pike, Scholastic, Inc. (New York, NY), 1998.

Abby's Un-Valentine, Scholastic, Inc. (New York, NY), 1998.

Claudia and the Little Liar, Scholastic, Inc. (New York, NY), 1999.

Kristy at Bat, Scholastic, Inc. (New York, NY), 1999.

Stacey's Movie, Scholastic, Inc. (New York, NY), 1999.

The Fire at Mary Anne's House, Scholastic, Inc. (New York, NY), 1999.

Graduation Day, Scholastic, Inc. (New York, NY), 2000.

"FRIENDS FOREVER" SERIES

Kristy's Big News, Scholastic, Inc. (New York, NY), 1999.

Stacey vs. Claudia, Scholastic, Inc. (New York, NY), 1999.

Mary Anne's Big Break Up, Scholastic, Inc. (New York, NY), 1999.

Claudia and the Friendship Feud, Scholastic, Inc. (New York, NY), 1999.

Kristy Power, Scholastic, Inc. (New York, NY), 1999.

Stacey and the Boyfriend Trap, Scholastic, Inc. (New York, NY), 1999.

Claudia Gets Her Guy, Scholastic, Inc. (New York, NY), 2000.

Mary Anne's Revenge, Scholastic, Inc. (New York, NY), 2000.

Kristy and the Kidnapper, Scholastic, Inc. (New York, NY), 2000.

Stacey's Problem, Scholastic, Inc. (New York, NY), 2000.

Welcome Home, Mary Anne, Scholastic, Inc. (New York, NY), 2000.

Claudia and the Disaster Date, Scholastic, Inc. (New York, NY), 2000.

"FRIENDS FOREVER SPECIAL" SERIES

Everything Changes, Scholastic, Inc. (New York, NY), 1999.

Graduation Day, Scholastic, Inc. (New York, NY), 2000.

"BABY-SITTERS CLUB MYSTERY" SERIES

Stacey and the Missing Ring, Scholastic, Inc. (New York, NY), 1991.

Beware, Dawn!, Scholastic, Inc. (New York, NY), 1991.

Mallory and the Ghost Cat, Scholastic, Inc. (New York, NY), 1992.

Kristy and the Missing Child, Scholastic, Inc. (New York, NY), 1992.

Mary Anne and the Secret in the Attic, Scholastic, Inc. (New York, NY), 1992.

The Mystery at Claudia's House, Scholastic, Inc. (New York, NY), 1992.

Dawn and the Disappearing Dogs, Scholastic, Inc. (New York, NY), 1993.

Jessi and the Jewel Thieves, Scholastic, Inc. (New York, NY), 1993.

Kristy and the Haunted Mansion, Scholastic, Inc. (New York, NY), 1993.

Stacey and the Mystery Money, Scholastic, Inc. (New York, NY), 1993.

Claudia and the Mystery at the Museum, Scholastic, Inc. (New York, NY), 1993.

Dawn and the Surfer Ghost, Scholastic, Inc. (New York, NY), 1993.

Mary Anne and the Library Mystery, Scholastic, Inc. (New York, NY), 1994.

Stacey and the Mystery at the Mall, Scholastic, Inc. (New York, NY), 1994.

Kristy and the Vampires, Scholastic, Inc. (New York, NY), 1994.

Claudia and the Clue in the Photograph, Scholastic, Inc. (New York, NY), 1994.

Dawn and the Halloween Mystery, Scholastic, Inc. (New York, NY), 1994.

Stacey and the Mystery at the Empty House, Scholastic, Inc. (New York, NY), 1994.

Kristy and the Missing Fortune, Scholastic, Inc. (New York, NY), 1995.

Mary Anne and the Zoo Mystery, Scholastic, Inc. (New York, NY), 1995.

Claudia and the Recipe for Danger, Scholastic, Inc. (New York, NY), 1995.

Stacey and the Haunted Masquerade, Scholastic, Inc. (New York, NY), 1995.

Abby and the Secret Society, Scholastic, Inc. (New York, NY), 1996.

Mary Anne and the Silent Witness, Scholastic, Inc. (New York, NY), 1996.

Kristy and the Middle School Vandal, Scholastic, Inc. (New York, NY), 1996.

Dawn Schafer, Undercover Baby-Sitter, Scholastic, Inc. (New York, NY), 1996.

Claudia and the Lighthouse Ghost, Scholastic, Inc. (New York, NY), 1996.

Abby and the Mystery Baby, Scholastic, Inc. (New York, NY), 1997.

Stacey and the Fashion Victim, Scholastic, Inc. (New York, NY), 1997.

Kristy and the Mystery Train, Scholastic, Inc. (New York, NY), 1997.

Mary Anne and the Music Box Secret, Scholastic, Inc. (New York, NY), 1997.

Claudia and the Mystery in the Painting, Scholastic, Inc. (New York, NY), 1997.

Stacey and the Stolen Hearts, Scholastic, Inc. (New York, NY), 1997.

Mary Anne and the Haunted Bookstore, Scholastic, Inc. (New York, NY), 1997.

Abby and the Notorious Neighbor, Scholastic, Inc. (New York, NY), 1997.

Kristy and the Cat Burglar, Scholastic, Inc. (New York, NY), 1997.

"BABY-SITTERS CLUB SUPER SPECIALS" SERIES

Baby-Sitters on Board!, Scholastic, Inc. (New York, NY), 1988.

Baby-Sitters Summer Vacation, Scholastic, Inc. (New York, NY), 1989.

Baby-Sitters Winter Vacation, Scholastic, Inc. (New York, NY), 1989.

Baby-Sitters Island Adventure, Scholastic, Inc. (New York, NY), 1990.

California Girls!, Scholastic, Inc. (New York, NY), 1990.

New York, New York!, Scholastic, Inc. (New York, NY), 1991.

Snowbound, Scholastic, Inc. (New York, NY), 1991.

Baby-Sitters at Shadow Lake, Scholastic, Inc. (New York, NY), 1992.

Starring the Baby-Sitters Club, Scholastic, Inc. (New York, NY), 1992.

Sea City, Here We Come!, Scholastic, Inc. (New York, NY), 1993.

The Baby-Sitters Remember, Scholastic, Inc. (New York, NY), 1994.

Here Come the Bridesmaids!, Scholastic, Inc. (New York, NY), 1994.

Aloha, Baby-Sitters!, Scholastic, Inc. (New York, NY), 1996.

"BABY-SITTERS LITTLE SISTERS" SERIES

Karen's Witch, Scholastic, Inc. (New York, NY), 1988.

Karen's Roller Skates, Scholastic, Inc. (New York, NY), 1988.

Karen's Worst Day, Scholastic, Inc. (New York, NY), 1989.

Karen's Kittycat Club, Scholastic, Inc. (New York, NY), 1989.

Karen's School Picture, Scholastic, Inc. (New York, NY), 1989.

Karen's Little Sister, Scholastic, Inc. (New York, NY), 1989.

Karen's Birthday, Scholastic, Inc. (New York, NY), 1990.

Karen's Haircut, Scholastic, Inc. (New York, NY), 1990.

Karen's Sleepover, Scholastic, Inc. (New York, NY), 1990.

Karen's Grandmothers, Scholastic, Inc. (New York, NY), 1990.

Karen's Prize, Scholastic, Inc. (New York, NY), 1990.

Karen's Ghost, Scholastic, Inc. (New York, NY), 1990.

Karen's Surprise, Scholastic, Inc. (New York, NY), 1990.

Karen's New Year, Scholastic, Inc. (New York, NY), 1991.

Karen's in Love, Scholastic, Inc. (New York, NY), 1991.

Karen's Goldfish, Scholastic, Inc. (New York, NY), 1991.

Karen's Brothers, Scholastic, Inc. (New York, NY), 1991.

Karen's Home Run, Scholastic, Inc. (New York, NY), 1991.

Karen's Good-Bye, Scholastic, Inc. (New York, NY), 1991.

Karen's Carnival, Scholastic, Inc. (New York, NY), 1991.

Karen's New Teacher, Scholastic, Inc. (New York, NY), 1991.

Karen's Little Witch, Scholastic, Inc. (New York, NY), 1992.

Karen's Doll, Scholastic, Inc. (New York, NY), 1992.

Karen's School Trip, Scholastic, Inc. (New York, NY), 1992.

Karen's Pen Pal, Scholastic, Inc. (New York, NY), 1992.

Karen's Ducklings, Scholastic, Inc. (New York, NY), 1992.

Karen's Big Joke, Scholastic, Inc. (New York, NY), 1992.

Karen's Tea Party, Scholastic, Inc. (New York, NY), 1992.

Karen's Cartwheel, Scholastic, Inc. (New York, NY), 1992.

Karen's Kittens, Scholastic, Inc. (New York, NY), 1992.

Karen's Bully, Scholastic, Inc. (New York, NY), 1992.

Karen's Pumpkin Patch, Scholastic, Inc. (New York, NY), 1992.

Karen's Secret, Scholastic, Inc. (New York, NY), 1992.

Karen's Snow Day, Scholastic, Inc. (New York, NY), 1993.

Karen's Doll Hospital, Scholastic, Inc. (New York, NY), 1993.

Karen's New Friend, Scholastic, Inc. (New York, NY), 1993.

Karen's Tuba, Scholastic, Inc. (New York, NY), 1993.

Karen's Big Lie, Scholastic, Inc. (New York, NY), 1993.

Karen's Wedding, Scholastic, Inc. (New York, NY), 1993.

Karen's Newspaper, Scholastic, Inc. (New York, NY), 1993.

Karen's School, Scholastic, Inc. (New York, NY), 1993.

Karen's Pizza Party, Scholastic, Inc. (New York, NY), 1993.

Karen's Toothache, Scholastic, Inc. (New York, NY), 1993.

Karen's Big Weekend, Scholastic, Inc. (New York, NY), 1993.

Karen's Twin, Scholastic, Inc. (New York, NY), 1994.

Karen's Baby-Sitter, Scholastic, Inc. (New York, NY), 1994.

Karen's Kite, Scholastic, Inc. (New York, NY), 1994.

Karen's Two Families, Scholastic, Inc. (New York, NY), 1994.

Karen's Stepmother, Scholastic, Inc. (New York, NY), 1994.

Karen's Lucky Penny, Scholastic, Inc. (New York, NY), 1994.

Karen's Big Top, Scholastic, Inc. (New York, NY), 1994.

Karen's Mermaid, Scholastic, Inc. (New York, NY), 1994.

Karen's School Bus, Scholastic, Inc. (New York, NY), 1994.

Karen's Candy, Scholastic, Inc. (New York, NY), 1994.

Karen's Magician, Scholastic, Inc. (New York, NY), 1994.

Karen's Ice Skates, Scholastic, Inc. (New York, NY), 1994.

Karen's School Mystery, Scholastic, Inc. (New York, NY), 1995.

Karen's Ski Trip, Scholastic, Inc. (New York, NY), 1995.

Karen's Leprechaun, Scholastic, Inc. (New York, NY), 1995.

Karen's Pony, Scholastic, Inc. (New York, NY), 1995.

Karen's Tattletale, Scholastic, Inc. (New York, NY), 1995.

Karen's New Bike, Scholastic, Inc. (New York, NY), 1995.

Karen's Movie, Scholastic, Inc. (New York, NY), 1995.

Karen's Lemonade Stand, Scholastic, Inc. (New York, NY), 1995.

Karen's Toys, Scholastic, Inc. (New York, NY), 1995.

Karen's Monsters, Scholastic, Inc. (New York, NY), 1995.

Karen's Turkey Day, Scholastic, Inc. (New York, NY), 1995.

Karen's Angel, Scholastic, Inc. (New York, NY), 1995.

Karen's Big Sister, Scholastic, Inc. (New York, NY), 1996.

Karen's Grandad, Scholastic, Inc. (New York, NY), 1996.

Karen's Island Adventure, Scholastic, Inc. (New York, NY), 1996.

Karen's New Puppy, Scholastic, Inc. (New York, NY), 1996.

Karen's Dinosaur, Scholastic, Inc. (New York, NY), 1996.

Karen's Softball Mystery, Scholastic, Inc. (New York, NY), 1996.

Karen's County Fair, Scholastic, Inc. (New York, NY), 1996.

Karen's Magic Garden, Scholastic, Inc. (New York, NY), 1996.

Karen's School Surprise, Scholastic, Inc. (New York, NY), 1996.

Karen's Half Birthday, Scholastic, Inc. (New York, NY), 1996.

Karen's Big Fight, Scholastic, Inc. (New York, NY), 1996.

Karen's Christmas Tree, Scholastic, Inc. (New York, NY), 1996.

Karen's Accident, Scholastic, Inc. (New York, NY), 1997.

Karen's Secret Valentine, Scholastic, Inc. (New York, NY), 1997.

Karen's Bunny, Scholastic, Inc. (New York, NY), 1997.

Karen's Big Job, Scholastic, Inc. (New York, NY), 1997.

Karen's Treasure, Scholastic, Inc. (New York, NY), 1997.

Karen's Telephone Trouble, Scholastic, Inc. (New York, NY), 1997.

Karen's Pony Camp, Scholastic, Inc. (New York, NY), 1997.

Karen's Puppet Show, Scholastic, Inc. (New York, NY), 1997.

Karen's Unicorn, Scholastic, Inc. (New York, NY), 1997.

Karen's Haunted House, Scholastic, Inc. (New York, NY), 1997.

Karen's Pilgrim, Scholastic, Inc. (New York, NY), 1997.

Karen's Sleigh Ride, Scholastic, Inc. (New York, NY), 1997.

Karen's Cooking Contest, Scholastic, Inc. (New York, NY), 1997.

Karen's Snow Princess, Scholastic, Inc. (New York, NY), 1997.

Karen's Promise, Scholastic, Inc. (New York, NY), 1997.

Karen's Big Move, Scholastic, Inc. (New York, NY), 1997.

Karen's Paper Route, Scholastic, Inc. (New York, NY), 1997.

Karen's Fishing Trip, Scholastic, Inc. (New York, NY), 1997.

Karen's Big City Mystery, Scholastic, Inc. (New York, NY), 1997.

Karen's Book, Scholastic, Inc. (New York, NY), 1997.

Karen's Chain Letter, Scholastic, Inc. (New York, NY), 1997.

Karen's Black Cat, Scholastic, Inc. (New York, NY), 1998.

Karen's Movie Star, Scholastic, Inc. (New York, NY), 1998.

Karen's Christmas Carol, Scholastic, Inc. (New York, NY), 1998.

Karen's Nanny, Scholastic, Inc. (New York, NY), 1998.

Karen's President, Scholastic, Inc. (New York, NY), 1998.

Karen's Copycat, Scholastic, Inc. (New York, NY), 1998.

Karen's Field Day, Scholastic, Inc. (New York, NY), 1998.

Karen's Show and Share, Scholastic, Inc. (New York, NY), 1998.

Karen's Swim Meet, Scholastic, Inc. (New York, NY), 1998.

Karen's Spy Mystery, Scholastic, Inc. (New York, NY), 1998.

Karen's New Holiday, Scholastic, Inc. (New York, NY), 1998.

Karen's Hurricane, Scholastic, Inc. (New York, NY), 1998.

Karen's Chicken Pox, Scholastic, Inc. (New York, NY), 1999.

Karen's Runaway Turkey, Scholastic, Inc. (New York, NY), 1999.

Karen's Reindeer, Scholastic, Inc. (New York, NY), 1999.

Karen's Mistake, Scholastic, Inc. (New York, NY), 2000.

Karen's Figure Eight, Scholastic, Inc. (New York, NY), 2000.

Karen's Yo-Yo, Scholastic, Inc. (New York, NY), 2000.

Karen's Easter Parade, Scholastic, Inc. (New York, NY), 2000.

Karen's Gift, Scholastic, Inc. (New York, NY), 2000.

Karen's Cowboy, Scholastic, Inc. (New York, NY), 2000.

"BABY-SITTERS LITTLE SISTERS SUPER SPECIAL" SERIES

Karen's Wish, Scholastic, Inc. (New York, NY), 1990.

Karen's Plane Trip, Scholastic, Inc. (New York, NY), 1991.

Karen's Mystery, Scholastic, Inc. (New York, NY), c. 1991.

Karen, Hannie, and Nancy: The Three Musketeers, Scholastic, Inc. (New York, NY), 1992.

Karen's Baby, Scholastic, Inc. (New York, NY), 1992.

Karen's Campout, Scholastic, Inc. (New York, NY), 1993.

"BABY-SITTERS CLUB PORTRAIT COLLECTION" SERIES

Dawn's Book, Scholastic, Inc. (New York, NY), 1993.

Stacey's Book, Scholastic, Inc. (New York, NY), 1994.

Claudia's Book, Scholastic, Inc. (New York, NY), 1995.

Mary Anne's Book, Scholastic, Inc. (New York, NY), 1996.

Kristy's Book, Scholastic, Inc. (New York, NY), 1996.

Abby's Book, Scholastic, Inc. (New York, NY), 1997.

"BABY-SITTERS CLUB SUPER MYSTERIES" SERIES

Baby-Sitters' Haunted House, Scholastic, Inc. (New York, NY), 1995.

Baby-Sitters Beware, Scholastic, Inc. (New York, NY), 1995.

Baby-Sitters' Fright Night, Scholastic, Inc. (New York, NY), 1996.

"BABY-SITTERS CLUB" SPECIAL EDITIONS

Logan Bruno, Boy Baby-Sitter, Scholastic, Inc. (New York, NY), 1993.

Baby-Sitters Little Sister School Scrapbook, Scholastic, Inc. (New York, NY), 1993.

Baby-Sitters Club Guide to Baby-sitting, Scholastic, Inc. (New York, NY), 1993.

Shannon's Story, Scholastic, Inc. (New York, NY), 1994.

Secret Santa, Scholastic, Inc. (New York, NY), 1994.

Baby-Sitters Little Sister Summer Fill-in Book, Scholastic, Inc. (New York, NY), 1995.

Baby-Sitters Little Sister Jump Rope Rhymes, Scholastic, Inc. (New York, NY), 1995.

Baby-Sitters Little Sister Playground Games, Scholastic, Inc. (New York, NY), 1996.

Complete Guide to the Baby-Sitters Club, Scholastic, Inc. (New York, NY), 1996.

The BSC Notebook, Scholastic, Inc. (New York, NY), 1996.

BSC Chain Letter, Scholastic, Inc. (New York, NY), 1996.

The Baby-Sitters Club Trivia and Puzzle Fun Book, Scholastic, Inc. (New York, NY), 1996.

The Baby-Sitters Club Postcard Book, Scholastic, Inc. (New York, NY), 1996.

Little Sister Photo Scrapbook, Scholastic, Inc. (New York, NY), 1997.

Baby-Sitters Little Sister Secret Diary, Scholastic, Inc. (New York, NY), 1997.

Baby-Sitters Little Sister Laugh Pack, Scholastic, Inc. (New York, NY), 1997.

"THE KIDS IN MS. COLMAN'S CLASS" SERIES; ILLUSTRATED BY CHARLES TANG

Teacher's Pet, Scholastic, Inc. (New York, NY), 1996.

Author Day, Scholastic, Inc. (New York, NY), 1996.

Class Play, Scholastic, Inc. (New York, NY), 1996.

The Second Grade Baby, Scholastic, Inc. (New York, NY), 1996.

Snow War, Scholastic, Inc. (New York, NY), 1997.

Twin Trouble, Scholastic, Inc. (New York, NY), 1997.

Science Fair, Scholastic, Inc. (New York, NY), 1997.

Summer Kids, Scholastic, Inc. (New York, NY), 1997.

Halloween Parade, Scholastic, Inc. (New York, NY), 1998.

Holiday Time, Scholastic, Inc. (New York, NY), 1998.

Spelling Bee, Scholastic, Inc. (New York, NY), 1998.

Baby Animal Zoo, Scholastic, Inc. (New York, NY), 1998.

"CALIFORNIA DIARIES" SERIES

Dawn, Scholastic, Inc. (New York, NY), 1997.

Sunny, Scholastic, Inc. (New York, NY), 1997.

Maggie, Scholastic, Inc. (New York, NY), 1997.

Amalia, Scholastic, Inc. (New York, NY), 1997.

Ducky, Scholastic, Inc. (New York, NY), 1997.

Dawn Diary Two, Scholastic, Inc. (New York, NY), 1998.

Sunny Diary Two, Scholastic, Inc. (New York, NY), 1998.

Maggie Diary Two, Scholastic, Inc. (New York, NY), 1998.

Amalia Diary Two, Scholastic, Inc. (New York, NY), 1998.

Ducky Diary Two, Scholastic, Inc. (New York, NY), 1998.

Dawn Diary Three, Scholastic, Inc. (New York, NY), 1999.

Sunny Diary Three, Scholastic, Inc. (New York, NY), 1999.

Maggie Diary Three, Scholastic, Inc. (New York, NY), 2000.

Amalia Diary Three, Scholastic, Inc. (New York, NY), 2000.

Ducky Diary Three, Scholastic, Inc. (New York, NY), 2001.

Martin's books have been translated into several foreign languages. The "Baby-Sitters Club" books have been translated into nineteen foreign languages.

ADAPTATIONS: The *Baby-Sitters Club* television series was produced by Scholastic Productions and broadcast on Home Box Office (HBO) and the Disney Channel; The Baby-Sitters Club Movie, co-produced by Scholastic Productions and Beacon Communications, was distributed by Columbia, 1995; a "Baby-Sitters Club"

board game has been released by Milton-Bradley; several "Baby-Sitters Club" stories have appeared on video and audio cassette.

SIDELIGHTS: When the curtain came down on the final act of the "Baby-Sitters Club" series in the year 2000, Ann M. Martin, series author and co-originator, had become one of the best-known names in juvenile publishing. What started in 1986 as an idea for a four-book series to be published over the course of one year had ballooned fourteen years later into a mini- publishing industry with several spin-off titles, a television series, a movie, games, and various "Baby-Sitters Club" (BSC) merchandise to satisfy the needs of legions of faithful BSC readers. With over 180 million books in print in nineteen languages, the "Baby-Sitters Club" had obviously, as Sally Lodge noted in *Publishers Weekly,* "struck a resounding chord with preteen girls all over the world." Martin bid adieu to her readers with the final BSC volume, *Graduation Day,* but not good- bye to publishing. She addressed her fans directly over the Internet on her Web site, *Ann Online,* telling them that "it still amazes me to see the incredible body of work that was a result of that original idea." Those spin-off titles include over 130 of the original "Baby-Sitters Club" editions as well as 120 more titles in the "Little Sisters" series, twenty-five books in the "Mystery" series, a baker's dozen in the "BSC Friends Forever" series, another fifteen in the "California Diaries" series, and dozens of titles in super editions, not to mention twelve books in the "Kids in Ms. Colman's Class" series—a spin-off of a spin-off. Millions of teens and pre-teens have grown up with the antics and adventures of Kristy, Mary Anne, Stacey, and Claudia, and then found new friends with whom to identify with the addition of Dawn, Jessi, Mallory, and Abby to the club. These perennial middle schoolers have found their way into the hearts of young girls worldwide.

Contrary to the way that most multi-volume children's book series are produced, Martin did much of the writing for both of the main series, rising at 5:30 each morning to start her writing day and completing nearly two books each month. As the number of series grew, however, it was impossible for Martin to keep up with the flow of books, and other writers were brought on to help write some of the titles. But after fourteen years both Martin and her publisher, Scholastic, were ready to move on to new projects. Martin already began such a move in 1998 with non-series titles aimed at older juvenile readers and written in collaboration with both Paula Danziger and Laura Godwin. Definitely Martin has not said farewell to writing. "While I am sad on one level to close this chapter of my writing life," Martin wrote, "I am also excited about the new projects that I will now have the time to explore. As you probably know, what I love to do most is write books for children."

Born in 1955, Martin grew up in Princeton, New Jersey, in a tight-knit family of parents and one younger sister, Jane. "I grew up in a very imaginative family," Martin once noted. "My mother was a preschool teacher and my father, an artist. Both liked fantasy and children's literature, so my world was one of circuses, animals, Beatrix Potter, *Winnie-the-Pooh, The Wizard of Oz,* elves and gnomes and fairies. It was a lot of fun, and it stayed with me. I'm often off in some other world, and all my daydreaming goes into my books." In an interview with Kristin McMurran of *People Weekly,* Martin further elaborated on her childhood: "I was moody and temperamental, but those were very happy years . . . because I had parents who would . . . teach us magic tricks and roast marshmallows in the woods with us. They never cared if we made a mess. My mother called our playroom 'toy soup.'" Martin was an enterprising child, running a library at one point and charging her friends overdue fines. She also was a babysitter; her oddest "client" was a snake which she had to tend one weekend. The reptile did not make it through the two days. The author subsequently modeled many of the events and characters of her popular series from those of her youth, including best friend Beth Perkins who informs much of the character of Kristy, leader of the Baby-Sitters Club.

Reading and writing were among her favorite childhood activities. Martin once commented, "I had always enjoyed writing, even as a child. Before I could write, I dictated stories to my mother. I took creative writing classes and that sort of thing as a kid, but I wanted desperately to be a teacher, so that was what I prepared for." At Smith College, Martin double-majored in psychology and early childhood education. Out of college, Martin taught elementary school for a year, working with students challenged by learning disabilities such as dyslexia. "Working with kids who had special problems or needs, plus seeing the natural way they got along with each other in school—the groups and rivalries that form among children—has all influenced me," Martin once noted.

Soon, however, Martin realized that she wanted to work in children's books rather than in education. Martin cut her literary teeth first on the "other" side of the desk, working as an editorial assistant, then assistant editor, and finally editor and senior editor at publishers including Pocket Books, Scholastic, and Bantam, from 1978 to 1985.

Martin published her first book, *Bummer Summer,* in 1983. A popular story for young readers, this debut is about a first overnight camp experience and paved the way for further teen and pre-teen books such as *Inside Out, Stage Fright,* and *Me and Katie (the Pest).* "Some of my books are based on actual experiences," Martin once said, "others are based more on imagination, and memories of feelings. *Me and Katie (the Pest)* is loosely based on riding lessons I took in the third grade. . . . *With You and without You* is about the death of a parent. *Inside Out* was based on my work as a therapist for autistic children; it wasn't really something that happened in my childhood. *Stage Fright* is probably the most autobiographical of my books. I had terrible stage fright when I was a kid, . . . and that was the inspiration for that book."

Increasingly Martin was coming to see herself as a writer rather than an editor. In 1985, Jean Feiwel, editor-in-chief of the book group at Scholastic, came up with the idea of a mini-series about a babysitting cooperative, and she asked Martin to write four stories. When the inaugural title, *Kristy's Great Idea* quickly sold out its 30,000-copy first printing, Feiwel and Martin thought they might just be on to something. The subsequent books were popular enough that Feiwel suggested Martin write two more stories for the series. "Scholastic decided the books were doing exceptionally well when the sixth book of the series hit number one on the B. Dalton Juvenile Bestseller list, sometime in 1987," Martin once noted. "That was when we decided that we really had something. We stepped up the schedule to one book every other month and eventually one every month."

From the outset the series was a collaborative effort, and Martin and Feiwel, as well other editors determined early on that the series—while sometimes dealing with serious issues such as death, racism, divorce, and peer pressure—would not deal with other hot button issues such as child abuse, alcohol or drug abuse, or the death of a parent. Geared at readers eight through about twelve, the series is intended as entertainment: light, breezy, and conversational. It has often been touted as the perfect introduction to books for reluctant readers. In all of the books, the characters remain the same age. "Two of them are permanently in the sixth grade, and the rest are permanently in the eighth grade," Martin once explained. "I can't let them grow up because the books come out too fast. I try not to allude to birthdays or summer vacations. . . . Otherwise the characters would soon be thirty-five." Martin was also careful to avoid slang and the use of time-fixers such as the names of current rock groups; the "Baby-Sitters Club" books take place in a time capsule, a sort of all-time and any-time. Neither does Martin talk down to readers in any of her books. "I suppose that somewhere in the back of my mind, I'm always thinking of the audience for whom I'm writing, but I don't talk down to kids, and I don't work with a controlled vocabulary. I just seem to fall into a young voice for Karen, the narrator of the 'Baby-Sitters Little Sister' series, and into older voices for the girls who narrate the 'Baby-Sitters Club' books."

Books in the series deal with the adventures of a group of girls who band together to operate a child-care business, and individual titles have explored a range of topics. *Kristy and the Secret of Susan* deals with an autistic savant, *Claudia and the Sad Good-bye* is about the death of a grandparent, *Kristy and the Snobs* relates the death of Kristy's pet, and *Jessi's Secret Language* finds Jessi baby-sitting for a deaf boy who communicates only in American Sign Language. Such books demonstrate Martin's own interests and proclivities. Her personal favorite among the books is *Kristy's Big Day.* Martin herself admitted in *Time* magazine that her books were "not great literature," but she has also noted that they "attract kids who are reluctant readers, if not children with definite learning problems such as dyslexia, and turn them into readers. And for kids who are already readers, I don't think there's anything wrong with picking up a series and reading it. I write the books as pure entertainment for myself as well as for the kids, but I am hoping that avid readers who are reading series are reading other things as well, and I also hope that reluctant readers who get hooked on reading through series reading, whether it's the 'Baby-Sitters Club' or another series, will then 'graduate' to other kinds of books."

Over the years, Martin and her editors added new series that would explore different age levels and that might update and enliven the series with a more modern approach. The last such addition was the "Baby-Sitters Club Friends Forever" series, ending with a title in a letters-and-journal-entries format in which the original four members of the club are left to carry on the traditions of their enterprise. The "California Diaries" series, inaugurated in 1997, features Dawn, one of the original baby-sitters, who moves to the West Coast to be with one of her divorced parents full-time. That series is, as the name implies, told in diary format. The eighth grade girls in this series are involved in somewhat edgier and more sophisticated activities than those found in the original "Baby-Sitters Club" books.

All good things, however, come to an end, and so too did the BSC finally call it a day with *Graduation Day.* Martin was prescient about such a demise. She once

noted that "as demographics and tastes change, kids do, too, and maybe in a few years they will find that they want pure fantasy and escape, like the C. S. Lewis books. That might signal the end of the 'Baby-Sitters Club'; I can't really think of the BSC characters traveling to an imaginary kingdom or another planet."

Martin continued publishing hardcover novels during the years she was churning out the BSC. One of her personal favorites of these is *Ten Kids, No Pets,* about the boisterous Rosso family. In a sequel to that book, *Eleven Kids, One Summer,* the Rossos spend the summer on New York's Fire Island. Each chapter puts the lens on the activities of one of the "amiable Rosso offspring," according to a *Publishers Weekly* reviewer, who range in age from six months to fifteen years. There is a movie being filmed on the island with a handsome star for eldest Rosso, Abbie, to form a friendship with; there is a house that the sensitive Candy thinks is haunted; and there are plenty of seashells for enterprising Woody to paint and then sell. "Martin . . . knows well what pleases young readers," the same reviewer concluded, "and this novel is filled with characters, escapades and dialogue that will do just that."

"One of the most important tools I use in my writing is my memory," Martin has said. "It is very clear. I can remember what that first day of kindergarten was like—the way the room looked, the children, how I felt when my mother left. And I remember my senior prom and my tenth birthday and vacations at the shore and junior high graduation just as clearly. Little things, too—making a bulletin board display in sixth grade and making doll clothes and playing statue after dinner on hot summer nights. It's just as important to be able to transport oneself back to childhood as it is to have a vivid imagination, in order to write believable children's books. When I speak through my young characters, I am remembering and reliving: redoing all those things one is never supposed to be able to redo, having a chance to play out the 'if onlys.'" Clarifying her use of the past in her writings, Martin once commented, "Some of my books have been based on past experiences, although very few of them have been based on actual events in my childhood. But I would say that while I write any book, I'm remembering how I felt when I was a kid. Those feelings definitely go into the books."

The author attributes the success of her books to a combination of humor and relevance. "Kids respond to humor and appreciate it. Secondly, I think the kids find characteristics they can relate to in all the main characters or the topic we've chosen. Whether I'm writing about a handicapped child or divorce, I believe in keeping it down-to-earth. I've received letters from children who have said that the characters in the books are their friends. So something in there makes these books seem real. Some kids have written me, asking for phone numbers because they want to call the characters in the books. Then I sort of sadly explain that they are not real, so they can't get in touch with them. I turned to writing as an outlet for both my emotions and humor. I feel I'm more articulate and funnier on paper, but the more I write, the more comfortable I become speaking. It's a delightfully vicious cycle. The marriage of my love for children's literature with this cycle makes for a continually gratifying creative process."

Humor takes center stage in Martin's picture book, *Leo the Magnificat,* a story based on an actual cat who adopted an entire church congregation. The cat in question sauntered into the yard of a Louisville, Kentucky, church one Sunday and remained there for the next twelve years. Martin, in her book, shows how this cat worms its way into the hearts of the entire congregation and surrounding neighborhood, insinuating itself into events from potlucks to church services. When Leo the cat passes on, he is buried in the church garden. A reviewer for *Publishers Weekly* dubbed this picture book effort a "charmer like its feline hero," and further noted that Martin is a "pro at age-appropriate writing." The same reviewer also praised the "polished, softly focused art" of Caldecott Medallist Emily Arnold McCully who illustrated the book. "An alluring choice for cat lovers of any age," this writer concluded. *Booklist*'s Stephanie Zvirin commented that "Martin's picture book reads just like what it is—a story drawn from life," and concluded that this "gently humorous, poignant (never sentimental)" tale "won't disappoint." Martin told Lodge of *Publishers Weekly* that she "had a wonderful time writing" *Leo the Magnificat,* and was hopeful that she would try the genre again.

In 1998 Martin teamed up with long-time friend and fellow children's book author, Paula Danziger, to write *P.S. Longer Letter Later.* In this book the two authors, who specialize in writing for young girls, blended their disparate writing styles to create an epistolary novel told from two points of view. When two seventh-grade girls, Elizabeth and Tara*Starr, are separated by a family move, they promise to maintain their friendship through letters. The two girls are a study in contrasts: Tara*Starr is the type to put purple streaks in her hair, to joke incessantly, to write scathingly funny columns for the school paper, while staid Elizabeth is into cross-stitching and poetry, and would never think of piercing her ears, let alone her nose. Suddenly Tara*Starr's free-

spirited parents become responsible, begin holding regular jobs, think about having another baby, and move to Ohio. Outrageous, flamboyant, creative Tara*Starr— whose letters are written by Danziger—cannot believe the overnight change and subsequently has a hard time of adjusting to a new school and finding new friends. Meanwhile the more reserved, introspective, and affluent Elizabeth—written by Martin—undergoes her own transformations. Her father loses his job, turns to alcohol, and then abandons the family as they are getting ready to move into a small apartment. In letters that are at once humorous and painful, the two girls maintain their long-distance friendship. They survive tiffs and personal crises and even silence when one or the other fails to write for a time.

"If Danziger and Martin had been childhood pen pals," commented a reviewer for *Publishers Weekly,* "their correspondence might have read much like this strikingly insightful epistolary novel." The same writer further observed that the "venerable authors here do a splendid job of creating a story based on . . . letters." *Booklist* contributor Hazel Rochman felt "the immediacy of the letters format will draw kids in, especially as the tension mounts in Elizabeth's home and her friend replies with humor and heartfelt sympathy." Lynda Drill Comerford, writing in *Publishers Weekly,* commented that the book, "a celebration of friendship, ends on a happy note, with characters overcoming personal conflicts and forgiving each other's shortcomings." Comerford concluded, "For characters and authors alike, it represents the unique meshing of two creative, witty and very different personalities." Renee Steinberg, reviewing the novel in *School Library Journal,* observed that the "authenticity of the well-drawn characters gives life and vitality to the story," and concluded that readers "will thoroughly enjoy this fast-paced story." Reviewing the audiocassette adaptation of the novel, a *Publishers Weekly* contributor noted that Martin and Danziger "breathe life into two of their most richly drawn characters," and that in "a satisfying ending" the two young girls are able to see each other face-to-face once again.

In concluding the review of the book version of *P.S. Longer Letter Later,* the writer for *Publishers Weekly* wished for more: "Given Danziger and Martin's penchant for continuing story lines, readers can only hope that this will be an ongoing correspondence." In 2000 such a hope became a reality with the publication of *Snail Mail No More,* a continuation of Elizabeth's and Tara*Starr's correspondence, this time by e-mail. *Booklist*'s Michael Cart dubbed the pair an "epistolary odd couple," and noted that in *Snail Mail No More* "it's business as usual." Martin continues to write the shy, conservative Elizabeth's letters, while Danziger creates Tara's letters. With her mother pregnant, Tara*Starr is not so sure she wants to be a sister. At the other end, Elizabeth's wayward father has shown up again with less than positive results. The girls now turn thirteen, and make new friends, including boys. The green-eyed monster pops up between the two girls for a time, but even jealousy is vanquished by their friendship. "Seasoned pros Danziger and Martin couldn't write a dull book if they tried," noted Cart, "and this one . . . is a funny, thought-provoking page-turner that will delight readers and leave them ready for more messages." While *School Library Journal* reviewer Linda Bindner found that *Snail Mail No More* "lacks the energy and freshness" of *P.S. Longer Letter Later,* she also commented that "fans will find it to be an enjoyable sequel." A contributor for *Publishers Weekly* felt *Snail Mail No More* was a "funny and poignant sequel," and concluded that the "two characters approach life differently enough that there will likely be a response or suggestion that resonates with every reader, and both heroines share one important trait: they are all heart."

Teaming up with Laura Godwin, Martin has also written *The Doll People,* the story of culture clash between members of a Victorian doll household who meet their new, plastic neighbors, the Funcrafts. The staid Victorian world of the doll people is turned upside down by the meeting. The Funcrafts are the birthday present of the younger sister of Kate, current owner of the Victorian dollhouse and its occupants. It's barbecues versus parlors now, but Tiffany, the Funcraft doll, is the same age as Annabelle, of the Victorian dollhouse, and the two opposites oddly enough hit it off. Together Annabelle and Tiffany hunt for the missing Auntie Sarah doll from the Victorian dollhouse. Kathie Meizner, writing in *School Library Journal,* commented that a "light-hearted touch and a dash of drama make this a satisfying read," while a writer for *Publishers Weekly* concluded that doll lovers "may well approach their imaginative play with renewed enthusiasm and a sense of wonder after reading this fun-filled adventure."

In addition to writing, Martin is also very active in supporting various community activities. She is co-founder of the Lisa Novak Community Libraries, and founder of the Ann M. Martin Foundation, which benefits children, education and literacy programs, and homeless people and animals. Even without the 'Baby-Sitters Club' on the back burner, it is clear that Martin will not be changing her early rising habits. "I love to feel that every week is full of a lot of different kinds of things," she told Lodge. "I've always worked better when I'm working on many things at one time."

BIOGRAPHICAL/CRITICAL SOURCES:

PERIODICALS

Booklist, September 1, 1996, Stephanie Zvirin, review of *Leo the Magnificat,* p. 143; June 1, 1998, Hazel Rochman, review of *P.S. Longer Letter Later,* p. 1765; November 1, 1999, p. 550; March 15, 2000, Michael Cart, review of *Snail Mail No More,* p. 1376, August, 2000, p. 2140.
Book Report, September-October, 1998, p. 51.
Curriculum Review, February, 1995, p. 13.
Emergency Librarian, March-April, 1991, p. 39.
Family Life, August, 1998, p. 89.
New York Times Book Review, April 27, 1986, p. 25; August 14, 1988, p. 28; April 30, 1989, p. 42; May 17, 1998, p. 27.
People Weekly, August 21, 1989, Kristin McMurran, "Ann Martin Stirs up a Tiny Tempest in Preteen Land with Her Bestselling 'Baby-Sitters Club,'" pp. 55-56.
Publishers Weekly, June 17, 1988, p. 37; August 23, 1991, review of *Eleven Kids, One Summer,* p. 62; September 13, 1993, p. 137; May 17, 1993, p. 34; November 21, 1994, p. 42; September 4, 1995, pp. 28-29; September 2, 1996, review of *Leo the Magnificat,* p. 131; September 1, 997, Sally Lodge, "Another Busy Season for Ann M. Martin," pp. 31-32; February 16, 1998, review of *P.S. Longer Letter Later,* p. 212; March 9, 1998, Lynda Drill Comerford, "A True Test of Friendship," p. 26; June 7, 1999, review of *P.S. Longer Letter Later,* p. 53; July 19, 1999, p. 197; January 10, 2000, review of *Snail Mail No More,* p. 68; March 6, 2000, p. 112; July 3, 2000, review of *The Doll People,* p. 71; October 30, 2000, p. 37.
School Library Journal, May, 1998, Renee Steinberg, review of *P.S. Longer Letter Later,* p. 141; March, 2000, Linda Bindner, review of *Snail Mail No More,* p. 234; November, 2000, Kathie Meizner, review of *The Doll People,* p. 128; December, 2000, p. 54.
Time, June 11, 1990, "Wake-up Call," p. 75.
U.S. News & World Report, November 13, 2000, p. 18.
Washington Post, August 17, 1995, p. C1.

OTHER

Ann Online, http://www.scholastic.com/annmartin/ (February 26, 2001).*

MAXWELL, Patricia 1942-

(Jennifer Blake, Maxine Patrick, Patricia Ponder; Elizabeth Treahearne, a joint pseudonym)

PERSONAL: Born March 9, 1942, in Winn Parish, LA (one source lists Goldonna, LA); daughter of John H. (an electrician) and Daisy (Durbin) Ponder; married J. R. Maxwell (a retail automobile dealer), August 1, 1957; children: Ronnie, Ricky, Delinda, Kathy. *Avocational interests:* Gardening, quilting.

ADDRESSES: Home—165 Maxwell Ln., Chatham, LA 71226.

CAREER: Writer. Writer-in-residence, University of Northeastern Louisiana.

MEMBER: National League of American Pen Women, Romance Writers of America (honorary member).

AWARDS, HONORS: Best Historical Romance Novelist of the Year citation, *Romantic Times,* 1985; Best Historical Romance with a Southern Background citations, Georgia Romance Writers/Waldenbooks, 1985, for *Midnight Waltz,* and 1987, for *Southern Rapture;* Golden Treasure Award, Romance Writers of America, 1987, for lifetime achievement in the romance genre; Reviewer's Choice designations, *Romantic Times,* 1994, for *Arrow to the Heart,* and 1995, for *Shameless;* Best Contemporary Romance, Affaire de Coeur, 1995, for *Shameless;* Romance Hall of Fame inductee, Affaire de Coeur, 1995; Frank Waters Award for excellence in fiction.

WRITINGS:

The Secret of Mirror House, Fawcett (New York, NY), 1970.
Stranger at Plantation Inn, Fawcett (New York, NY), 1971.
(With Carol Albritton, under joint pseudonym Elizabeth Treahearne) *Storm at Midnight,* Ace Books (New York, NY), 1973.
The Bewitching Grace, Popular Library (New York, NY), 1973.
Dark Masquerade, Fawcett (New York, NY), 1974.
The Court of the Thorn Tree, Popular Library (New York, NY), 1974.

Bride of a Stranger, Fawcett (New York, NY), 1974, reprinted under pseudonym Jennifer Blake, 1990.
Notorious Angel, Fawcett (New York, NY), 1977, reprinted under pseudonym Jennifer Blake, 1983.
(Under name Patricia Ponder) *Haven of Fear,* Manor Books (New York, NY), 1977.
(Under name Patricia Ponder) *Murder for Charity,* Manor Books (New York, NY), 1977.
Sweet Piracy, Fawcett (New York, NY), 1978.
Night of the Candles, Fawcett (New York, NY), 1978.

HISTORICAL ROMANCES; UNDER PSEUDONYM JENNIFER BLAKE

Love's Wild Desire, Popular Library (New York, NY), 1977.
Tender Betrayal, Popular Library (New York, NY), 1979.
The Storm and the Splendor, Fawcett (New York, NY), 1979.
Golden Fancy, Fawcett (New York, NY), 1980.
Embrace and Conquer, Fawcett Columbine (New York, NY), 1981.
Royal Seduction, Fawcett Columbine (New York, NY), 1983.
Surrender in Moonlight, Fawcett Columbine (New York, NY), 1984.
Midnight Waltz, Fawcett Columbine (New York, NY), 1985.
Fierce Eden, Fawcett Columbine (New York, NY), 1985.
Royal Passion, Fawcett Columbine (New York, NY), 1986.
Prisoner of Desire, Fawcett Columbine (New York, NY), 1986.
Southern Rapture, Fawcett Columbine (New York, NY), 1987.
Louisiana Dawn, Fawcett Columbine (New York, NY), 1987.
Perfume of Paradise, Fawcett Columbine (New York, NY), 1988.
Spanish Serenade, Fawcett Columbine (New York, NY), 1990.
Arrow to the Heart, Fawcett Columbine (New York, NY), 1993.
Silver-Tongued Devil, Fawcett Columbine (New York, NY), 1996.
Garden of Scandal, Mira Books (New York, NY), 1997.

UNDER PSEUDONYM JENNIFER BLAKE

Love and Smoke, Fawcett Columbine (New York, NY), 1989.
Joy and Anger, Fawcett Columbine (New York, NY), 1991.

Wildest Dreams, Fawcett Columbine (New York, NY), 1992.

Shameless, Fawcett Columbine (New York, NY), 1994.

Tigress, Fawcett Columbine (New York, NY), 1996.

(With Emilie Richards) *Southern Gentlemen,* Mira Books (New York, NY), 1998.

"LOUISIANA GENTLEMEN" SERIES; UNDER PSEUDONYM JENNIFER BLAKE

Kane, Mira Books (New York, NY), 1998.

Luke, Mira Books (New York, NY), 1999.

Roan, Mira Books (New York, NY), 2000.

Clay, Mira Books (New York, NY), 2001.

UNDER PSEUDONYM MAXINE PATRICK

The Abducted Heart, Signet (New York, NY), 1978.

Bayou Bride, Signet (New York, NY), 1979.

Snowbound Heart, Signet (New York, NY), 1979.

Love at Sea, Signet (New York, NY), 1980.

Captive Kisses, Signet (New York, NY), 1980.

April of Enchantment, Signet (New York, NY), 1981.

OTHER

Contributor to anthologies, under pseudonym Jennifer Blake, including *A Dream Come True,* Topaz (New York, NY), 1994; *Secrets of the Heart,* Topaz, 1994; *Stardust,* Avon (New York, NY), 1994; *Honeymoon Suite,* St. Martin's Press (New York, NY), 1995; *A Purrfect Romance,* Harper Monogram (New York, NY), 1995; *The Quilting Circle,* 1996; *A Joyous Season,* 1996; *Unmasked,* Harlequin (New York, NY), 1997; *Southern Gentlemen,* 1998; and *The Seven Deadly Sins.* Also contributor to *Vignettes of Louisiana History* and *Louisiana Leaders;* contributor of poetry, short stories, and articles to newspapers.

Maxwell's books have been translated into seventeen languages.

SIDELIGHTS: Patricia Maxwell is one of the most popular authors of modern romantic fiction. Writing under her own name and several pseudonyms—most frequently that of Jennifer Blake—she was one of the most prominent authors in the historical romance boom of the 1970s and 1980s. Her popularity has endured even as trends in the publishing industry have changed, and

she has proven her ability to write bestselling novels with contemporary settings as well as those with a historical background.

Maxwell was an avid reader as a child. Married at age fifteen and a mother of two by age nineteen, her urge to write was sparked by a vivid dream with a historical setting. She wrote down the dream, and that process encouraged her to take up writing as a hobby in 1963. Her first published work was a mystery suspense novel in the style of such established authors as Daphne Du Maurier and Victoria Holt. *The Secret of Mirror House* was accepted by the first editor who read the manuscript, and Maxwell's career was launched. She wrote several more books in the same genre before the market changed and this type of book went out of favor. Asked by an editor to write a proposal for a historical romance, she responded with *Love's Wild Desire,* which eventually made it to the *New York Times* bestseller list.

Many more successes followed in the historical romance genre, but when the market for that type of book slowed down, Maxwell proved herself equally adept at writing contemporary romances. Whether set in centuries past or in modern times, the author frequently uses her native Louisiana as the setting for her stories. Authenticity is so important to her that, when she penned the novels *Perfume of Paradise* and *Love and Smoke,* about a heroine whose trademark fragrance was called "Paradise," Maxwell actually worked with a New Orleans perfumer to create the scent. As a *Womens Wear Daily* contributor noted, in *Perfume of Paradise,* "the perfume plays a central role as a magical potion created by a Voodoo priestess, who uses it to enslave men." After readers wrote asking where to purchase the perfume, Maxwell decided to create it.

In her "Louisiana Gentelemen" series, which includes *Kane, Luke, Roan,* and *Clay,* Maxwell creates fast-paced stories with crime and suspense as well as romance, all set in the small Louisiana town of Turn-Coupe. In *Kane,* protagonists Kane Benedict and Regina Dalton begin their relationship when they are locked in a coffin together. Treachery, greed, and unscrupulous competition among funeral home directors all come together in a romance which, according to Kristin Ramsdell in *Library Journal,* is made "all the more intriguing by Blake's trademark overlay of sultry, deep-South charm." *Luke* features such contemporary elements as a drive-by shooting, threatening phone calls, and an escape on a luxury pontoon boat. April Halstead, the heroine, is a famous romance novelist, allowing Maxwell to offer her readers "countless insights into the joys and torments of being a popular author," according to a *Publishers Weekly* writer.

The romantic alliance in *Roan* has one of Maxwell's characteristically unlikely beginnings, as Sheriff Roan Benedict shoots and wounds a fugitive from a holdup, only to discover that his target is actually a woman, the wealthy and beautiful Victoria. Roan takes the injured woman to his home to recuperate, where she tells him she is on the run from her scheming father and fiancé. While he sometimes doubts her story, he can't deny his growing feelings for her. A *Publishers Weekly* reviewer praised the author for her sure touch with the "playful dialogue and sexy teasing [that] will keep readers turning the pages," while in *BookBrowser* Harriet Klausner praised the novel for its believable plot and characters. Maxwell "shows why she is so popular with a fast-paced romantic suspense that will keep reader's interest from start to finish," Klausner added. *Clay,* the fourth installment in the "Louisiana Gentlemen" series, finds Janna Kerr waging a battle to save her young daughter's life. In search of a kidney for her child, Janna becomes involved with a black-market doctor, murder, and kidnaping the handsome Clay Benedict. While a *Publishers Weekly* contributor noted that Maxwell's plot "treads the fine line between drama and melodrama," the critic added that "the lush setting . . . and [Maxwell's] vivid prose" would win new fans to the series.

Discussing her career with an interviewer for the Online *Die Romantische Bucherecke,* Maxwell commented: "'My life has changed immeasurably since I became a best selling author. . . . Suddenly I was expected to write a constant stream of best selling novels, and also to travel around the country making television and radio appearances, to attend booksignings at bookstores and in shopping malls, and generally to become much more of a business person and public personality. It was hard to do these things at first, though I came to accept and even to enjoy them after a while. But I still have times when I'd just as soon write my stories of life and love and let someone else promote them!'"

Maxwell once told *CA:* "I write for the classic reason, to entertain, but also for the joy of the mental exercise and for that rare moment of euphoria that comes when the writer's subconscious takes over and pours out the story with little interference from the conscious mind. The [Jennifer] Blake historical romances give me particular pleasure because of a love affair with history that is longstanding. I like to recreate the past as closely

as possible. If I can take readers with me back in time, if I can make them see what I see, feel what I feel, even if only for a brief moment, then I am satisfied."

BIOGRAPHICAL/CRITICAL SOURCES:

PERIODICALS

Booklist, June 15, 1992, Alice Joyce, review of *Wildest Dreams,* p. 1809; June 1, 1994, Melanie Duncan, review of *Shameless,* p. 1724; March 15, 1999, Ann Bouricius, review of *Luke,* p. 1293.
Kirkus Reviews, April 1, 1994, p. 411.
Library Journal, May 1, 1994, Margaret Hanes, review of *Shameless,* p. 135; May 15, 1994, Kristin Ramsdell, review of *Shameless,* p. 64; February 15, 1998, Kristin Ramsdell, review of *Kane,* p. 130.
Publishers Weekly, April 20, 1992, review of *Wildest Dreams,* p. 35; May 24, 1993, review of *Arrow to the Heart,* p. 68; April 18, 1994, review of *Shameless,* p. 43; December 4, 1995, review of *Silver-Tongued Devil,* p. 58; March 10, 1997, review of *Garden of Scandal,* p. 64; February 2, 1998, review of *Kane,* p. 87; April 6, 1998, review of *Southern Gentlemen,* p. 75; February 8, 1999, review of *Luke,* p. 210; June 19, 2000, review of *Roan,* p. 64; May 28, 2001, review of *Clay,* p. 57.
Womens Wear Daily, September 8, 1989, Sharon Donavan, "From Book to Bottle, Paradise Is a Literal Success," p. F50.

OTHER

All about Romance, http://www.likesbooks.com/ (February 1, 2002), Kate Smith, review of *Luke;* Ellen D. Micheletti, review of *Roan.*
BookBrowser, http://www.bookbrowser.com/ (February 8, 1998), Harriet Klausner, review of *Kane;* (April 24, 2000) Harriet Klausner, review of *Roan.*
Die Romantische Bücherecke, http://www.die-buecherecke.de (August 21, 2000), interview with Jennifer Blake.
Fictionwise, http://www.fictionwise.com/ (February 1, 2002), "Jennifer Blake."
Jennifer Blake Web site, http://www.jenniferblake.com (February 1, 2002).*

*   *   *

McCABE, John (Charles III) 1920-

PERSONAL: Born November 14, 1920, in Detroit, MI; son of Charles J. (an engineer) and Rosalie (Dropiewski) McCabe; married Vija Valda Zarina (a ballet teacher), October 19, 1958; children: Linard Peter, Sean Cahal,

John McCabe

Deirdre Rose. *Education:* University of Detroit, Ph.B., 1947; Fordham University, M.F.A., 1948; Shakespeare Institute of University of Birmingham, Stratford-upon-Avon, England, Ph.D., 1954. *Politics:* Liberal Unionist. *Religion:* Roman Catholic.

ADDRESSES: Home—Box 363, British Landing, Mackinac Island, MI 49757.

CAREER: Wayne University (now Wayne State University), Detroit, MI, instructor in theater, 1948-51; City College of New York (now City College of the City University of New York), New York, NY, instructor in speech, 1955-56; New York University, New York, NY, assistant professor, 1956-58, associate professor, 1958-63, professor of theater and chairman of department of educational theatre, 1963-67; Mackinac College, Mackinac Island, MI, professor of theater and chairman of department, 1967-70; Lake Superior State College, Sault Ste. Marie, MI, author-in-residence, 1970-86. Producer, writer, actor, and director of plays and films, 1943-62; founder, Sons of the Desert, 1963. *Military service:* U.S. Army Air Forces, 1943-45; became sergeant.

MEMBER: Actors Equity Association, Shakespeare Association of America, Catholic Actors Guild, Baker Street Irregulars, Lambs, Players.

WRITINGS:

Mr. Laurel and Mr. Hardy, Doubleday (New York, NY), 1961, revised edition, Grosset (New York, NY), 1967, reprinted as *Mr. Laurel and Mr. Hardy: An Affectionate Biography,* Robson/Parkwest (New York, New York), 2002.
George M. Cohan: The Man Who Owned Broadway, Doubleday (New York, NY), 1973.
The Comedy World of Stan Laurel, Doubleday (New York, NY), 1974, new edition, Moonstone Press (Beverly Hills, CA), 1990.
(With Al Kilgore and Dick Bann) *Laurel and Hardy,* Dutton (New York, NY), 1975.
(With G. B. Harrison) *Proclaiming the Word,* Pueblo Press, 1976.
Charlie Chaplin, Doubleday (New York, NY), 1978.
Grand Hotel: Mackinac Island, Unicorn Press (Detroit, MI), 1987.
Babe: The Life of Oliver Hardy, Carol Publishing (New York, NY), 1990.
The High, 1992.
Cagney, Knopf (New York, NY), 1997.

Also contributor to *Variety* and *Detroit News.* Consultant to James Cagney for *Cagney by Cagney* (autobiography), Doubleday (New York, NY), 1976.

SIDELIGHTS: John McCabe has worked professionally as a stage and film actor in addition to his careers as a theater instructor and author. His lifelong love of movies has led him to write several books about Stan Laurel and Oliver Hardy and other screen legends. His favorite actor of all time, though, is James Cagney. McCabe ghostwrote Cagney's 1976 autobiography, *Cagney by Cagney,* and in 1997, McCabe wrote the full-length, authorized biography of the legendary actor based on his previous interviews with him, called simply *Cagney.*

Cagney recounts the actor's poverty-stricken childhood on the streets of New York. The son of a hard-drinking Irishman and a stalwart, soft-spoken mother, Cagney sought to better himself and attended Columbia University before being plucked from obscurity by movie mogul Jack Warner in the early 1930s. He starred in such classics as *The Public Enemy* and *White Heat,* but resented being typecast as a hotheaded gangster and largely stayed out of the Hollywood limelight. More inscrutable than most movie stars, Cagney was called "the faraway fella" by his best friend, the actor Pat

O'Brien. By the 1960s, Cagney quietly slipped into retirement and concentrated on other interests, notably painting and living a country life in upstate New York.

Reviewers noted that *Cagney* is the work of an unabashed fan who is well-versed in the craft of acting. "Cagney exceeds the typical standards of celebrity biography," wrote James T. Fisher in *Commonweal*, "because McCabe is fully attentive to the many dimensions of his subject's artistry." Bonnie Smothers of *Booklist* wrote that "what McCabe has done with his book is to bring back vividly those old, golden images; he has written a reverent and good book." Though "written from the point of view of a devoted fan," wrote Wilborn Hampton in the *New York Times Book Review*, "McCabe makes no attempt to hide the occasional irascibility and eccentricity of his subject. . . . Often, the author simply opens his interview notebooks and lets the actor speak for himself."

Some criticism was leveled against McCabe for his "lack of analysis about Cagney's personal life," as Jeff Brown of *People* put it. For example, Cagney and his wife (to whom he was married for 64 years) had long hoped to have children, but when medical problems prevented it, the couple adopted two children. But they built a separate house on their property for the children and their housekeeper, and removed themselves from the day-to-day tasks of raising them. Further references to the children in the book are few. "You can sense McCabe sweeping the few handfuls of dirt under the rug," wrote Ty Burr in *Entertainment Weekly*. Yet McCabe is careful to distinguish between the actor and the roles he played. "As McCabe brings to light in his revealing biography," said David Hajdu in the *New York Times Book Review*, "Cagney the man was hardly interchangeable with his hard-nosed screen persona, and he was anything but the philistine he professed to be."

McCabe once told *CA*: "The theater—into which I was born—became for me (perhaps inevitably) a paradigm of what life should be. As my years increased, I never saw essential reason to alter that view, and indeed in my maturity that opinion is constantly being reaffirmed. Our dear Will [Shakespeare] put life's outline clearly in the Seven Ages speech, and Christ set forth its best functional impulses in the Sermon on the Mount. Everything that I have experienced in life—both as a man and writer—reassures me that this pattern of life is not only drama unending but the deepest truth as well.

"The theater—and in that I include film, radio, television, journalism, and all writing—when it does its job

best both entertains and tells the truth. This is what I have tried to do as a writer.

"I love good wine, O. Henry, classic chili, the word 'grape,' blue, the songs of Noel Coward, Mackinac Island, water, the plays of Shaw, O'Casey, Shakespeare, and W. S. Gilbert, *The Tavern* by George M. Cohan, 104 of the 105 films made by Laurel and Hardy, ['Twice Two' being the exception], James Cagney, most Jesuits, London, potato salad, Stratford-upon-Avon, Mozart, draught beer, Dublin, God, and my family."

BIOGRAPHICAL/CRITICAL SOURCES:

PERIODICALS

Booklist, October 15, 1997, Bonnie Smothers, a review of *Cagney*, p. 362.
Commonweal, April 10, 1998, James T. Fisher, review of *Cagney*, p. 33.
Entertainment Weekly, December 19, 1997, Ty Burr, a review of *Cagney*, p. 69.
New York Times Book Review, May 14, 1978; December 7, 1997, David Hajdu, "Yankee Doodle Dandy"; January 2, 1998, Wilborn Hampton, "A Master at Making Gansters Likable."
New Yorker, March 31, 1973.
People, January 26, 1998, Jeff Brown, a review of *Cagney*, p. 33.
Publishers Weekly, October 27, 1997, a review of *Cagney*, p. 59.
Variety, March 14, 1973.

*   *   *

McKILLIP, Patricia A(nne) 1948-

PERSONAL: Born February 29, 1948, in Salem, OR; daughter of Wayne T. and Helen (Roth) McKillip. *Education:* San Jose State University, B.A., 1971, M.A., 1973. *Avocational interests:* Music.

ADDRESSES: Home—2661 California, No. 14, San Francisco, CA 94115.

CAREER: Writer.

AWARDS, HONORS: World Fantasy Award for best novel, 1975, and American Library Association notable book selection, both for *The Forgotten Beasts of Eld*; Hugo Award nomination, World Science Fiction Convention, 1979, for *Harpist in the Wind*.

WRITINGS:

FANTASY

The House on Parchment Street, Atheneum (New York, NY), 1973.

The Throme of the Erril of Sherill, Atheneum (New York, NY), 1973.

The Forgotten Beasts of Eld, Atheneum (New York, NY), 1974.

The Night Gift, Atheneum (New York, NY), 1976.

The Riddle-Master of Hed (first book in trilogy), Atheneum (New York, NY), 1976.

Heir of Sea and Fire (second book in trilogy), Atheneum (New York, NY), 1977.

Harpist in the Wind (third book in trilogy), Atheneum (New York, NY), 1979.

Riddle of the Stars (trilogy; contains *The Riddle-Master of Hed, Heir of Sea and Fire,* and *Harpist in the Wind*), Doubleday (Garden City, NY), 1979, published as *Chronicles of Morgan, Prince of Hed,* Future Publications (London, England), 1979, published as *Riddle-Master: The Complete Trilogy,* Ace (New York, NY), 1999.

The Changeling Sea, Atheneum (New York, NY), 1988.

The Sorceress and the Cygnet, Ace (New York, NY), 1991.

The Cygnet and the Firebird, Ace (New York, NY), 1993.

Something Rich and Strange ("Brian Froud's Faerielands" series), illustrated by Brian Froud, Bantam (New York, NY), 1994.

Winter Rose, Ace (New York, NY), 1996.

Song for the Basilisk, Ace (New York, NY), 1998.

The Tower at Stony Wood, Ace (New York, NY), 2000.

SCIENCE FICTION

Moon-Flash, Atheneum (New York, NY), 1984.

The Moon and the Face, Atheneum (New York, NY), 1985.

Fool's Run, Warner (New York, NY), 1987.

The Book of Atrix Wolfe, Ace (New York, NY), 1995.

OTHER

Stepping from the Shadows (young adult novel), Atheneum (New York, NY), 1982.

Contributor of short fiction to anthologies, including *Xanadu 2.*

SIDELIGHTS: Patricia A. McKillip is a critically acclaimed author of works in three literary genres: fantasy, science fiction, and the young adult novel. Of her most ambitious project, *Riddle of Stars,* a fantasy adventure in three parts, Roger C. Schlobin wrote in *Science Fiction and Fantasy Book Review:* "The canon of excellent women fantasists must now be expanded to include another superb effort. . . . McKillip's series delves deeply into the rich earth of full human characterization and creates a world elaborate in both magic and mythology." The concentration on basic human traits and themes is a common characteristic of all of McKillip's works, which include such novels as *The Cygnet and the Firebird, The Forgotten Beasts of Eld,* and *Song of the Basilisk.* Noting that McKillip imbues her fantasy worlds with music and a "sense of history and culture," an essayist in *Children's Books and Their Creators* added that "the main attraction to [her] . . . books . . . remains the irresistible and timeless combination of adventure, magic, and romance."

McKillip was born in Salem, Oregon, in 1948. The second of six children, she soon found she had a talent for storytelling, which helped because, as she recalled, "the baby-sitting duties were pretty constant. I don't know how old I was when I started telling stories to my younger siblings to while away the boredom of sitting in a car waiting while our parents shopped." She began working on her first novel, *The House on Parchment Street,* as a teenager. "I started to write when I was fourteen," she once stated, "during one of those 'moody' periods teenagers have when they know they want something, but don't quite know what it is. I was living in England at the time (my father was stationed at a local air base) in a big old house facing a graveyard: the 'house on Parchment Street.' The countryside was very peaceful, and evocative of all kinds of tales. I spent that summer, between eighth grade and high school, writing fairy tales, reading them to my younger brothers and sisters, and feeling that I had at least found one of the things I didn't know I wanted."

She wrote constantly after that discovery, "all through high school and college—anything and everything—poems, plays, novels, short stories, fantasies. What I really wanted to be was a musician, a pianist, but I realized finally that I was far better at writing. Since I didn't think I was capable of holding down a full-time job, I thought I'd better get published before I left college, so I could support myself." As she recalled, "no one discouraged me, and I rarely made writing as a career a subject for discussion. I knew the kinds of things I'd hear, so I just kept quiet about it and wrote. My parents never chased me outside when I wanted to write—which was most of the time. They let me grow at my own speed, which strikes me now as an extraordinary way for modern parents to behave."

Although she was determined to be a writer, McKillip did not initially plan to become a children's author. "I never deliberately decided to write for children," she once explained; "I just found them particularly satisfying to write about, and *The House on Parchment Street* happened to be the first thing I sold."

Many reviewers of McKillip's work have noted her ability, regardless of the genre in which she is writing, to touch on basic human traits and themes. *The Forgotten Beasts of Eld,* published in 1974, is filled with the trappings of the fantasy adventure novel: dragons, talking animals, doorless towers, and glass mountains. *New York Times Book Review* contributor Georgess McHargue wrote that "*The Forgotten Beasts of Eld* works on a strictly human level. Trust, loneliness, love's responsibilities and the toxicity of fate are the themes that underlie the fantasy love story." *Riddle of the Stars,* McKillip's famous fantasy trilogy, garnered similar praise. The plot follows the fortunes of Morgan from his beginnings as ruler of Hed, a peaceful, sleepy kingdom, to his ultimate destiny as a trained "riddle-master." Referring to the first volume in the trilogy, *The Riddle-Master of Hed,* Glenn Shea stated in the *New York Times Book Review,* "She understands that we spend much of our time choosing, not between good and evil, but the lesser of two ills."

In 1982 McKillip published the young adult novel *Stepping from the Shadows,* in an apparent departure from her usual fantasy adventure format. Discussing her switch across literary genres, she explained to Charles L. Wentworth in a *Contemporary Authors* interview: "I don't think the changes have been abrupt, but I can't look at it as a reader. I knew while I was writing the trilogy that I wanted to write the modern novel afterward, so to me it was a natural thing to do; it didn't seem like an abrupt switch." *Stepping from the Shadows,* in terms of its concentration on universal human themes, develops naturally from McKillip's earlier work. The book revolves around the private torments of Frances, a young girl who shares, through conversation and writing, her rich fantasy life with an imaginary sister. "McKillip has put an imaginary playmate on paper and the more sophisticated truth that we all have an outside view of ourselves as well as an inside view,"

noted Charles Champlin in a *Los Angeles Times* review; "McKillip's memory of the coming of age of an author is rich, particular and extremely appealing."

With the publication of *Moon-Flash, The Moon and the Face,* and *Fool's Run,* McKillip achieved distinction in yet another literary genre: science fiction. She explained to Wentworth what she sees as the differences between fantasy adventure and science fiction: "For my own purposes, I try to keep the two separate. If I'm writing fantasy I use elements of epic, fantasy, myth, legend; and if I put magic in it, it's magic out of the imagination and out of the heart. When I write science fiction, . . . I try to turn my back on traditional fantasy elements and extrapolate a plot from history, or daily life, or whatever science happens to stick in my head. I am probably more successful at keeping science fiction out of my fantasy than keeping fantasy out of my science fiction. The heritage, the roots and background of science fiction are very different from those of fantasy. The language is different; the images I find in my mind when I contemplate a science fiction plot are different. The stars in *Riddle-Master* are a symbol. The stars in science fiction are real."

In 1991 McKillip returned to fantasy with the debut volume of another series, *The Sorceress and the Cygnet.* The story of Corleu, a young man who is different in appearance and interests from his Wayfolk kin, is "a richly imagined tale of enchantment, intrigue, and romance," according to *Voice of Youth Advocates* contributor Carolyn Shute. The fantasy world of *The Sorceress and the Cygnet* also serves as the backdrop for McKillip's 1993 novel *The Cygnet and the Firebird,* as a mage's plot to steal an ancient, magical key is thwarted after a firebird appears that magically transforms things around it into gold and precious gems but whose mystery grows deeper still when it is discovered to be a young warrior who returns to his own shape under certain circumstances, but has no knowledge of his name or his past. Sorceresses, dragons, and the power of the dead also figure into this story, which a *Kirkus Reviews* critic dubbed "often charming and inventive." "McKillip weaves a magic spell of words almost as intoxicating as a drug," noted *School Library Journal* contributor Cathy Chauvette, while adding the caveat that while some would like her lush style, others "will be confused and long for a breath of fresh air."

Fantasy has continued to capture most of McKillip's attention. In 1995's *The Book of Atrix Wolfe,* she weaves shape-shifting, the lust for power, and magecraft into the mix as Prince Talis, a student of wizardry, finds a book the spells of which have undisclosed meanings. Returning home, Talis meets a Queen in search of her daughter, Sorrow, and joins with Mage Atrix Wolfe to discover the young woman's whereabouts and dispel a dark power that threatens both the world of humans and that of faerie. Praising McKillip's "masterfully evocative" language, a *Publishers Weekly* contributor maintained that "connoisseurs of fine fantasy will delight in this expertly wrought tale." *Song for the Basilisk* follows a young man named Rook as he survives an uprising that killed the rest of his family and travels to another land to lead a quiet life. However, he is haunted by violent dreams that force him to confront the evils in the land of his childhood, and he discovers his destiny as Caldrius, and his fate: to demand justice from the Prince who killed his family. While calling the novel "a trifle cerebral" for some fantasy fans, *Booklist* contributor Roland Green noted that McKillip works her usual magic, bringing her "archetypal characters and plot . . . to life with dozens of subtle touches." And in *Winter Rose,* a young woman who falls in love with a man trapped in a magical otherworld pines away for lack of him, leaving her determined sister Rois to solve the murder that caused him to become a captive in this perpetual dreamworld. Calling her prose a "delightful, delicate filigree," a *Kirkus Reviews* contributor noted that the "frail and undeveloped" plot seemed inadequate by comparison, while in *Booklist,* a reviewer labeled *Winter Rose* "compelling."

In her discussion with Wentworth, McKillip spoke of her strategy as a writer: "I'd like to do more of everything. . . . There are so many backgrounds and people I'd like to write about—not in any personal way, but just people I know who suggest stories that might be nice to write."

BIOGRAPHICAL/CRITICAL SOURCES:

BOOKS

McKillip, Patricia A., interview with Charles L. Wentworth in *Contemporary Authors New Revision Series,* Volume 18, Gale (Detroit, MI), 1986.

Silvey, Anita, editor, *Children's Books and Their Creators,* Houghton (Boston, MA), 1995.

St. James Guide to Fantasy Writers, St. James Press (Detroit, MI), 1996.

St. James Guide to Young Adult Writers, St. James Press (Detroit, MI), 1999.

PERIODICALS

Analog, January, 1980.

Booklist, August, 1995, Sally Estes, review of *The Book of Atrix Wolfe,* p. 1936; January, 1997, review of *Winter Rose,* p. 763; August, 1998, Roland Green, review of *Song for the Basilisk,* pp. 1978- 1979.

Bulletin of the Center for Children's Books, January, 1975, p. 82; July, 1979, p. 196; September, 1984, p. 10.

Christian Science Monitor, November 2, 1977, p. B2.

Fantasy Review, November, 1985.

Kirkus Reviews, July 15, 1993, review of *The Cygnet and the Firebird,* p. 898; May 15, 1996, review of *Winter Rose,* p. 718.

Locus, January, 1990, p. 52.

Los Angeles Times, March 26, 1982, Charles Champlin, review of *Stepping from the Shadows.*

New York Times Book Review, October 13, 1974, Georgess McHargue, review of *The Forgotten Beasts of Eld,* p. 8; March 6, 1977, Glenn Shea, review of *The Riddle-Master of Hed,* p. 29.

Publishers Weekly, October 3, 1994, review of *Brian Froud's Faerielands,* p. 54; June 26, 1995, review of *The Book of Atrix Wolfe,* p. 90.

School Library Journal, October, 1991, p. 160; May, 1994, Cathy Chauvette, review of *The Cygnet and the Firebird,* p. 143.

Science Fiction and Fantasy Book Review, May, 1979, Roger C. Schlobin, review of "Riddlemaster" trilogy, pp. 37-38.

Science Fiction Chronicle, July, 1991, p. 30.

Voice of Youth Advocates, October, 1982, p. 32; June, 1991, Carolyn Shute, review of *The Sorceress and the Cygnet,* p. 112; December, 1993, Esther Sinofsky, review of *The Cygnet and the Firebird,* p. 311; April, 1999, review of *Song for the Basilisk,* p. 14.

Washington Post Book World, January 9, 1986; October 23, 1994, Gregory Feeley, review of *Something Rich and Strange,* p. 6.

*   *   *

MORGENSTERN, S.
See GOLDMAN, William (W.)

*   *   *

MYLES, Eileen 1949-

PERSONAL: Born December 9, 1949, in Cambridge, MA; daughter of Terrence Myles (a mail carrier) and Genevieve Preston Hannibal (a secretary). *Education:* University of Massachusetts, B.A., 1971; studied at St.

Mark's Poetry Project, 1975-77. *Politics:* Democrat. *Religion:* "None." *Avocational interests:* "Visiting zoos, studying economic trends."

ADDRESSES: Home and office—86 East Third St., New York, NY 10003. *E-mail*—Easter8@aol.com.

CAREER: Poet, editor, and reviewer. Instructor at St. Mark's Poetry Project, 1980, New York University School of Continuing Education, 1987-88, Parsons School of Design, 1991-92, Baruch College, 1993—, and New School University, 1994—. Artistic director at St. Mark's Poetry Project, 1984-86; writer-in-residence, Pratt Institute, 2001. Conducts workshops at institutions, including School of Visual Arts, 1981-84 and 1989-91, Rochester Institute of Technology, 1982, Detroit Institute of Arts, 1985, California Institute of the Arts, 1991 and 1992, Maryland Art Institute, 1992, Bard College, 1993, Art Center (Pasadena), 2000, and Otis College of Art and Design, 2000. Gives poetry readings and solo performances at various locations, including the Museum of Modern Art, Detroit Institute of Arts, School of Visual Arts, Yale University, San Diego State University, Poetry Center at San Francisco State University, and Rutgers University.

MEMBER: PEN, Poets and Writers.

AWARDS, HONORS: New York State Creative Artist's Public Services grant, 1980; Fund for Poetry grant, 1988 and 1990; National Endowment for the Arts interarts grant, 1989; MacDowell Colony fellow, summer, 1991 and 1996; Djerassi Foundation fellow, 1994; Rex Foundation grant, 1994; Blue Mountain Center grant, 1997; New York Foundation for the Arts grant, 1999.

WRITINGS:

The Irony of the Leash, Jim Brodey Books (New York, NY), 1978.
A Fresh Young Voice from the Plains, Power Mad (New York, NY), 1981.
Sappho's Boat, Little Caesar (Los Angeles, CA), 1982.
Bread and Water (short stories), Hanuman Books (New York, NY), 1987.
Feeling Blue, Parts 1, 2 and 3 (play), first produced in New York at P.S. 122, 1988.
1969, Hanuman Books (New York, NY), 1989.

Modern Art (play), first produced in New York at P.S. 122, 1990.
Not Me (poetry), Semiotext(e) (New York, NY), 1991.
Chelsea Girls (short stories), Black Sparrow Press (Santa Rosa, CA), 1994.
Maxfield Parrish (poetry), Black Sparrow Press (Santa Rosa, CA), 1995.
(Editor, with Liz Kotz) *The New Fuck You: Adventures in Lesbian Reading,* Semiotext(e) (New York, NY), 1995.
School of Fish, Black Sparrow Press (Santa Rosa, CA), 1997.
Cool for You (novel), Soft Skull Press (New York, NY), 2000.

Work represented in several anthologies, including *Women on Women 2,* edited by Joan Nestle, Dutton (New York, NY), 1993; *Postmodern Poetry Anthology,* edited by Paul Hoover, Norton (New York, NY), 1994; and *The World in Us,* edited by Michael Lassell and Elena Georgiou, St. Martin's Press (New York, NY), 2000. Contributor of articles and reviews to periodicals, including *Art in America* and *Village Voice.* Contributor of poetry to *City Lights Anthology, Santa Monica Review, Kenyon Review,* and *Paris Review.*

Myles has recorded several poetry readings, including *Big Ego,* Giorno Poetry Systems (New York, NY), 1979, *Sugar, Alcohol and Meat,* Giorno Poetry Systems, 1980, *The World Record,* The Poetry Project (New York, NY), 1981, and *A Sheep on the Bus,* New York, 1993.

SIDELIGHTS: A veteran of New York's downtown poetry scene, prolific author Eileen Myles has enjoyed a long association with St. Mark's Poetry Project, where she has studied her craft with Ted Berrigan, Alice Notley, Bill Zavatsky, and Paul Violi. In addition to authoring such poetry volumes as *Not Me,* Myles has written and presented several pieces for the stage, issued sound recordings of other works, produced a volume of short stories, and has a novel in the making. "I regard all forms of writing as an extension of speech and cinematic narration," she explained to *CA,* adding, "I have been most inspired by Gertrude Stein (her *Lectures*), Henry Miller, Violette Leduc, James Schuyler, Frank O'Hara, and Christopher Isherwood."

Myles often celebrates her own authenticity in her poems, writing from the viewpoint of woman, poet, and lesbian. In a *Voice Literary Supplement* review of *Not*

Me, C. Carr described Myles as "an observer-poet more than a philosopher-poet. . . . In an essay at the end of *Not Me,* she speaks of 'going out to get a poem, like hunting.' Indeed, I finished the book with an impression of a peripatetic poet on a mission to find . . . herself? No. To amplify herself. To live large. A good quality in a woman, an excellent quality in a lesbian."

While many of Myles's poems are autobiographical, the author has also written a collection of largely autobiographical short stories titled *Chelsea Girls.* Examining universal themes of life, death, love, and loneliness, these stories discuss Myles's alcoholic father, her experimentation with alcohol, drugs, and sex, and her triumphant emergence as a writer. *Publishers Weekly* critic Maria Simson commented on Myles's stark prose, noting that the "accounts of her life are so harsh that they stick with the reader as closely as they stick with her."

BIOGRAPHICAL/CRITICAL SOURCES:

PERIODICALS

New York Times, May 30, 2001, arts section.
New York Times Book Review, September 25, 1994, p. 24.
Publishers Weekly, June 27, 1994, Maria Simson, review of *Chelsea Girls,* p. 71.
Voice Literary Supplement, June, 1991, C. Carr, review of *Not Me,* p. 29.

N-O

NIELSEN HAYDEN, Patrick (James) 1959-

PERSONAL: Born January 2, 1959; son of James (an artist and designer) and Jeanette (an artist and designer) Hayden; married Teresa Nielsen (a writer and editor), March 23, 1979.

ADDRESSES: Office—c/o Tor Books, 175 Fifth Ave., New York, NY 10010. *E-mail*—pnh@panix.com.

CAREER: Editor and writer. Literary Guild, New York, NY, editorial assistant, 1984; Chelsea House, New York, NY, associate editor, 1984-87; Tor Books, New York, NY, editor, 1988-90, senior editor, 1990-96, manager of science fiction and editor of *Starlight,* 1996—. Editor of fanzines, including *Twibbet,* 1975; *Thangorodrim,* 1975-77; (with Gary Farber, Seth McEvoy, and AnneLaurie Logan) *Tweek,* 1977; *Ecce Fanno,* 1977-81; (with Teresa Nielsen Hayden) *Telos,* 1980-82; (with Teresa Nielsen Hayden) *Zed,* 1981-86; *Flash Point,* 1981-87; and (with Teresa Nielsen Hayden) *Izzard,* 1982-87. Cofounder, *New York Review of Science Fiction;* cofounder, Babble-17 discussion club.

AWARDS, HONORS: Hugo Awards, finalist for best fanzine (with Teresa Nielsen Hayden), 1984, for *Izzard,* for best fanwriter, 1986 and 1987, for best semi-prozine (with others), 1989, for *New York Review of Science Fiction,* finalist for best professional editor, 1997; TAFF winner (with Teresa Nielsen Hayden), 1985; *Science Fiction Chronicle* Readers' Award for best fanzine (with Teresa Nielsen Hayden), 1987, for *Izzard;* World Fantasy Award for best anthology, 1997, for *Starlight 1; Science Fiction Chronicle* Readers' Award for best book editor, 1997.

WRITINGS:

EDITOR

Starlight 1, Tor (New York, NY), 1996.
(With Mike Resnick) *Alternate Skiffy,* Wildside (Berkeley Heights, NJ), 1997.
Starlight 2, Tor (New York, NY), 1998.
Starlight 3, Tor (New York, NY), 2001.

Contributor to books, including *The New Encyclopedia of Science Fiction,* edited by James Gunn, 1988; *The Encyclopedia of Science Fiction,* edited by Clute and Nicholls, 1993; and *Writers' Digest Science-Fiction and Fantasy Writers' Source Book,* edited by David H. Borcherding, Writer's Digest Books (Cincinnati, OH), 1996. Contributor to anthologies, including *The Map: Rediscovering Rock and Roll,* by Paul Williams, And Books (South Bend, IN), 1988; *Aladdin: Master of the Lamp,* edited by Mike Resnick, DAW Books (New York, NY), 1992; *Xanadu 1,* edited by Jane Yolen, Tor (New York, NY), 1993; and *More Whatdunits,* edited by Mike Resnick, DAW Books, 1993. Contributor to periodicals, including *Mainstream, Energumen, Warhoon, Prevert, Hyphen, Crawdaddy,* and *Mississippi Review.*

WORK IN PROGRESS: UP, a science-fiction anthology, for Tor.

SIDELIGHTS: Patrick Nielsen Hayden, called by Janice M. Eisen in the *Washington Post Book World* "one of the most literate and historically aware editors in science fiction," has been an editor with Tor Books since

1988. In 1996, Nielsen Hayden inaugurated a new science-fiction original anthology series with *Starlight 1.* This first volume, which featured new work from, among others, Michael Swanwick, Maureen F. McHugh, John M. Ford, Jane Yolen, Susan Palwick, Robert Reed, and Martha Soukup, went on to win the World Fantasy Award for best anthology. Of the collection's twelve never-before-published stories, many were finalists for a variety of science-fiction and fantasy AWARDS, HONORS: McHugh and Swanwick's stories were nominated for the Hugo Award; Ford, McHugh, Swanwick, and Yolen's stories were all Nebula Award finalists; and Palwick's story was a finalist for the World Fantasy Award. A *Library Journal* reviewer said the book features "science-by-god . . . fantasy" and "magical realism." A long-lost earth colony is rediscovered in Maureen F. McHugh's "The Cost to Be Wise," while Gregory Feeley's "The Weighing of Ayre" revolves around the seventeenth-century glass technology of telescopes and microscopes. Michael Swanwick proposes zombies as a future labor force in "The Dead."

A *Kirkus Reviews* contributor listed other themes found in *Starlight 1* as: "Emily Dickinson, Josef Mengele and quantum theory, miracle cures, weird water, magicians, and angels," and dubbed the collection a "well-crafted work with broad appeal." *Booklist* reviewer Roland Green felt that Nielsen Hayden's collection also provides "a promising venue for experimentation by the authors of such fare." A *Publishers Weekly* reviewer wrote that each story "is stellar, and together they show the fullest range of writing in the field."

Starlight 2, published in 1998, contains "gems of the genre" and equals the quality of *Starlight 1,* with "original and powerful stories with an overall darker, grimmer cast than the ones that came before," according to a reviewer for *Publishers Weekly.* Stories in *Starlight 2* also won several awards, and touch on a number of different topics in speculative fiction. In M. Shayne Bell's "Lock Down," time travelers try to change history and the racist treatment of black singer Marian Anderson. Geoffrey A. Landis presents the character of a homeless, unmarried mother whose intelligence matches that of Einstein in "Snow," while in Jonathan Lethem's "Access Fantasy" the rich abuse the poor and disenfranchised, then retreat behind a translucent barrier. Ellen Kushner offers up an erotic adult fairy tale, and Susanna Clarke's fantasy is set in Victorian England. *Booklist* reviewer Roberta Johnson called *Starlight 2* "some of the best new writing in speculative fiction." "Dynamic, often exceptional work," was the conclusion of a writer in *Kirkus Reviews.* Nielson Hayden continued the series with *Starlight 3,* which prompted a *Pub-lishers Weekly* contributor to note: "The fine writing of many of the stories indicates that the genre is as vivid and alive at the beginning of the 21st century as it was in the 20th."

In 1997 Wildside Press published *Alternate Skiffy,* which Nielsen Hayden co-edited with Mike Resnick. This small-press anthology consists of original stories set in alternate worlds. A forthcoming anthology, *UP,* has been dubbed by Nielsen Hayden "a *Dangerous Visions* for optimists."

Nielsen Hayden once told CA: "Someone once asked Damon Knight what kind of science fiction stories he wanted for his original anthology series Orbit. He replied 'I'm trying to keep you confused about that.' I feel much the same way about Starlight, which I founded because I missed the great original anthology series of science fiction's past—Frederik Pohl's Star Science Fiction, Terry Carr's Universe, Robert Silverberg's New Dimensions, and of course Orbit. Some of the fiction in Starlight is there because it 'stretches the boundaries of the genre'; some of it is there because it reminds us of how much life remains in the genre's established conventions. Everyone's always looking for the next new revolutionary thing; sometimes that comes from the edges where we tend to look for it, and sometimes it emerges from the center when we aren't looking."

BIOGRAPHICAL/CRITICAL SOURCES:

PERIODICALS

Booklist, September 1, 1996, Roland Green, review of *Starlight 1,* p. 69; October 15, 1998, Roberta Johnson, review of *Starlight 2;* June 1, 2001, Roland Green, review of *Starlight 3,* p. 1856.
Kirkus Reviews, July 15, 1996, review of *Starlight 1,* p. 1013; September 15, 1998, review of *Starlight 2.*
Library Journal, August, 1996, review of *Starlight 1,* p. 119; July, 2001, Jackie Cassada, review of *Starlight 3,* p. 131.
Publishers Weekly, September 2, 1996, review of *Starlight 1,* p. 120; October 26, 1998, review of *Starlight 2,* p. 48; June 18, 2001, review of *Starlight 3,* p. 64.

OTHER

Nielsen Hayden's Web site, http://www.panix.com/~pnh/ (February 8, 1999).

Science Fiction Writers of America Web site, http://www.sfwa.org/ (February 1, 2002), Darrell Schweitzer, "An Interview with Patrick Nielsen Hayden."*

*   *   *

NISKANEN, William Arthur, Jr. 1933-

PERSONAL: Born March 13, 1933, in Bend, OR; son of William Arthur (a businessman) and Nina McCord (a teacher) Niskanen; married Helen Barr, August 3, 1957 (divorced, 1978); married Kathryn Washburn; children: Lia Anne, Pamela Cay, Jaime. *Education:* Harvard University, B.A., 1954, University of Chicago, M.A., 1955, Ph.D., 1962. *Politics:* Republican.

ADDRESSES: Home—638 A St. South East, Washington, DC 20003. *Office*—Cato Institute, 1000 Massachusetts Ave NW, Washington, DC 20001-5400. *E-mail*—wniskan@cato.org.

CAREER: RAND Corp., Santa Monica, CA, economist, 1957-62; Office of Secretary of Defense, Arlington, VA, director of special studies, 1962-64; Institute for Defense Analyses, Arlington, VA, division director, 1964-70; Office of Management and Budget, Washington, DC, assistant director, 1970-72; University of California, Berkeley, professor of economics, 1972-75; Ford Motor Company, Dearborn, MI, director of economics, 1975-80; University of California, Los Angeles, professor of economics, 1980-81; Council of Economic Advisors, Washington, DC, member, 1981-85; Cato Institute, Washington, DC, chair, 1985—.

MEMBER: American Economic Association, Public Choice Society (past president), Atlantic Economic Association (past president).

AWARDS, HONORS: Reaganomics: An Insider's Account of the Policies and the People selected by *Business Week* as one of the ten best books of the year, 1998; Aaron B. Wildavsky Award, 2001, for lifetime scholarly achievement in the field of public budgeting and finance.

WRITINGS:

Bureaucracy and Representative Government, Aldine-Atherton (Hawthorne, NY), 1971.
Structural Reform of the Federal Budget Process, American Enterprise Institute (Washington, DC), 1973.

Bureaucracy—Servant or Master?: Lessons from America, Institute of Economic Affairs (London, England), 1973.
Reaganomics: An Insider's Account of the Policies and the People, Oxford University Press (New York, NY), 1988.
(Editor, with James A. Dorn) *Dollars, Deficits and Trade,* Kluwer Academic (Boston, MA), 1989.
Bureaucracy and Public Economics, E. Elgar (Brookfield, VT), 1994.
Policy Analysis and Public Choice, E. Elgar (Northhampton, MA), 1998.
(With Robert E. Litan) *Going Digital!: A Guide to Policy in the Digital Age,* Brookings Institution Press and Cato Institute (Washington, DC), 1998.

Editor of *Regulation Magazine,* 1990-96.

WORK IN PROGRESS: Research on fiscal choices and economic outcomes of alternative political regimes.

SIDELIGHTS: William Arthur Niskanen, Jr.'s expertise in the field of economics has led him to a successful and prestigious career in education, business, and government. Not only has Niskanen held professorships at major universities, such as the University of California at Berkeley, but he has served as director of economics for the Ford Motor Company and as a member of the Council of Economic Advisors under President Ronald Reagan. In 1985 Niskanen joined the Cato Institute in Washington, D.C., a libertarian research foundation that emphasizes "the traditional American principles of limited government, individual freedom, and free markets."

Niskanen's *Going Digital!: A Guide to Policy in the Digital Age,* written in collaboration with Robert E. Litan of the Brookings Institute, draws on a conference cosponsored by the Cato and Brookings Institutes in 1997. The book examines the impact of the information-age technological revolution on fundamental economic activities, and suggests some consequent changes government should consider in terms of regulating such activities. Some of the topics covered are antitrust enforcement, intellectual property laws, professional licensing requirements, and laws regulating privacy, content, and standards.

Niskanen's other books include studies of budget reform, bureaucracy, taxation, and international trade. His 1988 volume, *Reaganomics: An Insider's Account of the Policies and the People,* was selected as one of the ten best books of the year by *Business Week,* and was also republished in Japanese.

BIOGRAPHICAL/CRITICAL SOURCES:

PERIODICALS

Government Finance Review, December, 1999, Betsy Bucy, review of *Going Digital!: A Guide to Policy in the Digital Age,* p. 50.
Journal of Economic Literature, December, 1998, review of *Policy Analysis and Public Choice,* p. 2221.
Reference & Research Book News, August, 1998, review of *Policy Analysis and Public Choice,* p. 66.

OTHER

CTPS Staff: William Niskanen, http://www.freetrade.org/ (June 24, 1998).

*   *   *

OAKLEY, Ann (Rosamund) 1944-
(Rosamund Clay)

PERSONAL: Born January 17, 1944, in London, England; daughter of Richard Morris (a university professor) and Kathleen (a social worker; maiden name, Miller) Titmuss; children: Adam, Emily, Laura. *Education:* Somerville College, Oxford, M.A. (with honors), 1965; Bedford College, London, Ph.D., 1974. *Politics:* "Feminist."

ADDRESSES: Office—Social Science Research Unit, 18 Woburn Sq., London WC1H 0NS, England. *Agent*—Tessa Sayle Ltd., 11 Jubilee Place, London SW3, England.

CAREER: University of London, Bedford College, London, England, research officer in Social Research Unit, 1974-79; Radcliffe Infirmary, National Perinatal Epidemiology Unit, Oxford, England, Wellcome research fellow, 1980-83; University of London, professor of sociology and social policy, 1991—, deputy director of Thomas Coram Research Unit, 1985-90, director of Social Science Research Unit, 1990—.

WRITINGS:

Sex, Gender, and Society, Maurice Temple Smith, 1972, Harper (New York, NY), 1973.
The Sociology of Housework, Martin Robertson, 1974, Pantheon (New York, NY), 1975.
Housewife, Allen Lane (London, England), 1974, published as *Woman's Work: A History of the Housewife,* Pantheon (New York, NY), 1975.
(Editor, with Juliet Mitchell) *The Rights and Wrongs of Women,* Penguin (London, England), 1976.
Becoming a Mother, Martin Robertson, 1979, Schocken (New York, NY), 1980.
Women Confined, Schocken (New York, NY), 1980.
Subject Women, Pantheon (New York, NY), 1981.
(With A. McPherson and H. Roberts) *Miscarriage,* Fontana (London, England), 1984.
Taking It like a Woman, Random House (New York, NY), 1984.
The Captured Womb: A History of the Medical Care of Pregnant Women, Blackwell (London, England), 1984, Oxford University Press (New York, NY), 1985.
Telling the Truth about Jerusalem, Blackwell (London, England), 1986.
(Editor, with Juliet Mitchell) *What Is Feminism,* Blackwell (London, England), 1986.
The Men's Room (fiction), Virago (London, England), 1988.
(Under pseudonym Rosamund Clay) *Only Angels Forget* (fiction), Virago (London, England), 1990.
Matilda's Mistake (fiction), Virago (London, England), 1990.
(With S. Houd) *Helpers in Childbirth: Midwifery Today,* Hemisphere Books (London, England), 1990.
The Secret Lives of Eleanor Jenkinson (fiction), HarperCollins (London, England), 1992.
Social Support and Motherhood: The Natural History of a Research Project, Blackwell (Oxford, England), 1992.
Essays on Women, Medicine, and Health, Edinburgh University Press (Edinburgh, Scotland), 1992.
Scenes Originating in the Garden of Eden (fiction), HarperCollins (London, England), 1993.
(With J. Brannen, K. Dodd, and P. Storey) *Young People, Health, and Family Life,* Open University Press (Buckingham, England), 1994.
(Editor, with S. Williams) *The Politics of the Welfare State,* University College Press (London, England), 1994.
A Proper Holiday, HarperCollins (London, England), 1996.
Man and Wife: Richard and Kay Titmuss: My Parents' Early Years, HarperCollins (London, England), 1996.
(Editor, with Juliet Mitchell) *Who's Afraid of Feminism? Seeing through the Backlash,* Hamish Hamilton (London, England), 1998.

(Editor, with F. Williams and J. Popay) *Welfare Research: A Critical Review,* University College Press (London, England), 1998.

Overheads, HarperCollins (London, England), 2000.

Experiments in Knowing: Gender and Method in the Social Sciences, Polity Press (Cambridge, England), 2000.

Contributor to books, including *Medical Sociology,* edited by David Tuckett, Tavistock (London, England), 1975.

BIOGRAPHICAL/CRITICAL SOURCES:

PERIODICALS

Globe & Mail (Toronto), April 13, 1985.
Newsweek, January 20, 1975.
New York Times Book Review, June 3, 1984.
Spectator, January 21, 1984.
Times (London), January 12, 1984; January 17, 1985.
Times Literary Supplement, March 2, 1972; February 28, 1975; June 28, 1985.
Village Voice, November 4, 1981.

P

PAGET-LOWE, Henry
See LOVECRAFT, H(oward) P(hillips)

* * *

PARKER, J(ohn) Carlyle 1931-

PERSONAL: Born October 14, 1931, in Ogden, UT; son of Levi C. (a farmer and security guard) and Marietta (a maker of sewn goods; maiden name, Parkinson) Parker; married Janet C. Greene, May 31, 1956; children: Denise, Nathan, Bret. *Ethnicity:* "White." *Education:* Brigham Young University, B.A., 1957; University of California, Berkeley, M.L.S., 1958; Humboldt State College (now University), graduate study, 1959-60. *Politics:* Democrat. *Religion:* Church of Jesus Christ of Latter-day Saints (Mormons). *Avocational interests:* Birding, travel, singing "solos, duets, and in choirs."

ADDRESSES: Home—2115 North Denair Ave., Turlock, CA 95382.

CAREER: Humboldt State College (now University), Arcata, CA, librarian, 1958-60; Church College of Hawaii (now Brigham Young University, Hawaii), Laie, assistant librarian, 1960-62, acting librarian, 1962-63; California State University, Stanislaus, Turlock, head of public services for university library, 1963-83 and 1985-86, assistant director, 1968-83 and 1984-90, acting director, 1983-84, university archivist, 1990-94, librarian and university archivist emeritus, 1994—. Modesto California Branch Genealogical Library, founder and librarian, 1968-90; Marietta Publishing Co., editor, 1985—; Turlock Family History Center, founder and director, 1990-97. Turlock Centennial Foundation Board, secretary, 1971-75; Turlock Community Concert Board, president, 1973-75. *Military service:* U.S. Army, chaplain's assistant, 1953-55.

MEMBER: American Library Association (fellow; chair of genealogy committee, Reference and Adult Services Division of the History Section, 1989-92), National Genealogical Society, California Library Association, California State Genealogical Alliance (historian, 1991—), Utah Genealogical Association (fellow), Stanislaus County Historical Society, Genealogical Society of Stanislaus County (honorary member), Turlock Historical Society.

AWARDS, HONORS: Award of Merit, National Genealogical Society, 1984; Meritorious Performance and Professional Promise Award, California State University, Stanislaus, 1986 and 1990; Genealogical Publishing Company Award, History Section, Reference and Adult Services Division, American Library Association, 1994.

WRITINGS:

An Annotated Bibliography of the History of Del Norte and Humboldt Counties, Humboldt State College Library (Arcata, CA), 1960.
Sources of Californiana: From Padron to Voter Registration, Genealogical Society of Utah (Salt Lake City, UT), 1969.
A Personal Name Index to Orton's "Records of California Men in the War of the Rebellion, 1861 to 1867," Gale (Detroit, MI), 1978.
City, County, Town, and Township Index to the 1850 Federal Census Schedule, Gale (Detroit, MI), 1979.

An Index to the Biographees in 19th-Century California County Histories, Gale (Detroit, MI), 1979.

Library Service for Genealogists, Gale (Detroit, MI), 1981.

(Editor) *Genealogy in the Central Association of Libraries: A Union Catalog Based on Filby's "American and British Genealogy and Heraldry,"* California State College Library, Stanislaus (Turlock, CA), 1981.

(Compiler) *Directory of Archivist and Librarian Genealogical Instructors,* Marietta Publishing (Turlock, CA), 1985, second edition, 1990.

Pennsylvania and Middle Atlantic States Genealogical Manuscripts: A User's Guide to the Manuscript Collections of the Genealogical Society of Pennsylvania, as Indexed in Its Manuscript Materials Index, Microfilmed by the Genealogical Department, Salt Lake City, Marietta Publishing (Turlock, CA), 1986.

(With wife, Janet G. Parker) *Nevada Biographical and Genealogical Sketch Index,* Marietta Publishing (Turlock, CA), 1986.

Music Directors' and Accompanists' Index to "Hymns" (1985) and "Simplified Accompaniments (1986), Marietta Publishing (Turlock, CA), 1988.

Rhode Island Biographical and Genealogical Sketch Index, Marietta Publishing (Turlock, CA), 1991.

Going to Salt Lake City to Do Family History Research, 2nd edition, Marietta Publishing (Turlock, CA), 1993, 3rd edition, 1996.

Documents of Library History, California State University, Stanislaus and Other Whatnots and War Stories from the Career of the Author, California State University Library, Stanislaus (Turlock, CA), 1994.

Contributor to books, including *The Craft of Public History: An Annotated Select Bibliography,* edited by David F. Trask and Robert W. Pomeroy III, Greenwood Press (Westport, CT), 1983. Editor of "Genealogy and Local History" series, Gale (Detroit, MI), 1978-81. Contributor of articles and reviews to genealogy, history, and library journals.

WORK IN PROGRESS: A fourth edition of *Going to Salt Lake City to Do Family History Research;* a second edition of *Library Service for Genealogists;* several additional biographical sketch indexes and genealogical reference works, for Marietta Publishing (Turlock, CA).

SIDELIGHTS: J. Carlyle Parker once told *CA:* "The majority of my early writing was an attempt to assist librarians in their understanding of how to help patrons in biographical, genealogical, and local history research;

how to use and obtain these research materials; and to make some of these research materials easier to use and more accessible. Some time ago my attention also turned to helping genealogists do their research through the preparation of indexes, guides, book and microform reviews, and how-to-do-it works."

*   *   *

PARKER, Nancy Winslow 1930-

PERSONAL: Born October 18, 1930, in Maplewood, NJ; daughter of Winslow Aurelius (a textile executive) and Beatrice McCelland (Gaunt) Parker. *Education:* Mills College, B.A., 1952; additional study at Art Students League, 1956, 1957, and School of Visual Arts, 1966-67. *Avocational interests:* Carpentry, tennis, gardening, genealogy.

ADDRESSES: Home—51 East 74th St., Apt. 3R, New York, NY 10021. *E-mail*—nwparker@aol.com.

CAREER: Author and illustrator. National Broadcasting Co., Inc. (NBC), New York, NY, sales promoter, 1956-60; New York Soccer Club, New York, NY, sports promoter, 1961-63; Radio Corp. of America (RCA), New York, NY, sales promoter, 1964-67; Appleton-Century-Crofts, Inc. (publisher), New York, NY, art director, 1968-70; Holt, Rinehart & Winston, Inc. (publisher), New York, NY, graphic designer, 1970-72; freelance writer and illustrator of children's books, 1972—.

MEMBER: Authors Guild, Authors League of America, Mills College Club of New York.

AWARDS, HONORS: Jane Tinkham Broughton fellowship, Bread Loaf Writers' Conference, 1975; Notable Children's Book in the field of social studies designations, 1975, for *Warm as Wool, Cool as Cotton: The Story of Natural Fibers,* and 1976, for *The Goat in the Rug; Saturday Review* best of the season citation, 1976, for *The Goat in the Rug; Philadelphia Inquirer* year's best children's book citation, 1976, for *Willy Bear;* Christopher awards, 1976, for *Willy Bear,* and 1981, for *My Mom Travels a Lot;* American Library Association notable book designation, 1980, for *Poofy Loves Company; New York Times* selection as one of ten best illustrated books, 1981, for *My Mom Travels a Lot;* honorable mention, New York Academy of Science, 1981, and placement on Sequoyah Children's Book Award Masterlist, Oklahoma Library Association, 1983-84, both for *The President's Car;* New York Public Library list of children's books, 1983, for *The Christmas Camel,* and 1985, for *The United Nations from A to Z;* Library of Congress' Books for Children, 1986, for *Paul Revere's Ride,* and 1988, for *Bugs;* Association of Booksellers for Children Choice Award, 1988, for *Bugs.*

WRITINGS:

SELF-ILLUSTRATED CHILDREN'S BOOKS

The Man with the Take-Apart Head, Dodd (New York, NY), 1974.
The Party at the Old Farm, Atheneum (New York, NY), 1975.
Mrs. Wilson Wanders Off, Dodd (New York, NY), 1976.
Love from Uncle Clyde, Dodd (New York, NY), 1977.
The Crocodile under Louis Finneberg's Bed, Dodd (New York, NY), 1978.
The President's Cabinet (nonfiction), Parents Magazine Press (New York, NY), 1978, revised edition, HarperCollins (New York, NY), 1991.
The Ordeal of Byron B. Blackbear, Dodd (New York, NY), 1979.
Puddums, the Cathcarts' Orange Cat, Atheneum (New York, NY), 1980.
Poofy Loves Company, Dodd (New York, NY), 1980.
The Spotted Dog, Dodd (New York, NY), 1980.
The President's Car (nonfiction), Crowell (New York, NY), 1981.
Cooper, the McNallys' Big Black Dog, Dodd (New York, NY), 1981.
Love from Aunt Betty, Dodd (New York, NY), 1983.
Christmas Camel, Dodd (New York, NY), 1983.
The United Nations from A to Z, Dodd (New York, NY), 1985.
(With others) *Bugs,* Greenwillow Press (New York, NY), 1987.
(With others) *Frogs, Toads, Lizards, and Salamanders,* Greenwillow Press (New York, NY), 1990.
Working Frog, Greenwillow Press (New York, NY), 1992.
Money, Money, Money: The Meaning of the Art and Symbols on United States Paper Currency, Greenwillow Press (New York, NY), 1995.
Locks, Crocs, and Skeeters: The Story of the Panama Canal, Greenwillow Press (New York, NY), 1996.
Land Ho! Fifty Glorious Years in the Age of Exploration with Twelve Important Explorers, Greenwillow Press (New York, NY), 2001.

ILLUSTRATOR

John Langstaff, *Oh, A-Hunting We Will Go!* (songbook), Atheneum (New York, NY), 1974.

Carter Hauck, *Warm as Wool, Cool as Cotton: The Story of Natural Fibers,* Seabury Press (New York, NY), 1975.
Blood and Link, *The Goat in the Rug,* Parents Magazine Press (New York, NY), 1976.
Mildred Kantrowitz, *Willy Bear,* Parents Magazine Press (New York, NY), 1976.
John Langstaff, *Sweetly Sings the Donkey* (songbook), Atheneum (New York, NY), 1976.
Lawler, *The Substitute,* Parents Magazine Press (New York, NY), 1977.
John Langstaff, *Hot Cross Buns and Other Old Street Cries* (songbook), Atheneum (New York, NY), 1978.
Jane Yolen, *No Bath Tonight,* Crowell (New York, NY), 1978.
Caroline Feller Bauer, *My Mom Travels a Lot,* Warne (New York, NY), 1981.
Henry Wadsworth Longfellow, *Paul Revere's Ride,* Greenwillow Press (New York, NY), 1985.
Rice, *Aren't You Coming Too?,* Greenwillow Price (New York, NY), 1988.
Field, *General Store,* Greenwillow Press (New York, NY), 1988.
Rice, *Peter's Pockets,* Greenwillow Press (New York, NY), 1989.
Shirley Nietzel, *The Jacket I Wear in the Snow,* Greenwillow Press (New York, NY), 1989.
Rice, *At Grammy's House,* Greenwillow Press (New York, NY), 1990.
Guy, *Black Crow,* Greenwillow Press (New York, NY), 1991.
Lillie, *When the Rooster Crowed,* Greenwillow Press (New York, NY), 1991.
Whittier, *Barbara Frietchie,* Greenwillow Press (New York, NY), 1991.
Shirley Nietzel, *The Dress I'll Wear to the Party,* Greenwillow Press (New York, NY), 1992.
T. B. Read, *Sheridan's Ride,* Greenwillow Press (New York, NY), 1993.
Charlotte Pomeranz, *Here Comes Henny,* Greenwillow Press (New York, NY), 1994.
Shirley Nietzel, *The Bag I'm Taking to Grandma's,* Greenwillow Press (New York, NY), 1995.
Shirley Nietzel, *We're Making Breakfast for Mother,* Greenwillow Press (New York, NY), 1996.
Shirley Nietzel, *The House I'll Build for the Wrens,* Greenwillow Press (New York, NY), 1997.
Shirley Nietzel, *I'm Taking a Trip on my Train,* Greenwillow Press (New York, NY), 1999.
Shirley Nietzel, *Our Class Took a Trip to the Zoo,* Greenwillow Press (New York, NY), 2000.
Shirley Nietzel, *I'm Not Feeling Well Today,* Greenwillow Press (New York, NY), 2001.

WORK IN PROGRESS: "Making wood constructions combining oils, electric lights, and found objects."

SIDELIGHTS: Nancy Winslow Parker is an award-winning children's book author and illustrator whose works, Dulcy Brainard writes in *Publishers Weekly,* "are marked by a fresh simplicity and an observant, ironic sense of humor that is particularly apparent in the unexpected ways her pictures expand on the text."

Parker often finds inspiration for her books in real-life situations. *Poofy Loves Company,* for example, is based on an actual incident in which Parker's overly friendly dog ambushed a visiting youngster, messing up her clothes and stealing her cookie. In the *Junior Literary Guild* Parker recalls that the story "took about fifteen minutes to write, the whole thing coming at once in a delicious outburst of creativity."

Animals, especially dogs, often figure into Parker's stories. In *Love from Uncle Clyde,* a boy named Charlie receives a three-thousand-pound hippopotamus as a Christmas present from his uncle. These same characters appear again in *The Christmas Camel,* in which Uncle Clyde sends Charlie a magical camel who takes the boy to Bethlehem on Christmas Eve.

Parker's nonfiction books have also achieved success. The award-winning *Bugs,* written with Joan R. Wright, examines the physical structure and habitats of several types of common insects. Patti Hagan, writing in the *New York Times Book Review,* claims that the book's "color illustrations, with precise anatomical tags, are a fine tool for introducing children" to the insects portrayed.

In addition to the books she has written, Parker has illustrated the works of other children's authors as well, including the Christopher Award-winning *Willy Bear* by Mildred Kantrowitz and *My Mom Travels a Lot* by Caroline Feller Bauer. Both of these works focus on children adjusting to new and sometimes frightening situations in their lives. *In Willy Bear* a youngster uses his teddy bear to act out his fear of going to school, and in *My Mom Travels a Lot,* a young girl reacts to her hectic mother's lack of time for her.

Parker once told *CA:* "I cannot remember when I have not been interested in children's literature. As a writer, the field has limitless potential for fantasy and the joy of creation. As an illustrator, the opportunity to let yourself go in wild interpretation is an artist's dream come true."

"[My] late-in-life effort to be up-to-date and more efficient [by using a computer instead of a typewriter] has only slowed me down (temporarily)," Parker later added, "and I am now inching towards books with pictures only.

"My next book will be about either houses, medicine or my great grandfather. If I do the art work first, by the time I am ready to do the manuscript, I may have cracked the code of my 'laptop' dragon."

BIOGRAPHICAL/CRITICAL SOURCES:

PERIODICALS

Booklist, May 1, 1991, p. 1710; June 15, 1992, p. 1851; October 15, 1994, Ilene Cooper, review of *Here Comes Henny,* p. 438; June 1, 1995, Hazel Rochman, review of *The Bag I'm Taking to Grandma's,* p. 1788, and Mary Harris Veeder, review of *Money, Money, Money,* p. 1757; May 15, 1996, Carolyn Phelan, review of *Locks, Crocs, and Skeeters,* p. 1583; March 1, 1997, C. Phelan, review of *We're Making Breakfast for Mother,* p. 1173; August, 1997, Stephanie Zvirin, review of *The House I'll Build for the Wrens,* p. 1899; April 15, 1999, Hazel Rochman, review of *I'm Taking a Trip on My Train,* p. 1537.
Horn Book Magazine, May-June, 1995, Margaret A. Bush, review of *The Bag I'm Taking to Grandma's,* p. 327; September-October, 1997, Ann A. Flowers, review of *The House I'll Build for the Wrens,* p. 562; May, 2001, review of *I'm Not Feeling Well Today,* p. 314.
Junior Literary Guild, March, 1980, p. 8.
Kirkus Reviews, April 1, 1992, p. 470.
Library Talk, November, 1991, p. 28.
New York Times Book Review, February 7, 1988, p. 29.
Publishers Weekly, February 22, 1985, pp. 161-162; May 4, 1992, p. 56.
Quill & Quire, July, 1992, p. 50.
Reading Teacher, September, 1993, p. 51.
School Library Journal, July, 1991, p. 84; August, 1992, p. 146; September, 1994, Sally R. Dow, review of *Here Comes Henny,* p. 192; April, 1995, Beth Irish, review of *The Bag I'm Taking to Grandma's,* p. 114; June, 1995, Jonathan Betz-Zall, review of *Money, Money, Money,* p. 124; April, 1996, review of *Locks, Crocs, and Skeeters,* p. 148; September, 1997, Carolyn Jenks, review of *The House I'll Build for the Wrens,* p. 188; March, 1999, Gay Lynn Van Vleck,

review of *I'm Taking a Trip on My Train,* p. 1537; July, 2001, Louie Lahana, review of *I'm Not Feeling Well Today,* p. 86; August, 2001, review of *Land Ho!,* p. 171.

Wilson Library Bulletin, January, 1995, review of *Here Comes Henny,* p. 119.

*   *   *

PATRICK, Maxine
   See MAXWELL, Patricia

*   *   *

PAYNE, Neil F. 1939-

PERSONAL: Born March 9, 1939, in Plymouth, WI; son of Forrest G. (a factory worker) and Ruth (a factory worker and homemaker; maiden name, Steinke) Payne; married Eileen Tagge, May 30, 1964 (divorced, 1984); married Jan Barberie (a professor of nursing), January 4, 1986; children: Adam, Mark, Erin. *Education:* University of Wisconsin—Madison, B.A., 1961; Virginia Polytechnic Institute and State University, M.S., 1964; Utah State University, Ph.D., 1975.

ADDRESSES: Home—4698 Pierce Dr., Plover, WI 54467. *E-mail*—npayne@uwsp.edu.

CAREER: Newfoundland Wildlife Division, St. Johns, Newfoundland, Canada, fur-bearer biologist, 1967-71; University of Washington, Seattle, research assistant professor, 1973-75; University of Wisconsin—Stevens Point, professor of wildlife, 1975-98. *Military service:* U.S. Marine Corps, 1964-67, served in Vietnam; became captain.

AWARDS, HONORS: University of Wisconsin—Stevens Point, College of Natural Resources, named outstanding faculty member, 1978, outstanding scholar, 1986, 1992, and 1998, and scholar of the year, 1992; annual publication award, book category, Texas chapter, Wildlife Society, 1994.

WRITINGS:

Techniques for Wildlife Habitat Management of Wetlands, McGraw-Hill (New York, NY), 1992, published as *Wildlife Habitat Management of Wetlands,* Krieger (Malabar, FL), 1998.

(With Fred C. Bryant) *Techniques for Wildlife Habitat Management of Uplands,* McGraw-Hill (New York, NY), 1994, published as *Wildlife Habitat Management of Forestlands, Rangelands, and Farmlands,* Krieger (Malabar, FL), 1998.

More Wildlife on Your Land: A Guide for Rural Landowners, Barberie (Plover, WI), 2001.

Contributor to periodicals.

WORK IN PROGRESS: Wildlife and Human Cultures in North America: The United States and Canada, with Richard D. Taber, publication by Krieger (Malabar, FL) expected in 2002.

SIDELIGHTS: A retired professor of wildlife, Neil F. Payne is the author of several research books on wildlife habitat management and ecology, including his 1992 publication *Techniques for Wildlife Habitat Management of Wetlands.* Reviewers have found Payne's volumes to be valuable reference works which include statistical tables, extensive appendixes, lists of common and scientific classifications, and, often, citations from previously unpublished sources.

In *Techniques for Wildlife Habitat Management of Wetlands,* Payne stresses the need to protect and manage unaltered wildlife habitats. The volume emphasizes the need to maintain biodiversity and to encourage population growth of endangered species. After focusing on species of waterfowl, and identifying various types of wetlands—from potholes to ponds, marshes, and other riparian sources—Payne discusses the importance of wetlands to the environment. IIe then describes the many techniques used to manage these areas, including the construction of dams, levees, and islands, erosion control, and the use of water manipulation, prescribed burns, and mechanical and other treatments to affect vegetation.

Payne, who drew from more than 700 references for the book, has been praised for presenting a wide scope on his subject, and wildlife specialists maintain that *Techniques for Wildlife Habitat Management of Wetlands* is an important addition to literature on the subject. Reviewer Roger L. Pederson, a representative of Ducks Unlimited in Minnesota, wrote in the *Journal of Wildlife Management:* "The greatest value of the book is the quantitative nature the author has used to describe a large variety of wetland management options. . . . I feel the author has accomplished his goal of producing a 'how-to' book of techniques used in wetland habitat management."

Similar comments were issued by David A. Haukos, of the United States Fish and Wildlife Service, in his review for *Ecology.* Haukos wrote: "Payne has successfully compiled a useful reference describing potential techniques for habitat management of the major wetland types of North America. He has met his purpose of producing a source book of ideas and a practical training guide for wetland managers." The critic added, "It will be a valuable shelf reference and idea source for many years to come." Robert G. Wetzel, writing in *Quarterly Review of Biology,* found Payne's "objectives are accomplished well," and predicted "the book will serve as a techniques manual for effective waterfowl management for many years."

Payne once told *CA:* "Although I've considered myself more of a population biologist than a habitat biologist, my frustration at teaching a habitat course every semester without a text stimulated me to develop one, especially after I became involved in writing on the subject for the U.S. Forest Service. With 700 references in *Techniques for Wildlife Habitat Management of Wetlands* and 1,500 in *Techniques for Wildlife Habitat Management of Uplands,* the two-volume set is a compendium of applied habitat management of wetlands, forestlands, rangelands, and farmlands."

Payne later added: "That led me to write a how-to wildlife habitat book for the rural landowner, so many of whom were interested in encouraging wildlife use of their land. I am also the junior author of the book *Wildlife and Human Cultures in North America: The United States and Canada,* with Richard D. Taber, who is a former graduate study of Aldo Leopold. We have taken to publication a book manuscript that Dick has been compiling for more than a quarter of a century on a subject that has influenced human cultural development."

BIOGRAPHICAL/CRITICAL SOURCES:

PERIODICALS

Choice, November, 1992, p. 493.
Ecology, March, 1993, David A. Haukos, review of *Techniques for Wildlife Habitat Management of Wetlands,* pp. 634-635.
Journal of Wildlife Management, January, 1993, Roger L. Pederson, review of *Techniques for Wildlife Habitat Management of Wetlands,* p. 190; March, 1994, pp. 589-590.

Quarterly Review of Biology, June, 1993, Robert G. Wetzel, review of *Techniques for Wildlife Habitat Management of Wetlands,* p. 291.

* * *

PHILLIPS, Ward
    See LOVECRAFT, H(oward) P(hillips)

* * *

PIERCE, Meredith Ann 1958-

PERSONAL: Born July 5, 1958, in Seattle, WA; daughter of Frank N. (a professor of advertising) and Jo Ann (an editor and professor of agriculture; maiden name, Bell) Pierce. *Education:* University of Florida, B.A., 1978, M.A., 1980. *Avocational interests:* Music (composition, harp, and voice), picture book collecting, film and theater, anthropology, archaeology, languages, folklore and mythology, cats, science fiction, fantasy.

ADDRESSES: Home—424-H Northeast Sixth St., Gainesville, FL 32601.

CAREER: Writer. University of Florida, instructor in creative writing, 1978-80; Bookland, Gainesville, FL, clerk, 1981; Waldenbooks, Gainesville, FL, clerk, 1981-87; Aluchua County Library District, FL, library assistant, 1987—. Treasurer, Children's Literature Association Conference, Gainesville, 1982.

MEMBER: Phi Beta Kappa.

AWARDS, HONORS: First prize, Scholastic/Hallmark Cards creative writing contest, 1973; Best Books for Young Adults citation and Best of the Best Books 1970-82 designation, both American Library Association (ALA), *New York Times* Notable Children's Book designation, and Parents' Choice Award Superbook citation, all 1982, Children's Book Award, International Reading Association, 1983, California Young Reader Medal, 1986, and Booklist Best Books of the Decade (1980-89) list, all for *The Darkangel;* Jane Tinkham Broughton Fellow in writing for children, Bread Loaf Writers' Conference, 1984; Best Books for Young Adults semifinalist, ALA, 1985, for *A Gathering of Gargoyles;* Parents' Choice Award for Literature citation, 1985, and New York Public Library Books for the Teen-Age citation, 1986, both for *The Woman Who*

Loved Reindeer; Individual Artist Fellowship special award for children's literature, Florida Department of State Division of Cultural Affairs, 1987; Best Books for Young Adults citation, ALA, 1991, for *The Pearl of the Soul of the World.*

WRITINGS:

YOUNG ADULT FANTASY NOVELS

The Darkangel (first novel in "Darkangel" trilogy; also see below), Little, Brown (Boston, MA), 1982, reprinted, Harcourt (San Diego, CA), 1998.

A Gathering of Gargoyles (second novel in "Darkangel" trilogy; also see below), Little, Brown (Boston, MA), 1984, reprinted, Harcourt (San Diego, CA), 1998.

Birth of the Firebringer (first novel of "Firebringer" trilogy), Macmillan (New York, NY), 1985.

The Woman Who Loved Reindeer, Little, Brown (Boston, MA), 1985, reprinted, Harcourt (San Diego, CA), 2000.

The Pearl of the Soul of the World (third novel in "Darkangel" trilogy; also see below), Little, Brown (Boston, MA), 1990.

The Darkangel Trilogy (contains *The Darkangel, A Gathering of Gargoyles,* and *The Pearl of the Soul of the World*), Doubleday (New York, NY), 1990.

Dark Moon (second novel in "Firebringer" trilogy), Little, Brown (Boston, MA), 1992.

The Son of Summer Stars (third novel in "Firebringer" trilogy), Little, Brown (Boston, MA), 1996.

Treasure at the Heart of Tanglewood, Viking (New York, NY), 2001.

OTHER

Where the Wild Geese Go (picture book), illustrated by Jamichael Henterly, Dutton (New York, NY), 1988.

Contributor of novella "Rampion" to *Four from the Witch World,* edited by André Norton, Tor Books (New York, NY), 1989. Contributor to anthologies and to periodicals, including *Mythlore, Horn Book, ALAN Review, Voice of Youth Advocates,* and *New Advocate.*

SIDELIGHTS: Meredith Ann Pierce's novels, which include the trilogies "Darkangel" and "Firebringer," are highlighted by their imaginative plots and settings, poetic language, and determined, independent characters.

Her most noted work, the "Darkangel" fantasy trilogy, relates a young girl's struggle to free herself, her friends, and her world from an evil witch. Pierce's fiction "combines a mythic inventiveness with such elemental themes as love, conflict, and quest," explained Joan Nist in the *ALAN Review.* As a *Publishers Weekly* contributor noted, Pierce's "imagination seems boundless and she writes with such assurance that readers believe in every magic being and occurrence."

Mary Corran noted in an essay for *St. James Guide to Fantasy Writers* that "the small quantity of Pierce's work is high in quality. There is a magic in the weaving of her tales which is deeply absorbing. The atmospheres she creates tend to linger in the mind, and there is a directness and lack of sentimentality about her characters which engender a powerful appeal." "Like good baklava, a work of fiction should be multilayered," Pierce herself once explained. "If it doesn't have its components properly situated in correct proportion, the taste and texture will be off. Plot is like the pastry: The body and support. Theme is the nut: The kernel and the heart. Style is the savor, blending honey and spice. Nothing is more delicious either to fashion or to devour,"

Several critics have noted the sophistication of Pierce's prose style, including her use of archaic language and advanced vocabulary. M. Jean Greenlaw, writing in *Twentieth-Century Young Adult Writers,* likened Pierce's novels to elaborate tapestries and commented that "when she is at her best, the tales are rich and evocative, stirring the reader to question as well as absorb. There are times, however, that her tellings become too intricate, and the reader loses the thread of the tapestry." Pierce, however, refuses to simplify her complex language. In an interview she defended her writing: "I can't change the way I think and I can't change my vocabulary and pretend that I don't know words that I know. . . . There are lots of word games in my stories, coined words and made up words, compound words, because I like doing that, it's very enjoyable."

Born in Seattle, Washington, in 1958, Pierce developed her considerable imagination by entertaining herself when she was a child. "I was a great collector of stuffed animals and had several entire imaginary lives," she admitted. "I would play with anything that was available whether it was animate or not. It would always be some sort of imagined environment—it was like role-playing games [such as Dungeons and Dragons] before role-playing games were invented." Books fueled her imagination after she began reading at age three, and the library became a favorite haunt. One book that

Pierce remembers fondly is Lewis Carroll's *Alice in Wonderland;* "*Alice in Wonderland* is like my religion," she revealed. "It was introduced into my system before my immune system was complete, so it's wired into my psyche. I can't distinguish between my own mythology and early influences like *Alice in Wonderland* or the movie *The Wizard of Oz.* Some of the stuff that I saw really impressed me when I was very little and just went straight into my neurons—it's inseparable from my way of thinking."

By the time she reached junior high, Pierce was scouring the shelves in the adult section of the library. She constantly wrote down ideas and stories, but she did not realize that people could actually make a living writing novels. She once said, "My parents always treated my writing as another one of those obsessive little hobbies. . . . Since they were the authority figures I had to pretend that this wasn't the most important thing in my life and find some other career." While attending the University of Florida, she encountered teachers who encouraged her talent and enthusiasm for writing, and at age twenty-three Pierce began work on what would be her first published novel, *The Darkangel.*

The Darkangel is a fantasy that takes place on the moon and follows the journey of Aeriel, a servant girl who sets out to rescue her mistress from a vampire who, while evil, is strangely compelling at the same time. The basic idea for the book was inspired by a real-life case Pierce encountered while reading the autobiography of noted psychiatrist Carl Jung. One of Jung's patients told him how she had once lived on the moon, where she met a handsome vampire who took her captive. "Jung's account of his patient and her fascinating delusion served as the germinal model for Aeriel and the first two chapters of *Darkangel,*" Pierce related in a *Horn Book* article. Later sections of the novel, as well as the rest of what developed as the "Darkangel" trilogy, draw from the fairy tale "Beauty and the Beast," the Greek myth of Psyche and Eros, and a host of other influences. While *Library Journal* contributor Paula M. Strain found *The Darkangel* to be somewhat "derivative," other critics thought otherwise. In her *New York Times Book Review* critique of the second volume of the "Darkangel" trilogy, *A Gathering of Gargoyles,* Eleanor Cameron commented that Pierce's novels "reflect the wellspring of myth and religion that have influenced her and have taken new form in her interpretation. The well-read adolescent or adult can revel in both the story that Pierce tells and the search for connections to other stories in the body of fantasy literature."

In the "Darkangel" trilogy—which includes *The Darkangel, A Gathering of Gargoyles,* and *The Pearl of the*

Soul of the World— Aeriel continues her battle against the evil White Witch that threatens the young woman's world. The close of the first volume finds Aeriel married to the vampire Irrylath, a son of the White Witch who is now humanized after she exchanges her heart for his. In *A Gathering of Gargoyles,* she discovers that Irrylath is still bound to the evil White Witch and cannot love another; she is a bride in name only. To release him, she searches the moon to find their world's Ions, ancient animal guardians who will help lead the battle against the witch's forces.

In the last novel of the series, *The Pearl of the Soul of the World,* Aeriel sets out to defeat the White Witch and persuade her to renounce evil: the classic showdown between good and evil. Her efforts are thwarted when a silver pin is driven into her skull, leaving Aeriel wandering through underground caves, mute and unaware of who she is. She is eventually rescued by Ravenna, last of the ancient creators, who removes the pin and places all her knowledge and powers into the luminous pearl Aeriel wears around her neck. Thus armed, Aeriel prepares for the final confrontation with her evil nemesis.

As Corran noted, while *The Darkangel* "possesses a fairy-tale—even an Arabian Nights—quality, . . . that is to underrate the extraordinarily evocative nature of the work, rich with the power of myth." *A Gathering of Gargoyles* contains a similar fairy-story feeling, although Corran found it "more rounded and more complex." Many critics have praised the entire trilogy for its well-developed characters, and Greenlaw also noted "the staunch love that Aeriel extends to the creatures and beings with whom she comes in contact." *The Signal Review* contributor Elizabeth Hammill found Aeriel "a brave and resourceful heroine—fascinating because she possesses that fairy-tale compassion for apparently base creatures which enables her to recognize their true nature and, hence, to redeem them."

Aeriel's determination to stand her ground in the face of danger is a reflection of Pierce's own childhood experiences, as the author wrote in her *Horn Book* article. Pierce once had to cope with an alcoholic and abusive relative who one day "had made up his mind to do me violence." But the author refused to be bullied by the relative who, faced with such determination, backed off. It was "a little bit of a revelation—that a lot of human relationships are bluff, and that's an important thing to know," she concluded.

Several critics have commented on Pierce's use of language in the "Darkangel" books, with Cameron describing Pierce's style as "intensely visual, even poetic," and

Fantasy Review critic Walter Albert pointing out that "one of her great strengths is her ability to capture the colors and textures of the physical world." Ann A. Flowers noted in a *Horn Book* review of *The Pearl of the Soul of the World,* that one of the novel's strengths was "the style, with shimmering, fragile textures and delicate, shadowy descriptions," while a *Publishers Weekly* reviewer commented on the "meticulous, creative use of language" in the concluding "Darkangel" novel.

Pierce's use of language is again praised in reviews of her "Firebringer" trilogy, which contains *Birth of the Firebringer, Dark Moon,* and *The Son of Summer Stars.* A contributor to *Kirkus Reviews* found the language in the opening volume "as elegant as the unicorn people it chronicles." In *Birth of the Firebringer,* an impulsive, outspoken young unicorn named Jan wants to prove his worth to his father, Prince of the Unicorns. He joins the unicorns' annual pilgrimage to a sacred lake, but finds himself challenged by an ancient enemy, the evil wyverns. Seeing no vision in the sacred well nearby, Jan runs away, and in his flight encounters a wyvern who tries to get him to betray his people. When Jan kills the wyvern, his noble deed results in his being able to see visions concerning his destiny as firebringer of the unicorns. Praising the novel for its "satisfying plot," *School Library Journal* contributor Holly Sanhuber noted that Pierce's talent for making her unicorn world believable is "enhanced by her stately use of language and the sense of [unicorn] history and culture which she creates and sustains."

The "Firebringer" trilogy continues with 1992's *Dark Moon,* which finds Jan falling in love with the unicorn Tek, whom he takes as his mate. However, Jan's happiness is cut short by an attack from harpies, and Jan lost at sea and believed dead. Crazed by grief, the unicorn prince— Jan's father—becomes ruthless in his dictatorship of the herd. Escaping the fury of Jan's father, Tek escapes to the home of her mother—a healer—in time to give birth to two foals. Meanwhile, Jan is still alive and in the care of humans who have taken him to their city and penned him up with a group of mares. One of the mares, Ryhenna, aids Jan in his escape and joins him in returning to his own land and attempt to make peace with the wyverns, harpies, and other creatures that besiege his land. *School Library Journal* critic JoAnn Rees noted that the novel would be must-reading for followers of the trilogy.

The Son of Summer Stars provides what *School Library Journal* reviewer Mary Jo Drungil called a "thrilling" and "deeply satisfying" conclusion to Pierce's second

trilogy by answering some of the questions left unanswered by the earlier books. In the novel, Jan leads his herd to its ancient homeland, finding a way to thwart the efforts of the wormlike wyverns and other creatures to do them harm. Jan's father, now living as a renegade, reveals that the rightful leader of the unicorns is Jan's mate, Tek, who is now a warrior, and this prophecy is proven true at a final showdown that takes place at the Hallow Hills. Although *The Son of Summer Stars* brings to an end much of the tension built during the previous novels, as *Booklist* contributor Chris Sherman noted, Pierce also includes "the encounters with exotic creatures and the adventures" that captured readers' attention in the first two "Firebringer" novels. Drungil concluded, "Readers of the earlier novels and fantasy addicts will be delighted with this compelling tale."

Inventing a new society like that of the unicorns is an aspect of fantasy-writing that Pierce particularly enjoys. "I'm very interested in environments, in worlds, civilizations, belief systems, societies, rules of society or religions. Both fantasy and science fiction tend to do a whole lot of world-building because they will build the environment, they will build the world, they'll get it all set up and then they'll say, 'What if?'" To develop all the details of a new world, Pierce draws on her wider reading experience: "lots of anthropology and mythology, religion and alternate cultures and books about animal behavior. All of that I read for pleasure, but it's also my research because it comes back in my stories, in shadows and echoes, distortions and amalgams. It refigures itself into a fantasy."

As with *Darkangel,* Pierce's *The Woman Who Loved Reindeer* resulted from an idea the author had during her high school years. As the author recalled in *Horn Book:* "As I stood looking out over the flat, barren, empty playing field, a vivid image came to mind of a woman dressed in doeskin standing stock still, her mouth open, her hands reaching out after a great stag that is carrying away her child. . . . The woman is speechless, but the child is screaming . . . with delight." Pierce developed her vision into a story by building on the Native American husk-myth in which an animal can cast off its skin to take human form, setting this story in an imagined world. In her novel, young Caribou, who lives alone after her father's death, is given her sister-in-law's baby, called Reindeer. Caribou takes herbs to cause her milk to flow, and nurtures the newborn despite qualms that the infant is not quite human. She eventually discovers that Reindeer is a "trangl"—a demon who can take human or reindeer form. Through her love and determination, Caribou earns the trust of the changeling and when he grows old enough to join his people, the other reindeer, he returns as a golden-eyed young man and becomes Caribou's lover. Discovering herself pregnant with Reindeer's child and finding her village threatened, Caribou eventually is forced to decide whether or not to follow Reindeer by becoming a trangl herself. *The Woman Who Loved Reindeer* is "a haunting story of great beauty," noted Patty Campbell in *Wilson Library Bulletin,* intensified by "a style both simple and poetic." "The author's imaginary world is an intriguing combination of realistic, folkloric, and fantastic elements," wrote Ann F. Flowers in *Horn Book,* adding that Pierce's style is "smooth, clear and elegant, with never a word in the wrong place." A reviewer in the *Bulletin of the Center for Children's Books* found the love story "convincing, the dangers . . . suspenseful."

Another self-contained novel, *Treasure at the Heart of Tanglewood* finds Hannah living alone in a forest known as Tanglewood, clad in brown leaves and surrounded by animals who serve as her sole companions. She has no recollection of how she came to this state, and is isolated, both feared and revered by nearby villagers for her powers as a healer. And Hannah does have a secret: she empowers a powerful but evil wizard who requires a drink made from flowers that blossom from Hannah's hair in order to perform his task as guard of a sacred treasure. Falling in love with a handsome knight, Hannah breaks the wizard's hold over her and goes on a journey to seek her ultimate purpose in life. Calling the book a "complex story with a strong mythical theme," Bruce Anne Shook noted in her *School Library Journal* review that the author successfully depicts "an ancient earth mother who is both life giver and sustainer." Commenting on the parallel to the myth of Demeter and Persephone, a *Horn Book* contributor found *Treasure at the Heart of Tanglewood* to be "romantic fantasy at its most lush and most rewarding," while in *Booklist* Sally Estes hailed the volume as "lyrical and magical, elegant in imagery, and memorable in characterization."

Pierce's picture book *Where the Wild Geese Go* found its source in a group of illustrations by artist Jamichael Henterly that the author was sent by an editor at Dutton. The illustrations featured a little girl with several animals, most in snowy settings. "I took about three seconds worth of a look at the pictures and said, 'Yes, there is a story'," Pierce related. *Where the Wild Geese Go* tells of Truzjka, a young girl who sets out to save her ailing grandmother by searching for the home of the wild geese. A careless girl by nature, Truzjka is forced to overcome her thoughtless ways during her quest in a book that a *Publishers Weekly* contributor praised as weaving "an enchanting aura, full of descriptive imag-

ery and mysterious allusions, all of which fit together into a cohesive whole." Noting that the story "combines elements of mystical fantasy and moral tale," *School Library Journal* contributor Eleanor K. MacDonald added that *Where the Wild Geese Go* "will appeal to . . . younger readers of fantasy."

In addition to her writing, Pierce works full-time at her local county library. As she once explained, she has "a reasonably good time telling little children to quit running on the stairs and helping them look for the shark books." But although she enjoys working in the library, she prefers writing, comparing it to "going to sleep and dreaming a wonderful dream." "To write a novel," she concluded in *Horn Book,* "is to be in love."

BIOGRAPHICAL/CRITICAL SOURCES:

BOOKS

Chambers, Nancy, editor, *The Signal Review: A Selective Guide to Children's Books,* Thimble Press (South Woodchester, England), 1984.
Children's Literature Review, Volume 20, Gale (Detroit, MI), 1990.
Pierce, Meredith Ann, interview with Diane Telgen for *Something about the Author,* Volume 67, Gale (Detroit, MI), 1992.
St. James Guide to Fantasy Writers, St. James Press (Detroit, MI), 1996.
St. James Guide to Young Adult Writers, second edition, St. James Press (Detroit, MI), 1999.
Twentieth Century Young Adult Writers, St. James Press (Detroit, MI), 1994.

PERIODICALS

ALAN Review, winter, 1986, p. 31.
Booklist, October 15, 1985, p. 330; February 15, 1986, p. 870; January 1, 1990; January 15, 1990, p. 991; March 1, 1990, p. 1356; May 15, 1992, p. 1674; April 15, 1996, Chris Sherman, review of *The Son of Summer Stars,* p. 1434; April 15, 2001, Sally Estes, review of *Treasure at the Heart of the Tanglewood,* p. 1557.
Book Report, May, 1986, p. 32; May, 1990, p. 49; March, 1999, Patsy Launspach, review of *A Gathering of Gargoyles,* p. 63.
Bulletin of the Center for Children's Books, July-August, 1982; February, 1985, p. 114; December, 1985, p. 75; January, 1986, p. 94.

English Journal, April, 1985, Beth Nelms, review of *A Gathering of Gargoyles,* p. 84; January, 1991, p. 80.

Fantasy Review, May, 1985, p. 20; April, 1986, p. 31.

Horn Book, August, 1982, p. 416; September, 1983, p. 245; October, 1984, p. 765; November-December, 1984, Ann A. Flowers, review of *A Gathering of Gargoyles,* p. 765; March-April, 1986, pp. 208-209; January-February, 1988, pp. 35-41; May-June, 1988, Ann A. Flowers, review of *Where the Wild Geese Go,* p. 349; May-June, 1990, p. 340; July, 2001, review of *Treasure at the Heart of the Tanglewood,* p. 460.

Horn Book Guide, January, 1990, p. 254; fall, 1996, Anne Deifendeifer, review of *The Son of Summer Stars,* p. 304.

Journal of Adolescent and Adult Literacy, November, 1999, Magda Gere Lewis, review of *A Gathering of Gargoyles,* pp. 300-301.

Journal of Reading, November, 1990, p. 234.

Kirkus Reviews, September 15, 1985, p. 992; October 1, 1985, p. 1090; February 1, 1988, p. 205; January 1, 1990, p. 49; May 15, 1992, review of *Dark Moon,* p. 674.

Library Journal, May 15, 1982, Paula M. Strain, review of *The Darkangel,* p. 1012.

Locus, January, 1990, p. 52; July, 1990, p. 15; October, 1990, p. 53; October, 1991, p. 52; June, 1992, p. 56.

Magazine of Fantasy and Science Fiction, November, 1984, p. 38.

New York Times Book Review, April 25, 1982, pp. 35, 47; November 30, 1982; December 5, 1982, review of *The Darkangel,* p. 16; December 30, 1984, p. 19; February 16, 1986, review of *Birth of the Firebringer,* p. 22.

Publishers Weekly, April 2, 1982, review of *The Darkangel,* p. 71; November 30, 1984, p. 92; June 7, 1985, p. 80; December 20, 1985, p. 65; February 12, 1988, review of *Where the Wild Geese Go,* p. 82; February 9, 1990, review of *The Pearl at the Soul of the World,* p. 63; May 29, 2000, review of *The Woman Who Loved Reindeer,* p. 84; May 7, 2001, review of *Treasure at the Heart of the Tanglewood,* p. 248.

School Library Journal, March, 1982, Ruth M. McConnell, review of *The Darkangel,* p. 160; December, 1984, review of *A Gathering of Gargoyles,* p. 94; December, 1985, p. 104; January, 1986, Holly Sanhuber, review of *Birth of the Firebringer,* p. 70; June-July, 1988, Eleanor K. MacDonald, review of *Where the Wild Geese Go,* p. 94; April, 1990, Ruth S. Vose, review of *The Pearl at the Soul of the World,* p. 145; June, 1992, JoAnn Rees, review of *Dark Moon,* pp. 139-140; April, 1996, Mary Jo Drungil, review of *The Son of Summer Stars,*

p. 157; June, 2001, Bruce Anne Shook, review of *Treasure at the Heart of the Tanglewood,* p. 153.

Voice of Youth Advocates, April, 1986, p. 41; June, 1990, p. 138; August, 1992, p. 178.

Wilson Library Bulletin, March, 1986, review of *The Woman Who Loved Reindeer,* pp. 50-51.*

* * *

POLLACK, Rachel (Grace) 1945-

PERSONAL: Born in 1945, in United States.

ADDRESSES: Home—Dutchess County, NY. *Office*—c/o Author's Mail, St. Martin's Press, 175 Fifth Ave., New York, NY 10010.

CAREER: Writer and Tarot card artist. Lectures widely on the modern interpretation of the Tarot.

AWARDS, HONORS: Arthur C. Clarke Award for best British science-fiction novel, 1988, for *Unquenchable Fire;* Nebula Award nomination, 1995, for *Temporary Agency;* World Fantasy Award for best novel, World Fantasy Convention, 1997, for *Godmother Night.*

WRITINGS:

NOVELS

Golden Vanity, Berkley (New York, NY), 1980.

Alqua Dreams, F. Watts (New York, NY), 1987.

Unquenchable Fire, Century (London, England), 1988, Overlook Press (Woodstock, NY), 1992.

Temporary Agency, St. Martin's Press (New York, NY), 1994.

Godmother Night, St. Martin's Press (New York, NY), 1996.

A Secret Woman, St. Martin's Press (New York, NY), 2001.

NONFICTION

Seventy-Eight Degrees of Wisdom: A Book of Tarot (two volumes), Aquarian Press (Wellingborough, England), 1980-1983, Borgo Press (San Bernardino, CA), 1986.

Salvador Dali's Tarot, Salem House (Salem, NH), 1985.

A Practical Guide to Fortune Telling: Palmistry, the Crystal Ball, Runes, Tea Leaves, the Tarot, Sphere/Rainbird (London, England), 1986, published as *Teach Yourself Fortune Telling,* Holt (New York, NY), 1986.

Tarot: The Open Labyrinth, Aquarian Press (Wellingborough, England), 1986, Borgo Press (San Bernardino, CA), 1989.

The New Tarot, Aquarian Press (Wellingborough, England), 1989, Overlook Press (Woodstock, NY), 1990.

Tarot Readings and Meditations, Aquarian Press (Wellingborough, England), 1990.

The Body of the Goddess: Sacred Wisdom in Myth, Landscape, and Culture, Element (Rockport, MA), 1997.

The Haindl Tarot: A Reader's Handbook, U.S. Games Systems (Stamford, CT), 1999.

The Complete Illustrated Guide to Tarot, Element (Boston, MA), 1999.

The Power of Ritual, Dell (New York, NY), 2000.

The Shining Tribe Tarot: Awakening the Universal Spirit, Llewellyn (St. Paul, MN), 2001.

OTHER

(Editor, with Caitlin Matthews) *Tarot Tales,* Legend (London, England), 1989.

(Editor, with Mary K. Greer) *New Thoughts on Tarot: Transcripts from the First International Newcastle Tarot Symposium,* Newcastle Publishing (North Hollywood, CA), 1989.

(With Gisela Gamper) *Fabrications,* Station Hill Arts (Tarrytown, NY), 1997.

Burning Sky (short stories), Cambrian (Miami, FL), 1998.

Author of short stories, including "Angel Baby," "The Protector," and "The Malignant One." Contributor to magazines and anthologies.

Pollack's work has been translated into Spanish, French, German, Italian, Portuguese, Dutch, and Danish.

SIDELIGHTS: Rachel Pollack has used her interest in the occult to establish literary careers both as a Tarot expert and as a science-fiction novelist. Her writing on the Tarot is considered by many to be authoritative, and her award-winning novels, including *Unquenchable Fire,* explore worlds in which magic is ordinary. In addition to writing, Pollack, who lived for almost twenty years in Europe before returning to her home state of New York, is an active Tarot reader and artist whose work is frequently sensual, philosophically minded, and feminist.

Pollack's first novel, *Golden Vanity,* initially attracted little attention when it was published in 1980; David V. Barrett, in *Twentieth-Century Science-Fiction Writers,* called it "neglected." *Golden Vanity,* according to Barrett, is a traditional science-fiction yarn with New Age overtones. While describing first contact between earthlings and aliens, it also delves into the terrain of meditation and religious self-deception.

Pollack's second novel, *Alqua Dreams,* also contains a traditional science-fiction premise, in this case an interstellar trader's attempt to establish trade with a new planet in order to obtain a mineral necessary for the operation of spaceships. Barrett considered the novel's philosophical theme to be "the age-old debate between Platonic and Aristotelian life-views," while *Analog* magazine reviewer Tom Easton noted the novel's "complex, difficult subtext of epistemological puzzling." The plot concerns space trader Jaimi Cooper, who visits Keela, a world whose inhabitants believe they are dead and that nothing is real. Because they believe they are dead, the Keelans also believe that Cooper's efforts to initiate commerce are unreal. In order to establish business with them, Cooper must convince them to abandon their beliefs. A *Publishers Weekly* critic enjoyed the novel's premise, but felt that it might have been explored more effectively as a short story. Barrett appreciated the "encyclopedic knowledge of religion and myth" that Pollack brings to *Alqua Dreams,* and considered the book's premise worthy and intriguing. Indeed, not since Philip Jose Farmer's *Night of Light,* a generation earlier, had Barrett found a more "disturbing and believable" exposition of an alien religion in a science fiction work.

Pollack's *Unquenchable Fire,* won the Arthur C. Clarke Award for best British science-fiction novel of 1988. Nevertheless, it was several years before the book found a U.S. publisher. Reviewer Gregory Feeley speculated in his review for the *Washington Post Book World* that the delay in acceptance by U.S. bookmakers resulted from Pollack's use of eclectic forms of magic as the basis for the book's fantasy, rather than the fairy tales and European folklore underlying most science-fiction novels. Aspects of the plot are familiar to fantasy and science-fiction readers, however, as a *Publishers Weekly* contributor pointed out, for the book describes a future United States—Dutchess County, New York, to be specific—in which the laws of the universe have changed and magic reigns. The twist is that the original sense of wonder has fallen away, and magic now seems routine.

The main character of *Unquenchable Fire,* Jennifer Mazdan, finds herself pregnant with a child who, according to magical signs, may be able to reawaken the lost sense of wonder at magic powers. This main plot is interwoven with tales of other aspects of life in the magical United States of America. Feeley found the novel's interpolations difficult and didactic, but called the main story "witty, absorbing and frequently funny." John Clute, reviewing the novel for the London *Observer,* went further and called it "dense, supple, and hilarious, by far her finest novel to date," and *Publishers Weekly* dubbed Pollack's third novel a "compelling, surrealistic fantasy." Barrett also liked the book. "It's by no means an easy book," he wrote, "but it is a very powerful and stimulating examination of the spiritual life."

Pollack's next novel, *Temporary Agency,* is comprised of two linked novellas, and acts as a sequel to *Unquenchable Fire* in that it assumes the reader is familiar with the characters from that novel, as well as with their magical powers. In the title novella, the main characters become involved with a being called a Malignant One and discover, according to a *Publishers Weekly* contributor, "what people will do in the name of pragmatism." In the second novella, "Benign Adjustments," characters Ellen and Alison find out "how the most benign intentions can be adulterated by human frailties." The settings of *Temporary Agency* include a Manhattan advertising agency and the floor of the New York Stock Exchange, where traders obtain assistance from magical robes and dolls.

A contributor to *Publishers Weekly* called *Temporary Agency* "a first-rate work" and commended it for combining rational speculation with an awareness that "the key to good fiction is people and what happens to them." *Library Journal* reviewer Jackie Cassada hailed the book as a "brilliant extrapolation of a spiritually awakened society" that "bears witness to [Pollack's] potent literary imagination," while Maureen F. McHugh praised the novel in the *Washington Post Book World* for being unsentimental and "full of ambiguity and loss." Pollack, McHugh concluded, "has written a fantasy book for grown-ups." *Temporary Agency* was a finalist for the 1994 Nebula Award.

Pollack's next novel, *Godmother Night,* is based on an ancient myth of a fantasy world that exists on the back of a giant turtle. The main characters are two young women, Laurie and Jaqe, who are lovers. Meeting Mother Night, who is really Death, enables the couple to overcome social obstacles in their path, but at the price of the early death of one of the women soon after the birth of their child. Mother Night then becomes a godmother figure to the child, easing its passage through life. Noting the novel's "resourceful and original" plot, a *Publishers Weekly* critic called *Godmother Night* "another fine outing by one of the most gifted and sensitive fantasists working today."

Burning Sky is a collection of twenty-seven short stories by Pollack, many previously unpublished, printed in a limited edition of 300 signed hardcover copies. Some of the stories are related to Pollack's previous novels, and most concern her central themes of sexuality, philosophy, and magic. Each story is followed by an afterword that discusses how Pollack came to write the story and what its themes are. Stories include "General All-Purpose Fairy Tale," which is exactly one-hundred words long, and "Is Your Child Using Drugs? Seven Ways to Recognize a Drug Addict," which is inspired by fear-inducing propaganda. Emily Streight, reviewing the book for *Rain Taxi,* noted that the stories range so widely that it often seems as if they were not written by the same author. Praising *Burning Sky,* the critic called the stories "polished performances of speculative fiction, effortlessly dancing on the tightrope between magic realism, social commentary, psychological portrait, and true science fiction."

Pollack's simultaneous careers as an occultist and novelist have won her acclaim. She has written a text for a Tarot deck illustrated by surrealist painter Salvador Dali, and has authored *The New Tarot,* which in "delightful and richly illustrated" fashion, according to Barrett, examines more than seventy commercial Tarot decks of the past generation. In 1986 Pollack published *A Practical Guide to Fortune Telling: Palmistry, the Crystal Ball, Runes, Tea Leaves, the Tarot,* which was issued in the United States as *Teach Yourself Fortune Telling.* Reviewing the work for the *Voice Literary Supplement,* Stacey D'Erasmo said: "I've been waiting for this book my whole life." Pollack's wide-ranging introduction to divination deals with palmistry, tea-leaf reading, Tarot, and other methods of foretelling the future, from the standpoint of character analysis rather than fortune telling in the strict sense. The author's thesis is that hidden patterns underlie the seemingly random events that occur in individuals' lives. Examining the apparent randomness, whether in a shuffled deck of cards or in the arrangement of leaves or in other phenomena, will unveil these patterns. D'Erasmo called Pollack "a gentle and learned guide" and singled out the Tarot section—the book's longest—for praise, saying, "amidst the flood of Tarot decks and guides now on the market, Pollack's is remarkably clear and free of gooeyness."

BIOGRAPHICAL/CRITICAL SOURCES:

BOOKS

Watson, Noelle, and Paul E. Schellinger, editors, *Twentieth-Century Science-Fiction Writers,* 3rd edition, St. James Press (Detroit, MI), 1991.

PERIODICALS

Analog, September, 1988, pp. 181-182; December, 1992, Tom Easton, review of *Unquenchable Fire,* p. 161; May, 1995, T. Easton, review of *Temporary Agency,* p. 162; June, 1997, T. Easton, review of *Godmother Night,* p. 145.
Booklist, August, 1994, Whitney Scott, review of *Temporary Agency,* p. 2030.
Library Journal, April 15, 1992, Jackie Cassada, review of *Unquenchable Fire,* p. 125; August, 1994, J. Cassada, review of *Temporary Agency,* p. 139.
Magazine of Fantasy and Science Fiction, September, 1995, Charles de Lint, review of *The Vertigo Tarot,* p. 29; June, 1997, C. de Lint, review of *Godmother Night,* p. 24.
Observer (London) December 18, 1988, p. 43.
Publishers Weekly, October 2, 1987, p. 87; March 23, 1992, p. 64; July 25, 1994, review of *Temporary Agency,* p. 38; August 26, 1996, p. 78.
Voice Literary Supplement, July/August, 1993, p. 20.
Washington Post Book World, April 26, 1992, p. 6; September 25, 1994, p. 14.

OTHER

Rain Taxi, http://wwww.raintaxi.com/ (December 14, 2000), Emily Streight, review of *Burning Sky.**

*   *   *

PONDER, Patricia
    See MAXWELL, Patricia

*   *   *

POWYS, John Cowper 1872-1963

PERSONAL: Surname is pronounced "*Po*-is"; born October 8, 1872, in Shirley, Derbyshire, England; came to United States, 1928; died June 17, 1963, in Merionethshire, Wales; son of Charles Francis (an Anglican

John Cowper Powys

clergyman) and Mary Cowper (Johnson) Powys; married Margaret Alice Lyon, 1896 (died, 1947); children: one son. *Education:* Corpus Christi College, M.A.

CAREER: Educator, critic, novelist, and poet. Lecturer in literature at universities in England, including Oxford and Cambridge; lecturer at universities in the United States, winters, c. 1904-34; lived in New York, NY, 1928-34; returned to Wales, 1934; full-time writer, c. 1934-60.

AWARDS, HONORS: Honorary doctor of letters from University of Wales.

WRITINGS:

Odes and Other Poems, Rider & Co. (London, England), 1896.
Poems, Rider & Co. (London, England), 1899.
The War and Culture: A Reply to Professor Münsterberg, G. A. Shaw, 1914, published as *The Menace of German Culture: A Reply to Professor Münsterberg,* Rider & Co. (London, England), 1915.

Visions and Revisions: A Book of Literary Devotions, G. A. Shaw, 1915, Core Collection (Great Neck, NY), 1978.

Wood and Stone: A Romance, G. A. Shaw, 1915.

Wolf's-Bane Rhymes (poems), G. A. Shaw, 1916.

Confessions of Two Brothers, Manas Press, 1916, reprinted, Scholarly Press (St. Clair Shores, MI), 1971.

One Hundred Best Books, G. A. Shaw, 1916.

Rodmoor: A Romance, G. A. Shaw, 1916, revised edition with preface by G. Wilson Knight, Colgate University Press (Hamilton, NY), 1973.

Suspended Judgments: Essays on Books and Sensations, G. A. Shaw, 1916, reprinted, Norwood Editions (Norwood, PA), 1977.

Mandragora (poems), G. A. Shaw, 1917.

The Complex Vision, Dodd (New York, NY), 1920.

T. Seltzer, Samphire, 1922.

The Art of Happiness, Haldeman-Julius, 1923, reprinted, Village Press (London, England), 1974.

Psychoanalysis and Morality, J. Colbert, 1923, reprinted, Village Press (London, England), 1975.

Ducdame (novel), Doubleday (New York, NY), 1925.

The Religion of a Sceptic (essays), Dodd (New York, NY), 1925, reprinted, Village Press (London, England), 1975.

The Secret of Self-Development, Haldeman-Julius, 1926, reprinted, Village Press (London, England), 1974.

The Art of Forgetting the Unpleasant, Haldeman-Julius, 1928, reprinted, Village Press (London, England), 1974.

The Meaning of Culture (essays), Norton (New York, NY), 1929, reprinted, Greenwood Press (Westport, CT), 1979.

Wolf Solent (novel), Simon & Schuster (New York, NY), 1929, reprinted, Vintage Books (New York, NY), 1998.

The Owl, the Duck, and—Miss Rowe! Miss Rowe! (short stories), Black Archer Press, 1930, reprinted, Village Press (London, England), 1975.

In Defence of Sensuality (essays), Simon & Schuster (New York, NY), 1930, reprinted, Village Press (London, England), 1974.

(With Bertrand Russell) *Debate: Is Modern Marriage a Failure?,* Discussion Guild (New York, NY), 1930, reprinted, Warren House (North Walsham, Norfolk, England), 1983.

Dorothy M. Richardson, Joiner & Steele, 1931.

A Glastonbury Romance (novel), Simon & Schuster (New York, NY), 1932, reprinted, Overlook Press (New York, NY), 1987.

A Philosophy of Solitude (essays), Simon & Schuster (New York, NY), 1933, reprinted, Village Press (London, England), 1974.

Weymouth Sands (novel), Simon & Schuster (New York, NY), 1934, reprinted with an introduction by Angus Wilson, Rivers Press, 1973, new edition, Overlook Press (Woodstock, NY), 1999.

Autobiography, Simon & Schuster (New York, NY), 1934, revised edition with introduction by J. B. Priestley and notes by R. I. Blackmore, Colgate University Press (Hamilton, NY), 1968.

Jobber Skald (novel), John Lane (London, England), 1935.

Maiden Castle (novel), Simon & Schuster (New York, NY), 1936, new edition, Overlook Press (Woodstock, NY), 2001.

Morwyn; or, The Vengeance of God (novel), Cassell (London, England), 1937, reprinted, Sphere (London, England), 1977.

Enjoyment of Literature (essays), Simon & Schuster (New York, NY), 1938, published as *The Pleasures of Literature,* Cassell (London, England), 1938.

Owen Glendower (novel), Simon & Schuster (New York, NY), 1940, reprinted, Chivers (London, England), 1974.

Mortal Strife, J. Cape (London, England), 1942, reprinted, Village Press (London, England), 1974.

The Art of Growing Old (essays), J. Cape (London, England), 1944.

Dostoievsky (essays), John Lane (London, England), 1946, reprinted, Haskell House, 1973.

Pair Dadeni; or, The Cauldron of Rebirth, Druid Press, 1946.

Obstinste Cymric: Essays 1935-1947, Druid Press, 1947, reprinted, Village Press (London, England), 1973.

Rabelais: His Life, the Story Told by Him, Selections Therefrom Here Newly Translated, and an Interpretation of His Genius and His Religion, Bodley Head (London, England), 1948, reprinted, Village Press (London, England), 1974.

The Inmates (novel), Philosophical Library (New York, NY), 1952.

In Spite Of: A Philosophy for Everyman (essays), Philosophical Library (New York, NY), 1953.

Atlantis (essays), Macdonald (London, England), 1954, reprinted, Chivers, 1973.

The Brazen Head (novel), Colgate University Press (Hamilton, NY), 1956.

Lucifer: A Poem, Macdonald (London, England), 1956.

Up and Out (contains "Up and Out" and "The Mountains of the Moon"), Macdonald (London, England), 1957, reprinted, Village Press (London, England), 1974.

Culture and Nature, edited by Ichiro Hara, Hokuseido Press, c. 1958.

Letters of John Cowper Powys to Louis Wilkinson, 1935-1956, Colgate University Press (Hamilton, NY), 1958.

Culture and Life, edited by Ichiro Hara, Hokuseido Press, c. 1958.

Homer and the Aether, Macdonald (London, England), 1959.

All or Nothing, Macdonald (London, England), 1960.

John Cowper Powys: A Selection from His Poems, edited with introduction by Kenneth Hopkins, Colgate University Press (Hamilton, NY), 1964.

Letters from John Cowper Powys to Glyn Hughes, edited by Bernard Jones, Ore Publications, 1971.

Letters to Nicholas Ross, edited by Arthur Uphill, Bertram Rota, 1971.

William Blake, Village Press (London, England), 1974.

John Cowper Powys: Letters, 1937-1954, edited with introduction and notes by Iorwerth C. Peate, University of Wales Press, 1974.

Romer Mowl and Other Stories (contains "Romer Mowl," "The Spot on the Wall," and "The Harvest Thanksgiving"), edited by Bernard Jones, Toucan Press, 1974.

Two and Two, Village Press (London, England), 1974.

An Englishman Up-State, Village Press (London, England), 1974.

Real Wraiths, Village Press (London, England), 1974.

Letters of John Cowper Powys to His Brother Llewellyn, edited by Malcolm Elwin, Volume 1: *1902-1925,* Volume 2: *1925-1939,* Village Press (London, England), 1975.

You and Me, Village Press (London, England), 1975.

After My Fashion (novel), Picador (New York, NY), 1980.

The Letters of John Cowper Powys to Sven-Erik Täckmark, C. Woolf (London, England), 1983.

Horned Poppies: New Poems, Warren House (North Walsham, Norfolk, England), 1983.

Three Fantasies, Carcanet (Manchester, England), 1985.

The Letters of John Cowper Powys to Ichiro Hara, edited by Anthony Head, C. Woolf (London, England), 1990.

The Letters of John Cowper Powys to Hal W. and Violet Trovillion, edited by Paul Roberts, introduction by Kenneth Hopkins, C. Woolf (London, England), 1990.

Porius: A Romance of the Dark Ages (novel), Macdonald, 1951, revised edition, Colgate University Press (Hamilton, NY), 1994.

Petrushka and the Dancer: The Diaries of John Cowper Powys, 1929-1939, edited by Morine Krissdóttir, St. Martin's Press (New York, NY), 1995.

The Letters of John Cowper Powys to Frances Gregg, C. Woolf (London, England), 1995.

The Dorset Year: The Diary of John Cowper Powys, 1934-July, 1935, Powys Press (Kilmersdon), 1998.

Contributor to periodicals, including *Dial, American Mercury,* and *Century.* Powys's manuscripts are collected at Churchill College, Cambridge Colgate University; and Humanities Research Center, University of Texas, Austin.

SIDELIGHTS: John Cowper Powys was a prodigious wordsmith—a novelist, lecturer, and philosopher whose works tackled spirituality and sensuality from an eclectic perspective. Powys authored both realistic and fantastic novels—some of which ran to thousands of pages—and is best known for his exploration of ancient Welsh and pre-Christian religions and myths. His writings attracted a wide audience during the middle decades of the twentieth century, and many remained in still in print or were reissued almost a half century later. In the *Atlantic Monthly,* Lawrence Millman called Powys "a maximalist writer in an increasingly minimalist age . . . an almost pathological celebrant of oddball sex and chthonic realms." His books, to quote *World Literature Today* correspondent Bernard F. Dick, are "overlong, repetitive, but undeniably brilliant . . . an exercise in the art of imagination, if not the art of fiction."

Powys belonged to a noted literary family. His mother was collaterally related to British poets William Cowper and John Donne. Of Powys's immediate family, six of his ten brothers and sisters also published books, although only two others, Llewellyn and Theodore Francis, achieved literary prominence. Powys published his first novel when he was forty-three years old, and continued a prolific writing career well into his eighties. Many of his works deal with myths, cosmic fantasies, and the elemental forces of nature. *A Glastonbury Romance,* for example, is an adaptation of the myth that Joseph of Arimathea possessed the Holy Grail. In his writings Powys seeks to convey his personal philosophies, and as a result the characters often seem to soliloquize instead of talk.

It has been said of Powys's lectures and writings that they reveal more about him than about the intended subject. No matter how odd the characters, "nobody in a novel by Mr. Powys is ever as interesting as the author himself," observed Mark Van Doren in his introduction to *The Private Reader: Selected Articles and Reviews.* "His best book is still his 'Autobiography,' which is completely and frankly about himself, and where to be sure he confesses that he has made an art out of acting as if he were even more interesting than he is." But despite the autobiographical nature of all his work, Glen Cavaliero insisted in *John Cowper Powys,*

Novelist, that "far from being narrowly egoistic and inward-turning, [it] is a projection of the self into an autonomous world of the imagination which is accessible to everyone."

An important theme in Powys's writing is man's sexual nature. In *Saturnian Quest: A Chart of the Prose Works of John Cowper Powys,* G. Wilson Knight assessed his treatment of the subject as "both unorthodox and traditional." Powys clearly presents man's obsession with the "bisexual . . . vision which, though transmitted through human figures, speaks from a dimension beyond the biological." His handling of human sexuality is strangely impersonal, according to Knight, in that "there is a divergence from ordinary desire to a more refined but impersonal and cerebral fascination." In Knight's opinion, "probably [Powys's] most important contribution to our religious tradition is his insistence that 'no religion that doesn't deal with sex-longing in some kind of way is much use to us.'"

Powys's writings tell us that he himself is "half a woman" and thus, he can understand sexual matters from a woman's point of view. But as Knight pointed out, Powys's fictional women are generally presented as stereotypical "normal" girls and are less individualized than the male characters. The only in-depth female characters are "those who have, or touch, boylike attributes, such as Gladys in *Wood and Stone,* Philippa in *Rodmoor,* and Persephone Spear in *A Glastonbury Romance.*"

Most of Powys's novels are extremely long and, as Knight explained, "his mastery of the long sentence, like the wielding of a giant's club, tempts him, on occasion, too far." A *Times Literary Supplement* reviewer called Powys a "self-indulgent writer . . . [who was] never fully master of the pace and cohesion of an entire novel," and complained about his "coyness or archness, his literary echoes, his use of capital letters, italics, hyphens, and exclamation marks to draw attention to what should be sufficiently challenging in itself." On the other hand, many of the same critics who panned Powys also praised him as a genius for his eloquence, humor, and cunning irony. Another *Times Literary Supplement* essayist explained this paradox: "Powys is rather like life itself: you can object strongly to parts of it, and be often baffled for a meaning, but the sum total impresses."

Powys's writing is usually divided into three periods: his early novels of contemporary life; his historical novels; and the futuristic, allegorical fantasies of his later years. Thematically linking the stories of these three eras of his work is the author's belief that modern civilization deters the individual from examining thoroughly the complexities of life. Written in 1920, Powys's posthumously published novel, *After My Fashion,* is considered among the most autobiographical of his novels. The protagonist of the work, Richard Storm, is a well-traveled literary critic who becomes romantically involved with a dancer named Elise Angel. Storm leaves Paris for his ancestral home in England—the village of Littlegate, in Sussex. "He is escaping from Elise, running away from an uncontrollable emotional situation, and he is coming to terms with England and the war," commented Charles Lock in *Listener.* "Powys's situation was similar." Originally published in 1935 as *Jobber Skald* and later published in a new edition, the novel *Weymouth Sands* exhibits both autobiographical elements and Powys's interest in the occult, incorporating many concepts of alchemy and other supernatural beliefs. The title comes from a coastal resort town that was the home of Powys's paternal grandmother. The work vividly evokes its coastal setting and reveals Powys's characteristic complexity and depth, exploring the experiences of several characters whose lives become intricately intertwined through romance, desire, and hatred.

Powys's *Three Fantasies* is often categorized as an example of the fantasy writing he produced during his later years. Contrasting with Powys's tendency toward longer forms, the collection of stories presents an example of his work in shorter forms. "Topsy Turvy" portrays a philosophical dialogue between two inanimate objects—a door handle and a child's painting. "Abertacklе" focuses on the ruminations and discussions of a group of villagers and presents a "philosophy of escape" in its assertion that "Life is a frantic struggle to escape from the old traditional legacies and myths and customs and convictions." "Abertackle" was viewed as "both bleaker and more bizarre" than "Topsy Turvy" by John Melmoth in his review for the *Times Literary Supplement.* Using a blend of science fiction, fantasy, and the absurd, "Cataclysm" depicts a war waged between two groups of fantastical characters.

Also revealing Powys's interest in magical themes is *Porius: A Romance of the Dark Ages.* Set in Arthurian Wales near the end of the fifth century, *Porius* revolves around conflicts and battles between various cults and nationalities during the Dark Ages and features many characters from the *Mabinogion,* Welsh history, and Arthurian legends. Critics emphasized the labyrinthine complexity of the work, frequently noting that it makes difficult, though linguistically fascinating, reading.

"Within the tradition of prose fiction, and of the novel in particular, certain books [including *Porius*] have been written . . . to explore and expose the scene of reading itself, of language as the defining state of human being," asserted Jerome McGann of *Times Literary Supplement*. "To enter any of these books is to be lost in wonder." Millman called *Porius* "Powys's masterpiece" and compared it to such classics of literature as *One Hundred Years of Solitude, Finnegan's Wake,* and *Alice in Wonderland*. The critic explained: "At times it reads like an extended study of what Powys called 'the three incomprehensibles': sex, religion, and nature. At other times it reads like a magical mystery extravaganza." *Porius* eventually reappeared in an unabridged version; 600 pages of the original manuscript were deleted prior to its initial publication in 1951.

Powys continued to write well into his eighties—as Millman put it, his "literary output in old age was so voluminous that upon learning he had died in his ninety-first year, in 1963, one is almost inclined to say 'Yes, but did he stop writing?'" His last fictions, some collected in *Three Fantasies,* were characterized as "the most eccentric works ever penned" by a contributor to the *St. James Guide to Fantasy Writers*. The critic concluded: "No other writer ever provided such a detailed account of his descent into mental incoherence, but it cannot be denied that Powys's account is of considerable interest and value precisely because it is unparalleled. There is a measure of real heroism in the desperate and obsessed groping for enlightenment and understanding which these stories represent."

BIOGRAPHICAL/CRITICAL SOURCES:

BOOKS

Brebner, John A., *The Demon Within: A Study of John Cowper Powys's Novels*, Macdonald (London, England), 1973.

Breckon, Richard, *John Cowper Powys: The Solitary Giant*, K. A. Ward, 1969.

Cavaliero, Glen, *John Cowper Powys, Novelist*, Clarendon Press (Oxford, England), 1973.

Churchill, R. C., *The Powys Brothers*, Longman (London, England), 1962.

Coates, C. A., *John Cowper Powys: In Search of a Landscape*, Macmillan (London, England), 1982.

Collins, Harold P., *John Cowper Powys: Old Earthman*, Barrie & Rockliff (London, England), 1966.

Contemporary Literary Criticism, Gale (Detroit, MI), Volume 7, 1977, Volume 9, 1978, Volume 15, 1980, Volume 46, 1988.

De Wet, Oloff, *A Visit to John Cowper Powys*, Village Press (London, England), 1974.

Dictionary of Literary Biography, Volume 15: *British Novelists, 1930-1959*, Gale (Detroit, MI), 1983.

Fawkner, H. W., *The Ecstatic World of John Cowper Powys*, Fairleigh Dickinson University Press (Rutherford, NJ), 1986.

Graves, Richard Perceval, *The Brothers Powys*, Routledge (London, England), 1983.

Hooker, Jeremy, *John Cowper Powys*, University of Wales Press (Cardiff, Wales), 1973.

Hooker, Jeremy, *Writers in a Landscape*, University of Wales Press (Cardiff, Wales), 1996.

Hopkins, Kenneth, *The Powys Brothers: A Biographical Appreciation*, Fairleigh Dickinson University Press (Rutherford, NJ), 1967.

Humtrey, Belinda, editor, *Essays on John Cowper Powys*, University of Wales Press (Cardiff, Wales), 1972.

Humtrey, Belinda, *John Cowper Powys's "Wolf Solent": Critical Studies*, University of Wales Press (Cardiff, Wales), 1990.

Knight, George Wilson, *Saturnian Quest: A Chart of the Prose Works of John Cowper Powys*, Barnes & Noble (New York, NY), 1964.

Knight, George Wilson, *Visions & Vices: Essays on John Cowper Powys*, C. Woolf (London, England), 1990.

Krissdöttir, Morine, *John Cowper Powys and the Magical Quest*, Macdonald & Jane's (London, England), 1980.

Lane, Denis, editor, *In the Spirit of Powys: New Essays*, with foreword by Jerome J. McGann, Bucknell University Press (Cranbury, NJ), 1990.

Marlowe, Louis, *Welsh Ambassadors: Powys Lives and Letters*, Chapman & Hall (London, England), 1936, revised edition, Colgate University Press (Hamilton, NY), 1971.

Miller, Henry, *The Immortal Bard*, Village Press (London, England), 1973.

Nordius, Janina, *"I Am Myself Alone": Solitude and Transcendence in John Cowper Powys*, Acta Universitatis Gothoburgensis, 1997.

Powys, John Cowper, *Autobiography*, Simon & Schuster (New York, NY), 1934, revised edition, Colgate University Press (Hamilton, NY), 1968.

Powys, *Confessions of Two Brothers*, Manas Press, 1916, reprinted, Scholarly Press, 1971.

Van Doren, Mark, *The Private Reader: Selected Articles and Reviews*, Holt (New York, NY), 1942.

PERIODICALS

American Scholar, spring, 1986, p. 248.

Atlantic Monthly, August, 2000, Lawrence Millman, "An Irresistible Long-winded Bore," p. 88.

Books and Bookmen, February, 1974; February, 1977; March, 1977.

British Book News, June, 1985, p. 364.

Chicago Tribune, December 21, 1987.

Choice, June, 1975; June, 1994, p. 1581.

Kirkus Reviews, February 15, 2001, review of *Maiden Castle,* p. 213.

Library Journal, July, 1985, p. 95.

Listener, August 7, 1980, p. 185.

London Magazine, February/March, 1973.

Modern Fiction Studies, summer, 1976.

New Statesman, October 10, 1980, p. 23.

New York Times Book Review, December 30, 1984; March 28, 1985, pp. 26-28.

Publishers Weekly, May 3, 1985, p. 69.

Science Fiction Studies, July, 1994, p. 251.

Spectator, April 22, 1995, p. 32; November 18, 1995, p. 49.

Times Literary Supplement, March 24, 1972; February 8, 1974; May 16, 1975; June 27, 1980, p. 726; June 14, 1985, p. 677; May 19, 1995, p. 3; December 1, 1995, p. 4.

Washington Post Book World, November 18, 1984, p. 12.

World Literature Today, autumn, 1994, Bernard F. Dick, review of *Porius: A Romance of the Dark Ages,* p. 813.*

*   *   *

PRESLEY, Priscilla (Ann Beaulieu) 1945-

PERSONAL: Born Priscilla Ann Wagner, May 24, 1945, in Brooklyn, NY; daughter of James (a Navy pilot) and Ann Wagner; married Elvis Presley (a singer and actor), May 1, 1967 (divorced, 1973); children: Lisa Marie, (with Marco Garibaldi) Navarone Anthony. *Education:* Studied acting with Milton Katselas, dance at Stephen Peck Theatre Art School, and karate at Chuck Norris Karate School. *Religion:* Scientologist.

ADDRESSES: Office—Graceland, P.O. Box 16508, Memphis, TN 38186. *Agent*—William Morris Agency, 151 El Camino Dr., Beverly Hills, CA 90212-2704.

CAREER: Actor, businesswoman, television personality, and author. Graceland, Memphis, TN, co-executor of estate; Bis and Beau (clothing design firm), founder; creator of signature fragrances "Moments," "Experiences," and "Indian Summer"; served as television spokesperson for beauty products. Member of board of directors, Metro Goldwyn Mayer, 2000—. Executive

producer of television movies, series, and specials, including *Elvis and Me,* ABC, 1988; (with others) *Elvis* (also known as *Elvis: Good Rockin' Tonight*), ABC, 1990; *Elvis: The Tribute,* ABC, 1994; *Elvis Aron Presley: The Tribute,* syndicated, 1994; and *The Road to Graceland,* 1998.

Actor in films, including *The Naked Gun—From the Files of Police Squad!,* Paramount, 1988; *The Adventures of Ford Fairlane* (also known as *Ford Fairlane*), Twentieth Century-Fox, 1990; *Naked Gun 2-1/2: The Smell of Fear,* Paramount, 1991; *Naked Gun 33-1/3: The Final Insult* (also known as *Naked Gun 3*), Paramount, 1994; (uncredited) *Austin Powers: International Man of Mystery,* New Line Cinema, 1997; and *Titanic Too: It Missed the Iceberg.*

Actor in television series, including *Those Amazing Animals,* ABC, 1980-81; and *Dallas,* CBS, 1983-88. Actor in television movies, including *Love Is Forever* (also known as *Comeback* and *Passion and Valour*), NBC, 1982; and *Breakfast with Einstein* (also known as *Fruhstuck mit Einstein*), 1998. Actor and host in television specials, including *The Barbara Walters Special,* ABC, 1985; *Night of 100 Stars II,* NBC, 1985; *Elvis' Graceland,* syndicated, 1987; *The 3rd Annual American Comedy Awards,* ABC, 1989; *Super Bloopers and New Practical Jokes,* NBC, 1989; *Naked Gun 2-1/2: Looking down the Barrel of Comedy,* HBO, 1991; *Rock the Vote,* Fox, 1992; *Elvis: The Great Performances,* CBS, 1992; *What Is This Thing Called Love?* (also known as *The Barbara Walters Special*), ABC, 1993; *Elvis: His Life and Times,* syndicated, 1993; *Elvis: The Tribute,* ABC, 1994; *Elvis Aron Presley: The Tribute,* syndicated, 1994; and *The Wonderful World of Disney: 40 Years of Television Magic,* ABC, 1994. Also guest actor in television series episodes, including (pilot) *Tom Snyder's Celebrity Spotlight,* NBC, 1980; *The Fall Guy,* ABC, 1981; *Tales from the Crypt,* HBO, 1993; and *Melrose Place,* Fox, 1996.

AWARDS, HONORS: Named a Fabulous Fashion Independent by Mr. Blackwell, 1980.

WRITINGS:

(As Priscilla Beaulieu Presley, with Sandra Harmon) *Elvis and Me* (memoir), Putnam (New York, NY), 1985.

SIDELIGHTS: Priscilla Presley will forever be connected with her ex-husband, legendary rock-and-roll singer Elvis Presley, but she has also made her own name as a savvy businesswoman. Though she began dating Elvis when she was just a freshman in high school, she picked up a good deal of business acumen along the way while watching his career rise and fall. After his death, she came into control of his estate once his father died, and as the executor of his estate, she transformed Graceland from a gaudy curiosity into a profitable, slick business. Presley also forged her own place in pop culture by appearing in the hilarious *Naked Gun* films with Leslie Neilsen and performing on prime-time television series. She has also dabbled in fashion design and fragrances. Presley recounted her years with the "King" in her 1985 autobiography, *Elvis and Me,* and in 2000 she was named to the Metro Goldwyn Mayer board of directors.

Presley was born on May 24, 1945, in Brooklyn, New York. She was the daughter of Lieutenant James Wagner, a Navy pilot who was killed when she was six months old. Her mother remarried when Presley was two-and-a-half, to career Air Force officer Joseph Paul Beaulieu, who adopted her. They had five more children together, Don, Michelle, Jeff, and twins Tim and Tom. The family moved to a new base every few years and had lived in six cities by the time Presley was eleven. Though she was exceptionally pretty, she was insecure.

In 1956, Presley's father gave her a copy of Elvis Presley's first album. She remarked in *Elvis and Me,* "Like almost every other kid in America, I liked Elvis but not as fanatically as many of my girlfriends at Del Valley Junior High." After finishing junior high, Presley's family moved to Wiesbaden, Germany, and her friends noted that Elvis Presley, who was serving in the military at the time, was stationed in nearby Bad Neuheim. At the time he entered the service, he was at the peak of his fame, with seventeen straight million-selling singles and four hit films to his credit.

One day at a club for military personnel and their families, Presley met a man who knew Elvis Presley and invited her to go to his house one evening. Elvis was drawn to the young American girl and they began dating. In March of 1960 he returned to the United States, and she remained in Germany. He called intermittently, and finally in 1962 she visited him in Los Angeles. She spent that Christmas with him, too, and they made plans for her to return and live with him.

At age sixteen, Presley moved to Memphis, where she enrolled at an all-girls Catholic high school and lived for a time with Elvis Presley's father and stepmother,

Vernon and Dee. But she soon moved into his twenty-three-room Georgian mansion, Graceland, and in the media earned the nickname "the live-in Lolita." During their courtship, he was intensely critical of her appearance and behavior. He insisted she wear heavy black eyeliner, as was the style of the 1960s, and a teased-up, dyed-black bouffant hairdo. Her posture and attitude were always under scrutiny as well. They also had many tender moments, though, frequently speaking baby talk to each other and calling each other pet names.

Despite Presley's efforts at pleasing Elvis, he nit-picked incessantly and they sometimes fought. She noted in her autobiography that his fury had a lot to with his reliance on prescription drugs, and she also began using pills to help her cope with the hectic schedule of dating a celebrity by night and trying to attend high school by day. In addition, Presley knew the star was having affairs with other women, including a much-publicized tryst with Ann-Margret during and after shooting *Viva Las Vegas.*

Nevertheless, Presley married her famous lover on May 1, 1967. To confuse reporters, they drove from Los Angeles to a rented home in Palm Springs, California, then left the next morning for Las Vegas, where they had a small ceremony at the Aladdin Hotel. Later, they celebrated at Graceland with their extended entourage of friends and family. In her autobiography, she made it clear that the two never consummated their relationship until their wedding night. Nine months later, she gave birth to Lisa Marie, and they both doted on her.

When they married, Elvis Presley's career had been on a downturn since the early 1960s, but by the late 1960s, he was entering his phase of headlining in Las Vegas. At the start things went well. His career was at a high point again, and he was in good physical shape. However, his family began to slip away. As Presley wrote in her book, "Thriving on all the excitement, glamour, and hysteria, he found it difficult to go home and resume his role as father and husband." He resumed touring, playing at huge arenas and staying away from home for long stretches of time.

Gradually, the Presley marriage disintegrated, and Presley herself began to have an affair with a karate expert in the early 1970s. Karate was one of Elvis Presley's longtime hobbies, and he had encouraged his wife to begin training as well. In addition to that, Presley was maturing and spreading her wings, taking art and dance classes. They separated in 1972 and divorced on October 9, 1973, but remained good friends, talking frequently on the phone and sharing custody of their daughter. "Elvis and I never treated the divorce as a divorce," Presley remarked to Jim Jerome in *Ladies Home Journal.* "We spent a lot of time together and remained very close. Lisa Marie remembers that vividly. She'll say, 'Mom, you and Dad never argued.' Those are the things you dream your kids will say. You don't have to divorce out of revenge or jealousy."

After the divorce, Elvis Presley's life entered a downward spiral. He was 80 pounds overweight, largely due to his continued drug abuse, and was the subject of much ridicule due to his appearance. His increasingly flashy stage outfits were to the point of being comical. In addition, his longtime manager, Colonel Tom Parker, had sold the rights to most of his songs in 1973.

Elvis Presley was found dead of a heart attack in his bathroom on August 16, 1977. He had named his father, Vernon, executor of his estate until his daughter, then nine, turned twenty-five. When Vernon Presley died in 1979, he named Presley executor. She found it increasingly difficult to keep up the fourteen-acre Graceland estate, where Elvis was buried alongside his parents and grandmother. He had squandered much of his wealth, and upkeep costs and taxes were too high.

By 1982, Presley decided to open the grounds of Graceland to the public. To handle this, she formed a business, Elvis Presley Enterprises (EPE), which became the operating arm of the trust that owns the Elvis Presley estate. Many fans were outraged. "The letters that came in, the phone calls, the threats," Presley told Suzanna Andrews in *Working Woman.* "I knew I wasn't really popular with them because we'd gotten a divorce, but I had no idea that there'd be so much opposition."

Presley felt she had no other option. First and foremost, she wanted to ensure the value of her daughter's inheritance. However, the mansion had been turned into "a carnival of crimes against good taste," as Andrews put it. Presley told her, "The first floor wasn't just red. It had feathers, it had teardrop lighting, it had leopard-skin pillows. It had fake-fur throw rugs. It was a Mae West type of look."

In addition, Elvis Presley had not died with dignity, and Presley wanted to deal with his memory respectfully. For ideas, she visited house museums and amusement parks such as San Simeon and the Smithsonian

Institution. Along with money manager Jack Soden, they decided to make the tours dignified yet personal. She also restored Graceland to its more tasteful blue, white, and gold furnishings that were present while she lived there.

By the early 1990s, the estate was a major tourist attraction worth more than $100 million, thanks in large part to Presley's management and marketing. When Lisa Marie Presley turned twenty-five, she became executor of the estate, but asked her mother to remain in control. Presley has all final approval on EPE merchandising decisions and also authorized the first official Elvis tribute, which was televised on pay-per-view in October of 1994. "We make an effort to keep his name and image alive," Presley told Vernon Scott in *Good Housekeeping.*

In addition to managing her ex-husband's estate and image, Presley forged some businesses on her own as well. In 1972, she opened her own clothing boutique, Bis and Beau, and attracted star clients like Barbra Streisand and Cher. She started the enterprise with the woman who designed her wardrobe, but Presley began to create and sell her own works as well. Four years later, she sold the operation to her partner. In the early 1990s for a brief time, Presley designed children's clothes under the name Gioco, which means "play" in Italian, and in the late 1990s, tried her hand again at apparel with the "River's Edge" Line.

Around 1987, Presley also began marketing her own fragrances. Concurrently, she sparked up a budding acting career, which went far in creating her own image apart from her ex-husband. In 1980, she hosted the television series *Those Amazing Animals,* and from 1983 to 1988, she created the sultry character of Jenna Wade on the highly rated prime-time drama *Dallas.* Then, she was a hit in the madcap *The Naked Gun—From the Files of Police Squad!,* released in 1988. She reprised her role of Jane Spencer in two sequels as well, in 1991 and 1994. After this, though, she traded the big screen for the small, appearing on episodes of *Melrose Place, Touched by an Angel,* and *Spin City* throughout the mid- to late-1990s.

The Presley name was in the spotlight once again in the summer of 1994 when Lisa Marie Presley announced she had married pop star Michael Jackson that May. Just one month earlier, her daughter announced her split from husband of six years, Danny Keough, a musician, with whom she had two children, Danielle and Benjamin. The wedding to Jackson was highly scrutinized in the media and short-lived, ending in early 1996.

Presley remained supportive of her daughter; she remarked to Scott in *Good Housekeeping,* "I learned a lot of vital things from my parents. . . . My parents and I are still friends because they allowed me to be myself. They did not try to control me when Elvis came into my life. It was too big and too powerful. You cannot fight love. You cannot." After her daughter's divorce from Jackson, Presley painted a picture of domestic tranquility for Jim Jerome in *Ladies Home Journal,* telling him, "Lisa Marie lives close by. We vacation together, baby-sit for each other and try to get the kids together as much as possible."

Presley and her daughter are also members of the Church of Scientology, a controversial religion founded by L. Ron Hubbard. Several top names in Hollywood are adherents, including Tom Cruise, Nicole Kidman, and John Travolta. Though her involvement with Scientology is often mentioned in the press, Presley rarely discusses it.

While working on *Dallas* in the mid-1980s, Presley met writer-director Marco Garibaldi, a Brazilian of Italian heritage who later became a computer programmer, and he became her longtime companion. They live in Bel-Air and had a son, Navarone, in 1987. She noted to Scott that it was difficult to enter a relationship after being with Elvis Presley for so long. "When you've been with someone that huge on a worldwide level," she stated, "it's hard to fill those shoes."

Presley's 1985 memoir, *Elvis and Me,* was long awaited, according to a *Booklist* reviewer. It charts the Elvis-Priscilla relationship from their first meeting, set up by a friend of Elvis's. Robert Hilburn, in the *Los Angeles Times Book Review,* complained that too much of *Elvis and Me* was consumed with the question of exactly when the couple consummated their love; he admitted, however, that given Priscilla's age at the time, "the date . . . does carry a certain fascination as pulp gossip." Hilburn also asserted that after the long buildup toward the wedding night, the book became "a rehash of what we already know about [Elvis's] life." Wrote Hilburn, "Elvis' rise and fall is a true American tragedy, one of the most fascinating stories of our time. As his ex-wife, Priscilla is uniquely qualified to shed some insight on this confused and complex figure." Hilburn said that she did not do this but asserted that "the larger question raised by the book is the obligation survivors have to famous loved ones." A *Booklist* reviewer offered a similar judgment, calling the memoir "more than a little disappointing," and claiming that in some ways, the book poses more questions than answers—for

example, why Priscilla's parents allowed her to go to Presley's house in the first place and why they kept allowing her to mix with a group of adults when she was a mere fourteen years old. The critic advised readers that the book's treatment of the Presleys' life together, and of their parting, did not convey powerful emotion. More positively, however, the reviewer noted that "some of the revelations in other Elvis biographies . . . are substantiated here."

BIOGRAPHICAL/CRITICAL SOURCES:

BOOKS

Contemporary Theatre, Film, and Television, Volume 16, Gale (Detroit, MI), 1997.
International Motion Picture Almanac 1996, Quigley Publishing (New York, NY), p. 308.
Legends in Their Own Time, Prentice-Hall (New York, NY), 1994.
Newsmakers, Gale (Farmington Hills, MI), 2001.
Presley, Priscilla, *Elvis and Me,* Putnam (New York, NY), 1985.

PERIODICALS

Booklist, September 15, 1993, p. 92.
Choice, April, 1992, p. 1192.
English Journal, January, 1988, p. 98.
Entertainment Weekly, May 1, 1992, p. 68; May 3, 1996, p. 67.
Good Housekeeping, November, 1994, pp. 135-136.
Harper's Bazaar, May, 1984, pp. 168-169; September, 1986, p. 84; May, 1990, p. 46.
Jet, August 15, 1994, pp. 56-57.
Ladies Home Journal, February, 1989, pp. 44-49; August, 1996, Jim Jerome, "My Daughter, Myself: Priscilla Presley Talks about Her Bond with Lisa Marie and the Tough Times They've Survived Together," pp. 108-113.
Library Journal, November 1, 1996, pp. 118-119.
Life, December, 1988, pp. 44-47; December, 1988, pp. 46-52.
London Review of Books, December 19, 1985, p. 19.
Los Angeles Magazine, June, 1985, p. 62; January, 1986, pp. 140-152; June, 1990, pp. 136-137; August, 1990, p. 241; July, 1991, p. 30.
Los Angeles Times Book Review, September 22, 1985, p. 3.
Maclean's, December 19, 1988, pp. 48-49.

McCall's, February, 1984, pp. 75-79; March, 1987, pp. 12-17; April, 1988, pp. 56-59; July, 1989, pp. 12-16; January, 1992, pp. 78-82; October, 1994, pp. 122-127.

Ms., May, 1986, p. 22.

National Catholic Reporter, August 2, 1991, p. 15.

New Statesman & and Society, June 28, 1991, p. 32.

Newsweek, December 12, 1988, pp. 74-75; August 18, 1997, Corie Brown, "Look Who's Takin' Care of Business: The King's Dead; the Daughter's Drifting, Priscilla and Elvis Inc. Are Rocking Out," p. 62.

New York, July 29, 1991, p. 49.

People Weekly, December 29, 1980, pp. 130-133; November 8, 1982, pp. 53-56; May 23, 1983, p. 9; January 14, 1985, pp. 48-55; September 8, 1986, pp. 90-94; August 17, 1987, p. 12; February 15, 1988, pp. 42-46; December 12, 1988, p. 19; July 15, 1991, p. 13; March 28, 1994, p. 18; February 12, 1996, p. 130.

Premiere, June, 1991, pp. 57-58.

Publishers Weekly, July 19, 1985, p. 43.

Redbook, January, 1987, pp. 8-10.

Rolling Stone, April 21, 1994, p. 93.

Time, October 14, 1985, p. 104; November 24, 1986, p. 79; August 4, 1997, S. C. Gwynne, "Love Me Legal Tender," pp. 62-67.

TV Guide, November 1, 1980, p. 1; February 17, 1990, pp. 4-11; September 24, 1994, p. 39.

Vanity Fair, July, 1991, pp. 100-106.

Variety, July 1, 1991, pp. 34-35; March 21, 1994, pp. 57-58.

Video Magazine, January, 1992, p. 68.

Video Review, February, 1991, p. 53; January, 1992, p. 74.

Vogue, October, 1985, p. 400.

Voice of Youth Advocates, October, 1991, p. 219.

Wall Street Journal, September 11, 1985, p. 30.

Woman's Day, November 27, 1990, pp. 42-47.

Working Woman, September, 1993, pp. 52-58.

OTHER

Internet Movie Database, http://www.imdb.com (1998).

Mr. Showbiz, http://www.mrshowbiz.com (1998).*

R

RALEIGH, Richard
    See LOVECRAFT, H(oward) P(hillips)

*   *   *

RAWLS, John (Bordley) 1921-

PERSONAL: Born February 21, 1921, in Baltimore, MD; son of William Lee (an attorney) and Anna Abel (Stump) Rawls; married Margaret Warfield Fox, June 28, 1949; children: Anne Warfield, Robert Lee, Alexander Emory, Elizabeth Fox. Education: Princeton University, A.B., 1943, Ph.D., 1950; fellowship student, Cornell University, 1947-48.

ADDRESSES: Office—Department of Philosophy, Harvard University, Cambridge, MA 02138.

CAREER: Princeton University, Princeton, NJ, instructor in philosophy, 1950-52; Cornell University, Ithaca, NY, assistant professor, 1953-56, associate professor, 1956-59; Harvard University, Cambridge, MA, visiting professor, 1959-60, professor of philosophy, 1962-74, John Cowles Professor, 1974-79, James B. Conant University Professor, 1979—, currently emeritus; Massachusetts Institute of Technology, Cambridge, professor of philosophy, 1960-62. Military service: U.S. Army, 1943-46, 32nd Infantry Division, served in Pacific theater.

MEMBER: American Philosophical Association (member of executive committee, Eastern division, 1959-62; vice president, 1973; president, 1974), American Academy of Arts and Sciences, American Association of Political and Legal Philosophy (president, 1970-72), American Philosophical Society, British Academy, Norwegian Academy of Sciences.

AWARDS, HONORS: Fulbright fellow at Christchurch College, Oxford University, 1952-53; fellowship at Center for Advanced Study in the Behavioral Sciences, Stanford University, 1969, 1970; visiting fellow, Institute for Advanced Study, Princeton University, fall, 1977; visiting fellow, All Souls College, Oxford University, spring, 1986; Phi Beta Kappa's Ralph Waldo Emerson Award, 1972, Ames Prize for outstanding work on legal subjects, Harvard Law School, 1985, and Brandeis University Award, 1990, all for A Theory of Justice; Spitz Book Prize, Conference for the Study of Political Thought, 1995, for Political Liberalism; National Humanities Medal, National Endowment for the Humanities, 1999; Rolf Schock Award for Logic and Philosophy, Royal Swedish Academy, 1999; honorary degrees from Oxford University, 1983, Princeton University, 1987, and Harvard University, 1997. French Colloquim on A Theory of Justice, March, 1987, at Ecole Polytechnique, Paris; symposium on "The Philosophy of John Rawls," October, 1995, Santa Clara University, CA, in honor of the twenty-fifth anniversary of A Theory of Justice.

WRITINGS:

A Theory of Justice, Harvard University Press (Cambridge, MA), 1971, revised edition, 1999.
Political Liberalism, Columbia University Press (New York, NY), 1993, paperback edition with additions, 1996.
Collected Papers, edited by Samuel Freeman, Harvard University Press (Cambridge, MA), 1999.

The Law of Peoples; with, The Idea of Public Reason Revisited, Harvard University Press (Cambridge, MA), 1999.

Lectures on the History of Moral Philosophy, edited by Barbara Herman, Harvard University Press, 2000.

Justice as Fairness, a Restatement, edited by Erin Kelly, Harvard University Press (Cambridge, MA), 2001.

Co-editor of *Philosophical Review,* 1956-59. Contributor to *The Tanner Lectures on Human Value, Volume III,* edited by Sterling M. McMurrin, University of Utah Press (Salt Lake City), 1982, and *Liberty, Equality, and Law: Selected Tanner Lectures on Moral Philosophy,* edited by Sterling M. McMurrin, University of Utah Press, 1987. Contributor to philosophy journals.

Rawls's work has been translated into twenty-six languages, including Chinese, Japanese, Korean, and several European languages.

SIDELIGHTS: The 1971 publication of John Rawls's *A Theory of Justice* has been perceived as a watershed moment in modern philosophy. *New Republic* correspondent Thomas Nagel described Rawls as "the most important political philosopher of the twentieth century," a writer whose work stimulated a revival of attention to moral philosophy in the American academy. In *Prospect,* a critic noted: "Since the appearance of Rawls's epoch-making *A Theory of Justice* . . . he has been acknowledged as America's—perhaps the world's—leading political philosopher. . . . Where once the foundations of Western civilisation went from Plato to Freud, nowadays it is from Plato to Rawls." The critic continued: "Rawls is a sophisticated and ambitious thinker. His arguments are informed by a deep sense of history and draw on an array of different disciplines. . . . Almost everything he has written is animated by an urgent concern with reviving and extending a neglected liberal tradition—the tradition of rights-based social contract thinking."

The expressed aim of *A Theory of Justice,* as C. F. Delaney explained in *Thinkers of the Twentieth Century,* is to present a fully elaborated alternative to the various utilitarian-inspired conceptions of justice that have been dominant in this century. Utilitarianism is the concept that a just society ought to work toward the greatest possible good for the greatest number of people. Among the theoretical shortcomings of this position are that by pursuing the greatest good of the majority, society may see fit to repress and abuse its minority citizens. Furthermore, the liberty of the individual is of only sec-

ondary importance, overshadowed by the majority's interests. Because these utilitarian principles violate Rawls's conception of justice, he sets out to propose a new theory. Rawls formulates the requirements of justice by asserting two principles. The first concerns individual liberty: each individual has a right to the most extensive basic liberty compatible with the same liberty for others. The second concerns the distribution of wealth and power. Social and economic inequalities are just, Rawls writes, only to the extent that they serve to promote the well-being of the least advantaged. But how would the members of a society come to agree upon structuring their public life in accordance with these principles? In answering this question, Rawls makes one of his most celebrated contributions to political philosophy. He revives the notion of the social contract, developed earlier by such thinkers as Thomas Hobbes, John Locke, and Jean Jacques Rousseau.

Rawls's theory is built around a hypothetical situation in which human beings choose the basic structure determining how they will live together. As a first step, he introduces the concept of a "veil of ignorance," which hides from each chooser the social and material position he or she will occupy in the world. The details of the chooser's life are hidden from him or her by the "veil of ignorance." The chooser must select a set of rules to live by, without knowing whether he or she will be prosperous or destitute in the society governed by those rules. Rawls calls this the "original position." Rawls asserts that choosers in the "original position" will choose the society in which the worst possible position—which, for all they know, will be theirs—is better than the worst possible position in any other system. Rawls argues that a system in which justice is defined by his two principles would most effectively protect the least fortunate. He believes that these principles guarantee a more livable social minimum—a higher bottom rung on society's ladder—than any other set of rules. His first principle, again, stipulates that individual liberty is the cornerstone of justice. This liberty is not unrestricted, however. Every citizen must have access to the same liberty; one person's freedom of action cannot be allowed to impinge upon another's. In keeping with Rawls's second principle, social and economic inequalities need not be abolished. But in order to be permitted, they must be just. That is, they must work out to the benefit of society's least fortunate members.

A Theory of Justice has profoundly affected the field of philosophy, refocusing thinking on the ancient questions of what justice is and what forms of government are likely to achieve it. Rawls's book, which *Times Literary Supplement* contributor Simon Blackburn hailed in 2001 as "not only the most important work of philosophy, but arguably of the humanities, in the past thirty years," has been passionately debated in the years since its publication. Some critics have challenged Rawls's willingness to sanction social inequalities; others have objected to his assertion that individual liberties must not be eroded to benefit the majority. Many writers have taken issue with various facets of Rawls's theory, urging the revision or rejection of his claims. In *National Review,* for instance, Damon Linker suggested that Rawls "is more concerned with telling us how the world ought to be than understanding how it is." Linker also faulted Rawls for "a condition of childlike innocence about the ways of the world." Thomas Nagel, however, praised the controversial aspects of Rawls's work: "His contribution was a large, intellectually rich theory—above all, a theory that had strong and highly contestable consequences," Nagel wrote in *New Republic.* "By showing that disagreements about how society should be ordered could be traced to differences in fundamental moral conceptions, he illuminated not only the views of those who agreed with him but also those of his opponents."

Rawls's 1993 book, *Political Liberalism,* is in part an attempt to respond to his critics, and to sharpen assertions he made in *A Theory of Justice.* In his introduction to the paperback edition of *Political Liberalism,* Rawls explains that the book tries to answer the question of how it is possible for those affirming a reasonable comprehensive religious, philosophical or moral doctrine—perhaps one based on religious authority—also to hold a reasonable political conception that supports a democratic regime, and for that condition to be stable over time in what he calls an "overlapping consensus." To do this he makes clear, as he says *A Theory of Justice* does not, that his conception of justice, which he calls "justice as fairness," is a purely political conception and not itself a comprehensive moral doctrine, or a part of one. This requires a series of adjustments in the basic theory to make it compatible with the fact of reasonable pluralism—the fact that any number of reasonable, often conflicting comprehensive doctrines will exist in any democracy.

In a review of *Political Liberalism* in *Times Literary Supplement,* Jeremy Waldron asserted: "At one level, this book is an extraordinarily well-reasoned commentary on *A Theory of Justice* by an author who takes seriously the obligation to respond to his critics. At another level it adds detail to the earlier book, particularly in his discussion of institutional stability and basic freedoms. But above all, this new book is a decisive turn towards *political* philosophy, as opposed to norma-

tive philosophizing on public affairs." John Gray, in *New York Times Book Review,* commented: "By any standards [*Political Liberalism*] must be ranked as one of the classics of political philosophy in English."

The Law of Peoples; with, The Idea of Public Reason Revisited contains two essays on the optimal principles of a constitutional democratic society. The latter essay, as Rawls explains in the introduction to the book, is his "most detailed account of why the constraints of public reason, as manifested in a modern democracy based on a liberal conception, are ones that holders of both religious and nonreligious comprehensive views can reasonably endorse." The ideal of public reason, first discussed in *Political Liberalism,* establishes an ideal of citizenship in a democratic regime. It involves the idea that in discussing constitutional essentials and matters of basic justice, we are not to appeal to comprehensive religious or philosophical doctrines, but our reasoning should rest on plain truths widely accepted or available to citizens generally. The idea of public reason is also integral to *The Law of Peoples,* which extends the idea of a social contract to the Society of Peoples, and lays out the principles that can and should be accepted by both liberal and nonliberal (but decent) societies as the standard for their behavior toward one another. As Nagel explained: "Rawls believes that hope for the future of humanity resides in the spread of liberal democratic societies, which have so far fulfilled Kant's remarkable prediction that they will not go to war with one another, and have left behind the worst forms of domestic oppression." The world Rawls envisions—which he calls a "realistic utopia"—cannot be achieved by force, but rather by investment in moral imperatives on an international scale. Nagel concluded: "Some may find these sentiments too noble to bear, but they give the spirit in which John Rawls's life work has been carried out."

Collected Papers, which brings together nearly all of Rawls's published papers, was hailed in *Prospect* as "an important event." The book reflects the development of Rawls's thought from his early career through *Political Liberalism* and beyond. "Rawls has thought hard about the moral, religious, cultural, and historical nuances that so often make utopic claims tragically optimistic," wrote Andrew Carpenter in *Antioch Review.* "His own vision of a realistic political uptopia rests in his faith in the idea of the social contract; the essays [in *Collected Papers*] present Rawls's lifework as a consistent project of extending and radicalizing this venerable idea."

Lectures on the History of Moral Philosophy contains lectures that Rawls gave at Harvard on Hume, Liebnitz, Kant, and Hegel. According to the editor, Barbara Herman, Rawls "had a profound influence on the approach to philosophical ethics of many generations of students, and through them, on the way the subject is now understood. In particular, his teaching conveyed an unusual commitment to the history of Moral philosophy." For many years, Rawls made photocopies of his lectures available to the class, and there exist many variations as he changed and improved the texts from year to year. These lectures are from the last offering of the course before Rawls retired in 1991.

Justice as Fairness, a Restatement was written, as Rawls says, "to rectify the more serious faults in *A Theory of Justice* that have obscured the main ideas of justice as fairness—and to connect into one unified statement the conception of justice presented in *Theory* and the main ideas in my essays beginning in 1974." At 202 pages, it is a short work, clarifying how justice as fairness is to be understood and justified as a political conception and not as part of a comprehensive religious, philosophical or moral doctrine. The book originated as lectures in a course on political philosophy, along with discussions of the work of historically important figures whose ideas had an impact on Rawls's thinking. As offered here, they are from the last time he gave the course, in 1994.

In Blackburn's view, *Justice as Fairness* is "the best and most comprehensive statement" of Rawls's mature philosophy, and is "an exemplary work in every way." The book, he added, is a "moving" work that "gives us a framework within which to think about justice to future generations, or to other nationalities who need our help. Above all, it is a testament to high moral seriousness, and to the quest for a space of public reason which that seriousness informs, that has survived thirty years during which both the culture in general and politics in particular have successfully stopped their ears to any such project." J. B. Schneewind, in a review of *Justice as Fairness* in *New York Times Book Review*, observed that "Rawls's brilliant, detailed and comprehensive defense of [justice as fairness] has made him the most important American political philosopher of the twentieth century."

BIOGRAPHICAL/CRITICAL SOURCES:

BOOKS

Berry, Brian M., *The Liberal Theory of Justice: A Critical Examination of the Principle Doctrines in "A Theory of Justice" by John Rawls,* Clarendon Press (Oxford, England), 1973.

Blocker, H. Gene, and Elizabeth H. Smith, editors, *John Rawls's Theory of Social Justice: An Introduction,* Ohio University Press (Athens, OH), 1980.

Daniels, Norman, editor, *Reading Rawls,* Blackwell (Oxford, England), 1975.

Davion, Victoria and Wolf, Clark, editors, *The Idea of Political Liberalism: Essays on Rawls,* Rowman and Littlefield (MD), 2000.

Gutmann, Amy, *Liberal Equality,* Cambridge University Press (Cambridge, England), 1980.

Kukathas, Chandran and Pettit, Philip, *Rawls: A Theory of Justice and Its Critics,* Stanford University Press (Stanford, CA), 1990.

Mandle, Jon, *What's Left of Liberalism? An Interpretation and Defense of Justice as Fairness,* Lexington Books (Lanham, MD), 2000.

Martin, Rex, *Rawls and Rights,* University Press of Kansas (Lawrence, KS), 1985.

Mulhall, Stephen, and Adam Swift, *Liberals and Communitarians,* Blackwell (Cambridge, MA), 1996.

Nelson, K., and R. Shiner, editors, *New Essays in Contract Theory,* Canadian Association for Publishing in Philosophy (Guelph, Ontario, Canada), 1977.

Pettit, Philip, *Judging Justice,* Routledge (London, England), 1980.

Pogge, Thomas, *Realizing Rawls,* Cornell University Press (Ithaca, NY), 1989.

Rao, A. P., *Distributive Justice: A Third-World Response to Rawls and Nozick,* International Scholars Publications (San Francisco, CA), 1997.

Rawls, John, *Justice as Fairness, a Restatement,* Harvard University Press (Cambridge, MA), 2001.

Rawls, John, *The Law of Peoples; with, The Idea of Public Reason Revisited,* Harvard University Press (Cambridge, MA), 1999.

Rawls, John, *Political Liberalism,* Columbia University Press (New York, NY), 1996.

Rawls, John, *A Theory of Justice,* Harvard University Press (Cambridge, MA), 1971.

Reath, Andrews, Barbara Herman and Christine Korsgaard, editors, *Reclaiming the History of Ethics: Essays for John Rawls,* Cambridge University Press (New York, NY), 1997.

Richardson, Henry S., and Paul J. Weithman, editors, *Philosophy of Rawls,* five volumes, Garland Publishing (New York, NY and London, England), 1999.

Schaefer, David Lewis, *Justice or Tyranny? A Critique of John Rawls's "A Theory of Justice,"* Kennikat (Port Washington, NY), 1979.

Talisse, Robert B., *On Rawls,* Wadsworth Philosophers Series/Thompson Learning Inc., 2001.

Thinkers of the Twentieth Century, St. James Press (Detroit, MI), 1987.

Von Dohlen, Richard, F., *Culture War and Ethical Theory,* University Press of America (Lanham, MD), 1997.

Wellbank, J. H., and others, *John Rawls and His Critics: An Annotated Bibliography,* Garland (New York, NY), 1982.

Wolff, Robert Paul, *Understanding Rawls: A Reconstruction and Critique of "A Theory of Justice,"* Princeton University Press (Princeton, NJ), 1977.

PERIODICALS

American Political Science Review, June, 1993, p. 348; September, 1997, p. 635.

Antioch Review, fall, 2000, Andrew Carpenter, review of *Collected Papers,* p. 523.

Business Week, December 1, 1975, "Egalitarianism."

Chronicle of Higher Education, July 20, 2001, Martha C. Nussbaum, "The Enduring Significance of John Rawls," p. B7.

Civilization, December 1999-January 2000, review of *The Law of Peoples,* p. 97.

Commonweal, September 25, 1998, Bernard G. Prusak, "Politics, Religion, and the Public Good: An Interview with Philosopher John Rawls," p. 12.

Economist, February 12, 2000, "The Social Contract," p. 88.

Esquire, March, 1983, Randall Rothenberg, "Robert Nozick vs. John Rawls," pp. 201-204.

Ethics, October, 1994, pp. 23, 44, 874; July, 1995, p. 874; October, 1995, p. 32; April, 2000, review of *Collected Papers,* p. 660.

Library Journal, May 1, 1993, p. 103; July, 1999, Robert Hoffman, review of *Collected Papers,* p. 93; November 1, 1999, Robert Hoffman, review of *The Law of Peoples; with, The Idea of Public Reason Revisited,* p. 88.

Listener, June 22, 1972, p. 837.

London Review of Books, May 13, 1993, p. 7; July 15, 1999, Jeremy Waldron, review of *Collected Papers,* p. 3.

Modern Age, fall, 2001, Wallace Matson, review of *A Theory of Justice,* p. 372.

Nation, September 11, 1972, p. 180.

National Review, July 5, 1993, p. 52; May 1, 2000, Damon Linker, "Higher Ignorance," p. 59.

New Republic, May 13, 1972, p. 24; October 11, 1993, Stephen Holmes, review of *Political Liberalism;* October 25, 1999, Thomas Nagel, "The Rigorous Compassion of John Rawls: Justice, Justice, Shalt Thou Pursue," p. 36; February 5, 2001, Charles Larmore, review of *Lectures on the History of Moral Philosophy.*

New Society, February 5, 1981, Alan Ryan, "John Rawls and His Theory of Justice."

New Statesman, May 5, 1972, p. 601; May, 1997, p. 126.

New York Review of Books, February 24, 1972, Stuart Hampshire, "What Is the Just Society?," pp. 34-39; August 12, 1993, Stuart Hampshire, review of *Political Liberalism,* p. 43; November 2, 1995, Stanley Hoffman, review of "On Human Rights: The Oxford Amnesty Lectures."

New York Times Book Review, July 16, 1972, Marshall Cohen, review of *A Theory of Justice,* pp. 1, 16, 18; December 3, 1972; May 16, 1993, John Gray, review of *Political Liberalism,* p. 35; June 24, 2001, J. B. Schneewind, review of *Justice as Fairness,* p. 21.

Observer (London, England), June 4, 1972, p. 32.

Prospect, June, 1999, "Portrait: John Rawls."

Review of Social Economy, John A. Edgren, "On the Relevance of John Rawls's Theory of Justice to Welfare Economics," p. 332.

Spectator, June 24, 1972, p. 972.

Times (London, England), June 10, 1986, "Rawls and Parfit—The Meeting of Two Masterminds."

Times Higher Education Supplement, December 10, 1999, John Dunn, review of *Collected Papers.* *Times Literary Supplement,* May 5, 1972, "The Good of Justice as Fairness," pp. 505-506; June 18, 1993, Jeremy Waldron, "Justice Revisited," pp. 5-6; September 10, 1999, Glen Newey, review of *Collected Papers,* p. 9; March 24, 2000, David Miller, review of *The Law of Peoples;* September 28, 2001, Simon Blackburn, review of *Justice as Fairness.* *Village Voice Literary Supplement,* June, 1988, p. 20.

Washington Post, April, 1977, p. 438.

*   *   *

REHNQUIST, William H(ubbs) 1924-

PERSONAL: Born October 1, 1924, in Milwaukee, WI; son of William Benjamin and Margery (Peck) Rehnquist; married Natalie Cornell, August 29, 1953 (died, October, 1991); children: James, Janet, Nancy. *Education:* Attended Kenyon College, 1943; Stanford University, B.A. and M.A., 1948, L.L.B., 1952; Harvard University, M.A., 1949. *Politics:* Republican. *Religion:* Lutheran.

ADDRESSES: Office—c/o Supreme Court of the United States, 1 First St. NE, Washington, DC 20543.

CAREER: U.S. Supreme Court, Washington, DC, law clerk for Justice Robert H. Jackson, 1952-53; called to the Bar of the state of Arizona, 1953; Evans, Kitchel & Jenckes, Phoenix, AZ, attorney, 1953-55; Ragan & Rehnquist, Phoenix, partner, 1956-57; Cunningham, Carson & Messenger, Phoenix, partner, 1957-60; Powers & Rehnquist, Phoenix, partner, 1960-69; U.S. Department of Justice, Office of Legal Counsel, assistant attorney, 1969-71; U.S. Supreme Court, justice, 1972-86, chief justice, 1986—. Member of the National Conference of Commissioners on Uniform State Laws, 1963-69. *Military service:* U.S. Army Air Corps, 1943-46; became sergeant, served in Weather Service in Africa-Middle East Theater.

MEMBER: Order of the Coif, Phi Beta Kappa, Phi Delta Phi.

WRITINGS:

The Supreme Court: How It Was, How It Is, Morrow (New York, NY), 1987, new edition, Knopf (New York, NY), 2001.
Grand Inquests: The Historic Impeachments of Justice Samuel Chase and President Andrew Johnson, Morrow (New York, NY), 1992.
All the Laws but One: Civil Liberties in Wartime, Knopf (New York, NY), 1998.

Contributor of articles to law journals.

SIDELIGHTS: The chief justice of the U.S. Supreme Court since 1986, William H. Rehnquist is noted for his conservative interpretation of the Constitution and for his strong leadership.

While a career in law or politics is often a family tradition, such was not the case with Rehnquist. He was born in Milwaukee in 1924; his father, William B. Rehnquist, was a paper salesman who never held an elected office and who, together with Rehnquist's mother, Margery, created a solidly middle-class home for his family. Rehnquist's trademark conservatism can be traced to family influence, however; his parents were staunch Republicans.

Rehnquist had just begun college in 1943 when World War II prompted him to enlist in the Air Force. He was trained as a weather observer, stationed in North Africa, and served three years, rising to the rank of sergeant.

Upon his return Rehnquist again took up his studies, this time with the assistance of the GI Bill, and graduated from Stanford University in 1948 with both a bachelor's and a master's degree in political science. One year later he earned a master's in government at Harvard, and in 1952 received his law degree from Stanford. Among his law-school classmates was another future Court justice, Sandra Day O'Connor.

During law school Rehnquist gained a reputation for excellence. His impressive academic performance earned him an interview with Justice Robert Jackson, who hired Rehnquist as a clerk, giving him his first taste of the inner workings of the Supreme Court. Rehnquist's conservatism remained undeterred even under the influence of the moderate Jackson. After completing his one-year clerkship, Rehnquist married his college sweetheart, Natalie Cornell; the two moved to Arizona where Rehnquist found both the actual and the political climates to be to his liking. The next few years brought three children: James, Janet, and Nancy. Rehnquist passed the Bar in Arizona and joined the law firm of Evans, Kitchel & Jenckes, where he practiced from 1953 through 1955. Three other firms were in his future—Ragan & Rehnquist, Cunningham, Carson & Messenger, and Powers & Rehnquist—and at each he was made a partner. During this time Rehnquist also joined and became active in the Republican Party. In 1969 he was made an assistant attorney with the U.S. Department of Justice, brought on board by Richard Kleindienst, deputy attorney general of President Richard Nixon's administration. In 1972 Rehnquist became an associate justice of the Supreme Court, nominated by Nixon to replace the retiring Justice John Marshall Harlan. Rehnquist was appointed chief justice upon the nomination of President Ronald Reagan in 1986, taking the place of Chief Justice Warren Burger upon his retirement.

Rehnquist proved an excellent administrator, lessening the Court's burgeoning case workload. Although he remained one of the most conservative justices, he also maintained a strong sense of independence. He had to endure charges that his opinions reflected his own personal politics more than actual judicial philosophy. However, when examined, it was noted that he often stood with the majority even if it crossed the established Republican line. In *Morrison v Olson* (1988) he upheld Congress' right to appoint independent counsel to investigate and prosecute government officials, over the strenuous objects of the Reagan administration, who had been responsible for his appointment to the Supreme Court. In 1996, he clashed openly with Republicans over their criticism of President Clinton's judicial appointments. In 1999, he oversaw the impeachment of President Bill Clinton, and in 2000, the presidential election controversy regarding invalid ballots cast in Florida. As Chief Justice, Rehnquist has brought order to the court and won striking support for judicial restraint from his colleagues. His belief that any move to weaken judicial independence would only serve to undermine the effectiveness of the federal courts is the cornerstone of his tenure at the Court.

Rehnquist has written three books concerning the American judiciary, *The Supreme Court: How It Was, How It Is, Grand Inquests: The Historic Impeachments of Justice Samuel Chase and President Andrew Johnson,* and *All the Laws but One: Civil Liberties in Wartime.* In *The Supreme Court,* Rehnquist offers a history of America's highest court from its beginnings to the mid-twentieth century and also reveals the inner workings of the institution today. Supreme Court justices, for instance, "read newspapers and magazines, we watch news on television, we talk to our friends about current events," Rehnquist writes in *The Supreme Court.* "No judge worthy of his salt would ever cast his vote in a particular case simply because he thought the majority of the public wanted him to vote that way, but that is quite a different thing from saying that no judge is ever influenced by the great tides of public opinion that run in a country such as ours." Additionally, the book includes an account of Rehnquist's own introduction to the Court as a clerk for Justice Robert H. Jackson in the 1950s. *The Supreme Court* was well received by critics, who considered it to be an engaging and readable volume appropriate for the general public.

In his 1992 book, *Grand Inquests,* Rehnquist concentrates on the impeachment trials of Supreme Court Justice Samuel Chase in 1805 and President Andrew Johnson in 1868. Both trials, Rehnquist notes, were motivated by politics rather than serious wrongdoing on the part of Chase or Johnson. The chief justice also points out that the acquittals of Chase and Johnson served to discourage future use of impeachment for political reasons and affirmed the political independence of the Supreme Court and the power of the executive branch. Published in 1992, the book and its premise became newly relevant as impeachment proceedings were successfully carried out (led, ironically, by Rehnquist's Court) against President Bill Clinton just a few years later, making Clinton the first president in U.S. history to be impeached. *Washington Post Book World* contributor Edwin M. Yoder commented that Rehnquist "brings fresh information and a fresh angle of vision" to his subject. *Grand Inquests,* according to Yoder, "is also incisive, readable and fair-minded. . . . The merits

of this engaging and informative book go well beyond its unusual authorship."

In *All the Laws but One: Civil Liberties in Wartime,* Rehnquist explored historical instances of violations of Constitutional rights during times of war, asserting that in many instances rights have been trampled or altogether ignored for less than adequate reasons. Cass R. Sunstein, writing in the *New Republic,* concluded that the book "seems in places like little more than a civics text, but in fact the Chief Justice has put forward the ingredients of a highly original account of the proper role of the Supreme Court, a role that makes most sense in times of war, but that has its attractions whenever the Court is embroiled in great social controversies."

In a 1996 speech Rehnquist stated: "Change is the law of life, and judiciary will have to change to meet the challenges which will face it in the future. But the independence of the federal judiciary is essential to its proper functioning and must be retained."

BIOGRAPHICAL/CRITICAL SOURCES:

BOOKS

Cushman, Claire, editor, *The Supreme Court Justices: Illustrated Biographies, 1789-1993,* Congressional Quarterly (Washington, DC), 1993.

Davis, Sue, *Justice Rehnquist and the Constitution: The Quest for a New Federalism,* Princeton University Press (Princeton, NJ), 1989.

Encyclopedia of World Biography, 2nd edition, Gale (Detroit, MI), 1998.

Newsmakers, Gale (Farmington Hills, MI), 2001.

Rehnquist, William H., *The Supreme Court: How It Was, How It Is,* Morrow (New York, NY), 1987.

Yarbrough, Tinsley E., *The Rehnquist Court and the Constitution,* Oxford University Press (New York, NY), 2000.

PERIODICALS

ABA Journal, October, 1996, David G. Savage, "Opinions on Rehnquist."

Arizona Republic, December 14, 2000, p. B11.

Commentary, March, 1999, Andrew C. McCarthy, review of *All the Laws but One,* p. 69.

Fortune, July 21, 1986, p. 8.

Insight on the News, July 28, 1997, David Wagner, "The Rehnquist High Court?," p. 8; January 25, 1999, David Wagner, "Rehnquist's Call," p. 10.

Library Journal, September 1, 1998, Steven Puro, review of *All the Laws but One,* p. 200; February 1, 2001, Steven Puro, review of *The Supreme Court,* p. 109.

Los Angeles Times Book Review, August 23, 1987, pp. 1, 13.

Mirror, December 14, 2000, pp. 4-5.

New Republic, November 9, 1998, Cass R. Sunstein, review of *All the Laws but One.*

New York Times Book Review, June 14, 1992, p. 9.

New York Times Magazine, March 3, 1985, John A. Jenkins, "The Partisan: A Talk with Justice Rehnquist"; October 6, 1996, David J. Garrow, "Rehnquist Reins."

People Weekly, January 25, 1999, Bill Hewitt, "Man in Black," p. 75.

Publishers Weekly, August 24, 1998, review of *All the Laws but One,* p. 33.

Time, January 11, 1999, J. F. O. McAllister, "A Very Public Trial for a Very Private Justice," p. 32; December 18, 2000, Charles Krauthammer, "The Winner in *Bush v. Gore?* It's Chief Justice Rehnquist, Who Runs the Most Trusted Institution in the U.S.," p. 104.

Vital Speeches, May 1, 1996, p. 418.

Washington Post Book World, July 12, 1992, p. 11.

Washington Times, January 1, 2001, p. A3.

Yale Law Journal, June, 1982, Jeff Powell, "The Complete Jeffersonian: Justice Rehnquist and Federalism."*

*   *   *

REICHART, Elisabeth 1953-

PERSONAL: Born November 19, 1953, in Steyregg, Austria; daughter of Alois (an engineer) and Herta (a tailor and homemaker; maiden name, Winkler) Reichart. *Education:* University of Salzburg, D.Phil., 1983.

ADDRESSES: Home—Ruckerg 12/20, 1120 Vienna, Austria.

CAREER: Writer.

MEMBER: Grazer Autoren Versammlung.

AWARDS, HONORS: Förderungspreis from the City of Vienna, 1983 and 1989; Austrian state grant, 1989-90; Austrian Wurdigunspreis 1999, 2000; Preis der Salzburger Wirtshopt; Anton Wied gans Preis.

WRITINGS:

Februarschatten (novel), Österreichische, 1984, translation by Donna L. Hoffmeister published as *February Shadows,* Ariadne Press (Riverside, CA), 1989.

Komm ber den See, S. Fischer, 1988.

Österreichische Dichterinnen, O. Müller (Salzburg, Germany), 1993.

Sakkorausch: ein Monolog, O. Müller (Salzburg, Germany), 1994.

Nachtmär (novel), O. Müller (Salzburg, Germany), 1995.

Das vergessene Lächeln der Amaterasu (novel), Aufbau-Verlag (Berlin, Germany), 1998.

La Valse [and] Foreign, translation and introduction by Linda C. DeMeritt, State University of New York Press (Albany, NY), 2000.

Also author of radio plays. Work represented in anthologies. Contributor of short stories, articles and essays to literary journals.

SIDELIGHTS: Elisabeth Reichart is, according to Linda C. DeMeritt in her introduction to *La Valse [and] Foreign,* "one of the most important and provocative writers to emerge in post-war Austria." Reichart, who is the author of several novels, a collection of short stories, and articles, essays, and radio plays, explained to Karl Müller in *Deutsche Bücher:* "All of my writing attempts to confront taboos or silence. The constant in my work is a concern with people. . . . without a language for the critical issues in their lives."

La Valse [and] Foreign is a collection of ten short stories, several of which deal with Austrians who cannot confront the nature of that country's past complicity in Nazi atrocities. The story "How Close Is Mauthausen?" tells of a woman betrayed to the Nazis by her husband. In "The Scar," a woman's husband, a plastic surgeon, reconstructs her burned face. But she comes to believe that by doing so, he has given her a face that is more his than hers. The critic for *Publishers Weekly* noted that although Reichert writes "uninflected feminist fiction," she "speaks ardently on the relationship between the ultimate horrors of the Holocaust and the everyday cruelty of late-20th-century patriarchal systems."

BIOGRAPHICAL/CRITICAL SOURCES:

BOOKS

Daviau, Donald G., *Austrian Writers and the Anschluss: Understanding the Past—Overcoming the Past,* Ariadne Press (Riverside, CA), 1991.

Gilbert, Sandra M., and Susan Gubar, *The Madwoman in the Attic,* Yale University Press (New Haven, CT), 1979.

Koonz, Claudia, *Mothers in the Fatherland: Women, the Family, and Nazi Politics,* St. Martin's Press (New York, NY), 1986.

Martin, Elaine, editor, *Gender, Patriarchy, and Fascism in the Third Reich: The Response of Women Writers,* Wayne State University Press (Detroit, MI), 1993.

Weedon, Chris, editor, *Post-War Women's Writing in German: Feminist Critical Approaches,* Berghahn Books (Providence, RI), 1997.

PERIODICALS

Deutsche Bücher, number 2, 1997, Karl Müller, "Gespräch mit Elisabeth Reichart," pp. 88-98.

Modern Austrian Literature, Volume 29, number 1, 1996, Linda DeMeritt and Peter Ensberg, "'Für mich ist die Sprache eigentlich ein Schatz': Interview mit Elisabeth Reichart," pp. 1-22.

Publishers Weekly, November 20, 2000, review of *La Valse [and] Foreign,* p. 47.

*   *   *

RICHIE, Donald 1924-

PERSONAL: Born April 17, 1924, in Lima, OH; son of Kent and Ona Richie; married Mary Evans (a writer), November, 1961 (divorced, 1965). *Education:* Attended Antioch College, 1942; attended U.S. Maritime Academy, 1943; Columbia University, B.S., 1953.

ADDRESSES: Home—Ueno 2, 12-18 (804), Taito-ku, Tokyo 110-0005, Japan.

CAREER: Pacific Stars and Stripes, Tokyo, film critic, 1947-49; *Saturday Review of Literature,* New York, NY, arts critic, 1950-51; *Japan Times,* Tokyo, film critic, 1953-69, literary critic, 1972—; *Nation,* New York, NY, arts critic, 1959-61; New York Museum of Modern Art, New York, NY, curator of film, 1968-73; *Newsweek,* New York, NY, arts critic, 1973-76. Lecturer in American literature, Waseda University, Tokyo, 1954-59; advisor to UniJapan Film, 1963—; Toyoda Chair, University of Michigan, 1993; designer and presenter of many film retrospectives, including Ozu retrospective, Berlin, 1961; Carte Blanche: Nantes Film Festival, 2000. *Military service:* U.S. Maritime Service, 1942-45.

AWARDS, HONORS: Citations from Japanese government, 1963, 1970; U.S. National Society of Film Critics citation, 1970; Kawakita Memorial Foundation Award, 1983; Presidential Citation, New York University, 1989; Novikoff Award, San Francisco Film Festival, 1990; Tokyo Metropolitan Government Cultural Award, 1993; John D. Rockefeller III Award, 1994; Japan Foundation Award, 1995; honorary doctorate, Maryland University, 1999; Japan Society Award, 2001.

WRITINGS:

(With Kenichi Ito) *The Erotic Gods* (bilingual edition), Sufushinsha (Tokyo, Japan), 1966.

Introducing Japan, Kodansha (Tokyo, Japan), 1978.

Where Are the Victors? (novel), Charles E. Tuttle (Tokyo, Japan), 1956, new edition, 1986.

(With Joseph L. Anderson) *The Japanese Film: Art and Industry,* Grove (London, England), 1959, expanded edition, Princeton University Press (Princeton, NJ), 1982.

The Japanese Movie: An Illustrated History, Kodansha (England), 1965, revised edition, 1982.

The Films of Akira Kurosawa, University of California Press (Berkeley, CA), 1965, revised edition, 1995.

Companions of the Holiday (novel), Weatherhill (Tokyo, Japan), 1968, new edition, Charles E. Tuttle (Tokyo, Japan), 1977.

(Editor) Akira Kurosawa, *Rashomon: A Film,* Grove (London, England), 1969.

George Stevens: An American Romantic, Museum of Modern Art (New York, NY), 1970.

The Inland Sea, Weatherhill (Tokyo, Japan), 1971, new edition, Kodansha (Tokyo, Japan), 1993.

Japanese Cinema, Doubleday (New York, NY), 1971.

Three Modern Kyogen, Charles E. Tuttle (Tokyo, Japan), 1972.

Ozu: The Man and His Films, University of California Press (Berkeley, CA), 1974.

(Editor and translator, with Eric Klestadt) Yasujiro Ozu, *Tokyo Story,* Knopf (New York, NY), 1977.

The Japanese Tatoo, photographs by Ian Buruma, Weatherhill (Tokyo, Japan), 1980.

Zen Inklings: Some Stories, Fables, Parables, Sermons, and Prints with Notes and Commentaries, Weatherhill (Tokyo, Japan), 1982.

A Taste of Japan: Food Fact and Fable; What the People Eat; Customs and Etiquette, Kodansha (England), 1985.

Viewing Film, Kenkyusha (Tokyo, Japan), 1986.

Introducing Tokyo, Kodansha (England), 1987.

Lateral View (collected essays), Stone Bridge Press (Berkeley, CA), 1987, new edition, 1992.

Different People: Pictures of Some Japanese, Kodansha (England), 1987.

Tokyo Nights, Harrap (London, England), 1988, new edition, Charles E. Tuttle (Tokyo, Japan), 1994.

Japanese Cinema: An Introduction, Oxford University Press (New York, NY), 1990.

The Honorable Visitors, Charles E. Tuttle (Tokyo, Japan), 1994.

The Temples of Kyoto, Charles E. Tuttle (Tokyo, Japan), 1995.

(Editor and Introduction) *Lafcadio Hearn's Japan: An Anthology of His Writings on the Country and Its People,* Charles E. Tuttle (Tokyo, Japan), 1997.

The Memoirs of the Warrior Kumagai, Charles E. Tuttle (Tokyo, Japan), 1999.

Tokyo: A View of the City, Reduktion Books (London, England), 1999.

The Donald Richie Reader: Fifty Years of Writing on Japan, edited with an introduction by Arturo Silva, Stonebridge Press (Berkeley, CA), 2001.

A Hundred Years of Japanese Film: A Short History and a Selective Guide to Videos and DVDs, Kodansha (Tokyo, Japan), 2001.

Also editor and translator of film scenarios *Ikiru,* Akira Kurosawa, 1968, new edition, Knopf, 1977; and *Seven Samurai,* Kurosawa, 1970, new edition, Faber (London, England), 1992. Editor, *International House of Japan Bulletin,* 1981—. Contributor of numerous articles, essays, and reviews to periodicals, including *New York Times, International Herald Tribune, San Francisco Chronicle, Los Angeles Times, Chicago Tribune, Christian Science Monitor, Wall Street Journal, Washington Post, Guardian, Times of India, Japan Times,* film journals, and major Japanese periodicals and newspapers.

Richie's collected papers are included in the Donald Richie Collection, in the Mugar Memorial Collected Film Criticism, Museum of Modern Art Library, New York, NY.

SIDELIGHTS: Donald Richie told *CA:* "Living as I do in Japan, for over fifty years now, I write mainly about this country and its people. It has become my subject, one which I seek to describe, understand, maybe even to illuminate. The experience of attempting to encompass an entire culture has given me, I think, a deeper insight than I might otherwise have had into my own. I came to the word through the picture—having spent much of my early years in movie theaters. It was through motion pictures that I first began to learn about life. Movies taught me to look around and consequently to begin to understand. When I came to Japan it was

film that became a paradigm for the country. And just as I had learned to see through the movies into the reality of small-town American life, so I now learned to decipher the language of Japanese film and reconstruct the realities of Japanese life. Having seen these I could then describe them."

BIOGRAPHICAL/CRITICAL SOURCES:

BOOKS

Contemporary Authors Autobiography Series, Volume 20, Gale (Detroit), 1994.

Japan Experience, Weatherhill (Tokyo, Japan), 1973.

Volkmer, Klaus, and Olaf Möller, editors, *Ricecar für Donald Richie,* Japanisches Kulturinstitute (Köln, Germany), 1997.

PERIODICALS

Communicator, December, 1988.

Comparative Literature Studies, Vol. 35, no. 2, 1998.

Daily Yomiuri, April, 1990; May 13, 1993.

East, winter, 2000.

Economist, June 20, 1984.

Hawaii Herald, December 16, 1983.

Honolulu Advertiser, September 20, 1979; December 8, 1984.

International Herald-Tribune, August 7, 1982.

Japan Times, April 25, 1991.

Kyoto Journal, summer, 1999.

Okura Lantern, summer, 1994.

St. Andrews Review, Vol. 1, no. 2, 1971.

Temple Voice, October 15, 1996.

Times Literary Supplement, July 3, 1987.

Tokyo Classified, June, 1999.

Tokyo Journal, March, 1992.

Toronto Star, October 9, 1989

Winds, November, 1985; October, 1996.

OTHER

Director's Cut: Donald Richie und der Japanische Film, direct by Brigitte Prinzgan, Navigator Film (Vienna, Austria), 2001.

*   *   *

ROBERTS, Randy (W.) 1951-

PERSONAL: Born January 8, 1951, in New Kensington, PA; son of Clifford Edwin and Bertha May (maiden name, Cable; present surname, Levarto) Roberts; married Susan Marie Rankin (a teacher), December 29, 1978; children: Alison Mackenzie, Kelly Rankin. *Edu-*

cation: Mansfield State College, B.A. (magna cum laude), 1972; University of Nebraska, M.A., 1973; Louisiana State University, Ph.D., 1978. *Politics:* Independent. *Religion:* Roman Catholic.

ADDRESSES: Office—Purdue University, West Lafayette, IN. *Agent*—Gerard McCauley, Gerard McCauley Agency, Inc., P.O. Box AE, Katonah, NY 10536. *E-mail*—rroberts@purdue.edu.

CAREER: Louisiana State University, Baton Rouge, LA, member of faculty, 1975-78; Louisiana State University at Alexandria, LA, assistant professor, 1978; University of Maryland at College Park, MD, lecturer, 1979-80; Sam Houston State University, Huntsville, TX, assistant professor, 1980-88; presently member of faculty of Purdue University, West Lafayette, IN. Instructor, Mansfield State College, 1977; visiting associate professor, University of Houston, 1987-88.

AWARDS, HONORS: Pulitzer Prize nominations, 1979 for *Jack Dempsey: The Manassa Mauler,* and 1983 for *Papa Jack: Jack Johnson and the Era of White Hopes;* grants from National Endowment for the Humanities, 1981 and 1984; Charles B. Murphy Outstanding Teaching Award, Purdue University, 1991.

WRITINGS:

Jack Dempsey: The Manassa Mauler, Louisiana State University Press (Baton Rouge, LA), 1979, revised edition, 1984.

Papa Jack: Jack Johnson and the Era of White Hopes, Free Press (New York, NY), 1983.

(With Robert A. Devine, T. H. Breen, and others) *America: Past and Present,* Scott, Foresman (Glenview, IL), 1985, 2nd edition, 1990.

(Editor, with James Stuart Olson) *American Experiences,* Volume I: *1607 to 1877,* Volume II: *From 1877,* Scott, Foresman (Glenview, IL), 1985, 4th edition, Longman (New York, NY), 1998.

(With Fred Harris and Margaret S. Elliston) *American Democracy,* Scott, Foresman (Glenview, IL), 1987.

(With James K. Martin, James Jones, and others) *America and Its People,* Scott, Foresman (Glenview, IL), 1988.

(With James Stuart Olson) *Winning Is the Only Thing: Sports in America since 1945,* Johns Hopkins University Press (Baltimore, MD), 1989.

(With James Stuart Olson) *Where the Domino Fell: America and Vietnam, 1945 to 1990,* St. Martin's (New York, NY), 1990, 2nd edition published as *Where the Domino Fell: American and Vietnam, 1945 to 1995,* 1996.

(Editor, with Elliott J. Gorn and Terry D. Bilhartz) *Constructing the American Past,* Volume I: *1607 to 1877,* Volume II: *1877 to Present,* Scott, Foresman (Glenview, IL), 1991, 2nd edition, HarperCollins (New York, NY), 1995.

(Editor, with James Stuart Olson and Ronald Fritze) *Reflections on Civilization,* Volume I: *Beginnings to Renaissance,* Volume II: *Renaissance to Present,* Scott, Foresman (Glenview, IL), 1991.

(With J. Gregory Garrison) *Heavy Justice: The State of Indiana v. Michael G. Tyson,* Addison-Wesley (Reading, MA), 1994, published as *Heavy Justice: The Trial of Mike Tyson,* University of Arkansas Press (Fayetteville, AR), 2000.

(With James Stuart Olson) *John Wayne: American,* Free Press (New York, NY), 1995.

(With James Stuart Olson) *My Lai: A Brief History with Documents,* Bedford Books (Boston, MA), 1998.

(Editor, with Benjamin G. Rader) John M. Carroll, *Red Grange and the Rise of Modern Football,* University of Illinois Press (Urbana, IL), 1999.

(Editor) *Pittsburgh Sports: Stories from the Steel City,* University of Pittsburgh Press (Pittsburgh, PA), 2000.

(With James Stuart Olson) *A Line in the Sand: The Alamo in Blood and Memory,* Free Press (New York, NY), 2001.

Also author of *But They Can't Beat Us,* 1999. Contributor to *Historical Dictionary of the New Deal* and *Encyclopedia of Southern Culture.* Coeditor of series "Studies of Sports and Society," University of Illinois Press, 1986—. Contributor to history and American studies journals. *Journal of Sport History,* book review editor, 1984-87, and presently member of editorial board; *Lamar Journal of the Humanities,* member of editorial board; *Arete: The Journal of Sport Literature,* advisory editor.

SIDELIGHTS: Randy Roberts has written extensively on American popular history and sports. Among his books are *Heavy Justice: The State of Indiana v. Michael G. Tyson, John Wayne: American,* and *A Line in the Sand: The Alamo in Blood and Memory.*

Heavy Justice, cowritten by Roberts and J. Gregory Garrison, examines the rape trial of American boxer Mike Tyson in 1991. Garrison was the prosecutor in the case. Charged with raping former beauty queen Desiree Washington, Tyson was found guilty and sentenced to six years in prison. According to Mary Carroll in *Booklist, Heavy Justice* "fleshes out the tabloid drama's dozens of characters . . . to produce an engrossing narrative."

Roberts cowrote *John Wayne: American,* a biography of the famous film actor, with James Stuart Olson. The two academics contend that although Wayne is one of the most popular of all film actors, he "has been marginalized by pop-culture elitists because of his political conservatism," as Gordon Flagg noted in *Booklist.* This argument, in the view of *New York Times Book Review* writer Julie Salamon, minimizes Wayne's flaws and glosses over the contradictions in his behavior, making the book "much more perceptive about [Wayne's] movies than about his life and politics." Desmond Ryan of the *Knight-Ridder/Tribune News Service,* too, found that Roberts and Olson "prove stronger on [Wayne's] films than on his controversial politics." Ryan concluded that, because of *John Wayne: American,* "we finally have the truth behind the legend." Woody West, reviewing the book for *Insight on the News,* called *John Wayne: American* "solid and a pleasure to read."

Roberts and Olson also wrote *A Line in the Sand,* a look at the place held by the battle of the Alamo in American mythology. The rebellion of Texans against Mexican dictator Antonio Lopez de Santa Anna in 1836 led to the tragic slaughter at the Alamo. "The authors' account of the continual conflicts over the physical and the mythical elements of the legend," wrote a critic for *Publishers Weekly,* "establishes the Alamo as a focal point of a wider struggle to define, and therefore to control, America's past." A *Kirkus Reviews* critic found *A Line in the Sand* to be an "engaging analysis of one of the most politically charged events in American history."

Roberts once told *CA:* "My goal is to write history for the widest possible audience. Although my interests change, the goal remains firmly fixed."

BIOGRAPHICAL/CRITICAL SOURCES:

PERIODICALS

Booklist, October 1, 1995, Gordon Flagg, review of *John Wayne: American,* p. 244.
Insight on the News, October 16, 1995, Woody West, review of *John Wayne,* p. 30.
Journal of American History, March, 1998, Luu doan Huynh, review of *Where the Domino Fell: America and Vietnam, 1945 to 1990,* p. 1464; June, 1999, Dennis Mills, review of *My Lai: A Brief History with Documents,* p. 315.
Journal of American Studies, April, 1999, review of *John Wayne,* p. 188.

Journal of Popular Culture, winter, 1997, review of *John Wayne,* p. 193.
Kirkus Reviews, November 1, 2000, review of *A Line in the Sand: The Alamo in Blood and Memory,* p. 1535.
Knight-Ridder/Tribune News Service, October 4, 1995, Desmond Ryan, review of *John Wayne,* p. 1004.
Library Journal, May 1, 1994, Sally G. Waters, review of *Heavy Justice: The State of Indiana v. Michael G. Tyson,* p. 1489; August, 1995, Thomas Wiener, review of *John Wayne,* p. 77; August, 1999, Tim Delaney, review of *Red Grange and the Rise of Modern Football,* p. 101.
New York Times Book Review, September 10, 1995, Julie Salamon, review of *John Wayne,* p. 28.
Publishers Weekly, March 14, 1994, review of *Heavy Justice,* p. 60; November 8, 1999, review of *But They Can't Beat Us,* p. 60; November 27, 2000, review of *A Line in the Sand,* p. 63.*

*   *   *

ROEMER, Kenneth Morrison 1945-

PERSONAL: Born June 6, 1945, in East Rockaway, NY; son of Arthur Kenneth (a senior publications engineer) and Mildred Hebert (an artist and teacher) Roemer; married Claire Marie O'Keefe (an educator and administrator), 1968; children: Yvonne, Michael. *Education:* Harvard University, B.A. (cum laude), 1967; University of Pennsylvania, M.A., 1968, Ph.D., 1971.

ADDRESSES: Home—3409 Halifax Dr., Arlington, TX 76013. *Office*—Department of English, Box 19035, University of Texas at Arlington, Arlington, TX 76019-0035; fax: 817-272-2718. *E-mail*—roemer@uta.edu.

CAREER: University of Texas—Arlington, assistant professor, 1971-74, associate professor, 1974-82, professor of English, 1982—, assistant dean of graduate school, 1975-77. Visiting professor, Shimane University, Japan, 1982-83, and at International Christian University, Tokyo, Japan, 1988; public speaker and lecturer, including venues in Austria, Brazil, Germany, Japan, Portugal, and Turkey, 1988—; Harvard University, Cambridge, MA, guest lecturer, 1993. University Catholic Community Choir, director, 1979-86; Education Creative Arts Theater and School, board member, 1989-2000, vice president, 1996-2000; affiliated with *What's the Word* (a Public Broadcasting Service [PBS] Utopias program), 1998; advisory board member for Utopias exhibit at Bibliotéque Nationale and New York Public Library, 2000-01.

MEMBER: Modern Language Association of America (chair, Late Nineteenth- and Early Twentieth-Century American Literature division and American Indian Literatures discussion group, both 1981; chair, American Indian Literatures division, 1995; executive committee, Science Fiction, Utopian, and Fantastic Literature discussion group, 1998-99), American Studies Association, American Historical Association, Melville Society, Association for the Study of American Indian Literatures (vice president, 1998), Society for Utopian Studies (member of steering committee, 1986—), Wordcraft Circle of Native Writers and Storytellers, American Studies Association of Texas.

AWARDS, HONORS: Research grants, summer stipends, and fellowship, University of Texas—Arlington, 1972, 1974, 1976, 1978, 1984, 1986, 1991, 1992, 1996, and 1999; nomination for Pulitzer Prize for American history, 1976, for *The Obsolete Necessity: America in Utopian Writings, 1888-1900;* Exxon Educational Foundation grant, 1977-78; ACLS travel grant, 1986; senior scientist fellowship, Japan Society for the Promotion of Science, 1988; Chancellor's Outstanding Teaching Award, University of Texas at Arlington, 1988; National Endowment for the Humanities grants to direct summer seminars, 1992, 1994, 1996, and 1998; finalist, Koizumi Yakumo Cultural Prize, 1995; Academy of Distinguished Teachers Award, 1998; Writer of the Year Award (reference work), Wordcraft Circle of Native Writers and Storytellers, 1998.

WRITINGS:

The Obsolete Necessity: America in Utopian Writings, 1888-1900, Kent State University Press, 1976.
(Author of introduction) King Camp Gillette, *The Human Drift* (reprint), Scholars' Facsimiles & Reprints, 1976.
(Editor and contributor) *America as Utopia,* B. Franklin, 1981.
Build Your Own Utopia: An Interdisciplinary Course in Utopian Speculation (textbook), University Press of America, 1981.
(Editor) *Approaches to Teaching Momaday's "The Way to Rainy Mountain,"* Modern Language Association of America, 1988.
(Editor, author of introduction, and contributor) *Native American Writers of the United States,* Gale (Detroit, MI), 1997.

Contributor to books, including *Studies in American Indian Literature,* edited by Paula Gunn Allen, Modern Language Association of America, 1983; *Smoothing the Ground: Essays on Native American Oral Literature,* edited by Brian Swann, University of California Press, 1983; *No Place Else: Explorations in Utopian and Dystopian Fiction,* edited by Eric Rabkin, Martin Greenberg, and Joseph Olander, Southern Illinois University Press, 1983; *Literarisch Utopien von Morus bis zur Gegenwart* (title means "Utopian Literature from More to the Present"), edited by Klaus L. Berghahn and Ulrich Seeber, Athenaum (Konigstein), 1983; *Reconstructing American Literature: Courses, Syllabi, Issues,* edited by Paul Lauter, Feminist Press, 1983; *Bibliographical Guide to the Study of the Literature of the U.S.A.,* 5th edition, edited by Clarence Gohdes and Sanford E. Marovitz, Duke University Press, 1984; *Utopian Thought in American Literature,* edited by Arno Heller, Gunter Narr Verlag, 1988; *Looking Backward: 1988-1888,* edited by Daphne Patai, University of Massachusetts Press, 1988; *Essays on Edward Bellamy,* edited by Daphne Patai, University of Massachusetts Press, 1988; *The Handbook of Native American Literature,* edited by Andrew Wiget, Garland, 1996; *Utopia e Modernita: Teorie e prassi utopiche nell'eta moderna e postmoderna,* edited by Giuseppa Saccaro Del Buffa, Casa del Libro (Rome, Italy), 1989; *Encyclopedia of American Literature,* edited by Continuum, Stephen Serafin, 1999; *Dictionary of Literary Utopias,* edited by Vita Fortunati, Skatkine, 2000.

Also contributor of articles, review, and essay reviews to periodicals, including *American Quarterly, American Literature, American Literary History, College English, Technology and Culture, Rising Generation, Prospects, Utopian Studies, ASAIL, American Historical Review, Chronicle of Higher Education, Japan Times, Paintbrush,* and *Here. American Quarterly,* assistant editor, 1969-70, *ALR,* managing editor, 1972-78, book review editor, 1978-86; *Utopus Discovered: A Most Informal Newsletter,* editor, 1975-88; *SAIL* (publication of the Association for the Study of American Indian Literatures), member of editorial board, 1989—; *Heath Anthology of American Literature,* contributing editor, 1990—.

WORK IN PROGRESS: Utopian Audiences: How Readers Locate Nowhere; A Sidewalker's Japan; and A Liberated Father's Survival Manual.

SIDELIGHTS: Kenneth Morrison Roemer told *CA:* "There are obvious drawbacks to writing about such 'unusual' topics as utopian and Indian literatures. People are always asking me to define what I mean and to justify what I do. But these disadvantages are actually advantages. If I were working in more conventional areas, I might be lulled into believing that grappling with fundamental questions of definition and value was unnecessary. My attitude about my writing is closely related to my decision to take my family to a very traditional area of Japan for a year. Living in Matsue, where our family of four accounted for approximately fifty percent of the American population in a city of 130,000, forced us to redefine and reevaluate ourselves. Too many voyages to utopias, Indian visions, and Matsue might lead to acute cases of dislocation, but without periodic, constructive dislocations we really do not know where we are."

BIOGRAPHICAL/CRITICAL SOURCES:

PERIODICALS

American Literature, November, 1976, October, 1982.
Japan Times, October 12, 1983.
Times Literary Supplement, September 10, 1976.
Village Voice Literary Supplement, February, 1982.

OTHER

Kenneth M. Roemer Web site, http://www.uta.edu/english/roemer/ (February 6, 2002).

*　　*　　*

ROSENBERG, Jane 1949-

PERSONAL: Born December 7, 1949, in New York, NY; daughter of Abner Emmanuel (a real estate developer) and Lily (Quittman) Rosenberg; married Michael B. Frankel, February 17, 1974 (divorced, 1978); married Robert F. Porter (a writer), May 30, 1982; children: (second marriage) Melo (stepdaughter), Ava Hermine, Eloise Pearl. *Education:* Attended City of London College and Sir John Cass College of Art, 1970; Beaver College, B.F.A., 1971; New York University, M.A., 1973.

ADDRESSES: Office—2925 Nichols Canyon Rd., Los Angeles, CA 90046; fax: 323-851-2532. *E-mail*—JaneRLA@aol.com.

CAREER: Daniel & Charles Associates, New York, NY, commercial artist, 1973; Ethical Culture School, New York, NY, art teacher, 1974-75; freelance illustrator and designer, 1975-81; art director of *New York News for Kids,* 1979-80; freelance illustrator. Exhibitions at galleries in New York, NY, including Master Eagle Gallery, 55 Mercer Gallery, and Judith Christian Gallery; in Los Angeles, CA, including Every Picture Tells a Story; and in Las Vegas, NV, including Summerlin Library and Performing Arts Center.

MEMBER: Authors Guild.

WRITINGS:

JUVENILES

(Self-illustrated) *Dance Me a Story: Twelve Tales from the Classic Ballets,* Thames & Hudson, 1985.
(Self-illustrated) *Sing Me a Story: The Metropolitan Opera's Book of Opera Stories for Children,* Thames & Hudson/Metropolitan Opera, 1989.
(Self-illustrated) *Play Me a Story: A Child's Introduction to Classical Music through Stories and Poems,* Knopf, 1994.

ILLUSTRATOR

Gloria Rothstein, *A Scholastic Skills Program: Vocabulary Skills,* Scholastic, 1980.
Rose Beranbaum, *Romantic and Classic Cakes,* Irena Chalmers, 1981.

Also illustrator of *Technology of the City,* edited by David Jacobs, for Abrams; and the "Four Opera Scenes" notecard series, for Metropolitan Opera Guild, 1986. Contributor of illustrations to magazines.

WORK IN PROGRESS: Author with others of pilot script, *The Flying Pizza Opera Company,* one-hour children's television series, for Public Broadcasting Service (PBS), 2001; *The Way up the Mountain* (stories from world religion), a one-half hour animated children's television series, for David Braun Productions, 2001.

SIDELIGHTS: Jane Rosenberg told *CA:* "Trained as a fine artist in New York City and exhibiting my paintings in downtown galleries, I turned to freelance illustration for income. I preferred illustrating to teaching or full-time commercial art, both of which demanded too much time away from the studio. The more my work appeared in magazines, newspapers, and books, the more appealing the notion of illustrating a project of my own became. Turning to a lifelong interest—the ballet—I retold the stories of the great classical ballets in the manner of fairy tales, attempting to offer the reader more than a program synopsis.

"Since childhood, illustrated books have held an irresistible attraction for me. Now I find myself painting and writing for children, telling tales of the ballet, opera, or the programmatic classical musical repertory; combining my art with my love of the performing arts into one of the most satisfying of all forms, the illustrated book. As parents face budget cutbacks in public schools and music programs are abandoned, it is more important than ever to expose young children to classical music. I attempt, in my books to convey the delights of great music through stories, poems and art. I am currently involved in the writing of a television series that will bring music to an even larger audience of children."

BIOGRAPHICAL/CRITICAL SOURCES:

PERIODICALS

Opera Quarterly, Volume 9, number 2, 1993.
Times Educational Supplement, April 11, 1986.

OTHER

KUSC radio, Los Angeles, CA, interview with Bonnie Grice, 1994.

*   *   *

ROTH, Klaus 1939-

PERSONAL: Born November 17, 1939, in Hamburg, Germany; son of Georg and Emma (Meyer) Roth; married Juliana Djendov (a lecturer), 1967; children: Maren M., Verena S. *Ethnicity:* "German." *Education:* Attended University of Freiburg, 1960-68, Ph.D., 1975; Indiana University—Bloomington, M.A., 1969. *Avocational interests:* "Ethnology, folklore, Southeast European studies, intercultural communication."

ADDRESSES: Home—Johann-von-Werth-strasse 1, D-80639 Munich, Germany. *Office*—Institut für deutsche und vgl. Volkskunde, University of Munich, Ludwigstrasse 25/0, D-80539 Munich, Germany; fax: 4989-13939079. *E-mail*—k.roth@lrz.uni-muenchen.de.

CAREER: High school teacher, Staufen, Germany, 1970-73; University of Münster, Münster, Germany, assistant professor, 1976-82; University of Munich, Munich, Germany, professor, 1982—. University of California—Berkeley, visiting professor, 1988 and 1991.

MEMBER: International Association for Southeast European Anthropology, Deutsche Gesellschaft für Volkskunde (vice president), Südosteuropa-Gesellschaft, American Folklore Society.

WRITINGS:

(With H. Mannheims) *Probate Inventories: An International Bibliography,* F. Coppenrath (Münster, Germany), 1984.
(Editor) *Southeast European Folk Culture in the Modern Era,* Südosteuropa-Gesellschaft (Munich, Germany), 1992.
(Editor and compiler, with Gabriele Wolf) *South Slavic Folk Culture: Bibliography of Literature in English, German, and French on Bosnian-Hercegovinian, Bulgarian, Macedonian, Montenegrin, and Serbian Folk Culture,* Slavica (Columbia, OH), 1993.
(Editor) *Radost Ivanova: Folklore of the Change: Folk Culture in Post-Socialist Bulgaria,* Academia Scientiarum Fennica (Helsinki, Finland), 1999.

Editor of journal, *Ethnologia Balkanica,* volumes 1-4, Waxmann (New York, NY), 1997-2000

IN GERMAN

Ehebruchschwänke in Liedform: Eine Untersuchung zur deutsch-und englischsprachigen Schwantballade, Fink (Munich, Germany), 1977.
(Editor with J. Roth) Lída and Tomás Micek, *Entdeckung Balkan: Jugoslawien, Griechenland, Bulgarien; Land und Menschen zwischen Adria, Ägäis und Schwarzem Meer,* Süddeutscher Verlag (Munich, Germany), 1987.
(Editor) *Handwerk im Mittel-und Südosteuropa: Mobilität, Vermittlung und Wandel im Handwerk des 18. bis 20. Jahrhunderts,* Südosteuropa-Gesellschaft (Munich, Germany), 1987.
(Editor) *Südosteuropäische Popularliteratur im 19. und 20. Jahrhunders,* Südosteuropa-Schriften (Munich, Germany), 1993.
(Editor and translator) *Typenverzeichnis der bulgarischen Volksmärchen, von L. Daskalova Perkowski, D. Dobreva, J. Koceva, E. Miceva,* FFC (Helsinki, Finland), 1995.

(Editor with Helge Gerndt) *Zeitschrift für Volkskunde: Gesamtregister Jahrgang 1-90 (1891-1994),* Schwartz (Göttingen, Germany), 1995s.

(Editor) *Mit der Differenz leben: Europäische Ethnologie und Interkulturelle Kommunikation,* Waxmann (New York, NY), 1996.

(Editor with Fr.-D. Grimm) *Das Dorf in Südosteuropa zwischen Tradition und Umbruch,* SOG (Munich, Germany), 1997.

(Editor with R. Alsheimer and A. Moosmüller) *Lokale Kulturen in einer globalisierenden Welt: Perspektiven auf interkulturelle Spannungsfelder,* Waxmann (New York, NY), 2000.

(Editor) *Nachbarschaft: Interkulturelle Beziehungen zwischen Deutschen, Polen und Tschechen,* Waxmann (New York, NY), 2001.

OTHER

Slike u glavama: Ogledi o narodnoj kulturi u jugoistocnoj Evropi (title means "Images in the Head: Perspectives on Southeast European Folk Cultures"; in Bulgarian or Serbian), translated by Alecksandra Bajazetov-Vucen, Biblioteka XX vek (Belgrade, Yugoslavia), 2000.

Editor with D. Dobreva, *Seloto mezdu promjana i tradicija* (title means "The Village between Change and Tradition"; No. 3-4 of the journal *Balgarski folklor* 23; in Bulgarian or Serbian), 1997. Contributor of about two hundred articles and reviews to academic journals.

WORK IN PROGRESS: Research on intercultural communication and on the folk culture of southeastern Europe.

*   *   *

ROTHENBERG, Jerome 1931-

PERSONAL: Born December 11, 1931, in New York, NY; son of Morris and Esther (Lichtenstein) Rothenberg; married Diane Brodatz (an anthropologist), December 25, 1952; children: Matthew. *Education:* College of the City of New York (now City College of the City University of New York), B.A., 1952; University of Michigan, M.A., 1953; Columbia University, graduate studies, 1956-59.

ADDRESSES: Home—1026 San Abella, Encinitas, CA 92024. *Office*—c/o New Directions, 80 Eighth Ave., New York, NY 10011.

CAREER: Poet, writer, teacher, and translator; Hawk's Well Press, New York, NY, founder, publisher, and editor, 1959-64; City College of New York, New York, NY, instructor, 1960-61; Mannes College of Music, instructor, 1961-70; University of California, San Diego, CA, Regents professor, 1971, professor of visual arts and literature, 1977-85 and 1989—, chairman, visual arts, 1990-93, head of creative writing, 1994-95; State University of New York, Binghamton, NY, professor, 1986-1988; visiting research professor, University of Wisconsin—Milwaukee, WI, 1974-75; visiting professor at New School for Social Research, 1971-72, San Diego State University, 1976-77, University of Southern California, 1983, and University of California, Riverside, CA, 1980; writer-in-residence, State University of New York, Albany, NY, 1986. *Military service:* U.S. Army, 1953-55.

MEMBER: PEN American Center, New Wilderness Foundation, World Academy of Poetry (UNESCO).

AWARDS, HONORS: Longview Foundation Award for Poetry, 1961; Wenner-Gren Foundation for Anthropological Research grant, 1968, for experiments in the translation of American Indian poetry; Guggenheim Foundation fellowship for poetry, 1974; National Endowment for the Arts fellowship in creative writing, 1976; American Book Award, Before Columbus Foundation, 1982, for *Pre-Faces and Other Writings;* PEN Center USA West Award in translation, 1994, PEN Oakland Josephine Miles Award, 1994, for *The Lorca Variations,* and 1996, for *Poems for the Millennium;* Doctor of Letters, State University of New York and the College at Oneota, 1997.

WRITINGS:

POETRY

White Sun Black Sun, Hawk's Well Press (New York, NY), 1960.

The Seven Hells of the Jigoku Zoshi, Trobar (New York, NY), 1962.

Sightings I-IX, Hawk's Well Press (New York, NY), 1964.

The Gorky Poems, El Corno Emplumado (Mexico City, Mexico), 1966.

Between: 1960-1963, Fulcrum Press (London, England), 1967.

Conversations, Black Sparrow Press (Los Angeles, CA), 1968.

Poems 1964-1967, Black Sparrow Press (Los Angeles, CA), 1968.

(With Ian Tyson) *Offering Flowers,* Circle Press (London, England), 1968.

(With Ian Tyson) *Sightings I-IX* [and] *Red Easy a Color,* Circle Press (London, England), 1968.

Poland/1931, Part I, Unicorn Press (Santa Barbara, CA), 1969.

(With Tom Phillips) *The Directions,* Tetrad Press (London, England), 1969.

Polish Anecdotes, Unicorn Press (Santa Barbara, CA), 1970.

Poems for the Game of Silence, 1960-1970, Dial Press (New York, NY), 1971.

A Book of Testimony, Tree Books (Bolinas, CA), 1971.

Net of Moon, Net of Sun, Unicorn Press (Santa Barbara, CA), 1971.

(With Ian Tyson and Richard Johnny John) *Poems for the Society of the Mystic Animals,* Tetrad Press (London, England), 1972.

A Valentine No a Valedictory for Gertrude Stein, Judith Walker (London, England), 1972.

(With Ian Tyson) *Three Friendly Warnings,* Tetrad Press (London, England), 1973.

Esther K. Comes to America, Unicorn Press (Greensboro, NC), 1973.

Seneca Journal 1: A Poem of Beavers, Perishable Press (Madison, WI), 1973.

Poland/1931 (complete), New Directions (New York, NY), 1974.

The Cards, Black Sparrow Press (Los Angeles, CA), 1974.

The Pirke and the Pearl, Tree Books (Berkeley, CA), 1975.

(With Philip Sultz) *Seneca Journal: Midwinter,* Singing Bone Press (St. Louis, MO), 1975.

A Poem to Celebrate the Spring and Diane Rothenberg's Birthday, Perishable Press (Madison, WI), 1975.

Book of Palaces: The Gatekeepers, Pomegranate Press (Boston, MA), 1975.

(With Ian Tyson) *I Was Going through the Smoke,* Tetrad Press (London, England), 1975.

Rain Events, Membrane Press (Milwaukee, WI), 1975.

The Notebooks, Membrane Press (Milwaukee, WI), 1976.

A Vision of the Chariot in Heaven, Hundred Flowers Bookshop (Boston, MA), 1976.

(With Ian Tyson) *Narratives and Realtheater Pieces,* Braad Editions (Bretenoux, France), 1977.

(With Philip Sultz) *Seneca Journal: The Serpent,* Singing Bone Press (St. Louis, MO), 1978.

A Seneca Journal (complete), New Directions (New York, NY), 1978.

Abulafia's Circles, Membrane Press (Milwaukee, WI), 1979.

B.R.M.Tz.V.H., Perishable Press (Madison, WI), 1979.

Letters and Numbers, Salient Seedling Press (Madison, WI), 1980.

Vienna Blood and Other Poems, New Directions (New York, NY), 1980.

For E. W.: Two Sonnets, Spot Press (London, England), 1981.

Imaginal Geography 9: Landscape with Bishop, Atticus Press (San Diego, CA), 1982.

The History of Dada as My Muse, Spot Press (London, England), 1982.

Altar Pieces, Station Hill Press, (Tarrytown, NY), 1982.

That Dada Strain, New Directions (New York, NY), 1983.

(With Harold Cohen) *15 Flower World Variations,* Membrane Press (Milwaukee, WI), 1984.

A Merz Sonata, illustrated by Debra Weier, Emanon Press (Easthampton, MA), 1985.

New Selected Poems, 1970-1985, New Directions (New York, NY), 1986.

Gematria 5, Bellevue Press (Binghamton, NY), 1987.

Khurbn and Other Poems, New Directions (New York, NY), 1989.

A Gematria for Jackson Mac Low, Imprints (London, England), 1991.

The Lorca Variations I-XXXIII, Zasterle Press (Tenerife, Spain), 1990, New Directions (New York, NY), 1993.

Gematria, Sun & Moon Press (Los Angeles, CA), 1994.

An Oracle for Delphi, illustrated by Demosthenes Agrafiotis, Light and Dust Books (Kenosha, WI), 1994.

Two Songs about Flowers & Where I Was Walking, privately printed, New College Book Arts (San Francisco, CA), 1995.

Pictures of the Crucifixion and Other Poems, drawings by David Rathman, typography by Philip Gallo, Granary Books (New York, NY), 1996.

A Flower like a Raven, translated from Kurt Schwitter's works, an artist's book edition by Barbara Fahrner, Granary Books (New York, NY), 1996.

Seedings and Other Poems, New Directions (New York, NY), 1996.

(With Ian Tyson) *Twin Gematria,* 1997.

Gematria 643, art by Ian Tyson, 1997.

Delight/Délices & Other Gematria, drawings by Ian Tyson, French translations by Nicole Peyrafitte, Editions Ottezec (Nimes, France), 1998.

At the Grave of Nakahara Chuya, Backwoods Broadsides (Ellsworth, ME), 1998.

The Treasures of Dunhuang, Graphic Arts Press (Bloomington, IN), 1998.

The Leonardo Project: 10+2 (visual poems), privately printed (San Diego, CA), 1998.

Paris Elegies and Improvisations, Meow Press (Buffalo, NY), 1998.

A Paradise of Poets: New Poems & Translations, New Directions (New York, NY), 1999.

(With Ian Tyson) *The Case for Memory, and Other Poems,* Granary Books (New York, NY), 2001.

A Book of Witness: Spells and Gris-Gris, New Directions (New York, NY), 2002.

RECORDINGS

Origins and Meanings, Folkways, 1968.

From a Shaman's Notebook, Folkways, 1968.

Horse Songs and Other Soundings, S-Press, 1975.

6 Horse Songs for 4 Voices, New Wilderness Audiographics, 1978.

Jerome Rothenberg Reads Poland/1931, New Fire, 1979.

Jerome Rothenberg, New Letters (Kansas City, MO), 1979.

Rothenberg, Turetsky: Performing, Blues Economique, 1984.

The Birth of the War God (with Charles Morrow) and *The Western Wind,* Laurel, 1988.

(With Charles Morrow) *Signature,* Granary, 2001.

PLAYS

The Deputy (adaptation of a play by Rolf Hochhuth; produced in New York, NY, 1964), Samuel French (New York, NY), 1965.

That Dada Strain, music by Bertram Turetsky, produced by Center for Theater Science and Research, San Diego, CA, 1985, produced in New York, NY, 1987.

Poland/1931, produced by The Living Theater, New York, NY, 1988.

(With Makoto Oda and Charles Morrow) *Khurbn/Hiroshima,* produced by Bread and Puppet Theater, Glover, VT.

OTHER

(Editor and translator) *New Young German Poets,* City Lights (San Francisco, CA), 1959.

(Editor) *Ritual: A Book of Primitive Rites and Events* (anthology), Something Else Press (New York, NY), 1966.

(Translator) *The Flight of Quetzalcoatl (Aztec),* Unicorn Bookshop (Brighton, England), 1967.

(Translator, with Michael Hamburger) Hans Magnus Enzenberger, *Poems for People Who Don't Read Poems,* Atheneum (New York, NY), 1968, published as *Selected Poems,* Penguin (New York, NY), 1968.

(Editor and author of commentaries) *Technicians of the Sacred: A Range of Poetries from Africa, America, Asia, and Oceania,* Doubleday (New York, NY), 1968, 2nd revised edition, University of California Press (Berkeley, CA), 1985.

(Translator) Eugen Gomringer, *The Book of Hours and Constellations,* Something Else Press (New York, NY), 1968.

(Translator) *The Seventeen Horse Songs of Frank Mitchell, Nos. X-XIII,* Tetrad Press (London, England), 1970.

(Editor) *Shaking the Pumpkin: Traditional Poetry of the Indian North Americans,* Doubleday (New York, NY), 1972, 2nd revised edition, University of New Mexico Press (Albuquerque, NM), 1991.

(Editor, with George Quasha) *America a Prophecy: A New Reading of American Poetry from Pre-Columbian Times to the Present,* Random House (New York, NY), 1973.

(Editor) *Revolution of the Word: A New Gathering of American Avant Garde Poetry 1914-1945,* Seabury-Continuum Books (New York, NY), 1974.

(Editor with Michel Benamou) *Ethnopoetics: A First International Symposium,* Alcheringa (Boston, MA), 1976.

(Translator, with Harris Lenowitz) *Gematria 27,* Membrane Press (Milwaukee, WI), 1977.

(Editor, with Harris Lenowitz and Charles Doria) *A Big Jewish Book: Poems and Other Visions of the Jews from Tribal Times to Present,* Doubleday (New York, NY), 1978, contents revised as *Exiled in the Word: Poems & Other Visions of the Jews from Tribal Times to the Present,* Copper Canyon Press (Port Townsend, WA), 1989.

Pre-Faces and Other Writings, New Directions (New York, NY), 1981.

(Editor and author of commentaries, with Diane Rothenberg) *Symposium of the Whole: A Range of Discourse toward an Ethnopoetics,* University of California Press (Berkeley, CA), 1983.

The Riverside Interviews 4: Jerome Rothenberg, edited by Gavin Selerie and Eric Mottram, Binnacle Press (London, England), 1984.

(Translator) *Four Lorca Suites,* Sun and Moon Press (Los Angeles, CA), 1989.

(Editor and co-translator) Kurt Schwitters, *Poems, Performance Pieces, Proses, Plays, Poetics,* Temple University Press (Philadelphia, PA), 1993.

(Editor, with Pierre Joris) *Poems for the Millennium: The University of California Book of Modern and Post-Modern Poetry,* University of California Press (Berkeley, CA), Volume One: *From Fin-de-Siècle to Negritude,* 1995, Volume Two: *From Postwar to Millennium,* 1998.

(Editor, with David Guss) *The Book, Spiritual Instrument,* Granary Books (New York, NY), 1996.

(Editor, with Steven Clay) *A Book of the Book: Some Works & Projections about the Book & Writing,* Granary Books (New York, NY), 2000.

(Translator, with Milos Sovak) Vitezslav Nexval, *Anti-lyrik and Other Poems,* Green Integer, 2001.

(Translator) Frederico García Lorca, *The Suites,* Green Integer, 2001.

(Co-editor with Pierre Joris, and translator) Pablo Picasso, *The Burial of the Count of Orgaz and Other Poems,* Exact Change, 2002.

"Writing Through": Translations and Variations, Wesleyan University Press, 2002.

Contributor of poetry to anthologies, including *A Controversy of Poets,* edited by Paris Leary and Robert Kelly, Doubleday-Anchor, 1965; *New Modern Poetry,* edited by M. L. Rosenthal, Macmillan, 1967; *Notations,* edited by John Cage, Something Else Press, 1969; *Caterpillar Anthology,* edited by Clayton Eshleman, Doubleday-Anchor, 1971; *East Side Scene,* edited by Allen DeLoach, Doubleday-Anchor, 1972; *New Directions Annual,* edited by James Laughlin, New Directions, 1973, 1975, 1976, 1978, 1980; *Preferences,* edited by Richard Howard, Viking, 1974; *The New Naked Poetry,* edited by Stephen Berg and Robert Mezey, Bobbs-Merrill, 1976; *Talking Poetics at Naropa,* edited by Anne Waldman and Marilyn Webb, Shambala Books, 1978; *Esthetics Contemporary,* edited by Richard Kostelanetz, Prometheus Books, 1979; *The New American Poetry,* edited by Donald M. Allen and George Butterick, Grove Press, 1980; *The Terror of Our Days: Four American Poets Respond to the Holocaust,* edited by Harriet L. Parmet, Lehigh University Press, 2001; and *Jewish American Literature: An International Anthology of Sound Poetry,* edited by J. Chametzky, J. Felstiner, H. Flanzbaum, and K. Hellerstein, W. W. Norton, 2001. Contributor to numerous journals, including *Caterpillar, Trobar, Kulchur, El Corno Emplumado, Action Poetique, American Book Review, American Poetry Review, Contact II, Boundary 2, Change, Dialectical Anthropology, Io, l-a-n-g-u-a-g-e, Partisan Review, Poetry Review, River Styx,* and *Vort.*

Founder and editor, Hawk's Well Press and *Poems from the Floating World* (magazine) 1959-64; co-editor, *Some/Thing,* 1965-69; ethnopoetics editor, *Stony Brook,* 1968-71; co-editor, *Alcheringa: A First Magazine of Ethnopoetics,* 1970-76; editor, *New Wilderness Letter,* 1976—. Rothenberg's manuscript collection is housed as the University of California, San Diego. Rothenberg's work has been translated into French, Swedish, Flemish, Spanish, Dutch, Italian, German, Serbian, Finnish, Portuguese, Latvian, Lithuanian, and Japanese.

WORK IN PROGRESS: Collected essays, interviews, and commentaries commissioned and in preparation for Granary Books.

SIDELIGHTS: Jerome Rothenberg's publishing career began in the late 1950s as a translator of German poetry, first for *Hudson Review* and then for City Lights Books. Founding Hawk's Well Press in 1959, Rothenberg used it as a venue to publish collections by some of the up-and-coming poets of the era, including Diane Wakoski and Robert Kelly. He also self-published his first book of poems, *White Sun Black Sun,* under the Hawk's Well imprint. From the beginning, his work embodied experimentation with syntax, image, and form that drew on varied influences and moved in diverse directions. Poetic and artistic forebears such as Gertrude Stein, James Joyce, Dali, the Dadaists, Ezra Pound, and Walt Whitman affected the voice and content of his early work. In a career that has already spanned half a century, including seventy books of his own poetry, plus plays, acclaimed anthologies, and other works, Rothenberg has gone on to explore primitive and archaic poetry, sound poetry, found poetry, visual poetry, collaborations, further translations, his own Jewish heritage, and much more.

In an interview with Michael Rodriguez for *Samizdat,* Rothenberg stated that he came to "believe early that poetry and art could make a difference . . . for the world-at-large at our most ambitious." However, Rothenberg also said that when he returned to writing at the end of his army servince in the mid-1950s, he "felt incredibly isolated as a writer," partly because of the wars during the previous decade (World War II and the Korean War) and partly because of the repressive spirit that permeated the United States due to McCarthyism. Rothenberg continued: "The emergence of the Beats at the same time was the first public signal that we weren't alone in the desire to assert or reassert what we thought of as a new revolution-of-the-word and a second awakening of a radical and unfettered modernism." For Rothenberg and other writers like himself, taking charge of their own publications was the primary means by which they were able to express their voice, and it was this realization that led him, in collaboration with David Antin and Diane Rothenberg, to found Hawk's Well Press.

Rothenberg identified with both the twentieth-century avant garde and with "a range of tribal and subterranean poetries" that can provide "a poetics big enough to account for human creativity, human language-making, over the broadest span available." Of his poetry and his experimental "anthology-assemblages," he once wrote: "My process has been like what Samuel Makindemewabe (per Howard Norman) said of the Cree Indian Trickster: 'to walk forward while looking backward.' With past and future up for grabs, the possibility opened up—by the late 1950s—to make a near-total change in poetry, perception, language, etc., tied up with earlier twentieth century 'revolutions of the word'. . . . My own contributions (nomenclature and praxis) have included 'deep image,' ethnopoetics, 'total translation,' poetics of performance, and assorted attempts 'to reinterpret the poetic past from the point of view of the present.'"

Rothenberg has been particularly interested in the poetry of the North American Indians, both verbal and non-verbal: a poetry that can often be expressed, according to Rothenberg, in "music, non-verbal phonetic sounds, dance, gesture and event, game, dream, etc." It is, he explained, "a high poetry and art, which only a colonialist ideology could have blinded us into labeling 'primitive' or 'savage.'" At the same time, he wrote, "I have been exploring ancestral sources of my own in the world of Jewish mystics, thieves and madmen," the latter resulting in works like *Poland/1931* and *A Big Jewish Book.*

Reviewing the collection titled *Seedings and Other Poems* for *Booklist,* Patricia Monaghan stated: "[He] evokes the dream in, of, and through language more effectively than any other contemporary poet," and she concluded by crediting his poems with being "simultaneously emotionally complex and linguistically experimental." A *Publishers Weekly* reviewer praised the title poem of the collection, an extended and personal contemplation on life and death, noting that its "plain style displays the influence of . . . primitive and oral tribal poetics." The same reviewer found the "Dada-influenced avant-garde" poems in *Seedings and Other Poems* to be less interesting, but was impressed with "'14 Stations' . . . a powerful and sad meditation on the Holocaust."

In 2000 Rothenberg published *A Paradise of Poets: New Poems and Translations,* a collection about which Rochelle Owens in *World Literature Today* observed: "In this volume the poet's stylistic mode, insistencies, and power to synthesize experience into a brilliant word-song orality are manifestations of his art and life where symbol, image, and events create new terminologies." As the titles indicates, the subject of *A Paradise of Poets* deals to a large extent with the lives and works of other poets (and artists) some of whom Rothenberg has known. The assemblage is international, including Garcia Lorca, Vitezslav Nezval, Paul Blackburn, Louis Zukofsky, Picasso, and Kurt Schwitters. Owens noted that "the illuminations and insights [of other poets and artists] . . . are revealed in their marvelous complexity by the poet/translator who renders the body of the poem into a transformational and personal journey of artistic risk and vitality of language."

Rothenberg is widely and highly respected as a consummate anthologist and poetic theorist as well as a poet. In the massive 1,700-page, two-volume *Poems for the Millennium: The University of California Book of Modern and Postmodern Poetry,* edited with Pierre Joris, Rothenberg presents what Hacsi Horvath of *Whole Earth* considered "a brilliant kaleidoscope of writing unstuck in time, both in English and in fine translation, from numerous archaic/modern/postmodern voices." Monaghan praises the editors for providing "the kind of critical guidance so sweeping a collection requires." The first volume, *From Fin-de-Siècle to Negritude,* covers the period from 1900 through World War II. The second volume, *From Postwar to Millennium,* encompasses the remainder of the twentieth century. Despite the length and worldwide scope of *Poems for the Millennium,* the anthology makes no attempt to be comprehensive with regard to twentieth-century poetry. Instead, it emphasizes what Rothenberg and Joris consider to be poems that point toward the future both in form and content, while passing over more conventional work. Beginning with a discussion of Rimbaud and Whitman, the editors present the poetry of Dadaism, Expressionism, Surrealism, and numerous other avant-garde movements, yet omit poets such as Frost, Auden, Derek Walcott, Sylvia Plath, and Robert Pinsky. Reviewing the first volume, a *Publishers Weekly* critic noted: "This invaluable collection, rather than gathering the most fully realized poetry of this century's first four decades, maps poetic possibility, thus demonstrating how poetry was literally remade during this period." Ray Olson of *Booklist* called it "a book to argue with, which is one of its strengths." Describing the second volume in *Publishers Weekly,* a reviewer stated: "This collection freely crosses national and aesthetic boundaries to include work by the Scottish concrete poet and garden designer Ian Hamilton Finlay, poems by the famed African novelist Chinua Achebe, and excerpts from *Dictée,* the only major writing project by the Korean American filmmaker Theresa Hak Kyung Cha," and went on to conclude: "As an introduction to the many avant-gardes of the second half of the century . . . the value of this international gatecrasher cannot be underestimated."

Writing in *Vort,* Kenneth Rexroth described Rothenberg and his poetry in the following way: "Jerome Rothenberg is one of the truly contemporary American poets who has returned U.S. poetry to the mainstream of international modern literature. At the same time, he is a true autochthon. Only here and now could have produced him—a swinging orgy of Martin Buber, Marcel Duchamp, Gertrude Stein, and Sitting Bull. No one writing poetry today has dug deeper into the roots of poetry." Introducing Rothenberg at a 1998 reading, Alan Filreis stated: "He has become the poet, critic, teacher, anthologist, translator, activist, archivist, assembler, organizer, and editor who has done as much as anyone of his generation to make a radical modernism available to readers."

BIOGRAPHICAL/CRITICAL SOURCES:

BOOKS

Anaya, José Vicente, *Los poetas que cayeron del cielo: La Generación Beat Comentada y en su propria voz,* Instituto de Cultura de Baja (Juan Pablos, Mexico), 1998.

Bardic Deadlines: Reviewing Poetry 1984-95, University of Michigan Press (Ann Arbor, MI), 1998.

Benet's Reader's Encyclopedia of American Literature, edited by George Perkins, Barbara Perkins, and Phillip Leininger, HarperCollins (New York, NY), 1991.

Contemporary Jewish-American Dramatists and Poets, edited by Michael Taub and Joel Shatsky, Greenwood Press, 1999.

Contemporary Literary Criticism, Volume VI, Gale (Detroit, MI), 1976.

Dictionary of Literary Biography, Volume 193: *American Poets since World War II,* edited by Joseph Conte, Gale (Detroit, MI), 1998.

Finkelstein, Norman, *Not One of Them in Place: Modern Poetry and Jewish-American Identity,* State University of New York Press, 2001.

Gilbert, Roger, *The Oxford Companion to Twentieth-Century Poetry,* edited by Ian Hamilton, Oxford University Press, 1994.

Opposing Poetries, Northwestern University Press Avante-Garde and Modernism Studies (Evanston, IL), 1996.

Ossman, David, editor, *The Sullen Art,* Corinth Books, 1963.

Packard, William, editor, *The Craft of Poetry,* Doubleday (New York, NY), 1974.

Parmet, Harriet L., *The Terror of Our Days: Four American Poets Respond to the Holocaust,* Lehigh University Press, 2001.

Poetics, Politics, Polemics, Marsilio Publishers (New York, NY), 1996.

Polkinhorn, Harry, *Jerome Rothenberg: A Descriptive Bibliography,* McFarland (Jefferson, NC), 1988.

Rational Geomancy: The Collected Research Reports of the Toronto Research Group, Talon Books (Vancouver, Canada), 1992.

Repositionings: Readings of Contemporary Poetry, Photography, and Performance Art, Pennsylvania State University Press, 1995.

Selerie, Gavin and Eric Mottram, editors, *Jerome Rothenberg,* Binnacle Press (London, England), 1984.

Sherman, Paul, *In Search of the Primitive: Reading David Antin, Jerome Rothenberg, and Gary Snyder,* Louisiana State University (Baton Rouge, LA), 1986.

PERIODICALS

Booklist, September 15, 1996, Patricia Monaghan, review of *Seedings and Other Poems,* p. 205; November 15, 1995, Patricia Monaghan, review of *Poems for the Millennium: The University of California Book of Modern and Postmodern Poetry,* Volume 1, p. 532; March 15, 1999, Ray Olsen, review of *Poems for the Millennium,* Volume 1, p. 1275.

Boundary 2, April, 1975.

New York Quarterly, winter, 1970.

Publishers Weekly, August 26, 1996, review of *Seedings and Other Poems,* p. 94; September 25, 1995, review of *Poems for the Millennium,* Volume 1, p. 50; March 30, 1998, review of *Poems for the Millennium,* Volume 2, p. 76.

Samizdat, winter, 2001, interview with Michael Rodriguez.

Vort, Volume 3, number 1, 1975.

Whole Earth, summer, 1997, Hacsi Horvath, review of *Poems for the Millennium,* p. 90.

World Literature Today, summer, 2000, Rochelle Owens, review of *A Paradise of Poets: New Poems and Translations,* p. 600.

OTHER

Alsop Review, http://www.alsopreview.com/ (April 20, 1998), Jack Foley, "Flowers Normally Irregular: An Interview with Jerome Rothenberg and Pierre Joris."

Jerome Rothenberg: Electronic Poetry Center, http://
  wings.buffalo.edu/epc/authors/rothenberg (February
  28, 2002).
Writers House, http://www.english/upenn.edu/
  (September 28, 1998), Alan Filreis, "Introduction to
  Jerome Rothenberg."
Jerome Rothenberg Papers: Biography/History, http://
  orpheus.ucsd.edu/ (January 21, 2001).

*   *   *

ROWLEY, Ames Dorrance
See LOVECRAFT, H(oward) P(hillips)

*   *   *

RYAN, Margaret 1950-

PERSONAL: Born June 23, 1950, in Trenton, NJ;
daughter of Thomas Michael (an accountant) and Anne
(a secretary; maiden name, Jansen) Ryan; married
Steven Lerner (a computer salesperson), August 29,
1974; children: Emily Ryan. *Education:* University of
Pennsylvania, B.A., 1972; Syracuse University, M.A.,
1974; attended Columbia University, 1976.

ADDRESSES: Home—250 West 104th St., No. 63, New
York, NY 10025. *E-mail*—margaret10025@yahoo.com.

CAREER: Ryan Business Writing, speechwriter and
owner, 1976—. New York State Poets in Public Service, teacher, 1987-91; 92nd Street YMHA-poetry, 60-
plus Program, teacher.

AWARDS, HONORS: College poetry prize, *Mademoiselle* magazine, 1972; Davidson Prize for Sonnets, Poetry Society of America, 1986; New York Foundation
for the Arts fellowship, 1987, 1993; "Best Books for
Young Readers" citation, New York Public Library,
1995, for *How to Give a Speech;* Emily Dickinson
Prize, Poetry Society of America, 1997.

WRITINGS:

So, You Have to Give a Speech!, F. Watts, 1987, 2nd
  edition published as *How to Give a Speech,* F.
  Watts, 1994.
Figure Skating, F. Watts, 1987.

How to Read and Write Poems, F. Watts, 1992.
How to Write a Poem, F. Watts, 1996.

POETRY

Filling out a Life, Front Street Press, 1981.
Black Raspberries, Parsonage Press, 1988.

SIDELIGHTS: Margaret Ryan once commented: "I
knew I wanted to be a writer from the time I was seven
years old. We were asked to write a composition about
spring during class; it was second grade. All my classmates struggled and chewed their pencils and thought
and wrote and scratched out. I closed my eyes, and
could see spring: a deep green lawn dotted with dande-
lions; lilacs in bloom at the edge of the lawn; a robin
foraging for worms. I wrote down what I saw. My
teacher read it out loud to the class . . . I liked the recognition of my talent; I was a shy child who rarely
spoke in class, so it was nice to have a voice, finally,
even if it was the teacher's voice reading my words. I
knew then that I would be a writer.

"I began to write poems when I was in high school. I
liked reading poems: Shakespeare's sonnets, e. e. cummings, Edna St. Vincent Millay, Ernest Downson, Edgar
Allan Poe. So I began trying to write poems of my own
when I was about fifteen. At that time, folk music was
very popular, and there was an emphasis on the lyrics
of popular songs. So writing poems seemed like a very
natural thing to do. Again, I learned that I was good at
it: I submitted works to my high school literary magazine, and they were published. It was a great pleasure
to see my poems in print.

"In college, I was lucky to have a wonderful Latin
teacher who taught Catullus and Ovid and Horace as
poems, real living poems, not as artifacts of a dead
language. Through him I learned much about the form
of poetry, its structure and subtlety. For a time I thought
I, too, would like to be a Latin teacher. But then when I
was a senior in college, I won the *Mademoiselle* magazine poetry contest and I knew I only wanted to be a
poet. So I went to graduate school in creative writing,
in Syracuse.

"I met my husband there. We were married in 1974 and
moved to New York City. Guess what? There were no
jobs for poets! In fact, it was the middle of a recession,
and there were very few jobs at all. I got work in an advertising agency that did ads and catalogs for art galler-

ies in New York. I was chosen because I knew how to spell the word 'Renaissance,' and no one else applying for the job could spell it!

"Eventually, I found work as a speechwriter. It is in many ways like writing poetry: you are writing for the voice; it must be rhythmical and interesting to the ear; it has to tell a story and be convincing. You also have to learn a lot of interesting facts, which can then be used in poems.

"Here's how I came to write a book about writing poetry: from a poetry workshop I was in, I knew an editor at Franklin Watts. He knew I was also a speechwriter, and asked me to do a book about it for high school students. So I wrote *So, You Have to Give a Speech!*

"Later, they asked me if I would like to write a book about something else, and I suggested *Figure Skating.* I have loved skating since I was a child, and it's always nice to write about something you love. Then a new editor came to Franklin Watts, and wanted to do a book about poetry. He called me because on the jacket of the speech book it said I was also a poet.

"I had then been teaching children how to read and write poems for several years, through a program called Poets in Public Service. I taught in schools all around New York City: kindergartens and high schools, middle schools and grade schools, in the city and in the suburbs, and everywhere I saw how much children liked poetry if they could just read it without too much emphasis on 'what it meant.' I had my own daughter by then, too, and I knew that making things—poems, pictures, puppets, cookies, anything creative—made kids feel better about themselves. So I agreed to write the book.

"It was hard to do, because I love poetry so much and know so much about it. I had trouble deciding what was most important to say in five thousand words—

which is hardly anything. I wanted to make sure I communicated some of the conventions of poetry, and the excitement of poetry, and answered the kinds of questions I had about poems when I was a child. Finding the pictures was fun. It was great to think up visual ways of representing ideas like repetition or metaphor.

"I still write poems and meet with a group of poets once a month or so to discuss what we've written. And I still write speeches for business executives. And I'm working on revising the first book I did for Franklin Watts, on giving speeches, to include some information on recent speeches, such as those given by Bill Clinton and George Bush during the election [in 1992].

"But poetry is my first love, and I am assembling a third collection of poems. They are mostly about love, but some are about growing up with my brother, others are about my daughter, and some are even about my work. But even in those poems, they are about how I love the things of this world, and love to name them, too."

BIOGRAPHICAL/CRITICAL SOURCES:

PERIODICALS

Booklist, April 15, 1987, p. 1270; February 1, 1988, p. 936.
Book Report, May, 1987, p. 56; March, 1988, p. 49.
Library Talk, May, 1993, p. 11.
School Library Journal, August, 1987, p. 98; March, 1988, p. 209; January, 1992, p. 132.
Voice of Youth Advocates, August, 1987, p. 139.
Wilson Library Journal, June, 1987, p. 65.

S

SABUDA, Robert (James) 1965-

PERSONAL: Born March 8, 1965, in Michigan; son of Bruce Edward (a tool and die maker) and Judith Elaine (a former singer; maiden name, Barnes) Sabuda; companion of Matthew Christian Reinhart (a writer and illustrator). *Education:* Pratt Institute, B.F.A. (summa cum laude), 1987.

ADDRESSES: Home—260 West End Ave., No. 15C, New York, NY 10023-3666. *Office*—155 West 72nd St., Suite 401, New York, NY 10023.

CAREER: Children's book author and illustrator, 1988—.

MEMBER: Society of Children's Book Writers and Illustrators, Movable Book Society.

AWARDS, HONORS: Notable Children's Trade Book in the Field of Social Studies citation, Children's Book Council, and Best Children's Book of the Year citation, New York Public Library, both 1990, both for *Walden;* Magic Reading Award, *Parenting,* and Children's Book of Distinction citation, *Hungry Mind Review,* both 1992, both for *Saint Valentine; Boston Globe-Horn Book* Honor Award, 1994, for *A Tree Place;* gold medal, Dimension Illustration Awards, 1994, for *A Christmas Alphabet.*

WRITINGS:

SELF-ILLUSTRATED

Saint Valentine, Atheneum (New York, NY), 1992.
Tutankhamen's Gift, Atheneum (New York, NY), 1994.

A Christmas Alphabet (pop-up book), Orchard Books, 1994.
Arthur and the Sword, Atheneum (New York, NY), 1995.
A Kwanzaa Celebration, Little Simon, 1996.
Cookie Count!, Little Simon, 1997.
Robert Sabuda's Disney ABC, Hyperion (New York, NY), 1998.
The Blizzard's Robe, Atheneum (New York, NY), 1999.
The Movable Mother Goose, Little Simon, 1999.
(With Matthew Reinhart) *Young Naturalist Pop-up Handbook: Butterflies,* Hyperion (New York, NY), 2001.
(With Matthew Reinhart) *Young Naturalist Pop-up Handbook: Beetles,* Hperion (New York, NY), 2001.

ILLUSTRATOR

Eugene (*the Fiddler's Son,* Green Tiger Press (La Jolla 988.
Eugene C *he Wishing Well,* Green Tiger Press (La Jolla, CA), 1988.
Henry David Thoreau, *Walden,* text selections by Steve Lowe, Putnam (New York, NY), 1990.
Walt Whitm , *I Hear America Singing,* Putnam (New York, N), 1991.
J. Patrick Lewis, *Earth Verses and Water Rhymes,* Atheneum (New York, NY), 1991.
Christopher Columbus, *The Log of Christopher Columbus,* text selections by Steve Lowe, Putnam (New York, NY), 1992.
Roy Owen, *The Ibis and the Egret,* Putnam (New York, NY), 1993.
Constance Levy, *A Tree Place,* McElderry Books, 1994.

Marguerite W. Davol, *The Paper Dragon,* Atheneum (New York, NY), 1997.

L. Frank Baum, *The Wonderful Wizard of Oz: A Commemorative Pop-up Book,* Little Simon, 2001.

WORK IN PROGRESS: Providence Traveler, for Atheneum, expected 2003.

SIDELIGHTS: Robert Sabuda once commented: "I always knew I would be an artist. I should have known I was going to be a children's book illustrator when I presented my mom with *The Wizard of Oz* ('a pop-up book complete with cyclone!') made with my own dirty little hands. My bedroom was a mess from all my projects. Now I get paid to make messes! My mother can't believe it (but of course she's thrilled, she was sure I'd starve to death)! I live in New York City and share a studio with my boyfriend, author/illustrator Matthew Reinhart."

BIOGRAPHICAL/CRITICAL SOURCES:

PERIODICALS

Booklist, November 15, 1992, Kathryn Broderick, review of *Saint Valentine,* p. 603; April 15, 1994, Ilene Cooper, review of *Tutankhamen's Gift,* p. 1537; November 1, 1995, Kathryn Broderick, review of *Arthur and the Sword,* p. 478; October 15, 1997, Susan Dove Lempke, review of *The Paper Dragon,* p. 402; December 15, 1997, Ilene Cooper, review of *Cookie Count!,* p. 700; December 15, 1999, Ilene Cooper, review of *The Movable Mother Goose,* p. 786; February 15, 2001, Henrietta M. Smith, review of *A Kwanzaa Celebration,* p. 1161.

Five Owls, January, 1993, p. 63.

Horn Book, spring, 1993, p. 87; November-December, 1994, Mary M. Burns, review of *A Christmas Alphabet,* p. 713; January-February, 1998, Hanna B. Zeiger, review of *The Paper Dragon,* p. 63; September, 2000, Michael Patrick Hearn, review of *The Wonderful Wizard of Oz: A Commemorative Pop-up Book,* p. 547.

Kirkus Reviews, November 15, 1992, p. 1447.

Library Talk, January, 1993, p. 17; May, 1993, p. 26.

New Advocate, spring, 1993, p. 140.

Publishers Weekly, October 26, 1992, review of *Saint Valentine,* p. 72; January 17, 1994, review of *Tutankhamen's Gift,* p. 434; September 19, 1994, review of *A Christmas Alphabet,* p. 28; November 6, 1995, review of *Arthur and the Sword,* p. 95;

September 29, 1997, review of *The Paper Dragon,* p. 88; November 29, 1999, review of *The Blizzard's Robe,* p. 637.

Reading Teacher, April, 1993, p. 592.

School Library Journal, November, 1992, Maria B. Salvatore, review of *Saint Valentine,* p. 86; May, 1994, Dot Minzer, review of *Tutankhamen's Gift,* p. 126; October, 1994, Jane Marino, review of *A Christmas Alphabet,* p. 43; November, 1995, Helen Gregory, review of *Arthur and the Sword,* p. 93; November, 1997, Margaret A. Chang, review of *The Paper Dragon,* p. 79; February, 2000, John Peters, review of *The Movable Mother Goose,* p. 97; November, 2000, John Peters, review of *The Wonderful Wizard of Oz: A Commemorative Pop-up Book,* p. 110.

* * *

SANFORD, John 1904-
   (John B. Sanford, Julian L. Shapiro)

PERSONAL: Born Julian Lawrence Shapiro, born May 31, 1904, in New York, NY; name legally changed, 1940; son of Philip D. (an attorney) and Harriet E. (a homemaker; maiden name, Nevins) Shapiro; married Marguerite Roberts (a screenwriter), December 30, 1938 (died February 17, 1989). *Education:* Attended Lafayette College, 1922-23; Fordham University, LL.B., 1927. *Politics:* "Democratic". *Religion:* Jewish.

ADDRESSES: Agent—c/o Sun & Moon Press, 6020 Wilshire Blvd., Los Angeles, CA, 90036.

CAREER: Poet, novelist, and historian, 1928—. Attorney, 1928-36.

AWARDS, HONORS: Award, Los Angeles chapter of PEN, 1986, for *The Color of the Air;* Kirsch Award, *Los Angeles Times,* 1999, for lifetime achievement.

WRITINGS:

Seventy Times Seven (novel), Knopf (New York, NY), 1939.

The People from Heaven (novel), Harcourt (San Diego, CA), 1943.

Every Island Fled Away (novel), Norton (New York, NY), 1964.

The $300 Man (novel), Prentice-Hall (Englewood Cliffs, NJ), 1967.

A More Goodly Country: A Personal History of America, Horizon Press (New York, NY), 1975.

Adirondack Stories, Capra (Santa Barbara, CA), 1976.

View from This Wilderness: American Literature as History, foreword by Paul Mariani, Capra (Santa Barbara, CA), 1977.

To Feed Their Hopes: A Book of American Women, foreword by Annette K. Baxter, University of Illinois Press (Champaign, IL), 1980, reprinted as *A Book of American Women,* University of Illinois Press, 1995.

The Winters of That Country: Tales of the Man-Made Seasons, Black Sparrow Press (Santa Barbara, CA), 1984.

(With William Carlos Williams) *A Correspondence,* foreword by Paul Mariani, Oyster (Santa Barbara, CA), 1984.

Scenes from the Life of an American Jew (autobiography), Black Sparrow Press (Santa Barbara, CA), Volume 1: *The Color of the Air,* 1985, Volume 2: *The Waters of Darkness,* 1986, Volume 3: *A Very Good Land to Fall With,* 1987, Volume 4: *A Walk in the Fire,* 1989, Volume 5: *The Season, It Was Winter,* 1991.

Maggie: A Love Story (autobiography), Barricade, 1993.

The View from Mt. Morris: A Harlem Boyhood (autobiographical), Barricade, 1994.

Intruders in Paradise, University of Illinois Press (Champaign, IL), 1995.

A Palace of Silver (autobiography), Sun & Moon Press (Los Angeles, CA), 2001.

UNDER NAME JOHN B. SANFORD

The Old Man's Place (novel), A. & C. Boni (New York, NY), 1935.

A Man without Shoes (novel), Plantin (Los Angeles, CA), 1951, published under name John Sanford, Black Sparrow Press (Santa Barbara, CA), 1982.

The Land That Touches Mine (novel), Doubleday (New York, NY), 1953.

We Have a Little Sister, Capra (Santa Barbara, CA), 1995.

OTHER

(Under name Julian L. Shapiro) *The Water Wheel* (novel), Dragon Press, 1933.

Contributor to periodicals, including *Contact, New Review, Pagany,* and *Tambour.*

WORK IN PROGRESS: Little Sister Spoken For; A Citizen of No Mean City; A Dinner of Herbs; and *The Sacco-Vanzetti Papers.*

SIDELIGHTS: Julian L. Shapiro had barely begun a career as a lawyer when a conversation with author Nathanael West, one of his old school friends, convinced him to become a writer. An increasing commitment to the art led Shapiro to leave the legal profession completely. Associated with what *New York Times Book Review* contributor Morris Dickstein labeled "the left-wing popular front" of the late 1930s and early 1940s, Shapiro has since written as John or John B. Sanford, adopting his pseudonym as his legal name in 1940. A writer of fiction, history, and autobiography, Sanford's work in all genres exhibits a concern for the poor and oppressed in America.

Sanford's first four novels were well received, but an increasingly conservative climate culminating with the 1950s U.S. Senate investigations of allegedly subversive activities headed by Senator Joseph McCarthy made it difficult to find a publisher for his fifth, *A Man without Shoes.* Though Sanford had the novel printed privately after approximately thirty rejections, the political atmosphere so disheartened him—he and his wife, screenwriter Marguerite Roberts, were blacklisted and therefore unable to get work—that he placed the printed copies in storage. In 1975 Sanford began rebuilding his literary reputation with the publication of his unusual historical work, *A More Goodly Country: A Personal History of America.* The critical acclaim accorded this and subsequent books in Sanford's historical series paved the way for the reissuance of *A Man without Shoes* by Black Sparrow Press in 1982, providing Sanford even wider exposure. In 1985 Sanford turned to autobiography, publishing *The Color of the Air,* the first volume of *Scenes from the Life of an American Jew,* which won him a PEN award in 1986.

A Man without Shoes is the story of Dan Johnson, a man born of working-class parents in New York City. Spanning the years from 1909 to 1938, the novel details Dan's growth from an innocent boy to a hardened crusader against injustice. He works in vain to stay the executions of political activists Nicola Sacco and Bartolomeo Vanzetti, then later marries and finds a job in depression-era New York at an employment agency. In the words of Robert W. Smith in the *Washington Post Book World,* "Dan finds that the sometime love and goodness he meets fail to mitigate the terrible distress permeating Depression-era America." The protagonist becomes increasingly concerned with the Spanish Civil

War of the late 1930s, but rather than leave to fight on the Loyalist side in that conflict—as other idealists of the time did—he elects to stay in America, depressed though it is. Calling the novel "a lyrical love affair with words and their arrangement," Smith praised Sanford's ability as an author, declaring, "compared to many writers today, his brilliance is a lantern on a dark lawn of lightning-bugs." Even Dickstein, who criticized the novel as "deeply flawed" because "Sanford lets his characters down when he allows them to fall into radical slogans, Marx for the masses," admitted that it is "beautifully written."

The applause that greeted the reissuing of *A Man without Shoes* added to the critical approval Sanford had begun to receive for his unique historical works, their titles taken from Puritan leader William Bradford's *History of Plymouth Plantation.* When the first of these, *A More Goodly Country,* was published during the U.S. Bicentennial, it sparked great enthusiasm. Paul L. Mariani announced in the *Nation* that a "very important literary work, dealing in a serious, deeply considered and profoundly imaginative way with [the American experience,] has entered the arena so modestly . . . that, like so much else that is truly in the American grain, it is in danger of being overlooked while all the hoopla goes merrily on its way." Richard M. Dorson, reviewing the novel in the *New Republic,* declared *A More Goodly Country* to be a "refreshing . . . relief from . . . historical monographs and literary studies of conventional scholarship." As Dorson put it, Sanford's method of writing history is "to relate [events] through the imagined tongues and eyes of its actors."

What results from Sanford's methodology is an often unconventional view of familiar historical events. General George Washington's crossing of the Delaware River with the Continental Army is presented by Sanford in the guise of an eyewitness: "Once over, they had nine white miles to Trenton [New Jersey], but the boozing . . . bastards made it, and even as the legend goes, they left bloody tracks in the snow. They lost four men to wounds (none died), but of the fancy-Dan Dutchmen [Hessians], some nine hundred never saw home. . . . *Fifty thousand pounds should not induce me again to undergo what I have done,* the C.-in-C. [Washington] said."

Aside from its originality, *A More Goodly Country* was praised for the power of its prose. Mariani lauded the book's approximately two hundred "independent sections," which are "executed in so masterful a manner, so extraordinary in lyric intensity, so without slack or

even brief sketches of uninspired writing, that one discovers very early on that he is reading a prose epic of America." Dorson averred that Sanford "has the [James] Joycean virtuosity with language" and asserted that the author "can assume the speech and posture of Americans in four centuries and from all walks, yet write his own prose, verse and dialogue, eloquent and searing, salted with slang and puns."

Sanford's other historical works, which include *View from This Wilderness: American Literature as History, To Feed Their Hopes: A Book of American Women,* and *The Winters of That Country: Tales of the Man-made Seasons,* also concern themselves with a wide variety of personalities. Not only do traditional historical figures such as presidents Washington, Thomas Jefferson, and Abraham Lincoln walk Sanford's pages, but also coal miners and authors. Each book spans a period beginning before the nation's political independence—one volume begins with the Viking exploration of North America—to modern times. Two books have a specialized focus: *View from This Wilderness* centers on literary figures, *To Feed Their Hopes* on women. Collectively, Sanford's historical novels have been compared to works by such writers as William Carlos Williams, John Dos Passos, and D. H. Lawrence. Robert Atwan concluded in the *Los Angeles Times Book Review* that "Sanford is completely at ease with the American idiom and—unlike most professional historians—he sees history as inseparable from the verbal texture of the past."

Though Sanford ostensibly turned from history after writing *The Winters of That Country* to work on his autobiography, *Scenes from the Life of an American Jew,* the first volume of the latter—*The Color of the Air*—exhibits similarities to his previous books. As Elaine Kendall noted in the *Los Angeles Times Book Review,* "Like his four volumes of American history, the autobiography is written as a series of compressed vignettes." Interspersed among incidents from Sanford's personal life are depictions of historical events that influenced his youth. *The Color of the Air* also contains commonplace elements of autobiography such as descriptions of family and friends, but, as Kendall pointed out, "everything [is] seen from an unexpected oblique angle, so even the familiar seems freshly invented. The method is metaphysical in its intensity, each image wrenching the imagination and forcing a new perspective upon the reader."

Sanford's vignette style also characterizes the second volume of his autobiography, *The Waters of Darkness,* which chronicles his early adult life against a backdrop of history. Discussed in this book are Sanford's fellow writers, who, deeply influenced by the Depression and the two World Wars, became part of what Kendall described in the *Los Angeles Times* as "a liberal 20th-Century consciousness." Sanford's friendship with novelist Nathanael West is particularly important to *The Waters of Darkness,* but, as Kendall explained, more "central to the book is the candid account of the making of a writer by trial and error, delight and disappointment, accolade and derogation, nothing spared or rationalized in the retelling."

Another of Sanford's autobiographical books is *Maggie: A Love Story,* about his wife Marguerite Roberts, who died in 1989. Sanford met her on a Hollywood film studio lot, after he moved to the West Coast in 1936 upon receiving a writing contract with Paramount Pictures. A successful screenwriter for Metro-Goldwyn-Mayer for thirteen years, Maggie was well known for many of her screenplays, including *True Grit,* which she produced upon her return to employment in the 1960s. She successfully supported Sanford and herself while her husband worked on his novels and memoirs. Maggie was officially blacklisted for ten years, following an appearance before McCarthy's House Un-American Activities Committee in 1951 during the senator's anti-communism investigations. She had attended socialist meetings with Sanford, and because they both pled the Fifth Amendment—so as not to incriminate other meeting attendees—during questioning the couple were censured. A *Publishers Weekly* reviewer remarked that Sanford's description of his wife's "courageous" appearance before the senate "is vividly told." Considering the book as a while, *Review of Contemporary Fiction* contributor Joe Napora described *Maggie: A Love Story* as "as honest a portrait of a writer at work as we have gotten," and labeled the Sanford's marriage as one "of life and literature."

The View from Mt. Morris: A Harlem Boyhood continues Sanford's autobiographical writings. The book "is both a boy's-eye view of adult life and homage to a distant age, an altogether charming collection of portraits from Jewish life in Harlem, between 1910 and 1920," commented Chris Goodrich in a review for the *Los Angeles Times Book Review.* A *Publishers Weekly* reviewer noted that the book "evokes the horsecar era" and captures Sanford's childhood neighborhood. Describing the author's characterizations of family and friends as "engaging," the reviewer further observed that Sanford's words "pay loving tribute" to his now-deceased wife, Maggie. Goodrich concludes that the reminiscences contain "much more than you typically find in a memoir, and with much less dross."

Sanford's five volumes of *Scenes from the Life of an American Jew* inspired Robert W. Smith to comment in the *Bloomsbury Review* on the overall impact and importance of the body of the author's work: "This wonderfully wrought autobiography caps Sanford's career by showing a man in love with a woman and words, doing beautifully for both. Undiminished by age, he continues to write with a brilliance that, compared to most writers today, is like a lantern on a dark lawn of lightning bugs."

BIOGRAPHICAL/CRITICAL SOURCES:

BOOKS

Sanford, John, *A More Goodly Country: A Personal History of America,* Horizon Press (New York, NY), 1975.

Sanford, John, *Scenes from the Life of an American Jew,* Black Sparrow Press (Santa Barbara, CA), Volume 1: *The Color of Air,* 1985, Volume 2: *The Waters of Darkness,* 1986, Volume 3: *A Very Good Land to Fall With,* 1987, Volume 4: *A Walk in the Fire,* 1989, Volume 5: *The Season, It Was Winter,* 1991.

Sanford, John, *Maggie: A Love Story,* Barricade, 1993.

Sanford, John, *The View from Mt. Morris: A Harlem Boyhood,* Barricade, 1994.

PERIODICALS

Bloomsbury Review, December, 1991, pp. 17-18.

Esquire, November 1, 1996, p. 140.

Los Angeles Times, August 22, 1986.

Los Angeles Times Book Review, July 15, 1984; November 24, 1985; December 25, 1994, p. 7.

Nation, September 13, 1975.

New Republic, February 14, 1976.

New York Times Book Review, July 7, 1982.

Publishers Weekly, August 2, 1993, p. 72; August 29, 1994, p. 57.

Review of Contemporary Fiction, summer, 1994, pp. 218-219.

Washington Post Book World, June 6, 1982; August 12, 1984.

*   *   *

SANFORD, John B.
   See SANFORD, John

SATYAMURTI, Carole 1939-

PERSONAL: Born August 13, 1939, in Farnborough, Kent, England; daughter of Charles (a manufacturer) and Rene (Walters) Methven; married T. V. Satyamurti, 1963 (divorced, 1982); children: Emma. *Ethnicity:* "Caucasian." *Education:* University of London, B.A. (with honors), 1960, Ph.D., 1978; University of Illinois at Urbana-Champaign, M.A., 1962; University of Birmingham, diploma in social work, 1965. *Politics:* Socialist. *Religion:* None.

ADDRESSES: Home—15 Gladwell Rd., London N8 911, England. *Office*—University of East London, Dept. of Human Relations, Longbridge Road, Dagenham, Essex RM8, England. *E-mail*—c.satyamurti@uel.ac.uk.

CAREER: University of Singapore, Singapore, lecturer in sociology, 1963-64; Save the Children Fund, Kampala, Uganda, trainer of volunteers, 1965-67; North-East London Polytechnic, London, England, lecturer, 1968-72, senior lecturer, 1972-81, principal lecturer in sociology, 1981—; University of Sussex, writer-in-residence, 1997. Part-time teacher of creative writing at various institutions, including Arvon Foundation.

MEMBER: National Association of Teachers in Further and Higher Education.

AWARDS, HONORS: Winner of England's National Poetry Competition, 1986, for "Between the Lines"; British Arts Council Writers' award, 1988; winner of Cholmondeley Award, Society of Authors, 2000.

WRITINGS:

(Editor, with Noel Parry and Michael Rustin) *Social Work, Welfare, and the State,* Edward Arnold (London, England), 1979.
Occupational Survival, Blackwell (Oxford, England), 1981.
Broken Moon (poetry), Oxford University Press (New York, NY), 1987.
Changing the Subject (poetry), Oxford University Press (New York, NY), 1990.
Striking Distance (poetry), Oxford University Press (New York, NY), 1994.
Selected Poems, Oxford University Press (New York, NY), 1998.

Love and Variations (poetry), Bloodaxe (Newcastle upon Tyne, England), 2000.

Work represented in anthologies, including *Poetry Book Society Anthology, 1987-1988,* Hutchinson, 1987; *PEN New Poetry II,* Quartet Books, 1988; and *First and Always,* Faber, 1988. Contributor of poems to magazines.

WORK IN PROGRESS: A novel.

SIDELIGHTS: One-time sociologist Carole Satyamurti is a poet whose work has appeared in a handful of single-author volumes, has been represented in anthologies, and has been published in magazines. Defining qualities of her work include evocative imagery and clear language. According to *Times Literary Supplement* contributor Sarah Maguire, Satyamurti's first two collections, *Broken Moon* and *Changing the Subject,* "established her reputation as a sensitive and careful chronicler of the strangled social mores of the Home Counties." Although, as *Booklist* contributor Ray Olson pointed out in review of *Selected Poems,* Satyamurti's subjects include frustration and grief, they can also become "occasions of balanced wisdom" in which "not a word . . . seems superfluous." Satyamurti told *Contemporary Women Poets,* "Many of the poems I write are concerned, from different points of view, with the way in which one life touches another. . . . There's a tension between the connectedness and separateness of lives, between sameness and difference, that several of the poems try to capture. The distance between people can be striking."

This tension is the frequent theme in *Striking Distance,* Satyamurti's third collection, which probes questions of relatedness and identity. The first section of the book explores the ways in which social constraints are used to define a self. In Maguire's view, the poems in this section are not wholly successful because they often lack "a certain degree of analysis." The critic found the book's second section more satisfying, noting that, at her best, Satyamurti "can write taut, graceful poems" that contain "commensurate linguistic inventiveness and poise."

In a later collection, *Love and Variations,* the poet ponders questions of love, identity, and sudden death. "A logical refinement of her earlier work" and a "pleasing collection" are the terms a *Kirkus Reviews* contributor used to describe the work.

Satyamurti once told *CA:* "I started writing poetry in 1983, after I attended a course run by the Arvon Foundation. Since then, writing has become my main activity, and although I teach sociology, I have largely stopped my research and writing in this field. I give frequent readings of my work and do some teaching of creative writing at the Arvon Foundation and elsewhere."

BIOGRAPHICAL/CRITICAL SOURCES:

BOOKS

Contemporary Women Poets, St. James Press (Detroit, MI), 1998.

PERIODICALS

Booklist, September 1, 1999, Ray Olson, review of *Selected Poems,* p. 59.
Kirkus Reviews, October 1, 2000, review of *Love and Variations,* p. 1399.
Times Literary Supplement, January 29, 1988, Simon Rae, review of *Broken Moon,* p. 115; July 5, 1991, Sarra Berkeley, review of *Changing the Subject,* p. 22; May 12, 1995, Sarah Maguire, review of *Striking Distance,* p. 23.*

*   *   *

SCHMID, Eleonore 1939-

PERSONAL: Born March 15, 1939, in Lucerne, Switzerland; daughter of Josef and Elise (Wunderli) Schmid; married Aja Iskander Schmidlin (a painter), 1969 (divorced, 1973); children: Caspar Iskander. *Education:* School of Arts and Crafts, Lucerne, Switzerland, degree in graphics, 1961.

ADDRESSES: Office—c/o Nord-Süd Books, Industriestrasse 837, CH-8625, Gossau, Zurich, Switzerland.

CAREER: Writer and illustrator of children's books. Worked in graphics in Zurich, Switzerland, 1961-64, in Paris, France, 1965, and in New York, NY, 1965-68.

AWARDS, HONORS: Award of Excellence, Society of Illustrators, first prize for illustration, Bologna Book Fair, and Biennale of Illustrations Bratislava medal, 1969, all for *The Tree;* Honor List for Picture Books, German Children's Book Prize, 1969, for *Fenny: Eine Wüstenfuchsgeschichte;* Award of Excellence, Society

of Illustrators, for *The Endless Party* and *Horns Everywhere;* Biennale of Illustrations Bratislava medal, for *Das schwarze Schaf.*

WRITINGS:

SELF-ILLUSTRATED

(With Etienne Delessert) *The Tree,* Quist (New York, NY), 1966.
(With Etienne Delessert) *The Endless Party,* Quist (New York, NY), 1967.
Horns Everywhere, Quist (New York, NY), 1968.
Tonia: Die Maus mit dem weissen Stein und was ihr begegnete auf der Reise zu Onkel Tobias, Betz, 1970, translated by Lone Thygesen-Blecher as *Tonia: The Mouse with the White Stone and What Happened on Her Way to See Uncle Tobias,* Putnam (New York, NY), 1974.
Das schwarze Schaf, Nord-Süd Verlag, 1976, translated as *Little Black Lamb,* Blackie, 1977.
Mein Kätzchen Sebastian, Nord-Süd Verlag, 1978, translated as *My Cat Smokey* Blackie, 1979.
Maerchenkatzen-Kaetzenmaerchen, Nord-Süd Verlag, 1981, translated as *Cats' Tales: Feline Fairy Tales from around the World,* North-South Books (New York, NY), 1985.
Suess, Sauer, Saftig, Nord-Süd Verlag, 1985, translated as *Sweet, Sour, Juicy,* Burke (New York, NY), 1985.
Wo ist der kleinste Kern, Nord-Süd Verlag, 1985, translated as *Seeds, Nuts, Kernels,* Burke (New York, NY), 1985.
Geschalt und Geschnitten, Nord-Süd Verlag, 1985, translated as *Raw, Cooked, Spicy,* Burke (New York, NY), 1985.
Kennst du uns?, Nord-Süd Verlag, 1985, translated as *Farm Animals,* North-South Books (New York, NY), 1985.
Allein in der Höhle, Nord-Süd Verlag, 1986, translated as *Alone in the Caves,* North-South Books (New York, NY), 1986.
Wach auf, Siebenschlaefer, Sankt Nikolaus ist da, Nord-Süd Verlag, 1989, translated by Elizabeth D. Crawford as *Wake up, Dormouse, Santa Claus Is Here,* North-South Books (New York, NY), 1989.
Eine Wasserreise, Nord-Süd Verlag, 1990, translated as *The Water's Journey,* North-South Books (New York, NY), 1990.
The Story of Christmas: From the Gospel according to Luke, North-South Books (New York, NY), 1990.
Winde wehen, vom Lufthauch bis zum Sturm, Nord-Süd Verlag, 1992, translated by J. Alison James as *The Air around Us,* North-South Books (New York, NY), 1992.

Erde lebt, Nord-Süd Verlag, 1994, translated as *The Living Earth,* North-South Books (New York, NY), 1994.

Eichhörnchen und der Mond, [Switzerland], translated by Rosemary Lanning as *The Squirrel and the Moon,* North-South Books (New York, NY), 1996.

Weihnachtshase, [Switzerland], translated by Rosemary Lanning as *Hare's Christmas Gift,,* North-South Books (New York, NY), 2000.

ILLUSTRATOR

Wendy Ann Kesselman, *Franz Tovey and the Rare Animals,* photographs by Norma Holt, Quist (New York, NY), 1968.

Hans Baumann, *Fenny: Eine Wüstenfuchsgeschichte,* Betz, 1968, adapted from the German by J. J. Curle as *Fenny: The Desert Fox,* Pantheon (New York, NY), 1970.

James Krüss, *Die Geschichte vom grossen A,* Thienemann (Stuttgart, Germany), 1972.

Robert Louis Stevenson, *Treasure Island,* McKay (New York, NY), 1977.

Marcel Aymé, *Les contes bleus du chat perché,* Gallimard (Paris, France), 1978.

Marcel Aymé, *Les contes rouges du chat perché,* Gallimard (Paris, France), 1978.

Chantal de Marolles, *Machs gut, Kleiner Wolf,* Nord-Süd Verlag, 1979, translated as *The Lonely Wolf,* North-South Books (New York, NY), 1986.

Jerzy Andrzejewski, *Der goldene Fuchs,* Huber Verlag, 1979.

Silja Walter, *Eine kleine Bibel,* Huber Verlag, 1980.

La Vue, Gallimard (Paris, France), 1981.

Le Chene, Gallimard (Paris, France), 1982.

Fritz Seuft, *Unter dem Wiehnachtsfärn,* Huber Verlag, 1982.

Jacob Grimm and Wilhelm Grimm, *Die drei Federn,* Middelhanre, 1984, translated as *The Three Feathers,* Creative Education (Mankato, MN), 1984.

Regine Schindler, *. . . und Sarah Lacht,* Kaufmann Verlag, 1984, translated by Renate A. Lass Porter as *A Miracle for Sarah,* Abingdon (Nashville, TN), 1984.

Regine Schindler, *Christophorus,* Kaufmann Verlag, 1985.

Regine Schindler, *Jesus teilt das Brot,* Kaufmann Verlag, 1986.

Regine Schindler, *Der Esel Napoleon,* [Switzerland], translated as *Napoleon the Donkey,* North-South Books (New York, NY), 1988.

Heinrich Wiesner, *Jaromir in einer mittelalterlichen Stadt: Schülerroman,* Zytglogge (Bern, Germany), 1990.

Andrienne Soutter-Perrot, *The Oak,* adapted and edited from the French by Kitty Benedict, Creative Education (Mankato, MN), 1993.

SIDELIGHTS: The works of Eleonore Schmid, a prolific illustrator and writer, span a variety of genres, from board books for very young children to elaborately illustrated picture books that present both clever tales and scientific facts. Many of her books have been published in German, and a number of them have appeared in English translation as well. *Farm Animals,* published in 1986, introduces very young children to various barnyard animals through large, colorful drawings in a board book format. A more recent work, *Wake up, Dormouse, Santa Claus Is Here,* presents the tale of Gus the dormouse, who longs to meet Santa Claus.

Some of Schmid's other popular works, including *The Water's Journey, The Air Around Us,* and *The Living Earth,* use the picture book format to focus on scientific and serious topics that concern the earth and its various components. The most consistent element of these various works, say reviewers, is Schmid's striking illustrations, which stretch across and fill the pages.

In these books, Schmid depicts the water cycle as it flows from the mountains to eventually reach the oceans, the different forms and qualities of the air as it flows over the earth, and the interactions of plants and animals in relation to the earth's surface. In her *School Library Journal* review of *The Water's Journey,* Kathy Piehl related: "Each two-page spread is a well-crafted painting that invites viewers to delight in the natural world."

In *The Living Earth,* Schmid sets out to inform young readers about the Earth's complex ecosystem and how humans can help keep it in balance. She discusses not only how nature continually renews itself, but also how pollution and misuse by humans potentially threaten the future of the planet. The author's ability to explain "these difficult subjects with ease," noted *Booklist* reviewer Lauren Peterson, "makes this third book about the environment a valuable addition to the 'easy' nonfiction shelf." A critic in *Junior Bookshelf* felt that Schmid's illustrations were the main focus of the book. "These are striking and wonderfully detailed," wrote the critic, "so that the scenes depicted seem to come alive." Writing in *School Library Journal,* Piehl similarly praised *The Living Earth,* writing that Schmid's illustrations "of panoramic views and poetic language emphasize the wonder and beauty of the natural world."

1996 saw the U.S. publication of *The Squirrel and the Moon,* a book about Tiff, a young squirrel, who learns about the rhythms of nature from the Moon. During her first year of life, Tiff is captivated by circles, particularly the beauty of the round moon. As the moon wanes, the young squirrel figures that it must be hungry and buries a store of hazelnuts for her distant friend. Tiff and her brothers do not disturb the nuts, even during the long winter months when food is scarce. For her loyalty, Tiff thinks, the moon repays her with a gift: a ring of trees that eventually grow to shelter her and her family. "A lovely story," observed *School Library Journal* critic Rosanne Cerny, who went on to say that the colored pencil illustrations "reflect the plant and animal life the squirrels encounter naturally."

Another small creature is the focus of Schmid's picture book *Hare's Christmas Gift.* After a brief rest, a young hare sets out to find a meal of herbs in the cool twilight air. However, he senses that something unusual is happening and sets off to investigate. Following the other animals, he finally arrives at a stable where baby Jesus has been born. The young hare wishes to offer the new child a gift and curls his furry body around the sleeping babe to keep him warm throughout the night. Writing in *Publishers Weekly,* a critic called *Hare's Christmas Gift* "an ideal introduction to the miracle of Christmas." According to a *School Library Journal* reviewer, "Children will delight in recognizing the Nativity story as it unfolds from the hare's perspective."

BIOGRAPHICAL/CRITICAL SOURCES:

PERIODICALS

Booklist, December 15, 1992, pp. 741-742; February 15, 1995, Lauren Peterson, review of *The Living Earth,* p. 1088.

Horn Book, June, 1980, pp. 280-281; January-February, 1990, Ethel R. Twichell, review of *Wake up, Dormouse, Santa Claus Is Here,* pp. 56-57.

Junior Bookshelf, February, 1986, review of *Cats' Tales: Feline Fairy Tales from around the World,* p. 20; February, 1995, review of *The Living Earth,* pp. 26-27.

Library Journal, October, 1968, p. 145.

New York Times Book Review, August 4, 1969, p. 20.

Publishers Weekly, April 8, 1974, review of *Tonia: The Mouse with the White Stone and What Happened on Her Way to See Uncle Tobias,* p. 83; September 25, 2000, review of *Hare's Christmas Gift,* p. 72.

School Library Journal, March, 1986, p. 158; October, 1989, p. 44; November, 1990, Kathy Piehl, review of *The Water's Journey,* p. 98; December, 1992, p. 107; December, 1994, Kathy Piehl, review of

Richard Selzer

The Living Earth, p. 102; September, 1996, Rosanne Cerny, review of *The Squirrel and the Moon,* p. 190; October, 2000, review of *Hare's Christmas Gift,* p. 63.*

*　　　*　　　*

SELZER, Richard 1928-

PERSONAL: Born June 24, 1928, in Troy, NY; son of Julius Louis (a family doctor) and Gertrude (Schneider) Selzer; married Janet White, February, 1955; children: Jonathan, Lawrence, Gretchen. *Education:* Union College, Schenectady, NY, B.S., 1948; Albany Medical College, M.D., 1953; postdoctoral study, Yale University, 1957-60.

ADDRESSES: Home—6 Saint Ronan Terr., New Haven, CT 06511. *Agent*—Georges Borchardt Inc., 136 East 57th St., New York, NY 10022. *E-mail*—richard. selzer@yale.edu.

CAREER: Private practice in general surgery, 1960-86. Yale University School of Medicine, associate professor of surgery, 1961-86; fellow of Ezra Stiles College. *Military service:* U.S. Army, 1955-57.

MEMBER: Elizabethan Club.

AWARDS, HONORS: National Magazine Award, Columbia University School of Journalism, 1975, for essays published in *Esquire;* Pushcart Prize, 1982; Guggenheim fellow, 1985; honorary degrees from Union College, Georgetown University, Albany Medical College, and Medical College of Pennsylvania.

WRITINGS:

Rituals of Surgery (short stories), Harper's Magazine Press (New York, NY), 1974.

Mortal Lessons: Notes on the Art of Surgery (essays), Simon & Schuster (New York, NY), 1976, with a preface, 1987, with new preface, Harcourt Brace (San Diego, CA), 1996.

Confessions of a Knife (essays), Simon & Schuster (New York, NY), 1979.

Letters to a Young Doctor (essays and fiction), Simon & Schuster (New York, NY), 1982, reprinted with new preface, Harcourt Brace (San Diego, CA), 1996.

Taking the World in for Repairs, William Morrow (New York, NY), 1986.

Imagine a Woman and Other Tales, Random House (New York, NY), 1990.

Down from Troy: A Doctor Comes of Age (memoir), William Morrow (New York, NY), 1992.

Raising the Dead: A Doctor's Encounter with His Own Mortality (memoir), Whittle Books (Knoxville, TN), 1993.

The Doctor Stories, Picador USA (New York, NY), 1998.

The Exact Location of the Soul: New and Selected Essays, Picador USA (New York, NY), 2001.

Contributor to magazines, including *Harper's, Esquire, Redbook, Mademoiselle, American Review, Antaeus,* and *New Choices.*

ADAPTATIONS: A Question of Mercy (play based on an essay by Selzer), by David Rabe, Grove Press (New York, NY), 1998. Works available in audio versions include *Confessions of a Knife, Taking the World in for Repairs,* and *Down from Troy: A Doctor Comes of Age.*

WORK IN PROGRESS: Editing diaries and letters for publication.

SIDELIGHTS: Richard Selzer draws upon his experience as a surgeon in his writing, both for the discipline it requires and for material. His stories and essays lead the reader through hospital wards, illuminating the world of medicine and surgery. Selzer's writing ranges from detailed descriptions of the human anatomy and operating techniques to discussions of patients' reactions to sickness and impending death. In the *New York Times Book Review,* Fitzhugh Mullan wrote of Selzer's work, "His marvelous insight and potent imagery make his tales of surgery and medicine both works of art and splendid tools of instruction."

Selzer first attracted serious literary attention with his second book, *Mortal Lessons: Notes on the Art of Surgery.* These essays, which J. F. Watkins in the *Times Literary Supplement* called "prose poems," open the human body to view. Examining the hair, skin, bones, liver, stomach, kidneys, and bladder, Selzer maintains that this visceral side of medicine has its own unique beauty. *Newsweek's* Peter S. Prescott, however, found the essays to be "grisly anecdotes" and contended that Selzer "aims to shock." Peter Stoler in *Time* wrote that Selzer's portrayal of the dark side of medicine "forces physicians to think about the morality of medicine." He added, "*Mortal Lessons* will not make any surgeon a better technician; but it just might make him a healer."

Selzer's *Confessions of a Knife,* another collection of essays, presents striking examples of what the surgeon encounters in his work. In "Raccoon," a woman suffering pain after an operation seeks relief by tearing open her stitches and reaching into her abdomen. In "Sarcophagus," a tumor-weakened aorta crumbles as Selzer works unsuccessfully to stop the rush of blood; the surgeon shares his failure with the reader. *New York Times* critic Christopher Lehmann-Haupt wrote of *Confessions,* "There may be some beauty in the way Dr. Selzer writes about these encounters with sickness and death, but to me the art of them seems gratuitous. It is quite enough that such things simply happen." Yet other reviewers commended Selzer for refusing to touch up the unpleasantries of his profession. As Henry McDonald wrote in the *Washington Post Book World,* Selzer reveals the dexterity of a surgeon when handling the complicated dichotomies he encounters: the physical and the mental, joy and pain, life and death. McDonald pointed out, "In all such pairs of opposites, Selzer refuses to settle for abstractions but probes deep within their single, sensuous source." In a *New York Times*

Book Review article, Lawrence Shainberg found that Selzer's representation of pain, failure, and death "forces the reader to confront and endure his terror, and acknowledge his own vulnerability." Elizabeth Peer stated in *Newsweek,* "By dwelling on the mechanics of death, [Selzer] celebrates life."

Letters to a Young Doctor, the fourth of Selzer's books, contains both essays and short fiction. Based on his own early experience in medicine, Selzer writes the book as a series of letters of advice to a young surgeon. In one piece, "Imelda," he relates the story of a medical tour through Central America on which he accompanied a plastic surgeon. An attempt to correct the cleft lip of a beautiful young girl ends tragically when she dies under anesthesia. Selzer awakens the next day to find that during the night the surgeon had returned to the corpse and corrected the deformity. Anna Fels saw in *Letters to a Young Doctor* the author's "need to grapple physically with the grotesque." In a *Nation* article, Fels stated, "Selzer is one of the few medical writers who take a hard look at the actual subjects of medicine: disease, deformity, and the human body in all its frailties."

Although a number of reviewers criticized Selzer's overly embellished prose style, David Black in the *Washington Post* pointed out that "when he forgets to be fancy, Selzer becomes a writer of great force. When he is colloquial, his prose is superior. And his anecdotes tend to be . . . dramatic." Concluded *Los Angeles Times* critic Elaine Kendall, "No one writes about the practice of medicine with Selzer's unique combination of mystery and wonder."

Tony Miksanek reviewed *Taking the World in for Repairs* in the *Journal of the American Medical Association.* Miksanek wrote that "love very much dominates this collection of stories. The author illustrates how love can isolate and torture as well as rejuvenate and exalt." "Fetishes" features a compassionate foreign intern whose patient doesn't want her husband to see her without her dentures. Miksanek called "Tom and Lily," the tragic romance of a sixteen-year-old boy and his fourteen-year-old girlfriend who is ill with tuberculosis, "one of the finest stories of this collection." In "How to Build a Slaughterhouse," Selzer describes his visit to the slaughterhouse killing floor. Diane Ackerman wrote in the *New York Times Book Review* that "a scrupulous observer, he misses none of the facts some might find ghoulish, but also none of the gestures and mannerisms of the men, or habits of the cows, or cadences of light. Workmen laugh and tidy up between moments of unselfconscious bloodletting, and it re-

minds you that nature neither gives nor expects mercy." The last, and title, essay relates the experiences of Selzer and other surgeons of INTERPLAST as they perform reconstructive surgery in Third World countries. Ackerman concluded by saying that "some readers are alarmed by the obvious sense of privilege Dr. Selzer feels when he writes about a patient's death or disease. That has never bothered me. Lifting up phenomena in the gleaming forceps of his imagination, he makes them viewable, poignant, and full of revelation. That's never more true than in this wonderful new collection."

Imagine a Woman and Other Stories contains six long stories. Merrill Joan Gerber wrote in the *New York Times Book Review* that in this fiction collection, Selzer "abandons the measured tone of his scientific observations and speaks with a wilder voice—deeply emotional, frankly melodramatic, and notably unmodern." "For the most part, these are gloomy narratives in which doctors and medicine appear only peripherally, and the few physicians who are portrayed seem either lifeless or artificially inflated," wrote Miksanek. "These bizarre stories are loaded with misery, obsession, madness, and loss. Hope is conspicuously absent in these pages, but fortunately love is not. Even love, however, appears convoluted and insufficient. In fact, Selzer suggests that there is a fine line separating acts of horror and acts of love." In "Whither Thou Goest," a woman wants to listen one last time to her husband's donated heart, now beating in the chest of another man. A gifted autistic boy lives in a bat cave in "Pipistrel." A young boy who scavenges in a Brazilian dump loses his fingers to a piece of radioactive material he thinks is a blessed star in "Luis." Sybil Steinberg noted in *Publishers Weekly* that Selzer based this last story on a true incident, "creating a parable of the tragic dichotomy between the high-minded ideals of science and the ignorance resulting from poverty."

Down from Troy: A Doctor Comes of Age is Selzer's memoir of growing up in Troy, New York, during the 1930s, to his retirement in 1985. Selzer writes of the Great Depression, his family, and his physician father, who died when Selzer was twelve. It was a time of rampant venereal disease, tuberculosis, poverty, and alcoholism. He recalls making a house call with his father in a rowboat during a flood and how his mother, a singer, opposed her husband and insisted that her son become a writer. But Selzer took up his father's profession, and he talks about the physician-patient relationship, saying that "it is trust, not gratitude or worship, that animates the physician. To palm a fevered brow, to feel a thin wavering pulse at the wrist, to draw down a pale lower lid—these simple acts cause a doctor's heart to expand. His own physical condition is altered by the presence of the patient. It is the sublime contagion of the diagnostic embrace. Add to this the possibility of the grace of healing, and there is no human contact more beautiful."

In a *New York Times Book Review* article, Lehmann-Haupt concluded from his reading of *Down from Troy* that Selzer has been most influenced by "his morbid outlook on life, a cast of mind suggestive of bloated corpses, dusty skeletons, and stuffed owls. The book is death-ridden. Bones break. Wounds gape. People keep keeling over. Children drown. . . . Needless to add, one of the author's favorite poems is 'The Raven,' by Edgar Allan Poe." Susan Cheever, writing in the *New York Times Book Review,* also referred to Poe, saying that "Dr. Selzer's vision of the world comes from the literary tradition of Hawthorne and Poe. His visit to the Gardner Earl Crematorium, where he goes as an adult to sign a document that will direct his own body into the flames when the time comes, reads like Madeline Usher's ghostly exit from the vault in Poe's masterpiece of dread and revulsion." Miksanek wrote that *Down from Troy* "is a wonderful book energized with characters, settings, and situations that remind us of the fragile balance between pain and joy with love as the fulcrum. . . . *Down from Troy* is an enduring work of art, which affirms the rapture of both literature and medicine." And a *Publishers Weekly* contributor said that Selzer's prose "breathes with life."

Raising the Dead: A Doctor's Encounter with His Own Mortality is a memoir of Selzer's 1991 brush with death as he lay in a coma for twenty-three days after being stricken with Legionnaires' disease. The title is a reference to his ten minutes of "certified death." Selzer begins by recounting the case of English writer Fanny Burney, who in 1811 underwent a mastectomy without anesthesia, then goes on to describe his own case history. A *Publishers Weekly* reviewer said Selzer relates his near-death experience "in a way that is at once odd, funny, and moving, written in an abstract, detached third-person narrative that is purposefully disquieting." Michael Vincent Miller wrote in the *New York Times Book Review* that "what is most remarkable about *Raising the Dead* is the foray it makes into uncharted autobiographical territory. . . . This is powerful writing, exemplifying Dr. Selzer's view that language is so closely knitted to the human body that it almost has a physical presence."

The Doctor Stories contains two new stories in addition to previously printed stories by Selzer. *Booklist* reviewer William Beatty said the debut stories "are worthy addi-

tions to the Selzer canon." Miksanek wrote that the collection "identifies strength in frailty, rapture in healing, and meaning in the single details of everyday life. Selzer's work is disturbing and biting, touching and uplifting. It is exactly the kind of literature that physicians should seek out and savor." *The Exact Location of the Soul: New and Selected Essays* contains several new stories, which Beatty said "will be worth the price of admission for Selzer's longtime fans." A *Kirkus Reviews* contributor called the volume "a passionate, unsentimental celebration of life's messiness."

BIOGRAPHICAL/CRITICAL SOURCES:

BOOKS

Josyph, Peter, *What One Man Said to Another: Talks with Richard Selzer,* Michigan State University Press (East Lansing, MI), 1994.

Selzer, Richard, *Down from Troy: A Doctor Comes of Age* (memoir), William Morrow (New York, NY), 1992.

Selzer, Richard, *Raising the Dead: A Doctor's Encounter with His Own Mortality* (memoir), Whittle Books (Knoxville, TN), 1993.

PERIODICALS

Bloomsbury Review, January, 1993, review of *Down from Troy: A Doctor Comes of Age,* p. 19.

Booklist, September 1, 1986, review of *Taking the World in for Repairs,* p. 15; November 15, 1990, review of *Imagine a Woman and Other Tales,* p. 601; May 15, 1992, William Beatty, review of *Down from Troy: A Doctor Comes of Age,* p. 1652; December 15, 1993, William Beatty, review of *Raising the Dead: A Doctor's Encounter with His Own Mortality,* p. 727; June 1, 1998, William Beatty, review of *The Doctor Stories,* p. 1729; January 1, 2001, William Beatty, review of *The Exact Location of the Soul: New and Selected Essays,* p. 901.

Chicago Tribune Book World, August 26, 1979.

Christianity Today, April 8, 1988, Rodney Clapp, review of *Taking the World in for Repairs,* p. 31.

Detroit News, January 9, 1983.

Journal of the American Medical Association, February 12, 1987, Louis Borgenicht, review of *Taking the World in for Repairs,* p. 419; June 17, 1988, Tony Miksanek, review of *Taking the World in for Repairs,* p. 3485; February 27, 1991, Tony Miksanek, review of *Imagine a Woman and Other Tales,*

p. 1032; October 21, 1992, Tony Miksanek, review of *Down from Troy: A Doctor Comes of Age,* p. 2107; October 28, 1998, Tony Miksanek, review of *The Doctor Stories,* p. 1457.

Kirkus Reviews, August 1, 1986, review of *Taking the World in for Repairs,* p. 1191; October 1, 1990, review of *Imagine a Woman and Other Tales,* p. 1349; May 15, 1992, review of *Down from Troy: A Doctor Comes of Age,* p. 660; November 15, 1993, review of *Raising the Dead: A Doctor's Encounter with His Own Mortality,* p. 1450; July 1, 1998, review of *The Doctor Stories,* p. 927; December 1, 2000, review of *The Exact Location of the Soul: New and Selected Essays,* p. 1668.

Kliatt, April, 1988, review of *Taking the World in for Repairs,* p. 32.

Library Journal, December, 1986, Jack Forman, review of *Taking the World in for Repairs,* p. 126; December, 1990, Francis Poole, review of *Imagine a Woman and Other Tales,* p. 165; June 15, 1992, Mark L. Shelton, review of *Down from Troy: A Doctor Comes of Age,* p. 84; December, 1993, review of *Raising the Dead: A Doctor's Encounter with His Own Mortality,* p. 160.

Los Angeles Times, August 27, 1982.

Los Angeles Times Book Review, December 9, 1990, review of *Imagine a Woman and Other Tales,* p. 3; July 19, 1992, review of *Down from Troy: A Doctor Comes of Age,* p. 6; February 13, 1994, review of *Raising the Dead: A Doctor's Encounter with His Own Mortality,* p. 6.

Medical Humanities Review, January, 1992, review of *Imagine a Woman and Other Tales,* p. 92; spring, 1993, review of *Down from Troy: A Doctor Comes of Age,* p. 28; fall, 1994, review of *Raising the Dead: A Doctor's Encounter with His Own Mortality,* p. 53; fall, 1998, review of *The Doctor Stories,* p. 119.

Nation, October 9, 1982; December 27, 1986, review of *Taking the World in for Repairs,* p. 747.

New England Journal of Medicine, Joel D. Howell, review of *Raising the Dead: A Doctor's Encounter with His Own Mortality,* p. 1835.

Newsweek, January 24, 1977; September 3, 1979.

New Yorker, August 17, 1992, review of *Down from Troy: A Doctor Comes of Age,* p. 87; February 28, 1994, Verlyn Klinkenborg, review of *Raising the Dead: A Doctor's Encounter with His Own Mortality,* p. 92.

New York Times, August 27, 1979; September 28, 1979.

New York Times Book Review, January 9, 1977; September 2, 1979; August 29, 1982; October 5, 1986, Diane Ackerman, "Science & Technology; Palpatating For Meaning," p. 42; April 26, 1987, Peggy

McCarthy, "M.D.'s Try Writing as Off-Duty Specialty," p. 3; May 3, 1987, Patricia O'Connor, review of *Confessions of a Knife,* p. 40; November 18, 1990, Merrill Joan Gerber, "Fighting for Their Lives," p. 32; July 20, 1992, Christopher Lehmann-Haupt, "When Both Parents Get Their Way"; July 26, 1992, Susan Cheever, "Dickie, the Doctor's Boy," p. 1; October 10, 1993, review of *Down from Troy: A Doctor Comes of Age,* p. 32; February 20, 1994, Michael Vincent Miller, "The Stranger in My Hospital Bed," p. 9; September 6, 1998, Tobin Harshaw, review of *The Doctor Stories,* p. 16; December 19, 1999, review of *The Doctor Stories,* p. 36.

People Weekly, October 5, 1992, Pam Lambert, review of *Down from Troy: A Doctor Comes of Age,* p. 32.

Publishers Weekly, July 25, 1986, review of *Taking the World in for Repairs,* p. 176; September 28, 1990, Sybil Steinberg, review of *Imagine a Woman and Other Tales,* p. 84; May 18, 1992, review of *Down from Troy: A Doctor Comes of Age,* p. 52; August 10, 1992, Sybil Steinberg, "Richard Selzer: The Surgeon/Writer Reflects on Youth in the Depression and His Two Careers" (interview), p. 48; August 9, 1993, review of *Down from Troy: A Doctor Comes of Age,* p. 473; January 24, 1994, review of *Raising the Dead: A Doctor's Encounter with His Own Mortality,* p. 49; July 17, 1995, review of *Raising the Dead: A Doctor's Encounter with His Own Mortality,* p. 227; June 1, 1998, review of *The Doctor Stories,* p. 50.

Saturday Review, August 4, 1979.

Sewanee Review, October, 1995, review of *Raising the Dead: A Doctor's Encounter with His Own Mortality,* p. 640.

Time, January 24, 1977.

Times Literary Supplement, May 29, 1981.

Tribune Books (Chicago), July 19, 1992, review of *Down from Troy: A Doctor Comes of Age,* p. 5; October 31, 1993, review of *Down from Troy: A Doctor Comes of Age,* p. 8.

Washington Post, August 14, 1982.

Washington Post Book World, August 5, 1979; September 21, 1986, review of *Taking the World in for Repairs,* p. 11; May 3, 1987, review of *Confessions of a Knife,* p. 12; May 24, 1987, review of *Rituals of Surgery,* p. 12; December 9, 1990, review of *Imagine a Woman and Other Tales,* p. 7; September 6, 1992, review of *Down from Troy: A Doctor Comes of Age,* p. 2; February 13, 1994, review of *Raising the Dead: A Doctor's Encounter with His Own Mortality,* p. 6; December 6, 1998, review of *The Doctor Stories,* p. 9.

OTHER

Teen Ink, http://www.teenpaper.org/ (December, 2000), "Interview with Doctor/Writer: Richard Selzer."

SHAPIRO, Julian L.
    See SANFORD, John

*   *   *

SHINDER, Jason (Scott) 1955-

PERSONAL: Born October 19, 1955, in Brooklyn, NY; son of Jack (a restaurateur) and Edith (a homemaker) Shinder. *Education:* Attended New School for Social Research and Cornell University; Skidmore College, B.A., 1976; University of California, Davis, M.A. (English), 1978; Naropa Institute, poetics certificate, 1979; National Psychological Association of Psychoanalysis, two-year certificate, 1982.

ADDRESSES: Home—2472 Broadway, #339, New York, NY 10025.

CAREER: Good Times, film critic, 1981-83; Writer's Voice of the West Side YMCA, New York, NY, founder and director, 1981-90; YMCA National Writer's Voice of the YMCA of the USA, founder and director, 1990—. Guggenheim Museum, lecturer, 1986-89; President's Commission on the Arts, member, 1994; core faculty member, graduate writing programs of Bennington College, Bennington, VT, 1994—, and the New School for Social Research (now New School University), New York, NY, 1995—. The Writing Program at Sundance Institute, director, 1999—. *American Poetry Review,* contributing editor; *Brim: An Arts Journal* and *Ithacan,* poetry editor; *California Quarterly,* member of editorial board.

MEMBER: Poetry Society of America (director, 1981-83).

AWARDS, HONORS: California State Arts Council poetry fellowship, 1980; Fine Arts Work Center, Provincetown, MA, poetry fellowship, 1980; notable best poetry book, New York Public Library, 1985; Yaddo poetry fellowship, 1989; National Endowment for the Arts fellowship, 1992.

WRITINGS:

(Editor) *The Imagining Head: Writing by Children,* Windless Orchard Press, 1978.
End of the Highest Balcony (poems), Indiana University Press, 1980.

(Editor) *Divided Light: Father and Son Poems: A Twentieth-Century American Anthology,* Sheep Meadow Press (Riverdale-on-Hudson, NY), 1983.
(Editor) *Eternal Light: Grandparent Poems,* Harcourt Brace (San Diego, CA), 1995.
(Editor) *The First-Book Market: Where and How to Publish Your First Book and Make It a Success,* Macmillan (New York, NY), 1988.
(Editor) *First Light: Mother and Son Poems: A Twentieth-Century American Selection,* Harcourt Brace (San Diego, CA), 1992.
Every Room We Ever Slept In (poems), Sheep Meadow Press (Riverdale-on-Hudson, NY), 1993.
(Editor) *More Light: Father and Daughter Poems: A Twentieth-Century American Selection,* Harcourt Brace (San Diego, CA), 1993.
(Editor) *Lights, Camera, Poetry!: American Movie Poems, the First Hundred Years,* Harcourt Brace (San Diego, CA), 1996.
(Series editor) *The Best American Movie Writing,* St. Martin's Griffin (New York, NY), beginning 1998.
(Editor) *Tales From the Couch: Writers on Therapy,* Morrow (New York, NY), 2000.
(With Jeff Herman and Amy Holman) *Get Your First Book Published: And Make It a Success,* Career Press (Franklin Lakes, NJ), 2000.
Among Women (poems), Graywolf Press (St. Paul, MN), 2001.
(Editor) *Birthday Poems,* Thunder Mouth Press (New York, NY), 2001.

Work represented in anthologies, including *Hudson River Anthology;* contributor to periodicals, including *Village Voice, Paris Review, New York Times, Kenyon Review, Michigan Quarterly Review, Newsday, American Poetry Review,* and *Agni.*

WORK IN PROGRESS: The Wizards of Ozone Park: The Letters between Allen Ginsberg and Jack Kerouac, 1944-1969; Poets on Poets of the Past; Conversations with Poets on Poets of the Past; First Death; Writers on Immortality.

SIDELIGHTS: Jason Shinder is a poet, writer, editor, teacher, and the founder of the YMCA National Writer's Voice programs of the Young Men's Christian Association (YMCA) and director of the YMCA Arts and Humanities for the United States. Shinder is a film fan, and for *Lights, Camera, Poetry!: American Movie Poems the First Hundred Years,* he collected more than one hundred poems, many of them odes to film stars such as James Dean, Jean Harlow, Errol Flynn, Marlene Dietrich, Bette Davis, Bela Lugosi, Marilyn Monroe,

John Wayne, and Harpo Marx. *USA Today* contributor Steven G. Kellman said that "the volume puts its best iambic feet forward first with 'Provide, Provide,'" Robert Frost's meditation on a faded movie star's transient glory. A few pages later comes Hart Crane's familiar depiction of Charlie Chaplin's tramp as modern human prototype, "Chaplinesque." Kellman wrote that the poems will "remind readers of the power of meticulous words and flickering images." "This collection is bliss," said Donna Seaman in *Booklist*.

In 1998, the first volume of *The Best American Movie Writing* was published with Shinder as series editor, working with editor George Plimpton in collecting the final twenty-two essays that would appear in the initial installment. Among the essays is Barbara Maltby's piece on her productions including *The American President, Ordinary People,* and *A River Runs through It*. A *Publishers Weekly* reviewer who felt Maltby's to be the best of the essays, called a number of other pieces "noteworthy," including Alice Walker's reflections on filming *The Color Purple* during her mother's final illness. In others, Garry Wills compares Oliver Stone to Dostoyevsky, Jill Robinson writes of Roman Polanski's exile, and Bonnie Friedman defines *The Wizard of Oz* as what the reviewer called "an anti-adventure story for girls, who if they go over the rainbow must relearn that 'there's no place like home.'"

Film Comment contributor Dale Thomajan felt the best essay to be Stephen Fry's thoughts on portraying Oscar Wilde, saying that "his prose is uncluttered and surprisingly adroit; his tone, continuously witty and civil." Thomajan said that Daniel Harris's "The Death Camp" "is invaluable as perhaps the first above ground attempt to explain and detail the mystifying obsession many gay men have with certain vintage Hollywood movies and actresses, as opposed to merely basking in it." Thomajan noted that few of the articles focus on specific movies, but added that Kathleen Murphy's commentary on Jane Campion's *Portrait of a Lady* is "an example of good, dense, descriptive-evocative criticism, carefully crafted in the form of hard poetry." *Booklist* reviewer Bonnie Smothers called Shinder's collection "solid."

Shinder worked with Peter Bogdanovich on the 1999 volume of the annual, in which the majority of essays are by men. A *Publisher Weekly* reviewer called the collection "an astonishingly wide array of page-turning articles," but found the "glaring flaw" to be the absence of women as contributors or subjects, "given the many excellent female voices . . . and the recent strides made by women in the film industry."

Tales from the Couch: Writers on Therapy is a collection of nineteen essays by authors who have been in therapy, most of whom relate how the process helped them in their private lives and with their writing. A *Publishers Weekly* reviewer noted that Adam Gopnik, "in a witty and entertaining piece, describes his therapy as 'one of the last, and easily one of the most unsuccessful, psychoanalyses that have ever been attempted.'" A *Kirkus Reviews* contributor wrote that "nonetheless, the majority of the therapists emerge as compassionate and insightful and critical to the success of the writers," and concluded by calling *Tales from the Couch* "intimate, intense, enlightening, and entertaining."

Shinder wrote *Get Your First Book Published: And Make It a Success* with Jeff Herman and Amy Holman, both poets. It is dedicated to Allen Ginsberg and focuses on poetry, but the suggestions can be applied to other genres. The book takes writers responses to a questionnaire on writing and illustrates their thoughts and experiences. *Get Your First Book Published: And Make It a Success* shows how writing contests and awards can help get a writer's work into print, gives suggestions on writers' organizations and possible markets for first-time book authors, and includes a list of suggested reading. Included are the experiences of first being published from such writers as Jack London and Robert Frost. Lee B. Roberts said in the *Writer* that "a few are almost instant success stories, while many offer lessons learned through the struggles of getting one's words into print. Either way, they prove to be inspirational." *Library Journal* contributor Robert Moore called the book "comforting, inspiring."

Shinder's collection *Among Women* is about love and sex, families, and men's perceptions of women. A *Publishers Weekly* reviewer called the poems "deliberate" and said that their "quiet language, slow pace, and emotional pitch" are reminiscent of the work of Stephen Dunn and Raymond Carver. The reviewer felt that the fans of those writers "may appreciate Shinder's frankness."

BIOGRAPHICAL/CRITICAL SOURCES:

PERIODICALS

Book, January, 2001, Jeff Ousborne, review of *Tales From the Couch: Writers on Therapy*, p. 75.
Booklist, April 1, 1992, Donna Seaman, review of *First Light: Mother and Son Poems: A Twentieth-Century American Selection*, p. 1425; March 1, 1996, Donna

Seaman, review of *Lights, Camera, Poetry!: American Movie Poems, the First Hundred Years,* p. 1117; April 15, 1998, Bonnie Smothers, review of *The Best American Movie Writing 1998,* p. 1413.

Film Comment, July, 1998, Dale Thomajan, review of *The Best American Movie Writing 1998,* p. 62.

Kirkus Review, November 1, 2000, review of *Tales from the Couch,* pp. 1535-1536.

Library Journal, June 1, 2001, Robert Moore, review of *Get Your First Book Published: And Make It a Success,* p. 176.

Publishers Weekly, March 16, 1984, review of *Divided Light: Father and Son Poems: A Twentieth-Century American Anthology,* p. 82; March 23, 1998, review of *The Best American Movie Writing 1998,* p. 89; October 11, 1999, review of *The Best American Movie Writing 1999,* p. 67; November 13, 2000, review of *Tales from the Couch,* p. 96; February 12, 2001, review of *Among Women,* p. 204.

USA Today, July, 1996, Steven G. Kellman, review of *Lights, Camera, Poetry!,* p. 80.

Voice Literary Supplement, November, 1984.

Writer, September, 2001, Lee B. Roberts, review of *Get Your First Book Published,* p. 47.

* * *

SHOWALTER, Elaine 1941-

PERSONAL: Born January 21, 1941, in Cambridge, MA; daughter of Paul (a wool merchant) and Violet (Rottenberg) Cottler; married English Showalter, Jr. (a professor of French), June 8, 1963; children: Vinca, Michael. *Education:* Bryn Mawr College, B.A., 1962; Brandeis University, M.A., 1964; University of California, Davis, Ph.D., 1970.

ADDRESSES: Office—Department of English, 22 McCosh Hall, Princeton University, Princeton, NJ 08544-0001. *E-mail*—elaines@princeton.edu; eshowalter@observer.com.

CAREER: University of California, 1967-78, began as instructor, became associate professor; Rutgers University, Douglass College, New Brunswick, NJ, assistant professor, 1970-74, associate professor, 1974-83, professor of English, 1983; Princeton University, Princeton, NJ, professor of English, 1984—, Avalon Foundation Professor of Humanities and chair, department of English. University of Delaware, visiting professor of English and women's studies, 1976-77; School of Criticism and Theory, Dartmouth College, visiting professor,

1986; Salzburg Seminars (Austria), professor, 1988; Oxford University (England), Clarendon lecturer, 1989; Phi Beta Kappa visiting scholar, 1993-94; director of National Endowment for the Humanities summer seminar for college teachers, 1984. Editor of *Women's Studies,* 1972—, and *Signs: Journal of Women, Culture, and Society,* 1975—.

MEMBER: Modern Language Association of America (vice president, 1996-97, president, 1998), National Organization for Women.

AWARDS, HONORS: Rutgers University Faculty Research fellow, 1972-73; Christian and Mary Lindbach Foundation Award for Distinguished Teaching, Rutgers University, 1976; Guggenheim fellow, 1977-78; Rockefeller humanities fellow, 1981-82; National Endowment for the Humanities fellow, 1988-89; Howard Behrman humanities award, Princeton University, 1989.

WRITINGS:

A Literature of Their Own: British Women Novelists from Brontë to Lessing, Princeton University Press (Princeton, NJ), 1977, revised edition, Virago (London, England), 1982, reprinted, Princeton University Press (Princeton, NJ), 1998.

(With others) *Women Who Dared to Write* (audio cassette), National Public Radio (Washington, DC), 1978.

The Female Malady: Women, Madness, and English Culture, 1830-1980, Pantheon (New York, NY), 1985, published as *Madness and the Wrongs of Women: Female Insanity and English Culture, 1830-1980,* Pantheon (New York, NY), 1985.

Sexual Anarchy: Gender and Culture at the Fin-de-Siècle, Viking (New York, NY), 1990.

Sister's Choice: Tradition and Change in American Women's Writing, Oxford University Press (New York, NY), 1991.

Hystories: Hysterical Epidemics and Modern Culture, Columbia University Press (New York, NY), 1997.

Inventing Herself: Claiming a Feminist Intellectual Heritage, Scribner (New York, NY), 2001.

Also author of *Guilt, Authority, and the Shadow of Little Dorrit,* 1979.

EDITOR

Women's Liberation and Literature, Harcourt (New York, NY), 1971.

(With Carol Ohmann) *Female Studies IV,* KNOW, 1971.

(And author of introduction) *These Modern Women: Autobiographical Essays from the Twenties,* Feminist Press (Old Westbury, NY), 1978, with revised introduction, Feminist Press at the City University of New York (New York, NY), 1989.

The New Feminist Criticism: Essays on Women, Literature, and Theory, Pantheon (New York, NY), 1985.

(And author of introduction) *Alternative Alcott,* Rutgers University Press (New Brunswick, NJ), 1988.

Speaking of Gender, Routledge (New York, NY), 1989.

Louisa May Alcott, *Little Women,* Penguin (New York, NY), 1989.

(With Lea Baechler and A. Walton Litz) *Modern American Women Writers,* Macmillan (New York, NY), 1991.

Daughters of Decadence: Women Writers of the Fin-de-Siècle, Rutgers University Press (New Brunswick, NJ), 1993.

Christina Rossetti, *Maude* [and] Dinah Mulock Craik, *On Sisterhoods: A Woman's Thoughts about Women,* New York University Press (New York, NY), 1993.

(And author of introduction) Joyce Carol Oates, *"Where Are You Going, Where Have You Been?,"* Rutgers University Press (New Brunswick, NJ), 1994.

(And author of introduction) Edith Wharton, *Ethan Frome,* Oxford University Press (New York, NY), 1996.

(And author of introduction) *Scribbling Women: Short Stories by Nineteenth-Century American Women,* Rutgers University Press (New Brunswick, NJ), 1997.

(Advisory editor, with Germaine Greer) *The Cambridge Guide to Women's Writing in English,* Cambridge University Press (New York, NY), 1999.

Contributor to *Victorian Studies, College English, Antioch Review, Women's Studies, Raritan, Feminist Studies, Women and Literature, Nineteenth-Century Fiction, Oxford Literary Review, New York Times Book Review,* and other publications.

SIDELIGHTS: Elaine Showalter is described by Marianne DeKoven in the *Dictionary of Literary Biography* as "one of the founders of feminist criticism and still one of its most important and influential practitioners." Showalter is known for her invention of gynocritics, the study of women as writers as distinct from the study of writing by women.

With the publication of *A Literature of Their Own: British Women Novelists from Brontë to Lessing,* Showalter first began to establish a reputation as a feminist literary critic. The study, Annmarie Pinarski noted in

Feminist Writers, "emphasizes the existence of a woman's tradition in literature to challenge the hegemony of the male-dominated literary canon." DeKoven found that "this groundbreaking (literally the first) history of the separate tradition of women's fiction in England is premised on the notions of a female subculture with its own 'values, conventions, experiences, and behaviors.'"

In the essay "Toward a Feminist Poetics," written in 1979, Showalter first introduced her term "gynocritics." "Gynocritics refers," Pinarski wrote, "to feminist criticism that is concerned with the woman writer 'as the producer of textual meaning' and with the 'history, themes, genres, and structures of literature by women.' With its focus on female culture, gynocritics aims to develop a critical framework appropriate for the specific study of women's literature." "Throughout her career," DeKoven wrote, "Showalter has been applying gynocritics to the analysis of specific texts as well as developing it as a feminist critical theory."

Showalter has applied gynocritics to several books of critical writing focused on nineteenth-century British authors. In *Daughters of Decadence: Women Writers of the Fin-de-Siècle,* an anthology of short fiction from the late nineteenth century, Showalter gathers examples of stories written by women from a period in which Victorian literature was dying out and Modernism was emerging. At this crucial time, the writers Showalter chooses were presenting "late 19th-century literary themes from a distinctly female perspective," as Pinarski pointed out. "The anthology provides, at the very least, a welcome corrective to the varieties of male narcissism that dominate our picture of the age," said Chris Baldick in the *Times Literary Supplement.* In *Alternative Alcott,* Showalter presents pseudonymous writings by Louisa May Alcott, best known for her children's classic, *Little Women.* Alcott's "dark, sultry, and melodramatic tales . . . initially published under her pseudonym A. M. Barnard . . . [provide] an expanded perspective on the well-known author," according to Pinarski.

In addition to her critical writings, Showalter is also the author of literary histories concerned with gender issues. In *Sexual Anarchy: Gender and Culture at the Fin de Siècle,* Showalter argues that the end of the nineteenth century saw a redefinition of masculine roles. "She analyzes," Pinarski wrote, "the rhetoric of popular periodicals, the vicissitudes of political discourse, and the themes and tensions in literature of the era; in the process, Showalter invents the term 'endism' to describe the social and sexual crisis that afflicts both 19th and 20th century fin de siecle's." Pinarski concluded that "with *Sexual Anarchy,* Showalter's contributions to literary, feminist, and cultural criticism and history merge to fortify her status as one of the foremost scholars of gender in the late 20th century." DeKoven noted that "in large part through Showalter's influence, gynocritics has become the predominant mode of feminist criticism practiced in the American academy."

Showalter's *Hystories: Hysterical Epidemics and Modern Culture* was called "a spirited Freudo-literary analysis of what she calls hysterical epidemics and what social scientists call emotional contagions or mass psychogenic illnesses," wrote Carol Tavris in the *New York Times Book Review.* Chronic fatigue syndrome, Gulf War syndrome, recovered memories of sexual abuse, multiple personality disorder, satanic ritual abuse, and alien abduction, are the six examples Showalter explores. "She knows full well that throwing the first three into the mix will 'infuriate thousands of people who believe they are suffering from unidentified organic disorders or the aftereffects of trauma,'" said Tavris, who added that Showalter "braves not only their wrath, but also that of the feminist therapists and writers whose 'credulous endorsements of recovered memory and satanic abuse' have contributed to these epidemics. This attitude alone is worth the price of the book." With the exception of Gulf War syndrome, each of Showalter's six examples are experienced primarily by women.

Showalter writes that hystories "are constructed by suffering patients, caring psychologists, dedicated clergy, devoted parents, hardworking police, concerned feminists, and anxious communities." Tavris said, "Indeed, but such narratives are also constructed by vested interests protecting their professions and incomes, ignorant psychologists, greedy opportunists who see a way to make a fast buck on the insecurities of the vulnerable, ideologues of the right and left, and clergy and politicians drunk on the elixir of moral righteousness. By not also identifying the venal motives that support epidemics, let alone their economic, social, and political supports, Ms. Showalter implies that they are merely psychological phenomena, reflecting people's efforts in scary times to reduce anxiety. So they are—but they are also big business."

Taner Edis and Amy Sue Bix reviewed *Hystories* for *Skeptical Inquirer.* They said that "Showalter's treatment of subjects like recovered memories, ritual abuse, and alien abductions reflects sources and themes from

the skeptical literature, and her direct and sympathetic style of writing makes her account attractive. Humor also helps, as when she skewers Harvard psychiatrist John Mack for his support of UFO abductions by coining 'Showalter's Law: As the hystories get more bizarre, the experts get more impressive.'" Edis and Bix felt Showalter's identification of chronic fatigue and Gulf War syndrome as hysterias to be "overly hasty," and noted that new findings are "still emerging about operations in the Gulf War." Edis and Bix added that "a physical ailment with unconventional, complex causes is not as outlandish a hypothesis as an alien abduction. Showalter should also have done more to acknowledge the non-paranoid reasons some women can be suspicious of our medical system. Medical science has produced real disasters like the Dalkon Shield and DES, and it has a history of neglecting women as research subjects."

In an interview with Pryde Brown of *Reason,* Showalter said that hysterias "usually begin in a fairly small, isolated community. . . . Then you need a charismatic doctor or scientist who begins to [define] it. That gets picked up by the media, and more and more doctors hear about it, and they pick up more and more patients. When it reaches some sort of critical mass, patient groups start to organize, and it politicizes." Showalter went on to note that the story is picked up on the evening news and the Internet, and is quickly the subject of a television movie. She compares her hystories to the Salem witch trials.

"Showalter does touch on many provocative subjects," wrote a *Publishers* Weekly reviewer. Library *Journal* contributor Kathleen L. Atwood called *Hystories* "a thought-provoking work." A *Kirkus Reviews* writer called the book "muscular, probably inflammatory, and elegantly expressed."

Inventing Herself: Claiming a Feminist Intellectual Heritage is Showalter's tribute to "feminist icons," called "a gracefully written analysis of several generations of notable women from the U.S., Britain, and France," by Mary Carroll in *Booklist.* It begins and ends with deaths—Mary Wollstonecraft's from childbirth in 1797, and Princess Diana's in the car crash that occurred two hundred years later. A *Kirkus Reviews* contributor said the collection "stirs together literary history, biography, personal reminiscence, and pop culture in a peculiar narrative that devotes as much time to female thinkers' dysfunctional private lives as to their public achievements." The book includes longer pieces, including those on Wollstonecraft, Margaret Fuller, Simone de Beauvoir, Susan Sontag, Germaine Greer, Camille Paglia, Charlotte Perkins Gilman, and Showalter herself. There are shorter sections about others, including Margaret Mead, Ann Douglas, Mary McCarthy, Oprah Winfrey, and Hillary Clinton.

Many reviewers were disappointed by the book's lack of academic rigor. *Nation* critic Deirdre English, who called *Inventing Herself* "sort of an Intellectual Feminists for Dummies," faulted Showalter's emphasis on celebrity over substance—a criticism also levelled by Jenny Turner in *New York Times Book Review* and Hermione Lee in *Times Literary Supplement.* "There is a tremendous amount of gossip," noted Lee, who observed that conflating the achievements of feminist heroines with those of mere celebrities "risks throwing away the whole concept" of feminist achievement. *American Prospect* contributor Nancy F. Cott raised similar concerns, adding that Showalter's neglect of class, race, and "structures of economic or social advantage or disadvantage" among her subjects further weakens the book's argument. "The flattening of complexity will leave most knowing readers unsatisfied," Cott concluded. Yet the book was also praised for its energy, scope, and appeal. Noting its "unabashedly romantic" style, Turner called the book "history as big, bold scribble." In *Book,* Eleanor J. Bader appreciated the "gossipy and entertaining" qualities in the work. And a *Publishers Weekly* contributor called *Inventing Herself* "engaging and blessedly free of both academic jargon and the weight of theory."

BIOGRAPHICAL/CRITICAL SOURCES:

BOOKS

Dictionary of Literary Biography, Volume 67: *Modern American Critics since 1955,* Gale (Detroit, MI), 1988.
Directory of American Scholars, 9th edition, Gale (Detroit, MI), 1999.
Feminist Writers, St. James Press (Detroit, MI), 1996.

PERIODICALS

American Journal of Psychology, spring, 1999, review of *Hystories: Hysterical Epidemics and Modern Culture,* p. 158.
American Prospect, June 4, 2001, Nancy F. Cott, review of *Inventing Herself: Claiming a Feminist Intellectual Heritage,* p. 46.

Antioch Review, spring, 1986, p. 242; winter, 1998, review of *Hystories,* p. 112.
Belles Lettres, spring, 1991, p. 43.
Bloomsbury Review, January, 1992, p. 15.
Book, May, 2001, Eleanor J. Bader, review of *Inventing Herself,* p. 74.
Booklist, May 15, 1985, p. 1289; January 1, 1986, p. 648; March 15, 2001, Mary Carroll, review of *Inventing Herself: Claiming a Feminist Intellectual Heritage,* p. 1337.
Choice, October, 1997, review of *Hystories,* p. 329; October, 1999, review of *A Literature of Their Own: British Women Novelists from Brontë to Lessing,* p. 331.
Commonweal, December 6, 1991, p. 728.
Contemporary Review, August, 1999, review of *A Literature of Their Own,* p. 108.
Encounter, September, 1988, p. 53.
Kirkus Reviews, February 1, 1997, review of *Hystories,* p. 208; December 15, 2000, review of *Inventing Herself,* p. 1750.
Lambda Book Report, September, 1991, p. 37.
Legacy, fall, 1993, p. 142.
Library Journal, April 15, 1997, Kathleen L. Atwood, review of *Hystories,* p. 103; January 1, 2001, Cynthia Harrison, review of *Inventing Herself,* p. 132.
London Review of Books, October 29, 1987, p. 14; December 10, 1987, p. 18; January 30, 1992, p. 19; July 17, 1997, review of *Hystories,* p. 20.
Los Angeles Times Book Review, September 2, 1990, p. 12; April, 1997, review of *Hystories,* p. 8.
Maclean's, May 20, 1991, p. 68.
Nation, June 11, 2001, Deirdre English, review of *Inventing Herself,* p. 44.
National Review, September 1, 1997, Steve Sailer, review of *Hystories,* p. 48.
Nature, July 17, 1997, review of *Hystories,* p. 239.
New Republic, March 10, 1986, p. 30; April 28, 1986, p. 34; May 12, 1997, Frederick Crews, review of *Hystories,* p. 35.
New Scientist, June 14, 1997, review of *Hystories,* p. 45.
New Statesman, June 13, 1997, review of *Hystories,* p. 48.
New York Times Book Review, June 16, 1985, p. 16; January 19, 1986, p. 7; December 29, 1991, p. 10; May 4, 1997, Carol Tavris, "Pursued by Fashionable Furies," p. 28; March 25, 2001, Jenny Turner, review of *Inventing Herself,* p. 30.
Nineteenth-Century Literature, December, 1997, review of *Scribbling Women: Short Stories by Nineteenth-Century American Women,* p. 410.
Observer (London), February 16, 1997, review of *Scribbling Women,* p. 15; June 1, 1997, review of *Hysto-*

ries, p. 15; April 5, 1998, review of *Scribbling Women,* p. 18.

Publishers Weekly, February 24, 1997, review of *Hystories,* p. 74; December 11, 2000, review of *Inventing Herself,* p. 69.

Punch, April 10, 1991, p. 46.

Rapport, March, 1998, review of *Hystories,* p. 37.

Reason, July, 1997, Pryde Brown, "Syndrome Syndrome" (interview), p. 21.

Signs, winter, 1994, p. 507.

Skeptic, March, 1997, review of *Hystories,* p. 102.

Skeptical Inquirer, September-October, 1997, Taner Edis and Amy Sue Bix, review of *Hystories,* p. 52.

Spectator, April 6, 1991, p. 28.

Times Literary Supplement, March 11, 1988, p. 283; April 12, 1991, p. 5; November 15, 1991, p. 8; September 3, 1993, pp. 20-21; March 21, 1997, review of *Scribbling Women,* p. 24; May 16, 1997, review of *Hystories,* p. 6; August 10, 2001, Hermione Lee, review of *Inventing Herself,* p. 22.

U.S. News & World Report, May 19, 1997, Wray Herbert, "The Hysteria over *Hystories,*" p. 14.

Washington Post, April 12, 1997, Linton Weeks, "Hysteria Book Hits a Raw Nerve; Sufferers Attack Author Who Says Its All in Their Heads," p. D1.

Women's Review of Books, August, 1985, p. 12; August, 1986, p. 1; November, 1991, p. 26; July, 2001, Brenda Wineapple, review of *Inventing Herself,* p. 34.*

*   *   *

SIMONT, Marc 1915-

PERSONAL: Born November 23, 1915, in Paris, France; naturalized citizen of the United States, 1936; son of Josep (an illustrator) and Dolors (Baste) Simont; married Sara Dalton (a teacher of handicapped children), April 7, 1945; children: Marc Dalton (Doc). *Education:* Studied art in Paris at Academie Ranson, Academie Julien, and Andre Lhote School, 1932-35, and in New York, NY, at National Academy of Design, 1935-37. *Avocational interests:* Country living, socializing, cigars, wine, skiing, soccer, and other sports.

ADDRESSES: Home—Town St., West Cornwall, CT 06796. *Office*—611 Broadway, New York, NY 10012.

CAREER: Artist and illustrator; since 1939 has worked in portraits, murals, sculpture, prints, and magazine and book illustration; translator and writer of children's

books, 1939—. Advocate of community soccer in West Cornwall, CT. *Military service:* U.S. Army, 1943-46; produced visual aids; became sergeant.

MEMBER: American Veterans Commission, Authors League of America, Authors Guild.

AWARDS, HONORS: Tiffany fellow, 1937; Caldecott Honor Book citation, 1950, for *The Happy Day; Book World* Spring Book Festival Award, and Child Study Association Book Award, both 1952, both for *Jareb;* Caldecott Medal, 1957, for *A Tree Is Nice;* Steck-Vaughn Award, 1957, for *The Trail-Driving Rooster;* Citation of Merit, Society of Illustrators, 1965; Best Book of the Season citation from *Today Show,* 1972, for *Nate the Great;* National Book Award finalist, 1976, for *The Star in the Pail;* Children's Younger Book Award, New York Academy of Sciences, 1980, for *A Space Story;* New Jersey Institute of Technology Award, 1981, for *Ten Copycats in a Boat and Other Riddles; New York Times* Outstanding Books citation, 1982, for *The Philharmonic Gets Dressed;* Garden State Children's Book awards, 1984, for *Nate the Great and the Missing Key,* and 1985, for *Nate the Great and the Snowy Trail;* American Institute of Graphic Arts certificate of excellence; Jefferson Cup, 1985, for *In the Year of the Boar and Jackie Robinson;* Parents' Choice award, 1986, for *The Dallas Titans Get Ready for Bed.*

WRITINGS:

SELF-ILLUSTRATED

Opera Soufflé: 60 Pictures in Bravura, Schuman, 1950.

Polly's Oats, Harper (New York, NY), 1951.

(With Red Smith) *How to Get to First Base: A Picture Book of Baseball,* Schuman, 1952.

The Lovely Summer, Harper (New York, NY), 1952.

Mimi, Harper (New York, NY), 1954.

The Plumber out of the Sea, Harper (New York, NY), 1955.

The Contest at Paca, Harper (New York, NY), 1959.

How Come Elephants?, Harper (New York, NY), 1965.

Afternoon in Spain, Morrow (New York, NY), 1965.

(With members of staff of Boston Children's Medical Center) *A Child's-Eye View of the World,* Delacorte (New York, NY), 1972.

The Goose That Almost Got Cooked, Scholastic (New York, NY), 1997.

The Stray Dog: From a True Story by Reiko Sassa, HarperCollins (New York, NY), 2001.

TRANSLATOR

Federico Garcia Lorca, *The Lieutenant Colonel and the Gypsy,* Doubleday, 1971.

Francesc Sales, *Ibrahim,* illustrations by Eulalia Sariola, Lippincott, 1989.

ILLUSTRATOR

Emma G. Sterne, *The Pirate of Chatham Square: A Story of Old New York,* Dodd, 1939.

Ruth Bryan Owens, *The Castle in the Silver Woods,* Dodd, 1939.

Albert Carr, *Men of Power,* Viking (New York, NY), 1940.

Mildred Cross, *Isabella, Young Queen of Spain,* Dodd, 1941.

Charlotte Jackson, *Sarah Deborah's Day,* Dodd, 1941.

Richard Hatch, *All Aboard the Whale,* Dodd, 1942.

Dougal's Wish, Harper (New York, NY), 1942.

Meindert DeJong, *Billy and the Unhappy Bull,* Harper (New York, NY), 1946.

Margaret Wise Brown, *The First Story,* Harper (New York, NY), 1947.

Iris Vinton, *Flying Ebony,* Dodd, 1947.

Robbie Trent, *The First Christmas,* Harper (New York, NY), 1948, new edition, 1990.

Andrew Lang, editor, *The Red Fairy Book,* new edition, Longmans, Green, 1948.

Ruth Krauss, *The Happy Day,* Harper (New York, NY), 1949.

Ruth Krauss, *The Big World and the Little House,* Schuman, 1949.

Red Smith, *Views of Sport,* Knopf (New York, NY), 1949.

Meindert DeJong, *Good Luck Duck,* Harper (New York, NY), 1950.

Ruth Krauss, *The Backward Day,* Harper (New York, NY), 1950.

James Thurber, *The Thirteen Clocks,* Simon & Schuster (New York, NY), 1951.

Marjorie B. Paradis, *Timmy and the Tiger,* Harper (New York, NY), 1952.

Alister Cooke, *Christmas Eve,* Knopf (New York, NY), 1952.

Miriam Powell, *Jareb,* Crowell (New York, NY), 1952.

The American Riddle Book, Schuman, 1954.

Elizabeth H. Lansing, *Deer Mountain Hideaway,* Crowell (New York, NY), 1954.

Jean Fritz, *Fish Head,* Coward (New York, NY), 1954.

Elizabeth H. Lansing, *Deer River Raft,* Crowell (New York, NY), 1955.

Fred Gipson, *The Trail-Driving Rooster,* Harper (New York, NY), 1955.

Julius Schwartz, *Now I Know,* Whittlesey House, 1955.

Janice May Udry, *A Tree Is Nice,* Harper (New York, NY), 1955.

Julius Schwartz, *I Know a Magic House,* Whittlesey House, 1956.

Thomas Liggett, *Pigeon Fly Home,* Holiday House, 1956.

Chad Walsh, *Nellie and Her Flying Crocodile,* Harper (New York, NY), 1956.

James Thurber, *The Wonderful "O",* Simon & Schuster (New York, NY), 1957.

Maria Leach, *The Rainbow Book of American Folk Tales and Legends,* World, 1958.

Alexis Ladas, *The Seal That Couldn't Swim,* Little, Brown (Boston MA), 1959.

James A. Kjelgaard, *The Duckfooted Hound,* Crowell (New York, NY), 1960.

Ruth Krauss, *A Good Man and His Wife,* Harper (New York, NY), 1962.

Julius Schwartz, *The Earth Is Your Spaceship,* Whitlesey House, 1963.

David McCord, *Every Time I Climb a Tree,* Little, Brown (New York, NY), 1967.

What To Do When There's Nothing to Do, Dell (New York, NY), 1967.

Charlton Ogburn, Jr., *Down, Boy, Down, Blast You!,* Morrow (New York, NY), 1967.

Janet Chenery, *Wolfie,* Harper (New York, NY), 1969.

Janice May Udry, *Glenda,* Harper (New York, NY), 1969.

Edward Fales, Jr., *Belts on, Buttons Down,* Dell, 1971.

David McCord, *The Star in the Pail,* Little, Brown (Boston MA), 1975.

Richard Kennedy, *The Contests at Cowlick,* Little, Brown (Boston, MA), 1975.

Eulalie Osgood Grover, *Robert Louis Stevenson, Teller of Tales,* Gale (Detroit, MI), 1975.

Beverly Keller, *The Beetle Bush,* Coward (New York, NY), 1976.

Karla Kuskin, *A Space Story,* Harper (New York, NY), 1978.

Joan Lowery Nixon, *Danger in Dinosaur Valley,* Putman (New York, NY), 1978.

Faith McNulty, *Mouse and Tim,* Harper (New York, NY), 1978.

Faith McNulty, *How to Dig a Hole to the Other Side of the World,* Harper (New York, NY), 1979.

Alvin Schwartz, editor, *Ten Copycats in a Boat, and Other Riddles,* Harper (New York, NY), 1979.

Faith McNulty, *The Elephant Who Couldn't Forget,* Harper (New York, NY), 1979.

Mitchell Sharmat, *Reddy Rattler and Easy Eagle,* Doubleday, 1979.

David McCord, *Speak Up: More Rhymes of the Never Was and Always Is,* Little, Brown (Boston, MA), 1980.

Charlotte Zolotow, *If You Listen,* Harper (New York, NY), 1980.

Marjorie Weinman Sharmat, *Chasing after Annie,* Harper (New York, NY), 1981.

Peggy Parish, *No More Monsters for Me!,* Harper (New York, NY), 1981.

Karla Kuskin, *The Philharmonic,* Harper (New York, NY), 1982.

Julie Delton, *My Uncle Nikos,* Crowell (New York, NY), 1983.

Mollie Hunter, *The Knight of the Golden Plain,* Harper (New York, NY), 1983.

Edward Davis, *Bruno the Pretzel Man,* Harper (New York, NY), 1984.

Bette Bao Lord, *The Year of the Boar and Jackie Robinson,* Harper (New York, NY), 1984.

Joan W. Blos, *Martin's Hats,* Morrow (New York, NY), 1984.

John Reynolds Gardiner, *Top Secret,* Little, Brown (Boston MA), 1984.

Franklyn Mansfield Branley, *Volcanoes,* Crowell (New York, NY), 1985.

Mollie Hunter, *The Three-Day Enchantment,* Harper (New York, NY), 1985.

Karla Kuskin, *The Dallas Titans Get Ready for Bed,* Harper (New York, NY), 1986.

Franklyn Mansfield Branley, *Journey into a Black Hole,* Crowell (New York, NY), 1986.

Wendell V. Tangborn, *Glaciers,* Crowell, 1988, revised edition, Harper (New York, NY), 1988.

Sing a Song of Popcorn, Scholastic, 1988.

Charlotte Zolotow, *The Quiet Mother and the Noisy Little Boy,* Harper (New York, NY), 1989.

Franklyn Mansfield Branley, *What Happened to the Dinosaurs?,* Harper (New York, NY), 1989.

James Thurber, *Many Moons,* Harcourt (New York, NY), 1990.

Willy Welch, *Playing Right Field,* Scholastic (New York, NY), 1995.

Ruth Krauss, *Happy Day,* Harper (New York, NY), 1995.

Betsy Cromer Byers, *My Brother, Ant,* Viking (New York, NY), 1996.

Betsy Cromer Byers, *Ant Plays Bear,* Viking (New York, NY), 1997.

Janice May Udry, *Glenda Glinka, Witch-at-Large,* HarperTrophy (New York, NY), 1997.

Marjorie Weinman Sharmat, *Richie and the Fritzes,* HarperCollins (New York, NY), 1997.

David McCord, *Every Time I Climb a Tree,* Little, Brown (Boston, MA), 1999.

ILLUSTRATOR; "NATE THE GREAT" SERIES BY MARJORIE WEINMAN SHARMAT

Nate the Great, Coward (New York, NY), 1972.

Nate the Great Goes Undercover, Coward (New York, NY), 1974.

Nate the Great and the Lost List, Coward (New York, NY), 1975.

Nate the Great and the Phony Clue, Coward (New York, NY), 1977.

Nate the Great and the Sticky Case, Coward (New York, NY), 1978.

Nate the Great and the Missing Key, Coward (New York, NY), 1981.

Nate the Great and the Snowy Trail, Coward (New York, NY), 1982.

Nate the Great and the Fishy Prize, Coward (New York, NY), 1985.

Nate the Great and the Boring Beach Bag, Coward (New York, NY), 1987.

Nate the Great Stalks Stupidweed, Coward (New York, NY), 1987.

Nate the Great Goes down in the Dumps, Coward (New York, NY), 1989.

Nate the Great and the Halloween Hunt, Coward (New York, NY), 1989.

(By Marjorie Weinman Sharmat and Craig Sharmat) *Nate the Great and the Musical Note,* Coward (New York, NY), 1990.

Nate the Great and the Stolen Base, Coward (New York, NY), 1992.

Nate the Great and the Pillowcase, Delacorte (New York, NY), 1993.

Nate the Great and the Mushy Valentine, Delacorte (New York, NY), 1994.

Nate the Great and the Tardy Tortoise, Delacorte (New York, NY), 1995.

Nate the Great and the Crunchy Christmas, Delacorte (New York, NY), 1996.

Nate the Great Saves the King of Sweden, Delacorte (New York, NY), 1997.

Nate the Great and Me: The Case of the Fleeing Fang, Delacorte (New York, NY), 1998.

ADAPTATIONS: Nate the Great Goes Undercover and *Nate the Great and the Sticky Case* were made into films. An excerpt from *Nate the Great* was adapted and is on permanent display at the Museum of Science and Industry, Chicago, Illinois.

SIDELIGHTS: Marc Simont was born in 1915 in Paris, France, to parents from the Catalonian region of northern Spain. He attended schools in Paris, Barcelona, Spain, and New York City, because his parents kept traveling. Simont's father came to the United States after World War I and decided to become an American citizen. Because that process took five years, Simont lived with his grandfather in Barcelona. During this time he sketched bullfighters and taught himself to draw by studying *El Ginesello,* a picture book.

This repeated relocation affected his performance as a student. "I was always more concerned with what a teacher looked like than what he said, which didn't do my algebra any good," the illustrator explained in *More Junior Authors.* Simont did not graduate from high school, although he became fluent in French, English, Spanish, and Catalonian. On the other hand, the traveling sharpened his skills as an observer—skills important for an artist. He studied art at the Academie Julian and the Academie Ranson in Paris, and in New York City at National Academy of Design. He also studied art with Andre Lohte, but he said his most important art teacher was his father, an illustrator for *L'Illustration* magazine. With a sister and two uncles also making a living as artists, he considers art the family trade.

When he returned to the United States, Simont worked odd jobs, painted portraits, and drew illustrations for advertising firms. Eventually he became an illustrator of picture books for children. Books by many notable children's writers, including James Thurber and Marjorie Weinman Sharmat, have been published with his illustrations. Simont illustrated Sharmat's book *Nate the Great,* featuring the boy detective who solves neighborhood mysteries, and has won several awards for books in the *Nate the Great* series; two were made into films. His illustrations for Janice May Udry's *A Tree Is Nice* won the Caldecott Medal in 1957, and his pictures for Ruth Krauss's *The Happy Day* earned him a Caldecott Honor.

Critics have pointed out that Simont's illustrations are perfectly suited to the text in books by a variety of children's authors. George A. Woods comments in the *New York Times Book Review* about Karla Kuskin's *The Philharmonic Gets Dressed:* "Simont has not missed a beat. His musicians are a varied band in terms of age, race and physique. He conveys the awkward stance as well as the graceful pose, the little scenes and moments that are all around us—the hole in the sock, the graffiti inside the subway car as well as the advertising posters." Kenneth Marantz, writing about the same book

in *School Library Journal,* notes that Simont's "ability to invest such convincing feelings of life using an almost cartoon- like simplicity is remarkable." *New York Times Book Review* contributor Nora Magid observes that Simont's illustrations in *How to Dig a Hole to the Other Side of the World* have terrific emotional power: "Simont's pictures break the heart. The child voyager is at once intrepid and vulnerable" as he takes an imaginary journey through the earth's crust to China. Other features of Simont's artistic style are a method of composition that gives continuity to the pictures in sequence, and humor that is inviting to readers of all ages.

In addition to illustrating books by other authors, Simont has also written and illustrated his own books for children. *The Goose That Almost Got Cooked* "is a rare treat" by this "veteran author/illustrator" noted Barbara Elleman in the *School Library Journal.* In this work, Simont blends his illustrations with a humorous and suspenseful tale of an adventurous goose who avoids the roasting pan with a narrow escape. A reviewer for *Publishers Weekly* noted that, "the superbly modulated art has no trouble getting this tale off the ground."

Another self-illustrated work, *The Stray Dog: From a True Story by Reiko Sassa,* appeared in 2001. Here, a family on a Saturday picnic finds a stray dog, names him Willy, and plays with him for the day. As the family prepares to leave, the parents will not let their new friend accompany them home, thinking that he probably belongs to someone else. But during the week, the family finds itself thinking about the dog and eventually return to the same picnic spot the next weekend. Here they save Willy from the dogcatcher and decide to keep him in the family permanently. "This picture book has all the earmarks of a classic," wrote a *Horn Book* contributor, who noted that the text is spare—"appropriately so, as the pictures are surprisingly eloquent." *School Library Journal* reviewer Mary Ann Carcich predicted that *The Stray Dog* would be "a great tale for any kid who's dreamed of adopting a pet."

"I believe that if I like the drawings I do, children will like them also," Simont told Lee Bennett Hopkins for *Books Are by People.* He continued, "The child in me must make contact with other children. I may miss it by ten miles, but if I am going to hit, it is because of the child in me."

BIOGRAPHICAL/CRITICAL SOURCES:

BOOKS

Caldecott Medal Books: 1938-1957, Horn Book, 1957.
Hopkins, Lee Bennett, *Books Are by People: Interviews with 104 Authors and Illustrators of Books for Young Children,* Citation Press, 1969.

Kingman, Lee, editor, *Newbery and Caldecott Medal Books: 1956-1965,* Horn Book, 1965.

Klemin, Diana, *The Art of Art for Children's Books,* Clarkson Potter, 1966.

More Junior Authors, H. W. Wilson, 1963.

PERIODICALS

Booklist, January 1, 2001, Hazel Rochman, review of *The Stray Dog: From a True Story by Reiko Sassa,* p. 974.

Book World, November 5, 1972, p. 4.

Christian Science Monitor, November 11, 1971.

Horn Book, February, 1980, p. 140; April, 1983, p. 158; February, 1984, p. 54; June, 1984, p. 318; May-June, 1985, p. 326; November-December, 1986, p. 737; November-December, 1989, p. 788; January, 2001, review of *The Stray Dog: From a True Story by Reiko Sassa,* p. 86.

New York Times Book Review, October 31, 1965, p. 56; November 18, 1979, Nora Magid, review of *How to Dig a Hole to the Other Side of the World;* October 17, 1982, George A. Woods, review of *The Philharmonic Gets Dressed,* p. 37; November 6, 1983, p. 43; May 20, 1984, p. 28; November 9, 1986, p. 40.

Publishers Weekly, April 20, 1992, review of *The Lovely Summer,* p. 55; June 23, 1997, review of *The Goose that Almost Got Cooked,* p. 91.

School Library Journal, August, 1982, Kenneth Marantz, review of *The Philharmonic Gets Dressed,* p. 99; August, 1984, p. 56; October, 1989, p. 100; June, 1992, Eve Larkin, review of *The Lovely Summer,* p. 103; August, 1997, Barbara Elleman, review of *The Goose that Almost Got Cooked,* p. 142; February, 2001, Mary Ann Carcich, review of *The Stray Dog: From a True Story by Reiko Sassa,* p. 106.

Science Books and Films, November-December, 1988, p. 95.

Time, December 4, 1978, p. 100; December 20, 1982, p. 79.*

*   *   *

SIMPSON, Helen 1957-

PERSONAL: Born in Bristol, England; married; children: one daughter. *Education:* Oxford University, M.Lit.

ADDRESSES: Office—c/o Random House, Attn: Crown Publishing Author Mail, 299 Park Ave., New York, NY 10171-0002.

CAREER: Staff writer for British edition of *Vogue;* freelance writer.

AWARDS, HONORS: Winner of British *Vogue* talent contest; Somerset Maugham award, and Young Writer of the Year award, *Sunday Times,* both 1990, for *Four Bare Legs in a Bed and Other Stories.*

WRITINGS:

The London Ritz Book of Afternoon Tea: The Art and Pleasure of Taking Tea, Arbor House (New York, NY), 1986.

The London Ritz Book of English Breakfasts, Arbor House (New York, NY), 1988.

Four Bare Legs in a Bed and Other Stories, Heinemann (London, England), 1990.

Flesh and Grass (suspense novella; bound with *The Strawberry Tree* by Ruth Rendell), Pandora Press, 1990.

Dear George and Other Stories, Heinemann (London, England), 1995.

Hey Yeah Right Get a Life (stories), Jonathan Cape, 2000, published as *Getting a Life,* Knopf (New York, NY), 2001.

Work also represented in anthologies. Contributor of articles and stories to magazines and newspapers. Author of the libretto for *Good Friday, 1663,* an opera for television, as well as plays for stage and radio.

SIDELIGHTS: Helen Simpson is a British short story writer whose works are acknowledged for their humor and jaundiced view of men, women, work, and relationships. "Simpson's special province is a certain female-seeming moodiness and temper," observed Anna Vaux in *Times Literary Supplement,* and these ill-tempered women are the targets of her satire as much as the mean-spirited or ineffectual men who fail them. Though her books are based in realism, critics noted that Simpson achieves her comic effects by the extreme actions of her characters, which push some of her later stories into the realm of fantasy. According to Rita Ciresi in *Library Journal,* such works are not as successful with the critics as those in which the female protagonists are "tough and true to life," but Simpson is still considered an accomplished short story writer.

The female characters in Simpson's first collection of short stories, *Four Bare Legs in a Bed and Other Stories,* are largely dissatisfied with themselves, their lives, and their relationships, but appear to exist in a world devoid of alternatives. "Ms. Simpson's dark vision deals directly enough with the battle of the sexes, but ultimately its most telling revelations are about the human soul and its tragic limitations," observed Richard Burgin in *New York Times Book Review*. In "A Shining Example," a wealthy older neighbor invites young Jane for lunch in order to instruct her about the necessity of selling herself in marriage only to the richest man she can find. In "What Are Neighbors For," a doctor surreptitiously interviews the women she has invited to tea as prospective babysitters for the child she plans to have, by the lover she intends to get rid of. In "Christmas Jezebels," a man attempts to convince his daughters to support him by prostituting themselves. In these stories and others, according to a reviewer for *Publishers Weekly*, the author "adroitly monitors [her] characters' minds and relationships, skirting the edges of empathetic realism and strident satire at the same time."

Dear George and Other Stories, Simpson's second collection of stories, features young women at odds with themselves, their mates, and often the world at large. This collection "is wonderfully caustic and sensual," according to a reviewer for *Books*, "displaying a boldness that only [Simpson] can get away with." And as in the earlier work, critics noted that the issue of children appears more than once. In "To Her Unready Boyfriend," a woman pressed for time by the ticking of her biological clock confronts her boyfriend in what Vaux called "a Marvellian exercise in persuasion." In the title story the reader is privy to a school girl's insights into Shakespeare, the topic of an assigned essay she is writing, and to her letters to George, a boy she has a crush on. The stories inspired Vaux to write, "There is a lot that is wayward and unpredictable about the stories here. . . . Simpson's ear and eye are gleefully alert, and there is something exuberant and charged in the detail." *Spectator*'s Charlotte Raven complained that Simpson's forays into the realm of fantasy lacked the imaginative humor of her more realistic pieces, and found *Dear George and Other Stories* to be less successful than *Four Bare Legs in a Bed and Other Stories*, but a reviewer for *Books* magazine concluded: "As she populates her stories with characters who often spend their time philosophizing about everyday insecurities in an extremely likeable and believable way, it's impossible to read [Simpson] without feeling uniquely satisfied."

Simpson is a writer whose main subject has been described as the plight of the generation of women charged with achieving the goals won by the feminist revolution, such as success in their careers and in their

relationships. The resulting scenarios are enlivened by what Ciresi called "Simpson's slick and funny prose," and have won awards and praise for the wicked humor and psychological acuity of the author's new versions of "age-old problems." While Simpson is sometimes accused of wandering too far into the realm of farcical fantasy, her most critically successful stories achieve effects both comic and horrific in their depiction of the lives of modern working-class women.

Simpson continued in the same vein with her third collection, known in England as *Hey Yeah Right Get a Life* and in the United States as *Getting a Life*. This book focuses on suburban mothers taking care of their children. Various characters, settings, and events appear and reappear among the stories. In "Café Society" two mothers confide while trying to keep under control a hyperactive youngster, and in "Hurrah for the Hols" a mother on the beach has had enough of demanding children and snaps at them sarcastically. In "Wurstigkeit" two women elude their family lives by shopping at a store so exclusive that it requires a secret password to enter. As in her other works, Simpson blends humor with emotional honesty, creating a "wise, gentle collection," to quote Lisa Allardice of *New Statesman and Society*. "All these stories are funny, even when their comedy is grotesque, grim or straight from the gallows," remarked a *Guardian* critic, who added, "Simpson also prevents her unfaltering lament from turning into the dirge of self-pity by her exceptionally perceptive writing and her gift for the arresting image." The stories, according to a *Publishers Weekly* reviewer, are "sharped-tongued and merciless." In the words of *Newsweek* contributor Jeff Giles, "It's exciting to see a fiction writer reclaim territory often left to sociologists—especially a fiction writer who can be both acidic and tender, who can, at her best, deliver some pretty serious shocks of recognition."

Jay McInerney stated in *New York Times Book Review* that *Getting a Life* is both comic and "frighteningly unsentimental about middle-class . . . family life." McInerney added that "Burns and the Bankers," in which a corporate banker and mother attends a hilariously dreadful mandatory celebration of the life of poet Robert Burns, "is a tour de force, one of the funniest and most ambitious stories I've read in years." Citing Simpson's "playful stylistic facility and her acute powers of observation and characterization," McInerney ventured that *Getting a Life* would cement Simpson's reputation in the United States. The book was equally admired in Britain, where Trev Broughton wrote in *Times Literary Supplement* that "Simpson's depiction of the maternal psyche in extremis is almost clinically discerning," adding that the stories impress "precisely because they allow the reader to share with their protagonists the tenderness that underpins the resentment, to see beyond the chronic fatigue and the bad-tempered coping, and to 'savour the deep romance and boredom' of childcare. Simpson's faithfulness to that daunting equation is a rare and beautiful feat."

BIOGRAPHICAL/CRITICAL SOURCES:

PERIODICALS

Books Magazine, summer, 1995, p. 14.

Guardian, October 7, 2000, review of *Hey Yeah Right Get a Life.*

Library Journal, January, 1992, p. 181.

New Statesman and Society, June 25, 2001, Lisa Allardice, "Paperback Reader," p. 56.

New York Times, June 12, 2001, Michiko Kakutani, "Women Stretched Thin in the 'Vanity-Free Zone,'" p. E7.

New York Times Book Review, March 8, 1992, p. 23; June 17, 2001, Jay McInerney, review of *Getting a Life,* p. 8.

Newsweek, June 25, 2001, Jeff Giles, review of *Getting a Life,* p. 91.

Publishers Weekly, November 22, 1991, p. 38; May 28, 2001, review of *Getting a Life,* p. 46.

Spectator, August 12, 1995, pp. 31-32.

Times Literary Supplement, July 13, 1990, p. 746; June 9, 1995, Anna Vaux, review of *Dear George and Other Stories,* p. 27; October 13, 2000, Trev Broughton, review of *Hey Yeah Right Get a Life,* p. 23.

Women's Review of Books, September, 2001, Rebecca Steinitz, review of *Getting a Life,* p. 19.*

*   *   *

SINGER, Isaac Bashevis 1904-1991

(Isaac Bashevis, Isaac Warshofsky)

PERSONAL: Born July 14, 1904, in Radzymin (some sources say Leoncin), Poland; immigrated to United States, 1935; naturalized U.S. citizen, 1943; died after several strokes, July 24, 1991, in Surfside, FL; buried at Beth-El Cemetery, New York, NY; son of Pinchos Menachem (a rabbi and author) and Bathsheba (Zylberman) Singer; married; wife's name, Rachel (divorced); married Alma Haimann, February 14, 1940; children: (first marriage) Israel Zamir. *Education:* Attended Tachkemoni Rabbinical Seminary, Warsaw, Poland, 1920-23. *Religion:* Jewish.

CAREER: Novelist, short story writer, children's author, and translator. *Literarishe Bletter,* Warsaw, Poland, proofreader and translator, 1923-33; *Globus,* Warsaw, associate editor, 1933-35; *Jewish Daily Forward,* New York, NY, member of staff, 1935-91. Founder of the literary magazine *Svivah.* Appeared in *Isaac in America* and *The Cafeteria* (based on one of his short stories), both Direct Cinema Limited Associates, both 1986.

MEMBER: Jewish Academy of Arts and Sciences (fellow), National Institute of Arts and Letters (fellow), Polish Institute of Arts and Sciences in America (fellow), American Academy of Arts and Sciences, PEN.

AWARDS, HONORS: Louis Lamed Prize, 1950, for *The Family Moskat,* and 1956, for *Satan in Goray;* National Institute of Arts and Letters and American Academy award in literature, 1959; Harry and Ethel Daroff Memorial Fiction Award, Jewish Book Council of America, 1963, for *The Slave;* D.H.L., Hebrew Union College, 1963; Foreign Book prize (France), 1965; National Council on the Arts grant, 1966; *New York Times* best illustrated book citation, 1966, Newbery Honor Book Award, 1967, International Board on Books for Young People (IBBY) honor list, 1982, *Horn Book* "Fanfare" citation, and American Library Association (ALA) notable book citation, all for *Zlateh the Goat and Other Stories;* National Endowment for the Arts grant, 1967; *Playboy* magazine award for best fiction, 1967; Newbery Honor Book Award, 1968, for *The Fearsome Inn;* Bancarella Prize, 1968, for Italian translation of *The Family Moskat;* Newbery Honor Book Award, 1969, ALA notable book citation, and *Horn Book* honor list citation, all for *When Schlemiel Went to Warsaw and Other Stories;* Brandeis University Creative Arts Medal for Poetry-Fiction, 1970; National Book Award for children's literature, 1970, and ALA notable book citation, both for *A Day of Pleasure;* Sydney Taylor Award, Association of Jewish Libraries, 1971; Children's Book Showcase Award, Children's Book Council, 1972, for *Alone in the Wild Forest;* D.Litt., Texas Christian University, 1972, Colgate University, 1972, Bard College, 1974, and Long Island University, 1979; Ph.D., Hebrew University, Jerusalem, 1973; National Book Award for fiction, 1974, for *A Crown of Feathers and Other Stories;* Agnon Gold Medal, 1975; ALA notable book citation, 1976, for *Naftali the Storyteller and His Horse, Sus, and Other Stories;* Nobel Prize for Literature, 1978; Kenneth B. Smilen/*Present Tense* Literary Award,

Present Tense magazine, 1980, for *The Power of Light; Los Angeles Times* fiction prize nomination, 1982, for *The Collected Stories of Isaac Bashevis Singer; New York Times* outstanding book citation, and *Horn Book* honor list citation, both 1982, Parents' Choice Award, Parents' Choice Foundation, 1983, and ALA notable book citation, all for *The Golem; New York Times* notable book citation, and ALA notable book citation, both 1984, both for *Stories for Children;* Handel Medallion, 1986; PEN/Faulkner Award nomination, 1989, for *The Death of Methuselah and Other Stories;* Gold Medal for Fiction, American Academy and Institute of Arts and Letters, 1989; *Mazel and Shlimazel; or, The Milk of a Lioness* and *The Wicked City* received ALA notable book citations.

WRITINGS:

NOVELS; ORIGINALLY IN YIDDISH

Der Satan in Gorey, [Warsaw, Poland], 1935, translation by Jacob Sloan published as *Satan in Goray,* Noonday, 1955, reprinted, Farrar, Straus (New York, NY), 1996.

(Under name Isaac Bashevis) *Di Familie Mushkat,* two volumes, [New York, NY], 1950, translation by A. H. Gross published under name Isaac Bashevis Singer as *The Family Moskat,* Knopf (New York, NY), 1950.

The Magician of Lublin, translation by Elaine Gottlieb and Joseph Singer, Noonday, 1960.

The Slave (also see below), translation by author and Cecil Hemley, Farrar, Straus (New York, NY), 1962.

The Manor, translation by Elaine Gottlieb and Joseph Singer, Farrar, Straus (New York, NY), 1967.

The Estate, translation by Elaine Gottlieb, Joseph Singer, and Elizabeth Shub, Farrar, Straus (New York, NY), 1969.

Enemies: A Love Story (first published in *Jewish Daily Forward* under title *Sonim, di Geshichte fun a Liebe,* 1966; also see below), translation by Aliza Shevrin and Elizabeth Shub, Farrar, Straus (New York, NY), 1972.

Shosha (also see below), translation by Joseph Singer, Farrar, Straus (New York, NY), 1978.

Reaches of Heaven: A Story of the Baal Shem Tov, Farrar, Straus (New York, NY), 1980.

Isaac Bashevis Singer, Three Complete Novels (includes *The Slave, Enemies: A Love Story,* and *Shosha*), Avenel Books, 1982.

The Penitent, Farrar, Straus (New York, NY), 1983.

The King of the Fields, limited edition, Farrar, Straus (New York, NY), 1988.

Scum, translation by Rosaline D. Schwartz, Farrar, Straus (New York, NY), 1991.

The Certificate, translation by Leonard Wolf, Farrar, Straus (New York, NY), 1992.

Meshugah, translation by Nili Wachtel, Farrar, Straus (New York, NY), 1994.

Shootns baym Hodson, translation by Joseph Sherman published as *Shadows on the Hudson,* Farrar, Straus (New York, NY), 1998.

SHORT STORY COLLECTIONS; ORIGINALLY IN YIDDISH

Gimpel the Fool, and Other Stories, translation by Saul Bellow and others, Noonday, 1957.

The Spinoza of Market Street, and Other Stories, translation by Elaine Gottlieb and others, Farrar, Straus (New York, NY), 1961.

Short Friday, and Other Stories, translation by Ruth Whitman and others, Farrar, Straus (New York, NY), 1964.

Selected Short Stories, edited by Irving Howe, Modern Library (New York, NY), 1966.

The Seance, and Other Stories, translation by Ruth Whitman, Roger H. Klein, and others, Farrar, Straus (New York, NY), 1968.

(And translator with others) *A Friend of Kafka, and Other Stories,* Farrar, Straus (New York, NY), 1970.

An Isaac Bashevis Singer Reader, Farrar, Straus (New York, NY), 1971.

(And translator with others) *A Crown of Feathers, and Other Stories,* Farrar, Straus (New York, NY), 1973.

Passions, and Other Stories, Farrar, Straus (New York, NY), 1975.

Old Love, and Other Stories, Farrar, Straus (New York, NY), 1979.

The Collected Stories of Isaac Bashevis Singer, Farrar, Straus (New York, NY), 1982.

The Image, and Other Stories, Farrar, Straus (New York, NY), 1985.

Gifts, Jewish Publication Society of America (Philadelphia, PA), 1985.

The Death of Methuselah, and Other Stories, Farrar, Straus (New York, NY), 1988.

FOR CHILDREN; ORIGINALLY IN YIDDISH; AND TRANSLATOR WITH ELIZABETH SHUB

Mazel and Shlimazel; or, The Milk of a Lioness, illustrated by Margot Zemach, Harper (New York, NY), 1966.

Zlateh the Goat, and Other Stories, illustrated by Maurice Sendak, Harper (New York, NY), 1966.

The Fearsome Inn, illustrated by Nonny Hogrogian, Scribner (New York, NY), 1967.

When Schlemiel Went to Warsaw, and Other Stories (also see below), illustrated by Margot Zemach, Farrar, Straus (New York, NY), 1968.

(Under pseudonym Isaac Warshofsky) *A Day of Pleasure: Stories of a Boy Growing up in Warsaw* (autobiography), photographs by Roman Vishniac, Farrar, Straus (New York, NY), 1969.

Elijah the Slave: A Hebrew Legend Retold, illustrated by Antonio Frasconi, Farrar, Straus (New York, NY), 1970.

Joseph and Koza; or, The Sacrifice to the Vistula, illustrated by Symeon Shimin, Farrar, Straus (New York, NY), 1970.

Alone in the Wild Forest, illustrated by Margot Zemach, Farrar, Straus (New York, NY), 1971.

The Topsy-Turvy Emperor of China, illustrated by William Pene du Bois, Harper (New York, NY), 1971.

The Wicked City, illustrated by Leonard Everett Fisher, Farrar, Straus (New York, NY), 1972.

The Fools of Chelm and Their History, illustrated by Uri Shulevitz, Farrar, Straus (New York, NY), 1973.

Why Noah Chose the Dove, illustrated by Eric Carle, Farrar, Straus (New York, NY), 1974.

A Tale of Three Wishes, illustrated by Irene Lieblich, Farrar, Straus (New York, NY), 1975.

Naftali the Storyteller and His Horse, Sus, and Other Stories (also see below), illustrated by Margot Zemach, Farrar, Straus (New York, NY), 1976.

The Power of Light: Eight Stories for Hanukkah (also see below), illustrated by Irene Lieblich, Farrar, Straus (New York, NY), 1980.

The Golem, limited edition, illustrated by Uri Shulevitz, Farrar, Straus (New York, NY), 1982.

Stories for Children (includes stories from *Naftali the Storyteller and His Horse, Sus, and Other Stories, When Schlemiel Went to Warsaw and Other Stories,* and *The Power of Light*), Farrar, Straus (New York, NY), 1984.

Shrewd Todie and Lyzer the Miser and Other Children's Stories, illustrated by Margot Zemach, Barefoot Books (Boston, MA), 1994.

AUTOBIOGRAPHY; ORIGINALLY IN YIDDISH; UNDER PSEUDONYM ISAAC WARSHOFSKY

Mayn Tatn's Bes-din Shtub, [New York, NY], 1956, translation by Channah Kleinerman-Goldstein published under name Isaac Bashevis Singer as *In My Father's Court,* Farrar, Straus (New York, NY), 1966.

A Little Boy in Search of God: Mysticism in a Personal Light (also see below), illustrated by Ira Moskowitz, Doubleday (Garden City, NY), 1976.

A Young Man in Search of Love (also see below), translation by Joseph Singer, Doubleday (Garden City, NY), 1978.

Lost in America (also see below), translation by Joseph Singer, paintings and drawings by Raphael Soyer, Doubleday (Garden City, NY), 1981.

Love and Exile: The Early Years: A Memoir (includes *A Little Boy in Search of God: Mysticism in a Personal Light, A Young Man in Search of Love,* and *Lost in America*), Doubleday (Garden City, NY), 1984.

More Stories from My Father's Court, translation by Curt Leviant, Farrar, Straus (New York, NY), 2000.

PLAYS; ORIGINALLY IN YIDDISH

The Mirror (also see below), produced in New Haven, CT, 1973.

(With Leah Napolin) *Yentl, the Yeshiva Boy* (adaptation of a story by Singer; produced on Broadway, 1974), Samuel French (New York, NY), 1978.

Schlemiel the First, produced in New Haven, CT, 1974.

(With Eve Friedman) *Teibele and Her Demon* (produced in Minneapolis at Guthrie Theatre, 1978, produced on Broadway, 1979), Samuel French (New York, NY), 1984.

A Play for the Devil (based on his short story "The Unseen"), produced in New York City at the Folksbiene Theatre, 1984.

TRANSLATOR INTO YIDDISH

Knut Hamsun, *Pan,* Wilno (Warsaw, Poland), 1928.

Knut Hamsun, *Di Vogler* (title means "The Vagabonds"), Wilno (Warsaw, Poland), 1928.

Gabriele D'Annunzio, *In Opgrunt Fun Tayve* (title means "In Passion's Abyss"), Goldfarb (Warsaw, Poland), 1929.

Karin Michaelis, *Mete Trap,* Goldfarb (Warsaw, Poland), 1929.

Stefan Zweig, *Roman Rolan,* Bikher (Warsaw, Poland), 1929.

Knut Hamsun, *Viktorya* (title means "Victoria"), Wilno (Warsaw, Poland), 1929.

Erich Maria Remarque, *Oyfn Mayrev-Front Keyn Nayes* (title means "All Quiet on the Western Front"), Wilno (Warsaw, Poland), 1930.

Thomas Mann, *Der Tsoyberbarg* (title means "The Magic Mountain"), four volumes, Wilno (Warsaw, Poland), 1930.

Erich Maria Remarque, *Der Veg oyf Tsurik* (title means "The Road Back"), Wilno (Warsaw, Poland), 1930.

Moshe Smilansky, *Araber: Folkstimlekhe Geshikhtn* (title means "Arabs: Stories of the People"), Farn Folk (Warsaw, Poland), 1932.

Leon S. Glaser, *Fun Moskve biz Yerusholayim* (title means "From Moscow to Jerusalem"), Jankowitz, 1938.

OTHER

(Editor with Elaine Gottlieb) *Prism 2*, Twayne (Boston, MA), 1965.

Visit to the Rabbinical Seminary in Cincinnati, [New York, NY], 1965.

(With Ira Moscowitz) *The Hasidim: Paintings, Drawings, and Etchings,* Crown (New York, NY), 1973.

Nobel Lecture, Farrar, Straus (New York, NY), 1979.

The Gentleman from Cracow; The Mirror, illustrated with water colors by Raphael Soyer, introduction by Harry I. Moore, Limited Editions Club, 1979.

Isaac Bashevis Singer on Literature and Life, University of Arizona Press (Tucson, AZ), 1979.

The Meaning of Freedom, United States Military Academy (West Point, NY), 1981.

My Personal Conception of Religion, University of Southwestern Louisiana Press (Lafayette, LA), 1982.

One Day of Happiness, Red Ozier Press, 1982.

Remembrances of a Rabbi's Son, translated by Rena Borrow, United Jewish Appeal-Federation Campaign, 1984.

(With Richard Burgin) *Conversations with Isaac Bashevis Singer,* Farrar, Straus (New York, NY), 1986.

The Safe Deposit and Other Stories about Grandparents, Old Lovers, and Crazy Old Men ("Masterworks of Modern Jewish Writing" series), edited by Kerry M. Orlitzky, Wiener, Markus (New York, NY), 1989.

Isaac Bashevis Singer: Conversations, edited by Grace Farrell, University Press of Mississippi (Jackson, MS), 1992.

Also author of works under name Isaac Singer. Author of the introduction for Knut Hamsun's *Hunger,* Farrar, Straus (New York, NY), 1967; of the preface for Ruth Whitman's *An Anthology of Modern Yiddish Poetry,* Workmen's Circle Education Department (New York, NY), 1979; and of the introduction and commentary for

Richard Nagler's *My Love Affair with Miami Beach,* Simon & Schuster (New York, NY), 1991. Contributor to books, including *Tully Filmus,* edited by Anatol Filmus, Jewish Publication Society of America (Philadelphia, PA), 1971; and *Miami Beach,* by Gary Monroe, Forest & Trees, 1989.

Also contributor of stories and articles to periodicals in the United States and Poland, including *Die Yiddische Welt, Commentary, Esquire, New Yorker, Globus, Literarishe Bletter, Harper's,* and *Partisan Review.* Sound recordings include *Isaac Bashevis Singer Reading His Stories* (contains *Gimpel the Fool* and *The Man Who Came Back*), and *Isaac Bashevis Singer Reading His Stories in Yiddish* (contains *Big and Little, Shiddah and Kuziba,* and *The Man Who Came Back*), both Caedmon Records, both 1967. Singer's works are housed in the Elman Collection, Arents Research Library, Syracuse University, and at the Butler Library, Columbia University.

ADAPTATIONS: Filmstrips based on Singer's short stories include: *Isaac Singer and Mrs. Pupko's Bread,* New Yorker, 1973, *Rabbi Leib and the Witch Cunnegunde,* Miller-Brody Productions, 1976, and *Shrewd Todie and Lyzer the Miser,* Miller-Brody Productions, 1976; works adapted into filmstrips by Miller-Brody Productions include *Zlateh the Goat and Other Stories, When Schlemiel Went to Warsaw,* and *Why Noah Chose the Dove,* all 1975, and *Mazel and Shlimazel,* 1976.

Zlateh the Goat and Other Stories was adapted into a film by Weston Woods, 1973, and broadcast on National Broadcasting Company (NBC-TV), 1973; *The Magician of Lublin* was adapted into a film starring Alan Arkin, produced by Menahem Golan, 1978; *Gimpel the Fool* was adapted for the stage by David Schechter and produced by the Bakery Theater Cooperative of New York, 1982; *Yentl, the Yeshiva Boy* was adapted into the movie *Yentl,* starring Barbra Streisand, Metro-Goldwyn-Mayer/United Artists, 1983; *Enemies: A Love Story* was adapted into a film by Paul Mazursky and Roger L. Simon and released by Twentieth Century-Fox, 1989.

Works adapted into recordings read by Eli Wallach include: *When Schlemiel Went to Warsaw and Other Stories,* Newbery Awards Records, 1974, *Zlateh the Goat and Other Stories,* Newbery Award Records, 1974, *Eli Wallach Reads Isaac Bashevis Singer* (contains *Zlateh the Goat and Other Stories* and *When Schlemiel Went to Warsaw and Other Stories*), Miller-Brody Productions, 1976, and *Isaac Bashevis Singer* (contains *The Seance* and *The Lecture*), Spoken Arts, 1979; *The Family Moskat, The Slave, Satan in Goray, Passions and Other Stories,* and *In My Father's Court* were adapted into audio cassettes; twenty of Singer's works have been adapted into Braille editions; twelve of Singer's works have been adapted into talking books.

SIDELIGHTS: Widely proclaimed to be one of the foremost writers of Yiddish literature, Isaac Bashevis Singer stood clearly outside the mainstream and basic traditions of both Yiddish and American literature. His work, translated into numerous languages, won him the Nobel Prize for Literature in 1978, as well as numerous other prestigious honors. "The river of words that flowed from Singer's pen is vast: hundreds of short stories, volumes of autobiography, a dozen novels and even more children's books," noted Lore Dickstein in the *New York Times Book Review.* Dickstein added, "He was embraced by a large, unlikely audience, including readers of *Playboy* and *The New Yorker,* most of them far removed from the lost world of Eastern European Jewry that Singer evoked so pungently." The critic also noted that Singer "is the most magical of writers, transforming reality into art with seemingly effortless sleight of hand. His deceptively spare prose has a pristine clarity that is stunning in its impact." Lee Siegel, also writing in the *New York Times Book Review,* deemed Singer "the creator of stories and novels that, at their best, are like hard diamonds of perfection."

Singer's writing has proven difficult to categorize, with critics attaching to the author various and sometimes contradictory labels in an attempt to define his work. He was called a modernist, although he personally disliked most contemporary fiction, and he was also accused of being captivated by the past, of writing in a dying language despite his English fluency, of setting his fiction in a world that no longer exists: the *shtetls* (Jewish ghettos) of Eastern Europe which were destroyed by Hitler's campaign against the Jews. And despite the attention called to the mysticism, the prolific presence of the supernatural, and the profoundly religious nature of his writing, Singer was called both a realist and a pessimist. Undeniably a difficult author to place in critical perspective, Singer addressed himself to the problems of labeling his work in an interview with Cyrene N. Pondrom for *Contemporary Literature:* "People always need a name for things, so whatever you will write or whatever you will do, they like to put you into a certain category. Even if you would be new, they would like to feel that a name is already prepared for you in advance. . . . I hope that one day somebody will find a new name for me, not use the old ones."

Whatever else he was, Singer was a storyteller. His works deal with crises of faith: having discarded their old traditions as inadequate to cope with modern society, his characters are engaged in a fruitless search for something to replace them. "Singer portrays men who are between faiths," Nili Wachtel explained in *Judaism.* "Having freed themselves from the bonds of God and community, they have also freed themselves from their very identities. With their God and their community, they knew who they were and what they were expected to do; now they know nothing as certain." Michael Wood similarly observed in the *New York Review of Books:* "Again and again in his fiction Singer evokes the destruction of a community, the crumbling of a whole social edifice, because people, one way or another, have averted their faces from a truth they used to know."

The key to Singer's work lies in his background, in his roots in the Polish, Yiddish-speaking, Jewish ghettos. "I was born with the feeling that I am part of an unlikely adventure, something that couldn't have happened, but happened just the same," Singer once remarked to a *Book Week* interviewer. Born in a small Polish town, Singer was the son of a Hassidic rabbi, and both his grandfathers were also rabbis. Visiting his maternal grandfather in the rural village of Bilgoray as a young boy, Singer learned of life in the *shtetl,* which would become the setting of much of his later work. The village was a "world of old Jewishness [in which] I found a spiritual treasure trove," the author was quoted as saying in the *Dictionary of Literary Biography Yearbook,* "Time seemed to flow backwards. I lived Jewish history."

The young Singer received a basic Jewish education, preparing him to follow his father's and grandfathers' steps into the rabbinical vocation. He studied the Torah, the Talmud, the Cabala, and other sacred Jewish books. An even stronger influence than his education and his parents' orthodoxy, however, was his older brother, the novelist I. J. Singer, who broke with the family's orthodoxy and began to write secular stories. Attempting to overcome the influence of his brother's rationalism and to strengthen the cause of religion, his parents told him stories of *dybbuks* (wandering souls in Jewish folklore believed to enter a human body and control its actions, possessions, and other spiritual mysteries). Singer once commented that he was equally fascinated by both his parents' mysticism and his brother's rationalism. Although this duality would come to characterize much of his writing, eventually Singer would break from both traditions.

At seventeen Singer entered a seminary in Warsaw, but he left two years later to follow his brother into the world of arts and letters. He got a proofreading job with a Yiddish literary magazine, worked as a translator, and at twenty-three had his first piece of fiction published. Concerned about German aggression and the policies of Adolph Hitler, Singer left Poland in 1935 and joined his brother in New York City. There he married and began a long career as a journalist and writer for the *Jewish Daily Forward.* The periodical would serve as the first publisher of many of Singer's works—short stories, articles, and serialized novels in Yiddish.

Singer continued to do all of his writing in Yiddish, and much of his large body of writing remains untranslated after his death in 1991. Before he felt sufficiently fluent in English, Singer had to rely on other people to do the translations; his nephew Joseph Singer was responsible for much of it. Toward the end of his career, though, Singer usually did a rough translation into English himself and then had someone help him polish the English version and work on the idioms. The English translations were often a "second original," according to Singer, differing structurally from the Yiddish. "I used to play with the idea [of writing in English]," Singer admitted in an interview with Joel Blocker and Richard Elman for *Commentary,* "but never seriously. Never. I always knew that a writer has to write in his own language or not at all."

Singer described Yiddish in his Nobel lecture as "a language of exile, without a land, without frontiers, not supported by any government, a language which possesses no words for weapons, ammunition, military exercises, war tactics; a language that was despised by both gentiles and emancipated Jews. . . . Yiddish has not yet said its last word. It contains treasures that have not been revealed to the eyes of the world. It was the tongue of martyrs and saints, of dreamers and cabalists—rich in humor and in memories that mankind may never forget. In a figurative way, Yiddish is the wise and humble language of us all, the idiom of the frightened and hopeful humanity."

Aside from believing that he must write in his native tongue, Singer also believed that the function of his fiction should be entertainment. "I never thought that my fiction—my kind of writing—had any other purpose than to be read and enjoyed by the reader," he commented to Sanford Pinsker in *The Schlemiel as Metaphor: Studies in the Yiddish and American Jewish Novel.* "I never sit down to write a novel to make a better world or to create good feelings towards the Jews or for any other purpose," he continued. "I knew this from the very beginning, that writing fiction has no other pur-

pose than to give enjoyment to a reader. . . . I consider myself an entertainer. . . . I mean an entertainer of good people, of intellectual people who cannot be entertained by cheap stuff. And I think this is true about fiction in all times."

Singer's first novel, *Satan in Goray,* was first published in Yiddish in 1935. The novel's action takes place in a small Hasidic community in Poland during the seventeenth century. Cossacks have raided the closely knit community, and the *shtetl* easily accepts the promises of a false messiah, Sabbatai Zevi. As violations of religious law take place, a rash of strange, demonic occurrences erupts, eventually concentrating themselves in Zevi's chosen bride, who becomes pregnant with Satan's child. According to Ted Hughes in the *New York Review of Books,* the novel is Singer's "weakest book—important, and with a stunning finish, but for the most part confusingly organized." Hughes added that the supernatural elements provide "an accurate metaphor for a cultural landslide that has destroyed all spiritual principles and duped an entire age into a cynical materialism emptied of meaning." In his critical work *Isaac Bashevis Singer: The Magician of West 86th Street* Paul Kresh described *Satan in Goray* as "rich in vivid, convincing descriptions of things, places and people [and] . . . haunting in its imagery."

The Family Moskat departs from its predecessor and offers a long, epic vision of a large family in a big Polish city. Radical changes are afoot, and the narrator, Asa Heshel, not only participates in them himself but also observes their effects upon the Moskat family. The story ends as the Nazis are about to invade, and Asa leaves his family behind to join the army. *Spectator* critic John Daniel called the work "a considerable novel" with "powerfully created characters; a deep sense of Warsaw as a city; and a real saturation in Jewish lore." *Yiddish Literature* contributor Charles A. Madison praised the novel's characterization, concluding that the book "is an intensely conceived narrative pulsating with human life and revealing the inner emotional recesses of the individuals involved."

Turning to yet another format, the picaresque adventure *The Magician of Lublin* follows magician and acrobat Yasha Mazur as he courts several women—even though he already has a devoted wife and family. According to *Critical Quarterly* contributor David Seed, this novel "is certainly one of Singer's most concentrated and unified works," mainly because the disordered setting of the Warsaw streets matches the emotional crisis suffered by Yasha, whose conscience pains him even as he involves himself in trouble. In addition, Nili Wachtel observed in *Judaism* that Yasha's profession—magician and tightrope walker—reflects the dilemma of rootless modern man: "He is afraid to be fixed by a single and permanent identity. . . . He has no peace, he feels himself dangling; he is walking his tightrope, he feels, but always on the verge of disaster." Yasha finally resolves his conscience with his actions by enclosing himself in a cell, locked away from the potential to misbehave. "That his singular behavior, which would normally seem queer, appears plausible is due to Singer's powers of exposition and characterization," Madison remarked, for the characters "are portrayed realistically, without affection or sympathy, but also without manipulation and artfulness."

Whether they feature sweeping historical events or the singular struggles of an individual, Singer's novels continued to express his concern with issues of faith and freedom. Set in Poland in the seventeenth century, *The Slave* features the religious crises the protagonist, Jacob, suffers as he experiences various forms of freedom and slavery, some of them mirroring Biblical events. *New York Times Book Review* contributor Milton Hindus found the novel "overburdened . . . with too much allegorical suggestiveness" but allowed that "there is a lovely lyricism in some of the descriptive passages which makes them partake of the quality of expressionist paintings." Madison hailed the appealing characters and setting, concluding that "all of this folklore, exotic atmosphere, and genuine emotion is depicted with an intimate knowledge and artistic sensuousness that combine to give the book major status as a work of fiction."

In *The Manor* and *The Estate,* originally published as a single work, Singer once again took an epic approach in portraying an era of Polish-Jewish history. The two volumes cover the last third of the nineteenth century, a time of dramatic change. "As in his earlier novels," Madison summarized, "Singer deals at length and significantly with the events and salient thoughts and ideas of the time in which his characters live and function." Nili Wachtel remarked in *Judaism* that the central character's experience "gives voice to what it is that ails modern man. Alone, independent, free of any single influence or direction, modern man becomes aware of a chaotic world alive within him, a churning chaos of conflicting drives and ambitions." These two novels, according to Seed, "raise various theoretical issues (usually in explicit discussion) and one of their central themes is the notion of progress."

Later Singer works reflect his experiences living not just as an exile from his homeland, but also as one of the few survivors of a culture that was exterminated by the Holocaust. In *Enemies: A Love Story* Herman Broder is a Polish refugee whose entire family has perished in the death camps. He has immigrated to America, where he lives in New York with Yadwiga, the Polish woman who saved him from the Nazis by hiding him in her hayloft. Although Yadwiga has converted to Judaism for him, Herman has taken a mistress, the divorced Masha, who lives with her mother, a bitter survivor of a concentration camp. When Herman discovers that the wife he thought had perished during the war is actually alive and living in New York, it sets in motion a tragicomic series of events. *Enemies* "is a bleak, obsessive novel that offers neither release nor hope," Dickstein claimed in the *New York Times Book Review*. Kresh, however, felt that the book "hangs together uncommonly well" and praised Singer's focus on the love story. He explained that the author concentrates "on the lines of force that bond his characters together, ironically, angrily, passionately, even though life has done everything to deprive them of their illusions and their appetites." *Newsweek* contributor Walter Clemons concluded, "Whether or not you accept its ending, *Enemies: A Love Story* is a brilliant, unsettling novel."

The author's most autobiographical novel, *Shosha*, "is filled with the usual Singer questions about demonic possession, free-floating souls, an archive of spirits, a world rife with secret powers and occult mysteries," to quote Edward Hirsch in the *Saturday Review*. "But mostly it is a testament to the haunting power of the past." Taking place in the Warsaw of the 1920s and 1930s, *Shosha* follows the developing relationship between a rabbi's son and the title character, a somewhat simple and innocent girl. As the protagonist looks for his place and for meaning in the world, he wanders from woman to woman until he returns to his childhood friend. "Singer conveys a sense of the teeming particularities of Polish-Jewish life," Robert Alter remarked in the *New Republic*. Alter added, "Singer, here as elsewhere, is so *beguiling* a writer that one readily forgives the flaws of his work." In *Harper's,* Paul Berman wrote that *Shosha* is "an entertaining novel, for though Singer is an earnest writer, his earnestness steps lightly." Kresh declared *Shosha* a "powerful and important work," adding that while the characters and themes are familiar ground for Singer, "*Shosha* casts a fresh light on them, making their story one of the most poignant Isaac has ever written."

Four more Singer novels have been translated and published posthumously: *Scum, The Certificate, Meshugah,* and *Shadows on the Hudson.* A *dybbuk* and Polish Jewry figure in *Scum.* In 1906 Max Barabander has returned to Warsaw from Argentina some twenty years after leaving. Because of shady dealings, he now is a wealthy man, but he is impotent after the sudden death of his teenage son and his wife's isolation. In Warsaw he becomes a womanizer, convinced he is possessed by a *dybbuk,* and a master of language. "There is, as Singer warns, little of God's wisdom and mercy in this book, but the display of human perversity and sheer cussedness is enthralling," Paul Gray remarked in *Time.*

Kenneth Turan stated in the *Los Angeles Times Book Review* that *The Certificate* "is a mildly engaging piece of work, more fictionalized memoir than anything else." The protagonist is unpublished writer David Bendinger, whose father is a rabbi and brother is a writer. After four years in the country, Bendinger returns to Warsaw seeking a certificate from the British government that will allow him to immigrate to Palestine. Through Bendinger's relationships with three very different women, Singer subtly criticizes the Zionists, Communists, and the religious Jewish community and reveals Bendinger's anxieties. "It is impossible not to feel the charm of this book, which may be the most Jewish of all Singer's works. The warmest and the saddest too," remarked Chicago *Tribune Books* reviewer Elie Wiesel.

Originally titled *Lost Souls, Meshugah* (Yiddish for "crazy") describes the encounters that Polish exile Aaron Greidinger has with Holocaust survivors in early-1950s Manhattan. "The various survivors, all mourning loved ones, are indeed 'lost souls,' subject to melancholy, poisonous dreams and thoughts of suicide," Joel Conarroe pointed out in the *New York Times Book Review.* "As for the concept of *meshugah,*" Conarroe added, "Singer weaves into his narrative references to the innate craziness not only of his high-strung men and women, but of the mad events that have shaped their behavior." George Packer commented in *Washington Post Book World* that in *Meshugah* Singer uses his "familiar bag of tricks: love triangles and quadrangles, sudden reversals from disaster to fulfillment and back, relentless questions about good and evil." However, concluded Packer, "the concoction lacks Singer's customary zest." According to Mark Shechner in Chicago *Tribune Books,* the previously serialized story "is reminiscent of daytime television" because it is episodic and contains licentiousness and pathos. However, stressed Shechner, "its licentiousness, far from being a commercial pandering to the market, is a tragic metaphysics, warranted by the apocalypses of the 20th Century."

Shadows on the Hudson once again is concerned with the lives of Jewish refugees in World War II-era Manhattan. Hertz Dovid Grein, a Polish native,

struggles to reconcile his simultaneous passions for three women while wrestling with theological, philosophical, and political issues pertinent to the times. The novel, like most of Singer's other works, was published serially in *The Jewish Daily Forward;* unlike the others, however, its publication in novel form does not include editing of redundant or repetitive passages. The work is therefore long and—some critics felt—tedious in places. Siegel noted in the *New York Times Book Review* that the "shapeless lump does a keen disservice to the author of 'Gimpel the Fool.'" Concluding that the novel "would have been a failure under any circumstances," Siegel determined that it "would have been a respectable failure if only Singer's editors had striven in the slightest degree."

Although his novels were frequently noteworthy, Singer was perhaps better known as a master of the short story. Story-writing was his most effective and favorite genre because, as he once explained, it was more possible to be perfect in the short story than in a longer work. Furthermore, Singer did not think that the supernatural—which was his main element—lent itself well to longer, novelistic writing. Singer's style in the short story was simple, spare, and in the tradition of the spoken tale. In his *Commentary* interview, the author remarked: "When I tell a story, I tell a story. I don't try to discuss, criticize, or analyze my characters." *Nation* reviewer Dan Isaac stated that Singer's short stories "are far superior to his novels" because they more closely follow the Jewish literary tradition of "the proverb, the parable and the folk tale." In *Studies in Short Fiction,* John Lawrence Abbott declared, "The short story continues to remain Singer's most congenial turf. It is here that the economy of style and the deceptive simplicity of his vision can be most richly felt." Hughes also observed that Singer's stories "give freer play to his invention than the novels. At their best, they must be among the most entertaining pieces extant. Each is a unique exercise in tone, focus, style, form, as well as an unforgettable re-creation of characters and life."

It was Singer's first collection of short fiction, *Gimpel the Fool, and Other Stories,* that first gained him a wider English-speaking audience. Part of the notoriety came from the collection's translator, for novelist Saul Bellow, himself a future Nobel laureate, was already critically acclaimed for his own fiction. But it was primarily the quality of the stories that captivated readers, particularly the title story about a supposed "fool" whose innocent faith protects him from the evil that harms others. Leon Wieseltier, writing in the *New York Review of Books,* felt that the collection "contains Singer's best work, his boldest and liveliest inventions.

And it belies at once his familiar disclaimer that he is only a storyteller. He is not. His tales are thick with speculation and prejudice, and both are damaging." The 1961 compilation *The Spinoza of Market Street, and Other Stories* also won notice for its title piece that concerns a Jewish scholar who eventually finds happiness in marriage, not philosophy. *New Republic* contributor Irving Howe remarked that the collection, while demonstrating nothing unexpected of Singer, is still the work of "a writer who has mastered his chosen form and keeps producing work often distinguished and always worthy of attention."

After his 1964 short story collection, *Short Friday, and Other Stories,* Singer's fiction began to show the influence of his adopted homeland. Many of the author's later stories feature Jews transplanted to America after World War II. The stories in *A Friend of Kafka,* for instance, "show this venerable master seriously extending his range," according to Jay L. Halio in *Southern Review.* Some stories still utilize Singer's popular Polish village settings, but there are many more following the lives of Jewish immigrants in America, Israel, and Argentina. *Time* correspondent Stefan Kanfer believed that "these twenty-one miraculous creations are, in the highest artistic tradition, true stories." Dan Isaac commented that the collection "is by far the best thing we have" from Singer, adding in his *Nation* review that the author "seems to go from strength to strength as though increasing age had become the generative force."

The National Book Award-winning collection *A Crown of Feathers* also demonstrates Singer's growing preoccupation with life in America. According to William Peden in *Sewanee Review,* "whether [Singer's] landscape be a Warsaw soup kitchen for intellectuals, an old world haunted by demons, imps, and *dybbuks* of the past, or a cafeteria in Coney Island, it is alive and vibrant with unforgettable people." While *Nation* writer Seymour Kleinberg found *A Crown of Feathers* "the least rewarding of Singer's . . . short-story collections," he acknowledged that "his literary craftsmanship and sophistication, and the special Singer voice, are here and gratifying; only in comparison with his past achievements does the book fall short." Crawford Woods concluded in his *New Republic* review, "These unusually fine stories take joy in paradox but not in irony, and they're often tragic but never sad. If their resemblance to each other makes the book seem long, it also makes it cut deep. What might be a sign of limitation in a lesser writer in Singer must be seen as wisdom. He is one of our best storytellers—'our' meaning everybody."

Later Singer collections garnered much the same praise as his previous works. In his *Studies in Short Fiction*

review of *Passions, and Other Stories,* Timothy Evans maintained, "Here is passion in the art, an imaginative providence as prodigal as ever, a talent in its prime, a writer to be rejoiced in." *New York Times* columnist John Gross observed of *The Image, and Other Stories* that while the themes and subjects are familiar, "in another sense, virtually every story in the book comes as a surprise, with the freshness of a bold conception firmly imagined and confidently executed." Singer, the critic concluded, "remains a true storyteller—at every stage, you want to know what happens next—and there has been no falling-off in the quality of his writing."

Even into his eighties Singer continued to produce new works of short fiction at a rapid pace. His final collection, *The Death of Methuselah, and Other Stories,* demonstrates that "like a vintage wine, Isaac Bashevis Singer gets better with time," to quote Lothar Kahn in *World Literature Today.* The stories include many of the same themes and supernatural occurrences that characterize his earlier fiction: an exorcist eventually gives in to his own demons; an artist discovers he has spent his creativity on love rather than art; and a Florida retiree cannot give up his wheeler-dealer lifestyle even though it jeopardizes his health. Believing that for Singer, the urge to create and learn was as tempting as sex, Robert Pinsky wrote in the *New York Times Book Review,* "Singer's stories both demonstrate the power and irresistible attraction of such [creative] secular arts, and question the moral force underneath the attraction."

In addition to his work for adult readers, Singer penned a number of acclaimed children's books. "Children are the best readers of genuine literature," Singer claimed in *Top of the News,* "In our epoch, when storytelling has become a forgotten art and has been replaced by amateurish sociology and hackneyed psychology, the child is still the independent reader who relies on nothing but his own taste. . . . Long after literature for adults will have gone to pieces, books for children will constitute that last vestige of storytelling, logic, faith in the family, in God and in real humanism."

Most of Singer's children's books are collections of short stories in which "religion and custom dominate life and a rich folktale tradition abounds," according to Sylvia W. Iskander in the *Dictionary of Literary Biography.* A number of his stories are set in the humorous Polish city of Chelm—a town that Yiddish people view as a place of fools. And they also include *schlemiel* (eternal loser) characters, who naturally reside in the city of Chelm. They are essentially fools, but are portrayed as being charming and engaging, as is the city itself. Aside from these humorous and silly tales, Singer also wrote about animals and such supernatural beings as witches, goblins, devils, and demons. "Certainly the union of stories by a Nobel laureate storyteller with illustrations by some of the finest artists in the field of children's literature has produced outstanding books," concluded Iskander. "But it is the content of the stories—the combination of folklore, fairy tale, religion, and imagination—that makes Singer's books unique and inimitable."

With so many of his fictional works finding a basis in the author's own experiences, it is not surprising that Singer also published several volumes of autobiography. These include *In My Father's Court, Little Boy in Search of God, A Young Man in Search of Love, Lost in America,* and *More Stories from My Father's Court.* "Singer makes vivid a world triply gone," observed Jonathan Rosen in the *New York Times Book Review.* "He is evoking the world of childhood, which is always a lost world, as well as the culture of Judaism that produced his father but that was already breaking apart under the weight of assimilation. He is also recording the transitional realm of Jewish Poland that Singer himself was born into in 1904—a world that was destroyed by the Nazis, who murdered the Jewish prostitutes and the rabbis without distinction. Writing in the aftermath of that destruction, Singer pays his characters the high honor of recreating them in all their low reality, which in some paradoxical way seems like an act of profound humanism."

Although Singer died in 1991, most of his work is still in print, and new translations of Yiddish prose and fiction are continuing to appear. Some critics have suggested that the author's use of a vanishing language, traditional folklore, and "old country" settings belie a modern consciousness that could address issues central to universal human emotion. "Singer repetitively and compellingly focuses on the individual's struggle to find a viable faith in the age possessed by this very problem," Linda G. Zatlin contended in *Critique.* "Thus, the stories, despite their setting, . . . portray and explore this predominant problem of modern man with all its accompanying apprehension and tension." For *Commentary* contributor Joseph Epstein it was Singer's skill at recreating eras that made him noteworthy. "No modern writer in any literature that I know is so adept at setting his stories anywhere he wishes temporally," Epstein wrote. "This ability sets much of Singer's writing finally beyond time, which is of course where everyone who thinks himself an artist wishes to be." "Singer is one of the great tale-tellers of this century," Sean French concluded in *New Statesman and Society.* "He has a

skill for the gripping short narrative, the 'yarn' that is almost without precedent since the time of Kipling. . . . Singer is better than anyone else on the surfaces, sounds and smells of life, about worldly things—lust, acquisitiveness, magic, superstition."

Julia O'Faolain summed up Singer's accomplishment in her *New Review* piece on the Nobel laureate. "My pleasure in Singer's work comes from no fact he imparts," she stated. "The virtue is in the tale itself and the tale is his response to those riddles which excite such passion in him that he had to elaborate a narrative method for dealing with it. It is *his* own method and fits his themes. In other words, he has a voice of his own." Noting that Singer was "a remarkable storyteller, at once swift and complex," Peter S. Prescott concluded in *Newsweek,* "I believe that Singer, in his short and humorous tales drawn from an old tradition, celebrates the dignity, mystery and unexpected joy of living with more art and fervor than any other writer."

BIOGRAPHICAL/CRITICAL SOURCES:

BOOKS

Alexander, Edward, *Isaac Bashevis Singer,* Twayne (Boston, MA), 1980.

Allentuck, Marcia, editor, *The Achievement of Isaac Bashevis Singer,* Southern Illinois University Press (Carbondale, IL), 1967.

Allison, Alida, *Isaac Bashevis Singer: Children's Stories and Memoirs,* Twayne (New York, NY), 1996.

Authors and Artists for Young Adults, Volume 29, Gale Group (Detroit, MI), 1999.

Authors in the News, Gale (Detroit, MI), Volume 1, 1976, Volume 2, 1976.

Biletzky, Israel Ch., *God, Jew, Satan in the Works of Isaac Bashevis-Singer,* University Press of America (Lanham, MD), 1995.

Buchen, Irving H., *Isaac Bashevis Singer and the Eternal Past,* New York University Press (New York, NY), 1968.

Children's Literature Review, Volume 1, Gale (Detroit, MI), 1976.

Concise Dictionary of American Literary Biography: The New Consciousness, 1941-1968, Gale (Detroit, MI), 1987.

Contemporary Literary Criticism, Gale (Detroit, MI), Volume 1, 1973, Volume 3, 1975, Volume 6, 1976, Volume 9, 1978, Volume 11, 1979, Volume 15, 1980, Volume 23, 1983, Volume 38, 1986, Volume 69, 1992.

Dictionary of Literary Biography, Gale (Detroit, MI), Volume 6: *American Novelists since World War II,* 1980, Volume 28: *Twentieth-Century American-Jewish Fiction Writers,* 1984, Volume 52: *American Writers for Children since 1960: Fiction,* 1986.

Dictionary of Literary Biography Yearbook 1991, Gale (Detroit, MI), 1992.

Farrell, Grace, editor, *Critical Essays on Isaac Bashevis Singer,* Hall (New York, NY), 1996.

Farrell Lee, Grace, *From Exile to Redemption: The Fiction of Isaac Bashevis Singer,* Southern Illinois University Press (Carbondale, IL), 1987.

Gibbons, Frances Vargas, *Transgression and Self-Punishment in Isaac Bashevis Singer's Searches,* Lang (New York, NY), 1995.

Goran, Lester, *The Bright Streets of Surfside: The Memoir of a Friendship with Isaac Bashevis Singer,* Kent State University Press (Kent, OH), 1994.

Hadda, Janet, *Isaac Bashevis Singer: A Life,* Oxford University Press (New York, NY), 1997.

Kazin, Alfred, *Bright Book of Life: American Novelists and Storytellers from Hemingway to Mailer,* Atlantic Monthly Press (New York, NY), 1973.

Kresh, Paul, *Isaac Bashevis Singer: The Magician of West 86th Street,* Dial (New York, NY), 1979.

Madison, Charles A., *Yiddish Literature: Its Scope and Major Writers,* Ungar (New York, NY), 1968.

Malin, Irving, editor, *Critical Views of Isaac Bashevis Singer,* New York University Press (New York, NY), 1969.

Malin, Irving, *Isaac Bashevis Singer,* Ungar (New York, NY), 1972.

Pearl, Lila, *Isaac Bashevis Singer: The Life of a Storyteller,* illustrated by Donna Ruff, Jewish Publication Society (Philadelphia, PA), 1994.

Pinsker, Sanford, *The Schlemiel as Metaphor: Studies in the Yiddish and American Jewish Novel,* Southern Illinois University Press (Carbondale, IL), 1971.

Ran-Moseley, Fay, *The Tragicomic Passion: A History and Analysis of Tragicomedy and Tragicomic Characterization in Drama, Film, and Literature,* Lang (New York, NY), 1994.

Short Story Criticism, Volume 3, Gale (Detroit, MI), 1989.

Siegel, Ben, *Isaac Bashevis Singer,* University of Minnesota Press (Minneapolis, MN), 1969.

Singer, Isaac Bashevis, *Nobel Lecture,* Farrar, Straus (New York, NY), 1979.

Telushkin, Dvorah, *Master of Dreams: A Memoir of Isaac Bashevis Singer,* Morrow (New York, NY), 1997.

St. James Guide to Children's Writers, 5th edition, St. James Press (Detroit, MI), 1999.

Tuszyanska, Agata, *Lost Landscapes: In Search of Isaac Bashevis Singer and the Jews of Poland,* translated *from the Polish by Madeline G. Levine,* Morrow (New York, NY), 1998.

Wirth-Nesher, Hana, *City Codes: Reading the Modern Urban Novel,* Cambridge University Press (New York, NY), 1996.

Zamir, Israel, and Barbara Harshav, *Journey to My Father, Isaac Bashevis Singer,* Little, Brown (Boston, MA), 1995.

PERIODICALS

American Spectator, September, 1985, Anita Susan Grossman, review of *The Image and Other Stories,* pp. 43-44.

Atlantic, August, 1962; January, 1965; July, 1970; January, 1979.

Best Sellers, October 1, 1970.

Books and Bookmen, October, 1973; December, 1974.

Book Week, July 4, 1965, interview with I. B. Singer.

Book World, October 29, 1967; March 3, 1968; September 1, 1968; November 25, 1979.

Chicago Review, spring, 1980.

Chicago Tribune, October 25, 1980; June 23, 1987; July 25, 1991.

Chicago Tribune Book World, July 12, 1981; March 21, 1982; November 6, 1983; July 21, 1985.

Christian Science Monitor, October 28, 1967; September 5, 1978; September 18, 1978.

Commentary, November, 1958; October, 1960; November, 1963; February, 1965; February, 1979; November, 1991, Joseph Epstein, "Our Debt to I. B. Singer," pp. 31-37; December, 1992.

Contemporary Literature, winter, 1969; summer, 1969, Cyrene N. Pondrom, interview with Singer.

Critical Quarterly, spring, 1976, David Seed, "The Fiction of Isaac Bashevis Singer," pp. 73-79.

Criticism, fall, 1963.

Critique, Volume 11, number 2, 1969, Linda G. Zatlin, "The Themes of Isaac Bashevis Singer's Short Fiction," pp. 40-46; Volume 14, number 2, 1972.

Detroit Free Press, July 25, 1991.

Globe & Mail (Toronto), May 3, 1980; November 23, 1985; June 13, 1988.

Harper's, October, 1965; September, 1978, Paul Berman, review of *Shosha,* p. 94.

Horn Book, September/October, 1991, p. 654.

Hudson Review, winter, 1966-67, Herbert Leibowitz, "A Lost World Redeemed," pp. 669-673; spring, 1974.

Jewish Currents, November, 1962.

Jewish Quarterly, winter, 1966-67; autumn, 1972.

Judaism, fall, 1962, J. A. Eisenberg, "Isaac Bashevis Singer: Passionate Primitive or Pious Puritan?," pp. 345-356; winter, 1974; spring, 1977, Nili Wachtel,

"Freedom and Slavery in the Fiction of Isaac Bashevis Singer," pp. 171-186; winter, 1979, Edward Alexander, "The Nobel Prize for I. B. Singer," pp. 8-13.

Kenyon Review, spring, 1964.

Library Journal, March 1, 1994, p. 120; August, 1999, Melody A. Moxley, p. 163.

London Review of Books, October 24, 1991, p. 17.

Los Angeles Times, November 8, 1978; December 28, 1981; November 18, 1983; March, 18, 1984; December 4, 1986; December 12, 1989.

Los Angeles Times Book Review, November 16, 1980; August 16, 1981; May 2, 1982; February 6, 1983; December 9, 1984; August 25, 1985; May 1, 1988; April 14, 1991, Jonathan Kirsch, "The Dybbuk Made Him Do It," p. 12; January 3, 1993, p. 7.

Nation, November 2, 1970, Dan Isaac, "The World of Jewish Gothic," pp. 438-440; November 19, 1973, Seymour Kleinberg, "The Last to Speak That Tongue," pp. 538-539; November 19, 1983.

New Republic, November 24, 1958; January 2, 1961; November 13, 1961, Irving Howe, "Stories: New, Old, and Sometimes Good," pp. 18-19, 22-23; June 18, 1962; November 3, 1973, Crawford Woods, "Worlds beyond Ours," pp. 28-29; October 25, 1975; September 16, 1978, Robert Alter, review of *Shosha,* pp. 20-22; October 21, 1978.

New Review, June, 1976, Julia O'Faolain, review of *Passions and Other Stories,* pp. 59-60.

New Statesman, September 13, 1974, Peter Straub, review of *A Crown of Feathers,* p. 355; April 19, 1985, Anne Smith, "Holy Fool," p. 30.

New Statesman & Society, July 14, 1989, Sean French, "Singer's Gods," pp. 42-43; October 18, 1991, p. 39.

Newsweek, June 26, 1972, Walter Clemons, "Herman's Three Wives," p. 86; November 12, 1973, Peter S. Prescott, "The Dance of Life," pp. 113-114; April 12, 1982; September 26, 1983; August 5, 1991.

New York, December 31, 1979.

New Yorker, August 17, 1981; December 21, 1992.

New York Review of Books, April 22, 1965, Ted Hughes, "The Genius of Isaac Bashevis Singer," pp. 8-10; February 7, 1974, Michael Wood, review of *A Crown of Feathers and Other Stories,* pp. 10-11; December 7, 1978, Leon Wieseltier, "The Revenge of I. B. Singer," pp. 6, 8.

New York Times, October 30, 1966; January 29, 1967; July 10, 1978; July 22, 1978; December 9, 1978; October 17, 1979; December 5, 1979; December 16, 1979; December 17, 1979; April 19, 1980; June 15, 1982; November 30, 1982; September 22, 1983; October 7, 1984; November 7, 1984; June 25, 1985, John Gross, review of *The Image and Other Stories,* pp. 43-44; October 30, 1985; November 17, 1985; June 24, 1986; September 28, 1986; November 8, 1986; July 6, 1987; April 12, 1988; May 18, 1989; July 30, 1989; December 10, 1989; December 13, 1989; April 9, 1991, Michiko Kakutani, "Trapped in a Somber Dialectic of Faith and Flesh," p. C14; July 26, 1991; May 30, 1996, p. B3; May 30, 1996, p. C13.

New York Times Book Review, December 29, 1957; June 26, 1960; October 22, 1961; June 17, 1962, Milton Hindus, "An Upright Man on an Eternal Landscape," p. 4; November 15, 1964; October 8, 1967, Hugh Nissenson, review of *The Fearsome Inn,* p. 38; February 1, 1970, Richard M. Elman, review of *A Day of Pleasure,* p. 30; June 25, 1972, Lore Dickstein, review of *Enemies: A Love Story,* pp.4-5, 10; November 4, 1973; November 2, 1975; April 30, 1978, Andrew Bergman, review of *A Young Man in Search of Love,* p. 59; July 23, 1978; October 28, 1979; January 18, 1981; June 21, 1981, Mark Harris, "A Storyteller's Story," pp. 7, 28-29; January 31, 1982; March 21, 1982; November 14, 1982; September 25, 1983; November 11, 1984; June 30, 1985; October 27, 1985; October 16, 1988, Ewa Kuryluk, "Nightmares of the Poles and Lesniks," pp. 12-13; March 24, 1991, Bette Pesetsky, "Looking for Love on Krochmaina Street," p. 7; November 1, 1992, Lore Dickstein, "An Account Book Full of Humiliations," p. 7; April 10, 1994, Joel Conarroe, "'The World Is One Vast Madhouse,'" p. 9; January 25, 1998, Lee Siegel, "West Side Story"; December 24, 2000, Jonathan Rosen, "A World Triply Lost."

Paris Review, fall, 1968.

Publishers Weekly, February 18, 1983, interview with Singer; September 18, 2000, review of *More Stories from My Father's Court,* p. 93.

San Francisco Review of Books, Summer, 1991, pp. 15-16.

Saturday Review, January 25, 1958; November 25, 1961; June 16, 1962; November 21, 1964; September 19, 1970, Curt Leviant, review of *A Friend of Kafka,* pp. 36-37, 46; July 22, 1972; July 8, 1978, Edward Hirsch, review of *A Young Man in Search of Love* and *Shosha,* pp. 34-35.

School Library Journal, September, 1991; June, 1996, p. 124.

Sewanee Review, fall, 1974, William Peden, review of *A Crown of Feathers,* pp. 718-719.

Southern Review, spring, 1972; spring, 1973, Jay L. Hallo, review of *A Friend of Kafka,* pp. 466-467.

Spectator, October 17, 1958; September 15, 1961; May 11, 1962; June 10, 1966, John Daniel, review of *The Family Moskat,* p. 734.

Studies in Short Fiction, summer, 1974, John Lawrence Abbott, review of *A Crown of Feathers,* pp. 311-312; fall, 1976, Timothy Evans, review of *Passions and Other Stories,* pp. 528-529.

Tikkun, September/October, 1994, p. 79.

Time, October 20, 1967; September 21, 1970, Stefan Kanfer, "Sammler's Planetarians," p. 101; October 27, 1975, Stefan Kanfer, "Fiddler," pp. 78, 80; November 3, 1975; June 15, 1981; April 5, 1982; October 17, 1983; October 28, 1984; July 15, 1985; May 2, 1988; March 25, 1991, p. 70; August 5, 1991.

Times (London), April 10, 1980; March 8, 1984.

Times Literary Supplement, January 2, 1959; May 4, 1962; April 11, 1980; July 16, 1982; July 22, 1983; March 23, 1984; October 19, 1984; May 3, 1985; April 4, 1986; May 1, 1987; October 21, 1988; September 1, 1989.

Top of the News, November, 1972.

Tribune Books (Chicago), April 10, 1988; November 6, 1988; June 7, 1992, p. 2; November 1, 1992, p. 6; May 8, 1994, p. 5.

Washington Post, October 6, 1978; October 16, 1979; October 26, 1979; November 4, 1981; September 17, 1984; July 26, 1991.

Washington Post Book World, November 30, 1980; June 28, 1981, Helen Epstein, "Isaac Singer in Pursuit of Love and Literature," p. 4; March 28, 1982 (interview); November 7, 1982; July 7, 1985; September 21, 1986; October 23, 1988; March 3, 1991, Jonathan Yardley, "The Ills of the Flesh," p. 3; April 3, 1994, p. 9; January 25, 1998, Franklin Foer, "Survivors and Café Philosophers," p. 8.

World Literature Today, spring, 1979, Lothar Kahn, "The Talent of I. B. Singer, 1978 Nobel Laureate for Literature," pp. 197-201; autumn, 1988, Lothar Kahn, review of *The Death of Methuselah and Other Stories,* pp. 675-676; summer-autumn, 2001, James Knudsen, review of *More Stories from My Father's Court,* p. 200.

OTHER

Books and Writers—Isaac Bashevis Singer, http://www.kirjasto.sci.fi/ (February 6, 2002).

Isaac Bashevis Singer (cassette), Tapes for Readers, 1978.

Meet the Newbery Author: Isaac Bashevis Singer (filmstrip with cassette), Miller-Brody Productions, 1976.

Nobel Museum, http://www.nobel.se/ (June 4, 2001), "Isaac Bashevis Singer."

OBITUARIES:

PERIODICALS

Boston Globe, July 26, 1991, p. 37.
Chicago Tribune, July 25, 1991, Section 1, p. 11.
Detroit Free Press, July 25, 1991, p. A4.
New York Times, July 26, 1991, p. B5.
Time, August 5, 1991, p. 61.
Washington Post, July 26, 1991, p. C4.*

*   *   *

SLICK, Grace (Wing) 1939-
(Grace Barnett Wing)

PERSONAL: Born October 30, 1939, in Chicago (some sources say Evanston), IL; daughter of Ivan W. (an investment banker) and Virginia (a singer and actress; maiden name, Barnett) Wing; married Gerald "Jerry" Robert Slick (a musician), August 26, 1961 (divorced, 1970); married Skip Johnson (a production manager), November 29, 1976 (marriage ended, 1994); children: (with Paul Kantner) China Kantner. *Education:* Attended Finch College, 1957-58, and University of Miami, 1958-59.

ADDRESSES: Home—Los Angeles, CA. *Office*—c/o Author Mail, Warner Books, 1271 Avenue of the Americas, New York, NY 10020.

CAREER: Singer, songwriter, and musician. Worked as model for I. Magnin's, 1960-63. Member of musical groups, including Grace Slick and the Great Society, 1965-66, Jefferson Airplane, 1966-72, Jefferson Starship, 1974-78, and Starship, 1981-88. Vocals on *Windows of Heaven,* with Starship, CMC International, 1999.

MEMBER: Guardians (founding member).

WRITINGS:

BIOGRAPHY

(With Andrea Cagan) *Somebody to Love?: A Rock-and-Roll Memoir,* Warner Books (New York, NY), 1998.

SOLO; SONG LYRICS ON ALBUMS

Dreams (includes songs "Dreams," "Diablo," "Face to the Wind," "Angel of Night Seasons," "Do It the Hard Way," "Full Moon Man," "Let It Go," and "Garden of Man"), RCA, 1981.

Welcome to the Wrecking Ball! (includes songs "Wrecking Ball," "Mistreater," "Shot in the Dark," "Round and Round," "Shooting Star," "Just a Little Love," "Sea of Love," "Lines," "Right Kind," and "No More Heroes"), RCA, 1981.

Software (includes songs "Call It Right Call It Wrong," "Me and Me," "All the Machines," "Fox Face," "Through the Window," "It Just Don't Stop," "Habits," "Rearrange My Face," and "Bikini Atoll"), RCA, 1984.

The Best of Grace Slick (compilation; includes songs "Somebody to Love," "White Rabbit," "Rejoyce," "Lather," "Eskimo Blue Day," "Sunrise," "Mexico," "Law Man," "Across the Board," "Better Lying Down," "Hyperdrive," "Fast Buck Freddie," "All the Machines," "Wrecking Ball," and "Do You Remember Me"), RCA, 1999.

WITH JEFFERSON AIRPLANE; SONG LYRICS ON ALBUMS

Surrealistic Pillow (includes songs "Somebody to Love" and "White Rabbit"), RCA, 1967.

After Bathing at Baxter's (includes songs "Rejoyce" and "Two Heads"), RCA, 1967.

Bless Its Pointed Little Head (includes songs "Somebody to Love," "Turn out the Lights," and "Bear Melt"), RCA, 1969.

The Worst of Jefferson Airplane (includes "Somebody to Love," "White Rabbit," and "Lather"), RCA, 1970.

Bark (includes songs "Crazy Miranda," "Law Man," and "Never Argue with a German If You're . . ."), RCA, 1971.

Thirty Seconds over Winterland (includes song "Milk Train"), RCA, 1973.

Early Flight (includes song "Mexico"), RCA, 1974.

Jefferson Airplane Loves You (boxed set; includes songs "Free Advice," "Somebody to Love," "White Rabbit," "Two Heads," "Lather," "Would You Like a Snack?," "Hey Fredrick," "Law Man," "Aerie (Gang of Eagles)," and "Dress Rap/You Wear Your Dresses Too . . ."), RCA, 1992.

Best Of, RCA, 1993.

(With others) *Woodstock—25th Anniversary Collection,* Atlantic, 1994.

WITH JEFFERSON STARSHIP; SONG LYRICS ON ALBUMS

Dragon Fly (includes songs "Ride the Tiger," "Be Young You," "Devil's Den," and "Hyperdrive"), 1974.

Red Octopus (includes songs "Fast Buck Freddie," "Ai Garimasu (There Is Love)," "Play on Love," and "I Want to See Another World"), RCA, 1975.

Spitfire (includes songs "Dance with the Dragon," "Hot Water," "Song to the Sun Ozymandias," and "Switchblade"), 1976.

Winds of Change (includes "Out of Control" and "Black Widow"), Grunt, 1982.

Nuclear Furniture, RCA, 1984.

At Their Best, RCA, 1992.

Deep Space/Virgin Sky, Intersound, 1995.

WITH STARSHIP; SONG LYRICS ON ALBUMS

Knee Deep in the Hoopla, RCA, 1985.

No Protection (includes songs "I Don't Know Why" and "Babylon"), RCA, 1987.

Love among the Cannibals, RCA, 1989.

Greatest Hits (Ten Years and Change, 1979-1991), RCA, 1991.

SIDELIGHTS: Grace Slick is a prominent rock musician who is probably best known for her work as a lead vocalist with the band Jefferson Airplane in the late 1960s. The band's hits include such rock classics as "Somebody to Love," "White Rabbit," and "Volunteers."

Grace Barnett Wing was born on October 30, 1939, in Chicago, Illinois. Her father, Ivan W. Wing, was an investment banker, and her mother, Virginia (Barnett) Wing, had given up a budding career as a singer and actress in order to marry and settle down. Slick's brother Chris was born in 1949, and after the family had moved to San Francisco for her father's job transfer. They relocated to the suburb of Palo Alto in the early 1950s.

Though Slick was a chubby blonde child, during adolescence her hair turned dark and she slimmed down. Not achieving the "Barbie doll" look that she had hoped for, she turned to sarcasm to fit in with the popular crowd at Jordan Junior High. However, this soon only served to alienate her. By high school, though, she had regained a social circle and was attending parties regularly at a girlfriend's house. She transferred to a private school, Castilleja School for Girls, to be with her friend. In her teens, Slick began encountering problems with consuming too much alcohol.

After graduation, Slick decided to attend Finch College in New York because another friend was attending there and she had always wanted to go to New York. After a year there, she transferred to the University of Miami in Florida. As she wrote in her autobiography *Somebody to Love?: A Rock-and-Roll Memoir,* "Obviously, none of my academic choices were designed to actually further my education. The most important attraction in selecting a school was how much fun might be involved."

Upon receiving a letter from another friend about the "hippie" scene in San Francisco, Slick moved back to the West Coast in 1958. Instead of diving into the counterculture, however, she entered a relationship with childhood pal Jerry Slick, whose parents were close friends of her parents. They were married in 1961 in a traditional ceremony. Soon, they moved to San Diego, where he attended college and Slick worked at a department store. They quickly returned to San Francisco, where she found work modeling for the I. Magnin couturier department.

Before long, Slick and her husband were associating with artistic friends, and she wrote her first song. She also wrote the music to accompany her husband's senior thesis at San Francisco State University, a satirical film called *Everybody Hits Their Brother Once.* It won first prize at the Ann Arbor Film Festival.

In 1965, Slick and her friends saw the band Jefferson Airplane at a local nightclub and decided to put together a group of their own. They called it Grace Slick and the Great Society. She wrote in her book that it was meant to "[make] fun of President Lyndon B. Johnson's grandiose moniker for the U.S. population."

The band consisted of Slick on vocals, piano, guitar, and improvisational organ; her husband on drums; his brother Darby on guitar and sitar; and Brad Du Pont on bass. Veering away from the pervasive love-story songs that had been popular for years, the Great Society began to perform original songs with sociopolitical content. One of the band's biggest numbers—"Somebody to Love"—was, in fact, about love, but as she explained in her autobiography, "The lyrics implied that rather than the loving you're whining about getting or not getting, a more satisfying state of heart might be the loving you're giving."

The Great Society often played the famous Fillmore Ballroom in San Francisco, sharing a bill with bands like Jefferson Airplane and Moby Grape. Slick and the band also began socializing with the Grateful Dead and Neal Cassady, the lead character in Jack Kerouac's novel *On the Road.* They also began to experiment widely with drugs, including peyote and LSD.

After the band played together for about a year, they broke up and Slick joined the Jefferson Airplane when their female singer quit to raise a family. They already had a contract with RCA and had released one album, *Jefferson Airplane Takes Off.* Meanwhile, Slick's marriage was generally over by 1967, though she didn't officially divorce until 1971. She was involved with music and her husband had a film career, so they did not see each other. In addition, Slick noted in her book that the marriage had never been one of passion to begin with.

In 1967 Slick and the Jefferson Airplane scored an immense success with the album *Surrealistic Pillow.* This recording featured Slick's vocals on "Somebody to Love" and "White Rabbit," two tunes that she had written and performed with the Great Society. Both songs were hits, and "White Rabbit," which songwriter Slick derived by mixing imagery from Lewis Carroll's tale *Alice in Wonderland* with rhythms from Maurice Ravel's composition *Bolero,* came to epitomize society's increasingly prevalent use of drugs in an attempt to expand consciousness.

Although Jefferson Airplane never matched the success of *Surrealistic Pillow* and its two hit singles, they continued to enjoy acclaim with recordings such as *Crown of Creation,* featuring Slick's lead vocals on the title track, and *Volunteers,* with both the crowd-rousing title track, in which Balin calls for revolution, and the more subdued Slick-Kantner-Crosby composition "Wooden Ships." By the early 1970s the band began fragmenting. Balin embarked on other projects, Kaukonen and Casady formed another band, Hot Tuna, and Slick and Kantner, who had become lovers, commenced a series of recordings—*Blows against the Empire, Sunfighter,* and *Baron von Tollbooth and the Chrome Nun*—in which they collaborated with other San Francisco musicians. The Airplane continued to record, but without sustaining the achievement of the earlier works.

When Kantner determined to restructure Jefferson Airplane as the Jefferson Starship, Slick reluctantly complied. By this time she had developed a problem with excessive alcohol consumption, which prompted her to behave obnoxiously with fellow band members and with audiences. It also contributed to her nearly fatal accident in which she smashed her speeding automobile into a concrete wall. Despite her alcoholism, Slick proved a key performer with Jefferson Starship, for which she continued to contribute characteristically quirky tunes reveling in sarcasm and mocking social convention.

In the mid-1970s, after Balin joined the band, Jefferson Starship enjoyed newfound popularity with such recordings such as *Red Octopus,* which was highlighted by Balin's romantic ballad "Miracles." Slick, however, regretted the band's commercial success, claiming that it compromised the group's artistic integrity. In 1978, after a harrowing performance in which she made insulting comments to a German audience, Slick abruptly quit the band. She entered a substance-abuse program that enabled her to stop drinking alcohol, though she continued her occasional drug use, and she produced two solo recordings, *Dreams* and *Welcome to the Wrecking Ball.* In the early 1980s, however, she suddenly rejoined the band, now simply known as the Starship, and she continued with the group as it enjoyed still another period of commercial success. In her new capacity as a supporting performer—Mickey Thompson having assumed the role of featured vocalist—Slick appeared on such popular tunes as "Find Your Way Back" and "We Built This City." But she eventually grew disconnected with the material, the audiences, and even her fellow band members, and in 1988, after recovering from a shoulder problem, she once again left the band.

Since quitting the Starship, Slick has rarely played concerts. She participated in a Jefferson Airplane reunion tour in 1989, and she appeared at a memorial concert for late bandmate Papa John Creech, but she has otherwise abstained from public performance. A website, *Grace Slick Biography,* containing a biography by Greg Gildersleeve quoted her as saying, "I don't like old people on a rock 'n' roll stage, including myself."

Instead of performing, Slick has devoted herself to campaigning against laboratory tests involving animals. "Biomedical research has to do with a few people making a lot of money on procedures that benefit human beings very little," she told *Vegetarian Times.* "Animals' metabolism is different from ours, so who are the real guinea pigs for the pharmaceutical industry? The animals *and* us." She added: "I started reading all this literature, and I became absolutely fascinated with they way human beings treat animals in a kind of philo-

sophical context. . . . But who do we think we are? And if we're so much better, how come the world is in such a mess?"

In 1998 Slick published a characteristically candid autobiography, *Somebody to Love?,* in which she recalls her career as a musician, relates her problems as a substance abuser, and reflects on her experiences in the 1960s counterculture. Prominent in the book are recollections of her romantic entanglements, including an encounter with Doors singer Jim Morrison, and revelations of some daring ventures, including her plot, concocted with radical leader Abbie Hoffman, to introduce LSD into punch being served at a White House function. The book, which Slick described for a website interview, *Grace Interview,* as "celebrity trash for cash," was appraised by Alex Kuczynski, writing in the *New York Times Book Review,* as "messy, muddled, indulgent, and occasionally amusing." *Library Journal* reviewer Richard Grefrath deemed the book "appealingly blunt and funny," and a *Kirkus Reviews* critic concluded that the course of Slick's life "makes for a fun and emblematic trip." Tom Sinclair, meanwhile, affirmed in *Entertainment Weekly* that on the basis of *Somebody to Love?* Slick is "not ready for the rock & roll nursing home yet."

Slick has recently begun an art career. In 2000, she sold about 60 pieces, ranging in style, sizes, and mediums, including oil paint, acrylic paint, pencil, and ink, and had an exhibit at Artrock Gallery in San Francisco late that year. Prices for her works ranged from $1,100 to $8,700, and Slick acknowledged that selling them helped pay her bills since she mainly was living off royalties from her music.

In an Associated Press report that ran in the *Charleston Gazette,* Kim Curtis wrote, "She knows that serious art critics probably won't like her work. And they don't." Slick admitted that many people probably buy art works from someone famous even if the work isn't very good, but also noted, "You don't have to be Rembrandt to make something that appeals to somebody else."

BIOGRAPHICAL/CRITICAL SOURCES:

BOOKS

Contemporary Musicians, Volume 5, Gale (Detroit, MI), 1991.
Newsmakers, Gale (Farmington Hills, MI), 2001.
Slick, Grace, and Andrea Cagan, *Somebody to Love: A Rock-and-Roll Memoir,* Warner Books, 1998.

PERIODICALS

Atlanta Journal-Constitution, November 1, 1998, p. L9.
Booklist, September 1, 1998, p. 49.
Charleston Gazette, November 23, 2000, p. D3.
Daily Telegraph, December 29, 1998.
Entertainment Weekly, August 21, 1998, p. 115.
Kirkus Reviews, July 15, 1998, p. 1025.
Library Journal, August, 1998.
Life, December 1, 1992, p. 70.
New York Daily News, September 24, 1998, p. C2.
New York Times, October 18, 1998.
New York Times Book Review, September 20, 1998
    p. 20.
Publishers Weekly, August 10, 1998, p. 382.
San Francisco Chronicle, September 6, 1998, pp. 3, 34;
    November 18, 2000, p. B1.
Vegetarian Times, July, 1993, pp. 56-61.

OTHER

Grace Interview, http://www.usaserve.net/users/
    fastbuckfreddie/book.htm.
Grace Slick 1997, http://www.geocities.com/
    SunsetStrip/Club/4220/gracenow.html.
Grace Slick Biography, http://www.mds.mdh.se/
    ~dal95son/starship/bio/grace, slick.htm.*

*   *   *

SLOBIN, Mark 1943-

PERSONAL: Born March 15, 1943, in Detroit, MI; son of Norval (a teacher) and Judith (a teacher; maiden name, Liepah) Slobin; married Greta Nachtjaler (a college teacher), June 11, 1966; children: Maya. *Education:* University of Michigan, B.A., 1964, M.A., 1966, Ph.D., 1969; attended Manhattan School of Music, 1962-64.

ADDRESSES: Office—Department of Music, Wesleyan University, Middletown, CT 06459. *E-mail*—mslobin@ wesleyan.edu.

CAREER: Educator and author. Wesleyan University, Middletown, CT, assistant professor, then professor of music and department chair, 1971—. Visiting member of faculty at Yiddish Scientific Institute's Institute for Jewish Research, 1979; research associate at University of Nebraska; consultant to General Learning Corp.

MEMBER: Society for Ethnomusicology (former president).

AWARDS, HONORS: Grants from Wenner-Gren Foundation, 1970, 1971, National Endowment for the Arts, 1976, 1979, and International Research and Exchanges Board, for the Soviet Union, 1976.

WRITINGS:

Kirgiz Instrumental Music, Society for Asian Music (New York, NY), 1969.
Central Asian Music, Wesleyan University Press (Middletown, CT), 1975.
Music in the Culture of Northern Afghanistan, University of Arizona Press (Tucson, AZ), 1976.
Tenement Songs: The Popular Music of the Jewish Immigrants (with recording), University of Illinois Press (Urbana, IL), 1982.
(Editor and translator) *Old Jewish Folk Music: The Collections and Writings of Moshe Beregovski,* University of Pennsylvania Press (Philadelphia, PA), 1982, reprinted, Syracuse University Press (Syracuse, NY), 2000.
Chosen Voices: The Story of the American Cantorate, University of Illinois Press (Urbana, IL), 1989.
Subcultural Sounds: Micromusics of the West, University Press of New England (Hanover, NH), 1993, second edition, 2000.
(Editor) *Yiddish Theater in America: "David's Violin" (1897) and "Shloyme Gorgl" (189-)* (printed music), Garland (New York, NY), 1994.
(Editor) *Retuning Culture: Musical Changes in Central and Eastern Europe,* Duke University Press (Durham, NC), 1996.
Fiddler on the Move: Exploring the Klezmer World ("American Musicspheres" series; with recording), Oxford University Press (New York, NY), 2000.
(Editor) *Klezmer: The Evolution of an American Micromusic,* University of California Press (Berkeley, CA), 2001.
(Translator and editor, with Robert A. Rothstein and Michael Alpert) *Jewish Instrumental Folk Music: The Collections and Writings of Moshe Beregovski,* foreword by Izaly Zemtsovsky (with recording), Syracuse University Press (Syracuse, NY), 2001.

Contributor to *Encyclopaedia Britannica, Grove's New Dictionary of Music, Oxford Companion to Music,* and to journals. Editor of *Asian Music,* 1972—.

SIDELIGHTS: Mark Slobin's writings concentrate on his field of interest and expertise as a professor of music, and include histories, studies of musicians such as

Russian folk musician Moshe Beregovski, and, in the case of *Yiddish Theater in America: "David's Violin" (1897) and "Shloyme Gorgl" (189-)*, translations of musical stage plays. Joseph Lateiner wrote the original text and Sigmund Mogulesco the music for *David's Violin*, a four-act musical drama first performed in New York City in 1897. A less-than-complete translation was possible for *Shloyme Gorgl*, presumed to be written during the same period by Lateiner but with only the opening scenes still available in manuscript form.

Notes contributor Judith Pinnolis Fertig explained that Yiddish theater "was an immensely important cultural, social, and psychological outlet for the masses of Jewish immigrants living in New York at the turn of [the twentieth] century. . . . The Yiddish theater provided relief, often playing to fonder memories of Europe in a confusing and frightening new world. The themes of these Yiddish plays resonated with issues central to immigrants' lives, including family, assimilation, changing mores, and religion. With themes addressing transformation, economic success, and reconciliation, *David's Violin* was just such a musical drama, standing perhaps as a metaphor for the secularization happening all around the new immigrant." Fertig added that Slobin's work is notable as the first modern edition of both plays, formatted to be enjoyed by the modern theatregoer. "Slobin has primarily reproduced previously unpublished vocal sheet music that is often difficult to locate," she added, "and the accessibility gained through Slobin's edition is perhaps its most important asset."

Fiddler on the Move: Exploring the Klezmer World is Slobin's 154-page study of the revival of klezmer and comes with a music CD of both contemporary and archived recordings referred to in the text. The book includes chapters titled "Klezmer as a Heritage Music," "Klezmer as an Urge," "Klezmer as Community," and "Klezmer Style as a Statement." *Library Journal* reviewer Larry Lipkis called *Fiddler on the Move* "well researched and rich in anecdotes," and added that the volume "makes a compelling case for the importance of Klezmer in American musical and cultural studies." Reviewing the volume in *Notes*, Alex Lubet explained that Slobin "investigates klezmer's social meaning and function" to show that the music "is similar to other Western micromusics in the ways it is made and displayed," yet "unique both historically and in its current revival." Lubet praised Slobin's work as "a beautifully written book on a timely topic by a well-informed author" and cited the volume as "important for anyone interested in contemporary Jewish and American studies."

Slobin once told *CA:* "My continuing interest is in how music is part of people's (individual and collective)

sense of who they are. To this end I have worked among people whose backgrounds are very different from mine (in Afghanistan and Central Asia) and on the music of my own background (Yiddish). This has involved considerable travel through Europe, the Soviet Union, Israel, and the Middle East and India, as well as work on the Lower East Side of New York. Since 1976 I have also been involved in producing and reproducing immigrant entertainment of the turn-of-the-[twentieth]-century period, and find I truly enjoy the show-business side of the work as much as the scholarship."

BIOGRAPHICAL/CRITICAL SOURCES:

PERIODICALS

American Anthropologist, June, 1990, review of *Chosen Voices: The Story of the American Cantorate,* p. 523.
American Jewish History, spring, 1990, Macy Nulman, review of *Chosen Voices,* p. 426.
Choice, October, 1982, review of *Tenement Songs: The Popular Music of the Jewish Immigrants,* p. 279; November, 1989, review of *Chosen Voices,* p. 498; July, 1997, review of *Retuning Culture: Musical Changes in Central and Eastern Europe,* p. 1814.
Journal of American Folklore, October, 1983, review of *Tenement Songs,* p. 472.
Journal of American Studies, April, 1985, review of *Tenement Songs,* p. 157.
Library Journal, August, 2000, Larry Lipkis, review of *Fiddler on the Move: Exploring the Klezmer World,* p. 108.
Notes, December, 1991, Peter Laki, review of *Chosen Voices,* p. 526; December, 1997, Judith Pinnolis Fertig, review of *Yiddish Theater in America: "David's Violin" (1897) and "Shloyme Gorgl" (189-),* p. 576; December, 2001, Alex Lubet, review of *Fiddler on the Move,* p. 380.
Religious Studies Review, July, 1984, review of *Old Jewish Folk Music: The Collection and Writings of Moshe Beregovski,* July, 1991, review of *Chosen Voices,* pp. 197, 201.
Times Literary Supplement, May 3, 1985, review of *Old Jewish Folk Music,* p. 504.*

*   *   *

SMITH, Huston (Cummings) 1919-

PERSONAL: Born May 31, 1919, in Soochow, China; son of Wesley (a Methodist minister) Moreland and Alice (Longden) Smith; married Eleanor Brunhilda Wieman, September 15, 1943; children: Karen, Gael, Robin,

Kimberly. *Education:* Central Methodist College, A.B., 1940; graduate study at University of California, Berkeley, 1944-45; University of Chicago, Ph.D., 1945.

ADDRESSES: Home—1151 Colusa Ave., Berkeley, CA 94707-2726.

CAREER: University of Denver, Denver, CO, assistant professor of philosophy, 1945-47; Washington University, St. Louis, MO, associate professor of philosophy, 1947-58; Massachusetts Institute of Technology, Cambridge, MA, professor of philosophy, 1958-73; Syracuse University, Syracuse, NY, professor of religion, 1973-83; University of California, Berkeley, CA, visiting professor religious studies, 1990—. Visiting lecturer, University of Colorado, 1944, 1947; visiting professor, Iliff School of Theology, 1947; Charles Strong Lecturer on World Religions to universities in Australia, 1961. Ordained minister in United Methodist Church, 1946. Producer of documentary films on Hinduism, Sufism, and Tibetan Buddhism. Subject of five-part Public Broadcasting System (PBS) series *The Wisdom of Faith with Huston Smith,* 1996.

MEMBER: World University Service (chairman of American committee, 1966-70), American Philosophical Association, Society for Religion in Higher Education (fellow), Phi Beta Kappa.

AWARDS, HONORS: D.Hum., Central Methodist College, 1958; D.Let., Concord College, 1961; L.H.D., Franklin College of Indiana, 1964; Sc.D., Lake Forest College, 1965; LL.D., MacMurray College, 1967; honorary degree, Alaska Pacific University, 1983; honorary degree, Hamline University, 1988; honorary degree, Syracuse University, 2000.

WRITINGS:

The Purposes of Higher Education, Harper (New York, NY), 1955, reprinted, Greenwood Press (Westport, CT), 1971.
The Religions of Man (also see below), Harper (New York, NY), 1958, revised as *The World's Religions: Our Great Wisdom Traditions,* HarperSanFrancisco (San Francisco, CA), 1991.
(Editor, with Richard T. Heffron and Eleanor Wieman Smith) *The Search for America,* Prentice-Hall (Englewood Cliffs, NJ), 1959.
Condemned to Meaning, Harper (New York, NY), 1964.

(With others) *Dialogue on Science,* Bobbs-Merrill (Indianapolis, IN), 1967.
(With others) *Great Religions of the World,* National Geographic Society (Washington, DC), 1971.
Forgotten Truth: The Primordial Tradition, Harper (New York, NY), 1976, published as *Forgotten Truth: The Common Vision of the World's Religions,* HarperSanFrancisco (San Francisco, CA), 1992.
Beyond the Post-Modern Mind, Crossroad (New York, NY), 1982.
(With David Ray Griffin) *Primordial Truth and Postmodern Society,* State University of New York (Albany, NY), 1989.
Essays on World Religion, Paragon House (New York, NY), 1992.
The Illustrated World's Religions: A Guide to Our Wisdom Traditions, HarperSanFrancisco (San Francisco, CA), 1994.
(Editor) *Gregorian Chant: Songs of the Spirit,* KQED Books (San Francisco, CA), 1996.
(Editor, with Reuben Snake) *One Nation under God: The Triumph of the Native American Church,* Clear Light (Santa Fe, NM), 1996.
Cleansing the Doors of Perception: The Religious Significance of Entheogenic Plants and Chemicals, J. P. Tarcher/Putnam (New York, NY), 2000.
Why Religion Matters: The Fate of the Human Spirit in an Age of Disbelief, HarperCollins (New York, NY), 2001.
Islam: A Concise Introduction, HarperSanFransisco, (San Fransisco, CA), 2001.

Contributor to *The Heart of Learning: Spirituality in Education,* J. P. Tarcher/Putnam, 1999.

SOUND RECORDINGS

Journeys into Civilization, Big Sur Recordings (Sausalito, CA), 1968.
Toward a World Civilization, Center for the Study of Democratic Institutions (Santa Barbara, CA), 1969.
(With Joseph Campbell) *Tibet,* Big Sur Recordings (Sausalito, CA), 1969.
Religions of the World, Sounds True Recordings, 1994.

SIDELIGHTS: Huston Smith is "one of the most productive and busiest scholars of religion in the world," to quote an *Amazon.com* interviewer. A highly visible expert on the world's religions, Smith is the author of *The World's Religions: Our Great Wisdom Traditions,* which has been the standard textbook in college-level comparative religion classes for almost half a century.

Smith was born to Methodist missionaries in China and has never ceased his affiliation with that particular church. Nevertheless, he has practiced Buddhism, prays five times a day in Arabic, and is fully conversant in Hindu rites as well. So well versed is he in the world's mystical and moral traditions that he was the subject of a five-part Public Broadcasting System (PBS) series, *The Wisdom of Faith with Huston Smith*. A *Publishers Weekly* contributor maintained that Smith's works are "marked by clarity, rare philosophical depth and a truly global perspective."

Smith is not a disinterested scholar who reports religious history without conviction. He is an ardent participant in faith-based practices and has experienced mysticism as well. As a young professor at Massachusetts Institute of Technology in the early 1960s, he ingested mind-altering substances with Timothy Leary before such elements became illegal. His own experiences while under their influence convinced him of the limited but real role "psychoactive sacraments" have played in the foundations and practices of certain world religions. This conviction prompted Smith to champion the rights of Native Americans to use peyote in their religious rites and led to the publication of such titles as *One Nation under God: The Triumph of the Native American Church* and *Cleansing the Doors of Perception: The Religious Significance of Entheogenic Plants and Chemicals*. *Christian Century* correspondent Craig B. Mousin called *One Nation under God* "a moving testament to the resiliency of a people's faith in the midst of a culture whose laws and mores restrict faithful participation in its traditions." David O'Reilly in the *Knight-Ridder/Tribune News Service* noted that when Smith describes his experience with mescaline in *Cleansing the Doors of Perception*, he "seems to be describing the same wondrous encounter with the divine that mystics have sung of for millennia. And perhaps he was."

Smith has also been vocal on the cynicism of scientists who "deny the existence of things other than those they can train their instruments on," as quoted in *Publishers Weekly*. He feels that science and religion need not be mutually exclusive, as "traditional metaphysics" does not contradict objective facts. In an interview with *Mother Jones* the scholar said, "I don't want to justify religion in terms of its benefits to us. I believe that, on balance, it does a lot of bad things too—a tremendous amount. But I don't think that the final justification of religion is the good it does for people. I think the final justification is that it's true, and truth takes priority over consequences. Religion helps us deal with what is most important to the human spirit: values, meaning, purpose, and quality."

BIOGRAPHICAL/CRITICAL SOURCES:

PERIODICALS

America, April 6, 1996, James Martin, review of *The Wisdom of Faith,* p. 18.
Booklist, January 1, 2001, Ray Olson, review of *Why Religion Matters: The Fate of the Human Spirit in an Age of Disbelief,* p. 881.
Christian Century, November 19, 1997, Craig B. Mousin, review of *One Nation under God: The Triumph of the Native American Church,* p. 1102.
Cross Currents, fall, 1989, Robert A. McDermott, "Philosophy and Evolution of Consciousness," p. 322.
Kirkus Reviews, December 1, 2000, review of *Why Religion Matters,* p. 1669.
Knight-Ridder/Tribune News Service, June 21, 2000, David O'Reilly, "Author Describes Experience with Divine through Mescaline," p. K2616.
Mother Jones, November-December, 1997, Marilyn Snell, "The World of Religion according to Huston Smith," p. 40.
Publishers Weekly, May 11, 1992, review of *Huston Smith: Essays on World Religions,* p. 62; September 12, 1994, review of *The Illustrated World's Religions,* p. 38; December 11, 2000, review of *Why Religion Matters,* p. 81; May 29, 2000, review of *Cleansing the Doors of Perception,* p.76.
U.S. Catholic, September, 1998, p.6.
Whole Earth, fall, 2000, Dale Pendell, Review of *Cleansing the Doors of Perception: The Religions Significance of Entheogenic Plants and Chemicals,* p. 95.

OTHER

Amazon.com, http://www.amazon.com/ (March 2, 2001), "How Blessed: An Interview with Huston Smith."
Thinking Aloud, http://www.thinkingallowed.com/ (March 6, 2001), Jeffrey Mishlove, "Huston Smith, Ph.D.: The Psychology of Religious Experience."

*   *   *

SMITH, William Jay 1918-

PERSONAL: Born April 22, 1918, in Winnfield, LA; son of Jay (with the U.S. Army) and Georgia Ella (Campster) Smith; married Barbara Howes (a poet), October 1, 1947 (divorced June, 1965); married Sonja Haussmann, September 3, 1966; children: (first

William Jay Smith

marriage) David Emerson, Gregory Jay. *Education:* Washington University, B.A., 1939, M.A., 1941; attended Institut de Touraine; Université de Poitiers, diplôme d'études françaises; graduate study at Columbia University, 1946-47, at Oxford University as a Rhodes Scholar, 1947-48, and at University of Florence, 1948-50. *Politics:* Democrat. *Religion:* Protestant. *Avocational interests:* Painting and travel.

ADDRESSES: Home—63 Luther Shaw Rd., Cummington, MA 01026-9787. *Agent*—George Nicholson, Sterling Lord Literistic, Inc., 65 Bleecker St., New York, NY 10012.

CAREER: Washington University, St. Louis, MO, assistant in French, 1939-41; Columbia University, New York, NY, instructor in English and French, 1946-47, visiting professor of writing and acting chair of writing division, 1973, 1974-75; Williams College, Williamstown, MA, lecturer in English, 1951, poet-in-residence and lecturer in English, 1956-64, 1966-67; Arena Stage, Washington, DC, writer-in-residence, 1964-65; Hollins University, Hollins, VA, writer-in-residence, 1965-66,

professor of English, 1970-80, professor emeritus, 1980—. Lecturer at Salzburg Seminar in American Studies, 1975; Fulbright lecturer, Moscow State University, 1981; poet-in-residence, Cathedral of St. John the Divine, 1985-88. Has lectured at colleges, clubs, writers' conferences, and book fairs, and has presented television programs on poetry for children. Vermont House of Representatives, Democratic member, 1960-62; Library of Congress, Washington, DC, consultant in poetry, 1968-70, honorary consultant, 1970-76. Staff member, University of Connecticut Writers Conference, 1951; Suffield Writer-Reader Conference, 1959-62; and University of Indiana Writers Conference, 1961. Jury member, National Book Award, 1962, 1970, 1975, Neustadt International Prize for Literature, 1978, and Pegasus Prize for Literature, 1979-2000. Chairman of board of directors, Translation Center, Columbia University. *Military service:* U.S. Naval Reserve, 1941-45; became lieutenant; awarded commendation by French Admiralty.

MEMBER: American Academy of Arts and Letters (vice president for literature, 1986-89), Association of American Rhodes Scholars, Authors Guild (member of council), PEN, Authors League of America, Academy of American Poets, Century Association.

AWARDS, HONORS: Young Poets Prize, *Poetry* magazine, 1945; alumni citation, Washington University, 1963; Ford fellowship for drama, 1964; Union League Civic and Arts Foundation prize, *Poetry* magazine, 1964; Henry Bellamann Major award, 1970; Russell Loines Award, American Academy and Institute of Arts and Letters, 1972; National Endowment for the Arts fellowship, 1972 and 1995; D.Litt., New England College, 1973; National Endowment for the Humanities fellowship, 1975 and 1989; Gold Medal of Labor, Hungary, 1978; New England Poetry Club Golden Rose, 1980; Ingram Merrill Foundation grant, 1982; California Children's Book and Video Awards recognition for excellence (preschool and toddlers category), 1990, for *Ho for a Hat!;* medal (médaille de vermeil) for service to the French language, French Academy, 1991; Pro Cultura Hungarica medal, 1993; René Vásquez Díaz prize, Swedish Academy, 1997.

WRITINGS:

POETRY

Poems, Banyan Press (New York, NY), 1947.
Celebration at Dark, Farrar, Straus (New York, NY), 1950.

Snow, Schlosser Paper, 1953.

The Stork: A Poem Announcing the Safe Arrival of Gregory Smith, Caliban Press, 1954.

Typewriter Birds, Caliban Press, 1954.

Poems 1947-57, Little, Brown (Boston, MA), 1957.

Two Poems, Mason Hill Press, 1959.

(With Richard Wilbur) *Prince Souvanna Phouma: An Exchange between Richard Wilbur and William Jay Smith,* Chapel Press, 1963.

The Tin Can, and Other Poems, Delacorte (New York, NY), 1966, title poem published as *The Tin Can,* Stone House Press (Roslyn, NY), 1988.

New and Selected Poems, Delacorte (New York, NY), 1970.

A Rose for Katherine Anne Porter, Albondocani Press (New York, NY), 1970.

At Delphi: For Allen Tate on His Seventy-fifth Birthday, 19 November 1974, Chapel Press, 1974.

Venice in the Fog, Unicorn Press (Greensboro, NC), 1975.

(With Richard Wilbur) *Verses on the Times,* Gutenberg Press, 1978.

Journey to the Dead Sea, illustrated by David Newbert, Abbatoir (Omaha, NE), 1979.

The Tall Poets, Palaemon Press, 1979.

The Traveler's Tree, New and Selected Poems, illustrated by Jacques Hnizdovsky, Persea Books (New York, NY), 1980.

Plain Talk: Epigrams, Epitaphs, Satires, Nonsense, Occasional, Concrete, and Quotidian Poems, Center for Book Arts (New York, NY), 1988.

Journey to the Interior, Stone House Press, 1988.

Collected Poems, 1939-1989, Macmillan (New York, NY), 1990.

The Cyclist, Stone House Press, 1995.

The World below the Window: Poems 1937-1997, Johns Hopkins University Press (Baltimore, MD), 1998.

The Cherokee Lottery: A Sequence of Poems, Curbstone Press (Willimantic, CT), 2000.

The Girl in Glass: Love Poems, Bootes and Company (New York, NY), 2002.

Also author of privately printed poems, including *The Bead Curtain: Calligrams,* 1957; *The Old Man on the Isthmus,* 1957; *A Minor Ode to the Morgan Horse,* 1963; *Morels,* 1964; *Quail in Autumn,* 1965; *A Clutch of Clerihews,* 1966; *Winter Morning,* 1967; *Imaginary Dialogue,* 1968; *Hull Boy, St. Thomas,* 1970; *Song for a Country Wedding,* 1976; and *Oxford Doggerel,* 1983. Author, with Barbara Howes, of privately printed Christmas card poems, including *Lachrymae Christi* and *In the Old Country,* 1948; *Poems: The Homecoming* and *The Piazza,* 1949; and *Two French Poems: The Roses of Saadi and Five-Minute Watercolor,* 1950.

Poetry is represented in numerous anthologies and textbooks, including *The War Poets,* Day, 1945; *The New Poets of England and America,* Meridian, 1957; *Modern Verse in English, 1900-1950,* Macmillan, 1958; *Poems for Seasons and Celebrations,* World Publishing, 1961; *Contemporary American Poets: American Poetry since 1940,* Meridian, 1969; and *Talking like the Rain,* Little, Brown, 1992.

POETRY FOR CHILDREN

Laughing Time (also see below), illustrated by Juliet Kepes, Little, Brown (Boston, MA), 1955, revised and enlarged edition published as *Laughing Time: Nonsense Poems,* illustrated by Fernando Krahn, Farrar, Straus (New York, NY), 1990.

Boy Blue's Book of Beasts, illustrated by Juliet Kepes, Little, Brown (Boston, MA), 1957.

Puptents and Pebbles: A Nonsense ABC, illustrated by Juliet Kepes, Little, Brown (Boston, MA), 1959.

(And illustrator) *Typewriter Town,* Dutton (New York, NY), 1960.

What Did I See?, illustrated by Don Almquist, Crowell-Collier (New York, NY), 1962.

My Little Book of Big and Little (Little Dimity, Big Gumbo, Big and Little), three volumes, illustrated by Don Bolognese, Macmillan (New York, NY), 1963.

Ho for a Hat!, illustrated by Ivan Chermayeff, Little, Brown (Boston, MA), 1964, revised edition published with illustrations by Lynn Munsinger, Joy Street Books (Boston, MA), 1989.

(Compiler, with Louise Bogan) *The Golden Journey* (anthology), Reilly & Lee, 1965, published with woodcuts by Fritz Kredel, Contemporary Books (Chicago, IL), 1990.

If I Had a Boat, illustrated by Don Bolognese, Macmillan (New York, NY), 1966.

(Compiler) *Poems from France,* illustrated by Roger Duvoisin, Crowell (New York, NY), 1967.

Mr. Smith, and Other Nonsense, illustrated by Don Bolognese, Delacorte (New York, NY), 1968.

Around My Room and Other Poems, illustrated by Don Madden, Lancelot (New York, NY), 1969.

Grandmother Ostrich and Other Poems, illustrated by Don Madden, Lancelot (New York, NY), 1969.

Laughing Time and Other Poems, illustrated by Don Madden, Lancelot (New York, NY), 1969.

(Compiler) *Poems from Italy,* illustrated by Elaine Raphael, Crowell (New York, NY), 1972.

The Key, Children's Book Council, 1982.

Birds and Beasts, illustrated by Jacques Hnizdovsky, Godine (Boston, MA), 1990.

Big and Little, illustrated by Don Bolognese, Wordsong (Honesdale, PA), 1991.

(Editor, with Carol Ra) *Behind the King's Kitchen,* illustrated by Jacques Hnizdovsky, Boyds Mills Press, 1992.

(Editor, with Carol Ra) *The Sun Is Up: A Child's Year of Poems,* Wordsong/Boyds Mills Press (Honesdale, PA), 1996.

Here Is My Heart: Love Poems, illustrated by Jane Dyer, Little, Brown (Boston, MA), 1999.

Around My Room, illustrated by Erik Blegvad, Farrar, Straus (New York, NY), 2000.

Hey Diddle, a Riddle, Winslow Press (Delray Beach, FL), 2002.

TRANSLATOR

Romualdo Romano, *Scirocco,* Farrar, Straus (New York, NY), 1951.

Valery Larbaud, *Poems of a Multimillionaire,* Bonacio & Saul/Grove (New York, NY), 1955.

(And editor) *Selected Writings of Jules Laforgue,* Grove (New York, NY), 1956.

Elsa Beskow, *The Children of the Forest* (for children), illustrated by Beskow, Delacorte (New York, NY), 1970.

Two Plays by Charles Bertin: Christopher Columbus and Don Juan, Minnesota University Press, 1970.

Lennart Hellsing, *The Pirate Book* (for children), illustrated by Poul Ströyer, Delacorte (New York, NY), 1972.

(With Max Hayward) Kornei Chukovsky, *The Telephone* (for children), illustrated by Blair Lent, Delacorte (New York, NY), 1977.

(With Leif Sjoeberg) Artur Lundkvist, *Agadir,* International Poetry Forum (Pittsburgh, PA), 1979, Ohio State University Press (Athens, OH), 1980.

(With Ingvar Schousboe) Thorkild Bjoernvig, *The Pact: My Friendship with Isak Dinesen,* Louisiana State University Press (Baton Rouge, LA), 1983.

(And editor, with James S. Holmes) *Dutch Interior: Postwar Poetry of the Netherlands and Flanders,* Columbia University Press (New York, NY), 1984.

Jules Laforgue, *Moral Tales,* New Directions (New York, NY), 1985.

(With Leif Sjoeberg) Henry Martinson, *Wild Bouquet: Nature Poems,* Bookmark Press, 1985.

Collected Translations: Italian, French, Spanish, Portuguese (poetry), New Rivers Press (St. Paul, MN), 1985.

(With Edwin Morgan and others) Sandor Weoeres, *Eternal Moment: Selected Poems,* New Rivers Press (St. Paul, MN), 1988.

(With wife, Sonja Haussmann Smith) Tchicaya U Tam'Si, *The Madman and the Medusa,* edited by A. James Arnold and Kandioura Drame, University Press of Virginia (Charlottesville, VA), 1989.

Jules Laforgue, *Berlin: The City and the Court,* Turtle Point Books, 1996.

(And editor and author of introduction) Gyula Illyés, *What You Have Almost Forgotten: Selected Poems,* Curbstone Press (Willimantic, CT), 1999.

Translations by Smith from the Russian, Hungarian, Swedish, and French—particularly of the poems of Jules Laforgue and Andrei Voznesensky—have appeared in periodicals and books.

OTHER

The Spectra Hoax (criticism), Wesleyan University Press (Middletown, CT), 1961, reprinted, Story Line Press (Ashland, OR), 2000.

Herrick, Dell (New York, NY), 1962.

The Straw Market (comedy), produced at Hollins University, 1965.

(With Virginia Haviland) *Children and Poetry: A Selective, Annotated Bibliography,* Library of Congress (Washington, DC), 1969, revised edition, 1979.

The Streaks of the Tulip, Selected Criticism, Delacorte (New York, NY), 1972.

(Editor and author of introduction) *Light Verse and Satires of Witter Bynner,* Farrar, Straus (New York, NY), 1976.

(Author of preface) Miklós Vajda, editor, *Modern Hungarian Poetry,* Columbia University Press (New York, NY), 1977.

Army Brat: A Memoir (also see below), Persea Books (New York, NY), 1980.

Army Brat: A Dramatic Narrative for Three Voices (play based upon Smith's memoir), produced in New York City, 1980.

(Compiler) *A Green Place: Modern Poems,* illustrated by Hnizdovsky, Delacorte (New York, NY), 1982.

(Editor, with Emanuel Brasil) *Brazilian Poetry,* Harper (New York, NY), 1984.

(Editor and author of introduction) Nina Cassian, *Life Sentence: Selected Poems,* Norton (New York, NY), 1990.

Contributor of poetry, reviews, translations, essays, and articles to major literary periodicals and national magazines, including *Harper's, Poetry, Nation, Harper's Bazaar, New Criterion, New Republic, Horn Book, Evergreen Review, Yale Review, New Yorker, Southern*

Review, and *Sewanee Review.* Poetry reviewer, *Harper's,* 1961-64; editorial consultant, Grove Press, 1968-70; editor, *Translation,* 1973-90.

A major collection of Smith's manuscripts is housed at Washington University; smaller collections are at the Berg Collection, New York Public Library, and at the University of Delaware; a collection of Smith's children's books are housed at Hollins University.

ADAPTATIONS: Smith's poetry has been recorded for the Library of Congress, Spoken Arts Treasury of Modern Poetry, Yale University, and Harvard University libraries.

SIDELIGHTS: William Jay Smith told *CA:* "I am a lyric poet, alert, I hope, as my friend Stanley Kunitz has pointed out, 'to the changing weathers of a landscape, the motions of the mind, the complications and surprises of the human comedy.' I believe that poetry should communicate: it is, by its very nature, complex, but its complexity should not prevent its making an immediate impact on the reader. Great poetry must have its own distinctive music; it must resound with the music of the human psyche."

Known for the diverse form and content of his work, Smith is the author of numerous poems for adults and children. He also has developed a reputation for his translations of French, Russian, Hungarian and Swedish poets' works. *Atlantic Monthly* reviewer Elizabeth Frank praised Smith for a "long and distinguished career" that included a term as Consultant in Poetry to the Library of Congress—a position known today as Poet Laureate.

In an era when most poets have chosen to craft free verse, Smith has created work, "which from its beginnings has been defined by a passionate and deeply informed commitment to traditional rhymed metrical-stanzaic forms," to quote Frank. Although he has also written free verse of his own, Smith is better known for his adherence to traditional styles. In 1973 in the *Sewanee Review,* Thomas H. Landess commended Smith's *New and Selected Poems* for the author's "considerable poetic achievement" and his "severe artistic conscience." Landess also mentioned with approval Smith's tendency to be "swayed by the shifting literary winds," seeing Smith's receptivity to his era as one of his poetic gifts. Writing in the *Southern Review* about the same collection, John T. Irwin pointed out what he saw as the volume's "two radically different kinds of poetry." As Irwin put it, "The poems published before

his 1966 volume are in closed forms; those in the 1966 volume and after are for the most part in open forms." Although Irwin commented that he himself preferred the earlier, closed-form poetry, he acknowledged that other readers might have precisely the opposite reaction.

Partisan Review contributor John Malcolm Brinnin deemed Smith "a poet whose credentials . . . give him title to distinction." Brinnin called "The Tin Can," the title poem in Smith's collection *The Tin Can, and Other Poems,* "superb." He defined the substance of the poem as "a Laocoon-like involvement in the toils of creative anxiety [and] a rage for freedom and identity." Brinnin considered the poem "at once a dispersion of forces and a gathering of strength . . . and so far superior to anything else in the book that it has the impact of a window smashed open . . . Wholly convincing, without a false syllable in its hundreds of lines, it is a recreation of experience. . . . To single out 'The Tin Can' is not to slight Smith's demonstrated talents, but to recognize a poem that comes from the depths with the awesome wholeness of a thing urged into being."

At a time in his life when his contemporaries had immersed themselves in retirement activities, Smith continued to publish poetry collections. *Collected Poems, 1939-1989* was received enthusiastically in 1990. The poet once again was praised for his range and variety. Writing in the *New York Times,* Herbert Mitgang claimed that "the far-reaching themes and variety of styles in William Jay Smith's poetry prove that commonplace ideas and everyday activities can be reinvented by lyrical language that enlightens and entertains the reader. His magical *Collected Poems* span a half-century of his life and the life of the nation, adding up to a literary and social history of our times in verse." A more comprehensive collection, *The World below the Window: Poems 1937-1997* was released in 1998. Frank felt that the volume "provides a welcome and generous retrospective of Smith's 'adult' work." The critic added: "With an artisan's care and conscience, Smith makes full use of all the aural and figurative resources of our language. His tetrameters, pentameters, and hexameters are as intricately crafted as Oriental rugs. . . . Smith is a singer rather than a prophet, and his voice tends toward the elegiac rather than the apocalyptic, the reflective rather than the incantatory. He is rooted in the concrete and the sensuous—in sight, sound, and touch."

Smith drew upon his Native American heritage—he is part Choctaw—for *The Cherokee Lottery: A Sequence of Poems,* published in 2000. In the work, Smith recounts a tragedy of American history: the forced relocation of five Native American tribes from their home-lands in the southeast to Oklahoma territory, an ordeal now known as "The Trail of Tears." "Smith accomplishes a remarkable poetry of fact and documentation . . . one whose art is artfully concealed," noted a critic in *Publishers Weekly*. Patricia Monaghan, reviewing *The Cherokee Lottery* in *Booklist*, called it "moving, unforgettable, humane."

In tandem with his serious poetry, translation, and literary criticism, Smith has published numerous volumes of rhymes and riddles for youngsters. Some of these, including *Laughing Time: Nonsense Poems*, and *Around My Room and Other Poems*, remained in print many decades after their first publication. In the *New York Times Book Review*, X. J. Kennedy called Smith "[one] of our most dependable poets for children." Reviewing Smith's *Laughing Time*, Kennedy wrote: "Mr. Smith reaches out to actual, laughter-prone kids." Commenting on *Puptents and Pebbles: A Nonsense ABC*, another of Smith's collections of verse for children, a *Saturday Review* critic recommended that "only sophisticated readers, like children and grownups, should be allowed such fun and wisdom." *Booklist* correspondent Hazel Rochman found Smith's work for children to be "generally true to the child's view of the universe, both immense and particular."

Smith's memoir, *Army Brat*, describes his experiences growing up on an Army base outside St. Louis in the years between the two world wars. Because Smith's father was an enlisted man, Smith was subject to the rigid discipline and hierarchy of military life at that time. Because *Army Brat* is a coming-of-age story, it evokes both a time gone by and a young writer's discovery of language, sexuality, and all the possibilities that the world might hold for him. In recalling his participation in a high school choral contest, Smith hints in *Army Brat* at his growing discovery of his own powers: "I had the odd, pleasing, and yet somehow terrifying sensation that while my voice was now only one among many, some day it would rise above the others and be heard in the vast realm represented by those stone towers and green lawns."

Washington Post reviewer Stephanie Vaughn declared *Army Brat* an "engaging book," adding: "The life of the military child has been so little documented that it is a pleasure to see it so fully handled in the poet William Jay Smith's memoir. . . . This is an uneven book, but it slides only occasionally into gush, and is for the most part a balanced and beguiling account of an unusual life lived in a little-known subculture." Other reviewers

praised Smith's sense of detail. "Mr. Smith has written a charming portrait of this forgotten world," wrote novelist Paul Zweig in the *New York Times Book Review*. "He evokes the sharp clink of the training rifles and the picnics on rough brown Army blankets overlooking the equally brown and muddy Mississippi. He evokes small things, like the V-shaped heavy cardboard his father hooked around the buttons on his uniform preparatory to buffing and polishing them. And he evokes the sometimes squalid living quarters, such as a two-room shack perched over a sinkhole, where he lived when he was six. . . . Mr. Smith himself is by no means absent from *Army Brat*, but we learn about him less in what he tells us about himself than by seeing what he sees and evokes with such intense simplicity." Carleton Jones was even more enthusiastic; writing in the Baltimore *Sun*, he commented: "The book may hover on the edge of being a minor classic. . . . but whatever its critical destiny, it is certainly a fine social document and an intimate picture of the pre-World War II army world."

During his tenure as consultant in poetry to the Library of Congress, Smith supervised the recorded readings of many notable American and foreign poets. He also has been recorded reading his poetry and lecturing on the works of others. A *Publishers Weekly* contributor described Smith's career as "formidable," noting that his poetic images "reveal the inescapability of memory, testifying to its enduring capacity to affirm the power of the imagination."

BIOGRAPHICAL/CRITICAL SOURCES:

BOOKS

Contemporary Literary Criticism, Volume 6, Gale (Detroit, MI), 1976.

Dickey, James, *Babel to Byzantium: Poets and Poetry Now*, Farrar, Straus (New York, NY), 1968.

Dictionary of Literary Biography, Volume 5: *American Poets since World War II*, Gale (Detroit, MI), 1980.

Nemerov, Howard, editor, *Poets on Poetry*, Basic Books (New York, NY), 1966.

Smith, William Jay, *Army Brat: A Memoir*, Persea Books (New York, NY), 1980.

Something about the Author Autobiography Series, Volume 22, Gale (Detroit, MI), 1996.

Untermeyer, Louis, editor, *Modern American Poetry*, Harcourt (New York, NY), 1962.

PERIODICALS

Atlantic Monthly, September, 1998, Elizabeth Frank, "The Pleasures of Formal Poetry."

Booklist, May 1, 1998, Ray Olson, review of *The World below the Window: Poems 1937-1997,* p. 1495; February 1, 2000, Hazel Rochman, review of *Around My Room,* p. 1026; May 15, 2000, Patricia Monaghan, review of *The Cherokee Lottery: A Sequence of Poems.*

Library Journal, April 15, 1964; April 15, 1998, Thomas F. Merrill, review of *The World below the Window: Poems 1937-1997,* p. 84; July, 2000, Louis McKee, review of *The Cherokee Lottery: A Sequence of Poems,* p. 99.

New Letters, summer, 1999, "William Jay Smith at Eighty" (interview), pp. 90-119.

New York Times, October 27, 1990.

New York Times Book Review, May 10, 1964; November 9, 1980, p. 51; November 16, 1980.

Partisan Review, winter, 1967.

Poetry, December, 1966; May, 1981.

Publishers Weekly, May 27, 1996, review of *Berlin: The City and the Court,* p. 73; April 27, 1998, review of *The World below the Window: Poems 1937-1997,* p. 63; February 14, 2000, review of *Around My Room,* p. 196; April 24, 2000, review of *The Cherokee Lottery: A Sequence of Poems.*

Quarterly Journal of the Library of Congress, April, 1970.

Saturday Review, November 7, 1959.

Sewanee Review, winter, 1973, pp. 144-145.

Southern Review, summer, 1973, pp. 729-731.

Sun (Baltimore), October 19, 1980, p. D5.

Voyages, winter, 1970.

Washington Post, December 1, 1990, p. D6.

*   *   *

SOFTLY, Edgar
   See LOVECRAFT, H(oward) P(hillips)

*   *   *

SOFTLY, Edward
   See LOVECRAFT, H(oward) P(hillips)

*   *   *

SOLLORS, Werner 1943-

PERSONAL: Born 1943; son of Ferdinand (a teacher) and Martha (a homemaker; maiden name, Bornitz) Sollors; children: David, Sara. *Education:* Attended Wake Forest College (now University), 1964-65, and Columbia University, 1969-70; Freie Universitaet Berlin, Ph. D., 1975; postdoctoral study at Harvard University, 1977-78.

ADDRESSES: Office—Department of English and American Language and Literature, Harvard University, Warren House, Cambridge, MA 02138. *E-mail*—sollors@fas.harvard.edu.

CAREER: Freie Universitaet Berlin, Berlin, West Germany, assistant professor of American studies, 1970-77; Columbia University, New York, NY, assistant professor, 1975-82, associate professor of English, 1982-83; Harvard University, Cambridge, MA, professor of American literature and Language and Afro-American Studies, 1983—, Henry B. and Anne M. Cabot Professor of English Literature, 1988—, director of undergraduate studies and chair of the committee on higher degrees in the history of American civilization.

MEMBER: Modern Language Association of America, American Studies Association (member of bibliography committee), Society for the Study of Multi-Ethnic Literature of the United States (MELUS), College Literature Association, Deutsche Gesellschaft für Amerikastudien.

AWARDS, HONORS: Andrew W. Mellon faculty fellow at Harvard University, 1977-78; Guggenheim fellow, 1981.

WRITINGS:

Amiri Baraka/LeRoi Jones: The Quest for a "Populist Modernism," Columbia University Press (New York, NY), 1978.

Beyond Ethnicity: Consent and Descent in American Literature, Oxford University Press (New York, NY), 1986.

(Editor) *The Invention of Ethnicity,* Oxford University Press (New York, NY), 1987.

(Editor) *The Return of Thematic Criticism,* Harvard University Press (Cambridge, MA), 1993.

(Coeditor) *Blacks at Harvard: A Documentary History,* New York University Press (New York, NY), 1993.

(Editor) *Theories of Ethnicity: A Classical Reader,* New York University Press (New York, NY), 1996.

Neither Black nor White yet Both: Thematic Explorations of Interracial Literature, Oxford University Press (New York, NY), 1997.

(Editor) *Multilingual America: Transnationalism, Ethnicity, and the Languages of American Literature,* New York University Press (New York, NY), 1998.

(Editor, with Marc Shell) *A Multilingual Anthology of American Literature: A Reader of Original Texts with English Translations,* New York University Press (New York, NY), 2000.

(Editor) *Interracialsm: Black-White Intermarriage in American History, Literature, and Law,* Oxford University Press (Oxford, England and New York, NY), 2000.

(Editor) Olaudah Equiano, *The Interesting Narrative of the Life of Olaudah Equiano; or, Gustavus Vassa, the African: An Authoritative Text, Written by Himself: Contexts, Criticism,* Norton (New York, NY), 2001.

Contributor to *Columbia History of American Literature,* Columbia University Press (New York, NY), 1988.

SIDELIGHTS: Werner Sollors has written extensively on racial themes in American literature. His books include *Amiri Baraka/LeRoi Jones: The Quest for a "Populist Modernism,"* a study of the avant garde black playwright; *Neither Black nor White yet Both: Thematic Explorations of Interracial Literature,* and *A Multilingual Anthology of American Literature: A Reader of Original Texts with English Translations.* According to Sally Baker in the *Harvard University Gazette,* "Sollors is among a small cadre of scholars who specialize in American literature written in languages other than English."

Amiri Baraka/LeRoi Jones examines the life and writings of Amiri Baraka, a central figure of the Afro-American avant-garde who has been called the "the committed artist par excellence." Beginning as a Beat poet in the late 1950s (as LeRoi Jones) and achieving fame with his plays *The Toilet, The Dutchman,* and *The Slave,* Baraka began to forge an ethnic and political art during the 1960s that culminated in the black cultural nationalist movement; he has since replaced racial exclusivity with the economic imperatives of socialism. "One of the virtues of Werner Sollors's thoughtful study is that he discovers consistency and order in all these dizzying swings and shifts," commented Nathan Irvin Huggins in *New Republic.* "Despite these radical changes, Baraka has remained constantly on the margin of the conventional and acceptable aesthetic and political thought . . . deliberately alienated from the disrupting center." Writing in *Washington Post Book World,* Jack Salzman concurred: "As Sollors brilliantly demonstrates, the very dynamic which led Baraka from beat

poetry to political and ethnic protest, from Cultural Nationalism to Maoism, 'has an element of constancy in Baraka's anti-bourgeois cultural strategy of populist modernism.'"

Similarly, both critics applauded Sollors's perceptive analysis of Baraka's thought within social and literary milieus. Salzman observed, "Of the numerous, almost voluminous, works written about Baraka, none has come as close to enabling us to understand the man." He added, "Werner Sollors allows us to see . . . that Baraka is an important figure in both political and aesthetic avant-gardism, that his 'eternal concern' has been a question of politics and literature." Sollors has "approached the subject both as a scholar of American studies and of comparative literature," Huggins noted. "This means that he sees Baraka in terms of the political, social and ethnic realities of American life, and at the same time places him within an international context of the literary 'isms' of the 19th and 20th centuries: Symbolism, Dadaism, Surrealism and Absurdism." Calling *Amiri Baraka/LeRoi Jones* "a definitive work," Huggins added, "It will also introduce American readers to Afro-American writers whose alienation from mainstream American letters has led them to produce some of the most lively and powerful literature around."

In *Neither Black nor White yet Both,* Sollors analyzes many examples of literary works from Europe and America and from ancient times to the present, in which interracial relationships are depicted. Though he acknowledged the book's impressive scholarship, *Journal of American Ethnic History* contributor Paul Spickard criticized the fact that Sollors includes only on relationships between whites and blacks, omitting references to Asians, Latinos, Native Americans, and others. In addition, Spickard felt that Sollors's thematic approach to his material "gives the book an elusive, unfocused quality." Many critics, however, hailed the book as an extraordinary achievement. Shelley Fisher Fishkin in *Modern Philology* found that Sollors draws "on his extraordinary command of languages and on his daunting familiarity with world literature and art [to produce] a book that is both magisterial and dazzling; it is certain to inspire and challenge generations to come." Writing in *Modern Language Quarterly,* Carla Kaplan called *Neither Black nor White yet Both* "one of the most comprehensive accounts to date of the history and workings of racial ideology."

In *A Multilingual Anthology of American Literature,* Sollors, who grew up near Frankfurt, Germany in an area occupied by American forces after World War II, compiled with coeditor Marc Shell a sampling of works in American literature originally written in such languages as Chinese, Polish, Spanish, Welsh, and Yiddish. Poetry, short stories, sermons, and other genres are represented; English translations of each selection are also provided. Morris Hounion in *Library Journal* found the anthology to be "the first compilation of American literature to collect works written in the United States from 1696 to 1994 in languages other than English." As Sollors points out, the earliest anthologies of American literature contained a diverse range of languages, from tales in French and Spanish to Puritan works written in Latin, Greek, and Hebrew; these works, he believes, offer important perspectives for continued study. Indeed, in an earlier book of essays which he edited, *Multilingual America: Transnationalism, Ethnicity, and the Languages of American Literature,* Sollors presents a range of critical commentary on multilingual literature in America. "Sollors and his colleagues clearly value expanding our historical and literary appreciation of the rich interplay between English and the mother-tongues of immigrants," wrote David W. Engstrom in *Journal of American Ethnic History.*

Sollors has continued his exploration of racial themes in two recent volumes which he edited: *Interracialism: Black-White Intermarriage in American History, Literature, and Law* and *The Interesting Narrative of the Life of Olaudah Equiano; or, Gustavus Vassa, the African: An Authoritative Text, Written by Himself: Contexts, Criticism,* an autobiography originally published in 1794 by an African who was enslaved in America.

Sollors once told *CA:* "One morning I woke up out of heavy dreams and found myself transformed into a literary critic. (I was more than three thousand miles away from Prague at the time.) Impressed by my new surroundings, I tried to find the meaning of the New World in literature. America seemed a wonderfully mixed-up place in which all sorts of new styles could flourish. My informants, however, told me about 'ethnic purity' (which I had not noticed). Was it all a dream?"

BIOGRAPHICAL/CRITICAL SOURCES:

PERIODICALS

American Literature, March, 1998, Elain K. Ginsberg, review of *Neither Black nor White yet Both: Thematic Explorations of Interracial Literature,* p. 204; March, 2000, Timothy Powell, review of *Multilingual America: Transnationalism, Ethnicity, and the Languages of American Literature,* p. 218.

American Studies International, October, 1999, Bernard Mergen, review of *Multilingual America,* p. 117.
Comparative Literature, summer, 1999, Henry B. Wonham, review of *Neither Black nor White yet Both,* p. 261.
Harvard University Gazette, February 25, 1999, Sally Baker, "America the Multilingual: Werner Sollors Shows That American Literature Was Not Always Written in English."
Journal of American Ethnic History, spring, 1999, John Higham, review of *Theories of Ethnicity,* p. 142; winter, 1999, Paul Spickard, review of *Neither Black nor White yet Both,* p. 153; winter, 2001, David W. Engstrom, review of *Multilingual America,* p.120.
Journal of American History, June, 1998, Peggy Pascoe, review of *Neither Black nor White yet Both,* p. 20.
Journal of American Studies, April, 1999, Sharon Monteith, review of *Neither Black nor White yet Both,* p. 183.
Journal of Modern Literature, spring, 1999, Steven G. Kellman, review of *Multilingual America,* p. 445.
Library Journal, July, 2000, Morris Hounion, review of *A Multilingual Anthology of American Literature: A Reader of Original Texts with English Translations,* p. 93.
Modern Language Quarterly, September, 1999, Carla Kaplan, review of *Neither Black nor White yet Both: Thematic Explorations of Interracial Literature,* p. 418.
Modern Philology, May, 2000, Shelley Fisher Fishkin, review of *Neither Black nor White yet Both,* p. 639.
New Republic, April 21, 1979, Nathan Irvin Huggins, review of *Amiri Baraka/LeRoi Jones: The Quest for a "Populist Modernism."*
Washington Post Book World, January 28, 1979, Jack Salzman, review of *Amiri Baraka/LeRoi Jones.**

*   *   *

SOLOVYOV, Vladimir Sergeyevich 1853-1900

PERSONAL: Born 1853; died 1900; son of S. M. Solovyov (a historian). *Education:* Moscow University, graduated in 1873; studied at Moscow Theological Academy. *Religion:* Orthodox Christian.

CAREER: Poet and philosopher. Moscow University, lecturer, 1876-1881.

WRITINGS:

L'idee russe, par Vladimir Soloviev, translated from the original Russian, Perrin (Paris, France), 1888.

Sobranie Sochinenii Vi Solovyova, 10 volumes, Pros-veshchenie (St. Petersburg, Russia), 1911-14.

War, Progress, and the End of History, Including a Short Story of the Anti-Christ: Three Discussions, translated by Alexander Bakshy, University of London Press (London, England), 1915.

(Contributor) *War and Christianity, from the Russian Point of View: Three Conversations,* G. P. Putnam's Sons (New York, NY), 1915.

The Justification of the Good: An Essay in Moral Philosophy, translated by Natalie A. Duddington, Macmillan (New York, NY), 1918.

Nationale und politische Bertrachtungen, Der Kommende Tag (Stuttgart, Germany), 1922.

Plato, translated by R. Gree, Stanley Nott (London, England), 1935.

God, Man, and the Church: The Spiritual Foundations of Life, translated by Donald Attwater, L. Clarke (London, England), 1938.

Godmanhood as the Main Idea of the Philosophy of Vladimir Solovyev, edited by Peter P. Zouboff, Harmon Printing House (Poughkeepsie, NY), 1944.

Vladimir Solovyev's Lectures on Godmanhood, International University Press (New York, NY), 1944.

The Meaning of Love, translated by Jane Marshall, International University Press (New York, NY), 1947.

Lectures on God-Manhood, Dennis Dobson (London, England, and Dublin, Ireland), 1948.

Russia and the Universal Church, translated by Herbert Rees, G. Blessing (London, England), 1948.

The Meaning of Love, translated by Jane Marshall, International University Press (New York, NY), 1948.

A Solovyov Anthology, translated by Natalie Duddington, Scribner's (New York, NY), 1950.

A Solovyov Anthology, translated from the Russian by Natalie Duddington, Greenwood Press (Westport, CT), 1974.

The Meaning of Love: Vladimir Solovyov, edited with a revised translation by Thomas R. Beyer, Lindisfarne Press (West Stockbridge, MA), 1985.

Sochinenieilia v dvukh tomakh, Adademieilia nauk SSSR (Moscow, USSR), 1988.

Literaturnaelia kritika, Sovremennik (Moscow, USSR), 1990.

Nepodvizhno lishs solnetise leiliubvi—: stikhotvorenieiia, proza, pissma, vospominanieiiia sovremennikov, Moskovskiaei rabochiaei (Moscow, USSR), 1990.

Filosofieiia iskusstva I literaturnaeiia kritika, Iskusstvo (Moscow, USSR), 1991.

Magomet: ego zhizns I religioznoe uchenie, Lider (Bishkek), 1991.

O khristianskom edinstve, Rudomino (Moscow, Russia), 1994.

Lectures on Divine Humanity, revised and edited by Boris Jakim, Lindisfarne Press (Hudson, NY), 1995.

Dukhovnye osnovy zhizni, Magik-Press/Mars (St. Petersburg, Russia), 1995.

The Crisis of Western Philosophy: Against Positivism, translated and edited by Boris Jakim, Lindisfarne Press (Hudson, NY), 1996.

Master's thesis published as *Krisis Zapadnoy Filosofi* (translated as *The Crisis of Western Philosophy: Against Positivism*), 1874; published long poem "Three Meetings"; *Lectures on God-Manhood* first published in 1878; doctoral dissertation published as *Kritika otvlechennykh Nachal* (translated as *The Critique of Abstract Principles*), 1880. Also author of *Istoria I Budushee Teokratii,* 1886.

Author's works have been translated into several languages, including Spanish, French, and German.

SIDELIGHTS: Born in 1853, Vladimir Sergeyevich Solovyov was the son of the famous Russian historian, Sergei Solovyov. Young Solovyov had an upper middle-class upbringing with intense religious education. Solovyov would grow to become a poet, philosopher, and mystic, stimulating a renaissance in Russian religious philosophy. Solovyov's lectures on Russian philosophy would mark him as the first notable Russian academic philosopher.

At nine years old, Solovyov claimed to have experienced his first vision in a dream of Sophia. To Solovyov, Sophia was a real and godlike person. Solovyov thought of Sophia as Divine Wisdom and Eternal Womanhood. He would have three more visions of Sophia, during which he felt he actually met her, and recount his experiences in the long poem "Three Meetings."

In his early teenage years, Solovyov turned against religion and pronounced himself a socialist and materialistic. He enrolled at Moscow University, and while a student there, reclaimed his religious faith. Solovyov would become almost militant in his beliefs about Christianity; some scholars feel that his need to defend Christianity as the one and only truth is the basis for his entire philosophy.

Solovyov's poetry is metaphysical; it is highly intellectual and philosophical and contains much unusual imagery. Solovyov's philosophy reflects his feelings that the universe is endeavoring to return to a unity with God. Development is the way that the world can progress towards a higher reintegration. Sophia was also a part of this reintegration; Solovyov saw her as part of religious love for mankind and the world.

Solovyov also envisioned a utopian society in which all nations and religions came together under the leadership of the pope and the Russian tsar. Some of Solovyov's philosophies had definite Catholic leanings, which brought him in direct conflict with the Russian Orthodox Church. Some of his works, which supported his Catholic ideas, were not allowed to be published in socialist Russia. In later life, Solovyov would moderate both his ideas for a theocracy and his pro-Catholic tendencies.

Solovyov's master's dissertation, which he presented in 1874 at age twenty-one, was later translated as *The Crisis of Western Philosophy: Against the Positivists.* In this work, Solovyov rails against Western philosophy, which he interprets as rationalist. Terry Skeats, of the *Library Journal,* views the dissertation as evidence of a "powerful philosophical mind in evolution." Once published, his dissertation made Solovyov famous seemingly overnight. Upon graduating from Moscow University, Solovyov studied for a year at Moscow Theological Academy, and then took the position of lecturer at Moscow University. In 1878, Solovyov's *Lectures on God-Manhood* was published. Solovyov's doctoral dissertation *Kritika Otvlechennykh Nachal* ("The Critique of Abstract Principles") was released in 1880.

Solovyov worked at the University until he was forced to resign in 1881 after he made a speech in which he begged the current tsar, Alexander III, to forgive the men who assassinated his father, Alexander II. In addition to being released from his position, Solovyov was also forbidden to make any further public speeches. Solovyov dedicated the rest of his life to writing. In 1900, Solovyov published one of his most acclaimed works, *Three Conversations.* The book presents three philosophical discussions on the need to find a way to integrate progress and Christianity. Solovyov also published *The History of Antichrist* as a supplement, in which he outlines a vision of the coming of the Antichrist and the subsequent Second Coming of Christ as imminent.

BIOGRAPHICAL/CRITICAL SOURCES:

BOOKS

Dictionary of Russian Literature, Greenwood Press (Westport, CT), 1971.
The Oxford Companion to Philosophy, Oxford University Press, (Oxford, England), 1995.

PERIODICALS

Library Journal, June 15, 1996, Terry Skeats, review of *The Crisis of Western Philosophy: Against the Positivists,* p. 68.*

*   *   *

SOREL, Edward 1929-

PERSONAL: Surname originally Schwartz, legally changed to Sorel; born March 26, 1929, in Bronx, NY; son of Morris (a salesperson) and Rebecca (a factory worker; maiden name, Kleinberg) Schwartz; married Elaine Rothenberg, July 1, 1956 (divorced, 1965); married Nancy Caldwell (a writer), May 29, 1965; children: (first marriage) Madeline, Leo; (second marriage) Jenny, Katherine. *Education:* Cooper Union College, diploma, 1951.

ADDRESSES: Home—156 Franklin St., New York, NY 10013. *Office*—c/o Margaret K. McElderry Books, Simon & Schuster Children's Publishing, 1230 Avenue of the Americas, New York, NY 10020.

CAREER: Esquire, New York, NY, assistant art director, 1951-53; Push Pin Studios (commercial and graphic arts studio), New York, NY, cofounder, 1953, staff artist, 1953-56; Columbia Broadcasting System (CBS-TV), New York, NY, art director in promotion department, 1956-57; freelance artist, political satirist, cartoonist, and illustrator of children's books, 1958—. *Exhibitions:* The Push Pin Retrospective at the Louvre, Paris, France, 1970, and other European galleries, 1970-71; one-man shows at Graham Galleries, New York, NY, 1973 and 1978; New School for Social Research, New York, NY, 1974; Galerie Bartsch & Chariau, Munich, Germany, 1986; Davis and Langdale Galleries, New York, NY, 1998 and 2000; and National Portrait Gallery, Washington, DC, 1999-2000.

AWARDS, HONORS: Fifty books of the year selection, American Institute of Graphic Arts, 1958, for *King Carlo of Capri;* ten best illustrated books of the year selection, *New York Times,* 1959, for *Pablo Paints a Picture;* Spring Book Festival Award, 1961, and first prize for illustration of children's books, *New York Herald Tribune,* both for *Gwendolyn, the Miracle Hen;* ten best illustrated books of the year selection, *New York Times,* 1963, for *Gwendolyn and the Weather Cock;* fifty books of the year exhibition selection, American

Institute of Graphic Arts, 1972, and U.S. representative, Children's Book International Biennial of Illustrations in Bratislava, 1973, both for *Magical Storybook;* Augustus St. Gaudens Medal, Cooper Union, 1973, for professional achievement; George Polk Award, 1981, for satirical drawing; Page One Award, Newspaper Guild of New York, 1988, for best editorial cartoon (magazines); Notable Books of 1998 selection, *New York Times Magazine,* for *Unauthorized Portraits;* additional awards for illustration from Society of Illustrators, American Institute of Graphic Arts, and Art Directors Club of New York; elected into the Art Directors Hall of Fame, Art Directors Club of New York, 2001.

WRITINGS:

SELF-ILLUSTRATED

How to Be President: Some Hard and Fast Rules, Grove (New York, NY), 1960.
Moon Missing: An Illustrated Guide to the Future, Simon & Schuster (New York, NY), 1962.
Sorel's World Fair, New York, 1964, McGraw (New York, NY), 1964.
Making the World Safe for Hypocrisy: A Collection of Satirical Drawings and Commentaries, Swallow Press (Chicago, IL), 1972.
Superpen: The Cartoons and Caricatures of Edward Sorel, edited by Lidia Ferrara, Random House (New York, NY), 1978.
(With Nancy Caldwell Sorel) *First Encounters: A Book of Memorial Meetings,* Knopf (New York, NY), 1994.
Unauthorized Portraits, Knopf (New York, NY), 1997.

SELF-ILLUSTRATED; FOR CHILDREN

The Zillionaire's Daughter, Warner Books, 1989.
Johnny-on-the-Spot, Margaret K. McElderry Books (New York, NY), 1998.
(With Cheryl Carlesimo) *The Saturday Kid,* Margaret K. McElderry Books (New York, NY), 1999.

ILLUSTRATOR

Warren Miller, *King Carlo of Capri* (adapted from Charles Perrault's *Riquet with the Tuft of Hair*), Harcourt (New York, NY), 1958.
Warren Miller, *The Goings-on at Little Wishful,* Little, Brown (Boston, MA), 1959,

Warren Miller, *Pablo Paints a Picture,* Little, Brown (Boston, MA), 1959.
Nancy Sherman, *Gwendolyn, the Miracle Hen,* Golden Press, 1961.
Nancy Sherman, *Gwendolyn and the Weathercock,* Golden Press, 1963.
Joy Cowley, *The Duck in the Gun,* Doubleday (New York, NY), 1969.
William Cole, *What's Good for a Five-Year-Old?,* Holt (New York, NY), 1969.
Nancy Caldwell Sorel, *Word People,* American Heritage Press (New York, NY), 1970.
Jay Williams, *Magical Storybook,* American Heritage Press (New York, NY), 1972.
Ward Botsford, *The Pirates of Penzance* (adapted from the Gilbert and Sullivan operetta), Random House (New York, NY), 1981.
Eric Metaxas, *Jack and the Beanstalk* (with cassette), Rabbit Ears Books (Westport, CT), 1991.

OTHER

Author of introduction to Charles Le Brun's *Resemblances, Amazing Faces,* Harlin Quist (New York, NY), 1980. Contributing editor of *New York, Gentleman's Quarterly,* and *Village Voice.* Creator of syndicated feature "Sorel's News Service," for King Features, 1969-70, and of other cartoon features, including "The Spokesman," for *Esquire,* and "Unfamiliar Quotations," for *Atlantic.* Contributor of artwork and articles to additional periodicals, including *Village Voice, Rolling Stone, Realist, Ramparts, GQ, New York Times Book Review, Forbes, American Heritage, Atlantic Monthly, Nation, New Yorker,* and *Time.*

SIDELIGHTS: An award-winning political cartoonist and children's book illustrator, Edward Sorel is known for his pen and ink drawings that have a free flowing, almost scratchy style. In his art, Sorel generally works "direct," explains National Portrait Gallery curator Wendy Rick Reaves to Bruce Hathaway in *Smithsonian.* "That means no tracing or erasing, and little preliminary sketching. With this sudden death approach, Sorel's figures often emerge from a dense, wiry tangle of overlapping pen strokes that crackle with energy." Using this technique, Sorel has developed a unique style, creating satirical portraits and cartoons of world leaders that have graced the nation's top magazines, including *Time, Rolling Stone,* and *New Yorker.*

In his work for children, Sorel also captures this same energy, according to critics. Talking about his entry into the world of children's literature, Sorel said in *Ameri-*

can Artist, "I had for some time wanted to illustrate a children's book and realized that I could not tell a story, could not show those details of costume, expression, or movement which children love, unless I forgot all about style or manner and concentrated on telling a story in pictures. . . . This need to describe rather than decorate was one turning point in my development." Sorel illustrated his first children's book, the award-winning *King Carlo of Capri,* in 1958, and followed it the next year with *Pablo Paints a Picture,* another award winner.

Throughout the 1960s and 1970s, Sorel continued both paths of his career, illustrating children's books as well as creating humorous, sometimes controversial, political cartoons for an adult audience. In the 1980s, the artist and illustrator began to devote more time to his literary efforts, publishing articles in the *New York Times Book Review, Forbes,* and *GQ.* In 1989, he wrote his first children's book, *The Zillionaire's Daughter,* a self-illustrated work about a young French girl who sails across the Atlantic with her wealthy father. Claire, the daughter of zillionaire Max Maximillion, learns from a fortune teller that one day she will grow up to marry a saxophone player. Her distinguished father is aghast at the thought and spends his time on the ship worrying about the revelation. Claire, however, decides to enjoy herself and makes friends with an Englishman named Charlie. On the night of the Grand Masqued Ball, Charlie reveals himself not only as a superb sax man, but also as the third Duke of Harley, much to the pleasure of Max. Writing in *Booklist,* Barbara Elleman described *The Zillionaire's Daughter* as "a good-hearted spoof on the opulence of the rich that has at its heart a likable young heroine." A *Publishers Weekly* critic commented favorably on the artist's work, saying "brimming with gorgeous Art Deco touches, Sorel's resplendent pen and ink, color-enhanced drawings are perfectly matched by his effortless verse."

A young boy with a fondness for radio captures the attention of readers in Sorel's 1998 work *Johnny on the Spot.* When his family's radio is broken, Johnny takes it to be repaired by the eccentric inventor living in his apartment building's basement flat. Hoping to be able to listen to his favorite adventure programs again, Johnny is amazed when he discovers that the newly repaired radio now broadcasts news twenty-four hours in advance. Using his newfound knowledge of the next-day's events, Johnny begins to make a name for himself as "Johnny on the Spot," thwarting bank robberies and putting out fires. However, as Johnny becomes tempted to use his forward- seeing radio for shadowy rewards, the young boy's parents decide to junk the "broken" radio and purchase a new one. "Sorel . . . constructs an

enticing cinematic world of brownstones and sepia-tinted interiors," observed a *Publishers Weekly* contributor. While noting that the book's ending is "perhaps a bit too predictable," *Booklist* critic Michael Cart nonetheless thought that "Sorel's lively pen-and-ink watercolor pictures add panache to a story that is engaging."

Set in New York City during the 1930s, *The Saturday Kid* recalls a time when the last day of the week was spent at the movie cinema, inspiring daydreams about adventures fighting gangsters, flying airplanes, and becoming a pirate. Or at least that is what young Leo likes to do on his Saturdays. However, this pleasure is interrupted one afternoon after Morty, the neighborhood bully, gets Leo ejected from the theater. Longing to repay Morty, Leo brags that he can play the violin and has even shook hands with the mayor. Leo's boasts go unbelieved until a newsreel shows him, larger than life, meeting the mayor after entertaining him with a violin performance. Receiving congratulations from Morty's parents gives the young Leo a feeling that his days of being bullied are soon over. *School Library Journal* reviewer Julie Cummins predicted that "a lot of nostalgia, an appealing underdog, and good old-fashioned moxie will charm any child who dares to dream." Several reviewers applauded the way Sorel's illustrations created a feel for a New York City of yesteryear. A *Publishers Weekly* critic claimed that "Sorel captures old New York in galloping ribbons of ink and sepia-tinted watercolors," while *Booklist* reviewer Denise Wilms, noted "The dynamic pen-and-wash drawings are never static . . . their rush of detail captures the city with fond affection."

BIOGRAPHICAL/CRITICAL SOURCES:

PERIODICALS

American Artist, May, 1960, Frederic Whitaker, "Edward Sorel," pp. 40-58.

Booklist, May 15, 1990, Barbara Elleman, review of *The Zillionaire's Daughter,* p. 1806; August, 1998, Michael Cart, review of *Johnny on the Spot,* p. 2017; December 15, 2000, Denise Wilms, review of *The Saturday Kid,* p. 829.

Kirkus Reviews, August 15, 1997, review of *Unauthorized Portraits,* p. 1298.

New York Times Book Review, December 6, 1998, "Notable Books of 1998," p. 90.

Publishers Weekly, February 9, 1990, review of *The Zillionaire's Daughter,* p. 60; September 7, 1998, review of *Johnny on the Spot,* pp. 94-95; August 28, 2000, review of *The Saturday Kid,* p. 83.

School Library Journal, September, 2000, Julie Cummins, review of *The Saturday Kid,* p. 209.

Smithsonian, October, 1999, Bruce Hathaway, "The Gang's All Here," p. 124.

*   *   *

SPRINGER, Nancy 1948-

PERSONAL: Born July 5, 1948, in Montclair, NJ; daughter of Harry E. (in business) and Helen (an artist; maiden name, Wheeler) Connor; married Joel Springer (a fine art photographer), September 13, 1969; children: Jonathan, Nora. *Education:* Gettysburg College, B.A. (cum laude), 1970.

ADDRESSES: Home—417 Lake Meade Dr., East Berlin, PA 17316. *Agent*—Jean V. Naggar, 216 East 75th St., New York, NY 10021.

CAREER: Delone Catholic High School, McSherrystown, PA, teacher, 1970-71; writer, 1972—. University of Pittsburgh at Johnstown, PA, personal development plan instructor, 1983-85; York College of Pennsylvania, personal and professional growth instructor, 1986-90; Franklin and Marshall College, Et Cetera program instructor, 1987-91; part-time communications instructor at Bradley Academy for the Visual Arts, 1990-95; creative writing instructor, York College of Pennsylvania, 1995-97; faculty member, Seton Hill College master's degree program in popular fiction, 1997—.

MEMBER: Society of Children's Book Writers, Pennwriters (former president), Phi Beta Kappa.

AWARDS, HONORS: Iowa State Best Books for Young Adults citation, for *Chains of Gold;* International Reading Association Children's Book Council Children's Choice citation, 1988, Florida Master Reading List citation, 1988, and Georgia Master Reading List citation, 1989, all for *A Horse to Love;* New York Public Library Books for the Teen Age citation, Enoch Pratt Free Library Youth-to-Youth Books: A List for Imagination and Survival citation, and American Library Association Best Books for Young Adults citation, all for *The Hex Witch of Seldom;* Nebula Award nomination, for *Apocalypse;* Dorothy Canfield Fisher Award nomination, for *Red Wizard;* Joan Fassler Memorial Book Award, 1992, for *Colt;* Edgar Allan Poe awards, Mystery Writers of America, 1995, for *Toughing It,* and 1996, for *Looking for Jamie Bridger;* Carolyn W. Field Award, 1998, for *I Am Mordred.*

Nancy Springer

WRITINGS:

The Book of Suns, Pocket Books (New York, NY), 1977.

The White Hart, Pocket Books (New York, NY), 1979.

The Silver Sun (based on *The Book of Suns*), Pocket Books (New York, NY), 1980.

The Sable Moon, Pocket Books (New York, NY), 1981.

The Black Beast (also see below), Pocket Books (New York, NY), 1982.

The Golden Swan (also see below), Pocket Books (New York, NY), 1983.

The Book of Vale (contains *The Black Beast* and *The Golden Swan*), Doubleday (New York, NY), 1983.

Wings of Flame, Tor Books (New York, NY), 1985.

Chains of Gold, Arbor House, 1986.

Madbond (Volume 1 of "Sea King" trilogy), Tor Books (New York, NY), 1987.

Mindbond (Volume 2 of "Sea King" trilogy), Tor Books (New York, NY), 1987.

Chance: And Other Gestures of the Hand of Fate (short stories, poetry, and novellas), Baen Books (New York, NY), 1987.

Godbond (Volume 3 of "Sea King" trilogy), Tor Books (New York, NY), 1988.

The Hex Witch of Seldom, Baen Books (New York, NY), 1988.

Apocalypse, Baen Books (New York, NY), 1989.

Stardark Songs (fantasy poetry), New Establishment Press, 1993.

Larque on the Wing, Avon Books (New York, NY), 1994.

Fair Peril, Avon Books (New York, NY), 1996.

Plumage, Morrow (New York, NY), 1999.

CHILDREN'S BOOKS

A Horse to Love, Harper (New York, NY), 1987.

Not on a White Horse, Atheneum (New York, NY), 1988.

They're All Named Wildfire, Atheneum (New York, NY), 1989.

Red Wizard, Atheneum (New York, NY), 1990.

Colt, Dial Books for Young Readers (New York, NY), 1991.

The Friendship Song, Atheneum (New York, NY), 1992.

The Great Pony Hassle, Dial Books for Young Readers (New York, NY), 1993.

Music of Their Hooves (poetry), Boyds Mills Press (Honesdale, PA), 1993.

The Boy on a Black Horse, Atheneum (New York, NY), 1994.

Toughing It, Harcourt (San Diego, CA), 1994.

Looking for Jamie Bridger, Dial (New York, NY), 1995.

Secret Star, Philomel Books (New York, NY), 1997.

I Am Mordred: A Tale from Camelot, Philomel Books (New York, NY), 1998, published as *I Am Morgan LeFay: A Tale from Camelot,* 2001.

Sky Rider, Avon Books (New York, NY), 1999.

(Editor) *Ribbiting Tales: Original Stories About Frogs,* illustrated by Tony DiTerlizzi, Philomel Books (New York, NY), 2000.

Rowan Hood: Outlaw Girl of Sherwood Forest, Philomel Books (New York, NY), 2001.

Separate Sisters, Holiday House (New York, NY), 2001.

OTHER

Also author of novellas, including "Chance," in *Under the Wheel,* Baen Books, 1987; "Serenity," in the *Magazine of Fantasy and Science Fiction,* 1989; and "Damnbanna," in *Axolotl Press,* 1992. Contributor of short stories to periodicals, including *Magazine of Fantasy and Science Fiction, Ellery Queen Mystery Magazine,* and *Alfred Hitchcock Mystery Magazine;* also contributor of short stories to anthologies, including *I Believe in Water,* edited by Marilyn Singer, HarperCollins, 2000.

WORK IN PROGRESS: Fantasy novels based on the Atlantis mythos.

SIDELIGHTS: Nancy Springer's career as an author was cemented in 1977 with the publication of her first fantasy novel, *The Book of Suns.* She went on to write a dozen more titles over the next several years, then decided to try her hand at a work for younger readers, *A Horse to Love.* Her adult fantasy works have been described as "quest" novels, and "while the quest is never a mere journey," noted an essay on the writer for *St. James Guide to Science-Fiction Writers,* "the novels can certainly be read on one level as exciting, fast-paced adventure gently touched with magic and myth, and peopled by believable characters with realistic flaws and strengths."

Springer grew up in Gettysburg, Pennsylvania, where she also attended college. An English major, she taught for a time in the early 1970s before devoting her energies to a husband, home, and family. As she wrote on her Web site, Springer had conformed to the expectations of others for much of her life, and this seemed to catch up with her. Never one to harbor a negative thought, she wrote that "[I] began to hear 'voices' in my head. First they whispered 'divorce' (not permissible), and later they hissed 'suicide.' They scared me silly." Several doctors and therapies proved unsuccessful, but Springer had found success with her first two novels by 1980, and decided to begin writing for two hours each morning, and told her husband of the plan. "He had reached the point where he would agree with whatever to humor the neurotic wife. . . . But to me it was the most important sentence I ever spoke," Springer recalled on her Internet biography. "With that sentence I stopped being a housewife who sometimes stole time to write, and I started being a writer."

The first few books from Springer's pen were set in Isle, a mythical kingdom replete with royals, gods, and fairy-tale creatures. Her quest tales drew heavily upon Celtic mythology. By 1985, Springer had branched out and created two new kingdoms for her first hardcover book, *Wings of Flame. Chains of Gold,* which appeared a year later, chronicles the love affair between a virginal "winterking" and his "bride," who must be sacrificed to the gods to ensure fertility in the kingdom of Catena. The two fall in love and decide to flee, but are tracked by pursuers both human and otherworldly.

The success of her books enabled Springer to fulfill a lifelong dream: when she was thirty-three, she bought her own horse. She once likened this act to "a key that let me back into my own childhood in a more complete and realistic way than my fantasy heroes had. And once I started writing books for children, I finally started growing up." Her first work for young readers, *A Horse to Love,* appeared in 1987, the story of an introverted young teen who finds a measure of confidence in herself when she begins to take care of a horse. In her subsequent novels aimed at the same audience, Springer began to present more complex plots of character development. In *They're All Named Wildfire,* the bond between two teenagers from different backgrounds is forged through their mutual love of horses, but community prejudices threaten to destroy their friendship.

Springer continued to write fantasy novels for adult readers as well. She wrote her "Sea King" trilogy in the mid-1980s, a series of novels set in an fantasy world. "The books explore relationships, those between choices and consequences and those between people, and the relativity of good and evil," noted the essayist in *St. James Guide to Science-Fiction Writers.* "Again the quest is the mechanism employed as both illumination and catalyst. The trilogy is a pleasure to read, gracefully written and resonating with poetic imagery." In 1988, Springer decided to end her creative reliance on fantasy worlds and root her characters in modern-day Pennsylvania with *The Hex Witch of Seldom.* For this Springer drew upon folklore from her home state to lend drama to the story. "All her fantasy novels since then have been set in the contemporary world," observed a contributor in *St. James Guide to Fantasy Writers,* "and the vividness and familiarity of these settings have proved more conducive to the realistic writing style, strong yet subtle characterization, feminism and humour which had all been growing features of her work. Away from lands of the imagination she was able to abandon the traditional moral certainties of heroic fantasy and introduce stories filled with moral doubt and ambiguous characters."

Springer continued to earn critical praise for her works for young adults. In *The Boy on a Black Horse,* for example, a young girl named Gray learns that her new classmate, of Romany stock, is actually a runaway. Both share a love of horses, and Gray learns much about herself while trying to reach out to Chav and his brother. *Booklist* reviewer Julie Corsaro found that here Springer had written "a convincing portrait of an abused child."

Strong, feminist-minded heroines have been a commonplace feature throughout much of Springer's fantasy and science fiction novels. In *Plumage,* Sassy finds herself working as a hotel maid after her husband of twenty-seven years leaves her. One day a bird in the hotel's atrium soils Sassy's hair, and when she looks in the mirror, Sassy sees a bird instead of her own reflection. She begins to see everyone as a different type of avian species, and she and her new friend, a boutique owner, must embark upon a journey into a magical hidden world in order to bring forth their true identities. "With a touch of Alice Hoffmanesque magic, a colorfully painted avian world and a winning heroine, this is pure fun," opined a *Publishers Weekly* reviewer.

Springer told *CA:* "People often ask me how I can write novels for both children and adults. I can't understand why this should be such a strange idea to them. The way any fiction writer works is to get inside the main character, to see through the character's eyes, to walk around in the character's skin awhile—and when writing a novel for children the main character is a child, that's all. Style, vocabulary, subject matter, everything else follows naturally once the fundamental act of imagination takes place. It's no big deal.

"I think the reason I perplex people is that they have notions about children's book writers, rather as they have notions about nuns. Aren't children's book writers supposed to be set apart, different, teacherly, idealistic, morally pure? Don't they write for children because they are incapable of dealing with adult interests? Um, gee, sorry to disappoint, but my contemporary fantasies such as *Larque on the Wing* are quite adult in content. I write for children because I like kids.

"The biggest real difference between writing for adults and writing for children is the distance between me and the audience. In order to get a book anywhere near a child, I as the writer must run a gauntlet of adults—editors, librarians, teachers, reviewers, parents—many of whom are eager to censor out any bit of subversive mischief that might actually be of interest to a child. This is frustrating for me as a writer, that do-gooders are interfering between me and my readers.

"I am spoiled, perhaps, by having written fantasy for many years. In the fantasy/science fiction/speculative fiction field, I enjoyed a remarkable amount of creative liberty. I still write fantasy—for adults and children—but am more and more interested in writing about the real world in a fantastic way, integrating what I have learned from writing fantasy into what I want to say about contemporary life."

BIOGRAPHICAL/CRITICAL SOURCES:

BOOKS

Authors and Artists for Young Adults, Volume 32, Gale (Detroit, MI), 2000.

St. James Guide to Fantasy Writers, 1st edition, St. James Press (Detroit, MI), 1996.

St. James Guide to Science-Fiction Writers, 4th edition, St. James Press (Detroit, MI), 1996.

PERIODICALS

Booklist, April 15, 1994, Julie Corsaro, review of *The Boy on a Black Horse,* p. 1526; September 1, 1994, Mary Harris Veeder, review of *Toughing It,* p. 36; February 1, 1996, Susan Dove Lempke, review of *Camelot,* p. 931; April 1, 1997, Hazel Rochman, review of *Secret Star,* p. 1322; April 15, 1998, Sally Estes, review of *I Am Mordred: A Tale from Camelot,* p. 1545; January 1, 1999, review of *I Am Mordred,* p. 782; November 1, 2000, GraceAnne A. DeCandido, review of *Ribbiting Tales: Original Stories About Frogs,* p. 541.

Gettysburg Times, November 2, 1977.

Horn Book, March-April, 1998, Ann A. Flowers, review of *I Am Mordred,* p. 219; November, 1999, Kristi Beavin, review of *I Am Mordred,* p. 765.

Kirkus Reviews, November 1, 2000, review of *Plumage,* p. 1514.

Library Journal, August, 1986.

Publishers Weekly, February 27, 1987; February 12, 1988; January 31, 1994, review of *Larque on the Wing,* p. 80; July 11, 1994, review of *Toughing It,* p. 80; October 16, 1995, review of *Camelot,* p. 62; October 21, 1996, review of *Fair Peril,* p. 76; March 16, 1998, review of *I Am Mordred,* p. 65; June 26, 2000, review of *Prince of Thieves,* p. 77; November 6, 2000, review of *Plumage,* p. 71.

Susquehanna, May, 1978; April, 1980.

Voice of Youth Advocates, December, 1986; April, 1990.

Washington Post Book World, May 10, 1992.

York Daily Record, January 8, 1980.

OTHER

Nancy Springer Web site, http://www.stlf.org/ntc/11/nsbio.htm (January 29, 2002).

*   *   *

STAFFORD, Barbara Maria 1941-

PERSONAL: Born September 16, 1941, in Vienna, Austria; daughter of K. S. (a military officer) and Ingeborg Anna Davis; married Fred E. Stafford (a science administrator). *Education:* Northwestern University, B.A., 1963, M.A., 1966; attended Warburg Institute, 1968 and 1970; University of Chicago, Ph.D., 1972.

ADDRESSES: Office—Department of Art, University of Chicago, 5540 South Greenwood, Chicago, IL 60637; fax: 773-702-5902. *E-mail*—bms6@midway.uchicago.edu.

CAREER: Writer and critic. University of Delaware, Newark, 1973-81, began as assistant professor, became associate professor of art history; University of Chicago, Chicago, IL, professor, 1982-95, William B. Ogden Distinguished Service Professor of Art History, 1995—.

MEMBER: American Society for Eighteenth-Century Studies (president, 1995), College Art Association of America, Word and Image, Science, Literature, and Society, History of Science Society, Humboldt Society.

AWARDS, HONORS: Excellence-in-Teaching Award, University of Delaware, 1976; fellow, National Endowment for the Humanities, 1979-80; Clifford Prize, American Society for Eighteenth-Century Studies, 1979, and Clifford Lecturer; fellow, Center for Advanced Study in the Visual Arts, 1981-82; Millard Meiss Publication Award, CCA, 1983; fellow, Woodrow Wilson International Center for Scholars, Smithsonian Institution, 1984-85; Guggenheim fellowship, 1989-90; Humboldt senior fellowship, 1989-91; fellow, Humanities Research Institute, University of California, 1991; Getty scholarship, 1995-96.

WRITINGS:

Symbol and Myth: Humbert de Superville's Essay on Absolute Signs in Art, Associated University Presses (Cranbury, NJ), 1979.

Voyage into Substance: Art, Science, Nature, and the Illustrated Travel Account, 1760-1840, MIT Press (Cambridge, MA), 1984.

Body Criticism: Imaging the Unseen in Enlightenment Art and Medicine, MIT Press (Cambridge, MA), 1991.

Artful Science: Enlightenment Entertainment and the Eclipse of Visual Education, MIT Press (Cambridge, MA), 1994.

Good Looking (essays), MIT Press (Cambridge, MA), 1995.

Visual Analogy: Consciousness as the Art of Connecting, MIT Press (Cambridge, MA), 1999.

Contributor to periodicals, including *Eighteenth-Century Studies.*

WORK IN PROGRESS: (With Frances Terpak) *Devices of Wonder: From the World in a Box to Images on a Screen,* an exhibition and catalog, for Getty Museum of Art (Los Angeles, CA).

SIDELIGHTS: Barbara Maria Stafford is an art historian specializing in the eighteenth century. She told a *Sculpture* interviewer: "The wonderful thing about the eighteenth century is that it's postmodern in many ways. . . . The eighteenth century is an era of conversation, and what happens toward the end of the eighteenth century is a kind of intellectualizing process that is a trend toward abstraction." In the same *Sculpture* interview, Stafford described the 1990s as "the decade of the brain" and lamented: "Cerebralization is what's important; the body and handwork are demoded. We're surrounded by images, but they are debased. Bodies are everywhere, but they're in servitude." She added, "We need to be anchored in something that isn't merely simulated, degraded or cerebral; all these false dichotomies."

Stafford once told *CA:* "I was born in Vienna, Austria. My stepfather was an American military attache, so I was privileged to roam the world. My educational background was checkered—studies were interrupted every three years when my stepfather was assigned a new post. My mother was extremely talented: she restored antiques, designed and sewed clothing and wore the pieces—so I was always surrounded by strange and exciting artifacts.

"At Northwestern University I took a double degree in philosophy and comparative literature. My unconventional background meant I never fit into any traditional graduate program. The most decisive event for me was when I went to the Warburg Institute to study with Sir Ernst Gombrich. My dissertation and, eventually, first book, *Symbol and Myth: Humbert de Superville's Essay on Absolute Signs in Art,* plunged me into the arcana of the eighteenth century, which has been my intellectual home ever since.

"My long years of travel were re-experienced in *Voyage into Substance: Art, Science, Nature, and the Illustrated Travel Account, 1760-1840,* a ten-year project chronicling the late development, in the West, of what might be termed an environmental aesthetics. My concern about the contemporary denigration of images inspired me to write about the history of visual education, linking the early modern era to the online digital age, in *Artful Science: Enlightenment Entertainment and the Eclipse of Visual Education. Body Criticism: Imaging the Unseen in Enlightenment Art and Medicine* marks my continuing engagement with contemporary issues, technology, and new aspects of the history of science. The essays collected in *Good Looking* explore contemporary issues in visualization, public policy, and the need to study the past history of representation."

She added: "*Visual Analogy: Consciousness as the Art of Connecting* takes up the old problem of sameness and difference, and links it to the current consciousness debates. *Devices of Wonder: From the World in a Box to Images on a Screen* explores the connection."

BIOGRAPHICAL/CRITICAL SOURCES:

PERIODICALS

Sculpture, May-June, 1994, interview with Stafford, pp. 12-14.

*   *   *

STANTON, Mary 1947-
(Claudia Bishop)

PERSONAL: Born June 12, 1947, in Winter Park, FL; daughter of William Bishop (a naval officer) and Caroline (Bauman) Whitaker; married Robert Tom Nelson, September 24, 1966 (marriage ended, November, 1972); married Robert J. Stanton, December 26, 1974 (marriage ended, August, 2000); stepchildren: John, Harry, Julie. *Ethnicity:* "Caucasian." *Education:* Attended St. Olaf College, 1967; University of Minnesota—Twin Cities, B.A., 1969; attended William Mitchell College of Law, 1970. *Politics:* Liberal. *Religion:* Episcopalian. *Avocational interests:* Equestrian activities.

ADDRESSES: Home—3287 LeRoy Rd., Palmyra, NY 14522; (winters) 140 Inlet Way, No. 110, Palm Beach Shores, FL 33404. *Agent*—Merrilee Heifetz, Writers House, 21 West 26th St., New York, NY 10010. *E-mail*—mstanton@redsuspenders.com.

CAREER: Singer and actress in Minneapolis, MN, 1969-70; Crum & Forster Insurance Co., Minneapolis, claims adjuster, 1971-72; State of Minnesota, St. Paul, medical examiner, 1972-73; Aetna Life and Casualty Co., Rochester, NY, claims adjuster, 1974-78; copy writer for an agency in Rochester, 1978-82; Stanton & Hucko, Rochester, founder, 1983, president, 1983-92; writer, 1992—.

MEMBER: Science Fiction and Fantasy Writers of America, Mystery Writers of America.

WRITINGS:

The Heavenly Horse from the Outermost West (fantasy), Baen, 1988.
Piper at the Gate (fantasy), Baen, 1989.
The Unicorns of Balinor (young adult fantasy), Scholastic Inc. (New York, NY), 1999.
The Road to Balinor (young adult fantasy), Scholastic Inc. (New York, NY), 1999.
Sunchaser's Quest, Scholastic Inc. (New York, NY), 1999.
Valley of Fear, Scholastic Inc. (New York, NY), 1999.
By Fire, by Moonlight, Scholastic Inc. (New York, NY), 1999.
Shadows over Balinor (young adult fantasy), Scholastic Inc. (New York, NY), 2000.
Search for the Star, Scholastic Inc. (New York, NY), 2001.
Secrets of the Scepter, Scholastic Inc. (New York, NY), 2001.
Night of the Shifter's Moon, Scholastic Inc. (New York, NY), 2001.

Author of *My Aunt the Monster* and *Next Door to a Witch* (both young adult science fiction), Berkley Publishing (New York, NY). Writer for the television series *Princess Gwenevere and the Jewel Riders.* Work represented in anthologies, including *Hooves of Thunder, Manes of Gold,* Doubleday (New York, NY), 1992; and *Horse Fantastic,* DAW Books (New York, NY), 1992.

MYSTERY NOVELS, UNDER PSEUDONYM CLAUDIA BISHOP

A Taste for Murder, Berkley Publishing (New York, NY), 1994.
A Dash of Death, Berkley Publishing (New York, NY), 1995.
A Pinch of Poison, Berkley Publishing (New York, NY), 1996.
Murder Well-Done, Berkley Publishing (New York, NY), 1996.
A Touch of the Grape, Berkley Publishing (New York, NY), 1997.

Death Dines Out, Berkley Publishing (New York, NY), 1998.
A Steak in Murder, Berkley Publishing (New York, NY), 1999.
Marinade for Murder, Berkley Publishing (New York, NY), 2000.
Death Dines at 8:30, Berkley Publishing (New York, NY), 2001.
Just Desserts, Berkley Publishing (New York, NY), 2002.

SIDELIGHTS: Mary Stanton once told *CA:* "I write to invoke particular states of mind in myself: hilarity, affection, pity, astonishment, awe. My characters are animals, teenagers, eccentric adults, and they usually revolve around a sensible, centered protagonist. I like plots that are as extravagant as my imagination can make them.

"For me, writing fiction is like building a house, equipped only with a hammer, a saw, and a plumb line. It is arduous. I always feel as though my foundation is out of true. Once the plot, structure, and theme are constructed, I have a much easier time with dialogue.

"I spend a great deal of time thinking up excuses not to write. When I do write, I'll work for twelve hours at a stretch, seven days a week. I rewrite as little as possible—but when I do, it is with the fervor of a fundamentalist avoiding the pits of hell."

*   *   *

STEELE, Philip 1948-

PERSONAL: Born May 17, 1948, in Dorking, Surrey, England; son of Tim and Marion (Bundey) Steele; married Linda C. Rogers; children: Elin Rhiannon (daughter). *Ethnicity:* "European." *Education:* University College, Durham, B.A. (honors; German and French), 1971. *Avocational interests:* Travel, Gardening, photography, walking, cooking.

ADDRESSES: Home and office—Tŷ Cerrig Llangoed, Beaumaris, Ynys Môn, Wales LL58 8SA, United Kingdom; fax: 01248-490715. *E-mail*—phil@tycerrig1.freeserve.co.uk.

CAREER: English language teaching assistant, Köln, Germany, 1969-70; Hodder Group (ULP/EUP), London, England, educational promotions assistant,

1971-73; Hamlyn Children's Books, Feltham, England, assistant editor, 1973-76; Macdonald Educational, London, England, editor, 1977-79, senior editor, 1979-80; freelance writer and editor, 1981—.

MEMBER: National Union of Journalists, Society of Authors.

AWARDS, HONORS: Step-by-Step Collage was selected as a Children's Books of the Year, Young Book Trust, 1994; joint winner of Off-the-Cuff Award for favorite nonfiction title, *Publishers Weekly,* 1996, for *The Greek News;* ABC Children's Booksellers Choice Award, 1997, for *The Greek News; The Greek News* was named to US Children's Literature Choice List, 1997.

WRITINGS:

CHILDREN'S NONFICTION

(With Brenda R. Lewis and Lynne Williams) *1,000 Great Events,* Hamlyn, 1975.
Transport around the World (in "International Picture Library" series), Macmillan, 1982.
(With Keith Lye) *Pictorial Atlas,* Hamlyn, 1983-89.
Counting and Numbers: Blue Book, Piccolo, 1983.
Festivals around the World (in "International Picture Library" series), Macmillan, 1983.
Reading and Writing: Blue Book, Piccolo, 1983.
Counting and Numbers: Red Book, Piccolo, 1984.
Reading and Writing: Red Book, Piccolo, 1984.
Children's Picture Atlas, BHS, 1985.
Do You Know about Life in the Sea?, Piccolo, 1985.
Do You Know How Animals Live?, Piccolo, 1985.
Money (in "My First Library" series), Macdonald, 1986.
The Tactics of Terror (in "Debates" series), Macdonald, 1986.
Whatever the Weather, Purnell, 1988.
China (in "World in View" series), Macmillan, 1989.
First Book of Questions and Answers, Hamlyn, 1989.
Môn Mam Cymru: The Anglesey Guide, Magma, 1990.
(With others) *Children's World Atlas,* Ilex, 1991.
Food and Diet (in "Science Now" series), Heinemann, 1991.
Journey through China, Eagle Books, 1991.
Sharks and Other Monsters of the Deep (in "Windows on the World" series), Dorling Kindersley, 1991.
The People Atlas, Oxford University Press, 1991, published as *Peoples of the World,* Horus Editions, 1995.

(With others) *Children's Illustrated Atlas of the World,* Book Express, 1992.
Little Bighorn (in "Great Battles and Sieges" series), Zoë Books, 1992, Macmillan, 1993.
(With others) *Step-by-Step Collage,* Kingfisher, 1993.
50 Years Ago in Europe during WWII (part of "History Detectives" series), Zoë Books, 1993, published as *Europe in World War Two,* Macmillan, 1993.
First Atlas, Kibworth, 1993.
Heyerdahl and the Kon Tiki, Zoë Books, 1993, published as *Thor Heyerdahl and Kon-Tiki,* Macmillan/Dillon, 1993.
The Incas and Machu Picchu (in "Hidden Worlds" series), Macmillan, 1993.
Thermopylai (in "Great Battles and Sieges" series), Wayland, 1993.
Farming Village (in "Where I Live" series), Watts, 1994.
Flags (in "Little Library" series), Kingfisher, 1994.
Food and Feasts between the Two World Wars, New Discovery Books, 1994.
Food and Feasts in Ancient Rome, New Discovery Books, 1994.
The Egyptians and Valley of the Kings (in "Hidden Worlds" series), Zoë Books, 1994.
The Romans & Pompeii (in "Hidden Worlds" series), Zoë Books, 1994.
The Blue Whale (in "Fold out and Find out" series), Kingfisher, 1994.
The Giant Panda (in "Fold out and Find out" series), Kingfisher, 1994.
The Samurai Sword (in "Fold out and Find out" series), Kingfisher, 1994.
I Wonder Why Castles Had Moats? and Other Questions about Long Ago, Kingfisher, 1994.
I Wonder Why Countries Fly Flags? and Other Questions about People and Places, Kingfisher, 1995.
I Wonder Why the Pyramids Were Built? and Other Questions about Ancient Egypt, Kingfisher, 1995.
(With others) *Encyclopaedia of Lands and Peoples,* Kingfisher, 1995.
Best-Ever Book of Castles (also see below), Kingfisher, 1995.
Great Discoveries (in "What Happened Next?" series), Watts, 1995.
(With Anton Powell) *The Greek News,* Walker Books, 1996, Gareth Stevens Publishing, 2000.
Anglesey: Ynys Môn (in "Archive Photograph" series), Chalford, 1996.
Beaumaris, Story of the Town, Magma, 1996.
Black Holes and Other Space Phenomena (in "Young Observer" series), David West for Kingfisher, 1996.
The World of Festivals, McNally, 1996.

Vampire Bats and Other Creatures of the Night (in "Young Observer" series), David West for Kingfisher, 1996.

Crafts and Clothes in Ancient Rome, Zoë Books, 1996, Gareth Stevens Publishing, 2000.

Crafts and Clothes in Ancient Greece, Zoë Books, 1997, Gareth Stevens Publishing, 2000.

Clothes and Crafts in Victorian Times, Zoë Books, 1997, Gareth Stevens Publishing, 2000.

Best-Ever Book of Pirates, Kingfisher, 1997.

Freedom of Speech (in "What Do We Mean by Human Rights?" series), Watts, 1997.

Kingfisher Atlas of the World, Kingfisher, 1997.

Rocking and Rolling: The Earth, Walker Books, 1997, Candlewick Press, 1998.

Snow and Ice (in "Living with the Weather" series), Thunderbolt for Wayland, 1997, Raintree Steck-Vaughn, 1998.

Best-Ever Book of Knights (also see below), Kingfisher, 1998.

Censorship (in "Moral Dilemmas" series), Evans Bros., 1998.

Children's Atlas, Dempsey Parr, 1998.

My Best Book of Mummies, Kingfisher, 1998.

Wannabe an Explorer, Parragon, 1998.

(With others) *Ultimate Atlas of Almost Everything,* HarperCollins, 1998, Sterling Publishing, 1999.

(With others) *Ultimate Atlas of the World,* Parragon, 1999.

A Tidal Pool (in "Small Worlds" series), Moondrake, 1999.

Crime and Punishment (in "Moral Dilemmas" series), Evans Bros., 1999.

Pirates (in "Discovery" series), Anness/Lorenz Books, 1999, revised as *World of Pirates* (in "World of" series), Southwater, 2000.

Time Capsule of the Twentieth Century, Wayland, 1999.

Toys and Games (in "Everyday History" series), Watts, 1999.

Volcanoes, Barron's, 1999.

(With others) *Peoples of the Americas,* 10 volumes, Marshall Cavendish, 1999.

(With others) *Peoples of Africa,* 10 volumes, Marshall Cavendish, 2000.

Animal Matters (in "Life Files" series), Evans Bros., 2000.

Atlas of the World (Volume 6 of "Explore and Learn" series), Southwestern, 2000.

Going to School (in "Everyday History" series), Watts, 2000.

Mummies (in "Moving Model Books" series), Arcturus/Hodder Children's, 2000.

People in Place and Time (Volume 4 of "Explore and Learn" series), Southwestern, 2000.

The Human Race (Volume 8 of "Being Human" series), Grolier Educational, 2000.

The Medieval World (contains *Best-Ever Book of Knights* and *Best-Ever Book of Castles*), Kingfisher, 2000.

A History of the British Isles, Miles Kelly, 2001.

Atlas of the World, Ticktock for Grolier/Watts USA, 2001.

Citizenship, Evans Bros., 2001.

Jesse Owens, Heinemann Library, 2001.

Scholastic Atlas of the World, Scholastic, 2001.

The Aztec News, Walker Books, 1997, Gareth Stevens Publishing, 2001.

"POCKET FACTS" CHILDREN'S NONFICTION SERIES

Birds, Macmillan/Heinemann, 1991.
Insects, Macmillan/Heinemann, 1991.
Reptiles, Macmillan/Heinemann, 1991.
Wild Animals, Macmillan/Heinemann, 1991.
Astronomy, Macmillan/Heinemann, 1991.
Space Travel, Macmillan/Heinemann, 1991.
Deserts, Macmillan/Heinemann, 1991.
Mountains, Macmillan/Heinemann, 1991.
Trains, Macmillan/Heinemann, 1991.
Planes, Macmillan/Heinemann, 1991.
Boats, Macmillan/Heinemann, 1991.
Cars and Trucks, Macmillan/Heinemann, 1991.

"EXTINCT AND ENDANGERED" CHILDREN'S NONFICTION SERIES

Reptiles, Watts, 1991.
Birds, Watts, 1991.
Amphibians, Watts, 1991.
Insects, Watts, 1991.
Land Mammals, Watts, 1991.
Underwater Life, Watts, 1991.

"KILLERS!" CHILDREN'S NONFICTION SERIES

Birds, Heinemann, 1991.
Fish, Heinemann, 1991.
Insects, Heinemann, 1991.
Mammals, Heinemann, 1991.
Reptiles, Heinemann, 1991.
Prehistoric Animals, Heinemann, 1991.

"WEATHER WATCH" CHILDREN'S NONFICTION SERIES

Frost, Watts, 1991.
Heatwave, Watts, 1991.
Storm, Watts, 1991.
Wind, Watts, 1991.
Rain, Watts, 1991.
Snow, Watts, 1991.

"PAST AND PRESENT" CHILDREN'S NONFICTION SERIES

Censorship, Heinemann, 1993.
Terrorism, Heinemann, 1993.
Kidnapping, Heinemann, 1993.
Smuggling, Heinemann, 1993.
Riots, Heinemann, 1993.

"THROUGH THE AGES" CHILDREN'S NONFICTION SERIES

City, Eagle/Quarto Children's, 1993.
Road, Eagle/Quarto Children's, 1993.
Farm, Eagle/Quarto Children's, 1993.
House, Eagle/Quarto Children's, 1993.
River, Eagle/Quarto Children's, 1993.
Factory, Eagle/Quarto Children's, 1993.

"DISCOVERING" CHILDREN'S NONFICTION SERIES

Discovering Germany, Macmillan, 1993.
Discovering Great Britain, Zoë Books, 1993.

Also, author of *Discovering China, Discovering Ireland,* and *Discovering Greece,* all published by Zoë Books, c. 1993-97.

"GEOGRAPHY DETECTIVES" CHILDREN'S NONFICTION SERIES

Islands, Carolrhoda Books, 1996.
Grasslands, Carolrhoda Books, 1996.
Tundra, Carolrhoda Books, 1996.

Also, author of *Deserts, Islands, Grasslands,* and *Tundra,* all published by Zoë Books, c. 1996.

"STEP INTO" CHILDREN'S NONFICTION SERIES

Step into Ancient Rome, Anness, 1997, published as *Find out about Ancient Rome* (in "Find out About" series), Southwater, 2000.
Step into Ancient Egypt, Anness/Lorenz Books, 1997, published as *Find out about Ancient Egypt* (in "Find out About" series), Southwater, 2000.
Step into the Viking World, Anness/Lorenz Books, 1998.
Step into the Chinese Empire, Anness/Lorenz Books, 1999.
Step into the Inca World, Anness/Lorenz Books, 2000.

CHILDREN'S NARRATIVE

Joseph and His Coat of Many Colours, Macdonald, 1985.
Joseph and His Brothers, Macdonald, 1985.
Grandma Goosegog, Hutchinson, 1987.
Last of the Monsters, Hutchinson, 1987.
Rainbow's End, Hutchinson, 1987.
The Fairy Post Box, Hutchinson, 1987.
The Ghost Train, Hutchinson, 1987.
The Giving Book, Hutchinson, 1987.
The Goblins of Griddlestone Gap, Hutchinson, 1987.
The King Who Loved Yellow, Hutchinson, 1987.
The Witches Who Came to Stay, Hutchinson, 1987.
The Wizard and the Weasel, Hutchinson, 1987.
Eyes of the Skull, Henderson, 1996.

OTHER

America's Natural Beauty (adult travelogue), Crescent, 1986.

Steele's works have been translated into various languages, including Chinese, Portuguese, French, Italian, Spanish, and German.

SIDELIGHTS: Philip Steele told *CA:* "As a child, my favorite books were historical novels by authors such as Rosemary Sutcliff and factual books about the world of nature." Many children's information books in the 1950s seemed to be written in adult language accompanied by dull black-and-white plates. It was a delight to enter publishing in the 1970s, when information books for children at last began to come alive, with lively language, colorful illustrations and inventive design. Over the last twenty years, the spirit of innovation has continued. I still find the most exciting part of my work begins with the planning and visualization of a title, sitting around the table with designers, artists, and editors.

"I worked as an editor myself for ten years, learning every aspect of publishing. It was then that I first began to write, compiling reference works in-house. After working as senior editor at Macdonald Educational in London, I decided to move to Wales in 1981 to work as a freelance writer and editor. The move was a stimulating one. I learned to speak the Welsh language, made new friends, and relaxed in some of the most beautiful scenery in the British Isles. Contact with local primary schools has kept me in touch with children's interests—and their terrible jokes!

"My wife Linda is a teacher, working in the fields of dyslexia and theatre in education. We have a daughter, Elin Rhiannon, born in 1996.

"I have always enjoyed traveling, and with Wales as my base I continue to escape overseas whenever possible. In the past I have backpacked across the Middle East, India, the former Soviet Union, and China. I have spent periods in the United States, Canada, and Mexico, as well as in several regions of Africa. These experiences have provided invaluable background material for my children's books about countries, peoples, and natural history. They have also provided a useful perspective for several older children's books on social and international issues.

"I have had over sixty titles published in Britain, a large total which does include several series of very slim volumes! In recent years I have been able to work on some fascinating historical projects and would like to write a historical novel for younger readers—if I can ever find the time!"

BIOGRAPHICAL/CRITICAL SOURCES:

PERIODICALS

School Library Journal, July, 1994, p. 98.

*   *   *

STEELE, Valerie (Fahnestock) 1955-

PERSONAL: Born June 29, 1955, in Boston, MA; daughter of George S. (a judge) and Valerie (Noel) Steele; married John Stephen Major (an editor), August 25, 1979; children: Stephen Nicholas. *Education:* Dart-

mouth College, B.A. (summa cum laude), 1978; Yale University, M.A. and M.Phil., 1980, Ph.D., 1983. *Avocational interests:* Travel.

ADDRESSES: Office—The Museum, Fashion Institute of Technology, Seventh Avenue at 27th Street, New York, NY, 10001-5992.

CAREER: Smithsonian Institution, Washington, DC, fellow and consultant, 1984; Fashion Institute of Technology, New York, NY, adjunct professor in graduate program, 1985-1996; The Museum at The Fashion Institute of Technology, New York, NY, chief curator, 1997—. Editor of *Fashion Theory: The Journal of Dress, Body and Culture,* 1997—.

MEMBER: Fashion Group International, International Association of Costume.

WRITINGS:

Fashion and Eroticism: Ideals of Feminine Beauty from the Victorian Era to the Jazz Age, Oxford University Press (New York, NY), 1985.
Paris Fashion: A Cultural History, Oxford University Press (New York, NY), 1988, revised edition, 1998.
(Editor, with Claudia Brush Kidwell) *Men and Women: Dressing the Part,* Smithsonian Institution Press (Washington, DC), 1989.
Women of Fashion: Twentieth-Century Designers, Rizzoli (New York, NY), 1991.
Fetish: Fashion, Sex, and Power, Oxford University Press (New York, NY), 1996.
Fifty Years of Fashion: New Look to Now, with photographs by Irving Solero, Yale University Press (New Haven, CT), 1997.
(With Valerie Laird Borrelli) *Bags: A Lexicon of Style,* Scriptum Editions (London, England), 1999.
Shoes: A Lexicon of Style, Rizzoli (New York, NY), 1999.
(With John S. Major) *China Chic: East Meets West,* Yale University Press (New Haven, CT), 1999.
The Red Dress, Rizzoli (New York, NY), 2001.
The Corset: A Cultural History, Cycle University Press (New Haven, CT), 2001.

Contributor to periodicals, including *Vogue, Dress,* and *Costume.*

SIDELIGHTS: While working toward her graduate degrees, Valerie Steele had trouble being taken seriously because she was interested in fashion as a representation of culture. If the number of her publications since then is any indication, the world now takes Steele seriously. Each of her ten volumes has approached fashion history from different points of view, focusing on such topics as ideals of female beauty, fetishism, and dress as a cultural statement. For example, one work is a survey of a roughly ninety-year period, that addresses the correlation between the modes of an epoch and the status of women during that time. Another study takes a specific look at Paris, the world capital of style, and the factors involved in that city's dominance of fashion. While *Women of Fashion: Twentieth-Century Designers* explores the careers and attitudes of modern women fashion designers, *Fetish: Fashion, Sex, and Power* explores the existence and meaning of fetish clothing.

In her first book, *Fashion and Eroticism: Ideals of Feminine Beauty from the Victorian Era to the Jazz Age,* Steele attempts to reverse the popular illusion that the periods covered in the title are polar opposites in regard to women's dress and feminine roles in society. As the author explains, women in the late nineteenth century were tightly corseted and covered, and regarded as silent victims of the era's societal repression of sexuality. The flapper, a more liberated woman of the 1920s, was considered freed by the societal and economic changes brought on by World War I. Arguing against these views, Steele explains that women in the Victorian age were able to express their sexuality through aspects of their dress, and that fashion was less influenced by upheavals in world and national events than many historians believe. The author further expands this premise to offer the theory that clothing allows women to create an erotic "ideal self" within the conventions of their society. Critical reaction to *Fashion and Eroticism* was mixed. Marilyn Powell of the Toronto *Globe and Mail* charged that the ideas expressed in the volume depend too heavily on the theories of Austrian psychoanalyst Sigmund Freud, and that Steele failed to support her ideas with concrete examples. Mary Douglas, writing in the *Times Literary Supplement,* also disagreed with some of Steele's arguments, but admitted that the author was successful in supporting some of her contentions. She added, "Steele's book finds itself in distinguished company." Michael S. Kimmel in *Psychology Today* wrote that the book "adds several important dimensions to fashion history."

In her next work, Steele moved from an analytical approach to fashion toward a broader historical strategy. In *Paris Fashion: A Cultural History,* she examines how the French city became the headquarters of the fashion industry and has remained the originator of in-

novative styles. Full of facts and illustrations, *Paris Fashion* is loosely organized into chapters centered around themes. In researching the beginnings of the influential design houses, Steele finds that women were more involved in the creation of pace-setting fashions of bygone eras than chroniclers of cultural history originally thought. The author also comments on the role of fashion in the lives and works of the French writers Charles-Pierre Baudelaire, Honoré de Balzac, and Marcel Proust. *Paris Fashion* received a warmer critical reception than had Steele's previous book. Francesca Stanfill of the *Los Angeles Times Book Review* called the work "an original, gracefully written study," recommending it for travelers to France for its glimpse into the country's character. Writing in the *New York Times,* John Gross praised the author for including a remarkable amount of detail "without clogging her narrative," and commended Steele's "well chosen [and] well integrated" illustrations. He concluded that *Paris Fashion* "offers many insights and pleasures."

Drawing on a number of fields of inquiry, Steele looks at fetishistic sexual practices and analyzes their impact on fashion history in *Fetish: Fashion, Sex, and Power.* Among the topics she discusses are the fascination with such articles as corsets, underwear as outerwear, shoes, and unusual fabrics; the introduction of fetishist items into mainstream fashion; and the political and cultural implications of fetish-influenced fashions. *Fetish* caught reviewers' attention. A *Publishers Weekly* critic called Steele's analysis "sketchy" at times, yet judged the study to be "thought provoking." Albert Wong, reviewing the work for *Archives of Sexual Behavior,* wrote: "This book is an excellent overview of the history of fetish clothing from the perspective of fashion culture. Steele is often witty and entertaining, and she manages to integrate a diverse set of discourses . . . into a thoughtful and balanced book."

To coincide with exhibition openings at the Fashion Institute of Technology in New York City, Steele produced several works, including *Fifty Years of Fashion: New Look Now* and *China Chic: East Meets West.* The former is a survey of fashion history from the 1950s to the turn of the millennium. The latter, for which she teamed up with Chinese history scholar John S. Major, also includes six essays by experts in Chinese clothing.

BIOGRAPHICAL/CRITICAL SOURCES:

PERIODICALS

American Craft, August, 1998, review of *Fifty Years of Fashion: From New Look to Now,* p. 22.

Archives of Sexual Behavior, June, 2000, Albert Wong, review of *Fetish: Fashion, Sex, and Power,* p. 292.

Books Magazine, December, 1997, review of *Fetish,* p. 18.

Globe & Mail (Toronto), September 28, 1985.

Library Journal, October 1, 1995, review of *Fetish,* p. 80; November 1, 1997, Therese Duzinkiewicz, review of *Fifty Years of Fashion,* p. 74; April 15, 1999, Therese Duzinkiewicz, review of *China Chic: East Meets West,* p. 84.

Los Angeles Times Book Review, March 27, 1988, pp. 1, 12; June 11, 1989, p. 6.

New Statesman and Society, December, 1995, review of *Fetish,* p. 29.

New York Times, March 29, 1988.

New York Times Book Review, January 14, 1996 (late edition), Sarah Boxer, "Who Are the Real Perverts?," p. 24.

New York Times Magazine, November 14, 1999, Amy Finnerty, "Threads Bared: Anatomy of a Men's Suit," p.60.

Observer (London), October 19, 1997, review of *Fifty Years of Fashion,* p. 18; November 23, 1997, review of *Fetish,* p. 18.

Psychology Today, November 1985, p. 88; July-August, 1997, Hara Estroff Marano, "The 'F-word'," p. 22.

Publishers Weekly, August 28, 1995, review of *Fetish,* p. 95; September 22, 1997, review of *Fifty Years of Fashion,* p. 58.

Times Literary Supplement, November 8, 1985, p. 1254; June 14, 1996, review of *Fetish,* p. 11.

OTHER

Yale University Press, http://www.yale.edu/ (January 23, 2001), reviews of *Fifty Years of Fashion* and *China Chic.*

*　　*　　*

STEVERMER, C. J.
See STEVERMER, Caroline

*　　*　　*

STEVERMER, Caroline 1955-
(C. J. Stevermer)

PERSONAL: Surname is pronounced "*Steve*-er-mer"; born January 13, 1955, in Houston, MN; daughter of John Weaver (a farmer) and Carol Jean (a teacher; maiden name, Dahlstrom) Stevermer. *Education:* Bryn Mawr College, B.A., 1977.

ADDRESSES: Home—Minneapolis, MN. *Office*—*Star Tribune,* 425 Portland Ave., Minneapolis, MN 55488. *Agent*—Frances Collins Literary Agency, P.O. Box 33, Wayne, PA 19087-0033.

CAREER: Clerical worker, 1977-84; *Star Tribune,* Minneapolis, MN, 1984—, became editorial assistant.

MEMBER: Newspaper Guild.

WRITINGS:

(Under name C. J. Stevermer) *The Alchemist: Death of a Borgia,* Ace Books (New York, NY), 1980.

(Under name C. J. Stevermer) *The Duke and the Veil,* Ace Books (New York, NY), 1981.

The Serpent's Egg, Ace Books (New York, NY), 1988.

(With Patricia C. Wrede) *Sorcery and Cecelia,* Ace Books (New York, NY), 1988.

River Rats, Harcourt (San Diego, CA), 1992.

A College of Magics, Tor (New York, NY), 1994.

When the King Comes Home, Tor (New York, NY), 2000.

Work represented in anthologies, including *Liavek: Wizard's Row,* edited by Will Shetterly and Emma Bull, Ace Books (New York, NY), 1987; and a collection edited by Terri Windling, Morrow (New York, NY), 1992.

SIDELIGHTS: Caroline Stevermer found herself at home in the fantastic, first writing adult historical novels with a mild fantasy element, then focusing on fantasy and science fiction novels for young adult readers. During the 1980s she wrote *The Alchemist: Death of a Borgia, The Duke and the Veil,* and *The Serpent's Egg.* The *Alchemist* and *The Duke and the Veil,* which were published under the pseudonym C. J. Stevemer, are historical mysteries set in the Italian Renaissance, featuring an English alchemist as sleuth and poison as the means of murder. Similarly, *The Serpent's Egg* is a murder mystery, yet it is set in an alternative Elizabethan England where magic in the form of a fabulous crystal called the serpent's egg plays a main role. Stevermer's next work, the epistolary novel *Sorcery and Cecelia,* was co-written with Patricia Wrede, who has also written works for young adult readers.

During the 1990s, Steverner wrote several noteworthy novels for young adults. In the sci-fi adventure *River Rats,* she told the post-Apocalyptic story of a group of teenagers who ply the polluted Mississippi River in their restored steam-powered paddle-boat. The novel caught critics' attention. According to Ann A. Flowers of *Horn Book, River Rats* is "an unusual, compelling futuristic novel." Likewise, a *Publishers Weekly* reviewer praised the setting and premise of the story, and noted that the author's "unwavering interest in the individuals who live there distinguishes the novel from mere space opera." In *Kirkus Reviews* a contributor called it a "sturdy, not over-earnest sf adventure."

In contrast to *River Rats, A College of Magics* and *When the King Comes Home* take place in alternate worlds that resemble historical Europe. *A College of Magics* combines characteristics of fantasy and conventional romance and revolves around the activities of a teenage duchess, who discovers while at finishing school her role as a wielder of important magical powers. In the words of a *Publishers Weekly* contributor, it is "clever and witty at its best . . . generally a pleasant read." *When the King Comes Home* is also a tale of discovery by a young woman of special powers and responsibilities. The young daughter of a rich wool merchant who is apprenticed to an artist discovers a medal depicting a legendary king and becomes obsessed with it. *Library Journal* reviewer Jackie Cassada praised the "winsome" first-person narration, and *Booklist* reviewer Roland Green commented on the novel's humor. The novel is "beautifully rendered, if ultimately promising more than it delivers," concluded a critic for *Kirkus Reviews.*

Stevermer told *CA:* "I was born on a Minnesota dairy farm within ten miles of the Mississippi River, where an occasional steamboat still churned the muddy waters. I do try not to boast about the one-room country schoolhouse where I acquired four years of education before switching to the 'town school.' After a summer as an exchange student in Sao Paolo, Brazil, I went to Bryn Mawr College in Pennsylvania, where I majored in history of art and the *Million Dollar Movie* on Channel 49.

"After graduation, I tried like hell to live in New York City but found I had no aptitude. As soon as they would let me, I returned to Minnesota. I now speak fluent Minnesotan, take an avid interest in the weather, and spend countless hours every summer at the State Fair."

BIOGRAPHICAL/CRITICAL SOURCES:

BOOKS

St. James Guide to Fantasy Writers, St. James Press (Detroit, MI), 1996.

PERIODICALS

Analog Science Fiction & Fact, September, 1994, Tom Easton, review of *A College of Magics,* pp. 163-164.
Booklist, April 1, 1992, review of *River Rats,* p. 1440; October 1, 1992, review of *River Rats,* p. 341; March 15, 1993, review of *River Rats,* p. 1343; March 1, 1994, Roland Green, review of *A College of Magics,* p. 1185; November 15, 2000, Roland Green, review of *When the King Comes Home,* p. 625.
Book Report, November, 1992, review of *River Rats,* p. 46.
Bookwatch, June, 1994, review of *A College of Magics,* p. 11.
Bulletin of the Center for Children's Books, review of *River Rats,* p. 306.
Children's Book Review Service, July, 1992, review of *River Rats,* p. 156.
English Journal, January, 1993, John H. Bushman and Kay Parks Bushman, review of *River Rats,* p. 80.
Horn Book, September-October, 1992, Ann A. Flowers, review of *River Rats,* p. 589.
Horn Book Guide, fall, 1992, review of *River Rats,* p. 271.
Journal of Reading, September, 1993, review of *River Rats,* p. 72.
Kirkus Reviews, May 1, 1992, review of *River Rats,* p. 617; February 1, 1994, review of *A College of Magics,* p. 104; October 1, 2000, review of *When the King Comes Home,* p. 1394.
Kliatt, January, 1997, review of *River Rats,* p. 16.
Library Journal, November 15, 2000, Jackie Cassada, review of *When the King Comes Home,* p. 101.
Locus, April, 1994, review of *A College of Magics,* p. 50; February, 1995, review of *A College of Magics,* p. 39.
Magazine of Fantasy and Science Fiction, August, 1994, Charles de Lint, review of *A College of Magics,* pp. 29-30.
Publishers Weekly, March 16, 1992, review of *River Rats,* p. 81; February 14, 1994, review of *A College of Magics,* p. 84.
School Library Journal, August, 1992, Jack Forman, review of *River Rats,* p. 178; August, 1998, review of *River Rats,* p. 51.
Voice of Youth Advocates, June, 1992, review of *River Rats,* p. 115; August, 1994, review of *A College of Magics,* p. 160; April, 1998, review of *River Rats,* p. 42.
Washington Post Book World, February 27, 1994, review of *A College of Magics,* p. 11.

Wilson Library Bulletin, December, 1992, Gene La-Faille, review of *River Rats,* pp. 94-95; October, 1994, Fred Lerner, a review of *A College of Magics,* pp. 96-97.*

*   *   *

SULLIVAN, Walter (Laurence) 1924-

PERSONAL: Born January 4, 1924, in Nashville, TN; son of Walter Laurence and Aline (Armstrong) Sullivan; married Jane Harrison (a college teacher), August 30, 1947; children: Pamela Holmes (Mrs. James Gordon Chenery), Walter Laurence, Jr., John Harrison. *Ethnicity:* "Caucasian." *Education:* Vanderbilt University, B.A., 1947; University of Iowa, M.F.A., 1949. *Politics:* Independent. *Religion:* Roman Catholic.

ADDRESSES: Home—6104 Chickering Ct., Nashville, TN 37215. *Agent*—Emilie Jacobson, Curtis Brown, Ltd., 10 Astor Pl., New York, NY 10003. *E-mail*—sullivwl@ctrvax.vanderbilt.edu.

CAREER: Vanderbilt University, Nashville, TN, instructor, 1949-52, assistant professor, 1952-57, associate professor, 1957-63, professor of fiction writing and of modern British and American literature, 1963-2001. *Military service:* U.S. Marine Corps, 1943-46; became first lieutenant.

MEMBER: Fellowship of Southern Writers (vice chancellor, 1997-2001; chancellor, 2001—), University Club of Nashville.

AWARDS, HONORS: Literary Achievement Award, Southern Heritage Society, 1996, for *The War the Women Lived.*

WRITINGS:

Sojourn of a Stranger (novel), Holt, 1957.
The Long, Long Love (novel), Holt, 1959, reprinted in "Voices of the South" series, Louisiana State University Press, 2000.
Death by Melancholy (criticism), Louisiana State University Press, 1972.
A Requiem for the Renascence (criticism), University of Georgia Press, 1976.

(Editor, with William Havard) *A Band of Prophets* (criticism), Louisiana State University Press, 1982.
(With George Core) *Writing from the Inside* (textbook), Norton, 1983.
Allen Tate: A Recollection (memoir), Louisiana State University Press, 1988.
In Praise of Blood Sports (criticism), Louisiana State University Press, 1990.
A Time to Dance (novel), Louisiana State University Press, 1995.
The War the Women Lived (anthology of Civil War women's writings), J. S. Sanders, 1996.

Contributor of short stories and articles to literary journals.

WORK IN PROGRESS: The Penalty of Love, a book of short stories; *Confessions of an Old New Critic,* essays.

SIDELIGHTS: Walter Sullivan once told *CA:* "I began my career as a writer when the southern literary renascence was coming to a close, although we did not know at that time—the late 1950's—how soon the end of the renascence would come. The South was changing and southern attitudes were changing and the unified, although flawed, culture that had supported the renascence was becoming fragmented as the population of the South became less homogeneous. Among most southerners, social attitudes were also being redefined, and much of the tension that had informed the best work of the renascence—often based on the relationships that grew out of racial differences—were no longer available in the ways that they once had been. And there was the 'lion in the path,' [William] Faulkner, who had done so much so well that he intimidated us all.

"After my first two traditional southern novels were published, I experimented with various approaches to writing about the New South, none of which was successful. During that period, I mostly published criticism along with a short story now and then. In the seventies, I became interested in writing about characters who were Catholic and lived in a Catholic world. I knew that doing this was not likely to make me rich or famous, but like most poor souls who follow the literary trade, writing was not something I consciously chose to do. I was called to it, driven to it, obliged to do it—to do it as best I could and perhaps write something that people who were able to recognize good writing would consider good. I must be very careful to emphasize that the work I'm doing is not meant to proselytize, and the characters are not saintly characters. But I see two advantages to writing about Catholics. One is the possibility for bringing into the work a sense of the transcendent. I don't mean the miraculous, just the sense that Catholics have of a spiritual dimension of reality. Another advantage is that Catholics constitute a sub-culture that has established rules by which the characters know they should live. That most of them don't live by the rules is a source of dramatic and thematic tension in the fiction. My concept of fiction remains fairly traditional. I think nothing is as important as characterization: the great fiction writers of every time and place were all good at it. I am against allowing plot rather than character to drive a story.

"When I was young, I wrote at night. Now, I write in the morning, for about two hours, and then I'm through. But like most writers, the process goes on after you've left your computer. You continue to think about the work at hand."

Earlier Sullivan had told *CA* "that ours is a very bad age for art in general and for the creation of literature in particular." Because of this, Sullivan currently spends more time "trying to explain the age and the artist's relationship to it" than writing fiction. He is, however, "writing longish short stories which appear in literary quarterlies." Someday, he hopes to devote all of his time to writing fiction. Sullivan says, "I brood a lot, which may be, for me at least, the most essential step in the act of writing."

*   *   *

SWIFT, Augustus
    See LOVECRAFT, H(oward) P(hillips)

T-V

THEOBALD, Lewis, Jr.
See LOVECRAFT, H(oward) P(hillips)

*   *   *

TOWSE, Ruth 1943-

PERSONAL: Born August 4, 1943, in Lancashire, England; married Mark Blaug; children: Tristan Blaug. *Education:* University of Reading, B.A. (with honors), 1964; London School of Economics and Political Science, M.Sc.Econ., 1966; Erasmus University, Rotterdam, Netherlands, Ph.D., 2002. *Politics:* "Middle of the road." *Religion:* "Atheist."

ADDRESSES: Office—L2-025, Erasmus University Rotterdam, P.O. Box 1738, NL-3000 DR Rotterdam, Netherlands. *E-mail*—towse@fhk.eur.nl.

CAREER: University of Exeter, Exeter, England, lecturer in economics, 1990-99; Erasmus University Rotterdam, Rotterdam, Netherlands, senior lecturer in cultural industries, 1999—.

WRITINGS:

(Editor, with Abdul Khakee; and contributor) *Cultural Economics,* Springer (Heidelberg, Germany), 1992.
Singers in the Marketplace: The Economics of the Singing Profession, Oxford University Press (New York, NY), 1993.
Economics of Culture: Arts, Heritage, and the Media Industries, Edward Elgar (Cheltenham, England), 1997.
(Editor) *Baumol's Cost Disease: The Arts and Other Victims,* Edward Elgar (Cheltenham, England), 1997.
(Editor and contributor) *Cultural Economics: The Arts, the Heritage, and the Media Industries* (two volumes), Edward Elgar (Cheltenham, England), 1997.
Creativity, Incentive, and Reward: An Economic Analysis of Copyright and Culture in the Information Age, Edward Elgar (Cheltenham, England), 2001.

Contributor to books, including *Cultural Economics and Cultural Policies,* edited by A. Peacock and I. Rizzo, Kluwer (Boston, MA), 1994; *Cultural Economics and Cultural Value,* edited by A. Klamer, University of Michigan Press (Ann Arbor, MI), 1996; *Economics of the Arts: Essays,* edited by V. Ginsburg and P. M. Menger, [Amsterdam, Netherlands], 1996; *Innovation, Incentive, and Reward: Intellectual Property Law and Policy,* edited by H. Macqueen and B. Main, Edinburgh University Press, 1997; *Economics of Artists and Arts Policy,* edited by M. Heikkinen and T. Koskinen, Arts Council of Finland (Helsinki, Finland), 1998; *Dal vinile a Internet,* edited by G. Ramello and F. Silva, Fondazione Giovanni Agnelli (Torino, Italy), 1999. Also, contributor of articles and book reviews to various periodicals, including *Copyright Reporter, Cultural Economics* (Journal of the Japan ACE), *Cultural Policy, Economic Journal, International Journal of Arts Management, Journal of Cultural Economics, KYKLOS,* and *Society and Economy in Central and Eastern Europe.*

SIDELIGHTS: Ruth Towse once told *CA:* "I believe that economics is a useful tool for understanding how things work. I am less interested in economics in the abstract than when it is applied. Cultural economics is a fascinating field, testing our understanding of economics and extending our knowledge about the arts as an economic activity."

* * *

TREAHEARNE, Elizabeth
    See MAXWELL, Patricia

* * *

TURNER, Henry Ashby, Jr. 1932-

PERSONAL: Born April 4, 1932, in Atlanta, GA; son of Henry Ashby (in sales) and Katherine (a secretary; maiden name, Bradley) Turner; married Jane Swanger (a consultant), June 14, 1958; children: Bradley, Sarah, Matthew. *Ethnicity:* "Caucasian." *Education:* Washington and Lee University, B.A., 1954; attended University of Munich, 1954-55, and Free University of Berlin, 1955; Princeton University, M.A., 1957, Ph.D., 1960.

ADDRESSES: Home—468 Whitney Ave., New Haven, CT 06511. *Office*—Department of History, Yale University, P.O. Box 208324, New Haven, CT 06520. *Agent*—Writers' Representatives, Inc., 116 West 14th St., New York, NY 10011-7305. *E-mail*—henry.turner@yale.edu.

CAREER: Yale University, New Haven, CT, Stille Professor of History, 1958—.

AWARDS, HONORS: Honorary D.Litt, Washington and Lee University, 1978; Commander's Cross, Order of Merit, Federal Republic of Germany, 1989.

WRITINGS:

Stresemann and the Politics of the Weimar Republic, Princeton University Press (Princeton, NJ), 1963.
Faschismus und Kapitalismus in Deutschland, Vandenhoeck & Ruprecht (Göttingen, Germany), 1972.
German Big Business and the Rise of Hitler, Oxford University Press (New York, NY), 1985.
The Two Germanies since 1945, Yale University Press (New Haven, CT), 1987.
Geissel des Jahrhunderts, Siedler Verlag (Berlin, Germany), 1989.
Hitler's Thirty Days to Power, Addison-Wesley (Reading, MA), 1996.

Contributor to various publications, including *History and Theory, New York Times Book Review,* and *Journal of Interdisciplinary History.**

* * *

URBAN, William L(awrence) 1939-

PERSONAL: Born December 31, 1939, in Monroe, LA; married March 28, 1965; children: Ilsabe, Elke, Karl. *Education:* Attended Baylor University, 1957-59; University of Texas at Austin, B.A., 1961, M.A., 1963, Ph.D., 1967; also attended University of Hamburg, 1964-65, Jagiellonian University, Cracow, 1973, Brown University, 1977, University of Illinois, 1978, University of North Carolina at Chapel Hill, 1981, and U.S. Military Academy, 1985. *Religion:* Society of Friends (Quaker).

ADDRESSES: Home—1062 East Second St., Monmouth, IL 61462. *Office*—Department of History, Monmouth College, Monmouth, IL 61462; fax: 309-457-2310. *E-mail*—urban.monm.edu.

CAREER: University of Kansas, Lawrence, assistant professor of history, 1965-66; Monmouth College, Monmouth, IL, assistant professor, 1966-71, associate professor, 1971-78, professor of history, 1978—, Lee L. Morgan Professor of History and International Studies. Visiting professor at Fort Hays Kansas State College, 1971, and at Knox College, 1971-72. Director of program in Florence, Italy, Associated Colleges of the Midwest, 1974-75; director of translation project, National Endowment for the Humanities, 1978-79; on sabbatical at J. G. Herder Institut, 1979 and 1983. Coach of varsity soccer team at Monmouth College, 1969-81; Associated Colleges of the Midwest, director of programs in Yugoslavia, 1986, and the Czech Republic, 1994; Eastern Michigan University Cultural Studies programs in Europe, summers of 1998-2000.

MEMBER: American Historical Association, Association for the Advancement of Baltic Studies, Kommission für ost und westpreussische Landeskunde (corresponding member), Baltische Historische Kommission (corresponding member).

AWARDS, HONORS: Fulbright grants, 1964-65 and 1975-76; citation, Zeta Beta Tau, 1972; outstanding educator award, 1975; National Endowment for the Humanities grants, 1977 and 1981-85; University of Chicago faculty fellow, 1978 and 1982-83; Dr. Arthur Puksow Foundation award for original research publication, 1983; Deutsche Akademische Austauschdient grant, 1983; Burlington Northern award for outstanding teaching, 1985.

WRITINGS:

Juvenal-Juvinall-Juvenile: A Family History, Interstate, 1972.

The Baltic Crusade, Northern Illinois University Press, 1975, revised and enlarged edition, Lithuanian Research and Studies Center (Chicago, IL), 1994.

(Translator, with Jerry Smith) *The Livonian Rhymed Chronicle,* University of Illinois Press, 1977.

The Prussian Crusade, University Press of America, 1980, 2nd edition, revised and enlarged, Lithuanian Research and Studies Center (Chicago, IL), 2000.

The Livonian Crusade, University Press of America, 1981.

The Samogitian Crusade, Lithuanian Research and Studies Center (Chicago, IL), 1989.

Dithmarschen: A Medieval Peasant Republic, Edwin Mellen Press (Lewiston, NY), 1991.

(Editor, with Eberhard Demm and Roger Noel) *The Independence of the Baltic States: Origins, Causes, and Consequences: A Comparison of the Crucial Years 1918-1919 and 1990-1991,* Lithuanian Research and Studies Center (Chicago, IL), 1996.

(Translator, with Jerry C. Smith and J. Ward Jones) *Johannes Renner's Livonian History 1556-1561,* Edwin Mellen Press (Lewiston, NY), 1997.

(Translator, with Jerry C. Smith and J. Ward Jones) *Johannes Renner's Chronicle,* Edwin Mellen Press (Lewiston, NY), 1997.

Tannenberg and After, Lithuanian Research and Studies Center (Chicago, IL), 1999.

Also author of *Narcissus and the Faceless Man;* and, with Mary Crow and Charles Speel, of *A History of Monmouth College through Its Fifth Quarter-Century;* translator, with Jerry C. Smith, of *The Chronicle of Balthasar Russow.* Contributor to periodicals, including *Speculum, Frontier Times, Kansas Historical Quarterly, Educational Record, Chaucer Review,* and *Journal of Baltic Studies.*

WORK IN PROGRESS: Revised and enlarged second edition of *The Livonian Crusade;* with Jerry C. Smith, revised second edition of *The Livonian Rhymed Chronicle.*

SIDELIGHTS: William L. Urban told CA: "The rapid advances in technology have modified greatly the ways that I write. Once I did as taught in graduate school, amassing piles of note cards, cross-referencing them, stacking them next to the typewriter, and then beginning to write. About 1970, however, a friend in computer science said, 'someone in humanities has to learn how to use the computer, and you're it.' We had one keyboard, which I could use between 6 and 7 AM. It wasn't much more than a punchcard system, but loading proper tapes onto the machine was an impressively complex operation. I instructed a few students in the system, getting two interesting papers on local land sales at the time of settlement (1819-1830). But it wasn't until the early 1980s that I could require all students in my classes to write their papers on the computer, and not until the mid-1990s that I could require all of them to submit papers via e-mail.

"My own writing reflected these limitations. I published two books in 1980-1981 on what was state of the art desk publishing. In retrospect, these look very primitive. Even more primitive, though less noticeable—this technology hardly affected the way I wrote. That would come later. With the widespread availability of affordable xerox and highlighters, why write out the laborious notes? With more computer space, why wait until all the notes are complete before trying out a first draft?

"I would not recommend this to everyone. There are good reasons for doing the research before the writing. However, at a certain point in one's career, one should have acquired a feel for the direction any project will take. It is so easy to move material around, to revise, to cut, to add footnotes or delete them, that an experienced scholar should not hesitate to sit down and write out an initial narrative at one sitting, then work on the nuances and corrections later.

"Longer narratives present an intellectual challenge that resembles assembling puzzles. Long ago I played moderately good chess. I might have played better had I not sensed what Castiglione wrote in the sixteenth century, that a gentleman should know how to play, but that learning to play well required much time and effort; and in the end, what has one acquired but the ability to play a game? Still, that game (and bridge) help develop important mental skills. (I have argued that deans should be required to demonstrate some acquaintance with one game or the other, so that we can be certain they can plan more than one step in advance).

"In the end, however, the way words go onto the page is a mystery. I look back at a passage and wonder, 'how did that ever get there?' One has to believe in the existence of a muse. This belief becomes reinforced at the distance of the year or two between the completion of a manuscript and the appearance of a book or article. The product appears so strange and unfamiliar, that surely someone else must have written it. Perhaps the muse inside the machine."

* * *

Van der KISTE, John (Patrick Guy) 1954-

PERSONAL: Born September 15, 1954, in Wendover, Buckinghamshire, England; son of Guy (a wing commander in Royal Air Force) and Nancy (a homemaker; maiden name, Holman) Van der Kiste. *Education:* Attended Ealing Technical College (London), 1974-76. *Politics:* "Never." *Religion:* Church of England. *Avocational interests:* Reading, popular music, philately, numismatics, painting, visiting art galleries, cats, walking.

ADDRESSES: Office—c/o Sutton Publishing, Phoenix Mill, Far Thrupp, Stroud, Gloucestershire GL5 2BU, England.

CAREER: Devon Library Services, Plymouth, Devon, England, library assistant, 1972-77; Land Registry, Plymouth, clerical assistant, 1977-78; College of Further Education, Plymouth, library assistant, 1978—.

MEMBER: British Academy of Songwriters, Composers and Authors, Performing Right Society, Library Association.

AWARDS, HONORS: Named associate of the Library Association, 1983.

WRITINGS:

Frederick III: German Emperor, 1888 (biography), Sutton (Gloucestershire, England), 1981.
Roxeventies: Popular Music in Britain, 1970-79, Kawabata (Torpoint, England), 1982.
Queen Victoria's Family: A Select Bibliography, Clover (Biggleswade, England), 1982.
(With Bee Jordaan) *Dearest Affie: Alfred, Duke of Edinburgh, Queen Victoria's Second Son, 1844-1900* (biography), Sutton (Gloucestershire, England), 1984.
The Roy Wood Story (biography), A & F (Devon, England), 1986.

Singles File: The Story of the 45 R.P.M. Record (music), A & F (Devon, England), 1987.
Queen Victoria's Children (biography), Sutton (Gloucestershire, England), 1987.
Windsor and Habsburg: The British and Austrian Reigning Houses, 1848-1922 (history/biography), Sutton (Wolfeboro Falls, NH), 1987.
Edward VII's Children (biography), Sutton (Gloucestershire, England), 1989.
(With Derek Wadeson) *Beyond the Summertime: The Mungo Jerry Story* (biography), A & F (Devon, England), 1990.
Princess Victoria Melita: Grand Duchess Cyril of Russia, 1876-1936 (biography), Sutton (Gloucestershire, England), 1991.
George V's Children (biography), Sutton (Gloucestershire, England), 1991.
George III's Children (biography), Sutton (Gloucestershire, England), 1992.
Crowns in a Changing World: The British and European Monarchies, 1901-36 (history), Sutton (Gloucestershire, England), 1993.
Kings of the Hellenes: The Greek Kings, 1863-1974, Sutton (Gloucestershire, England), 1994.
Childhood at Court, 1819-1914 (biography), Sutton (Gloucestershire, England), 1995.
Northern Crowns: Kings of Modern Scandinavia (biography), Sutton (Gloucestershire, England), 1996.
King George II and Queen Caroline (biography), Sutton (Gloucestershire, England), 1997.
The Romanovs, 1818-1959: Alexander II of Russia and His Family (biography), Sutton (Gloucestershire, England), 1998.
Kaiser Wilholm II: Germany's Last Emperor (biography), Sutton (Gloucestershire, England), 1999.
The Georgian Princesses (biography), Sutton (Gloucestershire, England), 2000.
(Compiler) *Gilbert & Sullivan's Christmas* (anthology), Sutton (Gloucestershire, England), 2000.
The Man on the Moor (fiction), Netspace (e-publisher), 2000.

Editor of *Stamp Out* (Ealing Technical College School of Librarianship journal), 1974-76, and *County Magazines Index,* 1978-80; editor and publisher of *Keep on Rockin',* 1991-96. Contributor to *New Dictionary of National Biography,* Oxford University Press, Guinness Rockopedia, and Guinness PLC. Author of weekly records review column in South Hams (Devonshire) newspapers, 1977—, and book review column, 1998—. Contributor of articles to periodicals, including *Illustrated London News, Devon Life, Hampshire County*

Magazine, Cambridgeshire Life, Buckinghamshire Countryside, Gibbons Stamp Monthly, Record Collector, Royalty Digest, European Royal History Journal, and *Antique Collector.*

WORK IN PROGRESS: Emperor and Empress Frederick (working title), a biography to be published by Sutton in 2001.

SIDELIGHTS: John Van der Kiste told *CA* that he has been "fascinated by the Victorian Royal family since childhood and was keen on filling in the gaps of the much-neglected characters." As a result, he has issued several biographies of British and European royal families from the eighteenth century onwards, focusing especially on the children, among them a son and a granddaughter of Queen Victoria. *Dearest Affie: Alfred, Duke of Edinburgh, Queen Victoria's Second Son, 1844-1900* (written with Bee Jordaan) and *Princess Victoria Melita: Grand Duchess Cyril of Russia, 1876-1936,* depict the lives of the Queen's son, known as Affie, and of his daughter, Victoria Melita, who married a Russian first cousin to become Grand Duchess of Russia in 1909.

According to Van der Kiste's accounts, both the Duke of Edinburgh and Princess Victoria once enjoyed the pleasures afforded them by their positions, but endured numerous misfortunes in the last years of their lives. The duke, for example, inherited the Saxe-Coburg and Gotha dukedoms, but had no real power, essentially living as a landlord in the region. His only son died apparently by suicide, the duke was separated from his wife, and he finally died a painful death from throat cancer. Van der Kiste portrays Affie's daughter, Victoria, as an undisciplined princess, prone to neglecting her royal duties while married to the Grand Duke of Hesse. Their marriage ended when she fell in love with her Russian cousin, the Grand Duke Cyril. Eventually they married and Victoria became a Russian grand duchess, a position in which she thrived. Her happiness was short-lived, however, as she and her family were forced to flee St. Petersburg in 1917 with only the belongings they could carry. She lived the remainder of her life in poverty. "Van der Kiste tells the sad story conscientiously and readably," wrote Steven Runciman in *Times Literary Supplement,* although the critic found the author "a little indulgent towards his heroine. She must have been a difficult and selfish woman; but her later misfortunes were not of her making, and she bore them with dignity and courage."

Van der Kiste's interest in the lives of royal children is also evident in the volumes *Edward VII's Children* and *George III's Children,* in which he examines the lives

of royal offspring. In a critique of the latter book, a *Times Literary Supplement* reviewer commended Van der Kiste for presenting the biographies of princes and princesses chronologically rather than separately, so that the siblings' interactions are revealed, and found the book "informative and pleasantly written." *Edward VII's Children* earned praise from London *Times* reviewer Hugo Vickers, who wrote: "The more-or-less forgotten children of Edward VII make an excellent study for a composite biography, a subject most adroitly handled by John Van der Kiste."

Van der Kiste commented: "I was inspired to write *Dearest Affie* by the duke's Devonport connections, and the book began as a short article published in *Devon Life* in 1977. I was put in touch with my coauthor, Bee Jordaan (1915-90) as a result of an inquiry to John A. S. Phillips of the Prince Albert Society.

"Writing on musical topics (*Roxeventies: Popular Music in Britain, 1970-79,* biographies of Roy Wood and Mungo Jerry, record reviews, etc.) and booklet notes for CDs by artists including ELO, The Move, and London, reflects my regular spare-time music activities, such as working as a resident disc-jockey in clubs, writing songs, performing as a singer and guitarist in rock groups and as a solo performer, and writing the songs for a children's musical, *Looking for the Raingod,* which had its first public performance in 2000. My love of Dartmoor, south Devon, where I have lived since childhood, was reflected in my first novel, *The Man on the Moor,* a historical thriller set in 1913 on the eve of the Great War."

BIOGRAPHICAL/CRITICAL SOURCES:

PERIODICALS

Times (London), July 8, 1989.
Times Literary Supplement, February 1, 1985, p. 117; September 27, 1991, p. 5; January 15, 1993, p. 29.

*   *   *

VANZANT, Iyanla (Rhonda) 1952-

PERSONAL: First name is pronounced "ee-yon-la"; born September 13, 1952, in Brooklyn, NY; daughter of Horace Lester and Sarah (Jefferson) Harris; married Charles Vanzant, Jr. (died January, 1984); married Adeyemi Bandele, May, 1966; children: Damon Keith;

Iyanla Vanzant

(first marriage) Gemmia Lynnette; (second marriage) Nisa Camille. *Education:* Medgar Evers College, B.S. (summa cum laude), 1983; Queens College of the City University of New York, J.D., 1988; doctoral studies at Temple University. *Religion:* "Ordained as a Yoruba priestess in 1983." *Avocational interests:* Gourmet cooking, astrology, herbalism, metaphysical healing practices, sewing.

ADDRESSES: Office—Inner Visions Worldwide Network, Inc., 926 Philadelphia Ave., Silver Spring, MD 20910. *Agent*—Marie Brown Associates, 625 Broadway, New York, NY 10012.

CAREER: Federation of Addiction Agencies, Brooklyn, NY, drug rehabilitation counselor, 1972-79; Medgar Evers College, Brooklyn, NY, director of Alumni Affairs, 1983-85; Philadelphia Public Defender's Association, Philadelphia, PA, attorney, 1988-90; Inner Visions Spiritual Life Maintenance, Philadelphia, PA, founder; Inner Visions Institute for Spiritual Development, Silver Spring, MD, founder; ordained gospel minister, 1997. Talk show host, *Just between Us,* WHAT, Philadelphia, PA. Medgar Evers College Center for Women's Development, founding member; African Street Festival, board member, 1988—.

MEMBER: Association of Black Journalists, African Women's Sisterhood (Philadelphia branch), National Black Women's Health Project.

AWARDS, HONORS: Outstanding community service award, Brownsville Community Development Corporation, 1984; Oni (unsung hero) award, International Congress of Black Women, 1991; Alumni of the Year award, National Association for Equal Opportunity in Education, 1994; Blackboard Book of the Year, 1994, 1995, 1996; Excelle award, London, for best nonfiction.

WRITINGS:

Crowning Glory, Aaron Press, 1989.
Tapping the Power Within: A Path to Self-Empowerment for Black Women, Writers and Readers (New York, NY), 1992.
Acts of Faith: Daily Meditations for People of Color, Fireside (New York, NY), 1993, published as *Faith in the Valley: Lessons for Women on the Journey to Peace,* Simon & Schuster (New York, NY), 1996.
The Value in the Valley: A Black Woman's Guide through Life's Dilemmas, Simon & Schuster (New York, NY), 1995.
Interiors: A Black Woman's Healing in Progress (memoir), Writers and Readers (New York, NY), 1995.
The Spirit of a Man: A Vision of Transformation for Black Men and the Women Who Love Them, HarperSan Francisco (San Francisco, CA), 1996.
The Big Book of Faith, Simon & Schuster (New York, NY), 1997.
In the Meantime: Finding Yourself and the Love That You Want, Simon & Schuster (New York, NY), 1998.
Yesterday, I Cried: Celebrating the Lessons of Living and Loving (memoir), Simon & Schuster (New York, NY), 1999.
One Day My Soul Just Opened Up: 40 Days and 40 Nights toward Spiritual Strength and Personal Growth, Fireside Books, 1998.
Don't Give It Away!, Fireside (New York, NY), 1999.
Until Today!: Daily Devotions for Spiritual Growth and Peace of Mind, Simon & Schuster (New York, NY), 2000.
Every Day I Pray: Awakening to the Grace of Inner Communion, Simon & Schuster (New York, NY), 2001.
Living through the Meantime: Learning to Break the Patterns of the Past and Begin the Healing Process, Fireside (New York, NY), 2001.

(Author of introduction) *Best Black Women's Erotica* ("Best Black Women's Erotica" series), Cleis Press, 2001.

OTHER

Iyanla Live! (audio series), Simon & Schuster, 2000—, includes *Commitment, Faith, Love, Self-Value, Self Worth, Self-Love, Our Relationship with the World,* and *Our Relationship with Money.*

Contributor to periodicals, including *Essence* and *Health Quest.*

ADAPTATIONS: Books adapted as sound recordings by Simon & Schuster Audio include *Acts of Faith: Daily Meditations for People of Color,* 1996; *In the Meantime: Finding Yourself and the Love That You Want,* 1998; *The Value in the Valley: A Black Woman's Guide through Life's Dilemmas,* 1999; and *Yesterday I Cried: Celebrating the Lessons of Living and Loving,* 1999.

SIDELIGHTS: Iyanla Vanzant is the author of popular self-help books that offer spiritual advice to her followers and fans. She conducts workshops and has appeared on radio and television, including frequent guest appearances on the *Oprah Winfrey Show.* Vanzant is also a priestess of the Yoruba religion, which blends African spirituality with black American culture. Her adopted name, Iyanla, means "great mother."

Vanzant had a troubled childhood and adolescence. She was born in the back of a taxi to a mother who died when Vanzant was two years old. Vanzant, whose birth name is Rhonda Harris, lived with her paternal grandmother, then with her father and stepmother, and later with family friends, one of whom raped her when she was nine. Vanzant was pregnant by age sixteen and had three children by age twenty-one. She married when she was eighteen and suffered serious physical injuries at the hands of her abusive husband; Vanzant eventually fled with her three children. Depressed and destitute, she attempted suicide. After being treated in a psychiatric hospital, Vanzant was released and went on welfare. She eventually attended Medgar Evers College and graduated summa cum laude with a bachelor's degree in public administration. She went on to earn a law degree and worked as a criminal-defense attorney in the office of a public defender for three years, but she then chose a different path, one that would help provide

spiritual guidance to others. She began hosting a radio program, *Just between Us,* on WHAT-AM in Philadelphia, and started a successful career as an author.

Vanzant had faced racism and sexism, and she drew on her own experiences and beliefs in writing *Tapping the Power Within: A Path to Self-Empowerment for Black Women, Acts of Faith: Daily Meditations for People of Color,* her most popular volume, and *The Value in the Valley: A Black Woman's Guide through Life's Dilemmas.* Vanzant's first memoir, *Interiors: A Black Woman's Healing in Progress,* was part of a two-book deal with the Harlem-based publisher Writers and Readers, which had published *Tapping the Power Within.* A *Contemporary Black Biography* contributor wrote that Writers and Readers "took a first-time author and 'put her on the map,' when they published *Tapping the Power Within . . .* at a time when few inspirational works were marked specifically to African Americans."

Vanzant's books are primarily directed at women, but in *The Spirit of a Man: A Vision of Transformation for Black Men and the Women Who Love Them,* she turns her attention to men. Lillian Lewis wrote in *Booklist* that in *The Spirit of a Man,* Vanzant "succeeds in probing the many issues that confront black men in this society."

In the Meantime: Finding Yourself and the Love That You Want is Vanzant's prescription for love, first of oneself, then of another. She offers her advice for happiness to all women, and the "meantime" of the title is that period between seeking and actually finding love. A *Publishers Weekly* contributor wrote that Vanzant "offers useful, though hardly original, advice." Lewis said Vanzant's tips "are well worth following."

Yesterday, I Cried: Celebrating the Lessons of Living and Loving is Vanzant's account of how she overcame the difficulties of her past and achieved success, and in *One Day My Soul Just Opened Up: 40 Days and 40 Nights toward Spiritual Strength and Personal Growth,* she writes of her personal and spiritual growth. *Until Today!: Devotions for Spiritual Growth and Peace of Mind* is Vanzant's collection of daily affirmations, called "a truly inspirational read—perfect no matter where you start the book," by Imani Q'ryn in *Black Issues Book Review.* Vanzant's workshops conducted at the Apollo Theatre and the Aaron Davis Hall, both in New York City, are available on cassette in her *Iyanla Live!* series.

Vanzant lives with her husband, Adeyemi Bandele, and other family members in Maryland. At her Inner Visions Institute for Spiritual Development in Silver

Spring, she trains what she calls "life coaches," people who will go on to mentor others in spiritual principles. Thomas Bradley, former mayor of Los Angeles, once called Vanzant "an inspiration to all women, particularly young African American women growing through hardships in the inner city." Diane Weathers wrote in *Essence* that "if life is a series of lessons, Vanzant has earned a Ph.D. in triumphing over adversity."

Vanzant told *CA:* "My writing is dedicated to the evolution and empowerment of women throughout the world, particularly women of color. It is dedicated to my stepmother and best friend Lynnette Harris, who saved me from myself and loved me in spite of myself. It is the legacy I want to leave my grandchildren Oluwa and Asole."

BIOGRAPHICAL/CRITICAL SOURCES:

BOOKS

Contemporary Black Biography, Volume 17, Gale (Detroit, MI), 1998.

Vanzant, Iyanla, *Interiors: A Black Woman's Healing in Progress* (memoir), Writers & Readers (New York, NY), 1995.

Vanzant, Iyanla, *Yesterday, I Cried: Celebrating the Lessons of Living and Loving* (memoir), Simon & Schuster (New York, NY), 1999.

PERIODICALS

Black Enterprise, April, 1998, Robyn D. Clarke, "Five Great Business Motivators," p. 83; June, 1998, review of *Acts of Faith: Daily Meditations for People of Color,* p. 324.

Black Issues Book Review, November, 1999, review of *Don't Give It Away!,* p. 71; March, 2001, Imani Q'ryn, review of *Until Today!: Devotions for Spiritual Growth and Peace of Mind,* p. 68.

Booklist, June 1, 1996, Lillian Lewis, review of *The Spirit of a Man: A Vision of Transformation for Black Men and the Women Who Love Them,* p. 1650; February 15, 1998, Lillian Lewis, review of *In the Meantime: Finding Yourself and the Love That You Want,* p. 951.

Ebony, October, 1998, Kelly Starling, "New Directions in Black Spirituality," p. 92.

Entertainment Weekly, March 19, 1999, Lori L. Tharpes, "High Priestess: Best-Selling Author Iyanla Vanzant Has Been Championed by Oprah and Embraced by Fans," p. 96.

Essence, July, 1996, Diane Weathers, "At Home with Iyanla Vanzant," p. 104; March, 1997, Lise Funderburg, "Can Men and Women Share a Spiritual Life?" (interview), p. 62; July, 1997, Iyanla Vanzant and others, "The Love You Need: Keep the Faith," p. 65; January, 2000, Joy Duckett Cain, "Iyanla's Gift," p. 78.

Jet, September 22, 1997, "Why Do Women Tolerate Domestic Violence?," p. 14.

Library Journal, May 1, 1995, Carolyn M. Craft, review of *The Value in the Valley: A Black Woman's Guide through Life's Dilemma,* p. 120; September 1, 1999, Beth Farrell, review of *One Day My Soul Just Opened Up: 40 Days and 40 Nights toward Spiritual Strength and Personal Growth,* p. 255.

Los Angeles Times Book Review, April 2, 1995, review of *Acts of Faith: Daily Meditations for People of Color,* p. 11.

People Weekly, April 20, 1998, Jane Sims Podesta and Larry Hackett, "Now Hear This: Author Iyanla Vanzant's Commanding Inner Voice Leads Her to Self-Help Stardom," p. 83.

Publishers Weekly, January 29, 1996, Calvin Reid, "Black Author, Black Publisher in Contract Dispute," p. 16; November 10, 1997, review of *In the Meantime: Finding Yourself and the Love That You Want,* p. 62.*

W-Z

WADDINGTON, Patrick (Haynes) 1934-
(Isobel Garnett, W. P. Haynes, Alexander Marsden)

PERSONAL: Born June 28, 1934, in Barnehurst, Kent, England; son of Reginald Herbert (a sales manager) and Edith Lilian (a teacher) Waddington; divorced; children: Marian, Emma, Claire. *Education:* Queens' College, Cambridge, B.A. (with honors), 1956, M.A., 1960; University of Exeter, Certificate in Education, 1958; University of Belfast, Ph.D., 1972. *Politics:* "Sensible." *Religion:* "None, of course." *Avocational interests:* "Pottering about, reading poetry, drinking red wine, singing along with Bach, being kind to donkeys."

ADDRESSES: Home—57 Elmslie Rd., Pinehaven, Upper Hutt, New Zealand.

CAREER: Assistant teacher of English at secondary schools in Lausanne, Switzerland, 1956-57; teacher at a primary school in Kent, England, 1957, and a secondary school in Dorset, England, 1958; Stamford School, in Lincolnshire, England, teacher of English, Latin, and general studies and master in charge of Russian and advanced French, 1958-63; Queen's University, Belfast, Northern Ireland, began as lecturer, became senior lecturer in modern languages and Slavonic studies, 1963-73; Victoria University of Wellington, Wellington, New Zealand, visiting professor, 1973, professor of Russian literature and civilization, 1974-93, professor emeritus, 1993—, department head, 1974-91. University of Victoria, Canada, Lansdown visitor, 1983; University of Queensland, chair for review of the Russian department, 1986; Cambridge University, visiting fellow at Wolfson College, 1991-92; Armstrong Browning Library (Texas), visiting fellow, 1991-92; lecturer at colleges and universities in New Zealand and abroad, including University of Maryland at College Park, Yale University, Cornell University, and Baylor University; broadcaster for British Broadcasting Corp., Australian Broadcasting Co., and Radio New Zealand. Copyright Licensing Ltd., director, 1990-95. Northern Ireland Board, chief examiner in Russian, 1963-66. Stamford Civic Trust, founding member, 1960-63; Belfast Russian Circle, founder and organizer, 1965-73; New Zealand Historic Places Trust, member, 1982—; New Zealand Book Council, member, 1989-90; New Zealand Copyright Council, member, 1989-95.

MEMBER: British Association of Slavonic and East European Studies, British Humanities Research Association, New Zealand PEN (member of executive committee, 1986-90; acting president, 1990).

AWARDS, HONORS: Leverhulme faculty fellow in European studies, Fontainebleau, France, 1972; British Council travel grants, 1986.

WRITINGS:

A Basic Russian-English Vocabulary, Methuen (London, England), 1962, Crowell (New York, NY), 1963.

(With David Buckley) *"O" Level Tests in Russian,* Methuen (London, England), 1963, revised edition, 1965.

(Editor) Mikhail Sholokhov, *Sud'ba cheloveka* (title means "Destiny of a Man"), Collet (London, England), 1964.

(Editor) A. P. Chekhov, *Dama s sobachkoy* (title means "The Lady with the Dog"), Bradda Books (Letchworth, England), 1964.

Russian by Subjects, Bradda Books (Letchworth, England), 1965, revised edition, Basil Blackwell (Oxford, England), 1989.

Advanced Translation from Russian Prose, Pergamon (New York, NY), 1965.

(Editor) Ivan Sergeyevich Turgenev, *Dvoryanskoye gnezdo* (title means "A Nest of the Gentry"), Pergamon (New York, NY), 1969.

(Editor) Ivan Sergeyevich Turgenev, *Rudin,* Bradda Books (Letchworth, England), 1970.

The Dodillon Copies of Letters by Turgenev to Pauline and Louis Viardot, privately printed (Belfast, Northern Ireland), 1970.

Turgenev and England, New York University Press (New York, NY), 1980.

Turgenev and George Sand: An Improbable Entente, Barnes & Noble (Totowa, NJ), 1981.

A First Russian Vocabulary, Basil Blackwell (New York, NY), 1988.

From "The Russian Fugitive" to "The Ballad of Bulgarie": Episodes in English Literary Attitudes to Russia from Wordsworth to Swinburne, Berg Publishers (Providence, RI), 1994.

(Editor and contributor) *Ivan Turgenev and Britain,* Berg Publishers (Providence, RI), 1994.

"Theirs but to Die and Die": The Poetry of the Charge of the Light Brigade at Balaklava, 25 October 1854, Astra Press (Nottingham, England), 1995.

(Editor) Ivan Sergeyevich Turgenev, *Fathers and Children,* Everyman (Vermont), 1998.

Russian Interests of the Rossetti Family: Gabriele Pasquale Giuseppe (1783-1854), Dante Gabriel (1828-82), Christina Georgina (1830-94), William Michael (1829-1919), Whirinaki Press (Pinehaven, New Zealand), 1998.

Turgenev and Pavlovsky: A Friendship and a Correspondence, Whirinaki Press (Pinehaven, New Zealand), 1998.

The Origins and Composition of Turgenev's Novel "Dym" (Smoke), Whirinaki Press (Pinehaven, New Zealand), 1998.

A Catalogue of Portraits of Ivan Sergeyevich Turgenev (1818-83), Whirinaki Press (Pinehaven, New Zealand), 1999.

Turgenev's Mortal Illness: From Its Origins to the Autopsy, Whirinaki Press (Pinehaven, New Zealand), 1999.

Author of short works on Turgenev and other authors. Contributor to books, including *Issues in Russian Literature before 1917,* edited by J. Douglas Clayton, Slavica (Columbus, OH), 1989; *From Pushkin to "Palisandriia": Essays on the Russian Novel in Honour of Richard Freeborn,* edited by Arnold McMillin, [London, England], 1990; and *Vsevolod Garshin at the Turn of the Century: An International Symposium in Three Volumes,* edited by Peter Henry, Vladimir Porudominsky, and Mikhail Girshman, Northgate Press (Oxford, England), 1999-2000; contributor to bibliographies and dictionaries. Contributor of more than 100 articles and reviews to scholarly journals and newspapers, including *Studies in Browning and His Circle: Journal of Criticism, History, and Bibliography* and *Journal of the D. H. Lawrence Society.* Some writings appear under the pseudonyms Isobel Garnett, W. P. Haynes, or Alexander Marsden. Editor, *New Zealand Slavonic Journal,* 1974-92.

WORK IN PROGRESS: Continuing research on Turgenev and on nineteenth-century Anglo-Russian relations.

SIDELIGHTS: Patrick Waddington told *CA:* "My vocation is to write books that few will read, in the conviction that ninety-five percent of writing is actually of that nature and that, without it, literature cannot survive. I am sustained by the hope that a pale glimmer of a reflection of my love for true creative literature may shine through the gloom, and that great men like Turgenev may be better appreciated by my commentaries on their lives. My pet aversions are critics who write about critics, and all literary 'isms' and 'theories'. Life is the only true value, art its elucidation and fulfillment."

*　　*　　*

WAKOSKI, Diane 1937-

PERSONAL: Born August 3, 1937, in Whittier, CA; daughter of John Joseph and Marie (Mengel) Wakoski; married S. Shepard Sherbell (a magazine editor), October 22, 1965 (divorced); married Michael Watterlond, February 22, 1973 (divorced, 1975); married Robert J. Turney, February 14, 1982. *Education:* University of California, Berkeley, B.A., 1960. *Avocational interests:* Astrology, detective fiction, cooking, collecting American Art pottery, growing orchids.

ADDRESSES: Home—607 Division, East Lansing, MI 48823. *Office*—Michigan State University, 207 Morrill Hall, East Lansing, MI 48824-1036.

CAREER: Poet. British Book Centre, New York, NY, clerk, 1960-63; Junior High School 22, New York, NY, teacher, 1963-66; New School for Social Research, New

Diane Wakoski

York, NY, lecturer, 1969; writer-in-residence, California Institute of Technology, 1972, University of Virginia, 1972-73, Willamette University, 1974, University of California, Irvine, Irvine, CA, 1974, University of Wisconsin-Madison, Madison, WI, 1975, Michigan State University, 1975, Whitman College, 1976, University of Washington, 1977, University of Hawaii, 1978, and Emory University, 1980, 1981; member of faculty at Michigan State University, 1976—. *American Poetry Review,* columnist, 1972-74.

MEMBER: PEN, Authors Guild, Authors League of America, Poetry Society of America.

AWARDS, HONORS: Robert Frost fellowship, Bread Loaf Writers Conference, 1966; Cassandra Foundation award, 1970; New York State Council on the Arts grant, 1971; Guggenheim Foundation grant, 1972; National Endowment for the Arts grant, 1973; Fulbright grant, 1984; Michigan Arts Council grant, 1988; Michigan Arts Foundation award recipient, 1989; distinguished faculty award, Michigan State University, 1989, William Carlos Williams Prize, 1989, for *Emerald Ice: Selected Poems, 1962-1987;* university distinguished professor award, Michigan State University, 1990.

WRITINGS:

POETRY

Coins and Coffins (also see below), Hawk's Well Press (New York, NY), 1962.
(With Rochelle Owens, Barbara Moraff, and Carol Berge) *Four Young Lady Poets,* edited by LeRoi Jones, Totem-Corinth (New York, NY), 1962.
Dream Sheet, Software Press (New York, NY), 1965.
Discrepancies and Apparitions (also see below), Doubleday (New York, NY), 1966.
The George Washington Poems (also see below), River-run Press (New York, NY), 1967.
The Diamond Merchant, Sans Souci Press (Cambridge, MA), 1968.
Inside the Blood Factory, Doubleday (Garden City, NY), 1968.
(With Robert Kelly and Ron Loewinsohn) *The Well Wherein a Deer's Head Bleeds: A Play for Winter Solstice,* Black Sparrow Press (Los Angeles, CA), 1968.
Greed, Black Sparrow Press (Los Angeles, CA), Parts 1 and 2, 1968, Parts 3 and 4, 1969, Parts 5, 6, 7, 1971, Parts 8, 9, 11, 1973.
The Lament of the Lady Bank Dick, Sans Souci Press (Cambridge, MA), 1969.
The Moon Has a Complicated Geography, Odda Tala Press (Palo Alto, CA), 1969.
Poems, Key Printing Co., 1969.
Some Black Poems for the Buddha's Birthday, Pierripont Press, 1969.
Thanking My Mother for Piano Lessons, Perishable Press (Mount Horeb, WI), 1969.
Love, You Big Fat Snail, Tenth Muse (San Francisco, CA), 1970.
Black Dream Ditty for Billy "the Kid" M Seen in Dr. Generosity's Bar Recruiting for Hell's Angels and Black Mafia, Black Sparrow Press (Los Angeles, CA), 1970.
The Wise Men Drawn to Kneel in Wonder at the Fact So of Itself, Black Sparrow Press (Los Angeles, CA), 1970.
The Magellanic Clouds, Black Sparrow Press (Los Angeles, CA), 1970.
On Barbara's Shore, Black Sparrow Press (Los Angeles, CA), 1971.

(Contributor) *The Nest,* Black Sparrow Press (Los Angeles, CA), 1971.

The Motorcycle Betrayal Poems, Simon & Schuster (New York, NY), 1971.

This Water Baby: For Tony, Unicorn Press (Santa Barbara, CA), 1971.

Exorcism, My Dukes (Boston, MA), 1971.

The Purple Finch Song, Perishable Press (Mount Horeb, WI), 1972.

Sometimes a Poet Will Hijack the Moon, Burning Deck (Providence, RI), 1972.

Smudging, Black Sparrow Press (Los Angeles, CA), 1972.

The Pumpkin Pie: or, Reassurances Are Always False, Tho We Love Them, Only Physics Counts, Black Sparrow Press (Los Angeles, CA), 1972.

Winter Sequences, Black Sparrow Press (Los Angeles, CA), 1973.

Dancing on the Grave of a Son of a Bitch, Black Sparrow Press (Los Angeles, CA), 1973.

Stilllife: Michael, Silver Flute, and Violets, University of Connecticut Library (Storrs, CT), 1973.

The Owl and the Snake: A Fable, Perishable Press (Mount Horeb, WI), 1973.

(Contributor) Karl Malkoff, editor, *Crowell's Handbook of Contemporary American Poetry,* Crowell (New York, NY), 1973.

The Wandering Tatler, Perishable Press (Mount Horeb, WI), 1974.

Trilogy (includes *Coins and Coffins, Discrepancies and Apparitions,* and *The George Washington Poems*), Doubleday (Garden City, NY), 1974.

Looking for the King of Spain (also see below), Black Sparrow Press (Los Angeles, CA), 1974.

Abalone, Black Sparrow Press (Los Angeles, CA), 1974.

Virtuoso Literature for Two and Four Hands, Doubleday (Garden City, NY), 1975.

The Fable of the Lion and the Scorpion, Pentagram Press (Milwaukee, WI), 1975.

The Laguna Contract of Diane Wakoski, Crepuscular Press (Madison, WI), 1976.

George Washington's Camp Cups, Red Ozier Press (Madison, WI), 1976.

Waiting for the King of Spain, Black Sparrow Press (Santa Barbara, CA), 1976.

The Last Poem, Black Sparrow Press (Santa Barbara, CA), 1976.

The Ring, Black Sparrow Press (Santa Barbara, CA), 1977.

Spending Christmas with the Man from Receiving at Sears, Black Sparrow Press (Santa Barbara, CA), 1977.

Overnight Projects with Wood, Red Ozier Press (Madison, WI), 1977.

Pachelbel's Canon (also see below), Black Sparrow Press (Santa Barbara, CA) 1978.

The Man Who Shook Hands, Doubleday (Garden City, NY), 1978.

Trophies, (Black Sparrow Press) (Santa Barbara, CA), 1979.

Cap of Darkness (includes *Looking for the King of Spain* and *Pachelbel's Canon*), Black Sparrow Press (Santa Barbara, CA), 1980.

(With Ellen Lanyon) *Making a Sacher Torte: Nine Poems, Twelve Illustrations,* Perishable Press (Mount Horeb, WI), 1981.

Saturn's Rings, Targ Editions, (New York, NY), 1982.

Divers, Barbarian Press, 1982.

The Lady Who Drove Me to the Airport, Metacom Press (Worcester, MA), 1982.

The Magician's Feastletters, Black Sparrow Press (Santa Barbara, CA), 1982.

The Collected Greed, Parts 1-13, Black Sparrow Press (Santa Barbara, CA), 1984.

The Managed World, Red Ozier Press (New York, NY), 1985.

Why My Mother Likes Liberace: A Musical Selection, SUN/Gemini Press (Tucson, AZ), 1985.

Celebration of the Rose: For Norman on Christmas Day, Caliban (Montclair, NJ), 1987.

Roses, Caliban Press (Montclair, NJ), 1987.

Husks of Wheat, California State University, Northridge Library (Northridge, CA), 1987.

Emerald Ice: Selected Poems 1962-1987, Black Sparrow Press (Santa Rosa, CA), 1988.

Medea the Sorceress ("The Archaeology of Movies and Books" series), Black Sparrow Press (Santa Rosa, CA), 1991.

Jason the Sailor ("The Archaeology of Movies and Books" series), Black Sparrow Press (Santa Rosa, CA), 1993.

The Emerald City of Las Vegas ("The Archaeology of Movies and Books" series), Black Sparrow Press (Santa Rosa, CA), 1995.

Argonaut Rose ("The Archaeology of Movies and Books" series), Black Sparrow Press (Santa Rosa, CA), 1998.

The Butcher's Apron: New and Selected Poems, Including "Greed: Part 14," Black Sparrow Press (Santa Rosa, CA), 2000.

OTHER

Form Is an Extension of Content (essay), Black Sparrow Press (Los Angeles, CA), 1972.

Creating a Personal Mythology (essays), Black Sparrow Press (Los Angeles, CA), 1975.

Variations on a Theme (essay), Black Sparrow Press (Santa Barbara, CA), 1976.

(Author of introduction) Barbara Drake, *Love at the Egyptian Theatre,* Red Cedar Press (East Lansing, MI), 1978.

(Author of introduction) Lynne Savitt, *Lust in Twenty-eight Flavors,* Second Coming Press (San Francisco, CA), 1979.

Toward a New Poetry (essays), University of Michigan Press (Ann Arbor, MI), 1980.

Unveilings, photographs by Lynn Stern, Hudson Hill Press (New York, NY), 1989.

Contributor to "Burning Deck Post Cards: The Third Ten," Burning Deck and to periodicals.

SIDELIGHTS: Diane Wakoski, described as an "important and moving poet" by Paul Zweig in the *New York Times Book Review,* is frequently named among the foremost contemporary poets by virtue of her experiential vision and her unique voice. Wakoski's poems focus on intensely personal experiences—on her unhappy childhood, on the painful relationships she has had with men and, perhaps most frequently, on the subject of being Diane Wakoski.

A few critics have found Wakoski's thematic concerns difficult to appreciate, especially the recurring "anti-male rage" theme noted by Peter Schjeldahl in the *New York Times Book Review.* Wakoski's poems, according to Schjeldahl, "are professionally supple and clear . . . but their pervasive unpleasantness makes her popularity rather surprising. One can only conclude that a number of people are angry enough at life to enjoy the sentimental and desolating resentment with which she writes about it."

Many other critics, however, believed that it is through this very rage and resentment that Wakoski makes a significant statement in her work. James F. Mersmann, for example, commented in *Margins* that Wakoski's poetry "gives us a moving vision of the terrible last stages of a disintegrating personality and a disintegrating society, and it painfully embodies the schizophrenia, alienation, and lovelessness of our time." Douglas Blazek concluded in *Poetry* that Wakoski's poems have the "substance necessary to qualify them notches above the works of creative 'geniuses,' 'stylists,' and 'cultural avatars' who have little to say."

The stylistic and structural aspects of Wakoski's poetry are as unique as her poetic statement. Often described as prosy, her poems are usually written in the first person. Rosellen Brown wrote in *Parnassus* that Wakoski "is a marvelously abundant woman" who sounds in her poetry "like some friend of yours who's flung herself down in your kitchen to tell you something urgent and makes you laugh and respect her good old-fashioned guts at the same time."

"Diane's style of writing," said David Ignatow in *Margins,* "reminds me of the baroque style of dress . . . the huge flounces, furbelows, puffed sleeves, trailing skirts, tight waist, heaving bosoms and stylishly protruding buttocks, all carried off with great elegance of movement and poise." In *Mediterranean Review,* critic Robert DeMaria found that, "stylistically, [Wakoski] has a marvelous and distinctive voice. It lingers in one's mind after one has read her. . . . Her timing is excellent, so excellent that she can convert prose into poetry at times. And most of what she writes is really prose, only slightly transformed, not only because of its arrangement on the page, but because of this music she injects into it."

While the structure of Wakoski's poems appears to be informal and casually built, her artistic control is tight. As Hayden Carruth suggested in the *Hudson Review,* "Wakoski has a way of beginning her poems with the most unpromising materials imaginable, then carrying them on, often on and on and on, talkily, until at the end they come into surprising focus, unified works. With her it is a question of thematic and imagistic control; I think her poems are deeply, rather than verbally, structured." In *Contemporary Literature,* Marjorie G. Perloff spoke of Wakoski's purpose in writing nontraditionally structured poems, saying that "Wakoski strives for a voice that is wholly natural, spontaneous, and direct. Accordingly, she avoids all fixed forms, definite rhythms, or organized image patterns in the drive to tell us the Whole Truth about herself, to be *sincere.*"

"Although her poems are not traditional structures," said Debra Hulbert in *Prairie Schooner,* "she builds them solidly with words which feel chosen, with repetition of images throughout a poem." This repetition, an element that critics mention often, makes its own statement apart from the individual themes of the poems. "Repetition," remarked Gloria Bowles in *Margins,* "has become Wakoski's basic stylistic mode. And since form is an extension of content (et vice versa) Wakoski's poetic themes have become obsessive. Repetition is a formal fact of her poetry and, so she suggests, the basic structure of our lives."

Wakoski's poems often rely on digressions, on tangential wanderings through imagery and fantasy, to present ideas and themes. Blazek observed that "many of her poems sound as if they're constantly in trouble, falling into triteness, clumsiness, or indirection. She is constantly jumping into deep water to save a drowning stanza or into burning buildings to recover disintegrating meaning, always managing to pull these rescues off, sometimes with what appears to be a superhuman determination, drawing gasps from witnesses who never lose that initial impression of disaster." But, he said, these "imaginative excursions and side-journeys (she can get strung-out in just about any poem over a page long) are well-founded in her life—they're not just facile language cyclone-spinning itself to naught. They are doors into her psyche."

Toby Olson, writing in *Margins,* believed that "one of the central forces of [Wakoski's] poems proceeds from a fundamentally serious playfulness, an evident desire to spin out and open the image rather than to close the structure. . . . One of their most compelling qualities is their obsessiveness: the need at every turn to digress, to let the magic of the words take her where they will, because they are so beautiful, because the ability to speak out is not to be taken for granted, is to be wondered at in its foreignness, is to be followed."

The "magic" of Wakoski's words is also wrought through her use of imagery and through her creation of a consistent personal mythology. Commenting on two of the poet's earliest works, *Coins and Coffins* and *Discrepancies and Apparitions,* Sheila Weller wrote in *Ms.* that the books "established [Wakoski] as a poet of fierce imagination. She was at once an eerie imagist (always the swooping gulls, deciduating hands, the hawk that 'pecks out my eyes like two cherries'); and a rapt parablist, reworking Wild West legend and cosmological symbols, transmuting fairy-tale scenes ('three children dancing around an orange tree') into macaberie ('Do you see the round orange tree? . . . glinting through the leaves, / the hanged man'). These poems are vivid landscapes—as diabolic as Dali, as gauzy as Monet."

In *Poetry,* Sandra M. Gilbert described Wakoski as "a fabulist, a weaver of gorgeous webs of imagery and a teller of archetypically glamorous tales [who has] always attempted self-definition through self-mythologizing. 'The poems were a way of inventing myself into a new life,' she has said." "The myth of herself," said H. Zinnes in *World Literature Today,* is of "one 'clothed in fat,' with an ugly face, without wit, brilliance or elegance, but having some 'obsession for truth and history.' This plain seeker after love . . . is of course a poet with a great deal of wit. . . . a poet who in her work and life is not merely searching for a lover," although many of her poems touch on this theme.

Wakoski's personal mythology embraces many other archetypal figures as well, including George Washington, the King of Spain, the motorcycle mechanic, the "man in Receiving at Sears," Beethoven, the "man with the gold tooth," and the "man who shook hands." These characters, most of whom appear more than once in Wakoski's canon, serve as symbols, emblematic of emotional states, past experiences, fantasies, and, sometimes, of real people in the poet's life.

George Washington, for example, appears in *The George Washington Poems,* a collection that Weller called "witty, caustic takes on the male mystique. In a voice by turns consciously absurdist and tremulously earnest, she takes the first President as her 'mythical father-lover,' romanticizes and barbs 'the militaristic, penalizing, fact-over-feeling male mind that I've always been afraid of and fascinated by.'" Wakoski speaks to George Washington in the poems with various voices—as Martha Washington, as a bitter child whose father has left home, as a lover left behind in the Revolutionary War. As Norman Martien explained in *Partisan Review,* "the George Washington myths serve to express the failure of a woman's relations to her men, but the myths also give her a means of talking about it. Partly *because* 'George' is so distant, he can be a safe listener. . . . [and] he can allow her a voice that can reaffirm human connection, impossible at closer ranges." This theme of the failure of relationships, of betrayal by others (especially men), is a central concern of Wakoski's, and many of her mythological figures embody one or more of the facets of human relations in which she sees the possibility of betrayal or loss.

The figure of the motorcycle mechanic in *The Motorcycle Betrayal Poems* symbolizes, as Wakoski says in her dedicatory statement, "all those men who betrayed me at one time or another." According to Zweig, the book is "haunted by a curious mythology composed of mustached lovers, 'mechanics' who do not understand the engine humming under [the narrator's] skin, the great-grandfatherly warmth of Beethoven and George Washington, to whom she turns with humor but also with a sort of desperation." In this book, said Eric Mottram in *Parnassus,* Wakoski "operates in a world of women as adjuncts to men and the erotics of bikes; the poems are survival gestures." According to Weller, the book "made . . . women start at [Wakoski's] power to personalize the paradox" of male-female relationships—"their anger at the rejecting male archetype . . . yet their willing glorification of it . . . The book's theme is the mythology and confusions of . . . love, and the fury at betrayal by symbols, envy, lovers, and self."

The theme of betrayal, and its resulting pain, also appears in *Inside the Blood Factory.* Here, as Zweig observed, Wakoski writes "poems of loss. The loss of childhood; the loss of lovers and family; the perpetual loss a woman lives with when she thinks she is not beautiful. These losses [create] a scorched earth of isolation around her, which she [describes] harshly and precisely. . . . From this vulnerable retreat, a stream of liberating images [emerges] to grapple with the world and mythify it." Peter D. Zivkovic, writing in *Southwest Review,* believed that *Inside the Blood Factory* is "significantly more than a memorable reading experience. Perhaps the most remarkable thing about . . . [the book] is the consistent strength of the individual poems. There is not," Zivkovic concluded, "a single weak poem in the volume—an achievement worthy of Frost and other American giants."

Fourteen years after *Inside the Blood Factory,* Wakoski produced *Saturn's Rings* and *The Magician's Feastletters. Saturn's Rings* is a collection of surrealist poems loosely connected by the metaphorical theme of self-banishment and characteristic self-scrutiny. Holly Prado noted in the *Los Angeles Times Book Review,* "Fearing decay, ignorance, and the inevitability of death, Wakoski writes with the intensity of someone fiercely alive, who still wants to unscramble failures, loneliness, the image of herself as the homely girl who was never acceptable." Noting the limitations of her shorter pieces in the collection, Paul Oppenheimer commented in *American Book Review* on the concluding series of eleven poems from which the title of the collection derives: "*Saturn's Rings* . . . is an often captivating, often self-pitying cry from the depths. . . . The cry is especially moving when uttered in the bright, chromic voice of Wakoski's most surrealistic lines. She is fine at depicting the possibility that 'the world / is flying out of control,' and that we may be living in 'a disintegrating time.'" In *The Magician's Feastletters,* arranged in four sections which parallel the four seasons, Wakoski uses food as a metaphor for love and deprivation. Though tending toward abstraction, Clayton Eshleman noted the concreteness of Wakoski's imagery and description of everyday items. He wrote in the *Los Angeles Times Book Review,* "Wakoski [begins] to reverse a whole system of frozen values geared to affirm youth/sexuality/summer/product and to denigrate aging/impotence/winter/soul. Especially in the light of current fashions in American poetry (where empty description is as touted as pretentious nonsense), Wakoski's poetry is extremely valuable."

The Collected Greed, Parts 1-13 and *Emerald Ice: Selected Poems 1962-1987* bring together examples of Wakoski's finest writing over a twenty-five year period. *The Collected Greed* is an assemblage of poetry from

previous installments of *Greed* between 1968 and 1973, with the addition of two previously unpublished parts. In the *Los Angeles Times Book Review,* Kenneth Funsten offered high praise for "The Greed To Be Fulfilled," one of the new sections. Here Wakoski traces her personal quest for purpose and completion in a surreal glass house where she revisits George Washington and representations of Charles Bukowski and the King of Spain. Funsten wrote, "The confessional voice of the self-centered ego reaches a new plane of maturity when it decides that intellectual things, not emotional ones, are what matter." Throughout the collection Wakoski explores various manifestations of greed, defined by her as "an unwillingness to give up one thing / for another," as quoted in Funsten's review.

In the 1990s Wakoski produced *Jason the Sailor* and *The Emerald City of Las Vegas,* both belonging to "The Archaeology of Movies and Books" series that began with *Medea the Sorceress* in 1991. In *Jason the Sailor,* consisting of poems, letters to men, and excerpted texts by Camille Paglia, Nick Herbert, and Jeremy Bernstein, Wakoski explores archetypal love, betrayal, and the dynamics of male-female relationships, concluding, as quoted in a *Kliatt* review of the work, "Women need men, the other halves of ourselves." *The Emerald City of Las Vegas* similarly examines the mythology of modern America in casinos and through excerpts from Frank Baum's *The Wizard of Oz.* A *Publishers Weekly* reviewer concluded that the book represents Wakoski's "inner conversation about what it means to be a woman, to be no longer young, to be a poet." The fourth book in the series is *Argonaut Rose,* in which Wakoski writes of her own history and popular culture. *Library Journal* reviewer Graham Christian said that she "remains an interesting poet to watch."

The Butcher's Apron: New and Selected Poems, Including "Greed: Part 14," focuses on the purchase, preparation, and enjoyment of food. Some of the poems read as recipes, as in "Braised Short Ribs." Wakoski writes of food failures, such as a pumpkin pie that won't set, and food she ate as a child. *Library Journal* contributor Judy Clarence wrote that the volume is pervaded by Wakoski's "feminine gentility," and felt that it shouldn't be read in one sitting, but should "be dipped into now and then, as if one were sticking a finger into a pot of honey."

BIOGRAPHICAL/CRITICAL SOURCES:

BOOKS

Contemporary Literary Criticism, Gale (Detroit, MI), Volume 2, 1974, Volume 4, 1975, Volume 7, 1977, Volume 9, 1978, Volume 11, 1979, Volume 40, 1986.

Contemporary Poets, 6th edition, St. James Press (Detroit, MI), 1996.

Contemporary Women Poets, St. James Press (Detroit, MI), 1998.

Dictionary of Literary Biography, Volume 5: *American Poets after World War II,* Part 2, Gale (Detroit, MI), 1980.

Lauter, Estella, *Women as Mythmakers: Poetry and Visual Art by Twentieth-Century Women,* Indiana University Press (Bloomington, IN), 1984.

Roberts, Sheila, editor, *Still the Frame Holds,* Borgo Press (San Francisco, CA), 1993.

PERIODICALS

American Book Review, September-October, 1987, Paul Oppenheimer, review of *Saturn's Rings.*

Contemporary Literature, winter, 1975.

Hudson Review, summer, 1974.

Kliatt, September, 1993, p. 26, review of *Jason the Sailor.*

Library Journal, June 1, 1982, p. 1100; November 15, 1986, p. 100; December, 1988; February 1, 1991; August, 1993, p. 109; August, 1995, p. 80; March 1, 1998, Graham Christian, review of *Argonaut Rose,* p. 92; February 15, 2001, Judy Clarence, review of *The Butcher's Apron: New and Selected Poems, Including "Greed: Part 14,"* p. 172.

Los Angeles Times Book Review, July 18, 1982, p. 11; November 4, 1984, p. 4; October 26, 1986, p. 14.

Margins, January, 1976.

Mediterranean Review, spring, 1972.

Ms., March, 1976, Sheila Weller, reviews of *Coins and Coffins* and *Discrepancies and Apparitions.*

New York Times Book Review, December 12, 1971; August 13, 1978.

Parnassus, fall-winter, 1972; spring-summer, 1973.

Partisan Review, winter, 1971, Norman Martien, review of *The George Washington Poems.*

Poetry, June, 1974; August, 1976.

Prairie Schooner, spring, 1973.

Publishers Weekly, July 31, 1995, p. 74, review of *The Emerald City of Las Vegas;* February 23, 1998, review of *Argonaut Rose,* p. 71.

Southwest Review, spring, 1975, Peter D. Zivkovic, review of *Inside the Blood Factory.*

Virginia Quarterly Review, autumn, 1972.

World Literature Today, autumn, 1978.

Writer's Digest, November, 1991.

OTHER

Academy of American Poets, http://www.poets.org (June 4, 2001).

WALKER, Rebecca 1970-

PERSONAL: Born November 11, 1970, in Jackson, MS; daughter of Alice Walker (a writer) and Mel Leventhal (an attorney); partner of Meshell N'degeocello (a singer), beginning 1996; children: one son. *Education:* Yale University, B.A. (cum laude), 1992.

ADDRESSES: Home—Berkeley, CA. *Agent*—Penguin Putnam Inc., Attn: Riverhead Books, Author Mail, 375 Hudson St., New York, NY 10014. *E-mail*—minnie@nyo.com.

CAREER: Writer and activist. *Ms.* magazine, New York, NY, contributing editor, 1989—. Third Wave Direct Action Corporation, New York, NY, cofounder, 1992; Kokobar, Brooklyn, NY, co-owner, 1996.

AWARDS, HONORS: Pickens Prize, Yale University, 1992, for excellence in African American scholarship; Feminist of the Year award, Fund for the Feminist Majority, 1992; named as one of fifty future leaders by *Time* magazine, 1994; Paz y Justicia award, Vanguard Foundation; Champion of Choice award, California Abortion Rights Action League; Woman of Distinction award, Kingsborough Community College.

WRITINGS:

(Editor and author of introduction) *To Be Real: Telling the Truth and Changing the Face of Feminism,* Anchor (New York, NY), 1995.

(Contributor) Barbara Findlen, editor, *Listen Up: Voices from the Next Feminist Generation,* Seal Press (Seattle, WA), 1995.

Black, White, and Jewish: Autobiography of a Shifting Self, Riverhead Books (New York, NY), 2001.

Contributor to periodicals, including *Essence, Mademoiselle, Black Scholar, Ms., New York Daily News, Spin, Harper's,* and *Sassy.*

WORK IN PROGRESS: Editing an anthology on bisexuality.

SIDELIGHTS: Through both her activism and her writing, Rebecca Walker has become a role model for a new generation of feminists attempting to reinterpret the legacy of the women's movement. *Feminist Writers* contributor Barbara Stretchberry wrote that Walker "is becoming a rallying voice for young feminists. But rather than always speaking for them, she is working to create a forum where young women can speak for themselves and voice their own ideas." Walker's efforts include cofounding a national nonprofit organization, Third Wave Direct Action Corporation, and owning businesses aimed at encouraging and supporting women. Walker, daughter of acclaimed novelist Alice Walker, also contributes to a number of periodicals and is the editor of *To Be Real: Telling the Truth and Changing the Face of Feminism,* published in 1995.

Born in 1970 in Jackson, Mississippi, Walker was raised in New York City and San Francisco. After graduating from Yale University in 1992, she decided to devote her talents to social activism on behalf of women. To that end she cofounded, with friend Shannon Liss, a national organization called Third Wave, designed to inspire leadership and social activism among young women. Third Wave has been instrumental in registering young women voters in urban districts, an effort for which Walker was awarded the Feminist of the Year award from the Fund for the Feminist Majority in 1992. Stretchberry noted that "her other Third Wave projects include fighting young women's illiteracy levels by educating young women about technology, so that they are not left behind on the information superhighway. And in 1996, she became co-owner of Kokobar, a cybercafe and bookstore, bringing the Internet into a multicultural, inner-city community."

In addition to directing the activities of Third Wave, Walker recruited young writers from around the country as contributors to *To Be Real.* With each individual response to the question, "Is there more than one way to be a feminist?," *To Be Real* illustrates the movement of younger women away from traditional mainstream feminism. In an essay titled "Brideland," Naomi Wolf, author of the groundbreaking *The Beauty Myth,* writes about her attempts to incorporate her ardent feminist beliefs within a wedding ceremony. bell hooks's piece "Beauty Laid Bare" concerns the materialism of African-American culture, while in another essay, supermodel Veronica Webb discusses the conflicts between feminism and having a career as a model, noting that modeling allowed her a measure of economic power that she might not otherwise have had.

Walker frames *To Be Real* with an examination of the necessity for a "third generation" feminist movement. She cites alienation from a media focused on the older, baby boom generation, the perpetuation of traditional negative stereotypes, and the sometimes hidden resentment of older generations of feminists. Noting that a lack of understanding has caused many younger women not to recognize their debt to the women's movements of past decades, she encourages readers of *To Be Real* to become more informed before disavowing feminism altogether. While noting that *To Be Real* is hardly the definitive voice of younger North American feminists, a *Publishers Weekly* reviewer noted that "both its virtues and its flaws attest to the strength of our feminist inheritance—and its promise for the future."

A journalist, Walker has served as a contributing editor to *Ms.* magazine since 1989 and has also published articles in a number of periodicals. In 1994, *Time* magazine named her to its list of fifty future leaders in the United States, an acknowledgment of her energetic efforts to help provide young women direction as feminism undergoes a new incarnation. "Walker calls upon her peers to become angry, and then turn that anger into power. Anger can change the politics as usual. Her . . . writings encompass topics like domestic violence, reproductive freedom, sexuality, and, of course, feminism," wrote Stretchberry.

Walker's *Black, White and Jewish: Autobiography of a Shifting Self* describes her childhood, which became more difficult after her mother and her Jewish father divorced when she was eight. Her parents' union had been forged during the Civil Rights movement in the South where Walker was born, but after the marriage ended, they moved to separate coasts, and Walker made a cross-country trip every two years. Walker was confused as she attempted to fit into two worlds, and never felt comfortable or accepted in either. In an interview with Robert Fleming for *Publishers Weekly,* Walker said, "My mother, who created beautiful spaces for me to live in, always trusted that I could navigate this world. . . . While my parents' nurturing was very important and kept me from splintering, neither of them actively addressed the issue of my experience as a mixed person."

Walker writes that she first had sex in fifth grade, that she had an abortion at fourteen, and that she used drugs daily. Catherine Saint Louis wrote in the *New York Times Book Review* that besides being about growing up biracial, Walker's story "is also about how parental neglect forced her to become prematurely independent . . . One cannot help wondering if more parental bolstering would have made a difference." Toward the end of the book, Walker introduces another element of her makeup, bisexuality. "There's a shyness, a sudden discretion that emerges in these final pages that doesn't feel native to Walker, who is bold and unsparing elsewhere," wrote Austin Bunn in the *Advocate.* "She's a thoughtful 'translator,' but it's hard not to feel that, at least for now, this one part of her shifting self has been negotiated right out of the conversation." A *Publishers Weekly* contributor felt that "her artfulness in baring her psyche, spirit, and sexuality will attract a wealth of deserved praise."

BIOGRAPHICAL/CRITICAL SOURCES:

BOOKS

Feminist Writers, St. James Press (Detroit, MI), 1996.
Walker, Rebecca, *Black, White, and Jewish: Autobiography of a Shifting Self,* Riverhead Books (New York, NY), 2001.

PERIODICALS

Advocate, February 27, 2001, Austin Bunn, "Walker, in Her Own Shoes," p. 65.
American Prospect, September 10, 2001, E. J. Graff, review of *Black, White, and Jewish: Autobiography of a Shifting Self,* p. 42.
Booklist, December 15, 2000, Mary Carroll, review of *Black, White, and Jewish,* p. 784; February 15, 2001, Brad Hooper, review of *Black, White, and Jewish,* p. 1099.
Curve, June, 2001, Erin Raber, "All in the Mix: A Conversation with Rebecca Walker," p. 43.
Emerge, February, 1996, p. 12.
Feminist Studies, spring, 1997, Jennifer Drake, review of *To Be Real: Telling the Truth and Changing the Face of Feminism,* p. 97.
Girlfriends, May, 1996.
Harper's Bazaar, November, 1992.
Journal of Women's History, winter, 2001, Stephanie Gilmore, review of *To Be Real,* p. 215.
Library Journal, November 15, 1995, p. 91; November 1, 2000, Pam Kingsbury, review of *Black, White, and Jewish,* p. 92.
New York, September 11, 1995, p. 87.
New York Times Book Review, January 21, 2001, Catherine Saint Louis, review of *Black, White, and Jewish,* p. 19.
Publishers Weekly, October 2, 1995, review of *To Be Real,* p. 67; August 14, 2000, "Dichotomies," p. 243; November 6, 2000, review of *Black, White, and Jewish,* p. 77, Robert Fleming, "PW Talks with Rebecca Walker," p. 78.

Time, January 15, 2001, Lise Funderburg, "Identity Gap: A Memoir of Growing up Biracial Falls too Short," p. 136.*

*   *   *

WALLEY, Byron
See CARD, Orson Scott

*   *   *

WARNEKE, Sara 1953(?)-
(Sara Douglass)

PERSONAL: Born c. 1953, in Penola, South Australia; father, a sheep farmer and health and weeds inspector; mother, a sheep farmer; married (marriage ended). *Education:* Attended Methodist Ladies College, Adelaide, Australia; University of Adelaide, B.A., Ph.D. (history), c. 1991.

ADDRESSES: Home—Bendigo, Australia. *Office*—c/o HarperCollins, 25 Ryde Rd., Pymble, New South Wales 2073, Australia. *E-mail*—douglass@bendigo.net.au.

CAREER: Novelist and historian. Worked as a nurse for seventeen years; Latrobe University, Bendigo, Australia, senior lecturer in history, 1992-99.

AWARDS, HONORS: Aurealis Award, best fantasy novel, 1997, for *The Axis Trilogy.*

WRITINGS:

Images of the Educational Traveller in Early Modern England, E. J. Brill (Leiden, Netherlands), 1995.
(Translator) Robert Mannyng of Brunne, *Story of Arthur,* 1995.

Contributor of scholarly articles to *Encyclopedia of the Reformation,* edited by H. Hillebrand, Oxford University Press (New York, NY).

UNDER PSEUDONYM SARA DOUGLASS

Beyond the Hanging Wall (young-adult novel), Hodder Headline (Sydney, Australia), 1996.
Threshold (novel), HarperCollins (Pymble, Australia), 1997.

The Betrayal of Arthur (nonfiction), 1999.
The Nameless Day (novel; first volume of "Crucible" trilogy), HarperCollins (Pymble, Australia), 2001.

Contributor to books, including *The Best of Australian Fantasy and Science Fiction 1996,* edited by Jonathan Strahan and Jeremy Byrne, HarperCollins (Pymble, Australia), 1997.

UNDER PSEUDONYM SARA DOUGLASS; "AXIS TRILOGY"

BattleAxe, HarperCollins (Pymble, Australia), 1995.
Enchanter, HarperCollins (Pymble, Australia), 1996.
StarMan, HarperCollins (Pymble, Australia), 1997.

UNDER PSEUDONYM SARA DOUGLASS; "WAYFARER REDEMPTION" SERIES

Sinner, HarperCollins (Pymble, Australia), 1997.
Pilgrim, HarperCollins (Pymble, Australia), 1998.
Crusader, HarperCollins (Pymble, Australia), 1999.

WORK IN PROGRESS: Two more volumes of the "Crucible" trilogy, and a book about how to create a fantasy world.

SIDELIGHTS: After spending her first seven years on her parents' sheep farm in South Australia, and then receiving her later education at a Methodist girls' school in Adelaide, Australian writer Sara Warneke became a nurse. However, she found nursing to be an unsatisfying outlet for her aspirations and eventually went back to school to work toward her doctorate in history. Beginning in 1995, Warneke began making up for lost time in rapid order, publishing both her first fantasy novel as Sara Douglass, and her first scholarly book on early modern British history. By the end of 1998, she was the author of no fewer than eight published novels and a work of her short fiction had been anthologized in a mainstream year's best collection of fantasy and science fiction.

Warneke began writing fantasy simply because she wanted something good to read. Her first novel, *Battle-Axe,* was inspired by her discovery of a miniature axe, provenance unknown, in a shop in Adelaide. When she finished *BattleAxe,* Warneke looked up literary agents in the Yellow Pages and sent one of them a query. While her manuscript was sitting in the agent's office, the agent received a query from the Australian office of

HarperCollins asking whether the agent had any science-fiction or fantasy novels. The agent sent them Warneke's novel.

The success of novels like *BattleAxe* enabled Warneke to purchase a house in Bendigo, where she taught at Latrobe University until 1999. As she told readers of her Internet home page, the need "to pay the thing off" keeps her writing "assiduously." Under the Douglass pseudonym, *BattleAxe* was quickly followed by two more novels, comprising the "Axis" trilogy. These three volumes tell the story of the efforts of various peoples on the world of Tencendor to unite against a common enemy despite their history of conflicts. Their commander is Axis, a leader of a religious military force known as the Axe-Wielders.

Dennis Neville, reviewing *BattleAxe* in *OzLit,* said that Warneke "understands her characters and makes them very believable. . . . This is a cracker of a book and instantly lands Douglass among luminaries like Stephen Donaldson and David Eddings." In *Eidolon,* reviewer Martin Livings criticized the publisher's presentation of the book—a paperback original with a "very poor" cover—but added that in spite of some problems of characterization and an unoriginal premise, "*BattleAxe* is by far the most professionally written fantasy novel to be written in Australia to date." Another positive review came from *OzLit* contributor Karen Brooks, who approached the work as a literary critic but enjoyed it as a reader. Brooks found some of the characters to have "interesting psychological and sexual quirks," and added that the book's weaknesses, "if indeed these are weaknesses, lie in its strict adherence to the generic conventions of fantasy, though this can also be read positively as a subversive move against the irresistible forces of change."

The sequel to *BattleAxe, Enchanter* involves a conflict between hero Axis and his half-brother, Borneheld. The book was trimmed by almost 100,000 words in the editorial process according to its author, and was inspired in large part by a piece of classical music, Pachelbel's *Canon in D Major.* Reviewing the novel for *OzLit,* Brooks called it "a sequel par excellence"—a novel that "tantalizes AND delivers." Although the reviewer felt that the 700-page novel began slowly, she found herself drawn in by its unpredictability and its "lyrical, tight and imaginative prose." In *Australian Book Review,* Peter Nicholls assessed both *BattleAxe* and *Enchanter,* asserting that, despite the many familiar elements of the fantasy genre that were present in the books—a quest, rites of passage, a war of light against darkness, mages, kingdoms, princesses, and a prophecy—"There is no need to be cynical at all. This Axis trilogy . . . turns out to be a wonderfully quirky and intelligent romp, in the way it plays variations on familiar fantasy themes." Warneke's books, Nicholls added, "are a terrific read, compulsive page-turners"; her novels include a philosophical probing of the nature of religion "that is quite firmly worked out."

The concluding installment in the "Axis" trilogy, *Star-Man,* was greeted by Brooks with the exclamation, "The wait is over. *StarMan* has landed!" Applauding the many new characters and settings in the concluding volume, Brooks trumpeted, "The results are magnificent. . . . It has an energetic, dramatic, and surprising conclusion that will continue to delight and disturb readers long after they have turned the last page. . . . Douglass is, without a doubt, the finest fantasy writer in Australia today."

With the success of the "Axis" trilogy, Warneke initiated a new trilogy that takes place on the world of Tencendor. This trilogy, "The Wayfarer Redemption," begins some forty years after the conclusion of the "Axis" trilogy. Many characters from the first series, including Axis, reappear in the later books, though in secondary roles. The three "Wayfarer Redemption" novels are *Sinner, Pilgrim,* and *Crusader.*

Under the Douglass pseudonym, Warneke published two solo novels during the same period that her "Wayfarer" series reached bookstore shelves. One is the young-adult fantasy *Beyond the Hanging Wall,* which Geoff Bull, in *Australian Book Review,* praised for overcoming his bias against the fantasy genre. Warneke "goes far beyond the traditional low fantasy," opined Bull; the world of the novel is "cleverly" imagined and leads to possibilities for other intriguing worlds, in the opinion of the critic. Declaring that "finely drawn characters and different settings . . . are Sara Douglass's real talents," Bull hailed *Beyond the Hanging Wall* as a convincing, successful work "about the power of truth. . . . about the corruption of power and the power of the State over the individual."

Warneke's other 1997 novel is *Threshold,* a fantasy with Middle Eastern and mathematical themes rather than medieval European ones. In this work, mathematician magi rule the land of Ashdod, worshiping the numeral One. Several generations before the novel opens, mathematicians derived a mathematical formula enabling them to merge with One, which they viewed as

the Infinite. This formula they encoded into the design of a glass pyramid, called Threshold. The novel's characters are magi and slaves who work on the glass pyramid. One of the workers, a woman named Tirzah, is the first-person narrator. Through her eyes, readers learn how the pyramid is warping, becoming out of control. Instead of serving as a bridge from the world of Ashdod to Infinity, it serves as a bridge in the other direction, as something unknown crossed from Infinity to Ashdod. Terry Dowling, reviewing the novel for *Weekend Australian,* found elements of the novel interesting. With the qualification that, "any shortcomings are largely those of the epic fantasy form itself, as it is so often these days," the reviewer called Warneke "an assured and gifted storyteller."

BIOGRAPHICAL/CRITICAL SOURCES:

PERIODICALS

Aurealis, no. 15, p. 80.
Australian, January 22, 2000, article by Murray Waldren.
Australian Book Review, September, 1996, review by Peter Nicholls, pp. 63-64; December, 1996/January, 1997, pp. 89-90; December, 1999, review of *The Betrayal of Arthur,* p. 246.
Australian Magazine, January 22, 2000, Murray Waldren, "The Reality of Sara Douglass."
Booknews, August 1, 1995, review of *Images of the Educational Traveller in Early Modern England.*
Eidolon, October, 1995, Martin Livings, review of *BattleAxe,* pp. 101-102.
Kirkus Reviews, January 15, 2001, review of *BattleAxe,* p. 85.
Locus, December, 1999, review of *The Nameless Day,* p. 29.
On Dit, April, 1997.
Out of the Ashes, December, 1995.
OzLit, October 21, 1995, Dennis Neville, review of *BattleAxe;* March 6, 1996, Karen Brooks, review of *BattleAxe;* November 1, 1996, Karen Brooks, review of *Enchanter.*
Weekend Australian, April 12-13, 1997, Terry Dowling, review of *Threshold.*

OTHER

OzLit Reader's Review, http://dargo.vicnet.net.au/ozlit/ (May 21, 1998).
Sara Douglass Homepage, http://www.bendigo.net.au/~douglass (January 30, 2002).*

WARSHOFSKY, Isaac
   See SINGER, Isaac Bashevis

*   *   *

WATT, Ian (Pierre) 1917-1999

PERSONAL: Born March 7 (some sources say March 9), 1917, in Windermere, Westmorland, England; died December 13, 1999, in Menlo Park, CA; son of Thomas (a schoolmaster) and Renee Jeanne Gabrielle (Guitton) Watt; married Ruth Mellinkoff, July 14, 1947; children: George Hilary, Josephine. *Education:* St. John's College, Cambridge, B.A. (first-class honors), 1938, M.A., 1946; Ph.D., 1947; postgraduate study at the Sorbonne, University of California—Los Angeles, 1946, and Harvard University, 1947-48.

CAREER: St. John's College, Cambridge University, Cambridge, England, research fellow and supervisor, 1948-52, lecturer in English, 1949-50; University of California—Berkeley, assistant professor, 1952-55, associate professor, 1955-59, professor of English, 1959-62; University of East Anglia, Norwich, England, professor of English and dean of School of English Studies, 1962-64; Stanford University, Stanford, CA, faculty member of English department, 1964-71, Jackson Eli Reynolds Professor of Humanities, 1971-87, founding director of Stanford Humanities Center, 1980-85, professor emeritus, 1987-99. Visiting summer professor at Stanford University, 1956, University of British Columbia, 1960, University of Hawaii, 1965, 1967, and 1968, Williams College, 1970, University of Nice and University of Paris, 1975; delivered Alexander Lectures, University of Toronto, 1974, and Christian Gauss Seminar, Princeton University, 1980. Public lecturer on English literature and modern fiction, and broadcaster on literary topics for British Broadcasting Corporation. Editor, *Eagle* (magazine supported by members of St. John's College, Cambridge), 1949-52; advisory editor, *Nineteenth-Century Fiction,* 1959, *Eighteenth-Century Literature,* 1966-99, *Novel,* 1966-99, *Style,* 1967-99. *Military/wartime service:* British Army, 1939-46; became lieutenant; wounded and captured by Japanese in Singapore, 1942; prisoner of war, 1942-45.

MEMBER: American Academy of Arts and Sciences (fellow, 1972).

AWARDS, HONORS: Commonwealth Fund fellow in the United States, 1946-48; Guggenheim fellow in England, for work on Joseph Conrad, 1959 and 1972-73.

WRITINGS:

(Editor) *Wordsworth in Cambridge,* Cambridge University Press (Cambridge, England), 1950.

The Rise of the Novel: Studies in Defoe, Richardson, and Fielding, University of California Press (Berkeley, CA), 1957, reprinted, Pimlico (London, England), 2000.

(Editor) *Jane Austen: A Collection of Critical Essays,* Prentice-Hall (Englewood Cliffs, NJ), 1963.

(Editor and author of introduction and notes) *The Life and Opinions of Tristram Shandy, Gentleman,* Houghton Mifflin (Boston, MA), 1965.

(Editor and author of introduction and notes) *The Augustan Age: Approaches to Its Literature, Life, and Thought,* Fawcett Publications (Greenwich, CT), 1968.

(Editor) *The Victorian Novel: Modern Essays in Criticism,* Oxford University Press (New York, NY), 1971.

(Editor) *Conrad: The Secret Agent; A Casebook,* Macmillan (London, England), 1973.

(Compiler) *The British Novel: Scott through Hardy,* AHM Publishing (Northbrook, IL), 1973.

Conrad in the Nineteenth Century, University of California Press (Berkeley, CA), 1979.

Joseph Conrad: Nostromo, Cambridge University Press (New York, NY), 1988.

Myths of Modern Individualism: Faust, Don Quixote, Don Juan, Robinson Crusoe, Cambridge University Press (New York, NY), 1996.

Essays on Conrad, Cambridge University Press (New York, NY), 2000.

CONTRIBUTOR

The Age of Shakespeare, Pelican, 1955.

(Author of introduction) Henry Fielding, *An Apology for the Life of Mrs. Shamela Andrews,* Augustan Reprint Society, 1956.

From Dryden to Johnson, Pelican, 1957.

Harbrace College Reader, Harcourt, 1959.

Eighteenth-Century Studies, edited by James L. Clifford, Oxford University Press (New York, NY), 1959.

Mark Schorer, *Modern British Fiction,* Oxford University Press (New York, NY), 1961.

(Author of introduction) Jane Austen, *Sense and Sensibility,* Harper (New York, NY), 1961.

Robert Scholes, *Approaches to the Novel,* Chandler Publishing, 1961.

Fielding: A Collection of Critical Essays, edited by Ronald Paulson, Prentice-Hall (Englewood Cliffs, NJ), 1962.

The Novelist as Innovator, British Broadcasting Corporation (London, England), 1965.

Contributor to *Encyclopaedia Britannica* and of articles and reviews to *Listener, New Republic, Partisan Review, Essays in Criticism,* and other literary and language journals. Watt's papers are collected in the archives of Stanford University.

SIDELIGHTS: Literary critic and author Ian Watt was born and educated in England. He joined the British Army and served during World War II as an infantry lieutenant from 1939 to 1946, during which time he was taken prisoner by the Japanese and put to work on the construction of a railway across Thailand, a project that was the subject of the Pierre Boulle novel *Bridge over the River Kwai,* later filmed by David Lean. He suffered from malnutrition but survived, unlike the 12,000 prisoners who died, and spent his free time reading Shakespeare and the works of Swift and Dante, sometimes using the pages he had finished as cigarette papers.

Following the war, Watt returned to Cambridge to earn his doctorate, then studied in the United States. He taught at the University of California—Berkeley for ten years before returning to England to teach at the University of East Anglia, where he became the dean of the new School of English Studies. He returned to the United States in 1964 to teach at Stanford University. Watt guided the English department through the turbulence and student protests of the late 1960s and 1970s, and he himself led a department-wide strike protesting the U.S. invasion of Cambodia. He was named Jackson Eli Reynolds Professor of English and chaired the program in modern thought and literature. Watt taught until his retirement in 1987 and died in 1999 after a long illness.

Watt's *The Rise of the Novel: Studies in Defoe, Richardson, and Fielding* is considered one of the most influential works of literary criticism of the twentieth century. Watt began writing it before the war, at age twenty-one, and completed it during the three years he was a prisoner of war. Stanford's Senate of the Academic Council noted in a memorial resolution that "no modern work has been more important in generating, directly and indirectly, the critical study of fiction and its problematic relationship to life. This investigation of

the origins of the English novel has lasted in a way remarkable in literary criticism, and the most interesting studies of the development of the novel form still explicitly reckon with it." The resolution went on to say that Watt "played a crucial role in opening up for literary studies fields for scholars of all bents—fields consisting, to be sure, of turf to fight about. His interdisciplinary method was instrumental in bringing about the interaction of many critical practices and positions—structuralist, psychoanalytic, and feminist interpretation, reader-response theory, biography, neo-Marxism, and 'new historicism,' for instance, that have preoccupied critics of the last two decades." Watt was named founding director of the Stanford Humanities Center in 1980 and held that position until 1985. The resolution concluded by saying that Watt was "one of the greatest humanists in Stanford's history."

Among Watt's last books is *Myths of Modern Individualism: Faust, Don Quixote, Don Juan, Robinson Crusoe.* It was completed with the help of Watt's editor and family after he became gravely ill in 1994. Watt's subjects, with the exception of Robinson Crusoe, who appeared a century later, first surfaced in literature during the Counter-Reformation at the end of the sixteenth century and beginning of the seventeenth. Tzvetan Todorov noted in the *New Republic* that Watt was not interested in providing a history of the myths of modern individualism, but that his goal was "to understand the meaning of the larger cultural event. Why is it that these myths emerged at approximately the same time? And what evolution has their meaning undergone through the centuries, from the age of romanticism to the present? What do these myths and their transformations teach us about the identity of modern man? For the ubiquity and the persistence of these tales cannot be fortuitous. They at once reveal and affect the manner in which Europeans have conceived and imagined their own lives. They are both a product of and a driving force in our history."

Paula R. Backscheider wrote in *Studies in the Novel* that "part of the pleasure of this book is its revelation of Watt's mind and his lifetime of engagement with myth and individualism, concepts central not only to literature but to our nation's life. Watt treats the topics differently. He traces humankind's fear-punctuated love affair with individualism but probes the meaning and power of myth." Backscheider noted that Watt "tallies up the negative aspects of individualism; repeatedly he points out the lack of attachment and concern for family, the community, or any social group." "The strengths of the book are its balance and lines of vision—Watt turns the concepts of myth and individualism over and over in his mind," wrote Backscheider, "reveals new facets and new implications, never pronounces them wholly beneficial or destructive, and never loses sight of their magical appeal and their dangers."

Todorov wrote that Watt's *Conrad in the Nineteenth Century*, "and his other studies of his favorite writer, illuminate not only Conrad but also the ideological and social interactions that characterized the European situation at the end of the nineteenth century." Todorov called Watt "a perfectionist and a passionate teacher." In reviewing the collection *Essays on Conrad, Times Literary Supplement* contributor Giles Foden called Watt "the doyen of Conrad studies."

BIOGRAPHICAL/CRITICAL SOURCES:

PERIODICALS

Booklist, May 1, 1980, review of *Conrad in the Nineteenth Century,* p. 1250.

Book World, April 6, 1980, review of *Conrad in the Nineteenth Century,* p. 1.

British Book News, August, 1980, review of *Conrad in the Nineteenth Century,* p. 501; August, 1987, review of *The Rise of the Novel: Studies in Defoe, Richardson, and Fielding,* p. 521.

Choice, July, 1980, review of *Conrad in the Nineteenth Century,* p. 676; July, 1996, review of *Myths of Modern Individualism: Faust, Don Quixote, Don Juan, Robinson Crusoe,* p. 1788.

Criticism, fall, 1980, review of *Conrad in the Nineteenth Century,* p. 386.

Economist, May 24, 1980, review of *Conrad in the Nineteenth Century,* p. 126.

Guardian Weekly, May 11, 1980, review of *Conrad in the Nineteenth Century,* p. 18; December 21, 1980, review of *Conrad in the Nineteenth Century,* p. 22.

Hudson Review, winter, 1997, review of *Myths of Modern Individualism,* p. 675.

Journal of English and Germanic Philology, July, 1981, review of *Conrad in the Nineteenth Century,* p. 445.

Library Journal, January 15, 1980, Keith Cushman, review of *Conrad in the Nineteenth Century,* p. 207.

Listener, June 12, 1980, review of *Conrad in the Nineteenth Century,* p. 766.

London Review of Books, September 15, 1988, review of *Joseph Conrad: Nostromo,* p. 9.

Modern Fiction Studies, winter, 1980, review of *Conrad in the Nineteenth Century,* p. 704.

Modern Philology, November, 1981, review of *Conrad in the Nineteenth Century,* p. 177.

New Republic, March 15, 1980, Jack Beatty, review of *Conrad in the Nineteenth Century,* pp. 32-35; March 25, 1996, Tzvetan Todorov, review of *Myths of Modern Individualism,* pp. 34-37.

New Statesman, August 22, 1980, James Campbell, review of *Conrad in the Nineteenth Century,* pp. 17-18.

New Yorker, May 5, 1980, review of *Conrad in the Nineteenth Century,* p. 174.

New York Times Book Review, March 9, 1980, Edward W. Said, review of *Conrad in the Nineteenth Century,* pp. 1-3; November 30, 1980, review of *Conrad in the Nineteenth Century,* p. 14; September 13, 1981, review of *Conrad in the Nineteenth Century,* p. 55.

Observer (London), June 22, 1980, review of *Conrad in the Nineteenth Century,* p. 29; July 13, 1980, review of *Conrad in the Nineteenth Century,* p. 29; December 7, 1980, review of *Conrad in the Nineteenth Century,* p. 27.

Religious Studies Review, January, 1997, review of *Myths of Modern Individualism,* p. 52.

Review of English Studies, May, 1990, review of *Joseph Conrad: Nostromo,* p. 281.

Rocky Mountain Review of Language & Literature, February, 1996, review of *Myths of Modern Individualism,* p. 210.

Sewanee Review, October, 1980, review of *Conrad in the Nineteenth Century,* p. 610.

Sixteenth-Century Journal, summer, 1997, review of *Myths of Modern Individualism,* p. 530.

Studies in the Novel, summer, 1997, Paula R. Backscheider, review of *Myths of Modern Individualism,* pp. 262-264.

Times Literary Supplement, April 25, 1980, review of *Conrad in the Nineteenth Century,* p. 455; January 19, 2001, Giles Foden, "A Cold Moral Dusk," pp. 6-7.

Victorian Studies, winter, 1981, review of *Conrad in the Nineteenth Century,* p. 257.

Virginia Quarterly Review, summer, 1981, review of *Conrad in the Nineteenth Century,* p. 98.

Yale Review, winter, 1981, Tony Tanner, review of *Conrad in the Nineteenth Century,* pp. 267-272.

OBITUARIES:

OTHER

Stanford University Online Report, http://www.stanford.edu/dept/news/ (January 5, 2000), Diane Manuel, "Literary Critic, Author, and 'Great Humanist' Ian Watt Dies."

Stanford University, Senate of the Academic Council, http://facultysenate.stanford.edu/ (October 20, 2001), Bliss Carnochan and others, "Memorial Resolution: Ian Watt."*

* * *

WELCH, Kathryn E. 1956-

PERSONAL: Born April 30, 1956, in Coulburn, Australia; daughter of Alfred and Doris (O'Brian) Welch; married James Buckman, January 6, 1996. *Education:* University of Sydney, B.A., 1977, M.A., 1984; University of Queensland, Ph.D., 1991; University of New England, Diploma of Humanities, 1993.

ADDRESSES: Home—Newtown, Australia. *Office*— School of Ancient History and Classics, University of Sydney, Sydney, New South Wales 2006, Australia; fax: +61-2-9351-3918. *E-mail*—Kathryn.Welch@antiquity. usyd.edu.au.

CAREER: University of Sydney, Sydney, Australia, associate lecturer in ancient history.

WRITINGS:

(With Estelle Lazer and Jonathan Barlow) *The Romans,* Rizzoli (New York, NY), 1998.
(Editor, with Anton Powell) *Julius Caesar as Artful Reporter: The War Commentaries as Political Instruments,* Duckworth (London, England), 1999.
(Editor, with Anton Powell) *Sextus Pompeius,* The Classical Press of Wales/Duckworth (London, England), 2001.

BIOGRAPHICAL/CRITICAL SOURCES:

PERIODICALS

Times Literary Supplement, March 12, 1999, p. 30.*

* * *

WELTGE, Sigrid W(ortmann) 1935-
(Sigrid Weltge-Wortmann)

PERSONAL: Born October 31, 1935, in Bremen, Germany; daughter of Friedrich Wilhelm and Johanne (Tischer) Wortmann; married James E. Hassell (deceased); children: Karin Welles, Kirsten Weltge. *Edu-*

cation: Attended University of Geneva, 1958-60, and Moore College of Art, 1970-72; Goddard College, B.A. (history of art), M.A. (history of art), 1975; private studies in the history of art and textiles under Dr. C. Beer-Zorian of University of Geneva, Switzerland. *Politics:* "Democrat." *Religion:* "None."

ADDRESSES: Home—37 West Southampton Ave., Philadelphia, PA 19118. *Office*—Philadelphia University, Henry Ave., Philadelphia, PA 19144; fax: 215-951-2651. *E-mail*—weltges@philau.edu.

CAREER: Philadelphia University (formerly Philadelphia College of Textiles and Science), Philadelphia, PA, professor of art history, design, textiles, and costumes, 1978—. Artist/scholar-in-residence at Goddard College, 1977, Penland School of Crafts, 1994, Danmarks Design Skøle, and Kansas City Art Institute, 1996.

MEMBER: College Art Association, Costume Society of America, Mid-Atlantic Cultural Association, Phi Psi.

AWARDS, HONORS: Lilly Foundation fellow, University of Pennsylvania, 1980 and 1981; President's Award for Teaching Excellence, 1982; research grant, Deutsches Textilmuseum, Krefeld, Germany, 1985; travel grants from National Endowment for the Humanities, 1990 and 2000, and German Consulate General (for Berlin), 1991; award for outstanding teaching, Student Government Association, 1992; Lindback Distinguished Teaching Award, 1996.

WRITINGS:

Die Ersten Maler in Worpswede, Worpsweder Verlag, 1976, revised edition, 1984.
Bauhaus Textiles: Women Artists and the Weaving Workshop, Thames & Hudson (London, England), 1993, Thames & Hudson (New York, NY), 1998.
(Under name Sigrid Weltge-Wortmann) *Women's Work: Textile Art from the Bauhaus,* Chronicle Books (San Francisco, CA), 1993.
I Tessuti del Bauhaus: L'arte e l'artigianator di un laboratorio femminile, Avallardi Garzanti Editore, 1993.
Die Ersten Maler in Worpswede, Worpsweder Verlag, 1997.
Lore Kadden Lindenfeld: A Life in Textiles 1945-1997 (Black Mountain Dossier 3), Black Mountain College Museum and Arts Center (North Carolina), 1997.

Contributor to books, including *International Dictionary of Women Artists Born before 1900*, G. K. Hall (Boston, MA), 1984; *History of Clothing*, Hong Kong Polytechnic, 1989; *Dictionary of Women Artists*, Fitzroy Dearborn (Chicago, IL), 1997; and to periodicals, including *Interweave, Women's Studies Quarterly, Portfolio*, and *Arts Exchange*.

SIDELIGHTS: Sigrid W. Weltge once told *CA:* "My books to date reflect my interest and original research in artists' colonies and groups of people who worked together with a common goal in mind. As a German-American, I am also interested in elucidating commonalities found in both countries, and I am interested in the lives of immigrants. Currently I am working on reminiscences of my war-time childhood in Germany."

*   *   *

WELTGE-WORTMANN, Sigrid
  See WELTGE, Sigrid W(ortmann)

*   *   *

WIATER, Stanley 1953-

PERSONAL: Surname pronounced "*Wee*-otter"; born May 21, 1953, in Northampton, MA; son of Stanley and Ann (Misholovsky) Wiater; married Iris Arroyo (a social service director), September 21, 1985; children: Tanya. *Ethnicity:* "Polish." *Education:* University of Massachusetts, B.A., 1975. *Politics:* Democrat. *Religion:* Catholic.

ADDRESSES: Home and office—ShadoWind, Inc., 381 Upper Rd., Deerfield, MA 01342-9714. *Agent*—Lori Perkins Associates, 5800 Arlington Ave., Riverdale, NY 10471. *E-mail*—StanWiater@aol.com.

CAREER: Freelance writer, 1975—; owner of corporation, ShadoWind, Inc; co-creator, writer, and host of *Dark Dreamers* (weekly half-hour interview series), produced in Canada, 2000—.

MEMBER: National Writers Union, Horror Writers Association.

AWARDS, HONORS: Winner of competition judged by Stephen King, 1980, for short story, "The Toucher"; Bram Stoker Award for superior achievement in nonfic-

tion, Horror Writers Association, 1991, and Bram Stoker Award nomination, 1993, both for *Dark Visions: Conversations with the Masters of the Horror Film;* Master of Ceremonies, World Horror Convention III, 1993; Harvey Award nomination and Eisner Award nomination, both 1994, both for *Comic Book Rebels: Conversations with the Creators of the New Comics;* Bram Stoker Award for Best Nonfiction, Horror Writers Association, 1998, for *Dark Thoughts: On Writing: Advice and Commentary from Fifty Masters of Fear and Suspense.*

WRITINGS:

(Editor) *Night Visions 7,* Dark Harvest (Niles, IL), 1989.

Dark Dreamers: Conversations with the Masters of Horror, limited edition, Underwood/Miller, 1990, Avon (New York, NY), 1990.

The Official Teenage Mutant Ninja Turtles Treasury, Villard Books/Random House (New York, NY), 1991.

Dark Visions: Conversations with the Masters of the Horror Film, Avon (New York, NY), 1992.

(Editor) *After the Darkness,* Maclay & Associates, 1993.

(With Stephen R. Bissette) *Comic Book Rebels: Conversations with the Creators of the New Comics,* Donald I. Fine (New York, NY), 1993.

Mysteries of the Word, Crossroads Press (Holyoke, MA), 1994.

Dark Thoughts: On Writing: Advice and Commentary from Fifty Masters of Fear and Suspense, Underwood Books (Grass Valley, CA), 1997.

(Editor) *Richard Matheson's "The Twilight Zone" Scripts,* limited edition, Cemetery Dance Publications, 1998, revised edition, Gauntlet Press, 2001.

(With Christopher Golden and Hank Wagner) *The Stephen King Universe: A Guide to the Worlds of the King of Horror,* limited edition, Cemetery Dance Publications, 2001, Renaissance Books, 2001.

Dark Dreamers: Facing the Masters of Fear, photographs by Beth Gwinn, limited edition, Cemetery Dance Publications, 2001.

Also author of original scripts for comic books, including *Teenage Mutant Ninja Turtles,* Archie Comics, 1992-94; *TMNT Universe Sourcebook,* Archie Comics, 1992-94; and "Teenage Mutant Ninja Turtles" (syndicated daily comic strip), 1993. Contributor of short-story adaptations to *Goreshriek #5, Shriek #1,* and *Shriek #2.* Contributor to fiction anthologies, including *Masques II,* 1987, *Obsessions,* 1991, and *Voices from the Night,* 1994. Contributor to nonfiction texts, including *The Star Trek Files: Where No Man Has Gone Before,* 1985, *The Robert Bloch Companion,* 1989, *Stephen King & Clive Barker: The Masters of the Macabre,* 1990, *Famous Monsters Chronicles,* 1991, *The Complete Stephen King Encyclopedia,* 1991, *James Herbert: By Horror Haunted,* 1992, and *Bizarre Bazaar III,* 1994. Since 1970 has made more than 700 contributions to popular-culture periodicals and Online publications, including *Valley Advocate, Amherst Record, Fate, Fangoria, Horrorstruck, New Blood,* Amazon.com, and Barnes and Noble.com. Wiater's interviews, articles, reviews, short stories, comic book scripts, and essays have been published in numerous countries, including England, France, Spain, Mexico, Italy, and Germany.

WORK IN PROGRESS: The Films of Wes Craven, 2002; as editor, *The Brian Lumley Companion,* for Tor Books, 2002.

SIDELIGHTS: Stanley Wiater once told *CA:* "Although I've spent most of my career writing in—and about—the horror genre, I find that the most appreciative audiences for this field are children and young people in general. Even better than most adults, they understand the healing and therapeutic values which tales of horror (which are little more than fairy tales for grown-ups) can provide to the attentive reader. As a young child, I distinctly recall actor Vincent Price being interviewed on television. When asked if scary movies and books had a negative effect on the youth of America, he replied without hesitation: 'Why, monsters are *good* for you!' I like to think my studies of the horror genre, and of the even less respectable comic book medium, will help others to understand why monsters are, indeed, good for us all."

The creators of these monsters and heroes are the focus of Wiater's books *Dark Dreamers: Conversations with the Masters of Horror, Dark Visions: Conversations with the Masters of the Horror Film,* and *Comic Book Rebels: Conversations with the Creators of the New Comics.* In each work, Wiater interviews leaders in a particular field. Trends of both the past and present are explored in these interviews, and anecdotes, as well as philosophies, are related by the artists. Patrick S. Jones, reviewing *Dark Dreamers* in *Kliatt,* maintained that the work is "a fine collection for either leisure reading or use in research papers about any of these macabre masters." And in his review of *Dark Visions, Washington Post Book World* contributor Martin Morse Wooster asserted that "Wiater is an experienced interviewer," concluding that for "people who love horror movies, *Dark Visions* provides a good deal of chatty fun."

BIOGRAPHICAL/CRITICAL SOURCES:

PERIODICALS

Kirkus Reviews, June 1, 1993, p. 712.
Kliatt, January, 1991, p. 29.
Locus, October, 1990, p. 31.
Publishers Weekly, June 21, 1993, p. 98.
Tribune Books (Chicago), February 2, 1992, p. 8.
Washington Post Book World, March 29, 1992, p. 8.

OTHER

Stanley Wiater Web site, http://www.stanleywiater.com (January 20, 2002).

*   *   *

WICOMB, Zoë 1948-

PERSONAL: Born November 23, 1948, near Vredendal, Cape Province, South Africa; daughter of Robert and Rachel Wicomb; children: Hannah Palmer. *Education:* University of the Western Cape, B.A., 1968; University of Reading, B.A. (with honors), 1973; University of Strathclyde, MLitt., 1989. *Religion:* "None."

ADDRESSES: Home—Glasgow, Scotland. *Agent*—Shelley Power Literary Agency, P.O. Box 149A, Surbiton, Surrey KT6 5JH, England. *E-mail*—z.wicomb@strath.ac.uk.

CAREER: Writer and educator. University of Strathclyde, Glasgow, Scotland, senior lecturer in English studies.

AWARDS, HONORS: South African MNet Prize, 2001, for *David's Story.*

WRITINGS:

You Can't Get Lost in Cape Town (short stories), Pantheon (New York, NY), 1987.
David's Story (novel; "Women Writing Africa" series), Feminist Press at the City University of New York (New York, NY), 2001.

Author of several essays on South African fiction and culture. Contributor to *Southern African Review of Books* and *London* and to collections, including *The Penguin Book of Contemporary South African Short Stories,* edited by S. Gray, Penguin (Johannesburg, South Africa), *The Heinemann Book of South African Short Stories,* edited by D. Hirson, Heinemann (London, England), and *The Art of the Story: An International Anthology of Contemporary Short Stories,* edited by Daniel Halpern, Viking (New York, NY).

SIDELIGHTS: Zoë Wicomb is an author and educator, now living in Scotland, whose books include *You Can't Get Lost in Cape Town,* a collection of connected stories featuring mixed-race South Africans, called coloured, and their lives and experiences as they are lived somewhere between white and black society. The South African-born Wicomb was labeled "coloured" according to official government classification.

The stories in the collection take place between the 1950s and 1980s, and revolve around apartheid and actions that are unlawful because of the parties' racial makeup. Bharati Mukherjee wrote in the *New York Times Book Review* that the characters "do not condone the system of racial classification, even if some of them go along with the segregated seating in buses and the segregated waiting rooms in doctors' offices." Some attempt to elevate their positions by requiring their children to speak English. Wicomb's own parents spoke Afrikaans and encouraged their children to learn English. In the title story, a maid tells fellow riders on a bus that she steals chicken legs from the family she cooks for to make up for injustices. In "Ash on My Sleeve," Moira, a coloured housewife, hides black men without passes. Many of Wicomb's characters escape to Canada; in "When the Train Comes," Frieda is the first non-white to enter a previously all-white school, but moves to England following an interracial affair.

"Ms. Wicomb's subject isn't—as American readers might expect—simple apartheid," wrote Mukherjee. "It is the desperate search of the 'coloured' for identity in a harshly hierarchical society. In this 'acceptance' of apartheid and the desire to see beyond it, Ms. Wicomb follows Faulkner and certainly echoes her black countryman Njabulo Ndebele." Mukherjee called Wicomb's prose "vigorous, textured, lyrical. An alien landscape— the veld riotous with proteas, the tangled bush, the clearings for dingy townships, the hills aglow with light from the Southern Cross—is rendered vividly. The smallest gestures—the gyre of yellow mealiemeal boiling in a pot or a cook's fingers kneading pastry—are in-

vested with arrested images. . . . This is a sophisticated storyteller who combines the open-endedness of contemporary fiction with the . . . simplicity of family stories."

Dorothy Driver wrote in *World Literature Today* that if *You Can't Get Lost in Cape Town* "destabilizes and decentres the subject as part of its political engagement with the various discourses at work, the effect is not one of annihilation, for the social cross-currents or webbings of identity are recognized rather than repressed within the text and often comprise the characters' self-representations. And although the stories are mostly told through the medium of a single first-person narrator, the network of voices around her . . . as well as her own voices from the past—are given in dialogue and then also returned to, one way or another, as part of the narrator's consciousness."

Wicomb's first novel, *David's Story,* is set in 1991, as Nelson Mandela is being released from prison and the African National Congress has been legalized. A *Publishers Weekly* contributor said the story "unravels a long, fascinating family history." The protagonist is David Dirkse, a coloured anti-apartheid activist married to fellow protester Sally. He leaves his wife and children for Kokstad to research his roots and takes a lover, Dulcie, who has suffered torture and rape. The history of Griqualand is revealed through David's discovery that he is descended from Andries Abraham Stockenstrom Le Fleur, who brought the Griqua tribe into the desert during the nineteenth century. *New York Times Book Review* contributor Tom Beer called the novel "a kaleidoscopic book—its story is fragmented and colorful, its focus continuously shifting." *Library Journal* reviewer Ann Irvine wrote that *David's Story* is "more than a history lesson . . . or even an exciting adventure story," but rather it is "a huge step in the remaking of the South African novel." "There's no preaching," said Hazel Rochman in *Booklist.* "Wicomb is commenting on her own intricate narrative, showing how hard it is to tell the truth."

BIOGRAPHICAL/CRITICAL SOURCES:

BOOKS

Bardolph, J., editor, *Short Fiction in the New Literatures in English,* 1991.
Fletcher, Pauline, editor, *Black/White Writing: Essays on South African Literature,* Bucknell Review Press, 1993.

PERIODICALS

Booklist, May 1, 2001, Hazel Rochman, review of *David's Story,* p. 1669.

Kirkus Reviews, March 1, 2001, review of *David's Story,* pp. 288-289.

Library Journal, May 1, 2001, Ann Irvine, review of *David's Story,* p. 129.

New York Times Book Review, May 24, 1987, Bharati Mukherjee, "They Never Wanted to Be Themselves," p. 7, Kim Heron, "The 'Snob Value' of English" (interview), p. 8; May 27, 2001, Tom Beer, review of *David's Story,* p. 16.

Publishers Weekly, March 26, 2001, review of *David's Story,* p. 65.

Wall Street Journal, May 11, 1987, Lee Lescaze, review of *You Can't Get Lost in Capetown,* p. 25.

Washington Post, August 19, 2001, Anderson Tepper, "No Direction Home," p. T06.

World Literature Today, winter, 1996, Dorothy Driver, "Transformation through Art: Writing, Representation, and Subjectivity in Recent South African Fiction," p. 45.

*   *   *

WILDING, Michael 1942-

PERSONAL: Born January 5, 1942, in Worcester, England; son of Richard (an iron molder) and Dorothy Mary (Bull) Wilding; married Lyndy Abraham (a writer and scholar). *Ethnicity:* "Anglo-Celtic." *Education:* Lincoln College, Oxford, B.A. (with first class honors), 1963, M.A., 1967; University of Sydney, D.Litt., 1996.

ADDRESSES: Office—c/o School of English, University of Sydney, Sydney, New South Wales 2006, Australia; fax: +61-2-9351-2434. *E-mail*—Michael.Wilding@english.usyd.edu.au.

CAREER: Teacher at primary school in Spetchley, England, 1960; University of Sydney, Sydney, Australia, lecturer in English, 1962-66; University of Birmingham, Birmingham, England, assistant lecturer, 1967, lecturer in English, 1968; University of Sydney, senior lecturer, 1969-72, reader, 1973-92, professor of English and Australian literature, 1993-2000, professor emeritus, 2001—, Herbert Blaiklock Lecturer, 1985. Wild & Woolley Ltd. (publisher), director, 1974-79; Paper Bark Press, coeditor, 1987-97. University of California, Santa Barbara, visiting professor, 1987; University of Queen-sland, George Watson Visiting Fellow, 1990; James Cook University, Colin Roderick Lecturer, 1992; National University of Singapore, visiting professor at Centre for the Arts, 1996. Literature Board of Australia, member of council, 1975-76; member of international advisory board, Fourth and Fifth International Milton Symposia, 1992, 1995; Sydney Festival Writers' Week, committee member, 1994-97; New South Wales State Literary Awards judging panel, chair, 1994; New South Wales Writers' Centre, chair, 1997—.

MEMBER: Australian Academy of the Humanities (fellow), Japan Milton Society (member, international advisory board), Sydney Association for Studies in Society and Culture (chair, 1992—).

AWARDS, HONORS: Senior fellowship, Literature Board of Australia, 1978.

WRITINGS:

FICTION

Aspects of the Dying Process (short stories), University of Queensland Press (St. Lucia, Australia), 1972.

Living Together (novel), University of Queensland Press (St. Lucia, Australia), 1974.

The Short Story Embassy (novel), Wild & Woolley (Sydney, Australia), 1975.

The West Midland Underground (short stories), University of Queensland Press (St. Lucia, Australia), 1975.

Scenic Drive (novel), Wild & Woolley (Sydney, Australia), 1976.

The Phallic Forest (short stories), Wild & Woolley (Sydney, Australia), 1978.

Pacific Highway (novel), Hale & Iremonger (Sydney, Australia), 1981.

Reading the Signs (short stories), Hale & Iremonger (Sydney, Australia), 1984.

The Paraguayan Experiment (novel), Penguin Books (Melbourne, Australia), 1985.

The Man of Slow Feeling: Selected Short Stories, Penguin Books (Melbourne, Australia), 1985.

Under Saturn (short stories), Black Swan (Sydney, Australia), 1987.

Great Climate (short stories), Faber & Faber (London, England), 1990.

Her Most Bizarre Sexual Experience (short stories), W. W. Norton (New York, NY), 1991.

This Is for You, Angus & Robertson (Sydney, Australia), 1994.

Book of the Reading, Paper Bark Press (Sydney, Australia), 1994.

Somewhere New: New and Selected Stories, McBride's Books (Colwall, England), 1996.

Wildest Dreams, University of Queensland Press (St. Lucia, Australia), 1998.

Raising Spirits, Making Gold, and Swapping Wives: The True Adventures of Dr. John Dee and Sir Edward Kelly, Shoestring Press (Nottingham, England), 1999.

Author's work has been translated into Japanese, Bengali, and Serbo-Croatian.

NONFICTION

Milton's "Paradise Lost," Sydney University Press (Sydney, Australia), 1969.

(With Michael Green and Richard Hoggart) *Cultural Policy in Great Britain,* UNESCO (Paris, France), 1970.

Marcus Clarke, Oxford University Press (Melbourne, Australia), 1977.

Political Fictions (criticism), Routledge & Kegan Paul (London, England), 1980.

Dragons Teeth: Literature in the English Revolution (criticism), Clarendon Press (Oxford, England), 1986.

The Radical Tradition: Lawson, Furphy, Stead, Foundation for Australian Literary Studies (Townsville, Australia), 1993.

Social Visions, Sydney Studies in Society & Culture (Sydney, Australia), 1993.

Studies in Classic Australian Fiction, Shoestring Press (Nottingham, England), 1997.

Among Leavisites, privately printed (Sydney, Australia), 1999.

EDITOR

(With Charles Higham) *Australians Abroad,* F. W. Cheshire (Melbourne, Australia), 1967.

Henry James, *Three Tales,* Hicks Smith (Sydney, Australia), 1967.

Marvell: Modern Judgements, Macmillan (London, England), 1969, Aurora (Nashville, TN), 1970.

John Sheffield, *The Tragedy of Julius Caesar and Marcus Brutus,* Cornmarket (London, England), 1970.

(With Shirley Cass, Ros Cheney, and David Malouf) *We Took Their Orders and Are Dead: An Anti-War Anthology,* Ure Smith (Sydney, Australia), 1971.

The Portable Marcus Clarke, University of Queensland Press (St. Lucia, Australia), 1976, 2nd edition, 1988.

(With Stephen Knight) *The Radical Reader,* Wild & Woolley (Sydney, Australia), 1977.

The Tabloid Story Pocket Book, Wild & Woolley (Sydney, Australia), 1978.

William Lane, *The Workingman's Paradise,* Sydney University Press (Sydney, Australia), 1980.

Marcus Clarke, *Stories,* Hale & Iremonger (Sydney, Australia), 1983.

(With Rudi Krausmann) *Airmail from down Under* (short stories in German translation), Gangan (Vienna, Austria), 1990.

The Oxford Book of Australian Short Stories, Oxford (New York, NY), 1994.

(Editor, with Mabel Lee) *History, Literature, and Society: Essays in Honour of S. N. Mukherjee,* Sydney Association for Studies in Society and Culture (Leichhardt, Australia), 1997.

(With Irina Dunn and Brian Kiernan) *Sydney Stories,* New South Wales Writers' Centre, in press.

OTHER

Author of screenplays *The Phallic Forest* (film), Sydney Filmmakers Co-operative, 1972; and *Reading the Signs* (television film), Central Independent Television (Birmingham, England), 1988. Sydney correspondent, *Overland,* 1999—. General editor of "Asian and Pacific Writing" series, University of Queensland Press (St. Lucia, Australia), 1972-82. Contributor to periodicals, including *London, New Yorker, Harper's, Bananas,* and *Gargoyle.* Editor of *Isis,* 1962; coeditor of *Balcony: Sydney Review,* 1965-67, *Tabloid Story,* 1972-76, and *Post-Modern Writing,* 1979-81; Australian editor, *Stand* magazine, 1972-99; member of advisory board, *Australian Literary Studies, DotLit,* and *Literature and Aesthetics;* past member of advisory board, *Dissent, New Poetry, Outrider, Redoubt, Science Fiction, Sydney City Hub, Ulitarra,* and *World Literature Written in English.*

SIDELIGHTS: Michael Wilding told *CA:* "I began writing at school, an English grammar school with a very ancient foundation (1292), and the first piece of writing I sold was to a local paper, the oldest surviving newspaper in the world, *Berrow's Worcester Journal* (established 1690). I continued writing at Oxford, quite an old place in itself, where I read English literature up to the 1870s (where the syllabus stopped), edited the undergraduate paper *Isis,* and applied for a college traveling scholarship to the U.S.A., where I proposed to take an M.A. in creative writing. 'You are suggesting we support you for a year in America while you write a novel?' 'Yes,' I answered brightly. They didn't. They told me I was the best candidate, but they thought I should stay at Oxford and do graduate work. I didn't. I took up a lectureship in Sydney and never did do any graduate work. Nor did I study creative writing, though I taught it at Santa Barbara years later, and then introduced it to Sydney University—the first university course in creative writing in Australia—and taught it for ten years. In the end I received a D.Litt. on the basis of my academic publications and shortly afterwards took early retirement.

"Writing fiction has always been my first interest. I sold my first story to the British Broadcasting Corporation in 1960, and I have continued to publish stories, in *London* magazine, *Stand, New Yorker, Harper's, Bananas, Gargoyle,* and a host of Australian journals and little magazines up to the present. In the 1970s I coedited the journal *Tabloid Story,* which had an influential role in establishing new fictional modes in Australia.

"University teaching in the 1960s and 1970s was a good life, lively, enjoyable, optimistic. It gave me of necessity a thorough grounding in the traditions of literature, which is important for a writer, and in 'the moderns' and, in due course, the contemporary. The lectures provided the basis for articles, which I collected into books. The rest of the time I wrote fiction, stories to begin with, then novels. I enjoyed writing literary criticism, up to a point. Then, when it became tedious, I turned to fiction. When the fiction seized up, I returned to literary criticism. The choice of alternatives saved me from sitting around lamenting writers' block or academic accidie.

"The new world of Australia was very different from the traditions of provincial England. I loved it, and it provided me with my first materials: the bohemian world of Sydney with its writers and journalists, anarchists and leftists, filmmakers and poets. I moved from English psychological realism to a new world experimentalism—'new writing' as we called it at the time, for want of any other term. Now it is called postmodernism. It was fun to do. Experimental, spontaneous, in love with the fictionality of fiction. I collected the stories of this new life, together with recollections of the England I had left, in such volumes as *Aspects of the Dying Process, The West Midland Underground,* and *Reading the Signs. The Man of Slow Feeling: Selected Short Stories, Great Climate, Book of the Reading,* and *Somewhere New: New and Selected Stories* are selections from these and other earlier volumes.

"Things changed, of course, as they do. The bohemia of youth and love and sexuality and drugs and protest turned sour, or revealed its transitoriness and illusoriness. Postmodernism began to seem an empty formalism and exposed the need for social content. The disillusion and rethinking provided new materials, new struggles, new techniques. The joyfulness of *The Short Story Embassy* and *Pacific Highway* were succeeded by the paranoid explorations of *Under Saturn* and the sardonic reflections of *This Is for You.* I took an overview of it all in *Wildest Dreams,* a book I had wanted to call *The Literary Pages,* but the publisher said books with 'literary' in the title did not sell: in itself a sad sign of the new times, or new publishers.

"Australia had offered the new, the future. But I was still drawn to the past. Fiction had offered spontaneity, but I was also drawn to scholarly research. As well as chronicling the life around me, I began to turn to historical themes, themes that also cast some light on the present. In the novel *The Paraguayan Experiment* I wrote about an actual 1890s experiment in communal living, the New Australia Movement. I told of the attempt by Australian trade-unionists and radicals, defeated in the 1890s strikes, to set up a new communal society in South America. I drew firmly on the surviving documentary materials, letters, diaries, newspaper accounts, and government reports in Australia and Britain.

"More recently I turned to the sixteenth century with *Raising Spirits, Making Gold, and Swapping Wives: The True Adventures of Dr. John Dee and Sir Edward Kelly*—an account of the alchemists John Dee and Edward Kelly in England and Central Europe. This time the documentary nature of the material is even more substantial, drawing on the surviving records of dialogues with spirits and angels, on diaries, diplomatic correspondence, and reports to bankers and government from spies and informers. It is an astonishing story, and I chose to let the materials speak for themselves—after reducing the huge mass of documentation to a manageable 500 pages. My wife, Lyndy Abraham, has written a number of scholarly works on alchemy, which helped me considerably with the intellectual context. And Edward Kelly was born in my home town of Worcester, which helped in other mysterious ways. The account was a welcome change to write after the autobiographical explorations of my other fictions and the attendant psychic anxieties they can create. There are another four or five books in the pipeline, different again, but I prefer not to comment on them until they have appeared."

BIOGRAPHICAL/CRITICAL SOURCES:

BOOKS

Anderson, Don, *Hot Copy: Reading & Writing Now,* Penguin (Ringwood, Australia), 1986.

Capone, Givoanna, editor, *European Perspectives: Contemporary Essays on Australian Literature,* University of Queensland Press (St. Lucia, Australia), 1991.

Clancy, Laurie, *Readers' Guide to Australian Fiction,* Oxford University Press (New York, NY), 1992.

de Groen, Fran, and Ken Stewart, editors, *Australian Writing and the City,* Association for the Study of Australian Literature (Sydney, Australia), 2000.

Dutton, Geoffrey, editor, *Literature of Australia,* revised edition, Penguin Books (Ringwood, Australia), 1976.

Daniel, Helen, editor, *The Good Reading Guide,* McPhee Gribble (Melbourne, Australia), 1989.

Gelder, Ken, and Paul Salzman, *The New Diversity: Australian Fiction 1970-88,* McPhee Gribble (Melbourne, Australia), 1989.

Goodwin, Ken, *A History of Australian Literature,* Macmillan (New York, NY), 1986.

Hamilton, K. G., editor, *Studies in the Recent Australian Novel,* University of Queensland Press (St. Lucia, Australia), 1978.

Hergenhan, L. T., editor, *The New Literary History of Australia,* Penguin (Ringwood, Australia), 1988.

Kramer, L. J., editor, *The Oxford History of Australian Literature,* Oxford University Press (New York, NY), 1981.

Maver, Igor, *Contemporary Australian Literature between Europe and Australia,* Shoestring Press (Nottingham, England), 1999.

Ousby, Ian, editor, *Cambridge Guide to Literature in English,* Cambridge University Press (New York, NY)), 1988.

Wilde, W. H., Barry Andrews, and Joy Hooten, editors, *The Oxford Companion to Australian Literature,* Oxford University Press (New York, NY), 1985, 2nd edition, 1994.

Wilkes, G. A., *The Stockyard and the Croquet Lawn: Literary Evidence for Australia's Cultural Development,* Edward Arnold (Melbourne, Australia), 1981.

PERIODICALS

Antipodes, June, 1994, Nadezda Obradovic, "A Return to Narrative: Talking with Michael Wilding," pp. 9-13, and Frank Parigi, "Frank Moorhouse and Michael Wilding—and Internationalism," pp. 15-20; December, 1998, Igor Maver, "'My Beloved Mississippi River': Michael Wilding's Somewhere New," pp. 83-89.

Aspect, spring, 1975, Rudi Krausmann, "A Reluctant Moralist," pp. 21-24.

Australian Literary Studies, Vol. 9, 1980, interview by David Albahari, pp. 321-327; Vol. 11, 1983, Bruce Clunies Ross, "A New Version of Pastoral: The Fiction of Michael Wilding," pp. 182-194; May, 1988, Ian Syson, "Michael Wilding's Three Centres of Value," pp. 269-279, and Ian Syson, "After Libertarianism: An Interview with Michael Wilding," pp. 280-292.

Caliban, Vol. 14, 1977, Brian Kiernan, "Recent Developments in Australian Writing with Particular Reference to Short Fiction," pp. 123-134.

Campaign, Vol. 23, 1977, Martin Smith, "Author, Critic, Radical, Michael Wilding," pp. 23-24.

Cleo, June, 1975, Elizabeth Wynhausen, "Wild Man of Letters."

Imago, Vol. 11, no. 2, 1999, pp. 15-21.

Journal of the Short Story in English, Vol. 12, 1989, Simone Vauthier, "Lost and Found: Narrative and Description in Michael Wilding's 'What It Was Like, Sometimes,'" pp. 63-76.

Kunapipi, Vol. 1, no. 2, 1980, Bruce Clunies Ross, "Laszlo's Testament, or Structuring the Past and Sketching the Present in Contemporary Short Fiction," pp. 110-123.

Meanjin, Vol. 45, no. 1, 1986, Bruce Clunies Ross, "Paradise, Politics, and Fiction: The Writing of Michael Wilding," pp. 19-27.

Overland, Vol. 96, 1984, Hans Hauge, "Post-Modernism and the Australian Literary Heritage," pp. 50-51.

Southerly, Vol. 33, 1973, Carl Harrison-Ford, "The Short Stories of Wilding and Moorhouse," pp. 167-178; Vol. 46, 1986, interview by Giulia Giuffre, pp. 313-321.

Southwest Review, spring, 1993, Don Graham, "Koka Kola Culture: Reflections upon Things American down Under," pp. 231-244.

Stand, Vol. 33, no. 1, 1991, interview by Peter Lewis, pp. 44-47.

Sydney Morning Herald, February 8, 1986.

Washington Post Book World, March 20, 1983.

World Literature Written in English, Vol. 35, no. 1, 1996, Igor Maver, "O My America, My Newfoundland, Australia," pp. 3-11.

OTHER

Australian Writers: Michael Wilding (video), University of Sydney Television Service (Sydney, Australia), 1992.

Reading the Signs (documentary film), Central Independent Television (Birmingham, England), 1988.

*   *   *

WILLIAMS, C(harles) K(enneth) 1936-

PERSONAL: Born November 4, 1936, in Newark, NJ; son of Paul Bernard and Dossie (Kasdin) Williams; married Sarah Dean Jones, June, 1966 (divorced, 1975); married Catherine Mauger (an editor), April 13, 1975; children: (first marriage) Jessica Anne; (second marriage) Jed Mauger. *Education:* University of Pennsylvania, B.A., 1959. *Avocational interests:* Piano, guitar, drawing.

ADDRESSES: Home—82, Rue d'Hauteville, 75010 Paris, France; 71 Leigh Ave., Princeton, NJ 08542. *E-mail*—ckwilliams@compuserve.com.

CAREER: Poet. Columbia University, New York, NY, professor of writing, 1981-85; George Mason University, Fairfax, VA, professor of literature, 1982-95. Visiting professor of literature, Beaver College, Jenkintown, PA, 1975, Drexel University, Philadelphia, PA, 1976, University of California at Irvine, 1978, Boston University, 1979-80, Brooklyn College, 1982-83; Franklin and Marshall College, Lancaster, PA, Mellon visiting professor of literature, 1977; Halloway lecturer at University California—Berkeley, 1986; lecturer at Princeton University, Princeton, NJ, 1996—.

MEMBER: PEN, Poetry Society of America.

AWARDS, HONORS: Guggenheim fellowship, 1974; Pushcart Press Prize, 1982, 1983, and 1987; National Endowment for Arts fellowships, 1985 and 1993; National Book Critics Circle Award, 1987, for *Flesh and Blood;* Morton Dauwen Zabel Prize, American Academy of Arts and Letters, 1989; Harriet Monroe Prize, 1993; Lila Wallace-*Reader's Digest* grantee, 1993; Pulitzer Prize for poetry, 2000, for *Repair.*

WRITINGS:

POEMS

A Day for Anne Frank, Falcon Press (Philadelphia, PA), 1968.
Lies, Houghton Mifflin (Boston, MA), 1969.
I Am the Bitter Name, Houghton Mifflin, 1972.

C. K. Williams

With Ignorance, Houghton Mifflin, 1977.
The Lark, the Thrush, the Starling, Burning Deck (Providence, RI), 1983.
Tar, Random House (New York, NY), 1983.
Flesh and Blood, Farrar, Straus (New York, NY), 1987.
Poems 1963-1983, Farrar, Straus, 1988.
Helen, Orchises Press (Washington, DC), 1991.
A Dream of Mind, Farrar, Straus, 1992.
Selected Poems, Farrar, Straus, 1994.
The Vigil, Farrar, Straus, 1996.
Repair, Farrar, Straus, 1999.
Love about Love, Ausable Press (Keene, NY), 2001.

TRANSLATOR

(With Gregory Dickerson) Sophocles, *Women of Trachis,* Oxford University Press, 1978.
Euripides, *Bacchae,* Farrar, Straus, 1990.
(With Renata Gorczynski and Benjamin Ivry) Adam Zagajewski, *Canvas,* Farrar, Straus, 1991.
(With John Montague and Margaret Grissom) *Selected Poems of Francis Ponge,* Wake Forest University Press (Winston-Salem, NC), 1994.

EDITOR

(And author of introduction) Paul Zweig, *Selected and Last Poems,* Wesleyan University Press (Middletown, CT), 1989.
(And author of introduction) Gerard Manly Hopkins, *The Essential Hopkins,* Ecco (Hopewell, NJ), 1993.

Also contributing editor of *American Poetry Review,* 1972—.

OTHER

Poetry and Consciousness (criticism), University of Michigan Press (Ann Arbor, MI), 1998.
Misgivings: My Mother, My Father, Myself (autobiography), Farrar, Straus, 2000.

SIDELIGHTS: Hailed by poet Paul Muldoon in the *Times Literary Supplement* as "one of the most distinguished poets of his generation," C. K. Williams has created a highly respected body of work, including not only several collections of original poems but volumes of translations, editions of poem collections, a book of criticism, and a memoir. Readers and critics alike esteem him as an original stylist. His characteristic line is extraordinarily long, almost prose-like, and emphasizes characterization and dramatic development. His early work focused on overtly political issues, such as the Vietnam War and social injustice. Though often admired, this scathing material was sometimes considered "ruthless, even cruel," as reported in a retrospective sketch in the *New York Times* in 2000. In his more recent work, Williams has shifted from a documentary style toward a more introspective approach, writing descriptive poems that reveal the states of alienation, deception, and occasional enlightenment that exist between public and private lives in modern urban America.

Williams's second book, *Lies,* was published upon the recommendation of confessional poet Anne Sexton who, according to Allan M. Jalon in the *Los Angeles Times,* called Williams "the Fellini of the written word," and the book received strong critical acclaim. M. L. Rosenthal, reviewing the book in *Poetry,* described it as a collection of poems that portrays "psychic paralysis despite the need to make contact with someone." Fred Moramarco in *Western Humanities Review* noted that the poems "sound the grim notes of [William Blake's] *Songs of Experience,*" where "paradox is a quality central to almost each poem in the volume." The final poem in the book, "A Day for Anne Frank," which had been published separately a year earlier, was praised by Alan Williamson in *Shenandoah* as "a surprisingly moving poem, one of the best in the book."

Williams's next three books all met with continued critical success. *I Am the Bitter Name,* the title of which, as Jascha Kessler pointed out in *Poetry,* "is meant . . . to stand for Death," is largely a collection of protest poems about the fear and hatred nurtured by America's involvement in the Vietnam War, culminating in a long, final poem, "In the Heart of the Beast," about the shooting of students at Kent State University by the Ohio National Guard. In this poem, John Vernon stated in *Western Humanities Review,* "the language is like a whip that lashes out."

Williams's next book, *With Ignorance,* however, shows the first development of the poet's trademark style, where, as James Atlas explained in *Nation,* "the lines are so long that the book had to be published in a wide-page format, like an art catalogue," giving the poetry "an eerie incantatory power." Indeed, these long lines, which have drawn comparisons to the work of Whitman and Ginsberg, have generated much critical comment throughout Williams's career. A *Publishers Weekly* contributor, in a review of *The Vigil,* observed that Williams's "stanzas extend to and from the book spine like knobby, elongated hands grabbing for God, for relief from pain and for love," while a writer for *Booklist,* commenting on the same book, found the poet's long line "an admirable instrument indeed . . . an Offenbach Baracolc of a line." In the *Boston Review,* Richard Howard related Williams's lines to color-field painting, pointing out that such a technique creates a "field" so wide that it cannot be taken in by the viewer/reader, but instead takes the viewer/reader in. Though Howard found that "The lines [in *The Vigil*] have to array some of the most garish and clunky language assayed in recent poetry" and employ a "clattering languor and . . . mock-Jamesian cadences," he appreciated their suitability for narration and description, if not for philosophical or intellectual matters. "So vivid are Williams's successes with immediacy of sensation and of narration, so overwhelming his virtuosity . . . in revving up his chosen, his imposed machine," Howard concluded, "that I am most of the time transfixed by his gift." However, Brian Phillips, reviewing Williams's eighth collection, *Repair,* in *New Republic,* commented that "his long poetic line often dips its toe testingly into the waters of the prosaic," showing that line breaks work efficiently but "cannot be said to have much of a felt impact on the aesthetic experience of reading the poem."

Flesh and Blood is a collection of eight-line poems, each poem of twenty or twenty-five syllables and printed two poems to a page, making them comparable, as Michael Hofmann suggested in the *Times Literary Supplement,* to "[Robert] Lowell's sonnets, or [John] Berryman's Dreamsongs." The poems' subjects, the critic pointed out, are "the by-now familiar gallery of hobos and winos, children and old people, lovers and invalids; the settings, typically, public places, on holidays, in parks, on pavements and metro-stations." Hirsch commented that while these poems "lack the narrative scope and sheer relentless force of Mr. Williams's longer poems . . . together they have a strong cumulative energy and effectiveness." Hirsch described Williams's poetry as having a "notational, ethnographic quality" that presents "single extended moments intently observed." Even though these poems sometimes read "like miniature short stories, sudden fictions," Hirsch continued, they always present people in situations where they are "vulnerable, exposed, on the edge." The book won Williams the National Book Critics Circle Award in 1987.

Poems 1963-1983 collects selections from *Lies* and *I Am the Bitter Name,* and reproduces both *With Ignorance* and *Tar* in their entirety. Muldoon called it "the book of poems I most enjoyed this year," finding Williams to have "an enviable range of tone" and to be "by turns tender and troubling." Hofmann claimed that the book "has as much scope and truthfulness as any American poet since Lowell and Berryman."

A Dream of Mind received mixed reviews. William Logan criticized the book in the *New York Times Book Review* as one in which Williams's long-line style has "decayed" from his earlier works into "continual repetition, pointless variation and the automatic cloning of phrases," making the poems "little Xerox machines of technique" in which Williams is "most successful when purely voyeuristic, less when confessional, and least when meditative." Lawrence Norfolk, however, writing in the *Times Literary Supplement,* lauded Williams for his "stubbornness or refusal to turn away" from "uncomfortable or harrowing realities," such as those presented in "Helen," a husband's account of his wife's decline and death. Michael Dirda, writing in the *Washington Post Book World,* favorably judged Williams's "often plain language" that "keeps the reader fascinated as much by his storytelling power as by his telling phrases."

Selected Poems replaces the early poems with work from *Flesh and Blood* and *A Dream of Mind,* and contains thirteen new poems. Ashley Brown, in *World Lit-*

erature Today, suggested that "Williams has learned from [French novelist Marcel] Proust how to make the power of memory operate to maximum effect," and a reviewer for the *Times Literary Supplement* appreciated Williams's later work, which "strikes a more refined balance between social and individual responsibilities." Williams, in a *Los Angeles Times* interview with Jalon, stated that he believes "the drama of American poetry is based very much on experience. It's coming out of all the different cultures. We're an enormous nation and we have an enormous poetry." Stephen Dobyns, writing in *Washington Post Book World,* described a characteristic Williams poem as one in which there are "variations of meaning pushing toward the increasingly precise."

The poet's later work developed an increasingly intimate tone as well, particularly in *Repair,* for which he won the Pulitzer prize for poetry in 2000. Often personal and introspective, the poems consider such subjects as the birth of the poet's grandson, the death of a friend's child, love, or something as mundane as the flowered house dresses worn by his mother and the women of her generation. Yet Williams also included powerfully social material, such as the title poem, in which he points a righteous finger at a tyrant whose "henchmen had disposed of enemies . . . by hammering nails into their skulls / . . .—how not to be annihilated by it?—the preliminary tap . . . / the way you do with your nail when you're fixing something, making something, shelves, a bed." *Boston Globe* critic Cathleen Calbert cited this poem as an example of "the Jewish sense of tikkun olam (to repair or make whole the world)," noting that "there is a deathly meaning to this kind of 'fixing something,' which Williams will not smooth over." Despite finding *Repair* an extremely bleak book, Calbert admired its "exact, bewildering, slant rendering of raw emotion and careful thought" and its unflinching honesty. Phillips, however, found the book often prosaic and almost didactic, suggesting that the poet's "inspections of motive and meaning seem more fit to offer moral instruction than to summon aesthetic intensity." Acknowledging Willliams's skills at observation and description, though, Phillips observed that "his work reflects the moral self-questioning of Herbert, the plain-spokenness and the yearning toward nature of Wordsworth, the foul rag-and-bone shop of the heart of the later Yeats." In addition to winning the Pulitzer, *Repair* was a finalist for the National Book Award.

Though his praise for *Repair* was qualified, Phillips expressed wholehearted admiration for Williams's prose memoir, *Misgivings: My Mother, My Father, Myself.* "In his memoir, Williams plumbs few deep truths," he observed, "but he emerges as one of the most authoritative psychologists (or pop-psychologists) in contemporary prose." The book presents mostly painful memories of Williams's authoritarian and emotionally cold father and his ineffective mother. In each chapter, the poet sketches a memory, then sharply questions his parents—both deceased—on their behavior. In the process, according to Phillips, Williams "creates an increasingly vivid portrait of both parents, who become fully realized and plausible human beings." A contributor to *Publishers Weekly*, however, faulted Williams for only "faint attempts to be sympathetic to his parents," and dismissed the memoir as a "tedious" list of grievances that "come off as both petty and inflated." But David Kirby, in *Library Journal*, praised the volume for its poetic nuance, complex understanding, and powerful emotional images.

BIOGRAPHICAL/CRITICAL SOURCES:

BOOKS

Clark, LaVerne Harrell, editor, *Focus 101*, Heidelberg Graphics (Chico, CA), 1979.
Contemporary Literary Criticism, Gale (Detroit), Volume 33, 1985, Volume 56, 1989.
Contemporary Poets, fifth edition, St. James Press (Detroit), 1991.
Dictionary of Literary Biography, Volume 5: *American Poets since World War II*, Gale (Detroit, MI), 1980.
Hamilton, Ian, editor. *Oxford Companion to Twentieth-Century Poetry in English*, Oxford University Press, 1994.

PERIODICALS

America, October 30, 1993.
American Poetry Review, fall, 1972, p. 45; winter, 1977; January-February, 1978, pp. 21-32; July-August, 1979, pp. 12-13; May, 1988, p. 9; May-June, 1994, Alan Williamson, "Poems including Politics," p. 17.
Antioch Review, summer, 1984, pp. 363-374.
Booklist, July 15, 1969, p. 1254; September 1, 1983, p. 23; June 15, 1992, Frances Woods, review of *A Dream of Mind*, p. 1803; October 1, 1994, Elizabeth Gunderson, review of *Selected Poems*, p. 232; December 1, 1996, Ray Olson, review of *The Vigil*, p. 640; June 1, 1999, p. 1775.
Boston Globe, March 30, 1997; September 12, 1999, p. C1.

Chicago Tribune, December 16, 1987, p. 3; January 16, 1995, p. 10.
Choice, April, 1973, p. 293; September, 1977, p. 867.
Critical Survey, May, 1997, Maurice Rutherford, review of *The Vigil*, p. 164.
Economist (US), September 6, 1997, p. S19; March 18, 2000, "Whose Voice Is It Anyway?," p. 14.
Georgia Review, winter, 1983, p. 894; fall, 1993, Judith Kitchen, review of *A Dream of Mind*, p. 578.
Hudson Review, spring, 1970, p. 130; spring, 1984, p. 122; winter, 1988, Robert McDowell, review of *Flesh and Blood*, pp. 680-681; summer, 1995, Thomas M. Disch, review of *Selected Poems*, p. 339.
Kliatt Young Adult Paperback Book Guide, summer, 1988, p. 30.
Library Journal, June 1, 1969, p. 2239; February 1, 1972, p. 504; June 15, 1977, p. 1386; October 1, 1983, p. 1880; May 1, 1987, Thom Tammaro, review of *Flesh and Blood*, p. 72; June 1, 1990, p. 130; May 1, 1992, Louis McKee, review of *A Dream of Mind*, p. 86; June 1, 1999, Rochelle Ratner, review of *Repair*, p. 120; March 1, 2000, David Kirby, review of *Misgivings*, p. 92; January 1, 2001, Fred Muratori, review of *Love about Love*, p. 112.
Los Angeles Times, March 7, 1993, Allan M. Jalon, "The Poet as Witness," p. 30.
Los Angeles Times Book Review, January 22, 1984, p. 3.
Nation, June 18, 1977, pp. 763-766; December 24, 1983, p. 673; May 30, 1987, Dan Bogen, review of *Flesh and Blood*, pp. 734-736.
National Book Critics Circle Journal, May 15, 1988, pp. 3-4.
New England Review and Bread Loaf Quarterly, spring, 1984, pp. 489-492.
New Republic, August 17, 1992, Edward Hirsch, review of *A Dream of Mind*, p. 46; December 21, 1992; January 25, 1993, Robert Pinsky, review of *Canvas*, p. 43; September 18, 2000, Brian Phillips, review of *Repair* and *Misgivings: My Mother, My Father, Myself*, p. 42.
New Statesman & Society, December 23, 1988, Robert Sheppard, review of *Flesh and Blood*, p. 36; December 4, 1992, David Herd, review of *A Dream of Mind*, p. 40.
New Yorker, April 29, 1991, p. 42; October 21, 1991, p. 84; April 20, 1992, p. 38; January 11, 1993, review of *A Dream of Mind*, p. 111.
New York Times, April 11, 2000, p. A26; October 4, 2000, Alan Riding, "An American Bard in Paris Stokes the Poetic Home Fires," p. E1.
New York Times Book Review, July 10, 1977, p. 14; November 27, 1983, Louis Simpson, review of *Tar*, p. 13; August 23, 1987, Edward Hirsch, review of *Flesh and Blood*, p. 20; March 13, 1988, p. 34; No-

vember 15, 1992, William Logan, review of *A Dream of Mind*, p. 15; October 8, 2000, Laura Ciolkowski, review of *Misgivings*, p. 23.

Observer, January 8, 1989, p. 46.

Parnassus, fall-winter, 1972, pp. 125-129; January, 1990, p. 115; August, 1990, Sherod Santos, reviews of *Poems: 1963-1983* and *Flesh and Blood*, p. 115; fall, 1993, Bill Marx, review of *Canvas*, p. 100; January, 1995, p. 11.

Partisan Review, summer, 1985, p. 302; March, 1991, p. 565; summer, 1991, Michael Collier, review of *Poems: 1963-1983*, p. 565.

Poetry, November, 1971, pp. 99-104; February, 1973, pp. 292-303; September, 1984, Bruce Bawer, review of *Tar*, pp. 353-355; February, 1988, Linda Gregerson, review of *Flesh and Blood*, pp. 431-433; April, 1989, J. D. McClatchy, review of *Poems: 1963-1983*, p. 29; December, 1993, Ben Howard, review of *A Dream of Mind*, p. 164; May, 1997, Bruce Murphy, review of *Selected Poems*, p. 95; August 1999, Christian Whitman, review of *Poetry and Consciousness*, p. 286; August, 2001, Ian Tromp, reviews of *Poetry and Consciousness* and *Repair*, p. 288.

Publishers Weekly, April 14, 1969, p. 96; July 22, 1983, review of *Tar*, p. 126; May 11, 1992, review of *A Dream of Mind*, p. 58; August 29, 1994, review of *Selected Poems*, p. 66; November 7, 1994, p. 41; November 25, 1996, p. 71, November 25, 1996, review of *The Vigil*, p. 71; April 26, 1999, p. 76; March 13, 2000, review of *Misgivings*, p. 72; April 17, 2000, p. 10.

Reference and Research Book News, December, 1992, p. 34.

Salmagundi, spring-summer, 1997, Frederick Pollack, review of *The Vigil*, p. 205.

San Francisco Review of Books, February, 1987, p. 34.

Shenandoah, summer, 1970, Alan Williamson, review of *Lies*, pp. 89-93.

Stand, autumn, 1990, p. 18; winter, 1993, p. 77.

Threepenny Review, summer, 1984, p. 11; fall, 1989, p. 21.

Times Literary Supplement, December 2, 1988, p. 1342; January 20, 1989, p. 59; February 12, 1993, Lawrence Norfolk, review of *A Dream of Mind*, p. 11; October 8, 1993, Michael Parker, review of *Canvas*, December 8, 1995, p. 28; October 3, 1997, Jamie McKendrick, review of *The Vigil*, p. 25; March 10, 2000, William Logan, review of *Repair*, p. 23.

TriQuarterly, winter, 1988, Reginald Gibbons, review of *Flesh and Blood*, pp. 224-225; spring-summer, 1991, Alan Shapiro, "In Praise of the Impure," p. 5.

Village Voice, January 10, 1984, p. 44.

Virginia Quarterly Review, winter, 1992, p. 27; winter, 1993, review of *A Dream of Mind*, p. S27.

Washington Post, November 18, 1999, p. C01; July 23, 2000, Debra Dickerson, "The Parent Trap," p. X06.

Washington Post Book World, October 9, 1983, p. 8; January 3, 1993, p. 10; July 30, 1995, p. 8.

Western Humanities Review, spring, 1970, pp. 201-207; winter, 1973, pp. 101-10; summer, 1978, p. 269.

World Literature Today, autumn, 1989, Michael Leddy, review of *Poems: 1963-1983*, p. 685; winter, 1989, Ashley Brown, review of *Flesh and Blood*, p. 104; autumn, 1992, Joachim T. Baer, review of *Canvas*, p. 746; spring, 1993, Bernard F. Dick, review of *A Dream of Mind*, p. 387; summer, 1995, p. 589; autumn, 1997, Ashley Brown, review of *The Vigil*, p. 794.

Writer's Digest, February, 1984, p. 55.

Yale Review, October, 1977, p. 72; October 1999, Carol Muske, review of *Repair*, p. 154.

OTHER

Boston Review, http://bostonreview.mit.edu/ (February, 2001), Richard Howard, review of *The Vigil*.

Online News Hour, http://www.pbs.org/newshour/ (April 19, 2000), Jim Lehrer, interview with C. K. Williams.

Princeton University News, http://www.princeton.edu/ (February, 2001).*

*   *   *

WILLIAMS, Terry Tempest 1955-

PERSONAL: Born in 1955 in Corona, CA; daughter of John Henry III and Diane (Dixon) Tempest; married, husband's name Brooke. *Education:* Attended Teton Science School; University of Utah, B.A. (English), M.A. (environmental education).

ADDRESSES: Agent—Brandt & Brandt Literary Agency, 1501 Broadway, New York, NY 10036.

CAREER: Writer. Worked as teacher at Navajo Reservation in Montezuma Creek, UT; former naturalist in residence at Utah Museum of Natural History. Shirley Sutton Thomas Visiting Professor of English, University of Utah, 1999; visiting scholar and lecturer.

MEMBER: National Parks and Conservation Association, The Nature Conservancy, Southern Utah Wilderness Alliance.

AWARDS, HONORS: Children's Science Book Award in younger category from New York Academy of Sciences, for *The Secret Language of Snow;* named as one of the "Utne 100 Visionaries" by *Utne Reader;* Rachel Carson Honor Roll inductee; conservation award for special achievement from National Wildlife Federation; award for "distinguished contributions in literature, ecology, and advocacy for an environmentally sustainable world" from Physicians for Social Responsibility; Lannan Literary Fellowship, 1993; John Simon Guggenheim Foundation Fellowship, 1997; "Spirit of the West" award from Mountain-Plains Booksellers Association, 1999; Lila Wallace-*Reader's Digest* Writer's Award, 2000.

WRITINGS:

(With Ted Major) *The Secret Language of Snow* (for children), illustrations by Jennifer Dewey, Sierra Club (San Francisco, CA), 1984.

Pieces of White Shell: A Journey to Navajo Land, Scribner (New York, NY), 1984.

Between Cattails (verse; for children), illustrations by Peter Parnall, Scribner (New York, NY), 1985.

Coyote's Canyon, Gibbs Smith (Salt Lake City, UT), 1989.

Refuge: An Unnatural History of Family and Place, Random House (New York, NY), 1992.

The Graywolf Annual Ten: Changing Community, Graywolf Press (St. Paul, MN), 1993.

Stone Time, Southern Utah: A Portrait and a Meditation, Clear Light (Weehawken, NJ), 1994.

Atomic Ghost: Poets Respond to the Nuclear Age, Coffee House Press (Minneapolis, MN), 1995.

Desert Quartet: An Erotic Landscape, Pantheon (New York, NY), 1995.

An Unspoken Hunger: Stories from the Field (essays), Random House (New York, NY, 1995.

Sacred Land of the Southwest, Monacelli Press, 1996.

Testimony: Writers in Defense of the Wilderness, Milkweed Editions (Minneapolis, MN), 1996.

(Editor, with Willliam B. Smart and Gibbs M. Smith) *New Genesis: A Mormon Reader on Land and Community,* Gibbs Smith, 1998.

(Author of introduction) Katie Lee, *All My Rivers Are Gone: A Journey of Discovery through Glen Canyon,* Johnson Books (Boulder, CO), 1998.

Leap, Pantheon (New York, NY), 2000.

Red, Pantheon (New York, NY), 2001.

Work represented in anthologies, including *On Nature's Terms: Contemporary Voices,* edited by Rick Bass, Texas A & M University Press (College Station, TX), 1992; and *The Owl in Monument Canyon, and Other Stories from Indian Country,* edited by H. Jackson Clark, University of Utah Press (Salt Lake City), 1993. Contributor to periodicals, including *Northern Lights, Orion, National Parks, Whole Earth, Sunset, Nation, Sierra,* and *Wilderness.*

SIDELIGHTS: Terry Tempest Williams is a writer of nature books who uses her excursions into wild places as a starting point for meditations on matters spiritual, ecological, artistic, and interpersonal. Highly regarded for her advocacy of conservation in the American West, Williams is "fiercely environmentalist, feminist, aware," to quote a *Publishers Weekly* review. Williams is a fifth-generation Mormon who was raised in Salt Lake City and who still lives there, within view of the lake. Much of her intensely personal work deals with her place in the world—as a member of an animal species, as a member of a family and a community, and as a member of a body of religious faith.

Williams began her career as an author with *The Secret Language of Snow,* a children's book co-written with Ted Major, which explains snow's role in nature and explores its effects on both wildlife and plant life. A reviewer for *Scientific American* noted that the creators of *The Secret Language of Snow* "know their snow" and concluded, "Any good reader close enough to snow . . . will find this work a fine introduction." In *Pieces of White Shell: A Journey to Navajo Land,* Williams looks at Navajo culture, emphasizing folklore in explaining various aspects of Navajo life. *Between Cattails* is a free-verse children's book about marsh life, and *Coyote's Canyon* is an account of the American southwest.

Williams gained national attention as the author of *Refuge: An Unnatural History of Family and Place,* in which she writes of two seemingly disparate subjects: the rise of the Great Salt Lake and the death of her mother. She recounts how the rising of the lake threatens a bird sanctuary and the general stability of the area's rather fragile ecosystem. Interwoven among the environmental accounts are commentaries on her mother's experience with cancer, the same illness that had already claimed other members of the Williams family. Williams ties her mother's cancer to environmental changes, contending that the illness derived from nuclear tests conducted in the Nevada desert in the 1950s and 1960s. Williams notes the high rate of cancer among "downwinders," individuals so called because they lived downwind from the nuclear test sites and were, thus, at greater risk of exposure to dangerous radiation.

For Williams, a greater familiarity with nature leads to a greater understanding of death and, thus, a greater awareness of the life-death cycle. As she explained to a *Bloomsbury Review* interviewer, "That's the premise of *Refuge*—that an intimacy with the natural world initiates an intimacy with death, because life and death are engaged in an endless, inseparable dance."

Refuge prompted positive reactions from reviewers. Marilyn R. Chandler, writing in *Women's Review of Books,* described the book as "a chronicle of sadness and rage," further observing that the work serves as a testament "to the courage it takes to live through the sicknesses of our time." Julie J. Nichols, in a *Belles Lettres* appraisal, deemed *Refuge* "remarkable" and added: "In it we are privileged to experience the vision of a woman of unusually enlightened consciousness."

In 1994 Williams published one of her better-known works, *An Unspoken Hunger: Stories from the Field,* a collection of essays on subjects such as nuclear protesting, and on places such as the African Serengeti Plain and Utah's Great Basin. John Hanson Mitchell, writing in the *New York Times Book Review,* noted an inevitably feminist perspective to *An Unspoken Hunger,* declaring that "the idea of women as intermediary between earth and human conduct is interwoven throughout the book." Mitchell added that Williams "has a knack for integrating topical issues and detailed observations of nature into her narratives."

An Unspoken Hunger has been acknowledged as a rich and varied volume. *Newsweek* contributor James N. Baker wrote: "This is not an exercise in didacticism: these are wide-ranging pieces as varied in tone as they are in subject matter." Similarly, Jan Zita Grover reported in *Women's Review of Books* that *An Unspoken Hunger* constituted "a various collection," though she noted that Williams's family inevitably plays a prominent role in the various proceedings. A particularly enthusiastic appraisal was expressed by Stephen Lyons, who wrote in *Bloomsbury Review* that the "writings in *An Unspoken Hunger* are well-crafted stories that prove the maxim that what is most personal is often most universal." He described Williams's language as "lean and intimate." And Suzanne Koehler concluded in *Workbook* that Williams's book provides "a year-round reminder of what being human on a fragile planet is all about."

As a child Williams spent many hours gazing at the paintings of Paradise and Hell created by Hieronymus Bosch. Copies of the paintings had been tacked to the wall in Williams's grandmother's house, and they insinuated themselves into Williams's active imagination. Many decades later, when she was able to view the painting in Madrid's Prado Museum, Williams was shocked to discover that the panels of Paradise and Hell were meant to surround a center panel from which the painting derives its name, *The Garden of Earthly Delights.* Fascinated by the sensuous and erotic details of the panel, as well as by its depiction of a fantastic earth in which ecstasy commingles with despair, Williams devoted seven years to a study of the work and its personal message to her as an artist, a woman, and a Mormon. *Leap,* her book on her adventure, was published in 2000.

In a *Knight-Ridder/Tribune News Service* review of *Leap,* Steve Paul observed: "Reflecting counterpoints of art and spirituality, faith and passion, nature and culture, Williams' book is a wide-ranging combination of essay, meditation, prayer and dream journal, all occasioned by her close-up study of Bosch's 15th-century hallucinations in paint." Paul deemed the work evidence of "a wild mind at full throttle." *New York Times Book Review* correspondent Jillian Dunham characterized *Leap* as "a boggling mix of magic realism, religious dogma and scientific method." And in the *Christian Science Monitor,* a critic praised Williams for "diving into [Bosch's] symbol-laden tableau with a fanatic's fervor and using the painting as a springboard for an intensely introspective examination of her own Mormon faith."

In an interview with Scott London, published on the *Insight & Outlook* Web site, Williams mused about the creative life. "I know the struggle from the inside out and I would never be so bold as to call myself a writer," she said. "I think that is what other people call you. But I consider myself a member of a community in Salt Lake City, in Utah, in the American West, in this country. And writing is what I do. That is the tool out of which I can express my love. My activism is a result of my love. So whether it's trying to preserve the wilderness in Southern Utah or writing about an erotics of place, it is the same impulse—to try to make sense of the world, to try to preserve something that is beautiful, to ask the tough questions, to push the boundaries of what is acceptable."

BIOGRAPHICAL/CRITICAL SOURCES:

PERIODICALS

Belles Lettres, winter, 1991-92, pp. 60-61; spring, 1995, pp. 32-34.

Bloomsbury Review, December, 1991, pp. 8-9; November/December, 1994, p. 12; July/August, 2000, Reamy Jansen, review of Leap.

Booklist, April 1, 2000, Donna Seaman, review of Leap, p. 1412.

Christian Science Monitor, June 22, 2000, "Paradise Lost and Found in Three Old Panels," p. 18.

Georgia Review, fall, 1994, pp. 601-609.

Knight-Ridder/Tribune News Service, June 28, 2000, Steve Paul, review of Leap, p. K2674; June 28, 2000, Eils Lotozo, review of Leap, p. K5039.

Newsweek, May 2, 1994, p. 58.

New York Times Book Review, September 4, 1996, p. 6; July 23, 2000, Jillian Dunham, review of Leap.

Publishers Weekly, April 3, 2000, review of Leap, p. 69.

Rocky Mountain Review of Books, Volume 49, number 1, 1995, pp. 106-112.

Scientific American, December, 1984, pp, 27-30.

Whole Earth, spring, 2000, review of New Genesis: A Mormon Reader on Land and Community, p. 101.

Women's Review of Books, March, 1992, p. 10; June, 1995, pp. 17-18.

Workbook, winter, 1994-95, p. 176.

OTHER

Insight & Outlook, http://www.scottlondon.com/ (October 1, 2000), "The Politics of Place: An Interview with Terry Tempest Williams."

Previewport, http://www.previewport.com/ (May, 2000), preview of Leap.*

* * *

WILLIE, Frederick
　See LOVECRAFT, H(oward) P(hillips)

* * *

WING, Grace Barnett
　See SLICK, Grace (Wing)

* * *

WISER, William

PERSONAL: Born in Cincinnati, OH; son of Clarence F. (a salesman) and Ethel (Francis) Wiser; married Micheline Vandenschrieck (a Belgian-born artist), April 19, 1962; children: Eric Paul, Anne Karin. Education: Attended high school in Covington, KY.

ADDRESSES: Home—Chemin de la Moliere, Speracedes 06530, Peymeinade, France. Agent—c/o Carroll & Graf Author Mail, 19 West 21st St., Ste. 601, New York, NY 10010-6805.

CAREER: Worked as a bellboy, beach boy, and hotel clerk in Miami, FL, 1950-55, and as a bookstore clerk, census taker, and psychiatric aide in New York, NY, 1955-58; New York Public Library, New York, NY, clerk, 1958-60; writer, living in France, 1960—. Drake University, writer-in-residence, 1974-75; University of Texas, lecturer, 1977-78. Military service: U.S. Navy and U.S. Naval Reserve, 1949-54.

AWARDS, HONORS: Centro Mexicano de Escritores fellowship, 1962; Mary Roberts Rinehart Foundation award, 1964, to complete manuscript, "Short Sketches of Bohemia" (published as K); National Endowment for the Arts fellowship, 1978.

WRITINGS:

K (novel), Doubleday (Garden City, NY), 1971.

The Wolf Is Not Native to the South of France (novel), Harcourt, Brace, Jovanovich (New York, NY), 1978.

Disappearances (novel), Atheneum (New York, NY), 1980.

Ballads, Blues, and Swan Songs (stories), Atheneum (New York, NY), 1982.

The Crazy Years: Paris in the Twenties, Thames and Hudson (London, England), 1983, G. K. Hall (Boston, MA), 1985.

The Circle Tour, Atheneum (New York, NY), 1988.

The Great Good Place: American Expatriate Women in Paris, Norton (New York, NY), 1991.

The Twilight Years: Paris in the 1930s, Carroll and Graf (New York, NY), 2000.

Contributor to short story anthologies, including Best American Short Stories 1967. Short stories and articles have been published in Playboy, Cosmopolitan, Redbook, Harper's Bazaar, Cavalier, Reporter, Escapade, Antioch Review, Kenyon Review, Carleton Miscellany, Nugget, and other magazines.

SIDELIGHTS: William Wiser's The Wolf Is Not Native to the South of France is the story of American expatriates, and was described by Anatole Broyard in the New York Times Book Review as "one of those interesting, melancholy novels whose sadness seems to derive from the tears in things, as Virgil put it." Wiser's *Disappearances* is a blend of fantasy and horror, in which a journalist covering the trial of "Bluebeard" murderer Henri Desire Landru becomes friends with Gertrude Stein. Broyard called it "a wonderful novel in which the author allowed himself to fall in love with France again by placing his book in 1919. His portrait of Paris and the Parisians is one of the best by an American since Henry Miller's *Tropic of Cancer.*" Broyard found little to praise, however, in Wiser's collection, *Ballads, Blues, and Swan Songs,* and said that "I can only assume that the author had not yet found his voice and his subject when he wrote most of them."

New York Times Book Review contributor James R. Mellow called *The Crazy Years: Paris in the Twenties* "a book of historical reportage. . . . It is alive with people and events, and the style has the velocity of a high-speed train rushing past familiar scenery." The book, Mellow continued, "is full of gossip, anecdote, and the inspired bitchiness of the intelligentsia. It covers everything from the rags-to-riches saga of Coco Chanel and the heady dissipations of F. Scott and Zelda Fitzgerald to the hysterical excitement of Lindbergh's trans-Atlantic flight and the exquisite panhandling of the poor-mouthing James Joyce." Mellow concluded by calling *The Crazy Years* "an entertainment, and a thoroughly enjoyable one."

Richard Bernstein wrote in the *New York Times Book Review* that in *The Twilight Years: Paris in the 1930s,* Wiser "mostly follows the bohemian and literary elite that lived in Paris from roughly 1930 to 1940, tracing an arc that goes from the fireworks of hedonism to the fires of the war." Of particular note, said Bernstein, "is the relative invisibility of French people in [the book]. A few well-known figures, like Jean-Paul Sartre, Jean Cocteau, and Simone de Beauvoir, play walk-on roles . . . [but] Mr. Wiser's most important protagonists are the foreigners in Paris, or such figures of foreign origin as Anaïs Nin." Wiser begins the book during the period threatened by economic crisis and fascism with the suicide of painter Jules Pascin. He writes that Sylvia Beach, who had published Joyce's banned *Ulysses,* suffered hard times when Joyce failed to honor his contract with her. Wiser also provides a detailed account of the bohemian love affair between Henry Miller, June Miller, and Nin. Bernstein noted that much of what Wiser includes comes from other sources but said that the stories "are well retold by Mr. Wiser, whose distillation of a vast body of material produces a flavorful and instructive brew." A *Publishers Weekly* reviewer wrote that "Wiser allows the complex, vivid details to speak for themselves in this impressively researched work."

Wiser does his writing in a small stone house near a lake in France, adjacent to his home, a converted olive mill. He and his family spend summers on the North Sea in Belgium.

BIOGRAPHICAL/CRITICAL SOURCES:

PERIODICALS

Best Sellers, March 1, 1971.
Booklist, November 1, 2000, Jay Freeman, review of *The Twilight Years: Paris in the 1930s,* p. 516.
Economist, December 9, 1983, review of *The Crazy Years: Paris in the Twenties,* p. 104.
Interview, Mark Marvel, review of *The Great Good Place: American Expatriate Women in Paris,* p. 26.
Library Journal, June 1, 1980, Janet Boyarin, review of *Disappearances,* p. 1329; January 15, 1982, review of *Ballads, Blues, and Swan Songs,* p. 197; November 1, 1983, review of *The Crazy Years,* p. 2084; May 1, 1988, Elizabeth Guiney Sandvick, review of *The Circle Tour,* p. 94; July, 1991, Lesley Jorbin, review of *The Great Good Place,* p. 108; December, 2000, Gene Shaw, review of *The Twilight Years,* p. 161.
Nation, February 27, 1982, review of *Ballads, Blues, and Swan Songs,* p. 250.
New Statesman, October 21, 1983, Christopher Priest, review of *The Crazy Years,* p. 25.
New York Times Book Review, August 10, 1980, Richard P. Brickner, review of *Disappearances,* p. 14; January 16, 1982, Anatole Broyard, review of *Ballads, Blues, and Swan Songs,* p. 13; October 30, 1983, James R. Mellow, "'A Silly Life . . . I Miss It,'" p. 13; April 15, 1984, Richard P. Brickner, review of *Disappearances,* p. 38; March 27, 1988, MacDonald Harris, review of *The Circle Tour,* p. 11; September 8, 1991, Vanessa V. Friedman, review of *The Great Good Place,* p. 30; November 19, 2000, Anna Rohleder, review of *The Twilight Years,* p. 75; November 24, 2000, Richard Bernstein, "Cultural Cavalcade of Paris before Disaster Struck," p. B41.
Publishers Weekly, April 11, 1980, review of *Disappearances,* p. 74; September 9, 1983, Genevieve Stuttaford, review of *The Crazy Years,* p. 56; February 19, 1988, Sybil Steinberg, review of *The Circle Tour,* p. 70; October 30, 2000, review of *The Twilight Years,* p. 61.
Saturday Review, January, 1982, David Bell, review of *Ballads, Blues, and Swan Songs,* p. 64.*

WOJCIECHOWSKI, Susan
(Susan Albertson)

PERSONAL: Born in Rochester, NY; daughter of Michael and Regina (Stenclik) Osinski; married Paul Wojciechowski, November 26, 1966; children: Joel, Christian, Mary. *Education:* Nazareth College, B.A.

ADDRESSES: Home—York, PA. *Office*—c/o Author Mail, Candlewick Press, 2067 Massachusetts Ave., Cambridge, MA 02140.

CAREER: Elementary school teacher; freelance writer, 1981—; school librarian, 1986—.

MEMBER: Society of Children's Book Writers and Illustrators, Rochester Area Children's Authors and Illustrators.

AWARDS, HONORS: Best Books of the Year selection, Child Study Association, and Book for the Teen Age selection, New York Public Library, both 1988, both for *And the Other, Gold;* Best Books of the Year selection, Child Study Association, and Book for the Teen Age selection, New York Public Library, both for *Patty Dillman of Hot Dog Fame;* Best Books of the Year selection, Child Study Association, and Book for the Teen Age selection, New York Public Library, both for *Promises to Keep;* Notable Children's Books selection, American Library Association, 1996, Teachers' Choice Award, International Reading Association, Parent's Choice Honor Book, Christopher Medal, and PaLA Carolyn W. Field Medal, all for *The Christmas Miracle of Jonathan Toomey;* Parent's Choice Gold Award, and Best Books of the Year list, Child Study Book Committee at Bank Street College, both for *Beany (Not Beanhead) and the Magic Crystal.* Wojciechowski's books have been named to numerous state recommended reading lists.

WRITINGS:

And the Other, Gold, Orchard Books (New York, NY), 1987.
Patty Dillman of Hot Dog Fame, Orchard Books (New York, NY), 1989.
Promises to Keep, Crown (New York, NY), 1991.
The Best Halloween of All (picture book), illustrated by Susan Meddaugh, Crown (New York, NY), 1992.

Don't Call Me Beanhead!, illustrated by Susanna Natti, Candlewick Press (Cambridge, MA), 1994.
The Christmas Miracle of Jonathan Toomey, illustrated by P. J. Lynch, Candlewick Press (Cambridge, MA), 1995.
Beany (Not Beanhead) and the Magic Crystal, illustrated by Susanna Natti, Candlewick Press (Cambridge, MA), 1997.
Beany and the Dreaded Wedding, illustrated by Susanna Natti, Candlewick Press (Cambridge, MA), 2000.
Beany Goes to Camp, illustrated by Susanna Natti, Candlewick Press (Cambridge, MA), 2002.

Contributor to periodicals and professional journals, including *Baby Talk, Times Union, National Catholic Education Association,* and *Upstate Magazine.* Has published writings in England under the name Susan Albertson.

SIDELIGHTS: With her humorous, true-to-life portrayals of young adults, Susan Wojciechowski has been compared to such authors as Judy Blume and Paula Danziger. One of Wojciechowski's most familiar characters is thirteen-year-old Patty Dillman, a student at St. Ignatius Junior High. Wojciechowski's first three books, *And the Other, Gold, Patty Dillman of Hot Dog Fame,* and *Promises to Keep,* follow Patty's adventures as she discovers boys, learns to value her friends, and becomes involved with social issues.

Wojciechowski introduced another popular character in her 1994 work *Don't Call Me Beanhead!* Bernice Lorraine Sherwin-Hendricks, nicknamed Beany. She is a worrywart and in five chapter-length stories for beginning readers, the author chronicles Beany's troubles, from getting her parents to sign a quiz with a poor mark, to standing up to her bossy best friend, to pleading with her mother to keep her favorite out-grown sweater. With the help of her understanding parents, the young character eventually learns to relax a bit and enjoy life. Writing in *Booklist,* Mary Harris Veeder observed that the author "catches Beany's own style and credibly tracks her eventual mellowing." "Wojciechowski captures the feelings, thoughts, and concerns of early elementary-age children in Beany's witty, honest first-person narrative," remarked *School Library Journal* contributor Jacqueline Rose.

Beany's adventures continue in *Beany (Not Beanhead) and the Magic Crystal.* In this episode, a saleswoman gives Beany a crystal from an antique chandelier. Thinking the crystal has magical properties to grant one wish,

Beany decides to choose very carefully the one thing she wants to come true. Rejecting wishes for straight hair or finding a lost hamster, the young protagonist finally decides to share her wish with an elderly neighbor. A critic from *Kirkus Reviews* felt that Wojciechowski has created a character that "everyone wants for a friend. . . . She's likeable and well-intentioned without being a goody-goody." "The characters are nicely drawn," noted *School Library Journal* reviewer Christina Dorr, "and the plot moves along nicely."

Further tales of Beany are recorded in *Beany and the Dreaded Wedding* and *Beany Goes to Camp.* In the first, Beany worries about standing up as a flower girl in her cousin's wedding. She fears the dress will be wrong, or she will run out of flower petals before she reaches the end of the aisle, or that she will not be able to afford the wedding present she has picked out. As in previous books, Beany's concerns turn out to be unfounded, and as always, everything turns out fine. "Simple and satisfying," wrote *Booklist* reviewer Ilene Cooper, "this is a good choice to readers past the beginning-chapter book stage." *School Library Journal* contributor Julie G. Shatterly favorably compared Beany to Beverly Cleary's popular Ramona Quimby character, going on to comment that "Wojciechowski does have a solid grasp of modern-day children."

Other picture books by Wojciechowski include *The Christmas Miracle of Jonathan Toomey,* illustrated by P. J. Lynch. Called "Mr. Gloomy" by the town children, Jonathan Toomey is considered the best wood-worker in the valley despite his grumpy demeanor. What no one knows is that years before he arrived in the colonial American town, Toomey's wife and child died, leaving him heart broken and bitter. Then before one Christmas, a boy and his widowed mother ask the town woodcarver to make them a new Nativity to replace one lost during their travels. Though thinking that "Christmas is pish-posh," the carver nevertheless agrees to the job. As Toomey grows closer to the widow and her son, he discovers some joy in his life and finally begins to recover from the loss of his earlier family. "The story verges on the sentimental," noted *Booklist* reviewer Hazel Rochman, "but it's told with feeling and lyricism." In a *New York Times Book Review* article, James Howe suggested that "the miracle here . . . is that the tale is unfolded with such mastery, humor, and emotional force that we are entirely in its power."

Wojciechowski once commented, "As a mother, librarian, and former teacher as well as a children's author, I have always felt the need to touch the minds of children.

Through my writing, I try to reach children in a special way, by portraying them as real people—warts and all—and showing them that they are more or less alike, despite their differences."

BIOGRAPHICAL/CRITICAL SOURCES:

BOOKS

The Christmas Miracle of Jonathan Toomey, illustrated by P. J. Lynch, Candlewick Press (Cambridge, MA), 1995.

PERIODICALS

Booklist, October 15, 1994, Mary Harris Veeder, review of *Don't Call Me Beanhead!,* p. 429; September 15, 1995, Hazel Rochman, review of *The Christmas Miracle of Jonathan Toomey,* p. 173; March 15, 1996, "Notable Children's Books, 1996," p. 1288; July, 1997, April Judge, review of *Beany (Not Beanhead) and the Magic Crystal,* p. 1820; November 15, 2000, Ilene Cooper, review of *Beany and the Dreaded Wedding,* p. 643.
Kirkus Reviews, July 15, 1992, review of *The Best Halloween of All,* p. 928; June 1, 1997, review of *Beany (Not Beanhead) and the Magic Crystal,* p. 882.
New York Times Book Review, December 3, 1995, James Howe, review of *The Christmas Miracle of Jonathan Toomey,* p. 68.
Publishers Weekly, November 13, 1987, review of *And the Other, Gold;* review of *Patty Dillman of Hot Dog Fame,* May 19, 1989, p. 85.
School Library Journal, November, 1987, Marcia Hupp, review of *And the Other, Gold,* pp. 107-108; October, 1994, Jacqueline Rose, review of *Don't Call Me Beanhead!,* p. 106; July, 1997, Christina Dorr, review of *Beany (Not Beanhead) and the Magic Crystal,* p. 79; Julie G. Shatterly, October, 2000, review of *Beany and the Dreaded Wedding,* p. 142.*

* * *

X

See KENNAN, George Frost

* * *

YALOM, Marilyn K. 1932-

PERSONAL: Born March 10, 1932, in Chicago, IL; daughter of Samuel (in business) and Celia (a homemaker; maiden name, Katz) Koenick; married Irvin Yalom (a psychiatrist), June 26, 1954; children: four.

Education: Wellesley College, B.A., 1954; Harvard University, M.A.T., 1956; Johns Hopkins University, Ph.D., 1963.

ADDRESSES: Home—951 Matadero, Palo Alto, CA 94306. *Office*—Institute for Research on Women and Gender, Stanford University, Stanford, CA 94305.

CAREER: University of Hawaii at Manoa, Honolulu, HI, lecturer in French, 1961-62; California State University, Hayward, CA, assistant professor, 1963-67, associate professor, 1967-71, professor of French, 1971-76; Stanford University, Stanford, CA, Institute for Research on Women and Gender, deputy director, 1976-87, senior scholar, 1987—.

WRITINGS:

(Editor, with Hellerstein, Hume, Offen, and others) *Victorian Women,* Stanford University Press (Stanford, CA), 1981.
(Editor, with Barrie Thorne) *Rethinking the Family: Some Feminist Questions,* Longman (New York, NY), 1982, 2nd edition, Northeastern University Press (Boston, MA), 1992.
(Editor) *Women Writers of the West Coast: Speaking of Their Lives and Careers,* Capra (Santa Barbara, CA), 1983.
(Editor, with Diane Middlebrook) *Coming to Light: American Women Poets in the Twentieth Century,* University of Michigan Press (Ann Arbor, MI), 1985.
Maternity, Mortality, and the Literature of Madness, Pennsylvania State University Press (University Park, PA), 1985.
(Editor, with Susan Groag Bell) *Revealing Lines: Autobiography, Biography, and Gender,* State University of New York Press (Albany, NY), 1991.
Blood Sisters: The French Revolution in Women's Memory, Basic Books (New York, NY), 1993.
A History of the Breast, Knopf (New York, NY), 1997.
A History of the Wife, HarperCollins (New York, NY), 2001.

SIDELIGHTS: Marilyn K. Yalom is a scholar of French and feminist studies, best known for her work as part of the Institute for Research on Women and Gender at Stanford University. Yalom has principally studied the history of women as partners in marriage, but she has also published popular scholarly studies of such pertinent topics as a history of the female breast and a study

of the role women played in the French Revolution and its aftermath. In the *Journal of Comparative Family Studies,* Ann Goetting suggests that Yalom's body of work "is designed to draw readers into two decades of feminist thinking about the family."

Yalom drew a large audience with her 1997 title, *A History of the Breast.* The study covered thousands of years of history, from the Stone Age to the present, exploring how women's breasts have evolved from objects of infant nurture to objects of erotic desire. To quote Benjamin Roberts in the *Journal of Social History,* Yalom's book "takes her readers on an adventurous journey to the source of men's infatuation with the bosom which eventually evolved into what is crudely known as the tits and ass culture of the late 20th century Western society. With an eclectic range of sources varying from iconography, biblical scriptures, treatises by moralists, Yalom allows us in this innovative study to look at breasts from sacred, erotic, domestic, political, psychological, commercialized, medical, and liberated perspectives." Roberts found the book "fascinating and enlightening," noting that "Yalom's flare for telling and tongue-in-cheek humor offers an added enjoyment." In the *New York Times Book Review,* Natalie Angier described *A History of the Breast* as "a fascinating cultural, political and artistic history of our most symbolically freighted body part." Angier added: "Ms. Yalom's stately romp through history is variously enlightening, amusing and enraging. . . . This exhilarating burst of female takes on the breast underscores what is so lacking in the historical material: women's voices and women's vision." A *Publishers Weekly* reviewer concluded: "This enlightening, often surprising cultural history will compel men and women to think differently about the breast."

In *A History of the Wife,* Yalom again examines marriage in all its incarnations across the centuries, which is, according to Etelka Lehoczky in the *Washington Post,* "well-trodden but recently neglected ground." Lehoczky praised Yalom for "refurbishing the classic feminist deconstruction of marriage" in her "entertaining" book. The critic added that Yalom "would like to create a 'New Wife,' to quote one of her chapter headings, by buttressing the romantic side of wifehood while dismantling its connotations of subservience." A *Kirkus Reviews* contributor deemed *A History of the Wife* "a useful and refreshingly cheerful overview of women's changing roles in marriage and society."

Yalom once told *CA:* "My move from a traditional career as a French professor to the broader arena of feminist scholarship was motivated by the women's movement in the mid-seventies. My book *Maternity, Mortality, and the Literature of Madness* focuses on ways in which the option or experience of motherhood plugs into mental illness, as communicated by women writers."

"My . . . book [*Blood Sisters: The French Revolution in Women's Memory*] is a study of women's memoirs of the French Revolution, following on the heels of one written in French on the same subject for the bicentennial of the Revolution *Le Temps des orages,* Maren Sell (Paris, 1989)."

BIOGRAPHICAL/CRITICAL SOURCES:

PERIODICALS

Booklist, February 1, 1997, Donna Seaman, review of *A History of the Breast,* p. 912.
Journal of Comparative Family Studies, summer, 1995, Ann Goetting, review of *Rethinking the Family: Some Feminist Questions,* p. 289.
Journal of Social History, summer, 1999, Benjamin Roberts, review of *A History of the Breast,* p. 951.
Kirkus Reviews, December 15, 1996, review of *A History of the Breast;* December 15, 2000, review of *A History of the Wife,* p. 1754.
New York Times Book Review, September 12, 1993, Hilary Mantel, "Liberté, Egalité, Sororité," p. 9; February 23, 1997, Natalie Angier, "Goddesses, Harlots, and Other Male Fantasies," p. 4.
Publishers Weekly, May 24, 1993, review of *Blood Sisters: The French Revolution in Women's Memory,* p. 78; December 16, 1996, review of *A History of the Breast,* p. 47.
Washington Post Book World, February 18, 2001, Etelka Lehoczky, "Altared States," p. 13.

OTHER

AnnOnline, http://www.annonline.com/interviews/ (February 25, 1997), "Biography: Marilyn Yalom."
MetroActive Books, http://www.metroactive.com/ (February 27, 1997), Christina Waters, "Breast Intentions: An Historian Examines the Political and Sexual Legacy of the Creamy Orb."

*   *   *

YOUNG, Elizabeth

PERSONAL: Born in London, England; daughter of Bryan (a naval officer) and Audrey (Marshall) Adams; married Wayland Young, Lord Kennet (formerly a member of House of Lords); children: Easter Donatella,

Emily Tacita, Mopsa Mary, William Aldus Thoby, Audrey Louisa, Alice Matelda Zoe. *Education:* Received M.A. from Oxford University. *Politics:* Labour. *Religion:* Church of England.

ADDRESSES: Home—100 Bayswater Rd., London W2 3HJ, England.

CAREER: Writer. Member of Greenwich Forum advisory board for redundant churches, formerly member of advisory committee on Protection of the Sea, and Tibor Dery committee; chairman of Hawksmoor committee; trustee of Friends of Christchurch, Spitalfields, and Friends of St. George's, Bloomsbury; former manager of London schools; coopted member of Westminster City Council house committee. *Military service:* Women's Royal Naval Service, 1943-46.

MEMBER: International Institute for Strategic Studies, Royal United Service Institution, Royal Institute of International Affairs, British and International Studies Association.

WRITINGS:

(With husband, Wayland Young) *Old London Churches,* Faber (London, England), 1956.
Time Is as Time Does (poems), Putnam (New York, NY), 1958.
(Editor with Ritchie Calder, and contributor) *Quiet Enjoyment: Arms Control and Police Forces for the Ocean,* University of Malta Press, 1971.
A Farewell to Arms Control?, Penguin (New York, NY), 1972.
(With Brian Johnson) *Law of the Sea,* Fabian Society, 1973.
(With Peter Fricke) *Sea-Use Planning,* Fabian Society, 1975.
(With W. Young) *Neither Red nor Dead: The Case for Disarmament,* Social Democrat Party, 1981.
Men and Women: Equal but Not Interchangeable, Social Democrat Party, 1982.
(With W. Young) *London's Churches,* 1986.
The Gorbachev Phenomenon, 1987.
(With W. Kennet) *Northern Lazio: An Unknown Italy,* 1990.

Contributor to newspapers and journals in England, the United States, Canada, France, Italy, and Japan.

WORK IN PROGRESS: Research on Soviet uses of the Arctic, the use of insurance as a regulatory mechanism, women's work, and the concept of gross domestic product. Together with her husband, she is currently under contract to write a book on the role of the military in current global problems-political, environmental, economical, social, etc.

SIDELIGHTS: Elizabeth Young, Lady Kennet, commented: "I believe strongly that women have a natural right both to be good mothers and to have an interesting professional life. As my children began to grow up, I have been lucky enough, first to collaborate with my husband in fields of common interest (church architecture, disarmament, and arms control), and later to develop some expertise in a field of my own—maritime policy and sea-use planning.

"By sea-use planning I mean the recognition that many different interest groups are concerned with using the seas and oceans, and that they are all best able to do so under the rule of law. In the North Sea and English Channel, for instance, there are major fish stocks, substantial oil and gas fields, the biggest concentration of shipping in the world, pollution arriving down the Rhine and other heavily industrialized rivers (and dropping down from the air as well), sand and gravel extration for the building industries, and so on. Because fishing has not been properly regulated several fish stocks are endangered and a common fisheries policy is recognized as essential. All these various economic interest groups use the sea; add to them the people interested in historic wrecks, in sailing boats, in swimming and using the beaches, and all the people who work in and use the ports, the submarine pipelines and cables, and the need for planning at regional, national, and local levels becomes clear. There is also need for on-the-spot policing if the rule of law—what we in Britain call the Queen's Peace—is to be kept.

"I am interested in the idea of the GDP (gross domestic product) because this is the tool with which government statisticians and others measure the economic activity of countries. Mainly, it measures marketed transactions of one kind or another. What it does not measure are transactions in the so-called 'black' economy (those transactions conducted by people who want to avoid the tax net) and also that large variety of activities mainly, but not exclusively, performed by women which are not paid for or marketed: Cooking, cleaning, washing for their families, looking after their children, growing things in their gardens, repairing their houses, looking after their old or sick relations; a whole lot of activities which are in fact 'marketable'—other people earn money for doing these jobs—but not in fact 'marketed.'

"In judging the success of our own and other economies in terms of a rising or falling GDP we are almost certainly not judging the whole reality. This concentration on only part of the reality may contribute to the general lack of success that economies worldwide are now sharing.

"On the matter of equality between men and women, I have no doubt that they are, and must be, equal in law and in esteem. This does not mean that men and women are physically, emotionally, or intellectually the same as each other, let alone does this mean that women should be treated as men. (It is hardly ever suggested that men should be treated as women!)

"It follows, I think, that women have a right to a 'woman-shaped life': The right to the best education of which they are capable (equally with men); the right to be pregnant and look after their small children without being pushed by economic need to try and combine that with a full-time job (unless they themselves want that); the right to engage in part-time work while their families are growing up, without, if they are professional women, suffering professionally; and, the right as 'returners' to full-time work, to training and refresher courses of all kinds so that, at age thirty-five or forty, when their families no longer need their special attention, they can return to full-time work without loss of status or opportunities."

*   *   *

ZOILUS
See LOVECRAFT, H(oward) P(hillips)